THE Scholarship Handbook 1999

Second Edition

Foreword by Joseph A. Russo
Director of Financial Aid
University of Notre Dame

The College Board
New York

Founded in 1900, the College Board is a not-for-profit educational association that supports academic preparation and transition to higher education for students around the world through the ongoing collaboration of its member schools, colleges, universities, educational systems, and organizations.

In all of its activities, the Board promotes equity through universal access to high standards of teaching and learning and sufficient financial resources so that every student has the opportunity to succeed in college and work.

The College Board champions—by means of superior research; curricular development; assessment; guidance, placement, and admission information; professional development; forums; policy analysis; and public outreach—educational excellence for all students.

This publication contains material related to Federal Title IV student aid programs. While the College Board believes that the information contained herein is accurate and factual, this publication has not been reviewed or approved by the U.S. Department of Education.

The scholarship descriptions in this book are based on information supplied by the program sponsors themselves in response to the College Board's Annual Survey of Financial Aid Programs 1998-99. The survey was completed in the spring of 1998. Over 1,200 sponsoring organizations throughout the United States participated in this effort and the information they provided was reviewed and verified by a staff of College Board editors. While every effort was made to insure the completeness and accuracy of the information contained in this book, sponsors' policies and programs are subject to change without notice and the College Board cannot take responsibility for changes made by sponsoring organizations after the information was submitted. If users of this book find that any of the descriptions are inaccurate, please contact College Board Annual Survey of Financial Aid Programs, Att: Guidance Publishing, by mail at 45 Columbus Avenue, New York, NY 10023-6992 or by fax: 212-713-8309.

Copyright © 1998 by College Entrance Examination Board. All rights reserved.

Library of Congress Catalog Number: 97-76451
International Standard Book Number: 0-87447-594-5

College Board, AP, College Scholarship Service, PSAT, SAT, College Explorer, College Board Online, ASC, and the acorn logo are registered trademarks of the College Entrance Examination Board. Annual Survey of Colleges, FUND FINDER, and Annual Survey of Financial Aid Programs are trademarks owned by the College Entrance Examination Board.

Printed in the United States of America

Contents

Foreword i

Important Advice and Information v
   Ground Rules for College Planning. v
   What Does College Cost? vii
   How Much Will You Be Expected to Pay? vii
   Frequently Asked Questions ix
   How To Avoid Scholarship Scams. ix
   Glossary x
   How to Use This Book x
   Program Descriptions xi
   How to Use *FUND FINDER* CD-ROM xiii
   Personal Characteristics Checklist. xiv

Eligibility Indexes 1
   Disabilities 1
   Field of Study/Intended Career 2
   Gender 34
   International Students 36
   Military Participation 37
   Minority Status 38
   National/Ethnic Background 49
   Religious Affiliation 49
   Returning Adult 50
   Study Abroad 50

Federal and State Programs 53

Private Unrestricted Programs 247

Private Restricted Programs 621

Program Index 767

Sponsor Index 801

Foreword

A college education is understandably one of the more commonly sought-after goals of American families. The opportunities it provides are arguably the finest and most diverse in the world. Both access and wide choices are generally available to just about everyone who wants to pursue education beyond high school.

The Benefits

The benefits that come with additional schooling are clearly evident to individuals as well as to our society. Most college graduates enjoy a significantly higher economic status than those without the same level of education. In addition to the obvious financial advantages, statistics show that college-educated people often live healthier and longer lives, are more involved in their communities, and raise children who are more likely to attend college and share in the same intellectually and economically richer life style. Society as a whole benefits from a more involved citizenry, less crime and unemployment, and a strong tax base.

The Cost Factors

Steadily rising college costs have created much concern among students and parents about the affordability of this American dream. While it's true that the costs of college have been rising at a rate greater than the cost of living, media commentators have tended to exaggerate the impact of this escalation, making it appear much worse than it really is. The facts are that the vast majority (75%) of students pay less than $4,000 a year for college tuition and fees, while only 4% pay more than $20,000. As Donald M. Stewart, president of the College Board, pointed out recently in testimony before the U.S. Senate Hearing on Access and Costs, "the misinformation fosters public alarm and discourages many students and families from even considering the option of higher education and the chance of reaping the benefits enjoyed by those with a college degree."

The Challenge

Nonetheless, paying for college is a concern for most American families. While traditional need-based financial aid programs continue to help students afford the costs of higher education, those resources are limited and more than ever include troublesome levels of student loans. Current government efforts to provide additional resources lean heavily toward further borrowing opportunities. Although such programs offer generous provisions in the form of low interest rates and deferred repayment over lengthy periods of time, they leave students and families with the prospect of long-term debt. The challenge is to find ways of achieving college and graduate school goals in the face of limited financial aid resources.

The Options

The good news is that there are a number of things that families can do to position themselves to meet that challenge. The most basic step is finding out what their options are in order to make informed decisions about tailoring life style choices to the needs of educational priorities.

Every family makes decisions regarding lifestyle on a regular basis. Food, housing, transportation, clothing, and entertainment are fundamental expenses, but there's considerable latitude in how much income is earmarked for any of those categories. Even if there hasn't been much advance planning, as the college-going years approach, parents have the choice of reordering some of their priorities—spending less on clothing and entertainment, for example, so they can increase the amount of money they allocate for savings and investments, or take advantage of the benefits of a tuition prepayment plan. Students have comparable choices—cutting back on what they spend for CDs, movies, or the latest fad in clothes; forgoing afternoons at the mall in favor of an after-school job; taking AP courses that could reduce overall college costs by a full year's tuition and fees.

Financial Aid Eligibility versus Availability

Prior to the 1970s, before the federal government began to provide substantial aid to cover college costs, families had to depend almost entirely on their own resources. The need to save for college was paramount.

With the advent of financial aid and formulas for expected family contribution, it seemed to some that saving was counterproductive because it reduced student aid eligibility. If that point of view ever had validity, it certainly doesn't today. As families are discovering, often the hard way, *eligibility* does not automatically translate into *availability* of funds. And the funds that are available are more likely to be in the form of loans than gift aid so the results of not having saved are often a much more expensive set of options at best, or a very reduced set of college opportunities at worst. Recent legislation designed to help families through limited tax credits for tuition costs, although admirable, will fall far short of the resources needed by many families.

Incentives for Saving

What is encouraging and very positive about some of the new tax proposals are the incentives to save for college. These incentives may not be of immediate help to families with students about to enter college, but they can have an impact on future years so parents should certainly investigate these avenues and begin to take advantage of them. It goes without saying that the earlier a saving program begins, the better. But the type of program and the amount of money to be set aside will depend on individual family circumstances such as income, non-discretionary expenses, number of children, number of years remaining prior to college, and, of course, the choice of college and its actual cost when the time comes. There are simple ways of projecting costs, using an estimated inflation factor compounded by the number of years remaining before college.

Once you know the estimated costs, the next step is to develop a savings/investment plan that assumes a compounded rate of return and monthly amount to be saved. There are a number of educational and financial organizations that have developed methods for making those kinds of projections, among them the College Board and the National Association of Student Financial Aid Administrators (NASFAA). Information and guidelines are available on the Internet from those organizations as well as from a number of others.

Even with careful advance planning and saving, the majority of families need some financial aid, including loans, to help them cover the full annual costs of college. But that doesn't mean that the decision about where to apply should be based on cost of tuition and fees. Families should *not* be discouraged by the price tag, and should *never* rule out a college, no matter how expensive, before exploring every financial aid option available. All colleges and universities have a variety of programs to assist in paying the bill. Most of them include scholarship, grant, loan and work opportunities, often combined in "packages" based on individual family circumstances. Some colleges offer other financial products and services as well, so it's important to find out what the "net cost" will be after all financial aid has been factored in before making a decision.

The Role of Private Scholarships

The one additional source of funding that hasn't been addressed up to this point is private scholarship opportunities—and they can play a significant role in supplementing a family's personal resources. As this book demonstrates, there are substantial programs sponsored by foundations; civic, fraternal, veterans, and religious associations; corporations; the military; and other private and public sector organizations.

Eligibility for these programs often requires meeting some condition such as demonstrating special talents or skills; being a member of a particular organization or ethnic group; pursuing a specified major or career goal; or agreeing to fulfill some postgraduate obligation. Such programs can be very helpful, though their resources are not always adequate to meet the full demand. Applicants have to realize that they're competing for limited resources—so identifying potential programs and applying to them as early as possible offer the best chances for success.

A few words of caution—don't let common sense be overwhelmed by the glowing claims of some commercial scholarship search companies that offer, for hefty fees, to tap into "untold millions of scholarship dollars" that go unused each year because no one applies. The general rule is that if it sounds too good to be true, it probably is. If scholarships are guaranteed for a fee, then beware—and rely on your own search efforts using resources such as this book or one of the annually updated scholarship search software programs that may be available free of charge in your local library or high school. The Internet is also an up-to-date, accurate source of free scholarship information. The College Board's Web site is a good example. It can be accessed at:

www.collegeboard.org/fundfinder/bin/fundfind01.pl

Another reliable organization that offers free search capability is the National Association of Student Financial Aid Administrators (NASFAA). It can be accessed at:

www.finaid.org/

Students who want to explore scholarship prospects need to be especially diligent in their school work and extracurricular activities, because superior academic and personal credentials often are critical factors in awarding scholarships. Moreover, colleges tend to look particularly favorably on the awarding of outside scholarships as an indication of students' initiative and sense of responsibility, often adjusting those students' financial aid packages to reduce the loan and work study components rather than the gift aid portion. Scholarship awards clearly enhance students' credentials and, all things being equal, make them stronger candidates from the colleges' perspective.

Meeting the Challenge

Paying for college is indeed a major challenge for most families. But with resources such as this College Board publication, students and parents can expand their access to funding for college and move another step closer to their goals for the future.

Joseph A. Russo
Director of Financial Aid
University of Notre Dame

Important Advice and Information

Ground Rules for College Planning

- When it comes to planning for college, the very first rule to remember is: *Time is money!*

Experts suggest that parents start saving for college somewhere between the time they decide on a name for the baby and the start of middle school.

- The second rule is: *It's never too early to begin saving and planning but it's never too late to develop strategies and options if your savings aren't sufficient.*

Virtually all colleges and graduate schools have financial aid professionals on staff to help you bridge the gap between your resources and the cost of attending those institutions. Last year, over $50 billion in financial aid enabled millions of students to continue their education beyond high school.

- The third rule is: *The responsibility of paying for college begins with you and your family.*

While help comes from colleges and universities as well as federal and state governments, you are a partner in the effort to cover the costs of your higher education. You are expected to contribute an amount calculated by the federal government and/or the institution you're attending as a fair share based on your family financial situation.

- The fourth rule is: *The cost of a college or graduate degree is an investment in the future.*

An investment is money spent to earn a financial return—and for most people, one of the benefits of a college education is higher lifetime earnings potential. When you add to that some of the more subjective benefits such as broadened perspectives and interests, expanded knowledge, and friendships, college begins to look like one of the best, most reliable, and high-yield investments you can make.

Advice to Parents: The "Five C's" of Preparing for College and Graduate School Costs

1. **Collect** as much information as possible. Catalogs from colleges and graduate schools, federal government brochures, state education department publications, bank and credit union information, and, increasingly important, Web sites on the Internet, provide extensive information on college preparatory courses, college savings strategies, college costs, financial aid programs, and private sector scholarship opportunities.

2. **Coordinate** the information and develop a timetable for getting the most out of your own resources. Understand what colleges and graduate studies cost today, anticipate that those costs will continue to increase, and at least estimate what share of those costs you might be expected to pay. If you're starting the planning process several years before that first tuition bill is due, you have a number of options to consider in terms of savings and investment strategies. You also have time to explore need and non-need scholarship opportunities to get an idea of what supplemental funds may be available.

3. **Consider** all of your options and opportunities. Time can be your most important advantage if you have even modest resources to invest in the stock market, mutual funds, prepaid tuition plans, or in recently developed "Education IRA" savings plans. Remember that, although fifty billion dollars of financial aid was available to students last year, an increasing percentage of that money is in the form of education loans. Making your money work for you enables you to *earn* interest now rather than *pay* interest later.

4. **Communicate** with college or graduate school financial aid offices and with private sector scholarship programs. Find out in advance what their requirements and application deadlines are; get a sense of what typical college financial aid packages or private scholarship awards may consist of and whether they're renewable. This book is a good place to either start or continue your efforts. The extensive listing of award programs illustrates the extent to which support is available to supplement what you are able to contribute toward college costs.

5. **Copy** all scholarship applications and financial aid documents you submit and keep them on file so that you can refer to them if any questions arise or duplicate them if necessary. No matter how reliable the postal service and electronic communications systems are, sometimes things you've sent get lost in the mail, don't arrive by fax, or disappear on their way via e-mail. Don't risk having to start over from scratch if that should happen.

Take the time to collect, coordinate, consider, and communicate—you'll find that it's a wise investment of your time and your money.

> Jack Joyce
> Manager of Communications and Training
> College Scholarship Service

What Does College Cost? How Much Will You Be Expected To Pay?

Some of the best things in life may be free, but college is not one of them. The purpose of this book is to help you:

- understand the components of college costs
- get a sense of what you'll be expected to contribute toward those costs
- learn from financial aid experts about ground rules and strategies for paying for college
- find additional resources to cover the costs of your college education

The Components of College Costs

Whether you're an undergraduate or graduate student, part-time or full-time, commuting or living on campus, your outlay is going to include both direct educational expenses and living expenses. Typically, they fall into the following five categories:

- tuition and fees
- books and supplies
- room and board
- personal expenses
- transportation

Tuition and Fees

Tuition is the charge for instruction. Fees may be charged for services such as Internet access, student activities, or the health center. The amount of tuition and fees charged by a particular college varies considerably. Public colleges, because they're funded by tax dollars, are generally less expensive than private institutions, though out-of-state (or, in the case of community colleges, out-of-district) students usually pay higher tuition, which can make a public college as costly as a private one for nonresident students.

Books and Supplies

The amount you spend for books, pens, pencils, paper, and other basic supplies isn't affected by the *type* of college you're attending, but will vary considerably based on the courses you're taking. Science, engineering, and art courses, for example, require specialized equipment and materials.

Room and Board

Whether you live in a campus dorm or in a private apartment off-campus, you have to cover the basic living expenses of food and housing. Even students who live at home have to factor in meals and snacks at school and their parents still have the expense of providing them with living quarters and food.

Personal Expenses

You're probably used to paying for some of your personal expenses—clothes, toiletries, magazines, CDs, movies. But once you're at college, you're also going to be responsible for laundry and dry cleaning bills, phone bills, accessories and supplies for your living quarters, and a lot of other little incidentals, which can add up to anywhere from $600 to more than twice that.

Estimating Your Expected Family Contribution

As Jack Joyce of the College Board's College Scholarship Service pointed out in the preceding section, the responsibility of paying for college begins with you and your parents. The amount that you as a family are expected to pay is the sum of what your parents can contribute from their income and assets plus what you can contribute from earnings and savings. If you're curious about what that means in terms of dollars, the table on the following page gives you a sense of what parental contribution is expected at various income and asset levels. Pick the combination of annual income and asset figures that are closest to your family's and you'll have a very rough idea of what your parents' share might be.

Don't Panic!

While the expense of going to college or graduate school may seem like a heavy burden, the fact is that the majority of students get financial aid that covers at least a portion of the cost. Of the four basic potential sources, this book deals with the first three listed below:

1. Much of the aid comes from the federal government in the form of grants, work study programs, and subsidized loans.
2. State governments also dispense significant amounts of financial aid in various forms to state residents.

3. In addition, there are a number of private foundations and corporations that have established scholarship programs to help qualified students pay for college.

4. Financial aid awards sponsored and administered by colleges, universities, and graduate schools are another important resource. They include scholarships, fellowships, fee waivers, internships, and teaching and research assistantships. Because criteria and application procedures vary considerably, your best source of information is the institution's own catalog or financial aid bulletin.

In this book you'll find detailed descriptions of more than 3,300 federal, state, and private sector programs representing over a million awards, with eligibility indexes to help you zero in on the awards you're likely to qualify for.

1997-98 Estimated parents' contribution

Net assets	$25,000				$50,000			
Family size	3	4	5	6	3	4	5	6
1997 income before taxes								
$10,000	$0	$0	$0	$0	$0	$0	$0	$0
20,000	0	0	0	0	0	0	0	0
30,000	1,219	532	0	0	1,452	765	120	0
40,000	2,820	2,080	1,435	706	3,090	2,312	1,667	939
50,000	5,031	3,932	3,068	2,254	5,453	4,291	3,374	2,501
60,000	7,950	6,644	5,423	4,201	8,446	7,141	5,845	4,560
70,000	10,334	9,028	7,812	6,417	10,830	9,524	8,308	6,913
80,000	13,321	12,015	10,799	9,404	13,817	12,511	11,295	9,900
90,000	16,307	15,002	13,785	12,390	16,804	15,498	14,383	12,887
100,000	19,294	17,989	16,772	15,377	19,791	18,485	17,269	15,874

Net assets	$100,000				$150,000			
Family size	3	4	5	6	3	4	5	6
1997 income before taxes								
$10,000	$0	$0	$0	$0	$836	$62	$0	$0
20,000	1,224	537	0	0	2,567	1,857	1,207	391
30,000	2,826	2,085	1,440	711	4,649	3,624	2,812	2,031
40,000	5,039	3,939	3,074	2,259	7,715	6,247	5,017	3,856
50,000	8,201	6,734	5,431	4,208	11,021	9,554	8,175	6,618
60,000	11,266	9,961	8,662	7,105	14,086	12,781	11,482	9,925
70,000	13,650	12,344	11,128	9,733	16,470	15,164	13,948	12,553
80,000	16,637	15,331	14,115	12,720	19,457	18,151	16,935	15,540
90,000	19,624	18,318	17,102	15,707	22,444	21,138	19,922	18,527
100,000	22,611	21,305	20,089	18,694	25,431	24,125	22,909	21,514

Note: The figures shown are parents' contribution under Federal Methodology (FM), assuming the older parent is age 45; both parents are employed (equal wages); income is only from employment; no unusual circumstances; standard deductions on U.S. income tax; 1040 tax return filed; and one undergraduate child enrolled in college. Net assets exclude primary place of residence and family farms.

Frequently Asked Questions

Q When should I start looking for scholarships?

A It's never too early to start finding out about what kinds of scholarships are available. If you're a high school student, it's a good idea to start your research in sophomore or junior year, even if you can't apply until you're a senior. If you're in college and need financial aid for graduate school, there's no time like the present to start exploring your options.

Q Will going to college part-time lessen my chances of receiving aid?

A Depending on your personal circumstances, you could be eligible for a Pell Grant and a number of other forms of federal aid. Many of the private sector scholarships in this book make no distinction between full-time and part-time study in awarding funds.

Q Are international students eligible for financial aid?

A If you're an international student (a noncitizen from abroad), you're generally not eligible for tax-supported aid such as federal or state grants, but there are private sector awards included in this book that international students are eligible for. You'll find them listed in the index.

Q If I get a scholarship from a foundation or corporation, will the financial aid offered by the college be affected?

A Colleges' policies on outside scholarships vary a great deal, so you'd have to check with the financial aid officer at the college itself to find out.

Q Is it true that my college financial aid package could be reduced by as much as the full amount of any outside scholarship I receive?

A Probably yes if your financial aid package meets your full need (as measured by the college); probably no if your need has been only partially met. The other factor to take into consideration is that many colleges will reduce the loan or work-study component of your aid package rather than the gift aid portion.

Q Are there scholarships that cover the whole four years or are they only awarded for one year?

A That varies from sponsor to sponsor. Many undergraduate scholarships cover a single year of study but are renewable. Some graduate and postgraduate grants and fellowships cover the entire period required to earn the degree or complete a research project.

How To Avoid Scholarship Scams

As college costs continue to rise, families have begun to look beyond government and college sources of funding, which has given rise to a growing industry of scholarship search services. Some do a responsible job for a modest fee, but many make unrealistic claims, and charge substantial fees. Some are outright fraudulent in their tactics.

Buyer Beware!

The Federal Trade Commission (FTC) recently launched Project $cholar$cam to alert consumers about potential scams and how to recognize them. Here are the FTC's six basic warning signs and advice:

"The scholarship is guaranteed or your money back."
> No one can guarantee that they'll get you a grant or a scholarship. Refund policies often have conditions or strings attached. Get refund policies in writing before you pay.

"You can't get this information anywhere else."
> Check with your school or library before you decide to pay someone to do the work for you.

"May I have your credit card or bank account number to hold this scholarship?"
> Don't give out your credit card or bank account number on the phone without getting information in writing first. It may be a set-up for an unauthorized withdrawal.

"We'll do all the work for you."
> Don't be fooled. There's no way around it. You must apply for scholarships or grants yourself.

The scholarship will cost some money.
> Don't pay anyone who claims to be "holding" a scholarship or grant for you. Free money shouldn't cost a thing.

"You've been selected by a national foundation to

receive a scholarship" or "You're a finalist" in a contest you never entered.

Before you send money to apply for a scholarship, check it out. Make sure the foundation or program is legitimate.

Glossary

Family contribution: The total amount that you and your family are expected to pay toward college costs from your income and assets. The amount is determined by a need analysis of your family's overall financial circumstances. A Federal Methodology is used to determine your eligibility for federal student aid. Colleges, state agencies, and private aid programs may use a different methodology in assessing eligibility for nonfederal sources of financial aid.

Federal Work-Study Program: A federally sponsored campus-based program. Participating colleges provide employment opportunities for students with demonstrated need who are enrolled at either the undergraduate or graduate level.

Fellowship: A form of graduate financial aid that usually requires service—often in the form of time devoted to a research project.

Financial aid package: The total financial aid award offered to you. It may be made up of a combination of aid that includes both gift aid (which doesn't have to be repaid) and self-help (work-study and/or loans). Many colleges try to meet a student's full financial need, but availability of funds, the institution's aid policies, and the number of students needing aid all affect the composition of a financial aid package.

Financial need: The difference between the cost of attending college and your expected family contribution.

Free Application for Federal Student Aid (FAFSA): A form you must complete to apply for federal student aid. In many states, completing the FAFSA is the way to establish your eligibility for state-sponsored aid programs. There is no charge to you for submitting this form, which is widely available in high schools and colleges and may be filed any time after January 1 of the year for which you're seeking aid.

Internship: A short-term, supervised work experience, usually related to your major, for which you earn academic credit. There are also internships included in this book for which you receive a stipend.

Need analysis form: The starting point in applying for financial aid. All students must file the FAFSA to apply for federal financial aid programs. To apply for state financial aid programs, the FAFSA may be all that you'll need to file, but check to be sure.

Research grants: Some scholarships are for research and require you to describe the project for which you're requesting funds. While most research grants are for graduate students, some in this book are available for undergraduates.

Scholarship or grant: A type of financial aid that doesn't have to be repaid. Grants are often based on financial need. Scholarships may be based on need, on need combined with other criteria, or solely on other criteria such as academic achievement, artistic ability, talent in the performing arts, and the like.

How to Use This Book

General Information

The opening sections of the *Scholarship Handbook* offer advice from financial aid experts, guidance on paying for college, tips for avoiding scholarship scams, answers to some of the most frequently asked questions about funding college or graduate studies, and a glossary of terms.

You may be tempted to go directly to the scholarship section and start browsing, but to get the most out of this book, start by reading the information and advice in those opening pages. They'll help you to get a realistic perspective on financial aid and give you useful guidelines for understanding and taking advantage of your college funding options.

Indexes

- Disabilities: This category covers students with disabilities. Most awards in this category, as well as other categories, have additional eligibility requirements.
- Field of Study/Intended Career: This category, by far the longest, identifies broad major and career

areas, so if you don't see your specific area of interest, look for the general area into which it might fit.

- Gender: While the vast majority of awards are not gender-specific, there are over 100 awards in this book exclusively for females, and more than 20 for males.
- International Students: If you're a citizen of another country and planning to study in the United States, this category will help you identify awards for which you may qualify.
- Military Participation: Many of the awards in this category are for the children, descendants, or spouses of members of the military, including the Reserves and National Guard, going back as far as the Civil War.
- Minority Status: There are seven groups within this category, representing a wide range of awards.
- National/Ethnic Background: The eleven national/ethnic groups in this category are determined by the sponsoring organizations that responded to our annual survey.
- Religious Affiliation: The ten groups in this category represent a broad range but, like the national/ethnic category, are determined by the respondents to our annual survey.
- Returning Adult: This category includes awards for undergraduate, graduate, and nondegree study. The age qualification varies but most often is for students 25 years or older.
- Study Abroad: There are several hundred U.S. government-sponsored Fulbright grants for study throughout the world in this category as well as a number of privately sponsored scholarships, fellowships, and internships for use outside the United States.

In addition to the eligibility indexes preceding the scholarship descriptions, there are program and sponsor indexes following the descriptions. These are helpful if you know the name of a scholarship program or sponsoring organization and want to go directly to it. In all of the indexes, awards that are offered only for graduate or nondegree study are identified by an asterisk.

Program Descriptions

The scholarship programs in this book are organized alphabetically by sponsor within three sections:

- Federal and State Programs: This section covers detailed information about the wide range of scholarships and loans sponsored by the U.S. Departments of Education, Interior Affairs, Vocational Rehabilitation, Defense, and other federal agencies, including Fulbright Program grants. There is also in-depth information about all the major state programs as well as awards sponsored by tribal, territorial, and commonwealth education assistance agencies.
- Unrestricted Private Programs: In this section are awards sponsored by private foundations, associations, and corporations that are open to all students who meet the eligibility requirements. There are no applicant limitations based on affiliation with the sponsoring organization.
- Restricted Private Programs: The awards described in this section are available only to applicants who in some way, either directly or through their parents or other relatives, have a specified affiliation with the sponsoring organization.

Each program description contains all of the information provided by the sponsor and verified for accuracy by a staff of editors at the College Board. A typical description includes:

Type of award: tells you whether the award is a scholarship, grant, internship, or loan, and whether it's renewable

Intended use: tells you the range and limitations of the award, such as level of study, full-time or part-time, at what kind of institution, whether in the United States or abroad

Eligibility: indicates the characteristics you must have to be considered for an award—for example, U.S. citizenship, specific state of residence, disability, membership in a particular organization, minority status

Basis for selection: may include major or career interest; personal qualities such as seriousness of purpose, high academic achievement, depth of character; financial need

Application requirements: outlines what you must provide in support of your application, such as recommendations, essay, transcript, interview, proof of eligibility, resume, references

Additional information: gives you any facts or requirements not covered in the categories above—for example, which test scores to submit, GPA level required, whether a particular type of student is given special consideration, when application forms are available, etc.

Amount of award: a single figure generally means the standard amount, but may indicate the maximum of a range of amounts; two figures indicate the range of awards from lowest to highest amounts

Number of awards: tells you how many awards are granted by the sponsor

Number of applicants: tells you how many students applied the previous year

Application deadline: the date by which your application must be submitted; some scholarships have two deadlines for considering applications

Notification begins: the earliest date that an award notification is sent; in some cases, all go out on the same date, in others, notification is on a rolling basis; if there are two application deadlines, there are usually two notification dates

Total amount awarded: tells you how much money is disbursed in the current award year, including renewable awards

Contact name, address, phone, fax, and Web site: gives you all available information on where to get application forms and further information. Where the contact name and address are identical for several different scholarship programs sponsored by the same organization, that information will appear at the end of the last scholarship in that group.

While some descriptions don't include all these details because they were either not applicable or not supplied by the sponsor, in every case all essential information is provided.

How to Use FUND FINDER CD-ROM

FUND FINDER is designed to quickly give you a list of awards for which your characteristics precisely match the eligibility requirements. Since many awards are linked to a specific level of study, it's essential for you to indicate that information before checking off other characteristics.

The more information you provide about yourself, the more scholarship options you're likely to have on your list. Be sure to check off every characteristic that applies to you.

- If you have a particular skill in one of the areas listed under "Awards based on competitions," include it in your personal profile.

- Demonstrated financial need is the difference between what it costs to attend a particular college and what you and your family can afford to pay toward those costs. To get detailed information about financial aid and how the federal government and colleges determine a student's eligibility, click on **College Board Online** and go to the financial aid services screen.

- Academic achievement doesn't necessarily mean that you have to be at the very top of your class. If your test scores, class rank, and/or grade point average are reasonably good, you may qualify for awards based on academic achievement. Don't underestimate your accomplishments or overestimate what scholarship sponsors may expect of you.

- The characteristics included in "Additional personal facts" are based on specific requirements for certain awards in *FUND FINDER*. You can make them part of your personal profile by clicking on any that apply to you.

- Many scholarships in *FUND FINDER* have no state residence requirements and a number of them are not restricted to United States residents. If you live outside the United States, you can ignore the state residence list. You will still be matched to any of the awards for which you meet eligibility requirements.

- If you have an interest or talent in one of the specialized areas listed here, you may be eligible for a related award. However, keep in mind that most scholarships have several requirements, all of which have to be met for them to appear on your list.

- If your family background includes several religious affiliations, minority groups, and/or nationalities, be sure to check *all* that apply.

- Many awards are linked to fields of study and/or careers. Even if you're not sure at this point what your major will be or what career you'll eventually pursue, don't let that stop you from checking any and *all* areas that you might be interested in considering.

- Scholarships related to the military aren't just for veterans. If one of your parents, a spouse, or even a distant ancestor was in military service, you may be eligible for funds to help you pay for college.

- Awards related to disabilities often have academic and/or field of study requirements as well so be sure to check all the characteristics that apply to you.

- Many corporations have generous higher education funding programs that are available exclusively for employees or their offspring. A large number of membership organizations have similar programs for their members. Check to see if any apply to your circumstances.

- The large majority of scholarships for study abroad are Fulbright grants for graduate students. But there are some awards for undergraduate study outside the United States, so don't overlook this possibility if you're interested in going to college in another country.

When you've completed all the information screens as fully as possible, click on "View scholarship list" to see how many award programs matched your search criteria. If the list is shorter than you expected, you can go back to the Main Menu and edit your personal profile or add more information to one or more of the eligibility screens.

Once you have your scholarship list, you can get basic facts about each one by clicking on the program name. You can also print the list and your search criteria. Then consult this book to get in-depth information.

Personal Characteristics Checklist

Disability:

☐ hearing ☐ learning ☐ physical ☐ visual

Field of study/intended career:

☐ Agricultural science, business, and natural resources conservation
☐ Architecture and design
☐ Area and ethnic studies
☐ Arts, visual and performing
☐ Biological and physical sciences
☐ Business, management, administration
☐ Communications
☐ Computer and information sciences
☐ Education
☐ Engineering and engineering technology
☐ English and literature
☐ Foreign languages

☐ Health professions and allied services
☐ Home economics
☐ Law
☐ Liberal arts and interdisciplinary studies
☐ Library science
☐ Mathematics
☐ Military science
☐ Mortuary science
☐ Protective services
☐ Philosophy, religion, and theology
☐ Social sciences and history
☐ Trade and industry

Gender: ☐ Female ☐ Male

International student: ☐   Returning adult: ☐

Military participation/affiliation:

☐ Air Force
☐ Army
☐ Marines

☐ Coast Guard
☐ Navy
☐ Reserves/National Guard

Minority status:

☐ African American
☐ Alaskan Native
☐ American Indian

☐ Asian American
☐ Hispanic American
☐ Mexican American
☐ Puerto Rican

National/ethnic background:

☐ Armenian
☐ Chinese
☐ Danish
☐ Greek

☐ Italian
☐ Japanese
☐ Mongolian
☐ Polish

☐ Swiss
☐ Ukrainian
☐ Welsh

Religious affiliation:

☐ Christian
☐ Eastern Orthodox
☐ Episcopal
☐ Jewish

☐ Lutheran
☐ Presbyterian (USA)
☐ Protestant
☐ Roman Catholic

☐ Unitarian Universalist
☐ United Methodist

Want to study abroad: ☐

Eligibility Indexes

Disabilities

Hearing impaired

Alexander Graham Bell Association for the Deaf Scholarship, 257

*American Speech-Language-Hearing Student with Disability Scholarship, 347

Elks Undergraduate Disabled Student Scholarship, 376

Geoffrey Foundation Undergraduate Scholarship, 412

Governor's Commission on People with Disabilities Scholarship Fund, 415

Louisiana Social Services Rehabilitation/Vocational Aid For Disabled Persons, 128

New York State Readers Aid Program, 188

Scholarship for People with Disabilities, 386

Sertoma Scholarships for Deaf and Hard of Hearing Students, 567

Texas Tuition Exemption for Blind and Deaf Students, 226

Tourism Foundation Yellow Ribbon Scholarship, 519

Virginia Rehabilitative Services College Scholarship, 239

Wisconsin Visual and Hearing Impaired Program, 244

Learning disabled

*American Speech-Language-Hearing Student with Disability Scholarship, 347

Easter Seal Society of Iowa Disability Scholarship, 395

Elks Undergraduate Disabled Student Scholarship, 376

Governor's Commission on People with Disabilities Scholarship Fund, 415

James L. & Lavon Maddon Mallory Disability Scholarship, 395

Learning Through Listening Award, 732

Louisiana Social Services Rehabilitation/Vocational Aid For Disabled Persons, 128

Marion Huber Learning Through Listening Award, 732

North Carolina Vocational Rehabilitation Award, 194

Scholarship for People with Disabilities, 386

Stanley E. Jackson Award for Gifted/Talented Minorities with Disabilities, 406

Stanley E. Jackson Scholarship Award for Ethnic Minority Students., 406

Stanley E. Jackson Scholarship Award for Gifted/Talented Students with Disabilities, 406

Virginia Rehabilitative Services College Scholarship, 239

Physically challenged

"Will to Win" Asthma Athlete Scholarship, 564

*American Speech-Language-Hearing Student with Disability Scholarship, 347

Billy Barty Financial Assistance Program, 368

Chairscholars Scholarship, 378

*Charles E. Culpeper Art Internship, 487

Easter Seal Society of Iowa Disability Scholarship, 395

Elks Undergraduate Disabled Student Scholarship, 376

Gore Family Memorial Foundation Scholarships, 415

Governor's Commission on People with Disabilities Scholarship Fund, 415

Grant Program for Physically Disabled Students in the Sciences, 407

James L. & Lavon Maddon Mallory Disability Scholarship, 395

Jean Driscoll Award, 532

Louisiana Social Services Rehabilitation/Vocational Aid For Disabled Persons, 128

Maryland Edward T. Conroy Memorial Grant--Disabled Public Safety Employees, 132

North Carolina Vocational Rehabilitation Award, 194

Scholarship for People with Disabilities, 386

Stanley E. Jackson Award for Gifted/Talented Minorities with Disabilities, 406

Stanley E. Jackson Scholarship Award for Ethnic Minority Students., 406

Stanley E. Jackson Scholarship Award for Gifted/Talented Students with Disabilities, 406

Tourism Foundation Yellow Ribbon Scholarship, 519

U.S. Department of Vocational Rehabilitation Scholarship, 231

Venture Clubs of America Student Aid Award, 608

Virginia Rehabilitative Services College Scholarship, 239

Visually impaired

Adult Undergraduate Incentive Award, 452

American Action Fund Scholarship, 483

*American Speech-Language-Hearing Student with Disability Scholarship, 347

Arthur E. Copeland Scholarship for Males, 607

Christian Record Services Scholarship, 380

College-Bound Incentive Award, 453

Computer Science Scholarship, 484

Delta Gamma Memorial Scholarship, 273

E.U. Parker Memorial Scholarship, 484

Educator of Tomorrow Award, 484

Elks Undergraduate Disabled Student Scholarship, 376

Federation of the Blind Humanities Scholarship, 484

Ferdinand Torres AFB Scholarship, 273

Florida Educational Assistance for the Blind, 76

Floyd Qualls Memorial Scholarship, 271

Frank Walton Horn Memorial Scholarship, 484

Frederick A. Downes Scholarship, 273

Gladys C. Anderson Memorial Scholarship, 274

Governor's Commission on People with Disabilities Scholarship Fund, 415

Helen Copeland Scholarship for Females, 607

Hermione Grant Calhoun Scholarship, 484

Howard Brown Rickard Scholarship, 484

*Graduate/nondegree study

1

Disabilities: Visually impaired

*Karen D. Carsel Memorial Scholarhip, 274
Kucher-Killian Scholarship, 485
Lazaroff Family Fund, 443
*Lighthouse Graduate Incentive Award, 453
Lighthouse Undergraduate Incentive Award, 453
Louisiana Social Services Rehabilitation/Vocational Aid For Disabled Persons, 128
Marion Huber Learning Through Listening Award, 732
*Mary P. Oenslager Scholastic Achievement Award, 732
Melva T. Owen Memorial Scholarship, 485
Mozelle Willard Gold Scholarship, 485
National Federation of the Blind Scholarship, 485
New York State Readers Aid Program, 188
R.L. Gillette Scholarship, 274
Rudolph Dillman Memorial Scholarship, 274
Rudolph Dillman Memorial Scholarship Based on Need, 274
Scholarship for People with Disabilities, 386
Scholastic Achievement Award, 732
Texas Tuition Exemption for Blind and Deaf Students, 226
Tourism Foundation Yellow Ribbon Scholarship, 519
Virginia Assistance for the Visually Handicapped, 238
Wisconsin Visual and Hearing Impaired Program, 244

Field of Study/Intended Career

Agricultural science, business, and natural resources conservation

1890 National Scholars Program, 228
A.T. Anderson Memorial Scholarship, 636
A.W. Bodine Memorial Scholarship, 595
Abbie Sargent Memorial Scholarship, 247
Aboriculture Internship, 469
Alaska Brindle Memorial Scholarship Loan, 257
*Alexander Hollaender Distinguished Postdoctoral Fellowship, 197
Alpine Club A.K. Gilkey and Putnam/Bedayn Research Grant, 259

American Academic Sanitarians Scholarship, 483
*American Indian Fellowship for Environmental Professionals, 597
Anne Seaman Memorial Scholarship, 553
Arnell BJUGSTAD Scholarship, 220
Barbara Carlson Scholarship, 363
Bok Tower Gardens Internship, 369
California Farm Bureau Scholarship, 374
Carl F. Dietz Memorial Scholarship, 364
*Catherine Beattie Fellowship, 410
Class Fund Scholarship Ornamental Horticulture Program, 450
*Conservation Internship, 520
Dairy Management Milking Marketing Scholarship, 482
Dairy Shrine Graduate Student Scholarship, 483
Dairy Shrine Student Recognition Scholarship, 483
Dosatron International Scholarship, 364
Earl J. Small Growers Scholarship, 364
Ed Markham International Scholarship, 364
EED Scholarship Program, 357
Eight-Month Gardener Internship, 529
Enology and Viticulture Scholarship, 339
Filoli Center Garden Internship, 404
Fran Johnson Non-traditional Scholarship, 364
Friends of the National Zoo Research Traineeships, 410
Garden Club of America Summer Environmental Awards, 411
*Garden in the Woods Horticultural Internship, 522
*Geography Research Grants, 489
*Gilbert F. White Postdoctoral Fellowship, 560
Grange Denise Scholarship, 720
Gulf Coast Research Laboratory Minority Summer Grant, 140
Harness Horse Youth Scholarship, 418
Harold Bettinger Memorial Scholarship, 365
Hopi Tribal Priority Scholarship, 428
*International Graduate Student Fellowship, 321
*J. Carew Memorial Scholarship, 365
J.K. Rathmell, Jr., Memorial for Work/Study Abroad, 365
Jacob Van Namen/Vans Marketing Scholarship, 365
Jane Demaree Internship, 549
Jerry Baker Scholarship, 365
Jerry Wilmot Scholarship, 366
*Joseph L. Fisher Dissertation Award, 560

Katherine M. Grosscup Scholarship, 411
Limouselle Scholarship, 723
Limousin Award of Excellence, 723
*Lindbergh Foundation Grant, 378
Loon Fund Grant Program, 528
Louisiana Rockefeller Wildlife Scholarship, 129
Maine Rural Rehabilitation Fund Scholarship, 221
Marshall E. McCullough Undergraduate Scholarship, 483
Martin McLaren-Interchange Fellowship in Horticulture and Landscape Design, 411
Masonic Range Science Scholarship, 583
*Meteorological Society Industry Graduate Fellowship, 320
Meteorological Society Industry Undergraduate Scholarship, 320
Meteorological Society Minority Scholarship, 320
Meteorological Society Undergraduate Scholarship, 320
Morris Arboretum Education Internship, 469
Morris Arboretum Horticulture Internship, 469
*NASA Space Grant Arizona Graduate Fellowship, 148
*NASA Space Grant Pennsylvania Graduate Fellowship, 167
*NASA Space Grant South Carolina Graduate Fellowship, 170
NASA Space Grant South Carolina Undergraduate Academic Year Research Program, 170
NASA Space Grant South Carolina Undergraduate Research Summer Scholarship, 170
NASA Space Grant South Carolina Undergraduate Scholarship Program, 170
National Future Farmers of America Scholarship Program, 716
*National Science Foundation Minority Postdoctoral Fellowship, 180
*National Science Foundation Postdoctoral Research Fellowship, 180
*Nicaragua: Full Grant (Fulbright), 100
*NNEMS Graduate Fellowship, 179
NNEMS Undergraduate Fellowship, 179
North Carolina Botanical Garden Internship Program, 192
*Oak Ridge Institute for Science and Education Magnetic Fusion Science Fellowship, 199
*Oak Ridge Institute for Science and Education Oak Ridge National Laboratory Postdoctoral Research, 200

*Graduate/nondegree study

Oak Ridge Institute for Science and Education Office of Biological and Environmental Research Historically Black Colleges and Universities Student Research Participation, 201
*Oak Ridge Institute for Science and Education Postgraduate Environmental Management Participation at the U.S. Army Environmental Center, 202
*Oak Ridge Institute for Science and Education Postgraduate Internship at the Office of Ground Water and Drinking Water, 202
*Oak Ridge Institute for Science and Education Postgraduate Internship at the U.S. Army Center for Health Promotion and Preventive Medicine, 202
*Oak Ridge Institute for Science and Education Postgraduate Research at the Centers for Disease Control and Prevention, 203
*Oak Ridge Institute for Science and Education Postgraduate Research at the National Exposure Research Laboratory, 204
*Oak Ridge Institute for Science and Education Postgraduate Research at the National Risk Management Research Laboratory, 204
*Oak Ridge Institute for Science and Education Postgraduate Research at the Oak Ridge National Laboratory, 204
*Oak Ridge Institute for Science and Education Postgraduate Research at the St. Louis District, U.S. Army Corps of Engineers, 205
*Oak Ridge Institute for Science and Education Postgraduate Research at the U.S. Army Aviation and Troop Command, 205
*Oak Ridge Institute for Science and Education Postgraduate Research at the U.S. Army Construction Engineering Research Laboratory, 205
*Oak Ridge Institute for Science and Education Postgraduate Research at the U.S. Army Depot, Anniston, 205
*Oak Ridge Institute for Science and Education Postgraduate Research at the U.S. Army Directorate of Environment-Fort McClellan, 205
*Oak Ridge Institute for Science and Education Postgraduate Research at the U.S. Army Edgewood Research, 206
*Oak Ridge Institute for Science and Education Postgraduate Research at the U.S. Army Garrison, Aberdeen, 206

Oak Ridge Institute for Science and Education Professional Internship Program at Federal Energy Technology Centers, 532
Oak Ridge Institute for Science and Education Professional Internship Program at the Oak Ridge National Laboratory, 207
Oak Ridge Institute for Science and Education Professional Internship Program at the Savannah River Site, 207
Oak Ridge Institute For Science and Education Student Environmental Management Participation for the U.S. Army Environmental Center, 208
Oak Ridge Institute for Science and Education Student Internship at the U.S. Army Center for Health Promotion and Preventive Medicine, 208
Oak Ridge Institute for Science and Education Student Research at the Agency for Toxic Substances and Disease Registry, 208
Oak Ridge Institute for Science and Education Student Research at the U.S. Army Aviation and Troop Command, 208
Oak Ridge Institute for Science and Education Student Research at the U.S. Army Environmental Policy Institute, 209
Oak Ridge Institute for Science and Education Student Research at the U.S. Army Garrison, Directorate of Safety, Health and the Environment, 209
Oak Ridge Institute for Science and Education Student Research Participation at the Centers for Disease Control and Prevention, 209
Oak Ridge Institute for Science and Education Student Research Participation at the U.S. Army Aviation and Troop Command, 210
Oak Ridge Institute for Science and Education Student Research Participation at the U.S. Army Edgewood Research, Development and Engineering Center, 210
Oak Ridge Institute for Science and Education U.S. Department of Energy/NAACP, 210
Oak Ridge Institute for Science and Education U.S. Geological Survey Earth Sciences Internship, 211
Oak Ridge Institute for Science and Education University Coal Research Internship, 211
*Orchid Research Grant, 328
Piancone Family Agriculture Scholarship, 500

Plant Propagation Internship, 469
Plant Protection Internship, 470
Procter-Channin Scholarship, 618
*Renew America Internship, 559
*Rob and Bessie Welder Wildlife Foundation Scholarship, 560
Rodolf Steiner Visiting Students Program, 561
Smithsonian Environmental Research Work/Learn Program, 218
*Soil and Water Conservation Research Scholarship, 745
Soil and Water Conservation Student Leader Scholarship, 746
Soil Conservation Scholarship, 746
Southface Internship, 590
Three-Month Gardener Internship, 529
Timothy Bigelow Scholarship, 429
*Trent R. Dames and William W. Moore Fellowship, 651
Tropical Garden Summer Internship, 403
Truman D. Picard Scholarship, 439
U.S. National Arboretum Internship, 601
United States EPA Tribal Lands Environmental Science Scholarship, 58
Upjohn Company Internship, 608
Urban and Community Forestry Internship, 470
*Van Schaik Dressage Scholarship, 320
Vocational Horticulture Scholarship, 366
Walt Disney World Horticulture Summer Internship, 610
Water Companies (NJ Chapter) Scholarship, 479
Yosemite National Park Internships, 245

Architecture and design

Aboriculture Internship, 469
*Aila/Yamagami/Hope Fellowship, 449
Air Force Four-Year Scholarships(Types # 1,2 and Targeted), 217
*American Academy in Rome/Rome Prize Fellowships in the School of Fine Arts, 57
American Institute of Architects Fellowship in Health Facilities Design, 282
American Institute of Architects for Professional Degree Candidates, 282
American Institute of Architects Minority/Disadvantaged Scholarship, 283
American Institute of Architects Scholarship, 523
*American Institute of Architects Scholarship for Advanced Study and Research, 283

*Graduate/nondegree study

Field of Study/Intended Career: Architecture and design

American Institute of Architects The RTKL Traveling Fellowship, 283
*American Schools of Oriental Research/Samuel H. Kress Fellowships, 335
*American Society Interior Designers Education Foundation/Dora Brahms Award, 342
*Architectural Study Tour Scholarship, 579
*Asian Humanities Fellowship Program, 356
Bechtel Corporation Summer Intern Program, 363
Black & Veatch Summer Internship in Engineering, Construction, and Architecture, 368
Bok Tower Gardens Internship, 369
Class Fund Internship Program, 449
Class Fund Scholarships, 450
Connecticut Building Congress Scholarship, 384
Cooperative Education Program, 363
David T. Woolsey Scholarship, 450
*Dora Brahms Interior Design Award, 342
*Edilia and Francois-Auguste de Montequin Fellowship, 579
Edith H. Henderson Scholarship, 450
Edward D. Stone, Jr., and Associates Minority Scholarship, 450
Eight-Month Gardener Internship, 529
Essay Contest, 414
Filoli Center Garden Internship, 404
Frank Walton Horn Memorial Scholarship, 484
*Fulbright Program/USIA - U.K. Calvin Klein/Harvey Nichols Award in Fashion, 410
*Gabriel Prize, 370
Gensler and Associates Intern Program, 412
Gianni Versace Scholarship in Fashion Design, 494
Golf Course Superintendents Association Scholars Program, 414
*Grant for Research in Venice, 413
Harriett Barnhart Wimmer Scholarship, 450
Howard Brown Rickard Scholarship, 484
J. Paul Getty Trust Internship Program, 440
J.K. Rathmell, Jr., Memorial for Work/Study Abroad, 365
Jane Demaree Internship, 549
Jerry Baker Scholarship, 365
*Kappa Omicrom Nu Fellowships and Grants, 698
*Lemmermann Scholarship, 451
*Mabelle Wilhelmina Boldt Interior Design Scholarship, 342

Martin McLaren-Interchange Fellowship in Horticulture and Landscape Design, 411
New Jersey Scholarship Foundation, 283
North East Roofing Contractors Association Scholarship, 716
Polsky-Fixtures Furniture Award, 342
*Polsky-Fixtures Furniture Prize, 343
Procter-Channin Scholarship, 618
Rain Bird Company Scholarship, 450
Raymond E. Page Scholarship, 451
*Rosann S. Berry Annual Meeting Fellowship, 580
ROTC/ Air Force Three-Year Scholarships Types 2 And Targeted, 217
*Rotch Traveling Scholarship, 370
S. Harris Memorial Interior Design Scholarship, 343
*Sally Kress Tompkins Fellowship, 580
*Samuel H. Kreiss/Alisa Mellon Bruce Paired Fellowship, 489
*Science and Technology Fellowship, 264
Scotts Company Scholars Program, 415
*Senior Fellowship Program, 489
Southface Internship, 590
*SSRC Dissertation Fellowship: South Asia, 576
Theodore Mazza Scholarship, 602
Thomas P. Papandrew Scholarship, 451
Three-Month Gardener Internship, 529
Timothy Bigelow Scholarship, 429
Urban and Community Forestry Internship, 470
Valderrama Award, 415
Walt Disney World Horticulture Summer Internship, 610
*Watson Fellowships, 415
William J. Locklin Scholarship, 451
*Winterthur Fellowship, 417
Women in Architecture Scholarship, 359
Yale R. Burge Interior Design Competition, 343

Area and ethnic studies

*Advanced Research Grants: Japan, 571
American Association of Japanese University Women Scholarship, 262
*American Schools of Oriental Research/Annual Professorship, 334
American Schools of Oriental Research/Endowment for Biblical Research and Travel Grant, 335
*American Schools of Oriental Research/Harrell Family Fellowship, 335

American Schools of Oriental Research/Jennifer C. Groot Fellowship, 335
*American Schools of Oriental Research/Kenneth W. Russell Fellowship, 267
*American Schools of Oriental Research/National Endowment for the Humanities Fellowship, 335
*American Schools of Oriental Research/United States Information Agency Fellowship, 336
Asia-Pacific Undergraduate Scholarship, 434
*Asian Language Fellowship, 369
Biblical Research Travel Grant, 336
Blossom Kalama Evans Memorial Scholarship, 419
*Council of Jewish Federations Scholarship, 385
*David Baumgardt Memorial Fellowship, 451
*Deutscher Akademischer Austausch Dienst Fellowship, 452
*Deutscher Akademischer Austausch Dienst Fellowship/Germany, 452
*Doctoral Dissertation Fellowship in Jewish Studies, 486
*Eastern Europe Postdoctorate Fellowship, 270
*Ethel Marcus Memorial Fellowship in American Jewish Studies, 285
*Fritz Halbers Fellowship, 452
*George A. Barton Fellowship, 267
*Helen M. Woodruff Fellowship, 352
*International Educational Exchange Graduate Scholarship/Russia, 68
International Educational Exchange Scholarship/China, 68
King Olav V Norwegian-American Heritage Fund, 589
Latino Summer Legislative Internship, 478
Lazaroff Family Fund, 443
*Lowenstein-Wiener Fellowship in American Jewish Studies, 285
Marguerite R. Jacobs Memorial Award in American Jewish Studies, 286
*Near and Middle East Research and Training Act Senior Post-Doctoral Research Grant, 336
*Postdoctoral Fellowship: Middle East, 574
*Predissertation Fellowship: Bangladesh, 574
*Predissertation Fellowship: Near-Middle East, 574
*Predissertation Fellowship: South Asia, 575
*Rabbi Frederic A. Doppelt Memorial Fellowship in American Jewish Studies, 286

*Graduate/nondegree study

Field of Study/Intended Career: Arts, visual and performing

* Rabbi Levi A. Olan Memorial Fellowship in American Jewish Studies, 286
* Rapoport Fellowships in American Jewish Studies, 286
Rose Basile Green Scholarship, 501
Smithsonian Native American Internship, 570
* SSRC Dissertation Fellowship: Eurasia, 576
* SSRC Dissertation Fellowship: Middle East, 576
* Starkoff Fellowship in American Jewish Studies, 286
* Study in Scandinavia Grant, 351
* Syria: Government Grant (Fulbright), 107
United States Holocaust Memorial Museum Internship, 232
* Vincent and Anna Visceglia Fellowship, 503

Arts, visual and performing

* Abe Schechter Graduate Scholarship, 555
Academy of Television Arts and Sciences Summer Student Internship, 247
Alabama Junior/Community College Performing Arts Scholarship, 55
Allen Lee Hughes Fellows Program, 353
* Allen Lee Hughes Internship, 353
* American Academy in Rome/Rome Prize Fellowships in the School of Fine Arts, 57
* American Academy in Rome/Rome Prize Pre- and Post-Doctoral Fellowship, 57
* American Art Dissertation Fellowship, 270
American Conservatory Theater Production Internships, 269
American Legion Maryland Auxiliary Scholarship, 297
American Legion Washington Auxiliary Florence Lemcke Fine Arts Scholarship, 312
* American Numismatic Society Frances M. Schwartz Fellowship, 326
American Numismatic Society Shaykh Hamad Fellowship in Islamic Numismatics, 326
* American Pen Women Award: Arts, 505
* American Pen Women Award: Music, 505
* American Schools of Oriental Research/Samuel H. Kress Fellowships, 335
* Andrew Mellon Fellowship, 487

* Andrew W. Mellon Conservation Fellowship, 462
* Andrew W. Mellon Fellowship, 463
Anna K. Meredith Fund Scholarship, 434
* Anne and Oliver C. Colburn Fellowship, 351
Artistic Internships, 269
Arts Recognition and Talent Search, 485
* Asian Art and Religion Fellowship Program, 356
* Asian Humanities Fellowship Program, 356
Association for Women in Communications Scholarship, 359
* Austrian Cultural Institute Fine Arts and Music Grant, 362
Broadcast Education Association Scholarship, 371
Broadcast News Pioneers Undergraduate Scholarships, 555
* Carillon Fellowship, 369
* Carmargo Foundation Fellowship, 376
Carole Fielding Video Grant, 607
Carole Simpson Scholarship, 555
Ceramic Manufacturers Scholarship, 377
* Charles E. Culpeper Art Internship, 487
* Chester Dale Fellowship, 463
* Chester Dale Fellowship, 487
* Chesterfield Writers Film Project, 379
Clare Brett Smith Scholarship, 434
* Classical Art Fellowship, 463
Cloisters Summer Internship for College Students, 463
Coca-Cola Internship, 509
Critical Studies Program, 613
Curatorial Program, 613
* David Finley Fellowship, 487
Dorice & Clarence Glick Classical Music Scholarship, 420
Ed Bradley Scholarship, 556
Elizabeth Dow Internship Program, 398
Elizabeth Greenshields Grant, 399
Employee Communication Internship, 391
Environmental and Science Reporting Fellowship, 556
ESPN Internship, 402
* Fellowship Grants to Asian Individuals, 356
Fisher Broadcasting Minority Scholarship, 405
Franklin D. Roosevelt Library/ Roosevelt Internship, 408
Geller Fellowship, 556
Gensler and Associates Intern Program, 412
* Getty Postdoctoral Fellowship, 413
* Gillian Award, 434

Gladys C. Anderson Memorial Scholarship, 274
* Grant for Research in Venice, 413
Grants-In-Aid for Research on the Roosevelt Years, 408
Guggenheim Foundation Internship, 588
Guggenheim Museum Internship, 588
* H.J. Swinney Internship, 594
* Hagley Museum and Library Grant-In-Aid, 417
* Harriet and Leon Pomerance Fellowship, 352
Hearst Journalism Award, 614
* Helen M. Woodruff Fellowship, 352
* Huntington Fellowship, 430
* Huntington National Endowment for the Humanities Fellowship, 431
* Huntington W.M. Keck Foundation Fellowship for Young Scholars, 431
Inroads Internship, 432
* Institut Francais de Washington Fellowship, 432
International Furnishings and Design Student Member Scholarship, 695
International Incentive Award, 434
* Italy: Miguel Vinciguerra Fund Grant (Fulbright), 93
* Ittleson Fellowship, 488
J. Paul Getty Trust Internship Program, 440
Jacque Minotte Health Reporting Fellowship, 556
* Jane and Morgan Whitney Fellowship, 463
* Japan-United States Arts Program, 356
John F. Kennedy Center Performing Arts Internship, 443
KCACTF/ Barbizon Awards for Theatrical Design Excellence, 443
KCACTF/ ChildrenÖs Theatre Foundation Award, 443
KCACTF/ Fourth Freedom Forum Playwriting Award, 443
KCACTF/ Irene Ryan Acting Scholarships, 444
KCACTF/ Lorraine Hansberry Playwriting Award, 444
KCACTF/ Musical Theater Award, 444
KCACTF/ National AIDS Fund/ CFDA - Vogue Initiative Award for Playwriting, 444
KCACTF/ National Student Playwriting Award, 444
KCACTF/ Short Play Awards Program, 445
KCACTF/ Short Play Awards Program, 445
* Kenan T. Erim Award, 352
KIMT Weather/News Internship, 447
* Kreiss Art History and Archaeology Fellowship, 333

*Graduate/nondegree study

Field of Study/Intended Career: Arts, visual and performing

* Kress Travel Fellowship, 563
* Kress Two-Year Research Fellowship at Foreign Institutions, 563
* Kurt Weill Foundation Dissertation Fellowships, 449
Lebovitz Internship, 509
Leiber and Stoller Scholarship, 355
* Lemmermann Scholarship, 451
Len Allen Award of Merit, 557
* Lester J. Cappon Fellowship in Documentary Editing, 525
Louis J. Salerno, M.D. Memorial Scholarship, 496
Marc A. Klein Playwriting Award, 377
* Mary Davis Fellowship, 488
Melon Minority Fellowship Program, 573
* Metropolitan Museum of Art Graduate Lecturing Internship, 463
* Metropolitan Museum of Art Nine-Month Art Internship, 464
Metropolitan Museum of Art Six-Month Art Internship, 464
Metropolitan Museum of Art Summer Art Internships for College Students, 464
* Metropolitan Museum of Art Summer Art Internships for Graduate Students, 464
Michelle Clark Fellowship, 557
* Morton Gould Young Composers Award, 355
* Mother Jones Art Internship, 470
Mother Jones MoJo Wire Internship, 470
Museum Internships in Washington DC, 510
Museum of Modern Art Internship Program, 471
Music Assistance Fund, 348
* NASA Space Grant South Carolina Graduate Fellowship, 170
NASA Space Grant South Carolina Undergraduate Academic Year Research Program, 170
NASA Space Grant South Carolina Undergraduate Research Summer Scholarship, 170
NASA Space Grant South Carolina Undergraduate Scholarship Program, 170
* National Art Gallery Diversity Internship Program, 476
* National Art Gallery Graduate Lecturing Fellowships, 476
* National Endowment for the Humanities Fellowship, 526
National Scholarship Trust Fund of the Graphic Arts, 513
* National Scholarship Trust Fund of the Graphic Arts Graduate Fellowships, 513

National Scholarship Trust Fund of the Graphic Arts Undergraduate Scholarships, 513
Nerone/NIAF Matching Art Scholarship, 497
New Dramatists Internship, 522
New England Graphic Arts Scholarship, 522
New Stage Theatre Internship, 524
Norfolk Chamber Music Festival Summer Fellowship Program, 527
Norfolk Chamber Music Festival Summer Internship Program, 527
* Numismatic Graduate Fellowship, 327
* Numismatic Graduate Seminar, 327
Oldfield National Security Reporter Fellowship, 557
* Olivia James Traveling Fellowship, 352
Oregon Broadcast Journalism Scholarship, 538
* Paul Mellon Fellowship, 488
Pavarotti Scholarship, 499
Peggy Guggenheim Internship, 588
Performing Arts Showcase 1999, 685
PGH Foundation Scholarship, 424
Playhouse on the Square Internship, 549
* Polaire Weissman Fund Fellowship, 464
* Postdoctoral Fellowship: Middle East, 574
* Predoctoral Clearinghouse Application Fee Waiver, 382
Presidential Memorial Scholarship, 557
Princess Grace Award, 552
R.L. Gillette Scholarship, 274
* Radio-Television News Capitol Hill News Internship, 557
Raychem Internship, 558
* Research and Travel Grants, 449
* Research Center in Egypt Fellowship, 59
* Robert and Clarice Smith Fellowship, 488
RTNDF Minority News Management Internship, 558
* S. Clawson Mills Scholarship, 465
* Sammy Cahn Award, 356
* Samuel H. Kreiss/Alisa Mellon Bruce Paired Fellowship, 489
Santavicca Scholarship, 501
Sculpture Society Scholarship, 514
* Senior Fellowship Program, 489
Sergio Franchi Music Scholarship/ Voice Performance, 502
Sherlee Barish Fellowship, 558
* Short-Term Resident Fellowship for Individual Research, 526
* Smithsonian Graduate Student Fellowship, 570
Smithsonian Minority Internship, 570

* Smithsonian Post-Doctoral Fellowship, 571
* Smithsonian Pre-Doctoral Fellowship, 571
* Smithsonian Senior Fellowship, 571
* South Central Modern Language Association Fellowship, 720
Southern Progress Corporation Summer Internship, 590
Spoleto Festival Production Internship, 593
* Starr Asian Painting Conservation Fellowship, 465
Studio Program, 613
* Study in Scandinavia Grant, 351
Technical Communication Scholarship Program, 577
Theodore Mazza Scholarship, 602
* Theodore Rousseau Fellowship, 465
Thomas Joseph Ambrosole Scholarship, 503
Unitarian Universalist Stanfield Art Scholarship, 602
United States Holocaust Memorial Museum Internship, 232
United States Information Agency Summer Internship, 232
Vincente Minelli Scholarship, 504
Virgin Islands Music Scholarship, 237
Virginia Museum of Fine Arts Fellowship, 609
* Weiss Brown Publication Subvention Award, 527
* Winterthur Fellowship, 417
Wolf Trap Performing Arts Internship, 615
* Wyeth Fellowship, 489
Young Composers Award, 490
Youth Entertainment Summer, 618

Biological and physical sciences

1890 National Scholars Program, 228
A.T. Anderson Memorial Scholarship, 636
Aboriculture Internship, 469
* Aerospace Graduate Research Fellowship Program, 172
Aerospace Undergraduate Scholarship Program, 173
* AFOSR Summer Research Program, 53
Aging Research Scholarship, 272
Air Force Four-Year Scholarships(Types # 1,2 and Targeted), 217
* Alexander Hollaender Distinguished Postdoctoral Fellowship, 197
* Alfred P. Sloan Foundation Fellowship in Molecular Evolution, 179
Alpine Club A.K. Gilkey and Putnam/ Bedayn Research Grant, 259

*Graduate/nondegree study

Field of Study/Intended Career: Biological and physical sciences

* American Association for the Advancement of Science Royer Revelle Fellowship in Global Stewardship, 261
American Electroplaters and Surface Finishers Society Scholarship, 272
* American Heart Association Grant-In-Aid, 278
* American Heart Association Predoctoral Fellowship, 279
American Heart Association Student Research Program, 279
American Legion Maryland Auxiliary Scholarship, 297
American Legion Maryland Science/Math Scholarship, 296
* American Museum of Natural History Graduate Student Fellowship Program, 321
* American Museum of Natural History Research Fellowships, 321
American Nuclear Society Environmental Sciences Division Scholarship, 322
American Physical Society Minorities Scholarship, 329
Amtrol Ground Water Research Scholarship, 277
Angelo S. Biseti Scholarship, 323
* Anne S. Chatham Fellowship in Medicinal Botany, 410
* Applied Health Physics Fellowship, 197
Arkansas Emergency Secondary Education Loan, 61
* Armed Forces Educational Foundation Fellowship, 353
Arthur and Doreen Parrett Scholarship, 355
* Atmospheric Research Graduate Fellowship, 177
Atmospheric Science Internship, 251
Barry M. Goldwater Scholarship, 62
* Basil O'Connor Starter Scholar Research Award, 459
BF Goodrich Collegiate Inventors Program, 363
Bluebird Research Grant, 528
Bok Tower Gardens Internship, 369
Burlington Northern Santa Fe Foundation Scholarship, 637
Career Advancement Scholarship, 372
Centenary Scholarship, 435
Chemical Society Minority Scholarship, 267
* Churchill Scholarship, 615
* CIC/GE Predoctoral Fellowship, 382
* Collection Study Grants, 321
Community College Scholarship Program, 173
Community College Transfer Scholarships, 173
Delayed Education Scholarship for Women, 323

Eastman Kodak Student Program, 395
* Edgar Pam Fellowship, 435
EED Scholarship Program, 357
Eight-Month Gardener Internship, 529
* Electrochemical Society Summer Fellowship, 397
Enology and Viticulture Scholarship, 339
Entomological Society Undergraduate Scholarship, 401
* Everitt P. Blizard Scholarship, 323
* Exploration Fund, 403
Explorers Club Youth Activity Fund, 403
F.M. Becket Summer Research Award, 397
F.M. Peacock Native Bird Habitat Scholarship, 411
Filoli Center Garden Internship, 404
* Florida Education Fund McKnight Doctoral Fellowship, 405
* Ford Foundation Dissertation Fellowship: Minorities, 510
* Ford Foundation Postdoctoral Fellowships for Minorities, 511
* Ford Foundation Predoctoral Fellowship: Minorities, 511
Fossil Energy Technology Internship, 197
* Frank M. Chapman Memorial Grants, 321
Fuel Cycle and Waste Management, 323
* Fulbright - USIA U.K. Zeneca Award, 87
* G. Vernon Hobson Bequest, 436
* Garden in the Woods Horticultural Internship, 522
* Gem Consortium Scholarship, 412
General Emmett Paige Scholarship, 353
General John A. Wickham Scholarship, 353
Geological Institute Minority Participation Program, 276
* Geological Society Research Grant, 413
* Gilbert F. White Postdoctoral Fellowship, 560
Grant Program for Physically Disabled Students in the Sciences, 407
Gulf Coast Research Laboratory Minority Summer Grant, 140
* H. Hughes Medical Institute Predoctoral Fellowship, 511
* Hagley Museum and Library Grant-In-Aid, 417
* Hertz Foundation Fellowship, 404
Hispanic Professional Engineers Educational Grant, 581
Horizons Foundation Scholarship, 429
* Horton Geophysical Research Grant, 276

Howard Brown Rickard Scholarship, 484
* Huntington Fellowship, 430
Inroads Internship, 432
Italian Cultural Society and NIAF Matching Scholarship, 495
* J. Carew Memorial Scholarship, 365
* James F. Schumar Scholarship, 323
James R. Vogt Scholarship, 323
* Jeppesen Meteorology Internship, 442
John and Muriel Landis Scholarship, 324
John R. Lamarsh Scholarship, 324
* John Randall Scholarship, 324
* Joseph L. Fisher Dissertation Award, 560
Joseph R. Dietrich Scholarship, 324
Kathleen S. Anderson Award, 459
Kathryn D. Sullivan Science and Engineering Undergraduate Fellowship, 169
KIMT Weather/News Internship, 447
* Lalor Postdoctoral Research Grants, 449
* Lerner-Gray Grants for Marine Research, 322
Loon Fund Grant Program, 528
* Louis Agassiz Fuertes Award, 614
* Louis N. and Arnold M. Katz Research Prize, 277
Louisiana Rockefeller Wildlife Scholarship, 129
* Luise Meyer-Schutzmeister Award, 360
* March of Dimes Request for Research Proposals, 459
* Margaret Morse Nice Award, 614
Maria Mitchell Internships for Astronomical Research, 460
Martin McLaren-Interchange Fellowship in Horticulture and Landscape Design, 411
Mass Media Science and Engineering Fellowship, 626
Massachusetts Biotechnology Scholars Program, 460
Melon Minority Fellowship Program, 573
Meteorological Society Father James B. MacElwane Annual Award, 319
* Meteorological Society Industry Graduate Fellowship, 320
Meteorological Society Industry Undergraduate Scholarship, 320
Meteorological Society Minority Scholarship, 320
Meteorological Society Undergraduate Scholarship, 320
Michigan Educational Opportunity Scholarship, 137
Microbiology Summer Research Fellowship for Minority Students, 339

*Graduate/nondegree study

Field of Study/Intended Career: Biological and physical sciences

Microscopy Presidential Student Award, 467
Microscopy Undergraduate Research Scholarship, 467
*Mining Club Award, 435
Mississippi Space Grant Consortium, 159
Morris Arboretum Education Internship, 469
*Myasthenia Gravis Foundation Kermit E. Osserman Fellowship, 471
Nancy Lorraine Jensen Memorial Scholarship, 746
NASA Academy Internship, 167
NASA Space Grant Alabama Graduate Fellowship, 146
NASA Space Grant Alabama Undergraduate Scholarship Program, 147
*NASA Space Grant Alaska Graduate Fellowship, 147
NASA Space Grant Alaska Undergraduate Scholarship, 147
*NASA Space Grant Arizona Graduate Fellowship, 148
NASA Space Grant Arizona Undergraduate Research Internship, 148
*NASA Space Grant Arkansas Graduate Fellowship, 148
NASA Space Grant Arkansas Undergraduate Scholarship, 148
*NASA Space Grant California Fellowship Program, 149
NASA Space Grant California Undergraduate Scholarship, 149
NASA Space Grant Colorado Graduate Fellowship, 149
NASA Space Grant Colorado Undergraduate Scholarship, 149
NASA Space Grant Connecticut Undergraduate Fellowship, 473
*NASA Space Grant Delaware Space Graduate Student Fellowship, 150
NASA Space Grant Delaware Undergraduate Summer Scholarship, 150
NASA Space Grant Delaware Undergraduate Tuition Scholarship, 150
NASA Space Grant District of Columbia Undergraduate Scholarship, 151
*NASA Space Grant District of Columbia Graduate Fellowship, 151
*NASA Space Grant Florida Fellowship Program, 151
*NASA Space Grant Florida Fellowship Program, 151
NASA Space Grant Florida Undergraduate Space Research Participation Program, 152
NASA Space Grant Georgia Fellowship Program, 152

*NASA Space Grant Hawaii Graduate Fellowship, 152
NASA Space Grant Hawaii Undergraduate Scholarship, 153
NASA Space Grant Hawaii Undergraduate Traineeship Program, 153
*NASA Space Grant Indiana Graduate Fellowship, 154
NASA Space Grant Indiana Summer Undergraduate Research Program, 154
NASA Space Grant Indiana Undergraduate Scholarship, 154
NASA Space Grant Kansas Graduate Fellowship, 155
NASA Space Grant Kansas Undergraduate Scholarship, 155
*NASA Space Grant Kentucky Graduate Fellowship, 155
NASA Space Grant Kentucky Undergraduate Scholarship, 156
NASA Space Grant Louisiana LaSPACE Graduate Fellowship Program, 156
NASA Space Grant Louisiana LaSPACE Undergraduate Scholarship Program, 156
*NASA Space Grant Maine Graduate Fellowship, 157
NASA Space Grant Maine Undergraduate Internship Award, 157
NASA Space Grant Maine Undergraduate Scholarship Program, 157
*NASA Space Grant Massachusetts Graduate Fellowships, 158
NASA Space Grant Massachusetts Summer Jobs for Students, 158
NASA Space Grant Massachusetts Undergraduate Research Opportunities, 158
*NASA Space Grant Michigan Graduate Fellowship, 158
NASA Space Grant Michigan Undergraduate Fellowship, 159
*NASA Space Grant Minnesota Graduate Fellowship, 159
NASA Space Grant Minnesota Internship Program, 159
NASA Space Grant Minnesota Undergraduate Scholarship, 159
*NASA Space Grant Missouri Summer Jobs for Students, 160
NASA Space Grant Missouri Summer Undergraduate Internship, 160
*NASA Space Grant Montana Graduate Fellowship, 160
NASA Space Grant Montana Undergraduate Scholarship Program, 160
*NASA Space Grant Nevada Graduate Fellowship, 161

NASA Space Grant Nevada Undergraduate Scholarship, 162
NASA Space Grant New Hampshire Undergraduate Scholarship, 162
*NASA Space Grant New Hampshire Graduate Fellowship, 162
NASA Space Grant New Jersey Undergraduate Summer Fellowship, 162
*NASA Space Grant New Mexico Graduate Fellowship, 163
NASA Space Grant New Mexico Undergraduate Scholarship, 163
NASA Space Grant New York Graduate Fellowship, 163
NASA Space Grant New York Undergraduate Internship, 163
*NASA Space Grant North Carolina Graduate Fellowship, 164
NASA Space Grant North Carolina Undergraduate Scholarship Program, 164
*NASA Space Grant North Dakota Graduate Fellowship, 164
NASA Space Grant North Dakota Undergraduate Scholarship, 164
*NASA Space Grant Oklahoma Space Grant Consortium Graduate Fellowship, 166
NASA Space Grant Oklahoma Undergraduate Scholarship, 166
*NASA Space Grant Oregon Graduate Fellowship, 166
NASA Space Grant Oregon Undergraduate Scholarship, 166
*NASA Space Grant Pennsylvania Graduate Fellowship, 167
NASA Space Grant Pennsylvania Undergraduate Scholarship, 167
*NASA Space Grant Puerto Rico Graduate Fellowship, 167
NASA Space Grant Puerto Rico Summer Internship Program, 168
NASA Space Grant Puerto Rico Undergraduate Scholarship, 168
*NASA Space Grant Rhode Island Graduate Fellowship, 168
NASA Space Grant Rhode Island Summer Undergraduate Scholarship Program, 168
NASA Space Grant Rhode Island Undergraduate Academic Year Scholarship Program, 169
NASA Space Grant Rocky Mountain Graduate Fellowship, 169
NASA Space Grant Rocky Mountain Undergraduate Scholarship, 169
*NASA Space Grant South Carolina Graduate Fellowship, 170
NASA Space Grant South Carolina Undergraduate Academic Year Research Program, 170

*Graduate/nondegree study

NASA Space Grant South Carolina Undergraduate Research Summer Scholarship, 170
NASA Space Grant South Carolina Undergraduate Scholarship Program, 170
*NASA Space Grant Tennessee Graduate Fellowship, 171
NASA Space Grant Tennessee Undergraduate Scholarship, 171
*NASA Space Grant Vermont Space Graduate Research Assistantship, 172
NASA Space Grant Vermont Undergraduate Scholarships, 172
*NASA Space Grant Washington Graduate Fellowships at the University of Washington, 174
NASA Space Grant Washington Undergraduate Scholarship Program, 174
*NASA Space Grant West Virginia Graduate Fellowship, 174
NASA Space Grant West Virginia Undergraduate Fellowship Scholarship, 175
NASA Space Grant West Virginia Undergraduate Scholarship, 175
*NASA Space Grant Wisconsin Graduate Fellowship, 175
NASA Space Grant Wisconsin Undergraduate Research Awards, 176
NASA Space Grant Wisconsin Undergraduate Scholarship, 176
*National Defense Science and Engineering Graduate Fellowship Program, 70
*National Science Foundation Graduate Fellowship, 179
*National Science Foundation Minority Graduate Fellowship, 180
*National Science Foundation Minority Postdoctoral Fellowship, 180
*National Science Foundation Postdoctoral Research Fellowship, 180
Native American Scholarship, 520
*Naval Architects and Marine Engineers Graduate Scholarship, 744
Naval Engineers Scholarship, 343
*Naval Research Laboratory - Postdoctoral Fellowship, 338
Network Internship or Summer Science Internship, 554
*New Jersey Minority Academic Career Program, 185
NIH Summer Internship Program, 178
NIH Undergraduate Scholarship Program, 178
*North American Bluebird Society General Research Grant, 528

North Carolina Botanical Garden Internship Program, 192
North Carolina Student Loans for Health/Science/Mathematics, 195
*Novartis Fellowship of the Immune Deficiency Foundation, 531
Nuclear Operations Division Scholarship, 324
Oak Ridge Institute for Science and Education Energy Research Undergraduate Laboratory Fellowship, 198
*Oak Ridge Institute for Science and Education Fossil Energy Postgraduate Research, 198
*Oak Ridge Institute for Science and Education Fusion Energy Postdoctoral Research, 198
Oak Ridge Institute for Science and Education Historically Black Building Technology Summer Research Participation, 199
Oak Ridge Institute for Science and Education Historically Black Colleges Nuclear Energy Training Program, 199
Oak Ridge Institute for Science and Education Historically Black Nuclear Energy Training Program, 199
*Oak Ridge Institute for Science and Education Magnetic Fusion Energy Technology Fellowship, 199
*Oak Ridge Institute for Science and Education Magnetic Fusion Science Fellowship, 199
Oak Ridge Institute for Science and Education National Oceanic and Atmospheric Administration Student Program, 200
*Oak Ridge Institute for Science and Education Nuclear Engineering Health Physics Fellowship, 200
*Oak Ridge Institute for Science and Education Oak Ridge National Laboratory Postdoctoral Research, 200
Oak Ridge Institute for Science and Education Office of Biological and Environmental Research Historically Black Colleges and Universities Student Research Participation, 201
Oak Ridge Institute for Science and Education Office of Civilian Radioactive Waste Management Historically Black Colleges and Universities Undergraduate Scholarship Program, 201
Oak Ridge Institute for Science and Education Office of Fossil Energy Historically Black Colleges and Universities Student Research Participation, 201

*Oak Ridge Institute for Science and Education Postgraduate Environmental Management Participation at the U.S. Army Environmental Center, 202
*Oak Ridge Institute for Science and Education Postgraduate Internship at the Office of Ground Water and Drinking Water, 202
*Oak Ridge Institute for Science and Education Postgraduate Internship at the U.S. Army Center for Health Promotion and Preventive Medicine, 202
*Oak Ridge Institute for Science and Education Postgraduate Research at the Agency for Toxic Substances and Disease Registry, 202
*Oak Ridge Institute for Science and Education Postgraduate Research at the Center for Biologics Evaluation and Research, 202
*Oak Ridge Institute for Science and Education Postgraduate Research at the Center for Devices and Radiological Health, 203
*Oak Ridge Institute for Science and Education Postgraduate Research at the Center for Drug Evaluation and Research, 203
*Oak Ridge Institute for Science and Education Postgraduate Research at the Centers for Disease Control and Prevention, 203
Oak Ridge Institute for Science and Education Postgraduate Research at the Department of Veterans Affairs, Birmingham Education Center, 203
*Oak Ridge Institute for Science and Education Postgraduate Research at the National Center for Toxicological Research, 204
*Oak Ridge Institute for Science and Education Postgraduate Research at the National Exposure Research Laboratory, 204
*Oak Ridge Institute for Science and Education Postgraduate Research at the National Risk Management Research Laboratory, 204
*Oak Ridge Institute for Science and Education Postgraduate Research at the Oak Ridge National Laboratory, 204
*Oak Ridge Institute for Science and Education Postgraduate Research at the Savanah River Site, 204
*Oak Ridge Institute for Science and Education Postgraduate Research at the St. Louis District, U.S. Army Corps of Engineers, 205

*Graduate/nondegree study

Field of Study/Intended Career: Biological and physical sciences

*Oak Ridge Institute for Science and Education Postgraduate Research at the U.S. Army Aviation and Troop Command, 205
*Oak Ridge Institute for Science and Education Postgraduate Research at the U.S. Army Construction Engineering Research Laboratory, 205
*Oak Ridge Institute for Science and Education Postgraduate Research at the U.S. Army Depot, Anniston, 205
*Oak Ridge Institute for Science and Education Postgraduate Research at the U.S. Army Directorate of Environment-Fort McClellan, 205
*Oak Ridge Institute for Science and Education Postgraduate Research at the U.S. Army Edgewood Research, 206
*Oak Ridge Institute for Science and Education Postgraduate Research at the U.S. Army Environmental Policy Institute, 206
*Oak Ridge Institute for Science and Education Postgraduate Research at the U.S. Army Garrison, Aberdeen, 206
*Oak Ridge Institute for Science and Education Postgraduate Research at the U.S. Army Medical Research Institute of Chemical Defense, 206
*Oak Ridge Institute for Science and Education Postgraduate Research at the U.S. Army National Guard Bureau, 207
*Oak Ridge Institute for Science and Education Postgraduate Research at the U.S. Navy Commander Fleet, Okinawa, 207
Oak Ridge Institute for Science and Education Professional Internship Program at Federal Energy Technology Centers, 532
Oak Ridge Institute for Science and Education Professional Internship Program at the Oak Ridge National Laboratory, 207
Oak Ridge Institute for Science and Education Professional Internship Program at the Savannah River Site, 207
Oak Ridge Institute For Science and Education Student Environmental Management Participation for the U.S. Army Environmental Center, 208
Oak Ridge Institute for Science and Education Student Internship at the U.S. Army Center for Health Promotion and Preventive Medicine, 208

Oak Ridge Institute for Science and Education Student Research at the Agency for Toxic Substances and Disease Registry, 208
Oak Ridge Institute for Science and Education Student Research at the U.S. Army Aviation and Troop Command, 208
Oak Ridge Institute for Science and Education Student Research at the U.S. Army Environmental Policy Institute, 209
Oak Ridge Institute for Science and Education Student Research at the U.S. Army Garrison, Directorate of Safety, Health and the Environment, 209
Oak Ridge Institute for Science and Education Student Research Participation at the Centers for Disease Control and Prevention, 209
Oak Ridge Institute for Science and Education Student Research Participation at the National Center for Toxicological Research, 209
Oak Ridge Institute for Science and Education Student Research Participation at the U.S. Army Aviation and Troop Command, 210
Oak Ridge Institute for Science and Education Student Research Participation at the U.S. Army Edgewood Research, Development and Engineering Center, 210
Oak Ridge Institute for Science and Education Student Research Participation at the U.S. Army Environmental Policy Institute, 210
Oak Ridge Institute for Science and Education U.S. Department of Energy/NAACP, 210
Oak Ridge Institute for Science and Education U.S. Geological Survey Earth Sciences Internship, 211
Oak Ridge Institute for Science and Education U.S. Nuclear Regulatory Commission Historically Black Colleges and Universities Student Research Participation, 211
Oak Ridge Institute for Science and Education University Coal Research Internship, 211
*Office of Naval Research - Postdoctoral Fellowship, 338
*Orchid Research Grant, 328
Oregon State Scholarship Commission/Howard Vollum American Indian Scholarship, 540
*Parenteral Research Grant, 544
Pathfinder Scholarship, 715
*Paul A. Greebler Scholarship, 324
Paul A. Stewart Award, 614
Pearl I. Young Scholarship, 165
*Pennsylvania Internship, 469

*Petroleum Geologists Grant-in-Aid, 263
*Pfizer Internships, 546
*Physical Science Graduate Fellowship: Minorities and Women, 510
Physics Students Leadership Scholarship, 744
Pittsburgh Local Section of the James R. Vogt Scholarship, 325
Plant Propagation Internship, 469
Plasma Physics National Undergraduate Fellowship Program, 216
Postdoctoral Fellowship in Nosocomial Infection Research and Training, 486
*Postdoctoral Microbiology Research Program, 339
Power Division Scholarship, 325
Raychem Internship, 558
Raymond DiSalvo Scholarship, 325
*Rennie Taylor/Alton Blakeslee Fellowship, 385
Research Experiences for Undergraduates, 322
Richard E. Merwin Award, 692
*Risk Assessment Science and Engineering Fellowships, 261
*Robert A. Dannels Scholarship, 325
*Robert D. Watkins Minority Graduate Fellowship, 651
Robert G. Lacey Scholarship, 325
Robert T. Liner Scholarship, 326
Rocky Mountain Coal Mining Scholarship, 561
ROTC Scholarships, 655
ROTC/ Air Force Three-Year Scholarships Types 2 And Targeted, 217
*Ruth Satter Memorial Award, 360
Schlumberger Internship, 564
Scholarships at Seattle Central Community College, 174
Scientific Research Grant-In-Aid, 569
*Scientific Study of Sexuality Student Grant, 579
Scripps Undergraduate Research Fellowship, 566
Smithsonian Environmental Research Work/Learn Program, 218
*Smithsonian Graduate Student Fellowship, 570
Smithsonian Minority Internship, 570
*Smithsonian Post-Doctoral Fellowship, 571
*Smithsonian Pre-Doctoral Fellowship, 571
*Smithsonian Senior Fellowship, 571
SOARS - Significant Opportunities in Atmospheric Research and Science, 233
Society of Exploration Geophysicists Scholarship, 581
*Stanley Elmore Fellowship Fund, 435

*Graduate/nondegree study

Field of Study/Intended Career: Business/management/administration

* Student Research Grant, 528
* Study in Scandinavia Grant, 351
* Syria: Government Grant (Fulbright), 107
Tandy Technology Students Award, 596
Teacher Education Scholarship Program, 173
* The GEM Consortium/Ph.D Science and Engineering Fellowship, 597
* Theodore Roosevelt Memorial Grants, 322
Three-Month Gardener Internship, 529
* Tropical Botany Award, 411
* U.S. Department of Energy Summer Research Fellowships, 398
U.S. National Arboretum Internship, 601
Undergraduate Microbiology Research Fellowship, 339
United States EPA Tribal Lands Environmental Science Scholarship, 58
Upjohn Company Internship, 608
Urban and Community Forestry Internship, 470
* Verne R. Dapp Scholarship, 326
Virginia Regional Contract Program, 238
Wal-Mart Competitive Edge Scholarship, 609
Walt Disney World Horticulture Summer Internship, 610
* Walter Meyer Scholarship, 326
Water Companies (NJ Chapter) Scholarship, 479
* Water Works Fellowship, 348
Weather Channel Meteorology Internship, 612
Willems Scholarship, 711
William and Dorothy Lanquist Foundation, 425
* Women in Science Education Research Grant, 360
Yosemite National Park Internships, 245

Business/management/administration

3M Internship, 247
* A.P. Giannini Scholarship, 491
A.T. Anderson Memorial Scholarship, 636
Actuarial Society Minority Scholarship, 579
Advertising/Public Relations Internship, 366
Alpha Beta Gamma International Scholarship, 625
American Express Card Scholarship Program, 280

* American Health Information Management Master's Program, 631
* American Institute of Certified Public Accountants' Minority Doctoral Fellowship, 284
American Legion California Auxiliary Department of Education Scholarship II, 289
American Legion Maryland Auxiliary Scholarship, 297
* Armenian Union U.S. Graduate Loan, 354
* Asian Language Fellowship, 369
* Aspen Systems Awards, 631
* Avis Rent-a-Car Travel Agents Scholarship, 345
Avon Products Foundation Career Empowerment Scholarship for Adult Women, 564
Barbara Thomas Enterprises Award, 632
Bechtel Corporation Summer Intern Program, 363
Bolla Wines Scholarship, 492
Burlington Northern Santa Fe Foundation Scholarship, 637
California Association of Realtors Scholarship, 374
CANFIT Program Undergraduate Scholarship, 374
* Certified Public Accountants' John L. Carey Scholarship, 284
Certified Public Accountants' Minorities Scholarship, 284
* Chartered Accountants Education Award Competition, 657
Coding Specialist Program Loan, 632
Colorado CPAs Ethnic Scholarship, 381
Colorado CPAs Ethnic-College and University Scholarship, 381
Colorado CPAs Gordon Scheer Scholarship, 381
Colorado CPAs High School Scholarship, 382
Colorado Society of CPAs Educational Foundation Scholarship, 382
Connecticut Building Congress Scholarship, 384
Construction Education and Research Scholarship, 481
Cooperative Education Program, 363
Cooperative Education Program, 62
Cooperative Education Program, 62
* Council of Jewish Federations Scholarship, 385
Curatorial Program, 613
Dairy Management Milking Marketing Scholarship, 482
Dairy Product Marketing Scholarship, 390
Deloitte And Touche Summer Internship Program, 392

* Doctoral Fellowship in Accounting, 392
Dolly Ching Scholarship Fund, 117
Duracell Internship Program, 393
Duracell/Gillette Minority Intern Scholarship, 520
Ecolah Scholarship Program, 280
Elizabeth Dow Internship Program, 398
Employee Communication Internship, 391
Ernst and Young Internship, 402
Executive Housekeepers Education Foundation Scholarship., 695
Executive Women International Scholarship, 403
Experiential Education Internship, 514
F.D. Stella Scholarship, 494
Federal Reserve Summer Internship, 71
Financial Women International Scholarship, 421
Fisher Broadcasting Minority Scholarship, 405
* Florida Education Fund McKnight Doctoral Fellowship, 405
Forbes Internship, 406
* FORE Graduate Scholarship, 632
* Fulbright - USIA U.K. Zeneca Award, 87
General Mills Internship Program, 412
George M. Brooker Collegiate Scholarship for Minorities, 435
Golf Course Superintendents Association Scholars Program, 414
GTE Internship Program, 416
Guggenheim Foundation Internship, 588
Guggenheim Museum Internship, 588
* H.J. Heinz Graduate Degree Fellowship, 512
* Hagley Museum and Library Grant-In-Aid, 417
Harold Bettinger Memorial Scholarship, 365
Harry Truman Scholarship, 117
Harwood Memorial Scholarship, 558
* Henry Belin DuPont Dissertation Fellowship, 417
HIM PROGRAM, 633
Hispanic Fund Scholarships, 491
HIT Program, 633
Hopi Tribal Priority Scholarship, 428
Horizons Foundation Scholarship, 429
Inroads Internship, 432
International Management Group Summer Intern Program, 436
* Investment Banking Internship, 549
J.W. Saxe Memorial Prize, 440
Jacob Van Namen/Vans Marketing Scholarship, 365
James A. Turner, Jr., Scholarship, 350
Jerry Wilmot Scholarship, 366

*Graduate/nondegree study

Field of Study/Intended Career: Business/management/administration

John F. Kennedy Center Performing Arts Internship, 443
*Juilliard Professional Intern Program, 446
Junior Achievement of Maine Scholarship, 447
*Kappa Omicrom Nu Fellowships and Grants, 698
Karla Scherer Foundation Scholarship, 447
Kemper Scholars Grant Program, 441
Latino Summer Legislative Internship, 478
Law/Social Sciences Summer Research Fellowship for Minority Undergraduates, 265
Lebovitz Internship, 509
*Lincoln Center for the Performing Arts Internships in Arts Administration, 454
Maine Innkeepers Association - Scholarships for Maine Residents, 705
Maine Innkeepers Association Affiliates Scholarship, 705
Merrill Lynch Scholarship, 496
Mexican American Grocers Association Scholarship, 465
*Mexico: Binational Business Grants (Fulbright), 98
*Miller Brewing Internship, 467
*Mississippi Public Management Graduate Internship, 143
Mobility Internship Program, 468
Mother Jones Publishing Internship, 470
Museum of Modern Art Internship Program, 471
NASA Space Grant Alabama Graduate Fellowship, 146
NASA Space Grant Alabama Undergraduate Scholarship Program, 147
National Association for Community Leadership, 476
National Organization for Women legal defense and Education fund Internships, 510
National Restaurant Association Undergraduate Scholarship, 512
National Scholarship Program, 712
National Society of Black Engineers/ GE African American Forum Scholarship, 718
National Space Society Internship Program, 515
Native American Scholarship, 520
Native Daughters of the Golden West Scholarship, 719
NBA Internship Program, 480
*NCAA Ethnic Minority Internship, 481
*NCAA Ethnic Minority Postgraduate Scholarship, 481

*NCAA Women's Enhancement Postgraduate Scholarship, 482
*NCAA Women's Internship, 482
Nerone/NIAF Matching Art Scholarship, 497
New Dramatists Internship, 522
*New York State Senate/Richard J. Ross Journalism Fellowship, 191
Norfolk Chamber Music Festival Summer Internship Program, 527
*North Carolina Community Arts Administrative Internship, 192
Octel Communications Internship, 532
Oregon Private 150 Scholarship, 539
*Peat Marwick Doctoral Scholarship Program, 448
PGA Minority Internship Program, 546
Plumbing, Heating, Cooling Contractors Education Foundation Scholarship, 478
Population Institute Internship, 550
*ProManagement Scholarship, 512
Public Accountants Scholarship, 514
Public Policy Internship Program, 460
Public Service Scholarship, 554
*Purchasing Management Doctoral Grant, 479
Raychem Internship, 558
*Robert L. Millender Sr. Memorial Fund Fellowship Program, 560
*Ron Brown Fellowship Program, 438
Russ Casey Scholarship, 458
Savvy Management Internship, 564
Schlumberger Internship, 564
Scotts Company Scholars Program, 415
*Sears-Roebuck Graduate Business Studies Loan Fund, 372
Secondary School Principals Leadership Award, 479
*Selected Professions Fellowship, 265
Service Merchandise Scholarship, 568
Sony Corporation of America Internship, 589
SONY Credited Internship, 590
Southern Progress Corporation Summer Internship, 590
Southface Internship, 590
Spoleto Festival Administrative Internship, 593
*St. Anthony Publishing Graduate Award, 633
*State Farm Companies Doctoral Disseration Award, 594
State Farm Companies Exceptional Student Fellowship, 594
*Teacher Work-Study Grant, 512
Texas Fifth-Year Accountancy Scholarship Program, 224
Think Automotive Scholarship, 362
Tourism Foundation Alabama-Birmingham Legacy, 517

Tourism Foundation California Scholarship, 517
Tourism Foundation Cleveland Legacy 1 Scholarship, 517
Tourism Foundation Cleveland Legacy 2 Scholarship, 517
Tourism Foundation Connecticut Scholarship, 517
Tourism Foundation Florida Scholarship, 517
Tourism Foundation Michigan Scholarship, 517
Tourism Foundation Montana Scholarship, 518
Tourism Foundation Nebraska-Lois Johnson Scholarship, 518
Tourism Foundation New Jersey 1 Scholarship, 518
Tourism Foundation New Jersey 2 Scholarship, 518
Tourism Foundation New York Scholarship, 518
Tourism Foundation North Carolina Scholarship, 518
Tourism Foundation Ohio Scholarship, 518
Tourism Foundation Quebec Scholarship, 518
Tourism Foundation Scholarship, 519
Tourism Foundation Tulsa Scholarship, 519
*Transcriptions Limited Graduate Scholarship, 634
U.S. Department of Commerce/Ron Brown Fellowship, 244
*United Kingdom: British-American Chamber of Commerce Award (Fulbright), 110
*United Kingdom: British-American Tobacco Industries Award (Fulbright), 110
*United Kingdom: Marks and Spencer Award (Fulbright), 111
Upjohn Company Internship, 608
USOC Student Intern Program, 607
Vennera Noto Scholarship, 503
Washington Crossing Foundation Scholarship, 611
Water Companies (NJ Chapter) Scholarship, 479
Wolf Trap Performing Arts Internship, 615
Women in Business Scholarship, 372
Women in Construction: Founders' Scholarship, 480
*Women's Research and Education Congressional Fellowship, 616
Woodrow Wilson Program in Public Policy and International Affairs, 618
Youth Entertainment Summer, 618

*Graduate/nondegree study

Communications

* Abe Schechter Graduate Scholarship, 555
Academy of Television Arts and Sciences Summer Student Internship, 247
Advertising Internship for Minority Students, 261
Advertising/Public Relations Internship, 366
American Legion New Jersey Press Club Scholarship, 645
American Legion New York Association Scholarship, 645
American Society of Magazine Editors Internship, 343
Archival Internships, 445
* Armenian Union U.S. Graduate Loan, 354
ARRL League Ph.D. Scholarship, 330
ARRL Mississippi Scholarship, 330
Associated Press/APTRA-CLETE Roberts Memorial Journalism Scholarship, 358
Association for Women in Communications Scholarship, 359
Black Journalists College Scholarship, 477
Black Journalists Summer Internship, 477
Black Journalists Sustaining Scholarship, 477
Bob Elliot - Channel 8 Journalism Scholarship, 615
* Boston Globe One-Year Internship, 369
Boston Globe Summer Internship, 370
Broadcast Education Association Scholarship, 371
Broadcast News Pioneers Undergraduate Scholarships, 555
Bucks County Courier Times Minority Internship, 371
* Carmargo Foundation Fellowship, 376
Carole Simpson Scholarship, 555
Center for Defense Information Internship, 377
* Charles E. Culpeper Art Internship, 487
Charles N. Fisher Memorial Scholarship, 331
Clarke Internship Program, 380
Coca-Cola Internship, 509
Communications Scholarship, 493
Dairy Product Marketing Scholarship, 390
* Dirksen Research Grant Program, 392
Dorothy Andrews Kabis Internship, 715
Dr. James L. Lawson Memorial Scholarship, 331
Duracell Internship Program, 393
Ed Bradley Scholarship, 556

Edward J. Nell Memorial Scholarship, 554
Employee Communication Internship, 391
Environmental and Science Reporting Fellowship, 556
ESPN Internship, 402
F. Charles Ruling N6FR Memorial Scholarship, 331
Fisher Broadcasting Minority Scholarship, 405
Food Service Communicators Scholarship, 436
Forbes Internship, 406
Fred R. McDaniel Memorial Scholarship, 331
Geller Fellowship, 556
General Mills Internship Program, 412
Harold K. Douthit Scholarship, 533
Hearst Journalism Award, 614
* Hoover Presidential Library Fellowship/Grant, 427
Indianapolis Newspapers Fellowship, 431
Inroads Internship, 432
Institute for Humane Studies Fellowship, 432
International Management Group Summer Intern Program, 436
Irving W. Cook WAOCGS Scholarship, 331
Irwin Scholarship Trust Fund, 422
J. Paul Getty Trust Internship Program, 440
Jacque Minotte Health Reporting Fellowship, 556
Joel Garcia Memorial Scholarship, 374
John F. Kennedy Center Performing Arts Internship, 443
John W. McDermott Scholarship, 423
KIMT Weather/News Internship, 447
L. Phil Wicker Scholarship, 332
L.M. Perryman Ethnic Minority Award, 606
Len Allen Award of Merit, 557
* Lester G. Benz Memorial College Journalism Scholarship, 555
Los Angeles Times Editorial Internships, 454
Mark Hass Journalism Scholarship, 538
Michelle Clark Fellowship, 557
* Mother Jones Editorial Internship, 470
Mother Jones MoJo Wire Internship, 470
Mother Jones Publishing Internship, 470
Museum Internships in Washington DC, 510
NASA Space Grant Alabama Graduate Fellowship, 146

NASA Space Grant Alabama Undergraduate Scholarship Program, 147
NASA Space Grant Delaware Undergraduate Tuition Scholarship, 150
* NASA Space Grant South Carolina Graduate Fellowship, 170
NASA Space Grant South Carolina Undergraduate Academic Year Research Program, 170
NASA Space Grant South Carolina Undergraduate Research Summer Scholarship, 170
NASA Space Grant South Carolina Undergraduate Scholarship Program, 170
National Association for Community Leadership, 476
National Journal Editorial Internship, 504
National Scholarship Trust Fund of the Graphic Arts, 513
* National Scholarship Trust Fund of the Graphic Arts Graduate Fellowships, 513
National Scholarship Trust Fund of the Graphic Arts Undergraduate Scholarships, 513
National Space Society Internship Program, 515
National Speakers Association Scholarship, 515
NCAA Freedom Forum Scholarship, 482
* Near and Middle East Research and Training Act Predoctoral Fellowship, 336
Nemal Electronics Scholarship, 332
New Republic Internship Program, 523
* New York State Senate/Richard J. Ross Journalism Fellowship, 191
New York Times Summer Internship Program for Minorities, 524
Newspaper Editing Intern Program, 393
Northwest Journalists of Color Scholarship Program, 530
* Oak Ridge Institute for Science and Education Postgraduate Research at the Centers for Disease Control and Prevention, 203
Oak Ridge Institute for Science and Education Student Research Participation at the Centers for Disease Control and Prevention, 209
Ohio Newspapers Minority Scholarship, 533
Oldfield National Security Reporter Fellowship, 557
Oregon Broadcast Journalism Scholarship, 538

*Graduate/nondegree study

Field of Study/Intended Career: Communications

Paul and Helen L. Grauer Scholarship, 332
Personnel Magazines Now Workforce Magazine Internship, 545
Polish Culture Scholarship, 285
Presidential Memorial Scholarship, 557
*Radio-Television News Capitol Hill News Internship, 557
Random House Internship, 558
*Rennie Taylor/Alton Blakeslee Fellowship, 385
*Ron Brown Fellowship Program, 438
RTNDF Minority News Management Internship, 558
San Francisco Chronicle Summer Internship Program, 563
San Francisco Chronicle Two-Year Internship Program, 563
School Division Internship, 429
Seventeen Magazine Journalism Internship, 568
Sherlee Barish Fellowship, 558
Southern Progress Corporation Summer Internship, 590
*Spain: Professional Grant in Journalism (Fulbright), 105
Stephen H. Gayle Essay Contest, 524
*Stoody-West Fellowship, 606
Technical Communication Scholarship Program, 577
Theodore C. Sorensen Research Fellowship, 446
*Univision-Mexican-American Legal Defense Fund Scholarship, 466
Wall Street Journal Internship, 610
Warwick, Baker and Fiore Internship Program, 610
Water Companies (NJ Chapter) Scholarship, 479
Wolf Trap Performing Arts Internship, 615
Young Feminist Scholarship Program, 593

Computer and information sciences

1890 National Scholars Program, 228
Actuarial Club Scholarship, 454
*Adelle and Erwin Tomash Fellowship, 378
Admiral Grace M. Hopper Scholarship, 583
*Aerospace Graduate Research Fellowship Program, 172
Aerospace Undergraduate Scholarship Program, 173
Air Force Four-Year Scholarships(Types # 1,2 and Targeted), 217
*American Health Information Management Master's Program, 631
American Heart Association Student Research Program, 279
*American Library Association Doctoral Dissertation Fellowship, 315
*Armed Forces Educational Foundation Fellowship, 353
ARRL League Ph.D. Scholarship, 330
*Aspen Systems Awards, 631
Avon Products Foundation Career Empowerment Scholarship for Adult Women, 564
Barbara Thomas Enterprises Award, 632
Bechtel Corporation Summer Intern Program, 363
Career Advancement Scholarship, 372
CIA Undergraduate Scholarship, 64
Coding Specialist Program Loan, 632
Community College Scholarship Program, 173
Computer Science Scholarship, 484
Computing Research Association Outstanding Undergraduate Award, 383
Cooperative Education Program, 363
Cooperative Education Program, 62
Cooperative Education Program, 62
Dell Computer Internship, 392
Experiential Education Internship, 514
*Ford Foundation Predoctoral Fellowship: Minorities, 511
*FORE Graduate Scholarship, 632
Fossil Energy Technology Internship, 197
Franklin D. Roosevelt Library/ Roosevelt Internship, 408
General Emmett Paige Scholarship, 353
General John A. Wickham Scholarship, 353
Grant Program for Physically Disabled Students in the Sciences, 407
Grants-In-Aid for Research on the Roosevelt Years, 408
GTE Internship Program, 416
HIM PROGRAM, 633
HIT Program, 633
Horizons Foundation Scholarship, 429
*I/ITSEC Graduate Student Scholarship Program, 520
IBM Internship & Co-Op Program, 431
Inroads Internship, 432
Kawasaki-McGaha Scholarship Fund, 423
Lance Stafford Larson Student Scholarship, 692
*Library and Information Science Grant, 438
Maria Mitchell Internships for Astronomical Research, 460
Mentor Graphics Scholarship, 538
Mother Jones MoJo Wire Internship, 470
NASA Space Grant Alabama Graduate Fellowship, 146
NASA Space Grant Alabama Undergraduate Scholarship Program, 147
*NASA Space Grant Florida Fellowship Program, 151
*NASA Space Grant Florida Fellowship Program, 151
NASA Space Grant Florida Undergraduate Space Research Participation Program, 152
NASA Space Grant Georgia Fellowship Program, 152
*NASA Space Grant Montana Graduate Fellowship, 160
NASA Space Grant Montana Undergraduate Scholarship Program, 160
NASA Space Grant New Hampshire Undergraduate Scholarship, 162
*NASA Space Grant New Hampshire Graduate Fellowship, 162
NASA Space Grant New Jersey Undergraduate Summer Fellowship, 162
*NASA Space Grant New Mexico Graduate Fellowship, 163
NASA Space Grant New Mexico Undergraduate Scholarship, 163
*NASA Space Grant North Dakota Graduate Fellowship, 164
*National Defense Science and Engineering Graduate Fellowship Program, 70
National Security Agency Undergraduate Tuition Assistance Program, 180
Native American Scholarship, 520
*Naval Research Laboratory - Postdoctoral Fellowship, 338
Oak Ridge Institute for Science and Education Energy Research Undergraduate Laboratory Fellowship, 198
*Oak Ridge Institute for Science and Education Fossil Energy Postgraduate Research, 198
*Oak Ridge Institute for Science and Education Postgraduate Research at the National Center for Toxicological Research, 204
*Oak Ridge Institute for Science and Education Postgraduate Research at the Oak Ridge National Laboratory, 204
*Oak Ridge Institute for Science and Education Postgraduate Research at the U.S. Army Directorate of Environment-Fort McClellan, 205

*Graduate/nondegree study

Field of Study/Intended Career: Education

* Oak Ridge Institute for Science and Education Postgraduate Research at the U.S. Army Edgewood Research, 206
Oak Ridge Institute for Science and Education Professional Internship Program at Federal Energy Technology Centers, 532
Oak Ridge Institute for Science and Education Professional Internship Program at the Oak Ridge National Laboratory, 207
Oak Ridge Institute For Science and Education Student Environmental Management Participation for the U.S. Army Environmental Center, 208
Oak Ridge Institute for Science and Education Student Internship at the U.S. Army Center for Health Promotion and Preventive Medicine, 208
Oak Ridge Institute for Science and Education Student Research at the U.S. Army Aviation and Troop Command, 208
Oak Ridge Institute for Science and Education Student Research Participation at the National Center for Toxicological Research, 209
Oak Ridge Institute for Science and Education Student Research Participation at the U.S. Army Aviation and Troop Command, 210
Oak Ridge Institute for Science and Education Student Research Participation at the U.S. Army Edgewood Research, Development and Engineering Center, 210
Oak Ridge Institute for Science and Education U.S. Department of Energy/NAACP, 210
Oak Ridge Institute for Science and Education U.S. Geological Survey Earth Sciences Internship, 211
Oak Ridge Institute for Science and Education U.S. Nuclear Regulatory Commission Historically Black Colleges and Universities Student Research Participation, 211
* Office of Naval Research - Postdoctoral Fellowship, 338
Oregon State Scholarship Commission/Howard Vollum American Indian Scholarship, 540
* Peat Marwick Doctoral Scholarship Program, 448
* Physical Science Graduate Fellowship: Minorities and Women, 510
Plasma Physics National Undergraduate Fellowship Program, 216
* Reforma Scholarship Program, 559
Richard E. Merwin Award, 692

ROTC Scholarships, 655
ROTC/ Air Force Three-Year Scholarships Types 2 And Targeted, 217
* Science and Technology Fellowship, 264
Silicon Graphics Computer Systems Internship Program, 569
Southern Progress Corporation Summer Internship, 590
* Special Libraries Institute for Scientific Information Scholarship, 748
* Special Libraries Plenum Scholarship, 748
* St. Anthony Publishing Graduate Award, 633
State Farm Companies Exceptional Student Fellowship, 594
Student Employment and Educational Program, 427
Tandy Technology Students Award, 596
* Transcriptions Limited Graduate Scholarship, 634
Upjohn Company Internship, 608
Upsilon Pi Epsilon Scholarships, 692
USOC Student Intern Program, 607
Wal-Mart Competitive Edge Scholarship, 609
Wolf Trap Performing Arts Internship, 615
Women Engineers Chrysler Corporation Re-entry Scholarship, 585
Women Engineers Chrysler Corporation Scholarship, 585
Women Engineers Chrysler Corporation Scholarship (Minorities), 585
Women Engineers GTE Foundation Scholarship, 586
Women Engineers Men's Auxiliary Memorial Scholarship, 587
Women Engineers Microsoft Corporation Scholarship, 587
* Women Engineers Microsoft Corporation Scholarship (Graduate), 587
Women Engineers Stone and Webster Scholarship, 588
Youth Entertainment Summer, 618

Education

* Aera/Spencer Research Training Fellowship, 591
Aerospace Undergraduate Scholarship Program, 173
* African-American Doctoral Teacher Loan / Scholarship, 140
* Alabama Technology Scholarship for Alabama Teachers, 53
Alaska Teacher Scholarship Loan, 56

Alma White--Delta Chapter, Delta Kappa Gamma Scholarship, 419
* American Health Information Management Master's Program, 631
American Legion California Auxiliary Department of Education Scholarship II, 289
American Legion Illinois Auxiliary Special Education Teaching Scholarship, 292
American Legion Iowa Auxiliary Harriet Hoffman Memorial Scholarship, 293
American Legion New Hampshire Christa McAuliffe Scholarship, 302
American Legion New Mexico Auxiliary Teachers of Exceptional Children Scholarship, 305
American Legion New York Auxiliary Medical & Teaching Scholarship, 305
American Legion New York Dr. Hannah K. Vuolo Memorial Scholarship, 645
* American Legion Wisconsin Auxiliary Child Welfare Scholarship, 313
Annis I. Fowler/Kaden Scholarship, 220
Applegate/Jackson/Parks Future Teacher Scholarship, 383
Arkansas Emergency Secondary Education Loan, 61
Arkansas Freshman/Sophomore Minority Grant, 61
* Arkansas Minority Master's Fellowship, 61
Arkansas Minority Teachers Loan, 62
* Armenian Union U.S. Graduate Loan, 354
* Aspen Systems Awards, 631
Barbara Thomas Enterprises Award, 632
Bethesda Lutheran Homes and Services Cooperative Program Internship, 368
* Bishop Greco Graduate Fellowship, 699
Burlington Northern Santa Fe Foundation Scholarship, 637
California Assumption Program Loans for Education, 63
California Child Development Teacher and Supervisor Grant Program, 63
California Teachers Association Martin Luther King, Jr., Memorial Scholarship, 667
Career Advancement Scholarship, 372
Coca-Cola Internship, 509
Coding Specialist Program Loan, 632
* Conservation Internship, 520
* CTA Scholarship for Members, 667
Cushman School Internship, 387
* David Levy Award, 627

*Graduate/nondegree study

Field of Study/Intended Career: Education

Delaware Christa McAuliffe Scholarship Loan, 69
Educator of Tomorrow Award, 484
Eight-Month Gardener Internship, 529
Experiential Education Internship, 514
*Fellowships for University Teachers, 177
Florida Critical Teacher Shortage Student Loan Forgiveness, 72
*Florida Critical Teacher Shortage Tuition Reimbursement, 72
Florida Teacher Scholarship and Forgivable Loan (Freshmen/Sophomores), 75
*Florida Teacher Scholarship and Forgivable Loan (Graduate), 75
Florida Teacher Scholarship and Forgivable Loan (Juniors/Seniors), 75
*FORE Graduate Scholarship, 632
Franklin D. Roosevelt Library/Roosevelt Internship, 408
*Georgia Hope Teacher Scholarship, 115
Georgia Promise Teacher Scholarship, 116
Georgia Service-Cancelable Stafford Loan, 116
Grants-In-Aid for Research on the Roosevelt Years, 408
*H.J. Swinney Internship, 594
Haines Memorial Scholarship, 219
Harry Truman Scholarship, 117
*Health Education Scholarship, 260
Henry and Dorothy Castle Memorial Scholarship, 421
HIM PROGRAM, 633
HIT Program, 633
Hopi Tribal Priority Scholarship, 428
Idaho Education Incentive Loan Forgiveness Program, 118
Illinois D.A. DeBolt Teacher Shortage Scholarship, 119
Illinois Minority Teachers Scholarship, 120
Indiana Minority Teacher Scholarship, 122
Indiana Special Education Services Scholarship, 122
International Educational Exchange Scholarship/China, 68
James Carlson Memorial Scholarship, 536
Kansas Teacher Scholarship, 126
Kentucky Teacher Scholarship, 127
Lazaroff Family Fund, 443
Lebovitz Internship, 509
*Lindbergh Foundation Grant, 378
Louisiana Innovative Professional Development/Teacher Tuition Exemption, 128
M.V. O'Donnell Memorial Teacher Training Award, 628

Mary Morrow-Edna Richards Scholarship, 528
Maryland Child Care Provider Scholarship, 130
Maryland Distinguished Scholar: Teacher Education Program, 131
Maryland Sharon Christa McAuliffe Memorial Teacher Education Award, 135
Mental Retardation Scholastic Achievement Scholarship, 368
*Miss America Education Scholarship for Post-Graduate Studies, 468
*Mississippi Graduate Teacher Summer Loan/Scholarship Program, 141
Mississippi William Winter Teacher Scholar Loan Program, 144
Missouri Minority Teaching Scholarship, 145
Missouri Teacher Education Scholarship, 145
Morris Arboretum Education Internship, 469
Museum Internships in Washington DC, 510
NASA Space Grant Alabama Graduate Fellowship, 146
NASA Space Grant Alabama Undergraduate Scholarship Program, 147
*NASA Space Grant Florida Fellowship Program, 151
*NASA Space Grant Florida Fellowship Program, 151
NASA Space Grant Florida Undergraduate Space Research Participation Program, 152
NASA Space Grant Georgia Fellowship Program, 152
*NASA Space Grant Idaho Graduate Fellowship, 153
NASA Space Grant Idaho Undergraduate Scholarship Program, 153
*NASA Space Grant Kentucky Graduate Fellowship, 155
NASA Space Grant Kentucky Undergraduate Scholarship, 156
*NASA Space Grant Pennsylvania Graduate Fellowship, 167
*NASA Space Grant South Carolina Graduate Fellowship, 170
NASA Space Grant South Carolina Undergraduate Academic Year Research Program, 170
NASA Space Grant South Carolina Undergraduate Research Summer Scholarship, 170
NASA Space Grant South Carolina Undergraduate Scholarship Program, 170
NASA Space Grant Texas Undergraduate Scholarship Program, 172

Native American Scholarship, 520
Native Daughters of the Golden West Scholarship, 719
New Mexico Minority and Handicapped Teachers Scholarship: Southeast, 186
*Newcombe Doctoral Dissertation Fellowship, 617
North Carolina Prospective Teacher Scholarship Loan, 193
North Carolina Teacher Assistant Scholarship Loan, 194
Oak Ridge Institute for Science and Education Postgraduate Research at the Department of Veterans Affairs, Birmingham Education Center, 203
Oklahoma Future Teachers Scholarship, 213
Oregon Alpha Delta Kappa/Harriet Simmons Scholarship, 538
*Phi Delta Kappa Graduate Fellowship, 727
Phillips Academy Summer Teaching Assistant Internship Program., 548
*Postdoctoral Sexuality Research Fellowship Program, 574
*Practitioner Research Communication and Mentoring Grant, 591
Retarded Citizens' Teachers Scholarship, 756
Rodolf Steiner Visiting Students Program, 561
*Rural Special Education Scholarship, 271
Scholarship Grant for Prospective Educators, 548
Secondary School Principals Leadership Award, 479
*Sexuality Research Dissertation Fellowship Program, 575
*Small Research Grants Program, 591
*Sociological Association Minority Fellowship, 60
South Carolina Teacher Loans, 219
*Spencer Dissertation Fellowship Program, 592
*Spencer Foundation Major Research Grants, 592
*Spencer Postdoctoral Fellowship Program, 474
*Spencer Professional Development Research and Documentation Program, 592
*St. Anthony Publishing Graduate Award, 633
Sutton Education Scholarship, 711
*Tandy Technology Teachers Award, 596
Teacher Education Scholarship Program, 173
Teacher Preparation Scholarship, 361
Tennessee Minority Teaching Fellows Program, 223
Tennessee Teaching Scholarship, 223

*Graduate/nondegree study

Field of Study/Intended Career: Engineering and engineering technology

Three-Month Gardener Internship, 529
*Transcriptions Limited Graduate Scholarship, 634
*Trent R. Dames and William W. Moore Fellowship, 651
United States Information Agency Summer Internship, 232
Utah Career Teaching Scholarship/ T.H. Bell Teaching Incentive Loan, 236
West Virginia Underwood-Smith Teacher Scholarship, 241
Wisconsin Minority Teacher Loan Program, 243
Wolf Trap Performing Arts Internship, 615
Yosemite National Park Internships, 245

Engineering and engineering technology

3M Internship, 247
A.T. Anderson Memorial Scholarship, 636
Admiral Grace M. Hopper Scholarship, 583
Aeronautics and Astronautics Undergraduate Scholarship, 281
*Aerospace Graduate Research Fellowship Program, 172
Aerospace Undergraduate Scholarship Program, 173
*AFOSR Summer Research Program, 53
AGC of Maine Scholarship Program, 357
Air Force Four-Year Scholarships(Types # 1,2 and Targeted), 217
Alwin B. Newton Scholarships, 341
*Amelia Earhart Fellowship, 619
American Electroplaters and Surface Finishers Society Scholarship, 272
American Engineers Longterm Member Scholarship, 744
American Legion California Auxiliary Department of Education Scholarship I, 289
American Legion California Auxiliary Department of Education Scholarship II, 289
American Nuclear Society Environmental Sciences Division Scholarship, 322
American Nuclear Society Washington Internship for Students of Engineering, 322
American Soc. Heating/Refrigeration/ Air-Conditioning Engineers Technical Scholarship, 337
American Soc. Heating/Refrigeration/ Air-Conditioning Engineers Undergraduate Scholarship, 337

Amtrol Ground Water Research Scholarship, 277
Angelo S. Biseti Scholarship, 323
Anne Maureen Whitney Barrow Memorial Scholarship, 583
*Applied Health Physics Fellowship, 197
*Armed Forces Educational Foundation Fellowship, 353
*Army Research Laboratory - Postdoctoral Fellowship, 338
ARRL League Ph.D. Scholarship, 330
ARRL Mississippi Scholarship, 330
Arthur and Doreen Parrett Scholarship, 355
*Arthur S. Tuttle Memorial National Scholarships, 340
ASM Foundation Undergraduate Scholarship, 357
ASME Student Loan Program, 652
Associated General Contractors James L. Allhands Essay Competition, 357
Automotive Engineers Engineering Scholarship, 580
B. Charles Tiney Memorial ASCE Student Chapter Scholarships, 340
Barry M. Goldwater Scholarship, 62
Bechtel Corporation Summer Intern Program, 363
Black & Veatch Summer Internship in Engineering, Construction, and Architecture, 368
BP America Internship, 665
California Farm Bureau Scholarship, 374
Capitol College Electronic Engineering Scholarship, 622
Career Advancement Scholarship, 372
Castleberry Instruments Scholarship, 252
Caterpillar Scholars Award, 582
Chemical Society Minority Scholarship, 267
*Churchill Scholarship, 615
CIA Undergraduate Scholarship, 64
*CIC/GE Predoctoral Fellowship, 382
*Civil Engineering Graduate Scholarship, 361
Community College Scholarship Program, 173
Community College Transfer Scholarships, 173
Computing Research Association Outstanding Undergraduate Award, 383
Connecticut Building Congress Scholarship, 384
Consulting Engineers Scholarship, 270
Cooperative Education Program, 363
Dam Safety Officials Scholarship, 361
David Arver Memorial Scholarship, 253
David J. Fitzmaurice Engineering Scholarship, 696

David Sarnoff Reseach Center Scholarship, 583
Delaware Engineering Society Undergraduate Scholarship Program, 392
Delayed Education Scholarship for Women, 323
*Denmark: Aalborg University Grant (Fulbright), 83
Dorothy Lemke Howarth Scholarship, 584
Duracell/Gillette Minority Intern Scholarship, 520
Dutch and Ginger Arver Scholarship, 253
Eastman Kodak Student Program, 395
Edmond A. Metzger Scholarship, 650
*Education and Research Junior Graduate Award, 358
*Education and Research Outstanding Educators Award, 358
Education and Research Undergraduate Scholarship, 358
Educational Optical Engineering Scholarship, 592
EED Scholarship Program, 357
*Electrochemical Society Summer Fellowship, 397
Ellison Onizuka Memorial Scholarship, 421
Engineers Foundation of Ohio Scholarship, 399
*EPSCoR Graduate Fellowship Program, 161
EPSCoR Undergraduate Scholarship Program, 161
*Everitt P. Blizard Scholarship, 323
F.M. Becket Summer Research Award, 397
F.W. and D.G. Miller Mechanical Engineering Scholarship, 652
F.W. Berchley Mechanical Engineering Scholarship, 652
*Florida Education Fund McKnight Doctoral Fellowship, 405
*Ford Foundation Dissertation Fellowship: Minorities, 510
*Ford Foundation Postdoctoral Fellowships for Minorities, 511
Fossil Energy Technology Internship, 197
Frank Walton Horn Memorial Scholarship, 484
*Freeman Fellowship, 340
Fuel Cycle and Waste Management, 323
*Fulbright - USIA U.K. Zeneca Award, 87
Fulfilling the Legacy Scholarship, 717
Garland Duncan Mechanical Engineering Scholarship, 652
*Gem Consortium Scholarship, 412
Gene Baker Honorary Scholarship, 253

*Graduate/nondegree study

17

Field of Study/Intended Career: Engineering and engineering technology

General Emmett Paige Scholarship, 353
General John A. Wickham Scholarship, 353
General Mills Internship Program, 412
Geography Students Internship, 490
Geological Institute Minority Participation Program, 276
Ginger and Fred Deines Canada Scholarship, 598
Ginger and Fred Deines Mexico Scholarship, 599
*Gordon C. Oates Award, 282
Grant Program for Physically Disabled Students in the Sciences, 407
GTE Internship Program, 416
Gulf Coast Avionics to Fox Valley Technical College Scholarship, 254
*Helicopter Mechanic Technician Scholarship, 426
Highway Engineers/Carolina Triangle Section Scholarship, 342
Hispanic Professional Engineers Educational Grant, 581
Hooper Memorial Scholarship, 599
Hopi Tribal Priority Scholarship, 428
Horizons Foundation Scholarship, 429
*Horton Geophysical Research Grant, 276
Howard Brown Rickard Scholarship, 484
*I/ITSEC Graduate Student Scholarship Program, 520
IBM Internship & Co-Op Program, 431
Inroads Internship, 432
*Integrated Manufacturing Fellowship, 512
*International Water Conference Merit Award Scholarship, 400
Ivy Parker Memorial Scholarship, 584
*Jack E. Leisch Memorial National Scholarships, 340
*James F. Schumar Scholarship, 323
John and Elsa Gracik Mechanical Engineering Scholarship, 653
John and Muriel Landis Scholarship, 324
John Cook Honorary Scholarship, 254
John R. Lamarsh Scholarship, 324
*John Randall Scholarship, 324
Joseph Levendusky Memorial Scholarship, 400
Joseph R. Dietrich Scholarship, 324
Judith Resnik Memorial Scholarship, 745
Junior/Senior Scholarship Program, 165
Kathryn D. Sullivan Science and Engineering Undergraduate Fellowship, 169
Kenneth Andrew Roe Mechanical Engineering Scholarship, 653

Lillian Moller Gilbreth Scholarship, 584
Lucile B. Kaufman Women's Scholarship, 582
M. & E. Walker Scholarship, 582
Maine Metal Products Scholarship, 456
Maine Society of Professional Engineers Scholarship Program, 458
Mass Media Science and Engineering Fellowship, 626
McDonnell Douglas Internship Program, 461
Mentor Graphics Scholarship, 538
*Meteorological Society Industry Graduate Fellowship, 320
Meteorological Society Industry Undergraduate Scholarship, 320
Meteorological Society Minority Scholarship, 320
Meteorological Society Undergraduate Scholarship, 320
*Mexico: Binational Business Grants (Fulbright), 98
Michigan Educational Opportunity Scholarship, 137
Michigan Society of Professional Engineers, 466
Mid-Continent Instrument Scholarship, 254
Mississippi Space Grant Consortium, 159
Monte R. Mitchell Global Scholarship, 255
Nancy Lorraine Jensen Memorial Scholarship, 746
NASA Academy Internship, 167
NASA Space Grant Alabama Graduate Fellowship, 146
NASA Space Grant Alabama Undergraduate Scholarship Program, 147
*NASA Space Grant Alaska Graduate Fellowship, 147
NASA Space Grant Alaska Undergraduate Scholarship, 147
*NASA Space Grant Arizona Graduate Fellowship, 148
NASA Space Grant Arizona Undergraduate Research Internship, 148
*NASA Space Grant Arkansas Graduate Fellowship, 148
NASA Space Grant Arkansas Undergraduate Scholarship, 148
*NASA Space Grant California Fellowship Program, 149
NASA Space Grant California Undergraduate Scholarship, 149
NASA Space Grant Colorado Graduate Fellowship, 149
NASA Space Grant Colorado Undergraduate Scholarship, 149

*NASA Space Grant Connecticut Graduate Fellowship, 150
NASA Space Grant Connecticut Undergraduate Fellowship, 473
*NASA Space Grant Delaware Space Graduate Student Fellowship, 150
NASA Space Grant Delaware Undergraduate Summer Scholarship, 150
NASA Space Grant Delaware Undergraduate Tuition Scholarship, 150
NASA Space Grant District of Columbia Undergraduate Scholarship, 151
*NASA Space Grant District of Columbia Graduate Fellowship, 151
*NASA Space Grant Florida Fellowship Program, 151
*NASA Space Grant Florida Fellowship Program, 151
NASA Space Grant Florida Undergraduate Space Research Participation Program, 152
NASA Space Grant Georgia Fellowship Program, 152
*NASA Space Grant Idaho Graduate Fellowship, 153
NASA Space Grant Idaho Undergraduate Scholarship Program, 153
*NASA Space Grant Illinois Graduate Fellowship, 154
NASA Space Grant Illinois Undergraduate Scholarship, 154
*NASA Space Grant Indiana Graduate Fellowship, 154
NASA Space Grant Indiana Summer Undergraduate Research Program, 154
NASA Space Grant Indiana Undergraduate Scholarship, 154
NASA Space Grant Kansas Graduate Fellowship, 155
NASA Space Grant Kansas Undergraduate Scholarship, 155
*NASA Space Grant Kentucky Graduate Fellowship, 155
NASA Space Grant Kentucky Undergraduate Scholarship, 156
NASA Space Grant Louisiana LaSPACE Graduate Fellowship Program, 156
NASA Space Grant Louisiana LaSPACE Undergraduate Scholarship Program, 156
*NASA Space Grant Maine Graduate Fellowship, 157
*NASA Space Grant Maine Research Acceleration Grant Program, 157
NASA Space Grant Maine Undergraduate Internship Award, 157

*Graduate/nondegree study

Field of Study/Intended Career: Engineering and engineering technology

NASA Space Grant Maine Undergraduate Scholarship Program, 157
*NASA Space Grant Massachusetts Graduate Fellowships, 158
NASA Space Grant Massachusetts Summer Jobs for Students, 158
NASA Space Grant Massachusetts Undergraduate Research Opportunities, 158
*NASA Space Grant Michigan Graduate Fellowship, 158
NASA Space Grant Michigan Undergraduate Fellowship, 159
*NASA Space Grant Minnesota Graduate Fellowship, 159
NASA Space Grant Minnesota Undergraduate Scholarship, 159
*NASA Space Grant Missouri Summer Jobs for Students, 160
NASA Space Grant Missouri Summer Undergraduate Internship, 160
*NASA Space Grant Montana Graduate Fellowship, 160
NASA Space Grant Montana Undergraduate Scholarship Program, 160
*NASA Space Grant Nevada Graduate Fellowship, 161
NASA Space Grant Nevada Undergraduate Scholarship, 162
NASA Space Grant New Hampshire Undergraduate Scholarship, 162
*NASA Space Grant New Hampshire Graduate Fellowship, 162
NASA Space Grant New Jersey Undergraduate Summer Fellowship, 162
*NASA Space Grant New Mexico Graduate Fellowship, 163
NASA Space Grant New Mexico Undergraduate Scholarship, 163
NASA Space Grant New York Graduate Fellowship, 163
NASA Space Grant New York Undergraduate Internship, 163
*NASA Space Grant North Carolina Graduate Fellowship, 164
NASA Space Grant North Carolina Undergraduate Scholarship Program, 164
*NASA Space Grant North Dakota Graduate Fellowship, 164
NASA Space Grant North Dakota Undergraduate Scholarship, 164
*NASA Space Grant Ohio Fellowship Program, 165
*NASA Space Grant Oklahoma Space Grant Consortium Graduate Fellowship, 166
NASA Space Grant Oklahoma Undergraduate Scholarship, 166
*NASA Space Grant Oregon Graduate Fellowship, 166

NASA Space Grant Oregon Undergraduate Scholarship, 166
*NASA Space Grant Pennsylvania Graduate Fellowship, 167
*NASA Space Grant Puerto Rico Graduate Fellowship, 167
NASA Space Grant Puerto Rico Summer Internship Program, 168
NASA Space Grant Puerto Rico Undergraduate Scholarship, 168
*NASA Space Grant Rhode Island Graduate Fellowship, 168
NASA Space Grant Rhode Island Summer Undergraduate Scholarship Program, 168
NASA Space Grant Rhode Island Undergraduate Academic Year Scholarship Program, 169
NASA Space Grant Rocky Mountain Graduate Fellowship, 169
NASA Space Grant Rocky Mountain Undergraduate Scholarship, 169
*NASA Space Grant South Carolina Graduate Fellowship, 170
NASA Space Grant South Carolina Undergraduate Academic Year Research Program, 170
NASA Space Grant South Carolina Undergraduate Research Summer Scholarship, 170
NASA Space Grant South Carolina Undergraduate Scholarship Program, 170
*NASA Space Grant Tennessee Graduate Fellowship, 171
NASA Space Grant Tennessee Undergraduate Scholarship, 171
*NASA Space Grant Texas Graduate Fellowship, 171
NASA Space Grant Texas Undergraduate Scholarship Program, 172
*NASA Space Grant Vermont Space Graduate Research Assistantship, 172
NASA Space Grant Vermont Undergraduate Scholarships, 172
*NASA Space Grant Washington Graduate Fellowships at the University of Washington, 174
NASA Space Grant Washington Undergraduate Scholarship Program, 174
*NASA Space Grant West Virginia Graduate Fellowship, 174
NASA Space Grant West Virginia Undergraduate Fellowship Scholarship, 175
NASA Space Grant West Virginia Undergraduate Scholarship, 175
*NASA Space Grant Wisconsin Graduate Fellowship, 175

NASA Space Grant Wisconsin Undergraduate Research Awards, 176
NASA Space Grant Wisconsin Undergraduate Scholarship, 176
*National Defense Science and Engineering Graduate Fellowship Program, 70
*National Science Foundation Graduate Fellowship, 179
*National Science Foundation Minority Graduate Fellowship, 180
National Security Agency Undergraduate Tuition Assistance Program, 180
National Society of Black Engineers Scholars Program, 718
National Society of Black Engineers/ GE African American Forum Scholarship, 718
National Space Society Internship Program, 515
Native American Scholarship, 520
*Naval Architects and Marine Engineers Graduate Scholarship, 744
Naval Engineers Scholarship, 343
*Naval Research Laboratory - Postdoctoral Fellowship, 338
North East Roofing Contractors Association Scholarship, 716
Nuclear Operations Division Scholarship, 324
Nuclear Training Educational Assistance Program, 473
O.H. Ammann Research Fellowship in Structural Engineering, 340
Oak Ridge Institute for Science and Education Energy Research Undergraduate Laboratory Fellowship, 198
*Oak Ridge Institute for Science and Education Fossil Energy Postgraduate Research, 198
*Oak Ridge Institute for Science and Education Fusion Energy Postdoctoral Research, 198
Oak Ridge Institute for Science and Education Historically Black Building Technology Summer Research Participation, 199
Oak Ridge Institute for Science and Education Historically Black Colleges Nuclear Energy Training Program, 199
Oak Ridge Institute for Science and Education Historically Black Nuclear Energy Training Program, 199
*Oak Ridge Institute for Science and Education Magnetic Fusion Energy Technology Fellowship, 199

*Graduate/nondegree study

Field of Study/Intended Career: Engineering and engineering technology

*Oak Ridge Institute for Science and Education Magnetic Fusion Science Fellowship, 199
Oak Ridge Institute for Science and Education National Oceanic and Atmospheric Administration Student Program, 200
*Oak Ridge Institute for Science and Education Nuclear Engineering Health Physics Fellowship, 200
*Oak Ridge Institute for Science and Education Oak Ridge National Laboratory Postdoctoral Research, 200
Oak Ridge Institute for Science and Education Office of Civilian Radioactive Waste Management Historically Black Colleges and Universities Undergraduate Scholarship Program, 201
Oak Ridge Institute for Science and Education Office of Fossil Energy Historically Black Colleges and Universities Student Research Participation, 201
Oak Ridge Institute for Science and Education Office of Nuclear Energy Undergraduate Scholarship, 201
*Oak Ridge Institute for Science and Education Postgraduate Environmental Management Participation at the U.S. Army Environmental Center, 202
*Oak Ridge Institute for Science and Education Postgraduate Internship at the Office of Ground Water and Drinking Water, 202
*Oak Ridge Institute for Science and Education Postgraduate Internship at the U.S. Army Center for Health Promotion and Preventive Medicine, 202
*Oak Ridge Institute for Science and Education Postgraduate Research at the Center for Devices and Radiological Health, 203
*Oak Ridge Institute for Science and Education Postgraduate Research at the National Exposure Research Laboratory, 204
*Oak Ridge Institute for Science and Education Postgraduate Research at the National Risk Management Research Laboratory, 204
*Oak Ridge Institute for Science and Education Postgraduate Research at the Oak Ridge National Laboratory, 204
*Oak Ridge Institute for Science and Education Postgraduate Research at the Savanah River Site, 204

*Oak Ridge Institute for Science and Education Postgraduate Research at the St. Louis District, U.S. Army Corps of Engineers, 205
*Oak Ridge Institute for Science and Education Postgraduate Research at the U.S. Army Aviation and Troop Command, 205
*Oak Ridge Institute for Science and Education Postgraduate Research at the U.S. Army Construction Engineering Research Laboratory, 205
*Oak Ridge Institute for Science and Education Postgraduate Research at the U.S. Army Depot, Anniston, 205
*Oak Ridge Institute for Science and Education Postgraduate Research at the U.S. Army Directorate of Environment-Fort McClellan, 205
*Oak Ridge Institute for Science and Education Postgraduate Research at the U.S. Army Edgewood Research, 206
*Oak Ridge Institute for Science and Education Postgraduate Research at the U.S. Army Environmental Policy Institute, 206
*Oak Ridge Institute for Science and Education Postgraduate Research at the U.S. Army Garrison, Aberdeen, 206
*Oak Ridge Institute for Science and Education Postgraduate Research at the U.S. Army National Guard Bureau, 207
*Oak Ridge Institute for Science and Education Postgraduate Research at the U.S. Navy Commander Fleet, Okinawa, 207
Oak Ridge Institute for Science and Education Professional Internship Program at Federal Energy Technology Centers, 532
Oak Ridge Institute for Science and Education Professional Internship Program at the Oak Ridge National Laboratory, 207
Oak Ridge Institute for Science and Education Professional Internship Program at the Savannah River Site, 207
Oak Ridge Institute For Science and Education Student Environmental Management Participation for the U.S. Army Environmental Center, 208
Oak Ridge Institute for Science and Education Student Internship at the U.S. Army Center for Health Promotion and Preventive Medicine, 208

Oak Ridge Institute for Science and Education Student Research at the U.S. Army Aviation and Troop Command, 208
Oak Ridge Institute for Science and Education Student Research at the U.S. Army Environmental Policy Institute, 209
Oak Ridge Institute for Science and Education Student Research at the U.S. Army Garrison, Directorate of Safety, Health and the Environment, 209
Oak Ridge Institute for Science and Education Student Research Participation at the U.S. Army Aviation and Troop Command, 210
Oak Ridge Institute for Science and Education Student Research Participation at the U.S. Army Edgewood Research, Development and Engineering Center, 210
Oak Ridge Institute for Science and Education Student Research Participation at the U.S. Army Environmental Policy Institute, 210
Oak Ridge Institute for Science and Education Technology Internship Program at the Oak Ridge National Laboratory, 210
Oak Ridge Institute for Science and Education U.S. Department of Energy/NAACP, 210
Oak Ridge Institute for Science and Education U.S. Geological Survey Earth Sciences Internship, 211
Oak Ridge Institute for Science and Education U.S. Nuclear Regulatory Commission Historically Black Colleges and Universities Student Research Participation, 211
Oak Ridge Institute for Science and Education University Coal Research Internship, 211
Octel Communications Internship, 532
*Office of Naval Research - Postdoctoral Fellowship, 338
Oklahoma Engineering Foundation Scholarship, 533
Olive Lynn Salembier Scholarship, 584
Oregon State Scholarship Commission/Howard Vollum American Indian Scholarship, 540
Oregon State Scholarship Commission/Oregon Building Industry Association Scholarship, 541
*Parenteral Research Grant, 544
*Paul A. Greebler Scholarship, 324
Paul and Blanche Wulfsberg Scholarship, 255
Pearl I. Young Scholarship, 165
*Pfizer Internships, 546

20

*Graduate/nondegree study

Field of Study/Intended Career: English and literature

* Pilot Training Scholarship, 255
Plane and Pilot Magazine/Garmin Scholarship, 255
Plasma Physics National Undergraduate Fellowship Program, 216
Plumbing, Heating, Cooling Contractors Education Foundation Scholarship, 478
Power Division Scholarship, 325
Professional Engineers of North Carolina Engineering Scholarship Program, 553
Raychem Internship, 558
Raymond DiSalvo Scholarship, 325
Reuben Trane Scholarship, 337
* Risk Assessment Science and Engineering Fellowships, 261
* Robert A. Dannels Scholarship, 325
Robert G. Lacey Scholarship, 325
Robert T. Liner Scholarship, 326
Rocket Program Internship, 147
Rockwell Internship Program, 561
Rocky Mountain Coal Mining Scholarship, 561
ROTC Scholarships, 655
ROTC/ Air Force Three-Year Scholarships Types 2 And Targeted, 217
* Ruth Satter Memorial Award, 360
* Samuel Fletcher Tapman ASCE Student Chapter/Club Scholarship, 340
Schlumberger Internship, 564
Scholarships at Seattle Central Community College, 174
* Science and Technology Fellowship, 264
Scripps Undergraduate Research Fellowship, 566
Smithsonian Environmental Research Work/Learn Program, 218
Society of Auto Engineers Engineering Scholarship, 596
* Society of Automotive Engineers Doctoral Scholars Loan, 580
Soil and Water Conservation Student Leader Scholarship, 746
Sony Corporation of America Internship, 589
Southface Internship, 590
Spence Reese Scholarship, 370
Stone Quarry Engineering Scholarship, 515
Student Employment and Educational Program, 427
Student Paper Competition, 400
* Tau Beta Pi Fellowship, 751
Teacher Education Scholarship Program, 173
Texas Transportation Scholarship, 599
* The GEM Consortium/Doctoral Bridge Projects, 597

* The GEM Consortium/M.S. Engineering Fellowship, 597
* The GEM Consortium/Ph.D Science and Engineering Fellowship, 597
* Trent R. Dames and William W. Moore Fellowship, 651
* U.S. Department of Energy Summer Research Fellowships, 398
* United Cerebral Palsy Clinical Fellowship, 603
* Verne R. Dapp Scholarship, 326
Vertical Flight Foundation Scholarship, 279
W.E. Weisel Scholarship, 582
W.J. and M.E. Adams, Jr., Mechanical Engineering Scholarship, 653
Wal-Mart Competitive Edge Scholarship, 609
* Walter Meyer Scholarship, 326
Washington Internships for Student of Engineering, 611
Water Companies (NJ Chapter) Scholarship, 479
* Water Works Fellowship, 348
* Wayne Kay Graduate Fellowship, 582
Wayne Kay Undergraduate Scholarship, 582
Westinghouse Bertha Lamme Scholarship, 584
Willems Scholarship, 711
* William T. Piper Award, 282
* Willis H. Carrier Graduate Fellowship, 341
Women Engineers Chevron Scholarship, 585
Women Engineers Chrysler Corporation Re-entry Scholarship, 585
Women Engineers Chrysler Corporation Scholarship, 585
Women Engineers Chrysler Corporation Scholarship (Minorities), 585
Women Engineers General Electric Foundation Scholarship, 586
* Women Engineers General Motors Foundation Graduate Scholarship, 586
Women Engineers General Motors Foundation Undergraduate Scholarship, 586
Women Engineers GTE Foundation Scholarship, 586
Women Engineers Men's Auxiliary Memorial Scholarship, 587
Women Engineers Microsoft Corporation Scholarship, 587
* Women Engineers Microsoft Corporation Scholarship (Graduate), 587
Women Engineers Northrop Corporation Founders Scholarship, 745

Women Engineers Rockwell International Corporation Scholarships, 587
Women Engineers Stone and Webster Scholarship, 588
Women Engineers Texaco Scholarship, 745
Women Engineers TRW Scholarship, 588
Women in Architecture Scholarship, 359
Women in Construction: Founders' Scholarship, 480
Women in Engineering Studies Loan Fund, 372
* Women in Science Education Research Grant, 360
* Wyeth-Ayerst Laboratories Scholarship, 373
Yanmar Scholarship, 580

English and literature

Advertising Internship for Minority Students, 261
American Numismatic Society Fellowship in Roman Studies, 326
* Anne and Oliver C. Colburn Fellowship, 351
* Antiquarian Society Short-Term Fellowship, 259
Archival Internships, 445
* Bulgarian Studies Grant, 438
* David Levy Award, 627
* Ecole des Chartes Exchange Fellowship, 525
Employee Communication Internship, 391
* English-Speaking Union Graduate Scholarship, 400
* Grant for Research in Venice, 413
* Harriet and Leon Pomerance Fellowship, 352
* Helen M. Woodruff Fellowship, 352
* Herzog August Bibliothek Wolfenbuttel Fellowship, 525
* Huntington British Academy Exchange Fellowship, 430
* Huntington Fellowship, 430
* Huntington National Endowment for the Humanities Fellowship, 431
* Huntington W.M. Keck Foundation Fellowship for Young Scholars, 431
* Institut Francais de Washington Fellowship, 432
Institute for Humane Studies Fellowship, 432
KCACTF/ ChildrenÖs Theatre Foundation Award, 443
KCACTF/ Fourth Freedom Forum Playwriting Award, 443
KCACTF/ Lorraine Hansberry Playwriting Award, 444
KCACTF/ Musical Theater Award, 444

*Graduate/nondegree study

21

Field of Study/Intended Career: English and literature

KCACTF/ National AIDS Fund/ CFDA - Vogue Initiative Award for Playwriting, 444
KCACTF/ National Student Playwriting Award, 444
KCACTF/ Short Play Awards Program, 445
KCACTF/ Short Play Awards Program, 445
*Kenan T. Erim Award, 352
*Korea: Teaching Assistantship (Fulbright), 95
Latin Honor Society Scholarship, 628
*Lemmermann Scholarship, 451
M.V. O'Donnell Memorial Teacher Training Award, 628
*Mali: Full Grant (Fulbright), 97
*Margaret P. Esmonde Memorial Scholarship, 670
*Mary Isabel Sibley Fellowship, 547
*Mary McEwen Schimke Scholarship, 612
*McKinlay Summer Award, 628
Melon Minority Fellowship Program, 573
*National Endowment for the Humanities Fellowship, 526
National Junior Classical League Scholarship, 628
*National Science Foundation Minority Postdoctoral Fellowship, 180
National Security Agency Undergraduate Tuition Assistance Program, 180
New Dramatists Internship, 522
*Numismatic Graduate Fellowship, 327
*Numismatic Graduate Seminar, 327
*Olivia James Traveling Fellowship, 352
*Postdoctoral Fellowship: Middle East, 574
R.L. Gillette Scholarship, 274
R.V. Gadabout Gaddis Charitable Fund, 455
*Short-Term Resident Fellowship for Individual Research, 526
*South Central Modern Language Association Fellowship, 720
*U.S. English Foundation Award (Fulbright), 109
Wall Street Journal Internship, 610
*Weiss Brown Publication Subvention Award, 527
*Woodrow Wilson Dissertation Grant in Women's Studies, 618
Young Feminist Scholarship Program, 593

Foreign languages

Alpha Mu Gamma Scholarship, 625
*American Academy in Rome/Rome Prize Pre- and Post-Doctoral Fellowship, 57
American Association of Japanese University Women Scholarship, 262
Arkansas Emergency Secondary Education Loan, 61
*Asian Language Fellowship, 369
*Austrian Research and Study Scholarship, 362
*Carmargo Foundation Fellowship, 376
CIA Undergraduate Scholarship, 64
Cultural Ambassadorial Scholarship, 562
*International Educational Exchange Graduate Scholarship/Russia, 68
International Educational Exchange Scholarship/China, 68
*Language Training Grant: Eastern Europe, 573
*Mary Isabel Sibley Fellowship, 547
Melon Minority Fellowship Program, 573
Mola Scholarship, 497
Paragano Scholarship, 499
Phi Sigma Iota Award, 548
*Predissertation Fellowship: Bangladesh, 574
*Predissertation Fellowship: South Asia, 575
*SSRC Dissertation Fellowship: Middle East, 576
*SSRC Dissertation Fellowship: Southeast Asia, 576
Turkish Language Summer Scholarship, 60

Health professions and allied services

1890 National Scholars Program, 228
A.T. Anderson Memorial Scholarship, 636
Abbie Sargent Memorial Scholarship, 247
ADHA Institute for Oral Health Minority Scholarship, 249
ADHA Institute for Oral Health Part-Time Scholarship, 249
*Advanced Predoctoral Pharmacology and Toxicology Fellowship, 546
Aging Research Scholarship, 272
Aiea General Hospital Association Scholarship, 419
*Alabama Chiropractic Scholarship, 256
Alabama Nursing Scholarship Program, 55
Ambucs Scholarship, 257
*Amer. Fdn. For Pharm. Educ./Clinical Pharmacy Post-Pharm.D. Fellowship In The Biomedical Research Sciences, 272
*American Foundation for Pharmaceutical Education Predoctoral Fellowship, 258
American Academic Sanitarians Scholarship, 483
American Association Of Medical Assistants Endowment (AAMA)/ Maxine Williams Scholarship Program, 262
American Association of Pharmaceutical Scientists Gateway Scholarship, 272
*American Cancer Society Doctoral Degree Scholarship in Cancer Nursing, 266
*American Foundation for Urologic Disease Health Policy Research Program, 274
*American Foundation for Urologic Disease Intramural Urologic Oncology Ph.D./ Post-Doctoral Research Training Program, 275
*American Foundation for Urologic Disease Intramural Urologic Oncology Research Training, 275
*American Foundation for Urologic Disease Intramural Urology Research Training Program, 275
*American Foundation for Urologic Disease MD Post-Resident Research Program, 275
*American Foundation for Urologic Disease MD/Ph.D. One Year Research Program, 275
*American Health Information Management Master's Program, 631
*American Heart Association Beginning Grant-in-Aid Program, 278
*American Heart Association Grant-In-Aid, 278
*American Heart Association Postdoctoral Fellowship, 279
*American Heart Association Predoctoral Fellowship, 279
American Legion Arizona Auxiliary Health Occupation Scholarship, 288
American Legion Arizona Auxiliary Nurses' Scholarship, 288
American Legion Arkansas Auxiliary Nurse Scholarship, 288
American Legion California Auxiliary Department of Education Scholarship I, 289
American Legion Colorado Auxiliary/ Past President's Parley Nurse's Scholarship, 290
American Legion Delaware Auxiliary Past President's Parley Nursing Scholarship, 290
American Legion Georgia Auxiliary Past President's Parley Nursing Scholarship, 291
American Legion Idaho Auxiliary Nursing Scholarship, 291
American Legion Illinois Auxiliary Student Nurse Scholarship, 292

22   *Graduate/nondegree study

Field of Study/Intended Career: Health professions and allied services

American Legion Indiana Auxiliary Past President's Parley Nursing Scholarship, 640
American Legion Iowa Auxiliary Mary Virginia Macrea Memorial Nurses Scholarship, 294
American Legion Kansas John and Geraldine Hobble Licensed Practical Nursing Scholarship, 294
American Legion Maine Auxiliary President's Parley Nursing Scholarship, 296
American Legion Maryland Auxiliary Nursing Scholarship, 297
American Legion Massachusetts Auxiliary Past President's Parley Scholarship, 298
American Legion Massachusetts Nursing Scholarship, 641
American Legion Michigan Auxiliary Scholarships For Nurses, Physical Therapists, and Respiratory Therapists, 299
American Legion Minnesota Auxiliary Past President's Parley Nursing Scholarship, 642
American Legion Missouri Auxiliary Past President's Parley Scholarship, 301
American Legion Missouri M.D. "Jack" Murphy Memorial Nursing Scholarship, 300
*American Legion National Eight and Forty Lung and Respiratory Nursing Scholarship Fund, 301
American Legion Nebraska Auxiliary Practical Nurse Scholarship, 302
American Legion New Hampshire Auxiliary Past President's Parley Nursing Scholarship, 303
American Legion New Jersey Auxiliary Past President's Parley Nursing Scholarship, 304
American Legion New York Auxiliary Medical & Teaching Scholarship, 305
American Legion New York Auxiliary Past President's Parley Nursing Scholarship, 305
American Legion North Dakota Auxiliary Past President's Parley Scholarship, 646
American Legion Ohio Auxiliary Scholarship For Nurse's Training or Medical Field, 307
American Legion Oregon Auxiliary Department Nurses Scholarship, 307
American Legion Puerto Rico Auxiliary Nursing Scholarship, 308
American Legion South Dakota Auxiliary Nurses Scholarship, 647
American Legion Tennessee Auxiliary Vara Gray Nursing Scholarship, 310

American Legion Texas Auxiliary Nurses Scholarship, 310
American Legion Washington Auxiliary Margarite McAlpin Nursing Scholarship, 312
American Legion Wisconsin Auxiliary Health Careers Award, 313
American Legion Wisconsin Auxiliary Registered Nurse Degree Award, 314
American Legion Wyoming Auxiliary Past Presidents' Parley Scholarship, 314
*American Liver Foundation Postdoctoral Fellowship, 317
*American Speech-Language-Hearing Graduate Scholarship, 347
*American Speech-Language-Hearing International/Minority Student Scholarship, 347
*American Speech-Language-Hearing Student with Disability Scholarship, 347
*American Speech-Language-Hearing Young Minority Scholars Award, 347
*Andrew M. Longley, Jr., D.O. Scholarship, 457
*Anne S. Chatham Fellowship in Medicinal Botany, 410
Arthur and Doreen Parrett Scholarship, 355
*Aspen Systems Awards, 631
Athletic Trainers Curriculum Scholarship, 713
Athletic Trainers Student Writing Contest, 713
Avon Products Foundation Career Empowerment Scholarship for Adult Women, 564
Barbara Thomas Enterprises Award, 632
*Beale Family Memorial Scholarship, 457
*Behavioral Sciences Research Fellowship, 401
Benedict Cassen Post-Doctoral Fellowship, 396
Bethesda Lutheran Homes and Services Cooperative Program Internship, 368
*Biotechnology Grant, 544
Black Nurse's Scholarship, 714
Black Nursing Faculty Scholarship, 360
*Brain Tumor Research Fellowship, 265
*Bristol-Myers Squibb Outstanding Resident Award, 329
Burlington Northern Santa Fe Foundation Scholarship, 637
*C.R. Bard Foundation Prize, 505
California Farm Bureau Scholarship, 374

*Cancer Research Fellowship, 441
*Cancer Society Postdoctoral Fellowship, 266
*CANFIT Program Graduate Scholarship, 373
CANFIT Program Undergraduate Scholarship, 374
*Cardiovascular Nursing Award, 634
*Carmela Gagliardi Fellowship, 493
*Carnegie Scholarship, 531
*Chinese American Medical Society Scholarship, 379
*Clinical Cancer Research Fellowship, 259
*Clinical Pathology Student Scholarship, 341
*Clinical Psychology Training Minority Fellowship, 58
*Clinical Rehabilitation Audiology Research Grant, 348
Coding Specialist Program Loan, 632
Colgate "Bright Smiles, Bright Futures" Minority Scholarships, 249
Colgate-Juliette A. Southard/ Oral B Laboratories Scholarship, 271
Colonial Dames of America Indian Nurse Scholarship, 515
Colorado Nursing Scholarship, 65
*Communicative Disorders Scholarships, 567
Connecticut Nursing Scholarship, 384
Cora Aguda Manayan Fund, 420
*Corning Inc. Optometric Scholarship, 328
*Cournand and Comroe Prize, 634
Crave To Be Your Best Scholarship, 532
Critical Care Nurses Education Advancement Scholarship, 262
Critical Care Nurses Education Advancement Scholarship (BSN), 627
*Critical Care Nurses Education Advancement Scholarship (Graduate), 627
*Cystic Fibrosis Clinical Research Grant, 387
*Cystic Fibrosis First and Second Year Clinical Fellowship, 387
*Cystic Fibrosis Pilot and Feasibility Award, 388
*Cystic Fibrosis Postdoctoral Research Fellowship, 388
*Cystic Fibrosis Research Grant, 388
Cystic Fibrosis Student Traineeship, 388
*Cystic Fibrosis Summer Scholarship in Epidemiology, 388
*Cystic Fibrosis Third and Fourth Year Clinical Fellowship, 389
*Damon Runyon Scholar Award, 376
*Deafness Research Foundation Otological Research Fellowship, 391

*Graduate/nondegree study

Field of Study/Intended Career: Health professions and allied services

Delaware Nursing Incentive Program, 70
*Delaware Speech Language Pathologist Incentive Program, 70
Delta Gamma Memorial Scholarship, 273
*Denmark: Aalborg University Grant (Fulbright), 83
Dental Assisting Scholarship, 271
Dental Hygiene Scholarship, 248
Dental Laboratory Technician Scholarship, 248
*Dental Student Research Fellowship, 260
*Dental Student Scholarship, 248
*Downeast Feline Fund, 455
Dr. Alfred C. Fones Scholarship, 249
Dr. Hans and Clara Zimmerman Foundation Health Scholarship, 420
Dr. Harold Hillenbrand Scholarship, 250
*Early Childhood Language Research Grant, 348
*Education and Reseach Foundation Tetalman Award, 582
Educational Optical Engineering Scholarship, 592
*Edward H. Hatton Awards Competition, 260
*Elizabeth Barrett-Connor Research Award, 635
*Elizabeth Glaser Scientist Award, 545
*Epilepsy Clinical Training Fellowship, 401
*Epilepsy Research Training Fellowship, 402
*Ethel Hausman Clinical Research Award, 603
*F. Maynard Lipe Scholarship, 267
*Fellowship in Infectious Diseases, 485
*Fellowship Program in Academic Medicine, 506
*Fight-For-Sight Postdoctoral Research Fellowship, 404
Fight-For-Sight Student Research Fellowship, 404
*Florida Occupational/Physical Therapist Loan Forgiveness Program, 73
Florida Occupational/Physical Therapist Scholarship Loan Program, 73
*Florida Occupational/Physical Therapist Tuition Reimbursement, 74
*FORE Graduate Scholarship, 632
*Franklin C. McLean Award, 506
Gateway Pharmaceutical Research Scholarship, 273
Geoffrey Foundation Undergraduate Scholarship, 412
*Georgia Osteopathic Medical Loan, 116

Georgia Service-Cancelable Stafford Loan, 116
*Gertrude Elion Cancer Research Award, 259
*Giargiari Fellowship, 494
*Graduate & Professional Degree Loan / Scholarship, 140
Grant Program for Physically Disabled Students in the Sciences, 407
*H. Hughes Medical Institute Predoctoral Fellowship, 511
*Harry Shwachman Clinical Investigator Award, 389
Hawaii Community Margaret Jones Memorial Nursing Scholarship, 421
Health Career Scholarship, 437
*Health Sciences Student Fellowship, 402
*Heed Ophthalmic Scholarship, 425
*Henry G. Award, 506
HIM PROGRAM, 633
*History of Pharmacy Grant-In-Aid, 285
HIT Program, 633
*HIV/AIDS Research Training Minority Fellowship, 58
Holistic Nursing Charlotte McGuire Scholarship, 636
*Holistic Nursing Charlotte McGuire Scholarship (Graduate), 636
*Holistic Nursing Research Grant, 636
Howard Brown Rickard Scholarship, 484
Idaho Education Incentive Loan Forgiveness Program, 118
Indiana Minority Teacher Scholarship, 122
Indiana Nursing Scholarship, 122
Indiana Special Education Services Scholarship, 122
Inroads Internship, 432
Irene E. Newman Scholarship, 250
*Irvine H. Page Arteriosclerosis Award, 277
*Irving Graef Memorial Scholarship, 506
J.A. Young Memorial Education Recognition Award, 333
*James H. Robinson Memorial Prize in Surgery, 506
Jean Driscoll Award, 532
*Jeanette Mowery Graduate Scholarship, 536
John Dawe Fund, 422
*John O. Butler Graduate Scholarships, 250
*John P. Utz Postdoctoral Fellowship in Medical Mycology, 486
Kaiser Permanente Dental Assistant Scholarship, 537
Kansas Nursing Scholarship, 125
*Kansas Optometry Program, 125
*Kansas Osteopathic Program, 125

Kansas State Scholarship, 126
Kappa Epsilon-Nellie Wakeman Fellowship, 631
Laura N. Dowsett Fund, 118
Lawrence R. Foster Memorial Scholarship, 537
Legal Medicine Student Writing Competition, 268
*Leroy Matthews Physician/Scientist Award, 389
*Lindbergh Foundation Grant, 378
*Liver Scholar Award, 317
*Louis N. and Arnold M. Katz Research Prize, 277
*Lung Association Career Investigator Award, 317
*Lung Association Clinical Research Grant, 318
*Lung Association Dalsemer Research Dissertation Grant, 318
*Lung Association Research Grant, 318
*Lung Association Research Training Fellowship, 318
*Lung Health Research Dissertation Grant, 318
*M.A. Cartland Shackford Medical Fellowship, 612
M.B. Duggan, Jr., Memorial Education Recognition Award, 333
*Maine Osteopathic Memorial Scholarship, 457
*Maine Osteopathic Scholarship, 457
Margaret E. Swanson Scholarship, 250
*Maryland Family Practice Medical Scholarship, 132
*Maryland Loan Assistance Repayment Program/Primary Care Services, 133
Maryland Physical/Occupational Therapists and Assistants Grant, 134
Maryland Professional School Scholarship, 134
Maryland Reimbursement of Firefighters, 134
Maryland State Nursing Scholarship and Living Expenses Grant, 135
Maryland Tuition Reduction for Out-of-State Nursing Students, 135
*Master's Degree Scholarship in Cancer Nursing, 266
Maxine Williams Scholarship, 263
McFarland Charitable Foundation Scholarship, 419
McKesson Pharmacy Scholarship Program, 707
*Medical Fellowships General Need-Based Scholarship, 507
*Medical Fellowships Special Awards Program, 507
*Medical Fellowships Technology Training Program, 507
*Medical Student Research Fellowship in Pharmacology/Clinical Pharmacology, 547

*Graduate/nondegree study

Medical Technologists Scholarship, 319
*Medical Women's Carroll L. Birch Award, 649
*Medical Women's Education Loan, 649
*Medical Women's Janet M. Glasgow Essay Award, 650
*Medical Women's Wilhelm-Frankowski Scholarship, 319
*Melvin Judkins Award, 635
*Melvin L. Marcus Award, 277
Mental Retardation Nursing Scholastic Achievement Scholarship, 367
*Merck Research Scholarship Program, 273
*Metropolitan Life Foundation Scholarship, 507
*Millipore/Charles P. Schaufus Grant, 544
Minnesota Nursing Grant for Persons of Color, 139
*Minority Dental Student Scholarship, 248
*Mississippi Dental Education Loan/Scholarship, 141
Mississippi Health Care Professional Loan/Scholarship, 141
*Mississippi Medical Education Loan/Scholarship, 142
Mississippi Nursing Education Loan/Scholarship, 142
*Mississippi Nursing Teacher Stipend Program, 142
*Mississippi Southern Regional Education Board Loan/Scholarship, 143
Missouri Nursing Scholarship, 468
*Morphology Fellowship, 547
*Myasthenia Gravis Foundation Kermit E. Osserman Fellowship, 471
Myasthenia Gravis Foundation Nursing Research Fellowship, 472
*NASA Space Grant Arkansas Graduate Fellowship, 148
NASA Space Grant Arkansas Undergraduate Scholarship, 148
*NASA Space Grant Florida Fellowship Program, 151
*NASA Space Grant Florida Fellowship Program, 151
NASA Space Grant Florida Undergraduate Space Research Participation Program, 152
National Health Services Corps Scholarship, 230
*National Hemophilia Foundation/Judith Graham Pool Postdoctoral Research Fellowship, 490
*National Hemophilia Foundation/Nursing Excellence Fellowship, 490
*National Institutes of Health Funding Award, 389

National Student Nurses Association Scholarship, 407
Native Daughters of the Golden West Scholarship, 719
*NCAA Ethnic Minority Internship, 481
*NCAA Ethnic Minority Postgraduate Scholarship, 481
*NCAA Women's Enhancement Postgraduate Scholarship, 482
*NCAA Women's Internship, 482
Nebraska Medical Student Scholarship Program, 181
*Neuromuscular Disease Research Grant, 471
*Neuroscience Training Minority Fellowship, 59
New Hampshire Nursing Scholarship Program, 183
*New Investigators Program, 273
New Mexico Allied Health Student Loan for Service Program, 186
New Mexico Medical Student Loan, 186
New Mexico Nursing Student Loan for Service, 187
New York Life Foundation Health Professions Scholarship, 372
New York State Primary Care Service, 189
*New York State Regents Health Care Professional Opportunity Scholarship, 190
*NIH Postgraduate Research Training Award, 178
NIH Summer Internship Program, 178
NIH Undergraduate Scholarship Program, 178
*North Carolina Board of Governors Dental Scholarship, 234
*North Carolina Board of Governors Medical Scholarship, 234
North Carolina Nurse Education Scholarship Loan, 195
North Carolina Nurse Scholars Program, 195
North Carolina Student Loans for Health/Science/Mathematics, 195
*Northwest Osteopathic Medical Scholarship, 530
*Northwest Osteopathic Medical Student Loan, 530
Northwest Pharmacists Pre-Pharmacy Scholarship, 530
*Novartis Fellowship of the Immune Deficiency Foundation, 531
*Nuclear Medicine Pilot Research Grant, 396
Nuclear Medicine Student Fellowship Award, 396
*Nurses Clinical Training Fellowship, 327
*Nurses Health Policy Research Institute Fellowship, 327

*Nurses Research Training Fellowship, 328
*Nurses Substance Abuse Fellowship, 328
*Oak Ridge Institute for Science and Education Nuclear Engineering Health Physics Fellowship, 200
*Oak Ridge Institute for Science and Education Postgraduate Environmental Management Participation at the U.S. Army Environmental Center, 202
*Oak Ridge Institute for Science and Education Postgraduate Internship at the U.S. Army Center for Health Promotion and Preventive Medicine, 202
*Oak Ridge Institute for Science and Education Postgraduate Research at the Agency for Toxic Substances and Disease Registry, 202
*Oak Ridge Institute for Science and Education Postgraduate Research at the Center for Devices and Radiological Health, 203
*Oak Ridge Institute for Science and Education Postgraduate Research at the Center for Drug Evaluation and Research, 203
*Oak Ridge Institute for Science and Education Postgraduate Research at the Centers for Disease Control and Prevention, 203
*Oak Ridge Institute for Science and Education Postgraduate Research at the National Center for Toxicological Research, 204
*Oak Ridge Institute for Science and Education Postgraduate Research at the U.S. Army Garrison, Aberdeen, 206
*Oak Ridge Institute for Science and Education Postgraduate Research at the U.S. Army Medical Research Institute of Chemical Defense, 206
Oak Ridge Institute for Science and Education Student Internship at the U.S. Army Center for Health Promotion and Preventive Medicine, 208
Oak Ridge Institute for Science and Education Student Research at the Agency for Toxic Substances and Disease Registry, 208
Oak Ridge Institute for Science and Education Student Research at the U.S. Army Garrison, Directorate of Safety, Health and the Environment, 209
Oak Ridge Institute for Science and Education Student Research Participation at the Centers for Disease Control and Prevention, 209

*Graduate/nondegree study

Field of Study/Intended Career: Health professions and allied services

Oak Ridge Institute for Science and Education Student Research Participation at the National Center for Toxicological Research, 209
Oak Ridge Institute for Science and Education Technology Internship Program at the Oak Ridge National Laboratory, 210
Ohio Nurse Education Assistance Loan Program, 212
*Oklahoma Chiropractic Education Assistance, 213
OMNE/Nursing Leaders of Maine Undergraduate Scholarship, 456
Oncology Nursing Bachelor's Scholarship, 533
*Oncology Nursing Doctoral Scholarship, 534
*Oncology Nursing Master's Scholarship, 534
*Oncology Nursing Post-Master's Nurse Practitioner Certificate, 534
*Oncology Nursing Research Grant, 534
*Oral and Maxillofacial Surgery Research Endowment Program, 725
Oral-B Laboratories Dental Hygiene Scholarship, 250
Oregon State Scholarship Commission/Bertha P. Singer Scholarship, 540
*Osborne Scholarship, 531
*Osteopathic Foundation Student Loan Program, 329
*Otologic Research Grant, 391
*Parenteral Research Grant, 544
Pathfinder Scholarship, 715
Paul Cole Scholarship, 397
*Pediatric AIDS Foundation Research Grants, 545
Pediatric AIDS Foundation Student Intern Award, 545
*Pediatric Nurses and Practitioners McNeil Scholarship, 478
*Periodontology Student Loan, 258
*Pfizer Internships, 546
*Phi Lambda Signa First Year Graduate Scholarship, 625
Physician's Assistants Scholarship, 626
*Physician's Research Development Grant, 317
*Postdoctoral Cancer Research Fellowship, 376
*Postdoctoral Fellowship in Emerging Infectious Diseases, 598
Postdoctoral Fellowship in Nosocomial Infection Research and Training, 486
*Postdoctoral Microbiology Research Program, 339
*Predoctoral Fellowship in Pharmaceutics, 547

*Presbyterian Grant Program for Medical Studies, 550
R.M. Lawrence Education Recognition Award, 334
*Ralph Lombardi Memorial Scholarship, 500
*Ralph W. Ellison Prize, 507
*Research Training Fellowships for Medical Students, 430
*Rho Chi First-Year Graduate Scholarship Program, 625
ROTC/Navy Nurse Corps Scholarship Program, 233
Rudolph Dillman Memorial Scholarship, 274
Rudolph Dillman Memorial Scholarship Based on Need, 274
*Russel C. McCaughan Education Fund Scholarship, 329
*Samuel A. Levine Young Clinical Award, 278
*Scholar Awards, 545
Scientific Research Grant-In-Aid, 569
*Selected Professions Fellowship, 265
*Short-Term Scientific Awards, 545
Sigma Phi Alpha Graduate Scholarship, 250
Sigma Phi Alpha Undergraduate Scholarship, 251
*Social Health Postdoctorate Research Fellowship in Sexually Transmitted Diseases, 338
*Sociological Association Minority Fellowship, 60
*Special Medical Education Loan / Scholarship, 144
Spence Reese Scholarship, 370
*Spencer Support for Scholars at Center for Advanced Study/Behavioral Sciences, 592
*St. Anthony Publishing Graduate Award, 633
*State Medical Education Board of Georgia Scholarship, 221
*Student Loan, 348
*Student Research Grant, 317
Surgical Technologists Scholarship Fund, 361
Texas General Scholarship for Nursing Students, 225
Texas Licensed Vocational Nurses Becoming Professional Nurses Scholarship, 225
Texas Outstanding Rural Scholar Program, 223
Texas Rural Bachelors or Graduate Nursing Students Scholarship, 226
Texas Rural Nursing Students Scholarship, 226
*The North Carolina Nurse Scholars Program MasterÖs Program, 195
Thz Fo Farm Fund, 118
*Transcriptions Limited Graduate Scholarship, 634

Undergraduate Research Fellowship in Pharmaceutics, 547
*United Cerebral Palsy Clinical Fellowship, 603
*United Cerebral Palsy Research Grant, 603
*Urologic Disease Ph.D. Research Scholarship, 276
*Veterinary Medicine Minority Loan / Scholarship, 144
*Veterinary Student Scholarship, 348
Viets Premedical/Medical Student Fellowship, 472
*Virginia Medical Scholarship Program, 222
Virginia Nursing Scholarship Program, 222
Virginia Regional Contract Program, 238
*Virginia Rural Dental Scholarship Program, 222
*Vision Awareness Educational Grant, 276
*Vivien Thomas Award, 635
*W.F. Miller Postgraduate Education Recognition Award, 334
*W.K. Kellog Community Medicine Training, 508
W.M. Burgin, Jr., Scholarship, 334
Walter and Marie Schmidt Scholarship, 543
Washington State Health Professions Loan/Scholarship, 240
*West Virginia Medical Student Loan Program, 241
*Whitney Postdoctoral Research Fellowship, 426
*William and Charlotte Cadbury Award, 508
Wisconsin Dental Association Scholarship, 615
*Wyeth-Ayerst Laboratories Prize, 508
*Wyeth-Ayerst Laboratories Scholarship, 373
Young Investigator Matching Grants, 486
*Young Investigator Prize in Thrombosis, 278
*Zecchino Postgraduate Orthopaedic Fellowship, 504
*Zeneca Pharmacy Underserved Healthcare Grant, 329

Home economics

1890 National Scholars Program, 228
*CANFIT Program Graduate Scholarship, 373
CANFIT Program Undergraduate Scholarship, 374
*ConAgra Fellowship in Child Nutrition, 738
Dairy Management Milking Marketing Scholarship, 482

*Graduate/nondegree study

Dairy Product Marketing Scholarship, 390
Dairy Shrine Graduate Student Scholarship, 483
Dairy Shrine Student Recognition Scholarship, 483
Enology and Viticulture Scholarship, 339
Food Engineering Division Junior/Senior Scholarship, 432
*Food Packaging Division Graduate Fellowship, 693
Food Service Communicators Scholarship, 436
General Mills Internship Program, 412
*H.J. Heinz Graduate Degree Fellowship, 512
*Hubert Humphrey Research Grant, 738
Institute of Food Technologists Freshman Scholarship, 433
*Institute of Food Technologists Graduate Fellowship, 433
Institute of Food Technologists Junior/Senior Scholarship, 433
Institute of Food Technologists Sophomore Scholarship, 433
*Kappa Omicrom Nu Fellowships and Grants, 698
*Lincoln Food Service Research Grant, 739
National Restaurant Association Undergraduate Scholarship, 512
*ProManagement Scholarship, 512
Quality Assurance Division Junior/Senior Scholarship, 433
*School Food Service Foundation Professional Growth Scholarship, 739
*Society of Flavor Chemists Memorial Graduate Fellowship, 433
*Teacher Work-Study Grant, 512
Tony's Food Service Scholarship, 739

Law

Alphonso Deal Scholarship, 480
*American Bar Doctoral Dissertation Fellowship, 265
American Legion California Auxiliary Department of Education Scholarship I, 289
American Legion California Auxiliary Department of Education Scholarship II, 289
Career Advancement Scholarship, 372
Cooperative Education Program, 62
Cooperative Education Program, 62
Dorothy Andrews Kabis Internship, 715
*Earl Warren Legal Training Program Scholarship, 472
*Federal Chancellor Scholarship, 56

*Florida Education Fund Minority Participation in Legal Education Law School Scholarship, 76
Florida Education Fund Minority Pre-law Scholarships, 76
*Grant for Research in Venice, 413
*H. Thomas Austern Writing Award, 405
*Harry Frank Guggenheim Dissertation Fellowship, 418
Hopi Tribal Priority Scholarship, 428
Horizons Foundation Scholarship, 429
Howard Brown Rickard Scholarship, 484
Institute for Humane Studies Fellowship, 432
*Jeanette Mowery Graduate Scholarship, 536
*Law Fellowships for Equal Justice, 476
*Law Internship Program, 198
Law/Social Sciences Summer Research Fellowship for Minority Undergraduates, 265
Legal Medicine Student Writing Competition, 268
Marion MacCarrell Scott Scholarship, 424
Maryland Professional School Scholarship, 134
*Mexican American Law School Scholarship, 465
*Mexico: Binational Business Grants (Fulbright), 98
NASA Space Grant Alabama Graduate Fellowship, 146
NASA Space Grant Alabama Undergraduate Scholarship Program, 147
Nathan Burkan Memorial Competition, 356
National Organization for Women legal defense and Education fund Internships, 510
*New Jersey C. Clyde Ferguson Law Scholarship, 183
*NIAF/FIERI D.C. Matching Scholarship, 498
*Oak Ridge Institute for Science and Education Postgraduate Research at the U.S. Army Environmental Policy Institute, 206
Oak Ridge Institute for Science and Education Student Research at the U.S. Army Environmental Policy Institute, 209
Oak Ridge Institute for Science and Education Student Research Participation at the U.S. Army Environmental Policy Institute, 210
Public Policy Internship Program, 460
*Puerto Rican Legal Defense & Educ. Fund-Father Joseph P. Fitzpatrick Scholarship, 554

*Ron Brown Fellowship Program, 438
*Scalia Scholarship, 501
*Selected Professions Fellowship, 265
Skadden, Arps, Slate, Meagher and Flom Law Internship, 569
Spence Reese Scholarship, 370
*SSRC Dissertation Fellowship: South Asia, 576
*Syria: Government Grant (Fulbright), 107
*Unitarian Universalist Stanfield Law Scholarship, 602
*Univision-Mexican American Legal Defense Fund Scholarship, 466
Youth Entertainment Summer, 618

Liberal arts and interdisciplinary studies

*Advanced Research Grants: Vietnam, 572
*Advanced Research Program, 437
*American Academy in Rome/Rome Prize Pre- and Post-Doctoral Fellowship, 57
American Society of Magazine Editors Internship, 343
*Andrew W. Mellon Fellowship in Humanistic Studies, 617
*Asian Humanities Fellowship Program, 356
*Austrian Research and Study Scholarship, 362
*Benin: Full Grant (Fulbright), 79
*Carmargo Foundation Fellowship, 376
Coca-Cola Internship, 509
*Council of Learned Societies Fellowship, 270
*Eastern Europe Dissertation Fellowship, 270
*Eastern Europe Postdoctorate Fellowship, 270
*Federal Chancellor Scholarship, 56
Federation of the Blind Humanities Scholarship, 484
*Fellowships for Postdoctoral Research: Eastern Europe, 572
*Florida Education Fund McKnight Doctoral Fellowship, 405
*Ford Foundation Postdoctoral Fellowships for Minorities, 511
*Ford Foundation Predoctoral Fellowship: Minorities, 511
Foreign Study/Minority Scholarship Strategic Studies Award, 281
*Graduate Scholarship in Lesbian Studies, 520
*Grant for Research in Venice, 413
*Hagley Museum and Library Grant-In-Aid, 417
*Harry Frank Guggenheim Dissertation Fellowships, 418
*Huntington British Academy Exchange Fellowship, 430

*Graduate/nondegree study

Field of Study/Intended Career: Liberal arts and interdisciplinary studies

* Huntington National Endowment for the Humanities Fellowship, 431
Indianapolis Newspapers Fellowship, 431
Institute for Humane Studies Fellowship, 432
* International Dissertation Field Research Fellowship Program, 572
International Educational Exchange/R.B. Bailey Minority Scholarship, 68
* International Research and Exchanges Board Travel Grant, 438
International Semester Scholarship, 281
International Summer Scholarship, 281
Italian Cultural Society and NIAF Matching Scholarship, 495
J. Paul Getty Trust Internship Program, 440
* Japan Foundation Doctoral Fellowship, 441
* Johnson and Johnson Dissertation Grants in Women's Health, 244
Lebovitz Internship, 509
* Mid Career Skills Enrichment Program for Tenured Faculty, 573
Museum Internships in Washington DC, 510
* National Endowment for the Humanities Postdoctoral Fellowship, 60
National Junior Classical League Scholarship, 628
Native American Scholarship, 520
* Near and Middle East Research and Training Act Senior Post-Doctoral Research Grant, 336
* New Jersey Minority Academic Career Program, 185
* Newcombe Doctoral Dissertation Fellowship, 617
* Postdoctoral Fellowship: Eurasia, 574
* Postdoctoral Sexuality Research Fellowship Program, 574
* Predissertation Fellowship: Bangladesh, 574
* Predissertation Fellowship: Near-Middle East, 574
* Predissertation Fellowship: South Asia, 575
* Research Institute in Turkey Fellowship, 333
* Ruth Strang Women's Research Awards, 522
* Sexuality Research Dissertation Fellowship Program, 575
* Spencer Postdoctoral Fellowship Program, 474
* SSRC Dissertation Fellowship: Bangladesh, 575
* SSRC Dissertation Fellowship: Eastern Europe, 575

* SSRC Dissertation Fellowship: Eurasia, 576
* SSRC Dissertation Fellowship: Middle East, 576
* SSRC Dissertation Fellowship: Middle East, 576
* SSRC Dissertation Fellowship: South Asia, 576
* SSRC Dissertation Fellowship: Southeast Asia, 576
* Study in Scandinavia Grant, 351
Thomas Joseph Ambrosole Scholarship, 503
* U.S. Information Agency Predoctoral/Postdoctoral Fellowship, 336
* Weiss Brown Publication Subvention Award, 527
* Women's Research and Education Congressional Fellowship, 616
* Woodrow Wilson Dissertation Grant in Women's Studies, 618
Young Feminist Scholarship Program, 593

Library science

* ALISE Dissertation Competition, 359
* ALISE Methodology Paper Competition, 359
* ALISE Research Grant Award, 656
* ALISE Research Paper Competition, 656
* American Library Association Doctoral Dissertation Fellowship, 315
Archival Internships, 445
AT&T Hispanic Division Fellowship, 452
* Beta Phi Mu Blanche E. Woolls Scholarship for School Library Media Service., 367
* Beta Phi Mu Doctoral Dissertation Scholarship, 367
* Bound to Stay Bound Books Scholarship, 315
* California Library Scholarship for Minority Students, 375
Coca-Cola Internship, 509
* David H. Clift Scholarship, 315
* David Rozkuszka Scholarship, 315
Experiential Education Internship, 514
* Frank B. Sessa Scholarship for Continuing Education, 661
Franklin D. Roosevelt Library/Roosevelt Internship, 408
* Frederic G. Melcher Scholarship, 316
Grants-In-Aid for Research on the Roosevelt Years, 408
* Harold Lancour Scholarship for Foreign Study, 661
* Library and Information Science Grant, 438
* Library and Information Technology Association/GEAC-CLSI Scholarship, 316

* Library and Information Technology Association/LSSI Minority Scholarship, 316
* Library and Information Technology Association/OCLC/Minority Scholarship, 316
Library of Congress Junior Fellows Internship, 127
* Louise Giles Minority Scholarship, 316
* Mary Adeline Connor Professional Development Scholarship, 748
* Medical Library Association Scholarship, 461
* Medical Library Doctoral Scholarship, 462
* Medical Library Rittenhouse Award, 462
* Medical Library Scholarship for Minority Students, 462
Museum Internships in Washington DC, 510
* Oak Ridge Institute for Science and Education National Library of Medicine Associate Fellowship, 200
* Reforma Scholarship Program, 559
* Sarah Rebecca Reed Scholarship, 367
* Special Libraries Association Affirmative Action Scholarship, 591
* Special Libraries Institute for Scientific Information Scholarship, 748
* Special Libraries Plenum Scholarship, 748
* Special Libraries Scholarship, 591
Virginia Regional Contract Program, 238

Mathematics

A.T. Anderson Memorial Scholarship, 636
Actuarial Club Scholarship, 454
Actuarial Society Minority Scholarship, 579
Aerospace Undergraduate Scholarship Program, 173
Air Force Four-Year Scholarships(Types # 1,2 and Targeted), 217
American Legion Maryland Science/Math Scholarship, 296
* Applied Health Physics Fellowship, 197
* Armed Forces Educational Foundation Fellowship, 353
Barry M. Goldwater Scholarship, 62
* Churchill Scholarship, 615
Community College Scholarship Program, 173
Community College Transfer Scholarships, 173
* Florida Education Fund McKnight Doctoral Fellowship, 405

*Graduate/nondegree study

Field of Study/Intended Career: Mathematics

*Ford Foundation Dissertation Fellowship: Minorities, 510
*Ford Foundation Postdoctoral Fellowships for Minorities, 511
*Ford Foundation Predoctoral Fellowship: Minorities, 511
Fossil Energy Technology Internship, 197
General Emmett Paige Scholarship, 353
General John A. Wickham Scholarship, 353
Grant Program for Physically Disabled Students in the Sciences, 407
Horizons Foundation Scholarship, 429
*I/ITSEC Graduate Student Scholarship Program, 520
Kathryn D. Sullivan Science and Engineering Undergraduate Fellowship, 169
Maria Mitchell Internships for Astronomical Research, 460
Melon Minority Fellowship Program, 573
Mississippi Space Grant Consortium, 159
NASA Academy Internship, 167
NASA Space Grant District of Columbia Undergraduate Scholarship, 151
*NASA Space Grant District of Columbia Graduate Fellowship, 151
*NASA Space Grant Idaho Graduate Fellowship, 153
NASA Space Grant Idaho Undergraduate Scholarship Program, 153
*NASA Space Grant Indiana Graduate Fellowship, 154
NASA Space Grant Indiana Summer Undergraduate Research Program, 154
NASA Space Grant Indiana Undergraduate Scholarship, 154
NASA Space Grant Kansas Graduate Fellowship, 155
NASA Space Grant Kansas Undergraduate Scholarship, 155
NASA Space Grant Louisiana LaSPACE Graduate Fellowship Program, 156
NASA Space Grant Louisiana LaSPACE Undergraduate Scholarship Program, 156
*NASA Space Grant Michigan Graduate Fellowship, 158
NASA Space Grant Michigan Undergraduate Fellowship, 159
*NASA Space Grant Nevada Graduate Fellowship, 161
NASA Space Grant Nevada Undergraduate Scholarship, 162

*NASA Space Grant New Mexico Graduate Fellowship, 163
NASA Space Grant New Mexico Undergraduate Scholarship, 163
*NASA Space Grant North Dakota Graduate Fellowship, 164
NASA Space Grant North Dakota Undergraduate Scholarship, 164
*NASA Space Grant Oregon Graduate Fellowship, 166
NASA Space Grant Pennsylvania Undergraduate Scholarship, 167
*NASA Space Grant Puerto Rico Graduate Fellowship, 167
NASA Space Grant Puerto Rico Summer Internship Program, 168
NASA Space Grant Puerto Rico Undergraduate Scholarship, 168
*NASA Space Grant Tennessee Graduate Fellowship, 171
NASA Space Grant Tennessee Undergraduate Scholarship, 171
*NASA Space Grant Vermont Space Graduate Research Assistantship, 172
NASA Space Grant Vermont Undergraduate Scholarships, 172
*NASA Space Grant Washington Graduate Fellowships at the University of Washington, 174
NASA Space Grant Washington Undergraduate Scholarship Program, 174
*National Defense Science and Engineering Graduate Fellowship Program, 70
*National Science Foundation Graduate Fellowship, 179
*National Science Foundation Minority Graduate Fellowship, 180
National Security Agency Undergraduate Tuition Assistance Program, 180
Native American Scholarship, 520
*New Jersey Minority Academic Career Program, 185
North Carolina Student Loans for Health/Science/Mathematics, 195
*Oak Ridge Institute for Science and Education Fossil Energy Postgraduate Research, 198
*Oak Ridge Institute for Science and Education Magnetic Fusion Energy Technology Fellowship, 199
*Oak Ridge Institute for Science and Education Magnetic Fusion Science Fellowship, 199
Oak Ridge Institute for Science and Education National Oceanic and Atmospheric Administration Student Program, 200

*Oak Ridge Institute for Science and Education Oak Ridge National Laboratory Postdoctoral Research, 200
Oak Ridge Institute for Science and Education Office of Civilian Radioactive Waste Management Historically Black Colleges and Universities Undergraduate Scholarship Program, 201
*Oak Ridge Institute for Science and Education Postgraduate Research at the National Center for Toxicological Research, 204
*Oak Ridge Institute for Science and Education Postgraduate Research at the Oak Ridge National Laboratory, 204
Oak Ridge Institute for Science and Education Professional Internship Program at Federal Energy Technology Centers, 532
Oak Ridge Institute for Science and Education Student Research Participation at the National Center for Toxicological Research, 209
Oak Ridge Institute for Science and Education U.S. Department of Energy/NAACP, 210
Oak Ridge Institute for Science and Education U.S. Nuclear Regulatory Commission Historically Black Colleges and Universities Student Research Participation, 211
Oregon State Scholarship Commission/Howard Vollum American Indian Scholarship, 540
Pearl I. Young Scholarship, 165
*Physical Science Graduate Fellowship: Minorities and Women, 510
Plasma Physics National Undergraduate Fellowship Program, 216
ROTC Scholarships, 655
ROTC/ Air Force Three-Year Scholarships Types 2 And Targeted, 217
Scholarships at Seattle Central Community College, 174
*Science and Technology Fellowship, 264
Scripps Undergraduate Research Fellowship, 566
State Farm Companies Exceptional Student Fellowship, 594
Tandy Technology Students Award, 596
Teacher Education Scholarship Program, 173
Think Automotive Scholarship, 362
Wal-Mart Competitive Edge Scholarship, 609
Willems Scholarship, 711

*Graduate/nondegree study

Field of Study/Intended Career: Military science

Military science

Center for Defense Information Internship, 377
Oak Ridge Institute for Science and Education Postgraduate Research at the Department of Veterans Affairs, Birmingham Education Center, 203
*U.S. Army Center of Military History Dissertation Fellowship, 227

Mortuary science

Mortuary Education Grant, 428

Philosophy, religion, and theology

*Bishop James C. Baker Award, 603
*Georgia Harkness Scholarship, 604
Ira Page Wallace Bible Scholarship, 550
Juliette M. Atherton Scholarship, 423
Lazaroff Family Fund, 443
Melon Minority Fellowship Program, 573
*Presbyterian Fund for Graduate Education, 550
*Presbyterian Native American Seminary Scholarship, 551
*Presbyterian Racial/Ethnic Leadership Supplemental Grant, 551
*Presbyterian Theological Continuing Education Loan, 552
*Presbyterian Theological Loan, 552
*Rabbi Marc H. Tannenbaum Foundation Fellowships, 286
*Rev. Charles W. Tadlock Scholarship, 604
*Student Ministry Fund, 437
*Theological Continuing Education Grant, 552

Protective services

Alphonso Deal Scholarship, 480
Captain James J. Regan Memorial Scholarship, 663
Former Agents of the U.S. Secret Service Scholarship, 657
*Harry Frank Guggenheim Dissertation Fellowship, 418
*Harry Frank Guggenheim Dissertation Fellowships, 418
Law/Social Sciences Summer Research Fellowship for Minority Undergraduates, 265
Maryland Reimbursement of Firefighters, 134
*National Institute of Justice Graduate Research Fellowship, 178
Sheryl A. Horak Law Enforcement Explorer Scholarship, 665
Virginia Regional Contract Program, 238

Social sciences and history

*Abe Fellowship Program, 571
Actuarial Club Scholarship, 454
*Adelle and Erwin Tomash Fellowship, 378
*Advanced Research Grants: Japan, 571
*Advanced Research Grants: Vietnam, 572
*Advanced Research Program, 437
*Aerospace Graduate Research Fellowship Program, 172
*Alice Smith Fellowship, 221
*Allport Intergroup Relations Prize, 577
*American Academy in Rome/Rome Prize Pre- and Post-Doctoral Fellowship, 57
*American Art Dissertation Fellowship, 270
American Association of Japanese University Women Scholarship, 262
*American Bar Doctoral Dissertation Fellowship, 265
*American Cancer Society Training Grants In Clinical Oncology Social Work (Tgcosw), 266
*American Heart Association Grant-In-Aid, 278
*American Heart Association Predoctoral Fellowship, 279
*American Museum of Natural History Research Fellowships, 321
American Nuclear Society Washington Internship for Students of Engineering, 322
American Numismatic Society Fellowship in Roman Studies, 326
American Numismatic Society Shaykh Hamad Fellowship in Islamic Numismatics, 326
*American Political Science Association Minority Fellows, 330
*American Schools of Oriental Research/Annual Professorship, 334
American Schools of Oriental Research/Endowment for Biblical Research and Travel Grant, 335
*American Schools of Oriental Research/Harrell Family Fellowship, 335
American Schools of Oriental Research/Jennifer C. Groot Fellowship, 335
*American Schools of Oriental Research/Kenneth W. Russell Fellowship, 267
*American Schools of Oriental Research/National Endowment for the Humanities Fellowship, 335

*American Schools of Oriental Research/Samuel H. Kress Fellowships, 335
*American Society for Eighteenth Century Studies Fellowship, 525
*Amy Louise Hunter Fellowship, 221
*Anne and Oliver C. Colburn Fellowship, 351
Anne U. White Fund, 656
*Antiquarian Society Short-Term Fellowship, 259
Archival Internships, 445
*Armenian Union U.S. Graduate Loan, 354
*Asian Humanities Fellowship Program, 356
*Association of American Geographers Dissertation Research Grant, 656
*Association of American Geographers General Research Grant, 656
*Audrey Lumsdem-Kouvel Fellowship, 525
*Austrian Research and Study Scholarship, 362
*Behavioral Sciences Research Fellowship, 401
Behavioral Sciences Student Fellowship, 401
*Benin: Full Grant (Fulbright), 79
*Berlin Program for Advanced German-European Studies, 572
Bethesda Lutheran Homes and Services Cooperative Program Internship, 368
Betty Rendel Scholarship, 715
Biblical Research Travel Grant, 336
Bolla Wines Scholarship, 492
*Bulgarian Studies Grant, 438
*Carmargo Foundation Fellowship, 376
Center for Defense Information Internship, 377
CIA Undergraduate Scholarship, 64
*Clara Mayo Grants-In-Aid, 577
*Clinical Psychology Training Minority Fellowship, 58
*Collection Study Grants, 321
Cooperative Education Program, 62
Cooperative Education Program, 62
*Council of Jewish Federations Scholarship, 385
*Council of Learned Societies Fellowship, 270
*Dirksen Research Grant Program, 392
*Doctoral Dissertation Fellowship in Jewish Studies, 486
Dorothy Andrews Kabis Internship, 715
Dupont Fellowship, 417
*Early American Industries Grants-In-Aid Program, 394
*Eastern Europe Dissertation Fellowship, 270
*Eastern Europe Postdoctorate Fellowship, 270

*Graduate/nondegree study

Field of Study/Intended Career: Social sciences and history

* Ecole des Chartes Exchange Fellowship, 525
* English-Speaking Union Graduate Scholarship, 400
* Exploration Fund, 403
* Federal Chancellor Scholarship, 56
  Federal Reserve Summer Internship, 71
* Fellowships for Postdoctoral Research: Eastern Europe, 572
* Ford Foundation Dissertation Fellowship: Minorities, 510
* Ford Foundation Postdoctoral Fellowships for Minorities, 511
* Ford Foundation Predoctoral Fellowship: Minorities, 511
* Frank M. Chapman Memorial Grants, 321
* Friedrich Ebert Advanced Graduate Fellowship, 409
* Friedrich Ebert Doctoral Research Fellowship, 409
* Friedrich Ebert Postdoctoral Fellowship, 409
* Fulbright - USIA U.K. Zeneca Award, 87
  Gary Merrill Memorial Scholarship Program, 455
* Geography Research Grants, 489
  Geography Students Internship, 490
* George A. Barton Fellowship, 267
* Graduate Scholarship in Lesbian Studies, 520
* Grant for Research in Venice, 413
* H.J. Swinney Internship, 594
* Harriet and Leon Pomerance Fellowship, 352
* Harry Frank Guggenheim Dissertation Fellowship, 418
* Harry Frank Guggenheim Dissertation Fellowships, 418
  Harry Truman Scholarship, 117
* Helen M. Woodruff Fellowship, 352
* Henry A. Murray Research Center Dissertation Award, 426
* Herbert Scoville Jr. Peace Fellowship, 566
  Herzog August Bibliothek Wolfenbuttel Fellowship, 525
* History of Pharmacy Grant-In-Aid, 285
* HIV/AIDS Research Training Minority Fellowship, 58
* Hoover Presidential Library Fellowship/Grant, 427
  Horizons Foundation Scholarship, 429
* Huntington British Academy Exchange Fellowship, 430
* Huntington National Endowment for the Humanities Fellowship, 431
* Huntington W.M. Keck Foundation Fellowship for Young Scholars, 431
* Institut Francais de Washington Fellowship, 432

  Institute for Humane Studies Fellowship, 432
* International Dissertation Field Research Fellowship Program, 572
* International Predissertation Fellowship Program, 573
* International Research and Exchanges Board Travel Grant, 438
* Jack E. Leisch Memorial National Scholarships, 340
* James Madison Memorial Junior Fellowship, 124
* James Madison Memorial Senior Fellowship, 124
* Japan Foundation Doctoral Fellowship, 441
* Jeanne Humphrey Block Dissertation Award, 426
* John C. Geilfuss Fellowship, 221
  John F. Kennedy Library Foundation/ Abba P. Schwartz Research Fellowship, 445
  John F. Kennedy Library Foundation/ Arthur M. Schlesinger Jr. Research Fellowships, 446
* Joint Fellowship with the American Antiquarian Society, 525
* Junior Investigator Epilepsy Research Grant, 402
  Karla Scherer Foundation Scholarship, 447
  Kawasaki-McGaha Scholarship Fund, 423
* Kenan T. Erim Award, 352
  Kennedy Library Research Grants, 446
* Klineberg Award, 578
* Kreiss Art History and Archaeology Fellowship, 333
  Latino Summer Legislative Internship, 478
  Law/Social Sciences Summer Research Fellowship for Minority Undergraduates, 265
* Lemmermann Scholarship, 451
* Lerner-Gray Grants for Marine Research, 322
* Lester J. Cappon Fellowship in Documentary Editing, 525
* Lloyd Lewis Fellowship in American History, 526
* Louise Kidder Early Career Award, 578
* Lung Association Clinical Research Grant, 318
* Lung Association Research Grant, 318
* Lung Health Research Dissertation Grant, 318
* Mali: Full Grant (Fulbright), 97
* Malyon-Smith Scholarship Award, 577
  Marion MacCarrell Scott Scholarship, 424

  Marjorie Kovler Research Fellowship, 446
* Mary Isabel Sibley Fellowship, 547
* Mary McEwen Schimke Scholarship, 612
  Mass Media Science and Engineering Fellowship, 626
  Melon Minority Fellowship Program, 573
  Mental Retardation Scholastic Achievement Scholarship, 368
* Metropolitan Museum of Art Graduate Lecturing Internship, 463
* Mexico: Binational Business Grants (Fulbright), 98
* Mid Career Skills Enrichment Program for Tenured Faculty, 573
  Mildred Towle Trust Fund Scholarship, 424
  Mississippi Health Care Professional Loan/Scholarship, 141
  Mississippi Psychology Apprenticeship Program, 142
  Mobility Internship Program, 468
  NASA Space Grant Alabama Graduate Fellowship, 146
  NASA Space Grant Alabama Undergraduate Scholarship Program, 147
* NASA Space Grant Delaware Space Graduate Student Fellowship, 150
  NASA Space Grant Delaware Undergraduate Tuition Scholarship, 150
* NASA Space Grant Kentucky Graduate Fellowship, 155
* NASA Space Grant Pennsylvania Graduate Fellowship, 167
  National Dean's List Scholarship, 700
* National Defense Science and Engineering Graduate Fellowship Program, 70
* National Endowment for the Humanities Fellowship, 526
  National Journal Editorial Internship, 504
* National Scholarship Award, 701
* National Science Foundation Minority Postdoctoral Fellowship, 180
  Native American Scholarship, 520
  Native Daughters of the Golden West Scholarship, 719
* Near and Middle East Research and Training Act Predoctoral Fellowship, 336
* Near and Middle East Research and Training Act Senior Post-Doctoral Research Grant, 336
  Network Internship or Summer Science Internship, 554
* New Jersey Minority Academic Career Program, 185
* Newcombe Doctoral Dissertation Fellowship, 617

*Graduate/nondegree study

31

Field of Study/Intended Career: Social sciences and history

* Nicaragua: Full Grant (Fulbright), 100
* Numismatic Graduate Fellowship, 327
* Numismatic Graduate Seminar, 327
* Nurses Research Training Fellowship, 328
* Nurses Substance Abuse Fellowship, 328
  Oak Ridge Institute for Science and Education Office of Civilian Radioactive Waste Management Historically Black Colleges and Universities Undergraduate Scholarship Program, 201
* Oak Ridge Institute for Science and Education Postgraduate Research at the Centers for Disease Control and Prevention, 203
* Oak Ridge Institute for Science and Education Postgraduate Research at the National Risk Management Research Laboratory, 204
* Oak Ridge Institute for Science and Education Postgraduate Research at the U.S. Army Environmental Policy Institute, 206
  Oak Ridge Institute For Science and Education Student Environmental Management Participation for the U.S. Army Environmental Center, 208
  Oak Ridge Institute for Science and Education Student Research at the U.S. Army Environmental Policy Institute, 209
  Oak Ridge Institute for Science and Education Student Research Participation at the Centers for Disease Control and Prevention, 209
  Oak Ridge Institute for Science and Education Student Research Participation at the U.S. Army Environmental Policy Institute, 210
  Oak Ridge Institute for Science and Education U.S. Geological Survey Earth Sciences Internship, 211
* Olivia James Traveling Fellowship, 352
  Pathfinder Scholarship, 715
  Patrick Murphy Internship, 516
* Postdoctoral Fellowship: Eurasia, 574
* Postdoctoral Fellowship: Middle East, 574
* Postdoctoral Sexuality Research Fellowship Program, 574
* Pre-Dissertation Fellowship for Research in Europe, 384
* Predissertation Fellowship: Bangladesh, 574
* Predissertation Fellowship: Near-Middle East, 574
* Predissertation Fellowship: South Asia, 575
* President Francesco Cossiga Fellowship, 526

* Presidential Management Program, 228
* Psychology Research Training Minority Fellowship, 59
* Purchasing Management Doctoral Grant, 479
* Radcliffe Research Support Program Award, 427
* Research Center in Egypt Fellowship, 59
* Research Institute in Turkey Fellowship, 333
  Rhode Island State Government Internship Program, 216
* Ron Brown Fellowship Program, 438
  Rosann S. Berry Annual Meeting Fellowship, 580
* Ruth Satter Memorial Award, 360
* Sally Kress Tompkins Fellowship, 580
* Scientific Study of Sexuality Student Grant, 579
  Secondary School Principals Leadership Award, 479
  Service Merchandise Scholarship, 568
* Sexuality Research Dissertation Fellowship Program, 575
* Short-Term Fellowship in the History of Cartography, 526
* Short-Term Resident Fellowship for Individual Research, 526
* Smithsonian Graduate Student Fellowship, 570
  Smithsonian Minority Internship, 570
* Smithsonian Post-Doctoral Fellowship, 571
* Smithsonian Pre-Doctoral Fellowship, 571
* Smithsonian Senior Fellowship, 571
* Social Issues Dissertation Award, 578
  Social Issues Internship Program, 578
* Social Issues Sages Program, 579
* Social Science Fellowship Program, 549
* Social Work Clinical Fellowship, 386
* Social Work Minority Research Fellowship, 386
* Sociological Association Minority Fellowship, 60
* South Central Modern Language Association Fellowship, 720
  Spence Reese Scholarship, 370
* Spencer Postdoctoral Fellowship Program, 474
* SSRC Dissertation Fellowship: Bangladesh, 575
* SSRC Dissertation Fellowship: Eastern Europe, 575
* SSRC Dissertation Fellowship: Eurasia, 576
* SSRC Dissertation Fellowship: Middle East, 576
* SSRC Dissertation Fellowship: Middle East, 576

* SSRC Dissertation Fellowship: South Asia, 576
* SSRC Dissertation Fellowship: Southeast Asia, 576
  State/County/Municipal Employees Jerry Clark Memorial Scholarship, 631
* Syria: Government Grant (Fulbright), 107
  Theodore C. Sorensen Research Fellowship, 446
* Theodore Roosevelt Memorial Grants, 322
  Think Automotive Scholarship, 362
* Trent R. Dames and William W. Moore Fellowship, 651
* U.S. Army Center of Military History Dissertation Fellowship, 227
  U.S. Department of State Foreign Affairs Fellowship, 245
* U.S. Information Agency Predoctoral/Postdoctoral Fellowship, 336
* United Kingdom: University College London Scholarship (Fulbright), 112
  United States Information Agency Summer Internship, 232
  Washington Crossing Foundation Scholarship, 611
* Weinberg Fellowship for Independent Scholars, 527
* Weiss Brown Publication Subvention Award, 527
* Winterthur Fellowship, 417
* Women in Science Education Research Grant, 360
* Women's Research and Education Congressional Fellowship, 616
* Woodrow Wilson Dissertation Grant in Women's Studies, 618
  Woodrow Wilson Program in Public Policy and International Affairs, 618
* Woodruff Dissertation Research Fellowship, 352
  Yosemite National Park Internships, 245

Trade and industry

A.J. "Andy" Spielman Travel Agents Scholarship, 344
AGC of Maine Scholarship Program, 357
Air Safety Foundation D.B. Burnside Scholarship, 256
Air Safety Foundation McAllister Memorial Scholarship, 256
Air Traffic Control Half/Full-Time Student Scholarship, 251
Air Travel Card Travel Agents Scholarship, 344
Airport Executives Scholarship, 261
Al and Art Murray Scholarship, 469
Alaska Airlines Travel Agents Scholarship, 344
Alwin B. Newton Scholarships, 341

*Graduate/nondegree study

Field of Study/Intended Career: Trade and industry

American Congress on Surveying and Mapping, 628
American Congress on Surveying and Mapping/Allen Chelf Scholarship, 268
American Congress on Surveying and Mapping/McDonnel Memorial Scholarship, 269
American Congress on Surveying and Mapping/National Society of Professional Surveyors Scholarship for Women, 629
American Express Travel Agents Scholarship, 344
American Soc. Heating/Refrigeration/Air-Conditioning Engineers Technical Scholarship, 337
American Soc. Heating/Refrigeration/Air-Conditioning Engineers Undergraduate Scholarship, 337
American Welding Society District Scholarship, 349
* American Welding Society Graduate Fellowship, 349
Arizona Chapter Gold Travel Agents Scholarship, 344
* Armed Forces Educational Foundation Fellowship, 353
ARRL Mississippi Scholarship, 330
Associated General Contractors James L. Allhands Essay Competition, 357
Aviation Distributors and Manufacturers Scholarship, 362
Aviation Scholarship and Work Studies Program, 394
Bernstein International Surveying Scholarship, 629
Bill Carpenter Memorial Certificate School Scholarship, 516
Black & Veatch Summer Internship in Engineering, Construction, and Architecture, 368
Bose Corporation Scholarship, 252
Bud Glover Memorial Scholarship, 252
CANFIT Program Undergraduate Scholarship, 374
Cartographic Association Scholarship, 629
Castleberry Instruments Scholarship, 252
Caterpillar Scholars Award, 582
Charles N. Fisher Memorial Scholarship, 331
Charlotte Woods Memorial Scholarship, 598
Chuck Peacock Honorary Scholarship, 252
College of Aeronautics Scholarship, 253
Community College Scholarship Program, 173
* ConAgra Fellowship in Child Nutrition, 738

Dairy Management Milking Marketing Scholarship, 482
Dairy Product Marketing Scholarship, 390
Dairy Shrine Graduate Student Scholarship, 483
Dairy Shrine Student Recognition Scholarship, 483
David Arver Memorial Scholarship, 253
* David Hallissey Memorial Travel Agents Scholarship, 345
Denny Lydic Scholarship, 598
Donald F. Hastings Scholarship, 349
Dr. James L. Lawson Memorial Scholarship, 331
Dr. Tom Anderson Memorial Scholarship, 516
Dutch and Ginger Arver Scholarship, 253
* Education and Research Junior Graduate Award, 358
Education and Research Undergraduate Scholarship, 358
Edward J. Brady Scholarship, 349
* EPSCoR Graduate Fellowship Program, 161
EPSCoR Undergraduate Scholarship Program, 161
Eric and Bette Friedhiem Scholarship, 516
F. Charles Ruling N6FR Memorial Scholarship, 331
Field Aviation Co., Inc. Scholarship, 253
Food Service Communicators Scholarship, 436
Fred R. McDaniel Memorial Scholarship, 331
Gene Baker Honorary Scholarship, 253
General John A. Wickham Scholarship, 353
* Geodetic Surveying Graduate Fellowship, 629
George Reinke Travel Agents Scholarship, 345
Ginger and Fred Deines Canada Scholarship, 598
Ginger and Fred Deines Mexico Scholarship, 599
Gulf Coast Avionics to Fox Valley Technical College Scholarship, 254
H. Neil Mecaskey Scholarship, 516
* H.J. Heinz Graduate Degree Fellowship, 512
Healy Travel Agents Scholarship, 345
Holland America Line-Westours Travel Agents Scholarship, 345
Hooper Memorial Scholarship, 599
* Hoover Presidential Library Fellowship/Grant, 427
Howard E. Adkins Memorial Scholarship, 350

* Hubert Humphrey Research Grant, 738
* Integrated Manufacturing Fellowship, 512
Irving W. Cook WAOCGS Scholarship, 331
J. Desmond Slattery Award: Student, 599
* Jack E. Leisch Memorial National Scholarships, 340
James A. Turner, Jr., Scholarship, 350
John C. Lincoln Memorial Scholarship, 350
John Cook Honorary Scholarship, 254
John W. McDermott Scholarship, 423
Joseph F. Dracup Scholarship, 629
Joseph R. Stone Travel Agents Scholarship, 346
L. Phil Wicker Scholarship, 332
Leica Surveying Scholarship, 629
Leon Harris/Les Nichols Memorial to Spartan School of Aeronautics, 254
* Lincoln Food Service Research Grant, 739
* Lindbergh Foundation Grant, 378
Louise Dessureault Memorial Scholarship, 516
Lowell Gaylor Memorial Scholarship, 254
Lucile B. Kaufman Women's Scholarship, 582
* Luray Caverns Grant, 516
M. & E. Walker Scholarship, 582
Maine Innkeepers Association - Scholarships for Maine Residents, 705
Maine Innkeepers Association Affiliates Scholarship, 705
Mary Macey Scholarship, 616
McAllister and Burnside Scholarship, 351
McDonnel Memorial Scholarship, 269
Mid-Continent Instrument Scholarship, 254
Miller Electric Manufacturing Company Ivic Scholarship, 350
Monte R. Mitchell Global Scholarship, 255
National Restaurant Association Undergraduate Scholarship, 512
National Society of Professional Surveyors Scholarship, 630
* Naval Research Laboratory - Postdoctoral Fellowship, 338
Nemal Electronics Scholarship, 332
North East Roofing Contractors Association Scholarship, 716
Northern Airborne Technical Scholarship, 255
Northern California/Epping Travel Agents Scholarship, 346
* Office of Naval Research - Postdoctoral Fellowship, 338

*Graduate/nondegree study

Field of Study/Intended Career: Trade and industry

Oregon State Scholarship Commission/Oregon Building Industry Association Scholarship, 541
*Parenteral Research Grant, 544
Patrick Murphy Internship, 516
Paul and Blanche Wulfsberg Scholarship, 255
Paul and Helen L. Grauer Scholarship, 332
*Pilot Training Scholarship, 255
Pioneers of Flight Scholarship Program, 474
Plane and Pilot Magazine/Garmin Scholarship, 255
Plumbing, Heating, Cooling Contractors Education Foundation Scholarship, 478
Pollard Travel Agents Scholarship, 346
Porter McDonnell Memorial Scholarship, 269
Praxair International Scholarship, 350
Princess Cruises and Tours Travel Agents Scholarship, 346
*ProManagement Scholarship, 512
Raychem Internship, 558
Reuben Trane Scholarship, 337
Rockwell Internship Program, 561
ROTC Scholarships, 655
Russ Casey Scholarship, 458
Russell Leroy Jones Memorial Scholarship (Colorado Aero Tech), 255
Schonstedt Surveying Scholarship, 630
*School Food Service Foundation Professional Growth Scholarship, 739
*Simmons Travel Agents Scholarship, 346
Southern California/Hawaiian Holidays Travel Agents Scholarship, 347
Spoleto Festival Production Internship, 593
Student Employment and Educational Program, 427
*Teacher Work-Study Grant, 512
Texas Transportation Scholarship, 599
Think Automotive Scholarship, 362
Tony's Food Service Scholarship, 739
Tourism Foundation Alabama-Birmingham Legacy, 517
Tourism Foundation California Scholarship, 517
Tourism Foundation Cleveland Legacy 1 Scholarship, 517
Tourism Foundation Cleveland Legacy 2 Scholarship, 517
Tourism Foundation Connecticut Scholarship, 517
Tourism Foundation Florida Scholarship, 517

Tourism Foundation Internship, 517
Tourism Foundation Michigan Scholarship, 517
Tourism Foundation Montana Scholarship, 518
Tourism Foundation Nebraska-Lois Johnson Scholarship, 518
Tourism Foundation New Jersey 1 Scholarship, 518
Tourism Foundation New Jersey 2 Scholarship, 518
Tourism Foundation New York Scholarship, 518
Tourism Foundation North Carolina Scholarship, 518
Tourism Foundation Ohio Scholarship, 518
Tourism Foundation Quebec Scholarship, 518
Tourism Foundation Scholarship, 519
Tourism Foundation Tulsa Scholarship, 519
Tourism Foundation Wyoming Scholarship, 519
Tourism Foundation Yellow Ribbon Scholarship, 519
*Travel and Tourism Student Research Award, 599
Travel Research Grant, 599
Treadway Inns, Hotels, and Resorts Scholarship, 519
Vertical Flight Foundation Scholarship, 279
W.E. Weisel Scholarship, 582
*Wayne Kay Graduate Fellowship, 582
Wayne Kay Undergraduate Scholarship, 582
Weeta F. Colebank Scholarship, 519
*William B. Keeling Dissertation Award, 599
*Willis H. Carrier Graduate Fellowship, 341
Women Engineers Rockwell International Corporation Scholarships, 587
Women in Construction: Founders' Scholarship, 480
*Women Pilots Airline Scholarship, 438
*Women Pilots Financial Scholarship, 439

Gender

Female

*AAUW Educational Foundation International Fellowship Program, 263
Admiral Grace M. Hopper Scholarship, 583

Agnes E. Vaghi-Cornaro Scholarship, 491
*Alice Smith Fellowship, 221
*Amelia Earhart Fellowship, 619
American Association of Japanese University Women Scholarship, 262
*American Association of University Women International Fellowship, 264
American Congress on Surveying and Mapping/McDonnel Memorial Scholarship, 269
American Congress on Surveying and Mapping/National Society of Professional Surveyors Scholarship for Women, 629
*American Dissertation Fellowship, 264
American Legion Florida Auxiliary Memorial Scholarship, 639
American Legion Georgia Auxiliary Past President's Parley Nursing Scholarship, 291
American Legion Indiana Auxiliary Past President's Parley Nursing Scholarship, 640
American Legion Iowa Auxiliary Mary Virginia Macrea Memorial Nurses Scholarship, 294
American Legion Kentucky Auxiliary Mary Barrett Marshall Scholarship, 295
American Legion Kentucky Auxiliary Mary Barrett Marshall Student Loan Fund, 295
American Legion Maryland Auxiliary Nursing Scholarship, 297
American Legion Maryland Auxiliary Scholarship, 297
American Legion Michigan Auxiliary Memorial Scholarship, 299
American Legion Missouri Lillie Lois Ford Girls Scholarship, 642
American Legion National Memorial Scholarship of the Twenty and Four, 643
American Legion New Hampshire Auxiliary Grace S. High Memorial Child Welfare Scholarship, 644
American Legion Washington Auxiliary Susan Burdett Scholarship, 312
American Legion Wisconsin Auxiliary M. Louise Wilson Educational Loan, 314
*American Pen Women Award: Arts, 505
*American Pen Women Award: Letters, 505
*American Pen Women Award: Music, 505
Anne Maureen Whitney Barrow Memorial Scholarship, 583

Gender: Female

Avon Products Foundation Career Empowerment Scholarship for Adult Women, 564
Betty Rendel Scholarship, 715
California Junior Miss Competition, 375
Career Advancement Scholarship, 372
*Career Development Grant, 264
Crave To Be Your Best Scholarship, 532
*Daughters of Penelope Graduate Student Award, 674
Daughters of Penelope Past Grand Presidents Award, 674
Daughters of Penelope Re-entry Grant, 390
Daughters of United States Army Scholarship, 581
David Sarnoff Reseach Center Scholarship, 583
Delaware Engineering Society Undergraduate Scholarship Program, 392
Delayed Education Scholarship for Women, 323
*Delta Gamma Fellowship, 676
Delta Gamma Scholarship, 677
Donna Brace Ogilvie-Zelda Gitlin Poetry Writing Award, 684
Dorothy Andrews Kabis Internship, 715
Dorothy Campbell Memorial Scholarship, 535
Dorothy Lemke Howarth Scholarship, 584
Financial Women International Scholarship, 421
*Georgia Harkness Scholarship, 604
Girls Incorporated Scholars Program, 684
Gladys C. Anderson Memorial Scholarship, 274
Harriett Barnhart Wimmer Scholarship, 450
Helen Copeland Scholarship for Females, 607
Hermione Grant Calhoun Scholarship, 484
Ivy Parker Memorial Scholarship, 584
J.B. Cornelius Foundation Grants Program, 440
Jean Driscoll Award, 532
Jean Fitzgerald Scholarship Fund, 422
*Jeanne Humphrey Block Dissertation Award, 426
Judith Resnik Memorial Scholarship, 745
Junior Miss Scholarship, 258
Kaiulani Home for Girls Trust Scholarship, 423
Karla Scherer Foundation Scholarship, 447
Kottis Family Award, 675

Lillian Moller Gilbreth Scholarship, 584
Lucile B. Kaufman Women's Scholarship, 582
*Luise Meyer-Schutzmeister Award, 360
*M.A. Cartland Shackford Medical Fellowship, 612
*Mary Isabel Sibley Fellowship, 547
Mary M. Verges Award, 675
*Mary McEwen Schimke Scholarship, 612
McDonnel Memorial Scholarship, 269
*Medical Women's Carroll L. Birch Award, 649
*Medical Women's Education Loan, 649
*Medical Women's Janet M. Glasgow Essay Award, 650
*Medical Women's Wilhelm-Frankowski Scholarship, 319
*Miss America Education Scholarship for Post-Graduate Studies, 468
Miss America Pageant, 468
*Monticello College Foundation Fellowship for Women, 526
Nancy Lorraine Jensen Memorial Scholarship, 746
National Scholarship Trust Fund of the Graphic Arts Undergraduate Scholarships and Graduate Fellowships, 717
*NCAA Women's Enhancement Postgraduate Scholarship, 482
*NCAA Women's Internship, 482
*New Mexico Graduate Scholarship: Minorities/Women, 186
New York Life Foundation Health Professions Scholarship, 372
NIAF/NOIAW Cornaro Scholarship, 498
Olive Lynn Salembier Scholarship, 584
Past Grand Presidents' Award, 675
Pathfinder Scholarship, 715
Pearl I. Young Scholarship, 165
Porter McDonnell Memorial Scholarship, 269
*Presbyterian Fund for Graduate Education, 550
R.L. Gillette Scholarship, 274
*Ruth Satter Memorial Award, 360
*Sears-Roebuck Graduate Business Studies Loan Fund, 372
*Selected Professions Fellowship, 265
Shannon Scholarship, 600
*Sonja Stefanadis Graduate Student Award, 675
*Student Aid Foundation Graduate Loan, 595
Student Aid Foundation Undergraduate Loan, 595

Supreme Guardian Council, International Order of Job's Daughters Scholarship, 750
Top Ten College Women Competition, 413
Uncommon Legacy Foundation Scholarship, 351
Westinghouse Bertha Lamme Scholarship, 584
Women Engineers Chevron Scholarship, 585
Women Engineers Chrysler Corporation Re-entry Scholarship, 585
Women Engineers Chrysler Corporation Scholarship, 585
Women Engineers Chrysler Corporation Scholarship (Minorities), 585
Women Engineers General Electric Foundation Scholarship, 586
*Women Engineers General Motors Foundation Graduate Scholarship, 586
Women Engineers General Motors Foundation Undergraduate Scholarship, 586
Women Engineers GTE Foundation Scholarship, 586
Women Engineers Men's Auxiliary Memorial Scholarship, 587
Women Engineers Microsoft Corporation Scholarship, 587
*Women Engineers Microsoft Corporation Scholarship (Graduate), 587
Women Engineers Northrop Corporation Founders Scholarship, 745
Women Engineers Rockwell International Corporation Scholarships, 587
Women Engineers Stone and Webster Scholarship, 588
Women Engineers Texaco Scholarship, 745
Women Engineers TRW Scholarship, 588
Women in Architecture Scholarship, 359
Women in Business Scholarship, 372
Women in Engineering Studies Loan Fund, 372
*Women in Science Education Research Grant, 360
Women of the Evangelical Lutheran Church in America Scholarship, 616
*Women Pilots Airline Scholarship, 438
*Women Pilots Financial Scholarship, 439
Women's Education Fund, 442
Women's Western Golf Foundation Scholarship, 617

*Graduate/nondegree study

Gender: Female

* Wyeth-Ayerst Laboratories Prize, 508
* Wyeth-Ayerst Laboratories Scholarship, 373
  Young Feminist Scholarship Program, 593

Male

American Legion Illinois Boy Scout Scholarship, 639
American Legion Indiana Frank W. McHale Memorial Scholarship, 639
American Legion Iowa Boy Scout of the Year Award, 640
American Legion Iowa Outstanding Citizen of Boys State, 640
American Legion Maryland Boys State Scholarship, 641
American Legion Missouri Lillie Lois Ford Boys Scholarship, 642
American Legion National Eagle Scout of the Year, 643
American Legion New Hampshire Boys State Scholarship, 644
American Legion Tennessee Eagle Scout Award, 648
American Legion Wisconsin Eagle Scout of the Year Scholarship, 648
American Nuclear Society Environmental Sciences Division Scholarship, 322
Arthur E. Copeland Scholarship for Males, 607
Boy Scouts of America/Eastern Orthodox Committee on Scouting Scholarship, 663
Boy Scouts of America/Eisenhower Memorial Scholarship, 663
Captain James J. Regan Memorial Scholarship, 663
Carter Scholarship Grants for New England Scouts, 664
E. Urner Goodman Scholarship, 664
Frank D. Visceglia Memorial Scholarship, 682
Frank L. Weil Memorial Scholarship, 664
* Henry G. Award, 506
National Eagle Scout Scholarship, 664
Sigma Alpha Epsilon Resident Educational Advisor, 741
Sigma Alpha Epsilon Scholarship, 742
Sons of the American Revolution Eagle Scout Scholarship, 718
Spence Reese Scholarship, 370
Willems Scholarship, 711

International Students

* AAUW Educational Foundation International Fellowship Program, 263
  Air Travel Card Travel Agents Scholarship, 344
* American Association of University Women International Fellowship, 264
  American Express Travel Agents Scholarship, 344
* American Schools of Oriental Research/Harrell Family Fellowship, 335
  American Schools of Oriental Research/Jennifer C. Groot Fellowship, 335
* American Schools of Oriental Research/Kenneth W. Russell Fellowship, 267
  American Welding Society District Scholarship, 349
* American Welding Society Graduate Fellowship, 349
* Andrew Mellon Fellowship, 487
  Armenian Union Awards for Students on Non-U.S. Soil, 354
* Armenian Union U.S. Graduate Loan, 354
  ASM Foundation Undergraduate Scholarship, 357
* Avis Rent-a-Car Travel Agents Scholarship, 345
* Beta Phi Mu Doctoral Dissertation Scholarship, 367
* Bound to Stay Bound Books Scholarship, 315
* Brain Tumor Research Fellowship, 265
* Chester Dale Fellowship, 487
* Civil Engineering Graduate Scholarship, 361
* Clinical Cancer Research Fellowship, 259
* Communicative Disorders Scholarships, 567
* Corning Inc. Optometric Scholarship, 328
* Daughters of Penelope Graduate Student Award, 674
  Daughters of Penelope Past Grand Presidents Award, 674
* David Finley Fellowship, 487
* David H. Clift Scholarship, 315
  Dr. Tom Anderson Memorial Scholarship, 516
* Edgar Pam Fellowship, 435
  Enology and Viticulture Scholarship, 339
  Eric and Bette Friedhiem Scholarship, 516

* Exploration Fund, 403
  Explorers Club Youth Activity Fund, 403
* Fellowship Grants to Asian Individuals, 356
  Foreign Postal Telegraph and Telephone International Affiliates Scholarship, 672
  Franklin D. Roosevelt Library/Roosevelt Internship, 408
* Frederic G. Melcher Scholarship, 316
  Ginger and Fred Deines Canada Scholarship, 598
  Ginger and Fred Deines Mexico Scholarship, 599
  H. Neil Mecaskey Scholarship, 516
* Hangin Memorial Scholarship, 468
* Harriet and Leon Pomerance Fellowship, 352
  Health Career Scholarship, 437
  Healy Travel Agents Scholarship, 345
* Herbert Scoville Jr. Peace Fellowship, 566
* International Graduate Student Fellowship, 321
* Ittleson Fellowship, 488
* Japan-United States Arts Program, 356
  John Lyons Scholarship, 694
  Joseph R. Stone Travel Agents Scholarship, 346
  Kottis Family Award, 675
  L.M. Perryman Ethnic Minority Award, 606
* Library and Information Science Grant, 438
* Library and Information Technology Association/GEAC-CLSI Scholarship, 316
* Library and Information Technology Association/LSSI Minority Scholarship, 316
* Library and Information Technology Association/OCLC/Minority Scholarship, 316
  Louise Dessureault Memorial Scholarship, 516
* Louise Giles Minority Scholarship, 316
* Lung Association Career Investigator Award, 317
* Lung Association Clinical Research Grant, 318
* Lung Association Research Grant, 318
* Lung Health Research Dissertation Grant, 318
  Martin McLaren-Interchange Fellowship in Horticulture and Landscape Design, 411
* Mary Davis Fellowship, 488
  Mary M. Verges Award, 675
* Medical Library Association Scholarship, 461

*Graduate/nondegree study

* Medical Library Doctoral Scholarship, 462
Medicus Student Exchange, 595
* Mining Club Award, 435
Monte R. Mitchell Global Scholarship, 255
* Naval Architects and Marine Engineers Graduate Scholarship, 744
Past Grand Presidents' Award, 675
Paul Cole Scholarship, 397
* Paul Mellon Fellowship, 488
* Periodontology Student Loan, 258
* Postdoctoral Cancer Research Fellowship, 376
Praxair International Scholarship, 350
* President Francesco Cossiga Fellowship, 526
* Ron Brown Fellowship Program, 438
* Sarah Rebecca Reed Scholarship, 367
* Scholar Exchange Program, 438
* Society of Automotive Engineers Doctoral Scholars Loan, 580
* Sonja Stefanadis Graduate Student Award, 675
* Student Ministry Fund, 437
Teamsters Scholarship Fund, 694
Texas American Hemisphere Student Scholarship, 224
Tourism Foundation Internship, 517
Tourism Foundation Quebec Scholarship, 518
Tourism Foundation Yellow Ribbon Scholarship, 519
Treadway Inns, Hotels, and Resorts Scholarship, 519
Valderrama Award, 415
* Wyeth Fellowship, 489
Yanmar Scholarship, 580
Young Investigator Matching Grants, 486

Military Participation

Air Force

Air Force Aid Society Education Grant, 251
Arkansas Missing/Killed in Action Dependents Scholarship, 62
Chief Master Sergeants of the Air Force Scholarship, 256
Katherine F. Gruber Scholarship, 369
Maria Jackson--General George White Scholarship, 537
Mary Baracco Scholarship, 721
New Jersey Tuition Credit Military and Veterans Affairs, 183
North Carolina Scholarships for Children of War Veterans, 194
Pentagon Federal Credit Union Grant, 721
Red River Valley Fighter Pilots Scholarship Program, 559
Retired Officers Educational Assistance Program, 734
Scholarship for Children of Members of the Non-Commissioned Officers Association, 722
West Virginia War Orphans Educational Assistance, 241
William T. Green Grant, 722

Army

1st Infantry Division/Lieutenant General C. R. Huebner Scholarship, 247
25th Infantry Division Educational Memorial Scholarship, 621
Arkansas Missing/Killed in Action Dependents Scholarship, 62
Army Emergency Relief Scholarship, 355
Daughters of United States Army Scholarship, 581
Katherine F. Gruber Scholarship, 369
Maria Jackson--General George White Scholarship, 537
Mary Baracco Scholarship, 721
Montgomery GI Bill (MGIB), 227
Montgomery GI Bill Plus Army College Fund, 227
New Jersey Tuition Credit Military and Veterans Affairs, 183
North Carolina Scholarships for Children of War Veterans, 194
Pentagon Federal Credit Union Grant, 721
Red River Valley Fighter Pilots Scholarship Program, 559
Retired Officers Educational Assistance Program, 734
Scholarship for Children of Members of the Non-Commissioned Officers Association, 722
Selected Reserve Montgomery GI Bill, 228
West Virginia War Orphans Educational Assistance, 241
William T. Green Grant, 722

Marines

Arkansas Missing/Killed in Action Dependents Scholarship, 62
First Marine Division Scholarship, 681
Katherine F. Gruber Scholarship, 369
Maria Jackson--General George White Scholarship, 537
Marine Corps Scholarship, 460
Mary Baracco Scholarship, 721
New Jersey Tuition Credit Military and Veterans Affairs, 183
North Carolina Scholarships for Children of War Veterans, 194
Pentagon Federal Credit Union Grant, 721
Red River Valley Fighter Pilots Scholarship Program, 559
Retired Officers Educational Assistance Program, 734
Scholarship for Children of Members of the Non-Commissioned Officers Association, 722
Second Marine Division Scholarship, 567
Third Marine Division Memorial Scholarship Fund, 753
Vice Admiral E.P. Travers Loan, 521
Vice Admiral E.P. Travers Scholarship, 521
West Virginia War Orphans Educational Assistance, 241
William T. Green Grant, 722

Coast Guard

Arkansas Missing/Killed in Action Dependents Scholarship, 62
Katherine F. Gruber Scholarship, 369
Maria Jackson--General George White Scholarship, 537
Mary Baracco Scholarship, 721
New Jersey Tuition Credit Military and Veterans Affairs, 183
North Carolina Scholarships for Children of War Veterans, 194
Pentagon Federal Credit Union Grant, 721
Red River Valley Fighter Pilots Scholarship Program, 559
Retired Officers Educational Assistance Program, 734
Scholarship for Children of Members of the Non-Commissioned Officers Association, 722
West Virginia War Orphans Educational Assistance, 241
William T. Green Grant, 722

Navy

Arkansas Missing/Killed in Action Dependents Scholarship, 62
Dolphin Scholarship, 393
Dolphin U.S. Submarine Veterans of World War II Scholarship, 678
Katherine F. Gruber Scholarship, 369
Maria Jackson--General George White Scholarship, 537
Mary Baracco Scholarship, 721
Navy Supply Corps Scholarship, 521
New Jersey Tuition Credit Military and Veterans Affairs, 183
North Carolina Scholarships for Children of War Veterans, 194
Pentagon Federal Credit Union Grant, 721
Red River Valley Fighter Pilots Scholarship Program, 559

*Graduate/nondegree study

Military Participatio: Navy

Retired Officers Educational Assistance Program, 734
Scholarship for Children of Members of the Non-Commissioned Officers Association, 722
Seabee Memorial Scholarship, 566
Vice Admiral E.P. Travers Loan, 521
Vice Admiral E.P. Travers Scholarship, 521
West Virginia War Orphans Educational Assistance, 241
William T. Green Grant, 722

Reserves/National Guard

Alabama National Guard Educational Assistance Award, 53
Arkansas Missing/Killed in Action Dependents Scholarship, 62
Chief Master Sergeants of the Air Force Scholarship, 256
Illinois National Guard Grant, 121
Iowa National Guard Tuition Aid Program, 123
Maria Jackson--General George White Scholarship, 537
Mary Baracco Scholarship, 721
New Jersey Tuition Credit Military and Veterans Affairs, 183
North Carolina Scholarships for Children of War Veterans, 194
Ohio National Guard Tuition Grant, 532
Pentagon Federal Credit Union Grant, 721
Red River Valley Fighter Pilots Scholarship Program, 559
Retired Officers Educational Assistance Program, 734
Scholarship for Children of Members of the Non-Commissioned Officers Association, 722
Selected Reserve Montgomery GI Bill, 228
South Dakota National Guard Tuition Assistance, 220
West Virginia War Orphans Educational Assistance, 241
William T. Green Grant, 722

Minority Status

African American

Actuarial Society Minority Scholarship, 579
Advertising Internship for Minority Students, 261
*African-American Doctoral Teacher Loan / Scholarship, 140
Allen Lee Hughes Fellows Program, 353

*Allen Lee Hughes Internship, 353
*American Dissertation Fellowship, 264
American Institute of Architects Minority/Disadvantaged Scholarship, 283
*American Institute of Certified Public Accountants' Minority Doctoral Fellowship, 284
American Physical Society Minorities Scholarship, 329
*American Political Science Association Minority Fellows, 330
*American Speech-Language-Hearing International/Minority Student Scholarship, 347
*American Speech-Language-Hearing Young Minority Scholars Award, 347
Arkansas Freshman/Sophomore Minority Grant, 61
*Arkansas Minority Master's Fellowship, 61
Arkansas Minority Teachers Loan, 62
Black Journalists College Scholarship, 477
Black Journalists Summer Internship, 477
Black Journalists Sustaining Scholarship, 477
Black Nurse's Scholarship, 714
Black Nursing Faculty Scholarship, 360
Bucks County Courier Times Minority Internship, 371
*C.R. Bard Foundation Prize, 505
*California Library Scholarship for Minority Students, 375
California Teachers Association Martin Luther King, Jr., Memorial Scholarship, 667
*CANFIT Program Graduate Scholarship, 373
CANFIT Program Undergraduate Scholarship, 374
*Career Development Grant, 264
*Carnegie Scholarship, 531
Carole Simpson Scholarship, 555
Certified Public Accountants' Minorities Scholarship, 284
*Charles E. Culpeper Art Internship, 487
Chemical Society Minority Scholarship, 267
*CIC/GE Predoctoral Fellowship, 382
*Clinical Psychology Training Minority Fellowship, 58
Colgate "Bright Smiles, Bright Futures" Minority Scholarships, 249
Colorado CPAs Ethnic Scholarship, 381
Colorado CPAs Ethnic-College and University Scholarship, 381

Congressional Black Caucus Foundation Spouses' Scholarship, 383
David and Dovetta Wilson Scholarship, 391
Duracell/Gillette Minority Intern Scholarship, 520
*Earl Warren Legal Training Program Scholarship, 472
Ed Bradley Scholarship, 556
Edward D. Stone, Jr., and Associates Minority Scholarship, 450
Experiential Education Internship, 514
*Fellowship Program in Academic Medicine, 506
Fisher Broadcasting Minority Scholarship, 405
*Florida Education Fund McKnight Doctoral Fellowship, 405
*Florida Education Fund Minority Participation in Legal Education Law School Scholarship, 76
Florida Education Fund Minority Pre-law Scholarships, 76
Florida Rosewood Family Scholarship, 74
*Ford Foundation Dissertation Fellowship: Minorities, 510
*Ford Foundation Postdoctoral Fellowships for Minorities, 511
*Ford Foundation Predoctoral Fellowship: Minorities, 511
Foreign Study/Minority Scholarship Strategic Studies Award, 281
*Franklin C. McLean Award, 506
*Gem Consortium Scholarship, 412
Geological Institute Minority Participation Program, 276
George M. Brooker Collegiate Scholarship for Minorities, 435
Golden State Minority Scholarship, 414
Gulf Coast Research Laboratory Minority Summer Grant, 140
*Henry G. Award, 506
Herbert Lehman Scholarship for African American Students, 472
*HIV/AIDS Research Training Minority Fellowship, 58
Illinois Minority Teachers Scholarship, 120
Indiana Minority Teacher Scholarship, 122
Indiana Nursing Scholarship, 122
Inroads Internship, 432
International Educational Exchange/ R.B. Bailey Minority Scholarship, 68
Ira Page Wallace Bible Scholarship, 550
*Irving Graef Memorial Scholarship, 506
Jackie Robinson Scholarship, 440

38

*Graduate/nondegree study

Minority Status: African American

* James H. Robinson Memorial Prize in Surgery, 506
Kansas Ethnic Minority Scholarship, 125
L.M. Perryman Ethnic Minority Award, 606
* Library and Information Technology Association/LSSI Minority Scholarship, 316
* Library and Information Technology Association/OCLC/Minority Scholarship, 316
* Louise Giles Minority Scholarship, 316
* Medical Fellowships General Need-Based Scholarship, 507
* Medical Fellowships Special Awards Program, 507
* Medical Fellowships Technology Training Program, 507
* Medical Library Scholarship for Minority Students, 462
Melon Minority Fellowship Program, 573
Meteorological Society Minority Scholarship, 320
* Metropolitan Life Foundation Scholarship, 507
* Metropolitan Museum of Art Nine-Month Art Internship, 464
Metropolitan Museum of Art Six-Month Art Internship, 464
Michelle Clark Fellowship, 557
Microbiology Summer Research Fellowship for Minority Students, 339
Minnesota Nursing Grant for Persons of Color, 139
* Minority Dental Student Scholarship, 248
Missouri Minority Teaching Scholarship, 145
Music Assistance Fund, 348
Nash Finch Scholarship Program, 711
National Achievement Scholarship, 508
* National Art Gallery Diversity Internship Program, 476
National Scholarship Program, 712
* National Science Foundation Minority Graduate Fellowship, 180
* National Science Foundation Minority Postdoctoral Fellowship, 180
National Society of Black Engineers Oratorical Contest, 717
National Society of Black Engineers Scholars Program, 718
National Society of Black Engineers/Boeing Flight Competition, 718
National Society of Black Engineers/GE African American Forum Scholarship, 718

National Society of Black Engineers/Undergraduate Students in Technical Research Awards Program, 718
* NCAA Ethnic Minority Internship, 481
* NCAA Ethnic Minority Postgraduate Scholarship, 481
* Neuroscience Training Minority Fellowship, 59
* New Jersey C. Clyde Ferguson Law Scholarship, 183
* New Jersey Minority Academic Career Program, 185
* New Mexico Graduate Scholarship: Minorities/Women, 186
* New Mexico Minority Doctoral Assistance Loan for Service, 187
New York Times Summer Internship Program for Minorities, 524
* Newhouse Graduate Newspaper Fellowship for Minorities, 527
Northwest Journalists of Color Scholarship Program, 530
Northwest Pharmacists Pre-Pharmacy Scholarship, 530
* Nurses Clinical Training Fellowship, 327
* Nurses Health Policy Research Institute Fellowship, 327
* Nurses Research Training Fellowship, 328
* Nurses Substance Abuse Fellowship, 328
Oak Ridge Institute for Science and Education Energy Research Undergraduate Laboratory Fellowship, 198
Oak Ridge Institute for Science and Education Office of Civilian Radioactive Waste Management Historically Black Colleges and Universities Undergraduate Scholarship Program, 201
Oak Ridge Institute for Science and Education Office of Fossil Energy Historically Black Colleges and Universities Student Research Participation, 201
Oak Ridge Institute for Science and Education U.S. Department of Energy/NAACP, 210
Ohio Newspapers Minority Scholarship, 533
* Oklahoma Minority Doctoral Study Grant, 214
* Oklahoma Minority Professional Study Grant, 214
* Osborne Scholarship, 531
* Peat Marwick Doctoral Scholarship Program, 448
PGA Minority Internship Program, 546

* Physical Science Graduate Fellowship: Minorities and Women, 510
* Predoctoral Clearinghouse Application Fee Waiver, 382
* Presbyterian Fund for Graduate Education, 550
* Presbyterian Racial/Ethnic Leadership Supplemental Grant, 551
Presbyterian Student Opportunity Scholarship, 551
Project Excellence Scholarship, 553
* Psychology Research Training Minority Fellowship, 59
* Ralph W. Ellison Prize, 507
* Regents Graduate/Professional Fellowship, 213
* Robert D. Watkins Minority Graduate Fellowship, 651
* Robert L. Millender Sr. Memorial Fund Fellowship Program, 560
RTNDF Minority News Management Internship, 558
Sachs Scholarship, 562
* Selected Professions Fellowship, 265
Smithsonian Minority Internship, 570
* Social Work Clinical Fellowship, 386
* Social Work Minority Research Fellowship, 386
* Sociological Association Minority Fellowship, 60
SONY Minority Internship, 590
* Special Libraries Association Affirmative Action Scholarship, 591
Stanley E. Jackson Award for Gifted/Talented Minorities with Disabilities, 406
Stanley E. Jackson Scholarship Award for Ethnic Minority Students., 406
Tennessee Minority Teaching Fellows Program, 223
* The GEM Consortium/Doctoral Bridge Projects, 597
* The GEM Consortium/M.S. Engineering Fellowship, 597
* The GEM Consortium/Ph.D Science and Engineering Fellowship, 597
Thomas P. Papandrew Scholarship, 451
United Methodist Ethnic Scholarship, 605
United Methodist Publishing House Merit Scholarship, 605
United Negro College Fund Scholarship, 607
* University of North Carolina Minority Grant: Doctor/Lawyer/Veterinary Medicine, 234
* Veterinary Medicine Minority Loan / Scholarship, 144
Virginia Transfer Grant, 239
Virginia Undergraduate Student Financial Aid, 239
* W.K. Kellog Community Medicine Training, 508

*Graduate/nondegree study

Minority Status: African American

*William and Charlotte Cadbury Award, 508
Wisconsin Minority Retention Grant, 243
Wisconsin Minority Teacher Loan Program, 243
Women Engineers Chrysler Corporation Scholarship (Minorities), 585
Women Engineers Stone and Webster Scholarship, 588
Women in Construction: Founders' Scholarship, 480
Woodrow Wilson Program in Public Policy and International Affairs, 618
*Wyeth-Ayerst Laboratories Prize, 508

Alaskan native

A.T. Anderson Memorial Scholarship, 636
Actuarial Society Minority Scholarship, 579
Allen Lee Hughes Fellows Program, 353
*Allen Lee Hughes Internship, 353
*American Dissertation Fellowship, 264
*American Indian Fellowship for Environmental Professionals, 597
*American Indian Graduate Fellowship, 280
American Institute of Architects Minority/Disadvantaged Scholarship, 283
*American Institute of Certified Public Accountants' Minority Doctoral Fellowship, 284
American Physical Society Minorities Scholarship, 329
*American Political Science Association Minority Fellows, 330
*American Speech-Language-Hearing International/Minority Student Scholarship, 347
*American Speech-Language-Hearing Young Minority Scholars Award, 347
Bucks County Courier Times Minority Internship, 371
Bureau of Indian Affairs-Oklahoma Area Grant, 371
Bureau of Indian Affairs-Oklahoma Area Scholarship, 63
Burlington Northern Santa Fe Foundation Scholarship, 637
*C.R. Bard Foundation Prize, 505
California Teachers Association Martin Luther King, Jr., Memorial Scholarship, 667
*Canada: Native North American Scholarship (Fulbright), 81
*CANFIT Program Graduate Scholarship, 373

CANFIT Program Undergraduate Scholarship, 374
*Career Development Grant, 264
Carole Simpson Scholarship, 555
Certified Public Accountants' Minorities Scholarship, 284
*Charles E. Culpeper Art Internship, 487
Chemical Society Minority Scholarship, 267
*CIC/GE Predoctoral Fellowship, 382
*Clinical Psychology Training Minority Fellowship, 58
Colorado CPAs Ethnic Scholarship, 381
Colorado CPAs Ethnic-College and University Scholarship, 381
Congressional Black Caucus Foundation Spouses' Scholarship, 383
Council of Energy Resource Tribes Summer Intern Program, 385
David and Dovetta Wilson Scholarship, 391
Duracell/Gillette Minority Intern Scholarship, 520
Ed Bradley Scholarship, 556
Edward D. Stone, Jr., and Associates Minority Scholarship, 450
Experiential Education Internship, 514
*Fellowship Program in Academic Medicine, 506
Fisher Broadcasting Minority Scholarship, 405
*Florida Education Fund Minority Participation in Legal Education Law School Scholarship, 76
Florida Education Fund Minority Pre-law Scholarships, 76
*Ford Foundation Dissertation Fellowship: Minorities, 510
*Ford Foundation Postdoctoral Fellowships for Minorities, 511
*Ford Foundation Predoctoral Fellowship: Minorities, 511
Foreign Study/Minority Scholarship Strategic Studies Award, 281
*Franklin C. McLean Award, 506
Geological Institute Minority Participation Program, 276
George M. Brooker Collegiate Scholarship for Minorities, 435
Golden State Minority Scholarship, 414
Gulf Coast Research Laboratory Minority Summer Grant, 140
Higher Education Undergraduate Grant Program, 58
*HIV/AIDS Research Training Minority Fellowship, 58
Illinois Minority Teachers Scholarship, 120
Indians Higher Education Grant Program, 231

Jackie Robinson Scholarship, 440
*James H. Robinson Memorial Prize in Surgery, 506
Kansas Ethnic Minority Scholarship, 125
L.M. Perryman Ethnic Minority Award, 606
*Library and Information Technology Association/LSSI Minority Scholarship, 316
*Library and Information Technology Association/OCLC/Minority Scholarship, 316
*Louise Giles Minority Scholarship, 316
*Medical Fellowships General Need-Based Scholarship, 507
Melon Minority Fellowship Program, 573
Meteorological Society Minority Scholarship, 320
*Metropolitan Museum of Art Nine-Month Art Internship, 464
Metropolitan Museum of Art Six-Month Art Internship, 464
Michelle Clark Fellowship, 557
Microbiology Summer Research Fellowship for Minority Students, 339
Missouri Minority Teaching Scholarship, 145
*National Art Gallery Diversity Internship Program, 476
National Scholarship Program, 712
*National Science Foundation Minority Graduate Fellowship, 180
*National Science Foundation Minority Postdoctoral Fellowship, 180
Native American Scholarship, 520
*NCAA Ethnic Minority Internship, 481
*NCAA Ethnic Minority Postgraduate Scholarship, 481
*Neuroscience Training Minority Fellowship, 59
*New Jersey C. Clyde Ferguson Law Scholarship, 183
*New Jersey Minority Academic Career Program, 185
*New Mexico Graduate Scholarship: Minorities/Women, 186
*New Mexico Minority Doctoral Assistance Loan for Service, 187
New York Times Summer Internship Program for Minorities, 524
*Newhouse Graduate Newspaper Fellowship for Minorities, 527
North American Indian Scholarship, 437
Northwest Journalists of Color Scholarship Program, 530
*Nurses Clinical Training Fellowship, 327

* Nurses Health Policy Research Institute Fellowship, 327
* Nurses Research Training Fellowship, 328
* Nurses Substance Abuse Fellowship, 328
  Oak Ridge Institute for Science and Education U.S. Department of Energy/NAACP, 210
  Ohio Newspapers Minority Scholarship, 533
* Oklahoma Minority Doctoral Study Grant, 214
* Oklahoma Minority Professional Study Grant, 214
* Peat Marwick Doctoral Scholarship Program, 448
  PGA Minority Internship Program, 546
* Physical Science Graduate Fellowship: Minorities and Women, 510
* Predoctoral Clearinghouse Application Fee Waiver, 382
* Presbyterian Fund for Graduate Education, 550
  Presbyterian Native American Education Grant, 551
* Presbyterian Native American Seminary Scholarship, 551
* Presbyterian Racial/Ethnic Leadership Supplemental Grant, 551
  Presbyterian Student Opportunity Scholarship, 551
* Psychology Research Training Minority Fellowship, 59
  Public Policy Internship Program, 460
* Ralph W. Ellison Prize, 507
* Regents Graduate/Professional Fellowship, 213
* Robert D. Watkins Minority Graduate Fellowship, 651
  RTNDF Minority News Management Internship, 558
  Schuyler Meyer Junior Scholarship, 280
* Selected Professions Fellowship, 265
  Smithsonian Minority Internship, 570
* Social Work Clinical Fellowship, 386
* Social Work Minority Research Fellowship, 386
* Sociological Association Minority Fellowship, 60
* Special Libraries Association Affirmative Action Scholarship, 591
  Stanley E. Jackson Award for Gifted/Talented Minorities with Disabilities, 406
  Tennessee Minority Teaching Fellows Program, 223
  Thomas P. Papandrew Scholarship, 451
  Truman D. Picard Scholarship, 439
  United Methodist Publishing House Merit Scholarship, 605

  United States EPA Tribal Lands Environmental Science Scholarship, 58
* Veterinary Medicine Minority Loan / Scholarship, 144
  Virginia Transfer Grant, 239
  Virginia Undergraduate Student Financial Aid, 239
* William and Charlotte Cadbury Award, 508
  Women Engineers Chrysler Corporation Scholarship (Minorities), 585
  Women Engineers Stone and Webster Scholarship, 588
  Women in Construction: Founders' Scholarship, 480
  Woodrow Wilson Program in Public Policy and International Affairs, 618
* Wyeth-Ayerst Laboratories Prize, 508

American Indian

  A.T. Anderson Memorial Scholarship, 636
  Actuarial Society Minority Scholarship, 579
  Advertising Internship for Minority Students, 261
  Allen Lee Hughes Fellows Program, 353
* Allen Lee Hughes Internship, 353
* American Dissertation Fellowship, 264
* American Indian Fellowship for Environmental Professionals, 597
* American Indian Graduate Fellowship, 280
  American Institute of Architects Minority/Disadvantaged Scholarship, 283
* American Institute of Certified Public Accountants' Minority Doctoral Fellowship, 284
  American Physical Society Minorities Scholarship, 329
* American Political Science Association Minority Fellows, 330
* American Speech-Language-Hearing International/Minority Student Scholarship, 347
* American Speech-Language-Hearing Young Minority Scholars Award, 347
  Arnell BJUGSTAD Scholarship, 220
  Bucks County Courier Times Minority Internship, 371
  Bureau of Indian Affairs-Oklahoma Area Grant, 371
  Bureau of Indian Affairs-Oklahoma Area Scholarship, 63
  Burlington Northern Santa Fe Foundation Scholarship, 637
* C.R. Bard Foundation Prize, 505

* California Library Scholarship for Minority Students, 375
  California Teachers Association Martin Luther King, Jr., Memorial Scholarship, 667
* Canada: Native North American Scholarship (Fulbright), 81
* CANFIT Program Graduate Scholarship, 373
  CANFIT Program Undergraduate Scholarship, 374
* Career Development Grant, 264
  Carole Simpson Scholarship, 555
  Certified Public Accountants' Minorities Scholarship, 284
* Charles E. Culpeper Art Internship, 487
  Chemical Society Minority Scholarship, 267
  Cheyenne-Arapaho Tribe Department of Education Scholarship, 379
  Cheyenne-Arapaho Tribe Higher Education Scholarship, 379
  Choctaw Nation Higher Eduation Grant, 65
* CIC/GE Predoctoral Fellowship, 382
* Clinical Psychology Training Minority Fellowship, 58
  Colgate "Bright Smiles, Bright Futures" Minority Scholarships, 249
  Colonial Dames of America Indian Nurse Scholarship, 515
  Colorado CPAs Ethnic Scholarship, 381
  Colorado CPAs Ethnic-College and University Scholarship, 381
  Congressional Black Caucus Foundation Spouses' Scholarship, 383
  Council of Energy Resource Tribes Summer Intern Program, 385
  David and Dovetta Wilson Scholarship, 391
  Duracell/Gillette Minority Intern Scholarship, 520
  Ed Bradley Scholarship, 556
  Edward D. Stone, Jr., and Associates Minority Scholarship, 450
  Experiential Education Internship, 514
* Fellowship Program in Academic Medicine, 506
  Fisher Broadcasting Minority Scholarship, 405
* Florida Education Fund Minority Participation in Legal Education Law School Scholarship, 76
  Florida Education Fund Minority Pre-law Scholarships, 76
  Florida Seminole and Miccosukee Indian Scholarship, 74
* Ford Foundation Dissertation Fellowship: Minorities, 510
* Ford Foundation Postdoctoral Fellowships for Minorities, 511

*Graduate/nondegree study

Minority Status: American Indian

* Ford Foundation Predoctoral Fellowship: Minorities, 511
Foreign Study/Minority Scholarship Strategic Studies Award, 281
* Franklin C. McLean Award, 506
* Gem Consortium Scholarship, 412
Geological Institute Minority Participation Program, 276
George M. Brooker Collegiate Scholarship for Minorities, 435
Golden State Minority Scholarship, 414
Gulf Coast Research Laboratory Minority Summer Grant, 140
Higher Education Undergraduate Grant Program, 58
* HIV/AIDS Research Training Minority Fellowship, 58
Hopi BIA Higher Education Scholarship, 428
Hopi Scholarship, 428
Hopi Supplemental Grant, 428
Hopi Tribal Priority Scholarship, 428
* Hopi Tuition-Book Scholarship, 429
Illinois Minority Teachers Scholarship, 120
Indians Higher Education Grant Program, 231
Inroads Internship, 432
International Educational Exchange/ R.B. Bailey Minority Scholarship, 68
* Irving Graef Memorial Scholarship, 506
Jackie Robinson Scholarship, 440
* James H. Robinson Memorial Prize in Surgery, 506
Kansas Ethnic Minority Scholarship, 125
L.M. Perryman Ethnic Minority Award, 606
* Library and Information Technology Association/LSSI Minority Scholarship, 316
* Library and Information Technology Association/OCLC/Minority Scholarship, 316
* Louise Giles Minority Scholarship, 316
* Medical Fellowships General Need-Based Scholarship, 507
* Medical Fellowships Technology Training Program, 507
* Medical Library Scholarship for Minority Students, 462
Melon Minority Fellowship Program, 573
Menominee Adult Vocational Training Scholarship, 136
Menominee Higher Education Scholarship, 462
Meteorological Society Minority Scholarship, 320

* Metropolitan Life Foundation Scholarship, 507
* Metropolitan Museum of Art Nine-Month Art Internship, 464
Metropolitan Museum of Art Six-Month Art Internship, 464
Michelle Clark Fellowship, 557
Microbiology Summer Research Fellowship for Minority Students, 339
Minnesota Nursing Grant for Persons of Color, 139
* Minority Dental Student Scholarship, 248
Missouri Minority Teaching Scholarship, 145
* National Art Gallery Diversity Internship Program, 476
National Scholarship Program, 712
* National Science Foundation Minority Graduate Fellowship, 180
* National Science Foundation Minority Postdoctoral Fellowship, 180
Native American Scholarship, 520
* NCAA Ethnic Minority Internship, 481
* NCAA Ethnic Minority Postgraduate Scholarship, 481
* Neuroscience Training Minority Fellowship, 59
* New Jersey C. Clyde Ferguson Law Scholarship, 183
* New Jersey Minority Academic Career Program, 185
* New Mexico Graduate Scholarship: Minorities/Women, 186
* New Mexico Minority Doctoral Assistance Loan for Service, 187
New York State Native American Student Aid Program, 191
New York Times Summer Internship Program for Minorities, 524
* Newhouse Graduate Newspaper Fellowship for Minorities, 527
North American Indian Scholarship, 437
North Dakota Indian Scholarship Program, 196
Northern Cheyenne Higher Education Program, 196
Northwest Journalists of Color Scholarship Program, 530
* Nurses Clinical Training Fellowship, 327
* Nurses Health Policy Research Institute Fellowship, 327
* Nurses Research Training Fellowship, 328
* Nurses Substance Abuse Fellowship, 328
Oak Ridge Institute for Science and Education U.S. Department of Energy/NAACP, 210

Ohio Newspapers Minority Scholarship, 533
* Oklahoma Minority Doctoral Study Grant, 214
* Oklahoma Minority Professional Study Grant, 214
Osage Tribal Education Scholarship, 543
* Peat Marwick Doctoral Scholarship Program, 448
PGA Minority Internship Program, 546
* Physical Science Graduate Fellowship: Minorities and Women, 510
* Predoctoral Clearinghouse Application Fee Waiver, 382
* Presbyterian Fund for Graduate Education, 550
Presbyterian Native American Education Grant, 551
* Presbyterian Native American Seminary Scholarship, 551
* Presbyterian Racial/Ethnic Leadership Supplemental Grant, 551
Presbyterian Student Opportunity Scholarship, 551
* Psychology Research Training Minority Fellowship, 59
Public Policy Internship Program, 460
* Ralph W. Ellison Prize, 507
* Regents Graduate/Professional Fellowship, 213
* Robert D. Watkins Minority Graduate Fellowship, 651
RTNDF Minority News Management Internship, 558
Schuyler Meyer Junior Scholarship, 280
* Selected Professions Fellowship, 265
Seneca Nation Higher Education Program, 567
Shoshone Tribal Scholarship, 569
Smithsonian Minority Internship, 570
Smithsonian Native American Internship, 570
* Social Work Clinical Fellowship, 386
* Social Work Minority Research Fellowship, 386
* Sociological Association Minority Fellowship, 60
SONY Minority Internship, 590
* Special Libraries Association Affirmative Action Scholarship, 591
Stanley E. Jackson Award for Gifted/ Talented Minorities with Disabilities, 406
Stanley E. Jackson Scholarship Award for Ethnic Minority Students., 406
Tennessee Minority Teaching Fellows Program, 223
* The GEM Consortium/Doctoral Bridge Projects, 597
* The GEM Consortium/M.S. Engineering Fellowship, 597

*Graduate/nondegree study

Minority Status: Asian American

* The GEM Consortium/Ph.D Science and Engineering Fellowship, 597
Thomas P. Papandrew Scholarship, 451
Truman D. Picard Scholarship, 439
United Methodist Ethnic Scholarship, 605
United Methodist Hana Scholarship, 605
United Methodist Publishing House Merit Scholarship, 605
United States EPA Tribal Lands Environmental Science Scholarship, 58
University of North Carolina Native American Incentive Graduate Scholarship, 235
University of North Carolina Native American Incentive Merit Scholarship, 235
University of North Carolina Native American Incentive Undergraduate Scholarship, 235
* Veterinary Medicine Minority Loan / Scholarship, 144
Virginia Transfer Grant, 239
Virginia Undergraduate Student Financial Aid, 239
* W.K. Kellog Community Medicine Training, 508
Washington State American Indian Endowed Scholarship, 239
* William and Charlotte Cadbury Award, 508
Wisconsin Minority Retention Grant, 243
Wisconsin Minority Teacher Loan Program, 243
Wisconsin Native American Student Grant, 244
Women Engineers Chrysler Corporation Scholarship (Minorities), 585
Women Engineers Stone and Webster Scholarship, 588
Women in Construction: Founders' Scholarship, 480
Woodrow Wilson Program in Public Policy and International Affairs, 618
* Wyeth-Ayerst Laboratories Prize, 508
Yakama Indian Nation Scholarship, 619

Asian American

Advertising Internship for Minority Students, 261
Allen Lee Hughes Fellows Program, 353
* Allen Lee Hughes Internship, 353
* American Dissertation Fellowship, 264
American Institute of Architects Minority/Disadvantaged Scholarship, 283

* American Institute of Certified Public Accountants' Minority Doctoral Fellowship, 284
* American Speech-Language-Hearing International/Minority Student Scholarship, 347
* American Speech-Language-Hearing Young Minority Scholars Award, 347
Arkansas Freshman/Sophomore Minority Grant, 61
* Arkansas Minority Master's Fellowship, 61
Arkansas Minority Teachers Loan, 62
Bucks County Courier Times Minority Internship, 371
* California Library Scholarship for Minority Students, 375
California Teachers Association Martin Luther King, Jr., Memorial Scholarship, 667
* CANFIT Program Graduate Scholarship, 373
CANFIT Program Undergraduate Scholarship, 374
* Career Development Grant, 264
Carole Simpson Scholarship, 555
Certified Public Accountants' Minorities Scholarship, 284
* Charles E. Culpeper Art Internship, 487
* Chinese American Medical Society Scholarship, 379
* Clinical Psychology Training Minority Fellowship, 58
Colgate "Bright Smiles, Bright Futures" Minority Scholarships, 249
Colorado CPAs Ethnic Scholarship, 381
Colorado CPAs Ethnic-College and University Scholarship, 381
Congressional Black Caucus Foundation Spouses' Scholarship, 383
Cora Aguda Manayan Fund, 420
David and Dovetta Wilson Scholarship, 391
Duracell/Gillette Minority Intern Scholarship, 520
Ed Bradley Scholarship, 556
Edward D. Stone, Jr., and Associates Minority Scholarship, 450
Experiential Education Internship, 514
Fisher Broadcasting Minority Scholarship, 405
* Ford Foundation Dissertation Fellowship: Minorities, 510
* Ford Foundation Postdoctoral Fellowships for Minorities, 511
* Ford Foundation Predoctoral Fellowship: Minorities, 511
Foreign Study/Minority Scholarship Strategic Studies Award, 281

George M. Brooker Collegiate Scholarship for Minorities, 435
Golden State Minority Scholarship, 414
Gulf Coast Research Laboratory Minority Summer Grant, 140
* HIV/AIDS Research Training Minority Fellowship, 58
Illinois Minority Teachers Scholarship, 120
International Educational Exchange/ R.B. Bailey Minority Scholarship, 68
Jackie Robinson Scholarship, 440
Kansas Ethnic Minority Scholarship, 125
L.M. Perryman Ethnic Minority Award, 606
* Library and Information Technology Association/LSSI Minority Scholarship, 316
* Library and Information Technology Association/OCLC/Minority Scholarship, 316
* Louise Giles Minority Scholarship, 316
* Medical Library Scholarship for Minority Students, 462
Meteorological Society Minority Scholarship, 320
* Metropolitan Museum of Art Nine-Month Art Internship, 464
Metropolitan Museum of Art Six-Month Art Internship, 464
Michelle Clark Fellowship, 557
Microbiology Summer Research Fellowship for Minority Students, 339
Minnesota Nursing Grant for Persons of Color, 139
Missouri Minority Teaching Scholarship, 145
* National Art Gallery Diversity Internship Program, 476
National Scholarship Program, 712
* NCAA Ethnic Minority Internship, 481
* NCAA Ethnic Minority Postgraduate Scholarship, 481
* New Jersey C. Clyde Ferguson Law Scholarship, 183
* New Jersey Minority Academic Career Program, 185
* New Mexico Graduate Scholarship: Minorities/Women, 186
* New Mexico Minority Doctoral Assistance Loan for Service, 187
New York Times Summer Internship Program for Minorities, 524
* Newhouse Graduate Newspaper Fellowship for Minorities, 527
Northwest Journalists of Color Scholarship Program, 530

*Graduate/nondegree study

Minority Status: Asian American

*Nurses Clinical Training Fellowship, 327
*Nurses Health Policy Research Institute Fellowship, 327
*Nurses Research Training Fellowship, 328
*Nurses Substance Abuse Fellowship, 328
Ohio Newspapers Minority Scholarship, 533
*Oklahoma Minority Doctoral Study Grant, 214
*Oklahoma Minority Professional Study Grant, 214
*Peat Marwick Doctoral Scholarship Program, 448
PGA Minority Internship Program, 546
*Physical Science Graduate Fellowship: Minorities and Women, 510
*Presbyterian Fund for Graduate Education, 550
*Presbyterian Racial/Ethnic Leadership Supplemental Grant, 551
Presbyterian Student Opportunity Scholarship, 551
*Psychology Research Training Minority Fellowship, 59
*Robert D. Watkins Minority Graduate Fellowship, 651
RTNDF Minority News Management Internship, 558
*Selected Professions Fellowship, 265
Smithsonian Minority Internship, 570
*Social Work Clinical Fellowship, 386
*Social Work Minority Research Fellowship, 386
*Sociological Association Minority Fellowship, 60
SONY Minority Internship, 590
*Special Libraries Association Affirmative Action Scholarship, 591
Stanley E. Jackson Award for Gifted/Talented Minorities with Disabilities, 406
Stanley E. Jackson Scholarship Award for Ethnic Minority Students., 406
Tennessee Minority Teaching Fellows Program, 223
United Methodist Ethnic Scholarship, 605
United Methodist Hana Scholarship, 605
United Methodist Publishing House Merit Scholarship, 605
*Veterinary Medicine Minority Loan / Scholarship, 144
Virginia Transfer Grant, 239
Virginia Undergraduate Student Financial Aid, 239
Wisconsin Minority Retention Grant, 243
Wisconsin Minority Teacher Loan Program, 243

Women Engineers Chrysler Corporation Scholarship (Minorities), 585
Women Engineers Stone and Webster Scholarship, 588
Women in Construction: Founders' Scholarship, 480
Woodrow Wilson Program in Public Policy and International Affairs, 618

Mexican American

Actuarial Society Minority Scholarship, 579
Advertising Internship for Minority Students, 261
Allen Lee Hughes Fellows Program, 353
*Allen Lee Hughes Internship, 353
*American Dissertation Fellowship, 264
American Institute of Architects Minority/Disadvantaged Scholarship, 283
*American Institute of Certified Public Accountants' Minority Doctoral Fellowship, 284
American Physical Society Minorities Scholarship, 329
*American Political Science Association Minority Fellows, 330
*American Speech-Language-Hearing International/Minority Student Scholarship, 347
*American Speech-Language-Hearing Young Minority Scholars Award, 347
Arkansas Freshman/Sophomore Minority Grant, 61
*Arkansas Minority Master's Fellowship, 61
Arkansas Minority Teachers Loan, 62
Bucks County Courier Times Minority Internship, 371
*C.R. Bard Foundation Prize, 505
*California Library Scholarship for Minority Students, 375
California Teachers Association Martin Luther King, Jr., Memorial Scholarship, 667
*CANFIT Program Graduate Scholarship, 373
CANFIT Program Undergraduate Scholarship, 374
*Career Development Grant, 264
Carole Simpson Scholarship, 555
Certified Public Accountants' Minorities Scholarship, 284
*Charles E. Culpeper Art Internship, 487
Chemical Society Minority Scholarship, 267
*CIC/GE Predoctoral Fellowship, 382
*Clinical Psychology Training Minority Fellowship, 58

Colgate "Bright Smiles, Bright Futures" Minority Scholarships, 249
Colorado CPAs Ethnic Scholarship, 381
Colorado CPAs Ethnic-College and University Scholarship, 381
Congressional Black Caucus Foundation Spouses' Scholarship, 383
Congressional Hispanic Caucus Internship, 383
David and Dovetta Wilson Scholarship, 391
Duracell/Gillette Minority Intern Scholarship, 520
Ed Bradley Scholarship, 556
Edward D. Stone, Jr., and Associates Minority Scholarship, 450
Experiential Education Internship, 514
*Fellowship Program in Academic Medicine, 506
Fisher Broadcasting Minority Scholarship, 405
*Florida Education Fund Minority Participation in Legal Education Law School Scholarship, 76
Florida Education Fund Minority Pre-law Scholarships, 76
Florida Jose Marti Scholarship Challenge Grant, 72
*Ford Foundation Dissertation Fellowship: Minorities, 510
*Ford Foundation Postdoctoral Fellowships for Minorities, 511
*Ford Foundation Predoctoral Fellowship: Minorities, 511
Foreign Study/Minority Scholarship Strategic Studies Award, 281
*Franklin C. McLean Award, 506
*Gem Consortium Scholarship, 412
Geological Institute Minority Participation Program, 276
George M. Brooker Collegiate Scholarship for Minorities, 435
Golden State Minority Scholarship, 414
Gulf Coast Research Laboratory Minority Summer Grant, 140
Hispanic Fund Scholarships, 491
*HIV/AIDS Research Training Minority Fellowship, 58
Illinois Minority Teachers Scholarship, 120
Indiana Minority Teacher Scholarship, 122
Indiana Nursing Scholarship, 122
Inroads Internship, 432
International Educational Exchange/R.B. Bailey Minority Scholarship, 68
*Investment Banking Internship, 549
*Irving Graef Memorial Scholarship, 506
Jackie Robinson Scholarship, 440

Minority Status: Mexican American

* James H. Robinson Memorial Prize in Surgery, 506
Joel Garcia Memorial Scholarship, 374
Kansas Ethnic Minority Scholarship, 125
L.M. Perryman Ethnic Minority Award, 606
Latino Summer Legislative Internship, 478
* Library and Information Technology Association/LSSI Minority Scholarship, 316
* Library and Information Technology Association/OCLC/Minority Scholarship, 316
* Louise Giles Minority Scholarship, 316
McDonald's RMHC-Hispanic American Commitment to Educational Resources H.S. Program, 461
* Medical Fellowships General Need-Based Scholarship, 507
* Medical Fellowships Technology Training Program, 507
* Medical Library Scholarship for Minority Students, 462
Melon Minority Fellowship Program, 573
Meteorological Society Minority Scholarship, 320
* Metropolitan Life Foundation Scholarship, 507
* Metropolitan Museum of Art Nine-Month Art Internship, 464
Metropolitan Museum of Art Six-Month Art Internship, 464
Mexican American Grocers Association Scholarship, 465
* Mexican American Law School Scholarship, 465
Michelle Clark Fellowship, 557
Michigan Educational Opportunity Scholarship, 137
Michigan Hispanic High School Graduate Award, 466
Microbiology Summer Research Fellowship for Minority Students, 339
Minnesota Nursing Grant for Persons of Color, 139
* Minority Dental Student Scholarship, 248
Missouri Minority Teaching Scholarship, 145
* National Art Gallery Diversity Internship Program, 476
National Scholarship Program, 712
* National Science Foundation Minority Graduate Fellowship, 180
* National Science Foundation Minority Postdoctoral Fellowship, 180

* NCAA Ethnic Minority Internship, 481
* NCAA Ethnic Minority Postgraduate Scholarship, 481
* Neuroscience Training Minority Fellowship, 59
* New Jersey C. Clyde Ferguson Law Scholarship, 183
* New Jersey Minority Academic Career Program, 185
* New Mexico Graduate Scholarship: Minorities/Women, 186
* New Mexico Minority Doctoral Assistance Loan for Service, 187
New York Times Summer Internship Program for Minorities, 524
* Newhouse Graduate Newspaper Fellowship for Minorities, 527
Northwest Journalists of Color Scholarship Program, 530
* Nurses Clinical Training Fellowship, 327
* Nurses Health Policy Research Institute Fellowship, 327
* Nurses Research Training Fellowship, 328
* Nurses Substance Abuse Fellowship, 328
Oak Ridge Institute for Science and Education U.S. Department of Energy/NAACP, 210
Ohio Newspapers Minority Scholarship, 533
* Oklahoma Minority Doctoral Study Grant, 214
* Oklahoma Minority Professional Study Grant, 214
* Peat Marwick Doctoral Scholarship Program, 448
PGA Minority Internship Program, 546
* Physical Science Graduate Fellowship: Minorities and Women, 510
* Predoctoral Clearinghouse Application Fee Waiver, 382
* Presbyterian Fund for Graduate Education, 550
* Presbyterian Racial/Ethnic Leadership Supplemental Grant, 551
Presbyterian Student Opportunity Scholarship, 551
* Psychology Research Training Minority Fellowship, 59
* Puerto Rican Legal Defense & Educ. Fund-Father Joseph P. Fitzpatrick Scholarship, 554
* Ralph W. Ellison Prize, 507
* Regents Graduate/Professional Fellowship, 213
* Robert D. Watkins Minority Graduate Fellowship, 651
* Robert L. Millender Sr. Memorial Fund Fellowship Program, 560

RTNDF Minority News Management Internship, 558
* Selected Professions Fellowship, 265
Smithsonian Minority Internship, 570
* Social Work Clinical Fellowship, 386
* Social Work Minority Research Fellowship, 386
* Sociological Association Minority Fellowship, 60
SONY Minority Internship, 590
* Special Libraries Association Affirmative Action Scholarship, 591
Stanley E. Jackson Award for Gifted/Talented Minorities with Disabilities, 406
Stanley E. Jackson Scholarship Award for Ethnic Minority Students., 406
Tennessee Minority Teaching Fellows Program, 223
* The GEM Consortium/Doctoral Bridge Projects, 597
* The GEM Consortium/M.S. Engineering Fellowship, 597
* The GEM Consortium/Ph.D Science and Engineering Fellowship, 597
Thomas P. Papandrew Scholarship, 451
United Methodist Ethnic Scholarship, 605
United Methodist Hana Scholarship, 605
United Methodist Publishing House Merit Scholarship, 605
* Univision-Mexican American Legal Defense Fund Scholarship, 466
* Veterinary Medicine Minority Loan / Scholarship, 144
Vikki Carr Scholarship, 609
Virginia Transfer Grant, 239
Virginia Undergraduate Student Financial Aid, 239
* W.K. Kellog Community Medicine Training, 508
* William and Charlotte Cadbury Award, 508
Wisconsin Minority Retention Grant, 243
Wisconsin Minority Teacher Loan Program, 243
Women Engineers Chrysler Corporation Scholarship (Minorities), 585
Women Engineers Stone and Webster Scholarship, 588
Women in Construction: Founders' Scholarship, 480
Woodrow Wilson Program in Public Policy and International Affairs, 618
* Wyeth-Ayerst Laboratories Prize, 508

*Graduate/nondegree study

Puerto Rican

Actuarial Society Minority Scholarship, 579
Advertising Internship for Minority Students, 261
Allen Lee Hughes Fellows Program, 353
*Allen Lee Hughes Internship, 353
*American Dissertation Fellowship, 264
American Institute of Architects Minority/Disadvantaged Scholarship, 283
*American Institute of Certified Public Accountants' Minority Doctoral Fellowship, 284
American Physical Society Minorities Scholarship, 329
*American Political Science Association Minority Fellows, 330
*American Speech-Language-Hearing International/Minority Student Scholarship, 347
*American Speech-Language-Hearing Young Minority Scholars Award, 347
Arkansas Freshman/Sophomore Minority Grant, 61
*Arkansas Minority Master's Fellowship, 61
Arkansas Minority Teachers Loan, 62
Bucks County Courier Times Minority Internship, 371
*C.R. Bard Foundation Prize, 505
*California Library Scholarship for Minority Students, 375
California Teachers Association Martin Luther King, Jr., Memorial Scholarship, 667
*CANFIT Program Graduate Scholarship, 373
CANFIT Program Undergraduate Scholarship, 374
*Career Development Grant, 264
Carole Simpson Scholarship, 555
Certified Public Accountants' Minorities Scholarship, 284
*Charles E. Culpeper Art Internship, 487
Chemical Society Minority Scholarship, 267
*CIC/GE Predoctoral Fellowship, 382
*Clinical Psychology Training Minority Fellowship, 58
Colgate "Bright Smiles, Bright Futures" Minority Scholarships, 249
Colorado CPAs Ethnic Scholarship, 381
Colorado CPAs Ethnic-College and University Scholarship, 381
Congressional Black Caucus Foundation Spouses' Scholarship, 383

Congressional Hispanic Caucus Internship, 383
David and Dovetta Wilson Scholarship, 391
Duracell/Gillette Minority Intern Scholarship, 520
Ed Bradley Scholarship, 556
Edward D. Stone, Jr., and Associates Minority Scholarship, 450
Experiential Education Internship, 514
*Fellowship Program in Academic Medicine, 506
Fisher Broadcasting Minority Scholarship, 405
*Florida Education Fund Minority Participation in Legal Education Law School Scholarship, 76
Florida Education Fund Minority Pre-law Scholarships, 76
Florida Jose Marti Scholarship Challenge Grant, 72
*Ford Foundation Dissertation Fellowship: Minorities, 510
*Ford Foundation Postdoctoral Fellowships for Minorities, 511
*Ford Foundation Predoctoral Fellowship: Minorities, 511
Foreign Study/Minority Scholarship Strategic Studies Award, 281
*Franklin C. McLean Award, 506
*Gem Consortium Scholarship, 412
Geological Institute Minority Participation Program, 276
George M. Brooker Collegiate Scholarship for Minorities, 435
Golden State Minority Scholarship, 414
Gulf Coast Research Laboratory Minority Summer Grant, 140
Hispanic Fund Scholarships, 491
*HIV/AIDS Research Training Minority Fellowship, 58
Illinois Minority Teachers Scholarship, 120
Indiana Minority Teacher Scholarship, 122
Indiana Nursing Scholarship, 122
Inroads Internship, 432
International Educational Exchange/ R.B. Bailey Minority Scholarship, 68
*Investment Banking Internship, 549
*Irving Graef Memorial Scholarship, 506
Jackie Robinson Scholarship, 440
*James H. Robinson Memorial Prize in Surgery, 506
Joel Garcia Memorial Scholarship, 374
Kansas Ethnic Minority Scholarship, 125
L.M. Perryman Ethnic Minority Award, 606

Latino Summer Legislative Internship, 478
*Library and Information Technology Association/LSSI Minority Scholarship, 316
*Library and Information Technology Association/OCLC/Minority Scholarship, 316
*Louise Giles Minority Scholarship, 316
McDonald's RMHC-Hispanic American Commitment to Educational Resources H.S. Program, 461
*Medical Fellowships General Need-Based Scholarship, 507
*Medical Fellowships Technology Training Program, 507
*Medical Library Scholarship for Minority Students, 462
Melon Minority Fellowship Program, 573
Meteorological Society Minority Scholarship, 320
*Metropolitan Life Foundation Scholarship, 507
*Metropolitan Museum of Art Nine-Month Art Internship, 464
Metropolitan Museum of Art Six-Month Art Internship, 464
Mexican American Grocers Association Scholarship, 465
*Mexican American Law School Scholarship, 465
Michelle Clark Fellowship, 557
Michigan Educational Opportunity Scholarship, 137
Michigan Hispanic High School Graduate Award, 466
Microbiology Summer Research Fellowship for Minority Students, 339
Minnesota Nursing Grant for Persons of Color, 139
*Minority Dental Student Scholarship, 248
Missouri Minority Teaching Scholarship, 145
*National Art Gallery Diversity Internship Program, 476
National Scholarship Program, 712
*National Science Foundation Minority Graduate Fellowship, 180
*National Science Foundation Minority Postdoctoral Fellowship, 180
*NCAA Ethnic Minority Internship, 481
*NCAA Ethnic Minority Postgraduate Scholarship, 481
*Neuroscience Training Minority Fellowship, 59
*New Jersey C. Clyde Ferguson Law Scholarship, 183

Minority Status: Hispanic American

* New Jersey Minority Academic Career Program, 185
* New Mexico Graduate Scholarship: Minorities/Women, 186
* New Mexico Minority Doctoral Assistance Loan for Service, 187
New York Times Summer Internship Program for Minorities, 524
* Newhouse Graduate Newspaper Fellowship for Minorities, 527
Northwest Journalists of Color Scholarship Program, 530
* Nurses Clinical Training Fellowship, 327
* Nurses Health Policy Research Institute Fellowship, 327
* Nurses Research Training Fellowship, 328
* Nurses Substance Abuse Fellowship, 328
Oak Ridge Institute for Science and Education U.S. Department of Energy/NAACP, 210
Ohio Newspapers Minority Scholarship, 533
* Oklahoma Minority Doctoral Study Grant, 214
* Oklahoma Minority Professional Study Grant, 214
* Peat Marwick Doctoral Scholarship Program, 448
PGA Minority Internship Program, 546
* Physical Science Graduate Fellowship: Minorities and Women, 510
* Predoctoral Clearinghouse Application Fee Waiver, 382
* Presbyterian Fund for Graduate Education, 550
* Presbyterian Racial/Ethnic Leadership Supplemental Grant, 551
Presbyterian Student Opportunity Scholarship, 551
* Psychology Research Training Minority Fellowship, 59
* Puerto Rican Legal Defense & Educ. Fund-Father Joseph P. Fitzpatrick Scholarship, 554
* Ralph W. Ellison Prize, 507
* Regents Graduate/Professional Fellowship, 213
* Robert D. Watkins Minority Graduate Fellowship, 651
* Robert L. Millender Sr. Memorial Fund Fellowship Program, 560
RTNDF Minority News Management Internship, 558
* Selected Professions Fellowship, 265
Smithsonian Minority Internship, 570
* Social Work Clinical Fellowship, 386
* Social Work Minority Research Fellowship, 386
* Sociological Association Minority Fellowship, 60

SONY Minority Internship, 590
* Special Libraries Association Affirmative Action Scholarship, 591
Stanley E. Jackson Award for Gifted/Talented Minorities with Disabilities, 406
Stanley E. Jackson Scholarship Award for Ethnic Minority Students., 406
Tennessee Minority Teaching Fellows Program, 223
* The GEM Consortium/Doctoral Bridge Projects, 597
* The GEM Consortium/M.S. Engineering Fellowship, 597
* The GEM Consortium/Ph.D Science and Engineering Fellowship, 597
Thomas P. Papandrew Scholarship, 451
United Methodist Ethnic Scholarship, 605
United Methodist Hana Scholarship, 605
United Methodist Publishing House Merit Scholarship, 605
* Univision-Mexican American Legal Defense Fund Scholarship, 466
* Veterinary Medicine Minority Loan / Scholarship, 144
Vikki Carr Scholarship, 609
Virginia Transfer Grant, 239
Virginia Undergraduate Student Financial Aid, 239
* W.K. Kellog Community Medicine Training, 508
* William and Charlotte Cadbury Award, 508
Wisconsin Minority Retention Grant, 243
Wisconsin Minority Teacher Loan Program, 243
Women Engineers Chrysler Corporation Scholarship (Minorities), 585
Women Engineers Stone and Webster Scholarship, 588
Women in Construction: Founders' Scholarship, 480
Woodrow Wilson Program in Public Policy and International Affairs, 618
* Wyeth-Ayerst Laboratories Prize, 508

Hispanic American

Actuarial Society Minority Scholarship, 579
Advertising Internship for Minority Students, 261
Allen Lee Hughes Fellows Program, 353
* Allen Lee Hughes Internship, 353
* American Dissertation Fellowship, 264
American Institute of Architects Minority/Disadvantaged Scholarship, 283

* American Institute of Certified Public Accountants' Minority Doctoral Fellowship, 284
American Physical Society Minorities Scholarship, 329
* American Political Science Association Minority Fellows, 330
* American Speech-Language-Hearing International/Minority Student Scholarship, 347
* American Speech-Language-Hearing Young Minority Scholars Award, 347
Arkansas Freshman/Sophomore Minority Grant, 61
* Arkansas Minority Master's Fellowship, 61
Arkansas Minority Teachers Loan, 62
Bucks County Courier Times Minority Internship, 371
* California Library Scholarship for Minority Students, 375
California Teachers Association Martin Luther King, Jr., Memorial Scholarship, 667
* CANFIT Program Graduate Scholarship, 373
CANFIT Program Undergraduate Scholarship, 374
* Career Development Grant, 264
Carole Simpson Scholarship, 555
Certified Public Accountants' Minorities Scholarship, 284
* Charles E. Culpeper Art Internship, 487
Chemical Society Minority Scholarship, 267
* Clinical Psychology Training Minority Fellowship, 58
Colgate "Bright Smiles, Bright Futures" Minority Scholarships, 249
Colorado CPAs Ethnic Scholarship, 381
Colorado CPAs Ethnic-College and University Scholarship, 381
Congressional Black Caucus Foundation Spouses' Scholarship, 383
Congressional Hispanic Caucus Internship, 383
David and Dovetta Wilson Scholarship, 391
Duracell/Gillette Minority Intern Scholarship, 520
Ed Bradley Scholarship, 556
Edward D. Stone, Jr., and Associates Minority Scholarship, 450
Experiential Education Internship, 514
Fisher Broadcasting Minority Scholarship, 405
* Florida Education Fund Minority Participation in Legal Education Law School Scholarship, 76

*Graduate/nondegree study

Minority Status: Hispanic American

Florida Education Fund Minority Pre-law Scholarships, 76
Florida Jose Marti Scholarship Challenge Grant, 72
Foreign Study/Minority Scholarship Strategic Studies Award, 281
*Gem Consortium Scholarship, 412
Geological Institute Minority Participation Program, 276
George M. Brooker Collegiate Scholarship for Minorities, 435
Golden State Minority Scholarship, 414
Gulf Coast Research Laboratory Minority Summer Grant, 140
Hispanic Fund Scholarships, 49†
*HIV/AIDS Research Training Minority Fellowship, 58
Illinois Minority Teachers Scholarship, 120
Indiana Minority Teacher Scholarship, 122
Indiana Nursing Scholarship, 122
Inroads Internship, 432
International Educational Exchange/R.B. Bailey Minority Scholarship, 68
*Investment Banking Internship, 549
*Irving Graef Memorial Scholarship, 506
Jackie Robinson Scholarship, 440
Joel Garcia Memorial Scholarship, 374
Kansas Ethnic Minority Scholarship, 125
L.M. Perryman Ethnic Minority Award, 606
Latino Summer Legislative Internship, 478
*Library and Information Technology Association/LSSI Minority Scholarship, 316
*Library and Information Technology Association/OCLC/Minority Scholarship, 316
*Louise Giles Minority Scholarship, 316
McDonald's RMHC-Hispanic American Commitment to Educational Resources H.S. Program, 461
*Medical Fellowships Technology Training Program, 507
*Medical Library Scholarship for Minority Students, 462
Melon Minority Fellowship Program, 573
Meteorological Society Minority Scholarship, 320
*Metropolitan Life Foundation Scholarship, 507
*Metropolitan Museum of Art Nine-Month Art Internship, 464

Metropolitan Museum of Art Six-Month Art Internship, 464
Mexican American Grocers Association Scholarship, 465
*Mexican American Law School Scholarship, 465
Michelle Clark Fellowship, 557
Michigan Educational Opportunity Scholarship, 137
Michigan Hispanic High School Graduate Award, 466
Microbiology Summer Research Fellowship for Minority Students, 339
Minnesota Nursing Grant for Persons of Color, 139
*Minority Dental Student Scholarship, 248
Missouri Minority Teaching Scholarship, 145
*National Art Gallery Diversity Internship Program, 476
National Scholarship Program, 712
*National Science Foundation Minority Graduate Fellowship, 180
*National Science Foundation Minority Postdoctoral Fellowship, 180
*NCAA Ethnic Minority Internship, 481
*NCAA Ethnic Minority Postgraduate Scholarship, 481
*Neuroscience Training Minority Fellowship, 59
*New Jersey C. Clyde Ferguson Law Scholarship, 183
*New Jersey Minority Academic Career Program, 185
*New Mexico Graduate Scholarship: Minorities/Women, 186
*New Mexico Minority Doctoral Assistance Loan for Service, 187
New York Times Summer Internship Program for Minorities, 524
*Newhouse Graduate Newspaper Fellowship for Minorities, 527
Northwest Journalists of Color Scholarship Program, 530
*Nurses Clinical Training Fellowship, 327
*Nurses Health Policy Research Institute Fellowship, 327
*Nurses Research Training Fellowship, 328
*Nurses Substance Abuse Fellowship, 328
Oak Ridge Institute for Science and Education U.S. Department of Energy/NAACP, 210
Ohio Newspapers Minority Scholarship, 533
*Oklahoma Minority Doctoral Study Grant, 214
*Oklahoma Minority Professional Study Grant, 214

*Peat Marwick Doctoral Scholarship Program, 448
PGA Minority Internship Program, 546
*Physical Science Graduate Fellowship: Minorities and Women, 510
*Presbyterian Fund for Graduate Education, 550
*Presbyterian Racial/Ethnic Leadership Supplemental Grant, 551
Presbyterian Student Opportunity Scholarship, 551
*Psychology Research Training Minority Fellowship, 59
*Puerto Rican Legal Defense & Educ. Fund-Father Joseph P. Fitzpatrick Scholarship, 554
*Regents Graduate/Professional Fellowship, 213
*Robert D. Watkins Minority Graduate Fellowship, 651
*Robert L. Millender Sr. Memorial Fund Fellowship Program, 560
RTNDF Minority News Management Internship, 558
*Selected Professions Fellowship, 265
Smithsonian Minority Internship, 570
*Social Work Clinical Fellowship, 386
*Social Work Minority Research Fellowship, 386
*Sociological Association Minority Fellowship, 60
SONY Minority Internship, 590
*Special Libraries Association Affirmative Action Scholarship, 591
Stanley E. Jackson Award for Gifted/Talented Minorities with Disabilities, 406
Stanley E. Jackson Scholarship Award for Ethnic Minority Students., 406
Tennessee Minority Teaching Fellows Program, 223
*The GEM Consortium/Doctoral Bridge Projects, 597
*The GEM Consortium/M.S. Engineering Fellowship, 597
*The GEM Consortium/Ph.D Science and Engineering Fellowship, 597
Thomas P. Papandrew Scholarship, 451
United Methodist Ethnic Scholarship, 605
United Methodist Hana Scholarship, 605
United Methodist Publishing House Merit Scholarship, 605
*Univision-Mexican American Legal Defense Fund Scholarship, 466
*Veterinary Medicine Minority Loan / Scholarship, 144
Vikki Carr Scholarship, 609
Virginia Transfer Grant, 239
Virginia Undergraduate Student Financial Aid, 239

*Graduate/nondegree study

Wisconsin Minority Retention Grant, 243
Wisconsin Minority Teacher Loan Program, 243
Women Engineers Chrysler Corporation Scholarship (Minorities), 585
Women Engineers Stone and Webster Scholarship, 588
Women in Construction: Founders' Scholarship, 480
Woodrow Wilson Program in Public Policy and International Affairs, 618

National/Ethnic Background

Armenian

* Armenian Relief Graduate Scholarship, 354
Armenian Relief Undergraduate Scholarship, 354
Armenian Union Awards for Students on Non-U.S. Soil, 354
* Armenian Union U.S. Graduate Loan, 354

Chinese

Thz Fo Farm Fund, 118

Danish

Danish Foundation Scholarship, 529

Greek

Daughters of Penelope Re-entry Grant, 390
Hellenic Progressive Association Scholarship, 534

Italian

* A.P. Giannini Scholarship, 491
Agnes E. Vaghi-Cornaro Scholarship, 491
Alyce M. Cafaro Scholarship, 491
Angela Scholarship, 491
Antonio and Felicia Marinelli Scholarships, 492
Antonio F. Marinelli Founders Scholarship, 492
Assunta Lucchetti Martino Scholarship for International Studies, 492
Bolla Wines Scholarship, 492
Capital Area Regional Scholarship, 493
* Carmela Gagliardi Fellowship, 493
Communications Scholarship, 493
Daniel Stella Scholarship, 493

Dr. William L. Amoroso Jr. Scholarship, 494
F.D. Stella Scholarship, 494
Gianni Versace Scholarship in Fashion Design, 494
* Giargiari Fellowship, 494
* GRI/ICIF Culinary Scholarship, 494
Henry Salvatori Scholarship, 589
Italian American Study Abroad Scholarship, 495
Italian Catholic Federation Scholarship, 439
Italian Cultural Society and NIAF Matching Scholarship, 495
Italian Regional Scholarship, 495
John A. Volpe Scholarship, 495
John Basilone Scholarship, 601
Louis J. Salerno, M.D. Memorial Scholarship, 496
Lower Mid-Atlantic Regional Scholarship, 496
Marija Bileta Scholarship, 496
Merrill Lynch Scholarship, 496
Mid-America Regional Scholarship, 497
Mid-Pacific Regional Scholarship, 497
Mola Scholarship, 497
NAIF/FIERI National Matching Scholarship, 497
Nerone/NIAF Matching Art Scholarship, 497
New England Regional Scholarship, 498
* NIAF/FIERI D.C. Matching Scholarship, 498
NIAF/NOIAW Cornaro Scholarship, 498
North Central Regional Scholarship, 498
North Central Regional Scholarship, 499
Paragano Scholarship, 499
Pavarotti Scholarship, 499
* Peter Sammartino Scholarship, 499
Piancone Family Agriculture Scholarship, 500
* President Francesco Cossiga Fellowship, 526
Rabbi Feinberg Scholarship, 500
* Ralph Lombardi Memorial Scholarship, 500
Recine Scholarship, 500
Robert J. Di Pietro Scholarship, 501
Rose Basile Green Scholarship, 501
Santavicca Scholarship, 501
* Scalia Scholarship, 501
Sergio Franchi Music Scholarship/ Voice Performance, 502
Silvio Conte Internship, 502
Sons of Italy National Leadership Grant, 589
South Central Regional Scholarship, 502
Southeast Regional Scholarship, 502

Southwest Regional Scholarship, 502
Thomas Joseph Ambrosole Scholarship, 503
Upper Mid-Atlantic Regional Scholarship, 503
Vennera Noto Scholarship, 503
* Vincent and Anna Visceglia Fellowship, 503
Vincente Minelli Scholarship, 504
West Virginia Italian Heritage Festival Scholarship, 504
William C. Davini Scholarship, 602
* Zecchino Postgraduate Orthopaedic Fellowship, 504

Japanese

Japanese American General Scholarship, 442
Japanese American Music Award Competition, 442

Mongolian

* Hangin Memorial Scholarship, 468

Polish

Kosciuszko Tuition Scholarship, 448
Polish Culture Scholarship, 285
Sons of Poland Scholarship, 657

Swiss

Achievement Award, 595
Medicus Student Exchange, 595
Pellegrini Scholarship, 596

Ukrainian

Eugene and Elinor Kotur Scholarship, 601
Ukrainian Fraternal Association Scholarship, 755

Welsh

Cymdeithas Gymreig (Welsh Society) Philadelphia Scholarship, 387
Saint David's Society Scholarship, 562

Arab or Jewish

* Interns for Peace Internship, 439

Religious Affiliation

Christian

L.M. Perryman Ethnic Minority Award, 606
* Stoody-West Fellowship, 606

*Graduate/nondegree study

Religious Affiliation: Episcopal

Episcopal

Shannon Scholarship, 600

Jewish

Frank L. Weil Memorial Scholarship, 664
JVS Jewish Community Scholarship Program, 447
Lazaroff Family Fund, 443
Samuel Lemberg Scholarship Loan, 563

Lutheran

Bethesda Lutheran Homes and Services Cooperative Program Internship, 368
Mental Retardation Nursing Scholastic Achievement Scholarship, 367
Mental Retardation Scholastic Achievement Scholarship, 368
Women of the Evangelical Lutheran Church in America Scholarship, 616

Presbyterian Church (USA)

Ira Page Wallace Bible Scholarship, 550
National Presbyterian College Scholarship, 550
Presbyterian Appalachian Scholarship, 550
*Presbyterian Fund for Graduate Education, 550
*Presbyterian Grant Program for Medical Studies, 550
Presbyterian Native American Education Grant, 551
*Presbyterian Native American Seminary Scholarship, 551
*Presbyterian Racial/Ethnic Leadership Supplemental Grant, 551
Presbyterian Service Loan for Undergraduates, 551
Presbyterian Student Opportunity Scholarship, 551
*Presbyterian Theological Continuing Education Loan, 552
*Presbyterian Theological Loan, 552
Presbyterian Undergraduate and Graduate Loan, 552
Samuel Robinson Award, 552
*Theological Continuing Education Grant, 552

Protestant

Juliette M. Atherton Scholarship, 423

Roman Catholic

*Bishop Greco Graduate Fellowship, 699
Italian Catholic Federation Scholarship, 439
Knights of Columbus Student Loan, 699
Matthews/Swift Educational Trust - Military Dependants, 699
Matthews/Swift Educational Trust - Police/Firefighters, 699
Pro Deo/Pro Patria Scholarship, 700

Unitarian Universalist

Unitarian Universalist Stanfield Art Scholarship, 602
*Unitarian Universalist Stanfield Law Scholarship, 602

United Methodist

*Bishop James C. Baker Award, 603
*E. Craig Brandenburg Graduate Award, 603
*Georgia Harkness Scholarship, 604
J.A. Knowles Memorial Scholarship, 604
*John Q. Schisler Award, 604
Priscilla R. Morton Scholarship, 604
*Rev. Charles W. Tadlock Scholarship, 604
United Methodist Bass Scholarship, 604
United Methodist Church Conference Merit Award, 605
*United Methodist Church Crusade Scholarship, 605
United Methodist Ethnic Scholarship, 605
United Methodist Hana Scholarship, 605
United Methodist Loan Program, 605
United Methodist Publishing House Merit Scholarship, 605
United Methodist Scholarship, 606
*United Methodist Seminary Award, 606

Eastern Orthodox

Boy Scouts of America/Eastern Orthodox Committee on Scouting Scholarship, 663

Returning Adult

A.J. "Andy" Spielman Travel Agents Scholarship, 344
Adult Undergraduate Incentive Award, 452
Air Traffic Control Full-Time Employee/Part-Time Student Scholarship, 623
*American Legion National Eight and Forty Lung and Respiratory Nursing Scholarship Fund, 301
Connecticut Tuition Waiver for Senior Citizens, 67
Consulting Engineers Scholarship, 270
Daughters of Penelope Re-entry Grant, 390
Delaware Engineering Society Undergraduate Scholarship Program, 392
*Mabelle Wilhelmina Boldt Interior Design Scholarship, 342
Montgomery GI Bill Plus Army College Fund, 227
NASA Space Grant North Carolina Undergraduate Scholarship Program, 164
New York State Vietnam Veteran Tuition Award/Persian Gulf Veteran Award, 191
Olive Lynn Salembier Scholarship, 584
Pollard Travel Agents Scholarship, 346
Royal Neighbors Non-Traditional Scholarship, 736
*Ruth Satter Memorial Award, 360
Women Engineers Chrysler Corporation Re-entry Scholarship, 585
Women of the Evangelical Lutheran Church in America Scholarship, 616
Women's Education Fund, 442

Study Abroad

*Abe Fellowship Program, 571
Academic-Year Ambassadorial Scholarship, 561
*Advanced Research Grants: Japan, 571
*Albania: Full Grant (Fulbright), 77
*Argentina: Full Grant (Fulbright), 77
*Australia: Full Grant (Fulbright), 77
*Austria: Full Grant (Fulbright), 77
*Austria: IFK Grants, 78
*Austria: Study Grant English Language Teaching Assistantship, 78
*Bahrain: Full Grant (Fulbright), 78
*Bangladesh: Full Grant (Fulbright), 78
*Belgium and Luxembourg: Full Grant (Fulbright), 79
*Belgium and Luxembourg: Teaching Assistantship (Fulbright), 79
*Belgum and Luxembourg: Center for European Studies Award, 79
*Benin: Full Grant (Fulbright), 79

*Graduate/nondegree study

Study Abroad

* Bolivia: Full Grant (Fulbright), 80
* Botswana: Full Grant (Fulbright), 80
* Brazil: Full Grant (Fulbright), 80
* Bulgaria: Full Grant (Fulbright), 80
* Burkina Faso: Full Grant (Fulbright), 81
* Cameroon: Full Grant (Fulbright), 81
* Canada: Full Grant (Fulbright), 81
* Canada: Native North American Scholarship (Fulbright), 81
* Carmargo Foundation Fellowship, 376
* Chad: Full Grant (Fulbright), 82
* Chile: Full Grant (Fulbright), 82
* Churchill Scholarship, 615
* Colombia: Full Grant (Fulbright), 82
* Costa Rica: Full Grant (Fulbright), 82
* Croatia: Full Grant (Fulbright), 83
  Cultural Ambassadorial Scholarship, 562
* Cyprus: Full Grant (Fulbright), 83
* Czech Republic: Full Grant (Fulbright), 83
* Denmark: Aalborg University Grant (Fulbright), 83
* Denmark: Full Grant (Fulbright), 84
* Dominican Republic: Full Grant (Fulbright), 84
* Ecuador: Full Grant (Fulbright), 84
* Egypt: Full Grant (Fulbright), 84
* El Salvador: Full Grant (Fulbright), 84
* Eritrea: Full Grant (Fulbright), 85
* Estonia: Full Grant (Fulbright), 85
* Ethiopia: Full Grant (Fulbright), 85
* European Union: Full Grant (Fulbright), 85
* Finland: Full Grant (Fulbright), 86
* Foreign Scholar Research Fellowships, 257
* France: Full Grant (Fulbright), 86
* France: Government Teaching Assistantship (Fulbright), 86
* France: Lusk Memorial Fellowship (Fulbright), 86
* Fulbright - USIA U.K. Zeneca Award, 87
* German Academic Exchange Service Grant (Fulbright), 87
* Germanistic Society of America Quadrille Grant (Fulbright), 87
* Germany: Bavarian State Government Grant (Fulbright), 87
* Germany: Full Grant (Fulbright), 88
* Germany: Government Teaching Assistantship (Fulbright), 88
* Germany: Travel Grant (Fulbright), 88
* Ghana: Full Grant (Fulbright), 88
* Greece: European Banking Grant (Fulbright), 89
* Greece: Full Grant (Fulbright), 89
* Guatemala: Full Grant (Fulbright), 89
* Guinea: Full Grant (Fulbright), 89
* Haiti: Full Grant (Fulbright), 90
* Honduras: Full Grant (Fulbright), 90

* Hong Kong: Full Grant (Fulbright), 90
* Hungary: Government Grant (Fulbright), 90
* Hungary: Teaching Assistantship (Fulbright), 91
* Hungary: Travel Grant (Fulbright), 91
* Huntington British Academy Exchange Fellowship, 430
* Iceland: Full Grant (Fulbright), 91
* Iceland: Travel Grant-Government Grant (Fulbright), 91
* India: Full Grant (Fulbright), 91
* Indonesia: Full Grant (Fulbright), 92
* Ireland: Full Grant (Fulbright), 92
* Israel: Full Grant (Fulbright), 92
* Israel: Postdoctoral Award (Fulbright), 93
* Italy: Full Grant (Fulbright), 93
* Italy: Miguel Vinciguerra Fund Grant (Fulbright), 93
* Italy: Travel Grant (Fulbright), 93
* Ivory Coast: Full Grant (Fulbright), 94
* Jamaica: Full Grant (Fulbright), 94
* Japan-United States Arts Program, 356
* Japan: Fellowship for Graduating Seniors (Fulbright), 94
* Japan: Full Grant (Fulbright), 94
* Jordan: Full Grant (Fulbright), 95
* Kenya: Full Grant (Fulbright), 95
* Korea: Full Grant (Fulbright), 95
* Korea: Teaching Assistantship (Fulbright), 95
* Korea: Travel Grant (Fulbright), 96
* Kuwait: Full Grant (Fulbright), 96
* Latvia: Full Grant (Fulbright), 96
* Lithuania: Full Grant (Fulbright), 96
* Madagascar: Full Grant (Fulbright), 97
* Malawi: Full Grant (Fulbright), 97
* Malaysia: Full Grant (Fulbright), 97
* Mali: Full Grant (Fulbright), 97
  Marshall Scholarship, 370
  Martin McLaren-Interchange Fellowship in Horticulture and Landscape Design, 411
* Mauritius: Full Grant (Fulbright), 98
  Medicus Student Exchange, 595
* Mexico: Binational Business Grants (Fulbright), 98
* Mexico: Garcia Robles Grant (Fulbright), 98
  Morocco: Full Grant (Fulbright), 98
* Mozambique: Full Grant (Fulbright), 99
  Multi-Year Ambassadorial Scholarship, 562
* Namibia: Full Grant (Fulbright), 99
* Nepal: Full Grant (Fulbright), 99
* Netherlands: America Foundation Grant (Fulbright), 99
* Netherlands: Full Grant (Fulbright), 100

* New Zealand: Full Grant (Fulbright), 100
* Nicaragua: Full Grant (Fulbright), 100
* Niger: Full Grant (Fulbright), 100
* Nigeria: Full Grant (Fulbright), 101
* Norway: Full Grant (Fulbright), 101
* Oman: Full Grant (Fulbright), 101
* Pakistan Studies Fellowship, 284
* Pakistan: Full Grant (Fulbright), 101
* Panama: Full Grant (Fulbright), 101
* Paraguay: Full Grant (Fulbright), 102
* Peru: Full Grant (Fulbright), 102
* Philippines: Full Grant (Fulbright), 102
* Poland: Government Grant (Fulbright), 102
  Portugal: Full Grant (Fulbright), 103
* Pre-Dissertation Fellowship for Research in Europe, 384
* Predissertation Fellowship: Bangladesh, 574
* Qatar: Full Grant (Fulbright), 103
* Research Center in Egypt Fellowship, 59
* Romania: Government Grant (Fulbright), 103
* Saudi Arabia: Full Grant (Fulbright), 103
* Senegal: Full Grant (Fulbright), 104
* Singapore: Full Grant (Fulbright), 104
* Slovak Republic: Full Grant (Fulbright), 104
* Slovenia: Full Grant (Fulbright), 104
* South Africa: Full Grant (Fulbright), 105
* Spain: Full Grant (Fulbright), 105
* Spain: Government Grant (Fulbright), 105
* Spain: Professional Grant in Journalism (Fulbright), 105
* Sri Lanka: Full Grant (Fulbright), 106
* Swaziland: Full Grant (Fulbright), 106
* Sweden: Full Grant (Fulbright), 106
* Switzerland: Government Grant (Fulbright), 106
* Switzerland: Seydel Fellowship (Fulbright), 107
* Syria: Government Grant (Fulbright), 107
* Taiwan: Full Grant (Fulbright), 107
* Taiwan: Teaching Assistantship-Internship (Fulbright), 107
* Tanzania: Full Grant (Fulbright), 108
* Thailand: Full Grant (Fulbright), 108
* Togo: Full Grant (Fulbright), 108
  Tourism Foundation Quebec Scholarship, 518
* Trinidad and Tobago: Full Grant (Fulbright), 108
* Tunisia: Full Grant (Fulbright), 109
* Turkey: Full Grant (Fulbright), 109
* Turkey: Teaching Assistantship (Fulbright), 109

*Graduate/nondegree study

* U.S. English Foundation Award (Fulbright), 109
* Uganda: Full Grant (Fulbright), 110
* United Arab Emirates: Full Grant (Fulbright), 110
* United Kingdom: British-American Chamber of Commerce Award (Fulbright), 110
* United Kingdom: British-American Tobacco Industries Award (Fulbright), 110
* United Kingdom: Cambridge University Research Scholarship (Fulbright), 111
* United Kingdom: Full Grant (Fulbright), 111
* United Kingdom: Marks and Spencer Award (Fulbright), 111
* United Kingdom: Oxford University Scholarship (Fulbright), 111
* United Kingdom: Sussex University Research Scholarship (Fulbright), 112
* United Kingdom: University College London Scholarship (Fulbright), 112
* United Kingdom: University of East Anglia Research Scholarship (Fulbright), 112
* Uruguay: Full Grant (Fulbright), 112
* Venezuela: Full Grant (Fulbright), 113
* Vietnam: Full Grant (Fulbright), 113
* Yemen: Full Grant (Fulbright), 113
* Zambia: Full Grant (Fulbright), 113
* Zimbabwe: Full Grant (Fulbright), 114

*Graduate/nondegree study

Federal and State

AFOSR/Air Force Office of Scientific Research

AFOSR Summer Research Program

Type of award: Internship.
Intended use: For graduate study at accredited graduate institution in United States. Designated institutions: Armstrong Laboratory (AL), Wilford Hall Medical Center (TX), Arnold Engineering Development Center (TN), Phillips Laboratory (NM), Air Logistics Centers (CA, UT, GA, OK & TX), Rome Laboratory (NY).
Eligibility: Applicant must be U.S. citizen or permanent resident.
Basis for selection: Major/career interest in science, general; physics; engineering; chemistry; biology; aerospace. Applicant must demonstrate depth of character and high academic achievement.
Application requirements: Recommendations, transcript and research proposal.
Additional information: Permanent Residents not eligible to participate at all locations. Contact sponsor for further information. Provides opportunities for graduate students to participate in scientific research at various Air Force laboratory facilities. Graduate students with bachelor's degrees earn $412 per week, graduate students with master's degree, $484 per week. Daily expense allowance for participants who live more than 50 miles from research facility.

Amount of award:	$3,296-$5,808
Application deadline:	March 6
Total amount awarded:	$100

Contact:
AFOSR/Air Force Office of Scientific Research
5800 Uplander Way
Culver City, CA 90230-6608
Website: www.rdi.com

Alabama Commission on Higher Education

Alabama National Guard Educational Assistance Award

Type of award: Scholarship, renewable.
Intended use: For undergraduate or graduate study at postsecondary institution in Alabama.
Eligibility: Applicant must be U.S. citizen residing in Alabama. Applicant must be in military service who served in the Reserves/National Guard. Active members in good standing with federally-recognized unit of Alabama National Guard.
Application requirements: Proof of eligibility.
Additional information: Award covers tuition, books, fees and supplies (minus any Federal Veterans' benefits) at Alabama public institution or up to $1,000 at private institution. Applications available from Alabama National Guard.

Amount of award:	$25-$1,000
Number of awards:	1,026
Number of applicants:	1,500
Total amount awarded:	$647,000

Alabama Student Assistance Program

Type of award: Scholarship, renewable.
Intended use: For full-time freshman, sophomore, junior or senior study at vocational, 2-year or 4-year institution in Alabama.
Eligibility: Applicant must be residing in Alabama.
Basis for selection: Applicant must demonstrate financial need.
Application requirements: Proof of eligibility.
Additional information: Contact high school guidance office or financial aid office of institution.

Amount of award:	$300-$2,500
Number of awards:	4,380
Total amount awarded:	$1,950,080

Alabama Student Grant

Type of award: Scholarship, renewable.
Intended use: For full-time or half-time undergraduate study at 2-year or 4-year institution in Alabama. Designated institutions: Birmingham-Southern College, Concordia College, Faulkner University, Huntingdon College, Judson College, Miles College, Mobile College, Oakwood College, Samford University, Southeastern Bible College, Spring Hill College, Stillman College, Southern Community College.
Eligibility: Applicant must be residing in Alabama.
Additional information: Contact financial aid office of institution for application.

Amount of award:	$136-$816
Number of awards:	8,717
Total amount awarded:	$5,502,628

Alabama Technology Scholarship for Alabama Teachers

Type of award: Scholarship, renewable.
Intended use: For non-degree study.
Eligibility: Applicant must be U.S. citizen residing in Alabama.
Basis for selection: Major/career interest in education.
Application requirements: Proof of eligibility.
Additional information: Applicant must be full-time regularly certified Alabama public school teacher. Grant may not exceed

cost of tuition and fees for approved courses in technology. Only available for up to three computer-based instructional technology courses.

Amount of award:	$334-$1,560
Number of awards:	1,374
Total amount awarded:	$1,170,857

Police/Firefighters' Survivors Educational Assistance

Type of award: Scholarship, renewable.
Intended use: For undergraduate study at vocational, 2-year or 4-year institution in Alabama. Designated institutions: Public postsecondary institutions.
Eligibility: Applicant must be residing in Alabama. Applicant's parent must have been killed or disabled in work-related accident as fire fighter or police officer.
Application requirements: Proof of eligibility.
Additional information: Grant covers full tuition, fees, books, and supplies at Alabama public institutions for dependents and eligible spouses of Alabama police officers and fire fighters killed in line of duty.

Amount of award:	$150-$3,000
Number of awards:	20
Number of applicants:	20
Total amount awarded:	$33,600

Contact:
Alabama Commission on Higher Education
P.O. Box 302000
Montgomery, AL 36130-2000

Alabama Department of Education

Alabama Robert C. Byrd Honors Scholarship

Type of award: Scholarship, renewable.
Intended use: For full-time undergraduate study at 2-year or 4-year institution.
Eligibility: Applicant must be high school senior. Applicant must be U.S. citizen residing in Alabama.
Basis for selection: Applicant must demonstrate high academic achievement.
Additional information: Contact high school guidance office or principal for application. Award continues through senior year if qualifications are met. Applicants are nominated by high school faculty for this award.

Amount of award:	$1,500
Number of awards:	315
Total amount awarded:	$472,500

Alabama Scholarship for Dependents of Blind Parents

Type of award: Scholarship, renewable.
Intended use: For undergraduate study at vocational, 2-year or 4-year institution in Alabama. Designated institutions: Public institutions.
Eligibility: Parent must be visually impaired. Applicant must be residing in Alabama.

Basis for selection: Applicant must demonstrate financial need.
Application requirements: Proof of eligibility.
Additional information: Award amount equals tuition costs at Alabama public institutions. Students may apply for this award up to years after completing high school studies.

| Number of awards: | 15 |

Contact:
Alabama Department of Education
P.O. Box 302101
50 North Ripley Street
Montgomery, AL 36130-2101

Alabama Department of Postsecondary Education

Alabama Junior/Community College Academic Scholarship

Type of award: Scholarship, renewable.
Intended use: For freshman, sophomore study at accredited 2-year institution in Alabama. Designated institutions: Two-year public institutions.
Eligibility: Applicant must be U.S. citizen or permanent resident residing in Alabama.
Basis for selection: Applicant must demonstrate financial need and high academic achievement.
Application requirements: Transcript.
Additional information: Contact any two-year public institution in Alabama.

Alabama Junior/Community College Athletic Scholarship

Type of award: Scholarship, renewable.
Intended use: For full-time freshman, sophomore study at 2-year institution in Alabama. Designated institutions: Two-year public institutions.
Eligibility: Applicant must be U.S. citizen or permanent resident residing in Alabama.
Additional information: Awards based on athletic ability determined through tryouts. Renewal dependent on continued athletic participation. Contact coach, athletic director, or financial aid officer of any Alabama junior or community college.

Alabama Junior/Community College Leadership Scholarship

Type of award: Scholarship.
Intended use: For freshman, sophomore study at accredited 2-year institution in Alabama. Designated institutions: Two-year public institutions.
Eligibility: Applicant must be U.S. citizen or permanent resident residing in Alabama.
Basis for selection: Applicant must demonstrate depth of character, leadership and service orientation.
Additional information: Must have proven leadership abilities through community service and campus community

involvement. Contact any Alabama junior or community college.

Alabama Junior/Community College Performing Arts Scholarship

Type of award: Scholarship.
Intended use: For full-time freshman, sophomore study at 2-year institution in Alabama. Designated institutions: Two-year public institutions.
Eligibility: Applicant must be residing in Alabama.
Basis for selection: Major/career interest in performing arts.
Application requirements: Audition.
Additional information: Awards based on demonstrated talent determined through competitive auditions. Contact financial aid office of any Alabama junior or community college.
Contact:
Alabama Department of Postsecondary Education
401 Adams Avenue
P.O. Box 302130
Montgomery, AL 36130-2130

Alabama Department of Veterans Affairs

Alabama GI Dependents Educational Benefit

Type of award: Scholarship, renewable.
Intended use: For full-time or half-time undergraduate or graduate study at postsecondary institution. Designated institutions: State-supported institution.
Eligibility: Applicant must be residing in Alabama. Applicant must be child of veteran, disabled veteran, deceased veteran or POW/MIA, spouse of veteran, disabled veteran, deceased veteran or POW/MIA. Veteran must have been involved in active military duties for at least 90 days prior to death or POW/MIA status. Hurt veterans must be rated at least 20% disabled due to service connected disabilities.
Application requirements: Proof of eligibility.
Additional information: Veteran parent/spouse must have been resident of Alabama at least one year prior to enlistment. Children of veterans must submit application before their 26th birthday. Spouses of veterans have no age limit.
   Number of awards: 936
   Number of applicants: 936
   Total amount awarded: $4,700,000
Contact:
Alabama Department of Veterans Affairs
P.O. Box 1509
Montgomery, AL 36102
Phone: 334-242-5077

Alabama Legislature

Alabama Nursing Scholarship Program

Type of award: Scholarship, renewable.
Intended use: For undergraduate study at 2-year or 4-year institution in Alabama.
Eligibility: Applicant must be residing in Alabama.
Basis for selection: Major/career interest in nursing.
Additional information: Contact financial aid office of participating institution for application and information.
   Amount of award: $600

Alaska Commission on Postsecondary Education

Alaska Educational Incentive Grant

Type of award: Scholarship, renewable.
Intended use: For full-time undergraduate, non-degree study. Designated institutions: Must be approved by U.S. Department of Education or Alaska Commission on Postsecondary Education.
Eligibility: Applicant must be U.S. citizen or permanent resident residing in Alaska.
Basis for selection: Applicant must demonstrate financial need.
Application requirements: Proof of eligibility.
   Amount of award: $100-$1,500
   Number of awards: 142
   Number of applicants: 1,565
   Application deadline: May 31
   Notification begins: June 30
   Total amount awarded: $213,000
Contact:
Alaska Commission on Postsecondary Education
Special Programs
3030 Vintage Boulevard
Juneau, AK 99801-7109
Phone: 800-441-2962

Alaska Family Education Loan

Type of award: Loan, renewable.
Intended use: For full-time undergraduate or graduate study. Designated institutions: Must be approved by U.S. Department of Education or Alaska Commission on Postsecondary Education.
Eligibility: Applicant must be U.S. citizen or permanent resident residing in Alaska.
Basis for selection: Applicant must demonstrate financial need.
Application requirements: Proof of eligibility.
Additional information: Recipients not eligible for Alaska Student Loan.
Contact:
Alaska Student Loan
3030 Vintage Boulevard
Juneau, AK 99801-7109
Phone: 800-441-2962

Alaska Student Loan

Type of award: Loan, renewable.
Intended use: For full-time or half-time undergraduate or graduate study. Designated institutions: Must be approved by U.S. Department of Education or Alaska Commission on Postsecondary Education.
Eligibility: Applicant must be U.S. citizen or permanent resident residing in Alaska.
Application requirements: Proof of eligibility.
Additional information: Undergraduates may borrow a maximum of $8,500 per year full-time, $5,000 per year half-time. Vocational students may borrow up to $5,500 per year full-time, $2,000 half-time, and graduate students may borrow $9,500 full-time, $4,500 half-time. Recipient not eligible for Family Education Loan. Contact office for interest rate information.

Amount of award:	$2,000-$9,500
Application deadline:	May 15
Notification begins:	July 15

Contact:
Alaska Student Loan Office
3030 Vintage Boulevard
Juneau, AK 99801-7109
Phone: 800-441-2962

Alaska Teacher Scholarship Loan

Type of award: Loan, renewable.
Intended use: For full-time undergraduate, non-degree study. Designated institutions: Must be approved by U.S. Department of Education or Alaska Commission on Postsecondary Education.
Eligibility: Applicant must be U.S. citizen or permanent resident residing in Alaska.
Basis for selection: Major/career interest in education, teacher; education, early childhood; education, special.
Application requirements: Recommendations and proof of eligibility.
Additional information: Must be graduate of Alaskan high school and have sponsorship of rural Alaskan school district. Loan forgiveness for teaching in rural Alaskan school district. May not borrow more than $37,500 in total. Minimum GPA of 2.0 required.

Amount of award:	$7,500
Number of awards:	227
Application deadline:	July 1
Notification begins:	June 1

Contact:
Alaska Commission on Postsecondary Education
Special Programs
3030 Vintage Boulevard
Juneau, AK 99801-7109
Phone: 800-441-2962

Alaska Division of Veterans Affairs

Alaska Educational Aid For Dependents of POWS/MIAs

Type of award: Scholarship, renewable.
Intended use: For full-time or half-time undergraduate study in Alaska.
Eligibility: Applicant must be U.S. citizen residing in Alaska. Applicant must be child of POW/MIA, spouse of POW/MIA. Parent or spouse must have been declared POW/MIA in southeast Asia conflict and a resident of Alaska.
Application requirements: Proof of eligibility.
Additional information: Award covers tuition and fees at three universities of the University of Alaska system. Student's parents must have been a resident of Alaska or born in the state of Alaska to be eligible for this award.

Application deadline:	August 29, January 17

Contact:
Scholarship Coordinator
P.O. Box 5800
Fort Richardson, AK 99505-5800

Alexander Von Humboldt Foundation

Federal Chancellor Scholarship

Type of award: Research grant.
Intended use: For graduate or non-degree study in Germany.
Eligibility: Applicant must be U.S. citizen.
Basis for selection: Major/career interest in economics; humanities/liberal arts; social and behavioral sciences; law. Applicant must demonstrate leadership and high academic achievement.
Application requirements: Interview, recommendations, transcript and research proposal.
Additional information: Applicants must be willing to spend a year in Germany while working on research projects.

Number of awards:	10
Number of applicants:	80
Application deadline:	October 31
Notification begins:	January 1

Contact:
Alexander Von Humboldt Foundation
1055 Thomas Jefferson Street, NW
Suite 2030
Washington, DC 20007
Phone: 202-296-2990
Fax: 202-833-8514

American Academy in Rome

American Academy in Rome/Rome Prize Fellowships in the School of Fine Arts

Type of award: Research grant.
Intended use: For master's, doctoral, first professional or postgraduate study outside United States in Rome, Italy.
Designated institutions: American Academy in Rome.
Eligibility: Applicant must be U.S. citizen.
Basis for selection: Major/career interest in landscape architecture; design; music; arts, general; architecture.
Application requirements: Interview, portfolio, recommendations, proof of eligibility and research proposal.
Additional information: For advanced study in Rome. Applicants for six-month and one-year fellowships must hold degree in field of application. Six-month applicants must also have at least seven years professional experience and be practicing in the applied field.

Amount of award:	$9,000-$15,000
Number of awards:	14
Application deadline:	November 15
Total amount awarded:	$186,000

Contact:
Research Grant Coordinator
7 East 60 Street
New York, NY 10022-1001
Phone: 212-751-7200
Fax: 212-751-7220
Website: www.aarome.org

American Academy in Rome/Rome Prize Pre- and Post-Doctoral Fellowship

Type of award: Research grant.
Intended use: For doctoral, postgraduate study in Rome, Italy.
Designated institutions: American Academy in Rome.
Eligibility: Applicant must be U.S. citizen or permanent resident.
Basis for selection: Major/career interest in archaeology; art; art history; Italian; humanities/liberal arts.
Application requirements: $40 application fee. Recommendations, proof of eligibility and research proposal.
Additional information: The application fee only applies to pre-doctoral applicants. Pre-doctoral applicants must be U.S. citizens.

Amount of award:	$15,000-$17,800
Number of awards:	12
Application deadline:	November 15
Total amount awarded:	$211,800

Contact:
American Academy in Rome
7 East 60 Street
New York, NY 10022-1001
Phone: 212-751-7200
Fax: 212-751-7220
Website: www.aarome.org

American Association for the Advancement of Science

Environmental Protection Agency Environmental Science and Engineering Fellowship

Type of award: Internship.
Intended use: For postgraduate study.
Eligibility: Applicant or parent must be member of American Association of Advancement of Science. Applicant must be U.S. citizen or permanent resident.
Basis for selection: Applicant must demonstrate depth of character, seriousness of purpose and service orientation.
Application requirements: Interview and recommendations.
Additional information: Fellows work for one year on an array of projects related to science policy and the environment. Applicant should be postdoctoral to mid-career scientist or engineer from any physical, biological, or social science, or in any field of engineering. Employees of AAAS are not eligible.

Amount of award:	$43,000
Number of awards:	10
Number of applicants:	50
Application deadline:	January 15
Total amount awarded:	$114,000

Science, Engineering, and Diplomacy Fellowship

Type of award: Research grant, renewable.
Intended use: For postgraduate study.
Eligibility: Applicant or parent must be member of American Association of Advancement of Science. Applicant must be U.S. citizen.
Basis for selection: Applicant must demonstrate depth of character, seriousness of purpose, service orientation and high academic achievement.
Application requirements: Interview and recommendations.
Additional information: For postdoctoral to mid-career scientists and engineers to come work at the State Department or U.S. Agency for International Development for one year. Applicants may be from any physical, biological, or social science, or any field of engineering.

Amount of award:	$46,000-$60,000
Number of awards:	16
Number of applicants:	130
Application deadline:	January 15

Contact:
American Association for the Advancement of Science
1200 New York Avenue, NW
Washington, DC 20005
Website: www.aaas.org

American Indian Graduate Center

Higher Education Undergraduate Grant Program

Type of award: Scholarship, renewable.
Intended use: For full-time undergraduate study at accredited 2-year or 4-year institution in United States.
Eligibility: Applicant must be Alaskan native or American Indian. Applicant must be U.S. citizen or permanent resident.
Basis for selection: Applicant must demonstrate depth of character, leadership, seriousness of purpose, service orientation and financial need.
Application requirements: Proof of eligibility. Proof of Native American Tribal Affiliation.
Additional information: Student must be accepted at/enrolled in a nationally accredited higher education institution for study toward an associate or bachelor's degree. Applicants must provide documentation that proves tribal affiliation (must be at least one quarter Native American) and must demonstrate financial need as determined by the financial aid officer of intended institution.
Contact:
American Indian Graduate Center
1849 C. ST. NW
MS 3512-MIB
Washington 20240

American Indian Science and Engineering Society

United States EPA Tribal Lands Environmental Science Scholarship

Type of award: Scholarship.
Intended use: For full-time junior, senior or graduate study at accredited 2-year, 4-year or graduate institution in United States.
Eligibility: Applicant must be Alaskan native or American Indian. Applicant must be U.S. citizen.
Basis for selection: Major/career interest in environmental science; chemistry; entomology; biology. Applicant must demonstrate depth of character, leadership, seriousness of purpose, service orientation and high academic achievement.
Application requirements: Recommendations, essay, transcript and proof of eligibility.
Additional information: Those studying biochemistry, environmental economics, toxicology, or related environmental disciplines also eligible. Must show demonstrated commitment to environmental protection on tribal lands. Must maintain a 2.0 GPA. Include SASE with all requests.

Amount of award:	$4,000
Number of awards:	76
Number of applicants:	90
Application deadline:	June 15
Notification begins:	August 31
Total amount awarded:	$304,000

Contact:
American Indian Science and Engineering Society
Attn: Scholarship Coordinator
5661 Airport Boulevard
Boulder, CO 80301-2339
Phone: 303-939-0023
Website: www.colorado.edu/AISES

American Psychological Association

Clinical Psychology Training Minority Fellowship

Type of award: Scholarship, renewable.
Intended use: For full-time doctoral study at accredited graduate institution in United States.
Eligibility: Applicant must be of minority background. Applicant must be U.S. citizen or permanent resident.
Basis for selection: Major/career interest in mental health/therapy; psychology. Applicant must demonstrate seriousness of purpose and high academic achievement.
Application requirements: Recommendations, essay, transcript and proof of eligibility. Clincial, counseling, and school psychology.
Additional information: Selection based on applicant's clinical and/or research potential, writing ability, knowledge of broad issues in psychology, and professional commitment.

Amount of award:	$10,008
Number of awards:	25
Number of applicants:	400
Application deadline:	January 15
Notification begins:	April 15
Total amount awarded:	$316,000

Contact:
American Psychological Association
Minority Fellowship Program
750 First Street NE
Washington, DC 20002-4242
Website: www.apa.org/mfp.

HIV/AIDS Research Training Minority Fellowship

Type of award: Scholarship.
Intended use: For full-time doctoral study at accredited graduate institution in United States.
Eligibility: Applicant must be of minority background.
Basis for selection: Major/career interest in psychology; public health; medicine (m.d.); mental health/therapy. Applicant must demonstrate seriousness of purpose and high academic achievement.
Application requirements: Recommendations, essay, transcript and proof of eligibility.
Additional information: Must be pursuing career as research

scientist in mental health issues related to minority populations in developmental, physiological, experimental, social, industrial/organizational, quantitative, or educational psychology. Students specializing in HIV prevention, AIDS treatment adherence, provider education, or psychoneuroimmunology are encouraged to apply.

Application deadline:	January 15
Notification begins:	April 15

Contact:
Minority Fellowship Program/APA
750 First Street NE
Washington, DC 20002-4242
Website: www.apa.org/mfp

Psychology Research Training Minority Fellowship

Type of award: Scholarship, renewable.
Intended use: For full-time doctoral study at accredited graduate institution in United States.
Eligibility: Applicant must be of minority background. Applicant must be U.S. citizen or permanent resident.
Basis for selection: Major/career interest in psychology. Applicant must demonstrate seriousness of purpose and high academic achievement.
Application requirements: Recommendations, essay, transcript and proof of eligibility.
Additional information: Must be pursuing career as research scientist in mental health issues related to minority populations in developmental, physiological, experimental, social, industrial/organizational, quantitative, or educational psychology.

Application deadline:	January 15
Notification begins:	, April 15

Contact:
American Psychological Association
Minority Fellowship Program
750 First Street NE
Washington, DC 20002-4242
Website: www.apa.org/mfp

American Psychological Association/MFP

Neuroscience Training Minority Fellowship

Type of award: Scholarship, renewable.
Intended use: For full-time doctoral study at accredited graduate institution in United States.
Eligibility: Applicant must be Alaskan native, American Indian, African American, Mexican American, Hispanic American or Puerto Rican. Asian Americans must be Pacific Islander. Applicant must be U.S. citizen or permanent resident.
Basis for selection: Major/career interest in neuroscience. Applicant must demonstrate seriousness of purpose and high academic achievement.
Application requirements: Recommendations, essay, transcript and proof of eligibility.
Additional information: Selection based on applicant's research experience and potential, writing ability, and professional commitment to neuroscience.

Amount of award:	$10,008
Number of awards:	30
Number of applicants:	50
Application deadline:	April 15
Notification begins:	March 15
Total amount awarded:	$490,000

Contact:
American Psychological Association
Minority Fellowship Program
750 First Street NE
Washington, DC 20002-4242
Website: www.apa.org

American Research Center in Egypt

Research Center in Egypt Fellowship

Type of award: Research grant.
Intended use: For doctoral, postgraduate study in Awards are for research in Egypt only. in Egypt.
Eligibility: Applicant must be U.S. citizen or permanent resident.
Basis for selection: Major/career interest in history; art, art history. Applicant must demonstrate seriousness of purpose and high academic achievement.
Application requirements: Recommendations, transcript and research proposal.
Additional information: Fellowship year runs from October 1, 1999 to September 30, 2000. Minimum stay: 3 months; maximum is 12 months. Fellowships are available to American pre-doctoral candidates who will be in the all-but-dissertation stage by the time the fellowship year begins. Fellowships for post-doctoral scholars are available to American citizens as well as permanent residents who have held a teaching position for a minimum of 4 years. The Kress fellowship in Egyptian art & architecture is available to pre-doctoral candidates of any nationality.

Amount of award:	$5,400-$30,000
Number of awards:	8
Number of applicants:	32
Application deadline:	October 1
Notification begins:	March 15
Total amount awarded:	$124,540

Contact:
American Research Center in Egypt
Fellowship Program
30 East 20Street, Suite 401
New York, NY 10003-1310
Phone: 212-529-6661
Fax: 212-529-6856
Website: www.arce.org

American Research Institute in Turkey

National Endowment for the Humanities Postdoctoral Fellowship

Type of award: Research grant.
Intended use: For postgraduate, non-degree study in Research in Turkey.
Eligibility: Applicant must be U.S. citizen or permanent resident.
Basis for selection: Major/career interest in humanities/liberal arts. Applicant must demonstrate high academic achievement.
Application requirements: Recommendations and research proposal. Permit to carry out research in Turkey.
- Amount of award: $10,000-$30,000
- Number of applicants: 15
- Application deadline: November 15
- Notification begins: January 25
- Total amount awarded: $45,000

Contact:
American Research Institute in Turkey
University of Pennsylvania Museum
33 and Spruce Streets
Philadelphia, PA 19104-6324
Phone: 215-898-3474
Fax: 215-898-0657

Turkish Language Summer Scholarship

Type of award: Scholarship.
Intended use: For senior, graduate or non-degree study outside United States. Designated institutions: Bosphorus University, Istanbul, Turkey.
Eligibility: Applicant must be U.S. citizen or permanent resident.
Basis for selection: Major/career interest in foreign languages. Applicant must demonstrate high academic achievement.
Application requirements: Recommendations, essay and transcript. Turkish proficiency exam.
Additional information: Turkish language required.
- Amount of award: $3,500
- Number of awards: 5
- Number of applicants: 25
- Application deadline: February 15
- Notification begins: April 15
- Total amount awarded: $5,000

Contact:
Washington University/American Research Institute in Turkey
Summer Fellowship Program
Center for the Study of Islamic Societies
Campus Box 1230/ One Brookings Drive
St. Louis, MO 63130-4899
Phone: 314-935-5166
Fax: 314-935-7462

American Sociological Association

Sociological Association Minority Fellowship

Type of award: Scholarship, renewable.
Intended use: For full-time doctoral study at graduate institution in United States.
Eligibility: Applicant must be of minority background. Applicant must be U.S. citizen or permanent resident.
Basis for selection: Major/career interest in mental health/therapy; sociology; education. Applicant must demonstrate seriousness of purpose, service orientation, financial need and high academic achievement.
Application requirements: Recommendations, essay and transcript.
Additional information: Applicants should be committed to teaching, research, and service careers related to sociological aspects of mental health issues.
- Amount of award: $11,469
- Number of awards: 15
- Number of applicants: 100
- Application deadline: December 31
- Notification begins: April 15
- Total amount awarded: $352,000

Contact:
American Sociological Association
Attn: Frances M. Foster
1722 N Street, NW
Washington, DC 20036
Phone: 202-833-3410
Fax: 202-785-0146

Arizona Board of Regents

Arizona Registration Fee Waiver Police/Fire Children

Type of award: Scholarship, renewable.
Intended use: For undergraduate study. Designated institutions: University of Arizona, Arizona State University, Northern Arizona University.
Eligibility: Applicant must be residing in Arizona. Applicant's parent must have been killed or disabled in work-related accident as fire fighter, police officer or public safety officer.
Application requirements: Proof of eligibility. Documentation of eligibilty.
Additional information: Eligible public safety categories include Emergency Medical Service and Conservation Corps. Apply at financial aid office of University of Arizona, Arizona State University, or Northern Arizona University.

Arizona Tuition and Registration Fee Waiver and Grant

Type of award: Scholarship.
Intended use: For undergraduate or graduate study.

Designated institutions: University of Arizona, Arizona State University, Northern Arizona University.
Eligibility: Applicant must be residing in Arizona.
Basis for selection: Applicant must demonstrate financial need.
Additional information: Funds for these programs provided by state of Arizona and student contributions at three participating institutions. Information and applications available from financial aid office of University of Arizona, Arizona State University, and Northern Arizona University.

Arizona Tuition Waiver Program

Type of award: Scholarship.
Intended use: For undergraduate or graduate study.
Designated institutions: University of Arizona, Arizona State University, Northern Arizona University.
Eligibility: Applicant must be residing in Arizona.
Basis for selection: Applicant must demonstrate financial need and high academic achievement.
Additional information: Apply to college financial aid office.

Arizona Commission for Postsecondary Education

Arizona State Student Incentive Grant

Type of award: Scholarship, renewable.
Intended use: For full-time or half-time undergraduate or graduate study at accredited postsecondary institution in Arizona.
Eligibility: Applicant must be residing in Arizona.
Basis for selection: Applicant must demonstrate financial need.
Additional information: Apply to college financial aid office. Application deadlines and notification dates are rolling.

Amount of award:	$100-$2,500
Number of awards:	4,985
Number of applicants:	4,985
Total amount awarded:	$2,975,410

Arkansas Department of Higher Education

Arkansas Emergency Secondary Education Loan

Type of award: Loan, renewable.
Intended use: For full-time sophomore, junior, senior or master's study at accredited 2-year, 4-year or graduate institution.
Eligibility: Applicant must be U.S. citizen or permanent resident residing in Arkansas.
Basis for selection: Major/career interest in education, teacher; education, special; foreign languages; science, general. Applicant must demonstrate high academic achievement.
Application requirements: Transcript and proof of eligibility.
Additional information: Must teach mathematics, the sciences, foreign languages or special education at the secondary level. Must be Arkansas resident for at least six months. Loan forgiveness for teaching at secondary level in Arkansas designated teacher shortage area: 20 percent of amount borrowed forgiven for each year of teaching.

Amount of award:	$2,500
Number of awards:	60
Number of applicants:	105
Application deadline:	April 1
Notification begins:	June 1
Total amount awarded:	$139,471

Arkansas Freshman/Sophomore Minority Grant

Type of award: Scholarship, renewable.
Intended use: For full-time freshman, sophomore study at accredited postsecondary institution.
Eligibility: Applicant must be Asian American, African American, Mexican American, Hispanic American or Puerto Rican. Applicant must be U.S. citizen or permanent resident residing in Arkansas.
Basis for selection: Major/career interest in education, teacher. Applicant must demonstrate high academic achievement.
Additional information: Students should contact education department of institution they plan to attend. Deadline set by participating institutions.

Amount of award:	$1,000
Number of awards:	300
Total amount awarded:	$250,000

Arkansas Law Enforcement Officers' Dependents Scholarship

Type of award: Scholarship, renewable.
Intended use: For full-time or half-time undergraduate study at accredited vocational, 2-year, 4-year or graduate institution.
Designated institutions: Arkansas public institutions.
Eligibility: Applicant must be U.S. citizen or permanent resident residing in Arkansas. Applicant's parent must have been killed or disabled in work-related accident as fire fighter, police officer or public safety officer.
Application requirements: Proof of eligibility. Documentation of eligibility.
Additional information: Children/spouses of Highway and Transportation Department employees disabled or killed in work related accident also eligible. Applicant must be Arkansas resident for at least six months. Dependent child applicant may be no older than 23; no age restriction for spouse. Application deadlines May 1 and July 1 for summer study.

Number of awards:	24
Number of applicants:	30
Application deadline:	August 1, December 1
Total amount awarded:	$47,613

Arkansas Minority Master's Fellowship

Type of award: Scholarship.
Intended use: For full-time post-bachelor's certificate, master's study at accredited graduate institution in Arkansas.
Eligibility: Applicant must be Asian American, African

American, Mexican American, Hispanic American or Puerto Rican. Applicant must be U.S. citizen or permanent resident residing in Arkansas.
Basis for selection: Major/career interest in education.
Application requirements: Transcript and proof of eligibility.
Additional information: Must be pursuing master's level teaching certification at an Arkansas institution in math, science or foreign language. Must have 2.75 GPA and agree to teach 2 years in Arkansas public school or institution of higher education following certification. Students can go part-time for 2 summers and receive $2,500 each summer.

Amount of award:	$1,250-$7,500
Number of awards:	19
Number of applicants:	27
Application deadline:	June 1
Total amount awarded:	$100,000

Arkansas Minority Teachers Loan

Type of award: Loan, renewable.
Intended use: For full-time junior, senior study at accredited 4-year institution in Arkansas.
Eligibility: Applicant must be Asian American, African American, Mexican American, Hispanic American or Puerto Rican. Applicant must be U.S. citizen or permanent resident residing in Arkansas.
Basis for selection: Major/career interest in education, teacher.
Application requirements: Transcript.
Additional information: Applicant must be pursuing course of study for teacher education and have completed at least 60 credit hours. Loan forgiveness for teaching five years in Arkansas public schools or three years in Arkansas teacher shortage area.

Amount of award:	$5,000
Number of awards:	108
Application deadline:	June 1
Total amount awarded:	$486,747

Arkansas Missing/Killed in Action Dependents Scholarship

Type of award: Scholarship, renewable.
Intended use: For full-time or half-time undergraduate, master's or non-degree study at accredited vocational, 2-year, 4-year or graduate institution.
Eligibility: Applicant must be U.S. citizen or permanent resident residing in Arkansas. Applicant must be child of deceased veteran or POW/MIA, spouse of deceased veteran or POW/MIA who served in the Army, Air Force, Marines, Navy, Coast Guard or Reserves/National Guard during Persian Gulf or Vietnam.
Application requirements: Proof of eligibility.
Additional information: Child/spouse of person killed in action or missing in action. Parent/spouse must have been Arkansas resident prior to enlistment. Applicant must be Arkansas resident for at least six months. Minimum 2.0 GPA required. Application deadlines for summer May 1 and July 1.

Number of awards:	1
Number of applicants:	2
Application deadline:	August 1, December 1
Total amount awarded:	$4,674

Contact:
Arkansas Department of Higher Education
114 East Capitol Street
Little Rock, AR 72201-3818
Phone: 8005478839

Barry M. Goldwater /Excellence In Education Foundation

Barry M. Goldwater Scholarship

Type of award: Scholarship.
Intended use: For full-time junior, senior study at accredited 4-year institution in United States.
Eligibility: Applicant must be U.S. citizen or permanent resident.
Basis for selection: Major/career interest in engineering; mathematics; natural sciences; science, general. Applicant must demonstrate depth of character, leadership, seriousness of purpose and high academic achievement.
Application requirements: Recommendations, essay, transcript, proof of eligibility and nomination by By college faculty representitive. Student's essay, of 600 words or less, must relate to the student's chosen career. Nominations from resident aliens must include a letter of nominee's intent to obtain U.S. citizenship and a photocopy of Alien Registration Card.
Additional information: Minimum GPA 3.0 required. Contact website to obtain the bulletin of information, nomination materials, and list of faculty representatives. Students must be nominated by their university's Goldwater Scholarship faculty representative. Award must be used to pursue careers as scientists, mathematicians, and engineers. Applicant must be a legal resident in the state from which he or she is a candidate.

Amount of award:	$7,500
Application deadline:	January 14
Notification begins:	April 1

Contact:
Barry M. Goldwater / Excellence In Education Foundation
6225 Brandon Avenue
Suite 315
Springfield 22150
Website: www.act.org/goldwater

Board of Governors of the Federal Reserve System

Cooperative Education Program

Type of award: Internship, renewable.
Intended use: For undergraduate or graduate study.
Basis for selection: Major/career interest in law; accounting; economics; information systems; finance/banking. Applicant must demonstrate high academic achievement.
Application requirements: Recommendations and transcript.
Contact:
Cooperative Education Program / Stop #129
Washington, DC 20551
Phone: 202-452-3850

Cooperative Education Program

Type of award: Internship, renewable.
Intended use: For undergraduate or graduate study.
Basis for selection: Major/career interest in law; accounting;

economics; information systems. Applicant must demonstrate high academic achievement.
Application requirements: Recommendations and transcript.
Additional information: Deadlines, compensation, and number of awards varies. Contact sponsor for more information.
Contact:
Cooperative Education Program
Stop #129
Washington, DC 20551
Phone: 202-452-3850

Bureau of Indian Affairs-Oklahoma Area Education Office

Bureau of Indian Affairs-Oklahoma Area Scholarship

Type of award: Scholarship.
Intended use: For full-time Designated institutions: Institutions outside United States only if credits can be transferred to an accredited college/university.
Eligibility: Applicant must be Alaskan native or American Indian. Must be enrolled member of a federally recognized Indian tribe. Applicant must be U.S. citizen.
Basis for selection: Applicant must demonstrate depth of character, leadership, patriotism and service orientation.
Application requirements: Recommendations, transcript and proof of eligibility.
Additional information: Applicant must have 2.0 GPA. Do not Contact BIA-Oklahoma. Applicant must contact his/her tribe for specific information.

Application deadline:	June 15, January 15
Notification begins:	September 1, June 1

California Student Aid Commission

California Assumption Program Loans for Education

Type of award: Loan, renewable.
Intended use: For full-time junior, senior or post-bachelor's certificate study in California. Designated institutions: Any California postsecondary institution with approved teacher program. Institution must have approved credential programs.
Eligibility: Applicant must be permanent resident residing in California.
Basis for selection: Major/career interest in education, teacher. Applicant must demonstrate high academic achievement.
Application requirements: Interview, recommendations, essay, transcript, proof of eligibility and nomination. Loan indebtedness; must not hold an initial teaching credential.
Additional information: Current educational loans must be in good status. Participants receive awards after providing eligible teaching service in a designated shortage area. Loans assumed for up to three years: up to $2,000 for first year and up to $3,000 for second and third years of consecutive eligible teaching service. Must complete 10 units per academic term.

Amount of award:	$2,000-$8,000
Number of awards:	897
Number of applicants:	1,100
Application deadline:	June 30
Notification begins:	August 14
Total amount awarded:	$2,321,000

Contact:
California Student Aid Commission
Specialized Programs
P.O. Box 510624
Rancho Cordova, CA 95741-9030

California Child Development Teacher and Supervisor Grant Program

Type of award: Loan.
Intended use: For full-time or half-time undergraduate study at accredited 2-year or 4-year institution in California.
Eligibility: Applicant must be permanent resident residing in California.
Basis for selection: Major/career interest in education, early childhood. Applicant must demonstrate financial need.
Application requirements: Recommendations. Recommendation from institution faculty.
Additional information: Applicants must attend a California public or private two-year or four year postsecondary institution with intent to teach or supervise in the field or child care and development in a licensed child care center. Recipients attending a two-year postsecondary institution will receive up to $1000 annually for up to two years. Recipients attending a four year institution will receive up to $ 2000 annually for up to two years. Recipients must agree to provide one full year of service in a licensed child care center for every year they receive the grant. The commission can award up to 100 new recipients each year.

Amount of award:	$1,000-$2,000
Number of awards:	100
Application deadline:	June 15
Notification begins:	September 1
Total amount awarded:	$12,000

Contact:
California Student Aid Commission
Specialized Programs
P.O. Box 510624
Rancho Cordova, CA 95741-9030

California Grant Program

Type of award: Scholarship, renewable.
Intended use: For full-time or half-time undergraduate study at 4-year institution in California.
Eligibility: Applicant must be U.S. citizen or permanent resident residing in California.
Basis for selection: Applicant must demonstrate financial need and high academic achievement.
Application requirements: Student Aid Commission Grade Point Average Verification Form.
Additional information: All potential freshman, sophomore

and junior undergraduates should submit a FAFSA to the federal processor and a GPA to the Commission by the March 2 deadline. Students with no available GPA can submit SAT I, ACT or GED scores. College seniors ineligible as first-time applicants.

Amount of award:	$700-$8,184
Number of awards:	97,600
Number of applicants:	419,000
Application deadline:	March 2
Notification begins:	May 1
Total amount awarded:	$309,703,000

Contact:
California Student Aid Commission
Grant Services Division
P.O. Box 510845
Rancho Cardova, CA 95741-9027
Website: www.csac.ca.gov

California Law Enforcement Personnel Dependents Scholarship

Type of award: Scholarship, renewable.
Intended use: For full-time or half-time undergraduate study at accredited 2-year or 4-year institution in California.
Eligibility: Applicant must be U.S. citizen residing in California. Applicant's parent must have been killed or disabled in work-related accident as fire fighter, police officer or public safety officer.
Basis for selection: Applicant must demonstrate financial need.
Application requirements: Proof of eligibility.
Additional information: Eligible public servant categories include law enforcement officers (peace officers, Highway Patrol, marshals, sheriffs, police officers); employees and officers of Departments of Corrections, Youth Authority, and permanent full-time firefighters employed by cities, counties, districts, etc. Contact Student Aid Commission for complete list and documentation requirements.

Amount of award:	$100-$8,184
Number of awards:	16
Number of applicants:	20
Total amount awarded:	$40,000

Contact:
Specialized Programs
P.O. Box 419029
Rancho Cordova, CA 95741-9029

California Robert C. Byrd Honors Scholarship

Type of award: Scholarship, renewable.
Intended use: For full-time undergraduate study at accredited 2-year or 4-year institution in United States.
Eligibility: Applicant must be high school senior. Applicant must be U.S. citizen or permanent resident residing in California.
Basis for selection: Applicant must demonstrate high academic achievement.
Application requirements: Nomination.
Additional information: Selection process begins at individual high schools. Contact guidance office for information. GED students may apply directly. Renewable up to four years.

Amount of award:	$1,500
Number of awards:	1,600
Number of applicants:	3,141
Application deadline:	April 15
Notification begins:	June 1
Total amount awarded:	$3,762,000

Contact:
California Student Aid Commission
Robert C. Byrd Honors Scholarship Program
P.O. Box 419029
Rancho Cordova, CA 95741-9030

California State Work-Study Program

Type of award: Internship, renewable.
Intended use: For full-time or half-time undergraduate or graduate study in California.
Eligibility: Applicant must be residing in California.
Basis for selection: Applicant must demonstrate financial need.
Additional information: Colleges identify jobs that relate to student's course of study, career goals, or exploration of careers. Contact financial aid office at participating postsecondary institutions.

Total amount awarded:	$663,000

Contact:
Specialized Programs
P.O. BOX 419029
Rancho Cordova, CA 95741-9029

Central Intelligence Agency

CIA Undergraduate Scholarship

Type of award: Scholarship, renewable.
Intended use: For full-time freshman, sophomore, junior or senior study at accredited 4-year institution in United States.
Eligibility: Applicant must be high school senior. Applicant must be U.S. citizen.
Basis for selection: Major/career interest in engineering; computer and information sciences; economics; foreign languages. Applicant must demonstrate financial need and high academic achievement.
Application requirements: Recommendations, essay and transcript.
Additional information: 2.7 GPA required. Applicants with family income over $70,000 not eligible. Applicants with family income between $60,000 and $70,000 accepted only if family has four or more dependents.

Amount of award:	$15,000
Number of awards:	6
Number of applicants:	300
Application deadline:	November 1
Notification begins:	June 30
Total amount awarded:	$60,000

Contact:
Central Intelligence Agency
Employment Center
PO Box 12727
Arlington, VA 22209-8727

Choctaw Nation of Oklahoma

Choctaw Nation Higher Eduation Grant

Type of award: Scholarship, renewable.
Intended use: For undergraduate or graduate study at accredited 2-year, 4-year or graduate institution in United States.
Eligibility: Applicant must be American Indian. Must be enrolled member of Choctaw Tribe and have Certificate Documenting Indian Blood (CDIB) or tribal membership card.
Basis for selection: Applicant must demonstrate financial need.
Application requirements: Transcript and proof of eligibility.
Additional information: Must first apply for federal financial assistance. Grant will assist with any unmet need. Must reapply for renewal.

Amount of award:	$1,600
Number of awards:	730
Number of applicants:	1,500
Application deadline:	March 15
Notification begins:	September 15

Contact:
Choctaw Nation of Oklahoma
Higher Education Department
P.O. Drawer 1210
Durant, OK 74702
Phone: 800-522-6170

College Foundation, Inc.

North Carolina Student Incentive Grant

Type of award: Scholarship, renewable.
Intended use: For full-time undergraduate study at vocational, 2-year or 4-year institution in North Carolina.
Eligibility: Applicant must be enrolled in high school. Applicant must be U.S. citizen or permanent resident residing in North Carolina.
Basis for selection: Applicant must demonstrate financial need.

Amount of award:	$200-$1,500
Number of awards:	3,900
Number of applicants:	60,500
Application deadline:	March 15
Notification begins:	July 15
Total amount awarded:	$2,300,000

Contact:
College Foundation, Inc.
2100 Yonkers Road
P.O. Box 12100
Raleigh, NC 27605-2100
Phone: 888-234-6400
Website: www.cfi-nc.org

Colorado Commission on Higher Education

Colorado Diversity Grant

Type of award: Scholarship, renewable.
Intended use: For full-time or half-time undergraduate study.
Eligibility: Applicant must be residing in Colorado.
Additional information: Must be member of underrepresented population at individual institution. Contact college financial aid office for information and application materials.

Amount of award:	$5,000

Contact:
Colorado Commission on Higher Education
1300 Broadway 2nd floor
Denver, CO 80203

Colorado Graduate Fellowship

Type of award: Scholarship.
Intended use: For full-time or half-time doctoral study.
Eligibility: Applicant must be residing in Colorado.
Basis for selection: Applicant must demonstrate high academic achievement.
Additional information: Contact college financial aid office for information and application. Nonresident awards are made at some institutions.

Amount of award:	$4,000
Number of awards:	560
Total amount awarded:	$1,211,369

Contact:
Colorado Commission on Higher Education
1300 Broadway 2nd floor
Denver, CO 80203

Colorado Graduate Grant

Type of award: Scholarship.
Intended use: For master's, first professional study.
Eligibility: Applicant must be residing in Colorado.
Basis for selection: Applicant must demonstrate financial need.
Additional information: Contact college financial aid office for information and application.

Amount of award:	$4,000
Number of awards:	1,080
Total amount awarded:	$1,257,013

Contact:
Colorado Commission on Higher Education
1300 Broadway 2nd Floor
Denver, CO 80203

Colorado Nursing Scholarship

Type of award: Loan.
Intended use: For undergraduate or graduate study.
Eligibility: Applicant must be residing in Colorado.
Basis for selection: Major/career interest in nursing. Applicant must demonstrate high academic achievement.
Additional information: Contact financial aid office of institution for information and application.

Amount of award: $2,500
Number of awards: 161
Total amount awarded: $192,143
Contact:
Colorado Commission on Higher Education
1300 Broadway, 2nd Floor
Denver, CO 80203

Colorado Part-time Student Grant

Type of award: Scholarship.
Intended use: For half-time or less than half-time undergraduate study.
Eligibility: Applicant must be residing in Colorado.
Basis for selection: Applicant must demonstrate financial need.
Additional information: Contact college financial aid office for information and application.
Amount of award: $2,500
Total amount awarded: $593,506
Contact:
Colorado Commission on Higher Education
1300 Broadway, 2nd floor
Denver, CO 80203

Colorado Student Grant

Type of award: Scholarship.
Intended use: For full-time or half-time undergraduate study.
Eligibility: Applicant must be residing in Colorado.
Basis for selection: Applicant must demonstrate financial need.
Additional information: Contact college financial aid office for information and application.
Amount of award: $5,000
Number of awards: 17,179
Total amount awarded: $14,835,793
Contact:
Colorado Commission on Higher Education
1300 Broadway 2nd floor
Denver, CO 80203

Colorado Student Incentive Grant

Type of award: Scholarship.
Intended use: For full-time or half-time undergraduate study.
Eligibility: Applicant must be residing in Colorado.
Basis for selection: Applicant must demonstrate financial need.
Additional information: Must demonstrate exceptional financial need, defined as $100 of need for each month of school attendance. Contact college financial aid office for information and application.
Amount of award: $5,000
Number of awards: 2,647
Total amount awarded: $1,927,290
Contact:
Colorado Commission on Higher Education
1300 Broadway 2nd floor
Denver, CO 80203

Colorado Undergraduate Merit Award

Type of award: Scholarship.
Intended use: For full-time or half-time undergraduate study.
Eligibility: Applicant must be residing in Colorado.
Basis for selection: Applicant must demonstrate high academic achievement.
Additional information: Amount of award cannot exceed tuition. Institutions may make awards for academic excellence or special talents, including music and athletics. Nonresidents may be eligible at some institutions. Contact college financial aid office for information and application.
Number of awards: 8,854
Total amount awarded: $7,966,876
Contact:
Colorado Commission on Higher Education
1300 Broadway 2nd floor
Denver, CO 80203

Colorado Work-Study Program

Type of award: Internship.
Intended use: For full-time or half-time undergraduate study.
Eligibility: Applicant must be residing in Colorado.
Basis for selection: Applicant must demonstrate financial need.
Additional information: Amount of award cannot exceed college cost. Contact college financial aid office for information and application.
Number of awards: 7,772
Total amount awarded: $11,190,722
Contact:
Colorado Commission on Higher Education
1300 Broadway 2nd floor
Denver, CO 80203

Connecticut Department of Higher Education

Connecticut Aid for Public College Students

Type of award: Scholarship, renewable.
Intended use: For undergraduate study in Connecticut.
Designated institutions: Public institutions in Connecticut.
Eligibility: Applicant must be U.S. citizen residing in Connecticut.
Basis for selection: Applicant must demonstrate financial need.
Additional information: Awards up to amount of unmet financial need. Apply at financial aid office at Connecticut public college.
Amount of award: $400-$1,900
Number of awards: 6,516
Total amount awarded: $5,492,653

Connecticut Aid to Dependents of Deceased/Disabled/MIA Veterans

Type of award: Scholarship.
Intended use: For undergraduate or graduate study.
Eligibility: Applicant must be U.S. citizen residing in Connecticut. Applicant must be child of disabled veteran, deceased veteran or POW/MIA, spouse of disabled veteran, deceased veteran or POW/MIA. Death or disability must be service related.
Basis for selection: Applicant must demonstrate financial need.
Application requirements: Proof of eligibility.
Additional information: Parent/spouse must have been Connecticut resident prior to enlistment.
    Amount of award: $400
    Number of awards: 6
    Number of applicants: 6
    Total amount awarded: $2,400

Connecticut Independent College Student Grant

Type of award: Scholarship, renewable.
Intended use: For undergraduate study at 4-year institution in Connecticut. Designated institutions: Private institutions in Connecticut.
Eligibility: Applicant must be U.S. citizen residing in Connecticut.
Basis for selection: Applicant must demonstrate financial need.
Additional information: Applications can be obtained at college financial aid office.
    Amount of award: $7,777
    Number of awards: 3,714
    Total amount awarded: $28,883,778

Connecticut Robert C. Byrd Honors Scholarship

Type of award: Scholarship, renewable.
Intended use: For freshman, sophomore, junior or senior study.
Eligibility: Applicant must be high school senior. Applicant must be U.S. citizen residing in Connecticut.
Basis for selection: Applicant must demonstrate high academic achievement.
Additional information: Must rank in top three percent of high school graduating class.
    Amount of award: $1,121
    Number of awards: 206
    Number of applicants: 700
    Total amount awarded: $306,060

Connecticut Scholastic Achievement Grant

Type of award: Scholarship, renewable.
Intended use: For undergraduate study.
Eligibility: Applicant must be high school senior. Applicant must be U.S. citizen or permanent resident residing in Connecticut.
Basis for selection: Applicant must demonstrate financial need and high academic achievement.
Additional information: Must rank in top fifth of class, and have SAT score of at least 1200 may be used at institutions in Conn, or at institutions that have reciprocity agreements with Conn. Applicants available through high school guidance office.
    Amount of award: $2,000
    Number of awards: 3,500
    Number of applicants: 7,500
    Application deadline: February 15
    Notification begins: June 30
    Total amount awarded: $3,000,000

Connecticut Tuition Set Aside Aid

Type of award: Scholarship, renewable.
Intended use: For undergraduate study at 2-year or 4-year institution in Connecticut. Designated institutions: Public institutions in Connecticut.
Eligibility: Applicant must be U.S. citizen residing in Connecticut.
Basis for selection: Applicant must demonstrate financial need.
Additional information: Awards up to unmet financial need. Apply at financial aid office of institution. Scholarship awarded through Connecticut public colleges.
    Total amount awarded: $21,371,316

Connecticut Tuition Waiver for Senior Citizens

Type of award: Scholarship.
Intended use: For undergraduate study. Designated institutions: Public two-year intitutions in Connecticut.
Eligibility: Applicant must be adult returning student. Applicant must be U.S. citizen residing in Connecticut.
Application requirements: Proof of eligibility.
Additional information: Waivers approved on space available basis. Apply through financial aid office of institution.
    Number of awards: 1,949
    Number of applicants: 1,949
    Total amount awarded: $448,292

Connecticut Tuition Waiver for Veterans

Type of award: Scholarship, renewable.
Intended use: For undergraduate study in Connecticut. Designated institutions: Public institution.
Eligibility: Applicant must be U.S. citizen residing in Connecticut. Applicant must be veteran. Must have served during time of conflict.
Application requirements: Proof of eligibility.
Additional information: Must have been Connecticut resident at time of enlistment.
    Number of awards: 4,213
    Number of applicants: 4,213
    Total amount awarded: $3,134,146

Connecticut Tuition Waiver for Vietnam MIA/POW Dependents

Type of award: Scholarship.
Intended use: For undergraduate study in Connecticut. Designated institutions: Public institutions.
Eligibility: Applicant must be U.S. citizen residing in

Connecticut. Applicant must be child of POW/MIA, spouse of POW/MIA during Vietnam.
Application requirements: Proof of eligibility.
Additional information: Apply at financial aid office of institution. Awarded through Connecticut public colleges.
Contact:
Connecticut Department of Higher Education
61 Woodland Street
Hartford, CT 06105-2391
Phone: 203-566-2618
Fax: 203-566-7865

Council on International Educational Exchange

International Educational Exchange Graduate Scholarship/Russia

Type of award: Scholarship.
Intended use: For master's, doctoral or postgraduate study at graduate institution outside United States in Russia. Designated institutions: Council Study Centers at St. Petersburg University, Russia.
Eligibility: Applicant must be U.S. citizen or permanent resident.
Basis for selection: Major/career interest in foreign languages; Russian studies. Applicant must demonstrate seriousness of purpose and high academic achievement.
Application requirements: Portfolio, recommendations, essay and transcript.
Additional information: Must be committed to field of Russian studies and have demonstrated proficiency in Russian language. Can be studying Russian language and literature.
    Amount of award: $1,000-$10,500
    Number of awards: 25
    Application deadline: April 1, November 1
    Notification begins: May 15, December 15
    Total amount awarded: $60,000
Contact:
Council On International Educational Exchange
205 East 42 Street
Attn: Program Registrar-Russia
New York, NY 10017
Phone: 888-268-6245
Website: www.ciee.org

International Educational Exchange Scholarship/China

Type of award: Scholarship.
Intended use: For junior, senior, master's, doctoral or postgraduate study at 4-year or graduate institution outside United States in China. Designated institutions: Council on International Educational Exchange Study Centers at Peking University or Nanjing University.
Eligibility: Applicant must be U.S. citizen or permanent resident.
Basis for selection: Major/career interest in foreign languages; education, teacher; Asian studies. Applicant must demonstrate financial need.
Application requirements: Transcript and proof of eligibility.
Additional information: Must have two years college-level Chinese and intend to teach language or area studies. Additional fields of study include ethnic and cultural studies, Asian studies, Chinese language and literature.
    Amount of award: $500-$5,000
    Number of awards: 15
    Number of applicants: 20
    Application deadline: April 1, November 1
    Notification begins: May 15, December 15
    Total amount awarded: $40,000
Contact:
Council On International Educational Exchange
205 East 42 Street
Attn: Program Officer - Asia
New York, NY 10017
Phone: 888-268-6245
Website: www.ciee.org

International Educational Exchange/ R.B. Bailey Minority Scholarship

Type of award: Scholarship.
Intended use: For undergraduate, master's, doctoral or postgraduate study at 2-year, 4-year or graduate institution.
Eligibility: Applicant must be American Indian, Asian American, African American, Mexican American, Hispanic American or Puerto Rican. May also be Arab American. Applicant must be U.S. citizen or permanent resident.
Basis for selection: Major/career interest in humanities/liberal arts. Applicant must demonstrate financial need.
Additional information: Must be applying to Council Study Center Program.
    Amount of award: $500
    Number of awards: 15
    Number of applicants: 150
    Application deadline: April 1, December 1
    Notification begins: May 1, December 1
    Total amount awarded: $7,500
Contact:
Council On International Educational Exchange
205 East 42 Street
Attn: Robert B. Bailey Scholarship Committee
New York, NY 10017
Phone: 888-268-6245
Website: www.ciee.org

Delaware Higher Education Commission

Delaware B. Bradford Barnes Scholarship

Type of award: Scholarship, renewable.
Intended use: For full-time freshman, sophomore, junior or senior study. Designated institutions: University of Delaware.
Eligibility: Applicant must be high school senior. Applicant must be residing in Delaware.
Basis for selection: Applicant must demonstrate high academic achievement.

Application requirements: Recommendations, essay, transcript and proof of eligibility.
Additional information: Must rank in top 25 percent of high school class. Minimum SAT score of 1100 (27 on ACT) required. Awards full tuition, fees, room and board at the University of Delaware.
   Number of awards: 1
   Number of applicants: 150
   Application deadline: February 1
   Notification begins: March 1
Contact:
Delaware Higher Education Commission
820 North French Street
Fourth Floor
Wilmington, DE 19801

Delaware Christa McAuliffe Scholarship Loan

Type of award: Loan, renewable.
Intended use: For full-time freshman, sophomore, junior or senior study at accredited 4-year institution in Delaware.
Eligibility: Applicant must be residing in Delaware.
Basis for selection: Major/career interest in education, teacher. Applicant must demonstrate high academic achievement.
Application requirements: Recommendations, essay, transcript and proof of eligibility.
Additional information: Loan forgiveness for teaching in Delaware public schools: one year for each year of financial assistance.
   Amount of award: $1,000-$3,500
   Number of awards: 80
   Application deadline: March 31
   Notification begins: May 1
   Total amount awarded: $170,000
Contact:
Delaware Higher Education Commission
820 North French Street
Fourth Floor
Wilmington, DE 19801

Delaware Diamond State Scholarship

Type of award: Scholarship, renewable.
Intended use: For full-time freshman, sophomore, junior or senior study at accredited vocational, 2-year or 4-year institution in United States.
Eligibility: Applicant must be high school senior. Applicant must be residing in Delaware.
Basis for selection: Applicant must demonstrate high academic achievement.
Application requirements: Recommendations, essay and transcript.
Additional information: Must rank in top 25 percent of high school class. Minimum SAT I score of 1100 (27 on ACT) required.

   Amount of award: $4,500
   Number of awards: 180
   Number of applicants: 256
   Application deadline: March 31
   Notification begins: May 1
   Total amount awarded: $180,000
Contact:
Delaware Higher Education Commission
820 North French Street
Fourth Floor
Wilmington, DE 19801

Delaware Education Fund for Children of Deceased Military Personnel/State Police

Type of award: Scholarship, renewable.
Intended use: For undergraduate, non-degree study in Delaware. Designated institutions: Public institutions in Delaware.
Eligibility: Applicant must be residing in Delaware. Applicant must be child of veteran or deceased veteran. Applicant's parent must have been killed or disabled in work-related accident as police officer.
Application requirements: Proof of eligibility.
Additional information: Parent must have been Delaware State Police officer killed in line of duty or veteran residing in Delaware at time of death. Awards full tuition and fees for four years at a Delaware public institution or reduced award for out-of-state school.
   Number of awards: 2
   Number of applicants: 2
Contact:
Delaware Higher Education Commission
820 North French Street
Fourth Floor
Wilmington, DE 19801

Delaware Herman M. Holloway, Sr. Memorial Scholarship

Type of award: Scholarship, renewable.
Intended use: For full-time freshman, sophomore, junior or senior study in Delaware. Designated institutions: Delaware State University.
Eligibility: Applicant must be high school senior. Applicant must be U.S. citizen residing in Delaware.
Basis for selection: Applicant must demonstrate high academic achievement.
Application requirements: Proof of eligibility.
Additional information: Minimum 3.25 GPA and acceptable SAT I or ACT scores required. Awards full tuition, room and board at Delaware State University.
   Amount of award: $6,300
   Number of awards: 1
   Number of applicants: 200
   Application deadline: March 15
   Notification begins: May 1
   Total amount awarded: $6,300
Contact:
Delaware Higher Education Commission
820 North French Street, 4th Floor
Wilmington, DE 19801

Delaware Nursing Incentive Program

Type of award: Loan, renewable.
Intended use: For full-time undergraduate, non-degree study at vocational, 2-year or 4-year institution in United States.
Eligibility: Applicant must be residing in Delaware.
Basis for selection: Major/career interest in nursing. Applicant must demonstrate high academic achievement.
Application requirements: Recommendations, essay, transcript and proof of eligibility.
Additional information: Minimum 2.5 GPA required. Loan forgiveness for practicing nursing at state-owned hospital: one year for each year of financial assistance.

Amount of award:	$2,000-$3,000
Number of awards:	10
Number of applicants:	20
Application deadline:	March 31
Notification begins:	May 1
Total amount awarded:	$150,000

Contact:
Delaware Higher Education Commission
820 North French Street
Fourth Floor
Wilmington, DE 19801

Delaware Scholarship Incentive

Type of award: Scholarship, renewable.
Intended use: For full-time freshman, sophomore, junior, senior, master's, doctoral or first professional study at accredited 2-year, 4-year or graduate institution in Delaware or Pennsylvania.
Eligibility: Applicant must be residing in Delaware.
Basis for selection: Applicant must demonstrate financial need.
Application requirements: Transcript.
Additional information: May be used outside of Delaware and Pennsylvania if program of study is not offered at tax-supported institution in either state.

Amount of award:	$700-$2,200
Number of awards:	1,300
Number of applicants:	13,000
Application deadline:	April 15
Notification begins:	July 1
Total amount awarded:	$1,100,000

Contact:
Delaware Higher Education Commission
820 North French Street
Fourth Floor
Wilmington, DE 19801

Delaware Speech Language Pathologist Incentive Program

Type of award: Loan.
Intended use: For master's study at accredited graduate institution in United States.
Eligibility: Applicant must be U.S. citizen or permanent resident residing in Delaware.
Basis for selection: Major/career interest in speech pathology/audiology. Applicant must demonstrate financial need and high academic achievement.
Application requirements: Proof of eligibility.
Additional information: Must spend two years for each year of financial assistance in Delaware public school system working in speech pathology.
Contact:
Delaware Higher Education Commission
820 North French Street, 4th Floor
Wilmington, DE 19801

Department of Defense

National Defense Science and Engineering Graduate Fellowship Program

Type of award: Scholarship, renewable.
Intended use: For full-time doctoral study at graduate institution in United States.
Eligibility: Applicant must be U.S. citizen.
Basis for selection: Major/career interest in physics; engineering, electrical and electronic; mathematics; social and behavioral sciences; chemistry; computer and information sciences. Applicant must demonstrate high academic achievement.
Application requirements: Recommendations, essay and transcript. GRE scores.
Additional information: A GPA of 3.0 required. Fellowships are renewable for up to three years. Applications from women and minority groups are encouraged. Tuition and fees are covered in addition to grant.

Amount of award:	$17,000-$19,000
Number of awards:	90
Number of applicants:	15,000
Application deadline:	January 21
Notification begins:	March 31

Contact:
Department of Defense National Defense Science and Engineering Graduate Fellowship Program
200 Park Drive, Suite 211
P.O. Box 13444
Research Triangle Park, NC 27709-3444
Phone: 919-549-8505
Fax: 919-549-8205
Website: www.battelle.org

District of Columbia Office of Postsecondary Education

District of Columbia Student Incentive Grant

Type of award: Scholarship, renewable.
Intended use: For full-time or half-time undergraduate, master's study at 2-year, 4-year or graduate institution in United States.
Eligibility: Applicant must be U.S. citizen or permanent resident residing in District of Columbia.
Basis for selection: Applicant must demonstrate financial need.

Application requirements: Proof of eligibility. Student Aid Report generated by FAFSA.
Additional information: Must apply for federal aid. Institution must be certified as eligible by U.S. Department of Education. Must be resident of D.C. for 15 months prior to application. Considered on a "first come, first served" basis for as long as funds are available.
    Amount of award: $1,000
    Application deadline: June 30
    Notification begins: October 15
Contact:
District of Comumbia Office of Postsecondary Education/Research/Assistance
2100 Martin Luther King, Jr. Avenue, S.E.
Suite 401
Washington, DC 20020

Environmental Protection Agency

National Network for Environmental Management Studies Internship

Type of award: Internship, renewable.
Intended use: For undergraduate or graduate study.
Application requirements: Interview and transcript.
Additional information: Open to all majors. Undergraduates are required to have at least four courses in environmental science. Graduate students must have completed at least one semester. Deadlines vary; contact sponsor for information. Interns may work in the following areas: environmental policy, environmental management, environmental science, public relations and media, and computer programming and development.
    Amount of award: $4,000-$7,000
    Number of awards: 88
    Number of applicants: 450
Contact:
Environmental Protection Agency
401 M Street, S.W.
Washington, DC 20460

Federal Reserve Bank of New York

Federal Reserve Summer Internship

Type of award: Internship.
Intended use: For full-time junior, master's study.
Eligibility: Applicant must be high school senior. Applicant must be U.S. citizen or permanent resident.
Basis for selection: Major/career interest in finance/banking; economics. Applicant must demonstrate leadership and high academic achievement.
Application requirements: Interview and transcript.
Additional information: Bachelor's level applicants should have completed their junior year of college before the beginning of the internship. Master's level applicants should have completed their first year of a graduate program. Minimum GPA of 3.5 is required.
    Amount of award: $3,000-$9,600
    Application deadline: January 31
Contact:
Federal Reserve Bank of New York
59 Maiden Lane
New York, NY 10038-4502
Website: www.ny.frb.org/job apps/summer html

Florida Department of Education

Florida Academic Scholars Award

Type of award: Scholarship, renewable.
Intended use: For full-time undergraduate study at postsecondary institution in Florida.
Eligibility: Applicant must be high school senior. Applicant must be U.S. citizen or permanent resident residing in Florida.
Basis for selection: Applicant must demonstrate high academic achievement.
Additional information: Part of the Bright Futures Scholarship Program. Scholarship covers full tuition and fees with up to $600 stipend. Check with Department of Education for current requirements. Must attend an eligible postsecondary institution in the state of Florida. Applications available from high school guidance office or Office of Financial Assistance.
    Application deadline: April 1
Contact:
Florida Department of Education
Office of Student Financial Assistance
255 Collins, 325 West Gaines Street
Tallahassee, FL 32399-0400
Phone: 904-487-0049
Website: www.firn.edu/doe

Florida Children of Deceased/Disabled Veterans/POW/MIA Scholarship

Type of award: Scholarship.
Intended use: For full-time undergraduate or graduate study at vocational, 2-year or 4-year institution.
Eligibility: Applicant must be U.S. citizen or permanent resident residing in Florida. Applicant must be child of disabled veteran or deceased veteran during Grenada, Korean War, Middle East War, Lebanon, Panama, Persian Gulf, WW I, WW II or Vietnam. Veterans or servicemen must have been residents of Florida during the period specified for the war, conflict or event in which they served. Consult Office of Student Financial Aid for additional details regarding specific conflicts and additional residency requirements.
Application requirements: Proof of eligibility.
Additional information: Award amount cover tuition/fees for one academic year..

Application deadline: April 1
Contact:
Florida Department of Veterans Affairs
Executive Director
P.O. Box 31003
St. Petersburg, FL 33731-8903
Phone: 813-898-4443
Website: www.firn.edu/doe

Florida Critical Teacher Shortage Student Loan Forgiveness

Type of award: Scholarship, renewable.
Intended use: For undergraduate certificate, post-bachelor's certificate or non-degree study at 4-year or graduate institution in United States.
Eligibility: Applicant must be U.S. citizen or permanent resident residing in Florida.
Basis for selection: Major/career interest in education, teacher.
Additional information: Must have graduated from an undergraduate or graduate teacher preparation program and been certified in a critical teacher shortage subject area. Awards are $2,500 for four years for undergraduate loans and $5,000 for up to two years for graduate loans. Applicants must apply within 12 months of certification and teach full-time in a critical subject for at least 90 days.
Amount of award: $2,500-$5,000
Application deadline: July 15
Contact:
Florida Department of Education
Office of Student Financial Assistance
255 Collins, 325 West Gaines Street
Tallahassee, FL 32399-0400
Phone: 904-487-0049
Website: www.firn.edu/doe

Florida Critical Teacher Shortage Tuition Reimbursement

Type of award: Scholarship, renewable.
Intended use: For post-bachelor's certificate study at 4-year or graduate institution.
Eligibility: Applicant must be U.S. citizen or permanent resident residing in Florida.
Basis for selection: Major/career interest in education, teacher; education; education, special.
Application requirements: Proof of eligibility.
Additional information: Must be eligible for certification and currently employed full-time in Florida public school system. Minimum GPA 3.0 required. Tuition reimbursement is for certification or graduate program in critical teacher shortage subject areas designated by State Board of Education. Reimbursement is $78 per credit hour for up to nine credit hours per academic year.
Amount of award: $702
Contact:
Florida Department of Education
Office of Student Financial Assistance
255 Collins, 325 West Gaines Street
Tallahassee, FL 32399-0400
Phone: 904-487-0049
Website: www.firn.edu/doe

Florida Exceptional Student Education Training Grant

Type of award: Scholarship, renewable.
Intended use: For post-bachelor's certificate, master's study.
Eligibility: Applicant must be U.S. citizen or permanent resident residing in Florida.
Basis for selection: Applicant must demonstrate high academic achievement.
Additional information: Provides reimbursement to those persons who are under contract to teach in an exceptional student education program and who need certification appropriate for the assignment. Awards cover $78 per credit hour for a maximum of nine credit hours per term.
Amount of award: $702
Contact:
Florida Department of Education
Office of Student Financial Assistance
255 Collins, 325 West Gaines Street
Tallahassee, FL 32399-0400
Phone: 904-487-0049
Website: www.firn.edu/doe

Florida Gold Seal Vocational Scholars Award

Type of award: Scholarship, renewable.
Intended use: For undergraduate study at vocational institution in Florida.
Eligibility: Applicant must be high school senior. Applicant must be U.S. citizen or permanent resident residing in Florida.
Basis for selection: Applicant must demonstrate high academic achievement.
Additional information: This scholarship is part of the Bright Futures Program. Check with Department of Education for current requirements. Award covers 75 percent of tuition and fees. Applications available from school guidance office or Office of Financial Assistance.
Contact:
Florida Department of Education
Office of Student Financial Assistance
255 Collins, 325 West Gaines Street
Tallahassee, FL 32399-0400
Phone: 904-487-0049
Website: www.firn.edu/doe

Florida Jose Marti Scholarship Challenge Grant

Type of award: Scholarship, renewable.
Intended use: For full-time undergraduate or graduate study at 2-year, 4-year or graduate institution.
Eligibility: Applicant must be Mexican American, Hispanic American or Puerto Rican. Applicant must be U.S. citizen or permanent resident residing in Florida.
Basis for selection: Applicant must demonstrate financial need and high academic achievement.
Application requirements: FAFSA.
Additional information: Seniors in high school or undergraduates applying to graduate school must have 3.0 cumulative, unweighted GPA and file Free Application for Federal Student Aid (FAFSA). Either applicant or parent must have been born in Mexico, Spain, or a Hispanic country of the

Caribbean, Central America, or South America. Must meet Florida eligibility criteria for state student aid. Award number is limited to the amount of available funds. High school seniors receive priority over undergraduates. Applications available from high school guidance office or college office of finacial aid.

Amount of award:	$2,000
Number of awards:	66
Number of applicants:	1,385
Application deadline:	April 1
Total amount awarded:	$123,000

Contact:
Florida Department of Education
Office of Student Financial Assistance
255 Collins, 325 West Gaines Street
Tallahassee, FL 32399-0400
Website: www.firn.edu/doe

Florida Limited Access Competitive Grant

Type of award: Scholarship.
Intended use: For full-time junior, senior study at 4-year institution in Florida. Designated institutions: Must be used at private institutions in Florida.
Eligibility: Applicant must be U.S. citizen or permanent resident residing in Florida.
Additional information: Provides enrollment opportunities for community college graduates or transfer students from state universities. Must plan to enroll in the limited access programs available at private institutions in Florida. The amount of the award is 50% of tuition/fees. Applications are available from the financial aid offices of the designated institutions.

Number of awards:	300

Contact:
Florida Department of Education
Office of Student Financial Assistance
255 Collins, 325 West Gaines Street
Tallahassee, FL 32399-0400
Phone: 904-487-0049
Website: www.firn.edu/doe

Florida Mary McLeod Bethune Scholarship

Type of award: Scholarship, renewable.
Intended use: For full-time undergraduate study. Designated institutions: Bethune-Cookman College, Edward Waters College, Florida A&M University, Florida Memorial College.
Eligibility: Applicant must be high school senior. Applicant must be residing in Florida.
Basis for selection: Applicant must demonstrate financial need and high academic achievement.
Additional information: Minimum 3.0 GPA required. Deadlines are established by participating institutions. Applications can be obtained from any of four designated institution's financial aid offices.

Amount of award:	$3,000
Number of awards:	265
Total amount awarded:	$250,500

Florida Merit Scholars Award

Type of award: Scholarship.
Intended use: For undergraduate study at 2-year or 4-year institution.
Eligibility: Applicant must be high school senior. Applicant must be U.S. citizen or permanent resident residing in Florida.
Basis for selection: Applicant must demonstrate high academic achievement.
Additional information: Part of the Bright Futures Program. Check with Department of Education for current requirements. Award covers 75 percent of tuition and fees assessed. Must meet Florida residency requirements. Applications available from school guidance office or Office of Financial Assistance.
Contact:
Florida Department of Education
Office of Student Financial Assistance
255 Collins, 325 West Gaines Street
Tallahassee, FL 32399-0400
Phone: 904-487-0049
Website: www.firn.edu/doe

Florida Occupational/Physical Therapist Loan Forgiveness Program

Type of award: Scholarship, renewable.
Intended use: For non-degree study.
Eligibility: Applicant must be residing in Florida.
Basis for selection: Major/career interest in occupational therapy; physical therapy.
Application requirements: Must be licensed or have a valid temporary permit as a therapist from Florida Department of Business and Professional Regulation; have been employed as a therapist in Florida public schools for at least half a school year, and declare intent to be employed for a minimum of 3 years.
Additional information: Awards are for loan payback. $2,500 a year for undergraduate loans and $5,000 a year for graduate loans for a maximum of four years or $10,000, whichever comes first. These awards are for licenced therapists with a valid temporary permit who have worked full-time in Florida public schools for one year and who intend to be employed in Florida public schools for a minimum of three years.

Amount of award:	$2,500-$5,000
Application deadline:	April 15

Contact:
Florida Department of Education
Bureau of Instructional Support/Com. Services
601 Florida Education Center-325 West Gaines Street
Tallahassee, FL 32399-0400
Phone: 904-488-1106
Website: www.firn.edu/doe

Florida Occupational/Physical Therapist Scholarship Loan Program

Type of award: Loan, renewable.
Intended use: For full-time undergraduate or graduate study at graduate institution in Florida.
Eligibility: Applicant must be residing in Florida.

Basis for selection: Major/career interest in physical therapy; occupational therapy.
Additional information: Applicant must be enrolled in a therapist assistant program, or an upper division or graduate level therapist program.
   Amount of award: $4,000
   Application deadline: April 15
Contact:
Florida Department of Education
Bureau of Instructional Support/Com. Services
601 Florida Education Center
Tallahassee, FL 32399-0400
Phone: 904-488-1106

Florida Occupational/Physical Therapist Tuition Reimbursement

Type of award: Scholarship, renewable.
Intended use: For non-degree study in Florida.
Eligibility: Applicant must be U.S. citizen or permanent resident residing in Florida.
Basis for selection: Major/career interest in occupational therapy; physical therapy.
Additional information: Provides assistance to licensed therapists who take courses to improve their skills and knowledge and have been employed as full-time therapists in Florida public schools for at least three years. Recipients receive $78 per credit hour for a maximum of nine credit hours per academic year.
   Amount of award: $702
Contact:
Florida Department of Education
Bureau of Instructional Support/Com. Services
601 Florida Education Center-325 West Gaines St.
Tallahassee, FL 32399-0400
Phone: 904-488-1106
Website: www.firn.edu/doe

Florida Resident Access Grant

Type of award: Scholarship, renewable.
Intended use: For full-time undergraduate study at accredited 4-year institution in Florida. Designated institutions: Non-profit institutions in Florida.
Eligibility: Applicant must be U.S. citizen or permanent resident residing in Florida.
Application requirements: Proof of eligibility.
Additional information: Applicant must not have previously received a bachelor's degree and may not use award for study of divinity or theology. Applications available from eligible institutions financial aid offices.
Contact:
Florida Department of Education
Office of Student Financial Assistance
325 West Gaines Street
Tallahassee, FL 32399-0400
Phone: 904-487-0049
Website: www.firn.edu/doe

Florida Robert C. Byrd Honors Scholarship

Type of award: Scholarship, renewable.
Intended use: For full-time undergraduate study at 2-year or 4-year institution in United States.
Eligibility: Applicant must be high school senior. Applicant must be U.S. citizen or permanent resident residing in Florida.
Basis for selection: Applicant must demonstrate high academic achievement.
Application requirements: Nomination by high school principal must nominate student.
Additional information: Application requires unweighted cumulative GPA and SAT I or ACT scores.
   Amount of award: $1,500
   Number of awards: 500
   Application deadline: April 15
   Total amount awarded: $800,000
Contact:
Florida Department of Education
Office of Student Financial Assistance
255 Collins, 325 West Gaines Street
Tallahassee, FL 32399-0400
Phone: 904-487-0049
Website: www.firn.edu/doe

Florida Rosewood Family Scholarship

Type of award: Scholarship.
Intended use: For full-time undergraduate study at vocational, 2-year or 4-year institution in Florida. Designated institutions: Must be public state schools in Florida.
Eligibility: Applicant must be African American. Applicant must be U.S. citizen or permanent resident residing in Florida.
Application requirements: FAFSA.
Additional information: Applicant must be descendant of African-American Rosewood families affected by the incidents of January 1923.
   Amount of award: $4,000
   Number of awards: 25
   Application deadline: April 1
   Total amount awarded: $100,000
Contact:
Florida Department of Education
Office of Student Financial Assistance
255 Collins, 325 West Gaines Street
Tallahassee, FL 32399-0400
Phone: 904-487-0049
Website: www.firn.edu/doe

Florida Seminole and Miccosukee Indian Scholarship

Type of award: Scholarship, renewable.
Intended use: For undergraduate or graduate study at vocational, 2-year, 4-year or graduate institution in Florida.
Eligibility: Applicant must be American Indian. Must be member of or eligible for membership in Seminole or Miccosukee Tribe in Florida. Applicant must be U.S. citizen or permanent resident residing in Florida.
Basis for selection: Applicant must demonstrate financial need.
Application requirements: Proof of eligibility.
Additional information: Award amount and deadline is

determined by tribe. Applications can be obtained from each tribes Higher Education Office.
Contact:
Florida Department of Education
Office of Student Financial Assistance
255 Collins, 325 West Gaines Street
Tallahassee, FL 32399-0400
Phone: 904-487-0049
Website: www.firn.edu/doe

Florida Student Assistance Grant

Type of award: Scholarship, renewable.
Intended use: For full-time undergraduate study at 2-year or 4-year institution in Florida.
Eligibility: Applicant must be U.S. citizen or permanent resident residing in Florida.
Basis for selection: Applicant must demonstrate financial need.
Application requirements: Proof of eligibility. FAFSA.
Additional information: FAFSA must be processed by May 15. Applicant must not have previously received a bachelor's degree. Applications available from high school guidance offices and at participating universities financial aid offices.
  Amount of award: $200-$1,500
  Application deadline: May 15
Contact:
Florida Department of Education
Office of Student Financial Assistance
325 West Gaines Street
Tallahassee, FL 32399-0400
Website: www.firn.edu/doe

Florida Teacher Scholarship and Forgivable Loan (Freshmen/Sophomores)

Type of award: Scholarship, renewable.
Intended use: For full-time freshman, sophomore study at accredited 4-year institution in Florida.
Eligibility: Applicant must be high school senior. Applicant must be U.S. citizen or permanent resident residing in Florida.
Basis for selection: Major/career interest in education, teacher; education. Applicant must demonstrate high academic achievement.
Application requirements: Proof of eligibility and nomination by High School staff nominates one student. Principal or dean must review application for eligibility before signing and submitting application to Office of Student Financial Assistance by April 1.
Additional information: Applicant must be member of Future Teaching Organization (if high school has one), be in top 25 percent of class, have 3.0 unweighted cumulative GPA, intend to teach in Florida. Fifteen percent of scholarships reserved for minorities.
  Amount of award: $1,500
  Application deadline: April 1
Contact:
Florida Department of Education
Office of Student Financial Assistance
255 Collins, 325 West Gaines Street
Tallahassee, FL 32399-0400
Phone: 904-487-0049
Website: www.firn.edu/doe

Florida Teacher Scholarship and Forgivable Loan (Graduate)

Type of award: Loan, renewable.
Intended use: For graduate study at accredited graduate institution in Florida.
Eligibility: Applicant must be U.S. citizen or permanent resident residing in Florida.
Basis for selection: Major/career interest in education, teacher; education. Applicant must demonstrate high academic achievement.
Application requirements: Dean must review application for eligibility before signing and submitting application to Office of Student Financial Assistance by April 1.
Additional information: Graduates must have 3.0 cumulative GPA or score 1000 on GRE; pursue degree in Florida Teaching Shortage Area. Loan can be paid back by teaching in designated areas or in cash.
  Amount of award: $8,000
  Application deadline: March 15
Contact:
Florida Department of Education
Office of Student Financial Assistance
255 Collins, 325 West Gaines Street
Tallahasee, FL 32399-0400
Phone: 904-487-0049
Website: www.firn.edu/doe

Florida Teacher Scholarship and Forgivable Loan (Juniors/Seniors)

Type of award: Loan, renewable.
Intended use: For junior, senior study at accredited 4-year institution in Florida.
Eligibility: Applicant must be U.S. citizen or permanent resident residing in Florida.
Basis for selection: Major/career interest in education, teacher; education. Applicant must demonstrate high academic achievement.
Application requirements: Proof of eligibility. Dean reviews application for eligibility before signing and submitting application to Office of Student Financial Assistance by April 1.
Additional information: Applicants must have 2.5 cumulative GPA, be in 40th percentile of ACT or SAT I, and pursue teaching in Florida Teaching Shortage Area. Loan forgiveness one year for each year of award for teaching anywhere in Florida and two years for teaching in teacher shortage area. Loans must be paid back in cash if student decides not to teach in designated areas.
  Amount of award: $4,000
  Application deadline: March 15
Contact:
Florida Department of Education
Office of Student Financial Assistance
255 Collins, 325 West Gaines Street
Tallahassee, FL 32399-0400
Phone: 904-487-0049
Website: www.firn.edu/doe

Florida Work Experience

Type of award: Internship, renewable.
Intended use: For undergraduate study at 2-year or 4-year

institution in Florida. Designated institutions: Participating institutions in Florida.
Eligibility: Applicant must be U.S. citizen or permanent resident residing in Florida.
Basis for selection: Applicant must demonstrate financial need.
Application requirements: Proof of eligibility. FAFSA. 2.0 GPA.
Additional information: Provides students with opportunity to be employed off-campus in jobs related to their academic major or area of career interest. Applications available from participating universities financial aid offices.
Contact:
Florida Department of Education
Office of Student Financial Assistance
1344 Florida Education Center
Tallahassee, FL 32399-0400
Phone: 904-487-0049
Website: www.firn.edu/doe

Florida Department of Health Professional Recruitment

Florida Nursing Loan Forgiveness

Type of award: Scholarship, renewable.
Intended use: For non-degree study.
Eligibility: Applicant must be residing in Florida.
Application requirements: Proof of eligibility.
Additional information: Must be licensed in state of Florida as a Licensed Practical, Registered Nurse, or Advanced Registered Nurse Practitioner but may have been trained elsewhere. Must work full-time at eligible employment site within Florida. Applications accepted quarterly (December 1, March 1, June 1, and September 1).

Amount of award:	$4,000
Number of awards:	150
Application deadline:	September 1, March 1
Total amount awarded:	$240,000

Contact:
Florida Nursing Student Loan Forgiveness Program
Florida Department of Health Professional Recruitment
1317 Winewood Boulevard
Tallahassee, FL 32399-0700
Phone: 800-342-8660

Florida Division of Blind Services

Florida Educational Assistance for the Blind

Type of award: Scholarship, renewable.
Intended use: For full-time undergraduate, graduate or non-degree study at vocational, 2-year, 4-year or graduate institution in United States.
Eligibility: Applicant must be visually impaired. Applicant must be U.S. citizen or permanent resident residing in Florida.
Basis for selection: Applicant must demonstrate seriousness of purpose and financial need.
Application requirements: Transcript and proof of eligibility. Must be a client of State of Florida Division of Blind Services. Applicant to first secure federal or state scholarships/grants/loans.
Additional information: In Florida, phone: 800-342-1828; out of state: 850-488-1330. Tuition, books, reader's service fees, and maintenance awarded for out-of-state institutions. Only tuition paid for in-state institutions. Deadline dates vary.
Contact:
Florida State Division of Blind Services
2551 Executive Center Circle
203 Douglas Building
Tallahassee, FL 32399
Phone: 800-342-1828

Florida Education Fund

Florida Education Fund Minority Participation in Legal Education Law School Scholarship

Type of award: Scholarship, renewable.
Intended use: For full-time first professional study.
Eligibility: Applicant must be Alaskan native, American Indian, African American, Mexican American, Hispanic American or Puerto Rican. Applicant must be U.S. citizen.
Basis for selection: Major/career interest in law. Applicant must demonstrate financial need and high academic achievement.
Application requirements: Recommendations, essay, transcript and proof of eligibility.
Additional information: Must be used at one of the following Florida institutions: Saint Thomas University, Stetson University, Nova Southeastern University, University of Florida, Florida State University, and the University of Miami. Must practice law in Florida for at least three years after graduating. Deadline varies; contact sponsor for information. Must submit LSAT scores, as well as LSDAS report.

Amount of award:	$19,000
Number of awards:	66

Florida Education Fund Minority Pre-law Scholarships

Type of award: Scholarship, renewable.
Intended use: For full-time junior, senior study at accredited 4-year institution in United States.
Eligibility: Applicant must be Alaskan native, American Indian, African American, Mexican American, Hispanic American or Puerto Rican. Applicant must be U.S. citizen residing in Florida.
Basis for selection: Major/career interest in law. Applicant must demonstrate financial need and high academic achievement.
Application requirements: Recommendations, essay, transcript and proof of eligibility.

Additional information: Deadline varies; contact sponsor for information. Must submit official report of GPA.
- **Amount of award:** $7,000
- **Number of awards:** 69

Contact:
The Florida Education Fund
15485 Eagle Nest Ln.
Suite 200
Miami Lakes, FL 33014
Website: www.fl-educ-fd.org

Fulbright Program/USIA- U.S. Student Programs

Albania: Full Grant (Fulbright)

Type of award: Research grant.
Intended use: For graduate or non-degree study at graduate institution in Albania.
Eligibility: Applicant must be U.S. citizen.
Basis for selection: Applicant must demonstrate seriousness of purpose.
Application requirements: Recommendations, transcript and research proposal.
Additional information: Preference given in the fields of history and linguistics. Working knowledge of Albanian strongly recommended, but not required. Not recommended to bring dependents. In the creative and performing arts, applicants who have not earned their BA, four years of professional experience meets the basic requirement. Applicants enrolled in U.S. academic institutions must apply through Fulbright Program Adviser on campus. All others must request application directly from IIE by October 8.
- **Number of awards:** 1
- **Application deadline:** October 23
- **Notification begins:** June 30

Contact:
Fulbright Program/USIA--U.S. Student Programs
Institute of International Education
809 United Nations Plaza
New York, NY 10017-3580
Website: www.iie.org/fulbright

Argentina: Full Grant (Fulbright)

Type of award: Research grant.
Intended use: For master's, doctoral or non-degree study in Argentina.
Eligibility: Applicant must be U.S. citizen.
Basis for selection: Applicant must demonstrate seriousness of purpose.
Application requirements: Recommendations, transcript and research proposal.
Additional information: Ph.D. candidates should propose specific research projects in support of their doctoral programs. Students working toward a master's degree will be considered. Academic year March to December. Grant period eight months. Spanish proficiency needed. Fulbright fellows assigned to university cities in the Argentinean interior when feasible. Applicants enrolled in U.S. academic institutions must apply through Fulbright Program Adviser on campus. All others must request application directly from IIE by October 8.
- **Number of applicants:** 56
- **Application deadline:** October 23
- **Notification begins:** June 30

Contact:
Fulbright Program/USIA--U.S. Student Programs
Institute of International Education
809 United Nations Plaza
New York, NY 10017-3580
Website: www.iie.org/fulbright

Australia: Full Grant (Fulbright)

Type of award: Scholarship.
Intended use: For master's, doctoral or non-degree study in Australia.
Eligibility: Applicant must be U.S. citizen.
Basis for selection: Applicant must demonstrate seriousness of purpose.
Application requirements: Recommendations, transcript and research proposal.
Additional information: U.S. students currently residing in Australia will not be considered. Academic year February to November. Grant period begins in July or February. Recipients negotiate waiving of affiliation and tuition fees. All fields are considered. Priority is given to candidates whose studies are particularly relevant to improving the bilateral relationship between the U.S. and Australia, and who include a statement to that effect in their applications. Applications are encouraged in international trade and investment, the visual and performing arts, environmental law and management, American studies, and information technology and telecommunications. It should be noted that whatever the discipline, profession or art field, all applications must meet the AAEF's primary criterion of substantial merit. In the creative and performing arts, applicants who have not earned their BA, four years of professional experience meets the basic requirement. Applicants enrolled in U.S. academic institutions must apply through Fulbright Program Adviser on campus. All others must request application directly from IIE by October 8. Tuition and fees vary from approximately US$6,100 to US$21,000.
- **Number of awards:** 10
- **Application deadline:** October 23
- **Notification begins:** June 30

Contact:
Fulbright Program/USIA--U.S. Student Programs
Institute of International Education
809 United Nations Plaza
New York, NY 10017-3580
Website: www.iie.org/fulbright

Austria: Full Grant (Fulbright)

Type of award: Research grant.
Intended use: For graduate or non-degree study in Austria.
Eligibility: Applicant must be U.S. citizen.
Basis for selection: Applicant must demonstrate seriousness of purpose.
Application requirements: Recommendations, transcript and research proposal.
Additional information: Academic year October to June.

Grant duration nine months. Stipend approximately AS 12,000 monthly, plus AS 16,000 travel expenses. Up to 12 commission-supported study grants and up to Ten study grants combined with English language teaching assistantships. Medicine and veterinary studies not recommended. German proficiency needed. In the creative and performing arts, applicants who have not earned their BA, four years of professional experience meets the basic requirement. Universities of music and the arts require auditions and/or entrance examinations, along with submission of a portfolio. Applicants should inquire about audition requirements and dates well in advance. The Fulbright Commission may require candidates to travel to Austria to audition as early as June. Grants are awarded only after acceptance by a music school. Applicants enrolled in U.S. academic institutions must apply through Fulbright Program Adviser on campus. All others must request application directly from IIE by October 8.

    Number of awards: 22
    Application deadline: October 23
    Notification begins: June 30

Contact:
Fulbright Program/USIA--U.S. Student Programs
Institute of International Education
809 United Nations Plaza
New York, NY 10017-3580
Website: www.iie.org/fulbright

Austria: IFK Grants

Type of award: Research grant.
Intended use: For doctoral study in Austria. Designated institutions: The Internationnales Forschungszentrum Kulturwissenschafter (IFK), Vienna.
Eligibility: Applicant must be U.S. citizen.
Basis for selection: Applicant must demonstrate seriousness of purpose.
Application requirements: Recommendations and transcript.
Additional information: Available to U.S. graduate students who are Ph.D candidates in cultural studies with fields of specialization thematically related to Austrian and Central European traditions and IFK's interest in the comparative dimensions of cultural studies. Applicants for Fulbright/IFK awards will simultaneously also be considered as candidates for traditional Fulbright student grants. Grant period nine months, October to June. Proficiency in spoken and written German is required. Grantees will have access to a work station at IFK and be expected to actively participate in IFK seminars, workshops, and symposia. Maintenance allowance approximately AS 15,000 per month. The Commission provides a fixed sum travel grant of approximately AS 10,000 covering round-trip travel to Austria.

    Number of awards: 2
    Application deadline: October 23

Contact:
Fulbright Program/USIA--U.S. Student Programs
Institute of International Education
809 United Nations Plaza
New York, NY 10017
Website: www.iie.org/fulbright

Austria: Study Grant English Language Teaching Assistantship

Type of award: Scholarship.
Intended use: For graduate study at graduate institution outside United States in Austria.
Eligibility: Applicant must be U.S. citizen.
Basis for selection: Applicant must demonstrate seriousness of purpose.
Application requirements: Recommendations and transcript.
Additional information: Ten study grants in German language, Austrian literature and culture supported by English teaching assistantships (12 hours per week) at secondary schools in university cities. Assistants receive a Ministry of Education salary of approximately AS 13,500 net per month. Includes full health and accident insurance, from October through May; for June, the Fulbright Commission pays a regular AS 12,000. Recent college and university graduates and future teachers of German are particularly encouraged to apply for these combined grants. Candidates who are willing to accept an English language teaching assistantship will have a better chance of getting an award. Students only interested in the Ministry of Education's English language teaching assistantships program should apply directly to the Austrian Fulbright Commission, Schmidgasse 14, A-1082 Vienna, by March 1, 1999.

    Number of awards: 10
    Application deadline: October 23

Contact:
Fulbright Program/USIA--U.S. Student Programs
Institute of International Education
809 United Nations Plaza
New York, NY 10017-3580
Website: www.iie.org/fulbright

Bahrain: Full Grant (Fulbright)

Type of award: Research grant.
Intended use: For graduate study in Bahrain.
Eligibility: Applicant must be U.S. citizen.
Basis for selection: Applicant must demonstrate seriousness of purpose.
Application requirements: Recommendations, transcript and research proposal.
Additional information: Ph.D. candidates preferred. A knowledge of Arabic sufficient to carry out the proposed research is required by the beginning date of the award. Applicants enrolled in U.S. academic institutions must apply through Fulbright Program Adviser on campus. All others must request application directly from IIE by October 8.

    Number of applicants: 1
    Application deadline: October 23
    Notification begins: June 30

Contact:
Fulbright Program/USIA--U.S. Student Programs
Institute of International Education
809 United Nations Plaza
New York, NY 10017-3580
Website: www.iie.org/fulbright

Bangladesh: Full Grant (Fulbright)

Type of award: Research grant.
Intended use: For graduate study in Bangladesh.
Eligibility: Applicant must be U.S. citizen.
Basis for selection: Applicant must demonstrate seriousness of purpose.
Application requirements: Recommendations, transcript and research proposal.
Additional information: M.A. and Ph.D. candidates preferred.

Candidates may arrive any time during July-June academic year with approval of supervising agency. English is spoken but knowledge of Bangla helpful. Applicants enrolled in U.S. academic institutions must apply through Fulbright Program Adviser on campus. All others must request application directly from IIE by October 8.

   Number of applicants: 5
   Application deadline: October 23
   Notification begins: June 30

Contact:
Fulbright Program/USIA--U.S. Student Programs
Institute of International Education
809 United Nations Plaza
New York, NY 10017-3580
Website: www.iie.org/fulbright

Belgium and Luxembourg: Full Grant (Fulbright)

Type of award: Research grant.
Intended use: For graduate or non-degree study in Belgium/Luxembourg.
Eligibility: Applicant must be U.S. citizen.
Basis for selection: Applicant must demonstrate seriousness of purpose.
Application requirements: Recommendations, transcript and research proposal.
Additional information: U.S. students residing in Belgium and Luxembourg ineligible. French or Dutch proficiency required for Belgium. French or German proficiency required for Luxembourg. Academic year late September to mid-July. Graduating seniors cannot be placed in Luxembourg. Conservatories grant Premier Prix-Eerste Prijs to musicians passing competitive examination. In the creative and performing arts, applicants who have not earned their BA, four years of professional experience meets the basic requirement. Applicants enrolled in U.S. academic institutions must apply through Fulbright Program Adviser on campus. All others must request application directly from IIE by October 8.

   Number of awards: 5
   Application deadline: October 23
   Notification begins: June 30

Contact:
Fulbright Program/USIA--U.S. Student Programs
Institute of International Education
809 United Nations Plaza
New York, NY 10017-3580
Website: www.iie.org/fulbright

Belgium and Luxembourg: Teaching Assistantship (Fulbright)

Type of award: Scholarship.
Intended use: For non-degree study in Belgium/Luxembourg.
Eligibility: Applicant must be U.S. citizen.
Basis for selection: Applicant must demonstrate seriousness of purpose.
Application requirements: Recommendations, transcript and research proposal.
Additional information: Assistants teach approximately 12 hours per week and may take limited courses. Preference given to future teachers of French, German, or Dutch. Applicants enrolled in U.S. academic institutions must apply through Fulbright Program Adviser on campus. Applicants enrolled in U.S. academic institutions must apply through Fulbright Program Adviser on campus. All others must request application directly from IIE by October 8.

   Number of awards: 2
   Application deadline: October 23
   Notification begins: June 30

Contact:
Fulbright Program/USIA--U.S. Student Programs
Institute of International Education
809 United Nations Plaza
New York, NY 10017-3580
Website: www.iie.org/fulbright

Belgum and Luxembourg: Center for European Studies Award

Type of award: Research grant.
Intended use: For doctoral study in Belgium/Luxembourg.
Eligibility: Applicant must be U.S. citizen.
Basis for selection: Applicant must demonstrate seriousness of purpose.
Application requirements: Recommendations, transcript and research proposal.
Additional information: Available to an advanced doctoral student during the academic year 1999/2000 for research at the CEPS in Brussels. The candidate's research interests should fit into one of the principal program units at CEPS. These are: European Economic Policy, European Policies and Business Strategy, Eurpoean Union Enlargement to the East and South, European Security or Politics and Institutions. The individual should take an active part in the life of the Centre. Monthly stipend, round-trip travel, and health and accident insurance included. The Centre for European Policy Studies provides supplementary funding of BF 40,000 per month. Applicants enrolled in U.S. academic institutions must apply through Fulbright Program Adviser on campus. All others must request application directly from IIE by October 8.

   Number of awards: 1
   Application deadline: October 23
   Notification begins: June 30

Contact:
Fulbright Program/USIA--U.S. Student Programs
Institute of International Education
809 United Nations Plaza
New York, NY 10017
Website: www.iie.org/fulbright

Benin: Full Grant (Fulbright)

Type of award: Research grant.
Intended use: For graduate study in Benin.
Eligibility: Applicant must be U.S. citizen.
Basis for selection: Major/career interest in political science/government; economics; womenÖs studies; archaeology. Applicant must demonstrate seriousness of purpose.
Application requirements: Recommendations, transcript and research proposal.
Additional information: Proficiency in French required; local languages (e.g., Fon, Yoruba, Bariba, Dendi, Hausa, etc.) may also be needed depending on the area of research. Academic year: November through July. Fields of study: Political Science (democratization in Africa); economics (development, effects of fiscal policy and devaluation); sociology (women's studies);

art history; archaeology; religion (Vodun and African expressions of Christianity and Islam). The study of Vodun requires lengthy development of personal contacts within this somewhat insular cultural milieu. Living conditions for researchers tend to be harsh, on a level with or slightly above that of Peace Corps volunteers. Applicants enrolled in U.S. academic institutions must apply through Fulbright Program Adviser on campus. All others must request application directly from IIE by October 8.

Number of applicants: 7
Application deadline: October 23
Notification begins: June 30
Contact:
Fulbright Program/USIA--U.S. Student Programs
Institute of International Education
809 United Nations Plaza
New York, NY 10017-3580
Website: www.iie.org/fulbright

Bolivia: Full Grant (Fulbright)

Type of award: Research grant.
Intended use: For graduate study in Bolivia.
Eligibility: Applicant must be U.S. citizen.
Basis for selection: Applicant must demonstrate seriousness of purpose.
Application requirements: Recommendations, transcript and research proposal.
Additional information: Proficient spoken and written Spanish required at the time of application. In rural areas, basic Aymara or Quechua will be needed for effective research. Academic year: February through November. Applicants in all fields will be considered. Ample opportunities exist in the social sciences (particularly anthropology, archaeology, linguistics, social and economic history); the natural sciences; the creative and performing arts; information science; health; the environment; and rain forest ecology. Applicants enrolled in U.S. academic institutions must apply through Fulbright Program Adviser on campus. All others must request application directly from IIE by October 8.

Number of applicants: 20
Application deadline: October 23
Notification begins: June 30
Contact:
Fulbright Program/USIA--U.S. Student Programs
Institute of International Education
809 United Nations Plaza
New York, NY 10017-3580
Website: www.iie.org/fulbright

Botswana: Full Grant (Fulbright)

Type of award: Research grant.
Intended use: For graduate study in Botswana.
Eligibility: Applicant must be U.S. citizen.
Basis for selection: Applicant must demonstrate seriousness of purpose.
Application requirements: Recommendations, transcript and research proposal.
Additional information: English is the official language. Researchers may need Setswana or other local languages. Academic year, August through May. Candidates should consider affiliation with the University of Botswana or the National Institute of Research. Applicants who wish to apply for admission to study at the University of Botswana are advised that application must be made one full year before the intended date of matriculation. Candidates obtain research approval from the Office of the President prior to arrival. Research clearance can be slow; apply one year in advance. Applicants enrolled in U.S. academic institutions must apply through Fulbright Program Adviser on campus. All others must request application directly from IIE by October 8.

Number of applicants: 9
Application deadline: October 23
Notification begins: June 30
Contact:
Fulbright Program/USIA--U.S. Student Programs
Institute of International Education
809 United Nations Plaza
New York, NY 10017-3580
Website: www.iie.org/fulbright

Brazil: Full Grant (Fulbright)

Type of award: Research grant.
Intended use: For graduate study in Brazil.
Eligibility: Applicant must be U.S. citizen.
Basis for selection: Applicant must demonstrate seriousness of purpose.
Application requirements: Recommendations, transcript and research proposal.
Additional information: Proficient spoken and written Portuguese required at the time of application. Academic year March to December. Candidates must initiate contacts with host institution of preference. The Commission can assist in locating a possible affiliation. Ph.D. candidates who plan to conduct dissertation research are preferred. Candidates must be mature and able to carry out independent research. M.A. candidates and recent graduates who present serious study projects will be considered. On a very selective basis, candidates in the creative and performing arts will be considered. Field priorities are the humanities and social sciences. However, the Commission is also interested in projects in the applied sciences. Applicants enrolled in U.S. academic institutions must apply through Fulbright Program Adviser on campus. All others must request applicationfrom IIE by October 8.

Number of applicants: 68
Application deadline: October 23
Notification begins: June 30
Contact:
Fulbright Program/USIA--U.S. Student Programs
Institute of International Education
809 United Nations Plaza
New York, NY 10017-3580
Website: www.iie.org/fulbright

Bulgaria: Full Grant (Fulbright)

Type of award: Research grant.
Intended use: For graduate study in Bulgaria.
Eligibility: Applicant must be U.S. citizen.
Basis for selection: Applicant must demonstrate seriousness of purpose.
Application requirements: Recommendations, transcript and research proposal.
Additional information: Academic year October to June. Proficiency in Bulgarian desirable. Applications will be

considered in the humanities, physical sciences, social sciences, and the arts. Applications in Slavic, Balkan, and East European studies are particularly welcome. Applicants enrolled in U.S. academic institutions must apply through Fulbright Program Adviser on campus. All others must request application directly from IIE by October 8.

Number of awards:	5
Number of applicants:	7
Application deadline:	October 23
Notification begins:	June 30

Contact:
Fulbright Program/USIA--U.S. Student Programs
Institute of International Education
809 United Nations Plaza
New York, NY 10017-3580
Website: www.iie.org/fulbright

Burkina Faso: Full Grant (Fulbright)

Type of award: Research grant.
Intended use: For graduate study in Burkina Faso.
Eligibility: Applicant must be U.S. citizen.
Basis for selection: Applicant must demonstrate seriousness of purpose.
Application requirements: Recommendations, transcript and research proposal.
Additional information: Proficient French required at the time of application. Academic year: Early October through early July, brief vacations in December and March. Ph.D. candidates with M.A. degrees preferred, especially those willing to teach courses at the University of Ouagadougou. To arrange affiliation with the University of Ouagadougou, applicants contact directly: Le Directeur des Relations Exterieures, Universite de Ouagadougou, 03 BP 7201, Ouagadougou 03, Burkina Faso. Tel: (226) 30-70-64/65; Fax: (226) 30-72-42. For affiliations with other educational, cultural or social institution, applicants should contact the heads of those institutions directly. Applicants enrolled in U.S. academic institutions must apply through Fulbright Program Adviser on campus. All others must request application directly from IIE by October 8.

Number of applicants:	3
Application deadline:	October 23
Notification begins:	June 30

Contact:
Fulbright Program/USIA--U.S. Student Programs
Institute of International Education
809 United Nations Plaza
New York, NY 10017-3580
Website: www.iie.org/fulbright

Cameroon: Full Grant (Fulbright)

Type of award: Research grant.
Intended use: For graduate study in Cameroon.
Eligibility: Applicant must be U.S. citizen.
Basis for selection: Applicant must demonstrate seriousness of purpose.
Application requirements: Recommendations, transcript and research proposal.
Additional information: Working knowledge of French needed. Academic year October through July. M.A. or Ph.D. candidates preferred. However, students at all levels will be considered. Applicants enrolled in U.S. academic institutions must apply through Fulbright Program Adviser on campus. All others must request application directly from IIE by October 8.

Number of applicants:	11
Application deadline:	October 23
Notification begins:	June 30

Contact:
Fulbright Program/USIA--U.S. Student Programs
Institute of International Education
809 United Nations Plaza
New York, NY 10017-3580
Website: www.iie.org/fulbright

Canada: Full Grant (Fulbright)

Type of award: Research grant.
Intended use: For graduate study in Canada.
Eligibility: Applicant must be U.S. citizen.
Basis for selection: Applicant must demonstrate seriousness of purpose.
Application requirements: Recommendations, transcript and research proposal.
Additional information: Applications in all fields relevant to Canada or U.S.-Canadian relations considered. Priority areas include: the environment, trade, energy and resource management, constitutional studies, government regulations, native studies, technology transfer, literacy and public policy, and studies that enhance U.S.-Canadian relations. U.S. students who have been in Canada over three years not considered. French proficiency needed at francophone universities. In the creative and performing arts, applicants who have not earned their BA, four years of professional experience meets the basic requirement. One award is reserved for students in all fields from the Buffalo, NY metropolitan area. One award is reserved for students in environmental studies who study or do their research at McMaster University. One award reserved for students in sustainable economic and social development of the Red River region of the Great Northern Plains, and who study or do their research at the University of Winnipeg. Applicants enrolled in U.S. academic institutions must apply through Fulbright Program Adviser on campus. All others must request application directly from IIE by October 8.

Number of awards:	25
Number of applicants:	65
Application deadline:	October 23
Notification begins:	June 30

Contact:
Fulbright Program/USIA--U.S. Student Programs
Institute of International Education
809 United Nations Plaza
New York, NY 10017-3580
Website: www.iie.org/fulbright

Canada: Native North American Scholarship (Fulbright)

Type of award: Scholarship.
Intended use: For graduate study in Canada.
Eligibility: Applicant must be Alaskan native or American Indian. Applicant must be U.S. citizen.
Basis for selection: Applicant must demonstrate seriousness of purpose.
Application requirements: Recommendations, transcript and research proposal.
Additional information: All fields of study considered. In the

creative and performing arts, applicants who have not earned their BA, four years of professional experience meets the basic requirement. Applicants enrolled in U.S. academic institutions must apply through Fulbright Program Adviser on campus. All others must request application directly from IIE by October 8.

   Number of awards: 2
   Application deadline: October 23
   Notification begins: June 30

Contact:
Fulbright Program/USIA--U.S. Student Programs
Institute of International Education
809 United Nations Plaza
New York, NY 10017-3580
Website: www.iie.org/fulbright

Chad: Full Grant (Fulbright)

Type of award: Research grant.
Intended use: For graduate study in Chad.
Eligibility: Applicant must be U.S. citizen.
Basis for selection: Applicant must demonstrate seriousness of purpose.
Application requirements: Recommendations, transcript and research proposal.
Additional information: French proficiency needed. Familiarity with local Arabic dialect or Sara language recommended. Academic year October to June. All fields of study considered. Special opportunities exist in anthropology and public health. Applicants enrolled in U.S. academic institutions must apply through Fulbright Program Adviser on campus. All others must request application directly from IIE by October 8.

   Number of applicants: 1
   Application deadline: October 23
   Notification begins: June 30

Contact:
Fulbright Program/USIA--U.S. Student Programs
Institute of International Education
809 United Nations Plaza
New York, NY 10017-3580
Website: www.iie.org/fulbright

Chile: Full Grant (Fulbright)

Type of award: Research grant.
Intended use: For graduate study outside United States in Chile.
Eligibility: Applicant must be U.S. citizen.
Basis for selection: Applicant must demonstrate seriousness of purpose.
Application requirements: Recommendations, transcript and research proposal.
Additional information: Proficient written and spoken Spanish required at time of application. Academic year March to December. Applications from well-qualified candidates at all degree levels encouraged. Grantees should plan to work independently. M.A. and Ph.D. candidates should consider attending regular classes in a Chilean university. Recent B.A.'s are expected to enroll in university courses. Cost of tuition may be covered by research allowance provided by grant. Research facilities are not open to students as a matter of course. Applicants enrolled in U.S. academic institutions must apply through Fulbright Program Adviser on campus. All others must request application directly from IIE by October 8.

   Number of applicants: 58
   Application deadline: October 23
   Notification begins: June 30

Contact:
Fulbright Program/USIA--U.S. Student Programs
Institute of International Education
809 United Nations Plaza
New York, NY 10017-3580
Website: www.iie.org/fulbright

Colombia: Full Grant (Fulbright)

Type of award: Research grant.
Intended use: For graduate study in Colombia.
Eligibility: Applicant must be U.S. citizen.
Basis for selection: Applicant must demonstrate seriousness of purpose.
Application requirements: Recommendations, transcript and research proposal.
Additional information: Open to Ph.D. candidates who plan research on topics approved by their U.S. universities as a basis for their doctoral dissertations; Graduating seniors and graduate students who will pursue course-work at a Colombian university and whose presentation meets university requirements for admission; Graduating seniors and graduate students with solid experience in the creative and performing arts who want to study and/or conduct research in Colombian institutions or with Colombian specialists. Security considerations preclude projects dealing with drug trafficking; guerrilla movements; violence. Grant period 12 months, beginning July or January. Spanish proficiency required at time of application. Applicants enrolled in U.S. academic institutions must apply through Fulbright Program Adviser on campus. All others must request application directly from IIE by October 8.

   Number of applicants: 15
   Application deadline: October 23
   Notification begins: June 30

Contact:
Fulbright Program/USIA--U.S. Student Programs
Institute of International Education
809 United Nations Plaza
New York, NY 10017-3580
Website: www.iie.org/fulbright

Costa Rica: Full Grant (Fulbright)

Type of award: Research grant.
Intended use: For graduate study outside United States in Costa Rica.
Eligibility: Applicant must be U.S. citizen.
Basis for selection: Applicant must demonstrate seriousness of purpose.
Application requirements: Recommendations, transcript and research proposal.
Additional information: Individuals who want to earn a Costa Rican university degree will not be considered. Spanish proficiency requireded at time of application. Academic year March to November. Grant period varies for independent research. Applicants enrolled in U.S. academic institutions must apply through Fulbright Program Adviser on campus. All others must request application directly from IIE by October 8.

Number of applicants: 23
Application deadline: October 23
Notification begins: June 30
Contact:
Fulbright Program/USIA--U.S. Student Programs
Institute of International Education
809 United Nations Plaza
New York, NY 10017-3580
Website: www.iie.org/fulbright

Croatia: Full Grant (Fulbright)

Type of award: Research grant.
Intended use: For graduate study in Croatia.
Eligibility: Applicant must be U.S. citizen.
Basis for selection: Applicant must demonstrate seriousness of purpose.
Application requirements: Recommendations, transcript and research proposal.
Additional information: Ph.D. candidates are preferred. Applications accepted in all fields. However, priority given to candidates in communications; economics/business administration; history; law; political science; sociology, and ecology. Academic year October to May. Working knowledge of Croatian helpful. Applicants enrolled in U.S. academic institutions must apply through Fulbright Program Adviser on campus. All others must request application directly from IIE by October 8.
Number of awards: 4
Number of applicants: 11
Application deadline: October 23
Notification begins: June 30
Contact:
Fulbright Program/USIA--U.S. Student Programs
Institute of International Education
809 United Nations Plaza
New York, NY 10017-3580
Website: www.iie.org

Cyprus: Full Grant (Fulbright)

Type of award: Research grant.
Intended use: For doctoral study in Cyprus.
Eligibility: Applicant must be U.S. citizen.
Basis for selection: Applicant must demonstrate seriousness of purpose.
Application requirements: Recommendations, transcript and research proposal.
Additional information: Only applicants conducting research for a Ph.D. are eligible. Interdisciplinary studies and candidates in the creative and performing arts are particularly welcome. Language skills must be commensurate with project requirements. Applicants enrolled in U.S. academic institutions must apply through Fulbright Program Adviser on campus. All others must request application directly from IIE by October 8..
Number of awards: 3
Number of applicants: 6
Application deadline: October 23
Notification begins: June 30
Contact:
Fulbright Program/USIA--U.S. Student Programs
Institute of International Education
809 United Nations Plaza
New York, NY 10017-3580
Website: www.iie.org/fulbright

Czech Republic: Full Grant (Fulbright)

Type of award: Research grant.
Intended use: For graduate study outside United States in Czech Republic.
Eligibility: Applicant must be U.S. citizen.
Basis for selection: Applicant must demonstrate seriousness of purpose.
Application requirements: Recommendations, transcript and research proposal. Applicants in the arts must submit a letter of support from their prospective tutor or host institution. Research applicants must present evidence of consultation with relevant scholars in the Czech Republic with regard to the feasibility of their proposed projects and the availability of related resources. Letters of support from Czech scholars must be included in the application.
Additional information: Language skills must be commensurate with project requirements. In the creative and performing arts, applicants who have not earned their BA, four years of professional experience meets the basic requirement. Applicants enrolled in U.S. academic institutions must apply through Fulbright Program Adviser on campus. All others must request application directly from IIE by October 8.
Number of awards: 7
Number of applicants: 27
Application deadline: October 23
Notification begins: June 30
Contact:
Fulbright Program/USIA--U.S. Student Programs
Institute of International Education
809 United Nations Plaza
New York, NY 10017-3580
Website: www.iie.org/fulbright

Denmark: Aalborg University Grant (Fulbright)

Type of award: Research grant.
Intended use: For full-time doctoral study in Denmark.
Eligibility: Applicant must be U.S. citizen.
Basis for selection: Major/career interest in engineering, biomedical; medicine (m.d.); dentistry; neuroscience. Applicant must demonstrate seriousness of purpose.
Application requirements: Recommendations, transcript and research proposal.
Additional information: M.S. degree in neuroscience, biomedical engineering, medicine or dentistry required. For an American student to pursue a Danish Ph.D. degree in Biomedical Sciences and Engineering at the Center for Sensory-Motor Interaction at Aalborg University. Applicants enrolled in U.S. academic institutions must apply through Fulbright Program Adviser on campus. All others must request application directly from IIE by October 8.
Number of awards: 1
Application deadline: October 23
Notification begins: June 30
Contact:
Fulbright Program/USIA--U.S. Student Programs
Institute of International Education
809 United Nations Plaza
New York, NY 10017
Website: www.iie.org/fulbright

Denmark: Full Grant (Fulbright)

Type of award: Research grant.
Intended use: For graduate study at graduate institution outside United States in Denmark.
Eligibility: Applicant must be U.S. citizen.
Basis for selection: Applicant must demonstrate seriousness of purpose.
Application requirements: Recommendations, transcript and research proposal.
Additional information: Danish recommended, but not required. Preference will be given to Ph.D. and M.A. degree students doing research for dissertations or theses. Placement for a few graduating seniors will be possible in fields where courses are taught in English. Grants are available in all fields of study; quality will be the main selection criterion. In the creative and performing arts, applicants who have not earned their BA, four years of professional experience meets the basic requirement. Applicants enrolled in U.S. academic institutions must apply through Fulbright Program Adviser on campus. All others must request application directly from IIE by October 8.

Number of awards:	8
Number of applicants:	23
Application deadline:	October 23
Notification begins:	June 30

Contact:
Fulbright Program/USIA--U.S. Student Programs
Institute of International Education
809 United Nations Plaza
New York, NY 10017-3580
Website: www.iie.org

Dominican Republic: Full Grant (Fulbright)

Type of award: Research grant.
Intended use: For graduate study in Dominican Republic.
Eligibility: Applicant must be U.S. citizen.
Basis for selection: Applicant must demonstrate seriousness of purpose.
Application requirements: Recommendations, transcript and research proposal.
Additional information: Spanish proficiency required. Academic year August to July. Areas of interest are humanities, economics, education, history, international commerce, marketing, environmental studies, and psychology. Mathematics, physical sciences, and law not recommended. Applicants enrolled in U.S. academic institutions must apply through Fulbright Program Adviser on campus. All others must request application directly from IIE by October 8.

Number of applicants:	14
Application deadline:	October 23
Notification begins:	June 30

Contact:
Fulbright Program/USIA--U.S. Student Programs
Institute of International Education
809 United Nations Plaza
New York, NY 10017-3580
Website: www.iie.org/fulbright

Ecuador: Full Grant (Fulbright)

Type of award: Research grant.
Intended use: For graduate study outside United States in Ecuador.
Eligibility: Applicant must be U.S. citizen.
Basis for selection: Applicant must demonstrate seriousness of purpose.
Application requirements: Recommendations, transcript and research proposal.
Additional information: Proficient spoken and written Spanish is required at the time of application. Ph.D. candidates preferred. Consideration given to recent graduates and M.A. candidates who present serious study projects. Applications will be accepted in all fields, particular interest in well-qualified students in anthropology; archaeology; architecture; biology; colonial art, particularly painting, sculpture and art restoration; environmental studies; Latin American and Ecuadorian literature and history; Quechua; sociology; vulcanology. Applicants enrolled in U.S. academic institutions must apply through Fulbright Program Adviser on campus. All others must request application directly from IIE by October 8.

Number of applicants:	21
Application deadline:	October 23
Notification begins:	June 30

Contact:
Fulbright Program/USIA--U.S. Student Programs
Institute of International Education
809 United Nations Plaza
New York, NY 10017-3580
Website: www.iie.org/fulbright

Egypt: Full Grant (Fulbright)

Type of award: Research grant.
Intended use: For graduate study in Egypt.
Eligibility: Applicant must be U.S. citizen.
Basis for selection: Applicant must demonstrate seriousness of purpose.
Application requirements: Recommendations, transcript and research proposal.
Additional information: Academic year October to June. Minimum stipend includes $1,430 per month, round-trip travel, $300 per month toward housing, $300 toward books and educational materials, and insurance. Language skills must be commensurate with project requirements. Not all fieldwork is permitted. Applicants enrolled in U.S. academic institutions must apply through Fulbright Program Adviser on campus. All others must request application directly from IIE by October 8.

Number of awards:	10
Number of applicants:	41
Application deadline:	October 23
Notification begins:	June 30

Contact:
Fulbright Program/USIA--U.S. Student Programs
Institute of International Education
809 United Nations Plaza
New York, NY 10017-3580
Website: www.iie.org/fulbright

El Salvador: Full Grant (Fulbright)

Type of award: Research grant.
Intended use: For graduate study in El Salvador.

Eligibility: Applicant must be U.S. citizen.
Basis for selection: Applicant must demonstrate seriousness of purpose.
Application requirements: Recommendations, transcript and research proposal.
Additional information: Proficient spoken and written Spanish is required at the time of application. Academic year January to September. Special opportunities for applicants studying administration of justice, drug abuse and rehabilitation, international trade, political science, sociology, international trade, media, political science, sociology, women's studies, or urban planning. Applicants enrolled in U.S. academic institutions must apply through Fulbright Program Adviser on campus. All others must request application directly from IIE by October 8.
   Number of applicants: 13
   Application deadline: October 23
   Notification begins: June 30
Contact:
Fulbright Program/USIA--U.S. Student Programs
Institute of International Education
809 United Nations Plaza
New York, NY 10017-3580
Website: www.iie.org/fulbright

Eritrea: Full Grant (Fulbright)

Type of award: Research grant.
Intended use: For graduate study at graduate institution outside United States in Eritrea.
Eligibility: Applicant must be U.S. citizen.
Basis for selection: Applicant must demonstrate seriousness of purpose.
Application requirements: Recommendations, transcript and research proposal.
Additional information: Academic year September to June. Researchers expected to teach at University of Asmara. Language skills must be commensurate with project requirements. Applicants enrolled in U.S. academic institutions must apply through Fulbright Program Adviser on campus. All others must request application directly from IIE by October 8.
   Number of applicants: 6
   Application deadline: October 23
   Notification begins: June 30
Contact:
Fulbright Program/USIA--U.S. Student Programs
Institute of International Education
809 United Nations Plaza
New York, NY 10017-3580
Website: www.iie.org/fulbright

Estonia: Full Grant (Fulbright)

Type of award: Research grant.
Intended use: For graduate study outside United States in Estonia.
Eligibility: Applicant must be U.S. citizen.
Basis for selection: Applicant must demonstrate seriousness of purpose.
Application requirements: Recommendations, transcript and research proposal.
Additional information: Working knowledge of Estonian recommended. Opportunities exist for study and research in terature. Hard sciences, medical sciences and agricultural sci oriental studies. Several archives, libraries and museums available for research in history and Estonian language and literature. Hard sciences, medical sciences and agricultural sciences not recommended. Applicants enrolled in U.S. academic institutions must apply through Fulbright Program Adviser on campus. All others must request application directly from IIE by October 8.
   Number of awards: 1
   Number of applicants: 5
   Application deadline: October 23
   Notification begins: June 30
Contact:
Fulbright Program/USIA--U.S. Student Programs
Institute of International Education
809 United Nations Plaza
New York, NY 10017-3580
Website: www.iie.org/fulbright

Ethiopia: Full Grant (Fulbright)

Type of award: Research grant.
Intended use: For graduate study outside United States in Ethiopia.
Eligibility: Applicant must be U.S. citizen.
Basis for selection: Applicant must demonstrate seriousness of purpose.
Application requirements: Recommendations, transcript and research proposal.
Additional information: Amharic or another local language is essential for some research topics. English is sufficient for other topics. Ph.D. candidates preferred. Visiting student researchers are required to find and finance their own housing. Applicants enrolled in U.S. academic institutions must apply through Fulbright Program Adviser on campus. All others must request application directly from IIE by October 8.
   Number of applicants: 3
   Application deadline: October 23
   Notification begins: June 30
Contact:
Fulbright Program/USIA--U.S. Student Programs
Institute of International Education
809 United Nations Plaza
New York, NY 10017-3580
Website: www.iie.org/fulbright

European Union: Full Grant (Fulbright)

Type of award: Research grant.
Intended use: For master's, doctoral study in European Union.
Eligibility: Applicant must be U.S. citizen.
Basis for selection: Applicant must demonstrate seriousness of purpose.
Application requirements: Recommendations, transcript and research proposal.
Additional information: Awards are offered to graduate students and advanced doctoral candidates with projects that focus on the new mechanisms for supranational governance emerging within the administrative framework of the European Union. Those in European Union internship program not eligible. Language skills must be commensurate with project requirements. Applicants enrolled in U.S. academic institutions

must apply through Fulbright Program Adviser on campus. All others must request application directly from IIE by October 8..

- **Number of awards:** 2
- **Number of applicants:** 23
- **Application deadline:** October 23
- **Notification begins:** June 30

Contact:
Fulbright Program/USIA--U.S. Student Programs
Institute of International Education
809 United Nations Plaza
New York, NY 10017-3580
Website: www.iie.org/fulbright

Finland: Full Grant (Fulbright)

Type of award: Research grant.
Intended use: For graduate study outside United States in Finland.
Eligibility: Applicant must be U.S. citizen.
Basis for selection: Applicant must demonstrate seriousness of purpose.
Application requirements: Recommendations, transcript and research proposal.
Additional information: Candidates can have an M.A. degree or be graduating seniors. A working knowledge of Finnish is not required but recommended by the beginning date of the grant. Stipend 5,900 Finnish marks per month for Fulbright Fellows with an M.A. Graduating seniors, FIM 4,100 per month, free tuition and free health and accident insurance. U.S. citizens currently residing in Finland not eligible. Applicants enrolled in U.S. academic institutions must apply through Fulbright Program Adviser on campus. All others must request application directly from IIE by October 8.

- **Number of awards:** 10
- **Number of applicants:** 22
- **Application deadline:** October 23
- **Notification begins:** June 30

Contact:
Fulbright Program/USIA--U.S. Student Programs
Institute of International Education
809 United Nations Plaza
New York, NY 10017-3580
Website: www.iie.org/fulbright

France: Full Grant (Fulbright)

Type of award: Research grant.
Intended use: For graduate study at graduate institution outside United States in France.
Eligibility: Applicant must be U.S. citizen.
Basis for selection: Applicant must demonstrate seriousness of purpose.
Application requirements: Recommendations, transcript and research proposal.
Additional information: Proficient spoken and written French is required at the time of application. Language study begun after applying is considered insufficient. Latin is needed for medieval studies. Academic year October to June. Special interest in projects in business research, communications systems and applications, comparative education, comparative immigration studies, economics, future development of computer science and its applications, history, nternational relations, philosophy, pure and applied sciences, and environmental studies. Applicants enrolled in U.S. academic institutions must apply through Fulbright Program Adviser on campus. All others must request application directly from IIE by October 8.

- **Number of awards:** 20
- **Application deadline:** October 23
- **Notification begins:** June 30

Contact:
Fulbright Program/USIA--U.S. Student Programs
Institute of International Education
809 United Nations Plaza
New York, NY 10017-3580
Website: www.iie.org/fulbright

France: Government Teaching Assistantship (Fulbright)

Type of award: Internship.
Intended use: For graduate study outside United States in France.
Eligibility: Applicant must be U.S. citizen.
Basis for selection: Applicant must demonstrate seriousness of purpose.
Application requirements: Recommendations and transcript.
Additional information: Strong preference for single students under 30 planning French teaching careers. Teaching assistantship duration eight months, beginning October 1. Stipend of 5,000-6,000 francs monthly. Recipient will teach English conversation in French secondary schools, mostly in provincial centers. No travel allowance provided. Candidates not eligible for Fulbright Travel Grant. Applicants enrolled in U.S. academic institutions must apply through Fulbright Program Adviser on campus. All others must request application directly from IIE by October 8.

- **Number of awards:** 35
- **Application deadline:** October 23
- **Notification begins:** June 30

Contact:
Fulbright Program/USIA--U.S. Student Programs
Institute of International Education
809 United Nations Plaza
New York, NY 10017-3580
Website: www.iie.org/fulbright

France: Lusk Memorial Fellowship (Fulbright)

Type of award: Research grant.
Intended use: For graduate study in France.
Eligibility: Applicant must be U.S. citizen.
Basis for selection: Applicant must demonstrate seriousness of purpose.
Application requirements: Recommendations, transcript and research proposal.
Additional information: Creative and performing arts only. For applicants who have not earned their BA, four years of professional experience meets the basic requirement. Stipend includes nine months maintenance, travel, and insurance. Applicants enrolled in U.S. academic institutions must apply through Fulbright Program Adviser on campus. All others must request application directly from IIE by October 8.

Number of awards: 1
Application deadline: October 23
Notification begins: June 30
Contact:
Fulbright Program/USIA--U.S. Student Programs
Institute of International Education
809 United Nations Plaza
New York, NY 10017-3580
Website: www.iie.org/fulbright

Fulbright - USIA U.K. Zeneca Award

Type of award: Research grant.
Intended use: For graduate study outside United States in United Kingdom.
Eligibility: Applicant must be U.S. citizen.
Basis for selection: Major/career interest in engineering; physical sciences; business; economics. Applicant must demonstrate seriousness of purpose.
Application requirements: Recommendations, transcript and research proposal.
Additional information: Offers the opportunity to learn the bio-science business with special emphasis on pharmaceuticals, biotechnology and agricultural sciences, along with specialty chemicals. Preference is for candidates with undergraduate degree in one of the following fields: engineering, physical sciences, biotechnology, business or economics. Prior work experience with an industrial company, consulting firm or bank, international work experience, second language capabilities and geographical flexibility are also important. Applicants enrolled in U.S. academic institutions must apply through Fulbright Program Adviser on campus. All others must request application directly from IIE by October 8.
Number of awards: 1
Application deadline: October 23
Notification begins: June 30
Contact:
Fulbright Program/USIA--U.S. Student Programs
Institute of International Education
809 United Nations Plaza
New York, NY 10017-3580

German Academic Exchange Service Grant (Fulbright)

Type of award: Research grant.
Intended use: For graduate study in Germany.
Eligibility: Applicant must be U.S. citizen.
Basis for selection: Applicant must demonstrate seriousness of purpose.
Application requirements: Recommendations, transcript and research proposal.
Additional information: Language skills must be commensurate with project requirements. Ph.D. candidates conducting research preferred. Applicants enrolled in U.S. academic institutions must apply through Fulbright Program Adviser on campus. All others must request application directly from IIE by October 8.

Number of awards: 30
Application deadline: October 23
Notification begins: June 30
Contact:
Fulbright Program/USIA--U.S. Student Programs
Institute of International Education
809 United Nations Plaza
New York, NY 10017-3580
Website: www.iie.org/fulbright

Germanistic Society of America Quadrille Grant (Fulbright)

Type of award: Research grant.
Intended use: For graduate study outside United States in Germany.
Eligibility: Applicant must be U.S. citizen.
Basis for selection: Applicant must demonstrate seriousness of purpose.
Application requirements: Recommendations, transcript and research proposal.
Additional information: Preference given to candidates with the minimum of an M.A. degree. For graduate study and research at a German university, primarily in art history, economics and banking, German language and literature, history, international law, philosophy, political science, public affairs. Language skills must be commensurate with project requirements. Candidates selected will be considered for Fulbright Travel Grant. Applicants enrolled in U.S. academic institutions must apply through Fulbright Program Adviser on campus. All others must request application directly from IIE by October 8.
Number of awards: 4
Application deadline: October 23
Notification begins: June 30
Contact:
Fulbright Program/USIA--U.S. Student Programs
Institute of International Education
809 United Nations Plaza
New York, NY 10017-3580
Website: www.iie.org/fulbright

Germany: Bavarian State Government Grant (Fulbright)

Type of award: Research grant.
Intended use: For graduate study in Germany. Designated institutions: Universities of Augsburg, Bamberg, Bayreuth, Erlangen-Nurnberg, Munich, Passau, Regensburg and Wurzburg; the Technical University of Munich; the music academies of Munich and Wurzburg; the art academies of Munich and Nurnberg; and the Television and Film Academy of Munich.
Eligibility: Applicant must be U.S. citizen.
Basis for selection: Applicant must demonstrate seriousness of purpose and financial need.
Application requirements: Recommendations, transcript and research proposal.
Additional information: Grant period of ten months begins October 1. Monthly stipend DM 950 plus tuition. Selected candidates considered for Fulbright Travel Grant. Candidates using veteran's benefits or with adequate private funds not eligible. Language skills must be commensurate with project

requirements. Applicants enrolled in U.S. academic institutions must apply through Fulbright Program Adviser on campus. All others must request application directly from IIE by October 8.

Number of awards:	2
Application deadline:	October 23
Notification begins:	June 30

Contact:
Fulbright Program/USIA--U.S. Student Programs
Institute of International Education
809 United Nations Plaza
New York, NY 10017-3580
Website: www.iie.org/fulbright

Germany: Full Grant (Fulbright)

Type of award: Research grant.
Intended use: For graduate study in Germany.
Eligibility: Applicant must be U.S. citizen.
Basis for selection: Applicant must demonstrate seriousness of purpose.
Application requirements: Recommendations, transcript and research proposal. Composers should submit scores and recordings of the same composition. Conductors must submit video tapes and perfromance recordings.
Additional information: German proficiency required. Applications considered in all fields. Engineering, law, natural, life and environmental sciences, media and communication studies, and social sciences encouraged. Grant duration ten months beginning September. Stipend between DM 1,185-2,030. All grantees matriculated at academic institutions. Music and arts academies limit age. Auditions held for music school. Applicants enrolled in U.S. academic institutions must apply through Fulbright Program Adviser on campus. All others must request application directly from IIE by October 8.

Number of awards:	91
Application deadline:	October 23
Notification begins:	June 30

Contact:
Fulbright Program/USIA--U.S. Student Programs
Institute of International Education
809 United Nations Plaza
New York, NY 10017-3580
Website: www.iie.org/fulbright

Germany: Government Teaching Assistantship (Fulbright)

Type of award: Internship.
Intended use: For graduate study in Germany.
Eligibility: Applicant must be U.S. citizen.
Basis for selection: Applicant must demonstrate seriousness of purpose.
Application requirements: Recommendations, transcript and research proposal.
Additional information: Few opportunities exist for married candidates or persons over 30 years of age. Assist teaching German high school students approximately 12 hours weekly in English language and American studies. Strong preference for students planning a career teaching German. Language skills must be commensurate with project requirements. Stipend of DM 1,150 monthly, plus insurance and transportation. Applicants enrolled in U.S. academic institutions must apply through Fulbright Program Adviser on campus. All others must request application directly from IIE by October 8.

Number of awards:	50
Application deadline:	October 23
Notification begins:	June 30

Contact:
Fulbright Program/USIA--U.S. Student Programs
Institute of International Education
809 United Nations Plaza
New York, NY 10017-3580
Website: www.iie.org/fulbright

Germany: Travel Grant (Fulbright)

Type of award: Research grant.
Intended use: For graduate study in Germany.
Eligibility: Applicant must be U.S. citizen.
Basis for selection: Applicant must demonstrate seriousness of purpose.
Application requirements: Recommendations, transcript and research proposal.
Additional information: Grant period one academic year. If supplementing award from Institute of International Education (IIE) source, or non-IIE sources not covering travel, or personal funds, travel grants cover round-trip transportation, limited health and accident insurance, and orientation. Those who apply for but do not receive full grant also considered. German proficiency needed. Applicants enrolled in U.S. academic institutions must apply through Fulbright Program Adviser on campus. All others must request application directly from IIE by October 8.

Number of awards:	10
Application deadline:	October 23
Notification begins:	June 30

Contact:
Fulbright Program/USIA--U.S. Student Programs
Institute of International Education
809 United Nations Plaza
New York, NY 10017-3580
Website: www.iie.org/fulbright

Ghana: Full Grant (Fulbright)

Type of award: Research grant.
Intended use: For graduate study in Ghana.
Eligibility: Applicant must be U.S. citizen.
Basis for selection: Applicant must demonstrate seriousness of purpose.
Application requirements: Recommendations, transcript and research proposal.
Additional information: Academic year from October to June. University affiliation, which provides research clearance, required. Applicants should initiate the African university affiliation process and research clearance procedure at the time of filing their IIE application, since in many countries a minimum of six months lead time may be required. Field researchers may need a local language. Copies of research deposited with university. Applicants enrolled in U.S. academic institutions must apply through Fulbright Program Adviser on campus. All others must request application directly from IIE by October 8.

Number of applicants: 50
Application deadline: October 23
Notification begins: June 30
Contact:
Institute of International Education
809 United Nations Plaza
New York, NY 10017-3580
Website: www.iie.org/fulbright

Greece: European Banking Grant (Fulbright)

Type of award: Internship.
Intended use: For graduate study in Greece.
Eligibility: Applicant must be U.S. citizen.
Basis for selection: Applicant must demonstrate seriousness of purpose.
Application requirements: Recommendations, transcript and research proposal.
Additional information: Foundation plans to award a grant on an internship basis to a U.S. student to come to Athens to learn EU banking practices, EMU and Maastricht guidelines, and banking practices in a country which plans to join the EU monetary union in 1999. Applicants enrolled in U.S. academic institutions must apply through Fulbright Program Adviser on campus. All others must request application directly from IIE by October 8.
Application deadline: October 23
Notification begins: June 30
Contact:
Fulbright Program/USIA--U.S. Student Programs
Institute of International Education
809 United Nations Plaza
New York, NY 10017
Website: www.iie.org

Greece: Full Grant (Fulbright)

Type of award: Research grant.
Intended use: For graduate study outside United States in Greece.
Eligibility: Applicant must be U.S. citizen.
Basis for selection: Applicant must demonstrate seriousness of purpose.
Application requirements: Recommendations, transcript and research proposal.
Additional information: One academic year or semester. All candidates must find placements and affiliations. Candidates in classical, Byzantine and contemporary Greek studies are particularly welcome, as are applicants in the social sciences. Language skills must be commensurate with project requirements. Applications are considered from advanced graduate students, graduating seniors in all fields, and creative and performing artists who have arranged their own affiliations. In the creative and performing arts, applicants who have not earned their BA, four years of professional experience meets the basic requirement. Applicants enrolled in U.S. academic institutions must apply through Fulbright Program Adviser on campus. All others must request application directly from IIE by October 8.

Number of awards: 8
Number of applicants: 31
Application deadline: October 23
Notification begins: June 30
Contact:
Fulbright Program/USIA--U.S. Student Programs
Institute of International Education
809 United Nations Plaza
New York, NY 10017-3580
Website: www.iie.org/fulbright

Guatemala: Full Grant (Fulbright)

Type of award: Research grant.
Intended use: For graduate study outside United States in Guatemala.
Eligibility: Applicant must be U.S. citizen.
Basis for selection: Applicant must demonstrate seriousness of purpose.
Application requirements: Recommendations, transcript and research proposal.
Additional information: Proficient spoken and written Spanish required at the time of application. Academic year January through November. Grant period ten months. Starting dates are flexible. Candidates in all fields will be considered. Guatemala offers opportunities of special interest in anthropology; archaeology; fine arts; history; journalism; law; linguistics; literature; political science; sociology; women's studies. Field research may be difficult for security reasons. Applicants seeking degree from Guatemalan university not considered. Applicants enrolled in U.S. academic institutions must apply through Fulbright Program Adviser on campus. All others must request application directly from IIE by October 8.
Number of applicants: 22
Application deadline: October 23
Notification begins: June 30
Contact:
Fulbright Program/USIA--U.S. Student Programs
Institute of International Education
809 United Nations Plaza
New York, NY 10017-3580
Website: www.iie.org/fulbright

Guinea: Full Grant (Fulbright)

Type of award: Research grant.
Intended use: For graduate study in Guinea.
Eligibility: Applicant must be U.S. citizen.
Basis for selection: Applicant must demonstrate seriousness of purpose.
Application requirements: Recommendations, transcript and research proposal.
Additional information: Proficiency in French is required at the time of application. A local language may be needed for field research. Academic year October through June. Preference will be given to master's or Ph.D. candidates capable of doing independent research. Affiliation can be arranged through institutions such as the University of Conakry, the National Museum or the National Archives. Applicants should initiate the African university affiliation process and research clearance procedure at the time of filing their IIE application, since in many countries a minimum of six months lead time may be required. Special opportunities

exist in anthropology; history; linguistics (local languages); sociology; art and music. Applicants enrolled in U.S. academic institutions must apply through Fulbright Program Adviser on campus. All others must request application directly from IIE by October 8.

   Number of applicants: 2
   Application deadline: October 23
   Notification begins: June 30

Contact:
Fulbright Program/USIA--U.S. Student Programs
Institute of International Education
809 United Nations Plaza
New York, NY 10017-3580
Website: www.iie.org/fulbright

Haiti: Full Grant (Fulbright)

Type of award: Research grant.
Intended use: For graduate study in Haiti.
Eligibility: Applicant must be U.S. citizen.
Basis for selection: Applicant must demonstrate seriousness of purpose.
Application requirements: Recommendations, transcript and research proposal.
Additional information: Proficiency in French or Haitian Creole is required at the time of application. Preference will be given to Ph.D. candidates capable of doing independent research. Fieldwork in rural areas possible, but can be very difficult due to lack of infrastructure. Applicants enrolled in U.S. academic institutions must apply through Fulbright Program Adviser on campus. All others must request application directly from IIE by October 8.

   Number of applicants: 8
   Application deadline: October 23
   Notification begins: June 30

Contact:
Fulbright Program/USIA--U.S. Student Programs
Institute of International Education
809 United Nations Plaza
New York, NY 10017-3580
Website: www.iie.org/fulbright

Honduras: Full Grant (Fulbright)

Type of award: Research grant.
Intended use: For graduate study outside United States in Honduras.
Eligibility: Applicant must be U.S. citizen.
Basis for selection: Applicant must demonstrate seriousness of purpose.
Application requirements: Recommendations, transcript and research proposal.
Additional information: Proficient spoken and written Spanish required at the time of application. Academic year February to December. Preference is given to applicants who plan independent research projects related to their theses or dissertations. Honduran Institute of History and Anthropology affiliation recommended for archaeology and anthropology applicants. Applicants seeking degree from National Autonomous University of Honduras not considered. Applicants enrolled in U.S. academic institutions must apply through Fulbright Program Adviser on campus. All others must request application directly from IIE by October 8.

   Number of applicants: 5
   Application deadline: October 23
   Notification begins: June 30

Contact:
Fulbright Program/USIA--U.S. Student Programs
Institute of International Education
809 United Nations Plaza
New York, NY 10017-3580
Website: www.iie.org/fulbright

Hong Kong: Full Grant (Fulbright)

Type of award: Research grant.
Intended use: For graduate study outside United States in Hong Kong.
Eligibility: Applicant must be U.S. citizen.
Basis for selection: Applicant must demonstrate seriousness of purpose.
Application requirements: Recommendations, transcript and research proposal.
Additional information: One year minimum of Mandarin or Cantonese Chinese recommended. Applications for research related to master's theses or Ph.D. dissertations preferred. Those studying sciences, social services, and Western medicine not recommended to apply. Applicants enrolled in U.S. academic institutions must apply through Fulbright Program Adviser on campus. All others must request application directly from IIE by October 8.

   Number of applicants: 26
   Application deadline: October 23
   Notification begins: June 30

Contact:
Fulbright Program/USIA--U.S. Student Programs
Institute of International Education
809 United Nations Plaza
New York, NY 10017-3580
Website: www.iie.org/fulbright

Hungary: Government Grant (Fulbright)

Type of award: Research grant.
Intended use: For graduate study in Hungary.
Eligibility: Applicant must be U.S. citizen.
Basis for selection: Applicant must demonstrate seriousness of purpose.
Application requirements: Recommendations, transcript and research proposal.
Additional information: Grant period starts with August/September orientation. Fulbright grant provides monthly stipend and round-trip transportation. Government grant provides monthly stipend and housing allowance. Tuition waivers not available for all programs. M.A. and Ph.D. students under 30 preferred. All fields of study welcomed. Preference will be given to subjects in arts and humanities (history, literature, music, folklore, and film); social sciences as they relate to the political, social and economic changes in Hungary (political science, comparative politics); the history and culture of East Central Europe; and in the sciences (e.g., Mathematics). Some Hungarian recommended. Applicants enrolled in U.S. academic institutions must apply through Fulbright Program Adviser on campus. All others must request application directly from IIE by October 8.

Number of awards: 10
Application deadline: October 23
Notification begins: June 30
Contact:
Fulbright Program/USIA--U.S. Student Programs
Institute of International Education
809 United Nations Plaza
New York, NY 10017-3580
Website: www.iie.org/fulbright

Hungary: Teaching Assistantship (Fulbright)

Type of award: Internship.
Intended use: For master's, doctoral study outside United States in Hungary.
Eligibility: Applicant must be U.S. citizen.
Basis for selection: Applicant must demonstrate seriousness of purpose.
Application requirements: Recommendations, transcript and research proposal.
Additional information: Applicants must be articulate native-English speakers. Knowledge of Hungarian is an advantage. Nine month grant period. 12 hours teaching English, 12 hours educational advising, plus 12 hours independent study and research per week. Those studying American literature, American studies, folklore, and educational advising also eligible. Applicants enrolled in U.S. academic institutions must apply through Fulbright Program Adviser on campus. All others must request application directly from IIE by October 8.
Number of awards: 2
Application deadline: October 23
Notification begins: June 30
Contact:
Fulbright Program/USIA--U.S. Student Programs
Institute of International Education
809 United Nations Plaza
New York, NY 10017-3580
Website: www.iie.org/fulbright

Hungary: Travel Grant (Fulbright)

Type of award: Scholarship.
Intended use: For graduate study in Hungary.
Eligibility: Applicant must be U.S. citizen.
Basis for selection: Applicant must demonstrate seriousness of purpose.
Application requirements: Recommendations, transcript and research proposal.
Additional information: Supplements awards from non-IIE source not covering travel expenses, or may also supplement personal funds. Those who apply for but do not receive full grants also considered. Language skills must be commensurate with project requirements. Applicants enrolled in U.S. academic institutions must apply through Fulbright Program Adviser on campus. All others must request application directly from IIE by October 8.
Number of awards: 3
Application deadline: October 23
Notification begins: June 30
Contact:
Fulbright Program/USIA--U.S. Student Programs
Institute of International Education
809 United Nations Plaza
New York, NY 10017-3580
Website: www.iie.org/fulbright

Iceland: Full Grant (Fulbright)

Type of award: Research grant.
Intended use: For graduate or non-degree study in Iceland.
Eligibility: Applicant must be U.S. citizen.
Basis for selection: Applicant must demonstrate seriousness of purpose.
Application requirements: Recommendations, transcript and research proposal.
Additional information: Icelandic, Old Norse, or another Scandinavian language needed for study of language, literature, and social sciences. English skills sufficient for sciences and arts. Advanced graduate students preferred. Graduating seniors may apply for Icelandic language study. Old Norse, modern Icelandic, Eddic poetry, and the sagas are recommended fields of study. Applicants enrolled in U.S. academic institutions must apply through Fulbright Program Adviser on campus. All others must request application directly from IIE by October 8.
Number of awards: 4
Number of applicants: 12
Application deadline: October 23
Notification begins: June 30
Contact:
Fulbright Program/USIA--U.S. Student Programs
Institute of International Education
809 United Nations Plaza
New York, NY 10017-3580
Website: www.iie.org/fulbright

Iceland: Travel Grant-Government Grant (Fulbright)

Type of award: Scholarship.
Intended use: For non-degree study in Iceland.
Eligibility: Applicant must be U.S. citizen.
Basis for selection: Applicant must demonstrate seriousness of purpose.
Application requirements: Recommendations, transcript and research proposal.
Additional information: Travel grants supplement award from non-IIE source that does not provide travel funds, or may also be used to supplement personal funds for academic year of study. Confirmed ability to support self while abroad may be required. Applicants enrolled in U.S. academic institutions must apply through Fulbright Program Adviser on campus. All others must request application directly from IIE by October 8.
Number of awards: 1
Application deadline: October 23
Notification begins: June 30
Contact:
Fulbright Program/USIA--U.S. Student Programs
Institute of International Education
809 United Nations Plaza
New York, NY 10017-3580
Website: www.iie.org/fulbright

India: Full Grant (Fulbright)

Type of award: Research grant.
Intended use: For graduate or non-degree study in the states of Jammu and Kashmir, India outside United States in India.
Eligibility: Applicant must be U.S. citizen.
Basis for selection: Applicant must demonstrate seriousness of purpose.
Application requirements: Recommendations, transcript and

research proposal. Ph.D. candidates to indicate if archival research at the National Archives, New Delhi, or state archives will be necessary.
Additional information: All fields of study are considered. However, candidates are encouraged to apply in business administration, public administration, environment, physical sciences, astronomy and astrophysics, humanities and social sciences, and the creative and performing arts. English is generally spoken. Additional language skills may be needed. Knowledge of Hindi is especially useful. Classical or modern Indian languages, or oral use of regional language, may be needed for specific research projects. Up to four grants for graduate students who are registered for their doctoral programs, with particular emphasis on Indian economy. Research on AIDS; problems relating to border and tribal areas; sensitive political, regional and social (including some communal and religious) themes is not recommended. Grantees will receive 17,000 Rupees per month towards maintenance, housing, and an incidental and internal transportation allowance. Applicants enrolled in U.S. academic institutions must apply through Fulbright Program Advisor on campus. All others must request application directly from IIE by October 8.
    Number of awards: 13
    Application deadline: October 23
    Notification begins: June 30
Contact:
Fulbright Program/USIA--U.S. Student Programs
Institute of International Education
809 United Nations Plaza
New York, NY 10017-3580
Website: www.iie.org/fulbright

Indonesia: Full Grant (Fulbright)

Type of award: Research grant.
Intended use: For master's, doctoral or non-degree study outside United States in Indonesia.
Eligibility: Applicant must be U.S. citizen.
Basis for selection: Applicant must demonstrate seriousness of purpose.
Application requirements: Recommendations, transcript and research proposal.
Additional information: Sufficient proficiency in Indonesian to carry out the proposed study or research is required. Open to M.A. and Ph.D. candidates currently enrolled in U.S. institutions, who want to conduct degree or nondegree study at Indonesian institutions and independent graduate-level research. Special consideration is given to proposals in the fields of Islamic studies; economics; international trade; ethnic studies (not Javanese or Balinese); the environment; journalism; international law; women's studies. Candidates must enroll at university or obtain research permit. Applicants enrolled in U.S. academic institutions must apply through Fulbright Program Adviser on campus. All others must request application directly from IIE by October 8.
    Number of awards: 9
    Application deadline: October 23
    Notification begins: June 30
Contact:
Fulbright Program/USIA--U.S. Student Programs
Institute of International Education
809 United Nations Plaza
New York, NY 10017-3580
Website: www.iie.org/fulbright

Ireland: Full Grant (Fulbright)

Type of award: Research grant.
Intended use: For non-degree study outside United States in Ireland.
Eligibility: Applicant must be U.S. citizen.
Basis for selection: Applicant must demonstrate seriousness of purpose.
Application requirements: Recommendations, transcript and research proposal.
Additional information: Specific research projects may require knowledge of the Irish language or linguistic training. Applicants establish their own affiliations with relevant scholars or academic institutions. Trinity College Dublin requires researchers to pay very high fees for affiliation. Students should note that these costs are not included in the grant. Applicants enrolled in U.S. academic institutions must apply through Fulbright Program Advisor on campus. All others must request application directly from IIE by October 8.
    Number of awards: 2
    Application deadline: October 23
    Notification begins: June 30
Contact:
Fulbright Program/USIA--U.S. Student Programs
Institute of International Education
809 United Nations Plaza
New York, NY 10017-3580
Website: www.iie.org/fulbright

Israel: Full Grant (Fulbright)

Type of award: Research grant.
Intended use: For graduate or non-degree study outside United States in Israel.
Eligibility: Applicant must be U.S. citizen.
Basis for selection: Applicant must demonstrate seriousness of purpose.
Application requirements: Recommendations, transcript and research proposal.
Additional information: A working knowledge of Hebrew is not required unless it is necessary for the proposed study or research. Advanced graduate students are preferred. Outstanding graduating seniors will be considered. Applications will be considered from well-qualified candidates in all fields. Applicants with little or no previous experience in Israel also receive preference. The stipend for the full academic year, including international travel and maintenance is $13,400 to $23,950. In addition, USIEF will cover tuition for the academic year and language study fees. Applicants enrolled in U.S. academic institutions must apply through Fulbright Program Advisor on campus. All others must request application directly from IIE by October 8.
    Number of awards: 12
    Application deadline: October 23
    Notification begins: June 30
Contact:
Fulbright Program/USIA--U.S. Student Programs
Institute of International Education
809 United Nations Plaza
New York, NY 10017-3580
Website: www.iie.org/fulbright

Israel: Postdoctoral Award (Fulbright)

Type of award: Research grant.
Intended use: For postgraduate, non-degree study outside United States in Israel. Designated institutions: Tel Aviv University; Weizmann Institute of Science, Rehovot; the Technion, Haifa; Bar Ilan University, Ramat Gan; Hebrew University, Jerusalem; Ben Gurion University of the Negev, Beersheva; and University of Haifa.
Eligibility: Applicant must be U.S. citizen.
Basis for selection: Applicant must demonstrate seriousness of purpose.
Application requirements: Recommendations, transcript and research proposal. Include estimated length of research and planned arrival date.
Additional information: Grant duration 10 to 21 months, depending on satisfactory progress. Stipend ranges from $22,100 to $78,550, according to number of dependents. Ph.D. must have been completed in last two years. Preferably no previous studies or research done in Israel by applicant. Applicants enrolled in U.S. academic institutions must apply through Fulbright Program Adviser on campus. Applicants enrolled in U.S. academic institutions must apply through Fulbright Program Advisor on campus. All others must request application directly from IIE by October 8.

  Number of awards: 3
  Application deadline: October 23
  Notification begins: June 30

Contact:
Fulbright Program/USIA--U.S. Student Programs
Institute of International Education
809 United Nations Plaza
New York, NY 10017-3580
Website: www.iie.org/fulbright

Italy: Full Grant (Fulbright)

Type of award: Research grant.
Intended use: For graduate or non-degree study outside United States in Italy.
Eligibility: Applicant must be U.S. citizen.
Basis for selection: Applicant must demonstrate seriousness of purpose.
Application requirements: Recommendations, transcript and research proposal.
Additional information: All fields of study are considered. Preference is given to projects that emphasize the history, political system, government, society, and culture of modern Italy. Must have proficiency in Italian necessary to carry out the proposed project. Students in the social sciences and other fields of the humanities should have a working proficiency, usually the equivalent of about two years of college level Italian. Courtesy level Italian is desirable for the sciences and arts. Latin is required for classical, medieval, and Renaissance history and philosophy, and applicants in these fields should give evidence in their applications of Latin proficiency. In addition to Fulbright full grants, two grants with comparable benefits are offered to advanced doctoral candidates in political science, history, law, social sciences, or international relations to study at the European University Institute, Florence. Applicants enrolled in U.S. academic institutions must apply through Fulbright Program Advisor on campus. All others must request application directly from IIE by October 8.

  Number of awards: 23
  Application deadline: October 23
  Notification begins: June 30

Contact:
Fulbright Program/USIA--U.S. Student Programs
Institute of International Education
809 United Nations Plaza
New York, NY 10017-3580
Website: www.iie.org/fulbright

Italy: Miguel Vinciguerra Fund Grant (Fulbright)

Type of award: Research grant.
Intended use: For graduate or non-degree study outside United States in Italy.
Eligibility: Applicant must be U.S. citizen.
Basis for selection: Major/career interest in theater (artistic). Applicant must demonstrate seriousness of purpose.
Application requirements: Recommendations, transcript and research proposal.
Additional information: For study in the creative and performing arts. Proficient spoken and written Italian is required at the time of application. Language study begun after applying for a grant will not be considered acceptable. Applicants enrolled in U.S. academic institutions must apply through Fulbright Program Advisor on campus. All others must request application directly from IIE by October 8.

  Number of awards: 1
  Application deadline: October 23
  Notification begins: June 30

Contact:
Fulbright Program/USIA--U.S. Student Programs
Institute of International Education
809 United Nations Plaza
New York, NY 10017-3580
Website: www.iie.org/fulbright

Italy: Travel Grant (Fulbright)

Type of award: Scholarship.
Intended use: For graduate or non-degree study outside United States in Italy.
Eligibility: Applicant must be U.S. citizen.
Basis for selection: Applicant must demonstrate seriousness of purpose.
Application requirements: Recommendations, transcript and research proposal.
Additional information: Supplements awards from non-Institute of International Education source not covering travel expenses, or may also supplement personal funds. Those who apply for but do not receive full grant also considered. Language skills must be commensurate with project requirements. Applicants enrolled in U.S. academic institutions must apply through Fulbright Program Adviser on campus. All others must request application directly from IIE by October 8.

  Number of awards: 2
  Application deadline: October 23
  Notification begins: June 30

Contact:
Fulbright Program/USIA--U.S. Student Programs
Institute of International Education
809 United Nations Plaza
New York, NY 10017-3580
Website: www.iie.org/fulbright

Ivory Coast: Full Grant (Fulbright)

Type of award: Research grant.
Intended use: For graduate or non-degree study outside United States in Ivory Coast.
Eligibility: Applicant must be U.S. citizen.
Basis for selection: Applicant must demonstrate seriousness of purpose.
Application requirements: Recommendations, transcript and research proposal.
Additional information: Apart from auditing classes in the universities and institutions which require a good knowledge of French, conversational French for researchers in other fields will be helpful. Teachers/researchers do not need to speak French. Offers numerous opportunities for research in African history and civilization, arts, anthropology, business, economics, ethnosociology, humanities and culture, law and public administration, linguistics, musicology, political science, tropical agriculture and architecture. Applicants enrolled in U.S. academic institutions must apply through Fulbright Program Advisor on campus. All others must request application directly from IIE by October 8.

Number of applicants:	9
Application deadline:	October 23
Notification begins:	June 30

Contact:
Fulbright Program/USIA--U.S. Student Programs
Institute of International Education
809 United Nations Plaza
New York, NY 10017-3580
Website: www.iie.org/fulbright

Jamaica: Full Grant (Fulbright)

Type of award: Research grant.
Intended use: For graduate or non-degree study outside United States in Jamaica.
Eligibility: Applicant must be U.S. citizen.
Basis for selection: Applicant must demonstrate seriousness of purpose.
Application requirements: Recommendations, transcript and research proposal.
Additional information: English is the official language. Study in technical fields which require the use of special equipment not recommended. Applicants enrolled in U.S. academic institutions must apply through Fulbright Program Advisor on campus. All others must request application directly from IIE by October 8.

Number of applicants:	11
Application deadline:	October 23
Notification begins:	June 30

Contact:
Fulbright Program/USIA--U.S. Student Programs
Institute of International Education
809 United Nations Plaza
New York, NY 10017-3580
Website: www.iie.org/fulbright

Japan: Fellowship for Graduating Seniors (Fulbright)

Type of award: Research grant.
Intended use: For non-degree study at graduate institution in Japan.
Eligibility: Applicant must be U.S. citizen.
Basis for selection: Applicant must demonstrate seriousness of purpose.
Application requirements: Recommendations, transcript and research proposal.
Additional information: Applications will be considered from students graduating who will receive a bachelor's degree between January and August 1999. Applications will be accepted in all fields, including the creative and performing arts and natural sciences. Although those with full academic year study abroad experience to Japan are eligible, preference will be given to those with living experience in Japan of six months or less. Future career and academic objectives are also important considerations and should be mentioned in the Curriculum Vitae in the IIE application. Language skills must be commensurate with project requirements. All students will be placed in institutions outside of Tokyo. Applicants enrolled in U.S. academic institutions must apply through Fulbright Program Adviser on campus. All others must request application directly from IIE by October 8.

Number of awards:	15
Application deadline:	October 23
Notification begins:	June 30

Contact:
Fulbright Program/USIA--U.S. Student Programs
Institute of International Education
809 United Nations Plaza
New York, NY 10017-3580
Website: www.iie.org/fulbright

Japan: Full Grant (Fulbright)

Type of award: Research grant.
Intended use: For graduate or non-degree study in Japan outside United States in Japan.
Eligibility: Applicant must be U.S. citizen.
Basis for selection: Applicant must demonstrate seriousness of purpose.
Application requirements: Recommendations, transcript and research proposal. Include evidence of preliminary contacts with relevant organizations.
Additional information: Applications are accepted only in social sciences and humanities . Applications from graduate students in the creative and performing arts will not be considered under any circumstances. Open to Ph.D. dissertation research candidates and graduate students enrolled in professional schools such as law, business, journalism, international relations, and public administration. Grants primarily for academic research, may be partly used for supplementary Japanese language study, or internship to supplement research. Japanese language study or internships are unacceptable as the major purpose of, or only activity for, the grant period. Awards are renewable for a maximum of nine months for Ph.D. dissertation grantees only, subject to satisfactory justification and progress. Applicants enrolled in U.S. academic institutions must apply through Fulbright Program Advisor on campus. All others must request application directly from IIE by October 8.

Number of awards:	10
Application deadline:	October 23
Notification begins:	June 30

Contact:
Fulbright Program/USIA--U.S. Student Programs
Institute of International Education
809 United Nations Plaza
New York, NY 10017-3580
Website: www.iie.org/fulbright

Jordan: Full Grant (Fulbright)

Type of award: Research grant.
Intended use: For graduate or non-degree study outside United States in Jordan.
Eligibility: Applicant must be U.S. citizen.
Basis for selection: Applicant must demonstrate seriousness of purpose.
Application requirements: Recommendations, transcript and research proposal.
Additional information: Candidates applying to study Arabic language must have at least two years of Arabic study. Applicants may come from any field/discipline. Preference is given to candidates who are currently enrolled in a master's or doctoral program and who have a primary focus on their thesis or dissertation research rather than language study. Grantees receive a one-time allowance of $5,150 for travel to and from Jordan; visa fee; approximate five-day stay at a hotel upon arrival; excess baggage and other miscellaneous fees. One-time payment of $1,500 provided as a research allowance. Monthly maintenance allowance, $800 to $1,200. Applicants enrolled in U.S. academic institutions must apply through Fulbright Program Advisor on campus. All others must request application directly from IIE by October 8.

Number of applicants:	25
Application deadline:	October 23
Notification begins:	June 30

Contact:
Fulbright Program/USIA--U.S. Student Programs
Institute of International Education
809 United Nations Plaza
New York, NY 10017-3580
Website: www.iie.org/fulbright

Kenya: Full Grant (Fulbright)

Type of award: Research grant.
Intended use: For graduate or non-degree study outside United States in Kenya.
Eligibility: Applicant must be U.S. citizen.
Basis for selection: Applicant must demonstrate seriousness of purpose.
Application requirements: Recommendations, transcript and research proposal.
Additional information: Academic year varies among institutions, often from year to year. Kiswahili proficiency useful outside Nairobi and needed by students of local languages. Travel and research grants to be applied for at same time as grant. Nonrefundable $500 fee for research permit. Applicants enrolled in U.S. academic institutions must apply through Fulbright Program Adviser on campus. Applicants enrolled in U.S. academic institutions must apply through Fulbright Program Adviser on campus. All others must request application directly from IIE by October 8.

Number of applicants:	27
Application deadline:	October 23
Notification begins:	June 30

Contact:
Fulbright Program/USIA--U.S. Student Programs
Institute of International Education
809 United Nations Plaza
New York, NY 10017-3580
Website: www.iie.org/fulbright

Korea: Full Grant (Fulbright)

Type of award: Research grant.
Intended use: For graduate or non-degree study outside United States in Korea.
Eligibility: Applicant must be single. Applicant must be U.S. citizen.
Basis for selection: Applicant must demonstrate depth of character and seriousness of purpose.
Application requirements: Recommendations, transcript and research proposal.
Additional information: Open to recent college graduates for Korean language study and/or independent study/research related to career objectives; young professionals and/or graduate students currently enrolled in, or recently graduated from, a master's level program (including those offered by professional schools), for study/research/internships related to their programs; and, Ph.D. candidates, especially those intending to pursue a career in Korean studies. Applicants enrolled in U.S. academic institutions must apply through Fulbright Program Advisor on campus. All others must request application directly from IIE by October 8.

Number of awards:	8
Application deadline:	October 23
Notification begins:	June 30

Contact:
Fulbright Program/USIA--U.S. Student Programs
Institute of International Education
809 United Nations Plaza
New York, NY 10017-3580
Website: www.iie.org/fulbright

Korea: Teaching Assistantship (Fulbright)

Type of award: Internship, renewable.
Intended use: For non-degree study outside United States in Korea.
Eligibility: Applicant must be single. Applicant must be U.S. citizen.
Basis for selection: Major/career interest in English as a second language. Applicant must demonstrate seriousness of purpose.
Application requirements: Recommendations, transcript and research proposal.
Additional information: No placements in Seoul. One year assistantship, renewals up to two years possible. Stipend approximately $1,000, plus travel and orientation fees. Teach conversational English, approximately 20 hours weekly, to middle and high school students. Independent study/research encouraged. Knowledge of Korean language unnecessary. Applicants enrolled in U.S. academic institutions must apply through Fulbright Program Adviser on campus. All others must request application directly from IIE by October 8.

Number of awards:	30
Application deadline:	October 23
Notification begins:	June 30

Contact:
Fulbright Program/USIA--U.S. Student Programs
Institute of International Education
809 United Nations Plaza
New York, NY 10017-3580
Website: www.iie.org/fulbright

Korea: Travel Grant (Fulbright)

Type of award: Scholarship.
Intended use: For graduate or non-degree study outside United States in Korea.
Eligibility: Applicant must be U.S. citizen.
Basis for selection: Applicant must demonstrate seriousness of purpose.
Application requirements: Recommendations, transcript and research proposal.
Additional information: Supplements awards from non-Institute of International Education source not covering travel expenses, or may also supplement personal funds. Those who apply for but do not receive full grant also considered. Language skills must be commensurate with project requirements. Applicants enrolled in U.S. academic institutions must apply through Fulbright Program Adviser on campus. All others must request application directly from IIE by October 8.

Number of awards:	2
Application deadline:	October 23
Notification begins:	June 30

Contact:
Fulbright Program/USIA--U.S. Student Programs
Institute of International Education
809 United Nations Plaza
New York, NY 10017-3580
Website: www.iie.org/fulbright

Kuwait: Full Grant (Fulbright)

Type of award: Research grant.
Intended use: For non-degree study outside United States in Kuwait.
Eligibility: Applicant must be U.S. citizen.
Basis for selection: Applicant must demonstrate seriousness of purpose.
Application requirements: Recommendations, transcript and research proposal.
Additional information: Arabic is required at the proficiency level needed for the proposed research. It is strongly recommended that candidates who want to study Arabic in Kuwait already have a minimum of two years of prior Arabic study at a recognized institution. All fields of study are considered. Candidates who are not proficient in Arabic should be aware that English language offerings are limited. These candidates should attempt an interdisciplinary program. Compared to U.S. standards, opportunities for social life outside the university are limited, particularly for women. Kuwaiti institutions typically do not authorize spouses or families to accompany students. Applicants enrolled in U.S. academic institutions must apply through Fulbright Program Advisor on campus. All others must request application directly from IIE by October 8.

Number of awards:	6
Application deadline:	October 23
Notification begins:	June 30

Contact:
Fulbright Program/USIA--U.S. Student Programs
Institute of International Education
809 United Nations Plaza
New York, NY 10017-3580
Website: www.iie.org/fulbright

Latvia: Full Grant (Fulbright)

Type of award: Research grant.
Intended use: For graduate or non-degree study outside United States in Latvia.
Eligibility: Applicant must be U.S. citizen.
Basis for selection: Applicant must demonstrate seriousness of purpose.
Application requirements: Recommendations, transcript and research proposal.
Additional information: A working knowledge of Latvian is recommended. Independent scholars may not need to have Latvian language skills, but students enrolled in Latvian institutions need to be able to follow lectures. Supervision by English-speaking professors is available. Applicants enrolled in U.S. academic institutions must apply through Fulbright Program Adviser on campus. All others must request application directly from IIE by October 8.

Number of awards:	2
Number of applicants:	9
Application deadline:	October 23
Notification begins:	June 30

Contact:
Fulbright Program/USIA--U.S. Student Programs
Institute of International Education
809 United Nations Plaza
New York, NY 10017-3580
Website: www.iie.org/fulbright

Lithuania: Full Grant (Fulbright)

Type of award: Research grant.
Intended use: For graduate or non-degree study outside United States in Lithuania.
Eligibility: Applicant must be U.S. citizen.
Basis for selection: Applicant must demonstrate seriousness of purpose.
Application requirements: Recommendations, transcript and research proposal.
Additional information: Graduating seniors are preferred. Lectures at the university level are in both Lithuanian and English. A working knowledge of Lithuanian is helpful, but not required. Knowledge of Russian, Polish or German may be helpful. Preference is given to research which addresses issues significant to contemporary Lithuania, especially to applicants in the arts, humanities, social and technical sciences. Applicants enrolled in U.S. academic institutions must apply through Fulbright Program Adviser on campus. All others must request application directly from IIE by October 8.

Number of awards: 4
Number of applicants: 27
Application deadline: October 23
Notification begins: June 30
Contact:
Fulbright Program/USIA--U.S. Student Programs
Institute of International Education
809 United Nations Plaza
New York, NY 10017-3580
Website: www.iie.org/fulbright

Madagascar: Full Grant (Fulbright)

Type of award: Research grant.
Intended use: For graduate or non-degree study outside United States in Madagascar.
Eligibility: Applicant must be U.S. citizen.
Basis for selection: Applicant must demonstrate seriousness of purpose.
Application requirements: Recommendations, transcript and research proposal.
Additional information: Proficiency in French is required at the time of application. A working knowledge of spoken Malagasy is needed by anyone planning anthropological, historical, ethnological, or other field research. Archival research requires reading Malagasy. French is not often spoken in rural areas. Ph.D. candidates conducting doctoral research who can work independently are preferred. Applicants enrolled in U.S. academic institutions must apply through Fulbright Program Adviser on campus. All others must request application directly from IIE by October 8.
Number of applicants: 6
Application deadline: October 23
Notification begins: June 30
Contact:
Fulbright Program/USIA--U.S. Student Programs
Institute of International Education
809 United Nations Plaza
New York, NY 10017-3580
Website: www.iie.org/fulbright

Malawi: Full Grant (Fulbright)

Type of award: Research grant.
Intended use: For graduate or non-degree study outside United States in Malawi.
Eligibility: Applicant must be U.S. citizen.
Basis for selection: Applicant must demonstrate seriousness of purpose.
Application requirements: Recommendations, transcript and research proposal. Indicate how research will directly benefit Malawi.
Additional information: English is the official language. Applicants at all academic levels will be considered, but graduating seniors are preferred. Special opportunities exist in agriculture and livestock. Applicants enrolled in U.S. academic institutions must apply through Fulbright Program Advisor on campus. All others must request application directly from IIE by October 8.

Number of applicants: 9
Application deadline: October 23
Notification begins: June 30
Contact:
Fulbright Program/USIA--U.S. Student Programs
Institute of International Education
809 United Nations Plaza
New York, NY 10017-3580
Website: www.iie.org/fulbright

Malaysia: Full Grant (Fulbright)

Type of award: Research grant.
Intended use: For graduate or non-degree study outside United States in Malaysia.
Eligibility: Applicant must be U.S. citizen.
Basis for selection: Applicant must demonstrate seriousness of purpose.
Application requirements: Recommendations, transcript and research proposal.
Additional information: Ph.D. candidates pursuing dissertation projects and those currently enrolled in master's degree or other graduate level programs are given preference in selection. English is the language of instruction for graduate level studies in Malaysian universities and is widely spoken within the academic context. Nevertheless, the language of undergraduate instruction at all major Malaysian universities is Malay. Applicants enrolled in U.S. academic institutions must apply through Fulbright Program Adviser on campus. All others must request application directly from IIE by October 8.
Number of awards: 2
Application deadline: October 23
Notification begins: June 30
Contact:
Fulbright Program/USIA--U.S. Student Programs
Institute of International Education
809 United Nations Plaza
New York, NY 10017-3580
Website: www.iie.org/fulbright

Mali: Full Grant (Fulbright)

Type of award: Research grant.
Intended use: For graduate or non-degree study outside United States in Mali.
Eligibility: Applicant must be U.S. citizen.
Basis for selection: Major/career interest in history; linguistics; archaeology. Applicant must demonstrate seriousness of purpose.
Application requirements: Recommendations, transcript and research proposal.
Additional information: Proficiency in written and spoken French is required at the time of application. Applications will be considered from well-qualified candidates in all fields in which relevant research can be carried out in Mali. There are many opportunities for historical, linguistic, archeological, and ethnographic research. Applicants enrolled in U.S. academic institutions must apply through Fulbright Program Adviser on campus. All others must request application directly from IIE by October 8.

Number of applicants:	6
Application deadline:	October 23
Notification begins:	June 30

Contact:
Fulbright Program/USIA--U.S. Student Programs
Institute of International Education
809 United Nations Plaza
New York, NY 10017-3580
Website: www.iie.org/fulbright

Mauritius: Full Grant (Fulbright)

Type of award: Research grant.
Intended use: For graduate or non-degree study outside United States in Mauritius.
Eligibility: Applicant must be U.S. citizen.
Basis for selection: Applicant must demonstrate seriousness of purpose.
Application requirements: Recommendations, transcript and research proposal.
Additional information: English is the official national language, principal language of instruction, and the only language needed for research on most contemporary topics. However, a working knowledge of French is useful. French is needed to conduct historical research. Creole is useful for field studies. Preference is given to projects that directly support Mauritius and/or enhance Mauritian-U.S. relations. Applicants enrolled in U.S. academic institutions must apply through Fulbright Program Adviser on campus. All others must request application directly from IIE by October 8.

Number of applicants:	6
Application deadline:	October 23
Notification begins:	June 30

Contact:
Fulbright Program/USIA--U.S. Student Programs
Institute of International Education
809 United Nations Plaza
New York, NY 10017-3580
Website: www.iie.org/fulbright

Mexico: Binational Business Grants (Fulbright)

Type of award: Research grant.
Intended use: For graduate study in Mexico.
Eligibility: Applicant must be U.S. citizen.
Basis for selection: Major/career interest in business; accounting; engineering; economics; international relations; business, international; law. Applicant must demonstrate seriousness of purpose.
Application requirements: Recommendations, transcript and research proposal.
Additional information: Proficient spoken and written Spanish is required at the time of application. Candidates must have a B.S. in business, accounting, engineering, economics and/or an MBA or MS in international business administration, international relations, engineering, economics, or a law degree from a U.S. university. Work experience is desirable. Applicants who are currently living in Mexico are discouraged from applying for all programs to Mexico. Applicants enrolled in U.S. academic institutions must apply through Fulbright Program Adviser on campus. All others must request application directly from IIE by October 8.

Number of awards:	12
Application deadline:	October 23
Notification begins:	June 30

Contact:
Fulbright Program/USIA--U.S. Student Programs
Institute of International Education
809 United Nations Plaza
New York, NY 10017-3580
Website: www.iie.org/fulbright

Mexico: Garcia Robles Grant (Fulbright)

Type of award: Research grant.
Intended use: For master's, doctoral or non-degree study outside United States in Mexico.
Eligibility: Applicant must be U.S. citizen.
Basis for selection: Applicant must demonstrate seriousness of purpose.
Application requirements: Recommendations, transcript and research proposal.
Additional information: Proficient spoken and written Spanish is required at the time of application. Candidates at all degree levels will be considered, but preference is given to M.A. and Ph.D. candidates with a 3.5 GPA. M.A. and Ph.D. applicants must present a thesis proposal approved by their U.S. university. Open to all fields in the social sciences and humanities, with preference for public policy, public administration, national business, international trade, international relations, education, environment, public health, demography, migration (domestic and international), criminology in an international environment, arts, arts administration and crafts. Medicine, odontology not recommended. Applicants enrolled in U.S. academic institutions must apply through Fulbright Program Adviser on campus. All others must request application directly from IIE by October 8.

Number of awards:	20
Number of applicants:	160
Application deadline:	October 23
Notification begins:	June 30

Contact:
Fulbright Program/USIA--U.S. Student Programs
Institute of International Education
809 United Nations Plaza
New York, NY 10017-3580
Website: www.iie.org/fulbright

Morocco: Full Grant (Fulbright)

Type of award: Research grant.
Intended use: For undergraduate, non-degree study outside United States in Morocco.
Eligibility: Applicant must be U.S. citizen.
Basis for selection: Applicant must demonstrate seriousness of purpose.
Application requirements: Recommendations, transcript and research proposal. Copy of research proposal in Arabic and/or French.
Additional information: Candidate must have either intermediate proficiency in Modern Standard Arabic (MSA) or spoken Moroccan Arabic (which differs considerably from MSA), or fluency in French. Applications will be considered

from well-qualified students in all fields related to Morocco. In addition to topics relating to social sciences and humanities, Morocco offers a range of fascinating topics relating to economics and commercial development, agriculture and other sciences. Applicants enrolled in U.S. academic institutions must apply through Fulbright Program Adviser on campus. All others must request application directly from IIE by October 8.
- **Number of awards:** 9
- **Application deadline:** October 23
- **Notification begins:** June 30

Contact:
Fulbright Program/USIA--U.S. Student Programs
Institute of International Education
809 United Nations Plaza
New York, NY 10017-3580
Website: www.iie.org/fulbright

Mozambique: Full Grant (Fulbright)

Type of award: Research grant.
Intended use: For graduate or non-degree study outside United States in Mozambique.
Eligibility: Applicant must be U.S. citizen.
Basis for selection: Applicant must demonstrate seriousness of purpose.
Application requirements: Recommendations, transcript and research proposal.
Additional information: A working knowledge of Portuguese is necessary. A knowledge of local languages (Macua, Changana, Makonde, Chuabo, Ndau) is useful for field study. Applicants at the graduate level or those who are professionals in a field are preferred. Social sciences, history, economics, and teaching of English as a second language. Other fields are possible depending on the grantee's level of Portuguese. Applicants enrolled in U.S. academic institutions must apply through Fulbright Program Adviser on campus. All others must request application directly from IIE by October 8.
- **Number of applicants:** 6
- **Application deadline:** October 23
- **Notification begins:** June 30

Contact:
Fulbright Program/USIA--U.S. Student Programs
Institute of International Education
809 United Nations Plaza
New York, NY 10017-3580
Website: www.iie.org/fulbright

Namibia: Full Grant (Fulbright)

Type of award: Research grant.
Intended use: For graduate or non-degree study outside United States in Namibia.
Eligibility: Applicant must be U.S. citizen.
Basis for selection: Applicant must demonstrate seriousness of purpose.
Application requirements: Recommendations, transcript and research proposal.
Additional information: Academic year February to December. University instruction in English. Research clearance required. Preference will be given to projects in media studies, business, community health, agriculture, water resource management and physics. Applicants enrolled in U.S. academic institutions must apply through Fulbright Program Adviser on campus. All others must request application directly from IIE by October 8.
- **Number of applicants:** 7
- **Application deadline:** October 23
- **Notification begins:** April 1

Contact:
Fulbright Program/USIA--U.S. Student Programs
Institute of International Education
809 United Nations Plaza
New York, NY 10017-3580
Website: www.iie.org/fulbright

Nepal: Full Grant (Fulbright)

Type of award: Research grant.
Intended use: For graduate or non-degree study outside United States in Nepal.
Eligibility: Applicant must be U.S. citizen.
Basis for selection: Applicant must demonstrate seriousness of purpose.
Application requirements: Recommendations, transcript and research proposal.
Additional information: Difficult living conditions. Grant period ten months, preferably beginning mid-September or early February. Nepali proficiency important for most research projects. Grantees do not take university classes and should affiliate with department or research center. Applicants enrolled in U.S. academic institutions must apply through Fulbright Program Adviser on campus. All others must request application directly from IIE by October 8.
- **Number of awards:** 5
- **Application deadline:** October 23
- **Notification begins:** June 30

Contact:
Fulbright Program/USIA--U.S. Student Programs
Institute of International Education
809 United Nations Plaza
New York, NY 10017-3580
Website: www.iie.org/fulbright

Netherlands: America Foundation Grant (Fulbright)

Type of award: Research grant.
Intended use: For graduate study outside United States in Netherlands.
Eligibility: Applicant must be U.S. citizen.
Basis for selection: Applicant must demonstrate seriousness of purpose.
Application requirements: Recommendations, transcript and research proposal.
Additional information: Candidates at all levels considered. Open to all academic fields of study, and projects in all disciplines in the creative and performing arts, will be considered with the understanding that the educational and cultural resources for the desired field of study are uniquely available in the Netherlands. Applicants enrolled in U.S. academic institutions must apply through Fulbright Program Adviser on campus. All others must request application directly from IIE by October 8.

Number of awards:	9
Application deadline:	October 23
Notification begins:	June 30

Contact:
Fulbright Program/USIA--U.S. Student Programs
Institute of International Education
809 United Nations Plaza
New York, NY 10017-3580
Website: www.iie.org/fulbright

Netherlands: Full Grant (Fulbright)

Type of award: Research grant.
Intended use: For master's, doctoral or non-degree study outside United States in Netherlands.
Eligibility: Applicant must be U.S. citizen.
Basis for selection: Applicant must demonstrate seriousness of purpose.
Application requirements: Recommendations, transcript and research proposal. Proof of acceptance from academic institution or letters of affiliation from appropriate Dutch specialists.
Additional information: Applications will be considered from well-qualified candidates in all fields if projects can be carried out in Dutch institutions of higher learning or by using Dutch archival sources. Applications in the humanities, arts and social sciences are particularly encouraged. A working knowledge of Dutch is useful at the time of arrival in the Netherlands. Applicants enrolled in U.S. academic institutions must apply through Fulbright Program Adviser on campus. All others must request application directly from IIE by October 8.

Number of awards:	11
Number of applicants:	92
Application deadline:	October 23
Notification begins:	June 30

Contact:
Fulbright Program/USIA--U.S. Student Programs
Institute of International Education
809 United Nations Plaza
New York, NY 10017-3580
Website: www.iie.org/fulbright

New Zealand: Full Grant (Fulbright)

Type of award: Research grant.
Intended use: For graduate or non-degree study outside United States in New Zealand.
Eligibility: Applicant must be U.S. citizen.
Basis for selection: Applicant must demonstrate seriousness of purpose.
Application requirements: Recommendations, transcript and research proposal.
Additional information: Applications will be considered from well-qualified applicants in all fields of study. Especially proposals that emphasize New Zealand or comparative studies with the U.S., i.e., in the fields of literature, education, political science and history. In addition, New Zealand is particularly strong in the geological and biological sciences, tourism and recreation management, resource management, public policy and public management. Familiarity with Maori may be needed. Applicants enrolled in U.S. academic institutions must apply through Fulbright Program Adviser on campus. All

Number of awards:	10
Number of applicants:	84
Application deadline:	October 23
Notification begins:	June 30

Contact:
Fulbright Program/USIA--U.S. Student Programs
Institute of International Education
809 United Nations Plaza
New York, NY 10017-3580
Website: www.iie.org/fulbright

Nicaragua: Full Grant (Fulbright)

Type of award: Research grant.
Intended use: For non-degree study outside United States in Nicaragua. Designated institutions: Sixteen total. See U.S. Student Program for 1998-99.
Eligibility: Applicant must be U.S. citizen.
Basis for selection: Major/career interest in history; political science/government; anthropology; archaeology; natural resources/conservation. Applicant must demonstrate seriousness of purpose.
Application requirements: Recommendations, transcript and research proposal.
Additional information: Proficient written and spoken Spanish is required at the time of application. Opportunities exist in research in socio-educational issues, Latin American literature, gender issues, ecology, archaeology and anthropology. Applicants enrolled in U.S. academic institutions must apply through Fulbright Program Adviser on campus. All others must request application directly from IIE by October 8.

Number of applicants:	13
Application deadline:	October 23
Notification begins:	June 30

Contact:
Fulbright Program/USIA--U.S. Student Programs
Institute of International Education
809 United Nations Plaza
New York, NY 10017-3580
Website: www.iie.org/fulbright

Niger: Full Grant (Fulbright)

Type of award: Research grant.
Intended use: For graduate or non-degree study outside United States in Niger.
Eligibility: Applicant must be U.S. citizen.
Basis for selection: Applicant must demonstrate seriousness of purpose.
Application requirements: Recommendations, transcript and research proposal.
Additional information: Academic year October/November to June/July. French proficiency needed. Hausa or another local language useful. Some localities restricted from research. Candidates required to provide synopsis of their proposals in French with their application. Applicants enrolled in U.S. academic institutions must apply through Fulbright Program Adviser on campus. All others must request application directly from IIE by October 8.

Number of applicants:	1

Contact:
Fulbright Program/USIA--U.S. Student Programs
Institute of International Education
809 United Nations Plaza
New York, NY 10017-3580
Website: www.iie.org/fulbright

Nigeria: Full Grant (Fulbright)

Type of award: Research grant.
Intended use: For graduate or non-degree study outside United States in Nigeria.
Eligibility: Applicant must be U.S. citizen.
Basis for selection: Applicant must demonstrate seriousness of purpose.
Application requirements: Recommendations, transcript and research proposal. Language skills commensurate with project requirements. Application to include confirmation that a Nigerian faculty member will sponsor university research, and that necessary office, studio or lab space will be available, plus written consent from university vice chancellor.
Additional information: Academic year October to November. Dates may vary by year and university and are subject to change without notice. Knowledge of local languages strongly recommended. Fellows affiliate with a university department and serve up to 50% of time as graduate assistants. High political sensitivity to research proposals. Severe logistical difficulties. Applicants enrolled in U.S. academic institutions must apply through Fulbright Program Adviser on campus. All others must request application directly from IIE by October 8.
   Number of applicants: 5
   Application deadline: October 23
   Notification begins: June 30
Contact:
Fulbright Program/USIA--U.S. Student Programs
Institute of International Education
809 United Nations Plaza
New York, NY 10017-3580
Website: www.iie.org/fulbright

Norway: Full Grant (Fulbright)

Type of award: Research grant.
Intended use: For master's, doctoral study outside United States in Norway.
Eligibility: Applicant must be U.S. citizen.
Basis for selection: Applicant must demonstrate seriousness of purpose.
Application requirements: Recommendations, transcript and research proposal.
Additional information: Academic year and grant period September to June. Knowledge of Norwegian recommended. Candidates can apply directly to their Norwegian institution of choice or the Foundation can help to expedite applications. Public universities and colleges generally do not charge tuition. Application deadline is February 1. Applicants enrolled in U.S. academic institutions must apply through Fulbright Program Adviser on campus. All others must request application directly from IIE by October 8.
   Number of awards: 9
   Application deadline: October 23
   Notification begins: June 30
Contact:
Fulbright Program/USIA--U.S. Student Programs
Institute of International Education
809 United Nations Plaza
New York, NY 10017-3580
Website: www.iie.org/fulbright

Oman: Full Grant (Fulbright)

Type of award: Research grant.
Intended use: For graduate study outside United States in Oman.
Eligibility: Applicant must be U.S. citizen.
Basis for selection: Applicant must demonstrate seriousness of purpose.
Application requirements: Recommendations, transcript and research proposal.
Additional information: Language skills must be commensurate with project requirements. Ph.D. candidates preferred. Projects in social sciences and humanities require approval from other ministries. Applicants enrolled in U.S. academic institutions must apply through Fulbright Program Adviser on campus. All others must request application directly from IIE by October 8.
   Number of applicants: 3
   Application deadline: October 23
   Notification begins: June 30
Contact:
Fulbright Program/USIA--U.S. Student Programs
Institute of International Education
809 United Nations Plaza
New York, NY 10017-3580
Website: www.iie.org/fulbright

Pakistan: Full Grant (Fulbright)

Type of award: Research grant.
Intended use: For graduate or non-degree study outside United States in Pakistan.
Eligibility: Applicant must be U.S. citizen.
Basis for selection: Applicant must demonstrate seriousness of purpose.
Application requirements: Recommendations, transcript and research proposal.
Additional information: Applications from candidates at all degree levels are encouraged. English is the official language. Knowledge of a local language may be needed. Affiliations arranged for all. Additional nine-month grant available for half-time internship as student adviser for students/researchers. Applicants enrolled in U.S. academic institutions must apply through Fulbright Program Adviser on campus. All others must request application directly from IIE by October 8.
   Number of awards: 5
   Number of applicants: 16
   Application deadline: October 23
   Notification begins: June 30
Contact:
Fulbright Program/USIA--U.S. Student Programs
Institute of International Education
809 United Nations Plaza
New York, NY 10017-3580
Website: www.iie.org/fulbright

Panama: Full Grant (Fulbright)

Type of award: Research grant.
Intended use: For graduate or non-degree study outside United States in Panama.
Eligibility: Applicant must be U.S. citizen.
Basis for selection: Applicant must demonstrate seriousness of purpose.

Application requirements: Recommendations, transcript and research proposal.
Additional information: Proficient spoken and written Spanish is required at the time of application. All applicants who present serious study or research projects and who can work independently are considered. Independent research projects are preferred. Research in physics not recommended. Applicants enrolled in U.S. academic institutions must apply through Fulbright Program Adviser on campus. All others must request application directly from IIE by October 8.
   Number of applicants: 9
   Application deadline: October 23
   Notification begins: June 30
Contact:
Fulbright Program/USIA--U.S. Student Programs
Institute of International Education
809 United Nations Plaza
New York, NY 10017-3580
Website: www.iie.org/fulbright

Paraguay: Full Grant (Fulbright)

Type of award: Research grant.
Intended use: For graduate or non-degree study outside United States in Paraguay.
Eligibility: Applicant must be U.S. citizen.
Basis for selection: Applicant must demonstrate seriousness of purpose.
Application requirements: Recommendations, transcript and research proposal.
Additional information: Proficient spoken and written Spanish is required at the time of application. Knowledge of Guarani is extremely helpful for research outside of Asuncion. Advanced graduate students working on doctoral dissertations are preferred. Recent graduates and M.A. candidates who present serious study projects and can work independently will be considered also. Candidates are encouraged to contact local sponsors before submitting applications. Applicants enrolled in U.S. academic institutions must apply through Fulbright Program Adviser on campus. All others must request application directly from IIE by October 8.
   Number of applicants: 3
   Application deadline: October 23
   Notification begins: June 30
Contact:
Fulbright Program/USIA--U.S. Student Programs
Institute of International Education
809 United Nations Plaza
New York, NY 10017-3580
Website: www.iie.org/fulbright

Peru: Full Grant (Fulbright)

Type of award: Research grant.
Intended use: For graduate or non-degree study outside United States in Peru.
Eligibility: Applicant must be U.S. citizen.
Basis for selection: Applicant must demonstrate seriousness of purpose.
Application requirements: Recommendations, transcript and research proposal.
Additional information: Academic year March to December. Grant period typically 12 months, beginning in August. Spanish proficiency recommended. Open to all fields of study. Candidates at all levels will be considered, with preference for recent graduates without extensive overseas experience. Grantees may conduct independent research, take university courses, or work as interns. Grantees are requested to give talks at universities and cultural organizations on topics in their fields. Border disputes, drug trade and delinquency are considered sensitive issues. The Commission does not approve grants to work in zones declared "emergency zones" by the Peruvian government. Affiliations needed. Research permits may be necessary. Applicants enrolled in U.S. academic institutions must apply through Fulbright Program Adviser on campus. All others must request application directly from IIE by October 8.
   Number of applicants: 49
   Application deadline: October 23
   Notification begins: June 30
Contact:
Fulbright Program/USIA--U.S. Student Programs
Institute of International Education
809 United Nations Plaza
New York, NY 10017-3580
Website: www.iie.org/fulbright

Philippines: Full Grant (Fulbright)

Type of award: Research grant.
Intended use: For graduate or non-degree study outside United States in Philippines.
Eligibility: Applicant must be U.S. citizen.
Basis for selection: Applicant must demonstrate seriousness of purpose.
Application requirements: Recommendations, transcript and research proposal.
Additional information: English is spoken throughout the country. Although not required, knowledge of Tagalog is useful. Doctoral candidates undertaking dissertation research are preferred, students pursuing master's degree projects and graduating seniors will be considered. Study in the fields of Philippine studies, including language and literature, history, government, culture, arts and humanities and education are preferred. Applicants enrolled in U.S. academic institutions must apply through Fulbright Program Adviser on campus. All others must request application directly from IIE by October 8.
   Number of awards: 10
   Number of applicants: 33
   Application deadline: October 23
   Notification begins: June 30
Contact:
Fulbright Program/USIA--U.S. Student Programs
Institute of International Education
809 United Nations Plaza
New York, NY 10017-3580
Website: www.iie.org/fulbright

Poland: Government Grant (Fulbright)

Type of award: Research grant.
Intended use: For graduate or non-degree study outside United States in Poland.
Eligibility: Applicant must be U.S. citizen.
Basis for selection: Applicant must demonstrate seriousness of purpose.

Application requirements: Recommendations, transcript and research proposal. List acceptable institutional placements.
Additional information: Academic year October to June. Grant period one academic year. Stipend approximately $350 monthly. Institutional affiliation required. Classroom attendance may be required. Lodz Film School students enroll in 3-year program; complete funding not possible. Applicants enrolled in U.S. academic institutions must apply through Fulbright Program Adviser on campus. All others must request application directly from IIE by October 8.

Number of awards:	10
Number of applicants:	32
Application deadline:	October 23
Notification begins:	June 30

Contact:
Fulbright Program/USIA--U.S. Student Programs
Institute of International Education
809 United Nations Plaza
New York, NY 10017-3580
Website: www.iie.org/fulbright

Portugal: Full Grant (Fulbright)

Type of award: Research grant.
Intended use: For undergraduate, non-degree study outside United States in Portugal.
Eligibility: Applicant must be U.S. citizen.
Basis for selection: Applicant must demonstrate seriousness of purpose.
Application requirements: Recommendations, transcript and research proposal.
Additional information: Proficiency in Portuguese at the level required by the proposed study necessary by the beginning date of the grant. Research in history, art history, literature, political science, archeology, anthropology or business recommended. Applicants enrolled in U.S. academic institutions must apply through Fulbright Program Adviser on campus. All others must request application directly from IIE by October 8.

Number of awards:	3
Number of applicants:	6
Application deadline:	October 23
Notification begins:	June 30

Contact:
Fulbright Program/USIA--U.S. Student Programs
Institute of International Education
809 United Nations Plaza
New York, NY 10017-3580
Website: www.iie.org/fulbright

Qatar: Full Grant (Fulbright)

Type of award: Research grant.
Intended use: For full-time graduate or non-degree study outside United States in Qatar. Designated institutions: The University of Qatar.
Eligibility: Applicant must be U.S. citizen.
Basis for selection: Applicant must demonstrate seriousness of purpose.
Application requirements: Recommendations, transcript and research proposal.
Additional information: Intermediate or advanced proficiency in Arabic is required. All undergraduate courses, except English and Engineering are taught in Arabic. Preference is given to candidates who are prepared to do self-directed, independent research. Applicants enrolled in U.S. academic institutions must apply through Fulbright Program Adviser on campus. All others must request application directly from IIE by October 8.

Application deadline:	October 23
Notification begins:	June 30

Contact:
Fulbright Program/USIA--U.S. Student Programs
Institute of International Education
809 United Nations Plaza
New York, NY 10017-3580
Website: www.iie.org/fulbright

Romania: Government Grant (Fulbright)

Type of award: Research grant.
Intended use: For graduate or non-degree study outside United States in Romania.
Eligibility: Applicant must be U.S. citizen.
Basis for selection: Applicant must demonstrate seriousness of purpose.
Application requirements: Recommendations, transcript and research proposal.
Additional information: Academic year October to June. Stipend approximately $150 monthly. Language skills in Romanian required. French useful, plus German and Hungarian in Transylvania and Banat. Advanced students who plan individual research/study preferred. Research approval for field studies can be difficult. Applicants enrolled in U.S. academic institutions must apply through Fulbright Program Adviser on campus. All others must request application directly from IIE by October 8.

Number of awards:	7
Number of applicants:	8
Application deadline:	October 23
Notification begins:	June 30

Contact:
Fulbright Program/USIA--U.S. Student Programs
Institute of International Education
809 United Nations Plaza
New York, NY 10017-3580
Website: www.iie.org/fulbright

Saudi Arabia: Full Grant (Fulbright)

Type of award: Research grant.
Intended use: For graduate or non-degree study outside United States in Saudi Arabia.
Eligibility: Applicant must be U.S. citizen.
Basis for selection: Applicant must demonstrate seriousness of purpose.
Application requirements: Recommendations, transcript and research proposal.
Additional information: Arabic is helpful but not necessary unless required by the project. Applications in all fields are acceptable. Some fields of particular interest are: computer science, earth sciences and ecology, education, English language (EFL), marine biology, mathematics, medicine, physics, special education and child development. Research

proposals in religion can be considered sensitive. Applicants enrolled in U.S. academic institutions must apply through Fulbright Program Adviser on campus. All others must request application directly from IIE by October 8.
- **Number of applicants:** 1
- **Application deadline:** October 23
- **Notification begins:** June 30

Contact:
Fulbright Program/USIA--U.S. Student Programs
Institute of International Education
809 United Nations Plaza
New York, NY 10017-3580
Website: www.iie.org/fulbright

Senegal: Full Grant (Fulbright)

Type of award: Research grant.
Intended use: For graduate or non-degree study outside United States in Senegal.
Eligibility: Applicant must be U.S. citizen.
Basis for selection: Applicant must demonstrate seriousness of purpose.
Application requirements: Recommendations, transcript and research proposal.
Additional information: Proficiency in French is required at the time of application. Study of Wolof or another Senegalese language is strongly recommended for in depth research. Opportunities for study in agriculture; architecture; art; business; computer/information science; culture; development studies, journalism; jurisprudence; law; literature; mathematics; medicine; natural sciences; and sociology. Applicants enrolled in U.S. academic institutions must apply through Fulbright Program Adviser on campus. All others must request application directly from IIE by October 8.
- **Number of applicants:** 21
- **Application deadline:** October 23
- **Notification begins:** June 30

Contact:
Fulbright Program/USIA--U.S. Student Programs
Institute of International Education
809 United Nations Plaza
New York, NY 10017-3580
Website: www.iie.org/fulbright

Singapore: Full Grant (Fulbright)

Type of award: Research grant.
Intended use: For graduate or non-degree study outside United States in Singapore.
Eligibility: Applicant must be U.S. citizen.
Basis for selection: Applicant must demonstrate seriousness of purpose.
Application requirements: Recommendations, transcript and research proposal. Applicants interested in National University of Singapore or Nanyang Technological University must apply directly to the registrar.
Additional information: English is the official language. A regional or local language may be needed for a specific project. Two programs are offered for postgraduate degrees by course work or research in the arts and social sciences only and non-graduating students. Postgraduate degree by course work begins at the end of July of each academic year and normally takes over two semesters to complete. The postgraduate degree by research may begin at any time and normally requires a minimum period of 18 months to complete. Non-graduating students - candidates must meet the entry requirements and be academically suitable to pursue undergraduate modules/courses or postgraduate research and /or modules/courses. Admission is for one academic year (course work) or on a 17-week basis (research). Applicants enrolled in U.S. academic institutions must apply through Fulbright Program Adviser on campus. All others must request application directly from IIE by October 8.
- **Number of applicants:** 22
- **Application deadline:** October 23
- **Notification begins:** June 30

Contact:
Fulbright Program/USIA--U.S. Student Programs
Institute of International Education
809 United Nations Plaza
New York, NY 10017-3580
Website: www.iie.org/fulbright

Slovak Republic: Full Grant (Fulbright)

Type of award: Research grant.
Intended use: For graduate or non-degree study outside United States in Slovakia.
Eligibility: Applicant must be U.S. citizen.
Basis for selection: Applicant must demonstrate seriousness of purpose.
Application requirements: Recommendations, transcript and research proposal.
Additional information: A knowledge of Slovak is required commensurate with the level needed for the proposed independent research or study in fields such as political science, history and anthropology by the beginning date of the grant. Applications in all fields will be considered; applications in the arts are encouraged. Applicants enrolled in U.S. academic institutions must apply through Fulbright Program Adviser on campus. All others must request application directly from IIE by October 8.
- **Number of awards:** 3
- **Number of applicants:** 7
- **Application deadline:** October 23
- **Notification begins:** June 30

Contact:
Fulbright Program/USIA--U.S. Student Programs
Institute of International Education
809 United Nations Plaza
New York, NY 10017-3580
Website: www.iie.org/fulbright

Slovenia: Full Grant (Fulbright)

Type of award: Research grant.
Intended use: For master's, doctoral or non-degree study outside United States in Slovenia.
Eligibility: Applicant must be U.S. citizen.
Basis for selection: Applicant must demonstrate seriousness of purpose.
Application requirements: Recommendations, transcript and research proposal.
Additional information: A working knowledge of the Slovenian language is desirable by the beginning date of the grant. Good command of the language is especially important

for Slovene studies. Consideration is given to recent graduates, M.A. and Ph.D. candidates who propose serious projects and can conduct independent study. Fellows should begin to seek housing well before anticipated departure from the U.S. Applicants enrolled in U.S. academic institutions must apply through Fulbright Program Adviser on campus. All others must request application directly from IIE by October 8.

> Number of awards: 2
> Number of applicants: 6
> Application deadline: October 23
> Notification begins: June 30

Contact:
Fulbright Program/USIA--U.S. Student Programs
Institute of International Education
809 United Nations Plaza
New York, NY 10017-3580
Website: www.iie.org/fulbright

South Africa: Full Grant (Fulbright)

Type of award: Research grant.
Intended use: For graduate or non-degree study outside United States in South Africa.
Eligibility: Applicant must be U.S. citizen.
Basis for selection: Applicant must demonstrate seriousness of purpose.
Application requirements: Recommendations, transcript and research proposal.
Additional information: Academic year February to November. English is the primary language. Knowledge of Afrikaans or African language may be needed. Preference given to research proposals that will strengthen relationships between U.S. and South African institutions. Prior arrangement of academic affiliation is required. Applicants enrolled in U.S. academic institutions must apply through Fulbright Program Adviser on campus. All others must request application directly from IIE by October 8.

> Number of applicants: 32
> Application deadline: October 23
> Notification begins: June 30

Contact:
Fulbright Program/USIA--U.S. Student Programs
Institute of International Education
809 United Nations Plaza
New York, NY 10017-3580
Website: www.iie.org/fulbright

Spain: Full Grant (Fulbright)

Type of award: Research grant.
Intended use: For graduate or non-degree study outside United States in Spain.
Eligibility: Applicant must be U.S. citizen.
Basis for selection: Applicant must demonstrate seriousness of purpose.
Application requirements: Recommendations, transcript and research proposal. Candidates desiring university component to submit copy of letter of acceptance. Music and fine arts students to establish contact with specialists before applying.
Additional information: Proficient spoken and written Spanish is required at the time of application. Knowledge of the Catalan and Basque languages is especially important for graduate students who will engage in course work in those regions. Projects in all fields will be considered. There is particular interest in contemporary issues. Preference is given to mature and self-motivated graduate students at all levels (graduating seniors, master's and Ph.D. candidates) who are able to work independently without immediate supervision. Awards are not offered for the sole purpose of study at universities or specialized institutions. Applicants enrolled in U.S. academic institutions must apply through Fulbright Program Adviser on campus. All others must request application directly from IIE by October 8.

> Number of awards: 30
> Number of applicants: 149
> Application deadline: October 23
> Notification begins: June 30

Contact:
Fulbright Program/USIA--U.S. Student Programs
Institute of International Education
809 United Nations Plaza
New York, NY 10017-3580
Website: www.iie.org/fulbright

Spain: Government Grant (Fulbright)

Type of award: Research grant.
Intended use: For graduate or non-degree study outside United States in Spain.
Eligibility: Applicant must be U.S. citizen.
Basis for selection: Applicant must demonstrate seriousness of purpose.
Application requirements: Recommendations, transcript and research proposal. Candidates desiring strong university component to submit copy of letter of acceptance. Music and fine arts students to establish contact with specialists before applying.
Additional information: Preference given to graduate students at all levels who are able to work independently. Academic year October to June. Grant period September 15 to June 14, unless otherwise approved. Spanish proficiency needed. Catalan and/or Basque may be important. Music and art students cannot base project on private study. In most cases, additional funds will be necessary. Applicants enrolled in U.S. academic institutions must apply through Fulbright Program Adviser on campus. All others must request application directly from IIE by October 8.

> Number of awards: 10
> Application deadline: October 23
> Notification begins: June 30

Contact:
Fulbright Program/USIA--U.S. Student Programs
Institute of International Education
809 United Nations Plaza
New York, NY 10017-3580
Website: www.iie.org/fulbright

Spain: Professional Grant in Journalism (Fulbright)

Type of award: Scholarship.
Intended use: For graduate or non-degree study outside United States in Spain.
Eligibility: Applicant must be U.S. citizen.
Basis for selection: Major/career interest in journalism. Applicant must demonstrate seriousness of purpose.
Application requirements: Recommendations, transcript and

research proposal. Professional Exchanges Application available through Fulbright Professional Exchanges Programs, U.S. Student Programs, Institute of International Education.
Additional information: Proficient spoken and written Spanish required at the time of application. Grant duration three months, beginning mid-September through April. Stipend 250,000 pesetas monthly and transportation. For early to mid-career professionals in print, broadcast, and business journalism. Affiliation with Spanish newspaper, radio or television station, or university communications department required. Applicants enrolled in U.S. academic institutions must apply through Fulbright Program Adviser on campus. All others must request application directly from IIE by October 8.

Number of awards:	2
Application deadline:	February 2
Notification begins:	June 30

Contact:
Fulbright Program/USIA--U.S. Student Programs
Institute of International Education
809 United Nations Plaza
New York, NY 10017-3580
Website: www.iie.org/fulbright

Sri Lanka: Full Grant (Fulbright)

Type of award: Research grant.
Intended use: For graduate or non-degree study outside United States in Sri Lanka.
Eligibility: Applicant must be U.S. citizen.
Basis for selection: Applicant must demonstrate seriousness of purpose.
Application requirements: Recommendations, transcript and research proposal.
Additional information: Proficiency in Sinhala/Tamil would be useful to those seeking to do field research. Applicants should present evidence of maturity and ability to adapt to conditions different from the U.S. While applications are accepted in all fields, preference is given to research proposals in the humanities and social sciences. Due to security concerns, study and research in northern and eastern areas of Sri Lanka are not recommended. Applicants enrolled in U.S. academic institutions must apply through Fulbright Program Adviser on campus. All others must request application directly from IIE by October 8.

Number of awards:	3
Number of applicants:	14
Application deadline:	October 23
Notification begins:	June 30

Contact:
Fulbright Program/USIA--U.S. Student Programs
Institute of International Education
809 United Nations Plaza
New York, NY 10017-3580
Website: www.iie.org/fulbright

Swaziland: Full Grant (Fulbright)

Type of award: Research grant.
Intended use: For graduate or non-degree study outside United States in Swaziland.
Eligibility: Applicant must be U.S. citizen.
Basis for selection: Applicant must demonstrate seriousness of purpose.
Application requirements: Recommendations, transcript and research proposal.
Additional information: English is the language of instruction at the University of Swaziland. Siswati needed for field research. Those desiring affiliation with University of Swaziland should contact registrar. Research assistantship and translator opportunities also available. M.A. and Ph.D candidates planning dissertation research are preferred. Applicants enrolled in U.S. academic institutions must apply through Fulbright Program Adviser on campus. All others must request application directly from IIE by October 8.

Application deadline:	October 23
Notification begins:	June 30

Contact:
Fulbright Program/USIA--U.S. Student Programs
Institute of International Education
809 United Nations Plaza
New York, NY 10017-3580
Website: www.iie.org/fulbright

Sweden: Full Grant (Fulbright)

Type of award: Research grant.
Intended use: For graduate study outside United States in Sweden.
Eligibility: Applicant must be U.S. citizen.
Basis for selection: Applicant must demonstrate seriousness of purpose.
Application requirements: Recommendations, transcript and research proposal.
Additional information: Academic year August to June. Grant period ten months. Large amount of course work in English. Swedish skills must be commensurate with project requirements. Advisor plus affiliation with university or research institute required. Consideration given to any project requiring presence in Sweden. Applicants enrolled in U.S. academic institutions must apply through Fulbright Program Adviser on campus. All others must request application directly from IIE by October 8.

Number of awards:	10
Number of applicants:	35
Application deadline:	October 23
Notification begins:	June 30

Contact:
Fulbright Program/USIA--U.S. Student Programs
Institute of International Education
809 United Nations Plaza
New York, NY 10017-3580
Website: www.iie.org/fulbright

Switzerland: Government Grant (Fulbright)

Type of award: Research grant.
Intended use: For full-time graduate or non-degree study outside United States in Switzerland.
Eligibility: Applicant must be U.S. citizen.
Basis for selection: Applicant must demonstrate seriousness of purpose.
Application requirements: Recommendations, transcript and research proposal. Arts/music candidates: sample artworks, sample cassette tapes, or scores.
Additional information: German or French proficiency required. Grant period coincides with nine-month academic year. Stipend SFr 1,450-1,650 monthly, plus tuition exemption (except some art schools), travel, and insurance. M.A. or

equivalent required, unless in music or fine arts. Grantees must be affiliated with an institution. Medical sciences not recommended. Applicants enrolled in U.S. academic institutions must apply through Fulbright Program Adviser on campus. All others must request application directly from IIE by October 8.

- **Number of awards:** 2
- **Application deadline:** October 23
- **Notification begins:** June 30

Contact:
Fulbright Program/USIA--U.S. Student Programs
Institute of International Education
809 United Nations Plaza
New York, NY 10017-3580
Website: www.iie.org/fulbright

Switzerland: Seydel Fellowship (Fulbright)

Type of award: Research grant.
Intended use: For graduate or non-degree study outside United States in Switzerland.
Eligibility: Applicant must be U.S. citizen.
Basis for selection: Applicant must demonstrate seriousness of purpose.
Application requirements: Recommendations, transcript and research proposal.
Additional information: Proficient French or German needed at time of application. Stipend provides allowance, transportation, and insurance. For graduating seniors with placements at Swiss universities. Applicants enrolled in U.S. academic institutions must apply through Fulbright Program Adviser on campus. All others must request application directly from IIE by October 8.

- **Application deadline:** October 23
- **Notification begins:** June 30

Contact:
Fulbright Program/USIA--U.S. Student Programs
Institute of International Education
809 United Nations Plaza
New York, NY 10017-3580
Website: www.iie.org/fulbright

Syria: Government Grant (Fulbright)

Type of award: Research grant.
Intended use: For graduate or non-degree study outside United States in Syria. Designated institutions: University of Damascus.
Eligibility: Applicant must be U.S. citizen.
Basis for selection: Major/career interest in history; law; Islamic studies; science, general. Applicant must demonstrate seriousness of purpose.
Application requirements: Recommendations, transcript and research proposal.
Additional information: Minimum two years of study Arabic is required at the time of application. Stipend/government grant covers living expenses, study and research, plus travel and insurance. Graduating seniors and Ph.D. dissertation research candidates preferred. Fellows audit at least two undergraduate classes, following typical Syrian course of studies. Modern social sciences not recommended field of study. Applicants enrolled in U.S. academic institutions must apply through Fulbright Program Adviser on campus. All others must request application directly from IIE by October 8.

- **Number of applicants:** 21
- **Application deadline:** October 23
- **Notification begins:** June 30

Contact:
Fulbright Program/USIA--U.S. Student Programs
Institute of International Education
809 United Nations Plaza
New York, NY 10017-3580
Website: www.iie.org/fulbright

Taiwan: Full Grant (Fulbright)

Type of award: Research grant.
Intended use: For non-degree study outside United States in Taiwan.
Eligibility: Applicant must be U.S. citizen.
Basis for selection: Applicant must demonstrate seriousness of purpose.
Application requirements: Recommendations, transcript and research proposal.
Additional information: Grant period up to ten months. Language skills must be commensurate with project requirements. Graduating seniors, recent graduates, and enrolled graduate students considered. No restrictions on field of study. However, up to four grants are available for MFA or doctoral students in the arts, including both performing and visual arts, and study related to the preservation, maintenance, and development of cultural assets. Projects may include language; arts and culture; independent research; enrollment in, or auditing of classes at a local university; or a combination. In addition to traditional Chinese studies, research projects related to contemporary Taiwan, such as the information industry, the social sciences, business and education, are also welcome. Applicants enrolled in U.S. academic institutions must apply through Fulbright Program Adviser on campus. All others must request application directly from IIE by October 8.

- **Number of awards:** 11
- **Number of applicants:** 83
- **Application deadline:** October 23
- **Notification begins:** June 30

Contact:
Fulbright Program/USIA--U.S. Student Programs
Institute of International Education
809 United Nations Plaza
New York, NY 10017-3580
Website: www.iie.org/fulbright

Taiwan: Teaching Assistantship-Internship (Fulbright)

Type of award: Internship.
Intended use: For graduate or non-degree study outside United States in Taiwan.
Eligibility: Applicant must be U.S. citizen.
Basis for selection: Applicant must demonstrate seriousness of purpose.
Application requirements: Recommendations, transcript and research proposal.
Additional information: Applicants must be articulate native English speakers with superior writing ability. Offered to those who have a bachelor's degree and are interested in the arts,

media, with emphasis on arts and cultural reporting; international education, cross-cultural counseling or TESL. The positions combine up to twenty hours per week of work at a nonprofit or governmental organization and another twenty hours per week devoted to language study or an independent study/research project. Applicants enrolled in U.S. academic institutions must apply through Fulbright Program Adviser on campus. All others must request application directly from IIE by October 8.

Number of awards:	5
Application deadline:	October 23
Notification begins:	June 30

Contact:
Fulbright Program/USIA--U.S. Student Programs
Institute of International Education
809 United Nations Plaza
New York, NY 10017-3580
Website: www.iie.org/fulbright

Tanzania: Full Grant (Fulbright)

Type of award: Research grant.
Intended use: For graduate or non-degree study outside United States in Tanzania.
Eligibility: Applicant must be U.S. citizen.
Basis for selection: Applicant must demonstrate seriousness of purpose.
Application requirements: Recommendations, transcript and research proposal.
Additional information: English sufficient for university admission but Kiswahili may be useful, and is necessary for field research. Clearance for independent research to be requested far in advance. In conducting research or studying, plan for difficult living conditions, high prices for consumer goods, unreliable in-country transportation, and the possibility of contracting malaria. Applicants enrolled in U.S. academic institutions must apply through Fulbright Program Adviser on campus. All others must request application directly from IIE by October 8.

Number of applicants:	32
Application deadline:	October 23
Notification begins:	June 30

Contact:
Fulbright Program/USIA--U.S. Student Programs
Institute of International Education
809 United Nations Plaza
New York, NY 10017-3580
Website: www.iie.org/fulbright

Thailand: Full Grant (Fulbright)

Type of award: Research grant.
Intended use: For graduate or non-degree study outside United States in Thailand.
Eligibility: Applicant must be U.S. citizen.
Basis for selection: Applicant must demonstrate seriousness of purpose.
Application requirements: Recommendations, transcript and research proposal.
Additional information: Some Thai language ability is desirable for life in Thailand. All fields are considered. Of particular interest are projects which deal with contemporary issues that have implications for cross-cultural understanding. Applications will be considered from graduating seniors, well-qualified M.A. and Ph.D. candidates for degree or nondegree study at Thai institutions, and/or independent graduate-level research in all fields of study. Professional internships can also be arranged. Applicants enrolled in U.S. academic institutions must apply through Fulbright Program Adviser on campus. All others must request application directly from IIE by October 8.

Number of awards:	5
Number of applicants:	28
Application deadline:	October 23
Notification begins:	June 30

Contact:
Fulbright Program/USIA--U.S. Student Programs
Institute of International Education
809 United Nations Plaza
New York, NY 10017-3580
Website: www.iie.org/fulbright

Togo: Full Grant (Fulbright)

Type of award: Research grant.
Intended use: For graduate or non-degree study outside United States in Togo.
Eligibility: Applicant must be U.S. citizen.
Basis for selection: Applicant must demonstrate seriousness of purpose.
Application requirements: Recommendations, transcript and research proposal.
Additional information: Academic year October to June. French proficiency needed at time of application. Those with M.A.s and Ph.D.s who can teach while studying are preferred. Applicants enrolled in U.S. academic institutions must apply through Fulbright Program Adviser on campus. All others must request application directly from IIE by October 8.

Number of applicants:	1
Application deadline:	October 23
Notification begins:	June 30

Contact:
Fulbright Program/USIA--U.S. Student Programs
Institute of International Education
809 United Nations Plaza
New York, NY 10017-3580
Website: www.iie.org/fulbright

Trinidad and Tobago: Full Grant (Fulbright)

Type of award: Research grant.
Intended use: For graduate or non-degree study outside United States in Trinidad & Tobago.
Eligibility: Applicant must be U.S. citizen.
Basis for selection: Applicant must demonstrate seriousness of purpose.
Application requirements: Recommendations, transcript and research proposal.
Additional information: Academic year August to May. All grantees affiliate with University of the West Indies. Applicants enrolled in U.S. academic institutions must apply through Fulbright Program Adviser on campus. All others must request application directly from IIE by October 8.

Number of applicants: 10
Application deadline: October 23
Notification begins: June 30
Contact:
Fulbright Program/USIA--U.S. Student Programs
Institute of International Education
809 United Nations Plaza
New York, NY 10017-3580
Website: www.iie.org/fulbright

Tunisia: Full Grant (Fulbright)

Type of award: Research grant.
Intended use: For graduate or non-degree study outside United States in Tunisia.
Eligibility: Applicant must be U.S. citizen.
Basis for selection: Applicant must demonstrate seriousness of purpose.
Application requirements: Recommendations, transcript and research proposal.
Additional information: Working knowledge of French or Arabic required. M.A. and Ph.D. candidates preferred. Enrollment in university classes not permitted. Researchers affiliate with State Secretariat for Scientific and Technological Research in the Prime Ministry. Applicants enrolled in U.S. academic institutions must apply through Fulbright Program Adviser on campus. All others must request application directly from IIE by October 8.
Number of applicants: 4
Application deadline: October 23
Notification begins: June 30
Contact:
Fulbright Program/USIA--U.S. Student Programs
Institute of International Education
809 United Nations Plaza
New York, NY 10017-3580
Website: www.iie.org/fulbright

Turkey: Full Grant (Fulbright)

Type of award: Research grant.
Intended use: For graduate or non-degree study outside United States in Turkey.
Eligibility: Applicant must be U.S. citizen.
Basis for selection: Applicant must demonstrate seriousness of purpose.
Application requirements: Recommendations, transcript and research proposal.
Additional information: Students who must attend lectures and/or make use of library facilities should have some degree of proficiency in Turkish. Instruction in the universities is in Turkish, with a few exceptions. Applicants enrolled in U.S. academic institutions must apply through Fulbright Program Adviser on campus. All others must request application directly from IIE by October 8.
Number of awards: 10
Number of applicants: 42
Application deadline: October 23
Notification begins: June 30
Contact:
Fulbright Program/USIA--U.S. Student Programs
Institute of International Education
809 United Nations Plaza
New York, NY 10017-3580
Website: www.iie.org/fulbright

Turkey: Teaching Assistantship (Fulbright)

Type of award: Internship.
Intended use: For graduate or non-degree study in Ankara or Izmir, Turkey outside United States in Turkey.
Eligibility: Applicant must be U.S. citizen.
Basis for selection: Applicant must demonstrate seriousness of purpose.
Application requirements: Recommendations, transcript and research proposal.
Additional information: Maximum 12 hours teaching weekly at university. Candidates should have bachelor's degree in English, American language, or literature. Applicants enrolled in U.S. academic institutions must apply through Fulbright Program Adviser on campus. All others must request application directly from IIE by October 8.
Number of awards: 1
Application deadline: October 23
Notification begins: June 30
Contact:
Fulbright Program/USIA--U.S. Student Programs
Institute of International Education
809 United Nations Plaza
New York, NY 10017-3580
Website: www.iie.org/fulbright

U.S. English Foundation Award (Fulbright)

Type of award: Research grant.
Intended use: For master's study outside United States in United Kingdom.
Eligibility: Applicant must be U.S. citizen.
Basis for selection: Major/career interest in English as a second language. Applicant must demonstrate seriousness of purpose.
Application requirements: Recommendations, transcript and research proposal. Fill out section on interest in special award.
Additional information: Offered to postgraduate students specializing in the Teaching of English as a Second Language to immigrant communities. Awards are for either an M.A. in Second Language Teaching focusing on practical methodology; or an M.A. in Language and Educational in Multilingual Society, focusing on the sociology of second language development. The award covers round-trip travel, maintenance allowance for 12 months, and approved tuition fees. Applicants enrolled in U.S. academic institutions must apply through Fulbright Program Adviser on campus. All others must request application directly from IIE by October 8.
Number of awards: 2
Application deadline: October 23
Notification begins: June 30
Contact:
Fulbright Program/USIA--U.S. Student Programs
Institute of International Education
809 United Nations Plaza
New York, NY 10017-3580
Website: www.iie.org/fulbright

Uganda: Full Grant (Fulbright)

Type of award: Research grant.
Intended use: For graduate or non-degree study outside United States in Uganda.
Eligibility: Applicant must be U.S. citizen.
Basis for selection: Applicant must demonstrate seriousness of purpose.
Application requirements: Recommendations, transcript and research proposal. Application for Permission to Conduct Research in Uganda, available through the Uganda National Council for Science and Technology (UNCST). Formal arrangements can be done through the Makerere Institute of Social Research (MISR). Affiliation fee $300.
Additional information: English is the official language. M.A. and Ph.D candidates are preferred. All research projects must be approved by the Uganda National Council for Science and Technology. Approval for AIDS research must go through the Uganda National AIDS Research Committee. Rebel and bandit activity in the areas along the Sundanese border and northern Uganda, and in the areas of western Uganda, have made these areas unstable and insecure. Applicants enrolled in U.S. academic institutions must apply through Fulbright Program Adviser on campus. All others must request application directly from IIE by October 8.

    Number of applicants: 15
    Application deadline: October 23
    Notification begins: June 30

Contact:
Fulbright Program/USIA--U.S. Student Programs
Institute of International Education
809 United Nations Plaza
New York, NY 10017-3580
Website: www.iie.org/fulbright

United Arab Emirates: Full Grant (Fulbright)

Type of award: Research grant.
Intended use: For graduate or non-degree study outside United States in United Arab Emirates.
Eligibility: Applicant must be U.S. citizen.
Basis for selection: Applicant must demonstrate seriousness of purpose.
Application requirements: Recommendations, transcript and research proposal.
Additional information: Arabic proficiency needed. Fellows will affiliate with academic institutions. Gender-segregated campuses. Applicants enrolled in U.S. academic institutions must apply through Fulbright Program Adviser on campus. All others must request application directly from IIE by October 8.

    Number of applicants: 2
    Application deadline: October 23
    Notification begins: June 30

Contact:
Fulbright Program/USIA--U.S. Student Programs
Institute of International Education
809 United Nations Plaza
New York, NY 10017-3580
Website: www.iie.org/fulbright

United Kingdom: British-American Chamber of Commerce Award (Fulbright)

Type of award: Scholarship.
Intended use: For full-time graduate or non-degree study at graduate institution in United Kingdom.
Eligibility: Applicant must be U.S. citizen.
Basis for selection: Major/career interest in business, management and administration; business; business, international. Applicant must demonstrate seriousness of purpose.
Application requirements: Recommendations, transcript and research proposal. Fill out section indicating interest in special award.
Additional information: Award covers round-trip travel, a maintenance allowance for 12 months and approved tuition fees. Candidates preferably must have two to three years relevant work experience and intend to pursue a UK, one-year program at an approved institution of higher education. If candidates choose a course which is longer in duration, the Fulbright Commission will fund the first year of study. Applicants enrolled in U.S. academic institutions must apply through Fulbright Program Adviser on campus. All others must request application directly from IIE by October 8.

    Number of awards: 2
    Application deadline: October 23
    Notification begins: June 30

Contact:
Fulbright Program/USIA--U.S. Student Programs
Institute of International Education
809 United Nations Plaza
New York, NY 10017-3580
Website: www.iie.org/fulbright

United Kingdom: British-American Tobacco Industries Award (Fulbright)

Type of award: Scholarship.
Intended use: For master's study in United Kingdom.
Eligibility: Applicant must be U.S. citizen.
Basis for selection: Major/career interest in business. Applicant must demonstrate seriousness of purpose.
Application requirements: Recommendations, transcript and research proposal. Fill out section indicating interest in special awards.
Additional information: One-year M.B.A. program for candidates interested in insurance. Award provides maintenance, tuition, and transportation. Information on TBA courses in the U.K can be obtained from The Association of MBA 15 Duncan Terrace, London N1 8B7. Applicants enrolled in U.S. academic institutions must apply through Fulbright Program Adviser on campus. All others must request application directly from IIE by October 8.

    Number of awards: 2
    Application deadline: October 23
    Notification begins: June 30

Contact:
Fulbright Program/USIA--U.S. Student Programs
Institute of International Education
809 United Nations Plaza
New York, NY 10017-3580
Website: www.iie.org/fulbright

United Kingdom: Cambridge University Research Scholarship (Fulbright)

Type of award: Research grant, renewable.
Intended use: For doctoral study at graduate institution in United Kingdom. Designated institutions: Cambridge University.
Eligibility: Applicant must be U.S. citizen.
Basis for selection: Applicant must demonstrate seriousness of purpose.
Application requirements: Recommendations, transcript and research proposal. Request consideration for jointly-funded scholarship and submit application for Overseas Research Student (ORS) award. For admission contact: Secretary, Board of Graduate Studies, University of Cambridge, 4 Mill Lane, Cambridge CB2 1RZ. Deadline 31 December.
Additional information: Provides funds for up to three years to outstanding students to pursue Ph.D. resource. Applicants enrolled in U.S. academic institutions must apply through Fulbright Program Adviser on campus. All others must request application directly from IIE by October 8.
   Number of awards: 3
   Application deadline: October 23
   Notification begins: June 30
Contact:
Fulbright Program/USIA--U.S. Student Programs
Institute of International Education
809 United Nations Plaza
New York, NY 10017-3580
Website: www.iie.org/fulbright

United Kingdom: Full Grant (Fulbright)

Type of award: Research grant.
Intended use: For non-degree study outside United States in United Kingdom.
Eligibility: Applicant must be U.S. citizen.
Basis for selection: Applicant must demonstrate leadership and seriousness of purpose.
Application requirements: Recommendations, transcript and research proposal. Both university and college acceptance needed for placement at Oxford or Cambridge. Auditions held for acting and music studies. Music students to provide sample on audio cassette. Letter of endorsement needed from proposed supervisor for independent research.
Additional information: Academic year October to June. Stipend includes nine months maintenance, travel, and tuition if not provided by another source. First or higher degree to have been earned within last five years. Plans for structured course work, or music or art study with a recognized teacher high priority. Recent U.K. residency or course work, or recent completion of Ph.D. low priority. In the creative and performing arts, applicants who have not earned their BA, four years of professional experience meets the basic requirement. Applicants enrolled in U.S. academic institutions must apply through Fulbright Program Adviser on campus. All others must request application directly from IIE by October 8.
   Number of awards: 32
   Number of applicants: 615
   Application deadline: October 23
   Notification begins: June 30
Contact:
Fulbright Program/USIA--U.S. Student Programs
Institute of International Education
809 United Nations Plaza
New York, NY 10017-3580
Website: www.iie.org/fulbright

United Kingdom: Marks and Spencer Award (Fulbright)

Type of award: Scholarship.
Intended use: For graduate or non-degree study outside United States in United Kingdom.
Eligibility: Applicant must be U.S. citizen.
Basis for selection: Major/career interest in business, international; business; business, management and administration. Applicant must demonstrate seriousness of purpose.
Application requirements: Recommendations, transcript and research proposal. Fill out section indicating interest in special award.
Additional information: One year award provides maintenance, tuition, and transportation. For M.B.A. candidate interested in retail, customer service, and international business. Applicants enrolled in U.S. academic institutions must apply through Fulbright Program Adviser on campus. All others must request application directly from IIE by October 8.
   Number of awards: 1
   Application deadline: October 23
   Notification begins: June 30
Contact:
Fulbright Program/USIA--U.S. Student Programs
Institute of International Education
809 United Nations Plaza
New York, NY 10017-3580
Website: www.iie.org/fulbright

United Kingdom: Oxford University Scholarship (Fulbright)

Type of award: Scholarship.
Intended use: For master's, doctoral study outside United States in United Kingdom. Designated institutions: Oxford University, U.K.
Eligibility: Applicant must be U.S. citizen.
Basis for selection: Applicant must demonstrate seriousness of purpose.
Application requirements: Recommendations, transcript and research proposal. Request consideration for jointly funded scholarship and submit application for Overseas Research Student (ORS) award. For admissions form contact: Graduate Admissions Office, University of Oxford, University Offices, Wellington Square, Oxford OXI 2JD. Deadline 31 January.
Additional information: Amount of award depends on evaluation of individual need. For Fulbright students proposing to follow a two- to three-year course leading to a higher degree. Applicants enrolled in U.S. academic institutions must apply through Fulbright Program Adviser on campus. All others must request application directly from IIE by October 8.

Number of awards: 3
Application deadline: October 23, January 31
Notification begins: June 30
Contact:
Fulbright Program/USIA--U.S. Student Programs
Institute of International Education
809 United Nations Plaza
New York, NY 10017-3580
Website: www.iie.org/fulbright

United Kingdom: Sussex University Research Scholarship (Fulbright)

Type of award: Scholarship.
Intended use: For master's study outside United States in United Kingdom.
Eligibility: Applicant must be U.S. citizen.
Basis for selection: Applicant must demonstrate seriousness of purpose.
Application requirements: Recommendations, transcript and research proposal.
Additional information: Reduction in tuition fees to enable a graduate to pursue a one year course for an M.A. degree at the University of Sussex. Students must apply for entry to an appropriate degree program at Sussex. Open for study in any M.A. program in the Graduate Research Centre in the Humanities. Strong preference for candidates whose application shows relevance to the field of study in the University's Cunliffe Research Centre for the study of constitutionalism and national identity; programs in areas including cultural and literary studies, post-colonialism, American history and contemporary history. Law, rhetoric and power are all likely to be relevant. For further information and advice, applicants should contact Dr. Vivien Hart, School of English and American studies, University of Sussex, Falmer, Brighton BN1 9QN; E-mail: v.m.hart@sussex.ac.uk. Applicants enrolled in U.S. academic institutions must apply through Fulbright Program Adviser on campus. All others must request application directly from IIE by October 8.
Number of awards: 1
Application deadline: October 23
Notification begins: June 30
Contact:
Fulbright Program/USIA--U.S. Student Programs
Institute of International Education
809 United Nations Plaza
New York, NY 10017-3580
Website: www.iie.org/fulbright

United Kingdom: University College London Scholarship (Fulbright)

Type of award: Scholarship.
Intended use: For full-time graduate study outside United States in United Kingdom. Designated institutions: University College London, U.K.
Eligibility: Applicant must be U.S. citizen.
Basis for selection: Major/career interest in geography. Applicant must demonstrate seriousness of purpose.
Application requirements: Recommendations, transcript and research proposal. Request consideration for jointly funded scholarship and submit application for Overseas Research student (ORS) award. For admission contact: Department of Geography, University College London, 26 Bedford Way, London WCIH OAP.
Additional information: University College London's Department of Geography offers an opportunity to study the "Environment, Space and Place." A reduction in tuition fees is offered to applicants choosing to take a 12 month taught master's degree in either, "Public Understanding of Environmental Change" or "Modernity, Space and Place." Application: Contact Postgraduate Tutor, Department of Geography, University College London, 26 Bedford Way, London WC1H 0AP. Applicants enrolled in U.S. academic institutions must apply through Fulbright Program Adviser on campus. All others must request application directly from IIE by October 8.
Number of awards: 1
Application deadline: October 23
Notification begins: June 30
Contact:
Fulbright Program/USIA--U.S. Student Programs
Institute of International Education
809 United Nations Plaza
New York, NY 10017-3580
Fax: (44) 171 380 7565
Website: www.ucl.ac.uk or www.iie.org/fulbright

United Kingdom: University of East Anglia Research Scholarship (Fulbright)

Type of award: Scholarship.
Intended use: For master's study outside United States in United Kingdom. Designated institutions: University of East Anglia, U.K.
Eligibility: Applicant must be U.S. citizen.
Basis for selection: Applicant must demonstrate seriousness of purpose.
Application requirements: Recommendations, transcript and research proposal.
Additional information: For a graduate student to pursue a one year taught master's course in any discipline at the University of East Anglia. For further information, applicants should contact: Academic Registrar, The Registry, University of East Anglia, Norwich NR4 7TJ. Applicants enrolled in U.S. academic institutions must apply through Fulbright Program Adviser on campus. All others must request application directly from IIE by October 8.
Number of awards: 1
Application deadline: October 23
Notification begins: June 30
Contact:
Fulbright Program/USIA--U.S. Student Programs
Institute of International Education
809 United Nations Plaza
New York, NY 10017-3580
Website: www.uea.ac.uk

Uruguay: Full Grant (Fulbright)

Type of award: Research grant.
Intended use: For graduate or non-degree study outside United States in Uruguay.
Eligibility: Applicant must be U.S. citizen.

Basis for selection: Applicant must demonstrate seriousness of purpose.
Application requirements: Recommendations, transcript and research proposal.
Additional information: Proficient spoken and written Spanish is required at the time of application. Advanced graduate student working on doctoral dissertations are preferred. Consideration will be given to recent graduates and M.A. candidates who present serious study or research projects and can work independently. Candidates in all fields of study will be considered, but students interested in working on projects or doing research on topics related to the MERCOSUR and NAFTA treaties are preferred. Applicants enrolled in U.S. academic institutions must apply through Fulbright Program Adviser on campus. All others must request application directly from IIE by October 8.
    Number of applicants: 3
    Application deadline: October 23
    Notification begins: June 30
Contact:
Fulbright Program/USIA--U.S. Student Programs
Institute of International Education
809 United Nations Plaza
New York, NY 10017-3580
Website: www.iie.org/fulbright

Venezuela: Full Grant (Fulbright)

Type of award: Research grant.
Intended use: For graduate or non-degree study outside United States in Venezuela.
Eligibility: Applicant must be U.S. citizen.
Basis for selection: Applicant must demonstrate seriousness of purpose.
Application requirements: Recommendations, transcript and research proposal.
Additional information: Proficient spoken and written Spanish are required at the time of application. Applications from master's-level graduate students who are enrolled in, or are recent graduates of professional schools of law/administration of justice, business, civic education, economics, environment/ecology, social communication, distance education/video conferencing for distance learning, international relations, political science, public policy and public administration are encouraged. Internships are typically arranged to supplement basic research proposals. Internships for the entire grant period are not acceptable. Applicants enrolled in U.S. academic institutions must apply through Fulbright Program Adviser on campus. All others must request application directly from IIE by October 8.
    Number of applicants: 16
    Application deadline: October 23
    Notification begins: June 30
Contact:
Fulbright Program/USIA--U.S. Student Programs
Institute of International Education
809 United Nations Plaza
New York, NY 10017-3580
Website: www.iie.org/fulbright

Vietnam: Full Grant (Fulbright)

Type of award: Research grant.
Intended use: For master's, doctoral or non-degree study outside United States in Vietnam.
Eligibility: Applicant must be U.S. citizen.
Basis for selection: Applicant must demonstrate seriousness of purpose.
Application requirements: Recommendations, transcript and research proposal.
Additional information: A working knowledge of Vietnamese is required at the time of application. All fields are considered. Applications are encouraged in transitional economics; environmental law and management; legal reform; educational reform. Grants are primarily intended for graduate students who require up to one year of supervised field work or who need to use Vietnamese research facilities to earn credit toward their U.S. master's or doctoral degrees. Applicants enrolled in U.S. academic institutions must apply through Fulbright Program Adviser on campus. All others must request application directly from IIE by October 8.
    Number of applicants: 22
    Application deadline: October 23
    Notification begins: June 30
Contact:
Fulbright Program/USIA--U.S. Student Programs
Institute of International Education
809 United Nations Plaza
New York, NY 10017-3580
Website: www.iie.org/fulbright

Yemen: Full Grant (Fulbright)

Type of award: Research grant.
Intended use: For graduate or non-degree study outside United States in Yemen.
Eligibility: Applicant must be U.S. citizen.
Basis for selection: Applicant must demonstrate seriousness of purpose.
Application requirements: Recommendations, transcript and research proposal.
Additional information: Knowledge of spoken Yemen recommended. Those studying sociology also eligible. Affiliations arranged. Applicants enrolled in U.S. academic institutions must apply through Fulbright Program Adviser on campus. All others must request application directly from IIE by October 8.
    Number of applicants: 5
    Application deadline: October 23
    Notification begins: June 30
Contact:
Fulbright Program/USIA--U.S. Student Programs
Institute of International Education
809 United Nations Plaza
New York, NY 10017-3580
Website: www.iie.org/fulbright

Zambia: Full Grant (Fulbright)

Type of award: Research grant.
Intended use: For graduate or non-degree study outside United States in Zambia.
Eligibility: Applicant must be U.S. citizen.

Basis for selection: Applicant must demonstrate seriousness of purpose.
Application requirements: Recommendations, transcript and research proposal.
Additional information: Academic year January/February to October/November. English is the official language but knowledge of local languages useful for field research. Researchers must affiliate with the University of Zambia. Study permits needed. Research findings to be presented. Applicants enrolled in U.S. academic institutions must apply through Fulbright Program Adviser on campus. All others must request application directly from IIE by October 8.
   Number of applicants: 2
   Application deadline: October 23
   Notification begins: June 30
Contact:
Fulbright Program/USIA--U.S. Student Programs
Institute of International Education
809 United Nations Plaza
New York, NY 10017-3580
Website: www.iie.org/fulbright

Zimbabwe: Full Grant (Fulbright)

Type of award: Research grant.
Intended use: For graduate or non-degree study outside United States in Zimbabwe.
Eligibility: Applicant must be U.S. citizen.
Basis for selection: Applicant must demonstrate seriousness of purpose.
Application requirements: Recommendations, transcript and research proposal. Occasional Student status may be needed for affiliation with University of Zimbabwe. Consult with departmental chairman first.
Additional information: Academic year January to March, May to July, and September to December. English is the official language. Knowledge of Shona and Ndebele useful in rural areas. Graduating seniors preferred. Land reform not recommended field of study. Affiliation required. Teaching responsibilities may be assigned. Research approval can take over a year. Research findings to be presented. Applicants enrolled in U.S. academic institutions must apply through Fulbright Program Adviser on campus. All others must request application directly from IIE by October 8.
   Number of applicants: 28
   Application deadline: October 23
   Notification begins: June 30
Contact:
Fulbright Program/USIA--U.S. Student Programs
Institute of International Education
809 United Nations Plaza
New York, NY 10017-3580
Website: www.iie.org/fulbright

General Motors Corporation

General Motors Corporation Education Relations Internship

Type of award: Internship.
Intended use: For undergraduate, graduate or postgraduate study.
Application requirements: Interview and transcript.
   Amount of award: $1,700-$1,800
Contact:
General Motors Corp.
3044 West Grand Boulevard., 8-162
Detroit, MI 48202-3091
Website: www.gm.com/careers

Georgia Student Finance Commission

Georgia Governor's Scholarship

Type of award: Scholarship, renewable.
Intended use: For full-time undergraduate or graduate study at accredited 2-year or 4-year institution in Georgia.
Eligibility: Applicant must be high school senior. Applicant must be U.S. citizen or permanent resident residing in Georgia.
Basis for selection: Applicant must demonstrate depth of character, leadership, patriotism, seriousness of purpose, service orientation and high academic achievement.
Application requirements: Transcript.
Additional information: Must be valedictorian, salutatorian, STAR Student, or Georgia Scholar. Minimum 3.75 GPA required.
   Amount of award: $1,575
   Number of awards: 2,689
   Number of applicants: 3,000
   Total amount awarded: $3,942,557
Contact:
Scholarship Committee
2082 East Exchange Place
Suite 100
Tucker, GA 30084
Website: www.gsfc.org

Georgia Hope Scholarship - GED Recipient

Type of award: Scholarship.
Intended use: For undergraduate study at accredited vocational, 2-year or 4-year institution in Georgia. Designated institutions: Any eligible public technical institute or public or private college or university in Georgia.
Eligibility: Applicant must be U.S. citizen or permanent resident residing in Georgia.
Application requirements: Proof of eligibility.
Additional information: Must have received GED from Georgia Department of Technical and Adult Education after June 30, 1993.

Amount of award:	$500
Number of awards:	4,785
Number of applicants:	4,785
Total amount awarded:	$2,376,639

Contact:
Hope Scholarship Program
Georgia Student Finance Commission
2082 East Exchange Place, Suite 100
Tucker, GA 30084
Website: www.gsfc.org

Georgia Hope Scholarship - Private Institution

Type of award: Scholarship, renewable.
Intended use: For full-time undergraduate study at accredited 2-year or 4-year institution in Georgia. Designated institutions: Georgia private college or university.
Eligibility: Applicant must be U.S. citizen or permanent resident residing in Georgia.
Basis for selection: Applicant must demonstrate high academic achievement.
Application requirements: Must complete Georgia Tuition Equalization Grant Application.

Amount of award:	$500-$3,000
Number of awards:	23,751
Total amount awarded:	$36,690,964

Contact:
Hope Scholarship Program
Georgia Student Finance Commission
2082 East Exchange Place, Suite 100
Tucker, GA 30084
Website: www.gsfc.org

Georgia Hope Scholarship - Public College or University

Type of award: Scholarship, renewable.
Intended use: For undergraduate study at accredited vocational, 2-year or 4-year institution in Georgia. Designated institutions: Any eligible Georgia public college or university.
Eligibility: Applicant must be U.S. citizen or permanent resident residing in Georgia.
Basis for selection: Applicant must demonstrate high academic achievement.
Application requirements: Proof of eligibility. FAFSA.
Additional information: Minimum GPA of 3.0. First-year HOPE assistance includes any tuition, mandatory fees and book allowance not covered by Pell or other federal grants for up to $100 per quarter.

Number of awards:	52,889
Total amount awarded:	$87,120,969

Contact:
Scholarship Committee
2082 East Exchange Place
Suite 100
Tucker, GA 30084
Phone: 770-414-3085
Website: www.gsfc.org

Georgia Hope Scholarship - Public Technical Institution

Type of award: Scholarship, renewable.
Intended use: For undergraduate certificate, non-degree study at accredited vocational institution in Georgia. Designated institutions: Georgia public technical institutes.
Eligibility: Applicant must be U.S. citizen or permanent resident residing in Georgia.
Application requirements: FAFSA.
Additional information: Scholarship covers tuition, mandatory fees and book allowance up to $50 per quarter for part-time students or $100 per quarter for full-time students.

Number of awards:	54,502
Total amount awarded:	$29,549,423

Contact:
Scholarship Committee
2082 East Exchange Place
Suite 100
Tucker, GA 30084
Phone: 770-414-3085
Website: www.gsfc.org

Georgia Hope Teacher Scholarship

Type of award: Loan, renewable.
Intended use: For graduate study at accredited graduate institution in Georgia. Designated institutions: Any Georgia public or private college or university currently offering advanced degree teacher education programs approved by Georgia Professional Standards Commission.
Eligibility: Applicant must be U.S. citizen or permanent resident residing in Georgia.
Basis for selection: Major/career interest in education; education, teacher.
Application requirements: Proof of eligibility. Signatures from selected institution's Department of Education teacher certification official and financial aid office.
Additional information: Must commit to teaching in Georgia public schools after earning advanced degree. For each $2,500 loaned, must agree to teach one academic year. Loan amount is dependent upon availability of funds.

Amount of award:	$10,000
Number of awards:	2,264
Total amount awarded:	$5,078,796

Contact:
Scholarship Committee
2082 East Exchange Place
Suite 100
Tucker, GA 30084
Phone: 770-414-3085
Website: www.gsfc.org

Georgia Law Enforcement Personnel Dependents Grant

Type of award: Scholarship, renewable.
Intended use: For full-time undergraduate study at accredited vocational, 2-year or 4-year institution. Designated institutions: Eligible postsecondary institutions in Georgia.
Eligibility: Applicant must be U.S. citizen or permanent resident residing in Georgia. Applicant's parent must have been killed or disabled in work-related accident as fire fighter, police officer or public safety officer.
Application requirements: Proof of eligibility.
Additional information: Must complete preliminary document that verifies claim with former employer and doctors.

Amount of award:	$2,000
Number of awards:	34
Number of applicants:	40
Total amount awarded:	$61,999

Contact:
Scholarship Committee
2082 East Exchange Place
Suite 100
Tucker, GA 30084
Website: www.gsfc.org

Georgia Osteopathic Medical Loan

Type of award: Loan, renewable.
Intended use: For full-time first professional study at accredited graduate institution in United States. Designated institutions: Must attend 1 of 15 eligible colleges of osteopathic medicine in United States.
Eligibility: Applicant must be U.S. citizen or permanent resident residing in Georgia.
Basis for selection: Major/career interest in medicine, osteopathic. Applicant must demonstrate depth of character, seriousness of purpose, service orientation and financial need.
Application requirements: Interview, recommendations, essay and transcript.
Additional information: Loan forgiveness for one year of financial assistance requires one year of practicing medicine in medically underserved area of Georgia.

Amount of award:	$10,000
Number of awards:	10
Number of applicants:	10
Application deadline:	May 15
Total amount awarded:	$100,000

Contact:
Loan Committee
2082 East Exchange Place
Suite 100
Tucker, GA 30084
Website: www.gsfc.org

Georgia Promise Teacher Scholarship

Type of award: Loan, renewable.
Intended use: For junior, senior study at accredited 4-year institution in Georgia. Designated institutions: Any public or private colleges and universities in Georgia currently offering teacher education programs approved by Georgia Professional Standards Commission.
Eligibility: Applicant must be U.S. citizen or permanent resident residing in Georgia.
Basis for selection: Major/career interest in education, teacher; education. Applicant must demonstrate seriousness of purpose and high academic achievement.
Application requirements: Transcript and proof of eligibility. 3.6 GPA at end of sophomore year; be academically classified as junior; have declared education as major and/or be accepted for enrollment into teacher education program leading to initial certification. Must obtain signatures from institution's Department of Education teacher certification official and financial aid office.
Additional information: Must commit to teach one year in Georgia public school for each $1,500 awarded. Teaching must be at preschool, elementary, middle or secondary level.

Amount of award:	$3,000
Number of awards:	327
Total amount awarded:	$934,157

Contact:
Scholarship Committee
2082 East Exchange Place
Suite 100
Tucker, GA 30084
Website: www.gsfc.org

Georgia Regents Scholarship

Type of award: Scholarship.
Intended use: For undergraduate or graduate study in United States. Designated institutions: University system of Georgia schools.
Eligibility: Applicant must be U.S. citizen or permanent resident residing in Georgia.
Basis for selection: Applicant must demonstrate financial need and high academic achievement.
Additional information: Contact the school's financial aid administrator regarding additional requirements and application procedures.

Amount of award:	$500-$1,000

Contact:
Georgia Student Finance Commission
2082 East Exchange Place
Suite 100
Tucker, GA 30084
Phone: 770-414-3000

Georgia Robert C. Byrd Scholarship

Type of award: Scholarship, renewable.
Intended use: For full-time undergraduate study at accredited 2-year or 4-year institution in United States.
Eligibility: Applicant must be high school senior. Applicant must be U.S. citizen or permanent resident residing in Georgia.
Basis for selection: Applicant must demonstrate depth of character, leadership, seriousness of purpose, service orientation and high academic achievement.
Application requirements: Recommendations, essay, transcript and proof of eligibility.

Amount of award:	$1,500
Number of awards:	645
Number of applicants:	800
Total amount awarded:	$699,515

Contact:
Scholarship Committee
Grants and Scholarships Section
2082 East Exchange Place, Suite 100
Tucker, GA 30084
Website: www.gsfc.org

Georgia Service-Cancelable Stafford Loan

Type of award: Loan.
Intended use: For full-time or half-time undergraduate, master's, doctoral or non-degree study at accredited postsecondary institution in Georgia. Designated institutions: GSFA-approved postsecondary schools.
Eligibility: Applicant must be U.S. citizen or permanent resident residing in Georgia.

Basis for selection: Major/career interest in education, teacher; health-related professions.
Additional information: Must have first applied for service-cancelable Stafford loan and been ineligible for maximum amount. Health professions students must have at least 2.0 GPA, education students at least 2.75 GPA. "Pre"-field programs such as pre-med are not eligible. Loan amount is dependent upon availabililty of funds.

Amount of award:	$300-$2,000
Number of awards:	1,403
Number of applicants:	1,891
Application deadline:	June 1
Total amount awarded:	$2,605,725

Contact:
Georgia Student Finance Commission
2082 East Exchange Place
Suite 100
Tucker, GA 30084

Georgia Student Incentive Grant

Type of award: Scholarship, renewable.
Intended use: For full-time freshman, sophomore, junior or senior study in United States. Designated institutions: Eligible post-secondary institutions in Georgia.
Eligibility: Applicant must be U.S. citizen or permanent resident residing in Georgia.
Basis for selection: Applicant must demonstrate financial need.
Additional information: Must have exceptional need. Apply at institution's financial aid office.

Amount of award:	$300-$5,000
Number of awards:	9,965
Number of applicants:	130,000
Total amount awarded:	$4,758,693

Contact:
Georgia Student Finance Commission
2082 East Exchange Place
Suite 100
Tucker, GA 30084
Phone: 770-414-3085
Website: www.gsfc.org

Georgia Tuition Equalization Grant

Type of award: Scholarship, renewable.
Intended use: For full-time undergraduate study at accredited 2-year or 4-year institution. Designated institutions: Approved private institutions in Georgia.
Eligibility: Applicant must be U.S. citizen or permanent resident residing in Georgia.
Application requirements: Proof of eligibility.

Amount of award:	$1,000
Number of awards:	30,168
Number of applicants:	30,168
Total amount awarded:	$25,896,943

Contact:
Grant Committee
2082 East Exchange Place
Suite 100
Tucker, GA 30084
Website: www.gsfc.org

Harry Truman Scholarship Foundation

Harry Truman Scholarship

Type of award: Scholarship.
Intended use: For full-time senior or graduate study at 4-year or graduate institution.
Eligibility: Applicant must be U.S. citizen.
Basis for selection: Major/career interest in public administration/service; governmental public relations; political science/government; education. Applicant must demonstrate leadership, service orientation, financial need and high academic achievement.
Application requirements: Recommendations, essay, transcript and nomination by participating institutions. Must have a signed Institution Nomination Form, a signed Nominee Information Form, and an analysis of a public policy issue.
Additional information: Applicants must participate in Truman Scholars Leadership Week, Awards Ceremony at the Harry S. Truman Library, and Truman Scholars Washington Summer Institute. Awardees receive $3,000 for senior year and $27,000 for graduate study. Open to all fields of study as long as candidate plans to use degree in public service. Must be in top 25% of class.

Amount of award:	$30,000
Number of awards:	78
Application deadline:	January 26

Contact:
Harry Truman Scholarship Foundation
712 Jackson Place NW
Washington, DC 20006
Website: www.truman.gov

Hawaii Community Foundation

Dolly Ching Scholarship Fund

Type of award: Scholarship.
Intended use: For full-time undergraduate study at accredited postsecondary institution in United States. Designated institutions: Any institution in the University of Hawaii system.
Eligibility: Applicant must be U.S. citizen or permanent resident residing in Hawaii.
Basis for selection: Major/career interest in business. Applicant must demonstrate depth of character, service orientation, financial need and high academic achievement.
Application requirements: Recommendations, essay and transcript.
Additional information: Applicants must have permanent address in Hawaii. Applicants who take up mainland residency must have relatives living in Hawaii. Other former Hawaii residents considered on a case by case basis. Must maintain a 3.0 GPA.

Amount of award:	$1,250
Number of awards:	2
Application deadline:	March 2

Laura N. Dowsett Fund

Type of award: Scholarship.
Intended use: For full-time undergraduate or graduate study at accredited 2-year or 4-year institution in Hawaii.
Eligibility: Applicant must be U.S. citizen or permanent resident residing in Hawaii.
Basis for selection: Major/career interest in occupational therapy. Applicant must demonstrate depth of character and financial need.
Application requirements: Recommendations, essay and transcript. At least one letter of recommendation should be from someone in the occupational therapy field.
Additional information: Applicants must have permanent address in Hawaii. Applicants who take up mainland residency must have relatives living in Hawaii. Other former Hawaii residents considered on a case by case basis. Notifications mailed in July.

Amount of award:	$800
Number of awards:	5
Application deadline:	March 2

Contact:
Hawaii Community Foundation
900 Fort Street Mall
Suite 1300
Honolulu, HI 96813
Phone: 808-556-5570

Thz Fo Farm Fund

Type of award: Scholarship.
Intended use: For full-time junior, senior study in Hawaii.
Eligibility: Applicant must be of Chinese heritage. Applicant must be permanent resident residing in Hawaii.
Basis for selection: Major/career interest in gerontology. Applicant must demonstrate financial need and high academic achievement.
Application requirements: Recommendations, essay and transcript.
Additional information: Applicants must have permanent address in Hawaii. Applicants who take up mainland residency must have relatives living in Hawaii. Other former Hawaii residents considered on a case by case basis. Notifications mailed out between April and July.

Amount of award:	$550
Number of awards:	8
Application deadline:	March 2

Contact:
Hawaii Community Foundation
900 Fort Street Mall
Suite 1300
Honolulu, HI 96813
Phone: 808-566-5570

Hawaii Postsecondary Education Commission

Hawaii Student Incentive Grant

Type of award: Scholarship, renewable.
Intended use: For full-time or half-time undergraduate or graduate study at accredited postsecondary institution in Hawaii. Designated institutions: Participating institutions in the Hawaii system.
Eligibility: Applicant must be U.S. citizen residing in Hawaii.
Basis for selection: Applicant must demonstrate financial need.
Application requirements: Applicant must be eligible for a Pell grant.
Additional information: Contact school's financial aid office for application.

Amount of award:	$2,000
Number of applicants:	600
Application deadline:	March 1, October 1
Notification begins:	July 1, November 1

Hawaii Tuition Waiver

Type of award: Scholarship, renewable.
Intended use: For undergraduate or graduate study at accredited postsecondary institution in Hawaii. Designated institutions: University of Hawaii campuses.
Eligibility: Applicant must be residing in Hawaii.
Basis for selection: Applicant must demonstrate financial need and high academic achievement.
Additional information: Contact financial aid office of University of Hawaii campus. Tuition waiver amount dependent upon applicant's resident or non-resident status and level of study. Deadline vary on each campus.

Amount of award:	$730-$6,090
Number of awards:	10,000
Total amount awarded:	$10,007,710

Idaho State Board of Education

Idaho Education Incentive Loan Forgiveness Program

Type of award: Loan, renewable.
Intended use: For full-time undergraduate study in Idaho.
Eligibility: Applicant must be residing in Idaho.
Basis for selection: Major/career interest in education, teacher; nursing.
Additional information: Loan forgiveness for teaching or nursing service in Idaho. Must have graduated from Idaho secondary school within last two years. Contact financial aid office of postsecondary institution for application materials and information.

Contact:
Idaho Stste Board of Education
P.O.Box 83720
Boise, ID 83720-0037

Idaho Minority and At-Risk Student Scholarship

Type of award: Scholarship.
Intended use: For full-time undergraduate study. Designated institutions: Boise State University, Idaho State University, North Idaho College, Eastern Idaho Technical College, Lewis-

Clark State College, University of Idaho, College of Southern Idaho, Albertson College.
Eligibility: Applicant must be residing in Idaho.
Basis for selection: Applicant must demonstrate financial need.
Additional information: Must be talented student at risk of failing to realize ambitions due to cultural, economic, or physical circumstances. Ethnic minority and first-generation college students given special consideration. Contact high school counselor or financial aid office of designated participating postsecondary institution for specific eligibility requirements and application.
  Amount of award: $2,700
  Number of awards: 40
  Total amount awarded: $108,000
Contact:
Idaho State Board of Education
P.O. Box 83720
Boise, ID 83720-0037

Idaho Paul A. Fowler Memorial Scholarship

Type of award: Scholarship.
Intended use: For full-time freshman study. Designated institutions: Public or private nonprofit institution.
Eligibility: Applicant must be high school senior. Applicant must be U.S. citizen or permanent resident residing in Idaho.
Basis for selection: Applicant must demonstrate seriousness of purpose and high academic achievement.
Application requirements: Transcript and proof of eligibility. ACT scores.
Additional information: Contact high school counselor for information and application materials.
  Amount of award: $3,000
  Number of awards: 2
  Number of applicants: 305
  Application deadline: January 31
  Total amount awarded: $6,000
Contact:
Idaho State Board of Education
P.O. Box 83720
Boise, ID 83720-0037

Idaho Robert C. Byrd Honors Scholarship

Type of award: Scholarship, renewable.
Intended use: For full-time freshman study at 2-year or 4-year institution.
Eligibility: Applicant must be high school senior. Applicant must be U.S. citizen or permanent resident residing in Idaho.
Basis for selection: Applicant must demonstrate high academic achievement.
Application requirements: Recommendations, transcript and proof of eligibility.
Additional information: Application and information available through high school guidance office.
  Amount of award: $1,500
  Application deadline: April 20
  Notification begins: , February
Contact:
Idaho State Department of Education
P.O. Box 83720
Boise, ID 83720-0027
Phone: 208-332-6946

Idaho Student Incentive Grant

Type of award: Scholarship, renewable.
Intended use: For full-time or half-time freshman, sophomore, junior, senior, master's or doctoral study at vocational, 2-year, 4-year or graduate institution in Idaho.
Eligibility: Applicant must be U.S. citizen or permanent resident residing in Idaho.
Basis for selection: Applicant must demonstrate financial need.
Application requirements: FAFSA.
Additional information: Institution makes recommendations to Idaho State Board of Education. Contact financial aid office of Idaho institution for materials or additional information.
  Number of awards: 1,900
  Total amount awarded: $698,900
Contact:
Idaho State Board of Education
P.O. Box 83720
Boise, ID 83720-0027

State of Idaho Scholarship

Type of award: Scholarship, renewable.
Intended use: For full-time undergraduate study at accredited vocational, 2-year or 4-year institution in Idaho. Designated institutions: Idaho Institutions.
Eligibility: Applicant must be enrolled in high school. Applicant must be U.S. citizen or permanent resident residing in Idaho.
Basis for selection: Applicant must demonstrate high academic achievement.
Application requirements: Recommendations. Must submit ACT scores and class rank.
Additional information: Contact high school guidance counselor for information and application materials. Must be in top ten percent of class. 25 percent of scholarships given to vocational students.
  Amount of award: $2,750-$2,750
  Number of awards: 20
  Number of applicants: 511
  Application deadline: January 31
  Total amount awarded: $300,329
Contact:
Idaho State Board of Education
P.O. Box 83720
Boise, ID 83720-0037

Illinois Student Assistance Commission

Illinois D.A. DeBolt Teacher Shortage Scholarship

Type of award: Scholarship, renewable.
Intended use: For full-time or half-time sophomore, junior or senior study at accredited 2-year or 4-year institution in Illinois. Designated institutions: Illinois public institution.
Eligibility: Applicant must be U.S. citizen or permanent resident residing in Illinois.
Basis for selection: Major/career interest in education.

Applicant must demonstrate financial need and high academic achievement.
Application requirements: FAFSA.
Additional information: Alternate phone (use outside of Illinois, Iowa, Indiana, Missouri, or Wisconsin): 847-948-8550. Must major in teacher shortage discipline. Recipients must agree to teach at an approved Illinois institution in an approved field for one year for each year of assistance received. Failure to complete requirement turns scholarship into loan.

Amount of award:	$5,000
Number of awards:	280
Number of applicants:	1,200
Application deadline:	May 1
Total amount awarded:	$1,307,001

Contact:
Illinois Student Assistance Commission
500 West Monroe, 3rd Floor
Springfield, IL 62704
Phone: 800-899-ISAC
Website: www.isac1.org

Illinois Descendents Grant Program

Type of award: Scholarship, renewable.
Intended use: For full-time or half-time undergraduate or graduate study at 2-year, 4-year or graduate institution in Illinois. Designated institutions: approved Illinois institutions.
Eligibility: Applicant must be U.S. citizen residing in Illinois. Applicant's parent must have been killed or disabled in work-related accident as fire fighter, police officer or public safety officer.
Application requirements: Proof of eligibility.
Additional information: Alternate phone (use outside of Illinois, Iowa, Indiana, Missouri, or Wisconsin): 847-948-8550. Grant for tuition and fees for spouse and children of policemen, firemen or corrections officers over 90 percent disabled or killed in line of duty.

Amount of award:	$4,000
Number of awards:	28
Number of applicants:	28
Total amount awarded:	$74,817

Contact:
Illinois Student Assistance Commission
Client Relations
1755 Lake Cook Road
Deerfield, IL 60015
Phone: 800-899-ISAC
Website: www.isac1.org

Illinois Incentive for Access

Type of award: Scholarship.
Intended use: For freshman study at 2-year or 4-year institution. Designated institutions: Illinois Institutions.
Eligibility: Applicant must be high school senior. Applicant must be U.S. citizen or permanent resident.
Additional information: Alternate phone (use outside of Illinois, Iowa, Indiana, Missouri, or Wisconsin):847-948-8550.

Amount of award:	$500
Number of awards:	19,469
Number of applicants:	46,359
Application deadline:	October 1
Total amount awarded:	$7,939,250

Contact:
Client Relations
1755 Lake Cook Road
Deerfield, IL 60015
Phone: 1-800-899-ISAC
Website: www.isac1.org

Illinois Merit Recognition Scholarship

Type of award: Scholarship.
Intended use: For full-time or half-time freshman study at 2-year or 4-year institution in Illinois. Designated institutions: Illinois institutions or a United States Service academy.
Eligibility: Applicant must be high school senior. Applicant must be U.S. citizen or permanent resident residing in Illinois.
Basis for selection: Applicant must demonstrate high academic achievement.
Application requirements: Proof of eligibility.
Additional information: Alternate phone (use outside of Illinois, Iowa, Indiana, Missouri, or Wisconsin): 847-948-8550. Must rank in top five percent of class. Contact high school guidance counselor to certify eligibility and request applications.

Amount of award:	$1,000
Number of awards:	2,168
Number of applicants:	2,168
Total amount awarded:	$2,156,835

Contact:
Illinois Student Assistance Commission
Client Relations
1755 Lake Cook Road
Deerfield, IL 60015
Phone: 800-899-ISAC
Website: www.isac1.org

Illinois Minority Teachers Scholarship

Type of award: Scholarship, renewable.
Intended use: For full-time sophomore, junior or senior study at 2-year or 4-year institution in Illinois. Designated institutions: Illinois institutions.
Eligibility: Applicant must be of minority background. Applicant must be U.S. citizen or permanent resident residing in Illinois.
Basis for selection: Major/career interest in education, teacher. Applicant must demonstrate high academic achievement.
Application requirements: Proof of eligibility.
Additional information: Alternate phone (use outside of Illinois, Iowa, Indiana, Missouri, or Wisconsin): 847-948-8550. Recipients agree to teach at an approved Illinois institution in an approved field for one year for each year of grant assistance received. Failure to complete requirement turns scholarship into loan.

Amount of award:	$5,000
Number of awards:	394
Number of applicants:	500
Application deadline:	May 1
Total amount awarded:	$1,738,341

Contact:
Illinois Student Assistance Commission
Client Relations
1755 Lake Cook Road
Deerfield, IL 60015
Phone: 800-899-ISAC
Website: www.isac1.org

Illinois Monetary Award

Type of award: Scholarship, renewable.
Intended use: For full-time or half-time undergraduate study at 2-year or 4-year institution in Illinois.
Eligibility: Applicant must be U.S. citizen or permanent resident residing in Illinois.
Basis for selection: Applicant must demonstrate financial need.
Application requirements: Must reapply when renewing scholarship.
Additional information: Alternate phone (use outside of Illinois, Iowa, Indiana, Missouri, or Wisconsin): 847-948-8550. Application deadline October 1 for first-time applicants, June 1 for continuing applicants.

Amount of award:	$300-$4,320
Number of awards:	127,607
Number of applicants:	400,056
Application deadline:	October 1
Total amount awarded:	$263,261,987

Contact:
Illinois Student Assistance Commission
Client Relations
1755 Lake Cook Road
Deerfield, IL 60015
Phone: 800-899-ISAC
Website: www.isac1.org

Illinois National Guard Grant

Type of award: Scholarship, renewable.
Intended use: For full-time or half-time undergraduate or graduate study at 2-year or 4-year institution in Illinois. Designated institutions: Illinois public only.
Eligibility: Applicant must be residing in Illinois. Applicant must be who served in the Reserves/National Guard.
Application requirements: Proof of eligibility.
Additional information: Alternate phone (use outside of Illinois, Iowa, Indiana, Missouri, or Wisconsin): 847-948-8550. Must have served at least one year in Illinois National Guard or Naval Militia. Only enlisted personnel or officers up to rank of captain currently serving with the Guard are eligible.

Number of awards:	2,488
Number of applicants:	2,488
Total amount awarded:	$3,369,879

Contact:
Illinois Student Assistance Commission
Client Relations
1755 Lake Cook Road
Deerfield, IL 60015
Phone: 800-899-ISAC
Website: www.isac1.org

Illinois Robert C. Byrd Honors Scholarship

Type of award: Scholarship, renewable.
Intended use: For full-time undergraduate study at accredited postsecondary institution in United States.
Eligibility: Applicant must be U.S. citizen or permanent resident residing in Illinois.
Basis for selection: Applicant must demonstrate high academic achievement.
Additional information: Must rank in top 5% of United States high school graduates. Alternate phone (use outside of Illinois, Iowa, Indiana, Missouri, or Wisconsin): 847-948-8550.

Amount of award:	$1,500
Number of awards:	1,102
Application deadline:	January 15
Total amount awarded:	$1,204,561

Contact:
Illinois Student Assistance Commission
500 West Monroe, 3rd Floor
Springfield, IL 62704
Phone: 800-899-ISAC
Website: www.isac1.org

Illinois Student-to-Student Grant

Type of award: Scholarship, renewable.
Intended use: For undergraduate study at 2-year or 4-year institution in Illinois. Designated institutions: Illinois Institutions that must participate in program.
Eligibility: Applicant must be U.S. citizen or permanent resident residing in Illinois.
Basis for selection: Applicant must demonstrate financial need.
Application requirements: Must reapply if renewing.
Additional information: Alternate phone (use outside of Illinois, Iowa, Indiana, Missouri, or Wisconsin): 847-948-8550.

Amount of award:	$1,000
Number of awards:	3,347
Number of applicants:	3,347
Application deadline:	October 1
Total amount awarded:	$1,696,714

Contact:
Illinois Student Assistance Commission
Client Relations
1755 Lake Cook Road
Deerfield, IL 60015
Phone: 800-899-ISAC
Website: www.isac1.org

Illinois Veteran Grant

Type of award: Scholarship, renewable.
Intended use: For full-time or half-time undergraduate or graduate study at 2-year, 4-year or graduate institution in Illinois. Designated institutions: Public Institutions in Illinois.
Eligibility: Applicant must be U.S. citizen or permanent resident residing in Illinois. Applicant must be veteran.
Application requirements: Proof of eligibility.
Additional information: Alternate phone (use outside of Illinois, Iowa, Indiana, Missouri, Wisconsin): 847-948-8550. Must have had at least one year of active duty. Contact field office of Illinois Department of Veterans Affairs or financial aid office of institution.

Number of awards:	15,024
Number of applicants:	15,024
Total amount awarded:	$201,223,795

Contact:
Illinois Student Assistance Commission
Client Relations
1755 Lake Cook Road
Deerfield, IL 60015
Phone: 800-899-ISAC
Website: www.isac1.org

Indiana Student Assistance Commission

Indiana Higher Education Grant

Type of award: Scholarship, renewable.
Intended use: For full-time undergraduate study at vocational, 2-year or 4-year institution in Indiana.
Eligibility: Applicant must be enrolled in high school. Applicant must be U.S. citizen or permanent resident residing in Indiana.
Basis for selection: Applicant must demonstrate financial need.
Application requirements: Proof of eligibility.
Additional information: Renewal recipients must maintain satisfactory academic progress. Summer work-study program available to recipients.

Amount of award:	$200
Number of awards:	57,426
Number of applicants:	150,000
Application deadline:	March 1
Notification begins:	July 1
Total amount awarded:	$129,646,575

Indiana Hoosier Scholar Program

Type of award: Scholarship.
Intended use: For full-time freshman study at accredited vocational, 2-year or 4-year institution in Indiana.
Eligibility: Applicant must be high school senior. Applicant must be U.S. citizen or permanent resident residing in Indiana.
Basis for selection: Applicant must demonstrate high academic achievement.
Application requirements: Proof of eligibility and nomination by high school. Nomination forms must be submitted by 3/1.
Additional information: List of eligible Indiana colleges provided with application. Applicant must be in top 20 percent of high school class.

Amount of award:	$500
Number of awards:	787
Number of applicants:	787
Application deadline:	March 1
Notification begins:	April 15
Total amount awarded:	$393,500

Indiana Minority Teacher Scholarship

Type of award: Scholarship, renewable.
Intended use: For full-time undergraduate or graduate study at accredited 4-year or graduate institution in Indiana.
Eligibility: Applicant must be African American, Mexican American, Hispanic American or Puerto Rican. Applicant must be U.S. citizen or permanent resident residing in Indiana.
Basis for selection: Major/career interest in education, special; occupational therapy; physical therapy. Applicant must demonstrate high academic achievement.
Application requirements: Proof of eligibility.
Additional information: Contact financial aid office of Indiana institution.

Amount of award:	$1,000-$4,000
Number of awards:	326
Number of applicants:	326
Total amount awarded:	$327,791

Indiana Nursing Scholarship

Type of award: Scholarship, renewable.
Intended use: For full-time or half-time undergraduate study at accredited vocational, 2-year or 4-year institution.
Eligibility: Applicant must be African American, Mexican American, Hispanic American or Puerto Rican. Applicant must be U.S. citizen residing in Indiana.
Basis for selection: Major/career interest in nursing. Applicant must demonstrate financial need and high academic achievement.
Application requirements: Proof of eligibility. FAF form.
Additional information: 2.0 GPA required. Deadline varies by institution. All students must be Indiana Residents attending eligible Indiana Institutions.

Amount of award:	$50-$5,000
Number of awards:	637
Number of applicants:	637
Total amount awarded:	$322,286

Indiana Special Education Services Scholarship

Type of award: Scholarship, renewable.
Intended use: For full-time undergraduate, master's study at accredited 4-year or graduate institution in Indiana. Designated institutions: Indiana institutions.
Eligibility: Applicant must be U.S. citizen residing in Indiana.
Basis for selection: Major/career interest in education; education, special; occupational therapy; physical therapy. Applicant must demonstrate high academic achievement.
Application requirements: Proof of eligibility.
Additional information: Scholarship selection made by individual schools. Minimum 2.0 GPA required to renew scholarship. All students must be Indiana Residents attending eligible Indiana Institutions.

Amount of award:	$1,000
Number of awards:	94
Number of applicants:	94
Total amount awarded:	$80,950

Robert C. Byrd Honors Scholarship

Type of award: Scholarship, renewable.
Intended use: For full-time freshman, sophomore, junior or

senior study at accredited 2-year or 4-year institution in United States.
Eligibility: Applicant must be high school senior. Applicant must be U.S. citizen or permanent resident residing in Indiana.
Basis for selection: Applicant must demonstrate high academic achievement.
Application requirements: Transcript and proof of eligibility.
Additional information: Contact high school guidance counselor for information.

Amount of award:	$1,110
Number of awards:	569
Number of applicants:	569
Application deadline:	April 24
Notification begins:	June 1
Total amount awarded:	$637,849

Contact:
Indiana Student Assistance Commission
150 West Market Street, Suite 500
Indianapolis, IN 46204

Iowa College Student Aid Commission

Iowa Grant

Type of award: Scholarship, renewable.
Intended use: For full-time or half-time freshman, sophomore, junior or senior study at vocational, 2-year or 4-year institution in Iowa.
Eligibility: Applicant must be high school senior. Applicant must be U.S. citizen or permanent resident residing in Iowa.
Basis for selection: Applicant must demonstrate financial need.
Application requirements: Proof of eligibility. Financial aid forms.

Amount of award:	$1,000
Number of awards:	1,889
Number of applicants:	2,300
Total amount awarded:	$1,531,336

Contact:
Iowa College Student Aid Commission
200 Tenth Street, Fourth Floor
Des Moines, IA 50309-3609
Website: www.state.ia.us/collegeaid

Iowa National Guard Tuition Aid Program

Type of award: Scholarship, renewable.
Intended use: For full-time or half-time undergraduate study.
Eligibility: Applicant must be U.S. citizen residing in Iowa. Applicant must be who served in the Reserves/National Guard.

Total amount awarded:	$625,000

Contact:
Iowa College Student Aid Commission
7700 NW Beaver Drive
Johnston, IA 50131
Website: www.state.ia.us/collegeaid/

Iowa Robert C. Byrd Honor Scholarship

Type of award: Scholarship.
Intended use: For full-time undergraduate study at accredited 2-year or 4-year institution in United States.
Eligibility: Applicant must be high school senior. Applicant must be U.S. citizen or permanent resident residing in Iowa.
Basis for selection: Applicant must demonstrate high academic achievement.
Application requirements: Recommendations, essay, transcript and proof of eligibility.

Amount of award:	$1,500
Number of awards:	214
Number of applicants:	850
Application deadline:	April 15
Notification begins:	June 1
Total amount awarded:	$321,727

Contact:
Iowa College Student Aid Commission
200 Tenth Street, Fourth Floor
Des Moines, IA 50309-3609
Website: www.state.ia.us/collegeaid/

Iowa Tuition Grant

Type of award: Scholarship, renewable.
Intended use: For full-time or half-time undergraduate study at accredited 2-year or 4-year institution in Iowa.
Eligibility: Applicant must be high school senior. Applicant must be U.S. citizen or permanent resident residing in Iowa.
Basis for selection: Applicant must demonstrate financial need.
Application requirements: Proof of eligibility. Financial aid forms.

Number of awards:	14,111
Number of applicants:	23,961
Application deadline:	June 1
Notification begins:	May 30
Total amount awarded:	$40,921,900

Contact:
Iowa College Student Aid Commission
200 Tenth Street, Fourth Floor
Des Moines, IA 50309-3609
Website: www.state.ia.us/collegeaid

Iowa Vocational-Technical Tuition Grant

Type of award: Scholarship, renewable.
Intended use: For full-time undergraduate study at accredited vocational institution in Iowa.
Eligibility: Applicant must be U.S. citizen or permanent resident residing in Iowa.
Basis for selection: Applicant must demonstrate financial need.
Application requirements: Proof of eligibility.
Additional information: Only vocational-technical career majors considered.

Amount of award:	$150-$600
Number of awards:	4,473
Number of applicants:	20,261
Application deadline:	June 1
Total amount awarded:	$1,811,426

Contact:
Iowa College Student Aid Commission
200 Tenth Street, Fourth Floor
Des Moines, IA 50309-3609
Website: www.state.ia.us/collegeaid/

Iowa Work Study

Type of award: Internship, renewable.
Intended use: For full-time or half-time undergraduate study at accredited vocational, 2-year or 4-year institution in Iowa.
Eligibility: Applicant must be enrolled in high school. Applicant must be U.S. citizen or permanent resident residing in Iowa.
Basis for selection: Applicant must demonstrate financial need.
Application requirements: Proof of eligibility.

Amount of award:	$871
Number of awards:	4,594
Application deadline:	June 1
Total amount awarded:	$3,147,976

Contact:
Iowa College Student Aid Commission
200 Tenth Street, Fourth Floor
Des Moines, IA 50309-3609
Website: www.state.ia.us/collegeaid/

State of Iowa Scholarship

Type of award: Scholarship.
Intended use: For full-time freshman study at accredited vocational, 2-year or 4-year institution in Iowa.
Eligibility: Applicant must be high school senior. Applicant must be U.S. citizen or permanent resident residing in Iowa.
Basis for selection: Applicant must demonstrate high academic achievement.
Application requirements: Proof of eligibility.
Additional information: Must rank in top 15 percent of class and have taken ACT test. For class ranking and other criteria for selection consult with high school guidance counselor.

Amount of award:	$400
Number of awards:	1,700
Number of applicants:	4,306
Application deadline:	November 1
Notification begins:	March 20
Total amount awarded:	$492,000

Contact:
Iowa College Student Aid Commission
200 Tenth Street, Fourth Floor
Des Moines, IA 50309-3609
Website: www.state.ia.us/collegeaid

James Madison Memorial Fellowship Foundation

James Madison Memorial Junior Fellowship

Type of award: Research grant.
Intended use: For master's, doctoral study at accredited 4-year or graduate institution in United States.
Eligibility: Applicant must be U.S. citizen or permanent resident.
Basis for selection: Major/career interest in American history; political science/government; history. Applicant must demonstrate depth of character, leadership, seriousness of purpose and service orientation.
Application requirements: Recommendations, essay, transcript and proof of eligibility.
Additional information: Award can only be used toward 2 years full-time graduate study. All fellows are required to attend a four-week, graduate level seminar in Washington, D.C. Junior fellows must possess a bachelor's degree no later than 8/31 of the year in which he or she is applying. James Madison fellows must agree to teach American History, American Government or Social Studies full time in a secondary school for no less than one year for each full academic year of study under a fellowship.

Amount of award:	$24,000
Application deadline:	March 1

James Madison Memorial Senior Fellowship

Type of award: Research grant.
Intended use: For master's, doctoral study at accredited 4-year or graduate institution in United States.
Eligibility: Applicant must be U.S. citizen or permanent resident.
Basis for selection: Major/career interest in political science/government. Applicant must demonstrate depth of character, leadership, seriousness of purpose and service orientation.
Application requirements: Recommendations, essay, transcript and proof of eligibility.
Additional information: Award can only be used toward a 1st or 2nd master's degree study, full-time or part-time. All fellows are required to attend a four-week, graduate level seminar in Washington, D.C. Senior fellows must be a full-time teacher of American History, Americn Government or Social Studies in grades 7-12 and be under contract or prospective contract to teach full time as a secondary school teacher. Senior fellows are eligible for a maximum of up to $24,000 for up to five years of part-time study, pro-rated over the period of study. James Madison fellows must agree to teach American History, American Government or Social Studies full time in a secondary school for no less than one year for each full academic year of study under a fellowship.

Amount of award:	$24,000
Application deadline:	March 1

Contact:
James Madison Memorial Fellowship Foundation
2201 N. Dodge St.
P.O. Box 4030
Iowa City, IA 52243-4030

Kansas Board of Regents

Kansas Ethnic Minority Scholarship

Type of award: Scholarship, renewable.
Intended use: For full-time freshman, sophomore, junior or senior study at 2-year or 4-year institution in Kansas.
Eligibility: Applicant must be of minority background. Applicant must be U.S. citizen or permanent resident residing in Kansas.
Basis for selection: Applicant must demonstrate financial need.
Application requirements: $10 application fee. Proof of eligibility.
Additional information: Must be recognized in National Merit Scholarship competition, or be designated Hispanic scholar, or have at least 3.0 GPA, ACT score of 21, SAT I score minimum 810, or rank in upper-third of high school graduating class. One-time $10 processing fee for any or all programs listed on application form.

Amount of award:	$1,500
Number of awards:	200
Number of applicants:	500
Application deadline:	April 1
Notification begins:	May 20
Total amount awarded:	$291,088

Contact:
Kansas Board of Regents
700 SW Harrison
Suite 1410
Topeka, KS 66603-3760

Kansas Nursing Scholarship

Type of award: Loan, renewable.
Intended use: For full-time undergraduate, master's or non-degree study at postsecondary institution in Kansas.
Eligibility: Applicant must be residing in Kansas.
Basis for selection: Major/career interest in nursing.
Application requirements: $10 application fee. Proof of eligibility.
Additional information: Must obtain sponsorship from hospital or long-term care facility. Loan forgiveness for nursing service with sponsoring facility: one year for each year of financial assistance. One time $10 processing fee for any or all programs listed on application form.

Amount of award:	$2,500-$3,500
Number of awards:	143
Number of applicants:	207
Application deadline:	May 1
Notification begins:	June 15
Total amount awarded:	$475,500

Contact:
Kansas Board of Regents
700 SW Harrison
Suite 1410
Topeka, KS 66603-3760

Kansas Optometry Program

Type of award: Scholarship.
Intended use: For full-time first professional study. Designated institutions: University of Missouri School of Optometry, University of Houston School of Optometry, Northeastern Oklahoma State University School of Optometry.
Eligibility: Applicant must be residing in Kansas.
Basis for selection: Major/career interest in optometry/ophthalmology.
Application requirements: $10 application fee. Proof of eligibility.
Additional information: Award helps pay difference between resident and non-resident tuition at eligible out-of-state institutions. Students at University of Houston and Northeastern Oklahoma State University must repay directly or through service as optometrist in Kansas; one year of practice for each year of financial assistance. One-time $10 processing fee for any or all programs listed on application form.

Number of awards:	36
Number of applicants:	62
Application deadline:	May 1
Total amount awarded:	$136,088

Contact:
Kansas Board of Regents
700 SW Harrison
Suite 1410
Topeka, KS 66603-3760

Kansas Osteopathic Program

Type of award: Loan, renewable.
Intended use: For full-time first professional study at graduate institution in United States.
Eligibility: Applicant must be residing in Kansas.
Basis for selection: Major/career interest in medicine, osteopathic. Applicant must demonstrate financial need.
Application requirements: $10 application fee. Interview, essay and proof of eligibility.
Additional information: Loan forgiveness for practicing primary care medicine in medically underserved area in Kansas. Must attend accredited school of osteopathy. One-time $10 processing fee for any or all programs listed on application form.

Amount of award:	$15,000
Number of awards:	36
Number of applicants:	41
Application deadline:	May 1
Total amount awarded:	$540,000

Contact:
Kansas Board of Regents
700 SW Harrison
Suite 1410
Topeka, KS 66603-3760

Kansas Regents Supplemental Grant

Type of award: Scholarship.
Intended use: For undergraduate study at 4-year institution in Kansas. Designated institutions: Public 4-year institutions in Kansas.
Eligibility: Applicant must be residing in Kansas.
Basis for selection: Applicant must demonstrate financial need.
Application requirements: $10 application fee. FAFSA.
Additional information: Obtain Free Application for Federal

Student Aid (FAFSA) from high school or college financial aid office. Award renewable--must reapply. One time $10 processing fee for any or all programs listed on application form.

Amount of award:	$200-$1,000
Number of awards:	3,648
Number of applicants:	12,943
Application deadline:	April 1
Notification begins:	May 31
Total amount awarded:	$3,105,887

Contact:
Kansas Board of Regents
700 SW Harrison
Suite 1410
Tokepa, KS 66603-3760

Kansas State Scholarship

Type of award: Scholarship, renewable.
Intended use: For full-time undergraduate study at postsecondary institution in Kansas.
Eligibility: Applicant must be high school senior. Applicant must be residing in Kansas.
Basis for selection: Major/career interest in nursing. Applicant must demonstrate financial need.
Application requirements: $10 application fee. Proof of eligibility.
Additional information: Must be designated by high school as Kansas State Scholar based on ACT scores. Notification of award decision in April or May. One-time $10 processing fee for any or all programs listed on application form.

Amount of award:	$50-$1,000
Number of awards:	1,478
Number of applicants:	1,500
Application deadline:	April 1
Total amount awarded:	$1,447,588

Contact:
Kansas Board of Regents
700 SW Harrison
Suite 1410
Topeka, KS 66603-3760

Kansas Teacher Scholarship

Type of award: Loan, renewable.
Intended use: For full-time freshman, sophomore, junior or senior study at 4-year institution in Kansas.
Eligibility: Applicant must be residing in Kansas.
Basis for selection: Major/career interest in education, teacher.
Application requirements: $10 application fee. Proof of eligibility.
Additional information: Must attend Kansas institution that offers education degree. Loan forgiveness for teaching in designated "hard-to-fill" subject areas in Kansas: one year for each year of financial assistance. Notification of award decision in April. One-time $10 processing fee for any or all programs listed on application form.

Amount of award:	$5,000
Number of awards:	71
Number of applicants:	242
Application deadline:	April 1
Total amount awarded:	$348,908

Contact:
Kansas Board of Regents
700 SW Harrison
Suite 1410
Topeka, KS 66603-3760

Kansas Tuition Grant

Type of award: Scholarship, renewable.
Intended use: For undergraduate study at 4-year institution in Kansas. Designated institutions: Kansas Board of Regents institutions.
Eligibility: Applicant must be residing in Kansas.
Basis for selection: Applicant must demonstrate financial need.
Application requirements: $10 application fee. FAFSA.
Additional information: One time $10 processing fee for any or all programs listed on application form.

Amount of award:	$200-$2,000
Number of awards:	3,035
Number of applicants:	3,602
Application deadline:	April 1
Notification begins:	May 1
Total amount awarded:	$5,523,233

Contact:
Kansas Board of Regents
700 SW Harrison
Suite 1410
Topeka, KS 66603-3760

Kansas Vocational Education Scholarship

Type of award: Scholarship, renewable.
Intended use: For full-time undergraduate study at vocational, 2-year or 4-year institution in Kansas.
Eligibility: Applicant must be residing in Kansas.
Application requirements: $10 application fee. Proof of eligibility. vocational examination.
Additional information: Must be among top 100 scorers on vocational examination. Funding for maximum two years of study in an approved vocational program. Register by mid-October for November examination; by mid-February for March examination. Award notification in May. One-time $10 processing fee for any or all programs listed on application form.

Amount of award:	$500
Number of awards:	135
Number of applicants:	344
Total amount awarded:	$67,500

Contact:
Kansas Board of Regents
700 SW Harrison
Suite 1410
Topeka, KS 66603-3760

Kentucky Higher Education Assistance Authority

Kentucky College Access Program (CAP) Grant

Type of award: Scholarship, renewable.
Intended use: For full-time or half-time undergraduate study at accredited vocational, 2-year or 4-year institution in Kentucky.

Eligibility: Applicant must be U.S. citizen or permanent resident residing in Kentucky.
Basis for selection: Applicant must demonstrate financial need.
Application requirements: Proof of eligibility. FAFSA; applicant ineligible if family contribution exceeds $1500.

Amount of award:	$100-$1,020
Number of awards:	24,650
Number of applicants:	178,550
Notification begins:	May 15
Total amount awarded:	$20,299,500

Contact:
Kentucky Higher Education Assistance Authority
Grant Programs
1050 U.S. 127 South
Frankfort, KY 40601-4323
Phone: 502-696-7393

Kentucky Teacher Scholarship

Type of award: Loan, renewable.
Intended use: For full-time undergraduate study at 2-year, 4-year or graduate institution in Kentucky.
Eligibility: Applicant must be U.S. citizen residing in Kentucky.
Basis for selection: Major/career interest in education, teacher. Applicant must demonstrate financial need.
Application requirements: Proof of eligibility.
Additional information: Must enroll in course of study leading to Kentucky teacher certification. Loan forgiveness for teaching in Kentucky schools: one year for each year of financial assistance, two years if service is in teacher shortage area. Cannot be enrolled in a program that leads to a degree, diploma or certificate in religion, divinity or theology.

Amount of award:	$5,000
Number of awards:	390
Number of applicants:	859
Application deadline:	May 8
Notification begins:	May 30
Total amount awarded:	$1,715,700

Contact:
Kentucky Higher Education Assistance Authority
Teacher Scholarship Program
1050 U.S. 127 South
Frankfort, KY 40601-4323
Phone: 502-696-7393

Kentucky Tuition Grant

Type of award: Scholarship, renewable.
Intended use: For full-time undergraduate study at 2-year or 4-year institution in Kentucky. Designated institutions: Private nonprofit institutions.
Eligibility: Applicant must be U.S. citizen residing in Kentucky.
Basis for selection: Applicant must demonstrate financial need.
Application requirements: Interview and proof of eligibility.
Additional information: Must file Free Application for Federal Student Aid (FAFSA).

Amount of award:	$200-$1,500
Number of awards:	6,260
Number of applicants:	13,530
Notification begins:	May 15
Total amount awarded:	$8,602,300

Contact:
Kentucky Higher Education Assistance Authority
Grant Programs
1050 U.S. 127 South
Frankfort, KY 40601-4323
Phone: 502-696-7393

Kentucky Work-Study Program

Type of award: Internship, renewable.
Intended use: For full-time or half-time undergraduate, master's, doctoral, first professional or postgraduate study at vocational, 2-year, 4-year or graduate institution in Kentucky.
Eligibility: Applicant must be U.S. citizen residing in Kentucky.
Application requirements: Interview and proof of eligibility.
Additional information: Job must be related to major course of study. Work study wage is at least the federal minimum wage. Cannot be enrolled in a religion, theology or divinity program.

Number of awards:	1,410
Total amount awarded:	$857,600

Contact:
Kentucky Higher Education Assistance Authority
KHEAA Work-Study Program
1050 U.S. 127 South
Frankfort, KY 40601-4323
Phone: 502-696-7393

Library of Congress

Library of Congress Junior Fellows Internship

Type of award: Internship.
Intended use: For undergraduate or graduate study in Washington, DC. Designated institutions: Library of Congress.
Basis for selection: Major/career interest in library science. Applicant must demonstrate seriousness of purpose.
Application requirements: Interview, recommendations and transcript. Cover letter indicating subject areas applicant is interested in, as well as any language abilities.
Additional information: One paid position at $300 per week for 14 weeks. There is also a variable number of unpaid positions. Applications from women, minorities, and people with disabilities encouraged. Those who have completed their degree since August 1998 also eligible. Also open to students in Hispanic/Latin American/Carribean studies.

Library of Congress: Library of Congress Junior Fellows Internship

Amount of award:	$4,200
Number of awards:	8
Number of applicants:	45
Notification begins:	1
Total amount awarded:	$4,200

Contact:
Library of Congress
Hispanic Division
Washington, DC 20540-4850
Phone: 202-707-8253
Website: lcweb.loc.gov/rr/hispanic

Louisiana Department of Education

Louisiana Innovative Professional Development/Teacher Tuition Exemption

Type of award: Scholarship.
Intended use: For undergraduate or graduate study in Louisiana.
Eligibility: Applicant must be U.S. citizen or permanent resident.
Basis for selection: Major/career interest in education, teacher.
Application requirements: Proof of eligibility. Authorization from applicant's principal and/or school system.
Additional information: Tuition exemption limited to courses directly relating to classroom teacher's job assignment. Applicant must be working as full-time teacher in Louisiana or on approved leave. Courses may be used toward graduate degree or to enhance knowledge of current job assignment. Application deadline April 15 for summer term. Contact Louisiana parish school system or non-public school system for application.

Number of awards:	500
Number of applicants:	5,000
Application deadline:	July 1, November 15

Louisiana Department of Social Services

Louisiana Social Services Rehabilitation/Vocational Aid For Disabled Persons

Type of award: Scholarship, renewable.
Intended use: For undergraduate, graduate or non-degree study.
Eligibility: Applicant must be visually impaired, hearing impaired, physically challenged or learning disabled. Applicant must be residing in Louisiana.
Basis for selection: Applicant must demonstrate financial need.
Application requirements: Proof of eligibility.
Additional information: Must have medically verifiable disability which constitutes substantial handicap to employment. Most severely disabled given preference. Mentally disabled also eligible. Provides monetary assistance for education leading to development of employable skill. Awards vary according to severity of disability.

Contact:
Louisiana Rehabilitation Services
8225 Florida Boulevard
Baton Rouge, LA 70818
Phone: 504-925-4166

Louisiana Department of Veterans Affairs

Louisiana Veterans Affairs Educational Assistance for Dependent Children

Type of award: Scholarship, renewable.
Intended use: For full-time undergraduate, graduate or non-degree study at vocational, 2-year, 4-year or graduate institution in Louisiana.
Eligibility: Applicant must be residing in Louisiana. Applicant must be child of veteran, disabled veteran or deceased veteran.
Application requirements: Proof of eligibility. Must obtain certification of eligibility and application from parish veterans assistance counselor.
Additional information: Disability must be 100 percent as rated by U.S. Department of Veterans' Affairs.

Louisiana Veterans Affairs Educational Assistance for Surviving Spouse

Type of award: Scholarship, renewable.
Intended use: For full-time undergraduate, graduate or non-degree study at postsecondary institution in Louisiana.
Designated institutions: Louisiana institutions.
Eligibility: Applicant must be single. Applicant must be residing in Louisiana. Applicant must be spouse of disabled veteran or deceased veteran.
Application requirements: Proof of eligibility. Must obtain certification of eligibility and application from parish veterans assistance counselor.
Additional information: Veteran must have been a Louisiana resident during time of conflict. Contact local Parish Veterans Service office for more information and application.

Contact:
Louisiana Department of Veterans Affairs
P.O. Box 94095, Capitol Station
Baton Rouge, LA 70804-9095

Louisiana Office of Student Financial Assistance

Louisiana Rockefeller Wildlife Scholarship

Type of award: Scholarship, renewable.
Intended use: For full-time undergraduate or graduate study at 4-year or graduate institution in Louisiana.
Eligibility: Applicant must be U.S. citizen or permanent resident residing in Louisiana.
Basis for selection: Major/career interest in wildlife/fisheries; forestry; oceanography/marine studies. Applicant must demonstrate high academic achievement.
Additional information: Must submit FAFSA by March 15. Minimum 2.5 GPA required. May not be in default on any educational loan or grant. Must be registered with Selective Service if required. Must attend public institution and graduate in eligible field or scholarship must be repaid with interest. Must maintain 2.5 GPA to renew scholarship and earn 24 hours credit. Recipients receive $500 for each semester. A cumulative amount of $7000 will be award over a five year period.
 Amount of award: $1,000
 Number of awards: 63
 Number of applicants: 150
 Application deadline: March 15
 Total amount awarded: $60,000

Louisiana State Student Incentive Grant

Type of award: Scholarship, renewable.
Intended use: For full-time freshman, sophomore, junior or senior study at vocational, 2-year or 4-year institution in Louisiana.
Eligibility: Applicant must be U.S. citizen or permanent resident residing in Louisiana.
Basis for selection: Applicant must demonstrate financial need.
Additional information: Must have minimum of 45 on GED, 20 on ACT, or high school or postsecondary GPA minimum of 2.00. May not be in default on any student loan or grant. May be used at state technical institutions or proprietary schools. Must be registered with Selective Service if required. Contact financial aid office of institution. Must reapply for annually award.
 Amount of award: $200-$2,000
 Number of awards: 3,500
 Total amount awarded: $1,479,021

Louisiana Tuition Opportunity Program Award

Type of award: Scholarship, renewable.
Intended use: For full-time undergraduate study at 2-year or 4-year institution in Louisiana.
Eligibility: Applicant must be U.S. citizen or permanent resident residing in Louisiana.
Basis for selection: Applicant must demonstrate financial need and high academic achievement.
Application requirements: Interview.
Additional information: All eligible students funded. Must have minimum GPA of 2.50, minimum ACT score of 20, and 17.5 high school core units (or meet two of these requirements and a third within 10 percent). Must enroll in public institution as first-time undergraduate within two years of high school graduation. Must not be in default on any student loan. Must not have criminal record. Awards vary by school depending upon tuition. Must be registered with Selective Service if required. Submit FAFSA by March 15. Formerly known as the Tuition Assistance Plan.
 Amount of award: $742-$2,645
 Application deadline: March 15
 Total amount awarded: $7,422,479

Louisiana Tuition Opportunity Program Performance Award

Type of award: Scholarship, renewable.
Intended use: For full-time undergraduate study at vocational, 2-year or 4-year institution in Louisiana. Designated institutions: Louisiana technical institutions, public or LAICU-approved private institutions.
Eligibility: Applicant must be high school senior. Applicant must be U.S. citizen or permanent resident residing in Louisiana.
Basis for selection: Applicant must demonstrate high academic achievement.
Application requirements: Proof of eligibility and nomination by principal/headmaster of nonpublic high school or school board superintendent of public high school.
Additional information: Must rank in top five percent of Louisiana public or approved nonpublic high school graduating class. Award must be used at public and approved private Louisiana college and university within two years of high school graduation. Must not be receiving financial assistance from public university or affiliated organization. Must maintain 3.0 GPA to renew scholarship and earn 24 hours credit. Award recipients receive an additional $400 for books and supplies. Formerly known as the Louisiana Honors Scholarship.
 Notification begins: August 1
 Total amount awarded: $9,200,000
Contact:
Louisiana Office of Student Financial Assistance
P.O. Box 91202
Baton Rouge, LA 70821-9202

Maine Division of Veterans Services

Maine Veterans Services Dependents Educational Benefits

Type of award: Scholarship.
Intended use: For undergraduate or graduate study at vocational, 2-year or 4-year institution. Designated institutions: For use at State of Maine supported institutions.
Eligibility: Applicant must be residing in Maine. Applicant must be child of disabled veteran, deceased veteran or POW/MIA, spouse of disabled veteran or deceased veteran. Must apply for program prior to 22nd birthday or before 26th birthday if applicant was enrolled in the U.S. Armed Forces.

Application requirements: Proof of eligibility.
Additional information: Parent or spouse must have been resident of Maine prior to enlistment or a resident of Maine for five years preceding application for aid. Provides tuition at all branches of the University of Maine system, all State of Maine vocational-technical colleges, and Maine Maritime Academy for eight semesters to be used within six years.
    Number of awards: 455
    Number of applicants: 499
Contact:
Maine Division of Veterans Services
State House Station 117
Augusta, ME 04333-0117

Maine Finance Authority

Maine Robert C. Byrd Honors Scholarship

Type of award: Scholarship, renewable.
Intended use: For full-time undergraduate study at 2-year or 4-year institution.
Eligibility: Applicant must be high school senior. Applicant must be U.S. citizen or permanent resident residing in Maine.
Basis for selection: Applicant must demonstrate high academic achievement.
Additional information: Information available through Maine high school guidance offices.
    Amount of award: $1,500
    Application deadline: April 15

Maryland Higher Education Commission/State Scholarship Administration

Maryland Child Care Provider Scholarship

Type of award: Loan, renewable.
Intended use: For full-time or half-time undergraduate study at accredited 2-year or 4-year institution in Maryland.
Eligibility: Applicant must be U.S. citizen or permanent resident residing in Maryland.
Basis for selection: Major/career interest in education, teacher; education, early childhood.
Application requirements: Interview, transcript and proof of eligibility. GED certificate may be submitted in place of transcript.
Additional information: Minimum 2.0 GPA. Must be enrolled in program leading to degree in child development or early childhood education. Must work as child care provider in Maryland one year for each year or portion thereof financial assistance was received beginning within six months of graduation.

    Amount of award: $500-$2,000
    Number of awards: 95
    Application deadline: June 15
    Notification begins: August 15
    Total amount awarded: $89,750
Contact:
Maryland Higher Education Commission/State Scholarship Administration
Child Care Provider Scholarship Program
16 Francis Street
Annapolis, MD 21401-1781
Phone: 410-974-5370
Website: www.ubalt.edu

Maryland Delegate Scholarship

Type of award: Scholarship, renewable.
Intended use: For full-time or half-time undergraduate or graduate study at vocational, 2-year, 4-year or graduate institution in Maryland.
Eligibility: Applicant must be U.S. citizen or permanent resident residing in Maryland.
Application requirements: Proof of eligibility. FAFSA may be required.
Additional information: Certain vocational programs eligible. Out-of-state institutions eligible only if major not offered in Maryland. Each State Delegate makes awards to students.
    Amount of award: $200-$3,480
    Number of awards: 2,428
    Application deadline: March 1
    Notification begins: July 1
    Total amount awarded: $1,639,837
Contact:
State Scholarship Administration
Delegate Scholarship
16 Francis Street
Annapolis, MD 21401-1781
Phone: 410-974-5370
Website: www.ubalt.edu

Maryland Distinguished Scholar: Academics

Type of award: Scholarship, renewable.
Intended use: For full-time undergraduate study at accredited vocational, 2-year or 4-year institution in United States. Designated institutions: Maryland public institutions.
Eligibility: Applicant must be high school junior. Applicant must be U.S. citizen or permanent resident residing in Maryland.
Basis for selection: Applicant must demonstrate high academic achievement.
Application requirements: Transcript and nomination by High school in second semester of junior year. PSAT or ACT scores.
Additional information: Nomination process through high school guidance counselor in the second semester of junior year. Must have a 3.7 GPA or higher.

Amount of award: $3,000
Number of awards: 1,447
Notification begins: June 30
Total amount awarded: $4,197,000
Contact:
Maryland Higher Education Commission/State Scholarship Administration
Distinguished Scholar Program
16 Francis Street
Annapolis, MD 21401-1781
Phone: 410-974-5370
Website: www.ubalt.edu

Maryland Distinguished Scholar: National Merit Finalists

Type of award: Scholarship, renewable.
Intended use: For full-time undergraduate study at accredited vocational, 2-year or 4-year institution in Maryland.
Eligibility: Applicant must be high school junior. Applicant must be U.S. citizen or permanent resident residing in Maryland.
Basis for selection: Competition in Performing arts.
Application requirements: Audition and nomination by High school in spring of junior year.
Additional information: Award based on quality of presentation as determined by the panel of judges. Nomination process by high school guidance counselor in the spring of junior year.
Amount of award: $3,000
Contact:
Maryland Higher Education Commission/State Scholarship Administration
Distinguished Scholar Program
16 Francis Street
Annapolis, MD 21401-1718
Phone: 410-974-5370
Website: www.ubalt.edu

Maryland Distinguished Scholar: Talent

Type of award: Scholarship, renewable.
Intended use: For full-time undergraduate study at accredited vocational, 2-year or 4-year institution in Maryland.
Eligibility: Applicant must be high school junior. Applicant must be U.S. citizen or permanent resident residing in Maryland.
Basis for selection: Competition in Writing/journalism.
Application requirements: Audition and nomination by High school in spring of junior year.
Additional information: Awards for dance, visual arts, and both vocal and instrumental music. Winners determined by the panel of judges. High school guidance counselor nominates individuals in the spring of the junior year.
Amount of award: $3,000
Contact:
Maryland Higher Education Commission/State Scholarship Administration
Distinguished Scholar Program
16 Francis Street
Annapolis, MD 21401-1781
Phone: 410-974-5370
Website: www.ubalt.edu

Maryland Distinguished Scholar: Teacher Education Program

Type of award: Loan, renewable.
Intended use: For full-time freshman, sophomore, junior or senior study at accredited 4-year institution in Maryland.
Eligibility: Applicant must be high school senior. Applicant must be U.S. citizen or permanent resident residing in Maryland.
Basis for selection: Major/career interest in education, teacher.
Additional information: Must enroll in course of study leading to teacher certification. Must agree to teach in Maryland public school one year for each year of financial assistance. Must be recipient of a Distinguished Scholar Award.
Amount of award: $3,000
Number of awards: 81
Application deadline: July 1
Notification begins: August 31
Total amount awarded: $237,000
Contact:
Maryland Higher Education Commission/State Scholarship Administration
Distinguished Scholar Teacher Ed. Program
16 Francis Street
Annapolis, MD 21401-1781
Phone: 410-974-5370
Website: www.ubalt.edu

Maryland Distinguished Scholar: Visual Arts

Type of award: Scholarship, renewable.
Intended use: For full-time undergraduate study at accredited vocational, 2-year or 4-year institution in Maryland.
Eligibility: Applicant must be high school junior. Applicant must be U.S. citizen or permanent resident residing in Maryland.
Basis for selection: Competition in Visual arts.
Application requirements: Interview, portfolio and nomination by High school in spring of junior year.
Additional information: There are only three ways to get a Distinguished Scholar award. National Merit Finalists will automatically qualify. Quality of talent demonstrated is judged in a competition. Scholastic achievement is measured with those with the highest G.P.A.
Amount of award: $3,000
Contact:
Maryland Higher Education Commission/State Scholarship Administration
Distinguished Scholar Program
16 Francis Street
Annapolis, MD 21401-1781
Phone: 410-974-5370
Website: www.ubalt.edu

Maryland Educational Assistance Grant

Type of award: Scholarship, renewable.
Intended use: For full-time undergraduate study at 2-year or 4-year institution in Maryland.
Eligibility: Applicant must be residing in Maryland.

Basis for selection: Applicant must demonstrate financial need.
Application requirements: Must file FAFSA before March 1.

Amount of award:	$200-$3,000
Number of awards:	20,743
Application deadline:	March 1
Notification begins:	April 15
Total amount awarded:	$26,554,462

Contact:
Maryland Higher Education Commission/State Scholarship Administration
Educational Assistance Grant
16 Francis Street
Annapolis, MD 21401-1781
Phone: 410-974-5370
Website: www.ubalt.edu

Maryland Edward T. Conroy Memorial Grant--Disabled Public Safety Employees

Type of award: Scholarship, renewable.
Intended use: For undergraduate or graduate study in Maryland. Designated institutions: Maryland.
Eligibility: Applicant must be physically challenged. Applicant must be residing in Maryland. Applicant's parent must have been killed or disabled in work-related accident as fire fighter, police officer or public safety officer.
Application requirements: Proof of eligibility.
Additional information: Children of POW/MIA declared after January 1, 1960 can also qualify. Parent must have been a Maryland resident when declared MIA/POW.

Amount of award:	$200-$3,480
Number of awards:	71
Application deadline:	July 15
Notification begins:	July 31
Total amount awarded:	$136,539

Contact:
Maryland Higher Education Commission/State Scholarship Administration
Edward T. Conroy Memorial Grant Program
16 Francis Street
Annapolis, MD 21401-1781
Phone: 410-974-5370
Website: www.ubalt.edu

Maryland Edward T. Conroy Memorial Scholarship Program

Type of award: Scholarship, renewable.
Intended use: For undergraduate or graduate study in Maryland. Designated institutions: Maryland institutions.
Eligibility: Applicant must be residing in Maryland. Applicant must be child of veteran, disabled veteran or deceased veteran, spouse of veteran, disabled veteran, deceased veteran or POW/MIA. Applicant's parent must have been killed or disabled in work-related accident as fire fighter, police officer or public safety officer.
Application requirements: Proof of eligibility.
Additional information: Also open to dependents of those who were permanently disabled or killed as direct result of military duty after December 7, 1941. Parent must have been resident of Maryland at time of death or disability rating.

Amount of award:	$200-$3,480
Number of awards:	67
Application deadline:	July 15
Notification begins:	July 31
Total amount awarded:	$151,378

Contact:
Maryland Higher Education Commission/State Scholarship Administration
Edward T. Conroy Memorial Grant Program
16 Francis Street
Annapolis, MD 21401-1781
Phone: 410-974-5370
Website: www.ubalt.edu

Maryland Family Practice Medical Scholarship

Type of award: Loan, renewable.
Intended use: For full-time first professional study in United States. Designated institutions: University of Maryland School of Medicine.
Eligibility: Applicant must be U.S. citizen or permanent resident residing in Maryland.
Basis for selection: Major/career interest in medicine (m.d.). Applicant must demonstrate financial need and high academic achievement.
Application requirements: Recommendations, essay and transcript. Must file FAFSA by March 1. Must file SSA application separately.
Additional information: Loan forgiveness is offered for work as a family practitioner in Maryland in a critical shortage area. The award forgives one year of financial assistance for each year worked. Must do residency in family practice.

Amount of award:	$7,500
Number of awards:	2
Number of applicants:	2
Application deadline:	March 1
Total amount awarded:	$15,000

Contact:
Maryland Higher Education Commission/State Scholarship Administration
Family Practice Scholarship Program
16 Francis Street
Annapolis, MD 21401-1781
Phone: 410-974-5370
Website: www.ubalt.edu

Maryland Guaranteed Access Grant

Type of award: Scholarship, renewable.
Intended use: For full-time undergraduate study at accredited postsecondary institution in Maryland. Designated institutions: Degree-granting institution or diploma school of nursing.
Eligibility: Applicant must be U.S. citizen or permanent resident residing in Maryland.
Basis for selection: Applicant must demonstrate financial need.
Application requirements: Proof of eligibility. File FAFSA by March 1 each award year.
Additional information: Applicant must have completed college preparatory program or vocational/technical program

and begin college within one year of completing high school. GPA 2.5. Must have total family income no greater than 130% above federal poverty level.

   Amount of award: $8,300
   Number of awards: 616
   Application deadline: March 1

Contact:
Maryland Higher Education Commission/State Scholarship Administration
16 Francis Street
Annapolis, MD 21401-1781
Phone: 410-974-5370
Website: www.ubalt.edu

Maryland Jack F. Tolbert Memorial Grant

Type of award: Scholarship, renewable.
Intended use: For full-time undergraduate certificate, non-degree study at vocational institution in Maryland. Designated institutions: Private career schools.
Eligibility: Applicant must be residing in Maryland.
Basis for selection: Applicant must demonstrate financial need.
Application requirements: Nomination by High school guidance counselor in the spring of the junior year.
Additional information: Must file Free Application for Federal Student Aid by March 1. Award can only be held for one semester per academic year.

   Amount of award: $200-$1,500
   Number of awards: 877
   Total amount awarded: $194,500

Contact:
Maryland Higher Education Commission/State Scholarship Administration
16 Francis Street
Annapolis
Maryland, MD 21401-1781
Phone: 410-974-5370

Maryland Loan Assistance Repayment Program

Type of award: Loan, renewable.
Intended use: For non-degree study in Maryland.
Eligibility: Applicant must be residing in Maryland.
Basis for selection: Applicant must demonstrate financial need.
Additional information: Program provides educational loan repayment assistance to graduates who received degree from a Maryland institution and are working for state or local government or the nonprofit sector in Maryland. Priority given to current critical shortage employment fields. Applications available March through July.

   Amount of award: $200-$7,500
   Number of awards: 94
   Application deadline: September 30
   Notification begins: October 31
   Total amount awarded: $226,578

Contact:
Maryland Higher Education Commission/State Scholarship Administration
Loan Assistance Repayment Program
16 Francis Street
Annapolis, MD 21401-1781
Phone: 410-974-5370
Website: www.ubalt.edu

Maryland Loan Assistance Repayment Program/Primary Care Services

Type of award: Loan, renewable.
Intended use: For first professional study in Maryland.
Eligibility: Applicant must be U.S. citizen or permanent resident residing in Maryland.
Basis for selection: Major/career interest in medicine (m.d.). Applicant must demonstrate financial need.
Additional information: Award amount ranges up to $30,000. Program provides educational loan repayment assistance to medical residency graduates in primary care services.

   Amount of award: $30,000
   Number of awards: 12
   Application deadline: July 31
   Notification begins: August 31
   Total amount awarded: $527,112

Contact:
Maryland Higher Education Commission/State Scholarship Administration
Loan Assist. Repayment Program-Medical Res.
16 Francis Street
Annapolis, MD 21401-1781
Phone: 410-974-5370
Website: www.ubalt.edu

Maryland Part-Time Grant Program

Type of award: Scholarship, renewable.
Intended use: For half-time freshman, sophomore, junior or senior study in Maryland.
Eligibility: Applicant must be residing in Maryland.
Basis for selection: Applicant must demonstrate financial need.
Additional information: Must be taking six to eleven credit hours. Apply through financial aid office of Maryland institution.

   Amount of award: $200-$1,000
   Number of awards: 2,053
   Total amount awarded: $750,000

Contact:
Maryland Higher Education/State Scholarship Administration
Part-Time Grant Program
16 Francis Street
Annapolis, MD 21401-1781
Phone: 410-974-5370
Website: www.ubalt.edu

Maryland Physical/Occupational Therapists and Assistants Grant

Type of award: Loan, renewable.
Intended use: For full-time undergraduate study at 2-year or 4-year institution in Maryland. Designated institutions: Institutions with approved programs.
Eligibility: Applicant must be residing in Maryland.
Basis for selection: Major/career interest in physical therapy; occupational therapy. Applicant must demonstrate high academic achievement.
Application requirements: Transcript.
Additional information: Loan forgiveness for service at public schools, state hospitals, or other approved sites: one year for each year of financial assistance.

Amount of award:	$200-$2,000
Number of awards:	95
Application deadline:	July 1
Notification begins:	August 1
Total amount awarded:	$87,250

Contact:
Maryland Higher Education Commission/State Scholarship Administration
Physical and Occupational Therapy Program
16 Francis Street
Annapolis, MD 21401-1781
Phone: 410-974-5370
Website: www.ubalt.edu

Maryland Professional School Scholarship

Type of award: Scholarship, renewable.
Intended use: For full-time undergraduate, first professional study.
Eligibility: Applicant must be residing in Maryland.
Basis for selection: Major/career interest in health-related professions; law; nursing; medicine (m.d.); dentistry; pharmacy/pharmaceutics/pharmacology. Applicant must demonstrate financial need.
Application requirements: File FAFSA and SSA application by March 1.
Additional information: Must file separate application available from the State Scholarship Administration. Contact sponsor for further information.

Amount of award:	$200-$1,000
Number of awards:	166
Application deadline:	March 1
Notification begins:	May 31
Total amount awarded:	$150,000

Contact:
Maryland Higher Education Commission/State Scholarship Administration
Professional School Scholarship Program
16 Francis Street
Annapolis, MD 21401-1781
Phone: 410-974-5370
Website: www.ubalt.edu

Maryland Reimbursement of Firefighters

Type of award: Scholarship, renewable.
Intended use: For undergraduate, graduate or non-degree study in Maryland.
Eligibility: Applicant must be residing in Maryland.
Basis for selection: Major/career interest in fire science and technology; medical emergency.
Application requirements: Transcript and proof of eligibility.
Additional information: Award amount may not exceed tuition rate and mandatory fees (approximately $4,100) for resident in-state student at University of Maryland College Park. Payment is made one year after completion of study if the recipient remains career or active volunteer firefighter/ambulance/rescue squad member during the intervening year.

Amount of award:	$200-$3,480
Number of awards:	182
Application deadline:	July 1
Total amount awarded:	$278,899

Contact:
Maryland Higher Education Commission/State Scholarship Administration
Reimbursement of Firefighters
16 Francis Street
Annapolis, MD 21401-1781
Phone: 410-974-5370
Website: www.ubalt.edu

Maryland Senatorial Scholarship

Type of award: Scholarship, renewable.
Intended use: For full-time or half-time freshman, sophomore, junior, senior, master's or doctoral study at postsecondary institution in Maryland.
Eligibility: Applicant must be residing in Maryland.
Basis for selection: Applicant must demonstrate financial need.
Application requirements: File FAFSA during January.
Additional information: SAT I or ACT required for freshmen at four-year institutions unless applicant graduated from high school five years prior to aid application. Only certain vocational programs and certain vocational institutions eligible. Out-of-state institutions eligible only if major not offered in Maryland. Each State Senator makes awards to students in his or her election district. Contact State Senator's office for further information and requirements.

Amount of award:	$200-$2,000
Number of awards:	6,998
Application deadline:	March 1
Total amount awarded:	$6,046,515

Contact:
Maryland Higher Education Commission/State Scholarship Administration
Senatorial Scholarship Program
16 Francis Street
Annapolis, MD 21401-1781
Phone: 410-974-5370
Website: www.ubalt.edu

Maryland Sharon Christa McAuliffe Memorial Teacher Education Award

Type of award: Loan, renewable.
Intended use: For full-time or half-time freshman, sophomore, junior, senior, master's or non-degree study at 4-year or graduate institution in Maryland.
Eligibility: Applicant must be residing in Maryland.
Basis for selection: Major/career interest in education, teacher; education, special. Applicant must demonstrate high academic achievement.
Application requirements: Essay and transcript.
Additional information: Must have 3.0 GPA.
    Amount of award: $200-$9,600
    Number of awards: 43
    Total amount awarded: $205,656
Contact:
Maryland Higher Education Commission/State Scholarship Administration
S.C. McAuliffe Mem. Teacher Education Award
16 Francis Street
Annapolis, MD 21401-1781
Phone: 410-974-5370
Website: www.ubalt.edu

Maryland State Nursing Scholarship and Living Expenses Grant

Type of award: Loan, renewable.
Intended use: For full-time or half-time undergraduate or graduate study at accredited 2-year, 4-year or graduate institution in Maryland.
Eligibility: Applicant must be residing in Maryland.
Basis for selection: Major/career interest in nursing. Applicant must demonstrate financial need and high academic achievement.
Additional information: Must have 3.0 GPA. Must file Free Application for Federal Student Aid by March 1 for Living Expenses Grant. Loan forgiveness for nursing service in Maryland shortage area: one year for each year of financial assistance.
    Amount of award: $200-$4,800
    Number of awards: 285
    Application deadline: March 1
    Notification begins: July 31
    Total amount awarded: $602,180
Contact:
Maryland Higher Education Commission/State Scholarship Administration
State Nursing Scholarship
16 Francis Street
Annapolis, MD 21401-1781
Phone: 410-974-5370
Website: www.ubalt.edu

Maryland Tuition Reduction for Out-of-State Nursing Students

Type of award: Scholarship, renewable.
Intended use: For undergraduate study in Maryland.
Eligibility: Applicant must be U.S. citizen.
Basis for selection: Major/career interest in nursing.
Additional information: Must serve as a nurse in the state of Maryland for one year for each year of the award.
    Amount of award: $3,000
Contact:
Maryland Higher Education Commission/State Scholarship Administration
16 Francis Street
Annapolis, MD 21401-1781
Phone: 410-974-5370
Website: www.ubalt.edu

Massachusetts Board of Higher Education

Massachusetts Christian A. Herter Memorial Scholarship Program

Type of award: Scholarship, renewable.
Intended use: For full-time undergraduate study at accredited vocational, 2-year or 4-year institution.
Eligibility: Applicant must be high school sophomore, junior. Applicant must be U.S. citizen or permanent resident residing in Massachusetts.
Basis for selection: Applicant must demonstrate depth of character, seriousness of purpose and financial need.
Application requirements: Interview, recommendations, essay, transcript and nomination by The student will be nominated based on GPA (a minimum of 2.75), leadership qualities, and financial need.
Additional information: Program provides grant assistance for students from low income or disadvantaged backgrounds who have had to overcome adverse circumstances. Selection made during sophomore and junior years in high school. Applicants must be nominated by high school principal, counselor, teacher, or social service agency.
    Amount of award: $2,500-$5,000
    Number of awards: 100
    Number of applicants: 211
    Application deadline: March 1
    Notification begins: March 31
    Total amount awarded: $650,000

Massachusetts Gilbert Grant

Type of award: Scholarship.
Intended use: For full-time undergraduate study at accredited 2-year or 4-year institution in Massachusetts. Designated institutions: Private institutions only or hospital schools of nursing.
Eligibility: Applicant must be residing in Massachusetts.
Basis for selection: Applicant must demonstrate financial need.
Additional information: Apply to college financial aid office.
    Amount of award: $2,500
    Number of awards: 4,900
    Total amount awarded: $10,000,000

Massachusetts Massgrant Program

Type of award: Scholarship, renewable.
Intended use: For full-time undergraduate study at accredited

vocational, 2-year or 4-year institution in Massachusetts or these states: Maine, New Hampshire, Vermont, Rhode Island, Connecticut, Pennsylvania, Maryland, or DC.
Eligibility: Applicant must be U.S. citizen or permanent resident residing in Massachusetts.
Basis for selection: Applicant must demonstrate financial need.
Additional information: Apply to college financial aid office.
Amount of award:	$250-$2,500
Number of awards:	30,943
Number of applicants:	250,000
Application deadline:	May 1
Notification begins:	June 15
Total amount awarded:	$32,179,000

Massachusetts No Interest Loan

Type of award: Loan.
Intended use: For full-time undergraduate study at accredited vocational, 2-year or 4-year institution in Massachusetts.
Eligibility: Applicant must be U.S. citizen or permanent resident residing in Massachusetts.
Basis for selection: Applicant must demonstrate financial need.
Application requirements: FAFSA.
Amount of award:	$1,000-$4,000
Number of applicants:	5,000
Application deadline:	March 13
Total amount awarded:	$9,200,000

Contact:
Massachusetts Board of Higher Education
330 Stuart Street
Boston, MA 02116-5292
Phone: 617-727-9420

Massachusetts Public Service Program

Type of award: Scholarship, renewable.
Intended use: For full-time undergraduate study at accredited 2-year or 4-year institution in Massachusetts.
Eligibility: Applicant must be U.S. citizen or permanent resident residing in Massachusetts. Applicant must be child of deceased veteran or POW/MIA, spouse of deceased veteran. Applicant's parent must have been killed or disabled in work-related accident as fire fighter, police officer or public safety officer.
Application requirements: Proof of eligibility.
Additional information: Child of deceased veteran or POW/MIA whose death was service related also eligible. Applicant must be a resident of Massachusetts at least one year prior to start of school.
Amount of award:	$972-$2,109
Number of awards:	42
Number of applicants:	42
Application deadline:	May 1
Notification begins:	June 1
Total amount awarded:	$61,039

Contact:
Massachusetts Office of Student Financial Assistance
330 Stuart Street
Boston, MA 02116-5292

Massachusetts Tuition Waver

Type of award: Scholarship.
Intended use: For undergraduate study at 2-year or 4-year institution in Massachusetts. Designated institutions: Public institutions.
Eligibility: Applicant must be residing in Massachusetts.
Basis for selection: Applicant must demonstrate financial need.
Additional information: Apply to financial aid office of institution.
Amount of award:	$972-$2,134
Number of awards:	11,493
Total amount awarded:	$9,876,186

Massachusetts Department of Education

Massachusetts Robert C. Byrd Honors Scholarship

Type of award: Scholarship, renewable.
Intended use: For full-time undergraduate study.
Eligibility: Applicant must be high school senior. Applicant must be residing in Massachusetts.
Basis for selection: Applicant must demonstrate leadership, service orientation and high academic achievement.
Additional information: 3.5 GPA.
Amount of award:	$1,120
Number of awards:	514
Number of applicants:	550
Application deadline:	June 1
Total amount awarded:	$576,194

Contact:
Massachusetts Department of Education
Scholarship Committee
350 Main Street
Malden, MA 02148-5023

Menominee Indian Tribe of Wisconsin

Menominee Adult Vocational Training Scholarship

Type of award: Scholarship, renewable.
Intended use: For undergraduate certificate, freshman, sophomore or non-degree study at accredited vocational institution in United States.
Eligibility: Applicant must be American Indian. Must be at least one-quarter degree, tribally enrolled Menominee.
Basis for selection: Applicant must demonstrate financial need.
Additional information: Must apply through college financial aid office.

Amount of award:	$100-$2,200
Number of awards:	35
Number of applicants:	35
Application deadline:	October 30, March 1

Contact:
Menominee Indian Tribe of Wisconsin
P.O. Box 910
Keshena, WI 54135
Phone: 715-799-5118

Michigan Educational Opportunity Fund, Inc.

Michigan Educational Opportunity Scholarship

Type of award: Scholarship.
Intended use: For full-time freshman study at accredited postsecondary institution in United States.
Eligibility: Applicant must be Mexican American, Hispanic American or Puerto Rican. Applicant must be residing in Michigan.
Basis for selection: Major/career interest in science, general; engineering. Applicant must demonstrate service orientation, financial need and high academic achievement.
Application requirements: Transcript. FAF.
Additional information: Minimum 3.0 GPA required.

Amount of award:	$1,000-$1,500
Number of awards:	12
Number of applicants:	100
Application deadline:	March 1
Total amount awarded:	$15,000

Contact:
Michigan Educational Opportunity Fund, Inc.
P.O. Box 19152
Lansing, MI 48901
Phone: 517-482-9699

Michigan Higher Education Assistance Authority

Michigan Adult Part-Time Grant

Type of award: Scholarship, renewable.
Intended use: For half-time or less than half-time undergraduate study at 2-year or 4-year institution in Michigan.
Eligibility: Applicant must be U.S. citizen or permanent resident residing in Michigan.
Basis for selection: Applicant must demonstrate financial need.
Application requirements: Proof of eligibility.
Additional information: Apply to college financial aid office.

Amount of award:	$600

Michigan Competitive Scholarship

Type of award: Scholarship, renewable.
Intended use: For full-time or half-time freshman, sophomore, junior or senior study at 2-year or 4-year institution in Michigan.
Eligibility: Applicant must be U.S. citizen or permanent resident residing in Michigan.
Basis for selection: Applicant must demonstrate financial need and high academic achievement.
Application requirements: FAFSA and ACT score.
Additional information:

Amount of award:	$100-$1,200
Number of awards:	28,200
Application deadline:	March 21
Total amount awarded:	$32,123,455

Michigan Educational Opportunity Grant

Type of award: Scholarship, renewable.
Intended use: For full-time undergraduate study at postsecondary institution in Michigan.
Eligibility: Applicant must be U.S. citizen or permanent resident residing in Michigan.
Basis for selection: Applicant must demonstrate financial need.
Application requirements: Proof of eligibility.
Additional information: Student must attend public institution. Apply through college financial aid office.

Amount of award:	$1,000

Michigan Robert C. Byrd Honors Scholarship

Type of award: Scholarship, renewable.
Intended use: For full-time freshman study in United States.
Eligibility: Applicant must be high school senior. Applicant must be U.S. citizen or permanent resident residing in Michigan.
Basis for selection: Applicant must demonstrate high academic achievement.
Application requirements: Nomination by high school guidance counselor.

Amount of award:	$1,110
Number of awards:	240
Total amount awarded:	$1,074,480

Michigan Tuition Grant

Type of award: Scholarship, renewable.
Intended use: For full-time or half-time freshman, sophomore, junior, senior, master's or doctoral study at 2-year, 4-year or graduate institution in Michigan.
Eligibility: Applicant must be U.S. citizen or permanent resident residing in Michigan.
Basis for selection: Applicant must demonstrate financial need.
Additional information: For use at private nonprofit education institutions. Deadline for college students: March 21.

Amount of award:	$100-$2,300
Number of awards:	31,000
Application deadline:	February 21, March 21
Total amount awarded:	$59,028,647

Michigan Work-Study Program

Type of award: Internship, renewable.
Intended use: For full-time or half-time undergraduate or graduate study at 2-year, 4-year or graduate institution in Michigan.
Eligibility: Applicant must be U.S. citizen or permanent resident residing in Michigan.
Basis for selection: Applicant must demonstrate financial need.
Application requirements: Proof of eligibility.
Additional information: Apply to college financial aid office.

Midwestern Higher Education Commission

Midwest Student Exchange Program

Type of award: Scholarship, renewable.
Intended use: For full-time undergraduate, master's, doctoral or first professional study at accredited 2-year, 4-year or graduate institution in United States. Designated institutions: Participating institutions in Kansas, Michigan, Minnesota, Missouri and Nebraska.
Eligibility: Applicant must be residing in Kansas or Michigan or Minnesota or Missouri or Nebraska.
Application requirements: Proof of eligibility.
Additional information: Reduced tuition rate for Kansas, Michigan, Minnesota, Missouri and Nebraska residents attending participating out-of-state institutions in one of the four other states in designated programs of study. For information, contact high school counselor or college admissions officer. For a list of participating institutions and programs contact either: (Kansas) Kansas Board of Regents, 700 SW Harrison, Suite 1410, Topeka, KS 66603 or 913-296-3422; (Michigan) Michigan Department of Education, Hannah Building, Second Floor, 608 West Allegan Street, Lansing, MI 48909, Phone: (517) 373-3360; Fax: (517) 373-2759; or Presidents Council, State Universities of Michigan, 230 North Washington Square 302, Lansing, MI 48933, or (517) 482-1563; Fax: 517-482-1241; (Minnesota) Minnesota Higher Education Services Office, Capitol Square, Suite 400, 550 Cedar Street, Suite 400, St. Paul, MN 55101 or (612) 296-3974; (Missouri) Coordinating Board for Higher Education, 3515 Amazonas Drive, Jefferson City, MO 65109-5717 Phone: (573)751-2361; Fax: (573) 751-6635; (Nebraska) Coordinating Commission for Postsecondary Education, 140 North Eighth Street, Suite 300, P.O. Box 95005, Lincoln, NE 68509-5005 Phone: (402) 471-0022; Fax (402) 471-2886; or Midwestern Higher Education Commission, 1300 South Second Street, Suite 130, Minneapolis, MN 55454-1015, Phone: (612) 626-8288.

Number of awards: 1,300
Contact:
Midwestern Higher Education Commission - MSEP Program Officer
1300 South 2nd Street
Suite 130
Minneapolis, MN 55454-1015
Phone: 612-626-8288
Fax: 612-626-8290
Website: www.umn.edu/mhec

Minnesota Department of Veteran's Affairs

Minnesota Educational Assistance for Veterans

Type of award: Scholarship.
Intended use: For undergraduate or graduate study at postsecondary institution in Minnesota. Designated institutions: All Minnesota institutions except the University of Minnesota.
Eligibility: Applicant must be residing in Minnesota. Applicant must be veteran.
Application requirements: Proof of eligibility.
Additional information: Must have exhausted eligible federal educational benefits. Information also available from institution or county veterans service officer.
Amount of award: $350

Minnesota Educational Assistance for War Orphans

Type of award: Scholarship, renewable.
Intended use: For full-time undergraduate study at accredited vocational, 2-year or 4-year institution in Minnesota. Designated institutions: Approved Minnesota schools.
Eligibility: Applicant must be residing in Minnesota. Applicant must be child of deceased veteran. Veteran's death must have been on active duty or service connected.
Application requirements: Proof of eligibility.
Additional information: All recipients receive stipend and tuition waiver. Program not accepted at University of Minnesota. Information also available from institution or county veterans service officer. Applicant must be a resident of Minnesota for 2 years prior to application. Available until recipients obtains bachelors degree or equvalent.
Amount of award: $350
Contact:
Minnesota Department of Veterans Affairs
Veterans Service Building, 2nd Floor
20 West 12 Street
St. Paul, MN 55155-2079

Minnesota Higher Education Services Office

Minnesota Non-Aid to Families with Dependent Children Child Care Grant

Type of award: Scholarship, renewable.
Intended use: For freshman, sophomore, junior or senior study at accredited vocational, 2-year or 4-year institution in Minnesota. Designated institutions: All Minnesota baccalaureate degree-granting institutions or public, non-profit vocational institutions.
Eligibility: Applicant must be U.S. citizen or permanent resident residing in Minnesota.
Basis for selection: Applicant must demonstrate financial need.
Additional information: Apply at college financial aid office, eligibility limited to applicants with children twelve years or younger. Award amount prorated upon enrollment. Maximum of $2,000 per eligible child per academic year. Applicant cannot receive Aid to Families with Dependent Children, Minnesota Family Investment Program, tuition reciprocity, or be in default of loan. Those with bachelor's degree or eight semesters or twelve quarters of credit, or equivalent, not eligible. Applicant must be enrolled at least half-time or have eight credits in nonsectarian program, and must be in good academic standing. Award based on family income and size. Application available at financial aid office of Minnesota institution. Deadlines established by individual institution.

Amount of award:	$2,000
Number of awards:	2,523
Number of applicants:	2,523

Minnesota Nursing Grant for Persons of Color

Type of award: Scholarship, renewable.
Intended use: For full-time or half-time undergraduate, master's study at accredited 2-year, 4-year or graduate institution in Minnesota.
Eligibility: Applicant must be American Indian, Asian American, African American, Mexican American, Hispanic American or Puerto Rican. Applicant must be U.S. citizen or permanent resident residing in Minnesota.
Basis for selection: Major/career interest in nursing. Applicant must demonstrate financial need.
Additional information: Must be enrolled in program leading to first licensure as registered nurse, baccalaureate degree or master's degree in nursing, or advanced nursing education program. Must enroll for at least six credits. For application materials or additional information contact yor institution's financial aid office.

Amount of award:	$2,000-$4,000
Number of awards:	65
Total amount awarded:	$150,000

Minnesota Safety Officers Survivors Program

Type of award: Scholarship.
Intended use: For undergraduate, non-degree study at accredited postsecondary institution in Minnesota.
Eligibility: Applicant must be residing in Minnesota. Applicant's parent must have been killed or disabled in work-related accident as fire fighter, police officer or public safety officer.
Application requirements: Proof of eligibility. Eligibility certificate.
Additional information: Must be enrolled in degree or certificate program at institution participating in State Grant Program. Obtain eligibility certificate from Department of Public Safety, 211 Transportation Building, St. Paul, MN 55155. Also eligible if parent or spouse, not officially employed in public safety, was killed while assisting public safety officer or offering emergency medical assistance. Apply through financial aid office.

Number of awards:	9
Number of applicants:	9
Total amount awarded:	$40,000

Minnesota State Grant Program

Type of award: Scholarship, renewable.
Intended use: For undergraduate study at accredited vocational, 2-year or 4-year institution in Minnesota.
Eligibility: Applicant must be U.S. citizen or permanent resident residing in Minnesota.
Basis for selection: Applicant must demonstrate financial need.
Application requirements: Proof of eligibility.
Additional information: Must not have completed four years of college. If not Minnesota high school graduate and parents not residents of Minnesota, applicant must be resident of Minnesota for at least one year. Can not be in default on loans or delinquent on child support payments. The Free Application for Federal Student Aid (FAFSA) is used as the application for Minnesota State Grant.

Amount of award:	$300-$6,180
Number of awards:	61,356
Number of applicants:	133,000
Application deadline:	June 30
Total amount awarded:	$88,838,785

Contact:
Minnesota Higher Education Services Office-State Grant Unit
400 Capitol Square
550 Cedar Street
St. Paul, MN 55101
Phone: 800-657-3866
Website: www.heso.state.mn.us/

Minnesota Student Educational Loan Fund

Type of award: Loan.
Intended use: For undergraduate or graduate study at vocational, 2-year, 4-year or graduate institution in Minnesota or eligible out-of-state institutions.
Eligibility: Applicant must be U.S. citizen or permanent resident residing in Minnesota.
Additional information: May be Minnesota resident attending

eligible out-of-state institution or student attending eligible Minnesota institution. Must seek aid from all other sources before applying, except Federal unsubsidized & subsidized Stafford loans, National Direct Student loans, HEAL loans, other private loans. Institution must approve application. Maximum eligibility for freshmen and sophomores $4,500; juniors, seniors and fifth year students $6,000; graduate students $9,000.

   Amount of award: $500-$9,000
   Number of awards: 8,354
   Total amount awarded: $21,074,292
Contact:
Minnesota Higher Education Services Office
400 Capitol Square
550 Cedar Street
St. Paul, MN 55101
Website: www.heso.state.mn.us/

Minnesota Work-Study Program

Type of award: Internship.
Intended use: For undergraduate or graduate study at accredited vocational, 2-year, 4-year or graduate institution in Minnesota.
Eligibility: Applicant must be U.S. citizen or permanent resident residing in Minnesota.
Basis for selection: Applicant must demonstrate financial need.
Application requirements: Interview.
Additional information: Work placement must be approved by school or non-profit agency. Apply to financial aid office. Must be used at a Minnesota college or for internship with non-profit or private sector employer located in Minnesota.

   Number of awards: 9,348
   Total amount awarded: $8,559,447
Contact:
Minnesota Higher Education Services Office
400 Capitol Square
550 Cedar Street
St. Paul, MN 55101
Website: www.heso.state.mn.us/

Mississippi Office of State Student Financial Aid

African-American Doctoral Teacher Loan / Scholarship

Type of award: Scholarship.
Intended use: For full-time doctoral study at accredited graduate institution in United States.
Eligibility: Applicant must be African American. Applicant must be U.S. citizen or permanent resident residing in Mississippi.
Basis for selection: Major/career interest in education, teacher.
Additional information: Supports full-time doctoral candidates who intent to teach at an accredited public Mississippi college or university. Obligation can be discharged on the basis of one yearÖs teaching service at an accredited public Mississippi college or universityi for one yearÖs support. In the event the recipient fails to fulfill the service obligation, repayment of principal and interest is required. The number of Awards and recipients are dependent upon availability of funds, and awards will be made on a first-come, first-served basis.

   Amount of award: $10,000
   Application deadline: April 30
Contact:
3825 Ridgewood Road
Jackson, MS 39211-6453
Phone: 601-982-6663

Graduate & Professional Degree Loan / Scholarship

Type of award: Scholarship.
Intended use: For first professional study at accredited graduate institution in United States.
Eligibility: Applicant must be U.S. citizen or permanent resident residing in Mississippi.
Basis for selection: Major/career interest in health-related professions.
Additional information: Program offers assistance to Mississippi residents who are seeking a professional degree not available at a Mississippi university and who, as a result, enroll full-time in one accredited out-of-state institution. Approved fields of study are limited to health-related professions including Chiropractic Medicine, Orthotics / Prosthetics and Podiatric Medicine. Obligation can be discharged on the basis of one yearÖs full-time service as a licensed professional in the approved profession in the State of Mississippi for one yearÖs support. In the event the recipient fails to fulfill the service obligation, repayment of principal and interest is required. The number of Awards and recipients are dependent upon availability of funds, and awards will be made on a first-come, first-served basis.

   Amount of award: $7,000
   Application deadline: April 30
Contact:
3825 Ridgewood Road
Jackson, MS 39211-6453
Phone: 601-982-6663

Gulf Coast Research Laboratory Minority Summer Grant

Type of award: Internship.
Intended use: For undergraduate study at accredited 4-year institution in United States. Designated institutions: Gulf Coast Research Laboratory.
Eligibility: Applicant must be of minority background. Applicant must be U.S. citizen or permanent resident residing in Mississippi.
Basis for selection: Major/career interest in oceanography/ marine studies; environmental science.
Additional information: Four to ten week program. Provides summer grants for minority students to attend classes or conduct independent study at the Gulf Coast Research Laboratory in the Gulf Coast Research laboratory Summer Academic Institute; to solicit, arrange and conduct field trips to introduce students to the marine environment and science community. The number of Awards and recipients are dependent upon availability of funds, and awards will be made on a first-come, first-served basis.

Amount of award: $250
Application deadline: May 18
Contact:
3825 Ridgewood Road
Jackson, MS 39211-6453
Phone: 601-982-6663

Higher Education Legislature Plan for Needy Students

Type of award: Scholarship.
Intended use: For full-time freshman, sophomore study at accredited 2-year institution in United States.
Eligibility: Applicant must be U.S. citizen residing in Mississippi.
Additional information: Minimum GPA 2.5. No criminal record. Student's family must have one child under age 21 and a two-year annual adjusted gross income of less than $30,000; or the family has two average annual adjusted gross income of less than $30,000 plus $5,000 for each additional child under 21. Award amounts vary. The number of Awards and recipients are dependent upon availability of funds, and awards will be made on a first-come, first-served basis.
Application deadline: May 1
Contact:
3825 Ridgewood Road
Jackson, MS 39211-6453
Phone: 601-982-6663

Mississippi Dental Education Loan/Scholarship

Type of award: Loan, renewable.
Intended use: For full-time first professional study. Designated institutions: University of Mississippi School of Dentistry.
Eligibility: Applicant must be U.S. citizen or permanent resident residing in Mississippi.
Basis for selection: Major/career interest in dentistry. Applicant must demonstrate high academic achievement.
Application requirements: Proof of eligibility.
Additional information: Loan forgiveness for service in geographical area of critical need or public health facility or community health center.
Amount of award: $4,000
Number of awards: 14
Application deadline: April 30
Notification begins: June 1
Total amount awarded: $56,000
Contact:
Student Financial Aid
3825 Ridgewood Road
Jackson, MS 39211-6453

Mississippi Eminent Scholars Grant

Type of award: Scholarship, renewable.
Intended use: For full-time undergraduate certificate, freshman study at accredited 2-year or 4-year institution in Mississippi. Designated institutions: Public and nonprofit institutions.
Eligibility: Applicant must be residing in Mississippi.
Basis for selection: Applicant must demonstrate high academic achievement.
Additional information: Must be resident of Mississippi for one year. Must be recognized as a semifinalist or finalist by the National Merit Scholarship Corporation or the National Achievement Scholarship Program. Must have 3.5 GPA or ACT of 29 or SAT combined score of 1280.
Amount of award: $2,500
Number of awards: 697
Application deadline: August 1
Contact:
3825 Ridgewood Road
Jackson, MS 39211-6453
Phone: 601-982-6663

Mississippi Graduate Teacher Summer Loan/Scholarship Program

Type of award: Scholarship, renewable.
Intended use: For master's study at accredited graduate institution in Mississippi.
Eligibility: Applicant must be residing in Mississippi.
Basis for selection: Major/career interest in education, teacher.
Additional information: Must be under contract as a full-time classroom teacher (K-12) at an accredited Mississippi public school. Must be accepted in program that leads to a master's degree and a Class AA teaching certificate.
Amount of award: $125-$1,500
Number of awards: 1,038
Application deadline: April 1
Notification begins: June 1
Total amount awarded: $1,132,732
Contact:
Mississippi Office of State Student Financial Aid
3825 Ridgewood Road
Jackson, MS 39211-6453
Phone: 601-982-6663

Mississippi Health Care Professional Loan/Scholarship

Type of award: Loan, renewable.
Intended use: For full-time junior, senior study.
Eligibility: Applicant must be residing in Mississippi.
Basis for selection: Major/career interest in physical therapy; occupational therapy; speech pathology/audiology; psychology. Applicant must demonstrate high academic achievement.
Application requirements: Proof of eligibility.
Additional information: Must be enrolled in accredited training program of critical need in Mississippi public institution. Loan forgiveness for service in Mississippi health care institution, one year for each year of financial assistance.
Amount of award: $1,500
Number of awards: 4
Application deadline: April 30
Notification begins: June 1
Total amount awarded: $6,000
Contact:
Mississippi Office of State Student Financial Aid
Student Financial Aid
3825 Ridgewood Road
Jackson, MS 39211-6453
Phone: 601-982-6578

Mississippi Law Enforcement Officers/Firemen Scholarship

Type of award: Scholarship, renewable.
Intended use: For full-time undergraduate study at 2-year or 4-year institution in Mississippi.
Eligibility: Applicant must be residing in Mississippi. Applicant's parent must have been killed or disabled in work-related accident as fire fighter, police officer or public safety officer.
Application requirements: Proof of eligibility.
Additional information: Award covers tuition, room, and lab fees and may be used only at a Mississippi public institution. Children entitled to award until age of 23. Spouses are also eligible.

Number of awards:	19
Total amount awarded:	$49,673

Contact:
Mississippi Office of State Student Financial Aid
Student Financial Aid
3825 Ridgewood Road
Jackson, MS 39211-6453
Phone: 601-982-6578

Mississippi Medical Education Loan/Scholarship

Type of award: Loan, renewable.
Intended use: For full-time first professional study. Designated institutions: University of Mississippi School of Medicine.
Eligibility: Applicant must be U.S. citizen or permanent resident residing in Mississippi.
Basis for selection: Major/career interest in medicine (m.d.). Applicant must demonstrate high academic achievement.
Application requirements: Proof of eligibility.
Additional information: Loan forgiveness for service in geographical area of critical need or health facility or community health center. Must specialize in primary care fields.

Amount of award:	$6,000
Number of awards:	20
Application deadline:	April 30
Notification begins:	June 1
Total amount awarded:	$120,000

Contact:
Mississippi Office of State Student Financial Aid
Student Financial Aid
3825 Ridgewood Road
Jackson, MS 39211-6453
Phone: 601-982-6578

Mississippi Nursing Education Loan/Scholarship

Type of award: Loan, renewable.
Intended use: For undergraduate, master's or doctoral study at accredited 4-year or graduate institution.
Eligibility: Applicant must be U.S. citizen or permanent resident residing in Mississippi.
Basis for selection: Major/career interest in nursing. Applicant must demonstrate high academic achievement.
Application requirements: Proof of eligibility.
Additional information: Students must attend school in Mississippi. Loan forgiveness for nursing service in Mississippi, one year for each year of financial assistance.

Amount of award:	$1,500-$5,000
Number of awards:	236
Application deadline:	April 30
Notification begins:	June 1
Total amount awarded:	$466,617

Contact:
Mississippi Office of State Student Financial Aid
Student Financial Aid
3825 Ridgewood Road
Jackson, MS 39211-6453
Phone: 601-982-6578

Mississippi Nursing Teacher Stipend Program

Type of award: Loan, renewable.
Intended use: For full-time master's, doctoral study in United States.
Eligibility: Applicant must be U.S. citizen or permanent resident residing in Mississippi.
Basis for selection: Major/career interest in nursing.
Application requirements: Recommendations.
Additional information: Must be recipient of the Nursing Education Loan/Scholarship Program administered by the Board of Trustees. Obligation can be discharged by full-time teaching in Mississippi in professional nursing for length of time equal to two academic years for one year's loan/scholarship amount.

Amount of award:	$12,000
Number of awards:	12
Application deadline:	April 30
Notification begins:	June 1
Total amount awarded:	$101,000

Contact:
Mississippi Office of State Student Financial Aid
3825 Ridgewood Road
Jackson, MS 39211-6453
Phone: (601) 982-6663

Mississippi Psychology Apprenticeship Program

Type of award: Internship.
Intended use: For freshman, sophomore, junior, senior, master's or doctoral study.
Eligibility: Applicant must be U.S. citizen or permanent resident residing in Mississippi.
Basis for selection: Major/career interest in psychology.
Application requirements: Recommendations and proof of eligibility.
Additional information: Summer training program in conjunction with Biloxi Veterans Affairs Medical Center.

Amount of award:	$500-$2,250
Number of awards:	2
Application deadline:	May 1
Notification begins:	May 1
Total amount awarded:	$1,500

Contact:
Mississippi Office of State Student Financial Aid
Student Financial Aid
3825 Ridgewood Road
Jackson, MS 39211-6453
Phone: 601-982-6578

Mississippi Public Management Graduate Internship

Type of award: Internship.
Intended use: For full-time master's study. Designated institutions: University of Mississippi, University of Southern Mississippi, Jackson State University, Mississippi State University.
Eligibility: Applicant must be U.S. citizen or permanent resident residing in Mississippi.
Basis for selection: Major/career interest in public administration/service. Applicant must demonstrate depth of character, leadership, service orientation and high academic achievement.
Application requirements: Interview, recommendations and proof of eligibility.
Additional information: Must plan to pursue career in Mississippi State Government.
    Amount of award: $3,000-$4,000
    Number of awards: 6
    Total amount awarded: $24,240
Contact:
Mississippi Office of State Student Financial Aid
Student Financial Aid
3825 Ridgewood Road
Jackson, MS 39211-6453
Phone: 601-982-6578

Mississippi Resident Tuition Assistance Grant

Type of award: Scholarship, renewable.
Intended use: For full-time freshman, sophomore, junior or senior study at accredited 2-year or 4-year institution in Mississippi.
Eligibility: Applicant must be U.S. citizen or permanent resident residing in Mississippi.
Application requirements: FAFSA.
Additional information: Must be resident of Mississippi for no less than one year. Must be receiving less than full Federal Pell Grant. 2.5 high school GPA and ACT score of 15 required. Must not be in default on an educational loan.
    Amount of award: $1,000
    Number of awards: 21,859
    Application deadline: August 1
Contact:
Grant Coordinator
3825 Ridgewood Road
Jackson, MS 39211-6453
Phone: 601-982-6663

Mississippi Southeast Asia POW/MIA Scholarship

Type of award: Scholarship, renewable.
Intended use: For full-time undergraduate study at 2-year or 4-year institution in Mississippi.
Eligibility: Applicant must be U.S. citizen or permanent resident residing in Mississippi. Applicant must be child of active service person or POW/MIA. MIA/POW must have been involved in the Southeast Asia conflict.
Application requirements: Proof of eligibility.
Additional information: Award covers cost of tuition, room, and lab fees and must be used at a Mississippi public institution. Notification upon receipt of required documents.
Contact:
Mississippi Office of State Student Financial Aid
Student Financial Aid
3825 Ridgewood Road
Jackson, MS 39211-6453
Phone: 601-982-6578

Mississippi Southern Regional Education Board Loan/Scholarship

Type of award: Loan, renewable.
Intended use: For full-time first professional study at graduate institution in Or Nova Southeastern University College of Osteopathic Med. Designated institutions: University of Houston, Southern College of Optometry, University of Alabama in Birmingham,.
Eligibility: Applicant must be U.S. citizen or permanent resident residing in Mississippi.
Basis for selection: Major/career interest in medicine, osteopathic.
Application requirements: Proof of eligibility.
Additional information: Loan forgiveness for service in Mississippi, one year for each year of financial assistance. Also covers study of optometry.
    Amount of award: $7,950
    Number of awards: 36
    Application deadline: April 30
    Notification begins: July 15
    Total amount awarded: $286,200
Contact:
Mississippi Office of State Student Financial Aid
Student Financial Aid Office
3825 Ridgewood Road
Jackson, MS 39211-6453
Phone: 601-982-6578

Mississippi Student Incentive Grant

Type of award: Scholarship, renewable.
Intended use: For full-time freshman, sophomore, junior or senior study at accredited 2-year or 4-year institution in Mississippi.
Eligibility: Applicant must be U.S. citizen or permanent resident residing in Mississippi.
Basis for selection: Applicant must demonstrate financial need and high academic achievement.
Application requirements: Recommendations and proof of eligibility.
Additional information: Must meet general requirements for participation in federal student aid program. Apply to college financial aid office.
    Amount of award: $200-$1,500
    Number of awards: 891
    Total amount awarded: $540,196
Contact:
Mississippi Office of State Student Financial Aid
3825 Ridgewood Road
Jackson, MS 39211-6453
Phone: 601-982-6578

Mississippi William Winter Teacher Scholar Loan Program

Type of award: Loan, renewable.
Intended use: For full-time undergraduate study at postsecondary institution in Mississippi.
Eligibility: Applicant must be U.S. citizen or permanent resident residing in Mississippi.
Basis for selection: Major/career interest in education, teacher. Applicant must demonstrate high academic achievement.
Application requirements: Proof of eligibility.
Additional information: Entering freshmen must have 3.0 GPA and ACT score of at least 21; undergraduate applicants must have 2.5 college GPA. Loan forgiveness for teaching service in Mississippi: one year for each year of financial assistance.

Amount of award:	$1,000-$3,000
Number of awards:	895
Application deadline:	April 1
Notification begins:	May 1
Total amount awarded:	$2,192,447

Contact:
Student Financial Aid
3825 Ridgewood Road
Jackson, MS 39211-6453
Phone: 601-982-6578

Special Medical Education Loan / Scholarship

Type of award: Scholarship.
Intended use: For full-time first professional study at accredited graduate institution in United States. Designated institutions: University of Mississippi Medical School.
Eligibility: Applicant must be U.S. citizen or permanent resident residing in Mississippi.
Basis for selection: Major/career interest in medicine (m.d.).
Application requirements: Transcript.
Additional information: Award is made on an annual basis with priority given to renewal students. Obligation can be discharged on the basis of one yearÖs full-time service in the State of Mississippi for one yearÖs support. In the event the recipient fails to fulfill the service obligation, repayment of principal and interest is required. The number of Awards and recipients are dependent upon availability of funds, and awards will be made on a first-come, first-served basis.

Amount of award:	$6,000
Application deadline:	April 30

Contact:
3825 Ridgewood Road
Jackson, MS 39211-6453
Phone: 601-982-6663

Veterinary Medicine Minority Loan / Scholarship

Type of award: Scholarship.
Intended use: For full-time first professional study at accredited graduate institution in United States. Designated institutions: Mississippi State University College of Veterinary Medicine.
Eligibility: Applicant must be of minority background. Applicant must be U.S. citizen or permanent resident residing in Mississippi.
Basis for selection: Major/career interest in veterinary medicine.
Application requirements: Transcript.
Additional information: Award is made on an annual basis with priority given to renewal students. Obligation can be discharged on the basis of one yearÖs full-time service as a licensed professional in the approved profession in the State of Mississippi for one yearÖs support. In the event the recipient fails to fulfill the service obligation, repayment of principal and interest is required. The number of Awards and recipients are dependent upon availability of funds, and awards will be made on a first-come, first-served basis.

Amount of award:	$6,000
Application deadline:	May 18

Contact:
3825 Ridgewood Road
Jackson, MS 39211-6453
Phone: 601-982-6663

Missouri Coordinating Board for Higher Education

Missouri Higher Education Academic Scholarship

Type of award: Scholarship, renewable.
Intended use: For full-time undergraduate study at accredited vocational, 2-year or 4-year institution in Missouri. Designated institutions: Approved Missouri institutions.
Eligibility: Applicant must be U.S. citizen or permanent resident residing in Missouri.
Basis for selection: Applicant must demonstrate high academic achievement.
Application requirements: Proof of eligibility. Academic progress important.
Additional information: May not be used for theology or divinity studies. SAT I or ACT test required for determining academic achievement.

Amount of award:	$2,000
Number of awards:	6,700
Number of applicants:	8,000
Application deadline:	July 31
Total amount awarded:	$13,000,000

Missouri Public Service Survivor Grant

Type of award: Scholarship, renewable.
Intended use: For full-time undergraduate study at accredited vocational, 2-year or 4-year institution in Missouri. Designated institutions: Institution must be approved.
Eligibility: Applicant must be U.S. citizen or permanent resident residing in Missouri. Applicant's parent must have been killed or disabled in work-related accident as fire fighter, police officer or public safety officer.
Application requirements: Proof of eligibility.
Additional information: For children of Missouri public safety officers, including law enforcement, firefighters, corrections, water safety, and conservation, killed in the line of

duty. Children of Missouri Dept. of Highway and Transportation employees also eligible if parent died during performance of job. May not be used for theology or divinity studies. Award amounts vary; contact sponsor for information.

- **Number of awards:** 8
- **Number of applicants:** 8
- **Total amount awarded:** $12,500

Missouri Student Grant

Type of award: Scholarship, renewable.
Intended use: For full-time undergraduate study at accredited vocational, 2-year or 4-year institution in Missouri.
Eligibility: Applicant must be U.S. citizen or permanent resident residing in Missouri.
Basis for selection: Applicant must demonstrate financial need.
Application requirements: Proof of eligibility. Any approved MDE or FAFSA may be used to apply.
Additional information: Must have resided in Missouri at least one year as non-student. May not be used for theology or divinity studies.

- **Amount of award:** $100-$1,500
- **Number of awards:** 9,400
- **Number of applicants:** 108,000
- **Application deadline:** April 1
- **Notification begins:** July 1
- **Total amount awarded:** $13,400,000

Contact:
Missouri Coordinating Board for Higher Education
3515 Amazonas Drive
Jefferson City, MO 65109

Missouri Department of Elementary and Secondary Education

Missouri Minority Teaching Scholarship

Type of award: Scholarship, renewable.
Intended use: For full-time undergraduate certificate, freshman, sophomore, junior, senior or master's study at accredited 2-year or 4-year institution in Missouri. Designated institutions: Missouri Institutions.
Eligibility: Applicant must be of minority background. Applicant must be high school senior. Applicant must be residing in Missouri.
Basis for selection: Major/career interest in education. Applicant must demonstrate high academic achievement.
Application requirements: Recommendations, transcript and proof of eligibility.
Additional information: Must rank in top 25 percent of class. Must score in top 25 percent on ACT or SAT. Must teach for five years in Missouri Public Schools or scholarship becomes loan. If in college, may have 3.0 GPA at 30 hours to qualify. If college graduate, may receive award if returning to a masters level math or science education program.

- **Amount of award:** $3,000
- **Number of awards:** 100
- **Application deadline:** February 15, February 15
- **Notification begins:** April 15
- **Total amount awarded:** $300,000

Contact:
Missouri Department of Elementary and Secondary Education
Teacher Recruitment and Retention, DESE
P.O. Box 480
Jefferson City, MO 65101
Phone: 573-751-1668

Missouri Robert C. Byrd Honors Scholarship

Type of award: Scholarship, renewable.
Intended use: For freshman, sophomore, junior or senior study at accredited 4-year institution in United States.
Eligibility: Applicant must be high school senior. Applicant must be U.S. citizen or permanent resident residing in Missouri.
Basis for selection: Applicant must demonstrate high academic achievement.
Application requirements: Transcript.
Additional information: Must be completing high school or GED in year of application. Must be in top 10 percent of class or have GED score at or above national 90th percentile. Final selection at each congressional district level based on SAT or ACT scores and GPA. High school guidance counselor must sign application. Award amount varies, contact sponsor for more information. The applicants high school guidance counselor must sign and verigy the application form.

- **Amount of award:** $1,500
- **Application deadline:** April 15
- **Notification begins:** October 1
- **Total amount awarded:** $355,500

Contact:
Missouri Department of Elementary and Secondary Education
Attn: Dr. Celeste Ferguson
P.O. Box 480
Jefferson City, MO 65102
Phone: 573-751-1668

Missouri Teacher Education Scholarship

Type of award: Scholarship.
Intended use: For full-time freshman, sophomore study at accredited 4-year institution in Missouri.
Eligibility: Fifteen percent of awards set aside for minorities. Applicant must be high school senior. Applicant must be U.S. citizen residing in Missouri.
Basis for selection: Major/career interest in education. Applicant must demonstrate high academic achievement.
Application requirements: Recommendations, transcript and proof of eligibility. ACT/SAT and class rank.
Additional information: Must rank in top 15 percent of graduating class or score in top 15 percent on ACT, SAT I or other standardized tests. Must teach in Missouri Public School for five years after graduation or scholarship becomes a loan.

Amount of award: $2,000
Number of awards: 240
Number of applicants: 500
Application deadline: February 15
Notification begins: April 15
Total amount awarded: $240,000
Contact:
Teacher Recruitment and Retention
P.O. Box 480
Jefferson City, MO 65102

Montana Board of Regents of Higher Education

Montana Student Incentive Grant

Type of award: Scholarship.
Intended use: For full-time undergraduate study in Montana.
Eligibility: Applicant must be residing in Montana.
Basis for selection: Applicant must demonstrate financial need.
Additional information: Contact college financial aid office for application information.
Amount of award: $900

Montana Tuition Fee Waiver for Dependents of POW/MIA

Type of award: Scholarship.
Intended use: For undergraduate or graduate study in Montana. Designated institutions: Montana University system institutions.
Eligibility: Applicant must be residing in Montana. Applicant must be child of POW/MIA, spouse of POW/MIA.
Additional information: Contact college financial aid office for application information.

Montana Tuition Fee Waiver for Veterans

Type of award: Scholarship.
Intended use: For undergraduate or graduate study in Montana. Designated institutions: Montana University system institutions.
Eligibility: Applicant must be residing in Montana. Applicant must be veteran. Must have been honorably discharged person who served with the United States forces during wartime.
Application requirements: Proof of eligibility.
Additional information: Must have used up all federal veterans educational assistance benefits. Contact college financial aid office.

Montana University System Community College Honor Scholarship

Type of award: Scholarship.
Intended use: For junior study at 4-year institution in Montana. Designated institutions: Montana University system institutions.
Eligibility: Applicant must be residing in Montana.
Basis for selection: Applicant must demonstrate high academic achievement.
Application requirements: Recommendations and proof of eligibility.
Additional information: Must be graduate of accredited Montana community college and be recommended by president and faculty. 3.5 GPA required. Award provides for tuition/fee waiver in any unit of Montana University System. For application, contact financial aid office of community college.
Number of awards: 15
Application deadline: June 30

Montana University System High School Honor Scholarship

Type of award: Scholarship.
Intended use: For freshman study at 4-year institution in Montana. Designated institutions: Montana University system institutions.
Eligibility: Applicant must be high school senior. Applicant must be U.S. citizen residing in Montana.
Basis for selection: Applicant must demonstrate high academic achievement.
Application requirements: Recommendations, transcript and proof of eligibility.
Additional information: Obtain information from high school guidance counselor who completes application for recommended students. Scholarships awarded to members of graduation classes fewer than 25. Must have 3.0 GPA. Terms of award and which fees are covered specified at time scholarship is awarded.
Contact:
Montana University System
PO Box 203101
Helena, MT 59620-3101

NASA Space Grant Alabama Space Grant Consortium

NASA Space Grant Alabama Graduate Fellowship

Type of award: Scholarship, renewable.
Intended use: For full-time senior or graduate study at accredited graduate institution in United States.
Eligibility: Applicant must be U.S. citizen or Must be U.S. Citizen.
Basis for selection: Major/career interest in aerospace;

astronomy; biology; business; communications; computer and information sciences; education; engineering; international relations; law. Applicant must demonstrate service orientation and high academic achievement.
Application requirements: Recommendations, essay, transcript, research proposal and by Through Campus Director on member institution campus. State applicant must attend college in Alabama.
Additional information: Awardees are expected to follow a multidisciplinary course of study. Applicants must include a resume and current transcript and GRE scores. Applicants must be sponsored by and must attend an Alabama Space Grant Consortium member institution. Consortium members include: Alabama A&M University, Auburn University, The University of Alabama, The University of Alabama at Birmingham, The University of Alabama in Huntsville, University of South Alabama. The Consortium actively encourages women, minority, and physically challenged students to apply.

Amount of award:	$20,000
Number of awards:	10
Number of applicants:	22
Application deadline:	, February 28
Notification begins:	, April 1
Total amount awarded:	$12

NASA Space Grant Alabama Undergraduate Scholarship Program

Type of award: Scholarship, renewable.
Intended use: For full-time undergraduate study at accredited 4-year institution in United States.
Eligibility: Applicant must be U.S. citizen.
Basis for selection: Major/career interest in aerospace; astronomy; biology; business; communications; computer and information sciences; education; engineering; international relations; law.
Application requirements: Recommendations, essay and transcript. State applicant must attend college in Alabama.
Additional information: Applicants must include a resume and have a GPA of 3.0 or greater. Awardees must attend an Alabama Space Grant Consortium member institution. Consortium members include: Alabama A&M University, Auburn University, The University of Alabama, The University of Alabama at Birmingham, The University of Alabama in Huntsville, University of South Alabama. The Consortium actively encourages women, minority, and physically challenged students to apply.

Amount of award:	$1,000
Number of awards:	27

Contact:
NASA Space Grant Alabama Space Grant Consortium
University of Alabama in Huntsville
Materials Science Building, 205
Huntsville, AL 35899
Website: www.uah.edu/agsc

NASA Space Grant Alaska Space Grant Consortium

NASA Space Grant Alaska Graduate Fellowship

Type of award: Research grant.
Intended use: For full-time master's, doctoral study at accredited graduate institution outside United States.
Eligibility: Applicant must be U.S. citizen.
Basis for selection: Major/career interest in aerospace; astronomy; engineering; physics.
Application requirements: Recommendations, transcript and research proposal. State applicant must attend college in Alaska.
Additional information: Must be used at a Alaska Consortium member institution. Member institutions include: The University of Alaska at Fairbanks, Southeast, and Anchorage, The International Space University, and Alaska Pacific University.

Amount of award:	$15,000
Application deadline:	April 1

NASA Space Grant Alaska Undergraduate Scholarship

Type of award: Scholarship.
Intended use: For full-time freshman, sophomore, junior or senior study at accredited 4-year institution in United States.
Eligibility: Applicant must be U.S. citizen.
Basis for selection: Major/career interest in aerospace; astronomy; engineering; physics.
Application requirements: Recommendations, essay and transcript. State applicant must attend college in Alaska.
Additional information: Must be used at an Alaska Space Grant Consortium member institution. Members include The University of Alaska at Fairbanks, Southeast, and Anchorage, The International Space University, and Alaska Pacific University. Number of scholarships and amount of funding varies; contact sponsor for information.

Application deadline:	April 1

Rocket Program Internship

Type of award: Internship.
Intended use: For freshman, sophomore, junior, senior, master's or doctoral study.
Eligibility: Applicant must be U.S. citizen.
Basis for selection: Major/career interest in aerospace; engineering.
Application requirements: Research proposal. State applicant must attend college in Alaska.
Additional information: Applicants must include resume and letter of intent. The deadline for letter of intent is: 4/28/99. The deadlines for proposals are: for Internships during September-December: 8/1/99; during January-April: 12/1/99; during May-August: 4/1/99.
Contact:
Project Director
Alaska Space Grant Program Office
University of Alaska - Fairbanks, P.O. Box 755919
Fairbanks, AK 99775-5919
Website: www.asyp.alaska.edu

147

NASA Space Grant Arizona Grant Consortium

NASA Space Grant Arizona Undergraduate Research Internship

Type of award: Internship.
Intended use: For full-time undergraduate study at accredited 2-year or 4-year institution in United States.
Eligibility: Applicant must be U.S. citizen.
Basis for selection: Major/career interest in aerospace; astronomy; engineering; physics; science, general.
Application requirements: State applicant must attend college in Arizona.
Additional information: Awardees must attend an Arizona Space Grant Consortium member institution. Members include: Arizona State University, Dine College, Embry-Riddle, Eastern Arizona University, Northern Arizona University, Pima Community College, Eastern Arizona College and University of Arizona.
Contact:
NASA Space Grant Arizona Space Grant Consortium
Lunar and Planetary Laboratory
University of Arizona, 1629 E. University Blvd.
Tucson, AZ 85721-0092
Website: www.seds.org/spacegrant/azfelann.htm

NASA Space Grant Arizona Space Grant Consortium

NASA Space Grant Arizona Graduate Fellowship

Type of award: Research grant, renewable.
Intended use: For full-time graduate study at accredited graduate institution in United States.
Eligibility: Applicant must be U.S. citizen.
Basis for selection: Major/career interest in aerospace; astronomy; atmospheric sciences/meteorology; biology; environmental science; geology/earth sciences; science, general; engineering, biomedical; engineering, chemical; engineering, electrical and electronic.
Application requirements: Essay, transcript, research proposal and nomination by Applicants must be nominated by their graduate departments. State applicant must attend college in Arizona.
Additional information: Awardees must attend an Arizona Space Grant Consortium with Graduate Program. Only two universities with Space Grant Graduate Fellowship Program are: Arizona State University and University of Arizona.

Amount of award:	$16,000
Number of awards:	6
Application deadline:	March 13

Contact:
NASA Space Grant Arizona Space Grant Consortium
Lunar and Planetary Laboratory
University of Arizona, 1629 E. University Blvd.
Tucson, AZ 85721-0092
Website: www.seds.org/spacegrant/azfelann.htm

NASA Space Grant Arkansas Space Grant Consortium

NASA Space Grant Arkansas Graduate Fellowship

Type of award: Scholarship.
Intended use: For full-time master's, doctoral study in United States.
Eligibility: Applicant must be U.S. citizen residing in Arkansas.
Basis for selection: Major/career interest in aerospace; astronomy; chemistry; engineering; physics; medicine (m.d.). Applicant must demonstrate high academic achievement.
Application requirements: Research proposal. State applicant must attend college in Arkansas.
Additional information: Members of the Arkansas Space Grant Consortium include: University of Arkansas at Little Rock, Arkansas State University, Arkansas Tech University, Harding University, Henderson State Universty, Hendrix College, Lyon College, Ouachita Baptist University, University of Arkansas at Fayetteville, University of Arkansas at Pine Bluff, University of Arkansas for Medical Sciences, University of Central Arkansas and University of the Ozarks. For any space-related research. Deadlines are usually in September; contact the Program Coordinator for up-to-date information. A GPA of at least 3.0 is preferred.

Amount of award:	$250-$5,000
Number of awards:	7
Total amount awarded:	$15,838

NASA Space Grant Arkansas Undergraduate Scholarship

Type of award: Scholarship.
Intended use: For full-time sophomore, junior or senior study in United States.
Eligibility: Applicant must be U.S. citizen residing in Arkansas.
Basis for selection: Major/career interest in aerospace; astronomy; chemistry; engineering; physics; medicine (m.d.). Applicant must demonstrate high academic achievement.
Application requirements: Research proposal. State applicant must attend college in Arkansas.
Additional information: Awards must be used at Consortium Member institutions. Members of the Arkansas Space Grant Consortium include: University of Arkansas at Little Rock, Arkansas State University, Arkansas Tech University, Harding University, Henderson State Universty, Hendrix College, Ouachita Baptist University, University of Arkansas at Fayetteville, University of Arkansas at Pine Bluff, University of Arkansas for Medical Sciences, University of Central Arkansas and University of the Ozarks. For any space-related research. Deadlines are usually in September; contact the Program Coordinator for up-to-date information. A GPA of at least 3.0 is preferred.

Amount of award:	$250-$5,000
Number of awards:	61
Total amount awarded:	$109,089

Contact:
NASA Space Grant Arkansas Space Grant Consortium
University of Arkansas, College of Science & Engineering Technology
2801 S. University Ave., ETAS 125
Little Rock, AR 72204-1099
Website: www.ualr.edu/~nasa/index.html

NASA Space Grant California Space Grant Consortium

NASA Space Grant California Fellowship Program

Type of award: Scholarship, renewable.
Intended use: For full-time graduate study at accredited graduate institution in United States.
Eligibility: Applicant must be U.S. citizen.
Basis for selection: Major/career interest in aerospace; engineering; science, general.
Application requirements: Nomination. State applicant must attend college in California.
Additional information: Awardees must attend a California Space Grant Consortium member institution. Consortium members include: The California State University: DQ University, San Diego Community College District, San Diego Unified School District; and University of California: Berkeley, Irvine, Los Angeles, Riverside, San Diego, Santa Barbara, and Santa Cruz. The San Francisco Art Institute, Paolomar Community College, Pomona College, Stanford University. The Consortium actively encourages women, minority, and physically challenged students to apply. Application dates and requirements vary by consortium member.

Amount of award:	$1,500-$12,200
Number of awards:	10
Total amount awarded:	$36,000

NASA Space Grant California Undergraduate Scholarship

Type of award: Scholarship, renewable.
Intended use: For full-time undergraduate study at accredited 4-year institution in United States.
Eligibility: Applicant must be U.S. citizen.
Basis for selection: Major/career interest in aerospace; engineering; science, general.
Application requirements: State applicant must attend college in California.
Additional information: Awardees must attend a California Space Grant Consortium member institution. Consortium members include: The California State University: DQ University, San Diego Community College District, San Diego Unified School District; and University of California: Berkeley, Irvine, Los Angeles, Riverside, San Diego, Santa Barbara, and Santa Cruz. The San Francisco Art Institute, Paolomar Community College, Pomona College, Stanford University. The Consortium actively encourages women, minority, and physically challenged students to apply. Application dates and requirements vary by consortium member.

Amount of award:	$1,500-$10,000
Number of awards:	34
Total amount awarded:	$65,400

Contact:
NASA Space Grant California Space Grant Consortium
University of San Diego: San Diego
California Space Institute, 9500 Gilman Dr., 0524
La Jolla, CA 92093
Website: deimos.uscd.edu/space_grant/fellowship.html

NASA Space Grant Colorado Space Grant Consortium

NASA Space Grant Colorado Graduate Fellowship

Type of award: Scholarship.
Intended use: For undergraduate study.
Eligibility: Applicant must be U.S. citizen.
Basis for selection: Major/career interest in science, general; engineering; aerospace.
Application requirements: State applicant must attend college in Colorado.
Additional information: Contact sponsor for program information. Must be used at a Colorado Space Grant Consortium member institution.

NASA Space Grant Colorado Undergraduate Scholarship

Type of award: Scholarship.
Intended use: For undergraduate study.
Eligibility: Applicant must be U.S. citizen.
Basis for selection: Major/career interest in science, general; engineering; aerospace.
Application requirements: State applicant must attend college in Colorado.
Additional information: Contact sponsor for program information. Must be used at a Colorado Space Grant Consortium member institution.

Contact:
Project Director
University of Colorado, Boulder
Engineering Center, Room 1B-76, Campus Box 520
Boulder, CO 80309-0520

NASA Space Grant Connecticut Space Grant Consortium

NASA Space Grant Connecticut Graduate Fellowship

Type of award: Research grant, renewable.
Intended use: For full-time master's, doctoral study at accredited graduate institution in United States.
Eligibility: Applicant must be U.S. citizen.
Basis for selection: Major/career interest in aerospace; engineering.
Application requirements: Recommendations, transcript, proof of eligibility and research proposal. State applicant must attend college in Connecticut.
Additional information: Must be used at a Connecticut Consortium member institution. Member institutions include: University of Connecticut, University of Hartford, University of New Haven, Trinity College. The Consortium actively encourages women, minority, and disabled students to apply.
    Amount of award: $6,250
    Number of awards: 4
    Number of applicants: 12
    Application deadline: October 15, April 1
    Total amount awarded: $25,000
Contact:
NASA Space Grant Connecticut Space Grant Consortium
200 Bloomfield Ave., UT Hall
West Hartford, CT 06117
Website: uhavax.hartford.edu/ctspgrant

NASA Space Grant Delaware Space Grant Consortium

NASA Space Grant Delaware Space Graduate Student Fellowship

Type of award: Research grant, renewable.
Intended use: For full-time master's, doctoral study at accredited graduate institution in United States.
Eligibility: Applicant must be U.S. citizen.
Basis for selection: Major/career interest in astronomy; engineering, chemical; engineering, mechanical; geography; physics.
Application requirements: Recommendations, transcript and research proposal.
Additional information: Awardees must attend a Delaware Space Grant Consortium member institution. Consortium members include: University of Delaware, Delaware Technical and Community College, Frranklin and Marshall College, Gettysburg College, Lehigh University, Lincoln University, Swathmore College, Delaware State University at Dover, University of Pennsylvania, Villanova College. Award amounts vary; contact Coordinator for specific information.
    Number of awards: 6
    Number of applicants: 6
    Application deadline: March 1

NASA Space Grant Delaware Undergraduate Summer Scholarship

Type of award: Scholarship, renewable.
Intended use: For full-time freshman, sophomore, junior or senior study at accredited 4-year institution in United States.
Eligibility: Applicant must be U.S. citizen.
Basis for selection: Major/career interest in aerospace; astronomy; engineering; physics.
Application requirements: Recommendations and transcript.
Additional information: Awardees must attend a Delaware Space Grant Consortium member institution. Consortium members include: University of Delaware, Delaware Technical and Community College, Frranklin and Marshall College, Gettysburg College, Lehigh University, Lincoln University, Swathmore College, Delaware State University at Dover, University of Pennsylvania, Villanova College.
    Amount of award: $3,000-$3,500
    Number of awards: 5
    Number of applicants: 7
    Application deadline: March 1
    Total amount awarded: $11,500

NASA Space Grant Delaware Undergraduate Tuition Scholarship

Type of award: Scholarship, renewable.
Intended use: For full-time undergraduate study at accredited 4-year institution in United States.
Eligibility: Applicant must be U.S. citizen.
Basis for selection: Major/career interest in aerospace; astronomy; communications; engineering; geography; geology/earth sciences; geophysics; physics.
Application requirements: State applicant must attend college in Delaware.
Additional information: Awardees must attend a Delaware Space Grant Consortium member institution. Consortium members include: University of Delaware, Delaware Technical and Community College, Frranklin and Marshall College, Gettysburg College, Lehigh University, Lincoln University, Swathmore College, Delaware State University at Dover, University of Pennsylvania, Villanova College.
    Amount of award: $4,000
    Number of awards: 5
    Number of applicants: 8
    Application deadline: March 1
    Total amount awarded: $20,000
Contact:
NASA Space Grant Delaware Space Grant Consortium
Delaware Space Grant Program Office
University of Delaware, 217 Sharp Lab
Newark, DE 19716
Website: www.bartol.udel.edu/~sherry/desgc

NASA Space Grant District of Columbia Space Grant Consortium

NASA Space Grant District of Columbia Undergraduate Scholarship

Type of award: Scholarship, renewable.
Intended use: For undergraduate study.
Eligibility: Applicant must be U.S. citizen.
Basis for selection: Major/career interest in science, general; mathematics; engineering. Applicant must demonstrate high academic achievement.
Application requirements: Recommendations, transcript and proof of eligibility. State applicant must attend college in Washington, D.C.
Additional information: Number of grants, amounts of funding, deadlines, and application requirements vary by year and by institutions; contact sponsor for more information. Must be used at a District of Columbia Consortium member institution. Consortium members that give funding include George Washington University, Howard University, and Gallaudet University.

NASA Space Grant District of Columbia Graduate Fellowship

Type of award: Scholarship, renewable.
Intended use: For graduate study.
Eligibility: Applicant must be U.S. citizen.
Basis for selection: Major/career interest in science, general; mathematics; engineering. Applicant must demonstrate high academic achievement.
Application requirements: Recommendations, transcript, proof of eligibility and research proposal. State applicant must attend college in Washington, D.C.
Additional information: Number of grants, amounts of funding, deadlines, and application requirements vary by year and by institutions; contact sponsor for more information. Must be used at a District of Columbia Consortium member institution. Consortium members that give funding include George Washington University, Howard University, and Gallaudet University. Funding also exists for applicants focusing on space policy.
Contact:
NASA Space Grant District of Columbia Space Grant Conrortium
2013 G St., Northwest
Stuart Hall, Suite 301
Washington, DC 20052
Website: www.gwu.edu/~spi/spacegrant

NASA Space Grant Florida Space Grant Consortium

NASA Space Grant Florida Fellowship Program

Type of award: Research grant, renewable.
Intended use: For full-time doctoral study at accredited graduate institution in United States.
Eligibility: Applicant must be U.S. citizen.
Basis for selection: Major/career interest in aerospace; astronomy; atmospheric sciences/meteorology; biology; computer and information sciences; education; engineering; geology/earth sciences; medical specialties/research; physics.
Application requirements: Recommendations, essay, transcript, research proposal and nomination. State applicant must attend college in Florida.
Additional information: Fellowship recipients will receive $12,000 for full-time doctoral study and a required summer traineeship in an industry, government, or non-profit laboratory. Applicants must append a c.v. and GRE scores; GPA should be 3.5 or higher. Awardees must attend a Florida Space Grant Consortium member institution. Consortium members include: Bethune-Cookman College, Eckerd College, Embry-Riddle Aeronautical University, Florida A&M University, Florida Atlantic University, Florida Community College, Florida Gulf Coast University, Florida Institute of Technology, Florida International University, Florida Southern College, Florida State University, University of Central Florida, University of Florida, University of Miami, University of North Florida, University of South Florida, University of West Florida. The Consortium actively encourages women, minority, and physically challenged students to apply.

Amount of award:	$12,000
Application deadline:	February 13
Notification begins:	March 15

NASA Space Grant Florida Fellowship Program

Type of award: Research grant, renewable.
Intended use: For full-time doctoral study at accredited graduate institution in United States.
Eligibility: Applicant must be U.S. citizen.
Basis for selection: Major/career interest in aerospace; astronomy; atmospheric sciences/meteorology; biology; computer and information sciences; education; engineering; geology/earth sciences; medical specialties/research; physics.
Application requirements: Recommendations, essay, transcript, research proposal and nomination. State applicant must attend college in Florida.
Additional information: Fellowship recipients will receive $12,000 for full-time doctoral study and a required summer traineeship in an industry, government, or non-profit laboratory. Applicants must append a c.v. and GRE scores; GPA should be 3.5 or higher. Awardees must attend a Florida Space Grant Consortium member institution. Consortium members include: Bethune-Cookman College, Eckerd College, Embry-Riddle Aeronautical University, Florida A&M University, Florida Atlantic University, Florida Community College, Florida Gulf Coast University, Florida Institute of

Technology, Florida International University, Florida Southern College, Florida State University, University of Central Florida, University of Florida, University of Miami, University of North Florida, University of South Florida, University of West Florida. The Consortium actively encourages women, minority, and physically challenged students to apply.

Amount of award:	$12,000
Number of awards:	8
Number of applicants:	9
Application deadline:	February 13
Notification begins:	March 15
Total amount awarded:	$100,000

NASA Space Grant Florida Undergraduate Space Research Participation Program

Type of award: Scholarship, renewable.
Intended use: For undergraduate study at accredited 2-year or 4-year institution in United States.
Basis for selection: Major/career interest in aerospace; astronomy; atmospheric sciences/meteorology; biology; computer and information sciences; education; engineering; geology/earth sciences; medical specialties/research; physics.
Application requirements: Recommendations, essay, transcript and nomination. State applicant must attend college in Florida.
Additional information: Scholarship receipients will receive up to $4,000 from FSGC (NASA). Equal amounts in matching required. The matching funds must be non-federal and can be cash or in-knd. Awardees must attend a Florida Space Grant Consortium member institution. Consortium members include: Bethune-Cookman College, Eckerd College, Embry-Riddle Aeronautical University, Florida A&M University, Florida Atlantic University, Florida Community College, Florida Gulf Coast University, Florida Institute of Technology, Florida International University, Florida Southern College, Florida State University, University of Central Florida, University of Florida, University of Miami, University of North Florida, University of South Florida, University of West Florida. The Consortium actively encourages women, minority, and physically challenged students to apply.

Amount of award:	$2,500-$4,000
Number of awards:	18
Number of applicants:	18
Application deadline:	February 13
Notification begins:	March 15
Total amount awarded:	$68,000

Contact:
NASA Space Grant Florida Space Grant Consortium
University of Florida, Department of Astronomy
211 SSRB, P.O. Box 112055
Gainesville, FL 32611-2055
Website: www.astro.ufl.edu/~fsgc

NASA Space Grant Georgia Space Grant Consortium

NASA Space Grant Georgia Fellowship Program

Type of award: Scholarship, renewable.
Intended use: For full-time junior, senior or graduate study at accredited postsecondary institution in United States.
Eligibility: Applicant must be high school junior, senior. Applicant must be U.S. citizen.
Basis for selection: Major/career interest in engineering; computer and information sciences; physics; chemistry; atmospheric sciences/meteorology; education. Applicant must demonstrate seriousness of purpose and service orientation.
Application requirements: Interview, portfolio, recommendations, essay and transcript. State applicant must attend college in Georgia.

Amount of award:	$550-$1,100
Number of applicants:	12
Total amount awarded:	$6,600

Contact:
NASA Space Grant Georgia Space Grant Consortium
Georgia Tech-Aerospace Engineering
Atlanta, GA 30332-0150
Website: www.cad.gatech.edu/~space/indes.html

NASA Space Grant Hawaii Space Grant Consortium

NASA Space Grant Hawaii Graduate Fellowship

Type of award: Scholarship, renewable.
Intended use: For full-time graduate study in United States.
Eligibility: Applicant must be U.S. citizen residing in Hawaii.
Basis for selection: Major/career interest in astronomy; geology/earth sciences; oceanography/marine studies; physics.
Application requirements: State applicant must attend college in Hawaii.
Additional information: Support for Fellows will include a stipend of $12,000 per nine-month period, and up to $1,000 for travel and supplies. Program offered at the University of Hawaii at Manoa. Additional fields include math, physics, engineering, computer sciences and life sciences that are concerned with the understanding, utilization, or exploration of space or with the investigation of Earth from space. Applicants must be sponsored by a faculty member who is willing to act as the student's advisor during the period of the award. Awards of Fellowships based on academic qualifications of the student, quality of the proposed research, relevance of the proposed research to NASA's programs, and feasibility of the prosposed research. Women, under-represented minorities (specifically Native Hawaiians, Filipinos, other Pacific Islanders, Native Americans, Blacks, and Hispanics), and physically challenged students who have interest in space-related fields are particularly encouraged to apply.

Amount of award: $13,000
Contact:
Project Director
2525 Correa Rd.
Honolulu, HI 96822
Website: www.soest.hawaii.edu/SPACEGRANT

NASA Space Grant Hawaii Undergraduate Scholarship

Type of award: Scholarship.
Intended use: For full-time junior, senior study in United States.
Eligibility: Applicant must be U.S. citizen residing in Hawaii.
Basis for selection: Major/career interest in astronomy; geology/earth sciences; oceanography/marine studies; physics.
Application requirements: State applicant must attend college in Hawaii.
Additional information: Additional fields include math, physics, engineering, computer sciences and life sciences that are concerned with the understanding, utilization, or exploration of space with the investigation of Earth from space. Applicants must be U.S. citizens and must be sponsored by a faculty member who is willing to act as the student's advisor during the period of the award. Full-time undergraduates at Manoa and Hilo who have declared a major can apply for two-semester fellowships that include a stipend of $1,750 per semester and up to $500 for supplies or travel. They are expected to work 10-15 hours per week on their projects. Recipients must attend Consortium member institutions. The Hawaii Consortium members are: University of Hawaii at Manoa and Hilo, Honolulu Community College, Kupiolani Community College, Leeward Community College, Maui Community College, and Windward Community College. Women, under-represented minorities (specifically Native Hawaiians, Filipinos, other Pacific Islanders, Native Americans, Blacks, and Hispanics), and physically challenged students who have interest in space-related fields are particularly encouraged to apply.

Amount of award: $200-$3,000
Number of awards: 20
Contact:
Project Director
2525 Correa Road
Honolulu, HI 96822
Website: www.soest.hawaii.edu/SPACEGRANT

NASA Space Grant Hawaii Undergraduate Traineeship Program

Type of award: Internship.
Intended use: For undergraduate study.
Eligibility: Applicant must be U.S. citizen.
Basis for selection: Major/career interest in science, general; astronomy; geology/earth sciences; oceanography/marine studies; physics.
Application requirements: State applicant must attend college in Hawaii.
Additional information: Deadlines, number of positions, and application criteria vary; contact sponsor for more information. Women, under-represented minorities (specifically Native Hawaiians, Filipinos, other Pacific Islanders, Native Americans, Blacks, and Hispanics), and physically challenged students who have interest in space-related fields are particularly encouraged to apply.

Amount of award: $1,000
Contact:
Project Director
2525 Correa Rd.
Honolulu, HI 96822
Website: www.soest.hawaii.edu/SPACEGRANT

NASA Space Grant Idaho Space Grant Consortium

NASA Space Grant Idaho Graduate Fellowship

Type of award: Research grant, renewable.
Intended use: For full-time master's, doctoral study.
Eligibility: Applicant must be U.S. citizen.
Basis for selection: Major/career interest in aerospace; engineering; mathematics; education.
Application requirements: Recommendations, transcript and research proposal. State applicant must attend college in Idaho.
Additional information: Applicants must attend an Idaho Space Grant Consortium member institution. Members include: Albertson College of Idaho, Boise State University, College of Southern Idaho, Idaho State University, Lewis Clark State College, North Idaho College, Northwest Nazarene College, Ricks College, and the University of Idaho. The application should include a resume, and GRE scores, if available. The Consortium actively encourages women, minority, and disabled students to apply. Out-of-state recipients are eligible for in-state tuition. The research proposal should not exceed 8 pages.

Amount of award: $3,000-$6,000
Number of awards: 6
Number of applicants: 6
Application deadline: February 26
Notification begins: March 26
Total amount awarded: $36,660

NASA Space Grant Idaho Undergraduate Scholarship Program

Type of award: Scholarship, renewable.
Intended use: For full-time undergraduate study at accredited 4-year institution in United States.
Eligibility: Applicant must be U.S. citizen.
Basis for selection: Major/career interest in engineering; mathematics; education.
Application requirements: Recommendations, essay and transcript. State applicant must attend college in Idaho.
Additional information: Applicants must attend an Idaho Space Grant Consortium member institution, and maintain a 3.0 GPA. Members include: Albertson College of Idaho, Boise State University, College of Southern Idaho, Idaho State University, Lewis Clark State College, North Idaho College, Northwest Nazarene College, Ricks College, and the

University of Idaho. The application should include ACT/SAT scores, if available. The Consortium actively encourages women, minority, and disabled students to apply. The application essay should not exceed 500 words.

> **Amount of award:** $350-$1,000
> **Number of awards:** 22
> **Number of applicants:** 40
> **Application deadline:** February 26
> **Notification begins:** March 26
> **Total amount awarded:** $22,000

Contact:
NASA Space Grant Idaho Space Grant Consortium
University of Idaho
College of Engineering
Moscow, ID 83844-1011
Website: www.vidaho.edu/nasa-isgc/

NASA Space Grant Illinois Space Grant Consortium

NASA Space Grant Illinois Graduate Fellowship

Type of award: Scholarship.
Intended use: For full-time graduate study.
Eligibility: Applicant must be U.S. citizen.
Basis for selection: Major/career interest in engineering; aerospace. Applicant must demonstrate high academic achievement.
Application requirements: Recommendations, transcript and research proposal. State applicant must attend college in Illinois.
Additional information: Contact sponsor for program deadline information. Must be used at an Illinois Space Grant Consortium member institution.

> **Amount of award:** $6,000-$12,000
> **Number of awards:** 3

Contact:
NASA Space Grant Illinois Space Grant Consortium
University of Illinois-Urbana, 306 Talbot Laboratory
104 S. Wright St.
Urbana, IL 61801-2935
Website: www.aae.uiuc.edu

NASA Space Grant Illinois Undergraduate Scholarship

Type of award: Scholarship, renewable.
Intended use: For full-time undergraduate study.
Eligibility: Applicant must be U.S. citizen.
Basis for selection: Major/career interest in engineering; aerospace.
Application requirements: Transcript. State applicant must attend college in Illinois.
Additional information: Must be used at an Illinois Space Grant Consortium member institutuion. Contact sponsor for deadline information. Recipient required to work on a research or design project and to participate in an outreach activity.

> **Amount of award:** $500-$1,000
> **Number of awards:** 3

Contact:
Project Director
University of Illinois-Urbana, 306 Talbot Laboratory
104 S. Wright St.
Urbana, IL 61801-2935
Website: www.aae.uiuc.edu

NASA Space Grant Indiana Space Grant Consortium

NASA Space Grant Indiana Graduate Fellowship

Type of award: Scholarship.
Intended use: For graduate study.
Eligibility: Applicant must be U.S. citizen.
Basis for selection: Major/career interest in science, general; mathematics; engineering; aerospace. Applicant must demonstrate high academic achievement.
Application requirements: State applicant must attend college in Indiana.
Additional information: Number of grants, amounts of funding, deadlines, and application requirements vary by institution; contact sponsor for more information. Must be used at an Indiana Space Grant Consortium member institution. Members include Purdue University at West Lafayette, Purdue University at Hammond, University of Notre Dame in South Bend, Indiana University in Bloomington, Ball State University, Taylor University, Valparaiso University. Funding available for summer research projects.

NASA Space Grant Indiana Summer Undergraduate Research Program

Type of award: Scholarship.
Intended use: For undergraduate study.
Eligibility: Applicant must be U.S. citizen.
Basis for selection: Major/career interest in science, general; mathematics; engineering; aerospace. Applicant must demonstrate high academic achievement.
Application requirements: State applicant must attend college in Indiana.
Additional information: Number of grants, amounts of funding, deadlines, and application requirements vary by institution; contact sponsor for more information. Must be used at an Indiana Space Grant Consortium member institution. Members include Purdue University at West Lafayette, Purdue University at Hammond, University of Notre Dame in South Bend, Indiana University in Bloomington, Ball State University, Taylor University, Valparaiso University. Funding available for summer research projects.

NASA Space Grant Indiana Undergraduate Scholarship

Type of award: Scholarship.
Intended use: For undergraduate study.

Eligibility: Applicant must be U.S. citizen.
Basis for selection: Major/career interest in science, general; mathematics; engineering; aerospace. Applicant must demonstrate high academic achievement.
Application requirements: State applicant must attend college in Indiana.
Additional information: Number of grants, amounts of funding, deadlines, and application requirements vary by institution; contact sponsor for more information. Must be used at an Indiana Space Grant Consortium member institution. Members include Purdue University at West Lafayette, Purdue University at Hammond, University of Nortre Dame in South Bend, Indiana University in Bloomington, Ball State University, Taylor University, Valparaiso University.
Contact:
NASA Space Grant Indiana Space Grant Consortium
Purdue University, School of Aeronautics and Astronautics
1282 Grissom Hall
West Lafayette, IN 47909-1282
Website: roger.ecn.purdue.edu/v1/isgc

NASA Space Grant Iowa Space Grant Consortium

Graduate and Undergraduate Fellowships

Type of award: Scholarship.
Intended use: For undergraduate or graduate study.
Additional information: The Iowa Space Grant Consortium offers graduate and undergraduate funding. Recipients are chosen by faculty nomination at the Consortium member institutions. Award amounts vary.
Contact:
NASA Space Grant Iowa Space Grant Consortium
Dept. of Aerospace/Engineering Mechanics
408 Iowa Engineering Building
Ames, IA 50011-3131

NASA Space Grant Kansas Space Grant Consortium

NASA Space Grant Kansas Graduate Fellowship

Type of award: Scholarship.
Intended use: For undergraduate study.
Eligibility: Applicant must be U.S. citizen.
Basis for selection: Major/career interest in mathematics; science, general; engineering.
Application requirements: State applicant must attend college in Kansas.
Additional information: Contact sponsor for all deadline, scholarhip application criteria information, and award amounts; these are determined locally by the member institution. Consortium members include: Emporia State University, Fort Hays State University, Kansas State University, Pittsburg State University, University of Kansas, and Wichita State University. Applicant must attend a Consortium member institution. Preference given to women and minorities.

NASA Space Grant Kansas Undergraduate Scholarship

Type of award: Scholarship.
Intended use: For undergraduate study.
Eligibility: Applicant must be U.S. citizen.
Basis for selection: Major/career interest in mathematics; science, general; engineering.
Application requirements: State applicant must attend college in Kansas.
Additional information: Contact sponsor for all deadline, scholarhip application criteria information, and award amounts; these are determined locally by the member institution. Consortium members include: Emporia State University, Fort Hays State University, Kansas State University, Pittsburg State University, University of Kansas, and Wichita State University. Applicant must attend a Consortium member institution. Preference given to women and minorities.
Contact:
NASA Space Grant Kansas Space Grant Consortium
2004 Leonard Hall
Lawrence, KS 66045
Website: www.ksgc.org

NASA Space Grant Kentucky Space Grant Consortium

NASA Space Grant Kentucky Graduate Fellowship

Type of award: Research grant, renewable.
Intended use: For full-time graduate study at accredited graduate institution in United States.
Eligibility: Applicant must be U.S. citizen.
Basis for selection: Major/career interest in aerospace; astronomy; education; engineering; physics; biology; chemistry; psychology.
Application requirements: Interview, recommendations, essay, transcript, research proposal and nomination. State applicant must attend college in Kentucky.
Additional information: Awardees must attend a Kentucky Space Grant Consortium member institution. Consortium members are: Centre College, Eastern Kentucky University, Kentucky Center for Space Enterprise, Kentucky State University, Morehead State University, Murray State University, Northern Kentucky University, Thomas More College, Transylvania University, University of Kentucky, University of Louisville, Western Kentucky University. Preference is given to schools that waive tuition for the recipient. The Consortium actively encourages women, minority, and physically challenged students to apply. The application deadline is in March of 1999. Call the Consortium coordinator for the exact date.

Amount of award:	$12,000-$16,000
Number of awards:	5
Number of applicants:	5

NASA Space Grant Kentucky Undergraduate Scholarship

Type of award: Scholarship, renewable.
Intended use: For full-time undergraduate study at accredited 4-year institution in United States.
Basis for selection: Major/career interest in aerospace; astronomy; education; engineering; physics.
Application requirements: Interview, recommendations, essay, transcript, research proposal and nomination. State applicant must attend college in Kentucky.
Additional information: Awardees must attend a Kentucky Space Grant Consortium member institution. Consortium members are: Centre College, Eastern Kentucky University, Kentucky Center for Space Enterprise, Kentucky State University, Morehead State University, Murray State University, Northern Kentucky University, Thomas More College, Transylvania University, University of Kentucky, University of Louisville, Western Kentucky University. Preference is given to schools that waive tuition for the recipient. The Consortium actively encourages women, minority, and physically challenged students to apply. The application deadline is in March of 1999. Call the Consortium coordinator for the exact date. Applicants doing work that is related to space exploration may qualify for funding, whatever their field of study may be.

Amount of award:	$3,000
Number of awards:	2
Number of applicants:	7

Contact:
NASA Space Grant Kentucky Space Grant Consortium
Western Kentucky University, Hardin Planetarium and Astrophysical Observatory
Dept. of Physics & Astronomy, TCCW 246, 1 Big Red Way
Bowling Green, KY 42101-3576
Website: www.wku.edu/ksgc

NASA Space Grant Louisiana Space Grant Consortium

NASA Space Grant Louisiana LaSPACE Graduate Fellowship Program

Type of award: Research grant, renewable.
Intended use: For full-time senior, master's or doctoral study at accredited graduate institution.
Eligibility: Applicant must be U.S. citizen residing in Louisiana.
Basis for selection: Major/career interest in aerospace; mathematics; science, general; engineering. Applicant must demonstrate depth of character, leadership and high academic achievement.
Application requirements: Recommendations, essay, transcript and proof of eligibility. State applicant must attend college in Louisiana.
Additional information: Members of the Louisiana Space Consortium: Dillard University, Grambling State University, LSU Agricultural Center, LSU and A&M Colege, Louisiana Tech University, Loyola University, McNeese State University, Northeast Louisiana University, Northwestern State University of Louisiana, Southern University and A&M College, Southern University at New Orleans, Southern University at Shreveport, Tulane University, The University of New Orleans, The University of Southwestern Louisiana, Xavier University of Louisiana. Matriculation must be at a member institution. Amounts awarded: Ph.D: $17,500 annually, terminal M.A.: $15,000 annually. Awardees must maintain a GPA of at least 3.0 and have GRE scores in excess of 1000 (with 600 minimum on the quantitative. Award recipients will be notified in April through May.

Amount of award:	$15,000-$17,500
Number of awards:	6
Number of applicants:	10
Application deadline:	February 6

NASA Space Grant Louisiana LaSPACE Undergraduate Scholarship Program

Type of award: Scholarship, renewable.
Intended use: For full-time undergraduate study at accredited 2-year or 4-year institution in United States.
Eligibility: Applicant must be high school senior. Applicant must be U.S. citizen residing in Louisiana.
Basis for selection: Major/career interest in aerospace; science, general; mathematics; engineering. Applicant must demonstrate depth of character, leadership and high academic achievement.
Application requirements: Recommendations, essay, transcript and proof of eligibility. State applicant must attend college in Louisiana.
Additional information: Applicant must be either a high school senior, a recent high school graduate, or a currently enrolled undergraduate. Must attend a Louisiana Space Consortium member university. Consortium members include: Dillard University, Grambling State University, LSU Agricultural Center, LSU and A&M Colege, Louisiana Tech University, Loyola University, McNeese State University, Northeast Louisiana University, Northwestern State University of Louisiana, Southern University and A&M College, Southern University at New Orleans, Southern University at Shreveport, Tulane University, The University of New Orleans, The University of Southwestern Louisiana, Xavier University of Louisiana. Scholarship funds are not available for summer school. Applicants must have a GPA of at least 3.0, high ACT/SAT scores, and pertinent science experiences and accomplishments. Award recipients will be notified in April through May.

Amount of award:	$2,500
Number of applicants:	36
Application deadline:	February 6
Total amount awarded:	$37,500

Contact:
NASA Space Grant Louisiana Space Grant Consortium
Louisiana State University
Dept. of Physics & Astronomy, 277 Nicholson Hall
Baton Rouge, LA 70803-4001
Website: phacts.phys.lsu.edu/scholars/program

NASA Space Grant Maine Space Grant Consortium

NASA Space Grant Maine Graduate Fellowship

Type of award: Research grant, renewable.
Intended use: For full-time master's, doctoral study at accredited graduate institution in United States.
Eligibility: Applicant must be U.S. citizen.
Basis for selection: Major/career interest in geology/earth sciences; aerospace; engineering.
Application requirements: Research proposal. State applicant must attend college in Maine.
Additional information: Must be used at a Maine Space Grant Consortium member institution. Contact sponsor for further information. Amount awarded: Ph.D. candidate: $15,000 annually, Master's candidate: $10,000 annually.

    Amount of award: $10,000-$15,000
    Application deadline: March 1
    Notification begins: April 1

NASA Space Grant Maine Research Acceleration Grant Program

Type of award: Research grant, renewable.
Intended use: For master's, doctoral or postgraduate study at accredited graduate institution in United States.
Eligibility: Applicant must be U.S. citizen.
Basis for selection: Major/career interest in aerospace; engineering.
Application requirements: Research proposal. State applicant must attend college in Maine.
Additional information: Must be used at a Maine Space Grant Consortium member institution. Contact sponsor for further information. Proposals may be sumitted by individuals in the public and private sectors in Maine; collaborations with other Maine institutions and with scientists at NASA research centers are encouraged but not required. A letter of intent and a summary of the proposed research project should be sent by November 1. Awards are available for projects which will take one year or less to complete; funds may be used for new projects or to supplement or complement ongoing research. A match of one dollar is required for every two dollars requested. Match can include cash or in-kind; for example: personnel time or waived indirect costs at the usual institutional rate. A related Travel Grant Program is available.

    Amount of award: $22,000
    Number of awards: 3
    Application deadline: December 13
    Total amount awarded: $66,000

NASA Space Grant Maine Undergraduate Internship Award

Type of award: Internship, renewable.
Intended use: For sophomore, junior or senior study at accredited 2-year or 4-year institution in United States.
Eligibility: Applicant must be U.S. citizen.
Basis for selection: Major/career interest in geology/earth sciences; aerospace; engineering.
Application requirements: Transcript and research proposal. State applicant must attend college in Maine.
Additional information: Students may work full-time during the summer for 10-12 weeks, or part-time during the academic year. Students must maintain a B average. Additional support, which may include salary, cost-of-living expenses, travel reimbursement, and housing accomodations, may be obtained from the host.

    Amount of award: $2,500
    Application deadline: March 15
    Notification begins: March 22

NASA Space Grant Maine Undergraduate Scholarship Program

Type of award: Scholarship, renewable.
Intended use: For full-time undergraduate study at accredited vocational, 2-year or 4-year institution in United States.
Eligibility: Applicant must be U.S. citizen.
Basis for selection: Major/career interest in geology/earth sciences; aerospace; engineering.
Application requirements: Research proposal. State applicant must attend college in Maine.
Additional information: Must be used at a Maine Space Grant Consortium member institution. Contact sponsor for further information.

    Amount of award: $2,000
    Number of awards: 9
    Application deadline: March 1
    Notification begins: April 1

Contact:
NASA Space Grant Maine Space Grant Consortium
87 Winthrop St.
Augusta, ME 04330
Website: www.mstf.org

NASA Space Grant Maryland Space Grant Consortium

NASA Space Grant Maryland Graduate Fellowship

Type of award: Scholarship.
Intended use: For graduate study.
Eligibility: Applicant must be U.S. citizen.
    Number of awards: 1

NASA Space Grant Maryland Undergraduate Scholarship

Type of award: Scholarship.
Intended use: For full-time undergraduate study.
Eligibility: Applicant must be U.S. citizen.

Number of awards: 4
Contact:
NASA Space Grant Maryland Space Grant Consortium
The John Hopkins University, Bloomburg Center for Physics and Astronomy
3400 N. Charles St., Rm. 203
Baltimore, MD 21218-2686
Website: msx4.pha.jhu.edu/ssip/contact.html

NASA Space Grant Massachusetts Space Grant Consortium

NASA Space Grant Massachusetts Graduate Fellowships

Type of award: Research grant, renewable.
Intended use: For graduate study at accredited graduate institution in United States.
Eligibility: Applicant must be U.S. citizen.
Basis for selection: Major/career interest in aerospace; astronomy; engineering; physics.
Application requirements: Recommendations, essay and transcript. State applicant must attend college in Massachusetts.
Additional information: Awardees must attend a Massachusetts Space Grant Consortium member institution. Consortium members include: Boston University, Harvard University, Massachusetts Institute of Technology, Tufts University, University of Massachusetts, Wellesley College, Worcester Polytechnic Institute, Charles Stark Draper Laboratory, and The Marine Biological Laboratory. Deadline in mid-February; call the coordinator for an exact date.
Amount of award: $20,000-$30,000
Number of awards: 3
Number of applicants: 17

NASA Space Grant Massachusetts Summer Jobs for Students

Type of award: Internship, renewable.
Intended use: For undergraduate or graduate study in United States.
Eligibility: Applicant must be U.S. citizen.
Basis for selection: Major/career interest in aerospace; astronomy; engineering; physics.
Application requirements: Interview and recommendations. State applicant must attend college in Massachusetts.
Additional information: Award amounts varie; contact sponsor. Awardees must attend a Massachusetts Space Grant Consortium member institution. Consortium members include: Boston University, Harvard University, Massachusetts Institute of Technology, Tufts University, University of Massachusetts, Wellesley College, Worcester Polytechnic Institute, Charles Stark Draper Laboratory, and The Marine Biological Laboratory. Deadline in mid-February; call the coordinator for an exact date.
Number of awards: 16
Number of applicants: 60

NASA Space Grant Massachusetts Undergraduate Research Opportunities

Type of award: Research grant, renewable.
Intended use: For full-time undergraduate study at accredited 4-year institution in United States.
Eligibility: Applicant must be U.S. citizen.
Basis for selection: Major/career interest in aerospace; astronomy; engineering; physics.
Application requirements: Recommendations and research proposal. State applicant must attend college in Massachusetts.
Additional information: Students working in any major and attending any Massachusetts Space Grant Consortium member institution may apply. Consortium members include: Boston University, Harvard University, Massachusetts Institute of Technology, Tufts University, University of Massachusetts, Wellesley College, Worcester Polytechnic Institute, Charles Stark Draper Laboratory, and The Marine Biological Laboratory.
Amount of award: $1,000
Number of awards: 10
Number of applicants: 10
Contact:
NASA Space Grant Massachusetts Space Grant Consortium
Massachusetts Institute of Technology, Aeronautics & Astronautics
77 Massachusetts Ave., Bldg. 33, Rm. 208
Cambridge, MA 02139
Website: www.mit.edu:8001/activities/magsc

NASA Space Grant Michigan Space Grant Consortium

NASA Space Grant Michigan Graduate Fellowship

Type of award: Scholarship.
Intended use: For graduate study.
Eligibility: Applicant must be U.S. citizen.
Basis for selection: Major/career interest in aerospace; engineering; science, general; mathematics. Applicant must demonstrate high academic achievement.
Application requirements: Recommendations, transcript and research proposal. State applicant must attend college in Michigan.
Additional information: Award may include tuition and fees waiver. Deadline varies between mid-November and early December; call coordinator for exact date.
Amount of award: $5,000-$12,000
Number of awards: 12
Number of applicants: 22

NASA Space Grant Michigan Undergraduate Fellowship

Type of award: Scholarship.
Intended use: For freshman, sophomore, junior or senior study.
Eligibility: Applicant must be U.S. citizen.
Basis for selection: Major/career interest in aerospace; engineering; science, general; mathematics. Applicant must demonstrate high academic achievement.
Application requirements: Recommendations, essay and transcript. State applicant must attend college in Michigan.
Additional information: Award may include tuition and fees waiver. Deadline varies between mid-November and early December; call coordinator for exact date.

Amount of award:	$2,500
Number of awards:	24
Number of applicants:	39

Contact:
NASA Space Grant Michigan Space Grant Consortium
University of Michigan, 2106 Space Physics Research Laboratory
2455 Hayward
Ann Arbor, MI 98109-2143

NASA Space Grant Minnesota Space Grant Consortium

NASA Space Grant Minnesota Graduate Fellowship

Type of award: Research grant, renewable.
Intended use: For full-time master's, doctoral study at accredited graduate institution in United States.
Eligibility: Applicant must be U.S. citizen.
Basis for selection: Major/career interest in aerospace; astronomy; atmospheric sciences/meteorology; biology; botany; chemistry; engineering, biomedical; engineering, chemical; engineering, civil; engineering, computer.
Application requirements: Interview, recommendations, transcript and research proposal. State applicant must attend college in Minnesota.

Amount of award:	$1,000-$2,000
Number of awards:	1
Number of applicants:	2
Application deadline:	April 1
Notification begins:	May 1

NASA Space Grant Minnesota Internship Program

Type of award: Internship.
Intended use: For full-time undergraduate study in United States.
Eligibility: Applicant must be U.S. citizen residing in Minnesota.
Basis for selection: Major/career interest in science, general.
Application requirements: Interview, recommendations, essay and transcript. State applicant must attend college in Minnesota.

Amount of award:	$600
Number of awards:	1
Number of applicants:	1
Application deadline:	May 1

NASA Space Grant Minnesota Undergraduate Scholarship

Type of award: Scholarship, renewable.
Intended use: For full-time undergraduate study at accredited 4-year institution in United States.
Eligibility: Applicant must be U.S. citizen.
Basis for selection: Major/career interest in aerospace; astronomy; atmospheric sciences/meteorology; biology; botany; chemistry; engineering, biomedical; engineering, chemical; engineering, civil; engineering, computer.
Application requirements: Recommendations and transcript. State applicant must college in Minnesota.
Additional information: Applicants must include a letter of intent and show a GPA of 3.2 or greater. Awardees must attend a Minnesota Space Grant Consortium member institution. Consortium members include: Augsburg College, Bethel College, Bemidji State University, Carleton College, College of St. Catherine, Fond de Lac Community College, Leech Lake Tribal College, Macalaser College, Normandale Community College, University of Minnesota - Duluth, University of Minnesota - Twin Cities, University of St. Thomas. The Consortium actively encourages women, minority, and physically challenged students to apply.

Amount of award:	$1,000-$2,500
Number of awards:	12
Number of applicants:	20
Application deadline:	March 15

Contact:
NASA Space Grant Minnesota Space Grant Consortium
University of Minnesota
Dept. of Aerospace Engineering & Mechanics
Minneapolis, MN 55455
Website: www.aem.umn.edu/other/msgc

NASA Space Grant Mississippi Space Grant Consortium

Mississippi Space Grant Consortium

Type of award: Scholarship, Internship, renewable.
Intended use: For full-time undergraduate or graduate study in United States.
Eligibility: Applicant must be U.S. citizen.
Basis for selection: Competition in Engineering/architecture. Varies by institution; most institutions consider grade point average, major and written essay. Most awards require research or public service activity. Major/career interest in engineering; mathematics; science, general. Applicant must

demonstrate leadership, seriousness of purpose and high academic achievement.
Application requirements: State applicant must attend college in the university awarding the scholarship.
Additional information: Award amounts vary; contact sponsor. Awardees must attend a Mississippi Space Grant Consortium member institution. Consortium members include: The University of Mississippi, The University of Southern Mississippi, Mississippi State University, Jackson State University, Alcron State University, Mississippi University for Women, Mississippi Valley State University, Delta State University, Coahoma Community College, Itawamba Community College, Pearl River Community College and Northeast Mississippi Community College.

Number of awards:	250
Number of applicants:	130
Total amount awarded:	$119,000

Contact:
NASA Space Grant Mississippi Space Grant Consortium
111 Somerville Hall
University, MS 38677

NASA Space Grant Missouri Space Grant Consortium

NASA Space Grant Missouri Summer Jobs for Students

Type of award: Research grant, renewable.
Intended use: For full-time master's, doctoral study at accredited graduate institution in United States.
Eligibility: Applicant must be U.S. citizen.
Basis for selection: Major/career interest in aerospace; astronomy; engineering; geology/earth sciences; physics.
Application requirements: Recommendations, essay, transcript and research proposal. State applicant must attend college in Missouri.
Additional information: Awardees are placed in space-related technical positions at ten industrial affiliates. Massachusetts Space Grant Consortium members include: Boston University, Harvard University, Massachusetts Institute of Technology, Tufts University, University of Massachusetts, Wellesley College, Worcester Polytechnic Institute, Charles Stark Draper Laboratory, and The Marine Biological Laboratory. The deadline varies; call coordinator for exact date.

Amount of award:	$12,500
Number of awards:	4
Application deadline:	March 7
Notification begins:	April 7
Total amount awarded:	$50,000

NASA Space Grant Missouri Summer Undergraduate Internship

Type of award: Internship, renewable.
Intended use: For full-time undergraduate study at accredited 4-year institution in United States.
Eligibility: Applicant must be U.S. citizen.
Basis for selection: Major/career interest in aerospace; astronomy; engineering; geology/earth sciences; physics.
Application requirements: Recommendations, essay and transcript. State applicant must attend college in Missouri.
Additional information: Awardees must attend a Missouri Space Grant Consortium member institution. Consortium members include: Southwest Missouri State University, University of Missouri - Columbia, University of Missouri - Rolla, University of Missouri - St. Louis, and Washington University in St. Louis. The Consortium actively encourages women, minority, and physically challenged students to apply.

Amount of award:	$2,000-$3,000
Number of awards:	20
Application deadline:	March 7
Notification begins:	April 7
Total amount awarded:	$55,000

Contact:
NASA Space Grant Missouri Space Grant Consortium
University of Missouri - Rolla
Dept. of Mechanical & Aerospace Engineering & Eng. Mech.,
101 Mechanical Engineering Bldg.
Rolla, MO 65401-0249
Website: www.umr.edu/~spaceg/

NASA Space Grant Montana Space Grant Consortium

NASA Space Grant Montana Graduate Fellowship

Type of award: Research grant, renewable.
Intended use: For full-time doctoral study at accredited graduate institution in United States.
Eligibility: Applicant must be U.S. citizen.
Basis for selection: Major/career interest in aerospace; biology; chemistry; geology/earth sciences; physics; astronomy; computer and information sciences; engineering, chemical; engineering, civil; engineering, electrical and electronic.
Application requirements: State applicant must attend college in Montana.
Additional information: Awardees must attend a Montana Space Grant Consortium member institution. Members include: Blackfeet Community College, Dull Knife Memorial College, Fort Belknap College, Fort Peck Community College, Little Big Horn College, Montana State University - Billings, Montana State University - Bozeman, Montana Tech, Rocky Mountain College, Salish Kootenai College, Stone Child College, University of Montana and Western Montana College.

Amount of award:	$10,000
Application deadline:	April 1

NASA Space Grant Montana Undergraduate Scholarship Program

Type of award: Scholarship, renewable.
Intended use: For full-time undergraduate study at accredited 2-year or 4-year institution in United States.

Eligibility: Applicant must be U.S. citizen.
Basis for selection: Major/career interest in aerospace; biology; chemistry; geology/earth sciences; physics; astronomy; computer and information sciences; engineering, chemical; engineering, civil; engineering, electrical and electronic.
Application requirements: State applicant must attend college in Montana.
Additional information: Awardees must attend a Montana Space Grant Consortium member institution. Members include: Blackfeet Community College, Dull Knife Memorial College, Fort Belknap College, Fort Peck Community College, Little Big Horn College, Montana State University - Billings, Montana State University - Bozeman, Montana Tech, Rocky Mountain College, Salish Kootenai College, Stone Child College, University of Montana and Western Montana College.
   Amount of award: $1,000
   Application deadline: April 1
Contact:
NASA Space Grant Montana Space Grant Consortium
261 EPS Building, Montana State University
P.O. Box 173835
Bozeman, MT 59717-3835
Website: www.montana.edu/~wwwmsgc

NASA Space Grant Nebraska Space Grant Consortium

EPSCoR Graduate Fellowship Program

Type of award: Research grant, renewable.
Intended use: For master's, doctoral study at accredited graduate institution in United States.
Eligibility: Applicant must be U.S. citizen.
Basis for selection: Major/career interest in aerospace; aviation.
Application requirements: Essay and transcript. State applicant must attend college in Nebraska.
Additional information: Awardees must attend a Nebraska Space Grant Consortium member institution. Member institutions include: Chadron State College, College of St. Mary, Creighton University, Grace University, Metro Community College, Nebraska Indian Community College, University of Nebraska - Lincoln, University of Nebraska at Kearney, University of Nebraska at Omaha, University of Nebraska Medical Center, Western Nebraska Community College, Hastings College and Little Priest Tribal College. Awards are up to $2,500 per semester. Fellowships for coursework which does not entail research are available, but award amounts are not as substantial. Awardees must maintain a 3.0 GPA upon receiving an award.
   Amount of award: $2,500
   Application deadline: September 30

EPSCoR Undergraduate Scholarship Program

Type of award: Scholarship, Research grant, renewable.
Intended use: For undergraduate study at accredited 2-year or 4-year institution in United States.
Eligibility: Applicant must be U.S. citizen.
Basis for selection: Major/career interest in aerospace; aviation.
Application requirements: Essay and transcript. State applicant must attend college in Nebraska.
Additional information: Awardees must attend a Nebraska Space Grant Consortium member institution. Member institutions include: Chadron State College, College of St. Mary, Creighton University, Grace University, Metro Community College, Nebraska Indian Community College, University of Nebraska - Lincoln, University of Nebraska at Kearney, University of Nebraska at Omaha, University of Nebraska Medical Center, Western Nebraska Community College, Hastings College and Little Priest Tribal College. Awards are up to $750 per semester. Fellowships for coursework which does not entail research are available, but award amounts are not as substantial. Awardees must maintain a 3.0 GPA upon receiving an award.
   Amount of award: $750
   Application deadline: September 30
Contact:
NASA Space Grant Nebraska Space Grant Consortium
Aviation Institute, Allwine Hall 422
6001 Dodge St.
Omaha, NE 68182-0406
Website: cid.unomaha.edu/~nasa

NASA Space Grant Nevada Space Grant Consortium

NASA Space Grant Nevada Graduate Fellowship

Type of award: Scholarship.
Intended use: For graduate study in United States.
Eligibility: Applicant must be U.S. citizen.
Basis for selection: Major/career interest in science, general; engineering; mathematics; aerospace.
Application requirements: State applicant must attend college in Nevada.
Additional information: Contact sponsor for scholarship information, such as deadlines, award amounts, and application requirements.
Contact:
John Gardner
Desert Research Institute
755 E. Flamingo Rd.
Las Vegas, NV 89132-0040

NASA Space Grant Nevada Undergraduate Scholarship

Type of award: Scholarship.
Intended use: For full-time undergraduate study in United States.
Eligibility: Applicant must be U.S. citizen residing in Nevada.
Basis for selection: Major/career interest in science, general; engineering; mathematics; aerospace.
Application requirements: State applicant must attend college in Nevada.
Additional information: Contact sponsor for scholarship information, such as deadlines, award amounts, and application requirements.
Contact:
NASA Space Grant Nevada Space Grant Consortium
Desert Research Institute
755 E. Flamingo Rd.
Las Vegas, NV 89132-0040

NASA Space Grant New Hampshire Space Grant Consortium

NASA Space Grant New Hampshire Undergraduate Scholarship

Type of award: Scholarship, renewable.
Intended use: For undergraduate study.
Eligibility: Applicant must be U.S. citizen.
Basis for selection: Major/career interest in astronomy; atmospheric sciences/meteorology; biology; computer and information sciences; engineering; geology/earth sciences; oceanography/marine studies; physics. Applicant must demonstrate high academic achievement.
Application requirements: Recommendations, essay, transcript and research proposal. State applicant must attend college in New Hampshire.
Additional information: Deadlines vary; contact sponsor for more information.

Amount of award:	$300-$3,000
Application deadline:	March 26
Notification begins:	April 29

Contact:
NASA Space Grant New Hampshire Space Grant Consortium
University of New Hampshire
Hood House, Room 209
Durham, NH 03824-3525
Website: www.nhsgc.sr.unh.edu

NASA Space Grant New Hampshire Graduate Fellowship

Type of award: Research grant.
Intended use: For full-time master's, doctoral study at accredited graduate institution in United States.
Eligibility: Applicant must be U.S. citizen.
Basis for selection: Major/career interest in astronomy; atmospheric sciences/meteorology; biology; computer and information sciences; engineering; geology/earth sciences; oceanography/marine studies; physics. Applicant must demonstrate high academic achievement.
Application requirements: Recommendations, essay, transcript and research proposal. State applicant must attend college in New Hampshire.
Additional information: New Hampshire Space Grant Graduate Fellowships are for study at the University of New Hampshire and Dartmouth College. Applicants must include GRE scores. Fellowships are not renewable except under unusual circumstances. The Consortium actively encourages women, minority, and disabled students to apply. At Dartmouth, outstanding students receive support for one or more academic quarters.

Amount of award:	$15,000
Number of awards:	3
Number of applicants:	11
Application deadline:	March 26
Notification begins:	April 29
Total amount awarded:	$45,000

Contact:
NASA Space Grant New Hampshire Space Grant Consortium
University of New Hampshire
Morse Hall
Durham, NH 03824-3525
Website: www.nhsgc.sr.unh.edu

NASA Space Grant New Jersey Space Grant Consortium

NASA Space Grant New Jersey Undergraduate Summer Fellowship

Type of award: Internship, renewable.
Intended use: For junior, senior study at accredited 4-year institution in United States.
Eligibility: Applicant must be U.S. citizen.
Basis for selection: Major/career interest in aerospace; biology; computer and information sciences; engineering, chemical; engineering, electrical and electronic; engineering, mechanical; physics.
Application requirements: Recommendations and essay. State applicant must attend college in New Jersey.
Additional information: The award is for ten week at $400 per week. Applicants must have completed at least two years of college, but preferable three. Applicants must submit a c.v. Awardees must attend a New Jersey Space Grant Consortium member insititution. Consortium members include: New Jersey Institute of Technology, Princeton University, Rutgers University, Seton Hall University, Stevens Institute of Technology and University of Medicine and Dentistry. The Consortium actively encourages women, minority, and physically challenged students to apply.

Amount of award:	$4,000
Number of awards:	12
Number of applicants:	30
Application deadline:	March 27
Notification begins:	April 24

Contact:
NASA Space Grant New Jersey Space Grant Consortium
Stevens Institute of Technology
Hoboken, NJ 07030-5991
Website: attila.stevens-tech.edu/njsgc

NASA Space Grant New Mexico Space Grant Consortium

NASA Space Grant New Mexico Graduate Fellowship

Type of award: Research grant, renewable.
Intended use: For full-time graduate study at accredited graduate institution in United States.
Eligibility: Applicant must be U.S. citizen.
Basis for selection: Major/career interest in astronomy; biology; chemistry; computer and information sciences; engineering, chemical; engineering, civil; engineering, electrical and electronic; engineering, mechanical; geology/earth sciences; mathematics.
Application requirements: Recommendations, transcript and research proposal. State applicant must attend college in New Mexico.
Additional information: Applicants must attend a New Mexico Space Grant Consortium member institute. Consortium members include: New Mexico State University, New Mexico Highlands University, University of New Mexico and New Mexico Institute of Mining and Technology. The Consortium actively encourages women, minority, and physically challenged students to apply.

Amount of award:	$4,000
Number of awards:	8
Application deadline:	October 15
Notification begins:	October 31
Total amount awarded:	$32,000

NASA Space Grant New Mexico Undergraduate Scholarship

Type of award: Scholarship, renewable.
Intended use: For full-time sophomore, junior or senior study at accredited 4-year institution in United States.
Eligibility: Applicant must be U.S. citizen.
Basis for selection: Major/career interest in astronomy; biology; chemistry; computer and information sciences; engineering, chemical; engineering, civil; engineering, electrical and electronic; engineering, mechanical; geology/earth sciences; mathematics.
Application requirements: Recommendations, transcript and research proposal. State applicant must attend college in New Mexico.
Additional information: Applicants must have 60 semester hours and a minimum GPA of 3.0. Preference is given to applicants who can show non-federal matching funds. Awardees must attend a New Mexico Space Grant Consortium member institute. Consortium members include: New Mexico Highlands University, University of New Mexico, New Mexico Institute of Mining and Technology and New Mexico State University. The Consortium actively encourages women, minority, and physically challenged students to apply.

Amount of award:	$2,000
Number of awards:	5
Application deadline:	October 15
Notification begins:	October 31
Total amount awarded:	$10,000

Contact:
NASA Space Grant New Mexico Space Grant Consortium
Program Office, New Mexico State University
Wells Hall, Bay 4, at Wells & Locust St.
Las Curces, NM 88003-0001
Website: spacegrant.nmsu.edu

NASA Space Grant New York Space Grant Consortium

NASA Space Grant New York Graduate Fellowship

Type of award: Scholarship, renewable.
Intended use: For full-time freshman, sophomore study at 4-year institution in United States. Designated institutions: Must be used only at Cornell University. Students must complete the Graduate School Application to Cornell University and be accepted.
Eligibility: Applicant must be U.S. citizen.
Basis for selection: Major/career interest in astronomy; engineering, electrical and electronic; geology/earth sciences; engineering, mechanical; aerospace. Applicant must demonstrate depth of character, leadership, seriousness of purpose and service orientation.
Application requirements: Recommendations, essay and transcript. State applicant must attend college in New York.
Additional information: Students must complete the Cornell University Graduate School application. Students who have been accepted in the following departments at Cornell will be considered: Astronomy, Electrical Engineering, Geological Sciences, and Mechanical and Aerospace Engineering.

Amount of award:	$11,460-$22,920
Number of applicants:	7
Application deadline:	February 1
Notification begins:	May 1
Total amount awarded:	$103,140

NASA Space Grant New York Undergraduate Internship

Type of award: Internship.
Intended use: For full-time undergraduate study in United States.
Eligibility: Applicant must be U.S. citizen.
Basis for selection: Major/career interest in astronomy;

engineering; engineering, electrical and electronic; engineering, mechanical; geology/earth sciences; aerospace. Applicant must demonstrate depth of character, leadership and seriousness of purpose.
Application requirements: Recommendations, essay and transcript. State applicant must attend college in New York.
Additional information: Students who are attending the following New York institutions are eligible to apply: Cornell, Colgate University, Barnard College, Columbia University, Clarkson University, Manhattan College, Syracuse University, City College of New York, Polytechnic University, SUNY Buffalo. Applications available only from Cornell University.

    Amount of award: $3,500

Contact:
NASA Space Grant New York Space Grant Consortium
Cornell University
517 Space Sciences Bldg.
Ithaca, NY 14853
Website: astrosun.tn.cornell.edu/spacegrant/spacegrant.html

NASA Space Grant North Carolina Space Grant Consortium

NASA Space Grant North Carolina Graduate Fellowship

Type of award: Scholarship, renewable.
Intended use: For full-time master's, doctoral study.
Eligibility: Applicant must be U.S. citizen.
Basis for selection: Major/career interest in science, general; engineering. Applicant must demonstrate high academic achievement.
Application requirements: Recommendations, transcript, research proposal and nomination by Faculty member. State applicant must attend college in North Carolina.
Additional information: Awardees must attend a North Carolina Space Grant Consortium member institution. Consortium members include: North Carolina State University, North Carolina Central University, Duke University, North Carolina A&T State University, Winston-Sales State University, University of North Carolina at Charlotte, University of North Carolina at Chapel Hill, University of North Carolina at Pembroke

    Amount of award: $2,000-$5,000
    Number of awards: 6
    Number of applicants: 11
    Application deadline: February 15
    Total amount awarded: $30,000

NASA Space Grant North Carolina Undergraduate Scholarship Program

Type of award: Scholarship, renewable.
Intended use: For full-time sophomore, junior or senior study.
Eligibility: Applicant must be adult returning student. Applicant must be U.S. citizen.
Basis for selection: Major/career interest in science, general; engineering. Applicant must demonstrate high academic achievement.
Application requirements: Recommendations, transcript, research proposal and nomination by Faculty member. State applicant must attend college in North Carolina.
Additional information: Awardees must attend a North Carolina Space Grant Consortium member institution. Consortium members include: North Carolina State University, North Carolina Central University, Duke University, North Carolina A&T State University, Winston-Sales State University, University of North Carolina at Charlotte, University of North Carolina at Chapel Hill, University of North Carolina at Pembroke

    Amount of award: $1,000-$4,000
    Number of awards: 8
    Number of applicants: 12
    Application deadline: , February 15
    Total amount awarded: $29,000

Contact:
NASA Space Grant North Carolina Space Grant Consortium
Box 7515
Raleigh, NC 27511

NASA Space Grant North Dakota Space Grant Consortium

NASA Space Grant North Dakota Graduate Fellowship

Type of award: Research grant, renewable.
Intended use: For full-time graduate study at accredited graduate institution in United States.
Eligibility: Applicant must be U.S. citizen.
Basis for selection: Major/career interest in aerospace; chemistry; computer and information sciences; engineering, chemical; engineering, electrical and electronic; engineering, mechanical; engineering, structural; geology/earth sciences; geophysics; mathematics.
Application requirements: Recommendations, transcript and research proposal. State applicant must attend college in North Dakota.
Additional information: The fellowships are only available at The University of North Dakota and North Dakota State University. A 3.0 GPA is required, and a 3.5 is highly recommended.

    Amount of award: $1,200-$1,600
    Application deadline: August 15, March 15

NASA Space Grant North Dakota Undergraduate Scholarship

Type of award: Scholarship, renewable.
Intended use: For full-time undergraduate study at accredited 2-year or 4-year institution in United States.
Eligibility: Applicant must be U.S. citizen.
Basis for selection: Major/career interest in aerospace; chemistry; engineering; mathematics; physics.

Application requirements: State applicant must attend college in North Dakota.
Additional information: Two awards of $500 are available at each of the two-year public and tribal colleges; three $750 scholarships are provided to the four-year public state univesities. Awardees must attend a North Dakota Space Grant Consortium member institution. Consortium members include all state-wide community colleges, public colleges and universities, and tribal colleges. Consortium actively encourages women, minority, and physically challenged students to apply. Deadlines vary. Contact the Consortium member directly.

    Amount of award: $500-$750
    Number of awards: 39

Pearl I. Young Scholarship

Type of award: Scholarship.
Intended use: For full-time undergraduate study at accredited 4-year institution in United States.
Eligibility: Applicant must be female. Applicant must be U.S. citizen.
Basis for selection: Major/career interest in aerospace; chemistry; engineering; mathematics; physics.
Application requirements: Nomination. State applicant must attend college in North Dakota.
Additional information: The Pearl I. Young Scholarship is awarded to a woman science student; she must attend the University of North Dakota. North Dakota Space Grant Consortium members include: Bismarck State College, Dickinson State University, Fort Berthold Community College, Little Hoop Community College, Mayville State University, Minot State University, Minot State University - Bottineau, North Dakota State University, Sitting Bull College, Turtle Mountain Community College, University of North Dakota - Lake Region, University of North Dakota - Williston, and Valley City State University. The Consortium actively encourages women, minority, and physically challenged students to apply. This scholarship only applies to those born, raised, and educated in North Dakota. Contact the coordinator for deadline information.

    Amount of award: $5,000
    Number of awards: 1
    Number of applicants: 1

Contact:
NASA Space Grant North Dakota Space Grant Consortium
University of North Dakota, Space Studies Department
P.O. Box 9008
Grand Forks, ND 58202-9008
Website: www.space.edu/projects/dakotah

NASA Space Grant Ohio Space Grant Consortium

Junior/Senior Scholarship Program

Type of award: Scholarship, renewable.
Intended use: For full-time junior, senior study at accredited 4-year institution in United States.
Eligibility: Applicant must be U.S. citizen.
Basis for selection: Major/career interest in aerospace; engineering.
Application requirements: Recommendations, essay and transcript. State applicant must attend college in Ohio.
Additional information: Ohio Space Grant Consortium members include: Air Force Institute of Technology, Case Western Reserve University, Cedarville College, Central State University, Cleveland State University, Marietta College, Ohio Northern University, Ohio University, The Ohio State University, The University of Akron, The University of Cincinnati, The University of Dayton, The University of Toledo, Wilberforce University, Wright State University, Youngstown State University, and Miami University. Awards are $2,000 for Juniors, $3,000 for Seniors.

    Amount of award: $2,000-$3,000
    Number of awards: 53
    Number of applicants: 212
    Application deadline: January 31
    Notification begins: April 30
    Total amount awarded: $130,000

NASA Space Grant Ohio Fellowship Program

Type of award: Research grant, renewable.
Intended use: For full-time master's, doctoral study at accredited graduate institution in United States.
Eligibility: Applicant must be U.S. citizen.
Basis for selection: Major/career interest in aerospace; engineering.
Application requirements: Recommendations, essay, transcript and research proposal. State applicant must attend college in Ohio.
Additional information: Ohio Space Grant Consortium members include: Air Force Institute of Technology, Case Western Reserve University, Cleveland State University, Ohio University, The Ohio State University, The University of Akron, The University of Cincinnati, The University of Dayton, The University of Toledo, Wright State University, Youngstown State University, and Miami University. Awards are Master's degree: $14,000, Doctorate: $18,000. Tuition waivers are provided by the university members.

    Amount of award: $14,000-$18,000
    Number of awards: 8
    Number of applicants: 24
    Application deadline: January 31, April 30

Contact:
NASA Space Grant Ohio Space Grant Consortium
The University of Toledo
Dept. of Chemical Engineering, 2801 W. Bancroft St.
Toledo, OH 43606
Website: www.osgc.org

NASA Space Grant Oklahoma Space Grant Consortium

NASA Space Grant Oklahoma Space Grant Consortium Graduate Fellowship

Type of award: Scholarship.
Intended use: For graduate study.
Eligibility: Applicant must be U.S. citizen.
Basis for selection: Major/career interest in science, general; engineering; aerospace.
Application requirements: State applicant must attend college in Oklahoma.
Additional information: Contact sponsor for information regarding award amounts, deadlines, and application requirements. Must be used at an Oklahoma Space Grant Consortium member institution. Member institutions include: Cameron University, Langston University, Oklahoma State University, and The University of Oklahoma.

NASA Space Grant Oklahoma Undergraduate Scholarship

Type of award: Scholarship.
Intended use: For undergraduate study.
Eligibility: Applicant must be U.S. citizen.
Basis for selection: Major/career interest in science, general; engineering; aerospace.
Application requirements: State applicant must attend college in Oklahoma.
Additional information: Contact sponsor for information regarding award amounts, deadlines, and application requirements.. Must be used at an Oklahoma Space Grant Consortium member institution. Member institutions include: Cameron University, Langston University, Oklahoma State University, and The University of Oklahoma.
Contact:
Oklahoma Space Grant Consortium
Univ. of Oklahoma, College of Geosciences
100 E. Boyd Ave., Ste. 1210
Norman, OK 73019-0628
Website: www.cameron.edui80/nasa.osgc

NASA Space Grant Oregon Space Grant Consortium

Community College Scholarship

Type of award: Scholarship.
Intended use: For full-time freshman, sophomore study at accredited 2-year institution in United States. Designated institutions: Must be used at Oregon Space Grant Program affiliated community colleges.
Eligibility: Applicant must be U.S. citizen.
Application requirements: Recommendations, essay and transcript. Student applicant must attend college in Oregon.

Amount of award:	$1,000
Number of awards:	1
Number of applicants:	45
Total amount awarded:	$5

NASA Space Grant Oregon Graduate Fellowship

Type of award: Research grant.
Intended use: For full-time graduate study at accredited graduate institution in United States.
Eligibility: Applicant must be U.S. citizen.
Basis for selection: Major/career interest in science, general; mathematics; engineering.
Application requirements: Interview, recommendations, essay, transcript and nomination. State applicant must attend college in Oregon.
Additional information: Applicants must be first-year graduate students. Awards are $14,000 plus tuition. Oregon Space Grant Consortium members include: Oregon State University Atmospheric Sciences, Oregon State University College of Engineering, Oregon State University College of Oceanographic and and Atmospheric Sciences, and Oregon State University College of Science. The Consortium actively encourages women, minority, and disabled students to apply. Application requirements may vary by institution.

Amount of award:	$14,000
Number of awards:	5
Number of applicants:	22
Application deadline:	February 27
Total amount awarded:	$70,000

NASA Space Grant Oregon Undergraduate Scholarship

Type of award: Scholarship.
Intended use: For full-time undergraduate study at accredited 2-year or 4-year institution in United States.
Eligibility: Applicant must be U.S. citizen.
Basis for selection: Major/career interest in science, general; engineering. Applicant must demonstrate high academic achievement.
Application requirements: Recommendations, essay and transcript. State applicant must attend college in Oregon.
Additional information: Affiliated undergraduate institutions include: Lynn Community College, Central Oregon Community College, University of Oregon, Portland State University, and Oregon Institute of Technology.

Amount of award:	$1,000
Number of awards:	10
Application deadline:	May 15, July 1
Total amount awarded:	$10,000

Contact:
NASA Space Grant Oregon Space Grant Consortium
Oregon State University
130 Radiation Center
Corvalis, OR 97331-5902
Website: www.ne.orst.edu/spcgrant

NASA Space Grant Pennsylvania Space Grant Consortium

NASA Academy Internship

Type of award: Internship.
Intended use: For full-time junior, senior study at accredited 4-year or graduate institution in United States.
Eligibility: Applicant must be U.S. citizen.
Basis for selection: Major/career interest in engineering; science, general; mathematics.
Application requirements: Interview, recommendations, essay, transcript and research proposal. State applicant must attend college in Pennsylvania.
Additional information: Awards are for ten-week periods. Applicants should be juniors, seniors, or first year graduate students. Awardees must attend a Pennsylvania Space Grant Consortium member institution. Consortium members include: Carnegie-Mellon University, Lincoln University, Penn State: University Park, Susquehanna University, Temple University, University of Pittsburgh, and West Chester University. The Consortium actively encourages women, minority, and physically challenged students to apply.

Amount of award:	$3,000-$4,000
Number of awards:	2
Number of applicants:	20
Application deadline:	January 30

NASA Space Grant Pennsylvania Graduate Fellowship

Type of award: Research grant, renewable.
Intended use: For full-time graduate study at accredited graduate institution in United States.
Eligibility: Applicant must be U.S. citizen.
Basis for selection: Major/career interest in aerospace; agriculture; astronomy; geology/earth sciences; engineering; physics; science, general; psychology; education.
Application requirements: Interview, recommendations, essay, transcript, research proposal and nomination. State applicant must attend college in Pennsylvania.
Additional information: Applicants must be admitted to the Penn State Graduate School. They must include a resume and GRE scores in their applications. Additional fellowships are given at Carnegie-Mellon University, and Temple University. Pennsylvania Space Grant Consortium members include: Carnegie-Mellon University, Lincoln University, Penn State at University Park, Susquehanna University, Temple University, University of Pittsburgh, and West Chester University. The Consortium actively encourages women, minority, and physically challenged students to apply.

Amount of award:	$5,000
Number of awards:	20
Application deadline:	February 27
Total amount awarded:	$100,000

NASA Space Grant Pennsylvania Undergraduate Scholarship

Type of award: Scholarship.
Intended use: For full-time sophomore study at accredited 4-year institution in United States.
Eligibility: Applicant must be U.S. citizen.
Basis for selection: Major/career interest in science, general; mathematics.
Application requirements: Interview, recommendations, essay and transcript. State applicant must attend college in Pennsylvania.
Additional information: Award will not be available until the 2000-2001 year. Scholarships are provided for undergraduates at Lincoln University, Susquehanna University, and West Chester University. The Sylvia Stein Memorial Space Grant Scholarship at Penn State University is awarded to an outstanding undergraduate with extensive community service. Awardees must attend a Pennsylvania Space Grant Consortium member institution. Consortium members include: Carnegie-Mellon University, Lincoln University, Penn State at University Park, Susquehanna University, Temple University, University of Pittsburgh, and West Chester University. The Consortium actively encourages women, minority, and physically challenged students to apply.
Contact:
NASA Space Grant Pennsylvania Space Grant Consortium
Penn State, University Park
101 S. Frear Laboratory
University Park, PA 16802
Website: eee.nasa-academy.masa.gov/sunner/html

NASA Space Grant Puerto Rico Space Grant Consortium

NASA Space Grant Puerto Rico Graduate Fellowship

Type of award: Research grant, renewable.
Intended use: For full-time graduate study at accredited graduate institution in United States.
Eligibility: Applicant must be U.S. citizen.
Basis for selection: Major/career interest in aerospace; atmospheric sciences/meteorology; biology; engineering, biomedical; engineering, chemical; engineering, computer; engineering, mechanical; mathematics; oceanography/marine studies; physics.
Application requirements: Interview, recommendations, essay, transcript and research proposal. State applicant must attend college in Puerto Rico.
Additional information: Awardees must attend a Puerto Rico Space Grant Consortium member institution. Consortium members include: University of Puerto Rico - Mayaguez, and University of Puerto Rico - Rio Pedras, Arecibo, and Humacao. Call the university for the latest additions to the Consortium. The Consortium actively encourages women, minority, and physically challenged students to apply. Call the university to get their web address.

Amount of award:	$7,000-$10,000
Number of applicants:	19
Application deadline:	April 25, June 1
Total amount awarded:	$68,225

NASA Space Grant Puerto Rico Summer Internship Program

Type of award: Internship.
Intended use: For full-time undergraduate study at accredited 4-year institution in United States.
Eligibility: Applicant must be U.S. citizen.
Basis for selection: Major/career interest in aerospace; atmospheric sciences/meteorology; biology; engineering, biomedical; engineering, chemical; engineering, computer; engineering, mechanical; mathematics; oceanography/marine studies; physics.
Application requirements: Recommendations, essay and transcript. State applicant must attend college in Puerto Rico.
Additional information: Awards are for a ten-week period. Awardees must attend a Puerto Rico Space Grant Consortium member institution. Consortium members include: University of Puerto Rico - Mayaguez, and University of Puerto Rico - Rio Pedras, Arecibo, and Humacao. Call the university for the latest additions to the Consortium. The Consortium actively encourages women, minority, and physically challenged students to apply. Call the university to get their web address.

Amount of award:	$2,500-$4,200
Number of awards:	5
Number of applicants:	35
Application deadline:	January 31, March 1
Total amount awarded:	$16,000

NASA Space Grant Puerto Rico Undergraduate Scholarship

Type of award: Scholarship, renewable.
Intended use: For full-time undergraduate study at accredited 4-year institution in United States.
Eligibility: Applicant must be U.S. citizen.
Basis for selection: Major/career interest in aerospace; atmospheric sciences/meteorology; biology; engineering, biomedical; engineering, chemical; engineering, computer; engineering, mechanical; mathematics; oceanography/marine studies; physics.
Application requirements: Interview, recommendations, essay, transcript and research proposal. State applicant must attend college in Puerto Rico.
Additional information: Awardees must attend a Puerto Rico Space Grant Consortium member institution. Consortium members include: University of Puerto Rico - Mayaguez, and University of Puerto Rico - Rio Pedras, Arecibo, and Humacao. Call the university for the latest additions to the Consortium. The Consortium actively encourages women, minority, and physically challenged students to apply. Call the university to get their web address.

Amount of award:	$6,000
Number of awards:	5
Number of applicants:	23
Application deadline:	September 14, June 2
Total amount awarded:	$30,000

Contact:
NASA Space Grant Puerto Rico Space Grant Consortium
University of Puerto Rico, Resource Center for Science and Engineering
P.O. Box 9027, College Station
Mayaguez, PR 00681

NASA Space Grant Rhode Island Space Grant Consortium

NASA Space Grant Rhode Island Graduate Fellowship

Type of award: Scholarship, renewable.
Intended use: For graduate study.
Eligibility: Applicant must be U.S. citizen residing in Rhode Island.
Basis for selection: Major/career interest in physics; engineering; biology; geology/earth sciences; aerospace. Applicant must demonstrate high academic achievement.
Application requirements: Interview, recommendations, essay, transcript and research proposal. State applicant must attend college in Rhode Island.
Additional information: Deadline is in April; call sponsor for exact date. Topics of study in the space sciences also funded. Must attend Brown University, the only Rhode Island Space Grant Consortium member institution.

NASA Space Grant Rhode Island Summer Undergraduate Scholarship Program

Type of award: Scholarship.
Intended use: For sophomore, junior or senior study.
Eligibility: Applicant must be U.S. citizen residing in Rhode Island.
Basis for selection: Major/career interest in physics; engineering; biology; geology/earth sciences; aerospace.
Application requirements: Interview, recommendations, essay and transcript. State applicant must attend college in Rhode Island.
Additional information: Deadline is in April; call sponsor for exact date. Topics of study in the space sciences also funded. Must attend Brown University, the only Rhode Island Space Grant Consortium member institution.

Amount of award:	$3,000
Number of awards:	3
Number of applicants:	6

NASA Space Grant Rhode Island Undergraduate Academic Year Scholarship Program

Type of award: Scholarship, renewable.
Intended use: For sophomore, junior or senior study.
Eligibility: Applicant must be U.S. citizen residing in Rhode Island.
Basis for selection: Major/career interest in physics; engineering; biology; geology/earth sciences; aerospace. Applicant must demonstrate high academic achievement.
Application requirements: Interview, recommendations, essay, transcript and research proposal. State applicant must attend college in Rhode Island.
Additional information: Deadline is in April; call sponsor for exact date. Topics of study in the space sciences also funded. Must attend Brown University, the only Rhode Island Space Grant Consortium member institution.

Amount of award:	$3,000
Number of awards:	3
Number of applicants:	6

Contact:
NASA Space Grant Rhode Island Space Grant Consortium
Brown University
Box 1846
Providence, RI 02912

NASA Space Grant Rocky Mountain Space Grant Consortium

NASA Space Grant Rocky Mountain Graduate Fellowship

Type of award: Scholarship, renewable.
Intended use: For full-time undergraduate or graduate study.
Eligibility: Applicant must be U.S. citizen.
Basis for selection: Major/career interest in science, general; aerospace; engineering. Applicant must demonstrate high academic achievement.
Application requirements: Recommendations, transcript and research proposal.
Additional information: Contact sponsor for deadline information. Must be used at a Rocky Mountain Space Grant Consortium member institution. Members include Utah State University, University of Utah, Brigham Young University, University of Denver, Weber State University, and Southern Utah University.

Amount of award:	$14,400

Contact:
NASA Space Grant Rocky Mountain Space Grant Consortium
Utah State University
EL Building, Room 302
Logan, UT 84322-3666
Phone: 435-797-3666
Website: www.rmc.sdl.usu.edu

NASA Space Grant Rocky Mountain Undergraduate Scholarship

Type of award: Scholarship, renewable.
Intended use: For full-time undergraduate study.
Eligibility: Applicant must be U.S. citizen.
Basis for selection: Major/career interest in science, general; aerospace; engineering. Applicant must demonstrate high academic achievement.
Application requirements: Recommendations, transcript and research proposal.
Additional information: Contact sponsor for deadline information. Must be used at a Rocky Mountain Space Grant Consortium member institution. Members include Utah State University, University of Utah, Brigham Young University, University of Denver, Weber State University, and Southern Utah University.

Amount of award:	$200-$1,000

Contact:
NASA Space Grant Rocky Mountain Space Grant Consortium
Utah State University
EL Building, Room 302
Logan, UT 84332-4140
Website: www.rmc.sdl.usu.edu

NASA Space Grant South Carolina Space Grant Consortium

Kathryn D. Sullivan Science and Engineering Undergraduate Fellowship

Type of award: Scholarship, renewable.
Intended use: For full-time senior study at accredited 4-year institution in United States.
Eligibility: Applicant must be U.S. citizen.
Basis for selection: Major/career interest in biology; geology/earth sciences; engineering; physics; astronomy; mathematics.
Application requirements: Recommendations, essay and transcript. State applicant must attend college in South Carolina.
Additional information: Applicants must attend a South Carolina Space Grant Consortium member institution. Consortium members include: Benedict College, The Citadel, Clemson University, Coastal Carolina University, Furman University, South Carolina State University, University of Charleston, University of South Carolina, University of the Virgin Islands, and Wofford College, The Medical University of South Carolina. Applicants must have sponsorship from a faculty advisor. Awards are $3,500 per semester. The Consortium actively encourages women, minority, and disabled students to apply.

Amount of award:	$7,000
Number of awards:	1
Number of applicants:	14
Application deadline:	February 15
Notification begins:	April 29

169

NASA Space Grant South Carolina Graduate Fellowship

Type of award: Research grant, renewable.
Intended use: For full-time graduate study at accredited graduate institution in United States.
Eligibility: Applicant must be U.S. citizen.
Basis for selection: Major/career interest in aerospace; arts, general; astronomy; education; engineering; environmental science; journalism; science, general.
Application requirements: Recommendations, essay, transcript and research proposal. State applicant must attend college in South Carolina.
Additional information: Applicants must attend a South Carolina Space Grant Consortium member institution. Consortium members include: Benedict College, The Citadel, Clemson University, Coastal Carolina University, Furman University, South Carolina State University, University of Charleston, University of South Carolina, University of the Virgin Islands, and Wofford College. Applicants must have sponsorship from a faculty advisor. The Consortium actively encourages women, minority, and disabled students to apply.
   Amount of award: $3,000
   Number of awards: 9
   Number of applicants: 11
   Application deadline: February 15

NASA Space Grant South Carolina Undergraduate Academic Year Research Program

Type of award: Research grant, renewable.
Intended use: For full-time junior, senior study at accredited 4-year institution in United States.
Eligibility: Applicant must be U.S. citizen.
Basis for selection: Major/career interest in aerospace; arts, general; astronomy; education; engineering; environmental science; geology/earth sciences; geophysics; journalism; science, general.
Application requirements: Recommendations, essay, transcript and research proposal. State applicant must attend college in South Carolina.
Additional information: Applicants must attend a South Carolina Space Grant Consortium member institution. Consortium members include: Benedict College, The Citadel, Clemson University, Coastal Carolina University, Furman University, South Carolina State University, University of Charleston, University of South Carolina, University of the Virgin Islands, and Wofford College. Applicants must have sponsorship from a faculty advisor. The Consortium actively encourages women, minority, and disabled students to apply.
   Amount of award: $2,500
   Number of awards: 1
   Application deadline: February 15

NASA Space Grant South Carolina Undergraduate Research Summer Scholarship

Type of award: Research grant, renewable.
Intended use: For full-time junior, senior study at accredited 4-year institution in United States.
Eligibility: Applicant must be U.S. citizen.
Basis for selection: Major/career interest in aerospace; arts, general; astronomy; education; engineering; environmental science; geology/earth sciences; geophysics; journalism; science, general.
Application requirements: Recommendations, essay, transcript and research proposal. State applicant must attend college in South Carolina.
Additional information: Applicants must attend a South Carolina Space Grant Consortium member institution. Consortium members include: Benedict College, The Citadel, Clemson University, Coastal Carolina University, Furman University, South Carolina State University, University of Charleston, University of South Carolina, University of the Virgin Islands, and Wofford College. Applicants must have sponsorship from a faculty advisor. The Consortium actively encourages women, minority, and disabled students to apply.
   Amount of award: $2,500
   Number of awards: 1
   Application deadline: February 15

NASA Space Grant South Carolina Undergraduate Scholarship Program

Type of award: Scholarship, renewable.
Intended use: For full-time junior, senior study at accredited 4-year institution in United States.
Eligibility: Applicant must be U.S. citizen.
Basis for selection: Major/career interest in aerospace; arts, general; astronomy; education; engineering; environmental science; geology/earth sciences; geophysics; journalism; science, general.
Application requirements: Recommendations, essay, transcript and research proposal. State applicant must attend college in South Carolina.
Additional information: Applicants must attend a South Carolina Space Grant Consortium member institution. Consortium members include: Benedict College, The Citadel, Clemson University, Coastal Carolina University, Furman University, South Carolina State University, University of Charleston, University of South Carolina, University of the Virgin Islands, and Wofford College. Applicants must have sponsorship from a faculty advisor. The Consortium actively encourages women, minority, and disabled students to apply.
   Amount of award: $750-$1,500
   Number of awards: 13
   Number of applicants: 50
   Application deadline: February 15
Contact:
NASA Space Grant South Carolina Space Grant Consortium
University of Charleston
Department of Geology
Charleston, SC 29424
Website: cofc.edu/~scsgrant

NASA Space Grant South Dakota Space Grant Consortium

NASA Space South Dakota Graduate Fellowship Space Grant

Type of award: Research grant, renewable.
Intended use: For full-time graduate study in United States.
Eligibility: Applicant must be U.S. citizen.
Basis for selection: Applicant must demonstrate depth of character, leadership, seriousness of purpose and high academic achievement.
Application requirements: Essay.
Additional information: Awardees must attend a South Dakota Space Grant Consortium member institution. Consortium members include: South Dakota School of Mines and Technology, South Dakota State University, and Augustana College. The deadline for 1999 will be in mid-August; contact coordinator for exact information. Award comes with a reduction of tuition by 2/3.
    Amount of award: $2,500-$5,000
    Number of awards: 3
    Number of applicants: 3
    Application deadline: August , February 29
    Notification begins: , April 1
    Total amount awarded: $15,000
Contact:
NASA Space Grant South Dakota Space Grant Consortium
South Dakota School of Mines & Technology
501 E. St. Joseph St.
Rapid City, SD 57701-3995
Website: www.sdsmt.edu/space/

NASA Space Grant Tennessee Space Grant Consortium

NASA Space Grant Tennessee Graduate Fellowship

Type of award: Scholarship, renewable.
Intended use: For full-time graduate study in United States.
Eligibility: Applicant must be U.S. citizen.
Basis for selection: Major/career interest in science, general; mathematics; engineering. Applicant must demonstrate seriousness of purpose and high academic achievement.
Application requirements: Research proposal.
Additional information: Topics related to space exploration in any field of study may qualify. Awardees must attend a Tennessee Space Grant Consortium member institution. Consortium members include: Vanderbilt University, University of Tennessee-Knoxville, Fisk University, Tennessee State University, Rhodes College, Autin Peay State University, Columbia State Community College. Application deadlines, criteria, and award amounts vary by member institutions. Contact the Consortium office for more specific information.
    Amount of award: $500-$15,000

NASA Space Grant Tennessee Undergraduate Scholarship

Type of award: Scholarship, renewable.
Intended use: For full-time undergraduate study in United States.
Eligibility: Applicant must be U.S. citizen.
Basis for selection: Major/career interest in science, general; mathematics; engineering. Applicant must demonstrate seriousness of purpose and high academic achievement.
Application requirements: Research proposal.
Additional information: Topics related to space exploration in any field of study may qualify. Awardees must attend a Tennessee Space Grant Consortium member institution. Consortium members include: Vanderbilt University, University of Tennessee-Knoxville, Fisk University, Tennessee State University, Rhodes College, Autin Peay State University, Columbia State Community College. Application deadlines, criteria, and award amounts vary by member institutions. Contact the Consortium office for more specific information.
    Amount of award: $100-$5,000
Contact:
NASA Space Grant Tennessee Space Grant Consortium
Vanderbilt University
Box 1592, Station B
Nashville, TN 37235
Website: www.vuse.vanderbilt.edu.80/~tnsg/homepage.html

NASA Space Grant Texas Space Grant Consortium

NASA Space Grant Texas Graduate Fellowship

Type of award: Scholarship, renewable.
Intended use: For full-time master's, doctoral study at accredited graduate institution outside United States.
Eligibility: Applicant must be U.S. citizen.
Basis for selection: Major/career interest in aerospace; engineering. Applicant must demonstrate high academic achievement.
Application requirements: Recommendations, essay, transcript and proof of eligibility. State applicant must attend college in Texas.
Additional information: Awardees must attend a Texas Space Grant Consortium member institution. Consortium members include: Baylor University, Lamar University, Prairie View A&M University, Rice University, Southern Methodist University, Sul Ross State University, Texas A&M University, Texas A&M University - Kingsville, Texas Christian University, Texas Southern University, Texas Tech University, University of Houston, University of Houston - Clear Lake, University of Houston - Downtown, University of Texas - Pan American, University of Texas at Arlington, University of Texas at Austin, University of Texas at Dallas, University of Texas at El Paso, University of Texas Houston State College - Houston, University of Texas at San Antonio, University of Texas Medical Branch - Galveston, University of Texas Southwestern Medical Center, West Texas A&M University.

Applicants must submit GRE scores. Each fellowship may be renewed for a maximum of three years, provided the recipient has spent no than two years as a master's candidate.

Amount of award:	$5,000
Number of awards:	20
Number of applicants:	45
Application deadline:	February 20
Total amount awarded:	$100,000

NASA Space Grant Texas Undergraduate Scholarship Program

Type of award: Scholarship.
Intended use: For full-time senior study at accredited 4-year institution in United States.
Eligibility: Applicant must be U.S. citizen.
Basis for selection: Major/career interest in aerospace; education.
Application requirements: Recommendations, essay, transcript and proof of eligibility. State applicant must attend college in Texas.
Additional information: Awardees must attend a Texas Space Grant Consortium member institution. Consortium members include: Baylor University, Lamar University, Prairie View A&M University, Rice University, Southern Methodist University, Sul Ross State University, Texas A&M University, Texas A&M University - Kingsville, Texas Christian University, Texas Southern University, Texas Tech University, University of Houston, University of Houston - Clear Lake, University of Houston - Downtown, University of Texas - Pan American, University of Texas at Arlington, University of Texas at Austin, University of Texas at Dallas, University of Texas at El Paso, University of Texas Houston State College - Houston, University of Texas at San Antonio, University of Texas Medical Branch - Galveston, University of Texas Southwestern Medical Center, West Texas A&M University.

Amount of award:	$1,000
Number of awards:	45
Number of applicants:	150
Application deadline:	February 27
Total amount awarded:	$45,000

Contact:
NASA Space Grant Texas Space Grant Consortium
University of Texas at Austin
Center for Space Research, 3925 W. Braker Ln., Suite 200
Austin, TX 78749-5321
Website: www.tsgc.utecas.edu/tsgc

NASA Space Grant Vermont Space Grant Consortium

NASA Space Grant Vermont Space Graduate Research Assistantship

Type of award: Scholarship, renewable.
Intended use: For full-time master's, doctoral study.
Eligibility: Applicant must be U.S. citizen residing in Vermont.
Basis for selection: Major/career interest in science, general; mathematics; aerospace.
Application requirements: Interview, recommendations, transcript and research proposal. State applicant must attend college in Vermont.
Additional information: Deadlines vary; contact coordinator for specific information.

Amount of award:	$16,000-$22,000
Number of awards:	5

NASA Space Grant Vermont Undergraduate Scholarships

Type of award: Scholarship, renewable.
Intended use: For full-time undergraduate study in United States.
Eligibility: Applicant must be U.S. citizen residing in Vermont.
Basis for selection: Major/career interest in science, general; mathematics; aerospace.
Application requirements: Recommendations, essay and transcript. State applicant must attend college in Vermont.
Additional information: Open to high school seniors as well as undergraduates who intend to be enrolled full time in the following year. Minimum GPA 3.0. Out-of-state recipients qualify for in-state tuition. Can be used at any accredited Vermont institution of higher education.

Amount of award:	$1,500
Number of awards:	14
Number of applicants:	14
Application deadline:	March 1, March 15

Contact:
NASA Space Grant Vermont Space Grant Consortium
Votey Building, College of Engineering and Mathematics
University of Vermont
Burlington, VT 05405-0156
Website: www.emba.uvm.edu/vsgc

NASA Space Grant Virginia Space Grant Consortium

Aerospace Graduate Research Fellowship Program

Type of award: Research grant, renewable.
Intended use: For full-time graduate study at accredited graduate institution in United States.
Eligibility: Applicant must be U.S. citizen.
Basis for selection: Major/career interest in aerospace; astronomy; computer and information sciences; engineering; physics; science, general; psychology.
Application requirements: Recommendations, essay, transcript and research proposal. State applicant must attend college in Virginia.
Additional information: Applicants must provide a resume, and show a GPA of 3.0 or higher. Awardees must attend a Virginia Space Grant Consortium member institution.

Qualifying Consortium members include: College of William and Mary, Hampton University, Old Dominion University, The University of Virginia, and Virginia Polytechnic Institute. The Consortium actively encourages women, minority, and physically challenged students to apply.

Amount of award:	$5,000
Number of awards:	14
Number of applicants:	35
Application deadline:	January 20
Notification begins:	March 1
Total amount awarded:	$70,000

Aerospace Undergraduate Scholarship Program

Type of award: Scholarship.
Intended use: For full-time junior, senior study at accredited 4-year institution in United States.
Eligibility: Applicant must be U.S. citizen.
Basis for selection: Major/career interest in aerospace; astronomy; biology; chemistry; computer and information sciences; education; engineering; geology/earth sciences; mathematics; physics.
Application requirements: Recommendations, essay, transcript and research proposal. State applicant must attend college in Virginia.
Additional information: Applicants must provide a resume, and show a GPA of 3.0 or greater. Awards can include $3,000 stipend plus $1,000 travel/research during the academic year, and $3,500 stipend plus $1,000 travel/research during the summer (ten weeks). Awardees must attend a Virginia Space Grant Consortium member institution. Qualifying Consortium members include: College of William and Mary, Hampton University, Old Dominion University, The University of Virginia, and Virginia Polytechnic Institute. The Consortium actively encourages women, minority, and physically challenged students to apply.

Amount of award:	$3,000-$8,500
Number of awards:	15
Number of applicants:	30
Application deadline:	January 27
Notification begins:	March 1

Community College Scholarship Program

Type of award: Scholarship.
Intended use: For sophomore study in United States.
Eligibility: Applicant must be U.S. citizen.
Basis for selection: Major/career interest in aerospace; computer and information sciences; electronics; engineering; mathematics; science, general.
Application requirements: Recommendations, essay and transcript. State applicant must attend college in Virginia.
Additional information: Awards are generally to full-time students (12 semester hours), but part-time students (6-9 hours) demonstrating academic achievements are also eligible. Applicants must provide a resume, photograph, and biographical information, and show a GPA of 3.0 or greater. The scholarship is open to students at all community colleges in Virginia. Application deadline may vary. The Consortium actively encourages women, minority, and physically challenged students to apply.

Amount of award:	$1,800
Number of awards:	11
Number of applicants:	18
Application deadline:	February 17
Notification begins:	May 1

Teacher Education Scholarship Program

Type of award: Scholarship.
Intended use: For full-time undergraduate study.
Eligibility: Applicant must be U.S. citizen.
Basis for selection: Major/career interest in aerospace; science, general; mathematics; education.
Application requirements: Recommendations, essay and transcript. State applicant must attend college in Virginia.
Additional information: Applicants must be enrolled in a program leading to teacher certification. The application deadline may vary. Awardees must attend a Virginia Space Grant Consortium member institution. Consortium members include: College of William and Mary, Hampton University, Old Dominion University, The University of Virginia, and Virginia Polytechnic Institute. The Consortium actively encourages women, minority, and physically challenged students to apply.

Amount of award:	$1,000
Number of awards:	11
Number of applicants:	20
Application deadline:	January 27
Notification begins:	March 1
Total amount awarded:	$11,000

Contact:
NASA Space Grant Virginia Space Grant Consortium
Old Dominion University Peninsula Center
2713-D Magruder Blvd.
Hampton, VA 23666
Website: www.vsgc.odu.edu

NASA Space Grant Washington Space Grant Consortium

Community College Transfer Scholarships

Type of award: Scholarship, renewable.
Intended use: For full-time undergraduate study at accredited 4-year institution in United States.
Eligibility: Applicant must be U.S. citizen residing in Washington.
Basis for selection: Major/career interest in engineering; mathematics; science, general.
Application requirements: Recommendations, essay and transcript. State applicant must attend college in Washington.
Additional information: The Washington Space Grant Consortium Community College Transfer Scholarships are for community college students who will transfer to the University of Washington. Consortium member institutions include:

Northwest Indian College, Office of the Superintendent of Public Education, Pacific Science Center, Seattle Central Community College, University of Washington, and Washington State University. The Consortium actively encourages women, minority, and disabled students to apply.

Amount of award:	$2,000
Number of awards:	5
Number of applicants:	35
Application deadline:	March 31
Notification begins:	May 1

NASA Space Grant Washington Graduate Fellowships at the University of Washington

Type of award: Research grant, renewable.
Intended use: For full-time graduate study at accredited graduate institution in United States.
Eligibility: Applicant must be U.S. citizen.
Basis for selection: Major/career interest in mathematics; science, general; engineering.
Application requirements: Recommendations, transcript and research proposal.
Additional information: The Washington Space Grant Consortium Graduate Fellowships are for students who will attend the University of Washington. Awards are for the first year of study. Applicants must include GRE scores. Consortium members include: Northwest Indian College, Office of the Superintendent of Public Education, Pacific Science Center, Seattle Central Community College, University of Washington, and Washington State University. The Consortium actively encourages women, minority, and disabled students to apply.

Amount of award:	$5,000
Number of awards:	5
Number of applicants:	20
Application deadline:	March 31

NASA Space Grant Washington Undergraduate Scholarship Program

Type of award: Scholarship, renewable.
Intended use: For full-time undergraduate study.
Eligibility: Applicant must be U.S. citizen.
Basis for selection: Major/career interest in mathematics; science, general; engineering.
Application requirements: Interview, recommendations, essay and transcript. State applicant must attend college in Washington.
Additional information: The Washington Space Grant Consortium member institutions are: Northwest Indian College, Office of the Superintendent of Public Education, Pacific Science Center, Seattle Central Community College, University of Washington, and Washington State University. The Consortium actively encourages women, minority, and disabled students to apply.

Amount of award:	$500-$5,000
Number of awards:	30
Number of applicants:	300
Application deadline:	January 15
Notification begins:	March 6

Scholarships at Seattle Central Community College

Type of award: Scholarship.
Intended use: For full-time undergraduate study at accredited 4-year institution in United States.
Eligibility: Applicant must be U.S. citizen.
Basis for selection: Major/career interest in mathematics; science, general; engineering.
Application requirements: Recommendations, essay and transcript. State applicant must attend college in Washington.
Additional information: The Washington Space Grant Consortium member institutions are: Northwest Indian College, Office of the Superintendent of Public Education, Pacific Science Center, Seattle Central Community College, University of Washington, and Washington State University. The Consortium actively encourages women, minority, and disabled students to apply.

Amount of award:	$500-$199
Number of awards:	3
Number of applicants:	35
Application deadline:	April 1
Total amount awarded:	$2,599

Contact:
NASA Space Grant Washington Space Grant Consortium
University of Washington
352 Johnson Hall, Box 351650
Seattle, WA 98125
Website: weber.u.washington.edu/~nasauw

NASA Space Grant West Virginia Consortium

NASA Space Grant West Virginia Graduate Fellowship

Type of award: Research grant, renewable.
Intended use: For full-time graduate study at accredited graduate institution in United States.
Eligibility: Applicant must be U.S. citizen residing in West Virginia.
Basis for selection: Major/career interest in engineering; science, general.
Application requirements: Research proposal. State applicant must attend college in West Virginia.
Additional information: Awardees must attend a West Virginia Space Grant Consortium member institution. Members include: Marshall University, West Virginia University, West Virginia University Institute of Technology, Wheeling-Jesuit University, Bethany College, Fairmont State College, Salem Teikyo University, Shepherd College, West Liberty State College, West Virginia State College, and West Virginia Wesleyan College.

Amount of award:	$1,000
Number of awards:	3
Number of applicants:	3
Application deadline:	August 31
Total amount awarded:	$3,000

NASA Space Grant West Virginia Undergraduate Fellowship Scholarship

Type of award: Scholarship, renewable.
Intended use: For full-time undergraduate study at accredited 4-year institution in United States.
Eligibility: Applicant must be U.S. citizen residing in West Virginia.
Basis for selection: Major/career interest in engineering; science, general.
Application requirements: Research proposal. State applicant must attend college in West Virginia.
Additional information: Awardees must attend a West Virginia Space Grant Consortium member institution. Members include: Marshall University, West Virginia University, West Virginia University Institute of Technology, Wheeling-Jesuit University, Bethany College, Fairmont State College, Salem Teikyo University, Shepherd College, West Liberty State College, West Virginia State College, and West Virginia Wesleyan College. Awards provide full tuition, fees, and room and board for four years. 3.0 GPA preferred.

Amount of award:	$1,000
Number of awards:	3
Number of applicants:	3
Application deadline:	August 31
Total amount awarded:	$3,000

NASA Space Grant West Virginia Undergraduate Scholarship

Type of award: Scholarship, renewable.
Intended use: For full-time undergraduate study at accredited 4-year institution in United States.
Eligibility: Applicant must be U.S. citizen residing in West Virginia.
Basis for selection: Major/career interest in engineering; science, general.
Application requirements: Research proposal. State applicant must attend college in West Virginia.
Additional information: Awardees must attend a West Virginia Space Grant Consortium member institution. Members include: Marshall University, West Virginia University, West Virginia University Institute of Technology, Wheeling-Jesuit University, Bethany College, Fairmont State College, Salem Teikyo University, Shepherd College, West Liberty State College, West Virginia State College, and West Virginia Wesleyan College.

Amount of award:	$1,000-$2,000
Number of awards:	16
Number of applicants:	16
Application deadline:	August 31
Total amount awarded:	$16,000

Contact:
NASA Space Grant West Virginia Space Grant Consortium
West Virginia University, NASA Space Grant Program
P.O. Box 6070
Morgantown, WV 26506-6070
Website: www.cemr.wvu.edu/~wwwnasa/

NASA Space Grant Wisconsin Space Grant Consortium

NASA Space Grant Wisconsin Graduate Fellowship

Type of award: Research grant, renewable.
Intended use: For full-time master's, doctoral study at accredited graduate institution in United States.
Eligibility: Applicant must be U.S. citizen.
Basis for selection: Major/career interest in aerospace; astronomy; engineering; physics; science, general.
Application requirements: Recommendations, transcript and research proposal. State applicant must attend college in Wisconson.
Additional information: Applicant must attend a Wisconsin Space Grant Consortium member institution. Members include: Alverno College, Astronatuics Corporation of America, Carroll College, College of the Menominee Nation, Lawrence University, Marquette University, Medical College of Wisconsin, Milwaukee School of Engineering, Ripon College, St. Norbert College, University of Wisconsin - Green Bay, University of Wisconsin - La Crosse, University of Wisconsin - Madison, Unviersity of Wisconsin - Milwaukee, University of Wisconsin - Oshkosh, Unviersity of Wisconsin - Parkside, University of Wisconsin - Whitewater, Wisconsin Association of CESA Administrators, Wisconsin Department of Public Instruction, Wisconsin Department of Transportation, and Wisconsin Space Business Roundtable. The Consortium actively encourages women, minority, and disabled students to apply. The application deadline is in February. Call the university for an exact date. The mailing address will change in the Fall of 1998. The new address will be available at the university web site.

Amount of award:	$1,500-$4,000
Number of awards:	10
Number of applicants:	20
Total amount awarded:	$20,000

Contact:
NASA Space Grant Wisconsin Space Grant Consortium
University of Wisconsin - Milwaukee
P.O. Box 413
Milwaukee, WI 53201-0413
Website: www.uwm.edu/dept/wsgc

NASA Space Grant Wisconsin Space Other Student Awards

Type of award: Research grant, renewable.
Intended use: For full-time undergraduate or graduate study.
Eligibility: Applicant must be U.S. citizen.
Additional information: The deadline and application requirements vary. Contact the University. The mailing address will change in the Fall of 1998. The new address will be available at the University web site.

Amount of award: $3,200
Number of awards: 3
Total amount awarded: $9,600
Contact:
NASA Space Grant Wisconsin Space Grant Consortium
University of Wisconsin - Milwaukee
P.O. Box 413
Milwaukee, WI 53201-0413
Website: www.uwm.edu/dept/wsgc

NASA Space Grant Wisconsin Undergraduate Research Awards

Type of award: Research grant, renewable.
Intended use: For full-time undergraduate study at accredited 4-year institution in United States.
Eligibility: Applicant must be U.S. citizen.
Basis for selection: Major/career interest in aerospace; astronomy; engineering; physics; science, general.
Application requirements: Recommendations, transcript and research proposal. State applicant must attend college in Wisconson.
Additional information: Applicant must attend a Wisconsin Space Grant Consortium member institution. Members include: Alverno College, Astronatuics Corporation of America, Carroll College, College of the Menominee Nation, Lawrence University, Marquette University, Medical College of Wisconsin, Milwaukee School of Engineering, Ripon College, St. Norbert College, University of Wisconsin - Green Bay, University of Wisconsin - La Crosse, University of Wisconsin - Madison, Unviersity of Wisconsin - Milwaukee, University of Wisconsin - Oshkosh, Unviersity of Wisconsin - Parkside, University of Wisconsin - Whitewater, Wisconsin Association of CESA Administrators, Wisconsin Department of Public Instruction, Wisconsin Department of Transportation, and Wisconsin Space Business Roundtable. Applicants must have a minimum of 3.0 GRE, and "good" SAT/ACT scores. Qualified students may apply for a summer session Undergraduate Research Award and an academic year Undergraduate Scholarship. The Consortium actively encourages women, minority, and disabled students to apply. The application deadline is in February. Call the university for an exact date.
Amount of award: $2,500
Number of awards: 4
Number of applicants: 10
Total amount awarded: $10,000
Contact:
NASA Space Grant Wisconsin Space Grant Consortium
Office of Research Infrastructure, SSEC/CIM5F
University of Wisconsin - Madison, 1225 W. Dayton St., Rm. 251
Madison, WI 53706-1380
Website: www.uwm.edu/dept/wsgc

NASA Space Grant Wisconsin Undergraduate Scholarship

Type of award: Scholarship, renewable.
Intended use: For full-time undergraduate study at accredited 4-year institution in United States.
Eligibility: Applicant must be U.S. citizen.
Basis for selection: Major/career interest in aerospace; astronomy; engineering; physics; science, general. Applicant must demonstrate high academic achievement.
Application requirements: Recommendations, essay and transcript. State applicant must attend college in Wisconsin.
Additional information: Applicant must attend a Wisconsin Space Grant Consortium member institution. Members include: Alverno College, Astronatuics Corporation of America, Carroll College, College of the Menominee Nation, Lawrence University, Marquette University, Medical College of Wisconsin, Milwaukee School of Engineering, Ripon College, St. Norbert College, University of Wisconsin - Green Bay, University of Wisconsin - La Crosse, University of Wisconsin - Madison, Unviersity of Wisconsin - Milwaukee, University of Wisconsin - Oshkosh, Unviersity of Wisconsin - Parkside, University of Wisconsin - Whitewater, Wisconsin Association of CESA Administrators, Wisconsin Department of Public Instruction, Wisconsin Department of Transportation, and Wisconsin Space Business Roundtable. Applicants must have a minimum of 3.0 GPA and must present their SAP/ACT scores. Qualified students may apply for an academic year. Undergraduate Scholarship and a summer session Undergraduate Research Award. The Consortium actively encourages women, minority, and disabled students to apply. The application deadline is in February. Call the university for an exact date. The mailing address will change in the Fall of 1998. The new address will be available at the university web site.
Amount of award: $500-$3,500
Number of awards: 23
Number of applicants: 33
Total amount awarded: $22,500
Contact:
NASA Space Grant Wisconsin Space Grant Consortium
University of Wisconsin - Milwaukee
P.O. Box 413
Milwaukee, WI 53201-0413
Website: www.uwm.edu/dept/wsgc

NASA Space Grant Wyoming Space Grant Consortium

NASA Space Grant Wyoming Space Graduate Research Fellowships

Type of award: Scholarship.
Intended use: For graduate or postgraduate study.
Eligibility: Applicant must be U.S. citizen.
Basis for selection: Applicant must demonstrate high academic achievement.
Application requirements: Transcript, proof of eligibility and research proposal. State applicant must attend college in Wyoming.
Additional information: Funding is not provided for travel, page charges, equipment or supplies. Proposals that cannot be funded from other sources are given priority. Research is expected to result in referred publications. Underrepresented groups are encouraged to apply. Deadline is in April; contact sponsor for exact date.
Amount of award: $10,500
Number of awards: 4

NASA Space Grant Wyoming Undergraduate Research Fellowships

Type of award: Scholarship.
Intended use: For undergraduate study.
Eligibility: Applicant must be U.S. citizen.
Basis for selection: Applicant must demonstrate high academic achievement.
Application requirements: Transcript, proof of eligibility and research proposal. State applicant must attend college in Wyoming.
Additional information: Funding is not provided for travel, page charges, equipment or supplies. Proposals that cannot be funded from other sources are given priority. Research is expected to result in referred publications. Underrepresented groups are encouraged to apply. Deadline is in April; contact sponsor for exact date.

Amount of award:	$4,000
Number of awards:	6
Number of applicants:	16

Contact:
NASA Space Grant Wyoming Space Grant Consortium
Planetary and Space Science Cener, University of Wyoming
Physics and Astronomy, P.O. Boxd 3905
Laramie, WY 82071
Website: faraday.uwyo.edu/space-grant

National Center for Atmospheric Research

Atmospheric Research Graduate Fellowship

Type of award: Scholarship.
Intended use: For doctoral study.
Basis for selection: Major/career interest in science, general. Applicant must demonstrate seriousness of purpose and high academic achievement.
Application requirements: Recommendations, transcript and research proposal.
Additional information: Student must intend to work on a doctoral thesis in cooperation with an National Center for Atmospheric Research program.

Amount of award:	$15,695
Number of awards:	4
Application deadline:	July 1
Notification begins:	August 1

Contact:
National Center for Atmospheric Research
P.O. Box 3000
Boulder, CO 80307-3000
Phone: 303-497-1601
Website: www.ncar.ucar.edu

National Endowment for the Humanities

Fellowships for College Teachers and Independent Scholars

Type of award: Research grant.
Intended use: For postgraduate study.
Eligibility: Applicant must be U.S. citizen or permanent resident.
Basis for selection: Applicant must demonstrate seriousness of purpose.
Application requirements: Research proposal. Resume.
Additional information: For college teachers working at an institution that does not offer a doctorate program. For specific information contact office or refer to website.

Amount of award:	$30,000
Application deadline:	May 1
Notification begins:	December 1

Contact:
National Endowment for the Humanities
Division of Research and Education - Fellowships
1100 Pennsylvania Ave. Room 318
Washington, DC 20506
Phone: 202-606-8467
Website: www.neh.fed.us

Fellowships for University Teachers

Type of award: Research grant.
Intended use: For postgraduate study.
Eligibility: Applicant must be U.S. citizen or permanent resident.
Basis for selection: Major/career interest in education.
Application requirements: Recommendations and research proposal. Resume.
Additional information: For university teachers who work at an institution that offers a doctoral program and hold a doctorate themselves. For specific information regarding this program, contact office or refer to website.

Amount of award:	$30,000
Application deadline:	May 1
Notification begins:	December 1

Contact:
National Endowment for the Humanities
Division of Research and Education - Fellowships
1100 Pennsylvania Avenue, NW Room 318
Washington, DC 20506
Phone: 202-606-8466
Website: www.neh.fed.us

National Endowment for the Humanities Summer Stipends Program

Type of award: Research grant.
Intended use: For postgraduate study.
Eligibility: Applicant must be U.S. citizen or permanent resident.
Basis for selection: Applicant must demonstrate seriousness of purpose.
Application requirements: Research proposal and

nomination by Must be nominated by applicants institution. Resume.
Additional information: For specific information regarding this program, refer to website or contact office.
 Amount of award: $4,000
 Application deadline: October 1
 Notification begins: April 1
Contact:
National Endowment for the Humanities
Division of Research and Education - Summer Stipends
1100 Pennsylvania Ave. Room 318
Washington, DC 20506
Phone: 202-606-8551
Website: www.neh.fed.us

National Institute of Justice

National Institute of Justice Graduate Research Fellowship

Type of award: Research grant.
Intended use: For doctoral study in United States.
Basis for selection: Major/career interest in criminal justice/law enforcement.
Application requirements: Recommendations and research proposal. Resume.
Additional information: Guidelines for application are explicit. Refer to web site or call for specific information. Deadline dates vary according to type of research.
 Amount of award: $35,000
 Number of awards: 4
 Number of applicants: 30
 Total amount awarded: $150,000
Contact:
National Institute of Justice
810 7 Street, NW
Washington, DC 20531
Phone: 202-307-2951
Website: www.ojp.usdoj.gov/nij

National Institutes of Health

NIH Postgraduate Research Training Award

Type of award: Research grant.
Intended use: For postgraduate study.
Eligibility: Applicant must be Must provide proof of visa held or sought.
Basis for selection: Major/career interest in medical specialties/research. Applicant must demonstrate seriousness of purpose and high academic achievement.
Application requirements: Recommendations and transcript. Curriculum vitae, Natioanl Board of Medical examiners test scores and United States Medical Licensing Examination scores. Foreign applicants must submit the Foreign Medical Graduate Examination in Medical Licensing scores.
Additional information: Applications accepted year-round.

Interested students should apply one to two years prior to start date. NIH seeks candidates for appointments in research training, clinical training or combined training in the field of biomedical research. Refer to web page or contact NIH for further information.
 Amount of award: $25,000-$70,000
Contact:
National Institutes of Health Office of Education
Building 10, Room 1C129
10 Center Drive, MSC 1158
Bethesda, MD 20892-1158
Phone: 301-496-2427
Website: www.training.nih.gov

NIH Summer Internship Program

Type of award: Internship, renewable.
Intended use: For full-time undergraduate or graduate study. Designated institutions: Research laboratories in Bethesda, Maryland.
Eligibility: Applicant must be U.S. citizen or permanent resident.
Basis for selection: Major/career interest in science, general; medicine (m.d.); medical specialties/research. Applicant must demonstrate high academic achievement.
Application requirements: Recommendations, essay, transcript and proof of eligibility. Cover letter, resume.
Additional information: Program offers a weekly research seminar featuring prominent National Institutes of Health scientists, workshops on career opportunities, and poster session which provides students an opportunity to conduct research in selected areas of laboratory investigation and to present their research. Program runs for approximately eight weeks, between June and August, but some adjustment in beginning and ending dates is possible. Send SASE with application request.
 Amount of award: $900-$1,600
 Number of awards: 1,000
 Number of applicants: 7,000
 Application deadline: March 1
 Notification begins: April 2
Contact:
National Institutes of Health
Building 10, Room 1C129
10 Center Drive MSC 1158
Bethesda, MD 20892-1158
Phone: 301-402-2176
Website: www.training.nih.gov

NIH Undergraduate Scholarship Program

Type of award: Scholarship.
Intended use: For full-time undergraduate study at accredited 4-year institution in United States.
Eligibility: Applicant must be U.S. citizen or permanent resident.
Basis for selection: Major/career interest in biology; bioengineering; medical specialties/research. Applicant must demonstrate seriousness of purpose, financial need and high academic achievement.
Application requirements: Recommendations, transcript and proof of eligibility.
Additional information: Must have 3.5 GPA or be within the

top 5% of class. For each year that scholarship is awarded, student must work 12 months as a full-time employee at NIH laboratories. Award covers tution/fees for up to $20,000.
- **Amount of award:** $20,000
- **Number of awards:** 20
- **Application deadline:** March 31

Contact:
National Institutes of Health Office of Loan Repayment and Scholarships
7550 Wisconsin Avenue
Room 604
Bethesda, MD 20892
Website: www.nih.gov

National Network for Environmental Management Studies

NNEMS Graduate Fellowship

Type of award: Research grant.
Intended use: For graduate study at accredited graduate institution in United States.
Eligibility: Applicant must be U.S. citizen or permanent resident.
Basis for selection: Major/career interest in environmental science. Applicant must demonstrate high academic achievement.
Application requirements: Recommendations, transcript and research proposal. Must submit resume.
Additional information: Stipends for fellowships based on level of education. Deadline dates vary. Must be studying in an academic program directly related to pollution abatement and have at least four undergraduate courses in environmental studies.

NNEMS Undergraduate Fellowship

Type of award: Research grant.
Intended use: For undergraduate study at accredited 4-year institution in United States.
Eligibility: Applicant must be U.S. citizen.
Basis for selection: Major/career interest in environmental science.
Application requirements: Recommendations, transcript and research proposal. Must submit resume.
Additional information: Stipends for fellowships based on level of education. Deadline dates vary. Must be studying in an academic program directly related to pollution abatement and have at least four undergraduate courses in environmental studies. Must have a 3.0 GPA.

Contact:
NNEMS
401 M Street, S.W.
Washington, DC 20460
Website: www.epa.gov

National Science Foundation

Alfred P. Sloan Foundation Fellowship in Molecular Evolution

Type of award: Research grant.
Intended use: For postgraduate study. Designated institutions: Non-profit research institution.
Eligibility: Applicant must be U.S. citizen or permanent resident.
Basis for selection: Major/career interest in microbiology; biology.
Application requirements: Recommendations and research proposal. Curriculum vitae.
Additional information: Must have earned doctorate degree no earlier than four years before the application deadline or expect to receive degree by June 30, 1999. Fellowships last two years with a stipend of $40,000/year. Additional fields of study include: Genetics, Systematics, Developmental Biology, Evolutionary Biology, Bacteriology and Biochemistry.
- **Amount of award:** $40,000
- **Application deadline:** November 4

Contact:
National Science Foundation
Sloan Molecular Evolu./Postdoc.Rsch. Fellow.
4201 Wilson Boulevard, BIR/BIO Room 615
Arlington, VA 22230
Phone: 703-306-1469
Website: www.fastlane.nsf.gov

National Science Foundation Graduate Fellowship

Type of award: Scholarship, renewable.
Intended use: For full-time master's, doctoral study at accredited graduate institution outside United States.
Eligibility: Applicant must be U.S. citizen or permanent resident.
Basis for selection: Major/career interest in engineering; mathematics; bioengineering; science, general; biology. Applicant must demonstrate seriousness of purpose and high academic achievement.
Application requirements: Recommendations and transcript. Proposed plan of study or research, general GRE scores required, as are subject test scores if one is available in the individual's discipline.
Additional information: Fellowships are for a maximum tenure of three years useable over a five year period. Must have completed no more than 20 semester hours, 30 quarter hours, or equivalent of graduate study at time of application. Recipient may apply for one-time $1,000 International Research Travel Allowance.
- **Amount of award:** $24,500
- **Application deadline:** November 6
- **Notification begins:** March 31

Contact:
National Science Foundation Graduate Research Fellowship Program
Oak Ridge Associated Universities (ORAU)
P.O. Box 3010
Oak Ridge, TN 37831-3010
Phone: 423-241-4300
Website: www.nsf.gov

National Science Foundation Minority Graduate Fellowship

Type of award: Scholarship.
Intended use: For full-time master's, doctoral study at accredited graduate institution.
Eligibility: Applicant must be Alaskan native, American Indian, African American, Mexican American, Hispanic American or Puerto Rican. Applicants of Asian descent must be Native Pacific Islanders(Polynesian or Micronesian). Alaskan Natives must be Eskimo or Aleut. Applicant must be U.S. citizen or permanent resident.
Basis for selection: Major/career interest in engineering; bioengineering; mathematics; science, general; biology. Applicant must demonstrate seriousness of purpose and high academic achievement.
Application requirements: Recommendations and transcript. Proposed plan of study or research, general GRE scores required, as are subject scores if test is available in individual's discipline.
Additional information: Fellowships are for a maximum tenure of three years useable over a five year period. Must have completed no more than 30 semester hours, 45 quarter hours, or equivalent of graduate study at time of application. Recipient may apply for one-time $1,000 International Research Travel Allowance. Applications available in September.

Amount of award:	$24,500
Application deadline:	November 6
Notification begins:	March 31

Contact:
National Science Foundation Graduate Research Fellowship Program
Oak Ridge Associated Universities (ORAU)
P.O. Box 3010
Oak Ridge, TN 37831-3010
Phone: 423-241-4300
Website: www.nsf.gov

National Science Foundation Minority Postdoctoral Fellowship

Type of award: Research grant.
Intended use: For postgraduate study.
Eligibility: Applicant must be Alaskan native, American Indian, African American, Mexican American, Hispanic American or Puerto Rican. Applicant must be U.S. citizen or permanent resident.
Basis for selection: Major/career interest in biology; social and behavioral sciences; environmental science; sociology; psychology; economics; linguistics; geography.
Application requirements: Recommendations and research proposal. Curriculum vitae.
Additional information: Must have earned doctorate degree no more than four years prior to the application deadline or will earn degree no more than one year after application deadline. Fellowships last two years and pay a stipend of $40,000/year. Additional fields of study include biochemistry, biological/life sciences, environmental studies, and genetics. Applications available in September.

Amount of award:	$40,000
Application deadline:	December 4

Contact:
National Science Foundation
4201 Wilson Boulevard, BIR/BIO Room 615
Minority Postdoctoral Research Fellowships
Arlington, VA 22230
Phone: 703-306-1469
Website: www.fastlane.nsf.gov

National Science Foundation Postdoctoral Research Fellowship

Type of award: Research grant.
Intended use: For postgraduate study. Designated institutions: Non-profit institution.
Eligibility: Applicant must be U.S. citizen or permanent resident.
Basis for selection: Major/career interest in science, general; biology; environmental science.
Application requirements: Research proposal.
Additional information: Additional fields of study: cell and molecular biology, ecology, and environmental studies. Applicants proposing tenure at Japanese institution must contact U.S.-Japan program, National Science Foundation Division of International Programs at 703-306-1701. Applications available in September.

Amount of award:	$80,000
Application deadline:	November 6
Notification begins:	April 1

Contact:
National Science Foundation
Postdoctoral Research Fellowship
4201 Wilson Boulevard, BIR/BIO Room 615
Arlington, VA 22230
Phone: 703-306-1469
Website: www.fastlane.nsf.gov

National Security Agency

National Security Agency Undergraduate Tuition Assistance Program

Type of award: Scholarship, renewable.
Intended use: For full-time undergraduate study at accredited 4-year institution in United States.
Eligibility: Applicant must be high school senior. Applicant must be U.S. citizen.
Basis for selection: Major/career interest in computer and information sciences; mathematics; linguistics; engineering, computer; engineering, electrical and electronic. Applicant must demonstrate depth of character, leadership, patriotism, seriousness of purpose, service orientation and high academic achievement.
Application requirements: Interview, recommendations, transcript and proof of eligibility. Must undergo polygraph and security screening. Must have at least 1200 on SAT and 27 on ACT.
Additional information: Must have 3.0 GPA.

Number of awards: 80
Number of applicants: 638
Application deadline: November 30
Notification begins: April 1
Contact:
National Security Agency Undergraduate Training Program
9800 Savage Road
S232-UTP, Suite 6840
Fort Meade, MD 20755-6840
Phone: 800-962-9398

Nebraska Coordinating Commission for Postsecondary Education

Nebraska Postsecondary Education Award

Type of award: Scholarship, renewable.
Intended use: For full-time or half-time undergraduate study at accredited 2-year or 4-year institution. Designated institutions: Private, nonprofit institutions in Nebraska.
Eligibility: Applicant must be residing in Nebraska.
Basis for selection: Applicant must demonstrate financial need.
Application requirements: Transcript.
Additional information: Applicant must be Pell Grant recipient. Dollar amount of award determined by institution. Application deadline are determined by the particular institution. Contact sponsor for more information.
   Total amount awarded: $895,000
Contact:
Coordinating Commission for Postsecondary Education
140 North 8 Street, Suite 300
P.O. Box 95005
Lincoln, NE 68509-5005
Phone: 402-471-6506

Nebraska Scholarship Assistance Program

Type of award: Scholarship, renewable.
Intended use: For full-time or half-time undergraduate study at accredited vocational, 2-year or 4-year institution in Nebraska.
Eligibility: Applicant must be high school senior. Applicant must be residing in Nebraska.
Basis for selection: Applicant must demonstrate financial need.
Application requirements: Transcript.
Additional information: Must be a Pell Grant recipient. Dollar amount of award determined by institution. Application deadlines determined by institution as well.
   Total amount awarded: $1,043,528
Contact:
The Nebraska Coordinating Commission for Postsecondary Education
140 North 8 Street, Suite 300
P.O. Box 95005
Lincoln, NE 68509-5005
Phone: 402-471-6506

Nebraska State Scholarship Award

Type of award: Scholarship, renewable.
Intended use: For full-time or half-time undergraduate study at accredited vocational, 2-year or 4-year institution in Nebraska.
Eligibility: Applicant must be high school senior. Applicant must be residing in Nebraska.
Basis for selection: Applicant must demonstrate financial need.
Application requirements: Transcript.
Additional information: Applicants must be eligible for a Pell Grant. Application deadlines are established by the institution the student has applied to.
   Total amount awarded: $1,268,336
Contact:
Coordinating Commission for Postsecondary Education
140 North 8 Street, Suite 300
P.O. Box 95005
Lincoln, NE 68509-5005
Phone: 402-471-6506
Website: www.nol.org/Nepostsecondaryed

Nebraska Department of Health and Human Services

Nebraska Medical Student Scholarship Program

Type of award: Scholarship, renewable.
Intended use: For full-time first professional study in Nebraska. Designated institutions: University of Nebraska Medical Center or Creighton University.
Eligibility: Applicant must be U.S. citizen or permanent resident residing in Nebraska.
Basis for selection: Major/career interest in physician assistant; medicine (m.d.). Applicant must demonstrate seriousness of purpose and service orientation.
Application requirements: Interview and proof of eligibility.
Additional information: Service-contingent awards to physician assistant students renewable once, to medical students renewable three times.
   Amount of award: $5,000-$10,000
   Number of awards: 21
   Number of applicants: 15
   Application deadline: June 1
   Notification begins: July 1
   Total amount awarded: $210,000
Contact:
Nebraska Department of Health & Human Services
Office of Rural Health
P.O. Box 95007
Lincoln, NE 68509

Nebraska State Department of Education

Nebraska Robert C. Byrd Honors Scholarship

Type of award: Scholarship, renewable.
Intended use: For full-time freshman study at accredited postsecondary institution.
Eligibility: Applicant must be high school senior. Applicant must be U.S. citizen or permanent resident residing in Nebraska.
Basis for selection: Applicant must demonstrate high academic achievement.
Application requirements: Transcript. ACT scores.
Additional information: Renewable up to three years with good academic standing.
  Amount of award: $1,500
  Number of awards: 130
  Application deadline: March 15
  Total amount awarded: $195,000
Contact:
Nebraska State Department of Education
Robert C. Byrd Scholarship
P.O. Box 94987
Lincoln, NE 68509-4987

Nevada Department of Education

Nevada Robert C. Byrd Honors Scholarship

Type of award: Scholarship, renewable.
Intended use: For undergraduate study.
Eligibility: Applicant must be high school senior. Applicant must be U.S. citizen or permanent resident residing in Nevada.
Basis for selection: Applicant must demonstrate high academic achievement.
Additional information: Contact high school guidance counselor. Minimum 3.5 GPA and SAT I score of 1100 or ACT score of 25 required. Applicants may postpone enrollment at an institution, they otherwise would have enrolled in, for up to one year after the institutions first day of classes. After this time period the award will be terminated.
  Amount of award: $1,500
  Number of awards: 114
  Number of applicants: 758
  Total amount awarded: $127,794

Nevada Student Incentive Grant

Type of award: Scholarship.
Intended use: For full-time or half-time undergraduate or graduate study at vocational, 2-year, 4-year or graduate institution in Nevada.
Eligibility: Applicant must be U.S. citizen or permanent resident residing in Nevada.
Basis for selection: Applicant must demonstrate financial need.
Additional information: Contact financial aid office of institution.
  Amount of award: $200-$5,000
  Number of awards: 613
  Total amount awarded: $376,995

New England Board of Higher Education

New England Regional Student Program

Type of award: Out-of-state tuition break
Intended use: New England residents enrolled in approved undergraduate or graduate programs at out-of-state New England public colleges or universities.
Eligibility: Applicant must be resident of Connecticut, Maine, Massachusetts, New Hampshire, Rhode Island or Vermont only.

Contact:
New England Regional Student Program
New England Board of Higher Education
41 Temple Place
Boston, MA 02111
Phone: 617-357-9620

New Hampshire Postsecondary Education Commission

New Hampshire Incentive Program

Type of award: Scholarship, renewable.
Intended use: For undergraduate study at accredited vocational, 2-year or 4-year institution in New England.
Eligibility: Applicant must be U.S. citizen or permanent resident residing in New Hampshire.
Basis for selection: Applicant must demonstrate financial need.
Application requirements: Proof of eligibility. Completed FAFSA form.
  Amount of award: $225-$1,000
  Number of awards: 3,000
  Number of applicants: 27,000
  Application deadline: May 1
  Total amount awarded: $1,400,000
Contact:
New Hampshire Postsecondary Education Commission
2 Industrial Park Drive
Concord, NH 03301-8512

New Hampshire Nursing Scholarship Program

Type of award: Loan, renewable.
Intended use: For full-time undergraduate, master's or postgraduate study at accredited vocational, 2-year, 4-year or graduate institution in New Hampshire.
Eligibility: Applicant must be U.S. citizen or permanent resident residing in New Hampshire.
Basis for selection: Major/career interest in nursing. Applicant must demonstrate financial need.
Application requirements: Transcript and proof of eligibility.
Additional information: Loan forgiveness for nursing practice in New Hampshire. Applicants must have a financial aid recommendation and maintain 2.0 GPA for renewal. Undergraduate awards must be used at public or private New Hampshire institution. Summer application deadline is May 1.
  Amount of award: $300-$2,000
  Number of awards: 105
  Number of applicants: 250
  Application deadline: June 1, December 15
  Notification begins: December 15
  Total amount awarded: $30,000
Contact:
Scholarship Committee
2 Industrial Park Drive
Concord, NH 03301-8512

New Hampshire Scholarship for Orphans of Veterans

Type of award: Scholarship, renewable.
Intended use: For full-time undergraduate or graduate study at vocational, 2-year, 4-year or graduate institution. Designated institutions: North Carolina institutions only.
Eligibility: Applicant must be U.S. citizen residing in New Hampshire. Applicant must be child of deceased veteran during Korean War, WW I, WW II or Vietnam.
Application requirements: Proof of eligibility.
Additional information: Parent must have been legal resident of New Hampshire at time of service-related death.
  Amount of award: $1,000
  Number of awards: 9
  Number of applicants: 10
  Total amount awarded: $9,000
Contact:
New Hampshire Postsecondary Education Commission
Patricia Edes
2 Industrial Park Drive
Concord, NH 03301-8512

New Jersey Department of Military and Veterans Affairs

New Jersey POW/MIA Program

Type of award: Scholarship, renewable.
Intended use: For full-time freshman, sophomore, junior or senior study at accredited 4-year institution in New Jersey.
Eligibility: Applicant must be residing in New Jersey. Applicant must be child of active service person or POW/MIA. Parent must have been officially declared Prisoner of War or Missing in Action after January 1, 1960.
Application requirements: Proof of eligibility.
  Number of awards: 4
  Application deadline: October 1, March 1
  Total amount awarded: $155,771

New Jersey Tuition Credit Military and Veterans Affairs

Type of award: Scholarship, renewable.
Intended use: For undergraduate or graduate study at postsecondary institution in United States.
Eligibility: Applicant must be residing in New Jersey. Applicant must be veteran who served in the Army, Air Force, Marines, Navy, Coast Guard or Reserves/National Guard during Vietnam. Must have served in Armed Forces between December 31, 1960 and May 7, 1975. Must have been New Jersey resident at time of induction or discharge, or for at least a year prior to application, excluding active duty time.
Application requirements: Proof of eligibility.
Additional information: Must be New Jersey resident for at least one year prior to application.
  Amount of award: $200-$400
  Number of awards: 119
  Application deadline: October 1, March 1
  Total amount awarded: $28,100
Contact:
New Jersey Department of Military and Veterans Affairs
DCVA-FO
Eggert Crossing Road, PO Box 340
Trenton, NJ 08625-0340
Phone: 609-530-6961

New Jersey Office of Student Assistance

New Jersey C. Clyde Ferguson Law Scholarship

Type of award: Scholarship.
Intended use: For first professional study. Designated institutions: Rutgers University School of Law--Newark, Rutgers University School of Law--Camden, or Seton Hall Law School.
Eligibility: Applicant must be of minority background. Applicant must be U.S. citizen or permanent resident.
Basis for selection: Major/career interest in law. Applicant must demonstrate financial need.
Additional information: Award minimum and maximum are established annually by Educational Opportunity Fund Board of Directors, and shall not exceed maximum of tuition, fees, room and board charged at Rutgers University School of Law--Newark. Applications can be obtained through Graduate Office and Educational Opportunity Fund Campus Director at college.

Amount of award:	$4,150
Number of awards:	39
Total amount awarded:	$199,999

Contact:
New Jersey Office of Student Assistance
4 Quakerbridge Plaza
PO Box 540
Trenton, NJ 08625
Phone: 800-792-8670
Website: www.state.nj.us/treasury/osa

New Jersey Class Loan Program

Type of award: Loan, renewable.
Intended use: For full-time or half-time freshman, sophomore, junior, senior, master's or doctoral study at accredited 2-year, 4-year or graduate institution in United States.
Eligibility: Applicant must be U.S. citizen or permanent resident residing in New Jersey.
Application requirements: Proof of eligibility.
Additional information: Must demonstrate credit-worthiness or provide co-signer. Parent or other eligible family member may borrow on behalf of student. Must have used maximum amount of Stafford loans or be ineligible for Stafford to apply. Maximum loan amount varies, may not exceed education cost (less all other financial aid). Average amount, $500.

Amount of award:	$500
Number of awards:	13,747
Number of applicants:	20,000
Total amount awarded:	$29,847,189

Contact:
State of New Jersey Office of Student Assistance
4 Quakerbridge Plaza, P.O. Box 540
Trenton, NJ 08625-0540
Phone: 800-792-8670
Website: www.state.nj.us/treasury/osa

New Jersey Educational Opportunity Fund Grant

Type of award: Scholarship, renewable.
Intended use: For full-time freshman, sophomore, junior, senior, master's or doctoral study at accredited 2-year, 4-year or graduate institution in New Jersey. Designated institutions: New Jersey Colleges and Universities.
Eligibility: Applicant must be U.S. citizen or permanent resident residing in New Jersey.
Basis for selection: Applicant must demonstrate financial need.
Additional information: For students from educationally disadvantaged backgrounds with demonstrated financial need. Must be New Jersey resident for at least 12 consecutive months prior to receiving grant. Students are admitted into the EOF program by the college. Program includes summer sessions, tutoring, and counseling. Contact financial aid office at institution.

Amount of award:	$200-$2,100
Number of awards:	13,553
Application deadline:	October 1, March 1
Total amount awarded:	$12,723,097

Contact:
New Jersey Office of Student Assistance
P.O. Box 540
Trenton, NJ 08625
Phone: 800-792-8670
Website: www.state.nj.us/treasury/osa

New Jersey Edward J. Bloustein Distinguished Scholars

Type of award: Scholarship, renewable.
Intended use: For full-time freshman, sophomore, junior or senior study at accredited 2-year or 4-year institution in New Jersey.
Eligibility: Applicant must be high school senior. Applicant must be U.S. citizen or permanent resident residing in New Jersey.
Basis for selection: Applicant must demonstrate high academic achievement.
Application requirements: Nomination by their high schools.
Additional information: Academic criteria: Open to students in top 10 percent of their class, SAT scores of 1260 or higher; and to students who rank first, second or third in their class at the end of their junior year. Must be New Jersey resident for at least 12 consecutive months prior to receiving award. Students demonstrating financial need may receive additional $1,000 per year. See guidance counselor for more information.

Amount of award:	$1,000
Number of awards:	4,475
Number of applicants:	15,000
Application deadline:	October 1
Total amount awarded:	$4,337,909

Contact:
New Jersey Office of Student Assistance
4 Quakerbridge Plaza, P.O. Box 540
Trenton, NJ 08625-0540
Phone: 800-792-8670
Website: www.state.nj.us/treasury/osa

New Jersey Garden State Scholars

Type of award: Scholarship, renewable.
Intended use: For full-time freshman, sophomore, junior or senior study at accredited 2-year or 4-year institution in New Jersey.
Eligibility: Applicant must be high school senior. Applicant must be U.S. citizen or permanent resident residing in New Jersey.
Basis for selection: Applicant must demonstrate high academic achievement.
Application requirements: Proof of eligibility and nomination by high school.
Additional information: Academic criteria: top 20 percent of class, minimum SAT of 1000. Number of awards depends on available funding. Must be New Jersey resident for at least 12 consecutive months prior to receiving award. See guidance counselor for more information.

Amount of award:	$500
Number of awards:	2,431
Number of applicants:	15,000
Application deadline:	October 1
Notification begins:	November 1
Total amount awarded:	$2,306,573

Contact:
New Jersey Office of Student Assistance
4 Quakerbridge Plaza
PO Box 540
Trenton, NJ 08625
Phone: 800-792-8670
Website: www.state.nj.us/treasury/osa

New Jersey Minority Academic Career Program

Type of award: Scholarship, renewable.
Intended use: For full-time doctoral study at accredited graduate institution. Designated institutions: Drew University, Fairleigh Dickinson University, New Jersey Institution of Technology, Princeton University, Rutgers, the State University, Seton Hall University, Stevens Institute of Technology, and the University of Medicine and Dentistry of New Jersey.
Eligibility: Applicant must be of minority background. Applicant must be U.S. citizen or permanent resident residing in New Jersey.
Basis for selection: Major/career interest in humanities/liberal arts; social and behavioral sciences; mathematics; science, general. Applicant must demonstrate financial need and high academic achievement.
Application requirements: Recommendations, essay, proof of eligibility and nomination by institution's MAC administrator and doctoral department. Nominees are reviewed by MAC advisory committee.
Additional information: MAC Fellow awarded annual financial support of at least $5,000 from the doctoral institution and may apply for loans through the MAC Program. Maximum loan value is $40,000 ($10,000 for four years). Recipient is eligible for redemption of 25 percent of his or her total indebtedness for each year of approved service. Must demonstrate strong commitment to college-level teaching in New Jersey.

Amount of award:	$10,000
Number of awards:	14
Total amount awarded:	$94,504

Contact:
State of New Jersey Office of Student Assistance
4 Quakerbridge Plaza, CN 540
Trenton, NJ 08625-0540
Website: www.state.nj.us/treasury/osa

New Jersey Public Tuition Benefits Program

Type of award: Scholarship, renewable.
Intended use: For full-time or half-time freshman, sophomore, junior or senior study at accredited 2-year or 4-year institution in New Jersey.
Eligibility: Applicant must be U.S. citizen or permanent resident residing in New Jersey. Applicant's parent must have been killed or disabled in work-related accident as police officer or public safety officer.
Application requirements: Proof of eligibility.
Additional information: Parent or spouse must have been New Jersey law enforcement or emergency service personnel killed in line of duty. Applications available by calling state of New Jersey Office of Student Assistance toll-free financial aid hotline.

Amount of award:	$4,378
Number of awards:	16
Number of applicants:	21
Application deadline:	October 1, March 1
Total amount awarded:	$65,000

Contact:
State of New Jersey Office of Student Assistance
4 Quakerbridge Plaza, PO Box 540
Trenton, NJ 08625-0540
Phone: 800-792-8670
Website: www.state.nj.us/treasury/osa

New Jersey Tuition and Grants

Type of award: Scholarship, renewable.
Intended use: For full-time freshman, sophomore, junior or senior study at accredited 2-year or 4-year institution in New Jersey.
Eligibility: Applicant must be U.S. citizen or permanent resident residing in New Jersey.
Basis for selection: Applicant must demonstrate financial need.
Application requirements: Proof of eligibility. FAFSA.
Additional information: Must have lived in New Jersey at least 12 consecutive months before receiving grant. Must maintain 2.0 GPA for renewals. Deadline for Fall and Spring awards June 1 for renewal students and October 1 for applicants who did not receive award during previous academic year. If state funds limited, priority given to students applying by these dates. Applications received after priority filing dates, but not later than March 1, considered on funds available basis for Spring.

Amount of award:	$786-$5,764
Number of awards:	58,049
Number of applicants:	218,393
Application deadline:	June 1, October 1
Total amount awarded:	$134,110,376

Contact:
State of New Jersey Office of Student Assistance
4 Quakerbridge Plaza, P.O. Box 540
Trenton, NJ 08625-0540
Phone: 800-792-8670
Website: www.state.nj.us/treasury/osa

New Jersey Urban Scholars

Type of award: Scholarship, renewable.
Intended use: For undergraduate study at postsecondary institution in New Jersey.
Eligibility: Applicant must be high school junior. Applicant must be U.S. citizen or permanent resident residing in New Jersey.
Basis for selection: Applicant must demonstrate financial need and high academic achievement.
Application requirements: Nomination by high school.
Additional information: Academic criteria: Open to students in top 10 percent of their class, with a minimum grade point average of 3.0 (or equivalent).

Amount of award: $1,000
Application deadline: October 1
Contact:
State of New Jersey Office of Student Assistance
4 Quakerbridge Plaza, CN 540
Trenton, NJ 08625-0540
Phone: 800-792-8670
Fax: 609-588-2228
Website: www.state.nj.us/treasury/osa

New Mexico Commission on Higher Education

New Mexico Allied Health Student Loan for Service Program

Type of award: Loan.
Intended use: For undergraduate or graduate study in New Mexico. Designated institutions: Public New Mexico postsecondary institutions.
Eligibility: Applicant must be U.S. citizen or permanent resident residing in New Mexico.
Basis for selection: Major/career interest in health-related professions; health sciences; medicine (m.d.); nursing. Applicant must demonstrate financial need.
Additional information: Loan forgiveness is offered to those who practice in medically underserved areas in New Mexico.
Amount of award: $12,000
Application deadline: July 1
Total amount awarded: $200,000
Contact:
New Mexico Commission on Higher Education
Financial Aid and Student Services
P.O. Box 15910
Santa Fe, NM 87506-5910

New Mexico Athlete Scholarship

Type of award: Scholarship, renewable.
Intended use: For full-time undergraduate study at accredited 2-year or 4-year institution in New Mexico. Designated institutions: Selected New Mexico public institutions.
Eligibility: Applicant must be U.S. citizen or permanent resident residing in New Mexico.
Additional information: For information and application contact athletic department of New Mexico public college or university.
Application deadline: March 1
Total amount awarded: $2,209,600

New Mexico Graduate Scholarship: Minorities/Women

Type of award: Scholarship, renewable.
Intended use: For graduate study at postsecondary institution in New Mexico. Designated institutions: New Mexico public institutions.
Eligibility: Applicant must be of minority background. Non-minority women also eligible. Applicant must be female. Applicant must be U.S. citizen or permanent resident residing in New Mexico.
Additional information: Contact New Mexico public institution dean of graduate studies for application. Program is targeted at underrepresented groups in graduate education, particularly minorities and women. Recipient must serve ten hours per week in unpaid internship or assistantship.
Amount of award: $7,200
Total amount awarded: $691,800
Contact:
New Mexico Commission on Higher Education
Financial Aid and Student Services
P.O. Box 15910
Santa Fe, NM 87506-5910

New Mexico Legislative Endowment Program

Type of award: Scholarship, renewable.
Intended use: For full-time or half-time undergraduate study. Designated institutions: Public postsecondary New Mexico institutions.
Eligibility: Applicant must be residing in New Mexico.
Basis for selection: Applicant must demonstrate financial need.
Additional information: Must submit Free Application for Federal Student Aid (FAFSA). Contact the Financial Aid Office of any public postsecondary institution in New Mexico.
Amount of award: $2,500
Contact:
New Mexico Commission on Higher Education
4068 Cerrillos Road
Santa Fe, NM 87501-4294
Phone: 800-279-9777
Website: www.nmche.org

New Mexico Medical Student Loan

Type of award: Loan, renewable.
Intended use: For undergraduate, first professional study.
Eligibility: Applicant must be U.S. citizen or permanent resident residing in New Mexico.
Basis for selection: Major/career interest in medicine (m.d.); physician assistant. Applicant must demonstrate financial need.
Additional information: Loan forgiveness for New Mexico residents to practice in medically underserved areas in New Mexico.
Amount of award: $12,000
Application deadline: July 1
Total amount awarded: $482,800
Contact:
New Mexico Commission on Higher Education
Financial Aid and Student Services
P.O. Box 15910
Santa Fe, NM 87506-5910

New Mexico Minority and Handicapped Teachers Scholarship: Southeast

Type of award: Scholarship.
Intended use: For full-time or half-time undergraduate, post-bachelor's certificate study at accredited postsecondary institution in New Mexico. Designated institutions: Any public postsecondary institution.
Eligibility: Applicant must be U.S. citizen or permanent resident residing in New Mexico.

Basis for selection: Major/career interest in education, teacher. Applicant must demonstrate financial need.
Additional information: Must be resident of Lea, Chaves, Roosevelt, Otero or Eddy counties. Loan forgiveness for qualified resident students who, after graduation, become teachers in any of the designated eligible counties.
- Amount of award: $4,000
- Application deadline: July 1
- Total amount awarded: $246,400

Contact:
New Mexico Commission on Higher Education
Financial Aid and Student Services
P.O. Box 15910
Santa Fe, NM 87506-5910

New Mexico Minority Doctoral Assistance Loan for Service

Type of award: Loan, renewable.
Intended use: For full-time doctoral study.
Eligibility: Applicant must be of minority background. Non-minority New Mexican women eligible. Applicant must be U.S. citizen residing in New Mexico.
Application requirements: Proof of eligibility.
Additional information: Award given for any academic disciplines in which ethnic minorities and women are underrepresented. Applicant must have received bachelor's and/or master's degree from a New Mexico four-year public institution, be sponsored by New Mexico four-year institution, and accepted for enrollment at eligible institution. Loan forgiveness for teaching in New Mexico colleges/universities. Contact any New Mexico four-year public postsecondary institution graduate dean's office for application.
- Amount of award: $25,000
- Application deadline: January 1
- Total amount awarded: $275,000

Contact:
New Mexico Commission on Higher Education
Financial Aid and Student Services
P.O. Box 15910
Santa Fe, NM 87506-5910

New Mexico Nursing Student Loan for Service

Type of award: Loan, renewable.
Intended use: For undergraduate or graduate study at accredited 2-year or 4-year institution in New Mexico.
Eligibility: Applicant must be U.S. citizen or permanent resident residing in New Mexico.
Basis for selection: Major/career interest in nursing. Applicant must demonstrate financial need.
Additional information: Loan forgiveness to New Mexico resident for practice in medically underserved areas in New Mexico.
- Amount of award: $12,000
- Application deadline: July 1
- Total amount awarded: $500,700

Contact:
New Mexico Commission on Higher Education
Financial Aid and Student Services
P.O. Box 15910
Santa Fe, NM 87506-5910

New Mexico Osteopathic Student Loan for Service

Type of award: Loan, renewable.
Intended use: For full-time first professional study at accredited graduate institution in United States. Designated institutions: Public school of osteopathy.
Eligibility: Applicant must be U.S. citizen or permanent resident residing in New Mexico.
Basis for selection: Applicant must demonstrate financial need.
Additional information: Loan forgiveness for New Mexico residents to practice in medically underserved areas in New Mexico. Fields of study: osteopathic physicians and physician's assistant.
- Amount of award: $12,000
- Application deadline: July 1
- Total amount awarded: $156,000

Contact:
New Mexico Commission on Higher Education
Financial Aid and Student Services
P.O. Box 15910
Santa Fe, NM 87506-5910

New Mexico Scholars Program

Type of award: Scholarship, renewable.
Intended use: For full-time or half-time undergraduate study at accredited 2-year or 4-year institution in New Mexico. Designated institutions: Private or public nonprofit institutions.
Eligibility: Applicant must be U.S. citizen or permanent resident residing in New Mexico.
Basis for selection: Applicant must demonstrate financial need and high academic achievement.
Additional information: Must be graduate of New Mexico high school. Maximum amount of award covers cost of tuition, fees and books. Must score at least 1020 on SAT I (25 on ACT) or rank in top five percent of high school graduating class and have family income no greater than $30,000 per year. Contact New Mexico post secondary institution of choice financial aid office for information and application.
- Amount of award: $2,324
- Application deadline: March 1
- Total amount awarded: $1,420,000

Contact:
New Mexico Commission on Higher Education
Financial Aid and Student Services
P.O. Box 15910
Santa Fe, NM 87506-5910

New Mexico Student Choice Program

Type of award: Scholarship, renewable.
Intended use: For full-time or half-time undergraduate study in New Mexico. Designated institutions: St. John's College, College of Southwest, College of Santa Fe.
Eligibility: Applicant must be U.S. citizen or permanent resident residing in New Mexico.
Basis for selection: Applicant must demonstrate financial need.
Additional information: Apply to financial aid office of one of the three colleges where award may be used.

Amount of award:	$2,168
Application deadline:	March 1
Total amount awarded:	$988,700

Contact:
New Mexico Commission on Higher Education
Financial Aid and Student Services
P.O. Box 15910
Santa Fe, NM 87506-5910

New Mexico Student Incentive Grant

Type of award: Scholarship, renewable.
Intended use: For full-time or half-time undergraduate study at accredited postsecondary institution in New Mexico. Designated institutions: Nonprofit New Mexico postsecondary institutions.
Eligibility: Applicant must be U.S. citizen or permanent resident residing in New Mexico.
Basis for selection: Applicant must demonstrate financial need.
Additional information: Must demonstrate exceptional financial need. Contact financial aid office of any New Mexico public postsecondary institution for information and application.

Amount of award:	$200-$2,500
Application deadline:	March 1
Total amount awarded:	$7,611,800

Contact:
New Mexico Commission on Higher Education
Financial Aid and Student Services
P.O. Box 15910
Santa Fe, NM 87506-5910

New Mexico Three Percent Scholarship

Type of award: Scholarship, renewable.
Intended use: For full-time or half-time undergraduate or graduate study in New Mexico. Designated institutions: New Mexico public institutions.
Eligibility: Applicant must be U.S. citizen or permanent resident residing in New Mexico.
Basis for selection: Applicant must demonstrate depth of character and leadership.
Application requirements: Transcript.
Additional information: One-third of scholarships awarded on basis of financial need. Contact school's financial aid office for details.

Application deadline:	March 1
Total amount awarded:	$3,525,700

New Mexico Vietnam Veteran's Scholarship

Type of award: Scholarship, renewable.
Intended use: For undergraduate, master's study at postsecondary institution in New Mexico. Designated institutions: Any New Mexico public institution.
Eligibility: Applicant must be U.S. citizen or permanent resident residing in New Mexico. Applicant must be veteran during Vietnam.
Application requirements: Proof of eligibility.
Additional information: Provides tuition/fees and book allowance on first come, first served basis. Eligibility must be certified by New Mexico Veterans Service Commission. Contact financial aid office of any New Mexico public postsecondary institution for information and application.

Amount of award:	$880
Application deadline:	March 1
Total amount awarded:	$105,642

Contact:
New Mexico Veteran's Service Commission
P.O. Box 2324
Santa Fe, NM 87503

New Mexico Work Study Program

Type of award: Internship, renewable.
Intended use: For full-time or half-time undergraduate or graduate study in New Mexico.
Eligibility: Applicant must be U.S. citizen or permanent resident residing in New Mexico.
Basis for selection: Applicant must demonstrate financial need.
Additional information: Limit of 20 hours per week, on-campus or off-campus in federal, state or local public agency. New Mexico residents receive state portion of funding. Contact financial aid office of any New Mexico public postsecondary institution for information and application.

Application deadline:	March 1
Total amount awarded:	$4,709,000

Contact:
New Mexico Commission on Higher Education
Financial Aid and Student Services
P.O. Box 15910
Santa Fe, NM 87506-5910

New York State Education Department

New York State Readers Aid Program

Type of award: Scholarship, renewable.
Intended use: For undergraduate, master's or doctoral study at 2-year, 4-year or graduate institution.
Eligibility: Applicant must be visually impaired or hearing impaired. Applicant must be residing in New York.
Application requirements: Proof of eligibility.
Additional information: Funds may be used for notetakers, readers, or interpreters. Applications available at degree-granting institutions.

Amount of award:	$100-$1,000
Number of awards:	700
Total amount awarded:	$300,000

Contact:
Scholarship Committee
Readers Aid Program
Room 1610, One Commerce Plaza
Albany, NY 12234

New York State Health Department

New York State Primary Care Service

Type of award: Internship, renewable.
Intended use: For undergraduate or graduate study at accredited postsecondary institution in New York.
Eligibility: Applicant must be residing in New York.
Basis for selection: Major/career interest in physician assistant; nurse practitioner; midwifery. Applicant must demonstrate high academic achievement.
   Amount of award: $7,500-$15,000
   Application deadline: April 8
Contact:
Intership Coordinator
New York State Primary Care Service Corps
Room 1602, Empire State Plaza
Albany, NY 12237
Phone: 518-473-7019

New York State Higher Education Services Corporation

City University Seek/College Discovery Program

Type of award: Scholarship.
Intended use: For undergraduate study at 2-year or 4-year institution in New York. Designated institutions: City University of New York campuses only.
Eligibility: Applicant must be U.S. citizen or permanent resident residing in New York.
Basis for selection: Applicant must demonstrate financial need.
Additional information: Available at City University of New York and community college campuses. Must be both academically and economically disadvantaged. Support services include pre-session summer program and tutoring, counseling, and special course work during academic year. Non-residents eligible to apply.
Contact:
City University of New York
Office of Admission Services
101 West 31 Street
New York, NY 10001-3503
Phone: 518-473-7087
Website: www.hesc.com

New York State Aid for Part-Time Study Program

Type of award: Scholarship, renewable.
Intended use: For less than half-time undergraduate study at accredited postsecondary institution in New York.
Eligibility: Applicant must be U.S. citizen or permanent resident residing in New York.
Basis for selection: Applicant must demonstrate financial need.
Application requirements: Proof of eligibility.
Additional information: Must fall within income limits. Campus-based program; recipients selected and award amount determined by school. Apply to financial aid office of institution.
   Amount of award: $2,000
Contact:
New York State Higher Education Services Corporation
99 Washington Avenue
Albany, NY 12255
Phone: 518-473-7087
Website: www.hesc.com

New York State Child of Correction Officer Award

Type of award: Scholarship, renewable.
Intended use: For full-time undergraduate study at accredited vocational, 2-year or 4-year institution in New York.
Eligibility: Applicant must be U.S. citizen residing in New York. Applicant's parent must have been killed or disabled in work-related accident as public safety officer.
Application requirements: Proof of eligibility.
Additional information: Parent must have been killed in line of duty.
   Amount of award: $450
   Application deadline: May 1
   Notification begins: May 1
Contact:
New York State Higher Education Services Corporation
99 Washington Avenue
Albany, NY 12255
Phone: 518-473-7087
Website: www.hesc.com

New York State Child of Veteran Award

Type of award: Scholarship.
Intended use: For full-time freshman, sophomore, junior, senior or non-degree study at 2-year or 4-year institution in New York.
Eligibility: Applicant must be residing in New York. Applicant must be child of veteran, disabled veteran or deceased veteran.
Application requirements: Proof of eligibility.
Additional information: Student's parents must have been a disabled or deaceased veteran, prisoner of war or classified as Missing In Action.
   Amount of award: $450
   Application deadline: May 1
Contact:
New York State Higher Education Services Corporation
Grants and Scholarships
99 Washington Avenue
Albany, NY 12255
Phone: 518-473-7087
Website: www.hesc.com

New York State Education Opportunity Program

Type of award: Scholarship.
Intended use: For full-time or half-time freshman, sophomore, junior or senior study at 2-year or 4-year institution in New York. Designated institutions: State University of New York colleges.
Eligibility: Applicant must be U.S. citizen or permanent resident residing in New York.
Basis for selection: Applicant must demonstrate financial need.
Additional information: Apply to campus financial aid office. Must be both academically and economically disadvantaged. Support services include pre-session summer program and tutoring, counseling, and special coursework during academic year. Non-residents eligible to apply.

New York State Higher Education Opportunity Program

Type of award: Scholarship.
Intended use: For full-time or half-time undergraduate study at 2-year or 4-year institution. Designated institutions: Private New York state institutions.
Eligibility: Applicant must be residing in New York.
Basis for selection: Applicant must demonstrate financial need.
Additional information: For use at private New York State institutions only. Apply to institution's financial aid office. Must be both academically and economically disadvantaged. Support services include pre-session summer program and tutoring, counseling, and special course work during academic year. Non-residents eligible to apply. Contact institution for application and additional information. Award amounts vary; contact sponsor for information.

New York State Memorial Scholarship for Families of Deceased Police/Firefighters

Type of award: Scholarship, renewable.
Intended use: For full-time undergraduate study at 2-year or 4-year institution in New York State.
Eligibility: Applicant must be U.S. citizen or permanent resident residing in New York. Applicant's parent must have been killed or disabled in work-related accident as fire fighter or police officer.
Application requirements: Proof of eligibility.
Additional information: Spouse and/or children of police officer/fire fighter who died as result of injuries in line of duty are eligible.
   Amount of award: $7,520-$9,710
   Application deadline: May 1
Contact:
New York State Higher Education Services Corporation
Grants and Scholarships
99 Washington Avenue
Albany, NY 12255
Phone: 518-473-7087
Website: www.hesc.com

New York State Regents Award for Children of Correction Officers

Type of award: Scholarship, renewable.
Intended use: For full-time undergraduate study at 2-year or 4-year institution in New York.
Eligibility: Applicant must be residing in New York. Applicant's parent must have been killed or disabled in work-related accident as public safety officer.
Application requirements: Proof of eligibility.
Additional information: Must be child of New York State correction officer who died as result of injuries sustained in line of duty.
   Amount of award: $450
   Application deadline: May 1
Contact:
New York State Higher Education Services Corporation
Grants and Scholarships
99 Washington Avenue
Albany, NY 12255

New York State Regents Health Care Professional Opportunity Scholarship

Type of award: Scholarship, renewable.
Intended use: For full-time first professional study at graduate institution in New York.
Eligibility: Applicant must be U.S. citizen or permanent resident residing in New York.
Basis for selection: Major/career interest in medicine (m.d.); dentistry. Applicant must demonstrate financial need.
Additional information: Underrepresented groups encouraged to apply.
   Amount of award: $1,000-$10,000
   Application deadline: March 1
Contact:
New York State Higher Education Services Corporation
Office of Postsecondary Grants
Cultural Education Center
Albany, NY 12220

New York State Robert C. Byrd Honors Scholarship

Type of award: Scholarship, renewable.
Intended use: For full-time undergraduate study at accredited 2-year or 4-year institution in United States.
Eligibility: Applicant must be high school senior. Applicant must be U.S. citizen or permanent resident residing in New York.
Basis for selection: Applicant must demonstrate high academic achievement.
Additional information: Must fall with in income limits. Submit free aplication for Federal Student Aid (FAFSA) and receive a prefilled Express TAP Application (ETA) to review, sign and return. Institution must be approved by the New York State Education Department to offer TAP eligible programs of study.
   Amount of award: $1,121
Contact:
New York State Higher Education Services Corporation
Education Building Annex
Albany, NY 12234

New York State Tuition Assistance Program

Type of award: Scholarship, renewable.
Intended use: For full-time undergraduate, graduate or non-degree study at accredited postsecondary institution in New York.
Eligibility: Applicant must be U.S. citizen or permanent resident residing in New York.
Basis for selection: Applicant must demonstrate financial need.
Application requirements: Proof of eligibility.
Additional information: Must fall with in income limits. Submit free aplication for Federal Student Aid (FAFSA) and receive a prefilled Express TAP Application (ETA) to review, sign and return. Institution must be approved by the New York State Education Department to offer TAP eligible programs of study.
    Amount of award: $75-$3,900
    Application deadline: May 1
Contact:
New York State Higher Education Services Corporation
99 Washington Avenue
Albany, NY 12255
Phone: 518-473-7087
Website: www.hesc.com

New York State Vietnam Veteran Tuition Award/Persian Gulf Veteran Award

Type of award: Scholarship, renewable.
Intended use: For undergraduate study at accredited vocational, 2-year or 4-year institution in New York.
Eligibility: Applicant must be adult returning student. Applicant must be U.S. citizen or permanent resident residing in New York. Applicant must be veteran during Persian Gulf or Vietnam. Must have served in armed forces in Indochina between December 1961 and May 1975 for VVTA. Must have served in hostilities beginning August 2, 1990 for Persian Gulf. Must have other than dishonorable discharge for either.
Application requirements: Proof of eligibility. Documentation of Indochina service.
    Amount of award: $500-$1,000
    Application deadline: May 1
Contact:
New York State Higher Education Services Corporation
99 Washington Avenue
Albany, NY 12255
Phone: 518-473-7087
Website: www.hesc.com

New York State Native American Education Unit

New York State Native American Student Aid Program

Type of award: Scholarship, renewable.
Intended use: For undergraduate study at accredited vocational, 2-year or 4-year institution in New York. Designated institutions: New York Institutions.
Eligibility: Applicant must be American Indian. Must be on official tribal roll of New York State tribe, or be child of enrolled member. Applicant must be U.S. citizen residing in New York.
Basis for selection: Applicant must demonstrate financial need.
Application requirements: Proof of eligibility. Tribal certification form, documentation of high school graduation and college acceptance letter.
Additional information: Minimum 2.0 semester GPA required. Summer application deadline May 20.
    Amount of award: $1,750
    Number of awards: 300
    Application deadline: July 15, December 31
Contact:
New York State Native American Education Unit
New York State Education Department
Room 543, Education Building
Albany, NY 12234

New York State Senate

New York State Senate Graduate/Post-Graduate Fellows Programs

Type of award: Internship.
Intended use: For full-time graduate or postgraduate study in New York.
Eligibility: Applicant must be single. Applicant must be U.S. citizen residing in New York.
Basis for selection: Applicant must demonstrate depth of character, seriousness of purpose and high academic achievement.
Application requirements: Interview, recommendations, essay, transcript and proof of eligibility.
Additional information: Students placed by the Director of the Senate Student Program and work onsite at the New York State Senate. Open to non-NY residents attending New York institutions and to NY residents, whether attending an in-state or out of state institution.
    Amount of award: $25,000
    Number of awards: 13
    Number of applicants: 120
    Application deadline: May 7
    Notification begins: July 15
Contact:
Dr. Russell J. Williams
New York State Senate
State Capitol c/o 90 South Swan Street/401
Albany, NY 12247
Phone: 518-455-2611
Fax: 518-432-5470

New York State Senate/Richard J. Ross Journalism Fellowship

Type of award: Scholarship.
Intended use: For full-time graduate or postgraduate study.

Eligibility: Applicant must be U.S. citizen residing in New York.
Basis for selection: Major/career interest in journalism; public relations; communications. Applicant must demonstrate depth of character, seriousness of purpose and high academic achievement.
Application requirements: Interview, recommendations, essay, transcript and proof of eligibility.
Additional information: College seniors with extraordinary experience in journalism may apply.

Amount of award:	$25,000
Number of awards:	1
Number of applicants:	10
Application deadline:	May 7
Notification begins:	July 15
Total amount awarded:	$25,000

Contact:
Dr. Russell J. Williams
State Capitol c/o 90 Southern St. #410
Albany, NY 12247
Phone: 518-455-2611

North Carolina Arts Council

North Carolina Community Arts Administrative Internship

Type of award: Internship.
Intended use: For non-degree study.
Basis for selection: Major/career interest in arts management.
Application requirements: Interview, recommendations and essay.
Additional information: Applicant must possess four-year college degree, have strong administrative and/or business capability, preferably demonstrated by work experience, have close familiarity with the arts, and be able to accept employment at end of program. Interns assigned to sponsoring North Carolina community arts council or cultural center for three months between September 1 and June 30. North Carolina residents preferred.

Amount of award:	$3,000
Number of awards:	4
Number of applicants:	35
Application deadline:	May 1
Notification begins:	June 15
Total amount awarded:	$12,000

Contact:
North Carolina Arts Council
Department of Cultural Resources
Raleigh, NC 27601-2807
Website: www.ncarts.org

North Carolina Botanical Garden

North Carolina Botanical Garden Internship Program

Type of award: Internship.
Intended use: For undergraduate, graduate or non-degree study.
Basis for selection: Major/career interest in horticulture; botany; forestry; environmental science.
Application requirements: Interview and essay.
Additional information: Full-time internship lasts from April 1 to October 30. Stipend of $7.50 an hour. Provides opportunity to gain experience in the maintenance of Southeastern U.S. plants and exotic species.

Amount of award:	$8,400
Application deadline:	February 14
Notification begins:	March 7

Contact:
North Carolina Botanical Garden
CB #3375 Totten Center, UNC-CH
Chapel Hill, NC 27599

North Carolina Department of Community Colleges

North Carolina Community College Scholarship

Type of award: Scholarship.
Intended use: For freshman, sophomore or non-degree study at 2-year institution in North Carolina.
Eligibility: Applicant must be residing in North Carolina.
Basis for selection: Applicant must demonstrate financial need.
Application requirements: Interview and transcript.
Additional information: High priority given to minority students. Apply to financial aid office of community college.

Amount of award:	$560
Number of awards:	600
Application deadline:	May 1
Notification begins:	August 1
Total amount awarded:	$502,600

North Carolina Community Colleges Masonry Contractors Scholarship

Type of award: Scholarship, renewable.
Intended use: For full-time freshman, sophomore or non-degree study at vocational or 2-year institution in North Carolina.
Eligibility: Applicant must be residing in North Carolina.
Basis for selection: Applicant must demonstrate financial need.
Additional information: Must enroll in degree or diploma

program at community college. Student must apply with financial aid office at institution.

Amount of award:	$750
Number of awards:	1
Total amount awarded:	$750

North Carolina Community Colleges Petroleum Marketers Association Scholarship

Type of award: Scholarship.
Intended use: For freshman, sophomore study at 2-year institution in North Carolina.
Eligibility: Applicant or parent must be employed by North Carolina Petroleum Marketers Association. Applicant must be residing in North Carolina.
Additional information: For employees and their children. Applications available at community colleges or offices of North Carolina Petroleum Marketers Association members.

Amount of award:	$500
Number of awards:	10
Number of applicants:	32
Application deadline:	July 30
Total amount awarded:	$5,000

North Carolina Community Colleges Southern Bell Telephone/Telegraph Scholarship

Type of award: Scholarship, renewable.
Intended use: For freshman, sophomore or non-degree study in North Carolina.
Eligibility: Applicant must be residing in North Carolina.
Basis for selection: Applicant must demonstrate financial need.
Additional information: Must enroll in degree or diploma program at one of 21 eligible community colleges located in Southern Bell service area. Must apply through financial aid office at institution.

Amount of award:	$500
Number of awards:	46
Total amount awarded:	$23,000

North Carolina Community Colleges Sprint College Transfer Scholarship

Type of award: Scholarship.
Intended use: For full-time freshman, sophomore study at 2-year institution in North Carolina.
Eligibility: Applicant must be residing in North Carolina.
Additional information: Must be enrolled in transfer program at community college in service area of Carolina Telephone and Telegraph Company. Apply through financial aid office of institution where enrolled. Priority given to African-American students.

Amount of award:	$500
Number of awards:	20
Total amount awarded:	$10,000

North Carolina Community Colleges Wachovia Technical Scholarship

Type of award: Scholarship.
Intended use: For full-time sophomore study at vocational or 2-year institution in North Carolina.
Eligibility: Applicant must be residing in North Carolina.
Basis for selection: Applicant must demonstrate financial need and high academic achievement.
Additional information: Must be enrolled in second year of two-year technical program. Apply through financial aid office of institution where enrolled.

Amount of award:	$500
Number of awards:	113
Total amount awarded:	$56,500

North Carolina Department of Public Instruction

North Carolina Prospective Teacher Scholarship Loan

Type of award: Loan, renewable.
Intended use: For full-time freshman, sophomore, junior or senior study at accredited vocational, 2-year or 4-year institution in North Carolina. Designated institutions: North Carolina public schools.
Eligibility: Applicant must be permanent resident residing in North Carolina.
Basis for selection: Major/career interest in education, teacher; education, special.
Application requirements: Transcript and proof of eligibility.
Additional information: One year of service in North Carolina public schools can be used for loan forgiveness for each year of financial assistance.

Amount of award:	$900-$2,500
Number of applicants:	1,127
Application deadline:	February 8
Total amount awarded:	$1,313,146

North Carolina Robert C. Byrd Honors Scholarship

Type of award: Scholarship, renewable.
Intended use: For undergraduate study in United States.
Eligibility: Applicant must be high school senior. Applicant must be U.S. citizen residing in North Carolina.
Basis for selection: Applicant must demonstrate high academic achievement.
Application requirements: Nomination by high school.
Additional information: Applications available from high school counselors in December. Minimum 3.0 GPA and SAT 1 score of 900 required.

Amount of award:	$1,110
Number of awards:	475
Number of applicants:	694
Application deadline:	February 1
Total amount awarded:	$707,070

North Carolina Teacher Assistant Scholarship Loan

Type of award: Loan, renewable.
Intended use: For less than half-time junior, senior study at 4-year institution in North Carolina.
Eligibility: Applicant must be residing in North Carolina.
Basis for selection: Major/career interest in education, teacher.
Application requirements: Recommendations and transcript. Formal admittance to teacher education program.
Additional information: Award is for part-time course of study leading to teacher certification. Must complete 12 semester hours in 12-month period. Must be employed as teacher assistant in North Carolina public school. Priority given to applicants with B.A. degree. Recommendation of district superintendent required. Loan forgiveness for teaching service in North Carolina.

Amount of award:	$1,200
Number of awards:	108
Application deadline:	January 1
Total amount awarded:	$83,500

Contact:
North Carolina Department of Public Instruction
Teacher Education
301 North Wilmington Street
Raleigh, NC 27601-2825

North Carolina Division of Veterans Affairs

North Carolina Scholarships for Children of War Veterans

Type of award: Scholarship, renewable.
Intended use: For undergraduate or graduate study at accredited postsecondary institution in North Carolina.
Eligibility: Applicant must be residing in North Carolina. Applicant must be descendant of veteran, child of veteran, disabled veteran, deceased veteran or POW/MIA who served in the Army, Air Force, Marines, Navy, Coast Guard or Reserves/National Guard.
Basis for selection: Applicant must demonstrate financial need and high academic achievement.
Application requirements: Interview, transcript and proof of eligibility. Birth certificate.
Additional information: Award is tuition waiver plus minimum room and board expenses. Parent must have been North Carolina resident at time of enlistment or child must have been born in and resided permanently in North Carolina.

Number of awards:	328
Number of applicants:	588
Application deadline:	May 31
Notification begins:	July 15
Total amount awarded:	$5,000,000

Contact:
North Carolina Division of Veterans Affairs
325 North Salisbury Street, Suite 1065
Raleigh, NC 27603

North Carolina Division of Vocational Rehabilitation Services

North Carolina Vocational Rehabilitation Award

Type of award: Scholarship, renewable.
Intended use: For full-time undergraduate study at vocational, 2-year or 4-year institution in North Carolina.
Eligibility: Applicant must be physically challenged or learning disabled. Applicant must be residing in North Carolina.
Application requirements: Interview and proof of eligibility.
Additional information: Applicants with mental disabilities also eligible.

Number of awards:	21,000
Total amount awarded:	$6,000,000

Contact:
North Carolina Division of Vocational Rehabilitation Services
P.O. Box 26053
Raleigh, NC 27611
Phone: 919-733-3364
Fax: 919-733-796

North Carolina State Education Assistance Authority

North Carolina Contractual Scholarship Fund

Type of award: Scholarship, renewable.
Intended use: For full-time or half-time undergraduate study at accredited 2-year or 4-year institution in North Carolina. Designated institutions: Private institutions.
Eligibility: Applicant must be residing in North Carolina.
Basis for selection: Applicant must demonstrate financial need.
Application requirements: Proof of eligibility.
Additional information: Theology/divinity students not eligible.

Total amount awarded:	$19,658,632

North Carolina Legislative Tuition Grant

Type of award: Scholarship, renewable.
Intended use: For full-time freshman, sophomore, junior or senior study at accredited 2-year or 4-year institution. Designated institutions: North Carolina private institutions.
Eligibility: Applicant must be permanent resident residing in North Carolina.
Application requirements: Proof of eligibility.
Additional information: Award is not applicable for theology, divinity, or religious education programs.

Amount of award:	$1,450
Number of awards:	27,275
Application deadline:	October 1
Total amount awarded:	$33,574,968

North Carolina Nurse Education Scholarship Loan

Type of award: Loan.
Intended use: For at accredited 2-year or 4-year institution in North Carolina.
Eligibility: Applicant must be U.S. citizen residing in North Carolina.
Basis for selection: Major/career interest in nursing. Applicant must demonstrate service orientation and financial need.
Application requirements: Proof of eligibility.
Additional information: Must attend specific participating North Carolina institutions. Recipient agrees to work for one year as a full-time nurse in North Carolina for each year of NESLP funding. Nontraditional students, including older individuals, ethnic minorities, male and individuals with previous careers and/or degree encouraged.

Amount of award:	$400-$5,000
Number of awards:	973
Total amount awarded:	$925,477

Contact:
Scholarship Loan Program
P.O. Box 14223
Research Triangle Park
Chapel Hill, NC 27709-1422
Website: www.ncseaa.edu

North Carolina Nurse Scholars Program

Type of award: Loan, renewable.
Intended use: For full-time freshman, sophomore, junior, senior or master's study at accredited postsecondary institution in North Carolina.
Eligibility: Applicant must be U.S. citizen residing in North Carolina.
Basis for selection: Major/career interest in nursing. Applicant must demonstrate leadership, service orientation and high academic achievement.
Application requirements: Recommendations, essay, transcript and proof of eligibility.
Additional information: Minimum 3.0 GPA required for undergraduate applicants and 3.2 for graduate applicants. Loan forgiveness for nursing service in North Carolina.

Amount of award:	$3,000-$6,000
Number of awards:	890
Number of applicants:	1,600
Application deadline:	February 15
Total amount awarded:	$3,193,000

Contact:
North Carolina Nurse Scholars Program
P.O. Box 14223
Research Triangle Park
Chapel Hill, NC 27709
Phone: 919-549-8614

North Carolina Student Loans for Health/Science/Mathematics

Type of award: Loan, renewable.
Intended use: For full-time freshman, sophomore, junior, senior, master's or first professional study at accredited postsecondary institution in North Carolina.
Eligibility: Applicant must be residing in North Carolina.
Basis for selection: Major/career interest in health-related professions; mathematics; science, general. Applicant must demonstrate financial need.
Application requirements: Transcript and proof of eligibility. FAFSA.
Additional information: Must express commitment to practice health professions or teach underserved populations in North Carolina. Loan forgiveness for service in North Carolina is one year for each year of financial assistance.

Amount of award:	$500-$8,500
Number of awards:	421
Number of applicants:	1,400
Application deadline:	April 1
Notification begins:	July 1
Total amount awarded:	$2,765,267

Contact:
North Carolina Student Loan Program
Health, Science and Mathematics
P.O. Box 20549
Raleigh, NC 27619-0549

The Governor James G. Martin College Scholarship

Type of award: Scholarship, renewable.
Intended use: For full-time freshman study at accredited 4-year institution in United States.
Eligibility: Applicant must be high school senior. Applicant must be U.S. citizen residing in North Carolina.
Additional information: The scholarship is renewable for up to five years of undergraduate study, provided the student continues to be enrolled full time, maintains at least a "C" average, and otherwise remains in good standing at an eligible school. Applications will be available in the financial aid offices of the 51 eligible institutions in North Carolina.

Amount of award:	$1,000
Number of awards:	25
Application deadline:	April 1

Contact:
North Carolina Nurse Education Scholarship Loan
Research Triangle Park
P.O. Box 14223
Chapel Hill, NC 27709
Website: www.ncseaa.edu

The North Carolina Nurse Scholars Program MasterÖs Program

Type of award: Scholarship, renewable.
Intended use: For full-time master's study at accredited graduate institution in United States. Designated institutions: Duke University; East Carolina University; University of North Carolina at Chapel Hill, School of Nursing and Public Health; University of North Carolina at Charlotte; University of North Carolina at Greensboro.

Eligibility: Applicant must be high school senior. Applicant must be U.S. citizen residing in North Carolina.
Basis for selection: Major/career interest in nursing. Applicant must demonstrate high academic achievement.
Application requirements: Transcript.
Additional information: Minimum 3.2 grade point average the last two years of an accredited BSN program (or 3.2 on the last 60 semester hours of a part-time program). Provides $6,000 per year for up to two years of Master's study, Recipient agrees to work as a Master's prepared nurse or to teach in a nurse education program in North Carolina for one year for each year of Manager, Scholarship and Grant Services-NSP funding. Recipients who withdraw from a nurse education program or who do not work or teach as an RN in North Carolina must begin cash repayment of the scholarship within 90 days.
    Amount of award: $1,000
    Application deadline: April 1
Contact:
North Carolina Nurse Education Scholarship Loan
Research Triangle Park
P.O. Box 14223
Chapel Hill, NC 27709
Website: www.ncseaa.edu

North Dakota University System

North Dakota Indian Scholarship Program

Type of award: Scholarship, renewable.
Intended use: For full-time undergraduate or graduate study.
Eligibility: Applicant must be American Indian. Must be enrolled member of an Indian tribe. Applicant must be U.S. citizen residing in North Dakota.
Basis for selection: Applicant must demonstrate financial need and high academic achievement.
Application requirements: Proof of eligibility.
    Amount of award: $700-$2,000
    Number of awards: 150
    Number of applicants: 560
    Application deadline: July 15
Contact:
Rhonda Schauer
North Dakota University System
600 East Boulevard - Dept. 215
Bismarck, ND 58505-0230

North Dakota Scholars Program

Type of award: Scholarship, renewable.
Intended use: For full-time undergraduate study at 2-year or 4-year institution in North Dakota.
Eligibility: Applicant must be high school senior. Applicant must be residing in North Dakota.
Basis for selection: Applicant must demonstrate high academic achievement.
Application requirements: Proof of eligibility.
Additional information: Must score in at least 95th percentile on ACT, rank in top fifth of class. Must maintain 3.5 GPA for renewal. The deadline for applications will be the October test date of the ACT. Contact sponsor for more information.
    Amount of award: $1,552-$2,360
    Number of awards: 50
    Number of applicants: 385
Contact:
North Dakota University System
600 East Boulevard
Bismarck, ND 58505-0230

North Dakota State Grant

Type of award: Scholarship, renewable.
Intended use: For full-time undergraduate study at vocational, 2-year or 4-year institution in North Dakota.
Eligibility: Applicant must be U.S. citizen or permanent resident residing in North Dakota.
Basis for selection: Applicant must demonstrate financial need.
Application requirements: Proof of eligibility.
    Amount of award: $600
    Number of awards: 3,700
    Number of applicants: 20,000
    Application deadline: April 15
    Total amount awarded: $2,220,000
Contact:
North Dakota University System
Student Financial Assistance Program
600 East Boulevard - Dept. 215
Bismarck, ND 58505-0230

Northern Cheyenne Tribal Education Department

Northern Cheyenne Higher Education Program

Type of award: Scholarship, renewable.
Intended use: For undergraduate study.
Eligibility: Applicant must be American Indian. Must be enrolled with the Northern Cheyenne Tribe. Applicant must be U.S. citizen.
Basis for selection: Applicant must demonstrate financial need.
Application requirements: Recommendations, essay, transcript and proof of eligibility. Northern Cheyenne Tribal Application and submit Federal Student Aid Form.
    Amount of award: $100-$6,000
    Number of awards: 70
    Number of applicants: 137
    Application deadline: March 1, October 1
    Notification begins: August 1, November 1
    Total amount awarded: $278,762
Contact:
Northern Cheyenne Tribal Education Department
Attn: Norma Bixby
Box 307
Lame Deer, MT 59043
Phone: 406-477-6602

Oak Ridge Institute for Science and Education

Alexander Hollaender Distinguished Postdoctoral Fellowship

Type of award: Internship, renewable.
Intended use: For postgraduate study in United States.
Basis for selection: Major/career interest in science, general; environmental science.
Application requirements: Recommendations, transcript and research proposal.
Additional information: Provides opportunities to participate in research in energy-related life, biomedical, and environmental sciences. Applicants must have completed Ph.D. within the last two years. Number of awards varies. Program available at: Ames Laboratory (Ames, IA), Argonne National Laboratory (Argonne, IL), Brookhaven National Laboratory (Upton, NY), Ernest Orlando Lawrence Berkeley National Laboratory (Berkeley, CA), Idaho National Engineering and Environmental Laboratory (Idaho Falls, ID), Lawrence Livermore National Laboratory (Livermore, CA), Los Alamos National Laboratory (Los Alamos, NM), Lovelace Respiratory Research Center (Albuquerque, NM), Oak Ridge National Laboratory (Oak Ridge, TN), Pacific Northwest National Laboratory (Richland, WA), Sandia National Laboratories (Albuquerque, NM and Livermore, CA); and appointment may also be served at a host laboratory under the guidance of a principal investigator who has an active research grant from the Office of Biological and Environmental Research.
   Amount of award: $37,500
   Application deadline: January 15
Contact:
Oak Ridge Institute of Science and Education
P.O. Box 117
Oak Ridge, TN 37831-0117
Website: www.orau.gov

Applied Health Physics Fellowship

Type of award: Scholarship.
Intended use: For full-time master's study at accredited graduate institution in United States.
Basis for selection: Major/career interest in engineering; mathematics; physical sciences.
Application requirements: Recommendations and transcript.
Additional information: Provides fellowships in applied health physics (radiation protection). Applicants must be pursuing mater's degrees in applied health physics at participating universities with practicums at various Department of Energy research facilities and not have completed more than one full-time academic term (semester or quarter) of graduate school (regardless of major) at the time of application, or have completed no more than one academic year of full-time graduate study when the Fellowhsip begins. Number of awards varies. No application will be reviewed without official GRE scores. $14,400 stipend; additional $300 per month during practicum; tuition and fees up to $9,000 per year. Recipient required to spend one year of full-time employment as a Department of Energy federal or contractor employee for each academic year of fellowship support.
   Amount of award: $47,700
   Application deadline: January 30
Contact:
Oak Ridge Institute of Science and Education
P.O. Box 117
Oak Ridge, TN 37831-0117
Website: www.orau.gov

Fossil Energy Technology Internship

Type of award: Internship.
Intended use: For freshman, sophomore study at accredited 2-year institution in United States. Designated institutions: Federal Energy Technology Center (Pittsburgh, PA., and Morgantown, WV).
Eligibility: Applicant must be U.S. citizen.
Basis for selection: Major/career interest in chemistry; computer and information sciences; engineering; mathematics; physics.
Application requirements: Recommendations and transcript.
Additional information: Minimum GPA 2.5. Provides opportunities to participate in fossil energy-related research. Three to 18 months in summer. Weekly stipend of $275 to $300; limited travel reimbursement (round-trip transportation expenses between facility and home or campus); off-campus tuition and fees if required by the home institution.
   Amount of award: $3,300-$23,400
   Number of awards: 5
Contact:
Fossil Energy Technology Internship
MS 36, Education Training Division
P.O. Box 117
Oak Ridge, TN 37831-0117
Website: www.orau.gov

Industrial Hygiene Graduate Fellowship Program

Type of award: Scholarship.
Intended use: For full-time master's study at accredited graduate institution in United States.
Eligibility: Applicant must be U.S. citizen.
Application requirements: Recommendations and transcript.
Additional information: Provides fellowships in industrial hygiene. Applicants must hold baccalaureate degree in physical sciences, life or health sciences, environmental sciences, or engineering. Program available at participating universities with practicums at various Department of Energy research facilities must not have completed more than one year (if currently enrolled in gradaute school) at the time the appointment becomes effective (normally in September). Number of awards varies. No application will be reviewed without official GRE scores. $15,600 stipend ($1,300 monthly); additional $400 monthly during practicum. Recipients are subject to a service obligation of year of full-time employment in a Department of Energy facility for each academic year of fellowship award, commencing immediately following the fellowship appointment.
   Amount of award: $28,200
   Application deadline: January 30
Contact:
Oak Ridge Institute of Science and Education
P.O. Box 117
Oak Ridge, TN 37831-0117
Website: www.orau.gov

Law Internship Program

Type of award: Internship.
Intended use: For first professional study at accredited graduate institution in United States. Designated institutions: Oak Ridge National Laboratory (Oak Ridge, TN.), Savannah River Site (Aiken, SC).
Eligibility: Applicant must be U.S. citizen or permanent resident.
Basis for selection: Major/career interest in law.
Application requirements: Recommendations and transcript.
Additional information: Provides opportunities to participate in research on legal aspects of energy-related techniques and procedures, national energy-related problems and efforts related to their solutions. U.S. citizens and permanent residents may work at Oak Ridge National Laboratory. Only U.S. citizens may work at the Savannah River Site. Three-month summer appointments; some appointments during the academic year. Weekly stipend of $465 to $490; limited travel reimbursement (round-trip transportation expenses between facility and home or campus). Must have completed first year of law school.
   Amount of award: $5,580-$5,880
   Application deadline: February 15
Contact:
Intership Coordinator
MS 36, Education Training Division
P.O. Box 117
Oak Ridge, TN 37831-0117
Website: www.orau.gov

Oak Ridge Institute for Science and Education Energy Research Undergraduate Laboratory Fellowship

Type of award: Internship.
Intended use: For full-time sophomore, junior or senior study at accredited 4-year institution in United States. Designated institutions: Ames Laboratory (Ames, Iowa); Argonne Laboratory (Argonne, Ill.); Brookhaven National Laboratory (Uptown, N.Y.); Ernest Orlando Lawrence Berkeley National Laboratory (Berkeley, Calif.); Fermi National Accelerator Laboratory (Batavia, Ill.); National Renewable Energy Laboratory (Golden, Colo.); Oak Ridge National Laboratory (Oak Ridge, Tenn.); Pacific Northwest National Laboratory (Richland, Wash.); Princeton Plasma Physics Laboratory (Princeton, N.J.); Stanford Linear Accelerator Center (Stanford, Calif.); Thomas Jefferson National Accelerator Laboratory (Newport News, Va.).
Eligibility: Applicant must be African American. Applicant must be U.S. citizen or permanent resident.
Basis for selection: Major/career interest in geology/earth sciences; ecology; engineering; computer and information sciences; physical sciences; life sciences.
Application requirements: Recommendations and transcript.
Additional information: Provides opportunities to participate in research relating to energy production, use, conservation, and societal implications. Ten-week summer appointments or 16-week fall semester appointments. Weekly stipend of $300; limited travel reimbursement (round-trip transportation expenses between facility and home or campus).
   Amount of award: $3,000-$4,800
   Application deadline: March 16, March 31
Contact:
Oak Ridge Institute for Science and Technology
P.O.Box 117
Oak Ridge, TN 37831-0117
Website: www.orau.gov

Oak Ridge Institute for Science and Education Fossil Energy Postgraduate Research

Type of award: Internship, renewable.
Intended use: For postgraduate study in United States. Designated institutions: Federal Energy Technology Center (Pittsburgh, PA and Morgantown, WV).
Eligibility: Applicant must be U.S. citizen.
Basis for selection: Major/career interest in science, general; engineering; computer and information sciences; mathematics; physical sciences.
Application requirements: Recommendations and transcript.
Additional information: Provides opportunities to participate in research in advanced fossil energy technologies and procedures. Applicants must have completed graduate degree within the last three years. Number of awards varies. Stipend based on research area and degree; limited reimbursement for inbound travel and moving.
   Application deadline: February 1
Contact:
Oak Ridge Institute of Science and Education
P.O. Box 117
Oak Ridge, TN 37831-0117
Website: www.orau.gov

Oak Ridge Institute for Science and Education Fusion Energy Postdoctoral Research

Type of award: Internship, renewable.
Intended use: For postgraduate study in United States.
Eligibility: Applicant must be U.S. citizen.
Basis for selection: Major/career interest in science, general; engineering; nuclear science.
Application requirements: Recommendations and transcript.
Additional information: Provides opportunities to participate in fusion energy research and development programs. Applicants must have completed doctoral degree within the last three years. Number of awards varies. Limited reimbursement for inbound travel and moving.
   Amount of award: $42,000
   Application deadline: February 1
Contact:
Oak Ridge Institute of Science and Education
P.O. Box 117
Oak Ridge, TN 37831-0117
Website: www.orau.gov

Oak Ridge Institute for Science and Education Historically Black Building Technology Summer Research Participation

Type of award: Internship.
Intended use: For full-time junior, senior study at accredited 4-year institution in United States. Designated institutions: Oak Ridge National Laboratory, Energy Division, Efficiency and Renewables Research Section (Oak Ridge, TN).
Eligibility: Applicant must be U.S. citizen or permanent resident.
Basis for selection: Major/career interest in physics; engineering; engineering, chemical; engineering, environmental; engineering, mechanical.
Application requirements: Recommendations and transcript.
Additional information: Minimum GPA 2.5. Provides opportunities for students from historically Black colleges and universities to participate in research on energy-related construction technologies. Ten to 12 weeks in summer. Stipend of $1,100 per month for juniors and $1,200 per month for seniors.
   Amount of award: $3,300-$3,600
   Application deadline: February 28
Contact:
Historically Black Colleges and Universities Building Technology Summer Research Participation
MS 36, Education Training Division
P.O. Box 117
Oak Ridge, TN 37831-0117
Website: www.orau.gov

Oak Ridge Institute for Science and Education Historically Black Colleges Nuclear Energy Training Program

Type of award: Scholarship, renewable.
Intended use: For full-time junior, senior study at accredited 4-year institution in United States. Designated institutions: Howard University (Washington, DC), North Carolina A&T State University, Lincoln University (PA), Virginia State University, South Carolina State University, Tennessee State University.
Eligibility: Applicant must be U.S. citizen or permanent resident.
Basis for selection: Major/career interest in nuclear science; engineering, electrical and electronic; engineering, mechanical; physics; chemistry.
Additional information: Provides competitive scholarships for study and research careers in nuclear energy-related technologies, including an off-campus research opportunity at a DOE-designated laboratory and a training institute at ORISE. Tuition and fees up to $9,600 per year in stipends; dislocation allowance during summer research appointment.
   Amount of award: $9,600
Contact:
Oak Ridge Institute of Science and Education
P.O. Box 117
Oak Ridge, TN 37831-0117
Website: www.orau.gov

Oak Ridge Institute for Science and Education Historically Black Nuclear Energy Training Program

Type of award: Internship.
Intended use: For full-time junior, senior study at 4-year institution in or outside United States. Designated institutions: Howard University (Washington, D.C.), North Carolina A&T State University, Lincoln University (Pa.), Virginia State University, South Carolina State University, Tennessee State University, and Virginia State University.
Eligibility: Applicant must be U.S. citizen or permanent resident.
Basis for selection: Major/career interest in nuclear science; engineering, electrical and electronic; engineering, mechanical; physics; chemistry; engineering; science, general.
Application requirements: Proof of health coverage.
Additional information: Provides competitive scholarships for study and research careers in nuclear energy-related technologies, including an off-campus research opportunity at a DOE-designated laboratory and a training institute at ORISE. Paid tuition and fees, up to $9,600 per year in stipends. Dislocation allowance during summer research appointment
   Amount of award: $9,600
   Application deadline: February 28
Contact:
Program Manager:Historically Black Colleges And Universities Nuclear Energy Training Program
P.O. Box 117
Oak Ridge, TN 37831-0117
Website: www.orau.gov

Oak Ridge Institute for Science and Education Magnetic Fusion Energy Technology Fellowship

Type of award: Research grant.
Intended use: For master's, doctoral study at accredited graduate institution in United States.
Eligibility: Applicant must be U.S. citizen.
Basis for selection: Major/career interest in engineering; physical sciences; mathematics; engineering, nuclear.
Application requirements: Recommendations and transcript.
Additional information: Offers fellowships for graduate work in magnetic fusion energy technology; application is usually made before receiving the bachelor's degree or during the first year of graduate school. $15,600 stipend, additional $200 per month during practicum, tuition and fees, some travel expenses. Deadline: last Monday in January.
Contact:
Magnetic Fusion Energy Technology Fellowship Program
P.O. Box 117
Oak Ridge, TN 37831-0117
Website: www.orau.gov

Oak Ridge Institute for Science and Education Magnetic Fusion Science Fellowship

Type of award: Research grant, renewable.
Intended use: For full-time master's study at accredited graduate institution in United States.

199

Eligibility: Applicant must be U.S. citizen or permanent resident. Applicant must be disabled while on duty.
Basis for selection: Major/career interest in engineering, nuclear; science, general; mathematics; environmental science. Applicant must demonstrate seriousness of purpose and high academic achievement.
Application requirements: Recommendations, essay, transcript, proof of eligibility and research proposal.
Additional information: Provides fellowships for graduate work in magnetic fusion energy technology. Application is usually made before receiving the bachelor's degree or during the first year of graduate school. Award provides 15,600 stipend; additional $200 per month during practicum, tuition and fees. Some travel expenses, access to study and research at Department of Energy laboratories. Renewable for up to four years. Must be working toward Ph.D.

Amount of award:	$15,600
Application deadline:	January 25
Notification begins:	May 1

Contact:
U.S. Department of Energy-ORISE
Education and Training Division
100 Mitchell Road
Oak Ridge, TN 37831-0117

Oak Ridge Institute for Science and Education National Library of Medicine Associate Fellowship

Type of award: Internship.
Intended use: For master's study in United States.
Eligibility: Applicant must be U.S. citizen.
Basis for selection: Major/career interest in library science.
Application requirements: Recommendations and transcript.
Additional information: Provides a one-year postgraduate training fellowship to prepare librarians for future leadership roles in health science libraries. Applicants must have an ALA accredited master's degree.

Amount of award:	$31,630
Number of awards:	6
Application deadline:	February 1

Contact:
Oak Ridge Institute of Science and Education
P.O. Box 117
Oak Ridge, TN 37831-0117
Website: www.orau.gov

Oak Ridge Institute for Science and Education National Oceanic and Atmospheric Administration Student Program

Type of award: Internship.
Intended use: For undergraduate or graduate study at 2-year, 4-year or graduate institution in United States.
Eligibility: Applicant must be U.S. citizen or permanent resident.
Basis for selection: Major/career interest in science, general; mathematics; engineering; physical sciences.
Additional information: Ten week Summer Internship. Weekly stipend of $300 to $500, depending on academic classification; limited travel reimbursement (round-trip

Amount of award:	$3,000-$5,000

Contact:
Oak Ridge Institute of Science and Education
P.O. Box 117
Oak Ridge, TN 37831-0117
Website: www.orau.gov

Oak Ridge Institute for Science and Education Nuclear Engineering Health Physics Fellowship

Type of award: Research grant, renewable.
Intended use: For full-time master's, doctoral study at accredited graduate institution in United States.
Eligibility: Applicant must be U.S. citizen or permanent resident.
Basis for selection: Major/career interest in engineering, nuclear; health sciences; physics; nuclear science. Applicant must demonstrate seriousness of purpose and high academic achievement.
Application requirements: Recommendations, essay, transcript and research proposal.
Additional information: offers fellowships master's or doctoral study in nuclear science and engineering and health physics; application usually made during the senior year of undergraduate school or during the first semester of graduate school; applicants may not have completed more than one-year or full-time graduate work by the time a fellowship appointment begins. $14,400 stipend; additional $300 per month during practicum; some travel expenses; tuition and fees Renewable for up to four years. Deadline: last Monday in January.
Contact:
ORISE
Oak Ridge Institute for Science and Education
P.O. Box 117
Oak Ridge, TN 37831-0117
Website: www.orau.gov

Oak Ridge Institute for Science and Education Oak Ridge National Laboratory Postdoctoral Research

Type of award: Internship, renewable.
Intended use: For postgraduate study in United States.
Eligibility: Applicant must be U.S. citizen.
Basis for selection: Major/career interest in engineering; environmental science; mathematics; physical sciences; science, general.
Application requirements: Recommendations and transcript.
Additional information: Provides opportunities to participate in research in a broad range of science and engineering activities related to basic sciences, energy, and the environment. Applicants must have completed doctoral degree within the last five years; others considered on a case-by-case basis. Number of awards varies. Stipend based on research area and degree; limited reimbursement for inbound travel and moving.
Contact:
Oak Ridge Institute of Science and Education
P.O. Box 117
Oak Ridge, TN 37831-0117
Website: www.orau.gov

Oak Ridge Institute for Science and Education Office of Biological and Environmental Research Historically Black Colleges and Universities Student Research Participation

Type of award: Internship.
Intended use: For freshman, sophomore, junior, senior or graduate study at accredited 4-year or graduate institution in United States. Designated institutions: Ames Laboratory (Ames, IA), Argonne National Laboratory (Argonne, IL), Brookhaven National Laboratory (Upton, NY), Lawrence Berkeley National Laboratory (Berkeley,CA), Lawrence Livermore National Laboratory (Livermore, CA.), Los Alamos National Laboratory (Los Alamos, NM), Oak Ridge National Laboratory (Oak Ridge, TN), Pacific Northwest National Laboratory (Richland, WA), Savannah River Site (Aiken, SC.), Oak Ridge Institute for Science and Education (Oak Ridge, TN), Savannah River Ecology Laboratory (Aiken, SC.).
Eligibility: Applicant must be U.S. citizen or permanent resident.
Basis for selection: Major/career interest in biology; environmental science; science, general.
Application requirements: Recommendations and transcript.
Additional information: Open to undergraduate and graduate students from historically black colleges and universities. Provides opportunities to participate in research relating to health and the environment. Ten- week Summer Internship. Stipend of $250 per week for undergraduate students, $1,800 per month stipend for graduate students. Limited travel reimbursement (round-trip transportation expenses between facility and home or campus. Deadline is usually third Tuesday in January. Contact sponsor for specific date.
   Amount of award: $2,500-$3,600
Contact:
Office of Biological and Environmental Research Historically Black Colleges and Universities Student Research Participation
MS 36, Education Training Division
P.O. Box 117
Oak Ridge, TN 37831
Website: www.orau.gov

Oak Ridge Institute for Science and Education Office of Civilian Radioactive Waste Management Historically Black Colleges and Universities Undergraduate Scholarship Program

Type of award: Scholarship.
Intended use: For junior study at accredited 4-year institution in United States. Designated institutions: Historically Black Colleges and Universities.
Eligibility: Applicant must be African American. Applicant must be U.S. citizen or permanent resident.
Basis for selection: Major/career interest in science, general; mathematics; social and behavioral sciences; engineering.
Additional information: Provides scholarships and practicum experience for students from historically black colleges and universities. Tuition and fees paid to maximum $8,000. Monthly stipend of $600.
   Amount of award: $8,000
   Number of awards: 10
   Application deadline: January 1
Contact:
Oak Ridge Institute of Science and Education
P.O. Box 117
Oak Ridge, TN 37831-0117
Phone: 423-576-9272
Website: www.orau.gov

Oak Ridge Institute for Science and Education Office of Fossil Energy Historically Black Colleges and Universities Student Research Participation

Type of award: Internship.
Intended use: For full-time sophomore, junior study at accredited 4-year or graduate institution in United States. Designated institutions: Federal Energy Technology Center.
Eligibility: Applicant must be African American. Applicant must be U.S. citizen.
Basis for selection: Major/career interest in engineering; physical sciences; geology/earth sciences.
Application requirements: Proof of health coverage.
Additional information: Provides opportunities for students from historically black colleges a three-month summer internship participating in ongoing fossil energy research and development. Weekly stipend of $225 to $250 for sophomores, juniors, and seniors; $1,600 per month for graduate students.
   Amount of award: $2,700-$4,800
   Application deadline: February 28
Contact:
Office of Fossil Energy Historically Black Colleges and Universities Student Research Participation
MS 36, Education Training Division MS 36, Education Training Division
P.O. Box 117
Oak Ridge, TN
Website: www.orau.gov

Oak Ridge Institute for Science and Education Office of Nuclear Energy Undergraduate Scholarship

Type of award: Scholarship, renewable.
Intended use: For full-time junior, senior study at accredited 4-year institution in United States.
Eligibility: Applicant must be U.S. citizen or permanent resident.
Basis for selection: Major/career interest in engineering, nuclear.
Additional information: Open to students majoring in or receiving a concentration in nuclear engineering; students should be planning to attend graduate school in nuclear engineering.

Amount of award: $2,000
Application deadline: January 1
Contact:
Project Manager
P.O. Box 117
Oak Ridge, TN 37831-0117
Website: www.orau.gov

Oak Ridge Institute for Science and Education Postgraduate Environmental Management Participation at the U.S. Army Environmental Center

Type of award: Internship, renewable.
Intended use: For graduate study in United States. Designated institutions: U.S. Army Environmental Center (Aberdeen Proving Ground, MD).
Eligibility: Applicant must be U.S. citizen.
Basis for selection: Major/career interest in engineering; environmental science; health sciences; physical sciences.
Application requirements: Recommendations and transcript.
Additional information: Provides opportunities to participate in research in environmental programs involving restoration, compliance, conservation, pollution prevention, validation, demonstration, transfer, quality assurance and quality control, training, information management and reporting, and related resource management and planning. Applicants must have completed bachelor's or graduate degree within the last three years; others considered on a case-by-case basis. Number of awards varies. Stipend based on research area and degree; limited reimbursement for inbound travel and moving.
Contact:
Oak Ridge Institute of Science and Education
P.O. Box 117
Oak Ridge, TN 37831-0117
Website: www.orau.gov

Oak Ridge Institute for Science and Education Postgraduate Internship at the Office of Ground Water and Drinking Water

Type of award: Internship, renewable.
Intended use: For graduate study in United States. Designated institutions: Office of Ground Water and Drinking Water (Cincinnati, OH).
Eligibility: Applicant must be U.S. citizen.
Basis for selection: Major/career interest in engineering; environmental science; physical sciences.
Application requirements: Recommendations and transcript.
Additional information: Provides opportunities to participate in studies related to development and implementation of drinking water regulations. Applicants must have completed bachelor's or graduate degree within the last three years; others considered on a case-by-case basis. Number of awards varies. Stipend based on research area and degree; limited reimbursement for inbound travel and moving.
Contact:
Oak Ridge Institute of Science and Education
P.O. Box 117
Oak Ridge, TN 37831-0117
Website: www.orau.gov

Oak Ridge Institute for Science and Education Postgraduate Internship at the U.S. Army Center for Health Promotion and Preventive Medicine

Type of award: Research grant, renewable.
Intended use: For graduate study. Designated institutions: Aberdeen Proving Ground, Maryland.
Eligibility: Applicant must be U.S. citizen.
Basis for selection: Major/career interest in environmental science; engineering; science, general; medicine (m.d.).
Application requirements: Recommendations and transcript.
Additional information: Provides opportunities to participate in applied clinical research in such areas as environmental health, engineering, entomology, ionizing and nonionizing radiation, occupational and environmental health, industrial hygiene and worksite hazards, environmental sanitation and hygiene, and laboratory services. Applicants must have completed bachelor's or graduate degree within the last three years; others considered on a case-by-case basis. Number of awards varies. Stipend based on research area and degree; limited reimbursement for inbound travel and moving.
Contact:
Project Manager
P.O. Box 117
Oak Ridge, TN 37831-0117
Website: www.orau.gov

Oak Ridge Institute for Science and Education Postgraduate Research at the Agency for Toxic Substances and Disease Registry

Type of award: Internship, renewable.
Intended use: For postgraduate study in United States. Designated institutions: Agency for Toxic Substances and Disease Registry (Atlanta, GA).
Eligibility: Applicant must be U.S. citizen.
Basis for selection: Major/career interest in public health; epidemiology; medicine (m.d.).
Application requirements: Recommendations and transcript.
Additional information: Provides opportunities to participate in research in exposure and disease registries, health investigations, public health assessments, toxicological profiles, emergency response, and health education. Applicants must have completed graduate degree within the last three years; others considered on a case-by-case basis. Number of awards varies. Stipend based on research area and degree; limited reimbursement for inbound travel and moving.
Contact:
Oak Ridge Institute of Science and Education
P.O. Box 117
Oak Ridge, TN 37831-0117
Website: www.orau.gov

Oak Ridge Institute for Science and Education Postgraduate Research at the Center for Biologics Evaluation and Research

Type of award: Internship, renewable.
Intended use: For postgraduate study in United States.

Designated institutions: Center for Biologics Evaluation and Research (Rockville, MD).
Eligibility: Applicant must be U.S. citizen.
Basis for selection: Major/career interest in bioengineering; life sciences; physical sciences.
Application requirements: Recommendations and transcript.
Additional information: Provides opportunities to participate in research concerning biologics. Applicants must have completed graduate degree within the last three years; others considered on a case-by-case basis. Number of awards varies. Stipend based on research area and degree; limited reimbursement for inbound travel and moving.
Contact:
Oak Ridge Institute of Science and Education
P.O. Box 117
Oak Ridge, TN 37831-0117
Website: www.orau.gov

Oak Ridge Institute for Science and Education Postgraduate Research at the Center for Devices and Radiological Health

Type of award: Internship, renewable.
Intended use: For graduate study in United States. Designated institutions: Center for Devices and Radiological Health (Rockville, MD).
Eligibility: Applicant must be U.S. citizen.
Basis for selection: Major/career interest in epidemiology; engineering; medical specialties/research; physics; medicine (m.d.).
Application requirements: Recommendations and transcript.
Additional information: Provides opportunities to participate in research concerning medical devices and radiation emissions from electronic products. Applicants must have completed bachelor's or graduate degree within the last three years; others considered on a case-by-case basis. Number of awards varies. Stipend based on research area and degree; limited reimbursement for inbound travel and moving.
Contact:
Oak Ridge Institute of Science and Education
P.O. Box 117
Oak Ridge, TN 37831-0117
Website: www.orau.gov

Oak Ridge Institute for Science and Education Postgraduate Research at the Center for Drug Evaluation and Research

Type of award: Internship, renewable.
Intended use: For graduate study in United States. Designated institutions: Center for Drug Evaluation and Research (Rockville, MD).
Eligibility: Applicant must be U.S. citizen.
Basis for selection: Major/career interest in bioengineering; medicine (m.d.); physical sciences.
Application requirements: Recommendations and transcript.
Additional information: Provides opportunities to participate in drug research. Applicants must have completed bachelor's or graduate degree within the last three years; others considered on a case-by-case basis. Number of awards varies.

Stipend based on research area and degree; limited reimbursement for inbound travel and moving.
Contact:
Oak Ridge Institute of Science and Education
P.O. Box 117
Oak Ridge, TN 37831-0117
Website: www.orau.gov

Oak Ridge Institute for Science and Education Postgraduate Research at the Centers for Disease Control and Prevention

Type of award: Internship, renewable.
Intended use: For graduate study in United States.
Eligibility: Applicant must be U.S. citizen.
Basis for selection: Major/career interest in communications; economics; environmental science; epidemiology; health sciences; physical sciences.
Application requirements: Recommendations and transcript.
Additional information: Provides opportunities to conduct research on infectious diseases. Applicants must have completed bachelor's or graduate degree within the last three years; others considered on a case-by-case basis. Number of awards varies. Stipend based on research area and degree; limited reimbursement for inbound travel and moving. Program administered at Division of AIDS, Sexually Transmitted Diseases, and Tuberculosis Laboratory Research, Division of Environmental Health Laboratory Sciences, Division of Media and Training Services, Division of Mycotic and Bacterial Diseases, Division of Prevention Research and Analytic Methods, Division of Sexually Transmitted Diseases and Prevention, Division of Viral and Rickettsial Diseases, Atlanta, GA and National Institute for Occupational Safety and Health Atlanta, GA; Cincinnati, OH; Morgantown, WV; Washington, D.C. Applications accepted on year-round basis except for the Division of Prevention Research and Analytic Methods-- contact sponsor for deadline.
Contact:
Oak Ridge Institute of Science and Education
P.O. Box 117
Oak Ridge, TN 37831-0117
Website: www.orau.gov

Oak Ridge Institute for Science and Education Postgraduate Research at the Department of Veterans Affairs, Birmingham Education Center

Type of award: Internship, renewable.
Intended use: For undergraduate study in United States. Designated institutions: Department of Veterans Affairs, Birmingham Education Center (Birmingham, AL).
Eligibility: Applicant must be U.S. citizen.
Basis for selection: Major/career interest in science, general; education; military science.
Application requirements: Recommendations and transcript.
Additional information: Provides opportunities to participate in research supportive of military training, education efforts and related issues. Applicants must have completed bachelor's or graduate degree within the last three years; others

considered on a case-by-case basis. Number of awards varies. Stipend based on research area and degree; limited reimbursement for inbound travel and moving.
Contact:
Oak Ridge Institute of Science and Education
P.O. Box 117
Oak Ridge, TN 37831-0117
Website: www.orau.gov

Oak Ridge Institute for Science and Education Postgraduate Research at the National Center for Toxicological Research

Type of award: Internship, renewable.
Intended use: For graduate study in United States. Designated institutions: National Center for Toxicological Research (Jefferson, AK).
Eligibility: Applicant must be U.S. citizen.
Basis for selection: Major/career interest in science, general; biology; chemistry; computer and information sciences; mathematics; medicine (m.d.).
Application requirements: Recommendations and transcript.
Additional information: Provides opportunities to participate in research on biological effects of potentially toxic chemicals and solutions to toxicology problems that have a major impact on human health and the environment. Applicants must have completed bachelor's or graduate degree within the last three years; others considered on a case-by-case basis. Number of awards varies. Stipend based on research area and degree; limited reimbursement for inbound travel and moving.
Contact:
Oak Ridge Institute of Science and Education
P.O. Box 117
Oak Ridge, TN 37831-0117
Website: www.orau.gov

Oak Ridge Institute for Science and Education Postgraduate Research at the National Exposure Research Laboratory

Type of award: Internship, renewable.
Intended use: For graduate study in United States. Designated institutions: National Risk Management Research Laboratory (Cincinnati, OH).
Eligibility: Applicant must be U.S. citizen.
Basis for selection: Major/career interest in science, general; engineering; environmental science; physical sciences.
Application requirements: Recommendations and transcript.
Additional information: Applicants must have completed bachelor's or graduate degree within the last three years; others considered on a case-by-case basis. Number of awards varies. Stipend based on research area and degree; limited reimbursement for inbound travel and moving.
Contact:
Oak Ridge Institute of Science and Education
P.O. Box 117
Oak Ridge, TN 37831-0117
Website: www.orau.gov

Oak Ridge Institute for Science and Education Postgraduate Research at the National Risk Management Research Laboratory

Type of award: Internship, renewable.
Intended use: For graduate study in United States. Designated institutions: National Risk Management Research Laboratory (Cincinnati, OH).
Eligibility: Applicant must be U.S. citizen.
Basis for selection: Major/career interest in science, general; engineering; environmental science; political science/government.
Application requirements: Recommendations and transcript.
Additional information: Provides opportunities to participate in research related to environmental and physical sciences concerns. Applicants must have completed bachelor's or graduate degree within the last three years; others considered on a case-by-case basis. Number of awards varies. Stipend based on research area and degree; limited reimbursement for inbound travel and moving.
Contact:
Oak Ridge Institute of Science and Education
P.O. Box 117
Oak Ridge, TN 37831-0117
Website: www.orau.gov

Oak Ridge Institute for Science and Education Postgraduate Research at the Oak Ridge National Laboratory

Type of award: Internship, renewable.
Intended use: For postgraduate study in United States.
Eligibility: Applicant must be U.S. citizen.
Basis for selection: Major/career interest in computer and information sciences; engineering; environmental science; mathematics; physical sciences.
Application requirements: Recommendations and transcript.
Additional information: Provides opportunities to participate in a broad range of energy research and engineering activities. Applicants must have completed graduate degree within the last three years. Number of awards varies. Stipend based on research area and degree; limited reimbursement for inbound travel and moving.
Contact:
Oak Ridge Institute of Science and Education
P.O. Box 117
Oak Ridge, TN 37831-0117
Website: www.orau.gov

Oak Ridge Institute for Science and Education Postgraduate Research at the Savanah River Site

Type of award: Internship, renewable.
Intended use: For postgraduate study in United States. Designated institutions: Savannah River Site (Aiken, SC).
Eligibility: Applicant must be U.S. citizen.
Basis for selection: Major/career interest in engineering, ceramic; geology/earth sciences; engineering, materials.
Application requirements: Recommendations and transcript.
Additional information: Provides opportunities to participate

in research that complements ongoing Savannah River research projects. Number of awards varies. Stipend based on research area and degree; limited reimbursement for inbound travel and moving. Immediate need for applicants.
Contact:
Oak Ridge Institute of Science and Education
P.O. Box 117
Oak Ridge, TN 37831-0117
Website: www.orau.gov

Oak Ridge Institute for Science and Education Postgraduate Research at the St. Louis District, U.S. Army Corps of Engineers

Type of award: Internship, renewable.
Intended use: For graduate study in United States. Designated institutions: St. Louis District, U.S. Army Corps of Engineers (St. Louis, MO).
Eligibility: Applicant must be U.S. citizen.
Basis for selection: Major/career interest in science, general; engineering; environmental science; physical sciences.
Application requirements: Recommendations and transcript.
Additional information: Provides opportunities to participate in research in applied anthropology including research concerning federal legislation and American archaeology; the history and status of collections curation at the national, regional, and Army installation levels; and the developing role of Native Americans, Hawaiians, and Alaskans in federal legislation. Applicants must have completed bachelor's or graduate degree within the last three years; others considered on a case-by-case basis. Number of awards varies. Stipend based on research area and degree; limited reimbursement for inbound travel and moving.
Contact:
Oak Ridge Institute of Science and Education
P.O. Box 117
Oak Ridge, TN 37831-0117
Website: www.orau.gov

Oak Ridge Institute for Science and Education Postgraduate Research at the U.S. Army Aviation and Troop Command

Type of award: Internship, renewable.
Intended use: For graduate study in United States. Designated institutions: U.S. Army Aviation and Troop Command (St. Louis, MO).
Eligibility: Applicant must be U.S. citizen.
Basis for selection: Major/career interest in science, general; engineering; environmental science.
Application requirements: Recommendations and transcript.
Additional information: Provides opportunities to participate in research related to aviation systems; safety, electrical and software engineering; and health physics. Applicants must have completed bachelor's or graduate degree within the last three years. Number of awards varies. Stipend based on research area and degree; limited reimbursement for inbound travel and moving.
Contact:
Oak Ridge Institute of Science and Education
P.O. Box 117
Oak Ridge, TN 37831-0117
Website: www.orau.gov

Oak Ridge Institute for Science and Education Postgraduate Research at the U.S. Army Construction Engineering Research Laboratory

Type of award: Internship, renewable.
Intended use: For graduate study in United States. Designated institutions: U.S. Army Construction Engineering Research Laboratory (Champaign, IL).
Eligibility: Applicant must be U.S. citizen.
Basis for selection: Major/career interest in science, general; engineering; environmental science.
Application requirements: Recommendations and transcript.
Additional information: Provides opportunities to participate in research supportive of military construction, environmental efforts and related issues. Applicants must have completed bachelor's or graduate degree within the last three years. Number of awards varies. Stipend based on research area and degree; limited reimbursement for inbound travel and moving.
Contact:
Oak Ridge Institute of Science and Education
P.O. Box 117
Oak Ridge, TN 37831-0117
Website: www.orau.gov

Oak Ridge Institute for Science and Education Postgraduate Research at the U.S. Army Depot, Anniston

Type of award: Internship, renewable.
Intended use: For graduate study in United States. Designated institutions: U.S. Army Depot (Anniston, AL).
Eligibility: Applicant must be U.S. citizen.
Basis for selection: Major/career interest in science, general; engineering; environmental science.
Application requirements: Recommendations and transcript.
Additional information: Provides opportunities to participate in research supportive of military environmental efforts and related issues. Applicants must have completed bachelor's or graduate degree within the last three years; others considered on a case-by-case basis. Number of awards varies. Stipend based on research area and degree; limited reimbursement for inbound travel and moving.
Contact:
Oak Ridge Institute of Science and Education
P.O. Box 117
Oak Ridge, TN 37831-0117
Website: www.orau.gov

Oak Ridge Institute for Science and Education Postgraduate Research at the U.S. Army Directorate of Environment-Fort McClellan

Type of award: Internship, renewable.
Intended use: For graduate study in United States. Designated institutions: U.S. Army Directorate of Environment-Fort McClellan (AL).
Eligibility: Applicant must be U.S. citizen.
Basis for selection: Major/career interest in biology; science, general; computer and information sciences; engineering; environmental science; physical sciences.

Application requirements: Recommendations and transcript.
Additional information: Provides opportunities to participate in research on cultural resources, natural resources, geographical information systems, and environmental fields. Applicants must have completed bachelor's or graduate degree within the last three years; others considered on a case-by-case basis. Number of awards varies. Stipend based on research area and degree; limited reimbursement for inbound travel and moving.
Contact:
Oak Ridge Institute of Science and Education
P.O. Box 117
Oak Ridge, TN 37831-0117
Website: www.orau.gov

Oak Ridge Institute for Science and Education Postgraduate Research at the U.S. Army Edgewood Research

Type of award: Internship, renewable.
Intended use: For graduate study in United States. Designated institutions: U.S. Army Edgewood Research, Development and Engineering Center (Aberdeen Proving Ground, MD).
Eligibility: Applicant must be U.S. citizen.
Basis for selection: Major/career interest in biology; science, general; computer and information sciences; engineering; environmental science; physical sciences.
Application requirements: Recommendations and transcript.
Additional information: Provides opportunities to participate in research and development in support of military missions. One year assignments. Applicants must have completed bachelor's or graduate degree within the last three years. Number of awards varies. Stipend based on research area and degree; limited reimbursement for inbound travel and moving.
Contact:
Oak Ridge Institute of Science and Education
P.O. Box 117
Oak Ridge, TN 37831-0117
Website: www.orau.gov

Oak Ridge Institute for Science and Education Postgraduate Research at the U.S. Army Environmental Policy Institute

Type of award: Internship, renewable.
Intended use: For graduate study in United States. Designated institutions: U.S. Army Environmental Policy Institute (Atlanta, GA).
Eligibility: Applicant must be U.S. citizen.
Basis for selection: Major/career interest in law; social and behavioral sciences; science, general; engineering.
Application requirements: Recommendations and transcript.

Additional information: Provides opportunities to participate in research in developing policies and strategies to address environmental issues that may have impacts on the Army and to assist the Army in its overall strategy for compliance, restoration, prevention, and conservation. One year assignments. Applicants must have completed bachelor's or graduate degree within the last three years; others considered on a case-by-case basis. Number of awards varies. Stipend based on research area and degree; limited reimbursement for inbound travel and moving.
Contact:
Oak Ridge Institute of Science and Education
P.O. Box 117
Oak Ridge, TN 37831-0117
Website: www.orau.gov

Oak Ridge Institute for Science and Education Postgraduate Research at the U.S. Army Garrison, Aberdeen

Type of award: Research grant, renewable.
Intended use: For graduate study. Designated institutions: Aberdeen Proving Ground, Maryland.
Eligibility: Applicant must be U.S. citizen.
Basis for selection: Major/career interest in engineering; environmental science; science, general; physical sciences; health sciences.
Application requirements: Recommendations and transcript.
Additional information: Provides opportunities to participate in research on issues related to safety, health, and the environment. One year assignments. Applicants must have completed bachelor's or graduate degree within the last three years; others considered on a case-by-case basis. Number of awards varies. Stipend based on research area and degree; limited reimbursement for inbound travel and moving. Also open to graduates in industrial hygiene and life sciences.
Contact:
Oak Ridge Institute of Science and Education
P.O. Box 117
Oak Ridge, TN 37831-0117
Website: www.orau.gov

Oak Ridge Institute for Science and Education Postgraduate Research at the U.S. Army Medical Research Institute of Chemical Defense

Type of award: Internship, renewable.
Intended use: For graduate study at accredited graduate institution in United States.
Eligibility: Applicant must be U.S. citizen.
Basis for selection: Major/career interest in biology; chemistry; medicine (m.d.); physical sciences; science, general.
Application requirements: Recommendations and transcript.

Additional information: Provides opportunities to participate in research related to protection against chemical warfare agents. One year assignments. Applicants must have completed bachelor's or graduate degree within the last three years. Stipend based on research area and degree; limited reimbursement for inbound travel and moving.
Contact:
Oak Ridge Institute of Science and Education
P.O. Box 117
Oak Ridge, TN 37831-0117
Phone: 423-576-4813
Website: www.orau.gov

Oak Ridge Institute for Science and Education Postgraduate Research at the U.S. Army National Guard Bureau

Type of award: Internship, renewable.
Intended use: For graduate study at accredited graduate institution in United States.
Eligibility: Applicant must be U.S. citizen.
Basis for selection: Major/career interest in science, general; engineering.
Application requirements: Recommendations and transcript.
Additional information: Provides opportunities to participate in research related to industrial hygiene issues. One year program. Applicants must have completed bachelor's or graduate degree within the last three years; others considered on a case-by-case basis. Stipend based on research area and degree; limited reimbursement for inbound travel and moving.
Contact:
Oak Ridge Institute of Science and Education
P.O. Box 117
Oak Ridge, TN 37831-0117
Website: www.orau.gov

Oak Ridge Institute for Science and Education Postgraduate Research at the U.S. Navy Commander Fleet, Okinawa

Type of award: Internship, renewable.
Intended use: For graduate study at accredited graduate institution in United States. Designated institutions: U.S. Navy Commander Fleet Activity (Okinawa, Japan).
Eligibility: Applicant must be U.S. citizen or permanent resident.
Basis for selection: Major/career interest in science, general; engineering.
Application requirements: Recommendations and transcript.
Additional information: Provides opportunities to participate in research and training supportive of military environmental efforts and related issues. One year assignments. Applicants must have completed bachelor's or graduate degree within the last three years. Stipend based on research area and degree; limited reimbursement for inbound travel and moving.
Contact:
Oak Ridge Institute of Science and Education
P.O. Box 117
Oak Ridge, TN 37831-0117
Website: www.orau.gov

Oak Ridge Institute for Science and Education Professional Internship Program at the Oak Ridge National Laboratory

Type of award: Internship.
Intended use: For undergraduate or graduate study. Designated institutions: Oak Ridge National Laboratory (Oak Ridge, Tenn.) and sites of the Hazardous Waste Remedial Actions Program.
Eligibility: Applicant must be U.S. citizen.
Basis for selection: Major/career interest in chemistry; environmental science; geology/earth sciences; hydrology; engineering, chemical; engineering, civil; engineering, environmental; engineering, mechanical; computer and information sciences; science, general.
Application requirements: Proof of health coverage.
Additional information: Provides opportunities for students to participate in energy-related research. Three to 18 consecutive months, full-time or part-time appointments. Weekly stipend of $260 to $350. Limited travel reimbursement (round-trip transportation expenses between facility and home or campus) Off-campus tuition and fees if required by the home institution. Deadlines are February 15, June 1, October 1.
Amount of award: $3,180-$27,300
Application deadline: February 15, June 1
Contact:
Intership Coordinator
MS 36, Education Training Division
P.O. Box 117
Oak Ridge, TN 37831-0117
Website: www.orau.gov

Oak Ridge Institute for Science and Education Professional Internship Program at the Savannah River Site

Type of award: Internship.
Intended use: For undergraduate or graduate study at accredited 2-year, 4-year or graduate institution in United States. Designated institutions: Savannah River Site (Aiken, SC).
Eligibility: Applicant must be U.S. citizen.
Basis for selection: Major/career interest in environmental science; chemistry; engineering; geology/earth sciences; physics; science, general.
Application requirements: Recommendations and transcript. Proof of health coverage.
Additional information: Provides opportunities to participate in energy-related and environmental research. Three to 18 consecutive months; full-time or part-time appointments. Weekly stipend of $307 to $620; limited travel reimbursement (round-trip transportation expenses between facility and home or campus) Deadlines are February 15, June 1, October 1. Minimum GPA 2.5.
Amount of award: $3,684-$48,360
Application deadline: February 15, June 1
Contact:
Professional Internship Program at the Savannah River Site
MS 36, Education Training Division
P.O. Box 117
Oak Ridge, TN 37831-0117
Website: www.orau.gov

Oak Ridge Institute For Science and Education Student Environmental Management Participation for the U.S. Army Environmental Center

Type of award: Internship, renewable.
Intended use: For undergraduate or graduate study at accredited 2-year, 4-year or graduate institution in or outside United States. Designated institutions: U.S. Army Environmental Center.
Eligibility: Applicant must be U.S. citizen.
Basis for selection: Major/career interest in anthropology; archaeology; biology; chemistry; computer and information sciences; zoology; ecology; engineering; entomology; environmental science.
Application requirements: Recommendations and transcript. Proof of health coverage.
Additional information: Provides opportunities to participate in research in environmental programs involving cultural and natural resources, restoration, compliance, conservation, pollution prevention, validation, demonstration, transfer, quality assurance and quality control, training, information management and reporting, and related programs. Three months to one year; full-time or part-time appointments. Stipend based on research area(s) and academic classification. Minimum GPA 2.5.
Contact:
Intership Coordinator
MS 36, Education Training Division
P.O. Box 117
Oak Ridge, TN 37831-0117
Website: www.orau.gov

Oak Ridge Institute for Science and Education Student Internship at the U.S. Army Center for Health Promotion and Preventive Medicine

Type of award: Internship, renewable.
Intended use: For undergraduate or graduate study at accredited 2-year, 4-year or graduate institution in United States. Designated institutions: U.S. Army Center for Health Promotion and Preventive Medicine.
Eligibility: Applicant must be U.S. citizen.
Basis for selection: Major/career interest in biology; chemistry; computer and information sciences; engineering; environmental science; physical sciences; science, general; health sciences.
Additional information: Provides opportunities to participate in applied research and development in the areas of occupational and environmental health engineering programs, health promotion projects, and activities. Three months to one year; full-time or part-time appointments. Stipend based on research area(s) and academic classification. Minimum GPA 2.5.
Contact:
Student Internship at the U.S. Army Center for Health Promotion and Preventive Medicine
MS 36, Education Training Division
P.O. Box 117
Oak Ridge, TN 37831-0117
Website: www.orau.gov

Oak Ridge Institute for Science and Education Student Research at the Agency for Toxic Substances and Disease Registry

Type of award: Internship.
Intended use: For undergraduate or graduate study at accredited 2-year, 4-year or graduate institution in United States. Designated institutions: Agency for Toxic Substances and Disease Registry (Atlanta, GA).
Eligibility: Applicant must be U.S. citizen or permanent resident.
Basis for selection: Major/career interest in biology; environmental science; public health; epidemiology; medicine (m.d.); pharmacy/pharmaceutics/pharmacology; physical sciences.
Application requirements: Recommendations and transcript.
Additional information: Provides opportunities to participate in research relating to exposure and disease registries, health investigations, public health assessments, toxicological profiles, emergency response and health education. Ten weeks to one year; full-time or part-time appointments. Stipend based on research area(s) and academic classification. Minimum GPA 2.5.
Application deadline: February 1
Contact:
Student Research Participation at the Agency for Toxic Substances and Disease Registry
MS 36, Education Training Division
P.O. Box 117
Oak Ridge, TN 37831-0117
Website: www.orau.gov

Oak Ridge Institute for Science and Education Student Research at the U.S. Army Aviation and Troop Command

Type of award: Research grant.
Intended use: For undergraduate or graduate study. Designated institutions: U.S. Army Aviation and Troop Command, St. Louis, MO.
Eligibility: Applicant must be U.S. citizen.
Basis for selection: Major/career interest in biology; computer and information sciences; engineering; environmental science; physical sciences; science, general.
Application requirements: Recommendations and transcript.
Additional information: Provides opportunities to participate in research related to aviation systems; safety, electrical and software engineering and health physics. Three months to one year; full-time or part-time appointments. Stipend based on research area(s) and academic classification.
Contact:
Project Manager
P.O. Box 117
Oak Ridge, TN 37831-0117
Website: www.orau.gov

Oak Ridge Institute for Science and Education Student Research at the U.S. Army Environmental Policy Institute

Type of award: Research grant.
Intended use: For undergraduate or graduate study.
Designated institutions: U.S. Army Environmental Policy Institute, Atlanta, GA.
Eligibility: Applicant must be U.S. citizen.
Basis for selection: Major/career interest in law; social and behavioral sciences; engineering; environmental science; physical sciences; science, general.
Application requirements: Recommendations and transcript.
Additional information: Provides opportunities to participate; additional information provided on web site. Three months to one year; full-time or part-time appointments. Stipend based on research area(s) and academic classification. Minimum GPA 2.5 required.
Contact:
Project Manager
P.O. Box 117
Oak Ridge, TN 37831-0117
Website: www.orau.gov

Oak Ridge Institute for Science and Education Student Research at the U.S. Army Garrison, Directorate of Safety, Health and the Environment

Type of award: Research grant.
Intended use: For undergraduate or graduate study.
Designated institutions: Aberdeen Proving Ground, Maryland.
Eligibility: Applicant must be U.S. citizen.
Basis for selection: Major/career interest in environmental science; science, general; physical sciences; health sciences; engineering.
Application requirements: Recommendations and transcript.
Additional information: Provides opportunities to participate in research on issues related to safety, health, and the environment. Three months to one year; full-time or part-time appointments. Stipend based on research area(s) and academic classification. Minimum GPA 2.5.
Contact:
Project Manager
P.O. Box 117
Oak Ridge, TN 37831-0117
Website: www.orau.gov

Oak Ridge Institute for Science and Education Student Research Participation at the Centers for Disease Control and Prevention

Type of award: Internship.
Intended use: For undergraduate or graduate study at accredited 2-year, 4-year or graduate institution in United States. Designated institutions: Centers for Disease Control and Prevention.
Eligibility: Applicant must be U.S. citizen or permanent resident.
Basis for selection: Major/career interest in epidemiology; health sciences; environmental science; communications; economics; science, general; life sciences; medicine (m.d.); physical sciences.
Application requirements: Recommendations and transcript.
Additional information: Provides opportunities to participate in research on infectious diseases, environmental health, epidemiology, or occupational safety and health. One month to one year; full-time or part-time appointments. Stipend based on research area(s) and academic classification. Minimum GPA 2.5. Program at the Centers for Disease Control and Prevention: Division of AIDS, Sexually Transmitted Diseases, and Tuberculosis Laboratory Research (Atlanta, Ga.), Division of Environmental Health Laboratory Sciences (Atlanta, Ga.) Division of Mycotic and Bacterial Diseases (Atlanta, Ga.) ,Division of Prevention Research and Analytic Methods (Atlanta, Ga.), Division of Viral and Rickettsial Diseases (Atlanta, Ga.) National Institute for Occupational Safety and Health (Atlanta, Ga.; Cincinnati, Ohio; Morgantown, W.Va.; Washington, D.C.) Applications accepted year-round except at Division of Prevention Research and Analytic Methods call for deadline.
Contact:
Student Research Participation at the Centers for Disease Control and Prevention
MS 36, Education Training Division Oak Ridge Institute for Science and Education
P.O. Box 117
Oak Ridge, TN 37831-0117
Website: www.orau.gov

Oak Ridge Institute for Science and Education Student Research Participation at the National Center for Toxicological Research

Type of award: Internship.
Intended use: For undergraduate or graduate study at accredited 2-year, 4-year or graduate institution in United States. Designated institutions: National Center for Toxicological Research (Jefferson, AK.).
Eligibility: Applicant must be U.S. citizen or permanent resident.
Basis for selection: Major/career interest in biology; chemistry; computer and information sciences; mathematics; pharmacy/pharmaceutics/pharmacology; science, general.
Application requirements: Recommendations and transcript.
Additional information: Provides opportunities to participate in research on biological effects of potentially toxic chemicals and solutions to toxicology problems that have a major impact on human health and the environment. Three months to one year; full-time or part-time appointments. Stipend based on research area(s) and academic classification. Minimum GPA 2.5. March 1, deadline for summer program. No deadline for academic year appointments.
Application deadline: April 1
Contact:
Student Research Participation at the National Center for Toxicological Research
MS 36, Education Training Division, Oak Ridge Institute for Science and Education
P.O. Box 117
Oak Ridge, TN 07831-0117
Website: www.orau.gov

Oak Ridge Institute for Science and Education Student Research Participation at the U.S. Army Aviation and Troop Command

Type of award: Internship, renewable.
Intended use: For undergraduate or graduate study at accredited 4-year or graduate institution in United States. Designated institutions: U.S. Army Aviation and Troop Command (St. Louis, Mo.).
Eligibility: Applicant must be U.S. citizen.
Basis for selection: Major/career interest in biology; computer and information sciences; engineering; environmental science; physical sciences.
Additional information: Provides opportunities to participate in research related to aviation systems; safety, electrical and software engineering and health physics. Three months to one year; full-time or part-time appointments. Stipend based on research area(s) and academic classification. Minimum GPA 2.5.
Contact:
P.O. Box 117
Oak Ridge, TN 37831-0117
Website: www.orau.gov

Oak Ridge Institute for Science and Education Student Research Participation at the U.S. Army Edgewood Research, Development and Engineering Center

Type of award: Internship.
Intended use: For undergraduate or graduate study at accredited 4-year or graduate institution in United States. Designated institutions: U.S. Army Edgewood Research, Development and Engineering Center.
Eligibility: Applicant must be U.S. citizen.
Basis for selection: Major/career interest in science, general; computer and information sciences; engineering; environmental science; physical sciences; biology.
Application requirements: Recommendations and transcript.
Additional information: Minimum GPA 2.5. Provides opportunities to participate in research and development in support of military missions. Three months to one year; full-time or part-time appointments. Stipend based on research area(s) and academic classification.
Contact:
Student Research Participation at the U.S. Army Edgewood Research, Development and Engineering Center
MS 36, Education Training Division
P.O. Box 117
Oak Ridge, TN 37831-0117
Website: www.orau.gov

Oak Ridge Institute for Science and Education Student Research Participation at the U.S. Army Environmental Policy Institute

Type of award: Internship.
Intended use: For undergraduate or graduate study at accredited 4-year or graduate institution in United States. Designated institutions: U.S. Army Environmental Policy Institute (Atlanta, Ga.).
Eligibility: Applicant must be U.S. citizen or permanent resident.
Basis for selection: Major/career interest in law; social and behavioral sciences; science, general; engineering.
Application requirements: Recommendations and transcript.
Additional information: Minimum GPA 2.5. Provides opportunities to participate in research in developing policies and strategies to address environmental issues that may have impacts on the Army and assist the Army in its overall strategy for compliance, restoration, prevention, and conservation. Three months to one year; full-time or part-time appointments. Stipend based on research area(s) and academic classification.
Contact:
Student Research Participation at the U.S. Army Environmental Policy Institute
MS 36, Education Training Division
P.O. Box 117
Oak Ridge, TN 37831-0117
Website: www.orau.gov

Oak Ridge Institute for Science and Education Technology Internship Program at the Oak Ridge National Laboratory

Type of award: Internship.
Intended use: For freshman, sophomore study at accredited 2-year institution in United States.
Eligibility: Applicant must be U.S. citizen or permanent resident.
Basis for selection: Major/career interest in engineering, chemical; engineering, electrical and electronic; health sciences; engineering, mechanical.
Application requirements: Recommendations and transcript.
Additional information: Provides opportunities to participate in energy-related research. Three to 18 months; full-time or part-time appointments. Weekly stipend of $300. Minimum GPA 2.5. Associate Degree Students only.
    Amount of award: $3,600-$23,400
    Number of awards: 10
Contact:
Internship Coordinator
MS 36, Education Training Division
P.O. Box 117
Oak Ridge, TN 37831-0117
Website: www.orau.gov

Oak Ridge Institute for Science and Education U.S. Department of Energy/NAACP

Type of award: Scholarship.
Intended use: For full-time freshman study at 4-year institution in United States.
Eligibility: Applicant must be Alaskan native, American Indian, African American, Mexican American, Hispanic American or Puerto Rican. Applicant must be high school senior. Applicant must be U.S. citizen or permanent resident.
Basis for selection: Major/career interest in computer and

information sciences; engineering; environmental science; mathematics; science, general.
Application requirements: Recommendations and transcript.
Additional information: Supports minority students who are pursuing undergraduate degrees in scientific and technical disciplines. Students are recruited during senior year in high school and supported for a four-year period while they are working toward their undergraduate degrees. Scholars will participate in internship assignments for the U.S. Department of Energy (DOE) or one of its contractors during the summers and will agree to work for DOE or one of its contractors for two years after graduation. Tuition/fees and stipend payments (not to exceed $10,000); additional allowance during summer internship assignments. Contact ORISE for deadlines and application.

   Amount of award: $10,000
Contact:
Oak Ridge Institute for Science and Technology
P.O.Box 117
Oak Ridge, TN 37831-0117
Website: www.orau.gov

Oak Ridge Institute for Science and Education U.S. Geological Survey Earth Sciences Internship

Type of award: Internship.
Intended use: For undergraduate or graduate study at accredited 4-year or graduate institution in United States. Designated institutions: U.S. Geological Survey Sites.
Eligibility: Applicant must be U.S. citizen or permanent resident.
Basis for selection: Major/career interest in geology/earth sciences; environmental science; computer and information sciences; geography; hydrology; biology; chemistry; engineering, environmental; engineering, civil; forestry.
Application requirements: Recommendations and transcript.
Additional information: Provides opportunities to participate in research in the earth sciences. Appointment lengths vary, up to two years. Stipend based on academic classification. Minimum GPA 2.5. Applicant must have graduated from a U.S. college or university within the past 12 months or have been enrolled full time in a U.S. college or university within the past year.

   Amount of award: $19,000-$38,000
Contact:
Ernestine Friedman
Oak Ridge Associated Universities
P.O. Box 117, MS 36
Oak Ridge, TN 37831-0117
Website: www.orau.gov

Oak Ridge Institute for Science and Education U.S. Nuclear Regulatory Commission Historically Black Colleges and Universities Student Research Participation

Type of award: Internship.
Intended use: For undergraduate or graduate study at accredited 4-year or graduate institution in United States. Designated institutions: Ames Laboratory (Ames, IA), Argonne National Laboratory (Argonne, IL), Brookhaven National Laboratory (Upton, N.Y.), Idaho National Engineering and Environmental Laboratory (Idaho Falls, Idaho), Lawrence Berkeley National Laboratory (Berkeley, Calif.), Lawrence Livermore National Laboratory (Livermore, CA) , Los Alamos National Laboratory (Los Alamos, N.M.), Oak Ridge National Laboratory (Oak Ridge, Tenn.), Pacific Northwest National Laboratory (Richland, Wash.), Sandia National Laboratories (Albuquerque, N.M. and Livermore, Calif.), Savannah River Site (Aiken, S.C.);.
Eligibility: Applicant must be U.S. citizen or permanent resident.
Basis for selection: Major/career interest in computer and information sciences; engineering; geology/earth sciences; mathematics; geophysics.
Application requirements: Recommendations and transcript.
Additional information: Minimum GPA 2.5. Provides opportunities for students from historically Black Colleges to participate in research relating to science and engineering. Ten to 12 weeks during the summer, some one-year appointments at participating facilities or on campus. Weekly stipend of $300 to $400. Limited travel reimbursement (round-trip transportation expenses between facility and home or campus). Some on-campus appointments during the academic year; an appointment can also be served at a host university under the guidance of a principal investigator who has an active research grant from the NRC

   Amount of award: $3,000-$4,800
   Application deadline: January 15
Contact:
U.S. Nuclear Regulatory Commission Historically Black Colleges and Universities Student Research Participation
P.O. Box 117
Oak Ridge,, TN 37831-0117
Website: www.orau.gov

Oak Ridge Institute for Science and Education University Coal Research Internship

Type of award: Internship.
Intended use: For junior, senior study at accredited 4-year institution in United States. Designated institutions: Federal Energy Technology Center, Pittsburgh (PA).
Eligibility: Applicant must be U.S. citizen or permanent resident.
Basis for selection: Major/career interest in chemistry; biology; environmental science; geology/earth sciences; engineering; physics; science, general.
Additional information: Provides opportunities to participate in coal-related research in an on-campus, graduate-level research environment. Ten weeks during the summer. Weekly stipend of $225. Limited travel reimbursement (round-trip transportation expenses between facility and home or campus). Housing. Minimum GPA 2.5.

   Amount of award: $2,250
   Number of awards: 25
   Application deadline: January 30
Contact:
Intership Coordinator
MS 36, Education Training Division
P.O. Box 117
Oak Ridge, TN 37831-0117
Website: www.orau.gov

Ohio Board of Regents

Ohio Academic Scholarship

Type of award: Scholarship, renewable.
Intended use: For full-time freshman, sophomore, junior or senior study at accredited 2-year or 4-year institution in Ohio.
Eligibility: Applicant must be high school senior. Applicant must be U.S. citizen or permanent resident residing in Ohio.
Basis for selection: Applicant must demonstrate high academic achievement.
Application requirements: ACT scores.
Additional information: Applications can be obtained from high school guidance counselor after December.

Amount of award:	$2,000
Number of awards:	4,000
Number of applicants:	4,500
Application deadline:	February 23
Notification begins:	May 1
Total amount awarded:	$7,000,000

Contact:
Ohio Student Aid Commission

Ohio Instructional Grant

Type of award: Scholarship.
Intended use: For full-time undergraduate study at accredited 2-year or 4-year institution in Ohio, and some select Pennsylvania schools.
Eligibility: Applicant must be U.S. citizen or permanent resident residing in Ohio.
Basis for selection: Applicant must demonstrate financial need.
Additional information: By completing the FAFSA form, you automatically apply for this scholarship.

Amount of award:	$252-$3,750
Number of awards:	90,000
Application deadline:	October 1
Notification begins:	March 1
Total amount awarded:	$93,600,000

Contact:
Ohio Student Aid Commission

Ohio Nurse Education Assistance Loan Program

Type of award: Loan, renewable.
Intended use: For full-time or half-time freshman, sophomore, junior, senior, post-bachelor's certificate or master's study in Ohio. Designated institutions: Ohio Hospital School of Nursing, public supported college or university, private nonprofit college or university, or vocational school with an approved nursing education program.
Eligibility: Applicant must be U.S. citizen or permanent resident residing in Ohio.
Basis for selection: Major/career interest in nursing. Applicant must demonstrate financial need.
Additional information: Must be accepted to or enrolled in approved pre- or post-licensure licensed practical nurse or registered nurse nursing education program. Debt cancellation at rate of 20 percent per year (for maximum of four years) if borrower is employed in clinical practice of nursing in Ohio after graduation. Applications available January. Contact college financial aid office for an application.

Amount of award:	$2,800
Number of awards:	98
Number of applicants:	446
Application deadline:	June 1
Notification begins:	July 15
Total amount awarded:	$271,103

Ohio Safety Officers College Memorial Fund

Type of award: Scholarship, renewable.
Intended use: For full-time or half-time freshman, sophomore, junior or senior study at vocational, 2-year or 4-year institution in Ohio.
Eligibility: Applicant must be U.S. citizen or permanent resident residing in Ohio.
Application requirements: Proof of eligibility.
Additional information: Parent must have been a firefighter or police officer killed in the line of duty. Apply at college financial aid office.

Number of awards:	46
Number of applicants:	46
Total amount awarded:	$121,068

Ohio Student Choice Grant

Type of award: Scholarship, renewable.
Intended use: For full-time freshman, sophomore, junior or senior study at 4-year institution in Ohio. Designated institutions: Award must be used at private nonprofit colleges or universities.
Eligibility: Applicant must be U.S. citizen or permanent resident residing in Ohio.
Additional information: Apply at college financial aid office.

Number of awards:	45,000
Total amount awarded:	$24,200,000

Ohio War Orphans Scholarship

Type of award: Scholarship, renewable.
Intended use: For full-time freshman, sophomore, junior or senior study at accredited 2-year or 4-year institution in Ohio.
Eligibility: Applicant must be U.S. citizen or permanent resident residing in Ohio. Applicant must be child of veteran, disabled veteran, deceased veteran or POW/MIA. Child of wartime veteran or POW/MIA in Asian war eligible.
Application requirements: Proof of eligibility.

Number of applicants:	341
Application deadline:	July 1
Notification begins:	July 1
Total amount awarded:	$3,600,000

Contact:
Sue Minturn, Program Administrator
P.O. Box 182452
Columbus, OH 43218-2452

Part-Time Student Instructional Grant Program

Type of award: Scholarship, renewable.
Intended use: For half-time or less than half-time freshman,

sophomore, junior or senior study at accredited 2-year or 4-year institution.
Eligibility: Applicant must be U.S. citizen residing in Ohio.
Basis for selection: Applicant must demonstrate financial need.
Additional information: For application contact college financial aid office.
    Number of awards: 30,000
    Total amount awarded: $10,000,000

Regents Graduate/Professional Fellowship

Type of award: Scholarship, renewable.
Intended use: For full-time master's study at accredited graduate institution in Ohio.
Eligibility: Applicant must be Alaskan native, American Indian, African American, Mexican American, Hispanic American or Puerto Rican. Applicant must be U.S. citizen or permanent resident residing in Ohio.
Basis for selection: Applicant must demonstrate high academic achievement.
Application requirements: Interview, recommendations, essay and transcript. GRE scores or scores from other graduate exam if required for Master's program.
Additional information: Must contact undergraduate institution for application. Must graduate with a bachelor's degree and start graduate school within the same year.
    Amount of award: $3,500
    Number of awards: 114
    Number of applicants: 114
    Application deadline: March 1
    Notification begins: April 1
    Total amount awarded: $399,000

Robert C. Byrd Honors Scholarship

Type of award: Scholarship, renewable.
Intended use: For full-time freshman study at accredited 2-year or 4-year institution in United States.
Eligibility: Applicant must be residing in Ohio.
Basis for selection: Applicant must demonstrate leadership and high academic achievement.
Application requirements: GPA, SAT I/ACT scores.
Additional information: Contact you undergraduate institution for application information.
    Amount of award: $1,100
    Number of awards: 200
    Number of applicants: 872
    Application deadline: March 10
    Total amount awarded: $415,000

Oklahoma State Regents for Higher Education

Oklahoma Academic Scholars Program

Type of award: Scholarship, renewable.
Intended use: For full-time freshman study at 2-year, 4-year or graduate institution.
Eligibility: Applicant must be high school senior. Applicant must be U.S. citizen residing in Oklahoma.
Basis for selection: Applicant must demonstrate high academic achievement.
Application requirements: Proof of eligibility.
Additional information: To support participation in a foreign study program sponsored by an Oklahoma institution. Must be graduating senior or first-time freshman entering within 27 months of high school graduation. Oklahoma resident must score in at least 99.5 percentile on SAT I or ACT or meet National Merit Scholarship finalist criteria. Out-of-state students eligible if National Merit Scholar, Presidential Awardee, or National Hispanic Awardee.
    Amount of award: $3,500-$5,500
    Number of awards: 1,208
Contact:
Academic Scholars Program
500 Education Building
Oklahoma City, OK 73105-4500

Oklahoma Chiropractic Education Assistance

Type of award: Scholarship, renewable.
Intended use: For full-time first professional study in United States.
Eligibility: Applicant must be U.S. citizen residing in Oklahoma.
Basis for selection: Major/career interest in chiropractic.
Application requirements: Proof of eligibility.
Additional information: Applications reviewed by Oklahoma State Board of Chiropractic Examiners, who make recommendations for acceptance.
    Amount of award: $898-$3,000
    Number of awards: 41
    Application deadline: July 1
    Notification begins: August 30
    Total amount awarded: $47,934
Contact:
Oklahoma State Regents For Higher Education
500 Education Building
Oklahoma City, OK 73105-4500

Oklahoma Future Teachers Scholarship

Type of award: Scholarship, renewable.
Intended use: For freshman, sophomore, junior, senior, master's or doctoral study at accredited 2-year, 4-year or graduate institution in Oklahoma.
Eligibility: Applicant must be U.S. citizen or permanent resident residing in Oklahoma.
Basis for selection: Major/career interest in education, teacher. Applicant must demonstrate high academic achievement.
Application requirements: Proof of eligibility.
Additional information: Requires ranking in top 15 percent of class or admission to a professional education program. Applications reviewed first by institutions, then sent to Regents Scholarship Committee with recommendations. Must pursue certification and plan to teach in critical teacher shortage area.

Amount of award:	$500-$1,500
Number of awards:	170
Number of applicants:	180
Application deadline:	July 1
Notification begins:	October 1
Total amount awarded:	$172,561

Contact:
Oklahoma State Regents For Higher Education
500 Education Building
State Capitol Complex
Oklahoma City, OK 73105-4500

Oklahoma Minority Doctoral Study Grant

Type of award: Scholarship, renewable.
Intended use: For full-time doctoral study at accredited graduate institution in Oklahoma.
Eligibility: Applicant must be of minority background. Applicant must be U.S. citizen residing in Oklahoma.
Basis for selection: Applicant must demonstrate high academic achievement.
Application requirements: Recommendations, transcript and proof of eligibility.
Additional information: Must be planning career teaching at institution of higher education. Award may be used at out-of-state institution only if program of study not offered in Oklahoma.

Amount of award:	$6,000
Number of awards:	19
Application deadline:	May 1
Notification begins:	June 15
Total amount awarded:	$114,000

Contact:
Oklahoma State Regents For Higher Education
500 Education Building
Oklahoma City, OK 73105-4500

Oklahoma Minority Professional Study Grant

Type of award: Scholarship, renewable.
Intended use: For full-time first professional study at accredited graduate institution in Oklahoma.
Eligibility: Applicant must be of minority background. Applicant must be U.S. citizen residing in Oklahoma.
Basis for selection: Applicant must demonstrate high academic achievement.
Application requirements: Proof of eligibility.
Additional information: Out-of-state students attending institutions in Oklahoma are eligible, but Oklahoma residents given priority.

Amount of award:	$4,000
Number of awards:	28
Number of applicants:	35
Application deadline:	June 1
Total amount awarded:	$112,000

Contact:
Oklahoma State Regents For Higher Education
500 Education Building
Oklahoma City, OK 73105-4500

Oklahoma Tuition Aid Grant

Type of award: Scholarship, renewable.
Intended use: For full-time or half-time undergraduate or graduate study at accredited vocational, 2-year, 4-year or graduate institution in Oklahoma. Designated institutions: Nonprofit vocational institutions only.
Eligibility: Applicant must be U.S. citizen or permanent resident residing in Oklahoma.
Basis for selection: Applicant must demonstrate financial need.
Application requirements: Proof of eligibility.
Additional information: Apply early as funding is limited. Must meet minimum standards of academic progress for financial aid recipients. Must be enrolled in a program leading to a degree or certificate.

Amount of award:	$200-$1,000
Number of awards:	19,061
Application deadline:	April 30
Total amount awarded:	$14,924,348

Contact:
Oklahoma State Regents For Higher Education
P.O. Box 3020
Oklahoma City, OK 73101-3020

Oregon State Scholarship Commission

Oregon Disabled Peace Officer Grant Program

Type of award: Scholarship.
Intended use: For full-time undergraduate study at accredited 2-year or 4-year institution in Oregon.
Eligibility: Applicant must be U.S. citizen or permanent resident residing in Oregon. Applicant's parent must have been killed or disabled in work-related accident as fire fighter, police officer or public safety officer.
Basis for selection: Applicant must demonstrate financial need.
Application requirements: Transcript and proof of eligibility.
Additional information: Send SASE.

Amount of award:	$2,500
Application deadline:	March 1

Contact:
Oregon State Scholarship Commission
1500 Valley River Drive, Suite 100
Eugene, OR 97401

Oregon Robert C. Byrd Honors Scholarship

Type of award: Scholarship, renewable.
Intended use: For full-time freshman study.
Eligibility: Applicant must be high school senior. Applicant must be U.S. citizen or permanent resident residing in Oregon.
Basis for selection: Applicant must demonstrate high academic achievement.
Application requirements: Essay and transcript.
Additional information: Graduating Oregon high school

seniors with 3.85+ cumulative GPA and combined SAT scores of 1250+ (or ACT composite of 28+) OR current Oregon GED recipients with 325+. 15 recipients per federal congressional district. Maximum 12 undergraduate quarters or equivalent.

 Amount of award: $1,110
 Number of awards: 75
 Application deadline: March 1
 Total amount awarded: $83,250

Contact:
Oregon State Scholarship Commission
1500 Valley River Drive, Suite 100
Attn: Private Awards
Eugene, OR 97401-2146
Website: www.ossc.state.or.us

Oregon State Need Grant

Type of award: Scholarship, renewable.
Intended use: For full-time undergraduate or graduate study at accredited 2-year or 4-year institution in Oregon.
Eligibility: Applicant must be U.S. citizen or permanent resident residing in Oregon.
Basis for selection: Applicant must demonstrate financial need.
Application requirements: Proof of eligibility. FAFSA.
Additional information: Students pursuing theology, divinity, or religious education degree not eligible. Contact high school guidance office, undergraduate financial aid office, or Commission (send SASE). Awards granted from January 1 until funds run out. TYY 541-687-7357.

 Amount of award: $936-$1,638
 Total amount awarded: $14,000,000

Contact:
Oregon State Scholarship Commission
Grant Department
1500 Valley River Drive, Suite 100
Eugene, OR 97401
Phone: 541-687-7400

Pennsylvania Higher Education Assistance Agency

Pennsylvania Grant Program

Type of award: Scholarship, renewable.
Intended use: For undergraduate study at accredited vocational, 2-year or 4-year institution in Pennsylvania.
Eligibility: Applicant must be residing in Pennsylvania.
Basis for selection: Applicant must demonstrate financial need.
Application requirements: Proof of eligibility. Must file FAFSA.
Additional information: Half-time students eligible for grant up to $1,350. Grants are portable to approved institutions located in other states.

 Amount of award: $200-$2,700
 Application deadline: May 1
 Total amount awarded: $244,000,000

Contact:
Pennsylvania Higher Education Assistance Agency
1200 North Seventh Street
Harrisburg, PA 17102-1444
Website: www.pheaa.org

Pennsylvania Robert C. Byrd Honors Scholarship

Type of award: Scholarship, renewable.
Intended use: For full-time freshman study at accredited 2-year or 4-year institution in United States.
Eligibility: Applicant must be high school senior. Applicant must be U.S. citizen or permanent resident residing in Pennsylvania.
Basis for selection: Applicant must demonstrate high academic achievement.
Application requirements: Transcript.
Additional information: Applicant must rank in top 5 percent of class, have a 3.5 GPA, a 1200 on the SAT combined score on SAT I (27 on ACT), or 289 on GED, and must enroll following graduation. Information available from high school guidance office.

 Amount of award: $1,500
 Number of awards: 1,130
 Number of applicants: 3,300
 Application deadline: May 1
 Total amount awarded: $1,695,000

Contact:
Pennsylvania Higher Education Assistance Agency
Robert C. Byrd Scholarship
P.O. Box 8114
Harrisburg, PA 17105-8114
Website: www.pheaa.org

Pennsylvania Work-Study Program

Type of award: Internship, renewable.
Intended use: For full-time freshman, sophomore, junior, senior, master's, doctoral or first professional study at accredited postsecondary institution in Pennsylvania.
Eligibility: Applicant must be U.S. citizen or permanent resident residing in Pennsylvania.
Basis for selection: Applicant must demonstrate financial need.
Application requirements: Interview and proof of eligibility.
Additional information: Student must demonstrate ability to benefit from career-related high tech or community service work experience. Funds earned must be used to pay school costs at PHEAA-approved postsecondary institution. All placements must be with PHEAA-approved Pennsylvania employers.

 Amount of award: $1,000-$3,600
 Number of applicants: 3,400
 Application deadline: October 1, January 15

Contact:
Pennsylvania Higher Education Assistance Agency
Grant Division, PHEAA
1200 North Seventh Street
Harrisburg, PA 17102
Phone: 717-720-2550
Website: www.pheaa.org

Princeton Plasma Physics Laboratory

Plasma Physics National Undergraduate Fellowship Program

Type of award: Internship.
Intended use: For junior study.
Eligibility: Applicant must be Must be attending US institution. This policy subject to change.
Basis for selection: Major/career interest in engineering; physics; mathematics; computer and information sciences. Applicant must demonstrate depth of character, leadership, seriousness of purpose, service orientation and high academic achievement.
Application requirements: Recommendations, essay and transcript.
Additional information: Student must have a 3.5 GPA. Internship is nine weeks in the summer.
    Amount of award: $4,800
    Number of awards: 15
    Number of applicants: 15
    Application deadline: February 25
    Notification begins: April 15
Contact:
Princeton Plasma Physics Laboratory
P.O. Box 451
Princeton, NJ 08543
Phone: 609-243-3049
Website: www.pppl.gov

Puerto Rico Department of Education

Puerto Rico Robert C. Byrd Honors Scholarship

Type of award: Scholarship, renewable.
Intended use: For full-time undergraduate study in United States.
Eligibility: Applicant must be high school senior. Applicant must be U.S. citizen residing in Puerto Rico.
Basis for selection: Applicant must demonstrate leadership and high academic achievement.
Application requirements: Recommendations, essay, transcript and proof of eligibility.
Additional information: Minimum required GPA of 3.5. One candidate selected by local committee from each of 100 Puerto Rican school districts; interviews required in most districts. Contact high school guidance office for information and application materials.
    Amount of award: $1,500
    Number of awards: 457
    Number of applicants: 109
    Total amount awarded: $685,000
Contact:
Departamento de Educacion
Orlando Valles, Becas Especiales
P.O. Box 190759
San Juan, PR 00919-0759

Rhode Island Higher Education Assistance Authority

Rhode Island Higher Education Assistance Authority State Grant

Type of award: Scholarship, renewable.
Intended use: For undergraduate study at accredited vocational, 2-year or 4-year institution in or outside United States.
Eligibility: Applicant must be U.S. citizen or permanent resident residing in Rhode Island.
Basis for selection: Applicant must demonstrate financial need.
Application requirements: Proof of eligibility.
    Amount of award: $250-$750
    Number of awards: 9,585
    Number of applicants: 36,813
    Application deadline: March 1
    Total amount awarded: $6,112,015
Contact:
Rhode Island Higher Education Assistance Authority
560 Jefferson Boulevard
Warwick, RI 02886
Phone: 401-736-1100
Fax: 401-732-3541

Rhode Island State Government

Rhode Island Government Intern Program

Type of award: Internship, renewable.
Intended use: For junior, senior or graduate study in United States.
Eligibility: Applicant must be residing in Rhode Island.
Application requirements: Interview and recommendations. Cover letter.
Additional information: Interns are placed in various state offices. Students from other states may work for academic credit in unpaid internships.
    Amount of award: $100-$800
    Number of awards: 180
    Application deadline: November 15
    Total amount awarded: $120,000
Contact:
Rhode Island State Government Intern Program
Room 8AA, State House
Providence, RI 02903
Phone: 401-277-6782

Rhode Island State Government Internship Program

Type of award: Internship.
Intended use: For undergraduate, postgraduate study.

Eligibility: Applicant must be residing in Rhode Island.
Basis for selection: Major/career interest in governmental public relations. Applicant must demonstrate depth of character, leadership, seriousness of purpose, service orientation and high academic achievement.
Application requirements: Interview, recommendations, essay, transcript and proof of eligibility.
Additional information: Minimum GPA 2.5, freshman and sophomores must be in participating RI schools. 8 weeks for spring, summer and fall. Fall application deadline is Rolling, and had no monetary compensation. $100 per week for spring and fall aprticipants will earn academic credit. Summer only. All located in Rhode Island.

    Amount of award: $800
    Application deadline: May 15, November 15

Contact:
Rhode Island State Government
State Capitol, Rm. 8AA
Providence, RI 02903

ROTC

Air Force Four-Year Scholarships(Types # 1,2 and Targeted)

Type of award: Scholarship.
Intended use: For freshman study at accredited 4-year institution in United States.
Eligibility: Applicant must be high school senior. Applicant must be U.S. citizen.
Basis for selection: Major/career interest in engineering; mathematics; physics; computer and information sciences; meteorology; architecture. Applicant must demonstrate high academic achievement.
Application requirements: Interview, recommendations and transcript.
Additional information: Minimum GPA 2.5 and be in top 40% of class. Minimum test scores: ACT Composite 24, Math 21, English 21. SAT Total 1100, Math 520, Verbal 530. Limited opportuntties in Chemistry, Business Administration, Accounting, Management, Economics, Geography, Political Science, Psychology and Foreign Language/Area Studies (focus should be in Central Europe-Russia/Slavic languages or Russian; Mideast/Arabic; Far East/Chinese Mandarin, Japanese, Korean, or a Southeast Asian language; Mideast/Persian Farsi). Applicants must not have been enrolled in college full-time prior to application. Type One provides full tuition, fees and textbook allowance, without restriction. $150 per month stipend during academic year. Type two provides full-tuition, fees and textbook allowance up to $9000 per year. $150 per month stipend during academic year. Payment increases to 80% of tuition with maintance of 3.0 GPA. Targeted scholarships provide full tuition and fees at a "low cost" school (mostly state institutions). $150 per month stipend during academic year. Scholarship board decides which type of scholarship is offered. Scholarship recipients agree to serve four years active duty.

    Application deadline: December 1

ROTC/ Air Force Three-Year Scholarships Types 2 And Targeted

Type of award: Scholarship.
Intended use: For sophomore study at accredited 4-year institution in United States.
Eligibility: Applicant must be U.S. citizen.
Basis for selection: Major/career interest in engineering; mathematics; physics; computer and information sciences; architecture. Applicant must demonstrate high academic achievement.
Application requirements: Interview, transcript and nomination.
Additional information: Minimum GPA 2.5 and be in top 40% of class. Minimum test scores: ACT Composite 24, Math 21, English 21. SAT Total 1100, Math 520, Verbal 530. Limited opportuntties in Chemistry, Business Administration, Accounting, Management, Economics, Geography, Political Science, Psychology and Foreign Language/Area Studies (focus should be in Central Europe-Russia/Slavic languages or Russian; Mideast/Arabic; Far East/Chinese Mandarin, Japanese, Korean, or a Southeast Asian language; Mideast/Persian Farsi). Applicants must not have been enrolled in college full-time prior to application. Type two provides full-tuition, fees and textbook allowance up to $9000 per year. $150 per month stipend during academic year. Payment increases to 80% of tuition with maintenance of 3.0 GPA. Targeted scholarships provide full tuition and fees at a "low cost" school (mostly state institutions). $150 per month stipend during academic year. ROTC scholarship board decides which type of scholarship is offered. Scholarship recipients agree to serve four years active duty.

    Application deadline: December 1

ROTC/United States Army Four-Year Historically Black College/ Univ. Scholarship

Type of award: Scholarship.
Intended use: For freshman study at accredited 4-year institution in United States. Designated institutions: Alabama A&M, Tuskegee University (AL), University of Arkansas-Pine Bluff (AR), Howard University (DC), Florida A&M University, Fort Valley State College (GA), Grambling State University, Southern University and A&M College (LA), Bowie State University (MD), Morgan State University (MD) Alcorn State University (MS), Jackson State University (MS), Lincoln University (MO), Elizabeth City State University (NC), North Carolina A&T State University (NC), Saint Augustine's College (NC), Central State University (OH), South Carolina State University, Prairie View A&M University (TX), Hampton University, Norfolk State University (VA), West Virginia State College (WV).
Eligibility: Applicant must be high school senior. Applicant must be U.S. citizen.
Basis for selection: Applicant must demonstrate depth of character and high academic achievement.
Application requirements: Interview and transcript.
Additional information: Minimum SAT score of 920 points (composite of Verbal and Math) or an ACT composite score of 19. Early Decision deadline July 15, notification November 1. Those applicants not selected for the Early Decision will

automatically be considered for the Regular Decision competition. Early Decision applicants may submit updates to their applications any time prior to December 15, 1998. Scholarships are offered at different levels up to $12,800 annually, providing college tuition and educational fees. All applicants are considered for each level. Designated book allowance. Tax-free subsistence allowance of $150 a month for up to 10 months each year the scholarship is in effect. Scholarships do not pay flight fees. To apply, complete item 11 on the first page of the application. You will still be considered for the national four-year scholarship program. Your first school choice must be one of the schools identified in the list of HBCUs. If your first school choice is not one of these schools, your application will not be considered for these dedicated HBCU scholarships. Contact your local ROTC recruiter for further information.

- **Amount of award:** $12,800
- **Application deadline:** November 15
- **Notification begins:** March 1

United States Army Four-Year Nursing Scholarship

Type of award: Scholarship.
Intended use: For freshman study at accredited 4-year institution in United States.
Eligibility: Applicant must be U.S. citizen.
Basis for selection: Applicant must demonstrate depth of character and high academic achievement.
Application requirements: Interview and transcript.
Additional information: Minimum SAT score of 920 points (composite of Verbal and Math) or an ACT composite score of 19. Early Decision deadline July 15, notification November 1. Those applicants not selected for the Early Decision will automatically be considered for the Regular Decision competition. Early Decision applicants may submit updates to their applications any time prior to December 15, 1998. Scholarships are offered at different levels up to $12,800 annually, providing college tuition and educational fees. All applicants are considered for each level. Designated book allowance. Tax-free subsistence allowance of $150 a month for up to ten months each year the scholarship is in effect. Scholarships do not pay flight fees. Limited numbers of 3- and 2- year scholarships are available once a student is on campus. Applicants should check with the Professor of Military Science once they are attending classes. Contact your local Army ROTC recruiter. Individuals applying for nurse program scholarships must indicate "JXX" as choice of major in item four of page eight of the four-year scholarship application; item three should include the PNES which applicant wishes to attend.

- **Amount of award:** $12,800
- **Application deadline:** November 15
- **Notification begins:** March 1

United States Army Four-Year Scholarship

Type of award: Scholarship.
Intended use: For freshman study at accredited 4-year institution in United States.
Eligibility: Applicant must be U.S. citizen.
Basis for selection: Applicant must demonstrate depth of character and high academic achievement.
Application requirements: Interview, transcript and nomination.
Additional information: Minimum SAT score of 920 points (composite of Verbal and Math) or an ACT composite score of 19. Early Decision deadline July 15, notification November 1. Those applicants not selected for the Early Decision will automatically be considered for the Regular Decision competition. Early Decision applicants may submit updates to their applications any time prior to December 15, 1998. Scholarships are offered at different levels up to $12,800 annually, providing college tuition and educational fees. All applicants are considered for each level. Designated book allowance. Tax-free subsistence allowance of $150 a month for up to 10 months each year the scholarship is in effect. Scholarships do not pay flight fees. Limited numbers of 3- and 2- year scholarships are available once a student is on campus. Applicants should check with the Professor of Military Science once they are attending classes. Contact your local Army ROTC recruiter.

- **Amount of award:** $12,800
- **Application deadline:** November 15
- **Notification begins:** March 1

Contact:
800-USA-ROTC

Smithsonian Environmental Research Center

Smithsonian Environmental Research Work/Learn Program

Type of award: Internship, renewable.
Intended use: For undergraduate or graduate study.
Designated institutions: Smithsonian Environmental Research Center in Edgewater, Maryland.
Basis for selection: Major/career interest in biology; chemistry; environmental science; engineering, environmental; ecology. Applicant must demonstrate seriousness of purpose.
Application requirements: Recommendations, essay and transcript.
Additional information: Stipends are from $240 to $300 per week. Available during spring and summer months. Projects are 40 hours per week, lasting from 12 weeks to four months. Dorm space is available for $60 per week on a limited basis.

- **Number of awards:** 15
- **Number of applicants:** 250
- **Application deadline:** March 1, November 1
- **Notification begins:** April 15, December 15
- **Total amount awarded:** $30,000

Contact:
Work/Learn Program
P.O. Box 28
Edgewater, MD 21037
Phone: 420-798-4424, ext. 215
Fax: 301-261-7954
Website: www.serc.si.edu

South Carolina Commission on Higher Education

South Carolina Teacher Loans

Type of award: Loan, renewable.
Intended use: For freshman, sophomore, junior, senior or graduate study at accredited 2-year, 4-year or graduate institution in South Carolina.
Eligibility: Applicant must be U.S. citizen residing in South Carolina.
Basis for selection: Major/career interest in education, teacher. Applicant must demonstrate high academic achievement.
Additional information: Master's or graduate study eligible only if required for initial teacher certification. Entering freshman must have minimum SAT I score of 838 (ACT 19.1); rank in top 40 percent of high school class. First-time undergraduate and entering graduate applicants must have 2.75 GPA and have passed Education Entrance Examination. Graduate applicant must have 3.5 GPA. Loan forgiveness for service in teacher shortage area in South Carolina public schools: 20 percent for each year of service, 33 percent if service in geographic and subject shortage area. $2,500 freshman and sophomore maximum; $5,000 junior, senior, graduate maximum.

Amount of award:	$5,000
Number of awards:	970
Number of applicants:	1,700
Application deadline:	June 1
Notification begins:	July 15
Total amount awarded:	$4,317,018

Contact:
South Carolina Student Loan Corporation
P.O. Box 21487
Columbia, SC 29221

South Carolina Higher Education Tuition Grants Commission

South Carolina Tuition Grants

Type of award: Scholarship, renewable.
Intended use: For full-time undergraduate study at accredited 2-year or 4-year institution in South Carolina. Designated institutions: Private, nonprofit institutions.
Eligibility: Applicant must be U.S. citizen residing in South Carolina.
Basis for selection: Applicant must demonstrate financial need.
Additional information: Recipient may reapply for up to four years of grant assistance. Incoming freshmen must score 900 on SAT or graduate in upper 3/4 of high school class. Upperclassmen must complete 24 semester hours and meet college's satisfactory progress requirements.

Amount of award:	$3,730
Number of awards:	9,340
Number of applicants:	16,385
Application deadline:	June 30
Total amount awarded:	$21,866,897

Contact:
South Carolina Higher Education Tuition Grants Commission
811 Keenan Building, 1310 Lady Street
P.O. Box 12159
Columbia, SC 29211

South Dakota Board of Regents

Haines Memorial Scholarship

Type of award: Scholarship.
Intended use: For sophomore, junior or senior study. Designated institutions: BHSU, DSU, NSU, SDSU, USD.
Eligibility: Applicant must be residing in South Dakota.
Basis for selection: Major/career interest in education. Applicant must demonstrate depth of character, leadership, seriousness of purpose and service orientation.
Application requirements: Essay, transcript and proof of eligibility.
Additional information: 2.5 GPA and typed resume of extracurricular activities, services, and memberships.

Amount of award:	$2,150
Number of awards:	1
Application deadline:	February 27
Notification begins:	March 27

Contact:
South Dakota Board of Regents Scholarship Committee
207 East Capitol Avenue
Pierre, SD 05750-3159
Phone: 605-773-3455

Marlin R. Scarborough Memorial Scholarship

Type of award: Scholarship.
Intended use: For full-time junior study. Designated institutions: SD Public University.
Eligibility: Applicant must be residing in South Dakota.
Basis for selection: Applicant must demonstrate depth of character, leadership, seriousness of purpose, service orientation and high academic achievement.
Application requirements: Essay, transcript and proof of eligibility.
Additional information: 3.5 GPA and have completed 3 full semesters at the same university.

Amount of award:	$1,500
Number of awards:	1
Application deadline:	February 27
Notification begins:	March 27

Contact:
South Dakota Board of Regents Scholarship Committee
207 East Capitol Avenue
Pierre, SD 57501-3159
Phone: 605-773-3455

South Dakota Board of Regents Scholarship Committee

Annis I. Fowler/Kaden Scholarship

Type of award: Scholarship.
Intended use: For freshman study. Designated institutions: USD, BHSU, DSU OR NSU.
Basis for selection: Major/career interest in education, early childhood. Applicant must demonstrate depth of character, leadership and seriousness of purpose.
Application requirements: Recommendations, essay, transcript and proof of eligibility.
- Amount of award: $1,000
- Number of awards: 1
- Application deadline: February 27
- Notification begins: March 27

Contact:
Lesta V. Turchen, Ph.D.
207 East Capitol Avenue
Pierre, South Dakota 57501-3159

Arnell BJUGSTAD Scholarship

Type of award: Scholarship.
Intended use: For freshman study.
Eligibility: Applicant must be American Indian. Federally-recognized Indian tribe in North Dakota or South Dakota. Applicant must be permanent resident residing in South Dakota or North Dakota.
Basis for selection: Major/career interest in agribusiness; agriculture; natural resources/conservation. Applicant must demonstrate depth of character, leadership and seriousness of purpose.
Application requirements: Recommendations, transcript and proof of eligibility.
Additional information: Verification of tribal enrollment required.
- Amount of award: $500
- Number of awards: 1
- Application deadline: February 27
- Notification begins: March 27

Contact:
Lesta V. Turchen, Ph.D.
207 East Capitol Ave.
Pierre, South Dakota 57502-3159

Martin R. Scarborough Memorial Scholarship

Type of award: Scholarship.
Intended use: For full-time junior study. Designated institutions: South Dakota public institutions.
Basis for selection: Applicant must demonstrate depth of character, leadership, seriousness of purpose, service orientation and high academic achievement.
Application requirements: Essay, transcript and proof of eligibility.
Additional information: 3.5 GPA and have completed 3 full semesters at the same university.
- Amount of award: $1,500
- Number of awards: 1
- Application deadline: February 27
- Notification begins: March 27

Contact:
Lesta V. Turchen, Ph.D.
207 East Capitol Avenue
Pierre, South Dakota 57501-3159

South Dakota Department of Education and Cultural Affairs

South Dakota National Guard Tuition Assistance

Type of award: Scholarship, renewable.
Intended use: For undergraduate study at vocational or 4-year institution in South Dakota.
Eligibility: Applicant or parent must be member of South Dakota National Guard. Applicant must be residing in South Dakota. Applicant must be who served in the Reserves/National Guard.
Application requirements: Proof of eligibility.
- Number of awards: 550
- Number of applicants: 550

South Dakota Robert C. Byrd Honors Scholarship

Type of award: Scholarship, renewable.
Intended use: For full-time undergraduate study in United States.
Eligibility: Applicant must be high school senior. Applicant must be U.S. citizen residing in South Dakota.
Basis for selection: Applicant must demonstrate high academic achievement.
Application requirements: Transcript. Must have ACT score of 24.
Additional information: Minimum 3.5 GPA and ACT score of 24 or above required.
- Amount of award: $1,500
- Number of awards: 83
- Number of applicants: 200
- Application deadline: May 1
- Notification begins: May 30
- Total amount awarded: $92,130

Contact:
South Dakota Department of Education and Cultural Affairs
700 Governors Drive
Pierre, SD 57501-2291
Phone: 605-773-5669

State Historical Society of Wisconsin

Alice Smith Fellowship

Type of award: Scholarship.
Intended use: For full-time master's, doctoral study at accredited graduate institution in or outside United States.
Eligibility: Applicant must be female.
Basis for selection: Major/career interest in history.
Application requirements: Research proposal. 4 copies of 2-page single-spaced letter of application giving summary of research project and history of research training background.
Additional information: Must do research on history of Wisconsin or the Midwest. Doctoral candidates preferred.

Amount of award:	$2,000
Number of awards:	1
Number of applicants:	35
Application deadline:	July 15
Notification begins:	October 1
Total amount awarded:	$2,000

Contact:
State Historical Society of Wisconsin
Office of State Historian
816 State Street
Madison, WI 53706-1488

Amy Louise Hunter Fellowship

Type of award: Scholarship.
Intended use: For full-time or half-time doctoral, first professional or non-degree study.
Basis for selection: Major/career interest in history.
Application requirements: Research proposal. Application letter describing current research work, personal background, historical research training. Resume.
Additional information: Award given in even-numbered years for research on topics related to the history of women and public policy. Preference given to those researching Wisconsin topics and/or using the society's collections.

Amount of award:	$2,500
Number of awards:	1
Number of applicants:	25
Application deadline:	May 1

Contact:
State Historical Society of Wisconsin
ATTN: Dr. Michael E. Stevens, State Historian
816 State Street
Madison, WI 53706-1488

John C. Geilfuss Fellowship

Type of award: Scholarship.
Intended use: For full-time graduate or postgraduate study at accredited graduate institution in or outside United States.
Basis for selection: Major/career interest in history; economics. Applicant must demonstrate high academic achievement.
Application requirements: Research proposal. Resume and letter of application.
Additional information: Award for research on Wisconsin business/economic history or U.S. business/economic history using society's collection. Doctoral candidates preferred over masters students.

Amount of award:	$2,000
Number of awards:	1
Number of applicants:	12
Application deadline:	February 1
Notification begins:	April 15
Total amount awarded:	$2,000

Contact:
State Historical Society of Wisconsin
Office of the State Historian
816 State Street
Madison, WI 53706-1488

State Medical Education Board of Georgia

State Medical Education Board of Georgia Scholarship

Type of award: Scholarship, renewable.
Intended use: For full-time first professional study in United States.
Eligibility: Applicant must be U.S. citizen residing in Georgia.
Basis for selection: Major/career interest in medicine (m.d.); surgical technology. Applicant must demonstrate depth of character, leadership, seriousness of purpose, service orientation and financial need.
Application requirements: Interview, recommendations, essay and transcript.
Additional information: Awards may be used only for medical school. Medical school service is "repayable." Intended medical careers may be in: family practice, general surgery, internal medicine, obstetrics/gynecology, and pediatrics.

Amount of award:	$10,000
Number of awards:	98
Number of applicants:	120
Application deadline:	May 1, September 1

Contact:
State Medical Education Board of Georgia
270 Washington St., NW, 7th Fl.
Atlanta, GA 30334

State of Maine-Department of Agriculture, Food and Rural Resources

Maine Rural Rehabilitation Fund Scholarship

Type of award: Scholarship.
Intended use: For undergraduate, graduate or postgraduate study at accredited postsecondary institution.
Eligibility: Applicant must be residing in Maine.
Basis for selection: Major/career interest in agriculture;

agribusiness. Applicant must demonstrate seriousness of purpose and financial need.
Application requirements: Transcript and proof of eligibility.
Additional information: Must meet at least one of the following qualifications. At least 50% of family's income is derived from farm or woodswork and/or applicant is the child of a deceased or physically impaired person who has operated a farm or woodswork occupation and/or the applicant is a FAA member who plans to pursue a career in agriculture or woodswork.

   Application deadline: June 16
Contact:
State of Maine-Department of Agriculture, Food and Rural Resources
28 State House Station
Augusta, ME 04333

State of Virginia

Virginia Medical Scholarship Program

Type of award: Scholarship.
Intended use: For first professional study at accredited graduate institution in United States.
Eligibility: Applicant must be U.S. citizen or permanent resident residing in Virginia.
Basis for selection: Major/career interest in medicine (m.d.).
Application requirements: Transcript.
Additional information: Provides funds to medical students studying to become primary care physicians who agree to practice in a medically under-served area or become employed with the State of Virginia in an approved department. Required repayment period of one year of service for each year of scholarship receipt. For more information, call the Virginia Department of Health at (804) 786-4891.

   Amount of award: $10,000

Virginia Nursing Scholarship Program

Type of award: Scholarship.
Intended use: For freshman, sophomore, junior, senior or master's study at accredited 4-year or graduate institution in United States.
Eligibility: Applicant must be U.S. citizen or permanent resident residing in Virginia.
Basis for selection: Major/career interest in nursing.
Application requirements: Transcript.
Additional information: Provides awards to students who agree to work in the nursing profession in Virginia at the rate of one month for every $100 of aid received. For more information, call the Virginia Department of Health (804) 371-4090.

Virginia Rural Dental Scholarship Program

Type of award: Scholarship.
Intended use: For first professional study at accredited graduate institution in United States.
Eligibility: Applicant must be U.S. citizen or permanent resident residing in Virginia.
Basis for selection: Major/career interest in dentistry.
Application requirements: Transcript.
Additional information: Recipients agree to work in an area of need or for the State of Virginia to repay the scholarship. For more information, call the Medical College of Virginia (804) 828-9196.

Amount of award:	$2,500
Number of awards:	10

Tennessee Student Assistance Corporation

Dependent Children Scholarship

Type of award: Scholarship, renewable.
Intended use: For full-time undergraduate study at accredited postsecondary institution in Tennessee.
Eligibility: Applicant must be single. Applicant must be U.S. citizen residing in Tennessee. Applicant's parent must have been killed or disabled in work-related accident as fire fighter, police officer or public safety officer.
Basis for selection: Applicant must demonstrate financial need.
Application requirements: Proof of eligibility. FAFSA.
Additional information: Applicant must be enrolled in a degree-granting program. Children of Emergency Medical Service personnel disabled or killed in work-related accident also eligible.

Amount of award:	$300-$10,000
Number of awards:	3
Number of applicants:	3
Application deadline:	July 15
Total amount awarded:	$20,500

Ned McWherter Scholarship

Type of award: Scholarship, renewable.
Intended use: For full-time freshman study at accredited 2-year or 4-year institution in Tennessee.
Eligibility: Applicant must be high school senior. Applicant must be U.S. citizen residing in Tennessee.
Basis for selection: Applicant must demonstrate leadership.
Application requirements: Transcript and proof of eligibility.
Additional information: Must score at 95th percentile on ACT or SAT I. Minimum 3.5 GPA. Difficulty level of high school courses is considered.

Amount of award:	$6,000
Number of applicants:	981
Application deadline:	February 15
Total amount awarded:	$1,290,000

Student Assistance Award

Type of award: Scholarship, renewable.
Intended use: For full-time or half-time undergraduate study in Tennessee. Designated institutions: Eligible Tennessee postsecondary institution.
Eligibility: Applicant must be U.S. citizen residing in Tennessee.

Basis for selection: Applicant must demonstrate financial need.
Application requirements: Proof of eligibility. FAFSA must be processed by May 1.
- **Amount of award:** $54-$3,450
- **Number of awards:** 22,000
- **Number of applicants:** 130,000
- **Application deadline:** May 1
- **Total amount awarded:** $19,400,000

Tennessee Minority Teaching Fellows Program

Type of award: Scholarship, renewable.
Intended use: For full-time freshman, sophomore, junior or senior study at accredited 2-year or 4-year institution in Tennessee.
Eligibility: Applicant must be of minority background. Applicant must be U.S. citizen residing in Tennessee.
Basis for selection: Major/career interest in education, teacher; education. Applicant must demonstrate seriousness of purpose and service orientation.
Application requirements: Recommendations, essay, transcript and proof of eligibility.
Additional information: Entering freshmen applicants have priority. Must rank in top 25 percent of class and score at least 18 on ACT (780 SAT), minimum 2.75 GPA. Must make commitment to teaching. Loan forgiveness given by teaching at designated schools.
- **Amount of award:** $5,000
- **Number of awards:** 106
- **Number of applicants:** 160
- **Application deadline:** April 15
- **Total amount awarded:** $530,000

Tennessee Robert C. Byrd Honors Scholarship

Type of award: Scholarship, renewable.
Intended use: For full-time freshman study at accredited vocational, 2-year or 4-year institution in United States.
Eligibility: Applicant must be high school senior. Applicant must be U.S. citizen or permanent resident residing in Tennessee.
Basis for selection: Applicant must demonstrate high academic achievement.
Application requirements: Transcript and proof of eligibility.
Additional information: Minimum 3.5 GPA or 3.0 GPA and score at 75th percentile on ACT/SAT I or score of 57 or above on GED.
- **Amount of award:** $1,500
- **Number of awards:** 488
- **Number of applicants:** 3,250
- **Application deadline:** April 1
- **Total amount awarded:** $732,000

Tennessee Teaching Scholarship

Type of award: Loan, renewable.
Intended use: For full-time or half-time junior, senior, post-bachelor's certificate or master's study at accredited 4-year institution in Tennessee.
Eligibility: Applicant must be U.S. citizen residing in Tennessee.
Basis for selection: Major/career interest in education; education, teacher; education, special. Applicant must demonstrate high academic achievement.
Application requirements: Recommendations, transcript and proof of eligibility. Must provide verification of standardized test score and be accepted into Teacher Licensure Program.
Additional information: Loan forgiveness for teaching in Tennessee public schools, K-12. Minimum 2.75 cumulative GPA and a standard test score adequate for admission to the Teacher Education Program in Tennessee schools.
- **Amount of award:** $1,500-$3,000
- **Number of awards:** 120
- **Number of applicants:** 500
- **Application deadline:** April 15
- **Total amount awarded:** $360,000

Contact:
Tennessee Student Assistance Corporation
Parkway Towers, Suite 1950
404 James Robertson Parkway
Nashville, TN 37243-0820
Phone: 615-741-1346
Website: www.highered.state.tn.us

Texas Center for Rural Health Initiatives

Texas Outstanding Rural Scholar Program

Type of award: Loan, renewable.
Intended use: For full-time or half-time undergraduate study in Texas.
Eligibility: Applicant must be U.S. citizen or permanent resident residing in Texas.
Basis for selection: Major/career interest in health-related professions. Applicant must demonstrate seriousness of purpose, financial need and high academic achievement.
Application requirements: Nomination by community, which agrees to provide half the tuition.
Additional information: Must reside in rural Texas. Must be in top 25 percent of high school class and/or have maintained a minimum 3.0 GPA. One year of work for the sponsoring community must be pledged for each year of support.

Contact:
Texas Center for Rural Health Initiatives
211 East 7th
Suite 915
Austin, TX 78701
Phone: 512-479-8891

Texas Higher Education Coordinating Board

Texas Aid to Families with Dependent Children (AFDC) Students Exemption

Type of award: Scholarship.
Intended use: For full-time or half-time undergraduate certificate, freshman or sophomore study in United States. Designated institutions: Texas public institutions.
Eligibility: Applicant must be U.S. citizen or permanent resident residing in Texas.
Basis for selection: Applicant must demonstrate financial need.
Application requirements: Proof of eligibility.
Additional information: Must have graduated from Texas public high school. Must have received financial assistance under Chapter 31 Human Resources Code (AFDC) for not less than six months during senior year in high school. Must enroll within one year of high school graduation. Contact school's financial aid office for application.

Texas American Hemisphere Student Scholarship

Type of award: Scholarship, renewable.
Intended use: For full-time or half-time undergraduate or graduate study in Texas. Designated institutions: Public institutions in Texas.
Eligibility: Applicant must be Native-born citizen of any Western Hemisphere country other than Cuba residing in Texas.
Application requirements: Proof of eligibility.
Additional information: Contact school's financial aid or international student office for application. Must attend a public, non-profit institution in Texas.
   Number of awards: 374
   Total amount awarded: $1,435,002

Texas Children of Disabled Firefighters/Peace Officers Tuition Exemption

Type of award: Scholarship, renewable.
Intended use: For undergraduate study at 2-year or 4-year institution in Texas. Designated institutions: Public Texas institutions.
Eligibility: Applicant must be residing in Texas. Applicant's parent must have been killed or disabled in work-related accident as fire fighter, police officer or public safety officer.
Application requirements: Proof of eligibility.
Additional information: Must be child of deceased or disabled firefighter, law enforcement officer, custodial employee of Department of Corrections, or game warden. Initial award must be granted prior to applicant's 21st birthday.

   Number of awards: 79
   Total amount awarded: $117,839
Contact:
Texas Higher Education Coordinating Board
Division of Student Services
Box 12788 Capitol Station
Austin, TX 78711

Texas College Work-Study Program

Type of award: Internship, renewable.
Intended use: For full-time or half-time undergraduate, graduate or non-degree study in Texas. Designated institutions: Public non-profit or independent institutions in Texas.
Eligibility: Applicant must be U.S. citizen or permanent resident residing in Texas.
Basis for selection: Applicant must demonstrate financial need.
Additional information: Apply through school's financial aid office. Not available at proprietary schools. Award amount based on need.
   Number of awards: 3,458
   Total amount awarded: $2,684,545

Texas Early High School Graduation Scholarship

Type of award: Scholarship, renewable.
Intended use: For full-time or half-time undergraduate study in Texas. Designated institutions: Public non-profit or independent institutions in Texas.
Eligibility: Applicant must be high school senior. Applicant must be U.S. citizen or permanent resident residing in Texas.
Application requirements: Proof of eligibility.
Additional information: Must have completed graduation requirements from a Texas public high school in less than 36 consecutive months. Applicants should contact the Board for copy of letter submitted by their high school counselor.
   Number of awards: 1,672
   Total amount awarded: $850,873
Contact:
Texas Higher Education Coordinating Board
Division of Student Services
Box 12788, Capitol Station
Austin, TX 78711

Texas Fifth-Year Accountancy Scholarship Program

Type of award: Scholarship.
Intended use: For full-time or half-time senior, post-bachelor's certificate or master's study in Texas. Designated institutions: Public non-profit or independent institutions in Texas.
Basis for selection: Major/career interest in accounting. Applicant must demonstrate financial need.
Application requirements: Proof of eligibility. Signed statement of intent to take CPA exam.
Additional information: Must be enrolled as fifth-year accounting student who has completed at least 120 credit hours. Contact college financial aid office for application.
   Amount of award: $3,000
   Number of awards: 572
   Total amount awarded: $1,014,854

Texas Foster Care Students Exemption

Type of award: Scholarship, renewable.
Intended use: For full-time or half-time undergraduate or graduate study at accredited vocational, 2-year, 4-year or graduate institution in United States. Designated institutions: Public institutions in Texas.
Eligibility: Applicant must be U.S. citizen or permanent resident residing in Texas.
Application requirements: Proof of eligibility.
Additional information: Must have been in foster or other residential care before one's 18th birthday. Must enroll in college before third anniversary of discharge from foster care. Contact college's financial aid office for application.
    Number of awards: 250
    Total amount awarded: $209,063

Texas General Scholarship for Nursing Students

Type of award: Scholarship, renewable.
Intended use: For full-time or half-time undergraduate or graduate study at accredited 2-year, 4-year or graduate institution in Texas. Designated institutions: Public institutions in Texas.
Eligibility: Applicant must be U.S. citizen or permanent resident residing in Texas.
Basis for selection: Major/career interest in nursing. Applicant must demonstrate financial need.
Application requirements: Proof of eligibility.
Additional information: Must be enrolled in program leading to license as a Licensed Vocational Nurse or a degree in professional nursing. Degree students must not be licensed as a Licensed Vocational Nurse. Apply through school's financial aid office.
    Amount of award: $1,500-$2,000
    Number of awards: 67
    Total amount awarded: $129,200

Texas Hazlewood Act Tuition Exemption: Dependents

Type of award: Scholarship, renewable.
Intended use: For undergraduate or graduate study at accredited 2-year, 4-year or graduate institution in Texas. Designated institutions: Public institutions in Texas.
Eligibility: Applicant must be residing in Texas. Applicant must be child of deceased veteran.
Application requirements: Proof of eligibility.
Additional information: Must have tuition and fee charges that exceed all federal education benefits. Apply through school's financial aid office. Parent must have been resident of Texas prior to enlistment.
    Number of awards: 19
    Total amount awarded: $8,474

Texas Hazlewood Act Tuition Exemption: Veterans

Type of award: Scholarship, renewable.
Intended use: For undergraduate or graduate study at accredited 2-year, 4-year or graduate institution in Texas. Designated institutions: Public institutions in Texas.
Eligibility: Applicant must be residing in Texas. Applicant must be veteran.
Application requirements: Proof of eligibility.
Additional information: Must have tuition and fee charges that exceed all federal education benefits. Must have been Texas resident when entered military service, served 180 days active duty, and been honorably discharged. Apply through school's financial aid office.
    Number of awards: 9,174
    Total amount awarded: $6,988,939

Texas Highest Ranking High School Graduate Tuition Exemption

Type of award: Scholarship.
Intended use: For freshman study at accredited 2-year or 4-year institution in Texas. Designated institutions: Any state-supported Texas institution.
Eligibility: Applicant must be U.S. citizen or permanent resident residing in Texas.
Basis for selection: Applicant must demonstrate high academic achievement.
Application requirements: Proof of eligibility.
Additional information: Must be valedictorian of accredited high school. Apply through school's financial aid office.
    Number of awards: 925
    Total amount awarded: $767,407

Texas Licensed Vocational Nurses Becoming Professional Nurses Scholarship

Type of award: Scholarship, renewable.
Intended use: For full-time or half-time undergraduate or graduate study at accredited 2-year, 4-year or graduate institution in Texas. Designated institutions: Public institutions in Texas.
Eligibility: Applicant must be U.S. citizen or permanent resident residing in Texas.
Basis for selection: Major/career interest in nursing. Applicant must demonstrate financial need.
Application requirements: Proof of eligibility.
Additional information: Must be licensed vocational nurse. Apply through school's financial aid office.
    Amount of award: $1,500-$2,500
    Number of awards: 58
    Total amount awarded: $106,519

Texas Public Educational Grant

Type of award: Scholarship.
Intended use: For full-time or half-time undergraduate or graduate study at accredited 2-year, 4-year or graduate institution in Texas. Designated institutions: Public institutions in Texas.
Eligibility: Applicant must be residing in Texas.
Basis for selection: Applicant must demonstrate financial need.
Additional information: Apply through school's financial aid office.
    Number of awards: 82,554
    Total amount awarded: $29,729,661

Texas Robert C. Byrd Honors Scholarship

Type of award: Scholarship, renewable.
Intended use: For full-time undergraduate study at vocational, 2-year or 4-year institution in United States.
Eligibility: Applicant must be high school senior. Applicant must be U.S. citizen residing in Texas.
Basis for selection: Applicant must demonstrate high academic achievement.
Additional information: Must be high school senior or person completing GED to receive initial award. Contact high school guidance office or GED center director who will submit applications of top candidates to Texas Higher Education Coordinating Board.
   Number of awards: 1,539
   Application deadline: March 15
   Total amount awarded: $1,541,059

Texas Rural Bachelors or Graduate Nursing Students Scholarship

Type of award: Scholarship, renewable.
Intended use: For full-time or half-time undergraduate or graduate study at accredited 4-year or graduate institution in Texas. Designated institutions: Public institutions in Texas.
Eligibility: Applicant must be U.S. citizen or permanent resident residing in Texas.
Basis for selection: Major/career interest in nursing. Applicant must demonstrate financial need.
Additional information: Must be from a rural county. Apply through school's financial aid office.
   Amount of award: $2,500
   Number of awards: 16
   Total amount awarded: $36,250

Texas Rural Nursing Students Scholarship

Type of award: Scholarship, renewable.
Intended use: For full-time or half-time undergraduate or graduate study at accredited vocational, 2-year, 4-year or graduate institution in Rural Texas. Designated institutions: Public institutions in Texas.
Eligibility: Applicant must be U.S. citizen or permanent resident residing in Texas.
Basis for selection: Major/career interest in nursing. Applicant must demonstrate financial need.
Application requirements: Proof of eligibility.
Additional information: Must be enrolled in program leading to license as an Licensed Vocational Nurse, or a degree program in professional nursing. Must be from a rural county. Apply through school's financial aid office.
   Amount of award: $1,500-$2,500
   Number of awards: 46
   Total amount awarded: $55,100

Texas Student Incentive Grant

Type of award: Scholarship, renewable.
Intended use: For full-time or half-time undergraduate or graduate study at accredited vocational, 2-year or 4-year institution in United States. Designated institutions: Public colleges in Texas.
Eligibility: Applicant must be U.S. citizen or permanent resident residing in Texas.
Basis for selection: Applicant must demonstrate financial need.
Application requirements: Proof of eligibility.
Additional information: For further information and application contact school's financial aid office.
   Amount of award: $50-$2,500
   Number of awards: 3,445
   Total amount awarded: $2,318,544

Texas Tuition Assistance Grant

Type of award: Scholarship.
Intended use: For full-time undergraduate study at accredited 2-year or 4-year institution in Texas. Designated institutions: Public non-profit and independant institutions in Texas.
Eligibility: Applicant must be U.S. citizen or permanent resident residing in Texas.
Basis for selection: Applicant must demonstrate financial need and high academic achievement.
Application requirements: Proof of eligibility.
Additional information: Minimum high school average 80. Initial award must be made within two years of high school graduation. Must not have been convicted of a felony. Contact college financial aid office for application.
   Number of awards: 264
   Total amount awarded: $167,466

Texas Tuition Equalization Grant

Type of award: Scholarship, renewable.
Intended use: For full-time or half-time undergraduate or graduate study at accredited 2-year, 4-year or graduate institution in United States. Designated institutions: Independent non-profit institutions in Texas.
Eligibility: Applicant must be U.S. citizen or permanent resident residing in Texas.
Basis for selection: Applicant must demonstrate financial need.
Application requirements: Proof of eligibility.
Additional information: Religion/Theology majors or athletic scholarship recipients not eligible. National Merit finalists who are not Texas residents also eligible. Apply through school's financial aid office.
   Amount of award: $2,834
   Number of awards: 21,551
   Total amount awarded: $37,200,337

Texas Tuition Exemption for Blind and Deaf Students

Type of award: Scholarship, renewable.
Intended use: For undergraduate or graduate study at accredited 2-year, 4-year or graduate institution in Texas. Designated institutions: Public Texas institution.
Eligibility: Applicant must be visually impaired or hearing impaired. Applicant must be U.S. citizen or permanent resident residing in Texas.
Basis for selection: Applicant must demonstrate depth of character.
Application requirements: Proof of eligibility. certification of disability.
Additional information: Must be certified by relevant state

vocational rehabilitation agency and have high school diploma or equivalent. Apply to financial aid office of institution.
Number of awards: 2,477
Total amount awarded: $2,172,740

Texas Tuition Exemption for Children of POW/MIAS

Type of award: Scholarship, renewable.
Intended use: For undergraduate study at accredited 2-year or 4-year institution in Texas. Designated institutions: Public non-profit institutions in Texas.
Eligibility: Applicant must be residing in Texas. Applicant must be child of POW/MIA.
Application requirements: Proof of eligibility. proof of parent's status from Department of Defense.
Additional information: If over age 20, must have received majority of support from parents. Award consists of exemption from cost of tuition and fees at certain public institutions. Apply through financial aid office of institution.
Number of awards: 3
Number of applicants: 3
Total amount awarded: $4,940
Contact:
Texas Higher Education Coordinating Board
Division of Student Services
Box 12788 Capitol Station
Austin, TX 78711

U.S. Army Center of Military History

U.S. Army Center of Military History Dissertation Fellowship

Type of award: Research grant.
Intended use: For doctoral study at accredited graduate institution outside United States.
Eligibility: Applicant must be U.S. citizen.
Basis for selection: Major/career interest in history; military science; social and behavioral sciences. Applicant must demonstrate depth of character, seriousness of purpose and high academic achievement.
Application requirements: Recommendations, essay, transcript, proof of eligibility and research proposal. Must obtain statement from academic director approving dissertation topic.
Additional information: Must be civilian graduate student who has completed all requirements for Ph.D. degree, except for dissertation. Dissertation must be on history of land war. Preference given to topics on history of U.S. Army. Military personnel and any student who has held or accepted equivalent fellowship from any other Department of Defense agency not eligible. No preference given to veterans.

Amount of award: $9,000
Number of awards: 2
Number of applicants: 32
Application deadline: February 1
Notification begins: April 1
Total amount awarded: $18,000
Contact:
U.S. Army Center of Military History-c/o Building 35
Executive Secretary Dissertation Fellowship
102 4th Ave, SW, FortMcNair
Washington, DC 20319-5058
Phone: 202-761-5364
Website: www.army.mil/cmh-pg

U.S. Army Recruiting Command

Montgomery GI Bill (MGIB)

Type of award: Scholarship.
Intended use: For undergraduate or graduate study at accredited postsecondary institution in the United States.
Eligibility: Applicant must be U.S. citizen or permanent resident. Applicant must be in military service who served in the Army.
Basis for selection: Applicant must demonstrate depth of character, leadership, patriotism, seriousness of purpose and service orientation.
Application requirements: Interview. Armed Services Vocational Aptitude Battery required.
Additional information: Enlistment in U.S. active Army for two to four years required.
Amount of award: $12,865-$15,834
Number of awards: 61,120
Contact:
U.S. Army Recruiting Command
P.O. Box 3219
Warminster, PA 18974-9844
Phone: 800-USA-ARMY

Montgomery GI Bill Plus Army College Fund

Type of award: Scholarship.
Intended use: For undergraduate or graduate study at accredited postsecondary institution.
Eligibility: Applicant must be adult returning student. Applicant must be U.S. citizen or permanent resident. Applicant must be in military service who served in the Army.
Basis for selection: Applicant must demonstrate depth of character, leadership, patriotism, seriousness of purpose and service orientation.
Application requirements: Interview. Armed Services Vocational Aptitude Battery required.
Additional information: Enlistment in active Army for two to four years required. Enrollment in colleges outside the United States must be approved by Veterans Administration.

Amount of award: $26,500-$40,000
Number of awards: 13,814
Contact:
U.S. Army Recruiting Command
P.O. Box 3219
Warminster, PA 18974-9844
Phone: 800-USA-ARMY

Selected Reserve Montgomery GI Bill

Type of award: Scholarship.
Intended use: For undergraduate or graduate study at accredited postsecondary institution.
Eligibility: Applicant must be U.S. citizen or permanent resident. Applicant must be veteran who served in the Army or Reserves/National Guard.
Basis for selection: Applicant must demonstrate depth of character, leadership, patriotism, seriousness of purpose and service orientation.
Application requirements: Interview. Armed Services Vocational Aptitude Battery (ASVAB) required.
Additional information: Enlistment in U.S. Army Reserve for minimum of six years required.
Amount of award: $7,521
Number of awards: 38,425
Contact:
U.S. Army
P.O. Box 3219
Warminster, PA 18974-9844
Phone: 800-USA-ARMY

U.S. Department of Agriculture

1890 National Scholars Program

Type of award: Scholarship.
Intended use: For full-time undergraduate study at 4-year institution in United States. Designated institutions: Must be used at one of the 17 Historically Black 1890 Institutions.
Basis for selection: Major/career interest in agriculture; agribusiness; agricultural education; agricultural economics; food science and technology; computer and information sciences; veterinary medicine; biology. Applicant must demonstrate financial need and high academic achievement.
Application requirements: Recommendations and transcript.
Additional information: Must have minimum 1000 SAT, 21 ACT and 3.0 GPA. Contact office for a list of eligible universities. Scholarship covers full tuition and fees for four year.
Number of awards: 34
Application deadline: January 15
Contact:
Scholarship Committee
14th & Independence Ave., SE, Room 301-W
Washington, DC 20250
Website: www.usda.gov

Hispanic Association of Colleges and Universities Internship

Type of award: Internship.
Intended use: For sophomore, junior, senior or graduate study.
Basis for selection: Applicant must demonstrate high academic achievement.
Application requirements: Recommendations and transcript.
Additional information: 10-week internship provides college students from institutions with significant numbers of Hispanic students the opportunity to explore a potential Federal Service career. Must be active in college and community service and possess at least a 3.0 GPA. Summer deadline March 1.
Amount of award: $3,900-$5,100
Contact:
Hispanic Association of Colleges and Universities
One Dupont Circle, NW, Suite 230
Washington, DC 20036
Website: www.hacu2000.org

Presidential Management Program

Type of award: Internship.
Intended use: For master's, first professional study.
Eligibility: Applicant must be U.S. citizen or permanent resident.
Basis for selection: Major/career interest in political science/government.
Application requirements: Nomination by Nomination from Dean or Department Chair of applicants institutuion.
Additional information: Graduate students and law students in last year of study are eligible. PMI Program is the Federal Government's premiere program for bringing individuals with advanced degrees into Federal service. Contact office for pay information.
Application deadline: October 31
Contact:
PMI Program Manager
Office of Personnel Management-Philadelphia Service Center
600 Arch St., Room 3256
Philadelpha, PA 19106
Website: www.usda.gov

U.S. Department of Agriculture Summer Intern Program

Type of award: Internship.
Intended use: For undergraduate study.
Eligibility: Applicant must be U.S. citizen.
Application requirements: Recommendations and transcript.
Additional information: Internships last approximately four months. Stipend amounts are based on level of education, prior experience and position. Open to undergraduates and high school graduates entering college. Applications available in January.
Application deadline: February 20
Contact:
United States Department of Agriculture
14th & Independence Ave., SW
Washington, DC 20250
Website: www.usda.gov

U.S. Department of Education

Federal Direct Student Loans

Type of award: Loan.
Intended use: For undergraduate or graduate study.
Eligibility: Applicant must be U.S. citizen or permanent resident.
Basis for selection: Applicant must demonstrate financial need.
Application requirements: Proof of eligibility. Free Application for Federal Student Aid (FAFSA).
Additional information: Must not have defaulted on federal grant or educational loan. Alternate phone number: 800-730-8913.
   Application deadline: June 30
   Notification begins: August 29
Contact:
Federal Student Aid Information Center
PO Box 84
Washington, DC 20044-0084
Phone: 800-4-FED-AID
Website: www.ed.gov

Federal Family Education Loan Program

Type of award: Loan.
Intended use: For full-time or half-time undergraduate or graduate study at postsecondary institution in Institution must be approved by the US Department of Education.
Eligibility: Applicant must be U.S. citizen or permanent resident.
Basis for selection: Applicant must demonstrate financial need.
Application requirements: Proof of eligibility. Student must take test. Free application for Federal Student Aid (FAFSA). Must not have defaulted on federal grant or educational loan.
Additional information: Subsidized and unsubsidized loans. Maximum: $23,000 (dependent undergraduates, $46,000 (independent undergraduates), and $138,500 (graduate or professional). Interest 7.66%. Repayment period 5-10 years. Alternate phone number: 800-730-8913.
   Amount of award: $46,000
   Application deadline: June 30
   Notification begins: August 29
Contact:
Federal Student Aid Information Center
PO Box 84
Washington, DC 20044-0084
Phone: 800-4-FED-AID
Website: www.ed.gov/offices/OPE

Federal Pell Grant Program

Type of award: Scholarship, renewable.
Intended use: For undergraduate study.
Eligibility: Applicant must be U.S. citizen or permanent resident.
Basis for selection: Applicant must demonstrate financial need.
Application requirements: Proof of eligibility. Free Application for Federal Student Aid (FAFSA). Must not have defaulted on federal grant or educational loan.
Additional information: Additional need analysis form may be required. Alternate phone number: 800-730-8913.
   Amount of award: $2,700
   Application deadline: June 30
   Notification begins: August 29
Contact:
Federal Student Aid Information Center
PO Box 84
Washington, DC 20044-0084
Phone: 800-4-FED-AID
Website: www.ed.gov

Federal Perkins Loan

Type of award: Loan, renewable.
Intended use: For undergraduate or graduate study.
Eligibility: Applicant must be U.S. citizen or permanent resident.
Basis for selection: Applicant must demonstrate financial need.
Application requirements: Proof of eligibility. Free Application for Federal Student Aid (FAFSA). Must not have defaulted on federal grant or educational loan.
Additional information: Loan limits: $15,000 for undergraduate study, $30,000 for graduate study--including undergraduate loan. Repayment begins nine months after course load drops below one half. Interest 5%. Alternate phone number: 800-730-8913.
   Amount of award: $3,000-$5,000
   Application deadline: June 30
   Notification begins: August 29
Contact:
Federal Student Aid Information Center
PO Box 84
Washington, DC 20044-0084
Phone: 800-433-3243
Website: www.ed.gov

Federal Plus Loan

Type of award: Loan.
Intended use: For undergraduate or graduate study.
Eligibility: Applicant must be U.S. citizen or permanent resident.
Basis for selection: Applicant must demonstrate financial need.
Application requirements: Free Application for Federal Student Aid (FAFSA). Must not have defaulted on federal grant or educational loan.
Additional information: Loans for parent of student, limited to full cost of education, minus financial aid or family contribution. Interest rate 8.72%. First payment within 60 days. Term up to ten years. Alternate phone number: 800-730-8913.
   Application deadline: June 30
   Notification begins: August 29
Contact:
Federal Student Aid Information Center
PO Box 84
Washington, DC 20044-0084
Phone: 800-4-FED-AID
Website: www.ed.gov

Federal Supplemental Educational Opportunity Grant Program

Type of award: Scholarship, renewable.
Intended use: For undergraduate study at vocational, 2-year or 4-year institution.
Eligibility: Applicant must be U.S. citizen or permanent resident.
Basis for selection: Applicant must demonstrate financial need.
Application requirements: Proof of eligibility. Free Application for Federal Student Aid (FAFSA).
Additional information: Priority given to Federal Pell Grant recipients with exceptional financial need. Must not have defaulted on federal grant or educational loan. Awards are not generally made to students enrolled for less than half-time.

Amount of award:	$100-$4,000
Application deadline:	June 30
Notification begins:	August 29

Contact:
Federal Student Aid Information Center
PO Box 84
Washington, DC 20044-0084
Phone: 800-4-FED-AID
Website: www.ed.gov

Federal Work-Study Program

Type of award: Internship.
Intended use: For undergraduate or graduate study at postsecondary institution in United States.
Eligibility: Applicant must be U.S. citizen or permanent resident.
Basis for selection: Applicant must demonstrate financial need.
Application requirements: Proof of eligibility. Free Application for Federal Student Aid (FAFSA). Must not have defaulted on federal grant/loan.
Additional information: On-campus and off-campus employment assignments based on health, class schedule, and academic progress. Students earn at least the minimum wage. Alternate phone number: 800-730-8913.

Application deadline:	June 30
Notification begins:	August 27

Contact:
Federal Student Aid Information Center
PO Box 84
Washington, DC 20044-0084
Phone: 800-4-FED-AID
Website: www.ed.gov

Paul Douglas Teacher Scholarship

Type of award: Scholarship, renewable.
Intended use: For undergraduate study at postsecondary institution in American Samoa, Guam, The North Mariana Islands, the Trust Territory of the Pacific Islands (Palua), the Virgin Islands.
Eligibility: Applicant must be high school senior. Applicant must be U.S. citizen.
Basis for selection: Applicant must demonstrate high academic achievement.
Application requirements: Proof of eligibility. Request application.
Additional information: For students graduating in top 10% of class and pursuing teaching careers. Up to $5,000 annually. Two years teaching generally required for each year of assistance received.

Amount of award:	$5,000
Number of awards:	54
Application deadline:	August 22
Total amount awarded:	$14,681,000

Contact:
U.S. Department of Education
400 Maryland Avenue SW
Washington, DC 20202-5329
Phone: 800-877-8339

U.S. Department of Education Robert C. Byrd Honors Scholarship

Type of award: Scholarship, renewable.
Intended use: For undergraduate study at postsecondary institution in United States.
Eligibility: Applicant must be U.S. citizen.
Basis for selection: Applicant must demonstrate high academic achievement.
Application requirements: Proof of eligibility. Minimun scores: SAT 1300, ACT composite score 31, or GED 65. Must be high school senior or receiving GED. Must not have defaulted on federal grant or educational loan or have received drug sentence.
Additional information: Merit-based. Renewable up to three years. Funds very limited. Selections by state agencies supervising public elementary/secondary schools.

Amount of award:	$1,500
Application deadline:	April 24

Contact:
Special Programs Division
State Student Assistance Commission of Indiana
150 West Market Street, Suite 500
Indianapolis, IN 46204-2811
Phone: 317-232-2350
Website: www.ed.gov/offices/OPE

U.S. Department of Health and Human Services

National Health Services Corps Scholarship

Type of award: Scholarship.
Intended use: For full-time undergraduate certificate, post-bachelor's certificate or postgraduate study at accredited 4-year or graduate institution in United States.
Eligibility: Applicant must be U.S. citizen.
Basis for selection: Major/career interest in midwifery; nursing; nurse practitioner; physician assistant; medicine, osteopathic. Applicant must demonstrate depth of character, seriousness of purpose and service orientation.
Application requirements: Interview.
Additional information: Award includes full tuition/fees, monthly stipend and other reasonable educational expenses. Must be studying within the fields indicated. One year of

service in underserved areas required for each year scholarship is granted.
- **Number of awards:** 326
- **Number of applicants:** 350
- **Application deadline:** March 26

Contact:
United States Department of Health and Human Services
National Health Service Corps
4350 East West Highway, 10th Floor
Bethesda, MD 20814
Phone: 8006380824

U.S. Department of Interior-Bureau of Indian Affairs

Indians Higher Education Grant Program

Type of award: Scholarship.
Intended use: For full-time undergraduate study at accredited 2-year or 4-year institution.
Eligibility: Applicant must be Alaskan native or American Indian. Applicant must be U.S. citizen.
Basis for selection: Applicant must demonstrate financial need.
Application requirements: Proof of eligibility. Member of tribal group served by bureau.
Additional information: Contact tribe or bureau agency serving tribe for application. For information only write the Department of the Interior/Bureau of Indian Affairs.
- **Application deadline:** June 30
- **Notification begins:** August 29

Contact:
U.S. Department of Interior-Bureau of Indian Affairs
Office of Education Programs MS 3512
1849 C Street, NW
Washington, DC 20240

U.S. Department of Vocational Rehabilitation

U.S. Department of Vocational Rehabilitation Scholarship

Type of award: Scholarship.
Intended use: For undergraduate or graduate study at postsecondary institution in United States.
Eligibility: Applicant must be physically challenged.
Application requirements: Proof of eligibility.

Additional information: Must have medically verifiable disability that constitutes substantial handicap to employment. Award may be used for programs of study leading to development of employable skills. Amounts vary depending on program. Contact nearest district office of U.S. Department of Rehabilitation.

Contact:
Scholarship Committee
Main Education Building
6000 Independence Ave., SW
Washington, DC 20202
Website: www.ed.gov/offices

U.S. Institute of Peace

National Peace Essay Contest

Type of award: Scholarship.
Intended use: For undergraduate study.
Eligibility: Applicant must be enrolled in high school.
Basis for selection: Competition in Writing/journalism. High school students must write an essay on a conflict resolution/international affairs topic chosen by USIP. Topic changes each year; the topic for applying in 1999 is "Preventing Violent International Conflict.".
Application requirements: Essay. Application.
Additional information: 1500 word limit to the essay.
- **Amount of award:** $1,000-$10,000
- **Number of awards:** 50
- **Number of applicants:** 1,500
- **Application deadline:** February 27
- **Notification begins:** April 28
- **Total amount awarded:** $50,250

Contact:
U.S. Institute of Peace
Attn: Heather Kerr-Stewart
1550 M Street NW, Suite 700
Washington, DC 20005
Website: www.usip.org/et/npec96.html

U.S. Navy-Marine Corps

NROTC Express Scholarship

Type of award: Scholarship.
Intended use: For full-time undergraduate study at 2-year or 4-year institution.
Eligibility: Applicant must be U.S. citizen.
Basis for selection: Applicant must demonstrate depth of character, leadership, patriotism, seriousness of purpose, service orientation and high academic achievement.
Application requirements: Interview, recommendations and transcript.
Additional information: NROTC scholarships must be used at schools hosting the NROTC Program or schools cross-enrolled with host school. Minimum four years reserve duty required plus 4 years in active reserve for commissioned officers. Applicants with previous active duty may be eligible for adjustments or waivers of the age limitations.

Number of awards:	2,419
Number of applicants:	6,058
Application deadline:	January 31

Contact:
Contact local Navy Recruiter

Phone: 800-628-7682

U.S. Navy-Marine Corps Immediate Selection Decision Scholarship

Type of award: Scholarship.
Intended use: For full-time undergraduate study.
Eligibility: Applicant must be U.S. citizen.
Basis for selection: Applicant must demonstrate depth of character, leadership, patriotism, seriousness of purpose, service orientation and high academic achievement.
Application requirements: Interview, recommendations and transcript.
Additional information: Program targets minorities and students who plan on taking technical majors. Immediate Selection Decision scholarships must be used at schools hosting NROTC program or cross-enrolled with a host school. Minimum of four years active duty and four years of reserve duty for commissioned officers.

Number of awards:	160
Number of applicants:	160
Application deadline:	December 1

Contact:
U.S. Navy-Marine Corps
Contact Local Recruiter

Phone: 800-628-7682

United States Department of State

United States Department of State Internships

Type of award: Internship.
Intended use: For junior, senior or master's study.
Eligibility: Applicant must be U.S. citizen.
Basis for selection: Applicant must demonstrate high academic achievement.
Additional information: Provides opportunities working in varied administrative branches of the Department of State. Departments include the Art Bank Program, Art in Embassies Program, Information Management, Bureau of African Affairs, Bureau of Inter-American Affairs, Bureau of Consular Affairs, Bureau of International Communications and Information Policy, Office of the Chief of Protocol, Bureau of Democracy, human Rights and Labor, 'Bureau of Diplomatic Security, Bureau of East Capitol Ave. Asian and Pacific Affairs, and Bureau of Economic and Business Affairs Deadlines: Summer, November1. Fall, March 1. Spring, July 1. Pay varies according to academic level. Contact the intern coordinator for further details.

Number of awards:	900

Contact:
Intern Coordinator Recruitment Division
PO Box 9317
Arlington, VA 22219
Website: www.state.gov/www/careers

United States Holocaust Memorial Museum

United States Holocaust Memorial Museum Internship

Type of award: Internship, renewable.
Intended use: For full-time undergraduate or graduate study.
Eligibility: Applicant must be enrolled in high school. Applicant must be U.S. citizen or permanent resident.
Basis for selection: Major/career interest in museum studies/administration; Jewish studies.
Additional information: Twelve week internship available in the summer, fall, and spring. Interns receive $260/week.

Amount of award:	$3,120
Number of awards:	35
Number of applicants:	250
Application deadline:	June 15, March 15

Contact:
100 Raoul Wallenberg Place, SW
Washington, DC 20024-2150
Phone: 202-488-0400
Fax: 202-488-2690

United States Information Agency

United States Information Agency Summer Internship

Type of award: Internship.
Intended use: For freshman, sophomore, junior or senior study.
Eligibility: Applicant must be U.S. citizen.
Basis for selection: Major/career interest in governmental public relations; arts, general; education.
Additional information: Prospective interns must obtain security clearance based on background and fingerprint check.

Application deadline:	June 30, September 30

Contact:
United States Information Agency
M/HRCO Room 518
301 4th St., SW
Washington, DC 20547

United States Navy/Marine NROTC College Scholarship Program

ROTC/Navy Marine Two-Year Scholarship Program

Type of award: Scholarship.
Intended use: For full-time junior, senior study at accredited 4-year institution in United States.
Eligibility: Applicant must be U.S. citizen.
Basis for selection: Applicant must demonstrate high academic achievement.
Application requirements: Interview and transcript.
Additional information: Provides tuition, fees, textbooks and uniforms for two academic years and a subsistence allowance for a maximum of 20 academic months. Open to college students who will complete their sophomore years or third years in a five-year curriculum. Students undergo six-and-a-half-week course at the Naval Science Institute on Newport, RI., during the summer between their freshman and sophomore years. Students who complete all NROTC Program requirements are commissioned ensigns, U.S. Naval Reserve, or second lieutenants, Marine Corps Reserve, upon graduation and incur four0years active duty obligations from the dates of their appointments. Total military service obligation is eight years of combined active and inactive duty. Students may apply for only one the three scholarship Program options-Navy, Marine Corps, or Nurse. Navy and Nurse-option applicants should apply through Navy recruiting offices; Marine Corps applicants should apply through Marine Corps recruiting offices. Contact your local recruiter for further details.
Contact:
Recruitment Officer
801 North Randolph
Arlington, VA 22203-9933
Website: www.navyjobs.com

ROTC/Navy Nurse Corps Scholarship Program

Type of award: Scholarship.
Intended use: For full-time freshman study at accredited 4-year institution in United States.
Eligibility: Applicant must be high school senior. Applicant must be U.S. citizen.
Basis for selection: Major/career interest in nursing. Applicant must demonstrate high academic achievement.
Application requirements: Interview and transcript.
Additional information: Four-year NROTC scholarships are available to students interested in pursuing bachelor of science degree in nursing (BSN). If selected for a scholarship, the selectee must major in a nursing degree program leading to a BSN. Upon Graduation, Nurse NROTC Scholarship Program midshipmen will be commissioned as reserve officers in the Navy Nurse Corps. Nurse NROTC eligibility and selection processes are the same as the regular four year NROTC Scholarship Program requirements. Academic, physical and military requirements differ slightly from regular NROTC. Contact you local recruiter for further details.
Contact:
Recruitment Officer
801 North Randolph
Arlington, VA 22203-9933
Website: www.navyjobs.com

ROTC/Navy/Marine Four-Year Scholarship

Type of award: Scholarship.
Intended use: For full-time freshman study at accredited 4-year institution in United States.
Eligibility: Applicant must be high school senior. Applicant must be U.S. citizen.
Application requirements: Interview and transcript.
Additional information: Minimum test scores: SAT Total 1050, Math 530, Verbal 520. ACT administered upon request. Applicants must not have been enrolled in college full-time prior to application. Provides full-tuition, fees and $150 per month stipend during academic year for four years to a maximum of $80,000. Scholarship recipients agree to serve four years active duty upon graduation. Students may apply for only one of the three scholarship program options-Navy, Marine Corps, or Nurse. Navy and Nurse-option applicants should apply through Navy recruiting offices; Marine Corps applicants should apply through Marine Corps recruiting offices. Contact your local recruiter for further details.
Contact:
United States Navy/Marine NROTC College Scholarship Program
801 North Randolph
Arlington, VA 22203-9933
Website: www.navyjobs.com

University Corporation for Atmospheric Research

SOARS - Significant Opportunities in Atmospheric Research and Science

Type of award: Internship.
Intended use: For full-time sophomore, junior or senior study.
Eligibility: Applicant must be U.S. citizen or permanent resident.
Basis for selection: Major/career interest in atmospheric sciences/meteorology.
Application requirements: Recommendations, essay and transcript.
Additional information: Applicant must be a member of a

group that is traditionally underrepresented in the atmospheric and related sciences. Compensation varies; contact the coordinator. Preference given to undergraduate applicants; graduate students may apply, but acceptance is unlikely.
- Number of awards: 17
- Application deadline: March 5, March 3

Contact:
University Corporation for Atmospheric Research
P.O. Box 3000
Boulder, CO 80307
Website: www.fin.ucar.edu/sours

University of North Carolina General Administration

North Carolina Board of Governors Dental Scholarship

Type of award: Scholarship, renewable.
Intended use: For full-time first professional study in North Carolina. Designated institutions: University of North Carolina School of Dentistry.
Eligibility: Applicant must be permanent resident residing in North Carolina.
Basis for selection: Major/career interest in dentistry. Applicant must demonstrate seriousness of purpose, service orientation and financial need.
Application requirements: Interview, recommendations, essay, transcript, proof of eligibility and nomination by University of North Carolina School of Dentistry. FAFSA form.
Additional information: Preference given to economically disadvantaged students. Must declare intent to practice in North Carolina. Award pays tuition, fees, instrument costs, and $5,000 stipend annually.
- Number of awards: 32
- Application deadline: April 1
- Notification begins: April 25
- Total amount awarded: $395,728

Contact:
University of North Carolina Dental School
Brauer Hall, CB 7450/UNC Chapel Hill
Chapel Hill, NC 27514

North Carolina Board of Governors Medical Scholarship

Type of award: Scholarship, renewable.
Intended use: For full-time first professional study in North Carolina medical schools.
Eligibility: Applicant must be permanent resident residing in North Carolina.
Basis for selection: Major/career interest in medicine (m.d.). Applicant must demonstrate seriousness of purpose, service orientation and financial need.
Application requirements: Recommendations, essay, transcript, proof of eligibility and nomination by one of the four North Carolina Medical Schools. need analysis form required by Medical School.
Additional information: Preference given to economically disadvantaged students who must declare intent to practice medicine in North Carolina. Award pays tuition, required fees, and $5,000 annual stipend.
- Number of awards: 80
- Total amount awarded: $1,212,953

University of North Carolina Incentive Scholarship

Type of award: Scholarship, renewable.
Intended use: For freshman, sophomore, junior or senior study at accredited 4-year institution in North Carolina. Designated institutions: Elizabeth City State University, Fayetteville State University, North Carolina Agricultural and Technical State University, North Carolina Central University, Pembroke State University, and Winston-Salem State University.
Eligibility: Applicant must be permanent resident residing in North Carolina.
Basis for selection: Applicant must demonstrate depth of character, leadership, service orientation, financial need and high academic achievement.
Additional information: At least six to eight hours public service required per week at university or in community.
- Amount of award: $3,000
- Total amount awarded: $1,750,979

Contact:
Office of Scholarships and Student Aid
P.O. Box 1080
Chapel Hill, NC 27514
Phone: 919-962-8396

University of North Carolina Minority Grant: Doctor/Lawyer/Veterinary Medicine

Type of award: Scholarship, renewable.
Intended use: For full-time doctoral, first professional study at accredited graduate institution in North Carolina. Designated institutions: East Carolina University, North Carolina State University, University of North Carolina at Chapel Hill and University of North Carolina Greensboro.
Eligibility: Applicant must be African American. Applicant must be residing in North Carolina.
Basis for selection: Applicant must demonstrate financial need.
Additional information: Priority given to students pursuing degrees in fields of study where African-American participation has been low historically.
- Amount of award: $500-$4,000
- Number of awards: 300
- Total amount awarded: $360,000

Contact:
Office of Scholarships and Student Aid
P.O. Box 1080
Chapel Hill, NC 27514
Phone: 919-962-8396

University of North Carolina Minority Presence Grant: General

Type of award: Scholarship, renewable.
Intended use: For undergraduate or graduate study at 4-year

institution in North Carolina. Designated institutions: University of North Carolina constituent institutions.
Eligibility: Applicant must be U.S. citizen or permanent resident residing in North Carolina.
Basis for selection: Applicant must demonstrate financial need.
Additional information: Grants available to students taking at least three hours of degree-credit course work per semester at a University of North Carolina constituent institution where their race is in the minority (black students at predominantly white institutions or white students at predominantly black institutions).

Amount of award:	$99-$2,000
Number of awards:	1,420
Total amount awarded:	$1,295,409

Contact:
Office of Scholarships and Student Aid
P.O. Box 1080
Chapel Hill, NC 27514
Phone: 919-962-8396

University of North Carolina Native American Incentive Graduate Scholarship

Type of award: Scholarship, renewable.
Intended use: For undergraduate study. Designated institutions: University of North Carolina constituent institutions.
Eligibility: Applicant must be American Indian. Must be member of tribe recognized by State of North Carolina or federal government. Applicant must be residing in North Carolina.
Additional information: Need-based doctoral awards. Merit-based awards have a public service component.

Amount of award:	$5,000
Total amount awarded:	$45,000

Contact:
Office of Scholarships and Student Aid
P.O. Box 1080
Chapel Hill, NC 27514
Phone: 919-962-8396

University of North Carolina Native American Incentive Merit Scholarship

Type of award: Scholarship, renewable.
Intended use: For undergraduate or graduate study. Designated institutions: University of North Carolina constituent institutions.
Eligibility: Applicant must be American Indian. Must be member of tribe recognized by State of North Carolina or federal government. Applicant must be residing in North Carolina.
Additional information: Award has a public service component.

Amount of award:	$3,000

Contact:
Office of Scholarships and Student Aid
P.O. Box 1080
Chapel Hill, NC 27514
Phone: 919-962-8396

University of North Carolina Native American Incentive Undergraduate Scholarship

Type of award: Scholarship, renewable.
Intended use: For undergraduate or graduate study. Designated institutions: University of North Carolina constituent institutions.
Eligibility: Applicant must be American Indian. Must be member of tribe recognized by State of North Carolina or federal government. Applicant must be residing in North Carolina.
Additional information: Need-based undergraduate award. Apply through financial aid office at institution. Merit-based awards have a public service component.

Amount of award:	$700
Total amount awarded:	$384,799

Contact:
Office of Scholarships and Student Aid
P.O. Box 1080
Chapel Hill, NC 27514
Phone: 919-962-8396

US Department of State

US Department of State Internships

Type of award: Internship.
Intended use: For junior, senior or master's study.
Eligibility: Applicant must be U.S. citizen.
Basis for selection: Applicant must demonstrate high academic achievement.
Additional information: Provides opportunities working in vareid administrative branches of the Department of State. Departments include the Art Bank Program, Art in Embassies Program, Information Management, Bureau of African Affairs, Bureau of Inter-American Affairs, Bureau of Consular Affairs, Bureau of International Communications and Information Policy, Office of the Chief of Protocol. Bureau of Democracy, Human Rights and Labor, Bureau of Diplomatic Security, Bureau of East Capitol Ave. Asian and Pacific Affairs, and Bureau of Economic and Business Affairs Deadline: Summer, November 1. Fall, March 1. Spring, July 1. Pay varies according to academic level. Contact the intern coordinator for further details.

Number of awards:	900

Contact:
US Department of State Internships
PO Box 9317
Arington, VA 22219
Website: www.state.gov/www/careers

Utah State Board of Regents

Utah State Student Incentive Grant

Type of award: Scholarship, renewable.
Intended use: For undergraduate study at vocational, 2-year or 4-year institution in Utah.
Eligibility: Applicant must be residing in Utah.
Basis for selection: Applicant must demonstrate financial need.
Additional information: Contact financial aid office for further information.
    Amount of award: $2,500

Utah State Office of Education

Utah Career Teaching Scholarship/ T.H. Bell Teaching Incentive Loan

Type of award: Loan, renewable.
Intended use: For full-time undergraduate study at accredited 4-year institution in Utah.
Eligibility: Applicant must be high school senior. Applicant must be U.S. citizen residing in Utah.
Basis for selection: Major/career interest in education, teacher.
Additional information: Provides tuition waiver with additional awards to limited number of qualified recipients. Loan forgiveness for teaching in Utah public schools. Contact high school counselor or financial aid adviser for application after Jan. 15.

Number of awards:	60
Number of applicants:	320
Application deadline:	March 31
Notification begins:	May 15

Utah Robert C. Byrd Honors Scholarship

Type of award: Scholarship, renewable.
Intended use: For undergraduate study.
Eligibility: Applicant must be high school senior. Applicant must be residing in Utah.
Basis for selection: Applicant must demonstrate high academic achievement.
Application requirements: Transcript.
Additional information: Contact high school counselor or financial aid adviser for application after Jan. 15.

Amount of award:	$1,500
Number of awards:	261
Number of applicants:	261
Application deadline:	March 31
Notification begins:	May 15
Total amount awarded:	$192,000

Vermont Student Assistance Corporation

Vermont Extra Loan (Supplemental)

Type of award: Loan.
Intended use: For undergraduate or graduate study at vocational, 2-year, 4-year or graduate institution in United States.
Eligibility: Applicant must be U.S. citizen residing in Vermont.
Additional information: Loan eligibility is based on credit and income requirements. Most borrowers need co-signer to meet income qualifications. Co-signer must be creditworthy and agree to be equally responsible for debt. Students must be Vermont residents or enrolled in a Vermont postsecondary institution. Students must be enrolled in a degree program. Students must first borrow maximum allowed under Federal loans. Award equals cost of admission minus other financial aid.
Contact:
Vermont Student Assistance Corporation
Education Loan Finance Department
P.O. Box 900
Winooski, VT 05404

Vermont Incentive Grant

Type of award: Scholarship.
Intended use: For full-time undergraduate study at vocational, 2-year or 4-year institution in or outside United States. Designated institutions: Any undergraduate institution or University of Vermont College of Medicine or veterinary school.
Eligibility: Applicant must be U.S. citizen residing in Vermont.
Basis for selection: Applicant must demonstrate financial need.
Application requirements: Proof of eligibility.
Additional information: Open to graduate students attending the University of Vermont Medical School and to state residents who are enrolled at an approved school of vetenirary medicine.

Amount of award:	$500-$5,200
Number of awards:	9,421
Number of applicants:	15,704
Application deadline:	March 1
Total amount awarded:	$9,964,276

Contact:
Vermont Student Assistance Corporation
Grant Department
P.O. Box 2000
Winooski, VT 05404

Vermont Non-Degree Program

Type of award: Scholarship.
Intended use: For non-degree study at postsecondary institution in United States.
Eligibility: Applicant must be U.S. citizen residing in Vermont or U.S. Territories.
Basis for selection: Applicant must demonstrate financial need.
Application requirements: Proof of eligibility. Available to

Vermont residents enrolled in a non-degree course that will improve employability or encourage further study. Must meet needs test.
Additional information: Maximum amount for this award is $350 for one course per semester.

    Number of awards: 1,278
    Number of applicants: 2,115
    Total amount awarded: $431,692

Contact:
Vermont Student Assistance Corporation
Grant Department
P.O. Box 2000
Winooski, VT 05404

Vermont Part-Time Grant

Type of award: Scholarship.
Intended use: For half-time or less than half-time undergraduate study at vocational, 2-year or 4-year institution in or outside United States.
Eligibility: Applicant must be U.S. citizen residing in Vermont.
Basis for selection: Applicant must demonstrate financial need.
Application requirements: Proof of eligibility.
Additional information: Must be taking fewer than 12 credits and have not received bachelor's degree Award amounts vary according to the number of credits the studunt is taking.

    Amount of award: $200-$3,900
    Number of awards: 2,747
    Number of applicants: 4,873
    Application deadline: January 31
    Total amount awarded: $887,358

Contact:
Vermont Student Assistance Corporation
Grant Department
P.O. Box 2000
Winooski, VT 05404

Vermont Robert C. Byrd Honors Scholarship

Type of award: Scholarship, renewable.
Intended use: For freshman study.
Eligibility: Applicant must be high school senior. Applicant must be U.S. citizen or permanent resident residing in Vermont.
Basis for selection: Applicant must demonstrate seriousness of purpose and high academic achievement.
Application requirements: Recommendations, essay, transcript and proof of eligibility. Application, SAT I/ACT scores, class rank, GPA.
Additional information: Applicant must rank in top 20 percent of high school graduating class, have very high GPA and very competitive SAT I and ACT scores. Grant may not exceed cost of attendance.

    Amount of award: $1,121
    Number of awards: 56
    Number of applicants: 187
    Application deadline: May 1
    Total amount awarded: $62,776

Contact:
Vermont Student Assistance Corporation Attn: Scholarships
Champlain Mill
P.O. Box 2000
Winooski, VT 05404-2601

Virgin Islands Board of Education

Virgin Islands Music Scholarship

Type of award: Scholarship, renewable.
Intended use: For full-time undergraduate study at accredited 2-year or 4-year institution in United States.
Eligibility: Applicant must be high school senior. Applicant must be residing in Virgin Islands.
Basis for selection: Major/career interest in music. Applicant must demonstrate financial need and high academic achievement.
Application requirements: Recommendations and transcript.
Additional information: Must be graduating from or a graduate of Virgin Islands high school. Minimum GPA 2.0.

    Amount of award: $2,000
    Number of awards: 8
    Number of applicants: 8
    Total amount awarded: $16,000

Contact:
Virgin Islands Board of Education
P.O. Box 11900
St. Thomas, VI 00801

Virgin Islands Student Incentive Grant

Type of award: Scholarship, renewable.
Intended use: For full-time undergraduate or graduate study.
Eligibility: Applicant must be residing in Virgin Islands.
Basis for selection: Applicant must demonstrate financial need and high academic achievement.
Application requirements: Recommendations and transcript.
Additional information: Minimum 2.0 GPA. Must agree to accept employment in Virgin Islands government one year for every year of award.

    Amount of award: $500-$3,000
    Number of applicants: 50

Contact:
Virgin Islands Board of Education-Financial Aid Office
P.O. Box 11900
St. Thomas, VI 00801

Virgin Islands Territorial Grants Scholarship

Type of award: Loan, renewable.
Intended use: For full-time undergraduate or graduate study at accredited graduate institution.
Eligibility: Applicant must be residing in Virgin Islands.
Basis for selection: Applicant must demonstrate financial need and high academic achievement.
Application requirements: Recommendations and transcript. Acceptance letter from institution for first time applicants or transfer students.
Additional information: Minimum required GPA 2.0. Must agree to accept employment in Virgin Islands government one year for every year of award upon completion of studies.

Amount of award:	$500
Number of applicants:	1,000

Contact:
Scolarship Committee
P.O. Box 11900
St. Thomas, VI 00801

Virgin Islands Territorial Loan Scholarship

Type of award: Loan, renewable.
Intended use: For full-time undergraduate or graduate study.
Eligibility: Applicant must be residing in Virgin Islands.
Basis for selection: Applicant must demonstrate financial need.
Application requirements: Recommendations and transcript. Acceptance letter from institution for first time applicants or transfer students.
Additional information: Minimum GPA 2.0.

Amount of award:	$500
Number of applicants:	1,000

Contact:
Virgin Islands Board of Education-Financial Aid Office
P.O. Box 11900
St. Thomas, VI 00801

Virginia Council of Higher Education

Virginia Academic Common Market Program

Type of award: Scholarship.
Intended use: For undergraduate study at 2-year or 4-year institution.
Eligibility: Applicant must be residing in Virginia.
Additional information: Awards Virginia residents in-state tuition at non-Virginia institutions in the South. Institution must offer programs unavailable in Virginia public institutions.

Virginia Assistance for the Visually Handicapped

Type of award: Scholarship.
Intended use: For undergraduate study.
Eligibility: Applicant must be visually impaired. Applicant must be residing in Virginia.
Additional information: Available only when need exist after federal, state and private funding have been used. (800) 622-2155. Contact Virginia Department for the Visually handicapped.

Virginia College Scholarship Assistance

Type of award: Scholarship, renewable.
Intended use: For undergraduate study at accredited 4-year institution in Virginia.
Eligibility: Applicant must be U.S. citizen or permanent resident residing in Virginia.
Basis for selection: Applicant must demonstrate financial need.
Application requirements: Proof of eligibility.
Additional information: Apply to financial aid office of institution. Theology or divinity majors not eligible. Must not be in default on any federal educational loans. Must satisfy draft registration requirements.

Amount of award:	$400-$5,000
Number of awards:	8,500
Number of applicants:	10,000
Total amount awarded:	$5,500,000

Virginia Eastern Shore Tuition Assistance

Type of award: Scholarship.
Intended use: For junior, senior study at 2-year or 4-year institution in Maryland. Designated institutions: University of Maryland-Eastern Shore or Salisbury State College (MD).
Eligibility: Applicant must be residing in Virginia.
Additional information: Award to Virginia residents living in Northampton or Accomack counties who are juniors or seniors commuting to the University of Maryland-Eastern Shore or Salisbury State College. Award amounts vary depending upon number of eligible applicants. Applications available from Maryland institutions, Eastern Shore Community College, and the Council.

Amount of award:	$2,000
Number of awards:	50

Virginia Graduate and Undergraduate Assistance

Type of award: Scholarship.
Intended use: For full-time undergraduate or graduate study at postsecondary institution in Virginia.
Eligibility: Applicant must be residing in Virginia.
Basis for selection: Applicant must demonstrate financial need.
Application requirements: $1 application fee.
Additional information: Must be used at state-supported college or university. Apply to financial aid office of institution. Award based on academic performance.

Number of awards:	750

Virginia Regional Contract Program

Type of award: Scholarship.
Intended use: For undergraduate or graduate study at accredited 2-year or 4-year institution.
Eligibility: Applicant must be residing in Virginia.
Basis for selection: Major/career interest in library science; science, general; optometry/ophthalmology; criminal justice/law enforcement.
Additional information: Provides assistance to Virginia residents studying library science, optometry, forensic science, paper and pulp technology at specific out-of-state institutions. Recipients are selected by the institution.

Amount of award:	$5,000
Number of awards:	60
Total amount awarded:	$300,000

Virginia Rehabilitative Services College Scholarship

Type of award: Scholarship.
Intended use: For undergraduate study.
Eligibility: Applicant must be hearing impaired, physically challenged or learning disabled. Applicant must be residing in Virginia.
Additional information: Funding available only if need remains after federal, state and other private sources are used. Provides aid to Virginians with disabilities. Award amounts and deadlines vary; contact sponsor for information. Contact Department of Rehabilitative Services office, Central Region (804) 367-1061, Northern Region (703) 569-4303, Southwest Region (540) 776-2720, or Tidewater Region (804) 858-6750. This program provides vocational rehabilitation and related services to Virginians with disabilities. The goal for this program is to provide individuals with the skills necessary to achieve greater self-sufficiency, independence, and employment. Individuals may apply by contacting on of the following Department of Rehabilitative Services offices: Central Region 2930 West Broad St., Suite 15 Richmond, VA 23230 1-804-367-1061 / Fax 1-804-367-0044 Northern Region 7411 Alban Station Court, Boy Scouts of America 255 Springfield, VA 22150-2292 703-569-4303 / Fax 703-569-3578 Southwest Region 3433 Brambleton Ave., SW Roanoke, VA 24018 540-776-2720 / Fax 540-776-2748 Tidewater Region 5365 Robin Hood Rd., Suite O Norfolk, VA 23513 804-858-6750 / Fax 804-858-6758

Virginia Student Financial Assistance Program

Type of award: Scholarship.
Intended use: For undergraduate or graduate study at postsecondary institution in Virginia.
Eligibility: Applicant must be residing in Virginia.
Basis for selection: Applicant must demonstrate financial need.
Additional information: Award ranges from $400 to tuition and fees. Award available to Virginia undergraduate with financial need. Graduate students eligible regardless of state residency or need. Additional award available for students who demonstrate above-average high school performance. Apply to financial aid office of institution.

Amount of award:	$400
Number of awards:	33,000
Total amount awarded:	$52,000,000

Virginia Transfer Grant

Type of award: Scholarship, renewable.
Intended use: For sophomore, junior or senior study at accredited 4-year institution in Virginia.
Eligibility: Applicant must be of minority background. Applicant must be residing in Virginia.
Basis for selection: Applicant must demonstrate financial need.
Application requirements: Transcript and proof of eligibility. transfer student.
Additional information: Awards up to full tuition and fees. Applicant must be minority transfer student enrolling in one of the Commonwealth's 13 traditionally white institutions or Commonwealth's two traditionally black institutions. Must qualify as first-time transfer student and meet minimum merit criteria. Contact financial aid office of institution for application/information.

Number of awards:	628
Total amount awarded:	$820,401

Virginia Tuition Assistance Grant

Type of award: Scholarship, renewable.
Intended use: For full-time undergraduate, master's, doctoral or first professional study at accredited postsecondary institution in Virginia. Designated institutions: Private, nonprofit institutions in Virginia.
Eligibility: Applicant must be residing in Virginia.
Application requirements: Proof of eligibility.
Additional information: Information and application available from financial aid office of qualifying private, nonprofit colleges and universities. Theology and divinity majors not eligible.

Amount of award:	$2,600
Number of awards:	13,000
Application deadline:	July 31
Total amount awarded:	$26,000,000

Virginia Undergraduate Student Financial Aid

Type of award: Scholarship.
Intended use: For freshman study at 2-year, 4-year or graduate institution in Virginia.
Eligibility: Applicant must be of minority background. Applicant must be residing in Virginia.
Basis for selection: Applicant must demonstrate financial need.
Additional information: Award varies from $400 to full tuition and fees. Apply to financial aid office of institution. Must be enrolled for the first time in a public Virginia institution.

Amount of award:	$400
Number of awards:	841

Washington State Higher Education Coordinating Board

Washington State American Indian Endowed Scholarship

Type of award: Scholarship.
Intended use: For full-time undergraduate study at accredited vocational, 2-year, 4-year or graduate institution in Washington.
Eligibility: Applicant must be American Indian. Must be member of American Indian tribe and affiliated with American Indian community within Washington State. Applicant must be U.S. citizen or permanent resident residing in Washington.
Basis for selection: Applicant must demonstrate financial need.

Additional information: Must be a member of a Native American Tribe to be eligible for this award.
    Amount of award: $2,000
    Number of awards: 15

Washington State Educational Opportunity Grant

Type of award: Scholarship, renewable.
Intended use: For full-time junior, senior study at accredited 4-year institution in Washington. Designated institutions: Must be accredited by NWASC and must be located in washington state.
Eligibility: Applicant must be U.S. citizen or permanent resident residing in Washington.
Basis for selection: Applicant must demonstrate financial need.
Application requirements: Essay and proof of eligibility.
Additional information: Must reside in specific counties and be transferring into a college (public or private) with existing unused capacity. Must be "placebound". Must be transfer students at junior or senior level.
    Amount of award: $2,500
    Number of awards: 900
    Application deadline: June 1
    Notification begins: July 1
    Total amount awarded: $2,000,000

Washington State Health Professions Loan/Scholarship

Type of award: Loan, renewable.
Intended use: For junior, senior or graduate study.
Eligibility: Applicant must be residing in Washington.
Basis for selection: Major/career interest in health-related professions; nursing; health sciences. Applicant must demonstrate seriousness of purpose and service orientation.
Application requirements: Recommendations, essay, transcript and proof of eligibility.
Additional information: Minimum three years service in Washington state primary care health professions fields required for loan forgiveness. Penalty for avoiding service is twice amount of loan plus interest. The listing of eligible health professions are subject to change on an annual basis.
    Amount of award: $20,000
    Number of awards: 38
    Application deadline: April 24
    Notification begins: June 30
    Total amount awarded: $305,117

Washington State Need Grant

Type of award: Scholarship.
Intended use: For full-time or half-time undergraduate study at vocational, 2-year or 4-year institution. Designated institutions: Eligible proprietary schools in Washington and some designated institutions in Oregon and Idaho.
Eligibility: Applicant must be U.S. citizen or permanent resident residing in Washington.
Basis for selection: Applicant must demonstrate financial need.
Application requirements: Proof of eligibility.
Additional information: Theology/religion majors not eligible. Use FAFSA to apply for grant at financial aid office of institution. Grants are only given to students that come from low income families.
    Amount of award: $1,450-$2,400
    Number of awards: 4,500
    Total amount awarded: $66,778,000

Washington State Scholars Program

Type of award: Scholarship, renewable.
Intended use: For undergraduate study at accredited vocational, 2-year or 4-year institution in Washington.
Eligibility: Applicant must be high school senior. Applicant must be U.S. citizen or permanent resident residing in Washington.
Basis for selection: Applicant must demonstrate depth of character, leadership, seriousness of purpose, service orientation and high academic achievement.
Application requirements: Transcript, proof of eligibility and nomination by high school principal. SAT I/ACT scores.
Additional information: Must rank in top one percent of class. May defer enrollment, but must begin use of award within three years of high school graduation. Students must be nominated by the school pricipal or guidance couselor to be eligible.
    Number of awards: 174
    Number of applicants: 560
    Application deadline: January 3
    Notification begins: February 28
    Total amount awarded: $736,916

Washington State Work-Study Program

Type of award: Internship.
Intended use: For full-time or half-time master's, doctoral study at accredited vocational, 2-year, 4-year or graduate institution in Washington.
Eligibility: Applicant must be residing in Washington.
Basis for selection: Applicant must demonstrate financial need.
Application requirements: Proof of eligibility.
Additional information: Must apply to financial aid office of institution. Priority given to Washington residents.
    Number of awards: 10,005
    Total amount awarded: $15,350,000

Contact:
Washington State Higher Education Coordinating Board
917 Lakeridge Way
P.O. Box 43430
Olympia, WA 98504-3430
Phone: 3607537843
Fax: 3607537808

West Virginia Division of Veterans Affairs

West Virginia War Orphans Educational Assistance

Type of award: Scholarship, renewable.
Intended use: For undergraduate, graduate or non-degree study in West Viriginia supported college or university.
Eligibility: Applicant must be U.S. citizen residing in West Virginia. Applicant must be descendant of veteran, child of deceased veteran who served in the Army, Air Force, Marines, Navy, Coast Guard or Reserves/National Guard. Applicant's parent must be veteran killed while on active duty during war time or died of an injury or illness resulting from war time service.
Application requirements: Proof of eligibility.
Amount of award:	$250
Number of awards:	35
Number of applicants:	35
Application deadline:	July 1, December 1
Notification begins:	July 15, December 15
Total amount awarded:	$1,500

Contact:
West Virginia Division of Veterans Affairs
1321 Plaza East-Suite 101
Charleston,, WV 25301-1400
Phone: 304-558-3661

West Virginia State College and University Systems

West Virginia Higher Education Grant

Type of award: Scholarship, renewable.
Intended use: For full-time undergraduate study at accredited 2-year or 4-year institution.
Eligibility: Applicant must be U.S. citizen residing in West Virginia or Pennsylvania.
Basis for selection: Applicant must demonstrate financial need and high academic achievement.
Application requirements: Proof of eligibility. FAFSA. ACT/SAT I test scores.
Additional information: Appicants can be residents of either West Virginia or Pennsylvania. Award restricted for use at non-profit institutions or hospital schools of nursing in West Virginia or Pennsylvania.
Amount of award:	$350-$2,348
Number of awards:	8,606
Number of applicants:	54,220
Application deadline:	March 1
Notification begins:	June 15
Total amount awarded:	$12,350,836

West Virginia Medical Student Loan Program

Type of award: Loan, renewable.
Intended use: For full-time first professional study at graduate institution in West Virginia.
Eligibility: Applicant must be U.S. citizen residing in West Virginia.
Basis for selection: Major/career interest in medicine (m.d.); medicine, osteopathic. Applicant must demonstrate high academic achievement.
Application requirements: Proof of eligibility.
Additional information: Students from other states attending West Virginia institutions also eligible. Loan forgiveness for service in medically underserved areas of West Virginia. May not be in default on any previous student loans.
Amount of award:	$500-$5,000
Number of awards:	233
Total amount awarded:	$865,390

West Virginia Robert C. Byrd Honors Scholarship

Type of award: Scholarship, renewable.
Intended use: For full-time freshman study at vocational, 2-year or 4-year institution in United States.
Eligibility: Applicant must be high school senior. Applicant must be U.S. citizen or permanent resident residing in West Virginia.
Basis for selection: Applicant must demonstrate high academic achievement.
Application requirements: Transcript, proof of eligibility and nomination by high school.
Additional information: SAT I or ACT required.
Amount of award:	$1,110
Number of awards:	1
Number of applicants:	309
Application deadline:	March 15
Notification begins:	June 1
Total amount awarded:	$198,690

West Virginia Underwood-Smith Teacher Scholarship

Type of award: Loan, renewable.
Intended use: For full-time undergraduate or graduate study at 2-year, 4-year or graduate institution in West Virginia.
Eligibility: Applicant must be U.S. citizen or permanent resident residing in West Virginia.
Basis for selection: Major/career interest in education, teacher. Applicant must demonstrate high academic achievement.
Application requirements: Essay and proof of eligibility.
Additional information: Must rank in top 10 percent of class. Must be permanent resident of West Virginia.

Amount of award:	$5,000
Number of awards:	78
Number of applicants:	85
Application deadline:	April 1
Notification begins:	July 1
Total amount awarded:	$279,052

Contact:
West Virginia State College and University Systems
Central Office
1018 Kanawha Boulevard East, Suite 700
Charleston, WV 25301-2827
Phone: 304-558-4618
Website: www.scusco.wvnet.edu

Wisconsin Department of Veterans Affairs

Wisconsin Veterans Affairs Economic Assistance Loan

Type of award: Loan.
Intended use: For undergraduate or graduate study at postsecondary institution in United States.
Eligibility: Applicant must be residing in Wisconsin. Applicant must be veteran, child of veteran or deceased veteran, spouse of veteran or deceased veteran during Grenada, Lebanon, Persian Gulf or Vietnam. Must meet WDVA Service requirements. Must have 90 days of active duty during wartime and/or two years of continuous active duty.
Application requirements: Applicant must either have been a resident of Wisconsin on entry into military service or a continuous resident of Wisconsin for at least 10 years immediately preceding the application date.
Additional information: Alternate phone: 800-947-8387. May be used for veteran's education and for the education of veteran's children. Annual interest rate is six to ten percent depending on income and has a five year term. The maximum qualifying income (veteran and spouse combined) is $60,000. Apply to your local county Veterans' Service Officer to establish eligibility.

Amount of award:	$10,000

Contact:
Wisconsin Department of Veterans Affairs
PO Box 7843
30 West Mifflin Street
Madison, WI 53703-7843
Phone: 800-947-8387
Website: badger.state.wi.us/agencies/dva

Wisconsin Veterans Affairs Part-Time Study Grant

Type of award: Scholarship.
Intended use: For half-time or less than half-time undergraduate study at accredited vocational, 2-year or 4-year institution in Wisconsin.
Eligibility: Applicant must be residing in Wisconsin. Applicant must be veteran, child of deceased veteran, spouse of deceased veteran. Two years of active duty during peacetime or 90 days of active duty during a specified wartime period.
Basis for selection: Applicant must demonstrate financial need.
Application requirements: Proof of eligibility.
Additional information: Alternate phone: 800-947-8387. Statutory combined income limit of $47,500. Limit increases by $500 for each dependent child in excess of two. Application deadline is 60 days after completion of semester/quarter.

Contact:
Wisconsin Department of Veterans Affairs
P.O. Box 7843
30 West Mifflin Street
Madison, WI 53703-7843
Phone: 608-266-1311
Website: badger.state.wi.us/agencies/dva

Wisconsin Veterans Affairs Retraining Grant

Type of award: Scholarship.
Intended use: For undergraduate study at vocational institution in Wisconsin.
Eligibility: Applicant must be residing in Wisconsin. Applicant must be veteran during Grenada, Lebanon, Persian Gulf or Vietnam. Two years of continuous active duty during peacetime or 90 days of active duty during designated wartime period.
Basis for selection: Applicant must demonstrate financial need.
Application requirements: Must have either have been a resident of Wisconsin on entry into military service or a continuous resident of Wisconsin for at least 10 years immediately preceding the application date.
Additional information: Alternate phone: 800-947-8387. Applicant must be unemployed veteran and registered for or enrolled in an education program that will lead to reemployment and completed within two years. Must have been employed for six consecutive months with the same employer or in the same or similar occupation. Certification and counseling is provided only at accredited Wisconsin schools. Training at other schools does not qualify. Apply at the local county Veterans' Service Office to establish eligibility.

Amount of award:	$3,000

Contact:
Wisconsin Department of Veterans Affairs
P.O. Box 7843
30 West Mifflin Street
Madison, WI 53703-7843
Phone: 608-266-1311
Website: badger.state.wi.us/agencies/dva

Wisconsin Veterans Affairs Tuition and Fee Reimbursement Grant

Type of award: Scholarship, renewable.
Intended use: For undergraduate study at vocational, 2-year or 4-year institution in Wisconsin.
Eligibility: Applicant must be U.S. citizen residing in Wisconsin. Applicant must be veteran.
Basis for selection: Applicant must demonstrate financial need.

Application requirements: Proof of eligibility. Federal Tax Return.
Additional information: Alternate phone: 800-947-8387. Family income limit of $47,500. Limit increases by $500 for each dependent child. Veterans may receive up to 50% reimbursement of the cost of tuition and fees. May receive reimbursement for up to 120 credits of part-time study or eight semesters of full-time study. Courses must be taken within 10 years of separation from active military service.
Contact:
Wisconsin Department of Veterans Affairs
PO Box 7843
30 West Mifflin Street
Madison, WI 53703-7843
Phone: 608-266-1311
Website: badger.state.wi.us/agencies/dva

Wisconsin Higher Educational Aid Board

Wisconsin Academic Excellence Scholarship

Type of award: Scholarship, renewable.
Intended use: For full-time undergraduate study at vocational, 2-year or 4-year institution in Wisconsin.
Eligibility: Applicant must be high school senior. Applicant must be residing in Wisconsin.
Basis for selection: Applicant must demonstrate high academic achievement.
Application requirements: Nomination by high school guidance counselor by February 15.
Additional information: 3.0 GPA must be maintained for renewal. Awards range from $2,250 to full tuition and fees.
   Amount of award: $2,250
   Application deadline: February 15
Contact:
Higher Education Aids Board
Attn: Alice Winters
131 West Wilson
Madison, WI 53707
Phone: 6082672213

Wisconsin Higher Education Grant

Type of award: Scholarship, renewable.
Intended use: For full-time or half-time undergraduate study at vocational or 4-year institution in Wisconsin. Designated institutions: University of Wisconsin and Wisconsin technical institutions.
Eligibility: Applicant must be residing in Wisconsin.
Basis for selection: Applicant must demonstrate financial need.
Application requirements: Proof of eligibility.
Additional information: Apply with FAFSA through high school guidance counselor or financial aid office of institution.

   Amount of award: $250-$1,800
Contact:
Higher Educational Aid Board
Attn: Sandra Thomas
131 West Wilson
Madison, WI 53707
Phone: 6082660888

Wisconsin Minority Retention Grant

Type of award: Scholarship, renewable.
Intended use: For sophomore, junior or senior study at vocational, 2-year or 4-year institution in Wisconsin. Designated institutions: Private and non-profit.
Eligibility: Applicant must be American Indian, Asian American, African American, Mexican American, Hispanic American or Puerto Rican. Asian American applicants must be former citizens or children of former citizens of Laos, Vietnam, or Cambodia admitted to United States after 12/31/75. Applicant must be residing in Wisconsin.
Basis for selection: Applicant must demonstrate financial need.
   Amount of award: $2,500
   Total amount awarded: $860,200
Contact:
Higher Educational Aid Board
Attn: May Lou Kuzdas
131 West Wilson
Wisconsin, WI 53707
Phone: 608-267-2206

Wisconsin Minority Teacher Loan Program

Type of award: Loan, renewable.
Intended use: For full-time junior, senior study at accredited 4-year institution in Wisconsin.
Eligibility: Applicant must be American Indian, Asian American, African American, Mexican American, Hispanic American or Puerto Rican. Asian American applicants must be either former citizens or descendants of former citizens of Laos, Vietnam, or Cambodia. Applicant must be residing in Wisconsin.
Basis for selection: Major/career interest in education; education, special; education, teacher. Applicant must demonstrate financial need.
Application requirements: Nomination by Nomination must come from Student Financial Aid Department.
Additional information: Recipient must agree to teach in Wisconsin school district where minority students constitute at least 29% of enrollment. For each year student teaches in an eligible district, 25% of loan is forgiven, otherwise loan must be repaid at an interest rate of 5%.
   Amount of award: $250-$2,500
Contact:
Higher Educational Aid Board
Attn: Mary Lou Kuzdas
131 West Wilson
Madison, WI 53707
Phone: 608-267-2212

Wisconsin Native American Student Grant

Type of award: Scholarship, renewable.
Intended use: For undergraduate or graduate study in Wisconsin.
Eligibility: Applicant must be American Indian. Must be at least one-quarter Native American. Applicant must be residing in Wisconsin.
Basis for selection: Applicant must demonstrate financial need.
Application requirements: Proof of eligibility. Application made through joint Board-BIA-Tribal form and needs analysis form.
   Amount of award: $1,100
   Total amount awarded: $779,800
Contact:
Higher Educational Aid Board
131 West Wilson
Madison, WI 53707
Phone: 608-267-2206

Wisconsin Talent Incentive Program

Type of award: Scholarship, renewable.
Intended use: For full-time or half-time freshman, sophomore, junior or senior study in Wisconsin.
Eligibility: Applicant must be residing in Wisconsin.
Basis for selection: Applicant must demonstrate financial need.
   Amount of award: $600-$1,800
Contact:
Higher Educational Aid Board
131 West Wilson
Madison, WI 53707
Phone: 608-267-2206

Wisconsin Tuition Grant

Type of award: Scholarship, renewable.
Intended use: For undergraduate study in Wisconsin.
Designated institutions: Independent, nonprofit institutions in Wisconsin.
Eligibility: Applicant must be residing in Wisconsin.
Basis for selection: Applicant must demonstrate financial need.
   Amount of award: $250-$2,300
   Total amount awarded: $16,050,200
Contact:
Higher Educational Aid Board
131 West Wilson
Madison, WI 53707
Phone: 608-267-2206

Wisconsin Visual and Hearing Impaired Program

Type of award: Scholarship, renewable.
Intended use: For undergraduate study.
Eligibility: Applicant must be visually impaired or hearing impaired. Applicant must be residing in Wisconsin.
Basis for selection: Applicant must demonstrate financial need.
Application requirements: Proof of eligibility.
Additional information: Study at out-of-state institution specializing in teaching blind or deaf is allowed if impairment prevents student from attending Wisconsin institution.
   Amount of award: $1,800
   Number of awards: 80
   Total amount awarded: $123,800
Contact:
Higher Educational Aid Board
131 West Wilson
P.O. Box 7885
Madison, WI 53707-7885
Phone: 608-267-2206

Woodrow Wilson National Fellowship Foundation

Johnson and Johnson Dissertation Grants in Women's Health

Type of award: Scholarship.
Intended use: For doctoral study in United States.
Basis for selection: Major/career interest in womenÖs studies.
Application requirements: Recommendations and transcript. Dissertation prospectus and selected bibliography, statement of interest in women's health, and timetable for dissertation completion.
Additional information: Candidates must have completed all predissertation requirements by October 30. Award is to be used for expenses connected with the dissertation.
   Amount of award: $2,000
   Application deadline: December 15
   Notification begins: February 2
Contact:
Woodrow Wilson National Fellowship Foundation
CN 5281
Princeton, NJ 08543-5281
Phone: 609-452-7007
Fax: 609-452-0066
Website: www.woodrow.org

U.S. Department of Commerce/Ron Brown Fellowship

Type of award: Scholarship.
Intended use: For junior, senior or master's study.
Eligibility: Applicant must be U.S. citizen or permanent resident.
Basis for selection: Major/career interest in business. Applicant must demonstrate depth of character, leadership, seriousness of purpose and high academic achievement.
Application requirements: Recommendations, essay, transcript and proof of eligibility.
Additional information: For students planning careers in international business and/or commerce. Must apply in sophomore year. Covers junior and senior years and the first year of graduate school. Incurs a four and a half year service commitment to the US department of Commerce as a trade specialist.

Number of awards:	5
Number of applicants:	90
Application deadline:	January 1
Notification begins:	May 1

Contact:
USDC Ronald H. Brown Commercial Fellowship
CN 5281
Princeton, NJ 08543-5281
Fax: 609-452-7007
Website: www.woodrow.org

U.S. Department of State Foreign Affairs Fellowship

Type of award: Scholarship, renewable.
Intended use: For full-time junior, senior or graduate study at accredited 4-year or graduate institution in United States. Designated institutions: Graduate portion of fellowship must be used at institutions affiliated with the Association of Professional Schools of International Affairs.
Eligibility: Applicant must be U.S. citizen.
Basis for selection: Major/career interest in international relations. Applicant must demonstrate depth of character, leadership, seriousness of purpose, service orientation, financial need and high academic achievement.
Application requirements: Recommendations, essay, transcript and proof of eligibility.
Additional information: Must have cumulative 3.2 GPA with intended career in foreign service. Covers tuition, room, and board during junior and senior years and during the first year of graduate study. Attendance is required between the junior and senior years at a junior year summer institute. Summer internships prior to graduate school an between first and second year of graduate school. Must apply in sophomore year. Cannot apply separately for senior year or graduate fellowship. Includes internships with State Department. Incurs a minimum four and a half year service commitment to U.S. Department of State as Foreign Service Officer.

Number of awards:	15
Number of applicants:	240
Application deadline:	March 2
Notification begins:	May 1

Contact:
Woodrow Wilson National Fellowship Foundation
U.S. Department of State Fellowship
CN 2437
Princeton, NJ 08543-2437
Phone: 609-452-7007
Website: www.woodrow.org

Wyoming Community College Commission

Wyoming State Student Incentive Grant

Type of award: Scholarship, renewable.
Intended use: For undergraduate study at 2-year or 4-year institution in Wyoming.
Eligibility: Applicant must be residing in Wyoming.
Basis for selection: Applicant must demonstrate financial need.
Additional information: Contact financial aid office of Wyoming institution.

Amount of award:	$200-$2,500
Number of awards:	400
Number of applicants:	1,200
Total amount awarded:	$198,000

Yosemite National Park

Yosemite National Park Internships

Type of award: Internship.
Intended use: For sophomore, junior, senior or graduate study in United States.
Eligibility: Applicant must be U.S. citizen or permanent resident.
Basis for selection: Major/career interest in environmental science; history; education; physical sciences.
Additional information: Full-time assignment of a minimum of 12 weeks. 15 to 30 Internship available during the summer (mid-June through Labor Day). Two Internships are available in the spring (one in education and one in wilderness) from March to June. One Internship is available in wilderness from August to November (exact dates for these three Internships are negotiable). $6.00 per day (or $30.00 per 40-hour week) to defray the cost of expenses during the working week. Each intern receive $1,000 scholarship at the end of 12-week commitment. Opportunities in park planning, archaeology, search and rescue resource management/research, wilderness management and interpretation.

Amount of award:	$1,360
Number of awards:	30

Contact:
Internship Coordinator
Wawona Ranger Office
PO Box 2027
Wawona, CA 95389
Website: www.nps.gov/yose/intern

Private Unrestricted

1st Infantry Division Foundation

1st Infantry Division/Lieutenant General C. R. Huebner Scholarship

Type of award: Scholarship.
Intended use: For freshman, sophomore, junior or senior study at 2-year or 4-year institution.
Eligibility: Applicant must be high school senior. Applicant must be U.S. citizen. Applicant must be child of veteran or deceased veteran who served in the Army. Must be dependent or grandchild of soldier who served in First Infantry Division Army.
Basis for selection: Applicant must demonstrate high academic achievement.
Application requirements: Recommendations, essay, transcript and proof of eligibility.
  Amount of award: $750
  Number of awards: 12
  Number of applicants: 80
  Application deadline: June 1
  Notification begins: August 30
  Total amount awarded: $9,000
Contact:
1st Infantry Division Foundation
1933 Morris Rd.
Blue Bell, PA 19422-1422
Phone: 215-233-5444
Fax: 215-233-9381

3M

3M Internship

Type of award: Internship.
Intended use: For sophomore, junior, senior or graduate study.
Eligibility: Applicant must be U.S. citizen or permanent resident.
Basis for selection: Major/career interest in engineering; finance/banking; marketing; business. Applicant must demonstrate depth of character, seriousness of purpose and high academic achievement.
Application requirements: Interview and transcript.
Additional information: 18-week internship. Minimum 3.0 GPA. Undergrads receive $440-$540 a week. Graduate students receive $550-$680 a week. Must submit resume and cover letter.
  Amount of award: $6,160-$9,520
  Application deadline: December 31
Contact:
3M
224-1W-02
3M Center
St. Paul, MN 55144

Abbie Sargent Memorial Scholarship Fund

Abbie Sargent Memorial Scholarship

Type of award: Scholarship, renewable.
Intended use: For full-time or half-time freshman, sophomore, junior, senior or graduate study at accredited 2-year or 4-year institution.
Basis for selection: Major/career interest in agriculture; veterinary medicine. Applicant must demonstrate depth of character, financial need and high academic achievement.
Application requirements: Transcript.
Additional information: Only New Hampshire residents should apply. The recepient may attend an out of state university. Send SASE for application.
  Number of awards: 3
  Number of applicants: 35
  Application deadline: March 15
  Notification begins: May 1
  Total amount awarded: $1,050
Contact:
Abbie Sargent Memorial Fund
295 Sheep Davis Road
Concord, NH 03301
Phone: 603-224-1934

Academy of Television Arts and Sciences

Academy of Television Arts and Sciences Summer Student Internship

Type of award: Internship.
Intended use: For full-time undergraduate or graduate study at accredited 2-year or 4-year institution in United States.
Basis for selection: Major/career interest in journalism; radio/television/film; communications; film/video.

Application requirements: Portfolio, recommendations, essay and transcript. Finalists prepare a videotaped interview.
Additional information: Eight-week internship in the television and film industry. Foreign applicants must be pursuing a degree at a college or university in the United States.

Amount of award:	$2,000-$2,400
Number of awards:	30
Number of applicants:	1,000
Application deadline:	March 31

College Television Award

Type of award: Scholarship.
Intended use: For full-time undergraduate, master's or doctoral study in United States.
Basis for selection: Competition in Visual arts. Excellence of work.
Application requirements: Must submit 3/4" cassette of originial film/tape made for course credit within the eligibility period. Must be student producer of record.
Additional information: Award for student videos and films in the categories of drama, comedy, music, documentary, news/sports/magazine shows, traditional and computer animation. Submissions must have been made for a college credit course. First-place winners chosen for their work on humanitarian concerns eligible for $2,000 Bricker Family College Award. First and Second place winners also receive grants in film stock from Kodak. Foreign applicants must be pursuing a degree at a college or university in the United States.

Amount of award:	$500-$2,000
Number of awards:	21
Number of applicants:	345
Application deadline:	December 15
Notification begins:	February 1
Total amount awarded:	$24,500

Contact:
Academy of Television Arts and Sciences
Educational Programs and Services
5220 Lankershim Boulevard
North Hollywood, CA 91601-3109
Website: www.emmys.org

ADA Endowment and Assistance Fund, Inc.

Dental Hygiene Scholarship

Type of award: Scholarship, renewable.
Intended use: For full-time sophomore study in United States. Designated institutions: Must be accredited by Commission on Dental Accreditation.
Eligibility: Applicant must be U.S. citizen.
Basis for selection: Major/career interest in dental hygiene. Applicant must demonstrate financial need and high academic achievement.
Application requirements: Recommendations and essay.
Additional information: 3.0 GPA, minimum 12 credit hours.

Amount of award:	$1,000
Number of awards:	75
Number of applicants:	200
Application deadline:	August 15
Notification begins:	October 23
Total amount awarded:	$75,000

Dental Laboratory Technician Scholarship

Type of award: Scholarship, renewable.
Intended use: For full-time freshman, sophomore study in United States. Designated institutions: Must be accredited by Commission on Dental Accreditation.
Eligibility: Applicant must be U.S. citizen.
Basis for selection: Major/career interest in dental laboratory technology. Applicant must demonstrate depth of character, seriousness of purpose, financial need and high academic achievement.
Application requirements: Recommendations and essay.
Additional information: 2.8 GPA, minimum 12 credit hours.

Amount of award:	$1,000
Number of awards:	10
Number of applicants:	60
Application deadline:	August 15
Notification begins:	October 23
Total amount awarded:	$30,000

Dental Student Scholarship

Type of award: Scholarship.
Intended use: For full-time doctoral study at accredited graduate institution in United States. Designated institutions: Institution must be accredited by Commission on Dental Accreditation.
Eligibility: Applicant must be U.S. citizen.
Basis for selection: Major/career interest in dentistry. Applicant must demonstrate depth of character, leadership, seriousness of purpose, financial need and high academic achievement.
Application requirements: Recommendations and essay.
Additional information: Must be second-year student at time of application. 3.0 GPA.

Amount of award:	$2,500
Number of applicants:	165
Application deadline:	July 31
Notification begins:	September 15
Total amount awarded:	$187,500

Minority Dental Student Scholarship

Type of award: Scholarship.
Intended use: For full-time doctoral study at accredited graduate institution in United States. Designated institutions: Must be accredited by Commission on Dental Accreditation.
Eligibility: Applicant must be American Indian, African American, Mexican American, Hispanic American or Puerto Rican. Applicant must be U.S. citizen.
Basis for selection: Major/career interest in dentistry. Applicant must demonstrate depth of character, leadership, seriousness of purpose, service orientation, financial need and high academic achievement.
Application requirements: Recommendations and essay.

Additional information: Must be entering second-year student at time of application. 3.0 GPA, minimum 12 credit hours.
- **Amount of award:** $2,000
- **Number of awards:** 46
- **Number of applicants:** 180
- **Application deadline:** July 31
- **Notification begins:** September 15
- **Total amount awarded:** $92,000

Contact:
ADA Endowment and Assistance Fund, Inc.
Scholarship Coordinator
211 East Chicago Avenue
Chicago, IL 60611

ADHA Institute for Oral Health

ADHA Institute for Oral Health Minority Scholarship

Type of award: Scholarship, renewable.
Intended use: For full-time undergraduate study at 4-year institution in United States.
Eligibility: Men are considered a minority in this field and are encouraged to apply for this program.
Basis for selection: Major/career interest in dental hygiene. Applicant must demonstrate depth of character, leadership, seriousness of purpose and service orientation.
Application requirements: Recommendations, essay, transcript, proof of eligibility and research proposal.
Additional information: Applicants must provide a statement of professional activities related to dental hygiene. Evidence of dental hygiene licensure eligibility must be provided. Applicants must be eligible for licensure in the academic year the award is being made.
- **Amount of award:** $2,000
- **Number of awards:** 2
- **Application deadline:** June 1

Contact:
ADHA Institute of Oral Health
444 N. Michigan Ave., Suite 3400
Chicago, IL 60611

ADHA Institute for Oral Health Part-Time Scholarship

Type of award: Scholarship, renewable.
Intended use: For half-time undergraduate, master's study at 4-year or graduate institution in United States.
Basis for selection: Major/career interest in dental hygiene. Applicant must demonstrate depth of character, leadership, seriousness of purpose and service orientation.
Application requirements: Recommendations, essay, transcript, proof of eligibility and research proposal.
Additional information: Awarded to applicants pursuing associate/certificate, baccalaureate or graduate degree enrolled part-time in accredited dental hygiene school.
- **Amount of award:** $2,000
- **Number of awards:** 1
- **Application deadline:** June 1

Contact:
ADHA Institute for Oral Health
444 N. Michigan Ave., Suite 3400
Chicago, IL 60611

Colgate "Bright Smiles, Bright Futures" Minority Scholarships

Type of award: Scholarship, renewable.
Intended use: For full-time junior, senior, master's or doctoral study at 4-year or graduate institution in United States.
Eligibility: Applicant must be American Indian, Asian American, African American, Mexican American, Hispanic American or Puerto Rican. Men are considered a minority in this field and do qualify.
Basis for selection: Major/career interest in dental hygiene. Applicant must demonstrate depth of character, leadership, seriousness of purpose, service orientation and high academic achievement.
Application requirements: Recommendations, essay, transcript, proof of eligibility and research proposal.
Additional information: Graduate applicants must provide a statement of professional activities related to dental hygiene. Evidence of dental hygiene licensure must be provided or applicant must be eligible for licensure in the academic year the award is being made. Graduate applicants must provide evidence of acceptance into a full time master's or doctoral degree program.
- **Amount of award:** $2,000
- **Number of awards:** 2
- **Application deadline:** June 1

Contact:
ADHA Institute for Oral Health
444 N. Michigan Ave., Suite 3400
Chicago, IL 60611

Dr. Alfred C. Fones Scholarship

Type of award: Scholarship, renewable.
Intended use: For full-time senior, master's study at 4-year or graduate institution in United States.
Basis for selection: Major/career interest in dental hygiene. Applicant must demonstrate depth of character, leadership, seriousness of purpose, service orientation, financial need and high academic achievement.
Application requirements: Recommendations, essay, transcript, proof of eligibility and research proposal.
Additional information: Evidence of dental hygiene license must be provided and applicant must hold the minimum of a baccalaureate degree or be granted such by the end of the current academic year. Undergraduate applicants must be eligible for licensure in the academic year the award is being made. Applicant must provide evidence of acceptance into a full time master's or doctoral degree program.
- **Amount of award:** $2,000
- **Number of awards:** 1
- **Application deadline:** June 1

Contact:
ADHA Institute for Oral Health
444 N. Michigan Ave., Suite 3400
Chicago, IL 60611

Dr. Harold Hillenbrand Scholarship

Type of award: Scholarship, renewable.
Intended use: For full-time undergraduate study at 4-year institution in United States.
Basis for selection: Major/career interest in dental hygiene. Applicant must demonstrate depth of character, leadership, seriousness of purpose, service orientation and high academic achievement.
Application requirements: Recommendations, essay, transcript, proof of eligibility and research proposal.
Additional information: Applicants must provide a statement of professional activities related to dental hygiene. Evidence of dental hygiene licensure eligibility must be provided. Applicants must be eligible for licensure in the academic year the award is being made. Minimum GPA 3.5.
    Amount of award: $2,000
    Number of awards: 2
    Application deadline: June 1
Contact:
ADHA Institute for Oral Health
444 N. Michigan Ave., Suite 3400
Chicago, IL 60611

Irene E. Newman Scholarship

Type of award: Scholarship, renewable.
Intended use: For full-time junior, senior, master's or doctoral study at 4-year or graduate institution in United States.
Basis for selection: Major/career interest in dental hygiene. Applicant must demonstrate depth of character, leadership, seriousness of purpose, service orientation, financial need and high academic achievement.
Application requirements: Recommendations, essay, transcript, proof of eligibility and research proposal.
Additional information: Awarded to an applicant who demonstrates strong potential in public health or community dental health. Evidence of dental hygiene licensure must be provided and applicant must hold the minimum of a baccalaureate degree or be granted such by the of the current academic year. Undergraduate applicants must be eligible for licensure in the academic year the award is being made. Applicant must provide evidence of acceptance into a full time master's or doctoral degree program.
    Amount of award: $2,000
    Number of awards: 1
    Application deadline: June 1
Contact:
ADHA Institute for Oral Health
444 N. Michigan Ave., Suite 3400
Chicago, IL 60611

John O. Butler Graduate Scholarships

Type of award: Scholarship, renewable.
Intended use: For full-time master's, doctoral study at graduate institution in United States.
Basis for selection: Major/career interest in dental hygiene. Applicant must demonstrate depth of character, leadership, seriousness of purpose, service orientation and financial need.
Application requirements: Recommendations, essay, transcript, proof of eligibility and research proposal.
Additional information: Evidence of dental hygiene licensure eligibility must be provided and applicant must hold the minimum of a baccalaureate degree. Applicant must provide evidence of acceptance in a full time master's or doctoral degree program.
    Amount of award: $2,000
    Number of awards: 7
    Application deadline: June 1
Contact:
ADHA Institute for Oral Health
444 N. Michigan Ave., Suite 3400
Chicago, IL 60611

Margaret E. Swanson Scholarship

Type of award: Scholarship, renewable.
Intended use: For full-time undergraduate, master's study at 4-year or graduate institution in United States.
Basis for selection: Major/career interest in dental hygiene. Applicant must demonstrate depth of character, leadership, seriousness of purpose and service orientation.
Application requirements: Recommendations, essay, transcript, proof of eligibility and research proposal.
Additional information: Awarded to an applicant who demonstrates excetional organizational leadership potential and is pursuing an associate/certificate, baccalaureate or graduate degree while enrolled at an accredited dental hygiene school.
    Amount of award: $2,000
    Number of awards: 1
    Application deadline: June 1
Contact:
ADHA Institute for Oral Health
444 N. Michigan Ave., Suite 3400
Chicago, IL 60611

Oral-B Laboratories Dental Hygiene Scholarship

Type of award: Scholarship, renewable.
Intended use: For full-time undergraduate study at 4-year institution in United States.
Basis for selection: Major/career interest in dental hygiene. Applicant must demonstrate depth of character, leadership, seriousness of purpose, service orientation and high academic achievement.
Application requirements: Recommendations, essay, transcript, proof of eligibility and research proposal.
Additional information: Evidence of dental hygiene licensure eligibility must be provided. Applicants must be eligible for licensure in the academic year the award is being made. Minimum GPA of 3.5
    Amount of award: $2,000
    Number of awards: 2
    Application deadline: June 1
Contact:
ADHA Institute for Oral Health
444 N. Michigan Ave., Suite 3400
Chicago, IL 60611

Sigma Phi Alpha Graduate Scholarship

Type of award: Research grant, renewable.
Intended use: For full-time senior, master's or doctoral study at 4-year or graduate institution in United States.
Basis for selection: Major/career interest in dental hygiene.

Applicant must demonstrate depth of character, leadership, seriousness of purpose, service orientation and high academic achievement.
Application requirements: Recommendations, essay, transcript, proof of eligibility and research proposal.
Additional information: Applicants must provide a statement of professional activities related to dental hygiene. Evidence of dental hygiene licensure must be provided and applicant must hold the minimum of a baccalaureate degree or be granted such by the end of the current application year and also provide evidence of acceptance into a full time master's or doctoral degree program. Applicants must be eligible for licensure in the academic year the award is being made.

Amount of award:	$2,000
Number of awards:	1
Application deadline:	June 1

Contact:
ADHA Institute for Oral Health
444 N. Michigan Ave., Suite 3400
Chicago, IL 60611

Sigma Phi Alpha Undergraduate Scholarship

Type of award: Scholarship, renewable.
Intended use: For full-time undergraduate study at 4-year institution in United States.
Basis for selection: Major/career interest in dental hygiene. Applicant must demonstrate depth of character, leadership, seriousness of purpose, service orientation and high academic achievement.
Application requirements: Recommendations, essay, transcript, proof of eligibility and research proposal.
Additional information: Awarded to applicants pursuing associate/certificate or baccalaureate degree at accredited dental hygiene school with an active chapter of the Sigma Alpha Dental Hygiene Honor Society.

Amount of award:	$2,000
Number of awards:	1
Application deadline:	June 1

Contact:
ADHA Institute for Oral Health
444 N. Michigan Ave., Suite 3400
Chicago, IL 60611

Aeromet, Inc.

Atmospheric Science Internship

Type of award: Internship.
Intended use: For senior or graduate study in United States.
Eligibility: Applicant must be U.S. citizen.
Basis for selection: Major/career interest in atmospheric sciences/meteorology. Applicant must demonstrate high academic achievement.
Application requirements: Recommendations and transcript. Resume, three references.
Additional information: Should have completed two years physics, two years calculus, four courses in atmospheric science or meteorology. Position from May 15 to September 1. Salary $9 to $11/hour, depending on experience.

Number of awards:	3
Application deadline:	May 1

Contact:
Aeromet, Inc.
P.O. Box 701767
Tulsa, OK 74170-1767
Phone: 918-299-2621
Website: www.aeromet.com

Air Force Aid Society

Air Force Aid Society Education Grant

Type of award: Scholarship, renewable.
Intended use: For full-time undergraduate study at accredited vocational, 2-year or 4-year institution in or outside United States.
Eligibility: Applicant must be child of active service person, veteran or deceased veteran, spouse of active service person or deceased veteran who served in the Air Force.
Basis for selection: Applicant must demonstrate financial need.
Application requirements: Proof of eligibility.
Additional information: Minimum 2.0 GPA. Veteran status alone not eligible. Veteran must either be retired reserve over age 60 and collecting retired pay, or retired with at least 20 years service in active duty Air Force. Applicant must be dependent of active, retired, or deceased serviceperson. Applicant may be spouse of active duty member stationed stateside. Air Force Reserve and Air National Guard not eligible.

Amount of award:	$1,500
Number of awards:	5,000
Number of applicants:	9,000
Application deadline:	March 20
Notification begins:	June 30
Total amount awarded:	$5,500,000

Contact:
Air Force Aid Society
Education Assistance Department
1745 Jefferson Davis Highway, Suite 202
Arlington, VA 22202
Website: www.afas.org

Air Traffic Control Association, Inc.

Air Traffic Control Half/Full-Time Student Scholarship

Type of award: Scholarship.
Intended use: For full-time freshman, sophomore, junior, senior, master's, doctoral or postgraduate study at accredited 4-year or graduate institution in United States.
Eligibility: Applicant must be U.S. citizen.
Basis for selection: Major/career interest in aviation.

Applicant must demonstrate depth of character, seriousness of purpose and financial need.
Application requirements: Recommendations, essay and proof of eligibility. 2 recommendations, 400 word essay on "How My Education Efforts Will Enhance My Potential Contribution To Aviation" and college transcript (and high school transcript if under 30 semester hours or 45 quarter hours completed).
Additional information: Minimum of 30 semester hours or 45 quarter hours still to be completed before graduation and attend at least half time (six hours).

Amount of award:	$1,500-$2,500
Number of awards:	3
Number of applicants:	200
Application deadline:	May 1
Notification begins:	September 30
Total amount awarded:	$4,500

Contact:
Air Traffic Control Association, Inc.
2300 Clarendon Boulevard, Suite 711
Arlington, VA 22201
Phone: 703-522-5717

Aircraft Electronics Association Educational Foundation

Bose Corporation Scholarship

Type of award: Scholarship, renewable.
Intended use: For full-time undergraduate study.
Eligibility: Applicant must be high school senior. Applicant must be U.S. citizen or permanent resident.
Basis for selection: Major/career interest in aviation. Applicant must demonstrate depth of character and seriousness of purpose.
Application requirements: Recommendations, transcript and proof of eligibility. Applicant must be planning to or is attending Embry-Riddle Aeronautical University.
Additional information: Scholarship can only be applied to individuals who are attending or plan to attend the Embry-Riddle Aeronautical University's avionics program.

Amount of award:	$1,500
Application deadline:	February 15

Contact:
Aircraft Electronics Association Educational Foundation
4217 S. Hocker
Independence, MO 64055
Website: www.aeaavneews.org/html/scholarship-info.html

Bud Glover Memorial Scholarship

Type of award: Scholarship, renewable.
Intended use: For full-time undergraduate study at vocational, 2-year or 4-year institution.
Eligibility: Applicant must be U.S. citizen or permanent resident.
Basis for selection: Major/career interest in aviation. Applicant must demonstrate depth of character and seriousness of purpose.
Application requirements: Recommendations, transcript and proof of eligibility. Must be at an accredited Avionics/Aircraft Repair School.
Additional information: Available to anyone attending or planning to attend an accredited school in an avionics or aircraft repair program.

Amount of award:	$1,000
Application deadline:	February 15

Contact:
Aircraft Electronics Association Educational Foundation
4217 S. Hocker
Independence, MO 64055
Website: www.aeaavneews.org/html/scholarship-info.html

Castleberry Instruments Scholarship

Type of award: Scholarship, renewable.
Intended use: For full-time undergraduate study at vocational, 2-year or 4-year institution.
Eligibility: Applicant must be U.S. citizen or permanent resident.
Basis for selection: Major/career interest in aviation; aviation repair. Applicant must demonstrate depth of character and seriousness of purpose.
Application requirements: Recommendations, transcript and proof of eligibility. Must be at an accredited Avionics/Aircraft Repair School.
Additional information: Available to anyone attending or planning to attend an accredited school in an avionics or aircraft repair program.

Amount of award:	$2,500
Application deadline:	February 15

Contact:
Aircraft Electronics Association Educational Foundation
4217 S. Hocker
Independence, MO 64055
Website: www.aeaavneews.org/html/scholarship-info.html

Chuck Peacock Honorary Scholarship

Type of award: Scholarship, renewable.
Intended use: For full-time undergraduate study at vocational, 2-year or 4-year institution.
Eligibility: Applicant must be U.S. citizen or permanent resident.
Basis for selection: Major/career interest in aviation. Applicant must demonstrate depth of character and seriousness of purpose.
Application requirements: Recommendations, transcript and proof of eligibility. Must be at an accredited Avionics/Aircraft Repair School.
Additional information: Available to anyone attending or planning to attend an accredited school in an avionics or aircraft repair program.

Amount of award:	$1,500
Application deadline:	February 15

Contact:
Aircraft Electronics Association Educational Foundation
4217 S. Hocker
Independence, MO 64055
Website: www.aeaavneews.org/html/scholarship-info.html

College of Aeronautics Scholarship

Type of award: Scholarship, renewable.
Intended use: For full-time undergraduate study.
Eligibility: Applicant must be U.S. citizen or permanent resident.
Basis for selection: Major/career interest in aviation. Applicant must demonstrate depth of character and seriousness of purpose.
Application requirements: Recommendations, transcript and proof of eligibility. Must be attending or planning to attend College of Aeronautics in Flushing, N.Y.
Additional information: Available to anyone attending or planning to attend the College of Aeronautics in Flushing, N.Y. Scholarship is for the duration of the two-year program, at $750 per semester with a maximum of $3,000 for four semesters.
   Amount of award: $6,000
   Number of awards: 3
   Application deadline: February 15
Contact:
Aircraft Electronics Association Educational Foundation
4217 S. Hocker
Independence, MO 64055
Website: www.aeaavneews.org/html/scholarship-info.html

David Arver Memorial Scholarship

Type of award: Scholarship, renewable.
Intended use: For full-time undergraduate study at vocational or 2-year institution.
Eligibility: Applicant must be U.S. citizen or permanent resident.
Basis for selection: Major/career interest in aviation; aviation repair. Applicant must demonstrate depth of character and seriousness of purpose.
Application requirements: Recommendations, transcript and proof of eligibility. Must be attending an accredited vocational/technical aviation school in AEA's region three.
Additional information: Available to anyone attending or planning to attend a school located in AEA region three (Illinois, Indiana, Iowa, Kansas, Michigan, Minnesota, Missouri, Nebraska, North Dakota, South Dakota or Wisconsin) for avionvics or aircraft repair program.
   Amount of award: $1,000
   Application deadline: February 15
Contact:
Aircraft Electronics Association Educational Foundation
4217 S. Hocker
Independence, MO 64055
Website: www.aeaavneews.org/html/scholarship-info.html

Dutch and Ginger Arver Scholarship

Type of award: Scholarship, renewable.
Intended use: For full-time undergraduate study at vocational, 2-year or 4-year institution.
Eligibility: Applicant must be U.S. citizen or permanent resident.
Basis for selection: Major/career interest in aviation; aviation repair. Applicant must demonstrate depth of character and seriousness of purpose.
Application requirements: Recommendations, transcript and proof of eligibility. Must be at an accredited Avionics/Aircraft Repair School.
Additional information: Available to anyone attending or planning to attend an accredited school in an avionics or aircraft repair program.
   Amount of award: $1,000
   Application deadline: February 15
Contact:
Aircraft Electronics Association Educational Foundation
4217 S. Hocker
Independence, MO 64055
Website: www.aeaavneews.org/html/scholarship-info.html

Field Aviation Co., Inc. Scholarship

Type of award: Scholarship, renewable.
Intended use: For full-time undergraduate study at vocational, 2-year or 4-year institution.
Eligibility: Applicant must be Must attend school in Canada.
Basis for selection: Major/career interest in aviation. Applicant must demonstrate depth of character and seriousness of purpose.
Application requirements: Recommendations, transcript and proof of eligibility. Must be at an accredited Avionics/Aircraft Repair School in Canada.
Additional information: Available to anyone attending or planning to attend an accredited school in an avionics or aircraft repair program in Canada.
   Amount of award: $1,000
   Application deadline: February 15
Contact:
Aircraft Electronics Association Educational Foundation
4217 S. Hocker
Independence, MO 64055
Website: www.aeaavneews.org/html/scholarship-info.html

Gene Baker Honorary Scholarship

Type of award: Scholarship, renewable.
Intended use: For full-time undergraduate study.
Eligibility: Applicant must be U.S. citizen or permanent resident.
Basis for selection: Major/career interest in aviation; aviation repair. Applicant must demonstrate depth of character and seriousness of purpose.
Application requirements: Recommendations, transcript and proof of eligibility.
Additional information: Available to all AEA members, their children, grandchildren or dependents. This award may be used for any field of study and will be applied directly to tuition costs.
   Amount of award: $1,500
   Application deadline: February 15
Contact:
Aircraft Electronics Association Educational Foundation
4217 S. Hocker
Independence, MO 64055
Website: www.aeaavneews.org/html/scholarship-info.html

Gulf Coast Avionics to Fox Valley Technical College Scholarship

Type of award: Scholarship, renewable.
Intended use: For full-time undergraduate study at vocational or 2-year institution.
Eligibility: Applicant must be U.S. citizen or permanent resident.
Basis for selection: Major/career interest in aviation; aviation repair. Applicant must demonstrate depth of character and seriousness of purpose.
Application requirements: Recommendations, transcript and proof of eligibility. Must be attending The Fox Valley Tech. College in Oshkosh, Wisconsin.
Additional information: Available to anyone attending or planning to attend Fox Valley Tech. College in Oshkosh, Wisconsin.
   Amount of award: $1,000
   Application deadline: February 15
Contact:
Aircraft Electronics Association Educational Foundation
4217 S. Hocker
Independence, MO 64055
Website: www.aeaavneews.org/html/scholarship-info.html

John Cook Honorary Scholarship

Type of award: Scholarship, renewable.
Intended use: For full-time undergraduate study.
Eligibility: Applicant must be high school senior. Applicant must be U.S. citizen or permanent resident.
Basis for selection: Major/career interest in aviation; aviation repair. Applicant must demonstrate depth of character and seriousness of purpose.
Application requirements: Recommendations, transcript and proof of eligibility.
Additional information: Available to all AEA members, their children, grandchildren or dependents. This award may be used to any field of study and will be applied directly to tuition costs.
   Amount of award: $1,500
   Application deadline: February 15
Contact:
Aircraft Electronics Association Educational Foundation
4217 S. Hocker
Independence, MO 64055
Website: www.aeaavneews.org/html/scholarship-info.html

Leon Harris/Les Nichols Memorial to Spartan School of Aeronautics

Type of award: Scholarship, renewable.
Intended use: For full-time undergraduate study.
Eligibility: Applicant must be U.S. citizen or permanent resident.
Basis for selection: Major/career interest in aviation. Applicant must demonstrate depth of character and seriousness of purpose.
Application requirements: Recommendations, transcript and proof of eligibility. Must be planning to attend The Spartan School of Aeronautics.
Additional information: Applicant may not be currently enrolled in the Avionics program at Spartan. Award will cover tuition expenses for eight quarters or until Associates Degree is completed--whichever comes first. All others expenses-- tools, living expenses, and fees must be covered by the student.
   Amount of award: $16,000
   Number of awards: 1
   Application deadline: February 15
Contact:
Aircraft Electronics Association Educational Foundation
4217 S. Hocker
Independence, MO 64055
Website: www.aeaavneews.org/html/scholarship-info.html

Lowell Gaylor Memorial Scholarship

Type of award: Scholarship, renewable.
Intended use: For full-time undergraduate study at vocational, 2-year or 4-year institution.
Eligibility: Applicant must be U.S. citizen or permanent resident.
Basis for selection: Major/career interest in aviation. Applicant must demonstrate depth of character and seriousness of purpose.
Application requirements: Recommendations, transcript and proof of eligibility. Must be an accredited Avionics/Aircraft Repair School.
Additional information: Available to anyone attending or planning to attend an accredited school in an avionics or aircraft repair program.
   Amount of award: $1,000
   Application deadline: February 15
Contact:
Aircraft Electronics Association Educational Foundation
4217 S. Hocker
Independence, MO 64055
Website: www.aeaavneews.org/html/scholarship-info.html

Mid-Continent Instrument Scholarship

Type of award: Scholarship.
Intended use: For full-time undergraduate study at vocational, 2-year or 4-year institution.
Eligibility: Applicant must be U.S. citizen or permanent resident.
Basis for selection: Major/career interest in aviation; aviation repair. Applicant must demonstrate depth of character and seriousness of purpose.
Application requirements: Recommendations, transcript and proof of eligibility. Must be at an accredited Avionics/Aircraft Repair School.
Additional information: Available to anyone attending or planning to attend an accredited school in an avionics or aircraft repair program.
   Amount of award: $1,000
   Application deadline: February 15
Contact:
Scholarship Coordinator
4217 S. Hocker
Independence, MO 64055
Website: www.aeaavneews.org/html/scholarship-info.html

Monte R. Mitchell Global Scholarship

Type of award: Scholarship, renewable.
Intended use: For full-time undergraduate study at accredited vocational or 2-year institution.
Eligibility: Applicant must be high school senior. Applicant must be European.
Basis for selection: Major/career interest in aviation; aviation repair. Applicant must demonstrate depth of character and seriousness of purpose.
Application requirements: Proof of eligibility. School may be located in Europe or the United States.
Additional information: Available to a European student pursuing a degree in aviation maintenance technology, avionics, or aircraft repair at an accredited school in Europe or the United States.
   Amount of award: $1,000
   Application deadline: February 15
Contact:
Aircraft Electronics Association Educational Foundation
4217 S. Hocker
Independence, MO 64055
Website: www.aeaavneews.org/html/scholarship-info.html

Northern Airborne Technical Scholarship

Type of award: Scholarship, renewable.
Intended use: For full-time undergraduate study at vocational, 2-year or 4-year institution.
Eligibility: Applicant must be Candian Citizen.
Basis for selection: Major/career interest in aviation. Applicant must demonstrate depth of character and seriousness of purpose.
Application requirements: Recommendations, transcript and proof of eligibility. Must be at an accredited Avionics/Aircraft Repair School in Canada.
Additional information: Available to anyone attending or planning to attend an accredited school in an avionics or aircraft repair program in Canada.
   Amount of award: $1,000
   Application deadline: February 15
Contact:
Aircraft Electronics Association Educational Foundation
4217 S. Hocker
Independence, MO 64055
Website: www.aeaavneews.org/html/scholarship-info.html

Paul and Blanche Wulfsberg Scholarship

Type of award: Scholarship, renewable.
Intended use: For full-time undergraduate study at vocational, 2-year or 4-year institution.
Eligibility: Applicant must be U.S. citizen or permanent resident.
Basis for selection: Major/career interest in aviation; aviation repair. Applicant must demonstrate depth of character and seriousness of purpose.
Application requirements: Recommendations, transcript and proof of eligibility. Must be at an accredited Avionics/Aircraft Repair School.
Additional information: Available to anyone attending or planning to attend an accredited school in an avionics or aircraft repair program.
   Amount of award: $1,000
   Application deadline: February 15
Contact:
Scholarship Coordinator
4217 S. Hocker
Independence, MO 64055
Website: www.aeaavneews.org/html/scholarship-info.html

Pilot Training Scholarship

Type of award: Scholarship, renewable.
Intended use: For full-time non-degree study.
Eligibility: Applicant must be U.S. citizen or permanent resident.
Basis for selection: Major/career interest in aviation; aviation repair. Applicant must demonstrate depth of character and seriousness of purpose.
Application requirements: Proof of eligibility.
Additional information: Available to an avionics technician who has been employed by an AEA member for at least one year. Scholarships are to be used to acquire a private pilot SEL license only.
   Amount of award: $1,000
   Number of awards: 3
   Application deadline: February 15
Contact:
Scholarship Coordinator
4217 S. Hocker
Independence, MO 64055
Website: www.aeaavneews.org/html/scholarship-info.html

Plane and Pilot Magazine/Garmin Scholarship

Type of award: Scholarship, renewable.
Intended use: For full-time undergraduate study at vocational, 2-year or 4-year institution.
Eligibility: Applicant must be U.S. citizen or permanent resident.
Basis for selection: Major/career interest in aviation; aviation repair. Applicant must demonstrate depth of character and seriousness of purpose.
Application requirements: Recommendations, transcript and proof of eligibility. Must be at an accredited Avionics/Aircraft Repair School.
Additional information: Available to anyone attending or planning to attend an accredited school in an avionics or aircraft repair program.
   Amount of award: $2,000
   Application deadline: February 15
Contact:
Scholarship Coordinator
4217 S. Hocker
Independence, MO 64055
Website: www.aeaavneews.org/html/scholarship-info.html

Russell Leroy Jones Memorial Scholarship (Colorado Aero Tech)

Type of award: Scholarship, renewable.
Intended use: For full-time undergraduate study.

Aircraft Electronics Association Educational Foundation: Russell Leroy Jones Memorial Scholarship (Colorado Aero Tech)

Eligibility: Applicant must be U.S. citizen or permanent resident.
Basis for selection: Major/career interest in aviation; electronics. Applicant must demonstrate depth of character and seriousness of purpose.
Application requirements: Recommendations, transcript and proof of eligibility. Must be attending or planning to attend Colorado Aero Tech School.
Additional information: Available to anyone attending or planning to attend Colorado Aero Tech. This award covers tuition only. Tools, fees, room and board must be paid for by the student.

Amount of award:	$6,000
Number of awards:	3
Application deadline:	February 15

Contact:
Aircraft Electronics Association Educational Foundation
4217 S. Hocker
Independence, MO 64055
Website: www.aeaavneews.org/html/scholarship-info.html

Aircraft Owners and Pilots Association Air Safety Foundation

Air Safety Foundation D.B. Burnside Scholarship

Type of award: Scholarship.
Intended use: For full-time or half-time junior, senior study at accredited 4-year institution in United States.
Eligibility: Applicant must be U.S. citizen.
Basis for selection: Major/career interest in aviation. Applicant must demonstrate high academic achievement.
Application requirements: Essay and transcript.
Additional information: Send SASE for application. Minimum 3.25 GPA.

Amount of award:	$1,000
Number of awards:	1
Number of applicants:	200
Application deadline:	March 31
Notification begins:	June 1
Total amount awarded:	$1,000

Air Safety Foundation McAllister Memorial Scholarship

Type of award: Scholarship.
Intended use: For full-time or half-time junior, senior study at accredited 4-year institution in United States.
Eligibility: Applicant must be U.S. citizen.
Basis for selection: Major/career interest in aviation.
Application requirements: Essay and transcript.
Additional information: Send SASE for application. Minimum 3.25 GPA.

Amount of award:	$1,000
Number of awards:	1
Number of applicants:	200
Application deadline:	March 31
Notification begins:	June 1
Total amount awarded:	$1,000

Contact:
Aircraft Owners and Pilots Association Air Safety Foundation
421 Aviation Way
P.O. Box 865
Frederick, MD 21701

Airmen Memorial Foundation

Chief Master Sergeants of the Air Force Scholarship

Type of award: Scholarship.
Intended use: For full-time undergraduate study at accredited vocational, 2-year or 4-year institution in or outside United States.
Eligibility: Applicant must be single. Applicant must be child of active service person or veteran who served in the Air Force or Reserves/National Guard. Must be child of active duty or retired enlisted member of U.S. Air Force, Air National Guard, or Air Force Reserves.
Basis for selection: Applicant must demonstrate depth of character, leadership and high academic achievement.
Application requirements: Recommendations, essay, transcript and proof of eligibility.
Additional information: Must be single dependent, including legally adopted child or stepchild, who will not reach 23rd birthday by September 1 of award year. Applications available November 1 to March 31. Send 9" x 12" SASE ($1.47).

Amount of award:	$1,000-$2,500
Number of awards:	35
Number of applicants:	200
Application deadline:	April 15
Notification begins:	August 1
Total amount awarded:	$24,000

Contact:
Airmen Foundation Scholarships
P.O. Box 50
Temple Hills, MD 20757-0050
Phone: 800-638-0591
Fax: 301-899-8136

Alabama State Chiropractic Association

Alabama Chiropractic Scholarship

Type of award: Scholarship, renewable.
Intended use: For full-time doctoral study.
Eligibility: Applicant must be U.S. citizen or permanent resident residing in Alabama.
Basis for selection: Major/career interest in chiropractic.

Applicant must demonstrate seriousness of purpose, service orientation, financial need and high academic achievement.
Application requirements: Transcript and proof of eligibility.
Additional information: Must have at least 2.5 GPA.

Amount of award:	$436-$3,000
Number of awards:	19
Number of applicants:	19
Application deadline:	September 30
Total amount awarded:	$37,000

Contact:
Alabama State Chiropractic Association
Dr. Sam Peavy, Scholarship Chair
1201 Ann Street
Montgomery, AL 36107-3004
Phone: 334-268-7123

Alaska Commission on Postsecondary Education

Alaska Brindle Memorial Scholarship Loan

Type of award: Loan, renewable.
Intended use: For full-time undergraduate or graduate study.
Designated institutions: Must be approved by U.S. Department of Education or Alaska Commission on Postsecondary Education.
Eligibility: Applicant must be U.S. citizen or permanent resident residing in Alaska.
Basis for selection: Major/career interest in wildlife/fisheries.
Application requirements: Proof of eligibility.
Additional information: Applicants with recommendation from an Alaskan fisheries business may be given priority. Minimum GPA of 2.0 required. Amounts of loans are based on budget. Contact office for more information.

Number of awards:	51
Number of applicants:	51
Application deadline:	May 15
Notification begins:	June 30
Total amount awarded:	$550,000

Contact:
Alaska Commission on Postsecondary Education
Special Programs
3030 Vintage Boulevard
Juneau, AK 99801-7109
Phone: 800-441-2962

Alexander Graham Bell Association for the Deaf

Alexander Graham Bell Association for the Deaf Scholarship

Type of award: Scholarship.
Intended use: For full-time undergraduate, master's, doctoral, first professional or postgraduate study at accredited 2-year, 4-year or graduate institution in or outside United States.
Eligibility: Applicant must be hearing impaired.
Basis for selection: Applicant must demonstrate financial need.
Application requirements: Recommendations, essay, transcript and proof of eligibility. Current audiogram.
Additional information: Must be prelingually deaf or hard of hearing, and use speech and residual hearing and/or speech-reading as customary form of communication. Must be accepted or enrolled in college or university program that primarily enrolls students with normal hearing.

Amount of award:	$200-$1,000
Number of awards:	77
Application deadline:	March 15
Notification begins:	June 11
Total amount awarded:	$82,000

Contact:
Alexander Graham Bell Association for the Deaf
Scholarship Awards Committee
3417 Volta Place, NW
Washington, DC 20007-2778

Alexander Von Humboldt Foundation

Foreign Scholar Research Fellowships

Type of award: Research grant.
Intended use: For postgraduate, non-degree study at graduate institution outside United States in Germany.
Basis for selection: Applicant must demonstrate high academic achievement.
Application requirements: Recommendations, transcript and research proposal. Must hold doctoral degree or equivalent. Must have published peer-reviewed publications.
Additional information: Must have good command of German. Award amounts vary; additional support available for travel and other expenses.

Number of awards:	500
Application deadline:	August 1, January 1

Contact:
Alexander Von Humboldt Foundation
1055 Thomas Jefferson Street, NW
Suite 2030
Washington, DC 20007
Phone: 202-296-2990
Fax: 202-833-8514

Ambucs Living Endowment Fund, Inc.

Ambucs Scholarship

Type of award: Scholarship, renewable.
Intended use: For full-time or half-time junior, senior or master's study at accredited 4-year or graduate institution in United States.

Eligibility: Applicant must be U.S. citizen.
Basis for selection: Major/career interest in occupational therapy; physical therapy; speech pathology/audiology. Applicant must demonstrate depth of character, service orientation, financial need and high academic achievement.
Application requirements: Essay and transcript.
Additional information: Minimum 3.0 GPA required, 3.5 recommended. Awards also in field of therapeutic recreation; not for therapist assistant, art therapy, respiratory therapy, special education, psychology, or social work. Program must be accredited by appropriate health therapy association. Applications available upon request, December 1, 1996 through March 15, 1997. Students must include a 1040 form from the previous year with applications. Send self-addressed, stamped envelope with request for application or with request for renewed scholarship.

Amount of award:	$500-$6,000
Application deadline:	April 15
Notification begins:	June 1

Contact:
Ambucs
P.O. Box 5127
High Point, NC 27262
Phone: 910-869-2166

America's Junior Miss Pageant, Inc.

Junior Miss Scholarship

Type of award: Scholarship.
Intended use: For undergraduate study.
Eligibility: Applicant must be single, female, high school junior, senior. Applicant must be U.S. citizen.
Basis for selection: Competition in Poise/talent/fitness. Scholastic evaluation, skill in creative and performing arts, physical fitness, presence and composure and panel interview.
Application requirements: Interview and transcript.
Additional information: Must compete in state of residence. State winners expected to compete at higher levels. Must never have been married. Only seniors can compete in finals but students are encouraged to begin application process during junior year. Contact office for application deadline information.

Amount of award:	$100-$30,000
Number of awards:	2,500
Number of applicants:	6,000
Total amount awarded:	$5,000,000

Contact:
America's Junior Miss Pageant
Contestant Inquiry
P.O. Box 2786
Mobile, AL 36652-2786
Phone: 334-438-3621
Fax: 334-431-0063
Website: www.ajm.org

American Foundation for Pharmaceutical Education

American Foundation for Pharmaceutical Education Predoctoral Fellowship

Type of award: Scholarship, renewable.
Intended use: For doctoral study.
Eligibility: Applicant must be U.S. citizen or permanent resident.
Basis for selection: Major/career interest in pharmacy/pharmaceutics/pharmacology.
Application requirements: Recommendations, essay, transcript and proof of eligibility. GRE scores.
Additional information: Must have completed at least three semesters of Ph.D. program and have no more than three years left to complete the Ph.D. One scholarship reserved for minority applicants; three reserved for those interested in teaching careers.

Amount of award:	$6,000-$10,000
Number of awards:	75
Number of applicants:	200
Application deadline:	March 1
Notification begins:	April 15

Contact:
American Foundation for Pharmaceutical Education
One Church Street
Suite 202
Rockville, MD 20850
Phone: 301-738-2160
Fax: 301-738-2161

American Academy of Periodontology

Periodontology Student Loan

Type of award: Loan.
Intended use: For full-time graduate study at graduate institution in United States or Canada.
Eligibility: Applicant must be U.S. citizen or Canadian citizen.
Basis for selection: Major/career interest in dentistry. Applicant must demonstrate financial need.
Application requirements: Recommendations. FAFSA, tax forms.
Additional information: Maximum $5,000 per year; limit $15,000 over three years. Must be a U.S. or Canadian citizen.

Amount of award: $5,000
Number of awards: 21
Number of applicants: 23
Application deadline: February 1
Notification begins: March 1
Total amount awarded: $105,000

Contact:
American Academy of Periodontology
Attn: Meetings & Membership Services Dept.
737 North Michigan Avenue, Suite 800
Chicago, IL 60611
Phone: 3127875518
Website: www.perio.org

American Alpine Club

Alpine Club A.K. Gilkey and Putnam/Bedayn Research Grant

Type of award: Research grant.
Intended use: For undergraduate or graduate study.
Eligibility: Applicant must be U.S. citizen.
Basis for selection: Major/career interest in science, general; biology; environmental science; forestry.
Application requirements: Recommendations and research proposal.
Additional information: Research proposals evaluated on scientific or technical quality and contribution to scientific endeavor germane to mountain regions.

Amount of award: $300-$1,000
Number of awards: 8
Number of applicants: 14
Application deadline: March 1
Notification begins: June 1
Total amount awarded: $4,476

Contact:
American Alpine Club
710 Tenth Street
Suite 100
Golden, CO 80401
Phone: 303-389-0110
Website: www.americanalpineclub.org

American Antiquarian Society

Antiquarian Society Short-Term Fellowship

Type of award: Research grant.
Intended use: For doctoral, postgraduate study at accredited graduate institution outside United States.
Basis for selection: Major/career interest in history; English literature. Applicant must demonstrate seriousness of purpose and high academic achievement.
Application requirements: Recommendations and research proposal.
Additional information: Fellowship intended for college teachers and Phd candidates. Award amount averages $950 per month; duration varies from one to three months.

Amount of award: $950-$2,850
Number of awards: 25
Number of applicants: 130
Application deadline: January 15
Notification begins: March 15

Contact:
American Antiquarian Society
185 Salisbury Street
Worcester, MA 01609
Phone: 508-754-9069

American Association for Cancer Research, Inc.

Clinical Cancer Research Fellowship

Type of award: Research grant.
Intended use: For postgraduate study.
Eligibility: Applicant must be U.S. citizen, permanent resident or Canadian citizen.
Basis for selection: Major/career interest in medical specialties/research.
Application requirements: Recommendations, proof of eligibility, research proposal and nomination by member of AACR, but not associate member.
Additional information: Fellowship sponsored by Bristol-Myers Squibb Oncology. Candidates must have completed M.D., Ph.D., or other doctoral degree. Candidates must currently be a postdoctoral or clinical research fellow and must have been a fellow for at least two years but not more than five years prior to the year of the award. Academic faculty holding the rank of assistant professor or higher, graduate or medical students, government employees, and employees of private industry are not eligible.

Amount of award: $30,000
Number of awards: 1
Application deadline: February 15
Total amount awarded: $30,000

Gertrude Elion Cancer Research Award

Type of award: Research grant.
Intended use: For postgraduate study. Designated institutions: In United States or Canada.
Basis for selection: Major/career interest in medical specialties/research.
Application requirements: Recommendations, proof of eligibility, research proposal and nomination by Must be nominated by an AACR member.

Amount of award: $30,000
Number of awards: 1
Application deadline: December 15
Total amount awarded: $30,000

Contact:
Research Grant Committee
Public Ledger Building, Suite 816
150 South Independence Mall West
Philadelphia, PA 19106-3483

American Association for Dental Research

Dental Student Research Fellowship

Type of award: Research grant, renewable.
Intended use: For full-time master's, doctoral or first professional study at accredited graduate institution in United States.
Basis for selection: Major/career interest in dentistry; dental hygiene. Applicant must demonstrate seriousness of purpose.
Application requirements: Recommendations, proof of eligibility and research proposal. Curriculum vitae, faculty sponsor's biographical sketch (or curriculum vitae).
Additional information: Must be enrolled ina n accredited dental institution in the U.S. and be sponsored by a faculty member.

Amount of award:	$3,000
Number of awards:	30
Number of applicants:	74
Application deadline:	January 15
Notification begins:	March 10
Total amount awarded:	$78,000

Contact:
American Association For Dental Research
Attn: Patricia J. Reynolds
1619 Duke Street
Alexandria, VA 22314-3406
Phone: 7035480066
Fax: 7035481883
Website: www.iadr.com

Edward H. Hatton Awards Competition

Type of award: Scholarship.
Intended use: For first professional, postgraduate study.
Eligibility: Applicant must be U.S. citizen or permanent resident.
Basis for selection: Competition in Research paper. Must exhibit potential for a productive career in dental research. Major/career interest in dental specialties (beyond dds/dmd); dentistry.
Application requirements: Research proposal.
Additional information: AADR sends ten individuals to compete in Vancouver, Canada. Entrants may not have been out of a full-time training program for more than one year. Faculty of AADR are not eligible.

Amount of award:	$250-$500
Number of awards:	10
Application deadline:	September 18

Contact:
American Association for Dental Research - Central Office
Gwynn Breckenridge
1619 Duke Street
Alexandria, VA 22314-3406
Phone: 703-548-0066
Fax: 703-548-1883
Website: www.iadr.com

American Association for Health Education

Health Education Scholarship

Type of award: Scholarship.
Intended use: For master's, doctoral study.
Basis for selection: Major/career interest in health education. Applicant must demonstrate high academic achievement.
Application requirements: Essay.
Additional information: Minimum GPA of 3.0. Must be currently enrolled in a health education program.

Amount of award:	$500
Number of awards:	2
Number of applicants:	26
Application deadline:	January 15
Notification begins:	January 15
Total amount awarded:	$1,000

Contact:
American Association for Health Education
1900 Association Drive
Reston, VA 20191-1599
Phone: 703-476-3437
Website: www.aahperd.org/aahe/aahe.html

American Association for the Advancement of Science

American Association for the Advancement of Science Risk Assessment Science & Engineering Fellows Program

Type of award: Research grant.
Intended use: For master's, doctoral study.
Eligibility: Applicant must be U.S. citizen.
Additional information: Applicants must have a Ph.D. or equivalent doctoral level degree. Persons with a master's dgree in Engineering and at least trhee years of post-degree professional experience may also apply. Federal employees are not eligible for the Fellowships. Fellows work for one year at either the U.S. Department of Agriculture or the U.S. Food and Drug Administration, providing scientific and technical input on issues relating to human health, economic, and environmental aspects of risk assessment or risk management. The annual stipend will be $42,000.

Application deadline:	January 15

Contact:
Fellowship Coordinator
1200 New York Ave., NW
Washington, DC 20005
Phone: 202-326-6700
Fax: 202-289-4950
Website: www.aaas.org

American Association for the Advancement of Science Royer Revelle Fellowship in Global Stewardship

Type of award: Scholarship.
Intended use: For postgraduate study.
Eligibility: Applicant must be U.S. citizen.
Basis for selection: Major/career interest in science, general. Applicant must demonstrate high academic achievement.
Application requirements: Must demonstrate sensitivity toward political and scoial issues.
Additional information: The Fellowship stipend is $45,000. All applicants must have a Ph.D. or equivalent doctoral level degree at the time of application (January 1999), and at least three years of post-degree professional experience. Persons with a master's degree in Engineering and six years of professional experience may apply. Federal employees are not eligible for the Fellowship. The Fellow will work for one year in the Congress, an executive branch agency, or elsewhere in the Washington DC policy community, on domestic or international environment issues encompassed under the umbrella of "global stewardship." The focus will be on human interaction with ecosystems, which includes, but is not limited to, population, sustainable development, food, oceans, global climate change and related environmental concerns.

Amount of award:	$45,000
Number of awards:	1
Application deadline:	January 15
Total amount awarded:	$45,000

Contact:
Fellowship Coordinator
1200 New York Ave., NW
Washington, DC 20005
Phone: 202-326-6700
Fax: 202-289-4950
Website: www.aaas.org

Risk Assessment Science and Engineering Fellowships

Type of award: Research grant.
Intended use: For postgraduate study.
Eligibility: Applicant must be U.S. citizen or permanent resident.
Basis for selection: Major/career interest in science, general; engineering.
Additional information: Deadline is in January; contact sponsor for exact date. Fellows serve one-year assignments at either the USDA or FDA. Fellowships will relate to the hazard/safety/risk assessment of possible contaminants in food.

Amount of award:	$42,000
Number of awards:	5
Total amount awarded:	$210,000

Contact:
AAAS Fellowship Programs
1200 New York Avenue, NW
Washington, DC 20005
Website: www.aaas.org

American Association of Advertising Agencies

Advertising Internship for Minority Students

Type of award: Internship, renewable.
Intended use: For full-time junior, senior or master's study at accredited 4-year or graduate institution.
Eligibility: Applicant must be American Indian, Asian American, African American, Mexican American, Hispanic American or Puerto Rican. Applicant must be U.S. citizen or permanent resident.
Basis for selection: Major/career interest in advertising; communications; journalism; English literature.
Application requirements: Interview, recommendations, essay and transcript.
Additional information: Must have completed junior year of college and have strong interest in advertising. Minimum 3.0 GPA required. Applicants with lesser GPA may be accepted on a case-by-case basis. Students are placed in member agency offices for ten weeks during the summer. Salary approximately $300 per week. 60 percent of housing and travel costs (if applicable) are provided. Can apply for following departments: account management, creative, media, or research.

Number of awards:	69
Number of applicants:	150
Application deadline:	January 30

Contact:
American Association of Advertising Agencies
Attn: Minority Advertising Intern Program
405 Lexington Avenue, 18th Floor
New York, NY 10174-1801
Website: www.commercepark.com/AAAA

American Association of Airport Executives

Airport Executives Scholarship

Type of award: Scholarship.
Intended use: For full-time junior, senior study at accredited 4-year institution.
Basis for selection: Major/career interest in aviation. Applicant must demonstrate financial need and high academic achievement.
Application requirements: Recommendations. Must apply through school scholarship or aviation management department. Only one recommendation per school.
Additional information: Must have 3.0 GPA. Extracurricular and community activities important. Applicant must have reached junior year in an aviation/airport management program.

Amount of award:	$1,000
Number of awards:	5
Application deadline:	May 15
Notification begins:	July 15
Total amount awarded:	$5,000

Contact:
Career Opportunities Through Education, Inc.
American Association of Airport Executives Scholarship
P.O. Box 2810
Cherry Hill, NJ 08034

American Association of Critical Care Nurses

Critical Care Nurses Education Advancement Scholarship

Type of award: Scholarship.
Intended use: For junior, senior study.
Eligibility: Applicant must be U.S. citizen or permanent resident.
Basis for selection: Major/career interest in nursing. Applicant must demonstrate seriousness of purpose and high academic achievement.
Additional information: For students who do not hold an RN license (applicants may hold degrees in other nursing fields). Must be currently enrolled in a NLN-accredited BSN program and have cumulative GPA of 3.0 or better. Must be member of National Student Nurses Association or American Association of Critical Care Nurses.

Amount of award:	$1,500
Application deadline:	February 1
Notification begins:	March 30

Contact:
National Student Nurses Association
555 West 57 Street
New York, NY 10019
Website: www.aacc.org

American Association of Japanese University Women

American Association of Japanese University Women Scholarship

Type of award: Scholarship.
Intended use: For full-time junior, senior or graduate study in United States.
Eligibility: Applicant must be female. Applicant must be residing in California.
Basis for selection: Major/career interest in foreign languages; Japanese studies; sociology. Applicant must demonstrate high academic achievement.
Application requirements: Recommendations, essay and transcript.
Additional information: Foreign student must be enrolled in U.S. institution prior to application, with stated intent regarding U.S.-Japan cultural exchange. Emphasis on southern California.

Amount of award:	$1,000
Number of awards:	3
Number of applicants:	8
Application deadline:	September 30
Notification begins:	November 15
Total amount awarded:	$3,000

Contact:
American Association of Japanese University Women c/o
Yasko Gamo
3812 Inlet Isle Drive
Corona del Mar, CA 92625
Phone: 714-720-0976

American Association of Medical Assistants Endowment

American Association Of Medical Assistants Endowment (AAMA)/ Maxine Williams Scholarship Program

Type of award: Scholarship, renewable.
Intended use: For undergraduate study at accredited 4-year institution in United States. Designated institutions: Must be enrolled or soon to be enrolled in a postsecondary medical assisting Program accredited by the commision of Accredation of Allied Education Programs (CAAHEP).
Basis for selection: Major/career interest in medical assistant. Applicant must demonstrate seriousness of purpose.
Application requirements: Essay, transcript and proof of eligibility.
Additional information: Must be committed to a medical assisting career, hold high school diploma or equivalent, and be enrolled or soon to be enrolled in a postsecondary medical assisting Program accredited by the Commission of Accreditation of Allied Education Programs (CAAHEP).

Amount of award:	$1,000
Number of applicants:	3
Application deadline:	June 1, February 1
Notification begins:	July 3
Total amount awarded:	$2,000

Contact:
20 North Wacker Dr.
Suite 1575
Chicago, IL 60606
Phone: 312-899-1500

American Association of Medical Assistants' Endowment

Maxine Williams Scholarship

Type of award: Scholarship.
Intended use: For undergraduate certificate, freshman or sophomore study at accredited vocational, 2-year or 4-year institution.
Basis for selection: Major/career interest in medical assistant. Applicant must demonstrate seriousness of purpose, financial need and high academic achievement.
Application requirements: Recommendations, essay, transcript and proof of eligibility. Must submit school catalog or published description of medical assisting program.
Additional information: Applicants must hold a high school diploma and be enrolled or soon to be enrolled in a postsecondary medical assistant program accredited by the CAAHEP.

Amount of award:	$1,000
Number of awards:	3
Number of applicants:	100
Application deadline:	February 1, June 1
Notification begins:	March 20, July 20
Total amount awarded:	$3,000

Contact:
American Association of Medical Assistants' Endowment
20 North Wacker Drive
Suite 1575
Chicago, IL 60606-2903
Phone: 312-899-1500

American Association of Petroleum Geologists Foundation

Petroleum Geologists Grant-in-Aid

Type of award: Research grant, renewable.
Intended use: For master's, doctoral study.
Eligibility: Applicant must be U.S. citizen.
Basis for selection: Major/career interest in geology/earth sciences. Applicant must demonstrate financial need and high academic achievement.
Application requirements: Recommendations, transcript, proof of eligibility and research proposal. Budget Development Worksheet.

Amount of award:	$500-$2,000
Number of awards:	61
Number of applicants:	178
Application deadline:	January 15
Notification begins:	April 1
Total amount awarded:	$96,500

Contact:
American Association of Petroleum Geologists Foundation
William A. Morgan/Grants-in-Aid
P.O. Box 979
Tulsa, OK 74101-0979
Phone: 918-560-2644
Website: www.aapg.org/fdn.html

American Association of School Administrators/ Discover Card, inc.

Discover Card Tribute Award

Type of award: Scholarship.
Intended use: For undergraduate study at accredited postsecondary institution in United States.
Eligibility: Applicant must be high school junior.
Basis for selection: Applicant must demonstrate leadership, service orientation and high academic achievement.
Application requirements: Recommendations, essay and transcript. Must describe future career plans in essay.
Additional information: Deadline is in January; call sponsor for exact date. Minimum 2.75 GPA. Pursuit of unique endeavors, evidence of having overcome difficult obstacles, and the possession of special talents important. Can also be used in Canadian universities.

Amount of award:	$1,000-$20,000
Number of awards:	437
Number of applicants:	11,000
Total amount awarded:	$993,000

Contact:
American Association of School Administrators
Discover Card Tribute Award
P.O. Box 9338
Arlington, VA 22209
Phone: 703-875-0708

American Association of University Women

AAUW Educational Foundation International Fellowship Program

Type of award: Scholarship.
Intended use: For full-time graduate or postgraduate study at graduate institution in United States.
Eligibility: Applicant must be female.
Basis for selection: Applicant must demonstrate seriousness of purpose, financial need and high academic achievement.

Application requirements: Recommendations and transcript.
Additional information: Fellowships last one year and offer stipend of $16,000. Six of 45 fellowships set aside for women from International Federation of University Women countries that can study anywhere except their home country. All others must study in the United States. Participants can apply for a supplemental community action grant for use in their home country.

Amount of award:	$16,000
Number of awards:	45
Number of applicants:	1,083
Application deadline:	January 15
Total amount awarded:	$720,000

Contact:
American Association of University Women
2201 North Dodge Street
Iowa City, IA 52243-4030
Phone: 319-337-1716
Website: www.aauw.org

American Association of University Women Educational Foundation

American Association of University Women International Fellowship

Type of award: Research grant.
Intended use: For full-time graduate study at graduate institution in or outside United States.
Eligibility: Applicant must be female.
Basis for selection: Applicant must demonstrate depth of character, leadership, seriousness of purpose, service orientation and high academic achievement.
Application requirements: Please send application via airmail from abroad. Applications available Aug.1 - Nov.15.
Additional information: Must be member of International Federation of University Women or AAUW Educational Foundation to study in any country other than their own. Applicant must have earned the equivalent of a U.S. bachelor's degree by December of 1998. Special consideration given to women who show prior commitment to the advancement of women and girls through civic, community, or professional work.

Amount of award:	$15,160
Number of awards:	45
Application deadline:	December 1

Contact:
AAUW Educational Foundation
Department 60
2201 N. Dodge St.
Iowa City, IA 52243-4030
Phone: 3193371716
Website: www.aauw.org

American Dissertation Fellowship

Type of award: Research grant, renewable.
Intended use: For doctoral study.
Eligibility: Applicant must be of minority background. Applicant must be female. Applicant must be U.S. citizen or permanent resident.
Basis for selection: Applicant must demonstrate depth of character, leadership, patriotism, seriousness of purpose, service orientation and high academic achievement.
Application requirements: Proof of eligibility and research proposal. Applications available Aug.1 - Nov.1.
Additional information: Applicants are expected to receive a doctoral degree by the end of the fellowship year. Open to applicants in all fields of study except engineering. Must have completed all course work and passed all preliminary exams.

Amount of award:	$14,500
Number of awards:	1
Application deadline:	November 17

Contact:
American Association of University Women Educational Foundation
2201 North Dodge Street
Iowa City, IA 52243-4030
Website: www.aauw.org

Career Development Grant

Type of award: Scholarship.
Intended use: For master's study at accredited vocational, 2-year, 4-year or graduate institution.
Eligibility: Applicant must be of minority background. Applicant must be female. Applicant must be U.S. citizen or permanent resident.
Basis for selection: Applicant must demonstrate depth of character, leadership, patriotism, seriousness of purpose, service orientation and high academic achievement.
Application requirements: Applications available Aug.1 - Dec.20.
Additional information: Must have earned a bachelor's degree and received last degree before June 30, 1994. Enroll in courses that are prerequisites for professional employment plans. Special consideration given to AAUW members, women of color, women pursuing their first terminal degree, and women pursuing degrees in nontraditional fields.

Amount of award:	$1,000-$5,000
Application deadline:	January 5

Contact:
AAUW Educational Foundation
Department 60
2201 N. Dodge St.
Iowa City, IA 52243-4030
Phone: 13193371716
Website: www.aauw.org

Science and Technology Fellowship

Type of award: Research grant.
Intended use: For master's study.
Eligibility: Applicant must be U.S. citizen or permanent resident.
Basis for selection: Major/career interest in architecture; computer and information sciences; engineering; mathematics. Applicant must demonstrate depth of character, leadership, patriotism, seriousness of purpose and service orientation.
Application requirements: Applications available Aug.1 - Dec.20.
Additional information: Applicants must be entering their

final year of a master's degree (including one-year programs). Special consideration given to applicants who show professional promise in innovative or neglected areas of research and/or practice in public interest concerns.
- **Amount of award:** $5,000-$12,000
- **Application deadline:** January 6

Contact:
AAUW Educational Foundation
Department 60
2201 N. Dodge St.
Iowa City, IA 52243-4030
Phone: 3193371716 ex. 60
Website: www.aauw.org

Selected Professions Fellowship

Type of award: Research grant.
Intended use: For master's, doctoral study.
Eligibility: Applicant must be of minority background. Applicant must be female. Applicant must be U.S. citizen or permanent resident.
Basis for selection: Major/career interest in business; law; medicine (m.d.). Applicant must demonstrate depth of character, leadership, patriotism, seriousness of purpose and service orientation.
Application requirements: Application available Aug.1 - Dec.20.
Additional information: Awarded to women from historically underrepresented ethnic minorities in business administration (M.B.A, two-year, and executive programs only), law (J.D.), and medicine (M.D. or D.O). Applicants must be entering their final year of study by September of 1999.
- **Amount of award:** $5,000-$12,000
- **Application deadline:** January 6

Contact:
AAUW Educational Foundation
2201 North Dodge Street
Iowa City, IA 52243-4030
Phone: 319-337-1716, ext. 98
Website: www.aauw.org

American Bar Foundation

American Bar Doctoral Dissertation Fellowship

Type of award: Research grant, renewable.
Intended use: For doctoral, postgraduate study.
Eligibility: Applicant must be U.S. citizen or permanent resident.
Basis for selection: Major/career interest in law; social and behavioral sciences. Applicant must demonstrate seriousness of purpose.
Application requirements: Recommendations, transcript and research proposal. Curriculumn vitae; sample of written work (optional).
Additional information: Applicant's dissertation must emphasize social scientific understanding of legal/law process. Minorities encouraged to apply. Deadline is usually on February 1st unless this date is on the weekend. Award amount of $15,000 is given to Doctoral fellows. Award amount of $30,000 is given to Postdoctoral fellows.

- **Amount of award:** $15,000-$30,000
- **Number of awards:** 2
- **Application deadline:** February 3
- **Notification begins:** April 1

Law/Social Sciences Summer Research Fellowship for Minority Undergraduates

Type of award: Internship.
Intended use: For sophomore, junior study.
Eligibility: Applicant must be U.S. citizen or permanent resident.
Basis for selection: Major/career interest in law; social and behavioral sciences; criminal justice/law enforcement; public administration/service. Applicant must demonstrate high academic achievement.
Application requirements: Recommendations, essay and transcript.
Additional information: Interns work ten 35-hour weeks as research assistants at American Bar Foundation in Chicago. Minimum 3.0 GPA.
- **Amount of award:** $3,500
- **Number of awards:** 4
- **Application deadline:** March 1
- **Notification begins:** April 15

Contact:
American Bar Foundation
750 North Lake Shore Drive
Chicago, IL 60611
Phone: 312-988-6500

American Brain Tumor Association

Brain Tumor Research Fellowship

Type of award: Research grant.
Intended use: For postgraduate study at graduate institution in United States.
Eligibility: Applicant must be U.S. citizen, permanent resident or Canadian citizen.
Basis for selection: Major/career interest in neurology; oncology.
Application requirements: Recommendations and research proposal. Curriculum vitae, list of publications.
Additional information: Must be used at graduate institutions in the U.S. or Canada. Award is $25,000 per year for two years.
- **Amount of award:** $50,000
- **Number of applicants:** 25
- **Application deadline:** January 5
- **Notification begins:** April 1
- **Total amount awarded:** $337,500

Contact:
American Brain Tumor Association
2720 River Road
Des Plaines, IL 60018
Phone: 847-827-9910
Website: www.abta.org

American Cancer Society

American Cancer Society Doctoral Degree Scholarship in Cancer Nursing

Type of award: Scholarship, renewable.
Intended use: For full-time doctoral study.
Eligibility: Applicant must be U.S. citizen or permanent resident.
Basis for selection: Major/career interest in nursing. Applicant must demonstrate seriousness of purpose and service orientation.
Application requirements: Research proposal.
Additional information: Must have applied to or be enrolled in graduate school at time of application. Must plan career in cancer nursing or a related area.

Amount of award:	$8,000
Number of awards:	5
Number of applicants:	8
Application deadline:	December 15
Notification begins:	May 1
Total amount awarded:	$40,000

Contact:
Extramural Grants Department
1599 Clifton Road NE
Atlanta, GA 30329-4251
Website: www.cancer.org

Cancer Society Postdoctoral Fellowship

Type of award: Scholarship, renewable.
Intended use: For postgraduate study.
Eligibility: Applicant must be U.S. citizen or permanent resident.
Basis for selection: Major/career interest in medical specialties/research. Applicant must demonstrate high academic achievement.
Application requirements: Recommendations, transcript, proof of eligibility and research proposal.
Additional information: Open to applicants with less than five years of postdoctoral research training.

Amount of award:	$78,000
Number of awards:	300
Number of applicants:	300
Application deadline:	March 1, October 1
Notification begins:	July 15, February 28
Total amount awarded:	$2,896,830

Contact:
American Cancer Society
Extramural Grants Department
1599 Clifton Road NE
Atlanta, GA 30329-4251
Phone: 404-329-7558, ext. 5734

Master's Degree Scholarship in Cancer Nursing

Type of award: Scholarship.
Intended use: For half-time master's study at accredited graduate institution in United States.
Eligibility: Applicant must be U.S. citizen or permanent resident.
Basis for selection: Major/career interest in nursing. Applicant must demonstrate seriousness of purpose and service orientation.
Application requirements: Proof of eligibility.
Additional information: Must have applied to or be enrolled in graduate nursing program at time of application. Master's degree program must have demonstrated integration of cancer nursing content.

Amount of award:	$8,000
Number of applicants:	18
Application deadline:	December 15
Notification begins:	May 1
Total amount awarded:	$88,000

Contact:
American Cancer Society
Extramural Grants Department
1599 Clifton Road, NE
Atlanta, GA 30329-4251
Website: www.cancer.org

American Cancer Society Extramural Grants

American Cancer Society Training Grants In Clinical Oncology Social Work (Tgcosw)

Type of award: Scholarship.
Intended use: For full-time master's, doctoral or postgraduate study.
Eligibility: Applicant must be U.S. citizen or permanent resident.
Basis for selection: Major/career interest in social work.
Application requirements: Recommendations, essay, transcript and proof of eligibility.
Additional information: For second year Master's students and post-Master's level social workers to provide psychosocial services to persons with cancer and their families. Awards are for $8,000 at the Master's level and $12,000 at the post-Master's level.

Amount of award:	$8,000-$12,000
Application deadline:	December 15

Contact:
American Cancer Society Extramural Grants Department
1599 Clifton Rd.
NE
Atlanta, GA 30329-4251
Website: www.cancer.org

American Center of Oriental Research

American Schools of Oriental Research/Kenneth W. Russell Fellowship

Type of award: Research grant.
Intended use: For master's, doctoral study at graduate institution in Jordan.
Eligibility: Applicant must be U.S. citizen, permanent resident or Any non-Jordanian.
Basis for selection: Major/career interest in archaeology; Middle Eastern studies; ancient Near Eastern studies.
Additional information: To assist a non-Jordanian graduate student of any nationality with travel expenses to join a field project or conduct independent archaeological or related research in Jordan.
   Amount of award: $1,500
   Application deadline: February 1
Contact:
Fellowship Coordinator
656 Beacon Street
Boston, MA 02215-2010
Phone: (617) 353-6570
Fax: (617) 353-6570

George A. Barton Fellowship

Type of award: Research grant.
Intended use: For full-time graduate study at postsecondary institution.
Basis for selection: Major/career interest in archaeology; Middle Eastern studies; ancient Near Eastern studies. Applicant must demonstrate seriousness of purpose, service orientation, financial need and high academic achievement.
Application requirements: Recommendations, essay, transcript and research proposal. Fellowship recipients must submit a report within one month of the conclusion of the award period. Recipient is expected to conduct a seminar or workshop based upon his/her research.
Additional information: $5000 award. The stipend is $2000, remainder for room and half board at the institution. Open to seminaries, pre-doctoral students, and recent recipients of Ph.D., specializing in Ancient Near Eastern studies, Archaeology, Geography, History and Biblical studies. Research period four to five months.
   Amount of award: $5,000-$5,000
   Application deadline: October 13, October 13
   Notification begins: January 15, January 15
Contact:
656 Beacon Street, 5th Floor
Boston, MA 02215-2010
Phone: (617) 353-6570
Fax: (617) 353-6575

American Chemical Society

Chemical Society Minority Scholarship

Type of award: Scholarship.
Intended use: For full-time undergraduate study at accredited 2-year or 4-year institution in United States.
Eligibility: Applicant must be Alaskan native, American Indian, African American, Mexican American, Hispanic American or Puerto Rican. Applicant must be high school senior. Applicant must be U.S. citizen or permanent resident.
Basis for selection: Major/career interest in chemistry; engineering, chemical. Applicant must demonstrate seriousness of purpose, service orientation, financial need and high academic achievement.
Application requirements: Recommendations and transcript. CSS PROFILE, FAFSA.
Additional information: Applicant must intend to pursue career in chemistry, biochemistry, or chemical engineering. Student must have minimum 3.0 GPA.
   Amount of award: $2,500
   Number of awards: 295
   Number of applicants: 1,200
   Application deadline: February 15
   Notification begins: March 5
   Total amount awarded: $650,000
Contact:
American Chemical Society
Scholars Program
1155 Sixteenth Street, NW
Washington, DC 20036
Phone: 800-227-5558
Website: www.acs.org

American College of Chiropractic Orthopedists

F. Maynard Lipe Scholarship

Type of award: Scholarship, renewable.
Intended use: For first professional study at accredited graduate institution in United States. Designated institutions: Must be an accredited school of chiropractic medicine.
Basis for selection: Competition in Writing/journalism. Article on orthopedics Major/career interest in chiropractic.
Application requirements: Recommendations and transcript.
Additional information: Must be in fifth trimester of chiropractic school and have an interest in orthopedic medicine.
   Amount of award: $500
   Number of awards: 1
   Application deadline: April 30
   Total amount awarded: $500
Contact:
American College of Chiropractic Orthopedists
5th St. & Montgomery Ave., Suite 100
Boyertown, PA 19512
Website: www.accoweb.com

# American College of Legal Medicine

Legal Medicine Student Writing Competition

Type of award: Scholarship.
Intended use: For undergraduate, post-bachelor's certificate, master's or doctoral study in . Designated institutions: In United States or Canada.
Basis for selection: Competition in Research paper. Scholarly writing in area of legal medicine. Major/career interest in medicine (m.d.); law; health sciences; dentistry.
Application requirements: Essay. Original uncollaborated research paper or essay (no less than 3,000 words) on legal medicine.
Additional information: Must be currently enrolled in accredited law, medical, dental, or allied health care school.
    Amount of award: $1,000
    Number of awards: 3
    Number of applicants: 70
    Application deadline: February 1
    Notification begins: April 1
    Total amount awarded: $3,000
Contact:
American College of Legal Medicine
611 East Wells Street
Milwaukee, WI 53202
Phone: 414-276-1881
Fax: 414-276-3349
Website: www.aclm.org

American College of Musicians/National Guild of Piano Teachers

American College of Musicians Musical Composition Test

Type of award: Scholarship.
Intended use: For non-degree study.
Basis for selection: Competition in Music performance/composition. Piano composition rated on imagination, originality, and skill.
Application requirements: Manuscript of composition.
Additional information: Teacher must be member of National Guild of Piano Teachers. Entry fees vary according to classification of students and length of composition.
    Amount of award: $200
    Number of awards: 1
    Number of applicants: 501
    Application deadline: March 1
    Total amount awarded: $200
Contact:
National Guild of Piano Teachers
International Headquarters
P.O. Box 2215
Austin, TX 78767-2215
Phone: 512-478-5775

Piano Teachers Scholarship

Type of award: Scholarship.
Intended use: For non-degree study.
Application requirements: Nomination by piano teacher.
Additional information: Student must have been in national or international solo auditions for ten years, be a Guild Paderewski winner, and be Guild High School Diploma recipient. Teacher must be member of National Guild of Piano Teachers.
    Amount of award: $200
    Number of awards: 150
    Application deadline: September 15
    Notification begins: October 31
    Total amount awarded: $3,000
Contact:
American College of Musicians/National Guild of Piano Teachers
International Headquarters
P.O. Box 1807
Austin, TX 78767-1807
Phone: 512-478-5775

Raissa Tselentis J. S. Bach Scholarship

Type of award: Scholarship.
Intended use: For non-degree study.
Basis for selection: Competition in Music performance/composition.
Application requirements: Audition and nomination.
Additional information: One award for early Bach; one for advanced Bach. Teacher must request entry for students. Teacher must be member of National Guild of Piano Teachers. Entry fees vary according to classification of students.
    Amount of award: $200
    Number of awards: 1
    Number of applicants: 96
    Application deadline: September 15
    Total amount awarded: $200
Contact:
National Guild of Piano Teachers
International Headquarters
P.O. Box 1807
Austin, TX 78767-1807
Phone: 512-478-5775

American Congress on Surveying and Mapping

American Congress on Surveying and Mapping/Allen Chelf Scholarship

Type of award: Scholarship.
Intended use: For full-time freshman, sophomore, junior or senior study at 4-year institution in United States.
Basis for selection: Major/career interest in surveying and mapping. Applicant must demonstrate seriousness of purpose and high academic achievement.

Application requirements: Recommendations, essay and transcript.
Additional information: Must be enrolled in a four-year program in surveying, geometics or surveying engineering in the United States.
    Amount of award: $1,500
    Number of awards: 1
    Application deadline: December 1
    Notification begins: January
    Total amount awarded: $250

American Congress on Surveying and Mapping/McDonnel Memorial Scholarship

Type of award: Scholarship.
Intended use: For full-time junior, senior study.
Eligibility: Applicant must be female. Applicant must be U.S. citizen.
Basis for selection: Major/career interest in surveying and mapping. Applicant must demonstrate leadership, seriousness of purpose and high academic achievement.
Application requirements: Recommendations, essay, transcript and proof of eligibility.
Additional information: Must be enrolled in a four-year program leading to surveying degree.
    Amount of award: $1,000
    Number of awards: 1
    Application deadline: December 1
    Total amount awarded: $1,000

McDonnel Memorial Scholarship

Type of award: Scholarship.
Intended use: For full-time junior, senior study.
Eligibility: Applicant must be female. Applicant must be U.S. citizen residing in Montana or Idaho or Oregon or Wyoming or Colorado or Utah or Nevada or California or Arizona or New Mexico or Alaska or Hawaii.
Basis for selection: Major/career interest in surveying and mapping. Applicant must demonstrate leadership, seriousness of purpose and high academic achievement.
Application requirements: Recommendations, essay, transcript and proof of eligibility.
Additional information: Must be enrolled in four-year program leading to surveying degree. Proof of residency must be submitted with application.
    Amount of award: $1,000
    Number of awards: 1
    Application deadline: December 1
    Total amount awarded: $1,000

Porter McDonnell Memorial Scholarship

Type of award: Scholarship, renewable.
Intended use: For full-time freshman, sophomore, junior or senior study.
Eligibility: Applicant must be female, high school senior. Applicant must be U.S. citizen.
Basis for selection: Major/career interest in surveying and mapping. Applicant must demonstrate leadership, seriousness of purpose, financial need and high academic achievement.
Application requirements: Transcript and proof of eligibility.
Additional information: Applicant must be enrolled in a four year degree in surveying, geomatics or surveying engineering.
    Amount of award: $1,000
    Number of awards: 1
    Application deadline: December 1
Web: www.landsurveyor.com

American Conservatory Theater

American Conservatory Theater Production Internships

Type of award: Internship.
Intended use: For undergraduate or graduate study.
Eligibility: Applicant must be Must have valid work permit.
Basis for selection: Major/career interest in performing arts; theater (artistic); theater (production/technical). Applicant must demonstrate high academic achievement.
Application requirements: $10 application fee. Interview, portfolio, recommendations and essay.
Additional information: Provides intern with practical experience in theater production. Work available in many different aspects. Stipends are $165/week, length of time depends on position. Placement based on past experience.
    Application deadline: April 15
    Notification begins: June 1
Contact:
American Conservatory Theater
Susan West - Intern Coordinator
30 Grant Avenue, 6th Floor
San Francisco, CA 94108
Phone: 4158343200
Website: www.act-sfbay.org

Artistic Internships

Type of award: Internship.
Intended use: For undergraduate or graduate study.
Eligibility: Applicant must be Must have valid work permit.
Basis for selection: Major/career interest in performing arts; theater (artistic); theater (production/technical). Applicant must demonstrate high academic achievement.
Application requirements: $10 application fee. Interview, portfolio, recommendations and essay.
Additional information: Provides intern with opportunity to work within the artistic and administrative fields of a theater company. There is no stipend. If intern needs paying employment, ACT will adjust hours. Different departments have available positions at different times of year. Application deadlines are rolling.
Contact:
American Conservatory Theater
Susan West - Intern Coordinator
30 Grant Avenue, 6th Floor
San Francisco, CA 94108
Phone: 4158343200
Website: www.act-sfbay.org

American Consulting Engineers Council

Consulting Engineers Scholarship

Type of award: Scholarship.
Intended use: For full-time junior, senior or graduate study at accredited 4-year or graduate institution in United States.
Eligibility: Applicant must be adult returning student. Applicant must be U.S. citizen.
Basis for selection: Major/career interest in engineering. Applicant must demonstrate depth of character, leadership and high academic achievement.
Application requirements: Recommendations, essay and transcript.
    Amount of award: $2,500-$5,000
    Number of awards: 6
    Application deadline: March 15
    Notification begins: June 10
Contact:
American Consulting Engineers Council
1015 15 Street, NW
Suite 802
Washington, DC 20005

American Council of Learned Societies

American Art Dissertation Fellowship

Type of award: Research grant.
Intended use: For doctoral study.
Eligibility: Minority and women applications are encouraged. Applicant must be U.S. citizen or permanent resident.
Basis for selection: Major/career interest in history; art, art history.
Application requirements: Recommendations, transcript and research proposal.
Additional information: Must be Ph.D. candidate who has completed all requirements except dissertation in an art history department. Award assists graduate students in any stage of Ph.D. dissertation research or writing focused on history of visual arts of U.S.
    Amount of award: $18,500
    Application deadline: November 14
    Notification begins: March 1
Contact:
ACLS Office of Fellowships & Grants
228 E. 45 Street
New York, NY 10017-3398
Website: www.acls.org

Council of Learned Societies Fellowship

Type of award: Research grant.
Intended use: For postgraduate, non-degree study.
Eligibility: Applicant must be U.S. citizen or permanent resident.
Basis for selection: Major/career interest in humanities/liberal arts; social and behavioral sciences.
Application requirements: Recommendations and research proposal. list of publications.
Additional information: Fellowships intended as salary replacements for six to twelve continuous months full-time research and writing. Must have had Ph.D. for two years by deadline date. At least five years must have elapsed between conclusion of the scholar's last supported research leave and July 1.
    Application deadline: September 30
    Notification begins: March 15

Eastern Europe Dissertation Fellowship

Type of award: Research grant, renewable.
Intended use: For doctoral study.
Eligibility: Applicant must be U.S. citizen or permanent resident.
Basis for selection: Major/career interest in humanities/liberal arts; social and behavioral sciences.
Application requirements: Recommendations, transcript and research proposal.
Additional information: For dissertation research or writing focused on Eastern Europe.
    Amount of award: $15,000
    Application deadline: November 1
    Notification begins: April 1
Contact:
ACLS Office of Fellowships & Grants
228 E. 45th Street
New York, NY 10017-3398
Website: www.acls.org

Eastern Europe Postdoctorate Fellowship

Type of award: Research grant.
Intended use: For postgraduate study.
Eligibility: Applicant must be U.S. citizen or permanent resident.
Basis for selection: Major/career interest in social and behavioral sciences; humanities/liberal arts; Russian studies.
Application requirements: Recommendations and research proposal.
Additional information: Must hold Ph.D. or equivalent as demonstrated by professional experience and publications and be working in Eastern European area studies. Fellowship for six to twelve consecutive months' research in East European studies in any country outside Eastern Europe.
    Amount of award: $30,000
    Application deadline: November 1
    Notification begins: April 1
Contact:
Office of Fellowships and Grants
228 East 45 Street
New York, NY 10017-3398

American Council of the Blind

Floyd Qualls Memorial Scholarship

Type of award: Scholarship, renewable.
Intended use: For full-time undergraduate or graduate study.
Eligibility: Applicant must be visually impaired. Applicant must be U.S. citizen or permanent resident.
Basis for selection: Applicant must demonstrate depth of character, leadership and high academic achievement.
Application requirements: Interview, recommendations, essay, transcript and proof of eligibility. Proof of legal blindness.
Additional information: One scholarship each reserved for residents of Colorado, Massachusetts, Pennsylvania, and South Dakota; two reserved for those with business-related degrees, and two more reserved for Virginia residents. Minimum 3.3 GPA for all applicants except vocational. Must be in or currently under consideration for postsecondary program. Applicants must be legally blind in both eyes.
  Amount of award: $500-$4,000
  Number of awards: 25
  Number of applicants: 300
  Application deadline: March 1
  Notification begins: June 1
Contact:
American Council of the Blind
Jessica Beach, Scholarship Administrator
1155 15 Street NW, Suite 720
Washington, DC 20005

American Council on Rural Special Education

Rural Special Education Scholarship

Type of award: Scholarship.
Intended use: For master's, non-degree study.
Eligibility: Applicant must be U.S. citizen.
Basis for selection: Major/career interest in education, special.
Application requirements: Recommendations and essay.
Additional information: Applicant must currently be (or have been) employed by a rural school district as a certified teacher in regular or special education for at least three years, or working with exceptional students or regular education students and preparing for work with students with disabilities.
  Amount of award: $1,000
  Number of awards: 1
  Number of applicants: 382
  Application deadline: December 10
  Notification begins: February 1
  Total amount awarded: $1,000
Contact:
ACRES Scholarship
Kansas State University
2323 Anderson Avenue, Suite 226
Manhattan, KS 66502
Website: www.ksu.edu/acres/scholar.html

American Dental Assistants Association/ Oral B Laboratories

Colgate-Juliette A. Southard/ Oral B Laboratories Scholarship

Type of award: Scholarship.
Intended use: For undergraduate study.
Basis for selection: Major/career interest in dental assistant. Applicant must demonstrate depth of character, leadership and high academic achievement.
Application requirements: Recommendations, transcript and proof of eligibility.
Additional information: Must be an American Dental Assistants Association member or American Dental Assistants Association student member.
  Amount of award: $500
  Number of awards: 10
  Application deadline: January 31
Contact:
American Dental Assistants Association
203 North LaSalle Street
Suite 1320
Chicago, IL 60601
Phone: 800-733-2322

American Dental Association Endowment and Assistance Fund, Inc..

Dental Assisting Scholarship

Type of award: Scholarship.
Intended use: For full-time freshman, sophomore study in United States. Designated institutions: Must be accredited by Commission on Dental Accreditation.
Eligibility: Applicant must be U.S. citizen.
Basis for selection: Major/career interest in dental assistant. Applicant must demonstrate financial need and high academic achievement.
Application requirements: Recommendations and essay.
Additional information: 2.8 GPA, minimum 12 credit hours.
  Amount of award: $1,000
  Number of awards: 25
  Number of applicants: 70
  Application deadline: September 15
  Notification begins: October 23
  Total amount awarded: $25,000
Contact:
ADA Endowment and Assistance Fund, Inc.
Scholarship Coordinator
211 East Chicago Avenue
Chicago, IL 60611

American Electroplaters and Surface Finishers Society Scholarship Committee

American Electroplaters and Surface Finishers Society Scholarship

Type of award: Scholarship, renewable.
Intended use: For full-time junior, senior or graduate study.
Basis for selection: Major/career interest in engineering, materials; engineering, chemical; engineering, environmental; chemistry.
Application requirements: Recommendations, essay and transcript. Resume.
Additional information: Additional fields of study: Any research related to plating and surface finishing technologies. Award notfication occurs between late July and early August.
    Amount of award: $1,500
    Number of awards: 7
    Number of applicants: 46
    Application deadline: April 15
    Total amount awarded: $7,000
Contact:
AESF Scholarship Committee
12644 Research Parkway
Orlando, FL 32826-3298
Phone: 407-281-6441

American Foundation for Aging Research

Aging Research Scholarship

Type of award: Research grant, renewable.
Intended use: For full-time freshman, sophomore, junior, senior, master's or doctoral study in United States.
Basis for selection: Major/career interest in neuroscience; medical specialties/research; biology; chemistry. Applicant must demonstrate high academic achievement.
Application requirements: $3 application fee. Recommendations, transcript, proof of eligibility and research proposal.
Additional information: Must be actively involved or planning active involvement in a specific biomedical or biochemical research project in field of aging. Number of awards varies. Call sponsor for information regarding deadline. SASE preferred.
    Amount of award: $500-$1,000
    Number of applicants: 5
    Total amount awarded: $4,000
Contact:
American Foundation for Aging Research
North Carolina State University
Biochemistry Dept., 128 Polk Hall, P.O. Box 7622
Raleigh, NC 27695-7622
Phone: 919-515-5679

American Foundation for Pharmaceutical Education

Amer. Fdn. For Pharm. Educ./ Clinical Pharmacy Post-Pharm.D. Fellowship In The Biomedical Research Sciences

Type of award: Research grant, renewable.
Intended use: For full-time postgraduate study.
Eligibility: Applicant must be U.S. citizen or permanent resident.
Basis for selection: Major/career interest in pharmacy/pharmaceutics/pharmacology.
Additional information: Must have received Pharm.D. within past ten years. Must have completed one or more one- or two-year postdoctoral residency/fellowship programs. Must provide evidence of acceptance for training by mentor at recognized academic/research institution.
    Amount of award: $27,500
    Number of awards: 2
    Application deadline: February 15
    Notification begins: April 15
    Total amount awarded: $27,500
Contact:
American Foundation for Pharmaceutical Education
One Church Street
Suite 202
Rockville, MD 20850
Phone: 301-738-2160
Fax: 301-738-2161

American Association of Pharmaceutical Scientists Gateway Scholarship

Type of award: Research grant.
Intended use: For sophomore, junior or senior study at accredited 4-year or graduate institution.
Basis for selection: Major/career interest in pharmacy/pharmaceutics/pharmacology.
Application requirements: Recommendations, essay, transcript and research proposal.
Additional information: Awards intended to encourage undergraduates from any discipline to pursue Ph.D. in pharmacy.
    Amount of award: $5,000
    Number of awards: 4
    Number of applicants: 25
    Application deadline: January 28
    Notification begins: April 15
    Total amount awarded: $17,000
Contact:
American Foundation for Pharmaceutical Education
AAPS-AFPE "Gateway" Scholarship Program
One Church Street, Suite 202
Rockville, MD 20850
Phone: 301-738-2160
Fax: 301-738-2161

Gateway Pharmaceutical Research Scholarship

Type of award: Research grant.
Intended use: For sophomore, junior or senior study at 4-year or graduate institution.
Eligibility: Applicant must be U.S. citizen or permanent resident.
Basis for selection: Major/career interest in pharmacy/pharmaceutics/pharmacology.
Application requirements: Recommendations, essay, transcript, proof of eligibility and research proposal. List of honors, awards, accomplishments, GRE, SAT I and/or other national achievement scores if available.
Additional information: Undergraduate research project done under supervision of faculty sponsor.
    Amount of award: $5,000
    Number of awards: 12
    Application deadline: January 28
    Notification begins: April 15
    Total amount awarded: $38,250
Contact:
American Foundation for Pharmaceutical Education
One Church Street
Suite 202
Rockville, MD 20850
Phone: 301-738-2160
Fax: 301-738-2161

Merck Research Scholarship Program

Type of award: Research grant.
Intended use: For doctoral, first professional study in United States.
Eligibility: Applicant must be U.S. citizen or permanent resident.
Basis for selection: Major/career interest in pharmacy/pharmaceutics/pharmacology. Applicant must demonstrate high academic achievement.
Application requirements: Recommendations, essay and transcript.
Additional information: Minimum GPA 3.0 required.
    Amount of award: $7,000
    Number of awards: 10
    Application deadline: January 28
    Notification begins: April 15
    Total amount awarded: $63,000
Contact:
American Association of Colleges of Pharmacy
Attn: Dr. Kenneth Miller
1426 Prince Street
Alexandria, VA 22314-2841
Phone: 703-739-2330 ext. 1039

New Investigators Program

Type of award: Research grant.
Intended use: For postgraduate study.
Basis for selection: Major/career interest in pharmacy/pharmaceutics/pharmacology.
Application requirements: Proof of eligibility and research proposal.
Additional information: Must have earned terminal degree and be in first through fifth year of academic faculty appointment in school of pharmacy and hold rank of assistant professor.
    Amount of award: $12,500
    Number of awards: 21
    Application deadline: June 6
    Notification begins: February 1
Contact:
American Association of Colleges of Pharmacy
1426 Prince Street, Attn: Kenneth Miller
Attn: Kenneth Miller
Alexandria, VA 22314
Phone: 703-739-2330 ext.1039

American Foundation for the Blind

Delta Gamma Memorial Scholarship

Type of award: Scholarship.
Intended use: For undergraduate or graduate study at accredited postsecondary institution.
Eligibility: Applicant must be visually impaired. Applicant must be U.S. citizen.
Basis for selection: Major/career interest in health-related professions. Applicant must demonstrate depth of character, seriousness of purpose, service orientation and high academic achievement.
Application requirements: Recommendations, essay, transcript and proof of eligibility.
Additional information: Applicant must be in a health related profession, in the fields of rehabilitation and/or education of blind or visually impaired persons.
    Amount of award: $1,000
    Number of awards: 1
    Application deadline: April 30
    Total amount awarded: $1,000

Ferdinand Torres AFB Scholarship

Type of award: Scholarship.
Intended use: For full-time undergraduate study.
Eligibility: Applicant must be visually impaired.
Basis for selection: Applicant must demonstrate leadership, patriotism, seriousness of purpose and financial need.
Application requirements: Recommendations, essay, transcript and proof of eligibility. State applicant must reside in USA.
Additional information: Preference given to residents of New York City metro-area and new immigrants to the USA.
    Amount of award: $1,000
    Number of awards: 1
    Application deadline: April 30
    Total amount awarded: $1,000

Frederick A. Downes Scholarship

Type of award: Scholarship.
Intended use: For undergraduate, graduate or postgraduate study at accredited postsecondary institution.

American Foundation for the Blind: Frederick A. Downes Scholarship

Eligibility: Applicant must be visually impaired. Applicant must be U.S. citizen.
Basis for selection: Applicant must demonstrate depth of character and seriousness of purpose.
Application requirements: Recommendations, essay, transcript and proof of eligibility.
Additional information: Must be 22 years of age or younger.
- Amount of award: $2,500
- Number of awards: 2
- Application deadline: April 30
- Total amount awarded: $5,000

Gladys C. Anderson Memorial Scholarship

Type of award: Scholarship.
Intended use: For undergraduate study at accredited postsecondary institution.
Eligibility: Applicant must be female. Must be visually impaired. Applicant must be U.S. citizen.
Basis for selection: Major/career interest in music. Applicant must demonstrate depth of character and seriousness of purpose.
Application requirements: Recommendations, essay, transcript and proof of eligibility.
Additional information: Provide sample performance tape under 30 minutes.
- Amount of award: $1,000
- Number of awards: 1
- Application deadline: April 30
- Total amount awarded: $1,000

Karen D. Carsel Memorial Scholarhip

Type of award: Scholarship.
Intended use: For full-time graduate study.
Eligibility: Applicant must be visually impaired. Applicant must be U.S. citizen.
Basis for selection: Applicant must demonstrate depth of character, seriousness of purpose and financial need.
Application requirements: Recommendations, essay, transcript and proof of eligibility.
- Amount of award: $500
- Number of awards: 1
- Application deadline: April 30
- Total amount awarded: $500

R.L. Gillette Scholarship

Type of award: Scholarship.
Intended use: For freshman, sophomore, junior or senior study.
Eligibility: Applicant must be female. Must be visually impaired. Applicant must be U.S. citizen.
Basis for selection: Major/career interest in music; literature.
Application requirements: Recommendations, essay, transcript and proof of eligibility.
Additional information: Provide sample performance tape not exceeding 30 minutes.
- Amount of award: $1,000
- Number of awards: 2
- Application deadline: April 30
- Total amount awarded: $2,000

Rudolph Dillman Memorial Scholarship

Type of award: Scholarship.
Intended use: For undergraduate or graduate study at accredited postsecondary institution in United States.
Eligibility: Applicant must be visually impaired. Applicant must be U.S. citizen.
Basis for selection: Major/career interest in health-related professions. Applicant must demonstrate depth of character, leadership, seriousness of purpose and service orientation.
Application requirements: Recommendations, essay, transcript and proof of eligibility. State applicant must attend college in USA.
Additional information: Applicant must be in a health related profession, in the fields of rehabilitation and/or education of blind or visually impaired persons.
- Amount of award: $2,500
- Number of awards: 3
- Application deadline: April 30
- Total amount awarded: $7,500

Rudolph Dillman Memorial Scholarship Based on Need

Type of award: Scholarship.
Intended use: For undergraduate or graduate study at accredited postsecondary institution in United States.
Eligibility: Applicant must be visually impaired. Applicant must be U.S. citizen.
Basis for selection: Major/career interest in health-related professions. Applicant must demonstrate depth of character, seriousness of purpose, service orientation and financial need.
Application requirements: Recommendations, essay, transcript and proof of eligibility. State applicant must attend college in USA.
Additional information: Applicant must be in a health related profession, in the fields of rehabilitation and/or education of blind or visually impaired persons.
- Amount of award: $2,500
- Number of awards: 1
- Application deadline: April 30
- Total amount awarded: $2,500

Contact:
American Foundation for the Blind
11 Penn Plaza, Suite 300
New York, NY 10001
Website: www.afb.org

American Foundation for Urologic Disease

American Foundation for Urologic Disease Health Policy Research Program

Type of award: Research grant.
Intended use: For full-time first professional study in United States.
Basis for selection: Major/career interest in medical

specialties/research. Applicant must demonstrate high academic achievement.
Application requirements: Proof of eligibility and research proposal.
Additional information: Must be committed to a career in academic urology and have interests and/or accomplishments in health economics, health service delivery, and health policy.
- Amount of award: $44,000
- Number of awards: 1
- Application deadline: September 4

Contact:
1128 North Charles St.
Baltimore, MD 21201-5559

American Foundation for Urologic Disease Intramural Urologic Oncology Ph.D./ Post-Doctoral Research Training Program

Type of award: Research grant.
Intended use: For full-time postgraduate study in United States.
Basis for selection: Major/career interest in medical specialties/research. Applicant must demonstrate high academic achievement.
Application requirements: Proof of eligibility and research proposal.
Additional information: Applications accepted year-round. A background in molecular biology, cell biology, or protein chemistry is preferred but not required. Must have less than five years of post-doctoral experience. For research on molecular genetics in cooperation with the National Cancer Institute (NCI).
- Amount of award: $28,700-$35,900

Contact:
1128 North Charles St.
Baltimore, MD 21201-5559

American Foundation for Urologic Disease Intramural Urologic Oncology Research Training

Type of award: Research grant.
Intended use: For full-time first professional study in United States.
Basis for selection: Major/career interest in medical specialties/research. Applicant must demonstrate high academic achievement.
Application requirements: Proof of eligibility and research proposal.
Additional information: Applications accepted year-round. Applicants must have less than five years of post-doctoral research experience. For research in laboratories at the National Cancer Institute (NCI) studying signal transduction, transgenic and knockout mice, and other aspects of onclolgic research, with a focus on tumor suppresser genes.
- Amount of award: $45,000-$52,000
- Number of awards: 4

Contact:
1128 North Charles St.
Baltimore, MD 21201-5559

American Foundation for Urologic Disease Intramural Urology Research Training Program

Type of award: Research grant.
Intended use: For full-time first professional study in United States.
Basis for selection: Major/career interest in medical specialties/research. Applicant must demonstrate high academic achievement.
Application requirements: Recommendations, transcript, proof of eligibility and research proposal.
Additional information: For Physicians who recently completed a urology residency; must have less than five years of post-doctoral research experience. For research utilizing basic molecular and cellular biologic techniques in projects relevant to urology. This intramural program involves collaboration with the National Institute of Diabetes and Digestive and Kidney Diseases (NIDDKD). Applications accepted year-round.
- Amount of award: $45,000-$52,000

Contact:
1128 North Charles St.
Baltimore, MD 21201-5559

American Foundation for Urologic Disease MD Post-Resident Research Program

Type of award: Research grant.
Intended use: For full-time first professional study in United States.
Basis for selection: Major/career interest in medical specialties/research. Applicant must demonstrate high academic achievement.
Application requirements: Proof of eligibility and research proposal.
Additional information: For a trained urologist within five years of post-residency who can dedicate two years to the Program. Compensation will be $44,000 for each of the two years.
- Amount of award: $44,000
- Number of awards: 1
- Application deadline: September 4

Contact:
1128 North Charles Street
Baltimore, MD 21201-5559

American Foundation for Urologic Disease MD/Ph.D. One Year Research Program

Type of award: Research grant.
Intended use: For full-time first professional study in United States.
Basis for selection: Major/career interest in medical specialties/research. Applicant must demonstrate high academic achievement.
Application requirements: Proof of eligibility and research proposal.
Additional information: For urologist who have completed their residency within five years of the date of application.

Amount of award: $25,000
Application deadline: September 4
Contact:
1128 North Charles St.
Baltimore, MD 21201-5559

Urologic Disease Ph.D. Research Scholarship

Type of award: Research grant.
Intended use: For full-time postgraduate study.
Basis for selection: Major/career interest in medical specialties/research.
Application requirements: Essay, research proposal and nomination. Medical research institution and senior Ph.D or M.D. must sponsor candidate.
Additional information: Must be postdoctoral basic scientist, full-time, with research interest in urology or related diseases and dysfunction's. Award consists of $23,000 from the AFVD and $23,000 for the sponsoring institution.
Amount of award: $4,600
Application deadline: September 4
Notification begins: February 16
Contact:
Research Grant Committee
Attn. Lesley Finney
1128 North Charles Street
Baltimore, MD 21201

American Foundation for Vision Awareness

Vision Awareness Educational Grant

Type of award: Scholarship.
Intended use: For first professional study.
Eligibility: Applicant must be U.S. citizen or permanent resident.
Basis for selection: Major/career interest in optometry/ophthalmology. Applicant must demonstrate service orientation and financial need.
Application requirements: Recommendations and transcript.
Amount of award: $1,000
Application deadline: February 1
Notification begins: June 15
Contact:
American Foundation for Vision Awareness
243 North Lindbergh Boulevard
St. Louis, MO 63141
Phone: 800-927-2382

American Geological Institute

Geological Institute Minority Participation Program

Type of award: Scholarship, renewable.
Intended use: For full-time undergraduate or graduate study at accredited 2-year, 4-year or graduate institution in United States.
Eligibility: Applicant must be Alaskan native, American Indian, African American, Mexican American, Hispanic American or Puerto Rican. Applicant must be U.S. citizen.
Basis for selection: Major/career interest in atmospheric sciences/meteorology; oceanography/marine studies; geology/earth sciences; hydrology. Applicant must demonstrate financial need and high academic achievement.
Application requirements: Recommendations, essay, transcript and proof of eligibility.
Additional information: Eskimos, Hawaiians, and Samoans eligible. Applicants are required to reapply each year.
Amount of award: $500-$10,000
Number of awards: 96
Number of applicants: 150
Application deadline: February 1
Notification begins: May 1
Total amount awarded: $170,000
Contact:
American Geological Institute
Minority Geoscience Scholarship - C/O Marilyn Suiter
4220 King Street
Alexandria, VA 22302-1507
Phone: 703-379-2480
Fax: 703-379-7563
Website: www.agiweb.org

American Geophysical Union

Horton Geophysical Research Grant

Type of award: Research grant.
Intended use: For half-time doctoral study at accredited graduate institution.
Basis for selection: Major/career interest in geophysics; hydrology.
Application requirements: Research proposal and nomination by committee of the Hydrology Section of the American Geophysical Union. Dissertation (includes title page, executive summary, statement of purpose, and two letters of recommendation for the award.

Amount of award:	$8,000-$10,000
Number of awards:	2
Application deadline:	March 1
Notification begins:	April 1

Contact:
American Geophysical Union
Horton Research Grant
2000 Florida Avenue, NW
Washington, DC 20009
Phone: 202-462-6900
Fax: 202-328-0566

American Ground Water Trust

Amtrol Ground Water Research Scholarship

Type of award: Scholarship.
Intended use: For undergraduate study at vocational, 2-year or 4-year institution.
Eligibility: Applicant must be high school senior. Applicant must be U.S. citizen.
Basis for selection: Major/career interest in engineering, environmental; geology/earth sciences. Applicant must demonstrate leadership, seriousness of purpose and service orientation.
Application requirements: Recommendations, essay and transcript.
Additional information: Must be entering field related to ground water, i.e. hydrology or hydrogeology.

Amount of award:	$1,000-$2,000
Number of awards:	2
Number of applicants:	100
Application deadline:	June 1
Notification begins:	August 1
Total amount awarded:	$2,000

Contact:
American Ground Water Trust Scholarship
16 Centre Street
P.O. Box 1796
Concord, NH 03301
Phone: 603-228-5444
Website: www.agwt.org

American Heart Association

Irvine H. Page Arteriosclerosis Award

Type of award: Research grant.
Intended use: For postgraduate study.
Basis for selection: Major/career interest in medical specialties/research.
Application requirements: Recommendations. Curriculum vitae, abstract of work, manuscript.
Additional information: Must have sustained research relating to arteriosclerosis and have at least one prior publication.

Amount of award:	$1,500
Number of awards:	1
Application deadline:	May 2
Notification begins:	September 1
Total amount awarded:	$1,500

Contact:
American Heart Association
Young Investigator Awards
7272 Greenville Avenue
Dallas, TX 75231
Phone: 214-706-1685
Fax: 214-373-3406
Website: www.americanheart.org

Louis N. and Arnold M. Katz Research Prize

Type of award: Research grant.
Intended use: For doctoral study.
Basis for selection: Major/career interest in medical specialties/research; medicine (m.d.); chemistry.
Application requirements: Recommendations. Curriculum vitae, abstract of work, manuscript.
Additional information: Faculty member must have been appointed after January 1, 1994. Must be pursuing research in basic biological or medical sciences or related fields.

Amount of award:	$500-$1,500
Number of awards:	5
Application deadline:	May 2
Notification begins:	September 1
Total amount awarded:	$3,500

Contact:
American Heart Association
Young Investigator Awards
7272 Greenville Avenue
Dallas, TX 75231-4596
Phone: 214-706-1685
Fax: 214-373-3406
Website: www.americanheart.org

Melvin L. Marcus Award

Type of award: Research grant.
Intended use: For postgraduate study.
Basis for selection: Major/career interest in medical specialties/research.
Application requirements: Recommendations. Curriculum vitae, abstract of work, manuscript.
Additional information: For applicants pursuing work in cardiovascular integrated physiology. Must have Doctoral or equivalent degree. Must rank no higher than Assistant Professor for three years. Women and minorities are encouraged to apply.

Amount of award:	$500-$1,500
Number of awards:	5
Application deadline:	May 2
Notification begins:	September 1
Total amount awarded:	$3,500

Contact:
American Heart Association
Young Investigator Awards
7272 Greenville Avenue
Dallas, TX 75231-4596
Phone: 214-706-1685
Fax: 214-373-3406
Website: www.americanheart.org

Samuel A. Levine Young Clinical Award

Type of award: Research grant.
Intended use: For postgraduate study.
Basis for selection: Major/career interest in medical specialties/research; medicine (m.d.).
Application requirements: Recommendations and essay. Curriculum vitae, abstract of work, manuscript.
Additional information: Must be within three years of completion of cardiovascular fellowship training. Candidates must be members, members in-training, or fellows of the Council on Clinical Cardiology.

Amount of award:	$500-$1,500
Number of awards:	5
Application deadline:	May 2
Notification begins:	September 1
Total amount awarded:	$3,500

Contact:
American Heart Association
Young Investigator Award
7272 Greenville Avenue
Dallas, TX 75231-4596
Phone: 214-706-1685
Fax: 214-373-3406
Website: www.americanheart.org

Young Investigator Prize in Thrombosis

Type of award: Research grant.
Intended use: For postgraduate study.
Basis for selection: Major/career interest in medical specialties/research.
Application requirements: Recommendations and nomination. Curriculum vitae, abstract of work, manuscript.
Additional information: Award for fundamental and applied research in thrombosis, including mechanism, detection, treatment, and prevention of thrombotic disorders. Award presented only in alternate years. Next award year, 2000. Must have completed postdoctoral training at least 2 years before nomination.

Amount of award:	$500-$1,500
Number of awards:	5
Application deadline:	May 7
Notification begins:	September 1
Total amount awarded:	$3,500

Contact:
American Heart Association
Young Investigator Awards
7272 Greenville Avenue
Dallas, TX 75231-4596
Phone: 214-706-1685
Fax: 214-373-3406
Website: www.americanheart.org

American Heart Association Western States Affiliate

American Heart Association Beginning Grant-in-Aid Program

Type of award: Research grant, renewable.
Intended use: For postgraduate study.
Basis for selection: Major/career interest in medical specialties/research (beyond m.d.); medical specialties/research.
Application requirements: Research proposal.
Additional information: Up to half can be used for P.I. salary. Two year grant of up to $60,000/year. For medical investigators holding a doctoral degree.

Amount of award:	$60,000
Application deadline:	October 15

Contact:
American Heart Association
Western States Affiliate
1710 Gilbreth Street
Burlingame, CA 94010-1713
Phone: 650-259-6725
Website: www.americanheart.org

American Heart Association Grant-In-Aid

Type of award: Research grant, renewable.
Intended use: For postgraduate study in California.
Eligibility: Applicant must be residing in California or Nevada or Utah.
Basis for selection: Major/career interest in medical specialties/research; science, general; social and behavioral sciences; public health.
Application requirements: Research proposal.
Additional information: Limited to faculty or staff (not research fellows) of nonprofit institutions in California, Utah or Nevada. Must have doctoral degree. Research must be broadly related to the cardiovascular area. Research term is two years. Participation by women and minorities encouraged.

Amount of award:	$60,000
Application deadline:	October 15

Contact:
American Heart Association
Western States Affiliate
1710 Gilbreth Road
Burlingame, CA 94010-1713
Phone: 650-259-6720
Website: www.americanheart.org

American Heart Association Postdoctoral Fellowship

Type of award: Research grant, renewable.
Intended use: For postgraduate study in California. Designated institutions: Nonprofit only.
Basis for selection: Major/career interest in medical specialties/research. Applicant must demonstrate seriousness of purpose, service orientation and high academic achievement.
Application requirements: Recommendations, proof of eligibility and research proposal.
Additional information: Must have doctoral degree by July 1 of award year. Must devote 80 percent of time to research. Must be pursuing career in biomedical research broadly related to cardiovascular area. Participation by women and minorities encouraged. Grant must be used at non-profit institutions in California, Utah or Nevada.

Amount of award:	$25,000-$33,000
Application deadline:	October 1
Notification begins:	May 10

Contact:
American Heart Association
Western States Affiliate
1710 Gilbreth Road
Burlingame, CA 94010-1713
Phone: 650-259-6720
Website: www.americanheart.org

American Heart Association Predoctoral Fellowship

Type of award: Research grant, renewable.
Intended use: For full-time doctoral, first professional study at accredited graduate institution in California. Designated institutions: Nonprofit only.
Basis for selection: Major/career interest in science, general; medical specialties/research; social and behavioral sciences; public health. Applicant must demonstrate seriousness of purpose, service orientation and high academic achievement.
Application requirements: Recommendations, transcript, proof of eligibility and research proposal.
Additional information: Must complete required doctoral course work by July 1. Must be doctoral candidate or medical student in basic or clinical biomedical sciences, social/behavioral sciences, epidemiology, or public health. Dissertation sponsor must be a faculty member at institution where research will be conducted. Must devote 80 percent of time to research. Participation by women and minorities encouraged. Must be enrolled in program in California, Nevada or Utah.

Amount of award:	$16,500
Application deadline:	October 1
Notification begins:	May 1

Contact:
American Heart Association
Western States Affiliate
1710 Gilbreth Road
Burlingame, CA 94010-1713
Phone: 650-259-6720
Website: www.americanheart.org

American Heart Association Student Research Program

Type of award: Research grant.
Intended use: For full-time junior, senior study.
Eligibility: Applicant must be residing in California or Nevada or Utah.
Basis for selection: Major/career interest in biology; chemistry; physics; computer and information sciences. Applicant must demonstrate depth of character, seriousness of purpose, service orientation and high academic achievement.
Application requirements: Recommendations, essay, transcript and proof of eligibility.
Additional information: Must have completed a combined total of at least four semesters or six quarters of biological sciences, physics or chemistry. Must have completed at least one quarter of calculus, statistics, computational methods or computer science. Students are assigned to scientist-supervised laboratories to work for ten weeks during the summer exploring careers in heart or stroke research. Must be attending institutions or be resident of California, Utah or Nevada.

Amount of award:	$2,500
Application deadline:	January 15
Notification begins:	April 1

Contact:
American Heart Association
Western States Affiliate
1710 Gilbreth Road
Burlingame, CA 94010-1317
Phone: 650-259-6720
Website: www.americanheart.org

American Helicopter Society, Inc.

Vertical Flight Foundation Scholarship

Type of award: Scholarship.
Intended use: For full-time junior, senior or graduate study at accredited postsecondary institution.
Basis for selection: Major/career interest in engineering; aerospace; aviation. Applicant must demonstrate depth of character, seriousness of purpose and high academic achievement.
Application requirements: Recommendations, essay and transcript. Academic endorsement.
Additional information: Must major in helicopter or vertical

flight engineering industry. Minimum GPA of 3.0 required, 3.5 recommended.
- **Amount of award:** $4,000
- **Number of awards:** 13
- **Number of applicants:** 300
- **Application deadline:** February 1
- **Notification begins:** June 30
- **Total amount awarded:** $2,500

Contact:
American Helicopter Society, Inc.
Vertical Flight Foundation
217 North Washington Street
Alexandria, VA 22314
Phone: 703-684-6777

American Hotel Foundation

American Express Card Scholarship Program

Type of award: Scholarship, renewable.
Intended use: For full-time or half-time undergraduate study at 2-year or 4-year institution.
Basis for selection: Major/career interest in hotel/restaurant management.
Application requirements: Essay and transcript. Copy of course curriculum, and copy of tax form 1040 or 1040EZ.
Additional information: Must work at a hotel 20 hours a week and have 12 months experience. The hotel must be a member of the American Hotel & Motel Association.
- **Amount of award:** $500-$2,000
- **Number of awards:** 8
- **Number of applicants:** 24
- **Application deadline:** May 1
- **Notification begins:** June 15

Ecolah Scholarship Program

Type of award: Scholarship.
Intended use: For full-time undergraduate study at 2-year or 4-year institution in United States.
Basis for selection: Major/career interest in hotel/restaurant management.
Application requirements: Essay and transcript. Copy of course curriculum, and copy of tax form 1040 or 1040EZ.
- **Amount of award:** $1,000
- **Number of awards:** 12
- **Application deadline:** June 1
- **Notification begins:** July 15

Contact:
American Hotel Foundation
1201 New York Avenue NW 600
Washington, DC 20005-3931
Phone: 202-289-3181
Fax: 202-289-3199

American Indian Graduate Center

American Indian Graduate Fellowship

Type of award: Scholarship, renewable.
Intended use: For master's, doctoral study.
Eligibility: Applicant must be Alaskan native or American Indian. Applicant must be U.S. citizen.
Basis for selection: Applicant must demonstrate financial need.
Additional information: Students should call in January for further information. Students must first apply for other aid through university financial aid office. Amount of award quoted is average only and subject to change.
- **Amount of award:** $250-$5,000
- **Number of awards:** 317
- **Number of applicants:** 1,280
- **Application deadline:** June 1
- **Notification begins:** July 15

Contact:
Scholarship Coordinator
4520 Montgomery Boulevard
Suite 1B
Albuquerque, NM 87109
Phone: 505-881-4584
Website: www.aigc.com

American Indian Science and Engineering Society

Schuyler Meyer Junior Scholarship

Type of award: Scholarship, renewable.
Intended use: For full-time undergraduate or graduate study at accredited postsecondary institution in United States.
Eligibility: Applicant must be Alaskan native or American Indian. Must have proof of enrollment with federally recognized tribe. Applicant must be single.
Basis for selection: Applicant must demonstrate depth of character, leadership, seriousness of purpose, service orientation and financial need.
Application requirements: Recommendations, essay, transcript and proof of eligibility.
Additional information: Must have at least one minor child residing in household. Include SASE with all application/information requests.
- **Amount of award:** $1,000
- **Number of awards:** 15
- **Application deadline:** June 15
- **Notification begins:** August 31
- **Total amount awarded:** $14,000

Contact:
Attn: Scholarship Coordinator
5661 Airport Blvd.
Boulder, CO 80301
Website: www.colorado.edu/AISES

American Institute for Foreign Study

Foreign Study/Minority Scholarship Strategic Studies Award

Type of award: Scholarship.
Intended use: For freshman, sophomore, junior or senior study outside United States in Australia, Czech Republic, Japan, Russia, South Africa, Western Europe.
Eligibility: Applicant must be of minority background. Applicant must be U.S. citizen.
Basis for selection: Major/career interest in humanities/liberal arts. Applicant must demonstrate financial need and high academic achievement.
Additional information: 3.0 GPA required. Deadlines are April 15 and October 15. Must be involved in multicultural/international activities. Average award $1,000. One full scholarship including round trip air fare awarded each year. Award must be used for an AIFS program.
    Amount of award: $15,000
    Number of awards: 6
    Number of applicants: 6
    Application deadline: April 15
    Total amount awarded: $20,000
Contact:
American Institute for Foreign Study
102 Greenwich Avenue
Attn: Bill Gertz
Greenwich, CT 06830

International Semester Scholarship

Type of award: Scholarship.
Intended use: For freshman, sophomore, junior or senior study at postsecondary institution outside United States in Australia, Czech Republic, Japan, Russia, South Africa, Western Europe.
Eligibility: Applicant must be U.S. citizen.
Basis for selection: Major/career interest in humanities/liberal arts. Applicant must demonstrate leadership and high academic achievement.
Application requirements: Transcript.
Additional information: 3.0 GPA required. Involvement in multicultural/international activities also needed. Minorities encouraged to apply. Award must be used on an AIFS program.
    Amount of award: $1,000
    Number of awards: 100
    Number of applicants: 700
    Application deadline: April 15, October 15
    Total amount awarded: $100,000
Contact:
American Institute for Foreign Study
102 Greenwich Avenue
Attn: Bill Gertz
Greenwich, CT 06830

International Summer Scholarship

Type of award: Scholarship.
Intended use: For freshman, sophomore, junior or senior study at postsecondary institution outside United States in Australia, Czech Republic, Japan, Mexico, Russia, South Africa, Western Europe.
Eligibility: Applicant must be U.S. citizen.
Basis for selection: Major/career interest in humanities/liberal arts. Applicant must demonstrate leadership and high academic achievement.
Application requirements: Essay. Must submit essay on benefits of study abroad.
Additional information: Minimum 3.0 GPA required. Involvement in multicultural/international activities a plus. Minorities strongly encouraged to apply. Award must be used on an AIFS program.
    Amount of award: $500
    Number of awards: 10
    Number of applicants: 100
    Application deadline: March 15
    Total amount awarded: $5,000
Contact:
American Institute for Foreign Study
Attn: Bill Gertz
102 Greenwich Avenue
Greenwich, CT 06830

American Institute of Aeronautics and Astronautics

Aeronautics and Astronautics Undergraduate Scholarship

Type of award: Scholarship, renewable.
Intended use: For full-time sophomore, junior or senior study at accredited 4-year institution.
Eligibility: Applicant must be U.S. citizen or permanent resident.
Basis for selection: Major/career interest in aerospace; engineering. Applicant must demonstrate high academic achievement.
Application requirements: Recommendations, essay, transcript and proof of eligibility. 500-1,000 word typewritten essay on how academic program supports career objectives.
Additional information: Institution must be accredited by Accreditation Board for Engineering and Technology. Must have completed at least one quarter or semester of full-time college work. Minimum 3.0 GPA. Must join American Institute of Aeronautics and Astronautics before receiving award. Not open to members of any American Institute of Aeronautics and Astronautics national committees or subcommittees. Applications must be requested by January 15.

Amount of award:	$2,000
Number of awards:	30
Number of applicants:	100
Application deadline:	January 31
Notification begins:	July 1
Total amount awarded:	$60,000

Contact:
American Institute of Aeronautics and Astronautics
Student Programs
1801 Alexander Bell Drive, Suite 500
Reston, VA 11091
Phone: 703-264-7506
Website: www.aiaa.org

Gordon C. Oates Award

Type of award: Scholarship.
Intended use: For full-time master's, doctoral study at accredited graduate institution.
Eligibility: Applicant must be U.S. citizen.
Basis for selection: Major/career interest in aerospace. Applicant must demonstrate high academic achievement.
Application requirements: Recommendations, essay, transcript, proof of eligibility and research proposal. 100-500 words on how academic program and associated research support candidate's career objectives.
Additional information: Department adviser approval of research activity in air breathing propulsion required. 3.0 GPA. Must join American Institute of Aeronautics and Astronautics before receiving award.

Amount of award:	$5,000
Number of awards:	1
Application deadline:	January 31
Notification begins:	July 1
Total amount awarded:	$5,000

Contact:
American Institute of Aeronautics and Astronautics Graduate
Awards
1800 Alexander Bell Drive, Suite 500
Reston, VA 22091
Website: www.aiaa.org

William T. Piper Award

Type of award: Scholarship.
Intended use: For full-time master's, doctoral study at accredited graduate institution.
Eligibility: Applicant must be U.S. citizen.
Basis for selection: Major/career interest in aerospace.
Application requirements: Recommendations, essay, transcript, proof of eligibility and research proposal. 500-1,000 word typewritten essay describing research objectives, approach, progress, expected results. 100-500 words on how academic program and associated research support candidate's career objectives. Three recommendations from area specialists.
Additional information: Must have department adviser approval of research activity in general aviation. Institution must be accredited by Accreditation Board for Engineering and Technology. Must have completed at least one year graduate work. Minimum 3.0 GPA required. Must join American Institute of Aeronautics and Astronautics before receiving award.

Amount of award:	$1,000
Number of awards:	1
Number of applicants:	1
Application deadline:	January 31
Notification begins:	July 1
Total amount awarded:	$1,000

Contact:
American Institute of Aeronautics and Astronautics Graduate
Awards
1801 Alexander Bell Drive, Suite 500
Reston, VA 22091
Phone: 703-264-7500
Website: www.aiaa.org

American Institute of Architects

American Institute of Architects Fellowship in Health Facilities Design

Type of award: Research grant.
Intended use: For senior or graduate study at accredited graduate institution in United States.
Eligibility: Applicant must be U.S. citizen or permanent resident.
Basis for selection: Major/career interest in architecture.
Additional information: Applicants must either have earned and received a professional degree from an accredited school of architecture or be in the final year of undergraduate work leading to a professional degree. Fellowships are available for study in any one of three settings: Graduate study for one academic year in any accredited school of architecture associated with a school of hospital administration or near hospital resources adequate to supplement prescribed graduate architecture courses in health facilities design. Independent Graduate-level study, research, or design in the health facilities field, to be completed within one calendar year. Travel with in-residence research at selected hospitals in a predetermined area, to be completed within one calendar year.

Amount of award:	$2,000
Number of awards:	1
Application deadline:	January 15

Contact:
Scholarship Coordinator
1735 New York Ave., NW
Washington, DC 20006-5292
Website: www.e-architect.com/institute/scholar

American Institute of Architects for Professional Degree Candidates

Type of award: Scholarship.
Intended use: For full-time junior, senior or master's study at accredited 4-year or graduate institution in United States.
Eligibility: Applicant must be U.S. citizen or permanent resident.
Basis for selection: Major/career interest in architecture.
Application requirements: Transcript and nomination.
Additional information: Assists students in one of the final

two years of a professional degree program in architecture. Student must be in one of the following: The third or fourth year of a five-year program resulting in a bachelor of architecture or equivalent degree. The fourth or fifth year of a six-year program (4 + 2 or other combination) that results in a master of architecture or equivalent degree. The second or third year of a three-to-four-year program that results in a master of architecture and who's undergraduate degree is in a discipline other than architecture.

Amount of award:	$500-$2,500
Application deadline:	February 1

Contact:
American Architectural Foundation
1735 New York Ave, NW
Washington, DC 20006-5292
Website: www.e-architect.com/institute/scholar

American Institute of Architects Minority/Disadvantaged Scholarship

Type of award: Scholarship, renewable.
Intended use: For full-time freshman study at accredited 2-year, 4-year or graduate institution in United States. Designated institutions: Institute must be NAAB accredited.
Eligibility: Applicant must be of minority background. Applicant must be high school senior. Applicant must be U.S. citizen or permanent resident.
Basis for selection: Major/career interest in architecture. Applicant must demonstrate financial need.
Application requirements: Transcript and nomination by An initial nomination by either a high school guidance counselor. AIA component, architect, or other individual who can speak for the students interest and aptitude for an architecture Program.
Additional information: An application is sent to eligible students after nomination screening. The nomination form is due December 12. Nomination forms are mailed upon request by calling (202) 626-7511. Open to high school seniors and college freshman who plan to enter a Program leading to a professional degree in architecture either bachelors or masters. Students who have completed a full year of undergraduate coursework are not eligible. Renewable up to three years.

Amount of award:	$500-$2,500
Number of awards:	25
Application deadline:	January 15

Contact:
American Architectural Foundation
1735
New York Ave, NW
Washington, DC 20006-5292
Website: www.e-architect.com/institute/scholar

American Institute of Architects Scholarship for Advanced Study and Research

Type of award: Research grant.
Intended use: For master's, doctoral study at accredited graduate institution in United States.
Eligibility: Applicant must be U.S. citizen or permanent resident.
Basis for selection: Major/career interest in architecture.
Additional information: Must be pursuing an advanced degree or conducting research under the direction of a U.S. university. Supports advanced study and research by those who have already earned a professional degree. Awards are based on the merits of a project proposal; not give for tuition assistance for and advanced degree.

Amount of award:	$1,000-$2,500
Number of awards:	1
Application deadline:	February 15

Contact:
1735 New York Ave.,NW
Washington, DC 20006-5292
Website: www.e-architect.com/institute/scholar

American Institute of Architects The RTKL Traveling Fellowship

Type of award: Research grant.
Intended use: For full-time senior, master's study at accredited 4-year or graduate institution in United States. Designated institutions: Institute must be NAAB accredited.
Eligibility: Applicant must be U.S. citizen or permanent resident.
Basis for selection: Major/career interest in architecture.
Application requirements: Recommendations, transcript and nomination.

Amount of award:	$500-$2,500
Number of awards:	1
Application deadline:	February 15

Contact:
American Architectural Foundation
1735 New York Ave, NW
Washington, DC 20006-5292
Website: www.e-architect.com/institute/scholar

New Jersey Scholarship Foundation

Type of award: Scholarship, renewable.
Intended use: For full-time sophomore, junior, senior, master's or first professional study at accredited postsecondary institution. Designated institutions: Accredited architectural school.
Eligibility: Applicant must be residing in New Jersey.
Basis for selection: Major/career interest in architecture. Applicant must demonstrate seriousness of purpose, financial need and high academic achievement.
Application requirements: $5 application fee. Portfolio, recommendations, essay, transcript and proof of eligibility. FAFSA.

Amount of award:	$1,000-$1,500
Number of awards:	12
Number of applicants:	25
Application deadline:	April 30
Notification begins:	July 15
Total amount awarded:	$12,000

Contact:
Scholarship Committee
New Jersey Scholarship Foundation Inc.
212 White Avenue
Old Tappan, NJ 07675

American Institute of Certified Public Accountants

American Institute of Certified Public Accountants' Minority Doctoral Fellowship

Type of award: Internship.
Intended use: For full-time doctoral study in United States.
Eligibility: Applicant must be of minority background. Applicant must be U.S. citizen.
Basis for selection: Major/career interest in accounting. Applicant must demonstrate financial need and high academic achievement.
Application requirements: Recommendations, essay and transcript. GRE or GMAT scores.
Additional information: Refer to Product Number 870110 when requesting application.

Amount of award:	$12,000
Number of awards:	13
Number of applicants:	21
Application deadline:	April 1
Notification begins:	May 1
Total amount awarded:	$122,000

Contact:
American Institute of Certified Public Accountants
AICPA Member Satisfaction Team
PO Box 2209
Jersey City, NJ 07303-2209
Phone: 212-596-6223
Fax: 800-362-5066
Website: www.aicpa.org

Certified Public Accountants' John L. Carey Scholarship

Type of award: Scholarship, renewable.
Intended use: For full-time master's study at graduate institution in United States.
Eligibility: Applicant must be U.S. citizen or permanent resident.
Basis for selection: Major/career interest in accounting. Applicant must demonstrate leadership, seriousness of purpose and high academic achievement.
Application requirements: Recommendations, essay and transcript. GRE or GMAT scores.
Additional information: Applicants must be accepted in or be in the process of applying to a graduate program in accounting that will enable them to sit for the CPA exam. Applicants must be liberal arts seniors/undergraduates of regionally accredited U.S. institution. Academic achievement, leadership, and future career interests important. Institution's business administration program must be accredited by the American Assembly of Collegiate Schools of Business.

Amount of award:	$5,000
Number of awards:	5
Number of applicants:	64
Application deadline:	April 1
Notification begins:	May 1
Total amount awarded:	$40,000

Contact:
American Institue of CPA's
1211 Avenue of the Americas
New York, NY 10036-8775
Phone: 212-596-6221
Fax: 212-596-6292
Website: www.aicpa.org

Certified Public Accountants' Minorities Scholarship

Type of award: Scholarship, renewable.
Intended use: For full-time undergraduate, master's study at accredited 4-year or graduate institution in United States.
Eligibility: Applicant must be of minority background. Applicant must be U.S. citizen.
Basis for selection: Major/career interest in accounting. Applicant must demonstrate financial need and high academic achievement.
Application requirements: Essay and transcript.
Additional information: Minimum GPA of 3.0 required. Must have completed thirty semester hours of college work, including six in accounting.

Amount of award:	$1,500-$5,000
Number of awards:	211
Number of applicants:	600
Application deadline:	July 1
Notification begins:	August 30
Total amount awarded:	$458,500

Contact:
American Institute of Certified Public Accountants
1211 Avenue of the Americas
New York, NY 10036-8775
Phone: 212-596-6223
Fax: 800-362-5066
Website: www.aicpa.org

American Institute of Pakistan Studies

Pakistan Studies Fellowship

Type of award: Research grant.
Intended use: For doctoral, postgraduate study outside United States in Pakistan.
Eligibility: Applicant must be U.S. citizen.
Basis for selection: Applicant must demonstrate depth of character, seriousness of purpose and high academic achievement.
Application requirements: Portfolio, recommendations, transcript and research proposal.
Additional information: Applicants from affiliated universities may apply without paying an application fee.

Applicants from non-affiliated universities must pay a $500 application fee. Contact sponsor for a list of affiliated universities.
- **Amount of award:** $3,400-$18,000
- **Number of awards:** 8
- **Number of applicants:** 14
- **Application deadline:** February 1
- **Notification begins:** April 1

Contact:
American Institute of Pakistan Studies
P.O. Box 7568
Wake Forest University
Winston-Salem, NC 27109
Phone: 336-758-5449
Fax: 910-759-6104

American Institute of Polish Culture

Polish Culture Scholarship

Type of award: Scholarship.
Intended use: For full-time undergraduate study.
Eligibility: Applicant must be of Polish heritage.
Basis for selection: Major/career interest in journalism; communications. Applicant must demonstrate high academic achievement.
Application requirements: $25 application fee. Recommendations, essay and transcript.
Additional information: SASE required.
- **Amount of award:** $1,000
- **Number of awards:** 10
- **Number of applicants:** 150
- **Application deadline:** February 15
- **Total amount awarded:** $10,000

Contact:
American Institute of Polish Culture
1440 79 Street Causeway, Suite 117
Miami, FL 33141

American Institute of the History of Pharmacy

History of Pharmacy Grant-In-Aid

Type of award: Research grant.
Intended use: For master's, doctoral study in United States.
Basis for selection: Major/career interest in history; pharmacy/pharmaceutics/pharmacology.
Application requirements: Proof of eligibility and research proposal. Must submit proposed expenses.

- **Amount of award:** $100-$5,000
- **Number of awards:** 4
- **Number of applicants:** 7
- **Application deadline:** February 1
- **Notification begins:** May 1
- **Total amount awarded:** $5,000

Contact:
American Institute of the History of Pharmacy
Pharmacy Building, 425 North Charter Street
Madison, WI 53706-1508
Website: www.wiscinfo.wisc.edu/pharmacy/aihp

American Jewish Archives

Ethel Marcus Memorial Fellowship in American Jewish Studies

Type of award: Research grant, renewable.
Intended use: For doctoral study.
Basis for selection: Major/career interest in Jewish studies. Applicant must demonstrate high academic achievement.
Application requirements: Recommendations and research proposal.
Additional information: Must be a doctoral student at the "all-but-dissertation" level. Must provide curriculum vitae. For one month of research or writing at the American Jewish Archives.
- **Amount of award:** $1,000
- **Application deadline:** April 1

Contact:
American Jewish Archives
3101 Clifton Avenue
Cincinnati, OH 45220
Website: home.fuse.net.aja.fellow.htm

Lowenstein-Wiener Fellowship in American Jewish Studies

Type of award: Research grant, renewable.
Intended use: For doctoral, postgraduate study.
Basis for selection: Major/career interest in Jewish studies. Applicant must demonstrate high academic achievement.
Application requirements: Research proposal.
Additional information: Available to post-doctoral or "all-but-dissertation" candidates for one month of research or writing at the American Jewish Archives. Stipend is $1,000 for "all-but-dissertation" recipients and $2,000 for post-doctoral recipients. Must provide a curriculum vitae and evidence of published research, where possible.
- **Amount of award:** $1,000-$2,000
- **Application deadline:** April 1

Contact:
American Jewish Archives
3101 Clifton Avenue
Cincinnati, OH 45220
Website: home.fuse.net.aja.fellow.htm

Marguerite R. Jacobs Memorial Award in American Jewish Studies

Type of award: Research grant, renewable.
Intended use: For freshman study.
Basis for selection: Major/career interest in Jewish studies. Applicant must demonstrate high academic achievement.
Application requirements: Recommendations and research proposal.
Additional information: Award is for one month a active research or writing at the American Jewish Archives. Must provide a curriculum vitage and evidence of published research, where possible.
   Amount of award: $2,000
   Application deadline: April 1
Contact:
American Jewish Archives
3101 Clifton Avenue
Cincinnati, OH 45220
Website: home.fuse.net.aja.fellow.htm

Rabbi Frederic A. Doppelt Memorial Fellowship in American Jewish Studies

Type of award: Research grant, renewable.
Intended use: For postgraduate study.
Basis for selection: Major/career interest in Jewish studies. Applicant must demonstrate high academic achievement.
Application requirements: Recommendations and research proposal.
Additional information: Preference given to candidates from Eastern Europe or those working on a topic related to Eastern European Jewry in the American context. Must provide a curriculum vitae. For one month of research or writing at the American Jewish Archives.
   Amount of award: $1,000
   Application deadline: April 1
Contact:
American Jewish Archives
3101 Clifton Avenue
Cincinnati, OH 45220
Website: home.fuse.net.aja.fellow.htm

Rabbi Levi A. Olan Memorial Fellowship in American Jewish Studies

Type of award: Research grant, renewable.
Intended use: For doctoral study.
Basis for selection: Major/career interest in Jewish studies. Applicant must demonstrate high academic achievement.
Application requirements: Recommendations and research proposal.
Additional information: Must be a doctoral student at the "all-but-dissertation" level. Must provide curriculum vitae. For one month of research or writing at the American Jewish Archives.
   Amount of award: $1,000
   Application deadline: April 1
Contact:
American Jewish Archives
3101 Clifton Avenue
Cincinnati, OH 45220
Website: home.fuse.net.aja.fellow.htm

Rabbi Marc H. Tannenbaum Foundation Fellowships

Type of award: Research grant, renewable.
Intended use: For doctoral, postgraduate study.
Basis for selection: Major/career interest in religion/theology. Applicant must demonstrate high academic achievement.
Application requirements: Recommendations and research proposal.
Additional information: Available to "all-but-dissertation" doctoral candidates and to applicants on the post-doctoral level. All research proposals must be in the field of interreligious affairs. Must provide a curriculum vitae and evidence of published research, where possible. The stipend is $1,000 for "all-but-dissertation" recipients and $2,000 for post-doctoral recipients, for one month of research or writing at the American Jewish Archives.
   Amount of award: $1,000-$2,000
   Application deadline: April 1
Contact:
American Jewish Archives
3101 Clifton Avenue
Cincinnati, OH 45220
Website: home.fuse.net.aja.fellow.htm

Rapoport Fellowships in American Jewish Studies

Type of award: Research grant, renewable.
Intended use: For postgraduate study.
Basis for selection: Major/career interest in Jewish studies. Applicant must demonstrate high academic achievement.
Application requirements: Recommendations and research proposal.
Additional information: Must provide a curriculum vitae and evidence of published research. For one month of research or writing at the American Jewish Archives.
   Amount of award: $2,000
   Application deadline: April 1
Contact:
American Jewish Archives
3101 CliftonAve.
Cincinnati, OH 45220
Website: home.fuse.net.aja.fellow.htm

Starkoff Fellowship in American Jewish Studies

Type of award: Research grant, renewable.
Intended use: For doctoral study.
Basis for selection: Major/career interest in Jewish studies. Applicant must demonstrate high academic achievement.
Application requirements: Recommendations and research proposal.
Additional information: Must be a doctoral student at the "all-but-dissertation" level. Must provide a curriculum vitae. For one month of research or writing at the American Jewish Archives.
   Amount of award: $1,000
   Application deadline: April 1
Contact:
American Jewish Archives
3101 Clifton Avenue
Cincinnati, OH 45220
Website: home.fuse.net.aja.fellow.htm

American Legion Alabama

American Legion Alabama Oratorical Contest

Type of award: Scholarship.
Intended use: For undergraduate study.
Eligibility: Applicant must be U.S. citizen residing in Alabama. Applicant must be descendant of veteran.
Basis for selection: Competition in Oratory/debate. Breadth of knowledge, originality, application of knowledge of topic, skill in selecting examples and analogies, logic, voice, diction, style of language, and delivery.
Application requirements: Proof of eligibility. Send 4" x 9 1/2" SASE with request. For children or grandchildren of veterans.
Additional information: Topic: U.S. Constitution and Citizenship.
Amount of award:	$1,000-$5,000
Number of awards:	3
Application deadline:	May 1
Total amount awarded:	$9,000

American Legion Alabama Scholarship

Type of award: Scholarship, renewable.
Intended use: For undergraduate study at postsecondary institution in Alabama.
Eligibility: Applicant must be U.S. citizen or permanent resident residing in Alabama. Applicant must be descendant of veteran, child of veteran during Korean War, Persian Gulf, WW I, WW II or Vietnam.
Additional information: Send 4" x 9 1/2" SASE. Four-year scholarships.
Amount of award:	$850
Number of awards:	130
Application deadline:	May 1

Contact:
American Legion Alabama
Department Adjutant
P.O. Box 1069
Montgomery, AL 36101-1069
Phone: 334-262-6638
Fax: 334-262-6638

American Legion Alabama Auxiliary

American Legion Alabama Auxiliary Scholarship

Type of award: Scholarship, renewable.
Intended use: For undergraduate or graduate study at postsecondary institution in Alabama. Designated institutions: State-supported institutions.
Eligibility: Applicant must be U.S. citizen or permanent resident residing in Alabama. Applicant must be descendant of veteran, child of veteran during Grenada, Korean War, Lebanon, Panama, Persian Gulf, WW I, WW II or Vietnam.
Application requirements: Proof of eligibility.
Additional information: Annual scholarships. Send SASE with request for application.
Amount of award:	$850
Number of awards:	40
Application deadline:	April 1
Total amount awarded:	$34,000

Contact:
American Legion Auxiliary, Department of Alabama
Department Headquarters
120 North Jackson Street
Montgomery, AL 36104
Phone: 334-262-1176

American Legion Alaska

American Legion Alaska Oratorical Contest

Type of award: Scholarship.
Intended use: For undergraduate study.
Eligibility: Applicant must be enrolled in high school. Applicant must be U.S. citizen or permanent resident residing in Alaska.
Basis for selection: Competition in Oratory/debate. Comprehensiveness of knowledge, originality, application of knowledge on topic, skill in selecting examples and analogies, logic, voice, diction, style of language and delivery.
Application requirements: Proof of eligibility.
Additional information: Topic: U.S. Constitution and citizenship.
Amount of award:	$500-$1,000
Number of awards:	2
Total amount awarded:	$1,500

Contact:
American Legion, Department of Alaska
Department Adjutant
519 West 8 Avenue, Suite 208
Anchorage, AK 99501
Phone: 907-278-8598
Fax: 907-278-0041

American Legion Alaska Auxiliary

American Legion Alaska Auxiliary Scholarship

Type of award: Scholarship.
Intended use: For undergraduate study.
Eligibility: Applicant must be high school senior. Applicant must be U.S. citizen or permanent resident residing in Alaska. Applicant must be descendant of veteran, child of veteran during Grenada, Korean War, Lebanon, Panama, Persian Gulf, WW I, WW II or Vietnam.

Basis for selection: Applicant must demonstrate high academic achievement.
Application requirements: Proof of eligibility. High school senior or graduate not having attended institution of higher learning.
Additional information: Scholarship funds apply toward tuition, matriculation, laboratory, or similar fees.
   Amount of award: $250-$1,000
   Application deadline: March 15
Contact:
American Legion Auxiliary, Department of Alaska
P.O. Box 220887
Anchorage, AK 99522-0887
Phone: 907-283-3222

American Legion Arizona Auxiliary

American Legion Arizona Auxiliary Health Occupation Scholarship

Type of award: Scholarship.
Intended use: For undergraduate study at accredited vocational, 2-year or 4-year institution in Arizona. Designated institutions: Arizona institution offering certificate or degree in health occupations.
Eligibility: Applicant must be U.S. citizen residing in Arizona.
Basis for selection: Major/career interest in health-related professions; health sciences.
Additional information: Must be resident of Arizona at least one year. Preference given to immediate family members of veterans.
   Amount of award: $300

American Legion Arizona Auxiliary Nurses' Scholarship

Type of award: Scholarship.
Intended use: For sophomore study at accredited 2-year institution in Arizona.
Eligibility: Applicant must be U.S. citizen residing in Arizona.
Basis for selection: Major/career interest in nursing.
Additional information: For student nurses enrolled at institutions awarding Registered Nurse degrees. Must be Arizona resident for at least one year. Preference given to immediate family members of veterans.
   Amount of award: $400
Contact:
American Legion Auxiliary, Department of Arizona
4701 North 19 Avenue, Suite 100
Phoenix, AZ 85015-3727

American Legion Arkansas

American Legion Arkansas Oratorical Contest

Type of award: Scholarship.
Intended use: For undergraduate study.
Eligibility: Applicant must be residing in Arkansas.
Basis for selection: Competition in Oratory/debate. Breadth of knowledge, originality, application of knowledge of topic, skill in selecting examples and analogies, logic, voice, diction, style of language and delivery.
Application requirements: Proof of eligibility. Must be a child, grandchild, or great-grandchild of an American Legion member.
Additional information: Topic: U.S. Constitution and citizenship.
   Amount of award: $100-$500
   Number of awards: 4
   Total amount awarded: $1,000
Contact:
American Legion Arkansas
Department Adjutant
Box 1751
Little Rock, AR 72203
Phone: 501-374-5836
Fax: 501-375-4236

American Legion Arkansas Auxiliary

American Legion Arkansas Auxiliary Academic Scholarship

Type of award: Scholarship.
Intended use: For undergraduate study in Arkansas.
Eligibility: Applicant must be residing in Arkansas. Applicant must be descendant of veteran, child of veteran during Grenada, Korean War, Lebanon, Panama, Persian Gulf, WW I, WW II or Vietnam.
Application requirements: Must be high school senior or graduate of accredited high school who has not yet attended an institution of higher learning.
   Amount of award: $1,000
   Number of awards: 1
   Total amount awarded: $1,000

American Legion Arkansas Auxiliary Nurse Scholarship

Type of award: Scholarship.
Intended use: For undergraduate study in Arkansas.
Eligibility: Applicant must be U.S. citizen or permanent resident residing in Arkansas. Applicant must be descendant of veteran, child of veteran during Grenada, Korean War, Lebanon, Panama, Persian Gulf, WW I, WW II or Vietnam.
Basis for selection: Major/career interest in nursing.

Amount of award: $500
Number of awards: 1
Total amount awarded: $500
Contact:
American Legion Arkansas Auxiliary
1415 West 7 Street
Little Rock, AR 72201
Phone: 501-374-5836

American Legion California

American Legion California Oratorical Contest

Type of award: Scholarship.
Intended use: For undergraduate study.
Eligibility: Applicant must be enrolled in high school. Applicant must be residing in California.
Basis for selection: Competition in Oratory/debate. Breadth of knowledge, originality, application of knowledge of topic, skill in selecting examples and analogies, logic, voice, diction, style of language and delivery. Applicant must demonstrate patriotism.
Application requirements: Proof of eligibility. See high school counselor.
Additional information: Topic: U.S. Constitution and Citizenship. Students selected by schools and participation in district contests, followed by area and departmental finals. Contact high school counselor.
Amount of award: $500-$1,200
Number of awards: 6
Total amount awarded: $4,600
Contact:
American Legion California
117 Veteran's War Memorial Building
San Francisco, CA 94102
Phone: 415-431-2400
Fax: 415-255-1571

American Legion California Auxiliary

American Legion California Auxiliary Department of Education Scholarship I

Type of award: Scholarship.
Intended use: For undergraduate certificate, freshman study at 4-year institution in California.
Eligibility: Applicant must be residing in California. Applicant must be descendant of veteran, child of veteran during Grenada, Korean War, Lebanon, Panama, Persian Gulf, WW I, WW II or Vietnam.
Basis for selection: Major/career interest in nursing; medicine (m.d.); engineering; law. Applicant must demonstrate financial need.
Application requirements: Proof of eligibility. For high school senior, or recent graduate prevented from enrolling due to illness or financial difficulty. Must have been a California resident for five years. If less, veteran parent must have been hospitalized in California or have been reported missing by the government. Submit E-21 application to local unit.
Additional information: Additional fields of study include: therapy, law enforcement, and business. Award paid in four installments.
Amount of award: $2,000
Number of awards: 1
Application deadline: March 15
Total amount awarded: $2,000

American Legion California Auxiliary Department of Education Scholarship II

Type of award: Scholarship.
Intended use: For undergraduate study.
Eligibility: Applicant must be high school senior. Applicant must be residing in California. Applicant must be descendant of veteran, child of veteran during Grenada, Korean War, Lebanon, Panama, Persian Gulf, WW I, WW II or Vietnam.
Basis for selection: Major/career interest in education; engineering; law; business.
Application requirements: Proof of eligibility. Must have been a California resident for 5 years. If less, veteran parent must have been hospitalized in California or have been reported missing by the government. Submit E-21 application to local unit.
Additional information: Additional field of study: law enforcement. Award paid in four annual installments of $250.
Amount of award: $1,000
Number of awards: 5
Total amount awarded: $5,000

American Legion California Auxiliary High School Scholarship

Type of award: Scholarship.
Intended use: For freshman study in California.
Eligibility: Applicant must be high school senior. Applicant must be residing in California. Applicant must be descendant of veteran, child of veteran during Grenada, Korean War, Lebanon, Panama, Persian Gulf, WW I, WW II or Vietnam.
Basis for selection: Applicant must demonstrate financial need.
Application requirements: Proof of eligibility. For high school senior or recent graduate prevented from enrolling due to illness or financial difficulty. Must have been a California resident for 5 years. If less, veteran parent must have been hospitalized in California or have been reported missing by the government. Submit E-21 application to local unit.
Amount of award: $500
Number of awards: 5
Total amount awarded: $2,500

American Legion California Auxiliary National President's Scholarship

Type of award: Scholarship.
Intended use: For undergraduate study.

Eligibility: Applicant must be residing in California. Applicant must be child of veteran.
Application requirements: Proof of eligibility. Submit special application.
Additional information: State winner competes in Western Division competition. Only one candidate from a unit; no elimination in the district. If California candidate does not win, $500 scholarship will be awarded by department of California.
- Amount of award: $1,500-$2,000
- Number of awards: 2
- Application deadline: March 11

Contact:
American Legion California Auxiliary
Headquarters
401 Van Ness, No. 113
San Francisco, CA 94102-4586
Phone: 415-861-5092

American Legion Colorado Auxiliary

American Legion Colorado Auxiliary/Past President's Parley Nurse's Scholarship

Type of award: Scholarship.
Intended use: For undergraduate study in Colorado.
Designated institutions: Any school of nursing.
Eligibility: Applicant must be residing in Colorado. Applicant must be veteran, child of veteran, spouse of veteran during Grenada, Korean War, Lebanon, Panama, Persian Gulf, WW I, WW II or Vietnam.
Basis for selection: Major/career interest in nursing.
- Number of awards: 1
- Application deadline: April 1
- Total amount awarded: $300

Contact:
American Legion Colorado Auxiliary
Department Headquarters
3003 Tejon Street
Denver, CO 80211
Phone: 303-477-5752
Fax: 303-477-2950

American Legion Delaware Auxiliary

American Legion Delaware Auxiliary Past President's Parley Nursing Scholarship

Type of award: Scholarship.
Intended use: For undergraduate study.
Eligibility: Applicant must be residing in Delaware. Applicant must be child of veteran.
Basis for selection: Major/career interest in nursing.

- Amount of award: $300
- Number of awards: 1
- Application deadline: February 28
- Total amount awarded: $300

Contact:
American Legion Auxiliary
Executive Secretary
43 Blades Drive
Dover, DE 19901

American Legion District of Columbia

American Legion District of Columbia Oratorical Contest

Type of award: Scholarship.
Intended use: For undergraduate study.
Eligibility: Applicant must be enrolled in high school. Applicant must be U.S. citizen residing in District of Columbia.
Basis for selection: Competition in Oratory/debate. Breadth of knowledge, originality, application of knowledge of topic, skill in selecting examples and analogies, logic, voice, diction, style of language and delivery.
Application requirements: Proof of eligibility.
Additional information: All awards in U.S. Savings Bonds. Topic: U.S. Constitution and citizenship.
- Amount of award: $50-$200
- Number of awards: 4
- Total amount awarded: $425

Contact:
American Legion, Department of District of Columbia
3408 Wisconsin Avenue NW, Suite 212
Washington, DC 20016
Phone: 202-362-9151

American Legion Florida

American Legion Florida Oratorical Contest

Type of award: Scholarship.
Intended use: For undergraduate study.
Eligibility: Applicant must be enrolled in high school. Applicant must be residing in Florida.
Basis for selection: Competition in Oratory/debate. Breadth of knowledge, originality, application of knowledge of topic, skill in selecting examples and analogies, logic, voice, diction, style of language and delivery.
Application requirements: Proof of eligibility.
Additional information: Topic: U.S. Constitution and citizenship. Oration will be on some aspect of the Constitution.

Amount of award: $1,000-$2,500
Number of awards: 6
Application deadline: October 1
Total amount awarded: $8,000
Contact:
American Legion Florida
Department Headquarters
P.O. Box 547936
Orlando, FL 32854-7936
Phone: 407-295-2631
Fax: 407-299-0901
Website: www.floridalegion.org

American Legion Florida Auxiliary

American Legion Florida Auxiliary Scholarship

Type of award: Scholarship.
Intended use: For undergraduate study at vocational, 2-year or 4-year institution in Florida.
Eligibility: Applicant must be residing in Florida. Applicant must be child of veteran.
Application requirements: Proof of eligibility. Must be sponsored by local auxiliary unit.
Additional information: $500 award for junior colleges and technical vocational school; $1,000 for four-year university.
Amount of award: $500-$1,000
Application deadline: January 1
Contact:
American Legion Auxiliary, Department of Florida
Department Secretary
P.O. Box 547917
Orlando, FL 32854-7917

American Legion Georgia Auxiliary

American Legion Georgia Auxiliary Past President's Parley Nursing Scholarship

Type of award: Scholarship.
Intended use: For undergraduate study at 2-year or 4-year institution.
Eligibility: Applicant must be female, high school senior. Applicant must be residing in Georgia. Applicant must be child of veteran.
Basis for selection: Major/career interest in nursing. Applicant must demonstrate high academic achievement.
Application requirements: Proof of eligibility. Student nurse.
Additional information: Amount of award and number of scholarships determined by available funds. Must be sponsored by local Auxiliary Unit. Daughter of deceased veteran preferred candidate.
Contact:
American Legion Georgia Auxiliary
Dept. Headquarters
3284 East Main Street
College Park, GA 30337

American Legion Georgia Auxiliary Scholarship

Type of award: Scholarship.
Intended use: For undergraduate study at postsecondary institution in Georgia.
Eligibility: Applicant must be high school senior. Applicant must be residing in Georgia. Applicant must be child of veteran.
Basis for selection: Applicant must demonstrate high academic achievement.
Application requirements: Essay, transcript and proof of eligibility. Must be sponsored by local auxiliary unit. Only one applicant per unit.
Additional information: Preference given to children of deceased veterans. Must be sponsored by local Auxiliary Unit. Information and application materials available through local American Legion Auxiliary units. Send stamped, self-addressed envelope with application request.
Amount of award: $1,000
Number of awards: 2
Total amount awarded: $2,000
Contact:
The American Legion Georgia Auxiliary
Dept. Headquarters
3284 East Main Street
College Park, GA 30337

American Legion Idaho Auxiliary

American Legion Idaho Auxiliary Nursing Scholarship

Type of award: Scholarship.
Intended use: For undergraduate study at 2-year or 4-year institution.
Eligibility: Applicant must be residing in Idaho. Applicant must be veteran, child of veteran.
Basis for selection: Major/career interest in nursing.
Application requirements: Idaho resident for at least 5 years.
Amount of award: $750
Application deadline: March 15
Total amount awarded: $750
Contact:
American Legion Auxiliary, Department of Idaho
Department Headquarters
905 Warren Street
Boise, ID 83706
Phone: 208-342-7066

American Legion Illinois

American Legion Illinois Oratorical Contest

Type of award: Scholarship.
Intended use: For undergraduate study.
Eligibility: Applicant must be enrolled in high school. Applicant must be U.S. citizen or permanent resident residing in Illinois.
Basis for selection: Competition in Oratory/debate. Breadth of knowledge, originality, application of knowledge of topic, skill in selecting examples and analogies, logic, voice, diction, style of language and delivery.
Application requirements: Proof of eligibility.
Additional information: Topic: U.S. Constitution and citizenship. Contest begins in January.

Amount of award:	$50-$1,600
Number of awards:	12
Total amount awarded:	$7,175

Contact:
American Legion Illinois
Department Headquarters
P.O. Box 2910
Bloomington, IL 61702
Phone: 309-663-0361
Fax: 309-663-5783

American Legion Illinois Auxiliary

American Legion Illinois Auxiliary Ada Mucklestone Memorial Scholarship

Type of award: Scholarship.
Intended use: For undergraduate study.
Eligibility: Applicant must be high school senior. Applicant must be residing in Illinois. Applicant must be child of veteran during Grenada, Korean War, Lebanon, Panama, Persian Gulf, WW I, WW II or Vietnam.
Application requirements: Unit sponsorship is required. Graduates of accredited high schools also eligible.
Additional information: Prizes: First $1,200; second $1,000; several $800.

Amount of award:	$800-$1,200
Application deadline:	March 15

American Legion Illinois Auxiliary Marie Sheehe Trade School Scholarship

Type of award: Scholarship.
Intended use: For undergraduate study. Designated institutions: Trade schools.
Eligibility: Applicant must be residing in Illinois. Applicant must be descendant of veteran, child of veteran.

Amount of award:	$800
Number of awards:	1
Application deadline:	March 15
Total amount awarded:	$800

American Legion Illinois Auxiliary Mildred R. Knoles Opportunity Scholarship

Type of award: Scholarship.
Intended use: For undergraduate study.
Eligibility: Applicant must be residing in Illinois. Applicant must be veteran, descendant of veteran, child of veteran during Grenada, Korean War, Lebanon, Persian Gulf, WW I, WW II or Vietnam.
Basis for selection: Applicant must demonstrate financial need.
Application requirements: Proof of eligibility. Unit sponsorship required.
Additional information: Awards: First-$1,200; several $800.

Amount of award:	$800-$1,200
Application deadline:	March 15

American Legion Illinois Auxiliary Special Education Teaching Scholarship

Type of award: Scholarship.
Intended use: For sophomore, junior study.
Eligibility: Applicant must be U.S. citizen or permanent resident residing in Illinois.
Basis for selection: Major/career interest in education, special.
Application requirements: Proof of eligibility. For students matriculating in the field of teaching retarded or handicapped children. Unit sponsorship is required.

Amount of award:	$1,000
Application deadline:	March 15
Total amount awarded:	$1,000

American Legion Illinois Auxiliary Student Nurse Scholarship

Type of award: Scholarship.
Intended use: For undergraduate study at 2-year or 4-year institution.
Eligibility: Applicant must be U.S. citizen or permanent resident residing in Illinois.
Basis for selection: Major/career interest in nursing.
Application requirements: Proof of eligibility. Unit sponsorship required.

Amount of award:	$1,000
Number of awards:	1
Total amount awarded:	$1,000

Contact:
American Legion Illinois Auxiliary
P.O. Box 1426
Bloomington, IL 61702-1426
Phone: 309-663-9366

American Legion Indiana

American Legion Indiana Oratorical Contest

Type of award: Scholarship.
Intended use: For undergraduate study.
Eligibility: Applicant must be enrolled in high school. Applicant must be residing in Indiana.
Basis for selection: Competition in Oratory/debate. Breadth of knowledge, originality, application of knowledge of topic, skill in selecting examples and analogies, logic, voice, diction, style of language, and delivery. Applicant must demonstrate patriotism.
Application requirements: Proof of eligibility.
Additional information: Topic: U.S. Constitution and citizenship.
    Amount of award: $250-$1,000
    Number of awards: 8
    Application deadline: December 1
    Total amount awarded: $3,200
Contact:
American Legion Indiana
Americanism Office, Department Headquarters
777 North Meridian Street
Indianapolis, IN 46204
Phone: 317-630-1263
Fax: 317-237-9891

American Legion Indiana Auxiliary

American Legion Indiana Auxiliary Edna M. Barcus Memorial Scholarship

Type of award: Scholarship.
Intended use: For undergraduate study at postsecondary institution in Indiana.
Eligibility: Applicant must be residing in Indiana. Applicant must be child of veteran during Civil War, Grenada, Korean War, Lebanon, Panama, Persian Gulf, Spanish/American War, WW I, WW II or Vietnam.
Basis for selection: Applicant must demonstrate high academic achievement.
Application requirements: Send SASE to departmental secretary.
    Amount of award: $500
    Application deadline: April 1
Contact:
American Legion Auxiliary, Department of Indiana
Department Secretary
777 North Meridian Street, Room 107
Indianapolis, IN 46204
Phone: 317-630-1390

American Legion Iowa

American Legion Iowa Oratorical Contest

Type of award: Scholarship.
Intended use: For undergraduate study.
Eligibility: Applicant must be enrolled in high school. Applicant must be U.S. citizen or permanent resident residing in Iowa.
Basis for selection: Competition in Oratory/debate. Breadth of knowledge, originality, application of knowledge of topic, skill in selecting examples and analogies, logic, voice, diction, style of language, and delivery.
Application requirements: Proof of eligibility.
Additional information: Topic: U.S. Constitution and citizenship.
    Amount of award: $400-$2,000
    Number of awards: 3
    Total amount awarded: $3,000

American Legion Iowa Outstanding Senior Baseball Player

Type of award: Scholarship.
Intended use: For undergraduate study.
Eligibility: Applicant must be high school senior. Applicant must be residing in Iowa.
Basis for selection: Applicant must demonstrate high academic achievement.
Application requirements: Recommendations. Participant in the Iowa American Legion Senior Baseball Program. Outstanding sportsmanship, team play, athletic ability, and proven academic achievments.
Additional information: Awarded on recommendation of State Baseball Committee.
    Amount of award: $1,000
    Number of awards: 1
    Total amount awarded: $1,000
Contact:
American Legion Iowa
720 Lyon Street
Des Moines, IA 50309
Phone: 515-282-5068
Fax: 515-282-7583

American Legion Iowa Auxiliary

American Legion Iowa Auxiliary Harriet Hoffman Memorial Scholarship

Type of award: Scholarship.
Intended use: For undergraduate study at postsecondary institution in Iowa.
Eligibility: Applicant must be residing in Iowa. Applicant must be descendant of veteran, child of veteran.

Basis for selection: Major/career interest in education; education, teacher.
Additional information: Teacher training scholarship. Preference given to deceased or disabled veteran's descendant.
    Amount of award: $400
    Number of awards: 1
    Application deadline: June 1
    Total amount awarded: $400

American Legion Iowa Auxiliary Mary Virginia Macrea Memorial Nurses Scholarship

Type of award: Scholarship, renewable.
Intended use: For undergraduate study at 2-year or 4-year institution in Iowa.
Eligibility: Applicant must be female. Applicant must be residing in Iowa. Applicant must be descendant of veteran, child of veteran, spouse of veteran or deceased veteran during Grenada, Korean War, Lebanon, Panama, Persian Gulf, WW I, WW II or Vietnam.
Basis for selection: Major/career interest in nursing.
Additional information: Also open to a veteran's mother or sister.
    Amount of award: $400
    Number of awards: 1
    Application deadline: June 1
    Total amount awarded: $400
Contact:
American Legion Auxiliary, Department of Iowa
720 Lyon Street
Des Moines, IA 50309
Phone: 515-282-5068
Fax: 515-282-7583

American Legion Kansas

American Legion Kansas Dr. Click Cowger Scholarship

Type of award: Scholarship.
Intended use: For freshman, sophomore or junior study at vocational, 2-year or 4-year institution in Kansas.
Eligibility: Applicant must be residing in Kansas.
Application requirements: Proof of eligibility. Must play or have played Kansas American Legion Baseball.
    Amount of award: $500
    Number of awards: 1
    Application deadline: July 15
    Total amount awarded: $500

American Legion Kansas John and Geraldine Hobble Licensed Practical Nursing Scholarship

Type of award: Scholarship.
Intended use: For undergraduate study at accredited 2-year or 4-year institution in Kansas.
Eligibility: Applicant must be residing in Kansas.
Basis for selection: Major/career interest in nursing.
Application requirements: Proof of eligibility. Kansas State Board Examination. Must attend accredited Kansas school that awards diploma for licensed practical nurse.
    Amount of award: $250
    Number of awards: 1
    Application deadline: February 15
    Total amount awarded: $250

American Legion Kansas Music Scholarship

Type of award: Scholarship.
Intended use: For freshman, sophomore or junior study at 2-year or 4-year institution in Kansas.
Eligibility: Applicant must be residing in Kansas.
Application requirements: Proof of eligibility.
    Amount of award: $1,000
    Number of awards: 1
    Application deadline: February 15
    Total amount awarded: $1,000
Contact:
American Legion Kansas
1314 Southwest Topeka Boulevard
Topeka, KS 66612-1886
Phone: 913-232-9315
Fax: 913-232-1399

American Legion Kansas Oratorical Contest

Type of award: Scholarship.
Intended use: For undergraduate study.
Eligibility: Applicant must be enrolled in high school. Applicant must be residing in Kansas.
Basis for selection: Competition in Oratory/debate. Breadth of knowledge, originality, application of knowledge of topic, skill in selecting examples and analogies, logic, voice, diction, style of language, and delivery.
Additional information: Topic: U.S. Constitution and citizenship.
    Amount of award: $150-$1,000
    Number of awards: 4
    Total amount awarded: $1,900
Contact:
American Legion Kansas
1314 Southwest Topeka Boulevard
Topeka, KS 66612-1886
Phone: 913-232-9315
Fax: 913-232-1399

American Legion Kansas Auxiliary

American Legion of Kansas General Scholarship

Type of award: Scholarship.
Intended use: For freshman study at vocational, 2-year or 4-year institution in Kansas. Designated institutions: Kansas institution.
Eligibility: Applicant must be high school senior. Applicant

must be residing in Kansas. Applicant must be child of veteran, spouse of veteran or deceased veteran during Grenada, Korean War, Lebanon, Panama, Persian Gulf, WW I, WW II or Vietnam.
Additional information: $500 total, $250 per year for two years.

Amount of award:	$500
Number of awards:	8
Application deadline:	April 1
Total amount awarded:	$4,000

Contact:
American Legion Kansas Auxiliary
1314 SW Topeka Boulevard
Topeka, KS 66612-1886
Phone: 913-232-1396

American Legion Kentucky Auxiliary

American Legion Kentucky Auxiliary Laura Blackburn Memorial Scholarship

Type of award: Scholarship.
Intended use: For undergraduate study.
Eligibility: Applicant must be high school senior. Applicant must be residing in Kentucky. Applicant must be descendant of veteran, child of veteran during Grenada, Korean War, Lebanon, Panama, Persian Gulf, WW I, WW II or Vietnam.
Application requirements: Proof of eligibility.

Amount of award:	$1,000
Number of awards:	1
Number of applicants:	1
Application deadline:	March 31
Total amount awarded:	$1,000

Contact:
American Legion Kentucky Auxiliary
PO Box 189
Greensburg, KY 42743

American Legion Kentucky Auxiliary Mary Barrett Marshall Scholarship

Type of award: Scholarship.
Intended use: For undergraduate study at vocational, 2-year or 4-year institution in Kentucky.
Eligibility: Applicant must be female. Applicant must be residing in Kentucky. Applicant must be descendant of veteran, child of veteran, spouse of veteran during Civil War, Grenada, Korean War, Lebanon, Panama, Persian Gulf, WW I, WW II or Vietnam.
Application requirements: Proof of eligibility. Female spouse or descendant of veteran eligible for membership in American Legion.
Additional information: Include SASE with request for application.

Amount of award:	$500
Number of awards:	1
Application deadline:	April 1
Total amount awarded:	$500

Contact:
American Legion Auxiliary, Department of Kentucky
Chair: Velma Greenleaf
1448 Leafdale Road
Hodgenville, KY 42748
Phone: 606-987-6864

American Legion Kentucky Auxiliary Mary Barrett Marshall Student Loan Fund

Type of award: Loan, renewable.
Intended use: For undergraduate study at vocational, 2-year or 4-year institution in Kentucky.
Eligibility: Applicant must be female. Applicant must be residing in Kentucky. Applicant must be descendant of veteran, child of veteran, spouse of veteran or deceased veteran.
Basis for selection: Applicant must demonstrate financial need.
Additional information: Maximum $800 per year, payable monthly, without interest after graduation or upon securing employment; 6% interest after five years.

Amount of award:	$800
Total amount awarded:	$800

Contact:
American Legion Auxiliary, Department of Kentucky
1448 Leafdale Road
Hodgenville, KY 42748
Phone: 606-987-6864

American Legion Maine

American Legion Maine Children and Youth Scholarship

Type of award: Scholarship.
Intended use: For undergraduate study.
Eligibility: Applicant must be high school senior. Applicant must be residing in Maine.
Basis for selection: Applicant must demonstrate depth of character, financial need and high academic achievement.
Additional information: High school seniors, college students, and veterans all eligible.

Amount of award:	$300
Number of awards:	7
Number of applicants:	300
Application deadline:	May 1
Total amount awarded:	$2,100

American Legion Maine Daniel E. Lambert Memorial Scholarship

Type of award: Scholarship.
Intended use: For undergraduate study at vocational, 2-year or 4-year institution.

Eligibility: Applicant must be high school senior. Applicant must be residing in Maine.
Basis for selection: Applicant must demonstrate depth of character and financial need.
   Application deadline: May 1
Contact:
American Legion Maine
Department Adjutant, State Headquarters
P.O. Box 900
Waterville, ME 04903
Phone: 207-873-3229

American Legion Maine Auxiliary

American Legion Maine Auxiliary General Scholarship

Type of award: Scholarship.
Intended use: For undergraduate study at vocational, 2-year or 4-year institution.
Eligibility: Applicant must be residing in Maine. Applicant must be child of veteran.
Basis for selection: Applicant must demonstrate financial need.
Additional information: Must be high school senior or graduate. Only residents of Maine qualify. Send SASE with application request.
   Amount of award: $300
   Number of awards: 2
   Application deadline: April 15
   Total amount awarded: $600

American Legion Maine Auxiliary President's Parley Nursing Scholarship

Type of award: Scholarship.
Intended use: For undergraduate study in Maine.
Eligibility: Applicant must be residing in Maine. Applicant must be descendant of veteran, child of veteran during WW I or WW II.
Basis for selection: Major/career interest in nursing.
Application requirements: Proof of eligibility.
Additional information: For training in an accredited nursing school.
   Amount of award: $300
   Number of awards: 1
   Application deadline: April 15
Contact:
American Legion Auxiliary, Department of Maine
Department Secretary
P.O. Box 887
Bucksport, ME 04416

American Legion Maryland

American Legion Maryland General Scholarship

Type of award: Scholarship.
Intended use: For undergraduate study.
Eligibility: Applicant must be residing in Maryland. Applicant must be child of veteran.
Application requirements: Transcript.
   Amount of award: $500
   Number of awards: 11
   Application deadline: March 31
   Total amount awarded: $5,500
Contact:
American Legion Maryland
Department Adjutant
War Memorial Building
Baltimore, MD 21202-1405
Phone: 301-752-3104

American Legion Maryland Oratorical Contest

Type of award: Scholarship.
Intended use: For undergraduate study.
Eligibility: Applicant must be residing in Maryland.
Basis for selection: Competition in Oratory/debate. Breadth of knowledge, originality, application of knowledge of topic, skill in selecting examples and analogies, logic, voice, diction, style of language and delivery.
Application requirements: Proof of eligibility.
   Amount of award: $500-$2,500
   Number of awards: 7
   Application deadline: October 1
   Total amount awarded: $6,000
Contact:
American Legion Maryland
War Memorial Building
101 North Gay Street
Baltimore, MD 21202-1405
Phone: 410-752-1405
Fax: 410-752-3822

American Legion Maryland Science/Math Scholarship

Type of award: Scholarship.
Intended use: For undergraduate study.
Eligibility: Applicant must be residing in Maryland. Applicant must be child of veteran.
Basis for selection: Major/career interest in science, general; mathematics.
Application requirements: Transcript.
Additional information: Must be between age 16 and 18.

Amount of award:	$500
Number of awards:	1
Application deadline:	March 31
Total amount awarded:	$500

Contact:
American Legion Maryland
Department Adjutant, War Memorial Building
101 North Gay Street
Baltimore, MD 21202-1405
Phone: 301-752-3104

American Legion Maryland Auxiliary

American Legion Maryland Auxiliary Nursing Scholarship

Type of award: Scholarship.
Intended use: For undergraduate study at 2-year or 4-year institution.
Eligibility: Applicant must be female. Applicant must be residing in Maryland. Applicant must be child of veteran.
Basis for selection: Major/career interest in nursing. Applicant must demonstrate financial need.
Application requirements: Recommendations. For daughter of ex-servicewoman or ex-serviceman. Submit application for department's Past President's Parley Scholarship.
Additional information: For the RN degree only.

Amount of award:	$1,000
Application deadline:	May 1
Total amount awarded:	$1,000

Contact:
American Legion Maryland Auxiliary
Chairman, Past President's Parley Fund
5205 East Drive, Suite R
Baltimore, MD 21227
Phone: 410-752-1405

American Legion Maryland Auxiliary Scholarship

Type of award: Scholarship.
Intended use: For undergraduate study at 2-year or 4-year institution in Maryland.
Eligibility: Applicant must be female, high school senior. Applicant must be residing in Maryland. Applicant must be child of veteran.
Basis for selection: Major/career interest in arts, general; science, general; business; public administration/service.
Additional information: Additional fields of study considered: education and medical sciences other than nursing.

Amount of award:	$2,000
Number of awards:	1
Application deadline:	May 1
Total amount awarded:	$2,000

Contact:
American Legion Auxiliary, Department of Maryland
Department Secretary
5205 East Drive, Suite R
Baltimore, MD 21227
Phone: 410-752-1405

American Legion Massachusetts

American Legion Massachusetts Oratorical Contest

Type of award: Scholarship.
Intended use: For undergraduate study.
Eligibility: Applicant must be enrolled in high school. Applicant must be residing in Massachusetts.
Basis for selection: Competition in Oratory/debate. Breadth of knowledge, originality, application of knowledge of topic, skill selecting examples and analogies, logic, voice, diction, style of language and delivery.
Application requirements: Proof of eligibility.
Additional information: Topic: U.S. Constitution and citizenship.

Amount of award:	$400-$1,000
Number of awards:	4
Application deadline:	December 15
Total amount awarded:	$2,500

Contact:
American Legion Massachusetts
Department Oratorical Chair
State House, Room 546-2
Boston, MA 02133-1044
Phone: 617-727-2966
Fax: 617-727-2969

American Legion Massachusetts Past County Commander's Scholarship

Type of award: Scholarship.
Intended use: For freshman study at 2-year or 4-year institution.
Eligibility: Applicant must be residing in Massachusetts. Applicant must be descendant of veteran, child of veteran.
Application requirements: Child or grandchild of paid-up living or deceased member of Hampden County American Legion Post. May be adopted or under legal guardianship.
Additional information: Awards: One-$500; additional $250 awards contingent on availability of funds.

Amount of award:	$250-$500
Application deadline:	April 15

Contact:
American Legion Massachusetts
Chairman
46 Brickett Street
Boston, MA 02133-1044
Phone: 617-727-2966
Fax: 617-727-2969

American Legion Massachusetts Auxiliary

American Legion Massachusetts Auxiliary Past President's Parley Scholarship

Type of award: Scholarship.
Intended use: For undergraduate study.
Eligibility: Applicant must be residing in Massachusetts. Applicant must be descendant of veteran, child of veteran.
Basis for selection: Major/career interest in nursing.
Application requirements: Child of living or deceased veteran not eligible for Federal or Commonwealth scholarships.

Amount of award:	$100
Number of awards:	1
Application deadline:	April 10
Total amount awarded:	$100

Contact:
American Legion Massachusetts Auxiliary
Department Secretary
Room 542-2, State House
Boston, MA 02133-1044
Phone: (617) 727-2966

American Legion Massachusetts Auxiliary Scholarship

Type of award: Scholarship.
Intended use: For undergraduate study at vocational, 2-year or 4-year institution.
Eligibility: Applicant must be residing in Massachusetts. Applicant must be descendant of veteran, child of veteran during Grenada, Korean War, Lebanon, Panama, Persian Gulf, WW I, WW II or Vietnam.
Application requirements: Related to living or deceased veteran.
Additional information: Awards: One-$500 and ten-$100.

Amount of award:	$100-$500
Number of awards:	11
Application deadline:	April 10
Total amount awarded:	$1,500

Contact:
American Legion, Department of Massachusetts
Department Secretary
Room 542-2 State House
Boston, MA 02133-1044
Phone: 617-727-2966

American Legion Michigan

American Legion Michigan Guy M. Wilson Scholarship

Type of award: Scholarship.
Intended use: For undergraduate study at 2-year or 4-year institution in Michigan.
Eligibility: Applicant must be residing in Michigan. Applicant must be child of veteran.
Application requirements: Proof of eligibility. Copy of living or deceased veteran's honorable discharge to be attached to application.

Amount of award:	$500
Number of awards:	20
Number of applicants:	500
Application deadline:	February 1
Total amount awarded:	$10,000

American Legion Michigan Oratorical Contest

Type of award: Scholarship.
Intended use: For undergraduate study.
Eligibility: Applicant must be enrolled in high school. Applicant must be residing in Michigan.
Basis for selection: Competition in Oratory/debate. Breadth of knowledge, originality, application of knowledge of topic, skill in selecting examples and analogies, logic, voice, diction, style of language and delivery.
Application requirements: Proof of eligibility.
Additional information: Topic: U.S. Constitution and citizenship.

Amount of award:	$600-$1,000
Number of awards:	3
Application deadline:	February 1
Total amount awarded:	$2,400

American Legion Michigan William D. Brewer--Jewell W. Brewer Scholarship Trusts

Type of award: Scholarship.
Intended use: For undergraduate study.
Eligibility: Applicant must be residing in Michigan. Applicant must be child of veteran.
Application requirements: Proof of eligibility. Copy of deceased or living veteran's honorable discharge.

Amount of award:	$500
Number of awards:	1
Application deadline:	February 1
Total amount awarded:	$500

Contact:
American Legion Michigan
212 North Verlinden Avenue
Lansing, MI 48915
Phone: 517-371-4720
Fax: 517-371-2401
Website: www.michiganlegion.org

American Legion Michigan Auxiliary

American Legion Michigan Auxiliary Memorial Scholarship

Type of award: Scholarship, renewable.
Intended use: For undergraduate study at postsecondary institution in Michigan.
Eligibility: Applicant must be female. Applicant must be residing in Michigan. Applicant must be descendant of veteran, child of veteran during Grenada, Korean War, Middle East War, Lebanon, Panama, Persian Gulf, WW I, WW II or Vietnam.
Basis for selection: Applicant must demonstrate financial need and high academic achievement.
Application requirements: Proof of eligibility. Must have been Michigan resident for one year preceding date of award.
Additional information: Can apply for renewal for second year.
   Amount of award: $500
   Application deadline: March 15
Contact:
American Legion Auxiliary, Department of Michigan
212 North Verlinden Avenue
Lansing, MI 48915
Website: www.michiganlegion.org

American Legion Michigan Auxiliary National President's Scholarship

Type of award: Scholarship.
Intended use: For undergraduate study.
Eligibility: Applicant must be residing in Michigan. Applicant must be descendant of veteran, child of veteran during Grenada, Korean War, Lebanon, Panama, Persian Gulf, WW I, WW II or Vietnam.
Additional information: Awards: Five-$2,000; five-$1,500.
   Amount of award: $1,500-$2,000
   Number of awards: 10
   Application deadline: March 11
   Total amount awarded: $17,500
Contact:
American Legion Michigan Auxiliary, Department of Michigan
212 North Verlinden Avenue
Lansing, MI 48915
Website: www.michiganlegion.org

American Legion Michigan Auxiliary Scholarships For Nurses, Physical Therapists, and Respiratory Therapists

Type of award: Scholarship.
Intended use: For freshman study at vocational, 2-year or 4-year institution in Michigan.
Eligibility: Applicant must be residing in Michigan. Applicant must be descendant of veteran, child of veteran, spouse of veteran or deceased veteran during Grenada, Korean War, Lebanon, Panama, Persian Gulf, WW I, WW II or Vietnam.
Basis for selection: Major/career interest in nursing; physical therapy; respiratory therapy. Applicant must demonstrate financial need and high academic achievement.
Application requirements: Proof of eligibility. Must be Michigan resident for one year preceding award.
Additional information: Applications available after November 15.
   Amount of award: $500
   Application deadline: March 15
Contact:
American Legion Auxiliary, Department of Michigan
212 North Verlinden Avenue
Lansing, MI 48915
Website: www.michiganlegion.org

American Legion Minnesota

American Legion Minnesota Legionnaire Insurance Trust Scholarship

Type of award: Scholarship.
Intended use: For undergraduate study at postsecondary institution in Minnesota institution or neighboring state with reciprocity agreement.
Eligibility: Applicant must be U.S. citizen residing in Minnesota. Applicant must be veteran, child of veteran.
Basis for selection: Applicant must demonstrate high academic achievement.
Application requirements: Veteran or child of veteran resident of Minnesota.
   Amount of award: $500
   Number of awards: 3
   Application deadline: April 1
   Total amount awarded: $1,500
Contact:
American Legion Minnesota
Education Committee
State Veterans Service Building
St. Paul, MN 55155
Phone: 612-291-1800
Fax: 612-291-1057

American Legion Minnesota Oratorical Contest

Type of award: Scholarship.
Intended use: For undergraduate study.
Eligibility: Applicant must be enrolled in high school. Applicant must be U.S. citizen residing in Minnesota.
Basis for selection: Competition in Oratory/debate. Breadth of knowledge, originality, application of knowledge of topic, skill in selecting examples and analogies, logic, voice, diction, style of language and delivery. Applicant must demonstrate financial need.
Application requirements: Proof of eligibility.
Additional information: Topic: U.S. Constitution and citizenship. Award amount varies. Contact sponsor for more information.

Amount of award:	$500-$1,200
Number of awards:	4
Application deadline:	December 15
Total amount awarded:	$3,300

Contact:
Department Oratorical Chair
State Veterans Service Building
St. Paul, MN 55155
Phone: 612-291-1800
Fax: 612-291-1057

American Legion Minnesota Auxiliary

American Legion Minnesota Auxiliary Department Scholarship

Type of award: Scholarship.
Intended use: For undergraduate study at postsecondary institution in Minnesota.
Eligibility: Applicant must be U.S. citizen residing in Minnesota. Applicant must be descendant of veteran, child of veteran. Applicant's parent or grandparent must have served during one of these eligibility dates: April 6, 1914 - November 11, 1918; December 7, 1941 - December 31, 1946; June 25, 1950 - January 31, 1955; December 22, 1961 - May 7, 1975; August 24, 1982 - July 31, 1984; December 20, 1989 - January 31, 1990.

Amount of award:	$500
Number of awards:	7
Application deadline:	March 15
Total amount awarded:	$3,500

Contact:
Scholarship Coordinator
State Veterans Service Building
St. Paul, MN 55155
Phone: 612-224-7634

American Legion Mississippi Auxiliary

American Legion Mississippi Auxiliary Scholarship

Type of award: Scholarship.
Intended use: For freshman study at postsecondary institution in Mississippi.
Eligibility: Applicant must be residing in Mississippi. Applicant must be descendant of veteran, child of veteran during Korean War, Lebanon, Panama, Persian Gulf, WW I, WW II or Vietnam.
Basis for selection: Applicant must demonstrate financial need.

Amount of award:	$500
Number of awards:	1
Application deadline:	March 10
Total amount awarded:	$500

Contact:
American Legion Mississippi Auxiliary
Department Headquarters
P.O. Box 1382
Jackson, MS 39215-1382

American Legion Missouri

American Legion Missouri M.D. "Jack" Murphy Memorial Nursing Scholarship

Type of award: Scholarship.
Intended use: For full-time undergraduate study at 2-year or 4-year institution.
Eligibility: Applicant must be single. Applicant must be residing in Missouri. Applicant must be descendant of veteran, child of veteran.
Basis for selection: Major/career interest in nursing. Applicant must demonstrate financial need.
Application requirements: Must be dependent child or grandchild of a resident veteran and not receiving any other scholarship.

Amount of award:	$600
Number of awards:	1
Total amount awarded:	$600

American Legion Missouri Oratorical Certificates

Type of award: Scholarship.
Intended use: For undergraduate study at vocational, 2-year or 4-year institution.
Eligibility: Applicant must be enrolled in high school. Applicant must be residing in Missouri.
Basis for selection: Competition in Oratory/debate.
Application requirements: Proof of eligibility. Must have won 1st, 2nd, 3rd, or 4th place at the Department of Missouri annual Oratorical contest.
Additional information: A total of four awards are offered, for the amounts of $2,000, $1,800, $1,600, and $1,400.

Amount of award:	$1,400-$2,000
Number of awards:	4
Total amount awarded:	$6,800

Contact:
American Legion Missouri
Department Adjutant
P.O. Box 179
Jefferson City, MO 65102
Phone: 573-893-2353

American Legion Missouri Auxiliary

American Legion Missouri Auxiliary Past President's Parley Scholarship

Type of award: Scholarship.
Intended use: For freshman study at vocational, 2-year or 4-year institution.
Eligibility: Applicant must be residing in Missouri. Applicant must be descendant of veteran, child of veteran.
Basis for selection: Major/career interest in nursing.
Application requirements: For nursing students.
    Amount of award: $1,000
    Number of awards: 1
    Application deadline: March 15
    Total amount awarded: $1,000
Contact:
American Legion Missouri Auxiliary
Department Secretary
210 West Dunklin Street
Jefferson City, MO 65101

American Legion Missouri Auxiliary Scholarship

Type of award: Scholarship.
Intended use: For freshman study.
Eligibility: Applicant must be high school senior. Applicant must be residing in Missouri. Applicant must be descendant of veteran, child of veteran during Korean War, Lebanon, Panama, Persian Gulf, WW I, WW II or Vietnam.
Application requirements: Cannot have attended an institution of higher learning.
    Amount of award: $500
    Number of awards: 2
    Application deadline: March 15
    Total amount awarded: $500
Contact:
American Legion Auxiliary, Department of Missouri
Department Secretary
210 West Dunklin Street
Jefferson City, MO 65101

American Legion National Headquarters

American Legion National Eight and Forty Lung and Respiratory Nursing Scholarship Fund

Type of award: Scholarship.
Intended use: For non-degree study.
Eligibility: Applicant must be adult returning student.
Basis for selection: Major/career interest in nursing.
Application requirements: Proof of eligibility. Contact Eight and Forty Scholarship Chairman or The American Legion Education Program.
Additional information: To assist registered nurses with advanced preparation for positions in supervision, administration or teaching. Must have full-time employment prospects on completion of education related to lung and respiratory control.
    Amount of award: $2,500
    Application deadline: May 15
    Notification begins: July 1
Contact:
American Legion Education Program
Eight and Forty Scholarships
P.O. Box 1055
Indianapolis, IN 46206

American Legion National High School Oratorical Contest

Type of award: Scholarship.
Intended use: For undergraduate study.
Eligibility: Applicant must be enrolled in high school.
Basis for selection: Competition in Oratory/debate.
Application requirements: Obtain oratorical contest rules from local legion post or state department headquarters.
Additional information: Scholarship awards: State winners participating in regional level win $1,500; second-round participants not advancing to national finals receive additional $1,500. Finalists win $18,000 (first place), $16,000 (runner-up), and $14,000 (third place).
    Amount of award: $1,500-$18,000
    Number of awards: 3
Contact:
American Legion National Headquarters
Education Programs Chair
P.O. Box 1055
Indianapolis, IN 46206

American Legion Nebraska

American Legion Nebraska Maynard Jensen Memorial Scholarship

Type of award: Scholarship.
Intended use: For undergraduate study at vocational, 2-year or 4-year institution in Nebraska.
Eligibility: Applicant must be residing in Nebraska. Applicant must be descendant of veteran.
Basis for selection: Applicant must demonstrate financial need and high academic achievement.
Application requirements: Must be descendant, adopted, or stepchild of American Legion member, POW, MIA, KIA, or any deceased veteran.
    Amount of award: $500
    Number of awards: 6
    Number of applicants: 500
    Total amount awarded: $30,000

American Legion Nebraska Oratorical Contest

Type of award: Scholarship.
Intended use: For undergraduate study.
Eligibility: Applicant must be enrolled in high school. Applicant must be residing in Nebraska.
Basis for selection: Competition in Oratory/debate. Breadth of knowledge, originally, application of knowledge of topic, skill in selecting examples and analogies, logic, voice, diction, style of language and delivery.
Application requirements: Proof of eligibility.
Additional information: Topic: U.S. Constitution and citizenship.
   Amount of award: $200-$1,000
   Number of awards: 4
   Total amount awarded: $2,200
Contact:
American Legion Nebraska
Department Headquarters
P.O. Box 5205
Lincoln, NE 68505-0205
Phone: 402-464-6338
Fax: 402-464-6330

American Legion Nebraska Auxiliary

American Legion Nebraska Auxiliary Practical Nurse Scholarship

Type of award: Scholarship.
Intended use: For undergraduate study at vocational, 2-year or 4-year institution.
Eligibility: Applicant must be residing in Nebraska. Applicant must be veteran, descendant of veteran, child of veteran, spouse of veteran.
Basis for selection: Major/career interest in nursing. Applicant must demonstrate financial need.
Application requirements: State resident for 3 years. Must be accepted at school of practical nursing.
   Amount of award: $400
   Application deadline: April 10
   Total amount awarded: $400

American Legion Nebraska Auxiliary Roberta Marie Stretch Memorial Scholarship

Type of award: Scholarship.
Intended use: For undergraduate, master's study at 4-year or graduate institution.
Eligibility: Applicant must be residing in Nebraska. Applicant must be descendant of veteran, child of veteran, spouse of veteran.
Application requirements: Must be enrolled or accepted in undergraduate or masters program.

Additional information: Preference given to former Nebraska Girls State citizens.
   Amount of award: $300
   Application deadline: April 10

American Legion Nebraska Auxiliary Student Aid Grant - Vocational Technical Scholarship

Type of award: Scholarship.
Intended use: For undergraduate study at vocational or 2-year institution in United States.
Eligibility: Applicant must be residing in Nebraska. Applicant must be veteran, child of veteran.
Basis for selection: Applicant must demonstrate financial need.
Application requirements: State resident for 5 years. Accepted at school of higher learning.
   Amount of award: $200-$300
   Application deadline: April 10
Contact:
American Legion Nebraska Auxiliary
Department Headquarters
P.O. Box 5227
Lincoln, NE 68505-2050
Phone: 402-466-1808

American Legion New Hampshire

American Legion New Hampshire Christa McAuliffe Scholarship

Type of award: Scholarship.
Intended use: For freshman study.
Eligibility: Applicant must be U.S. citizen residing in New Hampshire.
Basis for selection: Major/career interest in education.
Application requirements: State resident for 3 years. Send SASE to State House Annex.
   Amount of award: $1,000
   Number of awards: 1
   Application deadline: May 1
   Total amount awarded: $1,000
Contact:
American Legion New Hampshire
Department Adjutant
State House Annex, Rm 431
Concord, NH 03301-6312
Phone: 603-271-2211

American Legion New Hampshire Department Scholarship

Type of award: Scholarship.
Intended use: For freshman study at vocational, 2-year or 4-year institution.
Eligibility: Applicant must be U.S. citizen residing in New Hampshire.

Application requirements: Graduate of New Hampshire high school and state resident of 3 years.
- **Amount of award:** $1,000
- **Number of awards:** 2
- **Application deadline:** May 1
- **Total amount awarded:** $2,000

Contact:
Scholarship Coordinator
Department Adjutant
State House Annex, Room 431
Concord, NH 03301-6312
Phone: 603-271-2211

American Legion New Hampshire Department Vocational Scholarship

Type of award: Scholarship.
Intended use: For freshman study.
Eligibility: Applicant must be U.S. citizen residing in New Hampshire.
Application requirements: State resident for three years. State high school graduate.
- **Amount of award:** $1,000
- **Application deadline:** May 1
- **Total amount awarded:** $1,000

Contact:
American Legion New Hampshire
Department Adjutant
State House Annex, Room 431
Concord, NH 03301-6312

American Legion New Hampshire Oratorical Contest

Type of award: Scholarship.
Intended use: For undergraduate study.
Eligibility: Applicant must be enrolled in high school. Applicant must be residing in New Hampshire.
Basis for selection: Competition in Oratory/debate. Breadth of knowledge, originality, application of knowledge of topic, skill in selecting examples and analogies, logic, voice, diction, style of language and delivery.
Application requirements: Proof of eligibility.
Additional information: Subject: U.S. Constitution and citizenship.
- **Amount of award:** $100-$500
- **Number of awards:** 4
- **Total amount awarded:** $1,000

Contact:
American Legion New Hampshire
State House Annex, Room 431
Concord, NH 03301-6312
Phone: 603-271-2211
Fax: 603-271-2361

American Legion New Hampshire Auxiliary

American Legion New Hampshire Auxiliary Marion J. Bagley Scholarship

Type of award: Scholarship.
Intended use: For undergraduate study.
Eligibility: Applicant must be U.S. citizen residing in New Hampshire.
Application requirements: High school graduate or equivalent or attending school of higher learning.
- **Amount of award:** $1,000
- **Number of awards:** 1
- **Application deadline:** May 1
- **Total amount awarded:** $1,000

American Legion New Hampshire Auxiliary Past President's Parley Nursing Scholarship

Type of award: Scholarship.
Intended use: For undergraduate study at 2-year or 4-year institution.
Eligibility: Applicant must be U.S. citizen residing in New Hampshire.
Basis for selection: Major/career interest in nursing. Applicant must demonstrate financial need.
Application requirements: Must be high school graduate.
Additional information: Child of veteran given preference. Award amount varies; contact sponsor for information.
- **Application deadline:** May 10

Contact:
American Legion Auxiliary, Department of New Hampshire
Department Secretary, Room 432
State House Annex
Concord, NH 03301

American Legion New Jersey

American Legion New Jersey David C. Goodwin Scholarship

Type of award: Scholarship.
Intended use: For undergraduate study.
Eligibility: Applicant must be high school junior. Applicant must be residing in New Jersey.
Application requirements: Must be high school junior participating in New Jersey American Legion Baseball Program.

Amount of award: $2,000-$4,000
Number of awards: 2
Application deadline: September 1
Total amount awarded: $6,000
Contact:
American Legion New Jersey
Baseball Committee
War Memorial Building
Trenton, NJ 08608
Phone: 609-695-5418

American Legion New Jersey David C. Goodwin Scholarship

Type of award: Scholarship.
Intended use: For undergraduate study.
Eligibility: Applicant must be high school junior. Applicant must be residing in New Jersey.
Additional information: Award: One $4,000 scholarship ($1,000/year), one $2,000 scholarship ($500/year). Applications are mailed to players.
Amount of award: $2,000-$4,000
Number of awards: 2
Application deadline: September 1
Total amount awarded: $6,000
Contact:
American Legion New Jersey
Baseball Committee
War Memorial Building
Trenton Trenton, NJ 08608

American Legion New Jersey Oratorical Contest

Type of award: Scholarship.
Intended use: For freshman study.
Eligibility: Applicant must be enrolled in high school. Applicant must be residing in New Jersey.
Basis for selection: Competition in Oratory/debate. Breadth of knowledge, originality, application of knowledge of topic, skill in selecting examples and analogies, logic, voice, diction, style of language and delivery.
Application requirements: Proof of eligibility.
Additional information: Subject: U.S. Constitution and citizenship. See your high school counselor for additional information.
Amount of award: $500-$4,000
Number of awards: 5
Total amount awarded: $8,250
Contact:
American Legion New Jersey
135 West Hanover Street
Trenton, NJ 08618
Phone: 609-695-5418
Fax: 609-394-1532

American Legion New Jersey Auxiliary

American Legion New Jersey Auxiliary Claire Oliphant Memorial Scholarship

Type of award: Scholarship.
Intended use: For freshman study at vocational, 2-year or 4-year institution.
Eligibility: Applicant must be high school senior. Applicant must be U.S. citizen residing in New Jersey. Applicant must be child of veteran.
Application requirements: State residency of two years.
Additional information: Information can be obtained from high school guidance department.
Amount of award: $1,800
Number of awards: 1
Application deadline: March 15
Total amount awarded: $1,800

American Legion New Jersey Auxiliary Department Scholarship

Type of award: Scholarship.
Intended use: For freshman study at vocational, 2-year or 4-year institution.
Eligibility: Applicant must be high school senior. Applicant must be U.S. citizen residing in New Jersey. Applicant must be descendant of veteran, child of veteran.
Application requirements: State resident for two years.
Additional information: Several awards are offered. Award amounts and number of awards varies; contact sponsor for information.
Application deadline: March 15

American Legion New Jersey Auxiliary Past President's Parley Nursing Scholarship

Type of award: Scholarship.
Intended use: For freshman study at 2-year or 4-year institution.
Eligibility: Applicant must be high school senior. Applicant must be residing in New Jersey. Applicant must be descendant of veteran, child of veteran.
Basis for selection: Major/career interest in nursing.
Application requirements: State resident for two years.
Additional information: Applicant must be enrolled in a nursing program. Award amount varies. Contact sponsor for more information.
Application deadline: March 15
Contact:
American Legion Auxiliary, Department of New Jersey
Department Secretary
146 Route 130
Bordentown, NJ 08505-2226
Phone: 609-291-9338

American Legion New Mexico Auxiliary

American Legion New Mexico Auxiliary Teachers of Exceptional Children Scholarship

Type of award: Scholarship.
Intended use: For undergraduate, graduate or non-degree study at postsecondary institution in New Mexico.
Eligibility: Applicant must be residing in New Mexico.
Basis for selection: Major/career interest in education, special.
Additional information: Award provides up to $250 for additional special education training, plus $50 travel and miscellaneous expenses. To teach exceptional children for one year.
   Amount of award: $250
   Number of awards: 1
   Application deadline: March 1
   Total amount awarded: $250
Contact:
American Legion Auxiliary, Department of New Mexico
Department Secretary
1215 Mountain Road, N.E.
Albuquerque, NM 87102

American Legion New York

American Legion New York Oratorical Contest

Type of award: Scholarship.
Intended use: For undergraduate study.
Eligibility: Applicant must be enrolled in high school. Applicant must be residing in New York.
Basis for selection: Competition in Oratory/debate. Breadth of knowledge, originality, application of knowledge of topic, skill in selecting examples and analogies, logic, voice, diction, style of language, and delivery.
Application requirements: Proof of eligibility.
Additional information: Topic: U.S. Constitution and citizenship. Also open to junior high school students.
   Amount of award: $2,000-$6,000
   Number of awards: 5
   Total amount awarded: $16,500
Contact:
American Legion New York
Department Adjutant
112 State Street, Suite 400
Albany, NY 12207
Phone: 518-463-2215
Fax: 518-427-8443

American Legion New York Auxiliary

American Legion New York Auxiliary Medical & Teaching Scholarship

Type of award: Scholarship.
Intended use: For full-time freshman study.
Eligibility: Applicant must be residing in New York. Applicant must be descendant of veteran, child of veteran.
Basis for selection: Major/career interest in health-related professions; education, teacher. Applicant must demonstrate financial need.
Additional information: One scholarship in each of the ten New York judicial districts.
   Amount of award: $1,000
   Number of awards: 10
   Application deadline: March 25
   Total amount awarded: $10,000
Contact:
American Legion New York Auxiliary, Department of New York
Department Secretary
112 State Street, Suite 409
Albany, NY 12207-0003

American Legion New York Auxiliary Past President's Parley Nursing Scholarship

Type of award: Scholarship.
Intended use: For freshman study at 2-year or 4-year institution.
Eligibility: Applicant must be residing in New York. Applicant must be descendant of veteran, child of veteran during Korean War, WW I, WW II or Vietnam.
Basis for selection: Major/career interest in nursing. Applicant must demonstrate financial need.
Additional information: Applications can be secured from your local units.
   Amount of award: $500
   Number of awards: 1
   Application deadline: March 25
   Total amount awarded: $500
Contact:
American Legion Auxiliary, Department of New York
Department Secretary
112 State Street, Suite 409
Albany, NY 12207-0003

American Legion New York Auxiliary Scholarship

Type of award: Scholarship.
Intended use: For undergraduate study.
Eligibility: Applicant must be residing in New York. Applicant must be descendant of veteran, child of veteran or deceased veteran.
Additional information: May use other scholarships. Applications may be secured from your local unit.

Amount of award: $1,000
Number of awards: 1
Application deadline: March 25
Total amount awarded: $1,000
Contact:
American Legion Auxiliary, Department of New York
Department Secretary
112 State Street, Suite 409
Albany, NY 12207-0003

American Legion North Carolina Auxiliary

American Legion New York Auxiliary Nannie W. Norfleet Loan Fund

Type of award: Loan, renewable.
Intended use: For undergraduate study at 2-year or 4-year institution.
Eligibility: Applicant must be residing in North Carolina. Applicant must be child of veteran.
Application requirements: Child of deserving veterans.
Additional information: Preference given to children of auxiliary members.
  Amount of award: $1,500
  Application deadline: January 31
Contact:
American Legion Auxiliary, Department of North Carolina
Department Chairman of Education Committee
P.O. Box 25726
Raleigh, NC 27611

American Legion North Dakota

American Legion North Dakota Oratorical Contest

Type of award: Scholarship.
Intended use: For undergraduate study.
Eligibility: Applicant must be enrolled in high school. Applicant must be residing in North Dakota.
Basis for selection: Competition in Oratory/debate. Breadth of knowledge, originality, application of knowledge of topic, skill in selecting examples and analogies, logic, voice, diction, style of language and delivery.
Application requirements: Proof of eligibility.
Additional information: Topic: U.S. Constitution and citizenship. Top four contestants in North Dakota Oratorical Contest win $400, $300, $200, and $100. Contact your local legion post or the department headquarters after the start of the school year.

Amount of award: $100-$400
Number of awards: 6
Total amount awarded: $1,500
Contact:
American Legion North Dakota
Department Headquarters
Box 2666
Fargo, ND 58108-2666
Phone: 701-293-3120
Fax: 701-293-9951

American Legion North Dakota Auxiliary

American Legion North Dakota Auxiliary Scholarship

Type of award: Scholarship.
Intended use: For undergraduate study. Designated institutions: North Dakota only.
Eligibility: Applicant must be residing in North Dakota.
Additional information: Must be resident of North Dakota enrolled in university or college in state of North Dakota. Apply to your community auxiliary unit. Local unit addresses are available at the contact address.
  Amount of award: $350
  Application deadline: December 15
Contact:
American Legion Auxiliary
Department Secretary
P.O. Box 250
Beach, ND 58621

American Legion Ohio Auxiliary

American Legion Ohio Auxiliary Scholarship

Type of award: Scholarship.
Intended use: For freshman study.
Eligibility: Applicant must be high school senior. Applicant must be residing in Ohio. Applicant must be descendant of veteran, child of veteran or deceased veteran during Grenada, Korean War, Lebanon, Persian Gulf, WW I, WW II or Vietnam.
Additional information: Additional scholarship of $1,000 awarded to second place applicant.
  Amount of award: $1,000-$1,500
  Number of awards: 2
  Application deadline: April 1
  Total amount awarded: $2,500

American Legion Ohio Auxiliary Scholarship For Nurse's Training or Medical Field

Type of award: Scholarship.
Intended use: For undergraduate study at vocational, 2-year or 4-year institution.
Eligibility: Applicant must be residing in Ohio. Applicant must be descendant of veteran, child of veteran, spouse of veteran.
Basis for selection: Major/career interest in nursing; health-related professions.
Additional information: Ten awards of $300 and two $500 awards are available.
   Amount of award: $300-$500
   Number of awards: 12
   Application deadline: June 1
   Total amount awarded: $3,100
Contact:
American Legion Ohio Auxiliary
1100 Brandywine Boulevard, Building D
P.O. Box 2279
Zanesville, OH 43702-2279

American Legion Oklahoma Auxiliary

American Legion Oklahoma Auxiliary Student Education Loan

Type of award: Loan, renewable.
Intended use: For undergraduate study at vocational, 2-year or 4-year institution in Oklahoma.
Eligibility: Applicant must be residing in Oklahoma. Applicant must be child of veteran, spouse of veteran.
Additional information: Up to $1,000 per year. Loans available to sisters of veterans as well.
   Amount of award: $1,000
   Number of awards: 1
   Total amount awarded: $1,000
Contact:
American Legion Auxiliary, Department of Oklahoma
Department Headquarters
P.O. Box 26003
Oklahoma City, OK 73126-0003
Phone: 405-528-4061
Fax: 405-528-4208

American Legion Oregon

American Legion Oregon Oratorical Contest

Type of award: Scholarship.
Intended use: For undergraduate study.
Eligibility: Applicant must be enrolled in high school. Applicant must be U.S. citizen residing in Oregon.
Basis for selection: Competition in Oratory/debate. Breadth of knowledge, originality, application of knowledge of topic, skill in selecting examples and analogies, logic, voice, diction, style of language and delivery.
Application requirements: Proof of eligibility.
Additional information: Topic: U.S. Constitution and citizenship.
   Amount of award: $200-$500
   Number of awards: 4
   Total amount awarded: $1,400
Contact:
American Legion Department of Oregon
P.O. Box 1730
Wilsonville, OR 97070-1730
Phone: 503-685-5006
Fax: 503-685-5008

American Legion Oregon Auxiliary

American Legion Oregon Auxiliary Department Nurses Scholarship

Type of award: Scholarship.
Intended use: For undergraduate study at accredited 2-year or 4-year institution. Designated institutions: School of nursing.
Eligibility: Applicant must be residing in Oregon. Applicant must be child of veteran or disabled veteran, spouse of veteran, disabled veteran or deceased veteran.
Basis for selection: Major/career interest in nursing. Applicant must demonstrate depth of character, seriousness of purpose, service orientation and financial need.
Application requirements: Proof of eligibility.
   Amount of award: $1,500
   Number of awards: 1
   Application deadline: June 1
   Total amount awarded: $1,500

American Legion Oregon Auxiliary Department Scholarship

Type of award: Scholarship.
Intended use: For undergraduate study at vocational, 2-year or 4-year institution.
Eligibility: Applicant must be residing in Oregon. Applicant must be child of veteran or disabled veteran, spouse of veteran, disabled veteran or deceased veteran.
Additional information: One of three grants designated for vocational or business school.
   Amount of award: $1,000
   Number of awards: 3
   Application deadline: March 15
   Total amount awarded: $3,000

American Legion Oregon Auxiliary National President's Scholarship

Type of award: Scholarship.
Intended use: For undergraduate study.
Eligibility: Applicant must be residing in Oregon. Applicant

must be child of veteran during Grenada, Korean War, Lebanon, Panama, Persian Gulf, WW I, WW II or Vietnam.
Additional information: Two awards in each division: One-$2,000; and one-$1,500.
- Amount of award: $1,500-$2,000
- Number of awards: 10
- Application deadline: March 15

American Legion Oregon Auxiliary One-Time Grant

Type of award: Scholarship.
Intended use: For undergraduate or graduate study at accredited postsecondary institution in Oregon.
Eligibility: Applicant must be residing in Oregon. Applicant must be descendant of veteran, child of veteran, spouse of veteran or deceased veteran.
- Amount of award: $1,000
- Application deadline: March 15
- Total amount awarded: $1,000

Contact:
American Legion Auxiliary, Department of Oregon
Chairman of Education
P.O. Box 1730
Wilsonville, OR 97070-1730

American Legion Pennsylvania Auxiliary

American Legion Pennsylvania Auxiliary Scholarship

Type of award: Scholarship.
Intended use: For undergraduate study at postsecondary institution in Pennsylvania.
Eligibility: Applicant must be high school senior. Applicant must be residing in Pennsylvania. Applicant must be child of veteran.
Basis for selection: Applicant must demonstrate financial need.
Additional information: Award $600 per year for four years.
- Amount of award: $2,400
- Number of awards: 1
- Application deadline: March 15
- Total amount awarded: $2,400

American Legion Pennsylvania Auxiliary Scholarship For Children of Deceased/Disabled Veterans

Type of award: Scholarship.
Intended use: For undergraduate study at postsecondary institution in Pennsylvania.
Eligibility: Applicant must be high school senior. Applicant must be residing in Pennsylvania. Applicant must be child of disabled veteran or deceased veteran.
Basis for selection: Applicant must demonstrate financial need.
Additional information: Award is $600 per year for four years.

- Amount of award: $2,400
- Number of awards: 1
- Application deadline: March 15
- Total amount awarded: $2,400

Contact:
American Legion Auxiliary, Department of Pennsylvania
Department Education Chairman
P.O. Box 2643
Harrisburg, PA 17105
Phone: 717-763-7545

American Legion Puerto Rico Auxiliary

American Legion Puerto Rico Auxiliary Nursing Scholarship

Type of award: Scholarship.
Intended use: For undergraduate study at 2-year or 4-year institution in Puerto Rico.
Eligibility: Applicant must be residing in Puerto Rico.
Basis for selection: Major/career interest in nursing.
Application requirements: Interview. Must be in nurses training.
Additional information: Personal interview required. Award distributed in two yearly installments of $250.
- Amount of award: $500
- Number of awards: 2
- Application deadline: March 15
- Total amount awarded: $1,000

Contact:
American Legion Auxiliary, Department of Puerto Rico
Education Chairman
P.O. Box 11424
Caparra Heights, PR 00922

American Legion South Carolina

American Legion South Carolina Robert E. David Children's Scholarship

Type of award: Scholarship.
Intended use: For freshman, sophomore, junior or senior study.
Eligibility: Applicant must be residing in South Carolina. Applicant must be descendant of veteran, child of veteran during Grenada, Korean War, Lebanon, Panama, Persian Gulf, WW I, WW II or Vietnam.
Basis for selection: Applicant must demonstrate financial need and high academic achievement.

Application deadline: May 1
Contact:
American Legion South Carolina
Department Adjutant
P.O. Box 11355 132 Pickens Street
Columbia, SC 29211
Phone: 803-799-1992

American Legion South Carolina Scholarship

Type of award: Scholarship.
Intended use: For undergraduate study.
Eligibility: Applicant must be enrolled in high school. Applicant must be residing in South Carolina.
Basis for selection: Competition in Oratory/debate.
Application requirements: Zone winner of High School Oratorical Contest.
Additional information: Award totals: First-$1,600; second-$1,000; and third through fifth-$500. Distributed over four-year period.
   Amount of award: $500-$1,600
   Number of awards: 5
   Total amount awarded: $4,100
Contact:
American Legion South Carolina
P.O. Box 11355
Columbia, SC 29211
Phone: 803-799-1992

American Legion South Carolina Auxiliary

American Legion South Carolina Auxiliary Floyd Memorial Scholarship Fund

Type of award: Loan.
Intended use: For undergraduate study.
Eligibility: Applicant must be residing in South Carolina. Applicant must be descendant of veteran, child of veteran during Korean War, Persian Gulf, WW I, WW II or Vietnam.
Basis for selection: Applicant must demonstrate financial need.
Additional information: Loans $500/year with no interest due. To be repaid six months after graduation.
   Amount of award: $500
   Number of awards: 2
   Total amount awarded: $1,000
Contact:
American Legion Auxiliary, Department of South Carolina
Department Secretary
132 Pickens Street
Columbia, SC 29205
Phone: 803-799-6695

American Legion South Dakota

American Legion South Dakota Educational Loan

Type of award: Loan, renewable.
Intended use: For freshman, sophomore, junior or senior study at vocational, 2-year or 4-year institution.
Eligibility: Applicant must be residing in South Dakota. Applicant must be child of veteran.
Additional information: Loan ammount varies; up to $2000.
   Amount of award: $2,000

American Legion South Dakota Oratorical Contest

Type of award: Scholarship.
Intended use: For undergraduate study.
Eligibility: Applicant must be enrolled in high school. Applicant must be residing in South Dakota.
Basis for selection: Competition in Oratory/debate. Breadth of knowledge, originality, application of knowledge of topic, skill in selecting examples and analogies, logic, voice, diction, style of language and delivery.
Application requirements: Proof of eligibility.
Additional information: Topic: U.S. Constitution and citizenship.
   Amount of award: $100-$600
   Number of awards: 5
   Total amount awarded: $1,500
Contact:
American Legion South Dakota
Department Adjutant
P.O. Box 67
Watertown, SD 57201-0067
Phone: 605-886-3604
Fax: 605-886-2870

American Legion Tennessee

American Legion Tennessee Oratorical Contest

Type of award: Scholarship, renewable.
Intended use: For undergraduate study at postsecondary institution in United States.
Eligibility: Applicant must be enrolled in high school. Applicant must be residing in Tennessee.
Basis for selection: Competition in Oratory/debate.
Application requirements: Proof of eligibility. Winner of Tennessee High School Oratorical Contest.
Additional information: Application deadline: early January. Scholarship awarded to top three winners. Includes savings bonds as well.

Application deadline: January 1
Contact:
American Legion Tennessee
Department Adjutant
215 Eighth Avenue, North
Nashville, TN 37203-3583
Phone: 615-254-0568
Fax: 615-255-1551

American Legion Tennessee Auxiliary

American Legion Tennessee Auxiliary Vara Gray Nursing Scholarship

Type of award: Scholarship.
Intended use: For freshman study at vocational, 2-year or 4-year institution.
Eligibility: Applicant must be high school senior. Applicant must be residing in Tennessee. Applicant must be child of veteran.
Basis for selection: Major/career interest in nursing.
Application requirements: Nomination by American Legion Auxiliary Units.
- Amount of award: $500
- Number of awards: 3
- Application deadline: March 1
- Total amount awarded: $1,500

American Legion Tennessee Auxiliary Vara Gray Scholarship

Type of award: Scholarship.
Intended use: For undergraduate study.
Eligibility: Applicant must be high school senior. Applicant must be residing in Tennessee. Applicant must be child of veteran.
Application requirements: Nomination by local American Legion Auxiliary units.
- Amount of award: $500
- Number of awards: 3
- Application deadline: March 1
- Total amount awarded: $1,500

Contact:
American Legion Auxiliary, Department of Tennessee
1007 Murfreesboro Road, Suite 100
Nashville, TN 37217
Phone: 615-361-8822

American Legion Texas

American Legion Texas Oratorical Contest

Type of award: Scholarship.
Intended use: For undergraduate study.
Eligibility: Applicant must be enrolled in high school. Applicant must be residing in Texas.
Basis for selection: Competition in Oratory/debate. Breadth of knowledge, originality, application of knowledge of topic, skill in selecting examples and analogies, logic, voice, diction, style of language, and delivery. Applicant must demonstrate patriotism.
Application requirements: Proof of eligibility.
Additional information: Topic: U.S. Constitution and citizenship.
- Amount of award: $250-$1,000
- Number of awards: 4
- Total amount awarded: $2,500

Contact:
American Legion Texas
P.O. Box 789
Austin, TX 78767
Phone: 512-472-4183
Fax: 512-472-0603

American Legion Texas Auxiliary

American Legion Texas Auxiliary General Scholarship

Type of award: Scholarship.
Intended use: For undergraduate study at postsecondary institution in Texas.
Eligibility: Applicant must be residing in Texas. Applicant must be child of veteran.
Application requirements: Nomination by local units. Unit sponsorship.
- Amount of award: $500
- Application deadline: April 1
- Total amount awarded: $500

American Legion Texas Auxiliary Nurses Scholarship

Type of award: Scholarship.
Intended use: For undergraduate study.
Eligibility: Applicant must be residing in Texas. Applicant must be child of veteran.
Basis for selection: Major/career interest in nursing.
Application requirements: Nomination by local units. Unit sponsorship.
- Amount of award: $500
- Application deadline: April 1
- Total amount awarded: $500

Contact:
American Legion Texas Auxiliary
Department Headquarters
709 East 10 Street
Austin, TX 78701
Phone: 512-476-7278

American Legion Utah Auxiliary

American Legion Utah Auxiliary National President's Scholarship

Type of award: Scholarship.
Intended use: For undergraduate study.
Eligibility: Applicant must be high school senior. Applicant must be residing in Utah. Applicant must be child of veteran during Grenada, Korean War, Lebanon, Panama, Persian Gulf, WW I, WW II or Vietnam.
Basis for selection: Applicant must demonstrate financial need and high academic achievement.
    Amount of award: $1,500-$2,000
    Number of awards: 2
    Total amount awarded: $3,500
Contact:
American Legion Utah Auxiliary
Department Headquarters
B-61 State Capitol Bldg.
Salt Lake City, UT 84114
Phone: 801-538-1014

American Legion Vermont

American Legion Vermont Scholarship

Type of award: Scholarship.
Intended use: For undergraduate study at vocational, 2-year or 4-year institution.
Eligibility: Applicant must be high school senior. Applicant must be residing in Vermont.
Application requirements: Seniors of Vermont secondary school, or seniors from adjacent state whose parents are legal Vermont residents, or seniors from adjacent state attending Vermont schools.
Additional information: Awards: One-$250 annually for four years, four-$250 annually for two years.
    Amount of award: $500-$1,000
    Number of awards: 5
    Total amount awarded: $3,000

American Legion Vermont Scholarship Program

Type of award: Scholarship.
Intended use: For undergraduate study.
Eligibility: Applicant must be high school senior. Applicant must be residing in Vermont.
Basis for selection: Applicant must demonstrate financial need.
Application requirements: Parents must be citizens.
Additional information: Amount and number of grants vary. Contact your local legion post.
Contact:
American Legion Vermont
Education and Scholarship Committee
P.O. Box 396
Montpelier, VT 05601-0396
Phone: 802-223-7131

American Legion Virginia

American Legion Virginia Oratorical Contest

Type of award: Scholarship.
Intended use: For undergraduate study.
Eligibility: Applicant must be enrolled in high school. Applicant must be residing in Virginia.
Basis for selection: Competition in Oratory/debate. Breadth of knowledge, originality, application of knowledge of topic, skill in selecting examples and analogies, logic, voice, diction, style of language and delivery.
Application requirements: Proof of eligibility.
Additional information: Topic: U.S. Constitution and citizenship.
    Amount of award: $600-$1,100
    Number of awards: 3
    Application deadline: December 1
    Total amount awarded: $2,300
Contact:
American Legion Virginia
Department Adjutant
1805 Chantilly Street
Richmond, VA 23230
Phone: 804-353-6606
Fax: 804-358-1940

American Legion Washington Auxiliary

American Legion Washington Auxiliary Education Scholarship

Type of award: Scholarship.
Intended use: For undergraduate study.
Eligibility: Applicant must be residing in Washington. Applicant must be child of veteran, disabled veteran or deceased veteran.
    Amount of award: $300
    Number of awards: 3
    Application deadline: March 11
    Total amount awarded: $900

American Legion Washington Auxiliary Florence Lemcke Fine Arts Scholarship

Type of award: Scholarship.
Intended use: For undergraduate study at 2-year or 4-year institution.
Eligibility: Applicant must be residing in Washington.
Basis for selection: Major/career interest in arts, general.
Additional information: For use in the field of fine arts.
  Amount of award: $500
  Number of awards: 1
  Application deadline: March 11
  Total amount awarded: $500

American Legion Washington Auxiliary Margarite McAlpin Nursing Scholarship

Type of award: Scholarship.
Intended use: For undergraduate study.
Eligibility: Applicant must be residing in Washington. Applicant must be veteran.
Basis for selection: Major/career interest in nursing.
  Amount of award: $700
  Number of awards: 1
  Application deadline: March 11
  Total amount awarded: $700

American Legion Washington Auxiliary Susan Burdett Scholarship

Type of award: Scholarship.
Intended use: For undergraduate study.
Eligibility: Applicant must be female. Applicant must be residing in Washington.
Application requirements: Former Evergreen Girls State Citizen (WA).
  Amount of award: $400
  Number of awards: 1
  Application deadline: March 11
  Total amount awarded: $400
Contact:
American Legion Washington Auxiliary
Education Scholarships
P.O. Box 5867
Lacey, WA 98509-5867

American Legion West Virginia

American Legion West Virginia Oratorical Contest

Type of award: Scholarship.
Intended use: For freshman study in West Virginia.
Eligibility: Applicant must be enrolled in high school. Applicant must be residing in West Virginia.
Basis for selection: Competition in Oratory/debate. Breadth of knowledge, originality, application of knowledge of topic, skill in selecting examples and analogies, logic, voice, diction, style of language, and delivery.
Additional information: There will be nine district awards of $500 and three section awards of $300. The state winner will receive a 4-year scholarship to a WV university or state college under the control of the board of regents. The contest is held in January and February. Information may be obtained from local high school or American Legion Post.
Contact:
American Legion West Virginia
Department Adjutant
2016 Kanawha Boulevard East
Charleston, WV 25332
Phone: 304-343-7591

American Legion West Virginia Auxiliary

American Legion West Virginia Auxiliary Scholarship

Type of award: Scholarship.
Intended use: For freshman, sophomore, junior or senior study at vocational, 2-year or 4-year institution in West Virginia.
Eligibility: Applicant must be residing in West Virginia. Applicant must be child of veteran.
  Number of awards: 4
  Application deadline: March 1
Contact:
American Legion West Virginia Auxiliary
Secretary/Treasurer Mary Rose Yoho
RR 1 Box 144-A
Proctor, WV 26055-9616
Phone: 304-455-3449

American Legion Wisconsin

American Legion Wisconsin Baseball Player of the Year Scholarship

Type of award: Scholarship.
Intended use: For undergraduate study.
Eligibility: Applicant must be residing in Wisconsin.
Application requirements: Nomination. Selected by Board of Directors for the Baseball Program.
  Amount of award: $500
  Number of awards: 1
  Total amount awarded: $500
Contact:
American Legion Wisconsin
812 East State Street
Milwaukee, WI 53202
Phone: 414-271-1940

American Legion Wisconsin Auxiliary

American Legion Wisconsin Auxiliary Badger Girls State Scholarships

Type of award: Scholarship.
Intended use: For undergraduate study.
Eligibility: Applicant must be residing in Wisconsin. Applicant must be descendant of veteran, child of veteran, spouse of veteran or deceased veteran.
Basis for selection: Applicant must demonstrate financial need and high academic achievement.
Additional information: Citizen of WALA Badger Girls State of the previous year. Applications automatically mailed to eligible student each year. Minimum 3.2 GPA required. Grandchildren and Great-grandchildren of veterans eligible if members of American Legion Auxiliary.

Amount of award:	$500
Number of awards:	4
Application deadline:	March 15
Total amount awarded:	$2,000

Contact:
American Legion Wisconsin Auxiliary
Department Headquarters
812 East State Street
Milwaukee 53202-3493

American Legion Wisconsin Auxiliary Child Welfare Scholarship

Type of award: Scholarship.
Intended use: For graduate study.
Eligibility: Applicant must be residing in Wisconsin. Applicant must be spouse of veteran or deceased veteran.
Basis for selection: Major/career interest in education, special.
Application requirements: Transcript.
Additional information: Minimum 3.2 GPA required. Grandchildren and Great-grandchildren of veterans eligible if members of American Legion Auxiliary.

Amount of award:	$1,000
Number of awards:	1
Application deadline:	March 15
Total amount awarded:	$1,000

Contact:
American Legion Wisconsin Auxiliary
Department Headquarters
812 East State Street
Milwaukee, WI 53202-3493

American Legion Wisconsin Auxiliary H.S. and Angeline Lewis Scholarship

Type of award: Scholarship.
Intended use: For undergraduate, master's or doctoral study at accredited postsecondary institution.
Eligibility: Applicant must be residing in Wisconsin. Applicant must be spouse of veteran or deceased veteran.
Basis for selection: Applicant must demonstrate financial need and high academic achievement.
Additional information: One award for graduate study; five awards for undergraduate study.

Amount of award:	$1,000
Number of awards:	6
Application deadline:	March 15
Total amount awarded:	$6,000

Contact:
American Legion Wisconsin Auxiliary
Department Headquarters
812 East State Street
Milwaukee, WI 53202-3493

American Legion Wisconsin Auxiliary Health Careers Award

Type of award: Scholarship.
Intended use: For undergraduate, non-degree study at accredited postsecondary institution.
Eligibility: Applicant must be residing in Wisconsin. Applicant must be child of veteran or deceased veteran, spouse of veteran or deceased veteran.
Basis for selection: Major/career interest in health sciences; health-related professions. Applicant must demonstrate financial need and high academic achievement.
Application requirements: Transcript.
Additional information: Minimum GPA of 3.5 required. Grandchildren or great-grandchildren of veterans must be auxiliary members.

Amount of award:	$750
Number of awards:	2
Application deadline:	March 15
Total amount awarded:	$1,500

Contact:
American Legion Wisconsin Auxiliary
Department Headquarters
812 East State Street
Milwaukee, WI 53202-3493
Phone: 414-271-0124

American Legion Wisconsin Auxiliary King-Hahn Scholarship

Type of award: Scholarship.
Intended use: For undergraduate study.
Eligibility: Applicant must be residing in Wisconsin. Applicant must be spouse of veteran.
Basis for selection: Applicant must demonstrate financial need and high academic achievement.
Application requirements: Transcript.
Additional information: Applications automatically mailed to eligible students each year. Minimum 3.5 GPA required. Grandchildren and great-grandchildren of veterans must be auxiliary members.

Amount of award:	$500
Number of awards:	1
Application deadline:	March 15
Total amount awarded:	$500

Contact:
American Legion Wisconsin Auxiliary
Department Headquarters
812 East State Street
Milwaukee, WI 53202-3493
Phone: 414-271-0124

American Legion Wisconsin Auxiliary M. Louise Wilson Educational Loan

Type of award: Loan.
Intended use: For undergraduate study.
Eligibility: Applicant must be female. Applicant must be residing in Wisconsin. Applicant must be veteran, child of veteran, spouse of veteran during Grenada, Korean War, Lebanon, Panama, Persian Gulf, WW I, WW II or Vietnam.
Basis for selection: Applicant must demonstrate financial need and high academic achievement.
Additional information: $400 annually up to five years. No interest. Repayments begin three months after graduation at minimum of $35 per month.

Amount of award:	$2,000
Application deadline:	March 15
Total amount awarded:	$2,000

Contact:
American Legion Wisconsin Auxiliary
Department Headquarters
812 East State Street
Milwaukee, WI 53202-3493
Phone: 414-271-0124

American Legion Wisconsin Auxiliary Merit and Memorial Scholarship

Type of award: Scholarship.
Intended use: For undergraduate study.
Eligibility: Applicant must be residing in Wisconsin. Applicant must be spouse of veteran or deceased veteran.
Basis for selection: Applicant must demonstrate financial need and high academic achievement.
Application requirements: Transcript.
Additional information: 3.2 GPA required. Grandchildren and great-grandchildren of veterans must be auxiliary members.

Amount of award:	$1,000
Number of awards:	5
Application deadline:	March 15
Total amount awarded:	$5,000

Contact:
American Legion Wisconsin Auxiliary
Department Headquarters
812 East State Street
Milwaukee, WI 53202-3493
Phone: 414-271-0124

American Legion Wisconsin Auxiliary Registered Nurse Degree Award

Type of award: Scholarship.
Intended use: For undergraduate, non-degree study at accredited postsecondary institution.
Eligibility: Applicant must be residing in Wisconsin. Applicant must be child of veteran or deceased veteran, spouse of veteran or deceased veteran.
Basis for selection: Major/career interest in nursing. Applicant must demonstrate financial need and high academic achievement.
Additional information: Minimum 3.5 GPA. Grandchild or great-grandchild of veteran must be auxiliary member. Can be used at accredited hospital nursing program.

Amount of award:	$750
Number of awards:	2
Application deadline:	March 15
Total amount awarded:	$1,500

Contact:
American Legion Wisconsin Auxiliary
Department Headquarters
812 East State Street
Milwaukee, WI 53202-3493
Phone: 414-271-0124

American Legion Wyoming

American Legion Wyoming Oratorical Contest

Type of award: Scholarship.
Intended use: For undergraduate study.
Eligibility: Applicant must be enrolled in high school. Applicant must be residing in Wyoming.
Basis for selection: Competition in Oratory/debate. Breadth of knowledge, originality, application of knowledge of topic, skill in selecting examples and analogies, logic, voice, diction, style of language and delivery.
Application requirements: Proof of eligibility.
Additional information: Topic: U.S. Constitution and citizenship.

Amount of award:	$500
Number of awards:	1
Total amount awarded:	$500

Contact:
American Legion Wyoming
Department Adjutant
P.O. Box 545
Cheyenne, WY 82003
Phone: 307-634-3035
Fax: 307-635-7093

American Legion Wyoming Auxiliary

American Legion Wyoming Auxiliary Past Presidents' Parley Scholarship

Type of award: Scholarship.
Intended use: For undergraduate study at 2-year or 4-year institution.
Eligibility: Applicant must be residing in Wyoming.
Basis for selection: Major/career interest in nursing; health-related professions. Applicant must demonstrate high academic achievement.
Application requirements: Must be in 3rd quarter of training and have 3.0 GPA.

Additional information: Preference given to nursing students that are children of veterans.

Amount of award:	$300
Number of awards:	2
Total amount awarded:	$600

Contact:
American Legion Wyoming Auxiliary
Department Secretary
Torrington, WY 82240

American Library Association

American Library Association Doctoral Dissertation Fellowship

Type of award: Research grant.
Intended use: For doctoral study.
Basis for selection: Major/career interest in library science; computer and information sciences.
Application requirements: Recommendations and research proposal. Curriculum vitae.
Additional information: Must be specializing in academic librarianship area, have completed all course work, and have had dissertation proposal accepted by institution. Research may already have begun in fall term in which applicant is applying. Must submit cover letter from dissertation adviser endorsing research proposal.

Amount of award:	$1,500
Number of awards:	1
Application deadline:	April 1
Total amount awarded:	$1,500

Contact:
American Library Association
Association of College and Research Libraries
50 East Huron Street
Chicago, IL 60611
Phone: 800-545-2433
Website: www.ala.org

Bound to Stay Bound Books Scholarship

Type of award: Scholarship.
Intended use: For master's, doctoral study. Designated institutions: In United States or Canada.
Eligibility: Applicant must be U.S. citizen or Canadian citizen.
Basis for selection: Major/career interest in library science. Applicant must demonstrate leadership and high academic achievement.
Application requirements: Recommendations and essay. Photocopy of acceptance letter from institution.
Additional information: Recipient expected to work directly with children in any type of library for at least one year following completion of educational program. Library science program must be ALA accredited.

Amount of award:	$6,000
Number of awards:	2
Application deadline:	March 1
Total amount awarded:	$12,000

Contact:
American Library Association
Association for Library Service to Children
50 East Huron Street
Chicago, IL 60611
Website: www.ala.org

David H. Clift Scholarship

Type of award: Scholarship.
Intended use: For master's study at accredited graduate institution. Designated institutions: In United States or Canada.
Eligibility: Applicant must be U.S. citizen, permanent resident or Canadian citizen.
Basis for selection: Major/career interest in library science. Applicant must demonstrate leadership, seriousness of purpose and high academic achievement.
Application requirements: Recommendations, essay and transcript.
Additional information: Library science program must be ALA accredited. Applicant must not have completed more than 12 semester hours toward master's degree prior to June 1, 1996.

Amount of award:	$3,000
Number of awards:	1
Application deadline:	April 1
Total amount awarded:	$3,000

Contact:
American Library Association
Staff Liaison - ALA Scholarship Juries
50 East Huron Street
Chicago, IL 60611
Phone: 312-944-6780
Website: www.ala.org

David Rozkuszka Scholarship

Type of award: Scholarship.
Intended use: For master's study.
Basis for selection: Major/career interest in library science. Applicant must demonstrate high academic achievement.
Additional information: Applicant must be currently working in library, specifically with government documents, accepted into ALA accredited master's degree program, and show evidence of commitment to government documents librarianship.

Amount of award:	$3,000
Number of awards:	1
Application deadline:	December 1
Total amount awarded:	$3,000

Contact:
American Library Association
Scholarships Jury
50 East Huron Street
Chicago, IL 60611
Phone: 202-628-8410
Website: www.ala.org

Frederic G. Melcher Scholarship

Type of award: Scholarship.
Intended use: For master's study. Designated institutions: In United States or Canada.
Eligibility: Applicant must be U.S. citizen or Canadian citizen.
Basis for selection: Major/career interest in library science. Applicant must demonstrate leadership and high academic achievement.
Application requirements: Recommendations, essay and transcript. Photocopy of acceptance letter from institution.
Additional information: Library science program must be ALA-accredited. Upon graduation, recipient expected to work with children in any type of library for one year.

Amount of award:	$6,000
Number of awards:	2
Application deadline:	March 1
Total amount awarded:	$12,000

Contact:
American Library Association
Association for Library Service To Children
50 East Huron Street
Chicago, IL 60611
Phone: 800-545-2433
Fax: 312-944-7671
Website: www.ala.org

Library and Information Technology Association/GEAC-CLSI Scholarship

Type of award: Scholarship.
Intended use: For master's study at accredited graduate institution. Designated institutions: In United States or Canada.
Eligibility: Applicant must be U.S. citizen or Canadian citizens.
Basis for selection: Major/career interest in library science. Applicant must demonstrate leadership and high academic achievement.
Application requirements: Recommendations, essay and transcript.
Additional information: Library science program must be ALA accredited. Applicant must specialize in library automation and demonstrate strong commitment to career in library automation and information technology.

Amount of award:	$2,500
Number of awards:	1
Application deadline:	April 1
Total amount awarded:	$2,500

Contact:
American Library Association
Library and Information Technology Association
50 East Huron Street
Chicago, IL 60611
Website: www.ala.org

Library and Information Technology Association/LSSI Minority Scholarship

Type of award: Scholarship.
Intended use: For master's study at accredited graduate institution in Canadian institutions only.
Eligibility: Applicant must be of minority background. Applicant must be U.S. citizen, permanent resident or Canadian citizen.
Basis for selection: Major/career interest in library science. Applicant must demonstrate leadership and high academic achievement.
Application requirements: Recommendations, essay and transcript.
Additional information: Library science program must be ALA accredited. Applicant must specialize in library automation and demonstrate strong commitment to career in library automation and information technology.

Amount of award:	$2,500
Number of awards:	1
Application deadline:	April 1
Total amount awarded:	$2,500

Contact:
American Library Association
Library and Information Technology Association
50 East Huron Street
Chicago, IL 60611
Website: www.ala.org

Library and Information Technology Association/OCLC/Minority Scholarship

Type of award: Scholarship.
Intended use: For master's study at accredited graduate institution. Designated institutions: In United States or Canada.
Eligibility: Applicant must be of minority background. Applicant must be U.S. citizen, permanent resident or Canadian citizen.
Basis for selection: Major/career interest in library science. Applicant must demonstrate leadership and high academic achievement.
Application requirements: Recommendations, essay and transcript.
Additional information: Library science program must be ALA accredited. Applicant must specialize in library automation and demonstrate strong commitment to career in library automation and information technology.

Amount of award:	$2,500
Number of awards:	1
Application deadline:	April 1
Total amount awarded:	$2,500

Contact:
American Library Association
Library and Information Technology Association
50 East Huron Street
Chicago, IL 60611
Website: www.ala.org

Louise Giles Minority Scholarship

Type of award: Scholarship.
Intended use: For master's study at accredited graduate institution. Designated institutions: In United States or Canada.
Eligibility: Applicant must be of minority background. Applicant must be U.S. citizen, permanent resident or Canadian citizen.
Basis for selection: Major/career interest in library science. Applicant must demonstrate leadership, seriousness of purpose and high academic achievement.

Application requirements: Recommendations, essay and transcript.
Additional information: Must not have completed more than 12 semester hours towards a master's degree in library science prior to June 1, 1996.

Amount of award:	$3,000
Application deadline:	April 1
Total amount awarded:	$3,000

Contact:
American Library Association
Staff Liaison - ALA Scholarship Juries
50 East Huron Street
Chicago, IL 60611
Phone: 312-944-6780
Fax: 312-280-3256
Website: www.ala.org

American Liver Foundation

American Liver Foundation Postdoctoral Fellowship

Type of award: Research grant, renewable.
Intended use: For full-time doctoral, postgraduate study at accredited 4-year or graduate institution in United States.
Basis for selection: Major/career interest in medical specialties/research. Applicant must demonstrate depth of character, leadership, seriousness of purpose and service orientation.
Application requirements: Proof of eligibility and research proposal.
Additional information: This award is distributed during one year to qualifying postdoctoral candidates doing research in an accredited U.S. institution. Research proposal must be complete to qualify and research project can have already begun. This award qualifies as salary support.

Amount of award:	$10,000
Number of awards:	15
Application deadline:	January 15
Total amount awarded:	$1,000,000

Liver Scholar Award

Type of award: Research grant, renewable.
Intended use: For full-time master's, doctoral study at accredited 4-year or graduate institution in United States.
Basis for selection: Major/career interest in medical specialties/research. Applicant must demonstrate depth of character, leadership, seriousness of purpose and service orientation.
Application requirements: Recommendations, proof of eligibility and research proposal.
Additional information: This award is distributed over three years to qualifying junior faculty members doing research in an accredited U.S. institution. Research proposal must be complete to qualify and research project can have already begun. This award qualifies as salary support.

Amount of award:	$90,000
Number of awards:	15
Application deadline:	January 15
Total amount awarded:	$1,000,000

Physician's Research Development Grant

Type of award: Research grant, renewable.
Intended use: For full-time doctoral, postgraduate study at accredited 4-year or graduate institution in United States.
Basis for selection: Major/career interest in medical specialties/research. Applicant must demonstrate depth of character, leadership, seriousness of purpose and service orientation.
Application requirements: Recommendations, proof of eligibility and research proposal.
Additional information: This award is distributed during one year to qualifying physicians doing research in an accredited U.S. institution. Research proposal must be complete to qualify and research project can have already begun. This award qualifies as salary support.

Amount of award:	$200,000
Number of awards:	15
Application deadline:	January 15
Total amount awarded:	$1,000,000

Student Research Grant

Type of award: Research grant, renewable.
Intended use: For full-time first professional study at accredited 4-year or graduate institution in United States.
Basis for selection: Major/career interest in medical specialties/research. Applicant must demonstrate depth of character, leadership, seriousness of purpose and service orientation.
Application requirements: Proof of eligibility and research proposal.
Additional information: This award is distributed during one year to qualifying medical school students with clearance to do research in an accredited U.S. institution. Research proposal must be complete to qualify and research project can have already begun.

Amount of award:	$2,500
Application deadline:	January 15

Contact:
American Liver Foundation
1425 Pompton Avenue
Cedar Grove, NJ 07009

American Lung Association

Lung Association Career Investigator Award

Type of award: Research grant, renewable.
Intended use: For postgraduate study. Designated institutions: In United States or Canada.
Eligibility: Applicant must be U.S. citizen, permanent resident or Canadian citizens.
Basis for selection: Major/career interest in medical specialties/research; health sciences. Applicant must demonstrate high academic achievement.
Application requirements: Recommendations and research proposal.
Additional information: Must be M.D. or D.O. or have

doctoral degree in scientific discipline relevant to lung disease. Not available to full professors or those with more than eight years faculty experience. Awards are $35,000/year, may be renewed for up to two additional years.

Amount of award:	$35,000
Number of applicants:	44
Application deadline:	October 1

Contact:
American Lung Association
Research Program Administration
1740 Broadway
New York, NY 10019-4374
Website: www.lungusa.org

Lung Association Clinical Research Grant

Type of award: Research grant, renewable.
Intended use: For postgraduate study at graduate institution in United States.
Eligibility: Applicant must be U.S. citizen, permanent resident or Canadian citizens.
Basis for selection: Major/career interest in medical specialties/research; social and behavioral sciences; health sciences. Applicant must demonstrate high academic achievement.
Application requirements: Research proposal.
Additional information: Applicant must hold doctoral degree, faculty appointment with academic institution, and have completed two years of research training. These grants are for investigators working in clinical areas rlevant to lung disease. Awards are up to $25,000/year, may be renewed for up to one additional year.

Amount of award:	$25,000
Application deadline:	November 1

Contact:
American Lung Association
Research Program Administration
1740 Broadway
New York, NY 10019-4374
Website: www.lungusa.org

Lung Association Dalsemer Research Dissertation Grant

Type of award: Research grant, renewable.
Intended use: For postgraduate study.
Basis for selection: Major/career interest in medical specialties/research (beyond m.d.). Applicant must demonstrate high academic achievement.
Application requirements: Research proposal.
Additional information: Applicant must be physician who has completed graduate training in pulmonary disease and is beginning a faculty track in school of medicine. Award is intended to support research in interstitial lung disease. Award is up to $25,000/year, may be renewed for up to one additional year.

Amount of award:	$25,000
Application deadline:	November 1

Contact:
American Lung Association
Research Programs Administration
1740 Broadway
New York, NY 10019-4374
Website: www.lungusa.org

Lung Association Research Grant

Type of award: Research grant, renewable.
Intended use: For full-time postgraduate study at graduate institution in United States.
Eligibility: Applicant must be U.S. citizen, permanent resident or Canadian citizens.
Basis for selection: Major/career interest in medical specialties/research; social and behavioral sciences; health sciences. Applicant must demonstrate high academic achievement.
Application requirements: Research proposal.
Additional information: Must be instructor or assistant professor and have completed at least two years of research training. Grants provide seed money to new investigators working in areas relevant to the conquest of lung disease and promotion of lung health. Awards are up to $25,000/year, may be renewed for one additional year.

Amount of award:	$25,000
Number of applicants:	222
Application deadline:	November 1

Contact:
American Lung Association
Research Program Administration
1740 Broadway
New York, NY 10019-4374

Lung Association Research Training Fellowship

Type of award: Research grant, renewable.
Intended use: For full-time postgraduate study. Designated institutions: In United States or Canada.
Eligibility: Applicant must be U.S. citizen or permanent resident.
Basis for selection: Major/career interest in medical specialties/research. Applicant must demonstrate high academic achievement.
Application requirements: Recommendations and research proposal.
Additional information: Must be M.D., D.O., Ph.D., Sc.D., or equivalent. Candidates with other doctoral degrees eligible if interested in further training as scientific investigators in field relevant to prevention and control of lung disease. Awards are $32,500/year, may be renewed for one additional year.

Amount of award:	$32,500
Number of applicants:	106
Application deadline:	October 1

Contact:
American Lung Association
Research Programs Administration
1740 Broadway
New York, NY 10019-4374
Website: www.lungusa.org

Lung Health Research Dissertation Grant

Type of award: Research grant, renewable.
Intended use: For full-time doctoral study at graduate institution in United States.
Eligibility: Applicant must be U.S. citizen, permanent resident or Canadian citizens.
Basis for selection: Major/career interest in social and

behavioral sciences; health sciences; medical specialties/research; nursing. Applicant must demonstrate high academic achievement.
Application requirements: Research proposal.
Additional information: Must be doctoral student in field of science related to social, behavioral, epidemiological, psychological, and educational aspects of lung health. Nurses pursuing doctoral degree in any field in lung disease may apply. Individuals with an MD seeking a PhD are not eligible. Awards are up to $21,000/year/ and may be renewed for up to three years.

Amount of award:	$21,000
Number of applicants:	5
Application deadline:	October 1

Contact:
American Lung Association
research Program Administration
1740 Broadway
New York, NY 10019-4374
Website: www.lungusa.org

American Medical Technologists

Medical Technologists Scholarship

Type of award: Scholarship.
Intended use: For full-time undergraduate or graduate study at accredited postsecondary institution.
Eligibility: Applicant must be high school senior. Applicant must be permanent resident.
Basis for selection: Major/career interest in medical assistant; dental assistant. Applicant must demonstrate depth of character, leadership, service orientation, financial need and high academic achievement.
Application requirements: Recommendations, essay and transcript.
Additional information: Other major fields of study include medical technology, medical laboratory technician, phlebotomy or physician office laboratory.

Amount of award:	$250
Number of awards:	5
Number of applicants:	140
Application deadline:	April 1
Total amount awarded:	$250

Contact:
American Medical Technologists
710 Higgins Road
Park Ridge, IL 60068
Phone: 847-823-5169

American Medical Women's Association

Medical Women's Wilhelm-Frankowski Scholarship

Type of award: Scholarship.
Intended use: For full-time first professional study in United States.
Eligibility: Applicant must be female. Applicant must be U.S. citizen or permanent resident.
Basis for selection: Major/career interest in medicine (m.d,); medicine, osteopathic. Applicant must demonstrate service orientation.
Application requirements: First, second and third year students only.
Additional information: Criteria include community service; work, research and participation in women's health isues; participation in AMWA activities, participation in women in medicine or medical student groups other than AMWA.

Amount of award:	$4,000
Application deadline:	April 30

Contact:
American Medical Women's Association
Wilhelm-Frankowski Scholarship-American Medical Women's Association
801 North Fairfax Street, Suite 400
Alexandria, VA 22314
Phone: 703-838-0500
Fax: 703-549-3864

American Meteorological Society

Meteorological Society Father James B. MacElwane Annual Award

Type of award: Scholarship.
Intended use: For undergraduate study.
Eligibility: Applicant must be U.S. citizen or permanent resident.
Basis for selection: Competition in Writing/journalism. Major/career interest in atmospheric sciences/meteorology.
Application requirements: Transcript.
Additional information: Must submit atmospheric science research project description. Must have been undergraduate student when research was conducted and paper written; submit letter verifying this from department chair or adviser. Request application after November 1.

Amount of award:	$300
Number of awards:	1
Application deadline:	June 13
Notification begins:	October 31
Total amount awarded:	$300

Contact:
American Meteorological Society
Scholarship Coordinator
45 Beacon Street
Boston, MA 02108-3693

Meteorological Society Industry Graduate Fellowship

Type of award: Scholarship.
Intended use: For full-time master's study at accredited 4-year institution in United States.
Eligibility: Applicant must be U.S. citizen or permanent resident.
Basis for selection: Major/career interest in atmospheric sciences/meteorology; oceanography/marine studies; engineering, environmental; environmental science. Applicant must demonstrate high academic achievement.
Application requirements: Recommendations, essay, transcript and proof of eligibility. GRE scores.
Additional information: Must be entering first year of graduate study.

Amount of award:	$15,000
Number of awards:	12
Number of applicants:	70
Application deadline:	February 16
Notification begins:	April 30
Total amount awarded:	$180,000

Contact:
American Meteorological Society
Fellowship Coordinator
45 Beacon Street
Boston, MA 02108-3693
Website: www.ametsoc.org/ams

Meteorological Society Industry Undergraduate Scholarship

Type of award: Scholarship, renewable.
Intended use: For full-time junior, senior study at accredited 4-year institution in United States.
Eligibility: Applicant must be U.S. citizen or permanent resident.
Basis for selection: Major/career interest in atmospheric sciences/meteorology; oceanography/marine studies; environmental science; engineering, environmental. Applicant must demonstrate high academic achievement.
Application requirements: Recommendations, essay, transcript and proof of eligibility. GRE Scores.
Additional information: Must have minimum 3.0 GPA. Second year funding dependent upon academic performance and faculty adviser recommendation.

Amount of award:	$4,000
Number of applicants:	60
Application deadline:	February 23
Notification begins:	May 1
Total amount awarded:	$72,000

Contact:
American Meteorological Society
Scholarship Coordinator
45 Beacon Street
Boston, MA 02108-3693
Website: www.ametsoc.org/ams

Meteorological Society Minority Scholarship

Type of award: Scholarship.
Intended use: For full-time freshman, sophomore study at accredited 4-year institution in United States.
Eligibility: Applicant must be of minority background. Applicant must be high school senior. Applicant must be U.S. citizen or permanent resident.
Basis for selection: Major/career interest in atmospheric sciences/meteorology; oceanography/marine studies; engineering, environmental; environmental science. Applicant must demonstrate high academic achievement.
Application requirements: Recommendations, essay, transcript and proof of eligibility. SAT scores.
Additional information: Second year funding dependent upon successful completion of first academic year.

Amount of award:	$6,000
Number of applicants:	40
Application deadline:	January 30
Notification begins:	April 1
Total amount awarded:	$30,000

Contact:
American Meteorological Society
Fellowship Coordinator
45 Beacon Street
Boston, MA 02108-3693
Website: www.ametsoc.org/ams

Meteorological Society Undergraduate Scholarship

Type of award: Scholarship.
Intended use: For full-time senior study at accredited 4-year institution in United States.
Eligibility: Applicant must be U.S. citizen or permanent resident.
Basis for selection: Major/career interest in atmospheric sciences/meteorology; oceanography/marine studies; environmental science; engineering, environmental. Applicant must demonstrate high academic achievement.
Application requirements: Recommendations, essay, transcript and proof of eligibility.
Additional information: Minimum 3.0 GPA required.

Amount of award:	$700-$5,000
Number of awards:	7
Number of applicants:	50
Application deadline:	June 14
Notification begins:	October 1
Total amount awarded:	$18,000

Contact:
American Meteorological Society
Scholarship Coordinator
45 Beacon Street
Boston, MA 02108-3693
Phone: 617-227-2426
Fax: 617-742-8718
Website: www.ametsoc.org/ams

American Morgan Horse Institute

Van Schaik Dressage Scholarship

Type of award: Scholarship, renewable.
Intended use: For non-degree study.

Basis for selection: Major/career interest in dressage. Applicant must demonstrate seriousness of purpose.
Application requirements: Recommendations, essay and proof of eligibility.
Additional information: Applicant must be studying dressage, and must be a dressage rider using a Morgan horse. Send SASE for application.

Amount of award:	$1,000
Number of awards:	1
Number of applicants:	50
Application deadline:	December 1
Notification begins:	January 2
Total amount awarded:	$1,000

Contact:
American Morgan Horse Institute, Inc.
Van Schaik Dressage Scholarships c/o AMHA P.O. Box 960
Shelburne, VT 05482-0519
Phone: 802-985-4944
Website: www.morganhorse.com

Youth Scholarship

Type of award: Scholarship.
Intended use: For full-time undergraduate study.
Basis for selection: Applicant must demonstrate depth of character, leadership, seriousness of purpose, service orientation and high academic achievement.
Application requirements: Recommendations, essay and transcript. Achievement with horses.
Additional information: Application requests must include a SASE.

Amount of award:	$3,000
Number of awards:	5
Number of applicants:	200
Application deadline:	March 1
Notification begins:	May 1
Total amount awarded:	$15,000

Contact:
American Morgan Horse Institute, Inc.
P.O. Box 837
Shelburne, VT 05482-0519
Phone: 802-985-8477
Fax: 802-985-8430

American Museum of Natural History

American Museum of Natural History Graduate Student Fellowship Program

Type of award: Research grant, renewable.
Intended use: For master's, doctoral study at graduate institution in United States.
Basis for selection: Major/career interest in paleontology; entomology. Applicant must demonstrate seriousness of purpose and high academic achievement.
Application requirements: Interview, recommendations, transcript and research proposal.
Additional information: Applicants must have a bachelors degree. Must apply to the Museum and to one of four cooperating universities depending on field of study. These universities are Columbia, Cornell, City University of New York and Yale University.

American Museum of Natural History Research Fellowships

Type of award: Research grant.
Intended use: For first professional study.
Basis for selection: Major/career interest in zoology; paleontology; ornithology; anthropology.
Application requirements: Research proposal.
Additional information: Provides support to recent postdoctoral investigators and established scientists to carry out a specific project within a limited time period. Appointment as a Research Fellow is usually for one year, but two-year appointments are possible in the fields of vertebrae paleontology and ornithology.

Amount of award:	$29,000
Application deadline:	January 15

Collection Study Grants

Type of award: Research grant.
Intended use: For doctoral, first professional study.
Basis for selection: Major/career interest in anthropology; entomology.
Application requirements: Recommendations and research proposal.
Additional information: Award partially supports travel and expenses while visiting the museum. Applicant should submit application forms at least 2 months prior to intended visit.

Amount of award:	$500-$800

Frank M. Chapman Memorial Grants

Type of award: Research grant.
Intended use: For doctoral study.
Basis for selection: Major/career interest in zoology; paleontology; anthropology; ornithology. Applicant must demonstrate seriousness of purpose and high academic achievement.
Application requirements: Recommendations and research proposal.
Additional information: The Memorial Grants support research in orinthology, both neontological and paleontological. Candidates will not receive support from more than one grant for the same project during the same grant year.

Amount of award:	$200-$2,000
Application deadline:	January 15

International Graduate Student Fellowship

Type of award: Scholarship, renewable.
Intended use: For full-time doctoral study at accredited graduate institution in United States.
Basis for selection: Major/career interest in environmental science. Applicant must demonstrate seriousness of purpose and high academic achievement.
Application requirements: Recommendations and transcript.
Additional information: Provides an opportunity for non-U.S.

citizens to study a diversified curriculum in biodiversity, conservation, systematics and public policy. Students are able to choose among offering of 4 major universities to create a graduate program. Fellowship provides travel assistance, stipend support for 12 months and tuition. Applications are encouraged from students from developing countries. Colleges that museum cooperates with are Columbia University, City University of New York, Yale University and Cornell University. Application to university is based on field of interest.

Lerner-Gray Grants for Marine Research

Type of award: Research grant.
Intended use: For doctoral study.
Basis for selection: Major/career interest in zoology; paleontology; anthropology. Applicant must demonstrate seriousness of purpose.
Application requirements: Recommendations and research proposal.
Additional information: Awards are not made to support research in botany and biochemistry. Candidates will not receive support from more than one grant for the same project during the same grant year.
   Amount of award: $200-$2,000
   Application deadline: March 15

Research Experiences for Undergraduates

Type of award: Internship.
Intended use: For undergraduate study at accredited 4-year institution in United States.
Eligibility: Applicant must be U.S. citizen.
Basis for selection: Major/career interest in science, general; biology. Applicant must demonstrate seriousness of purpose and high academic achievement.
Application requirements: Recommendations and essay.
Additional information: Must have strong science background. Travel and research expenses reimbursed.
   Amount of award: $3,000
   Number of awards: 4
   Number of applicants: 65
   Application deadline: April 18
   Notification begins: May 1

Theodore Roosevelt Memorial Grants

Type of award: Research grant.
Intended use: For graduate study.
Basis for selection: Major/career interest in zoology; paleontology; anthropology. Applicant must demonstrate seriousness of purpose and high academic achievement.
Application requirements: Recommendations and research proposal.
Additional information: Projects dealing with ornithology should be submitted to The Frank M. Chapman Memorial Grants. Candidates will not receive support from more than one grant for the same project during the same grant year.
   Amount of award: $200-$2,000
   Application deadline: February 15
Contact:
American Museum of Natural History
Central Park West at 79th Street
New York, NY 10024-5192
Website: www.amnh.org

American Nuclear Society

American Nuclear Society Environmental Sciences Division Scholarship

Type of award: Scholarship, renewable.
Intended use: For full-time sophomore, junior or senior study at accredited 4-year institution.
Eligibility: Applicant must be male. Applicant must be U.S. citizen or permanent resident.
Basis for selection: Major/career interest in nuclear science; engineering, nuclear. Applicant must demonstrate depth of character, leadership, seriousness of purpose, service orientation and high academic achievement.
Application requirements: Recommendations, transcript and proof of eligibility.
Additional information: Application available online.
   Application deadline: March 1
Contact:
American Nuclear Society
555 North Kensington Avenue
La Grange Park, IL 60526
Website: www.ans.org

American Nuclear Society Washington Internship for Students of Engineering

Type of award: Internship.
Intended use: For junior study.
Eligibility: Applicant must be U.S. citizen or permanent resident.
Basis for selection: Major/career interest in engineering, nuclear; political science/government. Applicant must demonstrate high academic achievement.
Application requirements: Recommendations, transcript and proof of eligibility.
Additional information: Sixteen outstanding students will compete for two ten-week intern positions located in Washington, D.C. The internship is geared toward understanding how government officials/engineers work together in making legislative/regulatory policy decisions.
   Number of awards: 16
Contact:
American Nuclear Society
555 North Kensington Avenue
La Grange Park, IL 60526
Website: www.ans.org

Angelo S. Biseti Scholarship

Type of award: Scholarship, renewable.
Intended use: For full-time sophomore, junior or senior study at accredited 4-year institution.
Eligibility: Applicant must be U.S. citizen or permanent resident.
Basis for selection: Major/career interest in nuclear science; engineering, nuclear. Applicant must demonstrate depth of character, leadership, seriousness of purpose, service orientation, financial need and high academic achievement.
Application requirements: Recommendations, transcript and proof of eligibility.
Additional information: Application is available online.
   Application deadline: March 1
Contact:
American Nuclear Society
555 North Kensington Avenue
La Grange Park, IL 60526
Phone: 708-352-6611
Website: www.ans.org

Delayed Education Scholarship for Women

Type of award: Scholarship, renewable.
Intended use: For undergraduate study at accredited 4-year institution.
Eligibility: Applicant must be female. Applicant must be U.S. citizen or permanent resident.
Basis for selection: Major/career interest in nuclear science; engineering, nuclear. Applicant must demonstrate financial need and high academic achievement.
Application requirements: Interview, transcript and proof of eligibility.
Additional information: Application available online. This award is for mature women who have had a delay in their education in field of Nuclear Science and Engineering. One request and one application cover the D.E.W.S. Award and The John and Muriel Landis Award.
   Application deadline: March 1
Contact:
American Nuclear Society
555 Norh Kensington Avenue
La Grange Park, IL 60526
Website: www.ans.org

Everitt P. Blizard Scholarship

Type of award: Scholarship, renewable.
Intended use: For full-time master's, doctoral study at accredited graduate institution.
Eligibility: Applicant must be U.S. citizen or permanent resident.
Basis for selection: Major/career interest in nuclear science; engineering, nuclear. Applicant must demonstrate depth of character, leadership, seriousness of purpose, service orientation, financial need and high academic achievement.
Application requirements: Recommendations, transcript and proof of eligibility.
Additional information: Applicant must be studying radiation protection of shielding. Application available online.
   Application deadline: March 1
Contact:
American Nuclear Society
555 North Kensington Avenue
La Grange Park, IL 60526
Website: www.ans.org

Fuel Cycle and Waste Management

Type of award: Scholarship, renewable.
Intended use: For full-time sophomore, junior or senior study at accredited 4-year institution.
Eligibility: Applicant must be U.S. citizen or permanent resident.
Basis for selection: Major/career interest in nuclear science; engineering, nuclear. Applicant must demonstrate depth of character, leadership, seriousness of purpose, service orientation, financial need and high academic achievement.
Application requirements: Recommendations, transcript and proof of eligibility.
Additional information: Application available online.
   Application deadline: March 1
Contact:
American Nuclear Society
555 North Kensington Avenue
La Grange Park, IL 60526
Website: www.ans.org

James F. Schumar Scholarship

Type of award: Scholarship, renewable.
Intended use: For full-time post-bachelor's certificate, master's study at accredited graduate institution.
Eligibility: Applicant must be U.S. citizen or permanent resident.
Basis for selection: Major/career interest in materials science; nuclear science; engineering, nuclear. Applicant must demonstrate depth of character, leadership, seriousness of purpose, service orientation, financial need and high academic achievement.
Application requirements: Recommendations, transcript and proof of eligibility.
Additional information: Applicant must be studying materials science and technologies for nuclear applications. Application available online.
   Application deadline: March 1
Contact:
American Nuclear Society
555 North Kensington Avenue
La Grange Park, IL 60526
Website: www.ans.org

James R. Vogt Scholarship

Type of award: Scholarship, renewable.
Intended use: For full-time freshman, sophomore, junior, senior, master's or doctoral study at accredited 4-year or graduate institution.
Eligibility: Applicant must be U.S. citizen or permanent resident.
Basis for selection: Major/career interest in nuclear science. Applicant must demonstrate depth of character, leadership, seriousness of purpose, service orientation, financial need and high academic achievement.

Application requirements: Recommendations, transcript and proof of eligibility.
Additional information: Application available online. Applicants must be enrolled or proposing to enroll in a radioanalytical, analytical chemistry or analytical applications of nuclear science.
　Application deadline:　　March 1
Contact:
American Nuclear Society
555 North Kensington Avenue
La Grange Park, IL 60526
Website: www.ans.org

John and Muriel Landis Scholarship

Type of award: Scholarship.
Intended use: For undergraduate, master's or doctoral study at accredited 4-year or graduate institution in United States.
Eligibility: Applicant must be U.S. citizen or permanent resident.
Basis for selection: Major/career interest in nuclear science; engineering, nuclear. Applicant must demonstrate depth of character, leadership, seriousness of purpose, service orientation, financial need and high academic achievement.
Application requirements: Recommendations, transcript and proof of eligibility.
Additional information: Application available online.
　Number of awards:　　8
　Application deadline:　　March 1
Contact:
555 North Kensington Avenue
La Grange Park, IL 60526
Phone: 708-352-6611
Website: www.ans.org

John R. Lamarsh Scholarship

Type of award: Scholarship, renewable.
Intended use: For full-time sophomore, junior or senior study at accredited 4-year institution.
Eligibility: Applicant must be U.S. citizen or permanent resident.
Basis for selection: Major/career interest in nuclear science; engineering, nuclear. Applicant must demonstrate depth of character, leadership, seriousness of purpose, service orientation, financial need and high academic achievement.
Application requirements: Recommendations, transcript and proof of eligibility.
Additional information: Application available online.
　Application deadline:　　March 1
Contact:
American Nuclear Society
555 North Kensington Avenue
La Grange Park, IL 60526
Website: www.ans.org

John Randall Scholarship

Type of award: Scholarship, renewable.
Intended use: For full-time master's, doctoral study at accredited graduate institution.
Eligibility: Applicant must be U.S. citizen or permanent resident.
Basis for selection: Major/career interest in nuclear science; engineering, nuclear. Applicant must demonstrate depth of character, leadership, seriousness of purpose, service orientation, financial need and high academic achievement.
Application requirements: Recommendations, transcript and proof of eligibility.
Additional information: Application available online.
　Application deadline:　　March 1
Contact:
American Nuclear Society
555 North Kensington Avenue
La Grange Park, IL 60526
Website: www.ans.org

Joseph R. Dietrich Scholarship

Type of award: Scholarship, renewable.
Intended use: For full-time sophomore, junior or senior study at accredited 4-year institution.
Eligibility: Applicant must be U.S. citizen or permanent resident.
Basis for selection: Major/career interest in nuclear science; engineering, nuclear. Applicant must demonstrate depth of character, leadership, seriousness of purpose, service orientation, financial need and high academic achievement.
Application requirements: Recommendations, transcript and proof of eligibility.
Additional information: Application available online.
　Application deadline:　　March 1
Contact:
American Nuclear Society
555 North Kensington Avenue
La Grange Park, IL 60526
Website: www.ans.org

Nuclear Operations Division Scholarship

Type of award: Scholarship, renewable.
Intended use: For full-time sophomore, junior or senior study at accredited 4-year institution.
Eligibility: Applicant must be U.S. citizen or permanent resident.
Basis for selection: Major/career interest in nuclear science; engineering, nuclear. Applicant must demonstrate depth of character, leadership, seriousness of purpose, service orientation, financial need and high academic achievement.
Application requirements: Recommendations, transcript and proof of eligibility.
Additional information: Application available online.
　Application deadline:　　March 1
Contact:
American Nuclear Society
555 North Kensington Avenue
La Grange Park, IL 60526
Website: www.ans.org

Paul A. Greebler Scholarship

Type of award: Scholarship, renewable.
Intended use: For full-time master's, doctoral study at accredited graduate institution.
Eligibility: Applicant must be U.S. citizen or permanent resident.
Basis for selection: Major/career interest in physics; nuclear

science; engineering, nuclear. Applicant must demonstrate depth of character, leadership, seriousness of purpose, service orientation, financial need and high academic achievement.
Application requirements: Recommendations, transcript and proof of eligibility.
Additional information: Application is available online.
   Application deadline: March 1
Contact:
American Nuclear Society
555 North Kensington Avenue
La Grange Park, IL 60526
Website: www.ans.org

Pittsburgh Local Section of the James R. Vogt Scholarship

Type of award: Scholarship.
Intended use: For full-time freshman, sophomore, junior, senior, master's or doctoral study at accredited 4-year or graduate institution.
Eligibility: Applicant must be U.S. citizen or permanent resident.
Basis for selection: Major/career interest in nuclear science. Applicant must demonstrate depth of character, leadership, seriousness of purpose, service orientation, financial need and high academic achievement.
Application requirements: Recommendations, transcript and proof of eligibility.
Additional information: Application is available online. Applicants must live in Western Pennsylvania and be enrolled or have proposed to enroll in radio-analytical chemistry, or analytical chemistry or analytical applications of nuclear science program.
   Number of applicants: 1
   Application deadline: March 1
Contact:
American Nuclear Society
555 North Kensington Avenue
La Grange Park, IL 60526
Website: www.ans.org

Power Division Scholarship

Type of award: Scholarship, renewable.
Intended use: For full-time sophomore, junior or senior study at accredited 4-year institution.
Eligibility: Applicant must be U.S. citizen or permanent resident.
Basis for selection: Major/career interest in nuclear science; engineering, nuclear. Applicant must demonstrate depth of character, leadership, seriousness of purpose, service orientation, financial need and high academic achievement.
Application requirements: Recommendations, transcript and proof of eligibility.
Additional information: Application available online.
   Application deadline: March 1
Contact:
American Nuclear Society
555 North Kensington Avenue
La Grange Park, IL 60526
Website: www.ans.org

Raymond DiSalvo Scholarship

Type of award: Scholarship, renewable.
Intended use: For full-time sophomore, junior or senior study at accredited 4-year institution.
Eligibility: Applicant must be U.S. citizen or permanent resident.
Basis for selection: Major/career interest in nuclear science; engineering, nuclear. Applicant must demonstrate depth of character, leadership, seriousness of purpose, service orientation, financial need and high academic achievement.
Application requirements: Recommendations, transcript and proof of eligibility.
Additional information: Application available online.
   Application deadline: March 1
Contact:
American Nuclear Society
555 North Kensington Avenue
La Grange Park, IL 60526
Website: www.ans.org

Robert A. Dannels Scholarship

Type of award: Scholarship, renewable.
Intended use: For full-time master's, doctoral study at accredited graduate institution.
Eligibility: Applicant must be U.S. citizen or permanent resident.
Basis for selection: Major/career interest in nuclear science; engineering, nuclear. Applicant must demonstrate depth of character, leadership, seriousness of purpose, service orientation, financial need and high academic achievement.
Application requirements: Recommendations, transcript and proof of eligibility.
Additional information: Handicapped applicants are strongly encouraged. Application available online.
   Application deadline: March 1
Contact:
American Nuclear Society
555 North Kensington Avenue
La Grange Park, IL 60526
Website: www.ans.org

Robert G. Lacey Scholarship

Type of award: Scholarship, renewable.
Intended use: For full-time sophomore, junior or senior study at accredited 4-year institution.
Eligibility: Applicant must be U.S. citizen or permanent resident.
Basis for selection: Major/career interest in nuclear science; engineering, nuclear. Applicant must demonstrate depth of character, leadership, seriousness of purpose, service orientation, financial need and high academic achievement.
Application requirements: Recommendations, transcript and proof of eligibility.
Additional information: Application available online.
   Application deadline: March 1
Contact:
American Nuclear Society
555 North Kensington Avenue
La Grange Park, IL 60526
Website: www.ans.org/membership/services/scholarships.html

Robert T. Liner Scholarship

Type of award: Scholarship, renewable.
Intended use: For full-time sophomore, senior or post-bachelor's certificate study at accredited 4-year institution.
Eligibility: Applicant must be U.S. citizen or permanent resident.
Basis for selection: Major/career interest in nuclear science; engineering, nuclear. Applicant must demonstrate depth of character, leadership, seriousness of purpose, service orientation, financial need and high academic achievement.
Application requirements: Recommendations, transcript and proof of eligibility.
Additional information: Application available online.
   Application deadline: March 1
Contact:
American Nuclear Society
555 North Kensington Avenue
La Grange Park, IL 60526
Website: www.ans.org

Verne R. Dapp Scholarship

Type of award: Scholarship, renewable.
Intended use: For full-time master's, doctoral study at accredited graduate institution.
Eligibility: Applicant must be U.S. citizen or permanent resident.
Basis for selection: Major/career interest in nuclear science; engineering, nuclear. Applicant must demonstrate depth of character, leadership, seriousness of purpose, service orientation, financial need and high academic achievement.
Application requirements: Recommendations, transcript and proof of eligibility.
Additional information: This award is only offered in odd years. Application available online.
   Application deadline: March 1
Contact:
American Nuclear Society
555 North Kensington Avenue
La Grange Park, IL 60526
Website: www.ans.org

Walter Meyer Scholarship

Type of award: Scholarship, renewable.
Intended use: For full-time master's, doctoral study at accredited graduate institution.
Eligibility: Applicant must be U.S. citizen or permanent resident.
Basis for selection: Major/career interest in nuclear science; engineering, nuclear. Applicant must demonstrate depth of character, leadership, seriousness of purpose, service orientation, financial need and high academic achievement.
Application requirements: Recommendations, transcript and proof of eligibility.
Additional information: Application available online. This award is only offered in even years.
   Application deadline: March 1
Contact:
American Nuclear Society
555 North Kensington Avenue
La Grange Park, IL 60526
Website: www.ans.org

American Numismatic Society

American Numismatic Society Fellowship in Roman Studies

Type of award: Scholarship.
Intended use: For full-time undergraduate or graduate study.
Eligibility: Applicant must be U.S. citizen.
Basis for selection: Major/career interest in classics; history; archaeology. Applicant must demonstrate high academic achievement.
Application requirements: Recommendations, transcript, proof of eligibility and research proposal.
Additional information: Preference given to applicants seeking advanced degrees. Fellowship is intended to support extended residence in New York and work in the society's cabinet and library.
   Amount of award: $5,000
   Number of awards: 1
   Number of applicants: 5
   Application deadline: March 1
   Notification begins: April 1
Contact:
The American Numismatic Society
Broadway at 155th Street
New York, NY 10032
Phone: 212-234-3130
Fax: 212-234-3381
Website: www.amnumsoc2.org

American Numismatic Society Frances M. Schwartz Fellowship

Type of award: Scholarship.
Intended use: For full-time graduate study. Designated institutions: American Numismatic Society.
Basis for selection: Major/career interest in museum studies.
Application requirements: Recommendations, essay and transcript.
Additional information: Award amount varies up to $2,000.
   Amount of award: $2,000
   Application deadline: March 1
   Notification begins: April 1
Contact:
The American Numismatic Society
Broadway at 155 Street
New York, NY 10032
Phone: 212-234-3130
Fax: 212-234-3381
Website: www.amnumsoc2.org

American Numismatic Society Shaykh Hamad Fellowship in Islamic Numismatics

Type of award: Scholarship.
Intended use: For full-time undergraduate or graduate study. Designated institutions: American Numismatic Society.
Basis for selection: Major/career interest in history; art, art

history; archaeology. Applicant must demonstrate high academic achievement.
Application requirements: Recommendations and essay.
Additional information: Applicants are expected to have some graduate-level training in medieval near eastern history or a related field as well as some knowledge of Arabic.

Amount of award:	$3,000
Number of awards:	1
Number of applicants:	4
Application deadline:	March 1
Notification begins:	April 1
Total amount awarded:	$3,000

Contact:
The American Numismatic Society
Broadway at 155 Street
New York, NY 10032
Phone: 212-234-3130
Fax: 212-234-3381
Website: www.amnumsoc2.org

Numismatic Graduate Fellowship

Type of award: Research grant.
Intended use: For doctoral study at graduate institution in United States.
Eligibility: Applicant must be U.S. citizen or permanent resident.
Basis for selection: Major/career interest in classics; history; art, art history; archaeology. Applicant must demonstrate high academic achievement.
Application requirements: Recommendations, transcript and research proposal. Must have attended one of Society's Graduate Seminars, but requirement may be waived in exceptional circumstances.
Additional information: Must have completed general examination (or equivalent) for doctorate and be writing dissertation in which numismatic evidence plays significant part.

Amount of award:	$3,500
Number of awards:	1
Number of applicants:	5
Application deadline:	March 1
Notification begins:	April 1
Total amount awarded:	$3,500

Contact:
American Numismatic Society
Broadway at 155 Street
New York, NY 10032
Phone: 212-234-3130
Website: www.amnumsoc2.org

Numismatic Graduate Seminar

Type of award: Scholarship.
Intended use: For full-time master's, doctoral or postgraduate study at graduate institution in United States.
Eligibility: Applicant must be U.S. citizen or permanent resident.
Basis for selection: Major/career interest in art, art history; classics; history; archaeology. Applicant must demonstrate high academic achievement.
Application requirements: Recommendations, essay and transcript.
Additional information: An intensive nine-week summer seminar in New York City that provides $2,000 stipend. Attendance qualifies participants for additional financial aid. Applicant must have completed at least one year of graduate study at a North American institution of higher learning. Faculty members not above assistant professor rank also eligible.

Amount of award:	$2,000
Number of awards:	12
Number of applicants:	38
Application deadline:	March 1
Notification begins:	April 1
Total amount awarded:	$24,000

Contact:
Seminar Coordinator
Broadway at 155 Street
New York, NY 10032
Phone: 212-234-3130
Fax: 212-234-3388
Website: www.amnumsoc2.org

American Nurses Association

Nurses Clinical Training Fellowship

Type of award: Research grant, renewable.
Intended use: For doctoral study.
Eligibility: Applicant must be of minority background. Applicant must be U.S. citizen or permanent resident.
Basis for selection: Major/career interest in nursing; mental health/therapy. Applicant must demonstrate seriousness of purpose and service orientation.
Additional information: Must be member of ethnic or racial minority group and/or demonstrate commitment to career in psychiatric nursing related to ethnic minority mental health. Must be registered nurse enrolled in ANA-approved program. Students who accept award are obligated to provide clinical services to underserved populations within 24 months of completion of training and for period equal to length of award. Fellowships last three years with a maximum allowance of $10008/year plus $948 towards tuition.

Amount of award:	$30,024
Number of applicants:	53
Application deadline:	January 15
Notification begins:	June 30

Nurses Health Policy Research Institute Fellowship

Type of award: Research grant.
Intended use: For doctoral, postgraduate study.
Eligibility: Applicant must be of minority background. Applicant must be U.S. citizen or permanent resident.
Basis for selection: Major/career interest in nursing; health-related professions. Applicant must demonstrate seriousness of purpose and service orientation.
Application requirements: Recommendations and research proposal. Curriculum vitae.
Additional information: Applicant must be registered nurse

with Ph.D., teach in an academic setting or practice in a service delivery area and demonstrate an interest in health policy research regarding minority populations or issues. Must be member of ANA. Must be EMFP Alumnus. Health Policy Research Institute is a two year program. Fellowship promotes research conducted in the areas of health services and policy for ethnic/minority populations or issues.

Amount of award:	$10,000
Number of awards:	10
Application deadline:	December 1
Notification begins:	January 31

Nurses Research Training Fellowship

Type of award: Research grant, renewable.
Intended use: For full-time doctoral study.
Eligibility: Applicant must be of minority background. Applicant must be U.S. citizen or permanent resident.
Basis for selection: Major/career interest in nursing; social and behavioral sciences. Applicant must demonstrate seriousness of purpose and service orientation.
Application requirements: Research proposal.
Additional information: Must be member of ethnic or racial minority group and/or demonstrate commitment to career in research related to ethnic minority mental health. Must be registered nurse enrolled in ANA approved program and planning career as research scientist on issues of importance to minority populations. Award consists of stipend plus $948 toward tuition.

Amount of award:	$57,480
Number of applicants:	53
Application deadline:	January 15
Notification begins:	June 30

Nurses Substance Abuse Fellowship

Type of award: Research grant, renewable.
Intended use: For full-time doctoral, postgraduate study.
Eligibility: Applicant must be of minority background. Applicant must be U.S. citizen or permanent resident.
Basis for selection: Major/career interest in nursing; social and behavioral sciences. Applicant must demonstrate seriousness of purpose, service orientation and financial need.
Additional information: Must be member of ethnic or racial minority group and/or demonstrate commitment to career in research related to ethnic minority mental health. Applicants must be enrolled full-time in a National League for Nursing accredited school and be pursuing a doctoral degree in psychiatric/mental health nursing at the time the Fellowship is awarded. Award includes stipend of up to $10,008/year for three years.

Amount of award:	$30,024
Application deadline:	January 15
Notification begins:	June 30

Contact:
American Nurses Association
Ethnic/Racial Minority Fellowship Program
600 Maryland Avenue SW, Suite 100 West
Washington, DC 20024-2571
Phone: 202-651-7244
Fax: 202-657-7007
Website: www.nursingworld.org

American Optometric Foundation

Corning Inc. Optometric Scholarship

Type of award: Scholarship.
Intended use: For full-time first professional study at accredited graduate institution in United States.
Eligibility: Applicant must be U.S. citizen.
Basis for selection: Major/career interest in optometry/ophthalmology. Applicant must demonstrate depth of character, leadership, seriousness of purpose, service orientation and high academic achievement.
Application requirements: Essay and nomination by college or school committee; deadline, May 10. Curriculum vitae, personal career statement.
Additional information: For third-year optometry student attending institution fully accredited by Association of Schools and Colleges of Optometry. Applications due to individual school/college's awards committee April 19. This program is currently under review. Contact AOF for information regarding the availability of the scholarship.

Amount of award:	$2,000-$3,000
Number of awards:	2
Number of applicants:	20
Application deadline:	May 1
Total amount awarded:	$5,000

Contact:
Corning Inc. Scholarship
c/o American Optometric Foundation
6110 Executive Blvd. Suite 506
Rockville, MD 20852-4408
Website: www.aaopt.org

American Orchid Society

Orchid Research Grant

Type of award: Research grant.
Intended use: For graduate study at accredited graduate institution in or outside United States.
Basis for selection: Major/career interest in biology; horticulture; botany; environmental science.
Application requirements: Research proposal.
Additional information: Those studying taxonomy, genetics, anatomy, physiology, development, pathology, tissue culture, conservation, or ecology also eligible.

Amount of award:	$500-$12,000
Application deadline:	August 1
Notification begins:	January 1

Contact:
American Orchid Society
6000 South Olive Avenue
West Palm Beach, FL 33405
Phone: 561-585-8666
Fax: 561-585-0654

American Osteopathic Foundation

Bristol-Myers Squibb Outstanding Resident Award

Type of award: Scholarship.
Intended use: For postgraduate study. Designated institutions: Colleges of osteopathic medicine.
Basis for selection: Major/career interest in medicine, osteopathic. Applicant must demonstrate depth of character, leadership, seriousness of purpose and service orientation.
Application requirements: Recommendations and by Residency Director must submit nomination forms. Curriculum vitae.
Additional information: Eligible applicants are osteopathic physicians currently in 2nd or 3rd year of an AOA approved residency program.
   Amount of award: $2,000
   Number of awards: 8
   Number of applicants: 25
   Application deadline: April 15
   Notification begins: June 15
Contact:
American Osteopathic Foundation
Bristol-Myers Squibb Outstanding Resident Award
142 East Ontario Street
Chicago, IL 60611
Phone: 800-621-1773
Website: www.osteopathic.org

Osteopathic Foundation Student Loan Program

Type of award: Loan, renewable.
Intended use: For doctoral study at accredited graduate institution. Designated institutions: Colleges of osteopathic medicine.
Basis for selection: Major/career interest in medicine, osteopathic.
Additional information: Must be second, third or fourth year student at an AOA accredited college of osteopathic medicine. Applications for loans available directly through schools Financial Aid Office.
   Amount of award: $1,000-$5,000
   Number of awards: 100
   Number of applicants: 100
   Total amount awarded: $400,000
Contact:
American Osteopathic Foundation
142 East Ontario Street
Chicago, IL 60611
Phone: 800-621-1773
Website: www.osteopathic.org

Russel C. McCaughan Education Fund Scholarship

Type of award: Scholarship.
Intended use: For doctoral study in United States. Designated institutions: Colleges of osteopathic medicine.
Basis for selection: Major/career interest in medicine, osteopathic.
Application requirements: Recommendations and nomination by Dean of Students makes nomination.
   Amount of award: $400
   Number of awards: 17
   Number of applicants: 16
   Application deadline: May 1
Contact:
American Osteopathic Foundation
Russel C. McCaughn Education Fund Scholarship
142 East Ontario Street
Chicago, IL 60611
Phone: 800-621-1773
Website: www.osteopathic.org

Zeneca Pharmacy Underserved Healthcare Grant

Type of award: Scholarship.
Intended use: For full-time doctoral study in United States. Designated institutions: Colleges of osteopathic medicine.
Basis for selection: Major/career interest in medicine, osteopathic. Applicant must demonstrate service orientation.
Application requirements: Interview, recommendations and essay.
Additional information: Applicant must practice in underserved or minority community. Encourages minority applicants. Only third year osteopathic students eligible to apply. Award paid in two installments over two years, first for fourth year of school, second for first year of practice.
   Amount of award: $5,000-$10,000
   Application deadline: January 31
Contact:
American Osteopathic Foundation
Zeneca Pharmaceuticals Underserved Healthcare Grant
142 Ontario Street
Chicago, IL 60611
Phone: 800-621-1773
Website: www.osteopathic.org

American Physical Society

American Physical Society Minorities Scholarship

Type of award: Scholarship, renewable.
Intended use: For full-time freshman, sophomore or junior study at 4-year institution in United States.
Eligibility: Applicant must be Alaskan native, American Indian, African American, Mexican American, Hispanic American or Puerto Rican. Applicant must be U.S. citizen.
Basis for selection: Major/career interest in physics. Applicant must demonstrate high academic achievement.
Application requirements: Recommendations, essay, transcript and proof of eligibility. ACT/SAT scores.

Amount of award:	$2,500
Number of awards:	26
Number of applicants:	100
Application deadline:	February 5
Notification begins:	May 15
Total amount awarded:	$70,000

Contact:
American Physical Society
Minorities Scholarship Program
One Physics Ellipse
College Park, MD 20740
Phone: 301-209-0865
Website: www.aps.org

American Political Science Association

American Political Science Association Minority Fellows

Type of award: Scholarship.
Intended use: For doctoral study at accredited graduate institution in United States.
Eligibility: Applicant must be Alaskan native, American Indian, African American, Mexican American, Hispanic American or Puerto Rican. Applicant must be U.S. citizen.
Basis for selection: Major/career interest in political science/government. Applicant must demonstrate seriousness of purpose and high academic achievement.
Application requirements: Recommendations, essay, transcript and proof of eligibility.

Amount of award:	$6,000
Number of awards:	3
Application deadline:	November 1
Notification begins:	January 1

Contact:
American Political Science Association
1527 New Hampshire Avenue, NW
Washington, DC 20036
Phone: 202-483-2512
Fax: 202-483-2657
Website: www.apsanet.org

American Radio Relay League Foundation, Inc.

ARRL General Fund Scholarship

Type of award: Scholarship.
Intended use: For undergraduate or graduate study at accredited postsecondary institution in United States.
Basis for selection: Applicant must demonstrate financial need.
Application requirements: Recommendations and transcript.
Additional information: Must be amateur radio operator holding any class license.

Amount of award:	$1,000
Number of awards:	2
Application deadline:	February 1
Notification begins:	June 30
Total amount awarded:	$2,000

ARRL League Ph.D. Scholarship

Type of award: Scholarship.
Intended use: For undergraduate, graduate or non-degree study at accredited postsecondary institution in United States.
Eligibility: Applicant must be residing in Iowa or Kansas or Missouri or Nebraska.
Basis for selection: Major/career interest in journalism; computer and information sciences; engineering, electrical and electronic. Applicant must demonstrate financial need.
Application requirements: Recommendations and transcript.
Additional information: Must be amateur radio operator holding any class license. May be child of deceased radio amateur.

Amount of award:	$1,000
Number of awards:	1
Application deadline:	February 1
Notification begins:	June 30
Total amount awarded:	$1,000

ARRL Mississippi Scholarship

Type of award: Scholarship.
Intended use: For freshman, sophomore, junior, senior or graduate study at accredited 4-year or graduate institution in Mississippi.
Eligibility: Applicant must be residing in Mississippi.
Basis for selection: Major/career interest in communications; electronics; engineering, electrical and electronic. Applicant must demonstrate financial need.
Application requirements: Recommendations, transcript and proof of eligibility.
Additional information: Must be an amateur radio operator with any class license.

Amount of award:	$500
Number of awards:	1
Number of applicants:	2,500
Application deadline:	February 1
Notification begins:	June 30
Total amount awarded:	$500

Charles Clarke Cordle Memorial Scholarship

Type of award: Scholarship.
Intended use: For undergraduate or graduate study at accredited postsecondary institution in Georgia or Alabama.
Eligibility: Applicant must be residing in Alabama or Georgia.
Basis for selection: Applicant must demonstrate financial need.
Application requirements: Recommendations and transcript.
Additional information: Must have at least 2.5 GPA. Must be amateur radio operator holding any class license.

Amount of award:	$1,000
Number of awards:	1
Application deadline:	February 1
Notification begins:	June 30
Total amount awarded:	$1,000

Charles N. Fisher Memorial Scholarship

Type of award: Scholarship.
Intended use: For undergraduate, graduate or non-degree study at accredited postsecondary institution in United States.
Eligibility: Applicant must be residing in Arizona or California.
Basis for selection: Major/career interest in communications; electronics. Applicant must demonstrate financial need.
Application requirements: Recommendations and transcript.
Additional information: Must be amateur radio operator holding any class license. Candidates residing in Los Angeles, Orange, San Diego, and Santa Barbara, California, also eligible.
    Amount of award: $1,000
    Number of awards: 1
    Application deadline: February 1
    Notification begins: June 30
    Total amount awarded: $1,000

Chicago FM Club Scholarship

Type of award: Scholarship.
Intended use: For undergraduate study at accredited postsecondary institution in United States.
Eligibility: Applicant must be U.S. citizen residing in Illinois or Indiana or Wisconsin.
Basis for selection: Applicant must demonstrate financial need.
Application requirements: Recommendations and transcript.
Additional information: Must be amateur radio operator with technician license.
    Amount of award: $500
    Application deadline: February 1
    Notification begins: June 30

Dr. James L. Lawson Memorial Scholarship

Type of award: Scholarship.
Intended use: For undergraduate or graduate study at accredited postsecondary institution in New England or New York State.
Basis for selection: Major/career interest in communications; electronics. Applicant must demonstrate financial need.
Application requirements: Recommendations and transcript.
Additional information: Must be amateur radio operator holding general license.
    Amount of award: $500
    Number of awards: 1
    Number of applicants: 2,500
    Application deadline: February 1
    Notification begins: June 30
    Total amount awarded: $500

F. Charles Ruling N6FR Memorial Scholarship

Type of award: Scholarship.
Intended use: For undergraduate or graduate study at accredited postsecondary institution in United States.
Basis for selection: Major/career interest in electronics; communications. Applicant must demonstrate financial need.
Application requirements: Recommendations and transcript.
Additional information: Must be amateur radio operator holding general license.
    Amount of award: $1,000
    Number of awards: 1
    Application deadline: February 1
    Notification begins: June 30
    Total amount awarded: $1,000

Fred R. McDaniel Memorial Scholarship

Type of award: Scholarship.
Intended use: For undergraduate or graduate study at accredited postsecondary institution in Texas, Oklahoma, Alaska, Louisiana, Michigan, New Mexico.
Eligibility: Applicant must be residing in Texas or Oklahoma or Arkansas or Louisiana or Michigan or New Mexico.
Basis for selection: Major/career interest in electronics; communications. Applicant must demonstrate financial need.
Application requirements: Recommendations and transcript.
Additional information: Preference to students with 3.0 GPA. Must be amateur radio operator holding general license.
    Amount of award: $500
    Number of awards: 1
    Application deadline: February 1
    Notification begins: June 30
    Total amount awarded: $500

Irving W. Cook WAOCGS Scholarship

Type of award: Scholarship.
Intended use: For undergraduate, graduate or non-degree study at accredited postsecondary institution in United States.
Eligibility: Applicant must be residing in Kansas.
Basis for selection: Major/career interest in communications; electronics. Applicant must demonstrate financial need.
Application requirements: Recommendations and transcript.
Additional information: Must be amateur radio operator holding any class license. Preference to candidates for bachelor's or higher degree.
    Amount of award: $1,000
    Number of awards: 1
    Application deadline: February 1
    Notification begins: June 30
    Total amount awarded: $1,000

K2TEO Martin J. Green, Sr. Memorial Scholarship

Type of award: Scholarship.
Intended use: For undergraduate or graduate study at accredited postsecondary institution in United States.
Basis for selection: Applicant must demonstrate financial need.
Application requirements: Recommendations and transcript.
Additional information: Must be an amateur radio operator with a general license. Preference given to students who come from family of ham operators.
    Amount of award: $1,000
    Number of awards: 1
    Application deadline: February 1
    Notification begins: June 30
    Total amount awarded: $1,000

L. Phil Wicker Scholarship

Type of award: Scholarship.
Intended use: For undergraduate, graduate or non-degree study at accredited postsecondary institution in North Carolina, South Carolina, Virginia, West Virginia.
Eligibility: Applicant must be residing in North Carolina or South Carolina or Virginia or West Virginia.
Basis for selection: Major/career interest in communications; electronics. Applicant must demonstrate financial need.
Application requirements: Recommendations and transcript.
Additional information: Must be amateur radio operator holding general license. Preference to bachelor's or higher degree.
   Amount of award: $1,000
   Number of awards: 1
   Application deadline: February 1
   Notification begins: June 30
   Total amount awarded: $1,000

Mary Lou Brown Scholarship

Type of award: Scholarship.
Intended use: For undergraduate or graduate study at accredited postsecondary institution in United States.
Eligibility: Applicant must be residing in Alaska or Idaho or Montana or Oregon or Washington.
Basis for selection: Applicant must demonstrate financial need.
Application requirements: Recommendations and transcript.
Additional information: Must have at least 3.0 GPA. Must be an amateur radio operator with general license.
   Amount of award: $2,500
   Application deadline: February 1
   Notification begins: June 30

Michael J. Flosi Memorial Scholarship

Type of award: Scholarship.
Intended use: For undergraduate or graduate study at accredited postsecondary institution in United States.
Eligibility: Applicant must be high school junior, senior. Applicant must be U.S. citizen residing in Illinois or Indiana or Wisconsin.
Basis for selection: Applicant must demonstrate financial need.
Application requirements: Recommendations and transcript.
Additional information: Must be amateur radio operator holding technician license.
   Amount of award: $500
   Application deadline: February 1
   Notification begins: June 30

Nemal Electronics Scholarship

Type of award: Scholarship.
Intended use: For undergraduate or graduate study at accredited postsecondary institution in United States.
Basis for selection: Major/career interest in electronics; communications. Applicant must demonstrate financial need.
Application requirements: Recommendations, essay and transcript. Must write brief letter detailing background and future plans.
Additional information: Must have at least 3.0 GPA. Must be amateur radio operator holding general license.
   Amount of award: $500
   Number of awards: 1
   Application deadline: February 1
   Notification begins: June 30
   Total amount awarded: $500

New England Femara Scholarship

Type of award: Scholarship.
Intended use: For undergraduate, graduate or non-degree study at accredited postsecondary institution in United States.
Basis for selection: Applicant must demonstrate financial need.
Application requirements: Recommendations and transcript.
Additional information: Must be amateur radio operator holding technician license.
   Amount of award: $600
   Number of awards: 5
   Application deadline: February 1
   Notification begins: June 30
   Total amount awarded: $3,000

Paul and Helen L. Grauer Scholarship

Type of award: Scholarship.
Intended use: For undergraduate, graduate or non-degree study at accredited postsecondary institution in Iowa, Kansas, Missouri, Nebraska.
Eligibility: Applicant must be residing in Iowa or Kansas or Missouri or Nebraska.
Basis for selection: Major/career interest in communications; electronics. Applicant must demonstrate financial need.
Additional information: Must be amateur radio operator with novice license.
   Amount of award: $1,000
   Number of awards: 1
   Application deadline: February 1
   Notification begins: June 30
   Total amount awarded: $1,000

Senator Barry Goldwater Scholarship, K7UGA

Type of award: Scholarship.
Intended use: For undergraduate, graduate or non-degree study at accredited postsecondary institution in United States.
Basis for selection: Applicant must demonstrate financial need.
Application requirements: Recommendations and transcript.
Additional information: Must be amateur radio operator with novice license.
   Amount of award: $5,000
   Number of awards: 1
   Application deadline: February 1
   Notification begins: June 30
   Total amount awarded: $5,000

Contact:
ARRL Foundation Inc./Scholarship Program
225 Main Street
Newington, CT 06111
Phone: 860-594-0200
Fax: 860-594-0259
Website: www.arrl.org

Six Meter Club of Chicago Scholarship

Type of award: Scholarship.
Intended use: For undergraduate study at accredited vocational, 2-year or 4-year institution in Illinois.
Eligibility: Applicant must be residing in Illinois.
Basis for selection: Applicant must demonstrate financial need.
Application requirements: Recommendations and transcript.
Additional information: Must be amateur radio operator holding any class license.

Amount of award:	$500
Number of awards:	1
Application deadline:	February 1
Notification begins:	June 30

Contact:
ARRL Foundation Inc./Scholarship Program
225 Main Street
Newington, CT 06111
Phone: 860-594-0200
Fax: 860-594-0259
Website: www.arrl.org

American Research Institute in Turkey

Kreiss Art History and Archaeology Fellowship

Type of award: Research grant.
Intended use: For full-time doctoral study at accredited graduate institution outside United States in Turkey. Designated institutions: For research in Turkey.
Basis for selection: Major/career interest in art, art history; archaeology. Applicant must demonstrate high academic achievement.
Application requirements: Recommendations, transcript and research proposal. Permit from Turkish government to conduct research in Turkey.

Amount of award:	$13,500
Application deadline:	November 15
Notification begins:	January 25

Contact:
Fellowship Coordinator
University of Pennsylvania Museum
33rd and Spruce Street
Philadelphia, PA 19104-6324
Phone: 215-898-3474
Fax: 215-898-0657

Research Institute in Turkey Fellowship

Type of award: Research grant.
Intended use: For doctoral, postgraduate study. Designated institutions: Must be affiliated with U.S. or Canadian institution.
Basis for selection: Major/career interest in social and behavioral sciences; humanities/liberal arts. Applicant must demonstrate high academic achievement.
Application requirements: Recommendations, transcript and research proposal. Permit from Turkish government.

Amount of award:	$2,000-$10,000
Number of awards:	12
Number of applicants:	65
Application deadline:	November 15
Notification begins:	January 25
Total amount awarded:	$66,000

Contact:
American Research Institute in Turkey
University of Pennsylvania Museum
33rd and Spruce Street
Philadelphia, PA 19104-6324

American Respiratory Care Foundation

J.A. Young Memorial Education Recognition Award

Type of award: Scholarship, renewable.
Intended use: For sophomore, junior or senior study at accredited vocational, 2-year or 4-year institution.
Eligibility: Applicant must be U.S. citizen or permanent resident.
Basis for selection: Major/career interest in respiratory therapy. Applicant must demonstrate seriousness of purpose, service orientation and high academic achievement.
Application requirements: Recommendations, essay, transcript, proof of eligibility and by The foundation prefers that a nomination be made by a school or program representative.
Additional information: Minimum 3.0 GPA required. Must have completed at least one semester in an accredited respiratory care program. Preference will be given minority applicants. If a nomination cannot be obtained, student may request for sponsorship. The foundation prefers that nominations be made by a representative of the school or an accredited respiratory training program, however, any student may initiate an application. Preference3 will be given to nominees of minority origin.

Amount of award:	$1,000
Number of awards:	1
Application deadline:	June 30
Notification begins:	September 1
Total amount awarded:	$1,000

M.B. Duggan, Jr., Memorial Education Recognition Award

Type of award: Scholarship, renewable.
Intended use: For sophomore, junior or senior study at accredited 2-year or 4-year institution in United States.
Eligibility: Applicant must be U.S. citizen or permanent resident.
Basis for selection: Major/career interest in respiratory therapy. Applicant must demonstrate depth of character,

333

seriousness of purpose, service orientation and high academic achievement.
Application requirements: Recommendations, essay, transcript and proof of eligibility.
Additional information: Preference given to Georgia and South Carolina applicants. Minimum 3.0 GPA required. Must have at least one semester in Commission on Accreditation of Allied Health Education Programs-approved respiratory care program.

Amount of award:	$1,000
Number of awards:	1
Application deadline:	June 30
Notification begins:	September 1
Total amount awarded:	$1,000

R.M. Lawrence Education Recognition Award

Type of award: Scholarship.
Intended use: For full-time junior, senior study at accredited 4-year institution in United States.
Eligibility: Applicant must be U.S. citizen or permanent resident.
Basis for selection: Major/career interest in respiratory therapy. Applicant must demonstrate high academic achievement.
Application requirements: Recommendations, essay, transcript and proof of eligibility.
Additional information: Minimum 3.0 GPA. Must provide letter verifying enrollment in a Commission on Accreditation of Allied Health Education Programs respiratory care program leading to a Baccalaureate degree.

Amount of award:	$2,500
Number of awards:	1
Application deadline:	June 30
Notification begins:	September 1
Total amount awarded:	$2,500

W.F. Miller Postgraduate Education Recognition Award

Type of award: Scholarship.
Intended use: For master's, doctoral study at accredited graduate institution.
Eligibility: Applicant must be U.S. citizen or permanent resident.
Basis for selection: Major/career interest in health-related professions; respiratory therapy. Applicant must demonstrate depth of character, leadership, seriousness of purpose and high academic achievement.
Application requirements: Recommendations, essay, transcript and proof of eligibility.
Additional information: Must be respiratory care practitioner with bachelor's degree accepted into advanced degree program. Minimum 3.0 undergraduate GPA required. Must present three letters of reference and essay must be at least 1200 words.

Amount of award:	$1,000
Number of awards:	1
Application deadline:	June 30
Notification begins:	September 1
Total amount awarded:	$1,000

W.M. Burgin, Jr., Scholarship

Type of award: Scholarship.
Intended use: For full-time sophomore study at accredited 4-year institution in United States.
Eligibility: Applicant must be U.S. citizen or permanent resident.
Basis for selection: Major/career interest in respiratory therapy. Applicant must demonstrate high academic achievement.
Application requirements: Recommendations, essay, transcript and proof of eligibility.
Additional information: Minimum 3.0 GPA and letter verifying enrollment in a Commission on Accreditation of Allied Health Education Programs-accredited program required. Applicants may apply directly or be nominated by the school or educational program.

Amount of award:	$2,500
Number of awards:	1
Number of applicants:	10
Application deadline:	June 30
Notification begins:	September 1
Total amount awarded:	$2,500

Contact:
American Respiratory Care Foundation
11030 Ables Lane
Dallas, TX 75229
Phone: 972-243-2272
Website: www.aarc.org

American Schools of Oriental Research

American Schools of Oriental Research/Annual Professorship

Type of award: Research grant.
Intended use: For postgraduate study at postsecondary institution outside United States. Designated institutions: Awards require residence at the Albright Institute.
Eligibility: Applicant must be U.S. citizen.
Basis for selection: Major/career interest in ancient Near Eastern studies; archaeology; geography; history. Applicant must demonstrate leadership, seriousness of purpose, service orientation, financial need and high academic achievement.
Application requirements: Interview, recommendations, essay, transcript, proof of eligibility and research proposal. Recipient must submit a written report within one month of conclusion of the award period.
Additional information: This stipend is $10,000 plus room and half-board for appointee and spouse at the institution.

Amount of award:	$23,000-$23,000
Application deadline:	October 13
Notification begins:	January 15

Contact:
American Schools of Oriental Research
Research Grant Committee
656 Beacon Street, 5th Floor
Boston, MA 02215-2010

American Schools of Oriental Research/Endowment for Biblical Research and Travel Grant

Type of award: Research grant.
Intended use: For undergraduate, master's, doctoral, first professional or postgraduate study in Mesopotamia (Baghdad).
Basis for selection: Major/career interest in archaeology; Middle Eastern studies; ancient Near Eastern studies.
Application requirements: Research proposal.
Additional information: One research grant and six travel grants for a one to three month period. Open to seniors, undergraduates, graduate students or recent post-doctoral scholars.

Amount of award:	$1,000-$2,000
Number of awards:	7
Number of applicants:	100
Application deadline:	February 1
Notification begins:	April 15
Total amount awarded:	$10,500

Contact:
Research and Grant Committee
656 Beacon Street
Boston, MA 02215-2010
Phone: (617) 353-6570
Fax: (617) 353-6575

American Schools of Oriental Research/Harrell Family Fellowship

Type of award: Research grant.
Intended use: For master's, doctoral study.
Basis for selection: Major/career interest in archaeology; Middle Eastern studies; ancient Near Eastern studies.
Additional information: To support a graduate student for participation in an ACOR - supported archaeological project, which has passed an academic review process, or an ACOR - funded archaeological research project. Open to enrolled graduate students of any nationality.

Amount of award:	$1,500
Number of awards:	1
Application deadline:	February 1

Contact:
American Center of Oriental Research
Research Grant Committee
656 Beacon Street, 5th Floor
Boston, MA 02215-2010

American Schools of Oriental Research/Jennifer C. Groot Fellowship

Type of award: Research grant.
Intended use: For undergraduate or graduate study at 4-year or graduate institution in United States in Jordan.
Eligibility: Applicant must be U.S. citizen, permanent resident or Canadian citizen.
Basis for selection: Major/career interest in archaeology; Middle Eastern studies; ancient Near Eastern studies.
Additional information: Provides support for beginners in archaeological fieldwork who have been accepted as staff members on archaeological projects in Jordan with ASOR/CAP affiliation. Open to undergraduate and graduate students.

Amount of award:	$1,500
Number of awards:	2
Application deadline:	February 1

Contact:
American Center of Oriental Research
Reseach Grant Coordinator
656 Beacon Street
Boston, MA 02215-2010
Phone: (617) 353-6570
Fax: (617) 353-6575

American Schools of Oriental Research/National Endowment for the Humanities Fellowship

Type of award: Research grant.
Intended use: For full-time master's, doctoral, first professional or postgraduate study at accredited postsecondary institution outside United States in Cyprus. Designated institutions: Award must be used at the Residence at the institute. The research should be continuous without frequent trips outside the country.
Eligibility: Minorities and women are encouraged to apply. Applicant must be U.S. citizen or permanent resident.
Basis for selection: Major/career interest in archaeology; ancient Near Eastern studies; Middle Eastern studies. Applicant must demonstrate leadership, seriousness of purpose, service orientation, financial need and high academic achievement.
Application requirements: Interview, recommendations, essay, transcript and research proposal. Each recipient must submit a written report within a month of the conclusion of award period.
Additional information: This award is open to scholars in the fields of Near Eastern archaeology, anthropology, geography, ancient history, philology, opigraphy, Biblical studies, Islamic studies, religion, history, literature, philosophy, or related disciplines holding a Ph.D (or equivalent) as of February 1, 1998.

Amount of award:	$15,000-$30,000
Number of awards:	2
Number of applicants:	15
Application deadline:	October 13
Notification begins:	January 15
Total amount awarded:	$30,000

Contact:
656 Beacon Street, 5th Floor
Boston, MA 02215-2010
Phone: 617-353-6570
Fax: 617-353-6575

American Schools of Oriental Research/Samuel H. Kress Fellowships

Type of award: Research grant, renewable.
Intended use: For doctoral, postgraduate study outside United States. Designated institutions: Awards can only be used at the Albright Institute of Archaeological Research (AIAR).
Eligibility: Applicant must be U.S. citizen.
Basis for selection: Major/career interest in architecture; archaeology; art, art history. Applicant must demonstrate leadership, seriousness of purpose, service orientation, financial need and high academic achievement.
Application requirements: Interview, recommendations,

essay, transcript, proof of eligibility and research proposal. Each recipient must submit a written report within one month of the conclusion of the award period.
Additional information: This award is $12,500 and provides a stipend of $6,000. A dissertation research fellowship for students specializing in architecture, art history and archaeology. The research period is for ten months and should be continuous without frequent trips outside the country.

Amount of award:	$12,500-$12,500
Application deadline:	October 13, October 13

Contact:
American Schools of Oriental Research
Research Grant Committee
656 Beacon Street
Boston, MA 02215-2010

American Schools of Oriental Research/United States Information Agency Fellowship

Type of award: Research grant.
Intended use: For doctoral, postgraduate study at graduate institution in Israel.
Eligibility: Applicant must be U.S. citizen.
Basis for selection: Major/career interest in ancient Near Eastern studies. Applicant must demonstrate high academic achievement.
Application requirements: Recommendations, essay, transcript, proof of eligibility and research proposal.
Additional information: Fellows are expected to conduct a seminar on research at institute. Stipend for each award is $6,800 and remainder is for room and half-board at the institute. Research period is for nine months and must be continuous. This award may not be used in the summer.

Number of awards:	3
Number of applicants:	3
Application deadline:	October 13
Notification begins:	January 15
Total amount awarded:	$39,300

Contact:
656 Beacon Street, 5th Floor
Boston, MA 02215-2010
Phone: 617-353-6570
Fax: 617-353-6575

Biblical Research Travel Grant

Type of award: Research grant, renewable.
Intended use: For undergraduate, master's, doctoral, first professional or postgraduate study outside United States in Iraq.
Basis for selection: Major/career interest in archaeology; ancient Near Eastern studies.
Application requirements: Research proposal.
Additional information: Must be/become individual member of American Center of Oriental Research or be affiliated with corporate member. Students from Middle East and eastern Mediterranean not eligible. Nine travel grants for Biblical excavation or research, one for summer research.

Amount of award:	$1,000-$1,500
Number of awards:	10
Number of applicants:	100
Application deadline:	February 1
Notification begins:	April 15
Total amount awarded:	$10,500

Contact:
Research Travel Grant Committee
656 Beacon Street, 5th Floor
Boston, MA 02215-2010

Near and Middle East Research and Training Act Predoctoral Fellowship

Type of award: Research grant.
Intended use: For doctoral study outside United States in Jordan.
Eligibility: Applicant must be U.S. citizen.
Basis for selection: Major/career interest in anthropology; economics; history; international relations; journalism.
Additional information: Two or more two- to four-month fellowships in Jordan for predoctoral students with little or no previous experience in the Middle East.

Amount of award:	$10,100
Number of awards:	7
Application deadline:	February 1

Contact:
656 Beacon Street, 5th Floor
Boston, MA 02215-2010
Phone: 617-353-6570
Fax: 617-353-6575

Near and Middle East Research and Training Act Senior Post-Doctoral Research Grant

Type of award: Research grant.
Intended use: For postgraduate study outside United States in Jordan.
Eligibility: Applicant must be U.S. citizen.
Basis for selection: Major/career interest in humanities/liberal arts; social and behavioral sciences; Middle Eastern studies.
Additional information: Two or more four- to nine-month fellowships in Jordan for senior postdoctoral scholars pursuing research or publication projects related to Middle East. Preference given to scholars with limited experience in Middle East.

Amount of award:	$34,700
Number of awards:	2
Application deadline:	February 1

Contact:
656 Beacon Street, 5th Floor
Boston, MA 02215-2010
Phone: 617-353-6570
Fax: 617-353-6575

U.S. Information Agency Predoctoral/Postdoctoral Fellowship

Type of award: Scholarship.
Intended use: For doctoral, postgraduate study outside United States in Jordan.

Eligibility: Applicant must be U.S. citizen.
Basis for selection: Major/career interest in humanities/liberal arts; social and behavioral sciences.
Additional information: Five or more two- to six-month fellowships in Jordan for predoctoral students and postdoctoral scholars. Topics should contribute to scholarship in Near East studies.

Amount of award:	$14,000
Number of awards:	5
Application deadline:	February 1

Contact:
American Center of Oriental Research Fellowship Committee
656 Beacon Street
Fifth Floor
Boston, MA 02215
Phone: 617-353-6570
Fax: 617-353-6575

American Soc. Heating/Refrigeration/Air-Conditioning Engineers, Inc.

American Soc. Heating/Refrigeration/Air-Conditioning Engineers Technical Scholarship

Type of award: Scholarship, renewable.
Intended use: For full-time undergraduate or graduate study at accredited vocational or 2-year institution. Designated institutions: Engineering technology schools.
Basis for selection: Major/career interest in engineering; air conditioning, heating, and refrigeration technology. Applicant must demonstrate depth of character, leadership, financial need and high academic achievement.
Application requirements: Recommendations.
Additional information: For those seeking a 2 year associates degree at U.S. and Canadian Institutions. Minimum 3.0 GPA required or Dean's List. Curriculum must be accredited by American Board of Engineering Technologies.

Amount of award:	$3,000
Number of awards:	1
Application deadline:	May 1
Total amount awarded:	$3,000

Contact:
American Society of Heating/Refrigeration/Air-Conditioning Engineers, Inc.
Scholarship Program
1791 Tullie Circle NE
Atlanta, GA 30329
Phone: 404-942-8400
Fax: 404-321-5478
Website: www.ashrae.org

American Soc. Heating/Refrigeration/Air-Conditioning Engineers Undergraduate Scholarship

Type of award: Scholarship, renewable.
Intended use: For undergraduate study at accredited vocational, 2-year or 4-year institution in United States.
Basis for selection: Major/career interest in engineering; air conditioning, heating, and refrigeration technology. Applicant must demonstrate depth of character, leadership, financial need and high academic achievement.
Application requirements: Recommendations and transcript.
Additional information: Must have 3.0 GPA or Dean's List. Curriculum must be accredited by American Board of Engineering Technologies. May deadline for 2 year students, December deadline for 4 year students.

Amount of award:	$3,000
Number of awards:	2
Application deadline:	May 1, December 1
Total amount awarded:	$6,000

Contact:
American Society of Heating/Refrigeration/Air-Conditioning Engineers, Inc.
1791 Tullie Circle NE
Atlanta, GA 30329
Phone: 404-636-8400
Fax: 404-321-5478
Website: www.ashrae.org

Reuben Trane Scholarship

Type of award: Scholarship, renewable.
Intended use: For junior, senior study at accredited 4-year institution.
Basis for selection: Major/career interest in engineering; air conditioning, heating, and refrigeration technology. Applicant must demonstrate depth of character, leadership, financial need and high academic achievement.
Application requirements: Recommendations and transcript.
Additional information: Must have minimum 3.0 GPA or be on Dean's List. Curriculum must be accredited by American Board of Engineering Technologies. Award is per year for two years, for students with two years of undergraduate studies remaining.

Amount of award:	$5,000
Number of awards:	6
Application deadline:	December 1
Total amount awarded:	$30,000

Contact:
American Society of Heating/Refrigeration/Air-Conditioning Engineers, Inc.
1791 Tullie Circle NE
Atlanta, GA 30329
Phone: 404-636-8400
Fax: 404-321-5478
Website: www.ashrae.org

American Social Health Association

Social Health Postdoctorate Research Fellowship in Sexually Transmitted Diseases

Type of award: Research grant.
Intended use: For postgraduate study in United States.
Basis for selection: Major/career interest in medical specialties/research (beyond m.d.). Applicant must demonstrate high academic achievement.
Application requirements: Recommendations, essay and research proposal.
Additional information: For research into sexually transmitted diseases, with special attention to areas not currently receiving adequate funding. Research in basic science as well as clinical and behavioral issues. Awardees receive a monthly award. Total award amount is $27,500 the first year and $28,750 the second year.

Amount of award:	$56,250
Number of awards:	2
Number of applicants:	12
Application deadline:	October 15
Notification begins:	May 15
Total amount awarded:	$112,500

Contact:
American Social Health Association
Nancy Hearndon
P.O. Box 13827
Research Triangle Park, NC 27709
Phone: 919-361-8492
Fax: 919-361-8425
Website: www.ashastd.org

American Society for Engineering Education

Army Research Laboratory - Postdoctoral Fellowship

Type of award: Research grant, renewable.
Intended use: For full-time doctoral, postgraduate or non-degree study at 4-year or graduate institution in United States.
Eligibility: Applicant must be U.S. citizen or permanent resident.
Basis for selection: Major/career interest in engineering. Applicant must demonstrate depth of character, seriousness of purpose and service orientation.
Application requirements: Recommendations, transcript, proof of eligibility and research proposal.
Additional information: ASEE will provide full insurance and travel/relocation allowance. Fellows must be in-residence at a research site for the duration of their award. All quests are subject to security screening/Army regulations Governing Visiting Scientists. All proposals/applicants must be sponsored by an advisor at ARL. A list of advisors is available on ASEE's website. This is a rolling deadline. Award amount will be determined by the needs of the research proposal.

Amount of award:	$40,000-$50,000

Naval Research Laboratory - Postdoctoral Fellowship

Type of award: Research grant, renewable.
Intended use: For postgraduate, non-degree study.
Eligibility: Applicant must be U.S. citizen.
Basis for selection: Major/career interest in engineering; aerospace; chemistry; oceanography/marine studies; construction; computer and information sciences. Applicant must demonstrate depth of character, seriousness of purpose and service orientation.
Application requirements: Recommendations, transcript, proof of eligibility and research proposal.
Additional information: A travel and relocation allowance will be provided according to the needs of the applicant and what the ASEE deems appropriate. Full health insurance for the fellow and his/her dependents will be provided. Applicants must pass security clearance and all guests are subject to Army regulations governing visiting scientists. Fellowship is renewable up to three years. There are four deadlines as follows: January 1, 1999, March 1, 1999, April 1, 1999, and June 1, 1999.

Amount of award:	$42,000
Number of awards:	40
Application deadline:	June 1, January 1

Office of Naval Research - Postdoctoral Fellowship

Type of award: Research grant, renewable.
Intended use: For postgraduate, non-degree study.
Eligibility: Applicant must be U.S. citizen or permanent resident.
Basis for selection: Major/career interest in engineering; aerospace; chemistry; oceanography/marine studies; construction; computer and information sciences. Applicant must demonstrate depth of character, seriousness of purpose and service orientation.
Application requirements: Transcript, proof of eligibility and research proposal.
Additional information: A travel and relocation allowance will be provided according to the needs of the applicant and what the ASEE deems appropriate. Full health insurance for the fellow and his/her dependents will be provided. Applicants must pass security clearance and all guests are subject to Navy regulations governing visiting scientists. Fellowship is renewable up to three years. Fellows are selected based solely on their proposals addressing specific areas defined by the Naval Warfare Enter Divisions and Laboratories. Fellows will work in a Navy laboratory environment. The amount of award is determined by the level of experience of the applicant. There are four deadlines as follows: January 1, 1999, March 1, 1999, April 1, 1999, and June 1, 1999.

Amount of award:	$36,000-$52,000
Number of awards:	40
Application deadline:	June 1, January 1

Contact:
American Society for Engineering Education
1818 N St., NW, Suite 600
Washington, DC 20036

American Society for Enology and Viticulture

Enology and Viticulture Scholarship

Type of award: Scholarship, renewable.
Intended use: For full-time junior, senior, master's or doctoral study at 4-year or graduate institution.
Eligibility: Applicant must be U.S. citizen, permanent resident or Canadian or Mexican citizen.
Basis for selection: Major/career interest in agriculture; chemistry; food science and technology; horticulture. Applicant must demonstrate financial need and high academic achievement.
Application requirements: Recommendations, essay, transcript and proof of eligibility.
Additional information: Curriculum must emphasize enology, viticulture, or science basic to wine and grape industry. Graduate students must have minimum 3.2 GPA, undergraduates 3.0.

Amount of award:	$1,500-$3,000
Number of awards:	19
Number of applicants:	50
Application deadline:	March 1
Notification begins:	May 31
Total amount awarded:	$48,000

Contact:
American Society for Enology and Viticulture
P.O. Box 1855
Davis, CA 95617

American Society for Microbiology

Microbiology Summer Research Fellowship for Minority Students

Type of award: Research grant.
Intended use: For undergraduate study.
Eligibility: Applicant must be of minority background. Applicant must be U.S. citizen or permanent resident.
Basis for selection: Major/career interest in microbiology; biology; chemistry. Applicant must demonstrate leadership, seriousness of purpose and high academic achievement.
Application requirements: Personal statement.
Additional information: Fellowship lasts two to six weeks with a stipend of $2,000. In addition to stipend, award covers travel and housing expenses and one-year membership in American Society for Microbiology. Student will pursue project directed by a scientist in research lab. Must be majoring in fields of study indicated.

Amount of award:	$2,000
Application deadline:	February 1

Contact:
American Society for Microbiology
Office of Education and Training
1325 Massachusetts Avenue NW
Washington, DC 20005-4171
Phone: 202-942-9295
Website: www.asmusa.org

Postdoctoral Microbiology Research Program

Type of award: Research grant.
Intended use: For postgraduate study in Atlanta, Georgia. Designated institutions: National Center for Infectious Diseases.
Eligibility: Applicant must be Must speak fluent English.
Basis for selection: Major/career interest in microbiology; public health. Applicant must demonstrate seriousness of purpose and high academic achievement.
Application requirements: TOEFL score required.
Additional information: Must hold doctorate degree or have completed a primary residency within last three years. Fellowships last up to two years. In addition of up to $30,000 annual stipend, recipients receive up to $2,000 each year for professional development and up to $3,500 annually in health benefits. Research will be conducted at the NCID at the Center for Disease Control in Atlanta, Georgia.

Amount of award:	$71,000
Application deadline:	November 15

Contact:
American Society for Microbiology, NCID Program
Office of Education and Training
1325 Massachusetts Avenue NW
Washington, DC 20005-4171
Phone: 202-942-9295
Website: www.asmusa.org

Undergraduate Microbiology Research Fellowship

Type of award: Research grant.
Intended use: For full-time undergraduate study at vocational, 2-year or 4-year institution.
Eligibility: Applicant must be U.S. citizen or permanent resident.
Basis for selection: Major/career interest in microbiology. Applicant must demonstrate seriousness of purpose and high academic achievement.
Application requirements: Research proposal.
Additional information: Award for three to six months beginning June 1 with stipend of up to $2,500 and additional support of up to $800 for supplies. Another $700 in travel funds is awarded if student is eligible. Must have ASM member at institution willing to serve a mentor. Student may not be receiving financial support from any other scientific organization during fellowship. Must have succesful achievement in previous research experience.

Amount of award: $3,300
Application deadline: February 1
Contact:
American Society for Microbiology, URF Program
Office of Education & Training
1325 Massachusetts Avenue NW
Washington, DC 20005
Website: www.asmusa.org

American Society of Civil Engineers

Arthur S. Tuttle Memorial National Scholarships

Type of award: Scholarship, renewable.
Intended use: For full-time master's, doctoral study.
Basis for selection: Major/career interest in engineering, civil. Applicant must demonstrate depth of character, leadership, seriousness of purpose, service orientation, financial need and high academic achievement.
Application requirements: Recommendations, essay, transcript, proof of eligibility and research proposal.
Additional information: Application is available on-line. Membership applications may be submitted with scholarship and/or fellowship application. This award is to be used for tuition expenses only. Recipients must be enrolled at an accredited gratuate institution.
Amount of award: $3,000-$5,000
Application deadline: February 20

B. Charles Tiney Memorial ASCE Student Chapter Scholarships

Type of award: Scholarship, renewable.
Intended use: For freshman, sophomore or junior study at accredited 4-year institution.
Basis for selection: Major/career interest in engineering, civil. Applicant must demonstrate depth of character, leadership, seriousness of purpose, service orientation, financial need and high academic achievement.
Application requirements: Recommendations, essay, transcript, proof of eligibility and research proposal.
Additional information: Application is available on-line. Membership applications may be submitted with scholarship and/or fellowship application. This scholarship may only be used toward tuition expenses. If more than one recipient is chosen, the award will be split evenly between all recipients.
Amount of award: $2,000
Number of awards: 1
Application deadline: February 20

Freeman Fellowship

Type of award: Research grant, renewable.
Intended use: For full-time graduate, postgraduate or non-degree study.
Basis for selection: Major/career interest in engineering, civil. Applicant must demonstrate depth of character, leadership, seriousness of purpose, service orientation, financial need and high academic achievement.
Application requirements: Recommendations, essay, transcript, proof of eligibility and research proposal.
Additional information: Application is available on-line. Membership applications may be submitted with scholarship and/or fellowship application. Resume required. This fellowship is specifically for the study of hydraulic science and construction. For applicants under the age of 45, this fellowship can be used as a traveling scholarship. This award may also be used for assisting in the translation or publication into English of foreign books pertaining to hydraulics.
Amount of award: $3,000-$5,000
Application deadline: February 20

Jack E. Leisch Memorial National Scholarships

Type of award: Scholarship.
Intended use: For full-time master's, doctoral study.
Basis for selection: Major/career interest in engineering, civil; transportation; urban planning. Applicant must demonstrate depth of character, leadership, seriousness of purpose, service orientation, financial need and high academic achievement.
Application requirements: Recommendations, essay, transcript, proof of eligibility and research proposal.
Additional information: Application is available online. Membership applications may be submitted with scholarship and/or fellowship application. This award is to be used for tuition expenses only. Recipients must be enrolled at a university that is a member of the Council of University Transportation Centers.
Amount of award: $1,000
Number of awards: 1
Application deadline: February 20

O.H. Ammann Research Fellowship in Structural Engineering

Type of award: Research grant, renewable.
Intended use: For undergraduate, graduate, postgraduate or non-degree study.
Basis for selection: Major/career interest in engineering, structural. Applicant must demonstrate depth of character, leadership, seriousness of purpose, service orientation, financial need and high academic achievement.
Application requirements: Recommendations, essay, transcript, proof of eligibility and research proposal.
Additional information: Award recipients will show the ability to conceive and explore original ideas in the field of structural engineering.
Amount of award: $5,000
Number of awards: 1
Application deadline: February 20

Samuel Fletcher Tapman ASCE Student Chapter/Club Scholarship

Type of award: Scholarship, renewable.
Intended use: For full-time master's, doctoral study.
Basis for selection: Major/career interest in engineering, civil. Applicant must demonstrate depth of character, leadership, seriousness of purpose, service orientation, financial need and high academic achievement.
Application requirements: Recommendations, essay, transcript, proof of eligibility and research proposal.
Additional information: Application is available online.

Membership applications may be submitted with scholarship and/or fellowship application. Resume required. This award is to be used for tuition expenses only. Not more than one application from any student chapter of the ASCE may be submitted. 3 applicants for each zone will be chosen.

Amount of award:	$1,500
Number of awards:	12
Application deadline:	February 20

Contact:
American Society of Civil Engineers
1801 Alexander Bell Drive
Reston, VA 20191-4400
Website: www.asce.org

American Society of Clinical Pathologists

Clinical Pathology Student Scholarship

Type of award: Scholarship.
Intended use: For post-bachelor's certificate study.
Eligibility: Applicant must be U.S. citizen or permanent resident.
Basis for selection: Major/career interest in medical assistant; health sciences. Applicant must demonstrate depth of character, leadership, seriousness of purpose and high academic achievement.
Application requirements: Recommendations, essay, transcript and proof of eligibility.
Additional information: Must be in final year of study in a NAACLS or CAAHEP accredited program studying histotechnology, cytotechnology, medical laboratory technology, or medical technology.

Amount of award:	$1,000
Number of awards:	50
Number of applicants:	268
Application deadline:	October 31
Notification begins:	February 1
Total amount awarded:	$50,000

Contact:
American Society of Clinical Pathologists
2100 West Harrison Street
Chicago, IL 60612
Phone: 312-738-1336
Fax: 312-738-5807

American Society of Heating/Refrigeration/Air-Conditioning Engineers, Inc.

Alwin B. Newton Scholarships

Type of award: Scholarship, renewable.
Intended use: For undergraduate study in United States.
Basis for selection: Major/career interest in engineering; air conditioning, heating, and refrigeration technology. Applicant must demonstrate depth of character, leadership, financial need and high academic achievement.
Application requirements: Recommendations and transcript.
Additional information: Must have at least 3.0 GPA or be on Dean's List. Curriculum must be accredited by American Board of Engineering Technologies. May deadline for 2 year students, December deadline for 4 year students.

Amount of award:	$3,000
Number of awards:	1
Application deadline:	May 1, December 1
Total amount awarded:	$3,000

Contact:
American Society of Heating/Refrigeration/Air-Conditioning Engineers, Inc.
1791 Tullie Circle NE
Atlanta, GA 30329
Phone: 404-636-8400 ext.201
Fax: 404-321-5478
Website: www.ashrae.org

Willis H. Carrier Graduate Fellowship

Type of award: Research grant, renewable.
Intended use: For full-time graduate study at accredited graduate institution in United States. Designated institutions: Research at Purdue University.
Basis for selection: Major/career interest in engineering, environmental; air conditioning, heating, and refrigeration technology. Applicant must demonstrate depth of character, leadership, financial need and high academic achievement.
Application requirements: Recommendations, transcript, proof of eligibility and research proposal.
Additional information: Application must be submitted by faculty adviser on behalf of student. Relevance of research proposed considered. Should have 3.0 GPA or be on Dean's List. Curriculum must be accredited by American Board of Engineering Technologies.

Amount of award:	$20,000
Number of awards:	1
Application deadline:	December 15

Contact:
American Society of Heating/Refrigeration/Air-Conditioning Engineers, Inc.
Scholarship Program
1791 Tullie Circle NE
Atlanta, GA 30329
Phone: 404-636-8400
Fax: 404-321-5478
Website: www.ashrae.org

American Society of Highway Engineers

Highway Engineers/Carolina Triangle Section Scholarship

Type of award: Scholarship.
Intended use: For full-time or half-time undergraduate study in North Carolina.
Eligibility: Applicant must be U.S. citizen residing in North Carolina.
Basis for selection: Major/career interest in engineering, civil. Applicant must demonstrate leadership, seriousness of purpose and high academic achievement.
Application requirements: Transcript.
    Amount of award: $1,000
    Number of awards: 3
    Number of applicants: 14
    Application deadline: March 31
    Notification begins: May 1
    Total amount awarded: $3,000
Contact:
American Society of Highway Engineers
5800 Faringdon Place, Suite 105
Raleigh, NC 27609
Phone: 919-878-9560

American Society of Interior Designers Educational Foundation

American Society Interior Designers Education Foundation/Dora Brahms Award

Type of award: Scholarship.
Intended use: For graduate study.
Basis for selection: Major/career interest in interior design. Applicant must demonstrate seriousness of purpose.
Application requirements: Research proposal.
Additional information: Open to students studying historic preservation or restoration studies. Student must be in at least the second year of studies to be eligible.
    Amount of award: $3,000
    Number of awards: 1
    Application deadline: February 16
    Total amount awarded: $3,000
Contact:
Educational Foundation
608 Massachusetts Avenue, NE
Washington, DC 20002-6006
Phone: 202-546-3480
Website: www.asid.org

Dora Brahms Interior Design Award

Type of award: Scholarship.
Intended use: For graduate study.
Basis for selection: Major/career interest in interior design.
    Amount of award: $3,000
    Number of awards: 1
    Application deadline: February 16
    Total amount awarded: $3,000
Contact:
American Society of Interior Designers Educational Foundation
608 Massachusetts Avenue, NE
Washington, DC 20002-6006

Mabelle Wilhelmina Boldt Interior Design Scholarship

Type of award: Scholarship.
Intended use: For master's, doctoral study.
Eligibility: Applicant must be adult returning student.
Basis for selection: Major/career interest in interior design. Applicant must demonstrate high academic achievement.
Application requirements: Recommendations, essay and transcript.
Additional information: Must have been practicing designer for at least five years before beginning graduate work.
    Amount of award: $2,000
    Number of awards: 1
    Application deadline: March 5
    Total amount awarded: $2,000
Contact:
American Society of Interior Designers Educational Foundation
608 Massachusetts Avenue, NE
Washington, DC 20002-6006
Phone: 202-546-3480
Website: www.asid.org

Polsky-Fixtures Furniture Award

Type of award: Scholarship.
Intended use: For undergraduate, graduate or non-degree study.
Basis for selection: Competition in Engineering/architecture. Content, comprehensive coverage of topic, innovative subject matter, bibliography, and references. Major/career interest in interior design; architecture. Applicant must demonstrate financial need and high academic achievement.
Additional information: Award to recognize outstanding interior design research or thesis project.
    Amount of award: $1,000
    Number of awards: 1
    Application deadline: March 15
    Total amount awarded: $1,000
Contact:
American Society of Interior Designers Educational Foundation
608 Massachusetts Avenue, NE
Washington, DC 20002-6006
Phone: 202-546-3480
Website: www.asid.org

Polsky-Fixtures Furniture Prize

Type of award: Scholarship.
Intended use: For non-degree study.
Basis for selection: Competition in Engineering/architecture. Content, comprehensive coverage of topic, innovative subject matter, bibliography, and references. Major/career interest in interior design.
Additional information: Award to recognize outstanding contributions to the discipline of interior design through literature or visual communication.

    Amount of award: $1,000
    Number of awards: 1
    Application deadline: March 5
    Total amount awarded: $1,000

Contact:
American Society of Interior Designers Educational Foundation
608 Massachusetts Avenue, NE
Washington, DC 20002-6006
Phone: 202-546-3480
Website: www.asid.org

S. Harris Memorial Interior Design Scholarship

Type of award: Scholarship.
Intended use: For sophomore, junior or senior study.
Basis for selection: Major/career interest in interior design. Applicant must demonstrate financial need and high academic achievement.
Application requirements: Recommendations, essay and transcript.

    Amount of award: $1,500
    Number of awards: 2
    Application deadline: March 5
    Total amount awarded: $3,000

Contact:
American Society of Interior Designers Educational Foundation
608 Massachusetts Avenue, NE
Washington, DC 20002-6006

Yale R. Burge Interior Design Competition

Type of award: Scholarship.
Intended use: For senior study.
Basis for selection: Competition in Visual arts. Quality of portfolio: presentation, design and planning, conceptual creativity. Major/career interest in interior design; architecture.
Application requirements: $10 application fee. Portfolio. Presentations (on slides).
Additional information: Registration forms and fees are due by February 12; applications must be complete by March 12. Award amounts varie; please contact sponsor.

    Amount of award: $250-$500
    Number of awards: 2
    Application deadline: February 12
    Total amount awarded: $750

Contact:
American Society of Interior Designers Educational Foundation
608 Massachusetts Avenue, NE
Washington, DC 20002-6006
Phone: 202-546-3480
Website: www.asid.org

American Society of Magazine Editors

American Society of Magazine Editors Internship

Type of award: Internship.
Intended use: For junior study.
Basis for selection: Major/career interest in journalism; humanities/liberal arts. Applicant must demonstrate seriousness of purpose.
Application requirements: Recommendations, essay and nomination by dean, department head or professor from school of journalism. Must submit writing and editing samples.
Additional information: A 10-week summer internship. Emphasis on consumer magazine and business publication editing. Most assignments in New York City. Interns receive $300 weekly stipend. Dormitory housing is available at a cost of $165 per week. Obtain application from the dean, department head or a professor.

    Amount of award: $3,000
    Number of applicants: 150
    Application deadline: December 15
    Notification begins: March 1

Contact:
American Society of Magazine Editors
919 Third Avenue
New York, NY 10022
Phone: 212-872-3700
Fax: 212-906-0128

American Society of Naval Engineers

Naval Engineers Scholarship

Type of award: Scholarship.
Intended use: For full-time senior, master's study at accredited 4-year or graduate institution.
Eligibility: Applicant must be U.S. citizen.
Basis for selection: Major/career interest in engineering, marine; engineering, mechanical; engineering, electrical and electronic; physical sciences. Applicant must demonstrate high academic achievement.
Application requirements: Recommendations, essay and transcript.
Additional information: Interest in naval architecture, aeronautical engineering, civil engineering, or ocean engineering considered.

Amount of award:	$1,000-$3,000
Number of awards:	20
Number of applicants:	90
Application deadline:	February 15
Notification begins:	May 15
Total amount awarded:	$46,000

Contact:
American Society of Naval Engineers
1452 Duke Street
Alexandria, VA 22314
Phone: 703-836-6727
Fax: 703-836-7491
Website: www.jhuapl.edu/ASNE

American Society of Travel Agents Foundation

A.J. "Andy" Spielman Travel Agents Scholarship

Type of award: Scholarship, renewable.
Intended use: For full-time or half-time undergraduate certificate, non-degree study at accredited vocational institution. Designated institutions: Award may be used in an instituion in Canada as well as the U.S.
Eligibility: Applicant must be adult returning student.
Basis for selection: Major/career interest in tourism and travel. Applicant must demonstrate service orientation and high academic achievement.
Application requirements: Recommendations, essay, transcript and proof of eligibility.
Additional information: Must submit 500-word essay entitled "Why I Have Chosen the Travel Profession for My Reentry into the Work Force." Include SASE.

Amount of award:	$2,500
Number of awards:	2
Application deadline:	July 28

Air Travel Card Travel Agents Scholarship

Type of award: Scholarship, renewable.
Intended use: For full-time or half-time undergraduate study at accredited 2-year or 4-year institution. Designated institutions: In United States or Canada.
Eligibility: Applicant must be U.S. citizen, permanent resident or Canadian citizen.
Basis for selection: Major/career interest in tourism and travel. Applicant must demonstrate high academic achievement.
Application requirements: Recommendations, essay, transcript and proof of eligibility.
Additional information: Must submit 500-word essay defining the importance and challenges of managing business travel. Must also include brief description of career goals and why career in travel and tourism is desired. Must currently be enrolled in travel curriculum. Minimum 2.5 GPA required. Include SASE.

Amount of award:	$3,000
Number of awards:	1
Application deadline:	July 28
Total amount awarded:	$3,000

Alaska Airlines Travel Agents Scholarship

Type of award: Scholarship, renewable.
Intended use: For full-time or half-time sophomore, junior or senior study at accredited 4-year institution in United States.
Basis for selection: Major/career interest in tourism and travel. Applicant must demonstrate high academic achievement.
Application requirements: Recommendations, essay, transcript and proof of eligibility.
Additional information: Canadian citizens also eligible. Must submit 500-word essay on travel and tourism, describing travel industry today and forecasting expected changes and reasons for changes over next several years. Include two career goals and reasons for pursuing career in travel and tourism. Minimum 2.5 GPA required. Send SASE.

Amount of award:	$2,000
Number of awards:	1
Application deadline:	July 28
Notification begins:	December 1
Total amount awarded:	$2,000

American Express Travel Agents Scholarship

Type of award: Scholarship, renewable.
Intended use: For full-time or half-time undergraduate study at accredited vocational, 2-year or 4-year institution in United States in Canadian citizens also eligible.
Eligibility: Applicant must be U.S. citizen, permanent resident or Canadian citizen.
Basis for selection: Major/career interest in tourism and travel. Applicant must demonstrate high academic achievement.
Application requirements: Recommendations, essay, transcript and proof of eligibility.
Additional information: Must submit 500-word essay detailing applicant's plans in travel and tourism and view of travel industry's future. Minimum 2.5 GPA required. Must be enrolled in travel and tourism program. Send SASE. May be used at Canadian institutions.

Amount of award:	$2,500
Number of awards:	1
Application deadline:	July 28
Notification begins:	December 1
Total amount awarded:	$2,500

Arizona Chapter Gold Travel Agents Scholarship

Type of award: Scholarship, renewable.
Intended use: For full-time or half-time sophomore, junior or senior study at accredited 4-year institution in Arizona.
Eligibility: Applicant must be U.S. citizen or permanent resident residing in Arizona.
Basis for selection: Major/career interest in tourism and travel. Applicant must demonstrate seriousness of purpose, service orientation and high academic achievement.
Application requirements: Recommendations, essay, transcript and proof of eligibility.
Additional information: Must submit 500-word essay detailing applicant's plans in travel industry and interest in business of travel and tourism. Letter of recommendation must be from educator or employer regarding applicant's credentials. Minimum 2.5 GPA required. Send SASE.

Amount of award:	$3,000
Number of awards:	1
Application deadline:	July 28
Notification begins:	December 1
Total amount awarded:	$3,000

Avis Rent-a-Car Travel Agents Scholarship

Type of award: Scholarship, renewable.
Intended use: For full-time or half-time master's study at accredited graduate institution. Designated institutions: In United States or Canada.
Eligibility: Applicant must be U.S. citizen, permanent resident or Canadian citizen.
Basis for selection: Major/career interest in business. Applicant must demonstrate seriousness of purpose and high academic achievement.
Application requirements: Recommendations, essay, transcript and proof of eligibility.
Additional information: Must submit 500-750 word essay explaining how graduate program relates to his/her future carreer in the travel industry. Must have worked in travel industry for at least 4 years. Minimum 3.0 GPA required. Send SASE.

Amount of award:	$2,000
Number of awards:	1
Application deadline:	July 28
Notification begins:	December 1
Total amount awarded:	$2,000

David Hallissey Memorial Travel Agents Scholarship

Type of award: Research grant, renewable.
Intended use: For full-time or half-time master's, doctoral or non-degree study at accredited graduate institution in or outside United States.
Basis for selection: Major/career interest in tourism and travel. Applicant must demonstrate seriousness of purpose and high academic achievement.
Application requirements: Recommendations, transcript, proof of eligibility and research proposal.
Additional information: Must be graduate student or professor of tourism in recognized institution. Must submit 500-word abstract incorporating methodology and objectives of intended topic of research. Minimum 2.5 GPA required. Send SASE. Award may also be used at Canadian institutions.

Amount of award:	$2,000
Number of awards:	1
Application deadline:	July 28
Notification begins:	December 1
Total amount awarded:	$2,000

Contact:
American Society of Travel Agents Scholarship Foundation
1101 King Street
Alexandria, VA 22314-2944
Website: www.astanet.com

Healy Travel Agents Scholarship

Type of award: Scholarship, renewable.
Intended use: For full-time or half-time freshman, sophomore, junior or senior study at accredited 4-year institution in or outside United States.
Eligibility: Applicant must be U.S. citizen, permanent resident or Canadian citizen.
Basis for selection: Major/career interest in tourism and travel. Applicant must demonstrate service orientation and high academic achievement.
Application requirements: Recommendations, essay, transcript and proof of eligibility.
Additional information: Must submit 500-word essay suggesting improvements in travel industry. Minimum 2.5 GPA required. Send SASE.

Amount of award:	$2,000
Number of awards:	1
Number of applicants:	13
Application deadline:	July 28
Notification begins:	December 1
Total amount awarded:	$2,000

Contact:
American Society of Travel Agents Scholarship Foundation
1101 King Street
Alexandria, VA 22314-2944
Phone: 703-739-2782
Website: www.astanet.com

American Society of Travel Agents Scholarship Foundation

George Reinke Travel Agents Scholarship

Type of award: Scholarship, renewable.
Intended use: For full-time or half-time undergraduate certificate, freshman, sophomore or non-degree study at accredited vocational or 2-year institution in or outside United States.
Eligibility: Applicant must be U.S. citizen.
Basis for selection: Major/career interest in tourism and travel. Applicant must demonstrate seriousness of purpose, service orientation, financial need and high academic achievement.
Application requirements: Recommendations, essay, transcript and proof of eligibility.
Additional information: For travel agent training. Must submit 500-word essay entitled "My Objectives in Travel and Tourism Industry." Applicant should also address need for scholarship. Minimum 2.5 GPA required. Send SASE.

Amount of award:	$2,000
Number of awards:	10
Application deadline:	July 28, December 22
Notification begins:	December 1, March 1
Total amount awarded:	$10,000

Holland America Line-Westours Travel Agents Scholarship

Type of award: Scholarship, renewable.
Intended use: For full-time or half-time undergraduate study

at accredited vocational, 2-year or 4-year institution. Designated institutions: In United States or Canada.
Basis for selection: Major/career interest in tourism and travel. Applicant must demonstrate seriousness of purpose, service orientation and high academic achievement.
Application requirements: Recommendations, essay, transcript and proof of eligibility.
Additional information: Must submit 500-word essay on future of cruise industry. Minimum 2.5 GPA required. Send SASE. Open to Canadian citizens or residents as well. Applicant or parent must be employed by some aspect of the travel industry.

Amount of award:	$3,000
Number of awards:	3
Number of applicants:	40
Application deadline:	July 28
Notification begins:	December 1
Total amount awarded:	$6,000

Joseph R. Stone Travel Agents Scholarship

Type of award: Scholarship, renewable.
Intended use: For full-time or half-time freshman, sophomore, junior or senior study at accredited 2-year or 4-year institution. Designated institutions: In United States or Canada.
Eligibility: Applicant must be U.S. citizen, permanent resident or Canadian citizen.
Basis for selection: Major/career interest in tourism and travel. Applicant must demonstrate high academic achievement.
Application requirements: Recommendations, essay, transcript and proof of eligibility.
Additional information: Student or parent must be employed by some aspect of the travel industry. Must submit 500-word essay on applicant's goals in travel industry. Minimum 2.5 GPA required. Send SASE.

Amount of award:	$2,400
Number of awards:	3
Number of applicants:	10
Application deadline:	July 28
Notification begins:	December 1
Total amount awarded:	$4,800

Northern California/Epping Travel Agents Scholarship

Type of award: Scholarship, renewable.
Intended use: For full-time or half-time undergraduate study at accredited vocational, 2-year or 4-year institution in Northern California or Northern Nevada.
Eligibility: Applicant must be U.S. citizen or permanent resident residing in California or Nevada.
Basis for selection: Major/career interest in tourism and travel. Applicant must demonstrate depth of character, seriousness of purpose, service orientation and high academic achievement.
Application requirements: Recommendations, essay, transcript and proof of eligibility.
Additional information: Applicants must be residents of Northern California or Northern Nevada. Application deadlines and notification dates vary. Must submit 500-word essay entitled "Why I Desire a Profession in the Travel and Tourism Industry." Minimum 2.5 GPA required. Send SASE. Must be attending school in Northern California or Northern Nevada.

Amount of award:	$2,000
Number of awards:	1
Number of applicants:	10
Application deadline:	July 28
Notification begins:	December 1
Total amount awarded:	$2,000

Pollard Travel Agents Scholarship

Type of award: Scholarship, renewable.
Intended use: For full-time or half-time undergraduate certificate, freshman, sophomore or non-degree study at accredited vocational or 2-year institution. Designated institutions: In United States or Canada.
Eligibility: Applicant must be adult returning student.
Basis for selection: Major/career interest in tourism and travel. Applicant must demonstrate high academic achievement.
Application requirements: Recommendations, essay, transcript and proof of eligibility.
Additional information: Must be reentering job market by enrolling in travel and tourism program. Must submit 500-word essay on objectives in travel and tourism industry. Minimum 2.5 GPA required. Send SASE.

Amount of award:	$2,000
Number of awards:	2
Number of applicants:	30
Application deadline:	July 28, December 22
Notification begins:	December 1
Total amount awarded:	$4,000

Princess Cruises and Tours Travel Agents Scholarship

Type of award: Scholarship, renewable.
Intended use: For full-time or half-time undergraduate study at accredited vocational, 2-year or 4-year institution in or outside United States.
Basis for selection: Major/career interest in tourism and travel. Applicant must demonstrate seriousness of purpose, service orientation and high academic achievement.
Application requirements: Recommendations, essay, transcript and proof of eligibility.
Additional information: Must submit 300-word essay on two features cruise ships will need to offer passengers in next 10 years. Minimum 2.5 GPA required. Send SASE.

Amount of award:	$2,000
Number of awards:	2
Number of applicants:	30
Application deadline:	July 28
Notification begins:	December 11
Total amount awarded:	$4,000

Simmons Travel Agents Scholarship

Type of award: Scholarship, renewable.
Intended use: For full-time or half-time master's, doctoral study at accredited graduate institution. Designated institutions: In United States or Canada.
Basis for selection: Major/career interest in tourism and travel. Applicant must demonstrate high academic achievement.
Application requirements: Recommendations, essay, transcript and proof of eligibility.
Additional information: Must submit upper-level paper or

thesis (15-50 pages) on travel and tourism and how it affects travel agent community. Minimum 2.5 GPA required. Send SASE. Also open to Canadian citizens or residents.

Amount of award:	$2,000
Number of awards:	2
Application deadline:	July 28
Notification begins:	December 1

Southern California/Hawaiian Holidays Travel Agents Scholarship

Type of award: Scholarship, renewable.
Intended use: For full-time or half-time freshman, sophomore, junior or senior study at accredited 2-year or 4-year institution in United States.
Eligibility: Applicant must be U.S. citizen.
Basis for selection: Major/career interest in tourism and travel. Applicant must demonstrate seriousness of purpose, service orientation and high academic achievement.
Application requirements: Recommendations, essay, transcript and proof of eligibility.
Additional information: Must submit 1,000-word essay entitled "My Goals in the Travel Industry" and statement why applicant should receive award. Two awards; one for an applicant attending school in Los Angeles, Kern, Riverside, San Bernardino, San Luis Obispo, Santa Barbara, and Ventura counties; the other award for anywhere in the United States. Send SASE.

Amount of award:	$1,500
Number of awards:	2
Number of applicants:	5
Application deadline:	July 28
Notification begins:	December 1
Total amount awarded:	$3,000

Contact:
American Society of Travel Agents Scholarship Foundation
1101 King Street
Alexandria, VA 22314-2944
Website: www.astanet.com

American Speech-Language-Hearing Foundation

American Speech-Language-Hearing Graduate Scholarship

Type of award: Scholarship.
Intended use: For full-time master's, doctoral or postgraduate study.
Basis for selection: Major/career interest in speech pathology/audiology. Applicant must demonstrate high academic achievement.
Application requirements: Recommendations, essay, transcript and proof of eligibility.
Additional information: Priority given to foreign or minority student for one award; one award reserved for disabled student. Master's degree candidates must be in American Speech-Language-Hearing Association (ASHA) Education Standard Board (ESB) accredited program.

Amount of award:	$1,000-$4,000
Number of applicants:	155
Application deadline:	June 12
Notification begins:	November 14
Total amount awarded:	$22,000

American Speech-Language-Hearing International/Minority Student Scholarship

Type of award: Scholarship, renewable.
Intended use: For full-time graduate study at graduate institution in United States.
Eligibility: Applicant must be of minority background.
Basis for selection: Major/career interest in speech pathology/audiology. Applicant must demonstrate high academic achievement.
Application requirements: Recommendations, essay and transcript.

Amount of award:	$2,000
Number of applicants:	101
Application deadline:	June 12
Notification begins:	November 30

American Speech-Language-Hearing Student with Disability Scholarship

Type of award: Scholarship, renewable.
Intended use: For full-time graduate study at graduate institution in United States.
Eligibility: Applicant must be visually impaired, hearing impaired, physically challenged or learning disabled.
Basis for selection: Major/career interest in speech pathology/audiology. Applicant must demonstrate high academic achievement.
Application requirements: Recommendations, essay and transcript.

Amount of award:	$2,000
Number of applicants:	10
Application deadline:	June 12
Notification begins:	November 30

American Speech-Language-Hearing Young Minority Scholars Award

Type of award: Scholarship.
Intended use: For full-time master's study.
Eligibility: Applicant must be of minority background. Applicant must be U.S. citizen.
Basis for selection: Merit of content, organization, clarity, adherence to formal writing style. Major/career interest in speech pathology/audiology.
Application requirements: Recommendations, essay and transcript.

Amount of award:	$2,000
Number of awards:	1
Number of applicants:	6
Application deadline:	June 12
Notification begins:	November 30
Total amount awarded:	$2,000

Clinical Rehabilitation Audiology Research Grant

Type of award: Research grant, renewable.
Intended use: For master's, doctoral or postgraduate study at graduate institution in United States.
Basis for selection: Major/career interest in speech pathology/audiology.
Application requirements: Recommendations and research proposal.
   Amount of award: $2,000
   Application deadline: June 12
   Notification begins: November 30

Early Childhood Language Research Grant

Type of award: Research grant, renewable.
Intended use: For master's, doctoral or postgraduate study at graduate institution in United States.
Basis for selection: Major/career interest in speech pathology/audiology.
Application requirements: Recommendations and research proposal.
   Amount of award: $2,000
   Application deadline: June 12
   Notification begins: November 30
Contact:
Program Assistant
10801 Rockville Pike
Rockville, MD 20852
Phone: 301-897-5700
Website: www.asha.org

American Symphony Orchestra League

Music Assistance Fund

Type of award: Scholarship, renewable.
Intended use: For undergraduate, master's study in or outside United States.
Eligibility: Applicant must be African American. Applicant must be U.S. citizen.
Basis for selection: Major/career interest in music.
Application requirements: Audition, recommendations and essay.
Additional information: For music performance students ages 12 and up. Must play orchestra instrument. Piano, saxaphone, voice and conducting students are not eligible. Write or email for more information.
   Amount of award: $500-$3,500
   Number of applicants: 150
   Notification begins: May 30
Contact:
American Symphony Orchestra League
Nathan Newbrough
1156 15 Street NW, Suite 800
Washington, DC 20005-1704

American Veterinary Medical Foundation

Student Loan

Type of award: Loan, renewable.
Intended use: For post-bachelor's certificate study at accredited graduate institution. Designated institutions: Must be used at an AVMA accredited Veterinary schools.
Eligibility: Applicant must be U.S. citizen.
Basis for selection: Major/career interest in veterinary medicine. Applicant must demonstrate financial need.
Application requirements: $15 application fee. Recommendations and proof of eligibility.
Additional information: Preference given to 4th year students. Applicants must be either school chapter members or graduates who have become members of the AVMA.
   Amount of award: $8,000
   Number of awards: 177
   Number of applicants: 34
   Application deadline: March 31
   Total amount awarded: $182,000

Veterinary Student Scholarship

Type of award: Scholarship, renewable.
Intended use: For post-bachelor's certificate study at accredited graduate institution.
Basis for selection: Major/career interest in veterinary medicine. Applicant must demonstrate financial need.
Application requirements: Proof of eligibility.
Additional information: Students must be members of The Student Chapter of the AVMA at their school. Preference given to 3rd and 4th year students. Stipend is available, but must be applied for.
   Amount of award: $3,000
   Number of awards: 50
   Total amount awarded: $100,000
Contact:
American Veterinary Medical Foundation
1931 N. Meacham Road, Suite 100
Schaumburg, IL 60173
Website: www.avma.org/avmf

American Water Works Association

Water Works Fellowship

Type of award: Scholarship, renewable.
Intended use: For full-time master's, doctoral study at accredited graduate institution in United States.
Eligibility: Applicant must be U.S. citizen or permanent resident.
Basis for selection: Major/career interest in engineering, civil; chemistry; engineering, environmental. Applicant must demonstrate depth of character, seriousness of purpose and high academic achievement.

Application requirements: Portfolio, recommendations, transcript and research proposal.
Additional information: Deadlines vary between January and February; contact sponsor. Open to university students in the U.S., Canada, Guam, Puerto Rico, and Mexico.
    Amount of award: $3,000-$20,000
    Number of awards: 5
    Number of applicants: 50
    Notification begins: May 1
    Total amount awarded: $38,000
Contact:
American Water Works Association
6666 West Quincy Avenue
Denver, CO 80235
Phone: 303-347-6206
Website: www.awwa.org

American Welding Society Foundation, Inc.

American Welding Society District Scholarship

Type of award: Scholarship.
Intended use: For full-time or half-time undergraduate study at accredited vocational, 2-year or 4-year institution in United States.
Eligibility: Applicant must be U.S. citizen.
Basis for selection: Major/career interest in welding. Applicant must demonstrate depth of character, leadership, seriousness of purpose, financial need and high academic achievement.
Application requirements: Recommendations, transcript and proof of eligibility.
    Amount of award: $250-$3,000
    Number of awards: 150
    Application deadline: April 1
    Notification begins: July 1
    Total amount awarded: $110,000
Contact:
American Welding Society Foundation Inc.
Attn: Vicki Pinsky
550 Northwest LeJeune Road
Miami, FL 33126
Phone: 800-443-9353

American Welding Society Graduate Fellowship

Type of award: Research grant, renewable.
Intended use: For full-time master's, doctoral study at accredited graduate institution outside United States in Any academic institution located in North America.
Eligibility: Applicant must be U.S. citizen or May be a resident of any country in North America.
Basis for selection: Major/career interest in welding. Applicant must demonstrate seriousness of purpose and high academic achievement.
Application requirements: Research proposal.
Additional information: Award is renewable for up to 3 years.
    Amount of award: $20,000
    Number of applicants: 5
    Notification begins: March 15
Contact:
American Welding Society Foundation Inc.
Attn: Gricelda Manalich
550 Northwest LeJeune Road
Miami, FL 33126
Phone: 800-443-9353

Donald F. Hastings Scholarship

Type of award: Scholarship, renewable.
Intended use: For sophomore, junior or senior study at 4-year institution in United States.
Eligibility: Applicant must be U.S. citizen.
Basis for selection: Major/career interest in welding. Applicant must demonstrate seriousness of purpose and financial need.
Application requirements: Recommendations, transcript and proof of eligibility.
Additional information: Minimum of 2.5 GPA required. Priority given to residents of Ohio and California.
    Amount of award: $2,500
    Number of awards: 1
    Number of applicants: 16
    Application deadline: January 15
    Notification begins: March 15
    Total amount awarded: $2,500
Contact:
AWS Foundation, Inc.
Attn: Vicki Pinsky
550 NW LeJeune Road
Miami, FL 33126
Phone: 800-443-9353

Edward J. Brady Scholarship

Type of award: Scholarship, renewable.
Intended use: For full-time or half-time sophomore, junior or senior study.
Eligibility: Applicant must be U.S. citizen.
Basis for selection: Major/career interest in welding. Applicant must demonstrate seriousness of purpose and financial need.
Application requirements: Recommendations, essay, transcript and proof of eligibility. Proposed curriculum, brief biography, verification of hands-on welding experience.
Additional information: Minimum GPA of 2.5. Must have proof of hands-on welding experience.
    Amount of award: $2,500
    Number of awards: 1
    Number of applicants: 16
    Application deadline: January 15
    Notification begins: March 15
    Total amount awarded: $2,500
Contact:
American Welding Society Foundation Inc.
Attn: Vicki Pinsky
550 Northwest LeJeune Road
Miami, FL 33126
Phone: 800-443-9353

Howard E. Adkins Memorial Scholarship

Type of award: Scholarship, renewable.
Intended use: For full-time junior, senior study.
Eligibility: Applicant must be U.S. citizen.
Basis for selection: Major/career interest in welding. Applicant must demonstrate seriousness of purpose and high academic achievement.
Application requirements: Recommendations, transcript and proof of eligibility.
Additional information: Minimum GPA of 3.2 in the engineering scientific and technical subjects, and a 2.8 overall GPA. Priority given to residents of Kentucky and Wisconsin.
    Amount of award: $2,500
    Number of awards: 1
    Number of applicants: 12
    Application deadline: January 15
    Notification begins: March 15
    Total amount awarded: $2,500
Contact:
AWS Foundation Inc.
Attn: Vicki Pinsky
550 NW LeJeune Road
Miami, FL 33126
Phone: 800-443-9353

James A. Turner, Jr., Scholarship

Type of award: Scholarship, renewable.
Intended use: For full-time sophomore, junior or senior study at accredited 4-year institution.
Eligibility: Applicant must be U.S. citizen.
Basis for selection: Major/career interest in welding; business, management and administration. Applicant must demonstrate seriousness of purpose and financial need.
Application requirements: Recommendations, transcript and proof of eligibility. Verification of employment, brief biography, financial aid report, proposed curriculum.
Additional information: Minimum GPA of 2.5. Must have interest in pursuing a management career in welding. Must work a minimum of 10 hours per week at a welding store.
    Amount of award: $2,500
    Number of awards: 1
    Number of applicants: 4
    Application deadline: January 15
    Notification begins: March 15
    Total amount awarded: $2,500
Contact:
American Welding Society Foundation Inc.
Attn: Vicki Pinsky
550 Northwest LeJeune Road
Miami, FL 33126
Phone: 800-443-9353

John C. Lincoln Memorial Scholarship

Type of award: Scholarship, renewable.
Intended use: For sophomore, junior or senior study.
Eligibility: Applicant must be U.S. citizen.
Basis for selection: Major/career interest in welding. Applicant must demonstrate seriousness of purpose and financial need.
Application requirements: Recommendations, transcript and proof of eligibility.
Additional information: Minimun GPA of 2.5
    Amount of award: $2,500
    Number of awards: 1
    Application deadline: January 15, March 15
    Total amount awarded: $2,500
Contact:
AWS Foundation, Inc.
Attn: Vicki Pinsky
550 NW LeJeune Road
Miami, FL 33126
Phone: 800-443-9553

Miller Electric Manufacturing Company Ivic Scholarship

Type of award: Scholarship.
Intended use: For undergraduate study at accredited vocational, 2-year or 4-year institution in United States.
Eligibility: Applicant must be U.S. citizen.
Basis for selection: Competition in Engineering/architecture. AWS National Welding Trials Major/career interest in welding. Applicant must demonstrate depth of character, leadership and seriousness of purpose.
Additional information: Minimum GPA of 2.5.
    Amount of award: $40,000
    Number of awards: 1
Contact:
American Welding Society Foundation
Attn: Vicki Pinsky
550 Northwest LeJeune Road
Miami, FL 33126
Phone: 800-443-9353

Praxair International Scholarship

Type of award: Scholarship, renewable.
Intended use: For full-time sophomore, junior or senior study.
Eligibility: Applicant must be U.S. citizen or Canadian students may apply.
Basis for selection: Major/career interest in welding. Applicant must demonstrate leadership, service orientation and financial need.
Application requirements: Recommendations, transcript and proof of eligibility.
Additional information: Minimum GPA of 2.5.
    Amount of award: $2,500
    Number of awards: 1
    Number of applicants: 15
    Application deadline: March 15, January 15
    Total amount awarded: $2,500
Contact:
American Welding Society Foundation Inc.
Attn: Vicki Pinsky
550 NW Lejuene Road
Miami, FL 33126
Phone: 800-443-9353

American-Scandinavian Foundation

Study in Scandinavia Grant

Type of award: Research grant, renewable.
Intended use: For graduate or non-degree study outside United States in Denmark, Finland, Iceland, Norway, Sweden.
Basis for selection: Major/career interest in Scandinavian studies/research; humanities/liberal arts; arts, general; physical sciences.
Application requirements: $10 application fee. Recommendations, transcript and research proposal.
Additional information: Preference given to applicants who have not received ASF awards in the past. Must have well defined research project that makes stay in Scandinavia essential. Should have some knowledge of host country's language. Priority is given to candidates at the graduate level for dissertation related research. Funding is for research only.

Amount of award:	$3,000-$100,000
Number of awards:	25
Number of applicants:	125
Application deadline:	November 1
Notification begins:	March 15
Total amount awarded:	$195,500

Contact:
American-Scandinavian Foundation
725 Park Avenue
New York, NY 10021
Phone: 212-879-9779
Fax: 212-249-3444
Website: www.amscan.org

An Uncommon Legacy Foundation, Inc.

Uncommon Legacy Foundation Scholarship

Type of award: Scholarship, renewable.
Intended use: For full-time undergraduate, master's or doctoral study at accredited 4-year or graduate institution.
Eligibility: Must be a lesbian. Applicant must be female. Applicant must be U.S. citizen or permanent resident.
Basis for selection: Applicant must demonstrate depth of character, leadership, seriousness of purpose, service orientation, financial need and high academic achievement.
Application requirements: Recommendations, essay, transcript and proof of eligibility.
Additional information: Applicants must demonstrate a commitment or contribution to the lesbian community. Minimum GPA of 3.0. Application is also available online.

Amount of award:	$1,000
Application deadline:	May 1

Contact:
An Uncommon Legacy Foundation, Inc.
150 West 26th St., Suite 503
New York, NY 10001
Website: www.uncommonlegacy.org

Aopa Air Safety Foundation

McAllister and Burnside Scholarship

Type of award: Scholarship.
Intended use: For junior, senior study.
Eligibility: Applicant must be U.S. citizen.
Basis for selection: Major/career interest in aviation. Applicant must demonstrate seriousness of purpose and high academic achievement.
Application requirements: Essay and transcript.
Additional information: Send SASE. Must have 3.25 GPA or above.

Amount of award:	$1,000
Number of awards:	2
Number of applicants:	300
Application deadline:	March 31
Notification begins:	June 1
Total amount awarded:	$2,000

Contact:
Aopa Air Safety Foundation
421 Aviation Way
Frederick, MD 21701
Phone: 301-695-2170
Fax: 301-695-2375
Website: www.aopa.org

Archaeological Institute of America

Anne and Oliver C. Colburn Fellowship

Type of award: Scholarship.
Intended use: For master's, doctoral or postgraduate study in Greece. Designated institutions: American School of Classical Studies at Athens.
Eligibility: Applicant must be U.S. citizen, permanent resident or Canadian citizen.
Basis for selection: Major/career interest in archaeology; classics; anthropology; history; art, art history. Applicant must demonstrate high academic achievement.
Application requirements: Recommendations and proof of eligibility.

Amount of award:	$13,000
Number of awards:	1
Number of applicants:	13
Application deadline:	February 1
Notification begins:	April 1
Total amount awarded:	$13,000

Contact:
Archaeological Institute of America
656 Beacon Street Fourth Floor
Boston, MA 02215-2010
Phone: 617-353-936
Fax: 617-353-6550

Harriet and Leon Pomerance Fellowship

Type of award: Scholarship.
Intended use: For doctoral, postgraduate or non-degree study.
Eligibility: Applicant must be permanent resident or Canadian citizen.
Basis for selection: Major/career interest in archaeology; classics; anthropology; history; art, art history. Applicant must demonstrate seriousness of purpose and high academic achievement.
Application requirements: Recommendations, proof of eligibility and research proposal.
Additional information: Preference given to candidates who require travel to Mediterranean and those whose work relates to Aegean Bronze Age archaeology.

Amount of award:	$4,000
Number of awards:	1
Number of applicants:	7
Application deadline:	November 1
Notification begins:	February 1
Total amount awarded:	$4,000

Contact:
Archaeological Institute of America
656 Beacon Street Fourth Floor
Boston, MA 02215-2010
Phone: 617-353-9361

Helen M. Woodruff Fellowship

Type of award: Scholarship.
Intended use: For doctoral, postgraduate study.
Basis for selection: Major/career interest in archaeology; classics; Middle Eastern studies; art, art history.
Application requirements: Recommendations and proof of eligibility.
Additional information: This fellowship, combined with other funds from the American Academy in Rome, will support a Rome Prize Fellowship.

Amount of award:	$8,000
Number of awards:	1

Contact:
American Academy in Rome
7 East 60th Street
New York, NY 10022-8051
Phone: 212-751-7200

Kenan T. Erim Award

Type of award: Research grant.
Intended use: For doctoral, postgraduate or non-degree study.
Basis for selection: Major/career interest in archaeology; classics; anthropology; history; art, art history. Applicant must demonstrate seriousness of purpose and high academic achievement.
Application requirements: Recommendations.
Additional information: Fellowship for research/work at Aphrodisias archaeological site in Turkey. Must receive approval of field director.

Amount of award:	$4,000
Number of awards:	1
Number of applicants:	3
Application deadline:	November 1
Notification begins:	February 1
Total amount awarded:	$4,000

Contact:
Archaeological Institute of America
656 Beacon Street Fourth Floor
Boston, MA 02215-2010
Phone: 617-353-9361

Olivia James Traveling Fellowship

Type of award: Scholarship.
Intended use: For doctoral, postgraduate or non-degree study.
Eligibility: Applicant must be U.S. citizen or permanent resident.
Basis for selection: Major/career interest in archaeology; classics; anthropology; history; art, art history. Applicant must demonstrate seriousness of purpose and high academic achievement.
Application requirements: Recommendations, proof of eligibility and research proposal.
Additional information: Award for travel to and study in Greece, Aegean Islands, Sicily, southern Italy, Asia Minor or Mesopotamia.

Amount of award:	$20,000
Number of awards:	1
Number of applicants:	19
Application deadline:	November 1
Notification begins:	February 1
Total amount awarded:	$20,000

Contact:
Archaeological Institute of America
656 Beacon Street Fourth Floor
Boston, MA 02215-2010
Phone: 617-353-9361

Woodruff Dissertation Research Fellowship

Type of award: Research grant.
Intended use: For doctoral study in Italy or western Mediterranean.
Basis for selection: Major/career interest in archaeology.
Application requirements: Recommendations, proof of eligibility and research proposal.
Additional information: Preference given to field-oriented projects. Award is for research, not for work on the dissertation, and covers travel, room and board, and some other expenses.

Amount of award:	$5,000
Number of awards:	1
Number of applicants:	5
Notification begins:	November 1
Total amount awarded:	$5,000

Contact:
Archaeological Institute of America
656 Beacon Street Fourth Floor
Boston, MA 02215-2010
Phone: 617-353-9361
Fax: 617-353-6550

Arena Stage

Allen Lee Hughes Fellows Program

Type of award: Scholarship.
Intended use: For undergraduate, graduate, postgraduate or non-degree study.
Eligibility: Applicant must be of minority background. Applicant must be U.S. citizen.
Basis for selection: Major/career interest in theater (artistic); theater (production/technical). Applicant must demonstrate seriousness of purpose.
Application requirements: Interview, audition, portfolio, recommendations, essay and transcript.
Additional information: All majors welcome. Preference given to theater majors.
   Amount of award: $10,800
   Application deadline: April 1

Allen Lee Hughes Internship

Type of award: Internship.
Intended use: For graduate or postgraduate study.
Eligibility: Applicant must be of minority background.
Basis for selection: Major/career interest in theater (production/technical); theater (artistic). Applicant must demonstrate seriousness of purpose.
Application requirements: Interview, audition, portfolio, recommendations, essay and transcript.
Additional information: Applicants of all majors are considered, though preference is given to those with theater-related career goals.
   Amount of award: $10,800
   Application deadline: April 1
Contact:
Intership Coordinator
1101 Sixth Street, S.W.
Washington, DC 20024

Armed Forces Communications and Electronics Association

Armed Forces Educational Foundation Fellowship

Type of award: Scholarship.
Intended use: For full-time doctoral study in United States.
Eligibility: Applicant must be U.S. citizen.
Basis for selection: Major/career interest in engineering, electrical and electronic; electronics; computer and information sciences; physics; mathematics. Applicant must demonstrate depth of character, leadership, patriotism, seriousness of purpose, service orientation and high academic achievement.
Application requirements: Recommendations, transcript and nomination by Dean of the college of engineering at an accredited U.S. university; one candidate per university.
Additional information: Send SASE.
   Amount of award: $25,000
   Number of awards: 2
   Number of applicants: 22
   Application deadline: February 1
   Notification begins: April 1
   Total amount awarded: $50,000

General Emmett Paige Scholarship

Type of award: Scholarship.
Intended use: For full-time freshman, sophomore or junior study at accredited 4-year institution in United States.
Eligibility: Applicant must be U.S. citizen. Applicant must be in military service, veteran, child of active service person, veteran or POW/MIA, spouse of active service person, veteran or POW/MIA.
Basis for selection: Major/career interest in engineering, electrical and electronic; computer and information sciences; engineering, computer; physics; mathematics. Applicant must demonstrate depth of character, leadership, patriotism, seriousness of purpose, service orientation and high academic achievement.
Application requirements: Recommendations, transcript and proof of eligibility. Freshmen must have letters from employer or supervisor or copy of performance evaluation, fitness report or similar document. Proof of eligibility can be copy of discharge form DD214, certificate of service, facsimile of applicants current DOD or Coast Guard identification card.
Additional information: Send SASE.
   Amount of award: $2,000
   Number of awards: 15
   Number of applicants: 56
   Application deadline: March 1
   Notification begins: July 21
   Total amount awarded: $30,000

General John A. Wickham Scholarship

Type of award: Scholarship.
Intended use: For full-time sophomore, junior study at accredited 4-year institution in United States.
Eligibility: Applicant must be U.S. citizen.
Basis for selection: Major/career interest in engineering, electrical and electronic; electronics; computer and information sciences; physics; mathematics. Applicant must demonstrate depth of character, leadership, patriotism, seriousness of purpose, service orientation and high academic achievement.
Application requirements: Recommendations and transcript. Two letters of recommendation from faculty member having personal knowledge of candidate's program, achievements and potential.
Additional information: GPA 3.4. Additional fields of study include mathematics. Send SASE.

Amount of award:	$2,000
Number of awards:	15
Number of applicants:	41
Application deadline:	May 1
Notification begins:	July 21
Total amount awarded:	$30,000

Contact:
Armed Forces Communications and Electronics Association
4400 Fair Lakes Court
Fairfax, VA 22033-3899
Phone: 703-631-6147
Fax: 703-631-4693
Website: www.afcea.org

Armenian General Benevolent Union

Armenian Union Awards for Students on Non-U.S. Soil

Type of award: Scholarship, renewable.
Intended use: For full-time undergraduate or graduate study outside United States.
Eligibility: Applicant must be of Armenian heritage.
Basis for selection: Applicant must demonstrate depth of character, leadership, seriousness of purpose, service orientation, financial need and high academic achievement.
Application requirements: Recommendations, transcript and proof of eligibility. Enrollment verification.
Additional information: Students at first professional level must be pursuing degree in medicine. Must be living and planning to study outside U.S. Students must provide verification of enrollment. Must be of Armenian descent.

Amount of award:	$300-$1,200
Number of awards:	223
Number of applicants:	265
Application deadline:	May 15
Notification begins:	September 15
Total amount awarded:	$313,000

Armenian Union U.S. Graduate Loan

Type of award: Loan, renewable.
Intended use: For full-time master's study at accredited graduate institution.
Eligibility: Applicant must be of Armenian heritage. Applicant must be permanent resident or must be living and/or planning to study on U.S. soil.
Basis for selection: Major/career interest in education; public administration/service; international relations; journalism. Applicant must demonstrate depth of character, leadership, seriousness of purpose, service orientation and high academic achievement.
Application requirements: Recommendations, transcript and proof of eligibility. CSS Profile. Journalism/radio-TV-broadcast students must submit writing samples.
Additional information: Education major must be specifically educational administration. Armenian studies students must be in final two years of Ph.D. program. Students studying radio-TV-broadcasting or pursuing first professional degrees in medicine or law also considered. Students at highly competitive institutions preferred. Must be of Armenian descent.

Amount of award:	$2,500-$7,500
Number of awards:	12
Number of applicants:	35
Application deadline:	April 1
Notification begins:	July 15
Total amount awarded:	$77,000

Contact:
Armenian General Benevolent Union
Mrs. Maral Achian
55 E. 59th Street
New York, NY 10022-1112
Phone: 212-319-6383
Fax: 212-319-6507

Armenian Relief Society of North America, Inc.

Armenian Relief Graduate Scholarship

Type of award: Scholarship, renewable.
Intended use: For graduate study at accredited graduate institution.
Eligibility: Applicant must be of Armenian heritage.
Basis for selection: Applicant must demonstrate service orientation and financial need.
Application requirements: Recommendations, transcript and proof of eligibility. Parent's tax returns.
Additional information: Send SASE with request for application after January 1.

Amount of award:	$1,000
Number of awards:	10
Number of applicants:	100
Application deadline:	May 1
Total amount awarded:	$10,000

Contact:
Armenian Relief Society of North America, Inc.
80 Bigelow Avenue
Watertown, MA 02172

Armenian Relief Undergraduate Scholarship

Type of award: Scholarship, renewable.
Intended use: For freshman, sophomore, junior or senior study at accredited 4-year institution.
Eligibility: Applicant must be of Armenian heritage.
Basis for selection: Applicant must demonstrate service orientation and financial need.
Application requirements: Recommendations, transcript and proof of eligibility. Parent's tax returns.
Additional information: Must be currently enrolled in college and have completed at least one semester. Send SASE with request for application after January 1.

Amount of award:	$200
Number of awards:	15
Number of applicants:	100
Application deadline:	May 1
Total amount awarded:	$3,000

Contact:
Armenian Relief Society of North America, Inc.
Scholarship Committee
80 Bigelow Avenue
Watertown, MA 02172

Army Emergency Relief

Army Emergency Relief Scholarship

Type of award: Scholarship, renewable.
Intended use: For full-time freshman, sophomore, junior or senior study at accredited vocational, 2-year or 4-year institution.
Eligibility: Applicant must be single. Applicant must be U.S. citizen or permanent resident. Applicant must be child of active service person, veteran or deceased veteran who served in the Army.
Basis for selection: Applicant must demonstrate leadership, financial need and high academic achievement.
Application requirements: Essay, transcript and proof of eligibility.

Amount of award:	$600-$1,700
Number of awards:	1,000
Number of applicants:	1,850
Application deadline:	March 1
Notification begins:	May 15
Total amount awarded:	$1,025,000

Contact:
ARMY Emergency Relief
200 Stovall Street
Alexandria, VA 22332-0600
Website: www.aerhq.org

Arthur and Doreen Parrett Scholarship Trust Fund

Arthur and Doreen Parrett Scholarship

Type of award: Scholarship, renewable.
Intended use: For full-time sophomore, junior, senior, master's, doctoral or first professional study.
Eligibility: Applicant must be residing in Washington.
Basis for selection: Major/career interest in science, general; engineering; dentistry; medicine (m.d.). Applicant must demonstrate financial need and high academic achievement.
Application requirements: Recommendations, essay and transcript.
Additional information: Applicants must have completed first year of college.

Amount of award:	$2,000-$4,000
Number of awards:	15
Number of applicants:	485
Application deadline:	July 31
Notification begins:	September 1
Total amount awarded:	$42,000

Contact:
Arthur and Doreen Parrett Scholarship Trust Fund
P.O. Box 720
Seattle, WA 98111-7206
Phone: 800-505-4545
Fax: 206-344-3738

ASCAP Foundation

Leiber and Stoller Scholarship

Type of award: Scholarship.
Intended use: For full-time freshman, sophomore, junior or senior study. Designated institutions: Berkley College of Music.
Eligibility: Applicant must be high school senior.
Basis for selection: Major/career interest in music. Applicant must demonstrate financial need.
Application requirements: Audition, recommendations and proof of eligibility. Must submit a tape.
Additional information: Music can be of any genre.

Amount of award:	$10,000
Number of awards:	2
Number of applicants:	20
Application deadline:	April 1
Total amount awarded:	$20,000

Contact:
ASCAP Foundation
Leiber & Stoller Scholarship/ATTN. Kim Hargraves
One Lincoln Plaza
New York, NY 10023
Phone: 2126216219

Morton Gould Young Composers Award

Type of award: Scholarship, renewable.
Intended use: For non-degree study.
Eligibility: Applicant must be U.S. citizen or permanent resident.
Basis for selection: Competition in Music performance/composition. Major/career interest in music.
Application requirements: Recommendations and proof of eligibility. Must submit score or manuscript of one musical work, boigraphical information, list of compositions to date, and tape of submitted composition.

Amount of award:	$100-$1,850
Number of awards:	25
Number of applicants:	500
Application deadline:	March 15
Notification begins:	June 1
Total amount awarded:	$20,000

Contact:
ASCAP Foundation Morton Gould Young Composers Awards
c/o Fran Richard
One Lincoln Plaza
New York, NY 10023

Nathan Burkan Memorial Competition

Type of award: Scholarship.
Intended use: For junior, senior study. Designated institutions: ABA law school.
Basis for selection: Competition in Writing/journalism. Local awards: $500 for 1st place and $200 for 2nd place; on papers certified by deans of competing at ABA accredited law schools. National award: eligible to compete for five national awards starting from $500 to $3,000. Major/career interest in law.
Application requirements: Essay and nomination. Essay must be certified by law school dean.
Additional information: Competition open to third year students. With permission of dean, second year students may be eligible. An essay not to exceed 50 pages on any aspect of copyright law is also required.
    Amount of award: $200-$3,000
    Number of awards: 7
    Application deadline: June 30
Contact:
ASCAP Foundation
One Lincoln Plaza
New York, NY 10023
Phone: 212-621-6273

Sammy Cahn Award

Type of award: Scholarship.
Intended use: For non-degree study.
Basis for selection: Competition in Music performance/composition. Major/career interest in music.
Application requirements: Proof of eligibility.
Additional information: Open to any participant of the ASCAP foundation songwriter workshop series. The submission of a tape of an original song is required.
    Amount of award: $10,000
    Application deadline: September 1
    Notification begins: October 1
Contact:
ASCAP Foundation
One Lincoln Plaza
New York, NY 10023
Phone: 212-621-6219

Asian Cultural Council

Asian Art and Religion Fellowship Program

Type of award: Scholarship.
Intended use: For postgraduate study outside United States in Asia.
Eligibility: Applicant must be U.S. citizen or permanent resident.
Basis for selection: Major/career interest in arts, general; performing arts.
Application requirements: Research proposal. Letter of inquiry and introduction.
Additional information: For American scholars, specialists, and artists wishing to conduct research and undertake projects in south, southeast, and East Asia focusing on the relationship between artistic and religious traditions in Asia. Fellowships last one to twelve months. Amount of grants depend on individual needs.
    Application deadline: February 1
    Notification begins: July 1

Asian Humanities Fellowship Program

Type of award: Scholarship.
Intended use: For graduate study outside United States.
Eligibility: Applicant must be U.S. citizen or permanent resident.
Basis for selection: Major/career interest in performing arts; arts, general; humanities/liberal arts; architecture; archaeology; museum studies. Applicant must demonstrate seriousness of purpose.
Application requirements: Research proposal. Letter of inquiry.
Additional information: Fellowships last one to twelve months. Award is based upon individual need.
    Application deadline: February 1
    Notification begins: July 1

Fellowship Grants to Asian Individuals

Type of award: Scholarship.
Intended use: For master's, doctoral or postgraduate study in United States.
Eligibility: Applicant must be East or Southeast Asian citizen (those from India and Pakistan excluded).
Basis for selection: Major/career interest in performing arts; arts, general. Applicant must demonstrate seriousness of purpose.
Application requirements: Research proposal. letter of inquiry.
Additional information: For artists, scholars, and specialists from Asia seeking grant assistance to conduct research, study, receive specialized training, undertake observation tours, or pursue creative activity in the United States. Fellowships last one to twelve months. Award is based on individual need.
    Application deadline: February 1
    Notification begins: July 1

Japan-United States Arts Program

Type of award: Scholarship.
Intended use: For postgraduate, non-degree study in Japan.
Eligibility: Applicant must be U.S. citizen, permanent resident or residents of Japan.
Basis for selection: Major/career interest in arts, general; performing arts.
Application requirements: Letter of inquiry.
Additional information: Grants are awarded to enable Japanese artists, scholars, and arts specialists to visit the United States and to enable American artists, scholars, and arts specialists to visit Japan. Fellowships last one to twelve months. Awards based on individual needs.

Application deadline: February 1
Notification begins: July 1
Contact:
Asian Cultural Council
437 Madison Avenue
37th Floor
New York, NY 10022-7001

ASM Foundation for Education and Research

ASM Foundation Undergraduate Scholarship

Type of award: Scholarship.
Intended use: For full-time sophomore, junior or senior study at vocational, 2-year or 4-year institution in United States.
Eligibility: Applicant must be U.S. citizen or Canadian or Mexican citizen.
Basis for selection: Major/career interest in engineering, materials; engineering, mechanical; engineering, ceramic; engineering. Applicant must demonstrate depth of character, leadership, seriousness of purpose, service orientation and high academic achievement.
Application requirements: Recommendations, essay, transcript and proof of eligibility.
Additional information: Also open to those in polymer, metallurgical, industrial and aeronautical engineering. Applicant must be a member of ASM international.
Amount of award: $500-$5,000
Number of awards: 42
Number of applicants: 85
Application deadline: June 15
Notification begins: August 15
Total amount awarded: $41,000
Contact:
ASM Foundation for Education and Research
Scholarship Program
Materials Park, OH 44073-0002
Phone: 216-338-5151
Fax: 216-338-4634

ASQ EED

EED Scholarship Program

Type of award: Scholarship.
Intended use: For full-time undergraduate, master's, doctoral, first professional or postgraduate study at 2-year, 4-year or graduate institution in United States.
Basis for selection: Major/career interest in engineering; environmental science; science, general. Applicant must demonstrate depth of character, seriousness of purpose and high academic achievement.
Application requirements: Recommendations, transcript and proof of eligibility.
Additional information: 2.75 GPA required. Must have course work in quality related courses and be associated with the environmental science and/or engineering.
Amount of award: $1,000-$2,000
Number of awards: 1
Number of applicants: 2
Application deadline: March 31, July 31
Contact:
Advanced Systems, Inc.
P.O. Box 8032
Newark, DE 19714

Associated Constructors of Maine, Inc. Educational Foundation

AGC of Maine Scholarship Program

Type of award: Scholarship, renewable.
Intended use: For sophomore, junior or senior study.
Eligibility: Applicant must be residing in Maine.
Basis for selection: Major/career interest in construction; engineering, civil. Applicant must demonstrate financial need and high academic achievement.
Application requirements: Interview, recommendations, essay and transcript.
Additional information: Full-time enrolled students preferred.
Amount of award: $500-$2,500
Number of awards: 7
Number of applicants: 17
Application deadline: March 15
Total amount awarded: $10,000
Contact:
Associated Constructors of Maine, Inc. Educational Foundation
P.O. Box N
Augusta
Augusta, ME 04332
Phone: 207-622-4741

Associated General Contractors Education and Research Foundation

Associated General Contractors James L. Allhands Essay Competition

Type of award: Scholarship.
Intended use: For full-time senior study at accredited 4-year institution.
Basis for selection: Competition in Writing/journalism. Essay which demonstrates clarity of thought, completeness, specific examples supporting opinions, grammar, neatness, adherence to contest rules. Major/career interest in engineering, civil; engineering, construction; construction.

Application requirements: Essay.
Additional information: First prize is $1,000 and trip to AGC convention. Second prize is $500. Third prize is $300. Topic, selected each year by sponsor, related to construction or general contracting, is management oriented, not technical.

Amount of award:	$300-$1,000
Number of awards:	3
Number of applicants:	50
Application deadline:	November 2
Notification begins:	February 15
Total amount awarded:	$1,800

Contact:
Association of General Contractors
Attn: Director of Programs
1957 E Street, NW
Washington, DC 20006
Phone: 202-393-2040
Fax: 202-347-4004
Website: www.agc.org

Education and Research Junior Graduate Award

Type of award: Scholarship.
Intended use: For full-time master's, doctoral study.
Eligibility: Applicant must be U.S. citizen or permanent resident.
Basis for selection: Major/career interest in construction; engineering, civil; engineering, construction. Applicant must demonstrate seriousness of purpose, service orientation, financial need and high academic achievement.
Application requirements: Interview, recommendations, essay and transcript.
Additional information: Applications and specific information available September 1 from the office or via the internet.

Amount of award:	$7,500
Application deadline:	November 2
Notification begins:	March 31

Contact:
Association of General Contractors
Attn: Director of Programs
1957 E Street, NW
Washington, DC 20006
Phone: 202-393-2040.
Fax: 202-347-4004
Website: www.agc.org

Education and Research Outstanding Educators Award

Type of award: Scholarship.
Intended use: For non-degree study.
Basis for selection: Major/career interest in engineering, construction; engineering, civil. Applicant must demonstrate service orientation.
Application requirements: Recommendations, proof of eligibility and nomination by administrative faculty member and officer of AGC member construction company. Undergraduate teaching load sheet.
Additional information: Must be full-time teaching faculty member (at least five years experience) at an ACCE or ABET accredited university who teaches construction or civil engineering. Application and nomination forms available in August either through the office or via the internet.

Amount of award:	$5,000
Number of awards:	1
Number of applicants:	20
Application deadline:	November 2
Total amount awarded:	$5,000

Contact:
Director of Programs/AGC Education and Research Foundation
1957 E St., NW
Washington, DC 20006
Phone: 202-393-2040
Fax: 202-347-4004
Website: www.agc.org

Education and Research Undergraduate Scholarship

Type of award: Scholarship, renewable.
Intended use: For full-time freshman, sophomore or junior study at accredited 4-year institution.
Eligibility: Applicant must be U.S. citizen or permanent resident.
Basis for selection: Major/career interest in engineering, civil; engineering, construction; construction. Applicant must demonstrate seriousness of purpose, service orientation, financial need and high academic achievement.
Application requirements: Recommendations and transcript.
Additional information: Must be enrolled in an ABET or ACCE accredited program to be eligible. Applications are available September 1 either from the office or via the internet.

Amount of award:	$1,500
Application deadline:	November 2
Notification begins:	March 30

Contact:
Association of General Contractors
Attn: Director of Programs
1957 E St., NW
Washington, DC 20006
Phone: 202-393-2040
Fax: 2023474004
Website: www.agc.org

Associated Press

Associated Press/APTRA-CLETE Roberts Memorial Journalism Scholarship

Type of award: Scholarship.
Intended use: For undergraduate or graduate study at graduate institution in United States. Designated institutions: Students must be enrolled in a California or Nevada college or university.
Basis for selection: Major/career interest in journalism.
Application requirements: Recommendations and essay.
Additional information: For study in broadcast journalism.

Amount of award:	$1,500
Number of awards:	3
Application deadline:	December 12
Notification begins:	March 21
Total amount awarded:	$4,500

Contact:
Scholarship Committee
221 South Figueroa St., #300
Los Angeles, CA 90012
Phone: 213-628-1200

Association for Library and Information Science Foundation

ALISE Dissertation Competition

Type of award: Scholarship.
Intended use: For postgraduate study.
Basis for selection: Competition in Research paper. Significance of research problem, application of appropriate research methods, and clarity and organization of the presentation. Major/career interest in library science.
Application requirements: Proof of eligibility.
Additional information: Winners receive 1998 conference registration and membership to ALISE for 1997-98. Dissertation must be complete by December 1998 to be eligible.

Amount of award:	$400
Application deadline:	September 15

ALISE Methodology Paper Competition

Type of award: Scholarship.
Intended use: For non-degree study.
Basis for selection: Competition in Research paper. Description of the methodology or technique, relevance of methodology or techinique to library and information science, practical applications of technique towards library and information science research, and clarity and organization of presentation Major/career interest in library science.
Additional information: Papers completed in pursuit of master's or doctoral degrees are eligible, as are papers generated as a result of research grant or other source of funding. Must be a personal member of ALISE.

Amount of award:	$500
Number of awards:	1
Application deadline:	September 15
Total amount awarded:	$500

Contact:
Association for Library and Information Science Foundation
P.O. Box 7640
Arlington, VA 22207
Website: www.alise.org/awards_main.html

Association for Women in Architecture

Women in Architecture Scholarship

Type of award: Scholarship, renewable.
Intended use: For full-time junior, senior, master's, doctoral or first professional study at 4-year or graduate institution.
Eligibility: Applicant must be female.
Basis for selection: Major/career interest in architecture; interior design; engineering; landscape architecture. Applicant must demonstrate seriousness of purpose, financial need and high academic achievement.
Application requirements: Interview, portfolio, recommendations, essay and transcript. Student must have completed at least one year in architecture or related program leading to a degree.
Additional information: Additional field of study may include urban planning. Must be either California resident or attend California school to qualify.

Amount of award:	$1,000-$2,000
Number of awards:	3
Number of applicants:	60
Application deadline:	April 23
Notification begins:	February 1
Total amount awarded:	$4,500

Contact:
Association for Women in Architecture
2550 Beverly Boulevard.
Los Angeles, CA 90057
Phone: 213-389-6490

Association for Women in Communications

Association for Women in Communications Scholarship

Type of award: Scholarship.
Intended use: For full-time junior, senior or graduate study at accredited 4-year or graduate institution.
Basis for selection: Major/career interest in communications; journalism; radio/television/film; film/video. Applicant must demonstrate depth of character, service orientation, financial need and high academic achievement.
Application requirements: Recommendations, essay and transcript.
Additional information: Preference given to applicants attending school in Washington state.

Amount of award:	$1,000-$2,500
Number of awards:	2
Application deadline:	February 1

Contact:
Association for Women in Communications
217 9th Avenue North
Seattle, WA 98109
Phone: 206-298-4966

Association for Women in Science Educational Foundation

Luise Meyer-Schutzmeister Award

Type of award: Scholarship.
Intended use: For doctoral study at accredited graduate institution in or outside United States. Designated institutions: U.S. citizens may study abroad; non-citizens must be enrolled in U.S. institutions.
Eligibility: Applicant must be female.
Basis for selection: Major/career interest in physics. Applicant must demonstrate high academic achievement.
Application requirements: Recommendations, transcript and research proposal.
  Amount of award: $500-$1,000
  Number of awards: 1
  Number of applicants: 100
  Application deadline: January 15
  Notification begins: June 30
  Total amount awarded: $1,000
Contact:
Association for Women in Science Educational Foundation
1200 New York Avenue
Suite 650
Washington, DC 20005
Phone: 202-326-8940
Fax: 202-326-8960

Ruth Satter Memorial Award

Type of award: Scholarship.
Intended use: For doctoral study at accredited graduate institution in or outside United States. Designated institutions: U.S. citizens may study abroad; non-citizens must be enrolled in U.S. institutions.
Eligibility: Applicant must be female, adult returning student.
Basis for selection: Major/career interest in science, general; physics; engineering; social and behavioral sciences. Applicant must demonstrate high academic achievement.
Application requirements: Recommendations, transcript and research proposal.
Additional information: For women going back to school after at least three year absence.
  Amount of award: $250-$1,000
  Number of awards: 12
  Number of applicants: 100
  Application deadline: January 15
  Notification begins: June 15
  Total amount awarded: $3,000
Contact:
Association for Women in Science
1200 New York Avenue Suite 650
Suite 650
Washington, DC 20005
Phone: 202-326-8940

Women in Science Education Research Grant

Type of award: Research grant.
Intended use: For full-time doctoral study at accredited graduate institution in or outside United States.
Eligibility: Applicant must be female.
Basis for selection: Major/career interest in science, general; physics; engineering; social and behavioral sciences. Applicant must demonstrate high academic achievement.
Application requirements: Recommendations, transcript and research proposal.
Additional information: U.S. citizens may study abroad; non-citizens must be enrolled in U.S. institutions.
  Amount of award: $250-$1,000
  Number of awards: 10
  Number of applicants: 100
  Application deadline: January 15
  Notification begins: June 30
  Total amount awarded: $10,000
Contact:
Association for Women in Science
1200 New York Avenue
Suite 650
Washington, DC 20005
Phone: 202-326-8940
Fax: 202-326-8960

Association of Black Nursing Faculty

Black Nursing Faculty Scholarship

Type of award: Scholarship, renewable.
Intended use: For sophomore, junior, senior, post-bachelor's certificate, master's or doctoral study at accredited 4-year or graduate institution in United States.
Eligibility: Applicant must be African American. Applicant must be U.S. citizen or permanent resident.
Basis for selection: Major/career interest in nursing. Applicant must demonstrate depth of character, leadership, seriousness of purpose, service orientation, financial need and high academic achievement.
Application requirements: Recommendations, essay, transcript and research proposal.
Additional information: Graduate students must submit a research proposal.
  Amount of award: $500-$600
  Number of awards: 3
  Number of applicants: 57
  Application deadline: May 15
  Notification begins: June 15
  Total amount awarded: $11,100
Contact:
Association of Black Nursing Faculty, Inc.
Attn: Vanessa Fahie
9 Potomac School Court
Potomac, MD 20854
Phone: 410-706-7501
Fax: 410-706-0344

Association of Drilled Shaft Contractors

Civil Engineering Graduate Scholarship

Type of award: Scholarship.
Intended use: For full-time master's study at accredited graduate institution.
Eligibility: Applicant must be U.S. citizen or Canadian citizen.
Basis for selection: Major/career interest in engineering; engineering, civil; engineering, structural. Applicant must demonstrate seriousness of purpose.
Application requirements: Recommendations, essay and transcript.
Additional information: Must be senior currently enrolled in ABET or CEAB accredited civil engineering undergraduate program and plan to enter graduate school during current year. Work experience important.

Amount of award:	$2,000
Number of awards:	15
Number of applicants:	50
Application deadline:	March 15
Notification begins:	June 15
Total amount awarded:	$30,000

Contact:
Association of Drilled Shaft Contractors
International Association of Foundation Drilling
P.O. Box 280379
Dallas, TX 75228-1279
Phone: 214-343-2091
Fax: 214-343-2384

Association of State Dam Safety Officials

Dam Safety Officials Scholarship

Type of award: Scholarship, renewable.
Intended use: For junior, senior study in United States.
Eligibility: Applicant must be U.S. citizen.
Basis for selection: Major/career interest in engineering, civil. Applicant must demonstrate depth of character, leadership, seriousness of purpose, service orientation, financial need and high academic achievement.
Application requirements: Recommendations, essay and transcript.
Additional information: Decisions based on grades, career goals, and extracurricular activities.

Amount of award:	$2,500
Number of awards:	2
Number of applicants:	50
Application deadline:	February 15
Notification begins:	May 11
Total amount awarded:	$5,000

Contact:
Association of State Dam Safety Officials
450 Old Vine Street, 2nd Floor
Lexington, KY 40507
Phone: 606-257-5140
Fax: 606-323-1958
Website: members.aol.com/damsafety/homepage.htm

Association of Surgical Technologists

Surgical Technologists Scholarship Fund

Type of award: Scholarship.
Intended use: For freshman, sophomore or non-degree study at accredited vocational or 2-year institution in United States.
Basis for selection: Major/career interest in surgical technology. Applicant must demonstrate financial need and high academic achievement.
Application requirements: Recommendations, transcript and proof of eligibility.
Additional information: One scholarship of $500 awarded each year. Amount and number of additional scholarships determined on basis of merit and size of scholarship fund. Applicant must be currently enrolled in a surgical technology program accredited by the Accreditation Review Committee for Educational Programs in Surgical Technology.

Amount of award:	$250-$500
Application deadline:	March 1
Notification begins:	July 1

Contact:
Association of Surgical Technologists
Awards Committee
7108-C South Alton Way
Englewood, CO 80112-2106

Association of Washington School Principals/PEMCO Financial Center

Teacher Preparation Scholarship

Type of award: Scholarship, renewable.
Intended use: For full-time freshman study at accredited 2-year or 4-year institution.
Eligibility: Applicant must be high school senior. Applicant must be U.S. citizen residing in Washington.
Basis for selection: Major/career interest in education, teacher.

Applicant must demonstrate depth of character, leadership, patriotism, seriousness of purpose, service orientation and high academic achievement.
Application requirements: Interview, recommendations, essay and transcript.
Additional information: For application information contact high school guidance counselor or principal. An interview may be requested during the application process.

Amount of award:	$600
Number of awards:	10
Number of applicants:	277
Application deadline:	March 1
Notification begins:	May 15

Contact:
Association of Washington School Principals
Teacher Preparation Program
1021 8th Avenue SE
Olympia, WA 98501-1500
Phone: 360-357-7951

Austrian Cultural Institute

Austrian Cultural Institute Fine Arts and Music Grant

Type of award: Scholarship.
Intended use: For master's, doctoral study in Austria outside United States. Designated institutions: Arts academies.
Basis for selection: Major/career interest in arts, general; performing arts; music. Applicant must demonstrate high academic achievement.
Application requirements: Portfolio, recommendations and transcript. Final admission subject to artistic entrance exam. Curriculum vitae and health certificates required.
Additional information: Working knowledge of German required. Fields of study allowed include drama/theater arts, visual/performing arts. Award consists of up to nine monthly payments of ATS 7,400 (approx. $560).

| Amount of award: | $5,040 |
| Application deadline: | January 31 |

Austrian Research and Study Scholarship

Type of award: Scholarship.
Intended use: For master's, doctoral study outside United States in Austria.
Basis for selection: Major/career interest in foreign languages; humanities/liberal arts; political science/government; economics.
Additional information: Additional fields of study can include area, ethnic, and cultural studies, comparative literature, European studies, with emphasis on Austrian studies. Study or research project in Austria-related subjects preferred. Working knowledge of German recommended. Awards consist of up to nine monthly payments of ATS 7,400 (approx. $700) for students without a master's, ATS 8,100 (approximately $750) for graduate students, and ATS 9,600 (approximately $900) for young scholars.

| Amount of award: | $8,100 |
| Application deadline: | January 31 |

Contact:
Austrian Cultural Institute
950 Third Avenue 20th Floor
New York, NY 10022

Automotive Hall of Fame

Think Automotive Scholarship

Type of award: Scholarship, renewable.
Intended use: For full-time sophomore, junior or senior study at accredited 2-year, 4-year or graduate institution in United States.
Basis for selection: Major/career interest in automotive technology; mathematics; economics; accounting.
Application requirements: Recommendations and transcript.
Additional information: Applicant must have an interest in pursuing an automotive career upon graduation.

Amount of award:	$250-$2,000
Number of awards:	24
Application deadline:	June 30

Contact:
Automotive Hall of Fame
21400 Oakwood Blvd
Dearborn, MI 48124
Phone: 517-631-5760
Fax: 517-631-0524

Aviation Distributors and Manufacturers Association

Aviation Distributors and Manufacturers Scholarship

Type of award: Scholarship.
Intended use: For full-time junior, senior study at accredited 2-year or 4-year institution.
Eligibility: Applicant must be U.S. citizen.
Basis for selection: Major/career interest in aviation. Applicant must demonstrate depth of character, leadership, seriousness of purpose, service orientation, financial need and high academic achievement.
Application requirements: Recommendations, essay, transcript, proof of eligibility and by ADMA members.
Additional information: Must be pursuing career in aviation, pilot, or A/P mechanic industry. Applicants for the A/P mechanic scholarship must be second year students. For further information or an application contact ADMA International directly. Requests for application materials must be received by March 1.

Amount of award:	$1,000
Number of awards:	2
Application deadline:	March 15

Contact:
Aviation Distributors & Manufacturers Association
1900 Arch Street
Philadelphia, PA 19103
Phone: 215-564-3484

B.F. Goodrich Collegiate Inventors Program

BF Goodrich Collegiate Inventors Program

Type of award: Scholarship.
Intended use: For undergraduate or graduate study.
Basis for selection: Competition in Science project. Major/career interest in science, general.
Additional information: Project should be completed by students and advisors. Project cannot have been made available to public or have been patented.
   Amount of award: $3,000-$7,500
   Application deadline: June 2
Contact:
BF Goodrich Collegiate Inventors Program
c/o Inventure Pl.
221 S. Broadway St.
Akron, OH 44308
Website: www.invent.org

Baltimore Opera Company

Vocal Competition for North American Operatic Artists

Type of award: Internship, renewable.
Intended use: For non-degree study.
Eligibility: Applicant must be U.S. citizen.
Application requirements: $40 application fee. Audition, recommendations and proof of eligibility. Birth certificate for proof of age. Names of vocal coaches, past and present.
Additional information: Twelve week residency program offering performance and carreer development opportunities to talented North American young singers. Acceptance is determined by participation in the company's annual vocal competition in June. Must be a member in good standing of AGMA. For the full length of the program, residence in Baltimore is required.
   Amount of award: $3,600
   Number of awards: 6
   Number of applicants: 150
   Application deadline: May 1
Contact:
Baltimore Opera Company
110 West Mount Royal Avenue Suite 306
Baltimore, MD 21201
Phone: 410-625-1600
Fax: 410-727-7854
Website: www.baltimoreopera.com

Bechtel Corporation

Bechtel Corporation Summer Intern Program

Type of award: Internship.
Intended use: For sophomore, junior, senior or graduate study.
Basis for selection: Major/career interest in engineering; architecture; accounting; business; computer and information sciences.
Additional information: 4-12 week sessions with a stipend of $300-$500/week. Provides opportunity for intern to gain valuable construction and engineering experience, as well as learn the administrative workings of an international contractor. Contact office for a list of available positions and application deadlines.
   Amount of award: $1,200-$6,000

Cooperative Education Program

Type of award: Internship.
Intended use: For sophomore, junior, senior or graduate study.
Basis for selection: Major/career interest in engineering; architecture; accounting; business; computer and information sciences.
Additional information: At least two 4-month sessions with a stipend of $300-$500/week. Provides student with the opportunity to gain construction and engineering skills, as well as administrative workings of an international contracting company. Contct office for available positions and application deadline dates.
   Amount of award: $4,800-$8,000
Contact:
Bechtel Corporation
P.O. Box 193965
San Francisco, CA 94119-3965

Bedding Plants Foundation, Inc.

Barbara Carlson Scholarship

Type of award: Scholarship.
Intended use: For undergraduate or graduate study at vocational, 2-year, 4-year or graduate institution.
Basis for selection: Major/career interest in horticulture. Applicant must demonstrate financial need and high academic achievement.
Application requirements: Recommendations and transcript. Statement outlining academic and professional intentions.
Additional information: Must be an intern at any public garden to be eligible for award.
   Amount of award: $1,000
   Number of awards: 1
   Application deadline: June 1
   Total amount awarded: $1,000
Contact:
Bedding Plants Foundation, Inc.
P.O. Box 27241
Lansing, MI 48909
Phone: 5176948537
Website: www.bpfi.org

Carl F. Dietz Memorial Scholarship

Type of award: Scholarship.
Intended use: For full-time undergraduate study at accredited 2-year or 4-year institution.
Basis for selection: Major/career interest in horticulture. Applicant must demonstrate financial need and high academic achievement.
Application requirements: Recommendations and transcript. Statement of academic and professional intent.
Additional information: Must have an interest in bedding plants.
    Amount of award: $1,000
    Number of awards: 1
    Number of applicants: 45
    Application deadline: June 1
    Notification begins: July 30
    Total amount awarded: $1,000
Contact:
Bedding Plants Foundation, Inc.
P.O. Box 27241
Lansing, MI 48909
Phone: 517-694-8537
Website: www.bpfi.org

Dosatron International Scholarship

Type of award: Scholarship.
Intended use: For undergraduate or graduate study at 4-year or graduate institution.
Basis for selection: Major/career interest in horticulture. Applicant must demonstrate financial need and high academic achievement.
Application requirements: Recommendations and transcript. Statement of academic and professional intent.
    Amount of award: $1,000
    Number of awards: 1
    Application deadline: June 1
    Total amount awarded: $1,000
Contact:
Bedding Plants Foundation, Inc.
P.O. Box 27241
Lansing, MI 48909
Phone: 5176948537
Website: www.bpfi.org

Earl J. Small Growers Scholarship

Type of award: Scholarship.
Intended use: For full-time undergraduate study at accredited 4-year institution. Designated institutions: In United States or Canada.
Eligibility: Applicant must be Canadian citizens are eligible to apply.
Basis for selection: Major/career interest in horticulture. Applicant must demonstrate financial need and high academic achievement.
Application requirements: Recommendations and transcript. Statement of academic and professional intent.
Additional information: Must be interested in pursuing a career in greenhouse production.
    Amount of award: $2,000
    Number of awards: 2
    Number of applicants: 70
    Application deadline: June 1
    Notification begins: July 30
    Total amount awarded: $4,000
Contact:
Bedding Plants Foundation, Inc.
P.O. Box 27241
Lansing, MI 48909
Phone: 517-694-8537
Website: www.bpfi.org

Ed Markham International Scholarship

Type of award: Scholarship.
Intended use: For undergraduate or graduate study at 2-year, 4-year or graduate institution.
Basis for selection: Major/career interest in horticulture. Applicant must demonstrate financial need and high academic achievement.
Application requirements: Recommendations and transcript. Statement of academic and professional intent.
Additional information: For students in pursuit of a career in horticulture who wish to further their understanding of domestic and international marketing through horticulturally realted study.
    Amount of award: $1,000
    Number of awards: 1
    Application deadline: June 1
    Total amount awarded: $1,000
Contact:
Bedding Plants Foundation Inc.
P.O. Box 27241
Lansing, MI 48909
Phone: 5176948537
Website: www.bpfi.org

Fran Johnson Non-traditional Scholarship

Type of award: Scholarship.
Intended use: For full-time undergraduate or graduate study at accredited 4-year or graduate institution. Designated institutions: In United States or Canada.
Eligibility: Applicant must be Candian citizens are eligible to apply.
Basis for selection: Major/career interest in horticulture. Applicant must demonstrate financial need and high academic achievement.
Application requirements: Recommendations and transcript. Statement of academic and professional intent.
Additional information: Must have been out of an academic setting for at least five years and reentering school. Specific interest in bedding plants or floral crops required.

Amount of award: $500-$1,000
Number of awards: 1
Number of applicants: 25
Application deadline: June 1
Notification begins: July 30
Total amount awarded: $1,000

Contact:
Bedding Plants Foundation, Inc.
P.O. Box 27241
Lansing, MI 48909
Phone: 517-694-8537
Website: www.bpfi.org

Harold Bettinger Memorial Scholarship

Type of award: Scholarship.
Intended use: For full-time undergraduate or graduate study at 4-year or graduate institution.
Basis for selection: Major/career interest in horticulture; business; marketing. Applicant must demonstrate financial need and high academic achievement.
Application requirements: Recommendations and transcript. Statement of academic and professional intent.
Additional information: Must have 3.0 GPA.

Amount of award: $1,000
Number of awards: 1
Number of applicants: 50
Application deadline: June 1
Notification begins: July 30
Total amount awarded: $1,000

Contact:
Bedding Plants Foundation, Inc..
P.O. Box 27241
Lansing, MI 48909
Phone: 517-694-8537
Website: www.bpfi.org

J. Carew Memorial Scholarship

Type of award: Scholarship.
Intended use: For full-time graduate study at accredited graduate institution. Designated institutions: In United States or Canada.
Basis for selection: Major/career interest in horticulture; botany; agriculture. Applicant must demonstrate financial need and high academic achievement.
Application requirements: Recommendations and transcript. Statement of academic and professional intent.
Additional information: Must have interest in bedding or flowering potted plants.

Amount of award: $1,500
Number of awards: 1
Number of applicants: 70
Application deadline: June 1
Notification begins: July 30
Total amount awarded: $1,500

Contact:
Bedding Plants Foundation, Inc,
P.O. Box 27241
Lansing, MI 48909
Phone: 517-694-8537
Website: www.bpfi.org

J.K. Rathmell, Jr., Memorial for Work/Study Abroad

Type of award: Scholarship.
Intended use: For full-time junior, senior or graduate study at 4-year or graduate institution. Designated institutions: U.S. or Canadian institutions.
Basis for selection: Major/career interest in horticulture; landscape architecture. Applicant must demonstrate depth of character, seriousness of purpose, financial need and high academic achievement.
Application requirements: Recommendations, essay and transcript. Statement of academic and professional intent.
Additional information: Applicants must have worked abroad. Preference given to those planning to work or study for six months or longer. Must have interest in floriculture, ornamental horticulture, or landscape architecture. Must provide letter of invitation from host institution and statement of work-study purpose.

Amount of award: $2,000
Number of awards: 1
Number of applicants: 5
Application deadline: June 1
Notification begins: July 30
Total amount awarded: $2,000

Contact:
Bedding Plants Foundation, Inc.
P.O. Box 27241
Lansing, MI 48909
Phone: 517-694-8537
Website: www.bpfi.og

Jacob Van Namen/Vans Marketing Scholarship

Type of award: Scholarship.
Intended use: For undergraduate study at 2-year or 4-year institution.
Basis for selection: Major/career interest in agribusiness; marketing. Applicant must demonstrate financial need and high academic achievement.
Application requirements: Recommendations and transcript. Statement of academic and professional intent.
Additional information: For students involved in agribusiness marketing and distribution of floral products.

Amount of award: $1,250
Number of awards: 1
Application deadline: June 1
Total amount awarded: $1,250

Contact:
Bedding Plants Foundation, Inc.
P.O. Box 27241
Lansing, MI 48909
Phone: 5176948537
Website: www.bpfi.org

Jerry Baker Scholarship

Type of award: Scholarship.
Intended use: For full-time freshman study at accredited 4-year institution. Designated institutions: In United States or Canada.
Eligibility: Applicant must be high school senior.
Basis for selection: Major/career interest in horticulture;

landscape architecture. Applicant must demonstrate financial need and high academic achievement.
Application requirements: Recommendations and transcript. Statement of academic and professional intent.
    Amount of award: $1,000
    Number of awards: 2
    Number of applicants: 70
    Application deadline: June 1
    Notification begins: July 30
    Total amount awarded: $2,000
Contact:
Bedding Plants Foundation, Inc.
P.O. Box 27241
Lansing, MI 48909
Phone: 517-694-8537
Website: www.bpfi.org

Jerry Wilmot Scholarship

Type of award: Scholarship.
Intended use: For full-time undergraduate study at accredited 2-year or 4-year institution.
Basis for selection: Major/career interest in horticulture; business; finance/banking; business, management and administration. Applicant must demonstrate financial need and high academic achievement.
Application requirements: Recommendations and transcript. Statement of academic and professional intent.
Additional information: Must be pursuing career in garden center management.
    Amount of award: $2,000
    Number of awards: 1
    Number of applicants: 70
    Application deadline: June 1
    Notification begins: July 30
    Total amount awarded: $2,000
Contact:
Bedding Plants Foundation, Inc.
P.O. Box 27241
Lansing, MI 48909
Phone: 517-694-8537
Website: www.bpfi.org

Paris Fracasso Production Floriculture Scholarship

Type of award: Scholarship.
Intended use: For junior, senior study.
Basis for selection: Applicant must demonstrate financial need and high academic achievement.
Application requirements: Recommendations and transcript. Statement of academic and professional intent.
Additional information: Open to students in a floriculture production program at a recognized college or university.
    Amount of award: $2,000
    Number of awards: 1
    Application deadline: June 1
    Total amount awarded: $2,000
Contact:
Bedding Plants Foundation, Inc.
P.O. Box 27241
Lansing, MI 48909
Phone: 5176948537
Website: www.bpfi.org

Vocational Horticulture Scholarship

Type of award: Scholarship.
Intended use: For full-time undergraduate certificate, freshman, sophomore or non-degree study at vocational or 2-year institution. Designated institutions: In United States or Canada.
Eligibility: Applicant must be Canadian citizens are eligible to apply.
Basis for selection: Major/career interest in horticulture. Applicant must demonstrate financial need and high academic achievement.
Application requirements: Recommendations and transcript. Statement of academic and professional intent.
Additional information: Must have 3.0 GPA. Must have intentions of becoming floriculture plant producer and/or operations manager.
    Amount of award: $500-$1,000
    Number of awards: 4
    Number of applicants: 30
    Application deadline: June 1
    Notification begins: July 30
Contact:
Bedding Plants Foundation, Inc.
P.O. Box 27241
Lansing, MI 48909
Phone: 517-694-8537
Website: www.bpfi.org

Bernstein-Rein

Advertising/Public Relations Internship

Type of award: Internship.
Intended use: For junior, senior study.
Basis for selection: Major/career interest in advertising; public relations.
Application requirements: Interview, recommendations, essay and proof of eligibility.
Additional information: In order to qualify, the applicant must be either a second semester junior or a first semester senior.
    Amount of award: $2,250
    Number of awards: 8
    Number of applicants: 120
    Application deadline: January 1, March 1
    Total amount awarded: $18,000
Contact:
Bernstein-Rein
4600 Madison, Suite 1500
Kansas City, MO 64112

Beta Phi Mu

Beta Phi Mu Blanche E. Woolls Scholarship for School Library Media Service.

Type of award: Scholarship.
Intended use: For full-time master's study at accredited graduate institution outside United States. Designated institutions: Canada.
Basis for selection: Major/career interest in library science.
Application requirements: Recommendations, transcript and proof of eligibility.
Additional information: Must be accepted into an ALA accredited master's Program beginning the fall semester.
    Amount of award: $1,000
    Number of awards: 1
    Application deadline: March 15
    Notification begins: June 1
Contact:
School of Information Studies
Florida State University
Tallahassee, FL 32306-2100
Website: www.cas.usf.edu/lis/bpm

Beta Phi Mu Doctoral Dissertation Scholarship

Type of award: Scholarship.
Intended use: For full-time doctoral study at accredited graduate institution outside United States.
Eligibility: Applicant must be U.S. citizen, permanent resident or Canadian citizens.
Basis for selection: Major/career interest in library science.
Application requirements: Recommendations, transcript and proof of eligibility.
    Amount of award: $1,500
    Number of awards: 1
    Application deadline: March 15
    Notification begins: June 1
Contact:
Florida State University
School of Information Studies
Tallahassee, FL 32306-2100
Website: www.cas.usf.edu/lis/bpm

Sarah Rebecca Reed Scholarship

Type of award: Scholarship.
Intended use: For full-time master's study.
Eligibility: Applicant must be U.S. citizen, permanent resident or US or Canadian citizen.
Basis for selection: Major/career interest in library science.
Application requirements: Recommendations, transcript and proof of eligibility.
Additional information: Must be accepted into ALA accredited master's program beginning the fall semester. Must be used at U.S. or Canadian institutions.
    Amount of award: $1,500
    Number of awards: 1
    Number of applicants: 40
    Application deadline: March 15
    Notification begins: June 1
    Total amount awarded: $1,500
Contact:
Scholarship Committee
School of Information Studies
Florida State University
Tallahassee, FL 32306-2100
Website: www.cas.usf.edu/lis/bpm

Bethesda Lutheran Homes and Services

Mental Retardation Nursing Scholastic Achievement Scholarship

Type of award: Scholarship, renewable.
Intended use: For full-time junior, senior, master's or doctoral study at accredited 2-year, 4-year or graduate institution.
Eligibility: Applicant must be Lutheran.
Basis for selection: Major/career interest in nursing. Applicant must demonstrate seriousness of purpose, service orientation and high academic achievement.
Application requirements: Recommendations, essay, transcript and proof of eligibility.
Additional information: Must have 3.0 GPA. Must be working toward registered nurse (R.N.) degree. Preference given to those interested in working with mentally retarded persons.
    Amount of award: $1,000
    Number of awards: 1
    Number of applicants: 2
    Application deadline: March 15
    Notification begins: May 1
    Total amount awarded: $1,000
Contact:
Kevin Keller-NCRC-Coordinator/Outreach Programs and Services
Bethesda Lutheran Homes and Services, inc.
700 Hoffmann Drive
Watertown, WI 53094
Phone: 800-369-4636, ext. 525
Website: www.bethesdainfo.org

Bethesda Lutheran Homes and Services, inc.

Bethesda Lutheran Homes and Services Cooperative Program Internship

Type of award: Internship, renewable.
Intended use: For full-time junior, senior study at accredited postsecondary institution.
Eligibility: Applicant must be Lutheran.
Basis for selection: Major/career interest in social work; psychology; nursing; education. Applicant must demonstrate depth of character, seriousness of purpose, service orientation and high academic achievement.
Application requirements: Interview and recommendations.
Additional information: Must have 3.0 GPA. Housing is provided during 12-week summer internship in the form of hourly wage of $7.19/hour. Applicants can also be studying public relations or chaplaincy.

Amount of award:	$3,451
Number of awards:	10
Number of applicants:	22
Application deadline:	March 1
Total amount awarded:	$34,512

Contact:
Kevin Keller-NCRC- Coordinator/Outreach Programs and Services
Bethesda Lutheran Homes and Services, inc.
700 Hoffmann Drive
Watertown, WI 53094
Phone: 800-369-4636, ext. 525
Website: www.bethesdainfo.org

Mental Retardation Scholastic Achievement Scholarship

Type of award: Scholarship, renewable.
Intended use: For full-time junior, senior or master's study at accredited 4-year or graduate institution.
Eligibility: Applicant must be Lutheran.
Basis for selection: Major/career interest in social work; education; psychology. Applicant must demonstrate seriousness of purpose, service orientation, financial need and high academic achievement.
Application requirements: Recommendations, essay, transcript and proof of eligibility.
Additional information: Preference to those interested in working with mentally retarded persons. Minimum 3.0 GPA. Also available for students of Lutheran Theology.

Amount of award:	$1,000
Number of awards:	1
Number of applicants:	6
Application deadline:	March 15
Notification begins:	May 1
Total amount awarded:	$1,000

Contact:
Bethesda Lutheran Homes and Services, inc.
Attn: Coordinator, Outreach Programs
700 Hoffmann Drive
Watertown, WI 53094
Phone: 800-369-4636, ext. 525
Fax: 414-261-8441
Website: www.bethesdainfo.org

Billy Barty Foundation

Billy Barty Financial Assistance Program

Type of award: Scholarship, renewable.
Intended use: For full-time undergraduate study.
Eligibility: Little person or family member of little person. Applicant must be . Must be physically challenged. Applicant must be U.S. citizen.
Basis for selection: Applicant must demonstrate depth of character, leadership, seriousness of purpose, financial need and high academic achievement.
Application requirements: Audition, portfolio, recommendations, essay and transcript.

Amount of award:	$2,000
Number of awards:	5
Number of applicants:	50
Application deadline:	August 15, October 1
Total amount awarded:	$10,000

Contact:
Billy Barty Foundation
929 W. Olive Ave., Suite C
Burbank, CA 91506

Black & Veatch

Black & Veatch Summer Internship in Engineering, Construction, and Architecture

Type of award: Internship.
Intended use: For junior, senior study.
Basis for selection: Major/career interest in engineering; construction; architecture.
Application requirements: Transcript.
Additional information: Deadline is in late March; Contact sponsor for exact date. Internship compensation varies; Call sponsor for specific information.

Contact:
Black & Veatch
P.O. Box 8405
Kansas City, MO 64114

Blakemore Foundation

Asian Language Fellowship

Type of award: Scholarship.
Intended use: For graduate study at graduate institution outside United States in East or Southeast Asia. Designated institutions: Language study only.
Eligibility: Applicant must be U.S. citizen or permanent resident.
Basis for selection: Major/career interest in business; Asian studies; foreign languages. Applicant must demonstrate seriousness of purpose and high academic achievement.
Application requirements: Recommendations, essay and transcript.

Amount of award:	$15,000-$35,000
Number of awards:	22
Number of applicants:	101
Application deadline:	January 15
Notification begins:	April 1

Contact:
Blakemore Foundation
1201 Third Avenue, 40th Floor
ATTN: Griffith Way, Trustee
Seattle, WA 98101-3099
Phone: 206-583-8778

Blinded Veteran's Association

Katherine F. Gruber Scholarship

Type of award: Scholarship, renewable.
Intended use: For full-time freshman, sophomore, junior, senior or graduate study at accredited postsecondary institution in United States.
Eligibility: Parent must be visually impaired. Applicant must be high school senior. Applicant must be U.S. citizen. Applicant must be descendant of veteran, child of veteran or disabled veteran, spouse of veteran or disabled veteran who served in the Army, Air Force, Marines, Navy or Coast Guard.
Application requirements: Recommendations, essay and transcript.
Additional information: Applicants may not be on probation during their study.

Amount of award:	$1,000-$2,000
Number of awards:	16
Number of applicants:	40
Application deadline:	April 17
Notification begins:	June 1
Total amount awarded:	$24,000

Contact:
Blinded Veteran's Association Katherine F. Gruber Scholarship
477 H Street NW
Washington, DC 20001
Phone: 202-371-8880
Fax: 202-371-8258

Bok Tower Gardens

Bok Tower Gardens Internship

Type of award: Internship.
Intended use: For junior, senior study. Designated institutions: Bok Tower Gardens.
Basis for selection: Major/career interest in horticulture; landscape architecture; botany.
Application requirements: Interview, recommendations and transcript. Letter outlining interests, resume.
Additional information: Preference given to students who will receive college credit for internship. Program offers on-the-job 10-week training in horticulture and conservation professions. Intern receives $170 for 40-hour work week. Housing provided. Other application deadlines: Summer, April 15; Winter, October 15.

Amount of award:	$1,700
Application deadline:	January 15, July 15

Contact:
Selection Committee
Horticulture Intern Coordination
1151 Tower Boulevard
Lake Wales, FL 33853-3412

Carillon Fellowship

Type of award: Research grant.
Intended use: For postgraduate study. Designated institutions: Bok Tower Gardens.
Basis for selection: Major/career interest in music. Applicant must demonstrate seriousness of purpose.
Application requirements: Interview, recommendations, transcript and research proposal. letter outlining interests, resume.
Additional information: Carillon Scholar Program helps advance scholarly research, composition, performance and other activities relating to the carillon. Program duration from one to six months depending on scholar's needs. Honorary monthly stipend of $1,000, free housing and utilities. Deadline three months before proposed starting date.

Amount of award:	$1,000-$6,000

Contact:
Fellowship Committee
Selection Committee
1151 Tower Boulevard
Lake Wales, FL 33853-3412
Website: www.boktower.org

Boston Globe

Boston Globe One-Year Internship

Type of award: Internship.
Intended use: For non-degree study.
Eligibility: Members of minority groups and candidates with unusual cultural backgrounds are strongly encouraged to apply.
Basis for selection: Major/career interest in journalism.
Application requirements: Resume, writing samples.
Additional information: Award provides one-year full-time

employment at $703.24 per week. Applicants must have six months newspaper experience.

| Amount of award: | $36,560 |
| Number of awards: | 1 |

Boston Globe Summer Internship

Type of award: Internship.
Intended use: For freshman, sophomore or junior study.
Basis for selection: Major/career interest in journalism.
Application requirements: Interview and recommendations. Writing samples and clips.
Additional information: Award is for 13 weeks full-time summer employment at $550 per week.

Amount of award:	$7,150
Number of awards:	15
Application deadline:	November 15
Notification begins:	January 30

Contact:
The Boston Globe
P.O. Box 2378
Boston, MA 02107-2378
Phone: 617-929-3120

Boston Society of Architects

Gabriel Prize

Type of award: Research grant.
Intended use: For non-degree study.
Eligibility: Applicant must be U.S. citizen.
Basis for selection: Major/career interest in architecture. Applicant must demonstrate seriousness of purpose.
Application requirements: Portfolio, recommendations and research proposal.
Additional information: Must use stipend for travel and study to encourage personal investigative and critical studies of French architectural compositions completed between 1630 and 1830. Must submit a written request for an application by December first.

Amount of award:	$15,000
Number of awards:	1
Number of applicants:	96
Application deadline:	December 1
Notification begins:	February 28
Total amount awarded:	$15,000

Contact:
Boston Society of Architects
BSA Gabriel Prize
52 Broad Street
Boston, MA 02109

Rotch Traveling Scholarship

Type of award: Scholarship.
Intended use: For non-degree study.
Basis for selection: Competition in Engineering/architecture. Overall excellence in solving 2-stage design problem. Major/career interest in architecture.
Additional information: Must have degree from accredited school of architecture and one year of work experience in an architectural firm. Award for travel in foreign country for eight to twelve months. Must travel alone unless married or with dependent. Recipient must not work or study while traveling.

Amount of award:	$30,000
Number of awards:	1
Number of applicants:	90
Application deadline:	January 1
Notification begins:	April 30
Total amount awarded:	$30,000

Contact:
Boston Society of Architects
Rotch Traveling Scholarship
52 Broad Street
Boston, MA 02109

Boys and Girls Clubs of San Diego

Spence Reese Scholarship

Type of award: Scholarship, renewable.
Intended use: For full-time freshman, sophomore, junior or senior study at accredited 4-year institution in United States.
Eligibility: Applicant must be male, high school senior.
Basis for selection: Major/career interest in law; political science/government; engineering; medicine (m.d.). Applicant must demonstrate high academic achievement.
Application requirements: $10 application fee. Recommendations, essay and transcript. SAT.
Additional information: Include SASE with application request. Finalists interview in San Diego. Travel expenses will be reimbursed.

Amount of award:	$8,000
Number of awards:	16
Number of applicants:	200
Application deadline:	May 15
Notification begins:	June 1
Total amount awarded:	$32,000

Contact:
Boys and Girls Clubs of San Diego
1761 Hotel Circle South, 123
San Diego, CA 92108

British Government

Marshall Scholarship

Type of award: Scholarship, renewable.
Intended use: For full-time junior, senior or master's study in United Kingdom.
Eligibility: Applicant must be U.S. citizen.
Basis for selection: Applicant must demonstrate depth of character, leadership, seriousness of purpose, service orientation and high academic achievement.
Application requirements: Interview, recommendations, essay, transcript and proof of eligibility. Endorsement by President or Dean of educational institution, or employer.
Additional information: Must pursue British first (bachelor's)

or higher degree. Must have bachelor's from accredited U.S. institution by start of award year. Must have minimum 3.7 GPA in academic courses after freshman year. Award period is two academic years, but may be extended a year. Americans already studying for or holding British degree or degree-equivalent qualification not eligible. Applicant indicates two preferred universities, but may be placed elsewhere, if necessary. Requests to study at institutions other than Oxford, Cambridge, or University of London particularly welcome. Applications available after June 1.

Amount of award:	$24,000
Number of awards:	80
Number of applicants:	1,000
Application deadline:	October 12
Notification begins:	November 26
Total amount awarded:	$1,840,000

Contact:
British Information Services
845 Third Avenue
New York, NY 10022-6691
Phone: 212-752-5747
Website: www.britain-info.org

Broadcast Education Association

Broadcast Education Association Scholarship

Type of award: Scholarship.
Intended use: For full-time junior, senior or graduate study in or outside United States. Designated institutions: Member of BEA.
Basis for selection: Major/career interest in communications; radio/television/film. Applicant must demonstrate depth of character, leadership, seriousness of purpose and high academic achievement.
Application requirements: Recommendations, essay and transcript.
Additional information: SASE.

Amount of award:	$1,250-$5,000
Number of awards:	14
Number of applicants:	100
Application deadline:	January 15
Notification begins:	April 20
Total amount awarded:	$28,000

Contact:
Scholarship Coordinator
1771 N Street NW
Washington, DC 20036
Phone: 202-429-5354

Bucks County Courier Times

Bucks County Courier Times Minority Internship

Type of award: Internship.
Intended use: For junior, senior, graduate or postgraduate study.
Eligibility: Applicant must be of minority background. Applicant must be U.S. citizen.
Basis for selection: Major/career interest in journalism.
Application requirements: Resume, clips.
Additional information: Internship duration is 12 weeks. Applicant must have basic journalism skills. Interns work as news reporters, bureau reporters, copy desk assistants, phorographers, graphic artists, sports writers, and feature writers.

Amount of award:	$4,380
Number of awards:	5
Number of applicants:	100
Application deadline:	February 28

Contact:
Bucks County Courier Times
8400 Route 13
Levittown, PA 19057
Website: www.bcct-gpn.com

Bureau of Indian Affairs-Oklahoma Area Education Office

Bureau of Indian Affairs-Oklahoma Area Grant

Type of award: Scholarship.
Intended use: For undergraduate or graduate study.
Eligibility: Applicant must be Alaskan native or American Indian. Must be member of a federally recognized Indian tribe. Applicant must be U.S. citizen.
Application requirements: Recommendations, essay, transcript and proof of eligibility.
Additional information: Must maintain a 2.0 GPA. Do not contact BIA-Oklahoma. Applicant must contact his/her tribe for specific information.

Notification begins:	June 30, October 30

Business and Professional Women's Foundation

Career Advancement Scholarship

Type of award: Scholarship, renewable.
Intended use: For junior, senior, master's or first professional study at 2-year, 4-year or graduate institution in United States.
Eligibility: Applicant must be female. Applicant must be U.S. citizen.
Basis for selection: Major/career interest in science, general; education, teacher; engineering; law; computer and information sciences. Applicant must demonstrate financial need.
Application requirements: Recommendations, essay, transcript and proof of eligibility. Tax forms.
Additional information: Also for applicants in the fields of paralegal studies and science or professional degrees (J.D., D.D.S., M.D.) Must be within 24 months of receiving degree, demonstrate critical financial need and have definite career plan. Application available October 1 through April 1. Send business-size double-stamped SASE.

Amount of award:	$500-$2,000
Number of awards:	200
Number of applicants:	900
Application deadline:	April 15
Notification begins:	July 31

Contact:
Business and Professional Women's Foundation
Scholarship and Loan Programs
2012 Massachusetts Avenue NW
Washington, DC 20036
Website: www.bpwusa.org/foundation/foundation.html

New York Life Foundation Health Professions Scholarship

Type of award: Scholarship, renewable.
Intended use: For undergraduate study at 2-year or 4-year institution in United States.
Eligibility: Applicant must be female. Applicant must be U.S. citizen.
Basis for selection: Major/career interest in health-related professions; physical therapy; nursing. Applicant must demonstrate seriousness of purpose and financial need.
Application requirements: Recommendations, essay, transcript and proof of eligibility. Tax forms.
Additional information: Must be within 24 months of receiving degree, demonstrate critical financial need and have definite career plan. Award for one of the last two years of study at associate or bachelor's level. Must already be accepted into program of study, but need not be enrolled. Application available October 1 through April 1. Send business-size double-stamped SASE.

Amount of award:	$500-$2,000
Number of awards:	200
Number of applicants:	700
Application deadline:	April 15
Notification begins:	July 31

Contact:
Business and Professional Women's Foundation
Scholarship and Loan Program
2012 Massachusetts Avenue NW
Washington, DC 20036
Website: www.bpwusa.org/foundation/foundation.html

Sears-Roebuck Graduate Business Studies Loan Fund

Type of award: Loan, renewable.
Intended use: For master's study at accredited graduate institution in or outside United States.
Eligibility: Applicant must be female. Applicant must be U.S. citizen.
Basis for selection: Major/career interest in business. Applicant must demonstrate financial need.
Application requirements: Recommendations, essay, transcript and proof of eligibility. Tax forms.
Additional information: Must already be accepted into program of study, but need not be enrolled. Application available October 1 through April 1. Send business-size double-stamped SASE.

Amount of award:	$2,500
Number of awards:	21
Number of applicants:	29
Application deadline:	April 15
Notification begins:	July 31
Total amount awarded:	$52,500

Contact:
Business and Professional Women's Foundation
Scholarship and Loan Programs
2012 Massachusetts Avenue NW
Washington, DC 20036
Website: www.bpwusa.org/foundation/foundation.html

Women in Business Scholarship

Type of award: Scholarship, renewable.
Intended use: For junior, senior or master's study at 2-year, 4-year or graduate institution in United States.
Eligibility: Applicant must be female. Applicant must be U.S. citizen.
Basis for selection: Major/career interest in accounting; business; marketing; business, management and administration. Applicant must demonstrate financial need.
Application requirements: Recommendations, essay, transcript and proof of eligibility. 1040 form.
Additional information: Must be within 24 months of receiving degree, demonstrate critical financial need, and have definite career plan. Application available October 1 through April 1. Send double-stamped SASE.

Amount of award:	$500-$1,500
Number of awards:	200
Number of applicants:	5,000
Application deadline:	April 15
Notification begins:	July 31

Contact:
Business and Professional Women's Foundation
Scholarship and Loan Programs
2012 Massachusetts Avenue NW
Washington, DC 20036
Website: www.bpwusa.org/foundation/foundation.html

Women in Engineering Studies Loan Fund

Type of award: Loan, renewable.
Intended use: For junior, senior, master's or non-degree study at 2-year, 4-year or graduate institution in United States.

Eligibility: Applicant must be female. Applicant must be U.S. citizen.
Basis for selection: Major/career interest in engineering. Applicant must demonstrate financial need.
Application requirements: Recommendations, essay and transcript. Tax forms.
Additional information: Program must be accredited by Accreditation Board of Engineering and Technology. Award for one of last two years of study in engineering program or non-degree study limited to refresher courses and conversion programs. Must already be accepted into program of study, but need not be enrolled. Application available October 1 through April 1. Send business-size double-stamped SASE.

Amount of award:	$5,000
Number of awards:	5
Number of applicants:	7
Application deadline:	April 15
Notification begins:	July 31
Total amount awarded:	$25,000

Contact:
Loan and Scholar Coordinator
Scholarship and Loan Programs
2012 Massachusetts Avenue NW
Washington, DC 20036
Website: www.bpwusa.org/foundation/foundation.html

Wyeth-Ayerst Laboratories Scholarship

Type of award: Scholarship, renewable.
Intended use: For graduate study at accredited graduate institution in United States.
Eligibility: Applicant must be female. Applicant must be U.S. citizen.
Basis for selection: Major/career interest in engineering, biomedical; health sciences; medical specialties/research; public health; medicine (m.d.). Applicant must demonstrate financial need.
Application requirements: Recommendations, essay and transcript. Tax forms.
Additional information: Fields of study include pharmaceutical marketing, biomedical research, and public health policy. Must already be accepted into program. Application available October 1 through April 1. Send business-sized, double-stamped SASE. Must have critical financial need.

Amount of award:	$500-$2,000
Number of awards:	22
Application deadline:	April 15
Notification begins:	July 31
Total amount awarded:	$50,000

Contact:
Business and Professional Women's Foundation
Scholarship and Loan Programs
2012 Massachusetts Avenue NW
Washington, DC 20036
Website: www.bpwusa.org/foundation/foundation.html

C.G. Fuller Foundation

C.G. Fuller Foundation Scholarship

Type of award: Scholarship, renewable.
Intended use: For full-time undergraduate study at 4-year institution in South Carolina.
Eligibility: Applicant must be high school senior. Applicant must be residing in South Carolina.
Basis for selection: Applicant must demonstrate financial need and high academic achievement.
Application requirements: Interview, recommendations and transcript. SAT scores.
Additional information: Apply through financial aid office of university. Applications distributed between end of October and end of November. Minimum 3.0 GPA. Recipient must attend college in South Carolina.

Amount of award:	$2,000
Number of awards:	15
Number of applicants:	200
Application deadline:	April 15
Notification begins:	August 1
Total amount awarded:	$120,000

Contact:
C.G. Fuller Foundation
c/o NationsBank of South Carolina
P.O. Box 448
Columbia, SC 29202-0448

California Adolescent Nutrition and Fitness (CANFIT) Program

CANFIT Program Graduate Scholarship

Type of award: Scholarship, renewable.
Intended use: For master's, doctoral study at accredited graduate institution in United States. Designated institutions: California.
Eligibility: Applicant must be of minority background. Applicant must be U.S. citizen or permanent resident.
Basis for selection: Major/career interest in dietetics/nutrition; physical education; public health.
Application requirements: Recommendations, essay and transcript.
Additional information: Minimum GPA 3.0. Must have completed 12-15 units of Graduate work. Must be enrolled in approved masters or doctoral program in California.

Amount of award:	$1,000
Number of awards:	8
Number of applicants:	17
Application deadline:	March 1
Notification begins:	May 1

Contact:
Program Administration
2140 Shattuck Ave., Suite 610
Berkeley, CA 94704
Phone: 510-644-1533
Fax: 510-644-1535

CANFIT Program Undergraduate Scholarship

Type of award: Scholarship, renewable.
Intended use: For junior, senior study at accredited 4-year institution in United States. Designated institutions: California.
Eligibility: Applicant must be of minority background. Applicant must be U.S. citizen or permanent resident.
Basis for selection: Major/career interest in dietetics/nutrition; culinary arts; public health; hotel/restaurant management; physical education. Applicant must demonstrate seriousness of purpose, service orientation and financial need.
Application requirements: Recommendations, essay and transcript.
Additional information: Minimum GPA 2.5. Must be enrolled in WASC-accredited institution in California.
    Amount of award: $500
    Number of awards: 15
    Number of applicants: 17
    Application deadline: March 31
    Notification begins: May 1
    Total amount awarded: $10,000
Contact:
Program Administration
CANFIT Undergraduate Program Scholarship
2140 Shattuck Ave., Suite 610
Berkeley, CA 94704
Phone: 510-644-1533
Fax: 510-644-1535

California Association of Realtors Scholarship Foundation

California Association of Realtors Scholarship

Type of award: Scholarship.
Intended use: For undergraduate or graduate study.
Eligibility: Applicant must be U.S. citizen residing in California.
Basis for selection: Major/career interest in real estate. Applicant must demonstrate financial need.
Application requirements: Interview, recommendations, essay and transcript.
Additional information: Minimum GPA of 2.6.
    Amount of award: $1,000-$2,000
    Number of awards: 30
    Application deadline: May 15, August 29
    Notification begins: October 20, September 25
Contact:
California Association of Realtors Scholarship Foundation
525 South Virgil Avenue
Los Angeles, CA 90020
Phone: 213-739-8200

California Chicano News Media Association

Joel Garcia Memorial Scholarship

Type of award: Scholarship, renewable.
Intended use: For undergraduate or graduate study at accredited postsecondary institution.
Eligibility: Applicant must be Mexican American, Hispanic American or Puerto Rican. Applicant must be U.S. citizen or permanent resident residing in California.
Basis for selection: Competition in Writing/journalism. Major/career interest in journalism; communications. Applicant must demonstrate seriousness of purpose, service orientation, financial need and high academic achievement.
Application requirements: Interview, recommendations, essay, transcript and proof of eligibility. Applicant must include samples of work: newspaper clips, photographs, audio or television tapes.
Additional information: Applicant can be resident of California attending school in or out of state or non-residents attending school in California. Must provide proof of pursuit of degree and career in journalism and/or commmunications.
    Amount of award: $250-$2,000
    Number of awards: 28
    Number of applicants: 61
    Application deadline: April 2
    Notification begins: May 1
    Total amount awarded: $20,000
Contact:
California Chicano News Media Association
3716 S. Hope Street, Room 300
Los Angeles, CA 90007
Phone: 213-743-2440
Fax: 213-744-1809
Website: www.ccnma.org

California Farm Bureau

California Farm Bureau Scholarship

Type of award: Scholarship, renewable.
Intended use: For full-time freshman, sophomore, junior or senior study at accredited 4-year institution in California.
Eligibility: Applicant must be U.S. citizen.
Basis for selection: Major/career interest in agriculture; agribusiness; veterinary medicine; engineering, agricultural.
Application requirements: Recommendations, essay and transcript.
Additional information: Applications may be obtained from the local County Farm Bureau office. Applicant must be preparing for a career in the agricultural industry. Award must be used at a California 4-year school.

Amount of award:	$2,000-$2,750
Number of applicants:	236
Application deadline:	March 1
Notification begins:	May 30
Total amount awarded:	$63,500

Contact:
California Farm Bureau Scholarship Foundation

Phone: 916-924-4052

California Junior Miss Program

California Junior Miss Competition

Type of award: Scholarship.
Intended use: For full-time or half-time undergraduate or graduate study at accredited 2-year, 4-year or graduate institution.
Eligibility: Applicant must be single, female, high school junior. Applicant must be U.S. citizen residing in California.
Basis for selection: Competition in Performing arts. Interview, talent, scholastic achievement, fitness, presence and composure. Applicant must demonstrate high academic achievement.
Application requirements: Interview, essay and transcript.
Additional information: Contact should be made early during junior year in high school.

Amount of award:	$300-$15,000
Number of awards:	22
Number of applicants:	60
Application deadline:	December 31, March 1
Notification begins:	August 16
Total amount awarded:	$40,000

Contact:
California Junior Miss Program
P.O. Box 1863
Santa Rosa, CA 95402
Phone: 707-576-7505

California Library Association

California Library Scholarship for Minority Students

Type of award: Scholarship.
Intended use: For master's study. Designated institutions: American Library Association accredited California library schools.
Eligibility: Applicant must be American Indian, Asian American, African American, Mexican American, Hispanic American or Puerto Rican. Applicant must be U.S. citizen or permanent resident residing in California.
Basis for selection: Major/career interest in library science. Applicant must demonstrate financial need.
Application requirements: Interview, essay, transcript and proof of eligibility.
Additional information: Must be a college senior or college graduate who has been accepted into an accredited MLS program in California.

Amount of award:	$2,000
Number of awards:	2
Application deadline:	May 31
Total amount awarded:	$4,000

Contact:
California Library Association
717 K Street, Suite 300
Sacramento, CA 95814-3477
Phone: 916-447-8541

California Masonic Foundation

California Masonic Foundation Scholarship

Type of award: Scholarship, renewable.
Intended use: For full-time undergraduate study at accredited 2-year or 4-year institution.
Eligibility: Applicant must be high school senior. Applicant must be U.S. citizen residing in California.
Basis for selection: Applicant must demonstrate service orientation, financial need and high academic achievement.
Application requirements: Interview, recommendations, essay, transcript and proof of eligibility. 1040 tax return.
Additional information: GPA 3.0. SASE. Application requests accepted between October 1 and January 31.

Amount of award:	$2,000-$10,000
Number of awards:	175
Number of applicants:	1,100
Application deadline:	February 28
Notification begins:	May 15

Contact:
California Masonic Foundation
1111 California Street
San Francisco, CA 94108-2284
Phone: 415-292-9196

California Teachers Association

L. Gordon Bittle Memorial Scholarship for Student CTA

Type of award: Scholarship, renewable.
Intended use: For full-time freshman, sophomore, junior, senior, post-bachelor's certificate or master's study at accredited postsecondary institution.
Eligibility: Applicant must be U.S. citizen residing in California.
Basis for selection: Applicant must demonstrate high academic achievement.

California Teachers Association: L. Gordon Bittle Memorial Scholarship for Student CTA

Application requirements: Proof of eligibility.
Additional information: Intended for a teacher credential program. Minimum GPA of 3.0. Information may also be obtained from chapter presidents or any Regional Resource Center Office.

Amount of award:	$2,000
Number of awards:	3
Number of applicants:	20
Application deadline:	February 15
Notification begins:	March
Total amount awarded:	$6,000

Contact:
California Teachers Association
PO Box 921
Burlingame, CA 94011-0921
Website: www.cta.org/resources98/

California/Hawaii Elks Major Project, Inc.

Elks Undergraduate Disabled Student Scholarship

Type of award: Scholarship, renewable.
Intended use: For full-time undergraduate, non-degree study at accredited vocational, 2-year or 4-year institution.
Eligibility: Applicant must be high school senior. Must be visually impaired, hearing impaired, physically challenged or learning disabled. Applicant must be U.S. citizen residing in California or Hawaii.
Basis for selection: Applicant must demonstrate depth of character, leadership, patriotism, seriousness of purpose, service orientation, financial need and high academic achievement.
Application requirements: Interview, recommendations, essay, transcript and proof of eligibility.
Additional information: Application may be obtained from any elks lodge in California or Hawaii, after November 15. Applicant must be interviewed and signed at the lodge where he or she obtaines the application. Scholarship provides $1500 toward tuition and $500 toward books and fees for students in 4 year institutions, and $1000 for students in Junior colleges.

Amount of award:	$1,000-$2,000
Number of applicants:	28
Application deadline:	March 15
Notification begins:	May 15

Contact:
California/Hawaii Elks Major Project Inc.

Phone: 818-963-1636

Camargo Foundation

Carmargo Foundation Fellowship

Type of award: Research grant.
Intended use: For full-time master's, doctoral, first professional, postgraduate or non-degree study in France in France. Designated institutions: Camargo Foundation, Cassis Center/Cassis, France.
Basis for selection: Major/career interest in communications; arts, general; humanities/liberal arts; social and behavioral sciences; music; foreign languages. Applicant must demonstrate seriousness of purpose.
Application requirements: Recommendations and research proposal. Project must be approved by selection committee of foundation.
Additional information: Award includes housing and the ability to utilize the Carmago center in Cassis, France. There is no monetary award. Transportation is not included. Additional fields of study include area, ethnic and cultural studies. French language and literature, English creative writing, art making, music composition, and photography. Minorities and women encouraged to apply.

Number of awards:	22
Number of applicants:	100
Application deadline:	February 1
Notification begins:	April 1

Contact:
Grant Coordinator
125 Park Square Court
400 Sibley Street
St. Paul, MN 55101-1928

Cancer Research Fund

Damon Runyon Scholar Award

Type of award: Research grant.
Intended use: For full-time postgraduate study.
Basis for selection: Major/career interest in oncology. Applicant must demonstrate high academic achievement.
Application requirements: Recommendations, essay, research proposal and nomination.
Additional information: Total award is $100,000 per year for two years. International candidates must do research in the U.S.

Amount of award:	$100,000
Number of awards:	5
Number of applicants:	35
Application deadline:	July 1
Notification begins:	October
Total amount awarded:	$500,000

Contact:
Cancer Research Fund
675 Third Avenue
25th Floor
New York, NY 10017
Phone: 212-532-3888
Fax: 212-697-4950
Website: www.cancerresearchfund.org

Postdoctoral Cancer Research Fellowship

Type of award: Research grant, renewable.
Intended use: For postgraduate study in or outside United States.

Eligibility: Applicant must be U.S. citizen or Must do research in U.S.
Basis for selection: Major/career interest in medical specialties/research. Applicant must demonstrate high academic achievement.
Application requirements: Recommendations, proof of eligibility, research proposal and nomination by sponsoring university, hospital or research institution. Letter describing previous research and teaching experience, curriculum vitae including bibliography of published works, sponsor's curriculum vitae and bibliography of relevant publications, sponsor evaluation of applicant's qualifications for project, and reprints of sponsor's and candidate's work.
Additional information: Applicants must have completed one or more of the following degrees or its equivalent: M.D., Ph.D., D.D.S., D.V.M. International candidates must to do their research in the United States. Summer application deadline is March 15.

Amount of award:	$26,000-$50,000
Number of awards:	60
Number of applicants:	690
Application deadline:	August 15, December 15
Notification begins:	November 1, February 1
Total amount awarded:	$5,100,000

Contact:
Cancer Research Fund of the Damon Runyon-Walter Winchell Foundation
Fellowship Program
675 Third Avenue, 25th Floor
New York, NY 10017
Phone: 212-697-9550
Website: www.cancerresearchfund.org

Caremark Therapeutic Services

Eric Delson Memorial Scholarship

Type of award: Scholarship, renewable.
Intended use: For freshman, sophomore, junior or senior study at accredited vocational, 2-year or 4-year institution.
Additional information: For further information or application contact Caremark Therapeutic Services directly or request information at hemophilia treatment centers.

Amount of award:	$2,500

Case Western Reserve University

Marc A. Klein Playwriting Award

Type of award: Scholarship.
Intended use: For undergraduate or graduate study at 2-year or 4-year institution in United States.
Basis for selection: Competition in Performing arts. Creativity, originality Major/career interest in theater (artistic).
Application requirements: Stage manuscript.
Additional information: Manuscripts must be endorsed by a faculty member of a university theater or drama department. Only plays that have not been professionally produced can be entered. Musicals and children's plays will not be accepted. Playwright may submit as many scrjipts as she/he desires.

Amount of award:	$1,000
Application deadline:	May 15
Notification begins:	August 1

Contact:
Mark A. Klien
Department of Theater Arts
10900 Euclid Ave.
Cleveland, OH 44106

Center for Defense Information

Center for Defense Information Internship

Type of award: Internship.
Intended use: For undergraduate or graduate study.
Basis for selection: Major/career interest in political science/government; military science; international relations; communications. Applicant must demonstrate depth of character, leadership, seriousness of purpose, service orientation and high academic achievement.
Application requirements: Recommendations, essay, transcript and proof of eligibility. Must have a resume and cover letter stating interests and reasons for wanting to work at CDI.
Additional information: Students must work full time for the duration of the internship (three to five months) to receive the monthly stipend of $700. Deadline for summer application is March 15.

Amount of award:	$2,100-$3,500
Number of awards:	12
Application deadline:	July 1, October 15
Notification begins:	July 22, November 7

Contact:
Center for Defense Information
1779 Massachusetts Avenue
Washington, DC 20036
Phone: 202-332-0600
Website: www.cdi.org

Ceramic Manufacturers Association

Ceramic Manufacturers Scholarship

Type of award: Scholarship.
Intended use: For undergraduate or graduate study at postsecondary institution in United States.
Eligibility: Applicant must be U.S. citizen.
Basis for selection: Major/career interest in ceramics. Applicant must demonstrate financial need and high academic achievement.

Application requirements: Essay.
Additional information: Minimum 2.0 GPA.
   Amount of award: $50-$1,000
   Application deadline: August 1
Contact:
Ceramic Manufacturers Association
1100-H Brandywine Boulevard
P.O. Box 3388
Zanesville, OH 43702-3388
Phone: 740-452-4541
Fax: 740-452-2552

Chairscholars Foundation, Inc.

Chairscholars Scholarship

Type of award: Scholarship, renewable.
Intended use: For full-time freshman study.
Eligibility: Applicant must be single, high school senior. Must be physically challenged. Applicant must be U.S. citizen.
Basis for selection: Applicant must demonstrate depth of character, leadership, seriousness of purpose, service orientation and financial need.
Application requirements: Recommendations, essay, transcript and proof of eligibility. Photograph.
   Amount of award: $3,000
   Number of awards: 4
   Number of applicants: 60
   Application deadline: March 15
   Total amount awarded: $12,000
Contact:
Chairscholars Foundation, Inc.
16101 Carencia Ln.
Odessa, FL 33556

Charles A. and Anne Morrow Lindbergh Foundation

Lindbergh Foundation Grant

Type of award: Research grant.
Intended use: For non-degree study.
Basis for selection: Major/career interest in environmental science; aviation; natural resources/conservation; education; health sciences.
Application requirements: Research proposal.
Additional information: Applicant research or educational project should address the balance between technological advancement and environmental preservation.

   Amount of award: $1,000-$10,580
   Number of awards: 52
   Number of applicants: 250
   Application deadline: June 16
   Notification begins: April 15
Contact:
The Charles A. and Anne Morrow Lindbergh Foundation
708 South 3 Street
Suite 110
Minneapolis, MN 55415-1141
Phone: 612-338-1703
Website: www.mtn.org/lindfdtn

Charles Babbage Institute

Adelle and Erwin Tomash Fellowship

Type of award: Research grant.
Intended use: For doctoral study.
Basis for selection: Major/career interest in computer and information sciences; history. Applicant must demonstrate high academic achievement.
Application requirements: Recommendations, transcript and research proposal. Biographical data, 3 recommendations, graduate school transcript.
Additional information: Priority given to students who have completed all requirements for doctoral degree except research and writing of dissertation. Dissertation must address topic in history of computers and information processing.
   Amount of award: $12,000
   Number of awards: 1
   Number of applicants: 10
   Application deadline: January 15
   Total amount awarded: $12,000
Contact:
Charles Babbage Institute
University of Minnesota, 103 Walter Library
117 Pleasant Street SE
Minneapolis, MN 55455
Phone: 612-624-5050

Charter Fund

Charter Fund Scholarship

Type of award: Scholarship.
Intended use: For full-time freshman study.
Eligibility: Applicant must be high school senior. Applicant must be U.S. citizen residing in Colorado.
Basis for selection: Applicant must demonstrate financial need.
Application requirements: Interview.

Amount of award:	$250-$1,500
Number of awards:	100
Application deadline:	May 1
Notification begins:	December 1
Total amount awarded:	$75,000

Contact:
Charter Fund
370 17 Street, Suite 5300
Denver, CO 80202
Phone: 303-572-1727

Chesterfield Film Company

Chesterfield Writers Film Project

Type of award: Research grant.
Intended use: For non-degree study.
Basis for selection: Major/career interest in radio/television/film.
Application requirements: $40 application fee. Writing samples.
Additional information: Selection based solely on the basis of demonstrated writing ability. Fellowships last one year and fellows receive a $20,000 stipend.

Amount of award:	$20,000
Application deadline:	June 2
Notification begins:	December 15

Contact:
Chesterfield Film Company
8205 Santa Monica Boulevard., Suite 200
Los Angeles, CA 90046
Phone: (213) 633-3977

Cheyenne-Arapaho Tribe

Cheyenne-Arapaho Tribe Department of Education Scholarship

Type of award: Scholarship.
Intended use: For half-time or less than half-time undergraduate, graduate or non-degree study at accredited vocational, 2-year, 4-year or graduate institution in United States.
Eligibility: Applicant must be American Indian. Must be enrolled member of Cheyenne-Arapaho Tribe.
Basis for selection: Applicant must demonstrate financial need and high academic achievement.
Application requirements: Proof of eligibility.
Additional information: Student must live within service area. Covers adult vocational students' tuition, fees and books. Must be meber of Cheyenne-Arapaho tribe through ancestry. Summer application deadline is April 1.

Amount of award:	$1,000
Number of awards:	50
Number of applicants:	200
Application deadline:	June 1, November 1

Cheyenne-Arapaho Tribe Higher Education Scholarship

Type of award: Scholarship, renewable.
Intended use: For full-time or half-time undergraduate or graduate study at accredited 2-year, 4-year or graduate institution in United States.
Eligibility: Applicant must be American Indian. Must be enrolled member of Cheyenne-Arapaho Tribe.
Basis for selection: Applicant must demonstrate financial need and high academic achievement.
Application requirements: Transcript and proof of eligibility.
Additional information: Student receives $1,000 per semester. Must be member of Cheyenne-Arapaho Tribe through ancestry. Sumer application deadline is April 1.

Amount of award:	$1,000
Number of awards:	130
Number of applicants:	200
Application deadline:	June 1, November 1

Contact:
Cheyenne-Arapaho Tribe
Department of Education
P.O. Box 38
Concho, OK 73022
Phone: 405-262-0345

Chinese American Medical Society

Chinese American Medical Society Scholarship

Type of award: Scholarship.
Intended use: For first professional, postgraduate study in United States.
Eligibility: Applicant must be Asian American. Applicants of Chinese descent given preference.
Basis for selection: Major/career interest in medicine (m.d.); medical specialties/research (beyond m.d.); dentistry. Applicant must demonstrate financial need and high academic achievement.
Application requirements: Recommendations, essay and transcript.
Additional information: Award to assist students of Chinese descent pursuing M.D./D.M.D. or holding research position in approved institution. This includes undergraduate study in U.S. medical/dental school, or postgraduate medical study or research in institution involved with helping Chinese people abroad.

Amount of award:	$1,000-$1,500
Number of awards:	5
Application deadline:	March 31

Contact:
Chinese American Medical Society
Attn: Dr. H.H. Wang
281 Edgewood Avenue
Teaneck, NJ 07666
Phone: 201-833-1506

Choate Rosemary Hall

Choate Rosemary Hall Internship

Type of award: Internship.
Intended use: For full-time undergraduate or graduate study.
Basis for selection: Applicant must demonstrate depth of character and seriousness of purpose.
Application requirements: Interview.
Additional information: 5-week summer internship, includes free room and board, $320 a week for undergrads $340 a week for grad students.
    Amount of award: $1,600-$1,700
Contact:
Choate Rosemary Hall
333 Chouristian St.
Wallingford, CT 06492

Christian Record Services

Christian Record Services Scholarship

Type of award: Scholarship, renewable.
Intended use: For full-time undergraduate study in United States.
Eligibility: Applicant must be visually impaired.
Basis for selection: Applicant must demonstrate financial need and high academic achievement.
Application requirements: Recommendations and transcript.
Additional information: Awardees must reapply yearly.
    Amount of award: $500
    Number of awards: 10
    Number of applicants: 50
    Application deadline: April 1
    Notification begins: May 15
    Total amount awarded: $5,000
Contact:
Christian Record Services
4444 South 52 Street
Lincoln, NE 68516
Phone: 402-488-0981
Fax: 402-488-7582

Chronicle of the Horse

Chronicle of the Horse Summer Internship

Type of award: Internship.
Intended use: For freshman, sophomore, junior, senior, graduate or postgraduate study.
Eligibility: Applicant must be U.S. citizen.
Application requirements: Interview and transcript.
Additional information: A strong English background and a knowledge of English horse sports is required. Interest in journalism or communications talent for photography is helpful. Interns receive $6.50 an hour. All majors considered.
    Amount of award: $350-$700
    Number of awards: 3
    Number of applicants: 30
    Application deadline: July 1, March 1
Contact:
Intership Coordinator
P.O. Box 46
Middleburg, VA 20118

Clarke and Company

Clarke Internship Program

Type of award: Internship.
Intended use: For junior, senior or graduate study.
Basis for selection: Major/career interest in communications. Applicant must demonstrate depth of character, leadership and high academic achievement.
Application requirements: Interview.
Additional information: Internships last 12-20 weeks and pay $240/week. Provides opportunity to gain valuable communications and public relations skills at a leading firm. Interns write press releases, generate media lists and conduct research. Summer, fall, and spring internships available.
    Amount of award: $2,880-$4,800
    Number of awards: 10
    Number of applicants: 175
    Application deadline: May 1
Contact:
Clarke and Company
535 Boylston Street
Boston, MA 02116
Phone: 617-536-3003

Clyde Russell Scholarship Fund

Clyde Russell Scholarship Fund

Type of award: Scholarship.
Intended use: For undergraduate or graduate study at 4-year or graduate institution in United States.
Eligibility: Applicant must be U.S. citizen residing in Maine.
Basis for selection: Applicant must demonstrate depth of character, seriousness of purpose and service orientation.
Application requirements: Recommendations and transcript.
Additional information: Applicants can be either a graduating high school senior, undergraduates, or graduate students. There is also an award for pursuing further educational and cultural research. Please specify which type of scholarship applying for when requesting information. Applications available between November 2 and January 14, only.
    Amount of award: $500-$10,000
    Application deadline: February 1
Contact:
Clyde Russell Scholarship Fund
P.O. Box 2457
Augusta, ME 04338

Coca-Cola Scholars Foundation

Coca-Cola Scholars Program

Type of award: Scholarship, renewable.
Intended use: For full-time undergraduate study at accredited 2-year or 4-year institution in United States.
Eligibility: Applicant must be high school senior. Applicant must be U.S. citizen or permanent resident.
Basis for selection: Applicant must demonstrate depth of character, leadership, seriousness of purpose, service orientation and high academic achievement.
Additional information: Must be attending high school in participating bottler territories.

Amount of award:	$1,000-$5,000
Number of awards:	150
Number of applicants:	129,000
Application deadline:	October 31
Notification begins:	December 31
Total amount awarded:	$1,400,000

Contact:
Coca-Cola Scholars Foundation
P.O. Box 442
Atlanta, GA 30301-0442
Phone: 800-306-COKE

Colorado Masons Benevolent Fund Association

Colorado Masons Scholarship

Type of award: Scholarship, renewable.
Intended use: For full-time freshman study at accredited vocational, 2-year or 4-year institution in Colorado. Designated institutions: Can only be used at Colorado institutions.
Eligibility: Applicant must be high school senior. Applicant must be residing in Colorado.
Basis for selection: Applicant must demonstrate depth of character, financial need and high academic achievement.
Additional information: Contact high school college counselor or local Masonic chapter for application details. Do not contact Association directly.

Amount of award:	$5,000
Number of awards:	53
Application deadline:	March 15
Total amount awarded:	$265,000

Colorado Society of CPAs Educational Foundation

Colorado CPAs Ethnic Scholarship

Type of award: Scholarship, renewable.
Intended use: For freshman study at accredited 2-year or 4-year institution in Colorado. Designated institutions: Public colleges in Colorado.
Eligibility: Applicant must be of minority background. Applicant must be high school senior. Applicant must be U.S. citizen residing in Colorado.
Basis for selection: Major/career interest in accounting. Applicant must demonstrate financial need and high academic achievement.
Application requirements: Transcript and proof of eligibility.
Additional information: Minimum 3.0 GPA required.

Amount of award:	$750
Number of awards:	2
Number of applicants:	20
Application deadline:	March 1
Total amount awarded:	$1,500

Contact:
Colorado Society of CPA's Educational Foundation
7979 East Tufts Avenue, Suite 500
Denver, CO 80237
Phone: 8005239082

Colorado CPAs Ethnic-College and University Scholarship

Type of award: Scholarship, renewable.
Intended use: For undergraduate or graduate study at accredited 2-year, 4-year or graduate institution in Colorado. Designated institutions: List of 15 designated institutions provided by Society.
Eligibility: Applicant must be of minority background. Applicant must be U.S. citizen residing in Colorado.
Basis for selection: Major/career interest in accounting. Applicant must demonstrate financial need and high academic achievement.
Application requirements: Interview, transcript and proof of eligibility. Incude with application, parent's tax return (if they are assisting financially); and last year's Federal tax return. Applicant must be declared accounting major and have completed at least 8 semester hours.
Additional information: Must have completed eight semester hours of accounting courses to be eligible to apply. Minimum 3.0 GPA required.

Amount of award:	$750
Number of awards:	2
Application deadline:	June 30, November 30

Contact:
Colorado Society of CPAs Educational Foundation
7979 East Tufts Avenue Suite 500
Denver, CO 80237
Phone: 800-523-9082

Colorado CPAs Gordon Scheer Scholarship

Type of award: Scholarship, renewable.
Intended use: For junior, senior or graduate study at accredited 4-year or graduate institution in Colorado. Designated institutions: List of 15 designated institutions provided by Society.
Eligibility: Applicant must be U.S. citizen residing in Colorado.
Basis for selection: Major/career interest in accounting. Applicant must demonstrate financial need and high academic achievement.
Application requirements: Interview, recommendations,

transcript and proof of eligibility. Letter of reference from the accounting department head, one faculty member and one other of your choice, not family.
Additional information: Minimum 3.5 GPA required.
- Amount of award: $1,000
- Number of awards: 1
- Application deadline: June 30
- Total amount awarded: $1,000

Contact:
Colorado Society of CPA's Educational Foundation
7979 East Tufts Avenue, Suite 500
Denver, CO 80237
Phone: 800-523-9082

Colorado CPAs High School Scholarship

Type of award: Scholarship, renewable.
Intended use: For full-time or half-time freshman, sophomore or junior study at accredited 2-year or 4-year institution in Colorado. Designated institutions: List of 15 designated institutions provided by Society.
Eligibility: Applicant must be high school senior. Applicant must be U.S. citizen residing in Colorado.
Basis for selection: Major/career interest in accounting. Applicant must demonstrate financial need and high academic achievement.
Application requirements: Transcript and proof of eligibility.
Additional information: Minimum 3.75 GPA required.
- Amount of award: $750
- Number of awards: 10
- Number of applicants: 75
- Application deadline: March 1
- Total amount awarded: $7,500

Contact:
Colorado Society of CPA's Educational Foundation
7979 East Tufts Avenue, Suite 500
Denver, CO 80237
Phone: 8005239082

Colorado Society of CPAs Educational Foundation Scholarship

Type of award: Scholarship, renewable.
Intended use: For full-time or half-time junior, senior or graduate study at accredited 4-year or graduate institution in Colorado. Designated institutions: List of 15 designated institutions provided by Society.
Eligibility: Applicant must be U.S. citizen residing in Colorado.
Basis for selection: Major/career interest in accounting. Applicant must demonstrate financial need and high academic achievement.
Application requirements: Transcript and proof of eligibility.
Additional information: Must have completed eight semester hours in accounting to be eligible to apply. Minimum 3.0 GPA required.

- Amount of award: $750
- Number of awards: 14
- Number of applicants: 50
- Application deadline: June 30, November 30
- Total amount awarded: $8,500

Contact:
Colorado Society of CPA's Educational Foundation
7979 East Tufts Avenue, Suite 500
Denver, CO 80237
Phone: 800-523-9082

Committee on Institutional Cooperation

CIC/GE Predoctoral Fellowship

Type of award: Scholarship.
Intended use: For doctoral study at graduate institution in United States.
Eligibility: Applicant must be Alaskan native, American Indian, African American, Mexican American or Puerto Rican. Applicant must be U.S. citizen.
Basis for selection: Major/career interest in physical sciences; engineering. Applicant must demonstrate high academic achievement.
Application requirements: Recommendations, essay and transcript.
Additional information: Covers tution/fees in addition to $15,000 award. Must be admitted by a CIC institution into a doctoral program in the physical sciences or engineering. Application deadlines are determined by institution.
- Amount of award: $15,000
- Number of awards: 5
- Number of applicants: 15

Contact:
Committee on Institutional Cooperation
Attn: Jean Girves
302 East John Street, Suite 1705
Champaign, IL 61820
Phone: 800-457-4420
Website: www.cic.net/cic

Predoctoral Clearinghouse Application Fee Waiver

Type of award: Scholarship.
Intended use: For doctoral study at graduate institution in United States.
Eligibility: Applicant must be Alaskan native, American Indian, African American, Mexican American or Puerto Rican. Applicant must be U.S. citizen.
Basis for selection: Major/career interest in arts, general. Applicant must demonstrate high academic achievement.
Additional information: This awards is to provide an application fee waiver for graduate school applications. Must be applying for admission to a CIC doctoral program or Master of Fine Arts program. Undergraduate GPA must be at least 3.0.

Number of awards: 600
Number of applicants: 600
Application deadline: November 1
Contact:
Committee on Institutional Cooperation
302 East John Street
Suite 1705
Champaign, IL 61820
Phone: 800-457-4420
Website: www.cic.net/cic

Computing Research Association

Computing Research Association Outstanding Undergraduate Award

Type of award: Scholarship.
Intended use: For undergraduate study.
Basis for selection: Major/career interest in computer and information sciences; engineering, computer. Applicant must demonstrate high academic achievement.
Additional information: Program recognizes students who show exceptional promise in an area of computing research. The 2 winners are given travel assistance for the CRA conference.

Amount of award: $1,000
Number of awards: 2
Total amount awarded: $2,000
Contact:
1100 17th St. NW, Suite 507
Washington, DC 20036-4632
Website: www.cra.org

Concerned Educators Against Forced Unionism

Applegate/Jackson/Parks Future Teacher Scholarship

Type of award: Scholarship.
Intended use: For undergraduate or graduate study at accredited postsecondary institution in United States.
Basis for selection: Quality of essay, which must demonstrate knowledge of and interest in principle of compulsory unionism in education. Major/career interest in education.
Application requirements: Essay, transcript and proof of eligibility.
Additional information: Must be majoring in education. Department of Education FASF forms are required with application.

Amount of award: $1,000
Number of awards: 1
Number of applicants: 250
Application deadline: April 30
Notification begins: July 15
Total amount awarded: $1,000
Contact:
Concerned Educators Against Forced Unionism
Attn: Catherine Jones
5211 Port Royal Road
Springfield, VA 22151
Phone: 703-321-9606
Fax: 703-321-7342

Congressional Black Caucus Foundation, Inc.

Congressional Black Caucus Foundation Spouses' Scholarship

Type of award: Scholarship, renewable.
Intended use: For full-time undergraduate study at accredited 4-year institution.
Eligibility: Applicant must be of minority background. Applicant must be U.S. citizen or permanent resident.
Basis for selection: Applicant must demonstrate financial need.
Application requirements: Transcript.
Additional information: Minimum GPA 2.5. Must reside or attend school in congressional district represented by Black Caucus member. Selection made at district level. List of eligible districts and members' addresses provided by national office. Award amounts vary.

Application deadline: May 15
Notification begins: August 1
Contact:
Congressional Black Caucus Foundation, Inc.
1004 Pennsylvania Avenue, SE
Washington, DC 20003

Congressional Hispanic Caucus Institute

Congressional Hispanic Caucus Internship

Type of award: Internship.
Intended use: For freshman, sophomore or junior study.
Eligibility: Applicant must be Mexican American, Hispanic American or Puerto Rican.
Basis for selection: Applicant must demonstrate high academic achievement.
Application requirements: Recommendations, essay, transcript and proof of eligibility.
Additional information: Excellent writing skills, leadership potential and involvement in community affairs required.

Interns assigned to congressional offices. Work experience is complimented by leadership development curriculum. Application deadlines change annually.
- Amount of award: $2,000-$2,500
- Number of awards: 30
- Number of applicants: 150
- Application deadline: January 15

Contact:
Program Coordinator
504 C St., NE
Washington, DC 20002
Website: www.chci.org

Connecticut Building Congress Scholarship Fund

Connecticut Building Congress Scholarship

Type of award: Scholarship, renewable.
Intended use: For undergraduate study at 2-year or 4-year institution in United States.
Eligibility: Applicant must be residing in Connecticut.
Basis for selection: Major/career interest in engineering, construction; architecture; construction management. Applicant must demonstrate financial need and high academic achievement.
Application requirements: Recommendations and transcript. State applicant must reside in Connecticut.
- Amount of award: $500-$2,000
- Number of awards: 5
- Number of applicants: 85
- Application deadline: March 1, June 1
- Total amount awarded: $10,000

Contact:
Connecticut Building Congress Scholarship Fund
2600 Dixwell Ave.
Hamden, CT 06514

Connecticut Higher Education Supplemental Loan Authority

Family Education Loan Program

Type of award: Loan, renewable.
Intended use: For full-time or half-time undergraduate or graduate study in United States.
Eligibility: Applicant must be U.S. citizen residing in Connecticut.
Additional information: Alternate phone: 800-252-3357. Connecticut residents may attend any institution in the United States, Non-residents must attend a Connecticut institution to be eligible.
- Amount of award: $2,000-$125,000
- Number of awards: 1,219
- Total amount awarded: $10,549,115

Contact:
Connecticut Higher Education Supplemental Loan Authority
29 South Main Street
Town Center, 304N
West Hartford, CT 06107
Phone: 860-561-2180
Website: www.ctdhe.commnet.edu/chesla/default.htm

Connecticut League for Nursing

Connecticut Nursing Scholarship

Type of award: Scholarship.
Intended use: For full-time or half-time senior or graduate study at accredited postsecondary institution.
Eligibility: Applicant must be U.S. citizen residing in Connecticut.
Basis for selection: Major/career interest in nursing. Applicant must demonstrate leadership, seriousness of purpose, financial need and high academic achievement.
Application requirements: Recommendations, essay, transcript and proof of eligibility.
Additional information: Must have 20 credit hours in nursing courses to be eligible to apply.
- Amount of award: $500
- Number of awards: 3
- Number of applicants: 17
- Application deadline: October 1
- Notification begins: November 15
- Total amount awarded: $1,500

Contact:
Connecticut League for Nursing
P.O. Box 365
Wallingford, CT 06492
Phone: 203-265-4248

Council for European Studies

Pre-Dissertation Fellowship for Research in Europe

Type of award: Scholarship.
Intended use: For full-time doctoral study outside United States in Europe. Designated institutions: Award is for independent research. No institutional affiliation in Europe is required.
Eligibility: Applicant must be U.S. citizen or permanent resident.
Basis for selection: Major/career interest in anthropology; economics; geography; political science/government; history; sociology. Applicant must demonstrate high academic achievement.
Application requirements: Research proposal. Political

Science and Sociology are possible fields of study. Projects involving study of any part of Europe, including Eastern Europe (preferably in comparative perspective), but excluding the countries of the former Soviet Union are welcome. Award may be used to pursue language study, pay tuition or to supplement a larger grant for research.
Additional information: Award is for short-term (six to eight weeks), full-time, independent research in Europe to determine the feasibility of a projected doctoral dissertation.

Amount of award:	$3,000
Number of awards:	12
Number of applicants:	71
Application deadline:	February 1
Notification begins:	April 20
Total amount awarded:	$36,000

Contact:
Council for European Studies
807-807A International Affairs Building
420 West 118 Street
New York, NY 10027
Phone: 212-854-4172
Fax: 212-854-8808
Website: www.columbia.edu/cu/ces

Council for the Advancement of Science Writing, Inc.

Rennie Taylor/Alton Blakeslee Fellowship

Type of award: Scholarship.
Intended use: For full-time master's, doctoral study at accredited graduate institution in United States.
Eligibility: Applicant must be U.S. citizen or permanent resident.
Basis for selection: Major/career interest in science, general; journalism. Applicant must demonstrate financial need and high academic achievement.
Application requirements: Recommendations, essay and transcript. Resume and writing samples.

Amount of award:	$1,000-$2,000
Number of applicants:	24
Application deadline:	June 15
Notification begins:	August 15
Total amount awarded:	$6,000

Contact:
Council for the Advancement of Science Writing, Inc.
P.O. Box 404
Greenlawn, NY 11740
Phone: 516-757-5664
Website: www.nasw.org/users/casw

Council of Energy Resource Tribes

Council of Energy Resource Tribes Summer Intern Program

Type of award: Internship.
Intended use: For sophomore, junior, senior or graduate study.
Eligibility: Applicant must be Alaskan native or American Indian. Applicant must be U.S. citizen.
Application requirements: Interview, recommendations, transcript and proof of eligibility. Resume, cover letter, writing samples.
Additional information: Ten week summer internship. Interns receive $400/week stipend, free housing and round-trip trvel. Provides opportunity to work alongside CERT staff and tribal leaders on various scientific and political projects. Contact office for applications and application deadlines.

Amount of award:	$4,000
Number of awards:	10
Number of applicants:	100
Total amount awarded:	$40,000

Contact:
Council of Energy Resource Tribes
Attn: Intern Director
1999 Broadway, Suite 2600
Denver, CO 80202
Phone: 303-297-2378

Council of Jewish Federations

Council of Jewish Federations Scholarship

Type of award: Scholarship, renewable.
Intended use: For full-time master's study at graduate institution in United States. Designated institutions: University of Pennsylvania, University of Maryland, University of Toronto, University of Southern California, University of Michigan, Brandeis University, Columbia University, Baltimore Institute for Jewish Communal Services, Case Western Reserve University, Hebrew Union College, Baltimore Hebrew University, Jewish Theological Seminary, Yeshiva University.
Eligibility: Applicant must be U.S. citizen.
Basis for selection: Major/career interest in Jewish studies; social work; public administration/service. Applicant must demonstrate depth of character, leadership, service orientation and high academic achievement.
Application requirements: Interview, recommendations, essay and transcript.
Additional information: Focus of Jewish studies must be Jewish communal service. Minimum 3.0 GPA. Up to three full-tuition grants of $20,000, and up to seven partial tuition assistance grants, available each year. Those receiving full grants must work for Jewish Federation in North America

minimum three years postgraduate; those receiving partial grants minimum two years.

Amount of award:	$7,500-$20,000
Number of awards:	12
Number of applicants:	40
Application deadline:	February 1
Notification begins:	May 1
Total amount awarded:	$95,000

Contact:
Council of Jewish Federations
Personnel Services Department
730 Broadway
New York, NY 10003-9596
Phone: 212-598-3583

Council on Social Work Education

Social Work Clinical Fellowship

Type of award: Internship, renewable.
Intended use: For full-time doctoral study at accredited graduate institution in United States.
Eligibility: Applicant must be of minority background. Applicant must be U.S. citizen or permanent resident.
Basis for selection: Major/career interest in social work. Applicant must demonstrate leadership, service orientation, financial need and high academic achievement.
Application requirements: Recommendations, essay and transcript. Resume, scholarly paper.
Additional information: Award for career in mental health research. Brandeis University's Heller School for Advanced Studies in Social Welfare.

Amount of award:	$1,800
Number of awards:	10
Number of applicants:	50
Application deadline:	February 27
Notification begins:	June 1

Contact:
Council on Social Work Education
Clinical Fellowship Award
1600 Duke Street, Suite 300
Alexandria, VA 22314-3421
Phone: 703-683-8080
Fax: 703-683-8099
Website: www.cswe.org

Social Work Minority Research Fellowship

Type of award: Internship, renewable.
Intended use: For full-time doctoral study at accredited graduate institution in United States.
Eligibility: Applicant must be of minority background. Applicant must be U.S. citizen or permanent resident.
Basis for selection: Major/career interest in social work. Applicant must demonstrate leadership, service orientation, financial need and high academic achievement.
Application requirements: Recommendations, essay and transcript. Resume, scholarly paper, statement on area of mental health interest required.
Additional information: Must be accepted into a doctoral social work program or Brandeis University's Heller School for Advanced Studies in Social Welfare.

Amount of award:	$10,000-$12,000
Number of awards:	20
Number of applicants:	40
Application deadline:	February 28
Notification begins:	June 1
Total amount awarded:	$200,100

Contact:
Council On Social Work Education
Minority Fellowship Program
1600 Duke Street, Suite 300
Alexandria, VA 22314-3421
Phone: 703-683-8080
Fax: 703-683-8099
Website: www.cswe.org

Courage Center Vocational Services-United Way Organization

Scholarship for People with Disabilities

Type of award: Scholarship.
Intended use: For undergraduate study at accredited vocational, 2-year or 4-year institution.
Eligibility: Applicant must be visually impaired, hearing impaired, physically challenged or learning disabled. Applicant must be U.S. citizen.
Basis for selection: Applicant must demonstrate depth of character, leadership, seriousness of purpose and financial need.
Application requirements: Interview, essay and proof of eligibility.
Additional information: If the student is not a Minnesota resident then she/he must be a U.S. citizen participating in Courage Center services. Student must have a sensory impairment or physical disability. Selection emphasis is placed on the applicant's intentions and achievements.

Amount of award:	$1,000
Application deadline:	May 31, July 1

Contact:
Courage Center-A United Way Organization
3915 Golden Valley Rd.
Golden Valley, MN 55422

Creede Repertory Theatre

Creede Repertory Theatre Summer Internship

Type of award: Internship.
Intended use: For undergraduate, graduate, postgraduate or non-degree study.
Application requirements: Audition and recommendations. resume.
Additional information: Open to all majors. We offer

internships in costumes, scene shop, box office, business management. High school seniors may apply, but must graduate by summer, and are hired on the basis of qualification. We also hire an acting company and designers (set, costume, lights, etc.) and stage managers. People are hired on the basis of their qualification for the various jobs. Actors must audition. All others must fill out an internship application and/or send a resume. We will consider any age/sex/race applicant, however, we rarely hire people under the age of 17. Housing is free, interns receive $115 a week.

 Amount of award: $1,725
 Application deadline: March 1, March 16

Contact:
Creede Repertory Theatre
P.O. Box 269
Creede, CO 81130

Cushman School

Cushman School Internship

Type of award: Internship, renewable.
Intended use: For undergraduate study.
Basis for selection: Major/career interest in education. Applicant must demonstrate depth of character.
Additional information: 17-week internships for fall and spring. Interns receive $118 a week, foreign interns receive $175 a week. Must submit cover letter and resume.

 Amount of award: $2,000-$3,000
 Number of awards: 4
 Application deadline: May 1

Contact:
Cushman School
592 Northeast 60th St.
Miami, FL 33137

Cymdeithas Gymreig/Philadelphia

Cymdeithas Gymreig (Welsh Society) Philadelphia Scholarship

Type of award: Scholarship.
Intended use: For full-time freshman, sophomore or junior study at accredited 2-year or 4-year institution in United States. Designated institutions: Must attend institutions in Delaware, Maryland, New Jersey or Pennsylvania.
Eligibility: Applicant must be of Welsh heritage. Applicant must be residing in Delaware or Maryland or New Jersey or Pennsylvania.
Basis for selection: Applicant must demonstrate leadership, seriousness of purpose, service orientation and high academic achievement.
Application requirements: Recommendations, essay, transcript and proof of eligibility.
Additional information: Applicant or parent must be member of or be active in Welsh organization, church, or activities. Applicant may study in Wales if primary residence is within 150 miles of Philadelphia. Must rank in top third of class. Send SASE for application.

 Amount of award: $500-$1,000
 Number of awards: 5
 Number of applicants: 500
 Application deadline: March 1
 Notification begins: June 1
 Total amount awarded: $5,000

Contact:
Cymdeithas Gymreig/Philadelphia
Hen Dy Hapus 367 South River Street
Wilkes-Barre, PA 18702
Phone: 717-822-4871

Cystic Fibrosis Foundation

Cystic Fibrosis Clinical Research Grant

Type of award: Research grant, renewable.
Intended use: For full-time postgraduate study at accredited graduate institution in United States.
Basis for selection: Major/career interest in medical specialties/research (beyond m.d.). Applicant must demonstrate high academic achievement.
Application requirements: Recommendations and research proposal.
Additional information: Supports clinical research projects directly related to cystic fibrosis treatment and care. Projects may address diagnostic or therapeutic methods related to cystic fibrosis, or to the pathophysiology of cystic fibrosis.

 Amount of award: $80,000
 Application deadline: October 1
 Notification begins: February 1
 Total amount awarded: $150,000

Contact:
Cystic Fibrosis Foundation
Office of Grants Management
6931 Arlington Road
Bethesda, MD 20814
Phone: 301-951-4422
Fax: 301-951-6378

Cystic Fibrosis First and Second Year Clinical Fellowship

Type of award: Research grant, renewable.
Intended use: For full-time postgraduate study at accredited graduate institution in United States.
Eligibility: Applicant must be U.S. citizen or permanent resident.
Basis for selection: Major/career interest in medical specialties/research (beyond m.d.). Applicant must demonstrate high academic achievement.
Application requirements: Recommendations and research proposal.
Additional information: Must be eligible for Board certification in pediatrics or internal medicine by the time the fellowship begins. Award encourages training in diagnostic and therapeutic procedures, comprehensive care, and cystic fibrosis related research.

Amount of award:	$36,000-$37,500
Application deadline:	October 1
Notification begins:	February 1

Contact:
Cystic Fibrosis Foundation
Office of Grants Management
6931 Arlington Road
Bethesda, MD 20814
Phone: 301-951-4422
Fax: 301-951-6378

Cystic Fibrosis Pilot and Feasibility Award

Type of award: Research grant, renewable.
Intended use: For postgraduate study at accredited graduate institution in United States.
Basis for selection: Major/career interest in medical specialties/research (beyond m.d.). Applicant must demonstrate high academic achievement.
Application requirements: Recommendations and research proposal.
Additional information: Proposed work must be hypothesis-driven and must reflect innovative approaches to critical questions in cystic fibrosis research.

Amount of award:	$40,000
Application deadline:	September 1
Notification begins:	February 1

Contact:
Cystic Fibrosis Foundation
Medical Department
6931 Arlington Road
Bethesda, MD 20814
Phone: 301-951-4422
Fax: 301-951-6378

Cystic Fibrosis Postdoctoral Research Fellowship

Type of award: Research grant, renewable.
Intended use: For full-time postgraduate study at accredited graduate institution in United States.
Eligibility: Applicant must be U.S. citizen or permanent resident.
Basis for selection: Major/career interest in medical specialties/research (beyond m.d.). Applicant must demonstrate high academic achievement.
Application requirements: Recommendations and research proposal.
Additional information: For basic or clinical research.

Amount of award:	$30,000-$33,000
Application deadline:	September 1
Notification begins:	February 1

Contact:
Cystic Fibrosis Foundation
Office of Grants Management
6931 Arlington Road
Bethesda, MD 20814
Phone: 301-951-4422
Fax: 301-951-6378

Cystic Fibrosis Research Grant

Type of award: Research grant, renewable.
Intended use: For doctoral, first professional or postgraduate study at graduate institution in or outside United States.
Basis for selection: Major/career interest in medical specialties/research; medical specialties/research (beyond m.d.). Applicant must demonstrate high academic achievement.
Application requirements: Research proposal.
Additional information: To contribute to the understanding of the basic etiology and pathogenesis of cystic fibrosis. All proposals must be hypothesis-driven; preliminary data must be provided.

Amount of award:	$60,000
Application deadline:	September 1
Notification begins:	February 1

Contact:
Cystic Fibrosis Foundation
Office of Grants Management
6931 Arlington Road
Bethesda, MD 20814
Phone: 301-951-4422
Fax: 301-951-6378

Cystic Fibrosis Student Traineeship

Type of award: Research grant, renewable.
Intended use: For full-time senior, master's or doctoral study at accredited graduate institution in United States.
Basis for selection: Major/career interest in medical specialties/research; medical specialties/research (beyond m.d.).
Application requirements: Recommendations and research proposal.
Additional information: Trainees must work with a faculty sponsor on a research project related to cystic fibrosis.

Amount of award:	$1,500

Contact:
Cystic Fibrosis Foundation
Office of Grants Management
6931 Arlington Road
Bethesda, MD 20814
Phone: 301-951-4422
Fax: 301-951-6378

Cystic Fibrosis Summer Scholarship in Epidemiology

Type of award: Scholarship.
Intended use: For full-time postgraduate study at accredited graduate institution in United States.
Eligibility: Applicant must be U.S. citizen or permanent resident.
Basis for selection: Major/career interest in medicine (m.d.); medical specialties/research; medical specialties/research (beyond m.d.). Applicant must demonstrate high academic achievement.
Application requirements: Recommendations and research proposal.
Additional information: Award to increase skills in epidemiology for M.D.s currently working in cystic fibrosis.

Amount of award:	$2,000
Number of awards:	1
Application deadline:	April 1
Notification begins:	May 1
Total amount awarded:	$2,000

Contact:
Cystic Fibrosis Foundation
Office of Grants Management
6931 Arlington Road
Bethesda, MD 20814
Phone: 301-951-4422
Fax: 301-951-6378

Cystic Fibrosis Third and Fourth Year Clinical Fellowship

Type of award: Research grant, renewable.
Intended use: For full-time postgraduate study at accredited graduate institution in United States.
Eligibility: Applicant must be U.S. citizen or permanent resident.
Basis for selection: Major/career interest in medical specialties/research (beyond m.d.). Applicant must demonstrate high academic achievement.
Application requirements: Recommendations and research proposal.
Additional information: Applicants must be eligible for Board certification in pediatrics or internal medicine by the time the fellowship begins. Award for diagnostic and therapeutic procedures, comprehensive care, and cystic fibrosis related research.

Amount of award:	$55,000
Application deadline:	September 1
Notification begins:	February 1

Contact:
Cystic Fibrosis Foundation
Office of Grants Management
6931 Arlington Road
Bethesda, MD 20814
Phone: 301-951-4422
Fax: 301-951-6378

Harry Shwachman Clinical Investigator Award

Type of award: Research grant, renewable.
Intended use: For full-time postgraduate study at accredited graduate institution in United States.
Eligibility: Applicant must be U.S. citizen or permanent resident.
Basis for selection: Major/career interest in medical specialties/research (beyond m.d.). Applicant must demonstrate high academic achievement.
Application requirements: Recommendations and research proposal.
Additional information: Provides opportunity for clinically trained physicians to develop into independent biomedical research investigators.

Amount of award:	$60,000
Application deadline:	August 1
Notification begins:	February 1

Contact:
Cystic Fibrosis Foundation
Office of Grants Management
6931 Arlington Road
Bethesda, MD 20814
Phone: 301-951-4422
Fax: 301-951-6378

Leroy Matthews Physician/Scientist Award

Type of award: Research grant, renewable.
Intended use: For full-time postgraduate study at accredited graduate institution in United States.
Eligibility: Applicant must be U.S. citizen or permanent resident.
Basis for selection: Major/career interest in medical specialties/research (beyond m.d.). Applicant must demonstrate high academic achievement.
Application requirements: Recommendations and research proposal.
Additional information: Provides up to six years of support for newly trained pediatricians and internists to complete subspecialty training and initiate a research program.

Amount of award:	$46,000-$75,000
Application deadline:	September 1
Notification begins:	February 1

Contact:
Cystic Fibrosis Foundation
Office of Grants Management
6931 Arlington Road
Bethesda, MD 20814
Phone: 301-951-4422
Fax: 301-951-6378

National Institutes of Health Funding Award

Type of award: Research grant, renewable.
Intended use: For full-time postgraduate study at accredited graduate institution in United States.
Eligibility: Applicant must be U.S. citizen or permanent resident.
Basis for selection: Major/career interest in medical specialties/research (beyond m.d.). Applicant must demonstrate high academic achievement.
Application requirements: Recommendations and research proposal.
Additional information: Award supports cystic fibrosis-related research projects that have been approved by the NIH but cannot be supported by available NIH funds.

Amount of award:	$75,000-$125,000

Contact:
Cystic Fibrosis Foundation
Office of Grants Management
6931 Arlington Road
Bethesda, MD 20814
Phone: 301-951-4422
Fax: 301-951-6378

Dairy Management, Inc.

Dairy Product Marketing Scholarship

Type of award: Scholarship.
Intended use: For full-time junior, senior study at accredited 4-year institution.
Eligibility: Applicant must be U.S. citizen.
Basis for selection: Major/career interest in advertising; marketing; food production/management/services; food science and technology. Applicant must demonstrate leadership, seriousness of purpose and high academic achievement.
Application requirements: Recommendations and transcript.
Additional information: Applications available through the Food Science Department Chairperson or financial aid officer of applicant's institution. Must have a commitment to a career in dairy food related disciplines.

Amount of award:	$1,500
Number of awards:	20
Number of applicants:	35
Application deadline:	March 31
Notification begins:	June 1
Total amount awarded:	$30,000

Contact:
Dairy Management Inc.
10255 West Higgins Road
Suite 900
Rosemont, IL 60018
Website: www.dairycouncil.com

Datatel Scholars Foundation

Datatel Scholarship

Type of award: Scholarship, renewable.
Intended use: For undergraduate or graduate study.
Basis for selection: Competition in Writing/journalism. Applicant must demonstrate high academic achievement.
Application requirements: Recommendations, essay, transcript and proof of eligibility.
Additional information: Limited to institutions that are Datatel clients. When requesting application include institution name for determination of qualification. Apply through school's financial aid office.

Amount of award:	$700-$2,000
Number of awards:	129
Number of applicants:	306
Application deadline:	February 15
Notification begins:	May 15
Total amount awarded:	$172,000

Contact:
Datatel Scholars Foundation
4375 Fair Lakes Court
Fairfax, VA 22033
Phone: 703-968-9000
Website: www.datatel.com

Daughters of Penelope

Daughters of Penelope Re-entry Grant

Type of award: Scholarship.
Intended use: For full-time or half-time undergraduate study at accredited vocational, 2-year or 4-year institution.
Eligibility: Applicant must be female, adult returning student, of Greek heritage. Applicant must be U.S. citizen or permanent resident.
Basis for selection: Applicant must demonstrate financial need.
Application requirements: Recommendations and transcript. Self-reported GPA of previous eduation.
Additional information: This grant is for students returning to school after a leave of absence. Must be endorsed by Daughters of Penelope or American Hellenic Educational Progressive Association (AHEPA) chapter. Applicants with immediate relatives in AHEPA also eligible.

Amount of award:	$1,000
Number of awards:	1
Application deadline:	June 20
Notification begins:	July 30
Total amount awarded:	$1,000

Contact:
Daughters of Penelope
1909 Q Street, NW
Suite 500
Washington, DC 20009

Daughters of Union Veterans of the Civil War 1861-1865, Inc.

Grand Army of the Republic Living Memorial Scholarship

Type of award: Scholarship.
Intended use: For full-time junior, senior or graduate study at accredited 4-year institution in United States.
Eligibility: Applicant must be U.S. citizen. Applicant must be descendant of veteran during Civil War.
Basis for selection: Applicant must demonstrate depth of character, leadership, patriotism, seriousness of purpose, service orientation and high academic achievement.
Application requirements: Recommendations and transcript. Ancestor's military record required. Must send stamped, self-addressed envelope when requesting information.
Additional information: Must be lineal descendant of Union Veteran of Civil War. Minimum 3.75 GPA required. Request for information, application honored only when sent with stamped, self-addressed envelope. Applications available between October 1 and February 1 only. MUST request application by February 1.

Amount of award:	$300
Number of awards:	3
Number of applicants:	700
Application deadline:	April 30
Notification begins:	September 30
Total amount awarded:	$900

Contact:
Daughters of Union Veterans of the Civil War 1861-1865, Inc.
503 South Walnut Street
Springfield, IL 62704

David and Dovetta Wilson Scholarship Fund

David and Dovetta Wilson Scholarship

Type of award: Scholarship.
Intended use: For full-time freshman study at accredited postsecondary institution in or outside United States.
Eligibility: Applicant must be of minority background. Applicant must be U.S. citizen.
Basis for selection: Applicant must demonstrate depth of character, leadership, seriousness of purpose, service orientation and financial need.
Application requirements: $20 application fee. Portfolio, recommendations, essay, transcript and proof of eligibility.

Amount of award:	$250-$1,000
Number of awards:	9
Number of applicants:	9
Application deadline:	March 15
Notification begins:	May 1

Contact:
David and Dovetta Wilson Scholarship Fund
Attn: Timothy M. Wilson
115-67 237 St.
Elmont, NY 11003

Davis Hays and Company

Employee Communication Internship

Type of award: Internship, renewable.
Intended use: For undergraduate or graduate study.
Eligibility: Applicant must be U.S. citizen or permanent resident.
Basis for selection: Major/career interest in graphic arts and design; communications; journalism; marketing; English. Applicant must demonstrate depth of character.
Application requirements: Interview.
Additional information: 6-week internship. Interns receive $240 a week. Interns assist account executives in all aspects of their work.

Amount of award:	$1,440
Number of awards:	2
Total amount awarded:	$2,880

Contact:
Davis Hays and Company
80 Grand Ave.
River Edge, NJ 07661
Website: www.davishays.com

Deafness Research Foundation

Deafness Research Foundation Otological Research Fellowship

Type of award: Scholarship.
Intended use: For full-time first professional study.
Basis for selection: Major/career interest in medical specialties/research. Applicant must demonstrate high academic achievement.
Application requirements: Recommendations, transcript, proof of eligibility and research proposal.
Additional information: Must be a medical student. Funding available for a one-year block of time at the end of the third year of medical school. For otological research: related disciplines may include anatomy, physiology, pharmacology, or basic immunology.

Amount of award:	$10,000
Number of awards:	1
Application deadline:	March 15
Total amount awarded:	$10,000

Contact:
Deafness Research Foundation
15 West 39th St.
6th Floor
New York, NY 10016

Otologic Research Grant

Type of award: Scholarship, renewable.
Intended use: For doctoral, postgraduate study in United States.
Eligibility: Applicant must be U.S. citizen or permanent resident.
Basis for selection: Major/career interest in deafness studies.
Application requirements: Research proposal.
Additional information: Field of Study: Otology.

Amount of award:	$5,000-$15,000
Number of awards:	34
Number of applicants:	80

Contact:
Deafness Research Foundation
15 West 39 Street, 6th Floor
New York, NY 10016
Phone: 212-768-1181

Delaware Engineering Society (DES)

Delaware Engineering Society Undergraduate Scholarship Program

Type of award: Scholarship, renewable.
Intended use: For full-time sophomore, junior or senior study at 4-year institution in United States.
Eligibility: Applicant must be female, adult returning student. Applicant must be U.S. citizen residing in Delaware.
Basis for selection: Major/career interest in engineering. Applicant must demonstrate financial need.
Application requirements: Recommendations, essay, transcript and proof of eligibility.
   Amount of award: $300
   Application deadline: December 1
   Notification begins: June 30
Contact:
Scholarship Committee
1210 Arundel Dr.
Wilmington, DE 19808-2137

Dell Computer

Dell Computer Internship

Type of award: Internship.
Intended use: For undergraduate study.
Basis for selection: Major/career interest in computer and information sciences.
Additional information: Deadline and compensation amount varies. Contact sponsor for more information.
   Number of awards: 35
Contact:
Dell Computer
2214 W. Braker Ln.
Austin, TX 78758

Deloitte and Touche

Deloitte And Touche Summer Internship Program

Type of award: Internship.
Intended use: For full-time junior, senior or graduate study.
Eligibility: Applicant must be U.S. citizen or permanent resident.
Basis for selection: Major/career interest in business; accounting. Applicant must demonstrate depth of character and seriousness of purpose.
Application requirements: Interview, recommendations and transcript.
Additional information: Summer, Fall and Spring internships are available. A minimum 3.0 GPA is required. Overseas positions are available. Internships last 8-12 weeks.
   Amount of award: $4,000-$6,400
Contact:
Deloitte and Touche
P.O. Box 820
Wilton, CT 06897

Deloitte and Touche Foundation

Doctoral Fellowship in Accounting

Type of award: Scholarship.
Intended use: For doctoral study at accredited graduate institution.
Basis for selection: Major/career interest in accounting.
Application requirements: Recommendations, transcript, proof of eligibility and nomination.
Additional information: Applications available through the accounting department of applicant's school.
   Amount of award: $20,000
   Number of awards: 10
   Number of applicants: 30
   Application deadline: October 15
   Total amount awarded: $200,000
Contact:
Deloitte & Touche Foundation
Ten Westport Road
Wilton, CT 06897

Dirksen Congressional Center

Dirksen Research Grant Program

Type of award: Scholarship, renewable.
Intended use: For doctoral, postgraduate or non-degree study.
Basis for selection: Major/career interest in history; political science/government; journalism.
Application requirements: Recommendations and research proposal. Project description budget, curriculum vitae.
Additional information: Applicants must have a serious interest in studying Congress.
   Amount of award: $750-$3,000
   Number of awards: 12
   Number of applicants: 77
   Application deadline: April 30
   Notification begins: June 15
   Total amount awarded: $25,000
Contact:
Dirksen Congressional Center
301 South 4 Street
Suite A
Pekin, IL 61554
Phone: 309-347-7113
Fax: 309-347-6432

Dog Writers Educational Trust

Dog Writers Educational Trust Scholarship

Type of award: Scholarship, renewable.
Intended use: For undergraduate study at accredited postsecondary institution in United States.
Eligibility: Applicant must be U.S. citizen.
Basis for selection: Applicant must demonstrate depth of character, seriousness of purpose, financial need and high academic achievement.
Application requirements: $25 application fee. Essay, transcript and proof of eligibility.
Additional information: Must have dog related experience. Amounts of awards vary yearly. Send SASE when requesting application.

Amount of award:	$1,000
Number of awards:	10
Number of applicants:	80
Application deadline:	December 31
Notification begins:	June 1
Total amount awarded:	$10,000

Contact:
Dog Writers Educational Trust
Attn: Roger Au
PO Box 760
North Olmstead, OH 44070-0199

Dolphin Scholarship Foundation

Dolphin Scholarship

Type of award: Scholarship, renewable.
Intended use: For full-time undergraduate study at accredited 4-year institution.
Eligibility: Applicant must be single. Applicant must be U.S. citizen. Applicant must be descendant of veteran, child of active service person, veteran, disabled veteran or deceased veteran who served in the Navy. Must be dependent child or stepchild of (1) member/former member of Submarine Force who has qualified in submarines and has served at least 8 years or died while on active duty; or (2) Navy member who served minimum of 10 years active duty in submarine support activities.
Basis for selection: Applicant must demonstrate depth of character, leadership, patriotism, seriousness of purpose, service orientation, financial need and high academic achievement.
Application requirements: Recommendations, essay, transcript and proof of eligibility.

Amount of award:	$3,000
Number of awards:	102
Number of applicants:	250
Application deadline:	April 15
Notification begins:	May 25
Total amount awarded:	$300,000

Contact:
Dolphin Scholarship Foundation
1683 Dillingham Boulevard
Norfolk, VA 23511
Phone: 757-451-3660
Fax: 757-489-8578

Dow Jones Newspaper Fund

Newspaper Editing Intern Program

Type of award: Internship.
Intended use: For full-time junior, senior or master's study at 4-year or graduate institution.
Eligibility: Applicant must be U.S. citizen.
Basis for selection: Major/career interest in journalism. Applicant must demonstrate seriousness of purpose and high academic achievement.
Application requirements: Essay, transcript and proof of eligibility. Editing test.
Additional information: Applications available August 15 to November 1. Editing test administered by designated professor on applicant's campus. Telephone interview required for finalists. Paid summer internships as editors at daily newspapers, online newspapers, or real-time financial news services last ten to twelve weeks. Interns returning to school receive scholarship at end of summer to apply toward following year. All interns attend pre-internship training that lasts from one to two weeks.

Amount of award:	$1,000
Number of awards:	102
Number of applicants:	600
Application deadline:	November 15
Notification begins:	December 25
Total amount awarded:	$65,000

Contact:
Dow Jones Newspaper Fund
Editing Intern Program
P.O. Box 300
Princeton, NJ 08543-0300
Website: www.dowjones.com/newsfund

Duracell

Duracell Internship Program

Type of award: Internship.
Intended use: For junior, senior, master's or doctoral study.
Eligibility: Applicant must be U.S. citizen or permanent resident.

Basis for selection: Major/career interest in marketing; communications.
Application requirements: Recommendations and transcript.
Additional information: Deadline varies. 10-16 week programs. Compensation ranges from $200-$400 per week. Only fall and spring interns are eligible to receive academic credit. Applicants must submit cover letter and resume.
    Amount of award: $2,000-$6,400
Contact:
Human Resources Director
Berkshire Corporate Park
Bethel, CT 06801

EAA Aviation Foundation

Aviation Scholarship and Work Studies Program

Type of award: Scholarship.
Intended use: For undergraduate, graduate or non-degree study.
Basis for selection: Major/career interest in aviation. Applicant must demonstrate depth of character, leadership, patriotism, seriousness of purpose and service orientation.
Application requirements: $5 application fee. Proof of eligibility. Must complete application form.
    Number of applicants: 200
    Application deadline: May 1
    Notification begins: September 1
    Total amount awarded: $15,000
Contact:
EAA Aviation Foundation
P.O. Box 3065
Oshkosh, WI 54903-3065
Phone: 9204266815
Website: www.eea.org

Early American Industries Association

Early American Industries Grants-In-Aid Program

Type of award: Research grant.
Intended use: For postgraduate study.
Eligibility: Applicant must be U.S. citizen.
Basis for selection: Major/career interest in American history.
Application requirements: Research proposal.
Additional information: Research in use of early American tools, mechanical devices, and/or industrial technology must end in publication or exhibition. This is not a scholarship or an internship.

    Amount of award: $2,000
    Number of applicants: 6
    Application deadline: March 15
    Notification begins: May 1
    Total amount awarded: $6,000
Contact:
Early American Industries Association
1324 Shallcross Avenue
Wilmington, DE 19806
Phone: 302-652-7297

Easter Seal Society of Iowa, Inc.

E.L. Peterson Scholarship

Type of award: Scholarship, renewable.
Intended use: For full-time undergraduate, master's study at accredited 4-year or graduate institution in United States.
Eligibility: Applicant must be U.S. citizen or permanent resident residing in Iowa.
Basis for selection: Applicant must demonstrate depth of character, leadership, seriousness of purpose, service orientation, financial need and high academic achievement.
Application requirements: Recommendations, transcript, proof of eligibility and research proposal.
Additional information: Applicants must be a resident of Iowa. In medical or dental fields of study. The Curriculum must be either physical or psychological rehabilitation oriented. A student in the nursing field must be accepted or participating in a four year program. Minimum GPA of 2.8. Award letters and recommendation forms are due no later than April 30, 1999.
    Amount of award: $600
    Application deadline: April 15

Easter Seal Scholarship

Type of award: Scholarship, renewable.
Intended use: For full-time undergraduate, master's study at accredited 4-year or graduate institution in United States.
Eligibility: Applicant must be U.S. citizen or permanent resident residing in Iowa.
Basis for selection: Applicant must demonstrate depth of character, leadership, seriousness of purpose, service orientation, financial need and high academic achievement.
Application requirements: Recommendations, transcript, proof of eligibility and research proposal.
Additional information: Applicants must be a resident of Iowa. In medical or dental fields of study. The curriculum must be either physical or psychological rehabilitation oriented. A student in the nursing field must be accepted or participating in a four year program. Minimum GPA of 2.8. Award letters and recommendation forms are due no later than April 30, 1999.
    Amount of award: $400
    Number of awards: 3
    Application deadline: April 15

Easter Seal Society of Iowa Disability Scholarship

Type of award: Scholarship, renewable.
Intended use: For full-time freshman study at accredited 4-year institution in United States.
Eligibility: Applicant must be high school senior. Must be physically challenged or learning disabled. Applicant must be U.S. citizen or permanent resident residing in Iowa.
Basis for selection: Applicant must demonstrate depth of character, leadership, seriousness of purpose, service orientation, financial need and high academic achievement.
Application requirements: Recommendations, transcript, proof of eligibility and research proposal.
Additional information: Applicants must be a resident of Iowa. Applicants must have a permanent disability. Minimum GPA of 2.8. Award letters and recommendation forms are due no later than April 30, 1999.
- Amount of award: $750
- Number of awards: 1
- Application deadline: April 15

James L. & Lavon Maddon Mallory Disability Scholarship

Type of award: Scholarship, renewable.
Intended use: For full-time freshman study at accredited 4-year institution in United States.
Eligibility: Applicant must be high school senior. Must be physically challenged or learning disabled. Applicant must be U.S. citizen or permanent resident residing in Iowa.
Basis for selection: Applicant must demonstrate depth of character, leadership, seriousness of purpose, service orientation, financial need and high academic achievement.
Application requirements: Recommendations, transcript, proof of eligibility and research proposal.
Additional information: Applicants must be a resident of Iowa. Applicants must have a permanent disability. Minimum GPA of 2.8. Award letters and recommendation forms are due no later than April 30, 1999.
- Amount of award: $1,000
- Number of awards: 1
- Application deadline: April 15

Lynn Marie Vogel Scholarship

Type of award: Scholarship, renewable.
Intended use: For full-time undergraduate, master's study at accredited 4-year or graduate institution in United States.
Eligibility: Applicant must be U.S. citizen or permanent resident residing in Iowa.
Basis for selection: Applicant must demonstrate depth of character, leadership, seriousness of purpose, service orientation, financial need and high academic achievement.
Application requirements: Recommendations, transcript, proof of eligibility and research proposal.
Additional information: Applicants must be a resident of Iowa. In medical or dental fields of study. The curriculum must be either physical or psychological rehabilitation oriented. A student in the nursing field must be accepted or participating in a four year program. Minimum GPA of 2.8. Award letters and recommendation forms are due no later than April 30, 1999.
- Amount of award: $500
- Application deadline: April 15

Rolfe B. Karlsson Scholarship

Type of award: Scholarship, renewable.
Intended use: For full-time undergraduate, master's study at accredited 4-year or graduate institution in United States.
Eligibility: Applicant must be U.S. citizen or permanent resident residing in Iowa.
Basis for selection: Applicant must demonstrate depth of character, leadership, seriousness of purpose, service orientation, financial need and high academic achievement.
Application requirements: Recommendations, transcript, proof of eligibility and research proposal.
Additional information: Applicants must be a resident of Iowa. In medical or dental fields of study. The curriculum must be either physical or psychological rehabilitation oriented. A student in the nursing field must be accepted or participating in a four year program. Minimum GPA of 2.8. Award letters and recommendation forms are due no later than April 30, 1999.
- Amount of award: $550
- Application deadline: April 14

Contact:
The Easter Seal Society of Iowa, Inc.
P.O. Box 4002
Des Moines, IA 50333

Eastman Kodak Company

Eastman Kodak Student Program

Type of award: Internship.
Intended use: For undergraduate or graduate study.
Eligibility: Applicant must be U.S. citizen or permanent resident.
Basis for selection: Major/career interest in science, general; engineering. Applicant must demonstrate service orientation.
Application requirements: Interview and transcript.
Additional information: Internships last 10 weeks to a year. Available in summer, fall and spring. Undergrads receive $400 to $700 a week. Grad students receive $550 to $800 a week. Minimum grade point average is 2.8. Deadlines for summer session is April 1. Most positions are technical in nature.
- Amount of award: $4,000-$41,600
- Number of awards: 200
- Number of applicants: 2,200
- Application deadline: May 1, November 1

Contact:
Eastman Kodak Company
Staffing, Dept. H5TPG
343 State St.
Rochester, NY 14650-1139
Website: www.kodak.com

Edmund F. Maxwell Foundation

Edmund F. Maxwell Foundation Scholarship

Type of award: Scholarship, renewable.
Intended use: For full-time freshman study.
Eligibility: Applicant must be U.S. citizen or permanent resident residing in Washington.
Basis for selection: Applicant must demonstrate depth of character, leadership, seriousness of purpose, service orientation, financial need and high academic achievement.
Application requirements: Essay and transcript.
Additional information: Combined SAT I must be greater than 1200. College or university must be independent. Must submit financial need assessment with application. Only residents of Western Washington are eligible.

Amount of award:	$3,500
Number of awards:	105
Number of applicants:	250
Application deadline:	April 30
Notification begins:	June 1
Total amount awarded:	$374,500

Contact:
Edmund F. Maxwell Foundation
P.O. Box 22537
Seattle, WA 98122-0537
Website: www.maxwell.org

Education and Research Foundation, Society of Nuclear Medicine

Benedict Cassen Post-Doctoral Fellowship

Type of award: Scholarship, renewable.
Intended use: For full-time undergraduate, postgraduate study at graduate institution in United States.
Eligibility: Applicant must be U.S. citizen.
Basis for selection: Major/career interest in nuclear medicine. Applicant must demonstrate high academic achievement.
Application requirements: Recommendations, transcript and research proposal.
Additional information: Work must be done at a U.S. institution which is different from the place where the recipient's graduate degree is earned.

Amount of award:	$25,000
Number of awards:	2
Application deadline:	January 3
Total amount awarded:	$50,000

Contact:
Susan C. Weiss, Administrative Director
CNMT: Children's Memorial. Hospital.
2300 Children's Plaza, No. 242
Chicago, IL 60614
Phone: 773-880-4416
Fax: 773-880-3839
Website: www.pet.upenn.edu/snmerf

Nuclear Medicine Pilot Research Grant

Type of award: Research grant.
Intended use: For doctoral, first professional or postgraduate study.
Basis for selection: Major/career interest in nuclear medicine.
Application requirements: Research proposal.
Additional information: Investigators may apply for limited research funding for initial clinical and basic research while other major grant support is being sought. These grants will not support salaries, major equipment purchases, institutional overhead or travel, but will provide materials essential to testing innovative ideas.

Amount of award:	$5,000
Number of awards:	6
Number of applicants:	7
Application deadline:	December 15, April 15
Notification begins:	February 15, July 1
Total amount awarded:	$30,000

Contact:
Susan C. Weiss, Administrative Director
CNMT: Children's Memorial Hospital
2300 Children's Plaza, No. 242
Chicago, IL 60614

Nuclear Medicine Student Fellowship Award

Type of award: Research grant.
Intended use: For undergraduate, master's, doctoral or first professional study.
Basis for selection: Major/career interest in nuclear medicine.
Application requirements: Recommendations and research proposal. Curriculum vitae.
Additional information: For part-time summer research internship. Competence in physical and/or biological aspects of radioactivity essential. Will assist in clinical and basic research activities in nuclear medicine.

Amount of award:	$2,000-$3,000
Number of awards:	6
Number of applicants:	7
Application deadline:	December 15, April 15
Notification begins:	February 15, July 1
Total amount awarded:	$18,000

Contact:
Susan C. Weiss, Administrative Director
CNMT: Children's Memorial. Hospital
2300 Children's Plaza, No. 242
Chicago, IL 60614
Website: www.pet.upenn.edu/snmerf

Paul Cole Scholarship

Type of award: Scholarship.
Intended use: For full-time undergraduate study at accredited 2-year or 4-year institution in Canadian institutions.
Eligibility: Applicant must be U.S. citizen or Canadian Citizens are also eligible.
Basis for selection: Major/career interest in nuclear medicine. Applicant must demonstrate financial need and high academic achievement.
Application requirements: Recommendations, essay and transcript. Acceptance to nuclear medicine technology program.
Additional information: Application must be submitted by director of nuclear medicine technology program on behalf of student. Though financial need is not a prerequisite, special consideration is given to students who demonstrate such need.

Amount of award:	$1,000-$1,000
Number of awards:	12
Number of applicants:	95
Application deadline:	April 15
Notification begins:	July 1
Total amount awarded:	$12,000

Contact:
Susan C. Weiss, Administrative Director
CNMT: Children's Memorial. Hospital
2300 Children's Plaza, No. 242
Chicago, IL 60614
Phone: 773-880-4663
Website: www.pet.upenn.edu/snmerf

Educational Communications Scholarship Foundation

Educational Communications Scholarship

Type of award: Scholarship.
Intended use: For undergraduate study at accredited postsecondary institution.
Eligibility: Applicant must be enrolled in high school. Applicant must be U.S. citizen.
Basis for selection: Applicant must demonstrate leadership and high academic achievement.
Application requirements: $3 application fee. Must have taken the ACT or SAT.
Additional information: Recipients selected by independent committee of professional educators on basis of GPA, achievement test scores, work experience, financial need. Request application by March 15.

Amount of award:	$1,000
Number of awards:	200
Application deadline:	May 31
Notification begins:	August 5
Total amount awarded:	$200,000

Contact:
Educational Communications Scholarship Foundation
721 North McKinley Road
Lake Forest, IL 60045

Electrochemical Society, Inc.

Electrochemical Society Summer Fellowship

Type of award: Scholarship, renewable.
Intended use: For full-time master's, doctoral study at accredited graduate institution. Designated institutions: Study outside U.S. limited to Canada only.
Eligibility: Applicant must be Open to residents of North American countries.
Basis for selection: Major/career interest in engineering, chemical; chemistry; engineering. Applicant must demonstrate high academic achievement.
Application requirements: Recommendations, essay, transcript, proof of eligibility and research proposal.
Additional information: Research proposal must be in field of electrochemistry.

Amount of award:	$3,000
Number of awards:	3
Application deadline:	January 1
Notification begins:	April 1
Total amount awarded:	$9,000

Contact:
Electrochemical Society, Inc.
Society Summer Fellowships
10 South Main Street
Pennington, NJ 08534-2896
Phone: 609-737-1902
Website: www.electrochem.org

F.M. Becket Summer Research Award

Type of award: Research grant, renewable.
Intended use: For full-time senior or graduate study at accredited 2-year, 4-year or graduate institution outside United States. Designated institutions: Must be Electrochemical Society host institution.
Eligibility: Applicant must be Open to residents of North American countries.
Basis for selection: Major/career interest in chemistry; engineering, chemical; engineering. Applicant must demonstrate high academic achievement.
Application requirements: Recommendations, transcript and research proposal.
Additional information: Provides grant-in-aid toward summer research and study overseas to encourage active and continued participation in the field of electrochemical science and technology concerned with specialty materials and processes. Must be used at approved host institutions. Award given biannually; next deadline 1999.

Amount of award:	$3,500
Number of awards:	1
Application deadline:	January 1
Notification begins:	March 30
Total amount awarded:	$3,500

Contact:
Marc Cahay
ECECS Department, 832 Rhodes Hall, ML 30
University of Cincinnati
Cincinnati, OH 45221-0030
Phone: 609-737-1902
Website: www.electrochem.org

U.S. Department of Energy Summer Research Fellowships

Type of award: Research grant, renewable.
Intended use: For full-time master's, doctoral study at accredited 2-year, 4-year or graduate institution. Designated institutions: In United States or Canada.
Eligibility: Applicant must be Open to residents of North American countries.
Basis for selection: Major/career interest in chemistry; engineering, chemical; engineering. Applicant must demonstrate high academic achievement.
Application requirements: Recommendations, transcript and research proposal.
Additional information: Awards for continuing graduate work in summer in such fields as energy-related aspects of electrochemical science and engineering as well as solid state science and engineering involving batteries, fuel cells, photoelectrochemistry, photovoltaics and process of materials aimed at reducing energy consumption.

Amount of award:	$3,000
Number of awards:	5
Application deadline:	January 1
Notification begins:	April 1
Total amount awarded:	$15,000

Contact:
Dr. Johna Leddy
Department of Chemistry, University of Iowa
Iowa City, IA 52242
Phone: 609-737-1902
Website: www.electrochem.org

Eli Lilly & Company

Lilly for Learning Diabetes Scholarship

Type of award: Scholarship.
Intended use: For full-time undergraduate study at accredited vocational, 2-year or 4-year institution in United States.
Eligibility: Applicant must be high school senior. Applicant must be U.S. citizen.
Basis for selection: Applicant must demonstrate depth of character and high academic achievement.
Application requirements: Recommendations, essay and transcript.
Additional information: Applicant must be diagnosed with type 1 diabetes, must be or have been involved in the community, contributed to promotion of diabetes awareness, or have overcome specific obstacles relating to diabetes. Applicant must have 1 personal recomenndation, as well as a recommendation from a physician.

Amount of award:	$2,500
Number of awards:	50
Number of applicants:	750
Application deadline:	March 31, July 15
Total amount awarded:	$125,000

Contact:
Eli Lilly & Company
Lilly Corporate Center
Drop Code 1625
Indianapolis, IN 46285
Website: www.lilly.com/diabetes

Elie Wiesel Foundation for Humanity

Elie Wiesel Prize in Ethics

Type of award: Scholarship.
Intended use: For full-time junior, senior study at 4-year institution in United States.
Eligibility: Applicant must be Must be a full-time student at an American institution.
Basis for selection: Competition in Writing/journalism. Essay must address an ethical dilemma, issue or question related to the contest's theme.
Application requirements: Essay. Letter of support verifying full-time junior or senior status from college or university faculty or staff.
Additional information: Application date may change. Send SASE after September 15 for application materials and updates. Must request application by December 18.

Amount of award:	$500-$5,000
Number of awards:	5
Application deadline:	January 22
Notification begins:	May 31
Total amount awarded:	$10,000

Contact:
Elie Wiesel Foundation for Humanity Ethics Prize
450 Lexington Avenue
Suite 1920
New York, NY 10017
Phone: 212-450-8295

Elizabeth Dow Ltd.

Elizabeth Dow Internship Program

Type of award: Internship.
Intended use: For undergraduate, graduate, postgraduate or non-degree study.
Basis for selection: Major/career interest in accounting; arts, general; business, management and administration; design.

Application requirements: Interview, portfolio and recommendations.
Additional information: Internship lasts approximately 3 months during the summer. There is no stipend. Provides opportunity to gain experience in design and development. Applications accepted year-round.
Contact:
Elizabeth Dow Ltd.
155 6th Avenue, 4th Floor
New York, NY 10013

Elizabeth Greenshields Foundation

Elizabeth Greenshields Grant

Type of award: Scholarship, renewable.
Intended use: For undergraduate, graduate or non-degree study.
Basis for selection: Major/career interest in arts, general.
Application requirements: Slides.
Additional information: For young artists in the early stages of careers creating representational or figurative works through painting, drawing, printmaking or sculpture. Must make a commitment to making art a lifetime career. All amounts are in Canadian dollars.

Amount of award:	$10,000
Number of awards:	55
Number of applicants:	1,500
Total amount awarded:	$550,000

Contact:
Elizabeth Greenshields Foundation
1814 Sherbrooke Street West, Suite 1
Montreal
Quebec, Canada, H3H 1E4
Phone: 514-937-9225

Elks National Foundation

Elks Most Valuable Student Scholarship

Type of award: Scholarship.
Intended use: For full-time freshman, sophomore, junior or senior study at accredited 2-year or 4-year institution in United States.
Eligibility: Applicant must be high school senior. Applicant must be U.S. citizen.
Basis for selection: Applicant must demonstrate leadership, financial need and high academic achievement.
Application requirements: Recommendations and transcript. SAT I, ACT.
Additional information: Should have average grade of 90 or above and rank in top five percent of class. Contact local Benevolent and Protective Order of Elks Lodge or refer to web site for application.

Amount of award:	$1,000-$7,500
Number of awards:	500
Application deadline:	January 15
Notification begins:	May 15
Total amount awarded:	$2,092,000

Contact:
Elks National Foundation

Website: www.elks.org/enf

Embassy of France, Office of Science and Technology

Embassy of France Office for Science and Technology Chateaubriand Fellowship

Type of award: Scholarship.
Intended use: For doctoral, postgraduate study.
Eligibility: Applicant must be U.S. citizen or permanent resident.
Basis for selection: Applicant must demonstrate high academic achievement.
Additional information: For research in a French laboratory for a 6 to 12 month period.

Amount of award:	$10,800-$26,040
Number of awards:	25
Application deadline:	December 1

Contact:
Chateaubriand Fellowship Program
4101 Reservoir Rd. NW
Washington, DC 20007-2175
Phone: 202-944-6246
Fax: 202-944-6244
Website: www.chateaubriand.amb-wash.fr

Engineers Foundation of Ohio

Engineers Foundation of Ohio Scholarship

Type of award: Scholarship.
Intended use: For freshman study at accredited 4-year institution in United States. Designated institutions: Must be used at an ABET accredited school in Ohio or at Notre Dame University.
Eligibility: Applicant must be high school senior. Applicant must be U.S. citizen residing in Ohio.
Basis for selection: Major/career interest in engineering. Applicant must demonstrate leadership, seriousness of purpose, service orientation and high academic achievement.
Application requirements: Transcript. Must submit SAT or ACT scores.
Additional information: 3.0 GPA required.

Amount of award:	$500-$2,500
Number of awards:	25
Number of applicants:	300
Application deadline:	December 1

Contact:
Engineers Foundation of Ohio
236 E. Town Street
Suite 210
Columbus, OH 43215

Engineers Society of Western Pennsylvania

International Water Conference Merit Award Scholarship

Type of award: Scholarship, renewable.
Intended use: For graduate study at accredited graduate institution.
Basis for selection: Major/career interest in engineering, environmental. Applicant must demonstrate financial need.
Application requirements: Essay and transcript.
Additional information: Must have undergraduate degree in science or engineering. Must be enrolled or accepted at an institution in studies related to industial water technology.

Amount of award:	$5,000
Number of awards:	1
Application deadline:	May 31
Notification begins:	July 31
Total amount awarded:	$2,000

Contact:
Engineers' Society of Western Pennsylvania
Pittsburgh Engineers' Building
337 Fouth Avenue
Pittsburgh, PA 15222
Phone: 412-261-0710 x12
Fax: 412-261-1606
Website: www.eswp.com

Engineers' Society of Western Pennsylvania

Joseph Levendusky Memorial Scholarship

Type of award: Scholarship.
Intended use: For undergraduate study at accredited 4-year institution.
Basis for selection: Major/career interest in engineering, chemical.
Application requirements: Essay and transcript.
Additional information: Must have been employed in the field of water technology for at least one year prior to selection(environmental wastewater, water pollution control and water resource management not included).

Amount of award:	$7,000
Number of awards:	1
Number of applicants:	4
Application deadline:	May 1
Notification begins:	August 15

Contact:
Engineers' Society of Western Pennsylvania
Pittsburgh Engineers' Building
337 Fourth Avenue
Pittsburgh, PA 15222
Phone: 412-261-0710 x12
Fax: 412-261-1606
Website: www.eswp.com

Student Paper Competition

Type of award: Scholarship.
Intended use: For undergraduate or graduate study at 4-year or graduate institution in United States.
Basis for selection: Competition in Engineering/architecture. Paper on bridge-related topic. Major/career interest in engineering. Applicant must demonstrate seriousness of purpose.
Additional information: Winning graduate paper receives $1000. Winning undergraduate paper receives $250. One graduate and undergraduate paper per institution. Papers limited to ten pages, single spaced. Papers prepared for other purposes (e.g., thesis, project) are acceptable.

Amount of award:	$250-$1,000
Number of applicants:	2
Application deadline:	March 6
Notification begins:	April 24

Contact:
Engineers' Society of Western Pennsylvania
Pittsburgh Engineers' Building
Pittsburgh, PA 15222
Phone: 412-261-0710 x12
Fax: 412-261-1606
Website: www.eswp.com

English-Speaking Union

English-Speaking Union Graduate Scholarship

Type of award: Research grant.
Intended use: For graduate study outside United States. Designated institutions: Degree program at a United Kingdom institution or for independent dissertation related research.
Eligibility: Applicant must be U.S. citizen residing in Illinois.
Basis for selection: Major/career interest in English literature; history. Applicant must demonstrate depth of character, seriousness of purpose and high academic achievement.
Application requirements: Interview, recommendations, essay, transcript, proof of eligibility and research proposal. Submit a statement of interest (4-5 pages) detailing background, academic achievements, and career and life goals. Include reasons why studying in the United Kingdom will contribute toward these goals. Submit a proposed financial plan. Be available for an interview with our scholarship committee in Chicago on a mutually agreeable day.

Additional information: For dissertation-related research that requires time in the United Kingdom.
- **Amount of award:** $2,000-$4,000
- **Number of awards:** 4
- **Number of applicants:** 6
- **Application deadline:** December 12
- **Notification begins:** February 6
- **Total amount awarded:** $10,000

Contact:
English-Speaking Union
Teresa Concannon
30 North Michigan Street, Suite 715
Chicago, IL 60602
Phone: 312-425-9609
Fax: 312-425-9616

Entertainment Weekly

Entertainment Weekly Internship

Type of award: Internship.
Intended use: For undergraduate or graduate study.
Eligibility: Applicant must be U.S. citizen.
Basis for selection: Applicant must demonstrate seriousness of purpose and high academic achievement.
Application requirements: Interview and transcript. Resume, three or four writing samples.
Additional information: Provides opportunity to work in such departments as Editorial, Photo, Design and Multimedia. Internship lasts 12-18 weeks and pays $8/hour. Overtime is available. Deadlines are rolling for fall, spring and summer internships.
- **Number of awards:** 9
- **Number of applicants:** 180

Contact:
Entertainment Weekly
1675 Broadway
New York, NY 10019

Entomological Society of America

Entomological Society Undergraduate Scholarship

Type of award: Scholarship.
Intended use: For full-time sophomore, junior or senior study at 4-year institution in United States. Designated institutions: Award may also be used at recognized institutions in Canada or Mexico.
Basis for selection: Major/career interest in entomology; biology; science, general.
Application requirements: Recommendations, essay and transcript.
Additional information: Must have accumulated 30 semester hours by time award is given. Send SASE for application and information.
- **Amount of award:** $1,500
- **Number of awards:** 4
- **Number of applicants:** 315
- **Application deadline:** May 31
- **Notification begins:** September 30
- **Total amount awarded:** $6,000

Contact:
Entomological Society of America
Undergraduate Scholarship Application Request
9301 Annapolis Road
Lanham, MD 20706-3115

Epilepsy Foundation of America

Behavioral Sciences Research Fellowship

Type of award: Research grant.
Intended use: For postgraduate study in United States.
Basis for selection: Major/career interest in social and behavioral sciences; sociology; psychology; anthropology; nursing; political science/government; social work.
Additional information: For work in the study of epilepsy. Women and minorities are encouraged to apply.
- **Amount of award:** $30,000
- **Application deadline:** February 27

Behavioral Sciences Student Fellowship

Type of award: Research grant.
Intended use: For undergraduate, graduate or postgraduate study in United States.
Basis for selection: Major/career interest in social and behavioral sciences.
Application requirements: Research proposal.
Additional information: Three-month fellowship for work on an epilepsy study project. The fellowship is awarded to a student of vocational rehabilitation counseling. Women and minorities are especially encouraged to apply.
- **Amount of award:** $2,000
- **Application deadline:** February 27

Epilepsy Clinical Training Fellowship

Type of award: Research grant, renewable.
Intended use: For non-degree study.
Basis for selection: Major/career interest in medicine (m.d.).
Application requirements: Research proposal.
Additional information: For work in epilepsy. Research may be either basic or clinical, but there must be an equal emphasis on clinical training and clinical epileptology. Must have completed residency.
- **Amount of award:** $40,000
- **Application deadline:** September 1

Epilepsy Research Training Fellowship

Type of award: Research grant.
Intended use: For postgraduate study. Designated institutions: Must have ongoing epilepsy research program.
Basis for selection: Major/career interest in medicine (m.d.); neuroscience.
Application requirements: Research proposal.
Additional information: For research in epilepsy. Preference is given to applicants whose proposals have a pediatric or developmental emphasis.
    Amount of award: $40,000
    Application deadline: September 1

Health Sciences Student Fellowship

Type of award: Research grant.
Intended use: For postgraduate study in United States.
Basis for selection: Major/career interest in health sciences.
Application requirements: Research proposal.
Additional information: For work on an epilepsy study project. Applications from women and minorities are encouraged.
    Amount of award: $2,000
    Application deadline: February 27

Junior Investigator Epilepsy Research Grant

Type of award: Research grant.
Intended use: For postgraduate study.
Basis for selection: Major/career interest in social and behavioral sciences.
Application requirements: Research proposal.
Additional information: Priority is given to beginning investigators just entering the field of epilepsy research, to new or innovative projects, and to investigators whose research is relevant to developmental or pediatric aspects of epilepsy.
    Amount of award: $40,000
    Application deadline: September 1
Contact:
Epilepsy Foundation of America
4351 Garden City Drive
Landover, MD 20785-2267
Phone: 301-459-3700
Website: www.efa.org

Ernst and Young

Ernst and Young Internship

Type of award: Internship.
Intended use: For full-time undergraduate study.
Eligibility: Applicant must be U.S. citizen or permanent resident.
Basis for selection: Major/career interest in accounting.
Application requirements: Recommendations and transcript.
Additional information: 2-week summer and winter internships. Undergraduates receive $400-$550 a week, graduate students receive $550-$700 a week.
    Amount of award: $4,000-$6,600
Contact:
Ernst and Young
787 Seventh Ave.
New York, NY 10019

ESPN Inc.

ESPN Internship

Type of award: Internship.
Intended use: For full-time senior study.
Eligibility: Applicant must be U.S. citizen.
Basis for selection: Major/career interest in journalism; communications; radio/television/film; graphic arts and design. Applicant must demonstrate high academic achievement.
Application requirements: Transcript.
Additional information: ESPN will assist interns in finding housing.
    Amount of award: $2,500
    Number of awards: 5
    Number of applicants: 400
    Application deadline: March 1
    Total amount awarded: $12,500
Contact:
ESPN Inc.
935 Middle St.
Bristol, CT 06010
Phone: 203-585-2000

ESPN2 Sports Figures Scholarship

Type of award: Scholarship.
Intended use: For freshman study at accredited 2-year or 4-year institution outside United States.
Eligibility: Applicant must be high school senior.
Basis for selection: Applicant must demonstrate depth of character, leadership, service orientation and high academic achievement.
Application requirements: Transcript.
    Amount of award: $2,500
    Number of awards: 8
    Application deadline: March 20
    Total amount awarded: $20,000
Contact:
Scholarship Coordinator Sports Figures Scholarship
P.O. Box 8290
Manchester, CT 06040

Essence Magazine

Essence Internship

Type of award: Internship, renewable.
Intended use: For undergraduate study.
Eligibility: Applicant must be U.S. citizen.
Basis for selection: This internship is open to students of all majors. Applicant must demonstrate depth of character.
Application requirements: Interview.
Additional information: Six week summer internship.

Students receive $275 a week. Students of any race or ethnic group may apply for this internship.
- Amount of award: $1,259
- Number of awards: 8
- Number of applicants: 50
- Application deadline: September 1
- Total amount awarded: $10,000

Contact:
Essence Magazine
1500 Broadway, Suite 600
New York, NY 10036
Phone: 212-640-0600

Executive Women International

Executive Women International Scholarship

Type of award: Scholarship, renewable.
Intended use: For full-time freshman study at accredited 4-year institution in United States.
Eligibility: Applicant must be high school junior.
Basis for selection: Major/career interest in business. Applicant must demonstrate depth of character, leadership, seriousness of purpose, service orientation and high academic achievement.
Application requirements: Interview, recommendations and essay. Applicants must have sponsoring teacher at their school.
Additional information: Scholarship awarded each academic year, for up to five consecutive years, until student completes degree.
- Amount of award: $1,000-$2,500
- Number of awards: 6
- Application deadline: January 31
- Notification begins: May 31
- Total amount awarded: $26,000

Contact:
Executive Women International
515 South 700 East
Suite 2E
Salt Lake City, UT 84102

Explorers Club

Exploration Fund

Type of award: Scholarship.
Intended use: For graduate or non-degree study.
Eligibility: Applicant must be U.S. citizen.
Basis for selection: Major/career interest in natural sciences; anthropology; archaeology; botany. Applicant must demonstrate seriousness of purpose and financial need.
Application requirements: Essay and research proposal. Request application form from club.
Additional information: Send SASE when requesting application.

- Amount of award: $800-$1,500
- Number of awards: 18
- Number of applicants: 194
- Application deadline: January 30
- Notification begins: April 15
- Total amount awarded: $18,000

Contact:
Explorers Club
Georgeann Stakosch
46 East 70 Street
New York, NY 10021
Phone: 212-628-8383

Explorers Club Youth Activity Fund

Type of award: Scholarship.
Intended use: For undergraduate study.
Eligibility: Applicant must be U.S. citizen.
Basis for selection: Major/career interest in natural sciences. Applicant must demonstrate seriousness of purpose and financial need.
Application requirements: Recommendations, essay and research proposal. Request application form from club.
Additional information: Send SASE when requesting application.
- Amount of award: $300-$1,000
- Number of awards: 20
- Number of applicants: 130
- Application deadline: April 1
- Notification begins: June 30

Contact:
Explorers Club
46 East 70 Street
New York, NY 10021
Phone: 212-628-8383

Fairchild Tropical Garden

Tropical Garden Summer Internship

Type of award: Internship.
Intended use: For full-time junior, senior, master's or first professional study in Miami, FL. Designated institutions: Fairchild Tropical Garden.
Eligibility: Applicant must be Must have work visas and fulfill all U.S. legal requirements.
Basis for selection: Major/career interest in horticulture. Applicant must demonstrate depth of character, seriousness of purpose and high academic achievement.
Application requirements: Recommendations and transcript. Resume, letter outlining interests.
Additional information: Intern paid $200 per week for ten-week program that provides hands-on work experience in all areas of tropical botanical gardening. Interns encouraged to arrange for academic credit. Interns must arrange for housing and transportation. Horticultural experience preferred, botanical backround is acceptable. Must be willing to perform physical outdoor horticultural work in a humid and hot outdoor environment. Fairchild strongly encourages applicants from minority groups to apply.

Fairchild Tropical Garden: Tropical Garden Summer Internship

Amount of award:	$2,000
Number of awards:	2
Number of applicants:	35
Application deadline:	March 15
Notification begins:	April 15
Total amount awarded:	$4,000

Contact:
Fairchild Tropical Garden
Summer Intern Program
10901 Old Cutler Road
Miami, FL 33156
Phone: 3056671651

Fannie and John Hertz Foundation

Hertz Foundation Fellowship

Type of award: Scholarship, renewable.
Intended use: For full-time master's, doctoral study at accredited graduate institution in United States. Designated institutions: California Institute of Technology, University California, Carnegie-Mellon, University of Chicago, Cornell, Georgia Tech, Harvard, University of Illinois (Champaign-Urbana), John Hopkins, MIT, NYU, Polytechnic University, Princeton, RPI, Rice, University Rochester, Stanford, Texas A&M, University Texas-Austin, Vanderbilt, University of Washington, University of Wisconsin, University of Minnesota (Minneapolis).
Eligibility: Applicant must be U.S. citizen or permanent resident.
Basis for selection: Major/career interest in physical sciences. Applicant must demonstrate seriousness of purpose and high academic achievement.
Application requirements: Interview, recommendations and transcript.
Additional information: Must have minimum 3.75 GPA.

Amount of award:	$25,000-$40,000
Number of awards:	25
Number of applicants:	423
Application deadline:	October 23

Contact:
Fannie and John Hertz Foundation
Box 5032
Livermore, CA 94551-5032
Phone: 510-373-1642
Website: www.hertzfndn.org

Fight-For-Sight

Fight-For-Sight Postdoctoral Research Fellowship

Type of award: Research grant.
Intended use: For postgraduate study.
Basis for selection: Major/career interest in medicine (m.d.); optometry/ophthalmology.
Application requirements: Research proposal.
Additional information: Supports individuals with doctorate interested in basic or clinical research in ophthalmology, vision or related sciences. Fields of study accepted include medical clinical sciences, ophthalmic medical technologist, etc.

Amount of award:	$5,000-$14,000
Number of awards:	16
Application deadline:	March 1
Notification begins:	June 1

Fight-For-Sight Student Research Fellowship

Type of award: Internship.
Intended use: For undergraduate, master's, doctoral or first professional study. Designated institutions: In United States or Canada.
Eligibility: Applicant must be Open to Canadian citizens.
Basis for selection: Major/career interest in medicine (m.d.); optometry/ophthalmology.
Application requirements: Research proposal.
Additional information: For students interested in eye-related clinical or basic research. Fellowships last 60 to 90 days, usually during the summer months.

Amount of award:	$1,000-$1,500
Number of awards:	30
Application deadline:	March 1
Notification begins:	May 15
Total amount awarded:	$43,700

Contact:
Fight-For-Sight
500 East Remington Road
Prevent Blindness America, Program Coordinator
Schaumburg, IL 60173
Phone: 847-843-2020
Website: www.prevent-blindness.org

Filoli Center

Filoli Center Garden Internship

Type of award: Internship.
Intended use: For undergraduate, graduate or non-degree study in Woodside, CA. Designated institutions: Filoli Center.
Basis for selection: Major/career interest in horticulture; landscape architecture; botany. Applicant must demonstrate depth of character, leadership and seriousness of purpose.
Application requirements: Interview, recommendations and transcript. Cover letter outlining interests.
Additional information: Internships designed for students pursuing career in public garden management, landscape maintenance or landscape architecture. Students earn college credits and receive $2,400 stipend for ten-week program. Student must have at least fifteen units of horticulture classes, 3.0 GPA. Ability to work well with public and work teams essential. Application deadline for summer is March 1.

Amount of award:	$2,400
Number of awards:	12
Number of applicants:	17
Application deadline:	August 1, February 1
Total amount awarded:	$28,800

Contact:
Filoli Center
Filoli Garden Internships
86 Canada Road
Woodside, CA 94062
Phone: 650-364-8300
Website: www.filoli.org

Financial Markets Center

Financial Markets Center Henry B. Gonzalez Award

Type of award: Scholarship.
Intended use: For graduate study.
Basis for selection: Competition in Writing/journalism. Essay on the subject of central bank reform.
Application requirements: Proof of eligibility.
Additional information: Open to students enrolled in law school or graduate programs in finance, economics, government, public policy, and related fields. Entries should be no longer than 15,000 words, not including footnotes, endnotes, and references. Preference will be given to clearly written entries accessible to a broad variety of audiences. The essay should propose institutional reforms that make the central bank more open, accountable, and effective.

Amount of award:	$2,500
Number of awards:	1
Application deadline:	March 27, May 1
Total amount awarded:	$2,500

Contact:
Financial Markets Center
P.O. Box 334
Philomont, VA 20131

Fisher Broadcasting Inc.

Fisher Broadcasting Minority Scholarship

Type of award: Scholarship, renewable.
Intended use: For full-time undergraduate, graduate or non-degree study at accredited postsecondary institution in United States.
Eligibility: Applicant must be of minority background. Applicant must be U.S. citizen residing in Washington.
Basis for selection: Major/career interest in radio/television/film; journalism; communications; marketing. Applicant must demonstrate depth of character, seriousness of purpose, service orientation, financial need and high academic achievement.
Application requirements: Interview, recommendations, essay, transcript and proof of eligibility.
Additional information: Award totals vary each year.

Minimum 3.0 GPA. Also open to applicants from other states attending school in Washington state. Washington state residents may attend school in any state.

Number of applicants:	9
Application deadline:	April 30
Notification begins:	July 1
Total amount awarded:	$6,600

Contact:
Sherry Sharer, VP Administration
Fisher Broadcasting Inc.
100 Fourth Avenue North
Seattle, WA 98109
Phone: 206-443-4048

Florida Education Fund

Florida Education Fund McKnight Doctoral Fellowship

Type of award: Scholarship, renewable.
Intended use: For full-time doctoral study.
Eligibility: Applicant must be African American. Applicant must be U.S. citizen residing in Florida.
Basis for selection: Major/career interest in humanities/liberal arts; science, general; mathematics; business; engineering. Applicant must demonstrate high academic achievement.
Application requirements: Essay and transcript.
Additional information: Applicant must seek the Ph.D. at a qualifying Florida university. Qualifying universities include: Burry University, Florida A&M University, Florida Atlantic University, Florida Institute of Technology, Florida International University, Florida State University, University of Central Florida, University of Florida, University of Miami, and the University of South Florida. For students holding at least a bachelor's degree from accredited institution. Currently enrolled doctoral students are not eligible to apply. GRE or GMAT scores required.

Amount of award:	$16,000
Number of awards:	20
Number of applicants:	275
Application deadline:	January 15

Contact:
The Florida Education Fund
201 East Kennedy Blvd.
Suite 1525
Tampe, FL 33602
Website: www.fl-educ-fd.org

Food and Drug Law Institute

H. Thomas Austern Writing Award

Type of award: Scholarship.
Intended use: For full-time or half-time first professional study at accredited graduate institution in United States.
Basis for selection: Competition in Writing/journalism.

Manuscript on topic relevant to food and drug law field. Major/career interest in law.
Application requirements: Essay and proof of eligibility. Manuscript topic must be relevant to food and drug law field.
  Amount of award: $1,000-$3,000
  Number of awards: 3
  Number of applicants: 50
  Application deadline: May 15
  Notification begins: August 31
  Total amount awarded: $6,000
Contact:
Food and Drug Law Institute
Julia K. Ogden, Director of Academic Programs
1000 Vermont Avenue NW, Suite 200
Washington, DC 20005

Forbes Magazine

Forbes Internship

Type of award: Internship, renewable.
Intended use: For undergraduate or graduate study.
Eligibility: Applicant must be U.S. citizen.
Basis for selection: Major/career interest in business; journalism. Applicant must demonstrate depth of character.
Application requirements: Interview.
Additional information: Interns work in the editorial department, doing research and writing for Forbes 400 Magazine. Contact sponsor for deadline information.
  Amount of award: $3,960-$4,620
  Number of awards: 2
Contact:
Intership Coordinator
62 Fifth Ave.
New York, NY 10011

Foundation for Exceptional Children

Stanley E. Jackson Award for Gifted/ Talented Minorities with Disabilities

Type of award: Scholarship.
Intended use: For freshman study.
Eligibility: Applicant must be of minority background. Applicant must be high school senior. Must be physically challenged or learning disabled. Applicant must be U.S. citizen.
Application requirements: Recommendations, essay, transcript and proof of eligibility.
Additional information: A statement verifying disability from physician or school counselor.
  Amount of award: $500
  Number of awards: 8
  Number of applicants: 500
  Application deadline: February 1
  Total amount awarded: $4,000
Contact:
STANLEY E. JACKSON AWARD FOR GIFTED/ TALENTED MINORITIES WITH DISABILITIES
ATTN: Scholarship Award
1920 Association Dr.
Reston, VA 22091
Phone: 703-264-9494

Stanley E. Jackson Scholarship Award for Ethnic Minority Students.

Type of award: Scholarship.
Intended use: For full-time undergraduate study at vocational or 2-year institution in United States.
Eligibility: Applicant must be American Indian, Asian American, African American, Mexican American, Hispanic American or Puerto Rican. Applicant must be high school senior. Must be physically challenged or learning disabled.
Basis for selection: Applicant must demonstrate depth of character, leadership and financial need.
Application requirements: Recommendations, essay and transcript.
Additional information: A statement verifying disability from physician or school counselor.
  Amount of award: $500
  Number of awards: 8
  Number of applicants: 200
  Application deadline: February 1
Contact:
STANLEY E. JACKSON SCHOLARSHIP AWARD FOR ETHNIC MINORITY STUDENTS.
ATTN: Scholarship Award
1920 Association Dr.
Reston, VA 22091
Phone: 703-264-9494

Stanley E. Jackson Scholarship Award for Gifted/Talented Students with Disabilities

Type of award: Scholarship.
Intended use: For full-time freshman study at postsecondary institution in United States.
Eligibility: Applicant must be high school senior. Must be physically challenged or learning disabled. Applicant must be U.S. citizen or permanent resident.
Basis for selection: Applicant must demonstrate financial need and high academic achievement.
Application requirements: Recommendations, essay, transcript and proof of eligibility.
Additional information: A statement verifying disability from physician or school counselor, three letters of recommendation and a completed application from are required. Applicant must have demonstrated talented abilities in any one of the following categories: general intellect, high academic aptitude, creativity, leadership or visual/performing arts

Amount of award:	$500
Number of awards:	8
Number of applicants:	200
Application deadline:	February 1
Total amount awarded:	$4,000

Contact:
Stanley E. Jackson Scholarship Award for Gifted/Talented Students with Disabilities
ATTN: Scholarship Award
1920 Association Dr.
Reston, VA 22091
Phone: 703-620-1054
Fax: 703-264-9494

Foundation for Science and Disability

Grant Program for Physically Disabled Students in the Sciences

Type of award: Research grant, renewable.
Intended use: For full-time senior, master's study.
Eligibility: Applicant must be physically challenged.
Basis for selection: Major/career interest in mathematics; science, general; medicine (m.d.); engineering; computer and information sciences. Applicant must demonstrate depth of character, leadership, seriousness of purpose and service orientation.
Application requirements: Recommendations, essay, transcript, proof of eligibility, research proposal and nomination by A research or academic advisor must support the proposal.
Additional information: College seniors must be accepted into a graduate school with the intention of studying one of the specified fields of science.

Amount of award:	$1,000
Number of awards:	2
Number of applicants:	15
Application deadline:	December 1

Contact:
Foundation for Science and Disability
503 Northwest 89th St.
Gainesville, FL 32607-1400

Foundation of the National Student Nurses Association, Inc.

National Student Nurses Association Scholarship

Type of award: Scholarship.
Intended use: For full-time undergraduate study at accredited 2-year or 4-year institution.
Eligibility: Applicant must be U.S. citizen or permanent resident.
Basis for selection: Major/career interest in nursing. Applicant must demonstrate service orientation, financial need and high academic achievement.
Application requirements: $10 application fee. Recommendations, essay, transcript and proof of eligibility. Must be currently enrolled in nursing or pre-nursing program. National Student Nurses Association members must submit proof of membership.
Additional information: All applicants considered for the following scholarships: General Scholarships, Career Mobility Scholarships, Breakthrough to Nursing Scholarships for Ethnic People of Color, and Specialty Scholarships. Awards granted in spring for use in summer and following academic year. Include business-sized SASE with $.55 postage when requesting application. Applications available from August through January 15.

Amount of award:	$1,000-$2,000
Application deadline:	February 1
Notification begins:	March 31
Total amount awarded:	$65,000

Contact:
Foundation of the National Student Nurses Association, Inc.
Suite 1327
555 West 57 Street
New York, NY 10019
Phone: 212-581-2215
Website: www.nsna.org

Francis Ouimet Scholarship Fund

Francis Ouimet Scholarship

Type of award: Scholarship, renewable.
Intended use: For full-time undergraduate study.
Basis for selection: Applicant must demonstrate depth of character, leadership, service orientation, financial need and high academic achievement.
Application requirements: Interview, recommendations, essay, transcript and proof of eligibility.
Additional information: Student must work for three years at a Massachusetts golf course.

Amount of award:	$500-$5,000
Number of awards:	270
Number of applicants:	300
Application deadline:	December 1
Notification begins:	August 15

Contact:
Francis Ouimet Scholarship Fund
190 Park Road
Weston, MA 02193
Phone: 781-891-6400

Franklin and Eleanor Roosevelt Institute

Grants-In-Aid for Research on the Roosevelt Years

Type of award: Research grant.
Intended use: For undergraduate or graduate study at postsecondary institution outside United States.
Eligibility: Applicant must be International students must be from established democracies or emerging democracies of the third world.
Basis for selection: Major/career interest in library science; museum studies; education; information systems.
Application requirements: Research proposal.
Additional information: Preference given to those majoring in history, political science, archival, library or computer systems. Researcher must hava a viable plan of research.
    Amount of award: $2,500
    Application deadline: February 15, September 15
Contact:
The Franklin and Eleanor Roosevelt Institute
511 Albany Post Rd.
New Hyde Park, NY 12538

Franklin D. Roosevelt Library

Franklin D. Roosevelt Library/ Roosevelt Internship

Type of award: Internship.
Intended use: For full-time undergraduate, graduate or postgraduate study at postsecondary institution outside United States.
Eligibility: Applicant must be U.S. citizen.
Basis for selection: Major/career interest in library science; computer and information sciences; museum studies; education.
Application requirements: Interview, recommendations and transcript.
Additional information: International students must be from an established or emerging democracy. Some students may work on The New Deal Network Web site project in New York City. Four to six week internships available for summer, fall and spring. Interns receive $250 a week.
    Amount of award: $1,200-$1,400
    Number of awards: 3
    Number of applicants: 10
    Application deadline: February 15, September 15
Contact:
Franklin D. Roosevelt Library
511 Albany Post Rd.
New Hyde Park, NY 12538
Website: www.academic.edu/fdr/feri/htm

Franklin Lindsay Student Aid Fund

Franklin Lindsay Student Aid

Type of award: Loan, renewable.
Intended use: For full-time sophomore, junior, senior or graduate study at accredited postsecondary institution in United States. Designated institutions: Must be used at accredited institutions in Texas.
Eligibility: Applicant must be U.S. citizen residing in Texas.
Basis for selection: Applicant must demonstrate depth of character, seriousness of purpose, service orientation and financial need.
Application requirements: Interview. Loan package must be completed and must have a co-signer other than spouse.
Additional information: Must have a GPA of 2.0 for undergraduates and a GPA of 3.0 for graduates. Upon graduation or termination from school, loan goes to repayment structure at six percent.
    Amount of award: $3,000
    Number of awards: 346
    Application deadline: July 1
    Notification begins: July 15
    Total amount awarded: $1,006,200
Contact:
Franklin Lindsay Student Aid Fund
P.O. Box 550
Austin, TX 78789
Phone: 512-479-2645

Fred G. Zahn Foundation

Fred G. Zahn Foundation Scholarship

Type of award: Scholarship, renewable.
Intended use: For undergraduate or graduate study at accredited 2-year, 4-year or graduate institution in United States. Designated institutions: Must be an institution in Washington state.
Eligibility: Applicant must be residing in Washington.
Basis for selection: Applicant must demonstrate financial need and high academic achievement.
Application requirements: Essay and transcript.
Additional information: 3.75 GPA. May obtain additional information and/or application at any Washington State college. Please contact financial aid department. Do not contact foundation.
    Amount of award: $1,500
    Number of awards: 7
    Number of applicants: 250
    Application deadline: April 15
    Notification begins: June 1

Freedom from Religion Foundation

Blanche Fearn Memorial Award

Type of award: Scholarship.
Intended use: For full-time undergraduate study.
Eligibility: Applicant must be high school senior. Applicant must be U.S. citizen.
Basis for selection: Competition in Writing/journalism. Essay on why you are a freethinker. Applicant must demonstrate depth of character and seriousness of purpose.
Application requirements: Essay.
Additional information: Essay topics change annually. Send SASE in Spring of contest year for current list of topics.

Amount of award:	$250-$1,000
Number of awards:	3
Application deadline:	August 1
Notification begins:	September 1
Total amount awarded:	$1,750

Contact:
Freedom from Religion Foundation
P.O. Box 750
Madison, WI 53701
Website: www.infidels.org/org/ffrf/

Saul Jakel Memorial Award

Type of award: Scholarship.
Intended use: For full-time undergraduate study.
Eligibility: Applicant must be U.S. citizen.
Basis for selection: Competition in Writing/journalism. Essay on freethought concerning religion. Specific topics change annually. Applicant must demonstrate depth of character, leadership, patriotism, seriousness of purpose and service orientation.
Application requirements: Essay.
Additional information: Essay topics change annually. Send SASE for current list in spring of contest year.

Amount of award:	$250-$1,000
Number of awards:	3
Application deadline:	August 1
Notification begins:	September 1
Total amount awarded:	$1,750

Contact:
Freedom from Religion Foundation
Student Essay Contest
P.O. Box 750
Madison, WI 53701
Website: www.infidels.org/org/ffrf/

Friedrich Ebert Foundation

Friedrich Ebert Advanced Graduate Fellowship

Type of award: Research grant.
Intended use: For master's, doctoral study outside United States in Federal Republic of Germany.
Eligibility: Applicant must be U.S. citizen.
Basis for selection: Major/career interest in political science/government; sociology; history; economics.
Application requirements: Recommendations, proof of eligibility and research proposal.
Additional information: Applicants should have special interest in contemporary or past German or European affairs and/or German-American relations and will be expected to show an ability and willingness to engage in political dialogue. Must have appropriate knowledge of German. Must intend to pursue doctoral degree. Stipend of DM 1,250 per month, plus airfare, books, health insurance, and tuition and fees if applicable.

Application deadline:	February 28
Notification begins:	May 15

Friedrich Ebert Doctoral Research Fellowship

Type of award: Research grant.
Intended use: For doctoral study outside United States in Federal Republic of Germany.
Eligibility: Applicant must be U.S. citizen.
Basis for selection: Major/career interest in political science/government; sociology; history; economics.
Application requirements: Recommendations, proof of eligibility and research proposal.
Additional information: Applicants should have a special interest in contemporary or past German or European affairs and/or German-American relations and will be expected to show an ability and willingness to engage in political debate. Must be qualified Ph.D. candidate at American university and have appropriate knowledge of German. Stipend of DM 1,390 per month, plus airfare, health insurance, books, and tuition and fees if applicable.

Application deadline:	February 28
Notification begins:	May 15

Friedrich Ebert Postdoctoral Fellowship

Type of award: Research grant.
Intended use: For postgraduate study.
Eligibility: Applicant must be U.S. citizen.
Basis for selection: Major/career interest in political science/government; sociology; history; economics.
Application requirements: copies of relevant academic publications.
Additional information: Applicants should have a special interest in contemporary or past German or European affairs and/or German-American relations, and will be expected to show an ability and willingness to engage in political dialogue. Must indicate German counterpart who will be available for cooperation and assistance while in Germany. Must have appropriate knowledge of German and at least two years experience in research and/or teaching. Stipend of DM 1,700 per month, plus airfare, health insurance, books, and tuition and fees if applicable.

Application deadline:	February 28
Notification begins:	May 15

Contact:
Friedrich Ebert Foundation
342 Madison Avenue
Suite 1912
New York, NY 10173
Phone: 212-687-0208
Fax: 212-687-0261

Friends of the National Zoo

Friends of the National Zoo Research Traineeships

Type of award: Internship.
Intended use: For undergraduate or graduate study.
Basis for selection: Major/career interest in animal sciences.
Application requirements: Recommendations, essay and transcript.
Additional information: There will be at least ten traineeships and research traineeships offered. Responsibilities may include animal observation and handling, data recording, laboratory analysis, data processing, and report writing. Positions will also be available in public affairs, landscaping, and zoo photography. Duration is 12 weeks. Deadlines vary.
    Amount of award: $2,400-$3,000
    Application deadline: December 31
Contact:
Traineeship Program
FONZ Human Resources
National Zooligical Park
Washington, DC 20008

Fulbright Program/USIA - U.S. Student Program

Fulbright Program/USIA - U.K. Calvin Klein/Harvey Nichols Award in Fashion

Type of award: Scholarship.
Intended use: For graduate or non-degree study at graduate institution outside United States. Designated institutions: United Kingdom.
Eligibility: Applicant must be U.S. citizen.
Basis for selection: Major/career interest in fashion design. Applicant must demonstrate high academic achievement.
Application requirements: Recommendations, transcript and research proposal.
Additional information: Provides a grant of US $4,000 and economy airfare for a student of fashion design to spend a minimum of four months at an approved school of fashion in the UK to study fashion techniques and enhance design skills. Candidates may use the award money towards a full-time postgraduate course. Applicants enrolled in U.S. academic institutions must apply through Fulbright Program Adviser on campus. All others must request application directly from IIE by October 8.
    Amount of award: $4,000
    Application deadline: October 23
    Notification begins: June 30
Contact:
Fulbright Program/USIA--U.S. Student Programs
809 United Nations Plaza
New York, NY 10017-3580

Fund for Gay and Lesbian Scholarships Whitman-Brooks Scholarship Fund

Fund for Lesbian and Gay Students Scholarship

Type of award: Scholarship, renewable.
Intended use: For undergraduate study at vocational, 2-year or 4-year institution in United States.
Eligibility: Applicant must be U.S. citizen or permanent resident.
Basis for selection: Applicant must demonstrate depth of character, leadership, seriousness of purpose, service orientation and financial need.
Application requirements: Recommendations, transcript and proof of eligibility.
Additional information: Available to gay, lesbian and bisexual students for full or part-time study in a college, university or trade school. Send a SASE to the organization to receive an application.
    Application deadline: September 15
Contact:
Whitman-Brooks Fund for Lesbian and Gay Scholarships (FLAGS)
P.O. Box 48320
Los Angeles, CA 90048-0320
Phone: 213-650-5752

Garden Club of America

Anne S. Chatham Fellowship in Medicinal Botany

Type of award: Research grant.
Intended use: For full-time doctoral, postgraduate study.
Basis for selection: Major/career interest in medicine (m.d.); botany. Applicant must demonstrate seriousness of purpose.
Application requirements: Research proposal.
Additional information: Grant to enable study in medicinal botany. Open to Ph.D candidates as well as Ph.D's.
    Amount of award: $4,000
    Number of awards: 1
    Application deadline: January 15
Contact:
Missouri Botanical Garden
Dr. James S. Miller
P.O. Box 299
St. Louis, MO 63166-0299
Phone: 3145779503
Fax: 3145779596
Website: www.mobot.org

Catherine Beattie Fellowship

Type of award: Research grant.
Intended use: For graduate study at accredited graduate institution in United States.
Basis for selection: Major/career interest in horticulture.

Application requirements: Research proposal.
Additional information: Research should focus on preservation of rare and endangered flora in U.S. Preference given to projects on endangered flora of the Carolinas and southeastern U.S.

Amount of award:	$4,000
Number of awards:	1
Application deadline:	December 31
Total amount awarded:	$4,000

Contact:
Garden Club of America, Interchange Fellowship
Missouri Botanical Garden
P.O. Box 299, Attn: Ms. Anukriti Sud
St. Louis, MO 63166-0299
Phone: 314-577-9452
Fax: 314-577-9465
Website: www.mobot.org/cpc

F.M. Peacock Native Bird Habitat Scholarship

Type of award: Scholarship.
Intended use: For senior or graduate study.
Basis for selection: Major/career interest in ornithology.
Additional information: Grant for advanced study of U.S. winter/summer habitat of threatened or endangered native birds. No phone calls.

Amount of award:	$4,000
Number of awards:	1
Application deadline:	January 15
Total amount awarded:	$4,000

Contact:
Garden Club of America, Interchange Fellowship
Cornell Laboratory of Ornithology
159 Sapsucker Woods Road
Ithaca, NY 14850

Garden Club of America Summer Environmental Awards

Type of award: Scholarship.
Intended use: For freshman, sophomore or junior study.
Basis for selection: Major/career interest in environmental science.
Additional information: Two or more awards for summer study in field of ecology and environmental studies. For more information either call office or send a business-size SASE.

Amount of award:	$1,500
Application deadline:	February 15

Contact:
Garden Club of America
Attn: Scholarship Committee
14 East 60th Street
New York, NY 10022
Phone: 212-753-8287
Fax: 212-753-0134
Website: www.gcamerica.org

Katherine M. Grosscup Scholarship

Type of award: Scholarship.
Intended use: For junior, senior or master's study at accredited 4-year or graduate institution in United States.
Basis for selection: Major/career interest in horticulture. Applicant must demonstrate financial need and high academic achievement.
Application requirements: Transcript.
Additional information: Several scholarships available. Financial assistance to college juniors, seniors or graduate students. Preference given to residents of Pennsylvania, Ohio, West Virginia, Michigan, and Indiana. Please do not contact by phone.

Amount of award:	$3,000
Application deadline:	February 15

Contact:
Grosscup Scholarship Committee/Cleveland Botanical Garden
Attn: Mrs. Nancy Stevenson
11030 East Boulevard, Attn: Mrs. Nancy Stevenson
Cleveland, OH 44106
Website: www.gcamerica.org

Martin McLaren-Interchange Fellowship in Horticulture and Landscape Design

Type of award: Scholarship.
Intended use: For full-time undergraduate, graduate or non-degree study in Great Britain in United Kingdom. Designated institutions: Must study in Great Britain at the Institute of Horticulture of British Isles.
Eligibility: Applicant must be U.S. citizen or Open to residents of Great Britain.
Basis for selection: Major/career interest in botany; horticulture; landscape architecture; environmental science.
Application requirements: Interview and proof of eligibility.
Additional information: Covers tuition, housing, board and provides an allowance. Additional funds are the responsibility of the student. McLaren Fellowship for U.S. students to study in Great Britain and Interchange Fellowship for British students to study in U.S. Include business size SASE with application request.

Number of awards:	1
Application deadline:	November 15

Contact:
Garden Club of America, Interchange Fellowship
Attn: Ms. Burch
598 Madison Avenue
New York, NY 10022
Phone: 212-753-8287
Fax: 212-753-0134
Website: www.gcamerica.org

Tropical Botany Award

Type of award: Research grant.
Intended use: For full-time doctoral study at accredited graduate institution outside United States in research in tropics.
Basis for selection: Major/career interest in botany. Applicant must demonstrate high academic achievement.
Application requirements: Recommendations, transcript and research proposal.
Additional information: For doctoral candidates in botany to pursue independent field study in tropics.

Amount of award:	$5,500
Number of awards:	2
Application deadline:	December 31
Total amount awarded:	$11,000

Contact:
World Wildlife Fund
Attn: Ms. Marlar Oo
1250 24th Street, NW
Washington, DC 20037-1175
Phone: 202-778-9714
Fax: 202-293-921

Gay & Lesbian Education Commission

Peter Kaufman Memorial Scholarship

Type of award: Scholarship.
Intended use: For freshman study.
Eligibility: Applicant must be high school senior.
Additional information: Applicant must be a gay, lesbian, bisexual, or transgender high school senior who has worked in the community.

Amount of award:	$1,000

Contact:
Gay & Lesbian Education Commission
LA Unified School District, Rm. 242
450 N. Grand Ave.
Los Angeles, CA 90012

Gem Consortium

Gem Consortium Scholarship

Type of award: Scholarship, renewable.
Intended use: For full-time master's, doctoral study in United States. Designated institutions: Must be used at a Gem Consortium sponsored school.
Eligibility: Applicant must be American Indian, African American, Mexican American, Hispanic American or Puerto Rican. Applicant must be U.S. citizen.
Basis for selection: Major/career interest in engineering; science, general.
Application requirements: Recommendations and transcript.
Additional information: Minimum GPA for master's students 2.8. Minimum GPA for doctoral students 3.0. Stipend is $6,000 per year for master's fellowship, and $12,000 per year for doctoral fellowship.

Amount of award:	$6,000-$12,000
Number of awards:	225
Number of applicants:	600
Application deadline:	December 1
Notification begins:	February 15

Contact:
Gem Consortium
P.O. Box 537
Notre Dame, IN 46556
Phone: 219-631-7771

General Mills

General Mills Internship Program

Type of award: Internship, renewable.
Intended use: For sophomore, junior or senior study.
Eligibility: Applicant must be U.S. citizen.
Basis for selection: Major/career interest in marketing; advertising; food science and technology; engineering.
Additional information: 10-14 week internship. Manufacturing and engineering interns will be placed in plants. All others will intern at company headquarters. Undergraduates receive $500-$700 a week. Graduate students receive $800-$1,000 a week.

Amount of award:	$5,000-$14,000
Application deadline:	February 1

Contact:
Internship Coordinator
P.O. Box 1113
Minneapolis, MN 55440

Gensler and Associates/Architects

Gensler and Associates Intern Program

Type of award: Internship.
Intended use: For full-time sophomore, junior or senior study.
Eligibility: Applicant must be U.S. citizen or permanent resident.
Basis for selection: Major/career interest in architecture; interior design; graphic arts and design. Applicant must demonstrate seriousness of purpose and high academic achievement.
Application requirements: Interview, portfolio and transcript.
Additional information: Intern pay rates start at $9 per hour. Internship duration ranges from two months to one year.

Amount of award:	$2,880-$18,720
Application deadline:	February 24

Contact:
Gensler and Association Architects
600 California St.
San Francisco, CA 94108

Geoffrey Foundation

Geoffrey Foundation Undergraduate Scholarship

Type of award: Scholarship, renewable.
Intended use: For full-time undergraduate study at accredited 4-year institution in United States. Designated institutions: Must be a college for Hearing Students.
Eligibility: Applicant must be hearing impaired. Applicant must be U.S. citizen.
Basis for selection: Major/career interest in medical

specialties/research; speech pathology/audiology; physical therapy. Applicant must demonstrate depth of character and seriousness of purpose.
Application requirements: Recommendations and proof of eligibility.
Additional information: Applications must include a current aided and unaided audiogram; recommendations must highlight the applicant's use of Auditory-Verbal communication skills.

Amount of award:	$1,000
Number of awards:	5
Application deadline:	March 31, May 30

Contact:
The Geoffrey Foundation
PO Box 1112
Kennebunkport, ME 04046

Geological Society of America

Geological Society Research Grant

Type of award: Research grant, renewable.
Intended use: For master's, doctoral study at graduate institution in or outside United States.
Basis for selection: Major/career interest in geology/earth sciences.
Application requirements: Recommendations and research proposal.
Additional information: Applications available from geology departments of U.S., Canadian, Mexican, and Central American universities. Award must be used to provide partial support for doctoral or master's thesis research.

Amount of award:	$250-$2,500
Number of awards:	218
Number of applicants:	478
Application deadline:	February 1
Notification begins:	April 15
Total amount awarded:	$349,625

Contact:
Geological Society of America
Research Grants Administrator
P.O. Box 9140
Boulder, CO 80301-9140

Getty Grant Program

Getty Postdoctoral Fellowship

Type of award: Research grant.
Intended use: For postgraduate study.
Basis for selection: Major/career interest in art, art history.
Application requirements: Recommendations and research proposal.
Additional information: Reserved for scholars whose doctoral degrees have been conferred within the last six years.

Amount of award:	$30,000
Number of awards:	15
Number of applicants:	150
Application deadline:	November 1
Notification begins:	April 1
Total amount awarded:	$450,000

Contact:
Joan Weinstein, Program Officer
1200 Getty Center Drive
Suite 800
Los Angeles, CA 90049-1685
Phone: 310-440-7320
Website: www.getty.edu/grant

Gladys Krieble Delmas Foundation

Grant for Research in Venice

Type of award: Research grant.
Intended use: For doctoral, postgraduate study in Venice and the Veneto.
Eligibility: Applicant must be U.S. citizen or permanent resident.
Basis for selection: Major/career interest in social and behavioral sciences; art, art history; humanities/liberal arts; political science/government; archaeology; architecture; economics; history; law; literature. Applicant must demonstrate financial need and high academic achievement.
Application requirements: Recommendations and research proposal. Curriculum vitae, including degrees, awards, publications, and professional experience.
Additional information: Research in bibliography, history of science, music, religion, and theater are also funded.

Amount of award:	$500-$12,500
Number of awards:	21
Number of applicants:	50
Application deadline:	December 15
Notification begins:	April 1
Total amount awarded:	$118,730

Contact:
Gladys Krieble Delmas Foundation
521 5th Avenue
Suite 1612
New York, NY 10175-1699
Phone: 212-687-0011
Fax: 212-687-8877

Glamour Magazine

Top Ten College Women Competition

Type of award: Scholarship.
Intended use: For full-time junior study at accredited 4-year institution.
Eligibility: Applicant must be female. Applicant must be U.S. citizen.
Basis for selection: Competition in Writing/journalism. Based

on meritorious attributes. Applicant must demonstrate depth of character, leadership, seriousness of purpose, service orientation and high academic achievement.
Application requirements: Recommendations, essay and transcript.
Additional information: Must be a goal oriented female. Applications available September 1. Award is a cash prize. This is not a scholarship.

Amount of award:	$1,000
Number of awards:	10
Number of applicants:	10
Application deadline:	January 31
Notification begins:	June 1
Total amount awarded:	$10,000

Contact:
Glamour Magazine
350 Madison Avenue
New York, NY 10017
Phone: 800-244-4526

Golden Key National Honor Society

Golden Key Scholar Awards

Type of award: Scholarship.
Intended use: For full-time graduate study at accredited graduate institution.
Basis for selection: Applicant must demonstrate leadership, service orientation and high academic achievement.
Application requirements: Recommendations, essay, transcript and proof of eligibility.
Additional information: Must be member of Golden Key National Honors Society. Must hold baccalaureate degree at time scholarship is awarded

Amount of award:	$10,000
Number of awards:	10
Number of applicants:	200
Application deadline:	February 15
Notification begins:	May 15
Total amount awarded:	$100,000

Contact:
Golden Key National Honors Society
1189 Ponce De Leon Avenue
Atlanta, GA 30306-4624
Phone: 800-377-2401 x211
Website: gknhs.gsu.edu

Golden State Minority Foundation

Golden State Minority Scholarship

Type of award: Scholarship.
Intended use: For full-time junior, senior or graduate study at accredited 4-year or graduate institution in California.
Eligibility: Applicant must be of minority background. Applicant must be U.S. citizen or permanent resident residing in California.
Basis for selection: Applicant must demonstrate depth of character, leadership, seriousness of purpose, service orientation, financial need and high academic achievement.
Additional information: Award is given to all fields of study. Must have a minimum 3.0 GPA. Can be either a resident of or attending school in California.

Amount of award:	$100-$4,000
Number of awards:	20
Number of applicants:	200
Application deadline:	April 1
Notification begins:	May 1
Total amount awarded:	$4,000

Contact:
Golden State Minority Foundation
1055 Wilshire Boulevard
Suite 1115
Los Angeles, CA 90017
Phone: 213-482-6300

Golf Course Superintendents Association of America

Essay Contest

Type of award: Scholarship.
Intended use: For undergraduate or graduate study at accredited 2-year, 4-year or graduate institution.
Basis for selection: Competition in Writing/journalism. Seven to 12 page essay focusing on relationship between golf courses and the environment Major/career interest in turf management; landscape architecture.
Application requirements: Recommendations and transcript.
Additional information: Applicants must be pursuing degrees in turfgrass science, agronomy or any field related to golf course management.

Amount of award:	$200
Application deadline:	March 31

Contact:
Scholarships Coordinator Jonelle O'Neill
1421 Research Park Dr.
Lawrence, KS 66049
Phone: 800-472-7878
Website: www.gcsaa.org

Golf Course Superintendents Association Scholars Program

Type of award: Scholarship.
Intended use: For sophomore, junior or senior study at accredited 2-year or 4-year institution.
Basis for selection: Major/career interest in turf management; landscape architecture; sports/sports administration. Applicant must demonstrate high academic achievement.
Application requirements: Recommendations and transcript.
Additional information: Must be planning career as a golfcourse superintendent and have successfully completed at

least 24 credit hours or the equivalent of one year of full-time study.
   Amount of award: $1,500-$3,500
   Application deadline: June 1
Contact:
Scholarship Coordinator Jonelle O'Neill
1421 Research Park Dr.
Lawrence, KS 66049
Phone: 800-472-7878
Website: www.gcsaa.org

Scotts Company Scholars Program

Type of award: Scholarship.
Intended use: For freshman, sophomore or junior study at accredited 2-year or 4-year institution.
Basis for selection: Major/career interest in turf management; sports/sports administration; landscape architecture.
Application requirements: Recommendations and transcript.
Additional information: Five finalists are selected for summer internships, receive a $500 award and an opportunity to complete for two $2,500 scholarships. Applicants must be pursuing a career in the green industry and be either a graduating high school senior or collegiate freshman, sophomore or junior.
   Amount of award: $500-$2,500
   Number of awards: 7
   Application deadline: March 1
   Total amount awarded: $7,500
Contact:
Golf Course Superintendents Association of America
1421 Research Park Dr.
Lawrence, KS 66049
Phone: 800-472-7878
Website: www.gcsaa.org

Valderrama Award

Type of award: Scholarship.
Intended use: For undergraduate, graduate or postgraduate study at accredited 2-year, 4-year or graduate institution in United States.
Eligibility: Applicant must be Must be a citizen of Spain.
Basis for selection: Major/career interest in turf management; landscape architecture. Applicant must demonstrate leadership, seriousness of purpose and high academic achievement.
Additional information: This scholarship is awarded to a citizen of Spain who wishes to study golf/turfgrass management in the United States. Contact office for applications and deadline dates.
   Amount of award: $7,000
Contact:
Scholarship Coordinator Jonelle O'Neill
1421 Research Park Dr.
Lawrence, KS 66049
Phone: 800-472-7878
Website: www.gcsaa.org

Watson Fellowships

Type of award: Scholarship.
Intended use: For master's, doctoral study at accredited graduate institution.
Basis for selection: Major/career interest in turf management; landscape architecture.
Application requirements: Recommendations and transcript.
Additional information: Must be working towards a degree in field related to golf course management.
   Amount of award: $5,000
   Application deadline: October 1
Contact:
Scholarship Coordinator Jonelle O'Neill
1421 Research Park Dr.
Lawrence, KS 66049
Phone: 800-472-7878
Website: www.gcsaa.org

Gore Family Memorial Foundation

Gore Family Memorial Foundation Scholarships

Type of award: Scholarship.
Intended use: For undergraduate study.
Eligibility: Applicant must be physically challenged. Applicant must be U.S. citizen or permanent resident.
Basis for selection: Applicant must demonstrate financial need.
Application requirements: Proof of eligibility.
Additional information: Scholarships available for severely disabled students: Award amount varies depending on need. Grants average from $1000 to $3000. No deadline.
   Number of awards: 100
Contact:
Scholarship Coordinator
4747 Notre Dame Dr. #204
Ft. Lauderdale, FL 33302

Governor's Commission on People with Disabilities

Governor's Commission on People with Disabilities Scholarship Fund

Type of award: Scholarship.
Intended use: For full-time undergraduate, graduate or postgraduate study at accredited postsecondary institution in United States.
Eligibility: Must have a disability. Applicant must be . Must be visually impaired, hearing impaired, physically challenged or learning disabled. Applicant must be U.S. citizen residing in Arkansas.
Basis for selection: Applicant must demonstrate depth of character, leadership, seriousness of purpose, financial need and high academic achievement.
Application requirements: Recommendations, transcript and proof of eligibility.

Amount of award:	$500
Number of awards:	14
Number of applicants:	100
Application deadline:	April 15

Contact:
Governor's Commission on People with Disabilities
1616 Brookwook Drive
Little Rock, AR 72202

Grand Encampment of Knights Templar of the USA

Knights Templar Educational Foundation Loan

Type of award: Loan, renewable.
Intended use: For junior, senior, master's, doctoral, first professional or postgraduate study at vocational, 4-year or graduate institution.
Eligibility: Applicant must be U.S. citizen.
Basis for selection: Applicant must demonstrate depth of character and high academic achievement.
Application requirements: Recommendations.
Additional information: Personal dependability important. Send SASE for application.

Amount of award:	$6,000
Number of awards:	292
Total amount awarded:	$645,943

Contact:
Grand Encampment of Knights Templar of the USA
5097 North Elston Avenue
Chicago, IL 60630-2460

Granite State Management and Resources

New Hampshire Alternative Loans for Parents and Students

Type of award: Loan, renewable.
Intended use: For full-time or half-time undergraduate or graduate study.
Eligibility: Applicant must be residing in New Hampshire.
Additional information: Must be New Hampshire resident enrolled in institution anywhere in U.S. or non-resident enrolled in New Hampshire institution. Fee of five percent of principal borrowed charged upon application.

Amount of award:	$2,000-$20,000

Contact:
Granite State Management and Resources
P.O. Box 2287
Concord, NH 03302
Phone: 800-444-3796

Greater Kanawha Valley Foundation

Greater Kanawha Valley Scholarship Program

Type of award: Scholarship, renewable.
Intended use: For full-time undergraduate or graduate study at postsecondary institution.
Eligibility: Applicant must be residing in West Virginia.
Basis for selection: Applicant must demonstrate depth of character, leadership, financial need and high academic achievement.
Application requirements: Recommendations, essay and transcript.

Amount of award:	$1,000-$4,400
Number of awards:	335
Number of applicants:	1,511
Application deadline:	February 14
Notification begins:	May 1
Total amount awarded:	$489,000

Contact:
Greater Kanawha Valley Foundation
P.O. Box 3041
Charleston, WV 25331
Phone: 304-346-3620

GTE

GTE Internship Program

Type of award: Internship.
Intended use: For undergraduate study.
Eligibility: Applicant must be U.S. citizen or permanent resident.
Basis for selection: Major/career interest in accounting; business; computer and information sciences; engineering, electrical and electronic; marketing. Applicant must demonstrate seriousness of purpose and high academic achievement.
Application requirements: Interview and transcript.
Additional information: 12-week summer program. Minimum GPA of 3.0 is required. Undergraduates receive $400-$600 a week and graduates receive $750 a week compensation.

Number of awards:	225
Number of applicants:	5,000
Application deadline:	March 1

Contact:
GTE
One Stamford Forum
Stamford, CT 06904

Guideposts

Young Writers Contest

Type of award: Scholarship.
Intended use: For undergraduate study at accredited vocational, 2-year or 4-year institution.
Eligibility: Applicant must be high school junior, senior.
Basis for selection: Competition in Writing/journalism. Nonfiction article (maximum 1,200 words) must be in first-person, written in style of Guideposts magazine, and demonstrate writer's faith in God.
Application requirements: Essay.
Additional information: Prizes must be used within five years after high school. Only high school juniors and seniors may compete.
    Amount of award: $1,000-$8,000
    Number of awards: 8
    Number of applicants: 4,500
    Application deadline: November 30
    Notification begins: January 5
    Total amount awarded: $25,000
Contact:
Youth Writing Contest/ Guideposts
16 East 34 Street
New York, NY 10016

Hagley Museum and Library

Dupont Fellowship

Type of award: Research grant.
Intended use: For postgraduate study at graduate institution in United States. Designated institutions: Hagley Museum and Library.
Basis for selection: Major/career interest in American history.
Application requirements: Recommendations and research proposal. Curriculum vitae.
Additional information: Stipends are for two to six months at $425 per week. Research must be relevant to library's collection. Application deadlines are March 31, June 30 and October 30.
    Amount of award: $3,400-$10,200
    Application deadline: March 31, June 30

Hagley Museum and Library Grant-In-Aid

Type of award: Research grant, renewable.
Intended use: For graduate study. Designated institutions: Hagley Library.
Basis for selection: Major/career interest in womenÖs studies; business; science, general; arts, general.
Application requirements: Research proposal. Curriculum vitae.
Additional information: Stipends are for two weeks to two months at $300 per week. Research relevant to Hagley's collections.
    Amount of award: $600-$2,400
    Application deadline: March 31, June 30

Henry Belin DuPont Dissertation Fellowship

Type of award: Research grant.
Intended use: For doctoral study. Designated institutions: Hagley's Center for History of Business, Technology, and Society.
Basis for selection: Major/career interest in business.
Application requirements: Recommendations, transcript and research proposal. Writing samples are welcome.
Additional information: Residential fellowship with a term of four months. Must demonstrate superior intellectual quality and present a persuasive methodology for the project. Applicants are strongly encouraged to consult with Hagley staff prior to submitting their dossier.
    Amount of award: $6,000
    Application deadline: November 15

Winterthur Fellowship

Type of award: Research grant.
Intended use: For graduate study at graduate institution in United States. Designated institutions: Winterthur Museum and Gardens and Hagley Museum and Library.
Basis for selection: Major/career interest in history; art, art history; arts, general; architecture.
Application requirements: Recommendations and research proposal. Curriculum vitae.
Additional information: Stipends are for one to six months at $300 per week. Research must focus on historical and cultural relationships between economic life and the arts, including design, architecture, crafts, and the fine arts.
    Amount of award: $1,200-$7,200
    Application deadline: December 1
Contact:
Hagley Museum and Library
P.O. Box 3630
Wilmington, DE 19807
Phone: 302-658-2400
Fax: 302-655-3188
Website: www.hagley.lib.de.us

Hallmark Cards

Hallmark Corporate Staffing Program

Type of award: Internship, renewable.
Intended use: For full-time senior, master's study.
Eligibility: Applicant must be U.S. citizen.
Basis for selection: Applicant must demonstrate depth of character, leadership, service orientation and high academic achievement.
Application requirements: Interview, recommendations and transcript.
Additional information: Internships are open to students entering the final year of a graduate or undergraduate program. A resume and cover letter is required as part of the application. Graduates receive $3,800-$3,850 per month; undergraduates receive $2,100-$2,350 per month. Open to all majors. Deadlines vary; contact sponsor for information.

Amount of award:	$6,300-$15,400
Number of awards:	17

Contact:
Internship Coordinator
Mail Drop #112
P.O. Box 419580
Kansas City, MO 64141

Harness Horse Youth Foundation

Harness Horse Youth Scholarship

Type of award: Scholarship, renewable.
Intended use: For full-time undergraduate, non-degree study at vocational, 2-year or 4-year institution.
Basis for selection: Major/career interest in wildlife/fisheries. Applicant must demonstrate depth of character, leadership, patriotism, seriousness of purpose, service orientation, financial need and high academic achievement.
Application requirements: Recommendations, essay and transcript.
Additional information: Must pursue horse related career. Preference given to applicants under 24 years of age.

Amount of award:	$1,000-$3,500
Number of applicants:	700
Application deadline:	April 30
Notification begins:	July 1
Total amount awarded:	$16,000

Contact:
Harness Horse Youth Foundation
14950 Greyhound Court
Suite 210
Carmel, IN 46032
Phone: 317-848-5132
Website: www.hhyf.org

Harry Frank Guggenheim Foundation

Harry Frank Guggenheim Dissertation Fellowship

Type of award: Research grant.
Intended use: For doctoral study at accredited graduate institution.
Basis for selection: Major/career interest in anthropology; psychology; history; law; criminal justice/law enforcement. Applicant must demonstrate high academic achievement.
Application requirements: Recommendations and research proposal.
Additional information: Will only support the writing of dissertations related to the study of violence and aggression. Students must have completed all requirements for Ph.D. except writing of dissertation.

Amount of award:	$10,000
Number of awards:	10
Number of applicants:	190
Application deadline:	February 1
Notification begins:	June 15
Total amount awarded:	$100,000

Contact:
Guggenheim Foundation
527 Madison Avenue
New York, NY 10022-4304
Website: www.hfg.org

Harry Frank Guggenheim Dissertation Fellowships

Type of award: Research grant.
Intended use: For doctoral study.
Basis for selection: Major/career interest in criminal justice/law enforcement; social and behavioral sciences; humanities/liberal arts; sociology; psychology; social work; anthropology. Applicant must demonstrate seriousness of purpose and high academic achievement.
Application requirements: Interview, recommendations, essay, transcript, proof of eligibility and research proposal.
Additional information: Dissertation thesis must be completed within one year of receiving award. Funding is offered to projects related to violence, aggression or dominance, with priority given to research that increases understanding of these topics. The Foundation does not offer tuition support.

Amount of award:	$10,000
Number of awards:	10
Number of applicants:	180
Application deadline:	February 1
Notification begins:	June 30
Total amount awarded:	$100,000

Contact:
Harry Frank Guggenheim Foundation
527 Madison Avenue
New York, NY 10022
Phone: 2126444907
Website: www.hfg.org

Hattie M. Strong Foundation

Strong Foundation Interest-Free Student Loan

Type of award: Loan, renewable.
Intended use: For full-time senior, master's, doctoral or first professional study at accredited 4-year or graduate institution.
Eligibility: Applicant must be U.S. citizen or permanent resident.
Basis for selection: Applicant must demonstrate depth of character, leadership, seriousness of purpose, service orientation, financial need and high academic achievement.
Application requirements: Recommendations, essay, proof of eligibility and research proposal.
Additional information: Must be entering final year of

undergraduate or graduate degree program. Terms of repayment are based upon monthly income after graduation. Students may request an application between January 1 and March 31. Enclose SASE with application.

Amount of award:	$3,000
Number of awards:	247
Number of applicants:	587
Application deadline:	March 31
Notification begins:	July 1
Total amount awarded:	$486,000

Contact:
Hattie M. Strong Foundation
1620 Eye Street, NW
Suite 700
Washington, DC 20006-4005
Phone: 202-331-1619

Havana National Bank

McFarland Charitable Foundation Scholarship

Type of award: Scholarship, renewable.
Intended use: For full-time undergraduate, non-degree study at accredited vocational, 2-year or 4-year institution in United States.
Basis for selection: Major/career interest in nursing. Applicant must demonstrate seriousness of purpose.
Application requirements: $5 application fee. Interview, recommendations, transcript and proof of eligibility. Letter of acceptance to the RN program.
Additional information: Award recipients must contractually obligate themselves to return to Havana, IL and work as registered nurses for one year for each year of funding. Co-signer is required.

Amount of award:	$1,000-$12,000
Number of awards:	5
Number of applicants:	15
Application deadline:	May 1
Notification begins:	June 15
Total amount awarded:	$50,000

Contact:
Havana National Bank
112 South Orange
P.O. Box 200
Havana, IL 62644-0200
Phone: 309-543-3361

Hawaii Community Foundation

Aiea General Hospital Association Scholarship

Type of award: Scholarship, renewable.
Intended use: For full-time undergraduate or graduate study at accredited 2-year, 4-year or graduate institution in United States.
Eligibility: Applicant must be U.S. citizen or permanent resident residing in Hawaii.
Basis for selection: Major/career interest in health-related professions. Applicant must demonstrate depth of character, financial need and high academic achievement.
Application requirements: Recommendations, essay and transcript. Personal letter, Student Aid Report.
Additional information: Applicant must be resident of one of the following Leeward Oahu zip codes: 96701, 96706, 96707, 96782, 96792, or 98797. Amount of award varies. CSS PROFILE Application required. Notifications mailed between April and July.

Amount of award:	$1,000
Number of awards:	16
Application deadline:	March 2

Contact:
Hawaii Community Foundation
900 Fort Street Mall
Suite 1300
Honolulu, HI 96813
Phone: 808-566-5570

Alma White--Delta Chapter, Delta Kappa Gamma Scholarship

Type of award: Scholarship.
Intended use: For full-time undergraduate or graduate study at accredited postsecondary institution in United States.
Eligibility: Applicant must be U.S. citizen or permanent resident residing in Hawaii.
Basis for selection: Major/career interest in education. Applicant must demonstrate depth of character and high academic achievement.
Application requirements: Recommendations, essay and transcript.
Additional information: Applicants must have permanent address in Hawaii. Applicants who take up mainland residency must have relatives living in Hawaii. Other former Hawaii residents considered on a case by case basis. Notifications mailed between April and July. Must be enrolled in an Education Program.

Application deadline:	March 2

Contact:
Hawaii Community Foundation
900 Fort Street Mall
Suite 1300
Honolulu, HI 96813
Phone: 808-566-5570

Blossom Kalama Evans Memorial Scholarship

Type of award: Scholarship, renewable.
Intended use: For full-time junior, senior or graduate study at accredited 4-year or graduate institution in Hawaii.
Eligibility: Applicant must be U.S. citizen or permanent resident residing in Hawaii.
Basis for selection: Major/career interest in Hawaiian studies. Applicant must demonstrate depth of character, leadership, seriousness of purpose, service orientation, financial need and high academic achievement.
Application requirements: Recommendations, essay and transcript. Personal letter, Student Aid Report.
Additional information: Preference given to students of

Hawaiian ancestry. Hawaiian language students also eligible. CSS PROFILE Application required. Award amount varies with each case. Applicants must have permanent address in Hawaii. Applicants who take up mainland residency must have relatives living in Hawaii. Other former Hawaii residents considered on a case by case basis. Notifications mailed between April and July.

Amount of award:	$300
Number of awards:	9
Application deadline:	March 2

Contact:
Hawaii Community Foundation
900 Fort Street Mall, Suite 1300
Honolulu, HI 96813
Phone: 808-566-5570

Castle & Cooke George W.Y. Yim Scholarship Fund

Type of award: Scholarship.
Intended use: For full-time undergraduate or graduate study at accredited postsecondary institution in United States.
Eligibility: Applicant must be U.S. citizen or permanent resident residing in Hawaii.
Basis for selection: Applicant must demonstrate depth of character, financial need and high academic achievement.
Application requirements: Recommendations, essay and transcript.
Additional information: Must be dependent of an employee with at least one year of service with a Castle & Cooke Hawaii affiliated company. Applicants must have permanent address in Hawaii. Applicants who take up mainland residency must have relatives living in Hawaii. Other Hawaii residents considered on a case by case basis. Notifications mailed between April and July.

Amount of award:	$2,000
Number of awards:	1
Application deadline:	March 2

Contact:
Hawaii Community Foundation
900 Fort Street Mall
Suite 1300
Honolulu, HI 96813
Phone: 808-566-5570

Cora Aguda Manayan Fund

Type of award: Scholarship, renewable.
Intended use: For full-time undergraduate or graduate study at accredited postsecondary institution in United States.
Eligibility: Applicant must be Asian American. Must be of Filipino ancestry and studying in Hawaii. Applicant must be U.S. citizen or permanent resident residing in Hawaii.
Basis for selection: Major/career interest in health-related professions. Applicant must demonstrate depth of character.
Application requirements: Recommendations, essay and transcript. Minimum 3.0 GPA requirement.
Additional information: Amount of award varies. CSS PROFILE Application required. Applicants must have permanent address in Hawaii. Applicants who take up mainland residency must have relatives living in Hawaii. Other former Hawaii residents considered on a case by case basis. Notifications mailed between April and July. Minimum 3.0 GPA required.

Amount of award:	$650
Number of awards:	9
Application deadline:	March 2

Contact:
Hawaii Community Foundation
900 Fort Street Mall
Suite 1300
Honolulu, HI 96813
Phone: 808-566-5570

Dorice & Clarence Glick Classical Music Scholarship

Type of award: Scholarship.
Intended use: For full-time undergraduate or graduate study at accredited postsecondary institution in United States.
Eligibility: Applicant must be residing in Hawaii or Hawaii.
Basis for selection: Major/career interest in music. Applicant must demonstrate depth of character, financial need and high academic achievement.
Application requirements: Recommendations, essay and transcript.
Additional information: Notifications mailed between April and July. Must be majoring in classical music.

Amount of award:	$800
Number of awards:	4
Application deadline:	March 2

Contact:
Hawaii Community Foundation
900 Fort Street Mall
Suite 1300
Honolulu, HI 96813
Phone: 808-566-5570

Dr. Hans and Clara Zimmerman Foundation Health Scholarship

Type of award: Scholarship, renewable.
Intended use: For full-time undergraduate or graduate study at accredited postsecondary institution in United States.
Eligibility: Applicant must be U.S. citizen or permanent resident residing in Hawaii.
Basis for selection: Major/career interest in health-related professions; health sciences; health services administration. Applicant must demonstrate depth of character, leadership, seriousness of purpose, service orientation and financial need.
Application requirements: Recommendations, essay and transcript. Student Aid Report, personal letter.
Additional information: CSS PROFILE Application required. Award amount varies. Applicants must have permanent address in Hawaii. Applicants who take up mainland residency must have relatives living in Hawaii. Other former Hawaii residents considered on a case by case basis. Notifications mailed between April and July. Minimum 2.5 GPA at Community College, 3.0 at other.

Amount of award:	$1,600
Number of awards:	293
Application deadline:	March 2

Contact:
Hawaii Community Foundation
900 Fort Street Mall
Suite 1300
Honolulu, HI 96813
Phone: 808-566-5570

Ellison Onizuka Memorial Scholarship

Type of award: Scholarship.
Intended use: For full-time freshman, sophomore study at accredited 2-year or 4-year institution in United States.
Eligibility: Applicant must be high school senior. Applicant must be U.S. citizen or permanent resident residing in Hawaii.
Basis for selection: Major/career interest in aerospace. Applicant must demonstrate depth of character, leadership, seriousness of purpose, service orientation and financial need.
Application requirements: Recommendations, transcript and nomination by high school principal. Student Aid Report, personal letter.
Additional information: Award amount varies. Applicants must have permanent address in Hawaii. Applicants who take up mainland residency must have relatives living in Hawaii. Other former Hawaii residents considered on a case by case basis. Applicants are selected by nomination. Contact your high school principle.
   Application deadline: April 15
Contact:
Hawaii Community Foundation
900 Fort Street Mall, Suite 1300
Honolulu, HI 96813
Phone: 808-566-5570

Financial Women International Scholarship

Type of award: Scholarship, renewable.
Intended use: For full-time junior, senior or graduate study at accredited 4-year or graduate institution in United States.
Eligibility: Applicant must be female. Applicant must be U.S. citizen or permanent resident residing in Hawaii.
Basis for selection: Major/career interest in business; accounting. Applicant must demonstrate depth of character, leadership, seriousness of purpose, service orientation, financial need and high academic achievement.
Application requirements: Interview, recommendations, essay and transcript.
Additional information: Applicants must have permanent address in Hawaii. Applicants who take up mainland residency must have relatives living in Hawaii. Other former Hawaii residents considered on a case by case basis. CSS PROFILE Application required. Award amount varies. Minimum 3.5 GPA.
   Amount of award: $500
   Number of awards: 2
   Application deadline: March 2
Contact:
Hawaii Community Foundation
900 Fort Street Mall, Suite 1300
Honolulu, HI 96813
Phone: 808-566-5570

Hawaii Community Margaret Jones Memorial Nursing Scholarship

Type of award: Scholarship, renewable.
Intended use: For full-time freshman, sophomore, junior, senior, master's or doctoral study at accredited 2-year, 4-year or graduate institution in United States.
Eligibility: Applicant must be U.S. citizen or permanent resident residing in Hawaii.
Basis for selection: Major/career interest in nursing. Applicant must demonstrate depth of character, leadership, seriousness of purpose, service orientation, financial need and high academic achievement.
Application requirements: Recommendations and transcript.
Additional information: Preference given to members of Hawaii Nurses Association. CSS PROFILE Application required. Award amount varies. Applicants must have permanent address in Hawaii. Applicants who take up mainland residency must have relatives living in Hawaii. Other former Hawaii residents considered on a case by case basis. Notifications mailed between April and July.
   Amount of award: $500
   Number of awards: 13
   Application deadline: March 2
Contact:
Hawaii Community Foundation
900 Fort Street Mall, Suite 1300
Honolulu, HI 96813
Phone: 808-566-5570

Hawaii Veterans Memorial Fund

Type of award: Scholarship, renewable.
Intended use: For full-time graduate study at accredited graduate institution in United States.
Eligibility: Applicant must be U.S. citizen or permanent resident residing in Hawaii.
Basis for selection: Applicant must demonstrate depth of character, leadership, seriousness of purpose, service orientation, financial need and high academic achievement.
Application requirements: Recommendations, essay and transcript. Student Aid Report. Minimum 3.5 GPA.
Additional information: Applicants must have permanent address in Hawaii. Applicants who take up mainland residency must have relatives living in Hawaii. Other former Hawaii residents considered on a case by case basis. CSS PROFILE Application required. Award amount varies. Notifications mailed between April and July. Minimum GPA 3.5.
   Amount of award: $300
   Number of awards: 46
   Application deadline: March 2
Contact:
Hawaii Community Foundation
900 Fort Street Mall, Suite 1300
Honolulu, HI 96813
Phone: 808-566-5570

Henry and Dorothy Castle Memorial Scholarship

Type of award: Scholarship, renewable.
Intended use: For full-time undergraduate or graduate study at accredited postsecondary institution in United States.
Eligibility: Applicant must be U.S. citizen or permanent resident residing in Hawaii.
Basis for selection: Major/career interest in education, teacher. Applicant must demonstrate depth of character, leadership, seriousness of purpose, service orientation, financial need and high academic achievement.
Application requirements: Recommendations, essay and transcript.
Additional information: Must plan to pursue studies in early

childhood education. CSS PROFILE Application required. Award amount varies. Applicants must have permanent address in Hawaii. Applicants who take up mainland residency must have relatives living in Hawaii. Other former Hawaii residents considered on a case by case basis. Notifications mailed between April and May.

Amount of award:	$750
Number of awards:	23
Application deadline:	March 2

Contact:
Hawaii Community Foundation
900 Fort Street Mall, Suite 1300
Honolulu, HI 96813
Phone: 808-566-5570

Irwin Scholarship Trust Fund

Type of award: Scholarship, renewable.
Intended use: For full-time undergraduate or graduate study at accredited 2-year, 4-year or graduate institution in United States.
Eligibility: Applicant must be U.S. citizen or permanent resident residing in Hawaii.
Basis for selection: Major/career interest in journalism. Applicant must demonstrate depth of character, financial need and high academic achievement.
Application requirements: Recommendations, essay and transcript.
Additional information: Amount of award varies. CSS PROFILE Application required. Applicants must have permanent address in Hawaii. Applicants who take up mainland residency must have relatives living in Hawaii. Other former Hawaii residents considered on a case by case basis. Notifications mailed between April and July. Minimum GPA 2.7.

Amount of award:	$700
Number of awards:	30
Application deadline:	March 2

Contact:
Hawaii Community Foundation
900 Fort Street Mall
Suite 1300
Honolulu, HI 96813
Phone: 808-566-5570

Jean Fitzgerald Scholarship Fund

Type of award: Scholarship, renewable.
Intended use: For full-time freshman study at accredited 2-year or 4-year institution in United States.
Eligibility: Applicant must be female. Applicant must be U.S. citizen or permanent resident residing in Hawaii.
Application requirements: Recommendations, essay and transcript. Personal letter, Student Aid Report.
Additional information: Amount of award varies. Applicant must be active member of Hawaii Pacific Tennis Association for last four years. CSS PROFILE Application required. Applicants must have permanent address in Hawaii. Applicants who take up mainland residency must have relatives living in Hawaii. Other former Hawaii residents considered on a case by case basis. Notifications mailed between April and July.

Amount of award:	$2,000
Number of awards:	2
Application deadline:	March 2

Contact:
Hawaii Pacific Tennis Association
2619 8 King Street, Suite 2A
Honolulu, HI 96826
Phone: 808-566-5570

John Dawe Fund

Type of award: Scholarship, renewable.
Intended use: For full-time undergraduate or graduate study at accredited postsecondary institution in United States.
Eligibility: Applicant must be U.S. citizen or permanent resident residing in Hawaii.
Basis for selection: Major/career interest in dentistry; dental hygiene; dental laboratory technology; dental assistant. Applicant must demonstrate depth of character, leadership, seriousness of purpose, service orientation, financial need and high academic achievement.
Application requirements: Recommendations, essay and transcript.
Additional information: Students in dental technology also eligible. Award amount varies. Applicants must have permanent address in Hawaii. Applicants who take up mainland residency must have relatives living in Hawaii. Other former Hawaii residents considered on a case by case basis. Award amount varies. Notifications mailed between April and July.

Amount of award:	$950
Number of awards:	14
Application deadline:	March 2

Contact:
Hawaii Dental Association
1000 Bishop Street
Suite 805
Honolulu, HI 96813
Phone: 808-566-5570

John Ross Foundation

Type of award: Scholarship, renewable.
Intended use: For full-time undergraduate or graduate study at accredited postsecondary institution in United States.
Eligibility: Applicant must be U.S. citizen or permanent resident residing in Hawaii.
Basis for selection: Applicant must demonstrate depth of character, financial need and high academic achievement.
Application requirements: Recommendations, essay and transcript. Student Aid Report.
Additional information: Amount of award varies. Preference given to undergraduates born on and who have ancestors from the Big Island. CSS PROFILE Application required. Applicants must have permanent address in Hawaii. Applicants who take up mainland residency must have relatives living in Hawaii. Other former Hawaii residents considered on a case by case basis. CSS PROFILE Application required. Award amount varies. Notifications mailed between April and July.

Amount of award:	$1,000
Number of awards:	18
Application deadline:	March 2

Contact:
Hawaii Community Foundation
900 Fort Street Mall
Suite 1300
Honolulu, HI 96813
Phone: 808-566-5570

John W. McDermott Scholarship

Type of award: Scholarship, renewable.
Intended use: For full-time undergraduate study at accredited 2-year or 4-year institution in Hawaii.
Eligibility: Applicant must be U.S. citizen or permanent resident residing in Hawaii.
Basis for selection: Major/career interest in communications; tourism and travel. Applicant must demonstrate depth of character, leadership, seriousness of purpose, service orientation and financial need.
Application requirements: Recommendations, essay and transcript. Student Aid Report, personal letter.
Additional information: CSS PROFILE Application required. Award amount varies. Applicants must have permanent address in Hawaii. Applicants who take up mainland residency must have relatives living in Hawaii. Other former Hawaii residents considered on a case by case basis. Notifications mailed between April and July.

Amount of award:	$600
Number of awards:	3
Application deadline:	March 2

Contact:
Hawaii Community Foundation
900 Fort Street Mall, Suite 1300
Honolulu, HI 96813
Phone: 808-566-5570

Juliette M. Atherton Scholarship

Type of award: Scholarship, renewable.
Intended use: For full-time undergraduate, graduate or non-degree study at accredited postsecondary institution in United States.
Eligibility: Applicant must be Protestant. Applicant must be U.S. citizen or permanent resident residing in Hawaii.
Basis for selection: Major/career interest in religion/theology. Applicant must demonstrate depth of character, leadership, seriousness of purpose, service orientation and financial need.
Application requirements: Recommendations, essay and transcript.
Additional information: Please call Hawaii Community Foundation for further information. CSS PROFILE Application required. Award amount varies. Applicants must have permanent address in Hawaii. Applicants who take up mainland residency must have relatives living in Hawaii. Other former Hawaii residents considered on a case by case basis.

Amount of award:	$1,800
Number of awards:	55
Application deadline:	March 2

Contact:
Hawaii Community Foundation
900 Fort Street Mall, Suite 1300
Honolulu, HI 96813
Phone: 808-566-5570

K.M. Hatano Scholarship

Type of award: Scholarship, renewable.
Intended use: For full-time undergraduate or graduate study at accredited 2-year, 4-year or graduate institution in Hawaii.
Eligibility: Applicant must be enrolled in high school. Applicant must be U.S. citizen or permanent resident residing in Hawaii.
Application requirements: Recommendations, essay and transcript. Personal letter, Student Aid Report.
Additional information: Amount of award varies. Applicant must be resident of Maui county. CSS PROFILE Application required. Contact Hyatt Regency Maui address for more information.

Application deadline:	March 2

Contact:
Hyatt Regency Maui
200 Nohoa Kai Drive
Lahalna, HI 96761

Kaiulani Home for Girls Trust Scholarship

Type of award: Scholarship, renewable.
Intended use: For full-time undergraduate or graduate study at accredited postsecondary institution in United States.
Eligibility: Applicant must be female. Applicant must be U.S. citizen or permanent resident residing in Hawaii.
Basis for selection: Applicant must demonstrate depth of character, leadership, seriousness of purpose, service orientation, financial need and high academic achievement.
Application requirements: Recommendations, essay, transcript and proof of eligibility.
Additional information: Preference given to those of Hawaiian ancestry. Must submit birth certificate to verify ancestry. CSS PROFILE Application required. Award amount varies. Applicants must have permanent address in Hawaii. Applicants who take up mainland residency must have relatives living in Hawaii. Other former Hawaii residents considered on a case by case basis. Award amount varies. Notifications mailed between April and July.

Amount of award:	$500
Number of awards:	202
Application deadline:	March 2

Contact:
Hawaii Community Foundation
900 Fort Street Mall, Suite 1300
Honolulu, HI 96813
Phone: 808-566-5570

Kawasaki-McGaha Scholarship Fund

Type of award: Scholarship.
Intended use: For full-time undergraduate or graduate study at accredited postsecondary institution in United States.
Eligibility: Applicant must be permanent resident residing in Hawaii.
Basis for selection: Major/career interest in computer and information sciences; international relations. Applicant must demonstrate depth of character, financial need and high academic achievement.
Application requirements: Recommendations, essay and transcript.
Additional information: Applicants must have permanent

address in Hawaii. Applicants who take up mainland residency must have relatives living in Hawaii. Other former Hawaii residents considered on a case by case basis. Notifications mailed between April and July.
- **Amount of award:** $500
- **Number of awards:** 3
- **Application deadline:** March 2

Contact:
Hawaii Community Foundation
900 Fort Street Mall
Suite 1300
Honolulu, HI 96813
Phone: 808-566-5570

Koloa Scholarship

Type of award: Scholarship, renewable.
Intended use: For undergraduate or graduate study at accredited vocational, 2-year or 4-year institution in United States.
Eligibility: Applicant must be U.S. citizen or permanent resident residing in Hawaii.
Application requirements: Recommendations, essay and transcript. Personal letter, Student Aid Report.
Additional information: Applicant must be resident of one if the following Kauai areas in Hawaii: Koloa, including Omao and Poipu (96756), Lawai (96765) or Kalaheo (96741). Amount of award varies. CSS PROFILE Application required. Notifications mailed between April and July.
- **Amount of award:** $1,000
- **Number of awards:** 5
- **Application deadline:** March 2

Contact:
Hawaii Community Foundation
900 Fort Street Mall
Suite 1300
Honolulu, HI 96813
Phone: 808-566-5570

Marion MacCarrell Scott Scholarship

Type of award: Scholarship, renewable.
Intended use: For full-time undergraduate or graduate study at accredited postsecondary institution in United States.
Designated institutions: Institution on the U.S. Mainland.
Eligibility: Applicant must be U.S. citizen or permanent resident residing in Hawaii.
Basis for selection: Major/career interest in international relations; history; economics; sociology; political science/government; anthropology; geography; law; psychology. Applicant must demonstrate depth of character, leadership, seriousness of purpose, service orientation, financial need and high academic achievement.
Application requirements: Recommendations, essay and transcript. Personal letter, Student Aid Report.
Additional information: Must be public high school graduate and pursue studies on U.S. Mainland that promote international understanding and world peace. CSS PROFILE Application required. Award amount varies. Minimum GPA 2.8. Applicants must have permanent address in Hawaii. Applicants who take up mainland residency must have relatives living in Hawaii. Other former Hawaii residents considered on a case by case basis. Notifications mailed between April and July.
- **Amount of award:** $2,000
- **Number of awards:** 196
- **Application deadline:** March 2

Contact:
Hawaii Community Foundation
900 Fort Street Mall
Suite 1300
Honolulu, HI 96813
Phone: 808-566-5570

Mildred Towle Trust Fund Scholarship

Type of award: Scholarship, renewable.
Intended use: For full-time undergraduate or graduate study at accredited postsecondary institution in or outside United States.
Eligibility: Applicant must be residing in Hawaii.
Basis for selection: Major/career interest in social and behavioral sciences; international relations. Applicant must demonstrate depth of character, leadership, seriousness of purpose, service orientation, financial need and high academic achievement.
Application requirements: Recommendations, essay and transcript.
Additional information: Award for Hawaii residents studying either in foreign country or at Boston University. African-Americans or foreign students studying in Hawaii also eligible. CSS PROFILE Application required. Award amount varies. Minimum GPA 2.7.
- **Amount of award:** $450
- **Number of awards:** 101
- **Application deadline:** March 2

Contact:
Hawaii Community Foundation
900 Fort Street Mall, Suite 1300
Honolulu, HI 96813
Phone: 808-566-5570

PGH Foundation Scholarship

Type of award: Scholarship.
Intended use: For undergraduate or graduate study at accredited postsecondary institution in United States.
Eligibility: Applicant must be U.S. citizen or permanent resident residing in Hawaii.
Basis for selection: Major/career interest in arts, general. Applicant must demonstrate depth of character, financial need and high academic achievement.
Application requirements: Recommendations, essay and transcript.
Additional information: Not for students studying video, film, or the performing arts. Applicants must have permanent address in Hawaii. Applicants who take up mainland residency must have relatives living in Hawaii. Other former Hawaii residents considered on a case by case basis. Notifications mailed between April and July.
- **Amount of award:** $1,000
- **Number of awards:** 5
- **Application deadline:** March 2

Contact:
Hawaii Community Foundation
900 Fort Street Mall
Suite 1300
Honolulu, HI 96813
Phone: 808-566-5570

Troy Barboza Education Fund

Type of award: Scholarship, renewable.
Intended use: For full-time undergraduate, graduate or non-degree study at accredited postsecondary institution in United States.
Eligibility: Applicant must be U.S. citizen or permanent resident residing in Hawaii. Applicant's parent must have been killed or disabled in work-related accident as fire fighter, police officer or public safety officer.
Basis for selection: Applicant must demonstrate depth of character, leadership, seriousness of purpose, service orientation, financial need and high academic achievement.
Application requirements: Recommendations and transcript.
Additional information: For employees of a public department in Hawaii and their dependents, or immediate family members of public employees killed or injured in line of duty. Resident of Hawaii who performed heroic act for protection or welfare of others also eligible. CSS PROFILE Application required. Applicants must have permanent address in Hawaii. Applicants who take up mainland residency must have relatives living in Hawaii. Other former Hawaii residents considered on a case by case basis. Award amount varies. Notifications mailed between April and July.
    Application deadline: March 2
Contact:
Hawaii Community Foundation
900 Fort Street Mall, Suite 1300
Honolulu, HI 96813
Phone: 808-566-5570

William and Dorothy Lanquist Foundation

Type of award: Scholarship, renewable.
Intended use: For full-time undergraduate or graduate study at accredited 2-year or 4-year institution in United States.
Eligibility: Applicant must be U.S. citizen or permanent resident residing in Hawaii.
Basis for selection: Major/career interest in physical sciences. Applicant must demonstrate financial need and high academic achievement.
Application requirements: Recommendations, essay and transcript. Personal letter, Student Aid Report.
Additional information: Amount of award varies. Applicant may not be studying biological or social sciences. CSS PROFILE Application required Applicants must have permanent address in Hawaii. Applicants who take up mainland residency must have relatives living in Hawaii. Other former Hawaii residents considered on a case by case basis. Notifications mailed between April and July. Minimum GPA 2.7.
    Amount of award: $2,100
    Number of awards: 8
    Application deadline: March 2
Contact:
Hawaii Community Foundation
900 Fort Street Mall
Suite 1300
Honolulu, HI 96813
Phone: 808-566-5570

Hawk Mountain Sanctuary

Hawk Mountain Internship Program

Type of award: Internship.
Intended use: For undergraduate or graduate study.
Additional information: Internships last four months and pay $500 a month. Interns receive free housing and course credit. Provides opportunity to gain experience in such fields as Environmental Education, Ecological Research and Biological Survey and Monitoring.
    Amount of award: $2,000
    Application deadline: June 15, February 15
Contact:
Hawk Mountain Sanctuary
1700 Hawk Mountain Rd.
Kempton, PA 19529
Website: www.hawkmountain.org

Heed Ophthalmic Foundation

Heed Ophthalmic Scholarship

Type of award: Research grant.
Intended use: For postgraduate study in United States.
Eligibility: Applicant must be U.S. citizen.
Basis for selection: Major/career interest in optometry/ophthalmology. Applicant must demonstrate depth of character, leadership, seriousness of purpose, service orientation and high academic achievement.
Application requirements: Recommendations and proof of eligibility.
Additional information: Applicant must be a graduate of an AMA accredited medical school. Fellowship must be completed within three years of residency. Preference given to those who plan to teach or conduct research in the field of opthamology at a medical school.
    Amount of award: $15,000
    Number of awards: 27
    Number of applicants: 100
    Application deadline: January 15
    Notification begins: March 15
Contact:
Heed Ophthalmic Foundation C/O F.A. Gutman, MD
9500 Euclid Avenue
Division of Ophthalmology, A-31
Cleveland, OH 44195-5024
Phone: 216-445-8145

Helen Hay Whitney Foundation

Whitney Postdoctoral Research Fellowship

Type of award: Research grant, renewable.
Intended use: For doctoral, postgraduate study in or outside United States. Designated institutions: Only US citizens may train abroad.
Eligibility: Applicant must be Must be studying in North America.
Basis for selection: Major/career interest in medical specialties/research.
Application requirements: Interview, recommendations, transcript, proof of eligibility and research proposal.
Additional information: Stipend of $27,000 first year, $29,000 second year, and $31,000 third year plus $2,000 each year toward research expenses. Travel to and from fellowship location covered also. Field of research must be in biomedical sciences. Applications not accepted from students studying abroad.

Amount of award:	$27,000-$31,000
Number of awards:	21
Number of applicants:	330
Application deadline:	August 15
Notification begins:	October 15

Contact:
Administrative Director
The Helen Hay Whitney Foundation
450 East 63 Street
New York, NY 10021-7999

Helicopter Association International

Helicopter Mechanic Technician Scholarship

Type of award: Scholarship.
Intended use: For non-degree study. Designated institutions: U.S. helicopter manufacturers or engine manufacturers.
Basis for selection: Major/career interest in aviation repair. Applicant must demonstrate high academic achievement.
Application requirements: Recommendations and nomination by FAA-approved Airframe and Powerplant (A&P) school.
Additional information: For students who wish to study helicopter maintenance who have graduated within past year from FAA-approved Airframe and Powerplant (A&P) school.

Amount of award:	$500-$1,500
Number of applicants:	50
Application deadline:	September 25
Notification begins:	December 1
Total amount awarded:	$3,750

Contact:
Helicopter Association International
1635 Prince Street
Alexandria, VA 22314-2818
Phone: 703-683-4646
Website: www.rotor.com

Henry A. Murray Research Center

Henry A. Murray Research Center Dissertation Award

Type of award: Research grant.
Intended use: For doctoral study at 4-year or graduate institution.
Basis for selection: Major/career interest in social and behavioral sciences. Applicant must demonstrate high academic achievement.
Application requirements: Recommendations, proof of eligibility and research proposal. Proposals must be approved by an adviser or committee at the time of application; priority given to proposals that draw on Murray Research Center data.
Additional information: Applicants are notified of acceptance two to three months after deadline date.

Amount of award:	$2,500
Number of awards:	4
Number of applicants:	65
Application deadline:	April 1
Notification begins:	June 1

Contact:
Henry A. Murray Research Center
Radcliffe College
10 Garden Street
Cambridge, MA 02138
Phone: 617-495-8140
Website: www.radcliffe.edu/murray

Jeanne Humphrey Block Dissertation Award

Type of award: Research grant.
Intended use: For doctoral study at 4-year or graduate institution.
Eligibility: Applicant must be female.
Basis for selection: Major/career interest in social and behavioral sciences. Applicant must demonstrate high academic achievement.
Application requirements: Recommendations, proof of eligibility and research proposal. Proposals must be approved by an adviser or committee at the time of application; priority given to proposals that draw on Murray Research Center data.
Additional information: Applicants are notified of acceptance two to three months after deadline date.

Amount of award:	$2,500
Number of awards:	2
Number of applicants:	65
Application deadline:	April 1
Notification begins:	June 1

Contact:
Henry A. Murray Research Center
Radcliffe College
10 Garden Street
Cambridge, MA 02138
Phone: 617-495-8140
Website: www.radcliffe.edu/murray

Radcliffe Research Support Program Award

Type of award: Research grant.
Intended use: For postgraduate study at 4-year or graduate institution.
Basis for selection: Major/career interest in social and behavioral sciences. Applicant must demonstrate high academic achievement.
Application requirements: Recommendations, proof of eligibility and research proposal.
Additional information: Research proposal must use Murray Center data. Award recipients are notified two to three months after deadline date.

Amount of award:	$5,000
Number of awards:	6
Number of applicants:	25
Application deadline:	October 15
Notification begins:	June 1

Contact:
Henry A. Murray Research Center
Radcliffe College
10 Garden Street
Cambridge, MA 02138
Phone: 617-495-8140
Website: www.radcliffe.edu/murray

Herbert Hoover Presidential Library Association, Inc.

Hoover Presidential Library Fellowship/Grant

Type of award: Research grant, renewable.
Intended use: For master's, doctoral, postgraduate or non-degree study. Designated institutions: Herbert Hoover Presidential Library.
Basis for selection: Major/career interest in history; political science/government; journalism; aviation.
Application requirements: Recommendations, proof of eligibility and research proposal.
Additional information: Those studying communications also eligible. Priority to proposals with greatest likelihood of publication and subsequent use by educators, students, and policymakers.

Amount of award:	$1,400
Number of awards:	21
Number of applicants:	23
Application deadline:	March 1
Notification begins:	May 1
Total amount awarded:	$20,000

Contact:
Herbert Hoover Presidential Library Association, Inc.
P.O. Box 696
West Branch, IA 52358
Phone: 319-643-5327
Fax: 319-643-2391

Herschel C. Price Educational Foundation

Herschel C. Price Educational Scholarship

Type of award: Scholarship, renewable.
Intended use: For full-time or half-time undergraduate or graduate study in United States.
Eligibility: Applicant must be U.S. citizen residing in West Virginia.
Basis for selection: Applicant must demonstrate depth of character, leadership and financial need.
Application requirements: Interview and transcript.
Additional information: All students may apply. Preference is shown to undergraduates. A limited number of applications are released.

Amount of award:	$350-$2,500
Number of awards:	160
Number of applicants:	400
Application deadline:	April 1, October 1
Notification begins:	May 15, November 15
Total amount awarded:	$137,000

Contact:
Herschel C. Price Educational Foundation
P.O. Box 412
Huntington, WV 25708-0412

Hewlett-Packard

Student Employment and Educational Program

Type of award: Internship.
Intended use: For sophomore, junior, senior or graduate study.
Eligibility: Applicant must be U.S. citizen or permanent resident.
Basis for selection: Major/career interest in engineering; electronics; computer and information sciences. Applicant must demonstrate depth of character, seriousness of purpose and high academic achievement.
Application requirements: Interview and transcript.
Additional information: Ten to fourteen week summer

internship. $450-$625/week for undergrads and $700-$750 for graduates. Provides opportunity to work within different departments at a major computer hardware manufacturer. Benefits include a relocation allowance.

Amount of award:	$4,500-$13,300
Number of awards:	400
Number of applicants:	2,500
Application deadline:	April 30

Contact:
Hewlett-Packard
3000 Hanover St.
Mail Stop 20-AC
Palo Alto, CA 94304-1181

Hilgenfeld Foundation for Mortuary Education

Mortuary Education Grant

Type of award: Research grant, renewable.
Intended use: For sophomore, master's, doctoral or non-degree study at accredited vocational, 2-year, 4-year or graduate institution in United States.
Eligibility: Applicant must be U.S. citizen.
Basis for selection: Major/career interest in mortuary science. Applicant must demonstrate depth of character, leadership, seriousness of purpose, financial need and high academic achievement.
Application requirements: Transcript and research proposal.

Amount of award:	$300-$6,000
Number of applicants:	150
Total amount awarded:	$30,000

Contact:
Hilgenfeld Foundation for Mortuary Education
P.O. Box 1305
Brunswick, ME 04011
Phone: 714-525-8614

Hoffman-La Roche

Hoffman-La Roche Student Internship

Type of award: Internship.
Intended use: For full-time undergraduate or graduate study.
Application requirements: Interview.
Additional information: Applicant must be authorized to work in the U.S. Internship fields and topics vary; all majors are privileged to apply.

Number of awards:	30
Number of applicants:	2,000
Application deadline:	February 15

Contact:
University Relations Department
340 Kingsland St.
Nutley, NJ 07110-1199
Phone: 973-235-5000
Website: www.roche.com

Hopi Tribe Grants and Scholarship Program

Hopi BIA Higher Education Scholarship

Type of award: Scholarship.
Intended use: For full-time or half-time undergraduate or graduate study at accredited 2-year, 4-year or graduate institution.
Eligibility: Applicant must be American Indian. Must be an enrolled member of the Hopi Tribe.
Basis for selection: Applicant must demonstrate financial need and high academic achievement.
Additional information: Entering freshmen must have 2.0 GPA for high school course work or minimum composite score of 45% on GED Exam. Continuing students must have 2.0 CGPA for all graduate course work.

Amount of award:	$2,500
Application deadline:	July 31, November 30

Hopi Scholarship

Type of award: Scholarship.
Intended use: For full-time undergraduate or graduate study at accredited 4-year or graduate institution.
Eligibility: Applicant must be American Indian. Must be an enrolled member of the Hopi Tribe.
Basis for selection: Applicant must demonstrate high academic achievement.
Additional information: Entering freshmen must be in upper 10% of graduating class or have minimum of 21 on the ACT or 930 on the SAT. Undergraduate students must have and maintain a 3.0 CGPA, and graduate, postgraduate, and professional students must have a 3.2 CGPA for all graduate course work. $1,000 award given each semester.

Amount of award:	$1,000
Application deadline:	July 31

Hopi Supplemental Grant

Type of award: Scholarship, renewable.
Intended use: For full-time or half-time undergraduate or graduate study at accredited 2-year, 4-year or graduate institution.
Eligibility: Applicant must be American Indian. Must be an enrolled member of the Hopi Tribe.
Basis for selection: Applicant must demonstrate financial need.
Additional information: Entering freshmen must have 2.0 GPA for high school course work or minimum composite score of 45% on the GED Exam. Continuing students must have 2.0 CGPA for all college work. $1500 is awarded each semester.

Amount of award:	$1,500
Application deadline:	July 31, November 30

Hopi Tribal Priority Scholarship

Type of award: Scholarship.
Intended use: For junior, senior or graduate study at accredited graduate institution.

Eligibility: Applicant must be American Indian. Must be an enrolled member of the Hopi Tribe.
Basis for selection: Major/career interest in law; natural resources/conservation; education; business; engineering. Applicant must demonstrate high academic achievement.
Additional information: Those studying medicine/health are also eligible. Award is based on amount of tuition.
   Application deadline: July 31

Hopi Tuition-Book Scholarship

Type of award: Scholarship.
Intended use: For full-time or half-time graduate study at accredited postsecondary institution.
Eligibility: Applicant must be American Indian. Must be an enrolled member of the Hopi Tribe.
Basis for selection: Applicant must demonstrate financial need and high academic achievement.
Additional information: Must have high school GPA of 2.0 or minimum composite score of 45% on GED Exam. Undergraduates must have minimum 2.0 CGPA.
   Amount of award: $1,000
   Application deadline: July 31, November 30
Contact:
Hopi Tribe Grants and Scholarship Program
P.O. Box 123
Kykotsmovi, AZ 86039
Phone: 8007629630

Horizons Foundation

Horizons Foundation Scholarship

Type of award: Scholarship, renewable.
Intended use: For full-time junior, senior or graduate study at 4-year or graduate institution in United States.
Eligibility: Applicant must be U.S. citizen.
Basis for selection: Major/career interest in engineering; computer and information sciences; physics; mathematics; business; law; international relations; political science/government; economics. Applicant must demonstrate financial need and high academic achievement.
Application requirements: Interview, recommendations, essay and transcript.
   Amount of award: $500
   Number of awards: 6
   Number of applicants: 65
   Application deadline: July 1, November 1
   Total amount awarded: $4,000
Contact:
Scholarship Director
Women In Defense - c/o NDIA
2111 Wilson Blvd., Suite 400
Arlington, VA 22201-3061
Website: www.adpansia.org/wid/horizon/scholar.htm

Horticulture Research Institute

Timothy Bigelow Scholarship

Type of award: Scholarship.
Intended use: For full-time junior, senior or graduate study at accredited 2-year, 4-year or graduate institution.
Basis for selection: Major/career interest in landscape architecture; horticulture. Applicant must demonstrate financial need.
Application requirements: Recommendations and transcript. Applicant must submit a one-page resume of background, employment history, and education.
Additional information: Must have at least 2.25 GPA for undergraduates and a 3.0 GPA for graduate students.
   Amount of award: $2,500
   Number of awards: 3
   Application deadline: May 15
   Notification begins: June 1
   Total amount awarded: $2,500
Contact:
Ashby P. Rudey-Director of Horticultural Research
Horticulture Research Institute
1250 I Street NW Suite 500
Washington, DC 20005
Phone: 202-789-2900
Website: www.anla.org

Houghton Mifflin Company

School Division Internship

Type of award: Internship.
Intended use: For undergraduate or graduate study.
Basis for selection: Major/career interest in publishing.
Application requirements: Must submit resume and cover letter.
Additional information: Summer internships are full-time, last for 12 weeks and pay $8/hour. Interns will be assigned to work in one of the School Division's Editorial Departments.
   Amount of award: $3,840
   Application deadline: April 30
Contact:
Houghton Mifflin Company
222 Berkeley St.
Boston, MA 02116
Website: www.hmco.com

Howard Hughes Medical Institute

Research Training Fellowships for Medical Students

Type of award: Research grant.
Intended use: For full-time first professional study in United States. Designated institutions: Research must be conducted at non-profit academic and research institutions in the U.S.
Eligibility: Applicant must be Must have valid work permit and visa.
Basis for selection: Major/career interest in medicine (m.d.); medical specialties/research; medical specialties/research (beyond m.d.). Applicant must demonstrate seriousness of purpose and high academic achievement.
Application requirements: Interview, recommendations, essay, transcript, proof of eligibility and research proposal.
Additional information: Fellowship lasts one year or more. Dental and veterinary students not eligible. Research institue receives $11,000 for expenses. Students may apply during any year of medical studies. Applicants in fourth year must defer graduation until completion of fellowship year. Not available for students enrolled in Ph.D or Sc.D programs, or recipients thereof. Applications and detailed information available in September.

Amount of award:	$15,000
Number of awards:	60
Application deadline:	December 2
Notification begins:	April 1
Total amount awarded:	$900,000

Contact:
Howard Hughes Medical Institute
Office of Grants and Special Programs
4000 Jones Bridge Road
Chevy Chase, MD 20815-6789
Phone: 301-215-8889
Website: www.hhmi.org

Hungtington's Disease Society of America

HDSA Fellowship Program

Type of award: Research grant, renewable.
Intended use: For doctoral, postgraduate study at graduate institution in or outside United States.
Eligibility: Applicant must be U.S. citizen or permanent resident.
Application requirements: Proof of eligibility and research proposal.

Amount of award:	$35,000-$50,000
Number of awards:	6
Number of applicants:	20
Application deadline:	January 5
Total amount awarded:	$200,000

Contact:
Huntington's Disease Society of America
158 W. 29th St., 7th Floor
New York, NY 10001
Website: hdsa.mgh.harvard.edu

Huntington

Huntington British Academy Exchange Fellowship

Type of award: Research grant.
Intended use: For postgraduate study outside United States in United Kingdom. Designated institutions: The British Academy.
Basis for selection: Major/career interest in history; literature; humanities/liberal arts. Applicant must demonstrate high academic achievement.
Application requirements: Recommendations and research proposal. Curriculum vitae.
Additional information: One-month stipend of 900 pounds awarded to six scholars pursuing research in Great Britain.

Number of awards:	6
Application deadline:	December 15
Notification begins:	March 15

Contact:
The Huntington
Chair, Awards Committee
1151 Oxford Road
San Marino, CA 91108
Phone: 818-405-2194
Fax: 818-449-5703
Website: www.huntington.org

Huntington Fellowship

Type of award: Research grant.
Intended use: For doctoral, postgraduate study. Designated institutions: The Huntington.
Basis for selection: Major/career interest in literature; art, art history; botany. Applicant must demonstrate high academic achievement.
Application requirements: Recommendations and research proposal. Curriculum vitae.
Additional information: Monthly Stipends of $1,800 fund from one to five months of study. Those studying British and American history, history of science, photography, medieval studies, British drama, and Renaissance studies also eligible. Relevance to the Huntington's collections is important.

Amount of award:	$1,800-$9,000
Application deadline:	December 15
Notification begins:	March 15

Contact:
The Huntington
The Huntington Committee on Awards
1151 Oxford Road
San Marino, CA 91108
Phone: 818-405-2116
Fax: 818-449-5703
Website: www.huntington.org

Huntington National Endowment for the Humanities Fellowship

Type of award: Research grant.
Intended use: For postgraduate study. Designated institutions: The Huntington.
Basis for selection: Major/career interest in literature; art, art history; history; humanities/liberal arts. Applicant must demonstrate high academic achievement.
Application requirements: Recommendations and research proposal. Curriculam vitae. Non-citizens to have resided in the U.S. for three years.
Additional information: Awards up to $30,000 for four to 12 months of scholarship in residence. Preference given to scholars who have not held major awards for three years. Additional fields of study considered: British and American history, history of science, photography, medical studies, British drama, Renaissance studies, botany.

Amount of award:	$30,000
Application deadline:	December 15
Total amount awarded:	$30,000

Contact:
Huntington
The Huntington Committee on Awards
1151 Oxford Road
San Marino, CA 91108
Phone: 818-405-2194
Fax: 818-449-5703
Website: www.huntington.org

Huntington W.M. Keck Foundation Fellowship for Young Scholars

Type of award: Scholarship.
Intended use: For doctoral, non-degree study. Designated institutions: The Huntington.
Basis for selection: Major/career interest in literature; art, art history; history.
Application requirements: Recommendations and research proposal. Curriculum vitae.
Additional information: Award funds one to three months of dissertation research or a new project. Additional fields of study considered: British and American history, history of science, photography, Medieval studies, British drama, Renaissance studies.

Amount of award:	$2,300-$6,900
Application deadline:	December 15
Notification begins:	March 15

Contact:
The Huntington
The Huntington Committee on Awards
1151 Oxford Road
San Marino, CA 91108
Phone: 818-405-2194
Fax: 818-449-5703
Website: www.huntington.org

IBM

IBM Internship & Co-Op Program

Type of award: Internship.
Intended use: For sophomore, junior, senior or graduate study at accredited 2-year, 4-year or graduate institution in United States.
Basis for selection: Major/career interest in engineering, computer; engineering, electrical and electronic; computer and information sciences. Applicant must demonstrate high academic achievement.
Application requirements: Transcript.
Additional information: Salary is based upon number of credits completed toward degree. Application deadlines are rolling. Interships available at numerous IBM locations.

Amount of award:	$3,600-$9,100
Number of awards:	1,800
Number of applicants:	10,000

Contact:
Intership Coordinator
National Information Center; IBM Corporation
Dept. B01, Bldg. 101, 1001 W.T. Harris Blvd.
Charlotte, NC 28262-8563
Website: www.cyberblu.ibm.com

Indianapolis Newspapers, Inc.

Indianapolis Newspapers Fellowship

Type of award: Scholarship.
Intended use: For senior study.
Basis for selection: Competition in Writing/journalism. Quality of the editorial written for the competition. Major/career interest in humanities/liberal arts; journalism. Applicant must demonstrate depth of character, leadership, seriousness of purpose, service orientation and high academic achievement.
Application requirements: Portfolio, recommendations, essay, transcript and proof of eligibility. Writing samples.
Additional information: Ten recipients work in Indianapolis offices, ten in Phoenix offices. Fellowship lasts ten weeks. Must obtain college degree between August and June preceding the summer fellowship.

Amount of award:	$5,250
Number of awards:	20
Number of applicants:	140
Application deadline:	November 15
Notification begins:	April 1
Total amount awarded:	$105,000

Contact:
Indianapolis Newspapers, Inc.
P.O. Box 145
Indianapolis, IN 46206-0145
Phone: 317-633-9121

Inroads, Inc.

Inroads Internship

Type of award: Internship, renewable.
Intended use: For full-time freshman, sophomore study.
Eligibility: Applicant must be American Indian, African American, Mexican American, Hispanic American or Puerto Rican.
Basis for selection: Major/career interest in engineering; business; health-related professions; communications; science, general; arts, general; information systems. Applicant must demonstrate leadership and high academic achievement.
Application requirements: Interview, essay and transcript.
Additional information: Internship duration and compensation varies; contact sponsor for specific information.

Number of awards:	7,000
Number of applicants:	21,000
Application deadline:	December 31

Contact:
Inroads, Inc.
10 South Broadway Suite 700
St. Louis, MO 63102
Phone: 314-241-7488

Institut Francais de Washington

Institut Francais de Washington Fellowship

Type of award: Research grant.
Intended use: For doctoral, postgraduate study outside United States in France.
Basis for selection: Major/career interest in arts, general; economics; linguistics; literature.
Application requirements: Recommendations and research proposal. Curriculum vitae.
Additional information: All subjects, including social sciences and history of science, must be in the area of French studies. Postdoctoral applicants must have received their Ph.D. within the last six years. Research will last at least two months. Award does not cover travel expenses.

Amount of award:	$1,000
Number of awards:	3
Application deadline:	January 15

Contact:
Institut Francais de Washington
Department of Romance Languages, 238 Dey Hall
CB 3170
Chapel Hill, NC 27599-3170

Institute for Humane Studies

Institute for Humane Studies Fellowship

Type of award: Scholarship.
Intended use: For full-time junior, senior, master's, doctoral or first professional study at accredited 4-year or graduate institution outside United States.
Basis for selection: Major/career interest in humanities/liberal arts; social and behavioral sciences; communications; law; anthropology; economics; history; linguistics; literature. Applicant must demonstrate depth of character, seriousness of purpose and high academic achievement.
Application requirements: $25 application fee. Recommendations, essay and transcript. GRE scores.
Additional information: Fellowships last one year and provide stipend of up to $12,000. Other fields of study also considered: political science, sociology, journalism. Applicants should have a clearly demonstrated interest in classical liberal/libertarian ideas and intend to pursue an intellectual or scholarly career. Complete information and applications available in October.

Amount of award:	$12,000
Number of awards:	80
Application deadline:	December 31
Notification begins:	April 15

Contact:
Institute for Humane Studies at George Mason University
4084 University Drive, Suite 101
Fairfax, VA 22030-6812
Phone: 8006978799

Institute of Food Technologists

Food Engineering Division Junior/Senior Scholarship

Type of award: Scholarship, renewable.
Intended use: For full-time junior, senior study.
Basis for selection: Major/career interest in food science and technology. Applicant must demonstrate high academic achievement.
Application requirements: Recommendations, essay, transcript and proof of eligibility.
Additional information: Must be enrolled in Institute of Food

Technologists approved program, or in engineering program accredited by Accreditation Board for Engineering and Technology. Minimum 2.5 GPA required.

Amount of award:	$1,000
Number of awards:	1
Application deadline:	February 1
Notification begins:	April 15
Total amount awarded:	$1,000

Institute of Food Technologists Freshman Scholarship

Type of award: Scholarship, renewable.
Intended use: For full-time freshman study.
Eligibility: Applicant must be high school senior.
Basis for selection: Major/career interest in food science and technology. Applicant must demonstrate high academic achievement.
Application requirements: Recommendations, essay, transcript and proof of eligibility.
Additional information: Must enroll in IFT approved program (list of institutions and programs provided by Institute Scholarship Department). Second-time applicants must be IFT members. Minimum 2.5 GPA required.

Amount of award:	$1,000-$1,500
Number of awards:	25
Application deadline:	February 15
Notification begins:	April 15
Total amount awarded:	$25,500

Institute of Food Technologists Graduate Fellowship

Type of award: Scholarship, renewable.
Intended use: For full-time master's, doctoral study.
Basis for selection: Major/career interest in food science and technology. Applicant must demonstrate high academic achievement.
Application requirements: Recommendations, essay, transcript, proof of eligibility and research proposal.
Additional information: Second-time applicants must be IFT members. School must be conducting fundamental research in the area of food science. Minimum 2.5 GPA required.

Amount of award:	$1,500-$5,000
Number of awards:	29
Application deadline:	February 1
Notification begins:	April 15
Total amount awarded:	$78,000

Institute of Food Technologists Junior/Senior Scholarship

Type of award: Scholarship, renewable.
Intended use: For full-time junior, senior study.
Basis for selection: Major/career interest in food science and technology. Applicant must demonstrate high academic achievement.
Application requirements: Recommendations, essay, transcript and proof of eligibility.
Additional information: Must be enrolled in IFT approved program (list of institutions and programs provided by Institute Scholarship Department). Second-time applicants must be IFT members. Minimum 2.5 GPA required.

Amount of award:	$1,000-$2,000
Number of awards:	61
Application deadline:	February 1
Notification begins:	April 15
Total amount awarded:	$69,000

Institute of Food Technologists Sophomore Scholarship

Type of award: Scholarship, renewable.
Intended use: For full-time sophomore study.
Basis for selection: Major/career interest in food science and technology. Applicant must demonstrate high academic achievement.
Application requirements: Recommendations, essay, transcript and proof of eligibility.
Additional information: Must be enrolled in or plan to enroll in IFT approved program (list of institutions and programs provided by Institute Scholarship Department). Second time applicants must be IFT members. Minimum 2.5 GPA required.

Amount of award:	$1,000
Number of awards:	23
Application deadline:	March 1
Notification begins:	April 15
Total amount awarded:	$23,000

Quality Assurance Division Junior/Senior Scholarship

Type of award: Scholarship, renewable.
Intended use: For full-time junior, senior study.
Basis for selection: Major/career interest in food science and technology. Applicant must demonstrate high academic achievement.
Application requirements: Recommendations, essay, transcript and proof of eligibility.
Additional information: Must be enrolled in IFT approved program (list of institutions and programs provided by Institute Scholarship Department). Preference given to applicants who are taking or have taken at least one course in quality assurance and demonstrate definite interest. Second-time applicants must be IFT members. Minimum 2.5 GPA required.

Amount of award:	$1,000
Number of awards:	2
Application deadline:	February 1
Notification begins:	April 15
Total amount awarded:	$2,000

Contact:
Institute of Food Technologists
Scholarship Department
221 North LaSalle Street
Chicago, IL 60601

Society of Flavor Chemists Memorial Graduate Fellowship

Type of award: Research grant, renewable.
Intended use: For full-time master's, doctoral study.
Basis for selection: Major/career interest in food science and technology. Applicant must demonstrate high academic achievement.
Application requirements: Recommendations, essay, transcript, proof of eligibility and research proposal.
Additional information: Research must be in flavor chemistry

or food technology area involving some aspect of flavor chemistry. Second-time applicants must be IFT members. School must be involved in research dealing with the advancement of food science/technology. Minimum 2.5 GPA required.

Amount of award:	$2,000
Number of awards:	1
Application deadline:	February 1
Notification begins:	April 15
Total amount awarded:	$2,000

Contact:
Institute of Food Technologists
Scholarship Department
221 North LaSalle Street
Chicago, IL 60601

Institute of International Education

Anna K. Meredith Fund Scholarship

Type of award: Scholarship.
Intended use: For undergraduate study outside United States in Italy. Designated institutions: Studio Art Centers International (SACI).
Basis for selection: Major/career interest in arts, general. Applicant must demonstrate financial need.
Application requirements: Portfolio.
Additional information: Supports study at the Studio Art Centers International (SACI). Must submit portfolio of 20 labeled slides of own work and financial aid report from home school, or recent tax return if not currently enrolled.

Amount of award:	$500-$3,000
Number of awards:	10
Application deadline:	May 1, October 15

Contact:
Institute of International Education
809 United Nations Plaza
U.S. Student Programs, SACI Coordinator
New York, NY 10017-3580
Website: www.iie.org

Asia-Pacific Undergraduate Scholarship

Type of award: Scholarship.
Intended use: For sophomore, junior or senior study outside United States in Australia, New Zealand, or Pacific Island nations.
Eligibility: Applicant must be U.S. citizen or permanent resident.
Basis for selection: Major/career interest in Asian studies.
Application requirements: Proof of eligibility.
Additional information: Supports unique, innovative approaches to study abroad. Accepted fields of study include area, ethnic, and cultural studies and Pacific area studies. Must be currently enrolled in an IIE West Coast Region Education Associate college or university. Award amount varies and includes travel costs.

Amount of award:	$10,000
Number of awards:	10
Number of applicants:	57
Application deadline:	March 19
Notification begins:	May 1

Contact:
Institute of International Education- West Coast
Dr. Carl Zachrisson, Director
41 Sutter Street, Suite 510
San Francisco, CA 94102
Website: www.iie.org

Clare Brett Smith Scholarship

Type of award: Scholarship.
Intended use: For undergraduate or graduate study outside United States in Italy. Designated institutions: Studio Art Centers International (SACI).
Basis for selection: Major/career interest in arts, general.
Application requirements: Portfolio.
Additional information: For photography student. Must submit portfolio of 20 labeled slides of own work and financial aid report from home school, or recent tax return if not currently enrolled.

Amount of award:	$1,000-$2,000
Number of awards:	1
Application deadline:	May 1, October 15

Contact:
Institute of International Education
809 United Nations Plaza
U.S. Student Programs, SACI Coordinator
New York, NY 10017-3580
Website: www.iie.org

Gillian Award

Type of award: Scholarship.
Intended use: For master's, doctoral or postgraduate study outside United States in Italy. Designated institutions: Studio Art Centers International (SACI).
Basis for selection: Major/career interest in arts, general.
Application requirements: Portfolio. Portfolio of 20 labelled slides of own work. Financial aid report from home school, or if not currently enrolled, recent tax return.
Additional information: Supports study at the Studio Art Centers International (SACI), in Florence, Italy.

Amount of award:	$17,500
Number of awards:	1
Application deadline:	May 1, October 15

Contact:
Institute of International Education
809 United Nations Plaza
U.S. Student Programs, SACI Coordinator
New York, NY 10017-3580
Website: www.iie.org

International Incentive Award

Type of award: Scholarship.
Intended use: For sophomore, junior or senior study outside United States in Florence, Italy. Designated institutions: Studio Art Centers International (SACI).
Basis for selection: Major/career interest in arts, general. Applicant must demonstrate high academic achievement.
Additional information: Must be at least sophomore with

minimum 3.0 GPA. Fine/studio arts accepted fields of study. Special efforts are made to encourage applications from minorities and underrepresented groups.
- Amount of award: $12,000
- Number of awards: 2
- Application deadline: May 1, October 15

Contact:
Institute of International Education
809 United Nations Plaza
U.S. Student Programs, SACI Coordinator
New York, NY 10017-3580

Institute of Mining and Metallurgy

Bosworth Smith Trust Fund

Type of award: Research grant.
Intended use: For undergraduate, graduate or postgraduate study.
Application requirements: Research proposal.
Additional information: Award is 4,000 pounds sterling. This program provides funding for research in metal mining, non-ferrous extraction metallurgy or mineral dressing.
- Application deadline: March 15

Centenary Scholarship

Type of award: Scholarship.
Intended use: For freshman, sophomore study.
Basis for selection: Major/career interest in geology/earth sciences.
Additional information: Amount of Scholarship is 500 pounds sterling. Award is for projects, visits, etc., in furtherance of applicants career development.
- Application deadline: March 15

Mining Club Award

Type of award: Research grant.
Intended use: For postgraduate study.
Eligibility: Applicant must be Restricted to residents of the United Kingdom.
Basis for selection: Major/career interest in geology/earth sciences.
- Application deadline: March 15

Stanley Elmore Fellowship Fund

Type of award: Research grant.
Intended use: For postgraduate study outside United States in United Kingdom.
Basis for selection: Major/career interest in geology/earth sciences.
Application requirements: Research proposal.
Additional information: Awards range from 10000 to 14000 pounds sterling. Fellowships are for research in all branches of extractive metallurgy and mineral processing. Research must be conducted in the United Kingdom.
- Application deadline: March 15

Contact:
Secretary
44 Portland Place
London WIN4BR, ENGLAND

Institute of Real Estate Management Foundation

George M. Brooker Collegiate Scholarship for Minorities

Type of award: Scholarship.
Intended use: For full-time junior, senior, master's or doctoral study at accredited 4-year or graduate institution.
Eligibility: Applicant must be of minority background. Applicant must be U.S. citizen.
Basis for selection: Major/career interest in real estate; business; business, management and administration. Applicant must demonstrate depth of character, leadership, seriousness of purpose and high academic achievement.
Application requirements: Interview, recommendations, essay and transcript.
Additional information: Must have 3.0 GPA in major. Must intend to enter the field of real estate management. Undergraduate scholarships $1,000, graduate $2,500.
- Amount of award: $1,000-$2,500
- Number of awards: 3
- Application deadline: March 15
- Notification begins: July 1
- Total amount awarded: $4,500

Contact:
Institute of Real Estate Management Foundation
Attn: Gini S. Ohlson
430 North Michigan Avenue
Chicago, IL 60611
Phone: 312-329-6008
Website: www.irem.org

Institution of Mining and Metallurgy

Edgar Pam Fellowship

Type of award: Research grant.
Intended use: For postgraduate study.
Eligibility: Applicant must be Restricted to residents of Australia, Canada, New Zealand, South Africa, and the United Kingdom.
Basis for selection: Major/career interest in geology/earth sciences.
Application requirements: Research proposal.
Additional information: Fellowship is tenable for one year and pays 2250 pounds sterling. Fields of research include explorative geology and extractive metallurgy and is for post graduate study. Research must be conducted in the United Kingdom.
- Application deadline: March 15

Contact:
Institution of Mining and Metallurgy
44 Portland Place
London, WIN4BR, England

G. Vernon Hobson Bequest

Type of award: Research grant.
Intended use: For postgraduate study.
Basis for selection: Major/career interest in geology/earth sciences.
Additional information: This award was established for the advancement of teaching and practice of geology as applied to mining. The amount of award is 2,000 pounds sterling.
  Application deadline: March 15
Contact:
Secretary
44 Portland Place
London, WIN4BR, ENGLAND

Intel Corporation

Intel Science Talent Search

Type of award: Scholarship.
Intended use: For undergraduate study.
Eligibility: Applicant must be high school senior. Applicant must be U.S. citizen.
Basis for selection: Competition in Science project. Individual Research Project and overall knowledge of science.
Application requirements: Interview, transcript and proof of eligibility.
  Amount of award: $1,000-$40,000
  Number of awards: 40
  Number of applicants: 1,581
  Application deadline: December
  Total amount awarded: $205,000
Contact:
Science Service
1719 N St. NW
Washington, DC 20036
Website: www.sciserv.org

INTELSAT

INTELSAT Summer Intern Program

Type of award: Internship.
Intended use: For senior or graduate study.
Application requirements: Recommendations.
Additional information: Application requirements include a curriculum vitae and cover letter. INTELSAT has a diverse listing of intern positions. Contact the human resources department for these pertinent to your field of study. Strong preference will be given to international students attending U.S. colleges or universities.
  Amount of award: $4,800-$6,240
  Number of awards: 25
  Application deadline: March 13
Contact:
INTELSAT
Box 24 INT 3400 International Dr., NW
Washington, DC 20008-3098
Website: www.intelsat.int

International Food Service Editorial Council (IFEC)

Food Service Communicators Scholarship

Type of award: Scholarship.
Intended use: For full-time undergraduate, master's study at accredited postsecondary institution in United States.
Basis for selection: Major/career interest in food science and technology; food production/management/services; culinary arts; communications. Applicant must demonstrate depth of character, leadership, seriousness of purpose, service orientation, financial need and high academic achievement.
Application requirements: Recommendations, transcript and proof of eligibility.
Additional information: Applicant must be pursuing academic or experiencial work in both culinary arts and communications. Applications may be requested by email.
  Amount of award: $1,000-$2,500
  Number of awards: 5
  Number of applicants: 350
  Application deadline: March 15
  Notification begins: July 1
  Total amount awarded: $6,000
Contact:
International Food Service Editorial Council (IFEC)
P.O. Box 491
Hyde Park, NY 12538

International Management Group

International Management Group Summer Intern Program

Type of award: Internship.
Intended use: For undergraduate or graduate study.
Basis for selection: Major/career interest in business; business, management and administration; finance/banking; accounting; advertising; sports/sports administration.
Application requirements: Interview, recommendations and transcript.
Additional information: Full-time, 8-week program. No compensation, but credit given, for U.S. interns.. London interns receive $970 stipend. Provides an opportunity for interns to learn aspects of sports management. Must receive academic credit. For overseas positions, contact Cleveland office for addresses and phone numbers.
  Number of awards: 75
  Number of applicants: 800
  Application deadline: February 15
Contact:
International Management Group
One Erieview Plaza
Cleveland, OH 44114

International Order of the King's Daughters and Sons

Health Career Scholarship

Type of award: Scholarship, renewable.
Intended use: For full-time junior, senior, master's or first professional study at accredited 4-year or graduate institution. Designated institutions: In United States or Canada.
Eligibility: Applicant must be U.S. citizen or Canadian citizens may apply.
Basis for selection: Major/career interest in medicine (m.d.); dentistry; pharmacy/pharmaceutics/pharmacology; nursing; health sciences; health-related professions. Applicant must demonstrate depth of character, leadership, seriousness of purpose, service orientation, financial need and high academic achievement.
Application requirements: Recommendations, essay, transcript and proof of eligibility. Resume, Statement of professional intent.
Additional information: Physical/occupational therapy or other health-related majors also eligible, except for pre-med. Inquiries must include SASE. To request an application, state the field and present level of study and enclose SASE.
   Amount of award: $1,000
   Application deadline: April 1
Contact:
International Order of the King's Daughters and Sons
Mrs. Fred Cannon
PO Box 1310
Brookhaven, MS 39602

North American Indian Scholarship

Type of award: Scholarship, renewable.
Intended use: For full-time undergraduate study at accredited vocational, 2-year or 4-year institution in United States.
Eligibility: Applicant must be Alaskan native or American Indian. Proof of Native American heritage. Applicant must be U.S. citizen.
Basis for selection: Applicant must demonstrate depth of character, leadership, seriousness of purpose, service orientation and financial need.
Application requirements: Recommendations, essay, transcript and proof of eligibility. Photograph, reservation registration number.
Additional information: Only one award per year to a family. Must request application between October 1 and March 1. Include SASE.
   Amount of award: $500-$750
   Application deadline: April 15
   Notification begins: July 1
Contact:
Mrs. T.R. McConchie
Director of North American Indian Department
4831 Kempsville Green Pkwy.
Virginia Beach, VA 23462

Student Ministry Fund

Type of award: Scholarship, renewable.
Intended use: For full-time master's study at accredited graduate institution. Designated institutions: In United States or Canada.
Eligibility: Applicant must be U.S. citizen or Canadian citizens.
Basis for selection: Major/career interest in religion/theology. Applicant must demonstrate depth of character, leadership, seriousness of purpose, service orientation, financial need and high academic achievement.
Application requirements: Recommendations, essay, transcript and proof of eligibility.
Additional information: For Master of Divinity applicants only. Institution must be accredited by Association of Theological Schools. Inquiries must include SASE, institution name, graduation date, and how you found out about scholarship. Applications must be requested between January 1 and March 31. Preference to applicants with intention of becoming ministers of organized congregations. Financial aid officer must endorse budget. Must have 3.0 GPA.
   Amount of award: $500-$1,000
   Number of awards: 43
   Number of applicants: 60
   Application deadline: April 30
   Notification begins: July 15
   Total amount awarded: $42,500
Contact:
International Order of The Kings Daughters and Sons
Attn: Melrose Rich
3520 Wilmot Avenue
Columbia, SC 29205
Phone: 8032541586

International Research and Exchanges Board

Advanced Research Program

Type of award: Research grant.
Intended use: For master's, doctoral, first professional or postgraduate study outside United States in Central and Eastern Europe, Eurasia, and Mongolia.
Eligibility: Applicant must be U.S. citizen or permanent resident.
Basis for selection: Major/career interest in humanities/liberal arts; social and behavioral sciences.
Application requirements: Interview and research proposal.
Additional information: Applicants in modern foreign languages and area studies are encouraged to apply simultaneously for Department of Education Fulbright-Hays grants. Applications for Mongolia are only accepted in the humanities and social sciences. May be required to take language test of relevant country.
   Number of awards: 52
   Number of applicants: 240
   Application deadline: November 1
   Notification begins: March 1
Contact:
International Research and Exchanges Board
1616 H Street, NW
Washington, DC 20006
Phone: 202-628-8188
Fax: 202-628-8189
Website: www.irex.org

Bulgarian Studies Grant

Type of award: Scholarship.
Intended use: For graduate study at graduate institution outside United States in Sofia, Bulgaria.
Basis for selection: Major/career interest in history; literature.
Additional information: Applicants must have intermediate level of proficiency in Bulgarian language.
    Application deadline: November 1
    Notification begins: March 1
Contact:
International Research and Exchanges Board
1616 H Street, NW
Washington, DC 20006
Phone: 202-628-8188
Fax: 202-628-8189
Website: www.irex.org

International Research and Exchanges Board Travel Grant

Type of award: Research grant.
Intended use: For postgraduate study in Central and Eastern Europe, Eurasia, and Mongolia.
Eligibility: Applicant must be U.S. citizen or permanent resident.
Basis for selection: Major/career interest in humanities/liberal arts; social and behavioral sciences.
Application requirements: Research proposal. Must contact International Research & Exchange Board regarding eligibility for projects in Mongolia and Central and Eastern Europe before submitting an application.
    Amount of award: $3,000
    Number of awards: 43
    Number of applicants: 181
    Application deadline: February 1, June 1
    Notification begins: April 1, August 1
Contact:
International Research and Exchanges Board
1616 H Street, NW
Washington, DC 20006
Phone: 202-628-8188
Fax: 202-628-8189
Website: www.irex.org

Library and Information Science Grant

Type of award: Research grant.
Intended use: For graduate study outside United States in all countries in Eurasia.
Basis for selection: Major/career interest in library science; computer and information sciences.
Application requirements: Interview, proof of eligibility and research proposal.
Additional information: Non-American applicants must work with Americans and obtain letter(s) of support.
    Amount of award: $10,000
    Application deadline: March 31
    Notification begins: June 1
Contact:
International Research and Exchanges Board
1616 H Street, NW
Washington, DC 20006
Phone: 202-628-8188
Fax: 202-628-8189
Website: www.irex.org

Ron Brown Fellowship Program

Type of award: Research grant.
Intended use: For post-bachelor's certificate, master's or non-degree study at accredited 2-year institution in United States.
Eligibility: Applicant must be Central or Eastern European citizens.
Basis for selection: Major/career interest in business, management and administration; economics; journalism; law.
Additional information: Additional fields of study include: civic education, educational administration, environmental policy, mass communications, public administration and policy.
    Amount of award: $35,000
    Application deadline: January 31
Contact:
International Research and Exchanges Board
1616 H Street, NW
Washington, DC 20006
Phone: 202-628-8188

Scholar Exchange Program

Type of award: Research grant.
Intended use: For master's, doctoral, first professional or postgraduate study in United States.
Additional information: Places students from newly independent states into cooperating U.S. institutions.
    Number of awards: 150
    Application deadline: October 31
Contact:
International Research and Exchanges Board
1616 H Street NW
Washington, DC 20006
Phone: 202-628-8188

International Society of Women Airline Pilots

Women Pilots Airline Scholarship

Type of award: Scholarship.
Intended use: For non-degree study.
Eligibility: Applicant must be female.
Basis for selection: Major/career interest in aviation. Applicant must demonstrate depth of character, leadership, seriousness of purpose, service orientation and financial need.
Application requirements: Interview, recommendations and essay.
Additional information: Must have 1500 total flight hours, flight engineer written test, and an ATP certificate.

Amount of award:	$1,000-$2,000
Number of awards:	5
Number of applicants:	25
Application deadline:	April 1
Notification begins:	September 1

Women Pilots Financial Scholarship

Type of award: Scholarship.
Intended use: For non-degree study in or outside United States.
Eligibility: Applicant must be female.
Basis for selection: Major/career interest in aviation. Applicant must demonstrate depth of character, leadership, seriousness of purpose, service orientation, financial need and high academic achievement.
Application requirements: Interview, recommendations and essay.
Additional information: Must have 750 total flight hours and a commercial pilot's certificate.

Amount of award:	$1,000-$2,000
Number of awards:	4
Number of applicants:	14
Application deadline:	April 1
Notification begins:	September 1
Total amount awarded:	$5,000

Contact:
Scholarship Committee
2250 East Tropicana Avenue, Suite 19-395
Las Vegas, NV 89119-6594
Website: www.iswap.org

Interns For Peace

Interns for Peace Internship

Type of award: Internship, renewable.
Intended use: For non-degree study in Israel.
Eligibility: Applicant must be of Arab or Jewish heritage.
Basis for selection: Applicant must demonstrate depth of character, seriousness of purpose and service orientation.
Application requirements: Interview, recommendations, essay and proof of eligibility.
Additional information: Open to persons of either Arab or Jewish descent. Two-year internship on ethnic conflict resolution in assigned community in Israel for Jews, Israeli Arabs, and Arabs. Must have knowledge of and commitment to furthering Jewish-Arab relations. Must have B.A., M.A., or equivalent; prior residence in Israel for six months; proficiency in advanced level Hebrew or Arabic; work experience. Salary approximately $500 per month plus housing and health benefits. Internship begins in fall; applications accepted year-round. Travel expenses are the responsibility of intern.

Number of awards:	12
Number of applicants:	180

Contact:
Interns for Peace
475 Riverside Drive, 16th Floor
New York, NY 10115

Intertribal Timber Council

Truman D. Picard Scholarship

Type of award: Scholarship, renewable.
Intended use: For full-time undergraduate or graduate study at accredited 2-year, 4-year or graduate institution in United States.
Eligibility: Applicant must be Alaskan native or American Indian. Must be enrolled member of a federally recognized tribe. Applicant must be U.S. citizen.
Basis for selection: Major/career interest in natural resources/conservation. Applicant must demonstrate depth of character, leadership, patriotism, seriousness of purpose, service orientation, financial need and high academic achievement.
Application requirements: Recommendations and transcript. Resume.
Additional information: Additional fields of study include: forestry, and wildlife/fisheries.

Amount of award:	$1,500
Number of awards:	10
Number of applicants:	70
Application deadline:	February 20
Notification begins:	April 30
Total amount awarded:	$15,000

Contact:
Intertribal Timber Council
Education Committee
4370 N.E. Halsey Street
Portland, OR 97213-1566

Italian Catholic Federation

Italian Catholic Federation Scholarship

Type of award: Scholarship, renewable.
Intended use: For full-time freshman study at accredited vocational, 2-year or 4-year institution.
Eligibility: Applicant must be of Italian heritage, Roman Catholic. Applicant must be U.S. citizen residing in Illinois or California or Nevada.
Basis for selection: Applicant must demonstrate financial need and high academic achievement.
Application requirements: Recommendations, essay and transcript. Tax returns of family.
Additional information: Applicants must submit a copy of their parent's most recent tax return. Minimum GPA 3.2. Also open to non-Italian students whose parents are members of the Italian Catholic Federation.

Amount of award:	$400-$1,000
Number of awards:	200
Number of applicants:	600
Application deadline:	March 15
Notification begins:	May 1
Total amount awarded:	$70,000

Contact:
Italian Catholic Federation
675 Hegenberger Road 110
Oakland, CA 94621
Phone: 510-633-9058

J. Paul Getty Trust

J. Paul Getty Trust Internship Program

Type of award: Internship.
Intended use: For sophomore, junior, senior or graduate study.
Basis for selection: Major/career interest in arts, general; communications; humanities/liberal arts; architecture; museum studies/administration.
Application requirements: Interview, recommendations and transcript.
Additional information: Priority given to Los Angeles residents and out-of-state residents attending school in Los Angeles. Summer internship pay undergrads $300/week. Graduates receive $350/ week and $750 for expenses. Must have two semesters of college and cannot expect to graduate before December 1999.
   Amount of award: $3,000-$20,350
   Application deadline: March 1
Contact:
J. Paul Getty Trust
Department of Education and Academic Affairs
P.O. Box 2112
Santa Monica, CA 90407-2112
Phone: 3104406545
Website: www.getty.edu

J.B. Cornelius Foundation, Inc.

J.B. Cornelius Foundation Grants Program

Type of award: Scholarship, renewable.
Intended use: For undergraduate study at 4-year institution in United States. Designated institutions: Must be specific schools in North Carolina.
Eligibility: Applicant must be female. Applicant must be U.S. citizen or permanent resident.
Basis for selection: Applicant must demonstrate financial need.
Application requirements: Proof of eligibility.
Additional information: State applicants must attend college in North Carolina. Applicants must be entering or attending one of the following North Carolina Schools: Bennett College, Brevard College, Greensboro College, High Point University or Pfeiffer College.
   Amount of award: $1,000
   Number of awards: 90
   Number of applicants: 215
   Application deadline: May 15
   Total amount awarded: $85,000
Contact:
J.B. Cornelius Foundation, Inc.
2201 N. Dodge Street
P.O. Box 4030
Iowa City, IA 52243-4030

J.W. Saxe Memorial Fund

J.W. Saxe Memorial Prize

Type of award: Scholarship.
Intended use: For undergraduate or graduate study.
Basis for selection: Major/career interest in public administration/service. Applicant must demonstrate depth of character, leadership, patriotism, seriousness of purpose and service orientation.
Application requirements: Recommendations, essay and research proposal. Resume and supporting letter from faculty member.
Additional information: Award enables students to gain practical experience working no-pay or low-pay job or internship during summer or other term. Preference given to applicants who have already found a position, but who require additional funds.
   Amount of award: $1,000
   Number of awards: 10
   Application deadline: March 15
   Notification begins: May 1
   Total amount awarded: $10,000
Contact:
J.W. Saxe Memorial Fund
1524 31 St. N.W.
Washington, DC 20007

Jackie Robinson Foundation

Jackie Robinson Scholarship

Type of award: Scholarship, renewable.
Intended use: For full-time freshman, sophomore, junior or senior study at accredited 4-year institution in United States.
Eligibility: Applicant must be of minority background. Applicant must be high school senior. Applicant must be U.S. citizen.
Basis for selection: Applicant must demonstrate leadership, financial need and high academic achievement.
Application requirements: Interview, recommendations, essay and transcript.
Additional information: Applications sent November 1 through March 1 upon receipt of written request. Award amount varies up to $5,000.
   Amount of award: $5,000
   Number of awards: 152
   Number of applicants: 2,250
   Application deadline: April 1
   Notification begins: September 1
Contact:
Jackie Robinson Foundation
Scholarship Programs
3 West 35 Street, 11th Floor
New York, NY 10001
Website: www.jackierobinson.org

James F. Byrnes Foundation

James F. Byrnes Scholarship

Type of award: Scholarship.
Intended use: For full-time freshman, sophomore study at accredited 4-year institution.
Eligibility: Applicant must be U.S. citizen residing in South Carolina.
Basis for selection: Applicant must demonstrate depth of character, leadership, patriotism, seriousness of purpose, service orientation, financial need and high academic achievement.
Application requirements: Interview, recommendations, essay and transcript.
Additional information: One or both parents of applicant must be deceased.

Amount of award:	$2,500
Number of applicants:	200
Application deadline:	February 15
Notification begins:	April 20
Total amount awarded:	$170,000

Contact:
James F. Byrnes Foundation
P.O. Box 9596
Columbia, SC 29290
Phone: 803-254-9325
Fax: 803-254-9354

James S. Kemper Foundation

Kemper Scholars Grant Program

Type of award: Scholarship, renewable.
Intended use: For freshman study at 4-year institution in United States.
Eligibility: Applicant must be U.S. citizen.
Basis for selection: Major/career interest in business. Applicant must demonstrate depth of character, leadership, seriousness of purpose, service orientation, financial need and high academic achievement.
Application requirements: Interview, recommendations, essay and transcript.
Additional information: Must complete internship each summer to receive annual scholarship.

Amount of award:	$1,500-$7,000
Number of awards:	70
Total amount awarded:	$396,822

Contact:
James S. Kemper Foundation
1 Kemper Drive
Long Grove, IL 60049

Jane Coffin Childs Memorial Fund for Medical Research

Cancer Research Fellowship

Type of award: Scholarship, renewable.
Intended use: For full-time postgraduate study. Designated institutions: Only US citizens may study outside US.
Eligibility: Applicant must be Must be studying in the United States.
Basis for selection: Major/career interest in medical specialties/research. Applicant must demonstrate depth of character, leadership, seriousness of purpose and service orientation.
Application requirements: Recommendations, research proposal and nomination by proposed sponsor. Bibliography.
Additional information: Must be engaged in cancer research and hold either M.D. or Ph.D. in field of study, with no more than one year postdoctoral experience. Awards $26,000 first year, $27,000 second year and $28,000 third year. $1,500 research allowance. Additional $750 per year per dependent child.

Amount of award:	$26,000-$28,000
Number of awards:	75
Number of applicants:	375
Application deadline:	February 1
Notification begins:	May 1
Total amount awarded:	$2,000,000

Contact:
Jane Coffin Childs Memorial Fund for Medical Research
Director, Yale University School of Medicine
P.O. Box 208000
New Haven, CT 06520-8000

Japan Foundation

Japan Foundation Doctoral Fellowship

Type of award: Scholarship, renewable.
Intended use: For full-time doctoral study.
Basis for selection: Major/career interest in social and behavioral sciences; humanities/liberal arts. Applicant must demonstrate high academic achievement.
Application requirements: Recommendations and transcript. Evaluation of Japanese-language ability.
Additional information: Research projects that relate in substantial part to Japan are preferred. Canditates must have completed all requirements except dissertation and have the necessary Japanese language skills to undertake research in Japan. Non-U.S. citizens must apply to The Japan Foundation office in Tokyo. Award is only renewable after three years.

Number of awards:	14
Application deadline:	November 1

Contact:
Fellowship Coordinator
152 West 57th Street, 39th Floor
New York, NY 10019
Website: www.jfny.org

Japanese American Association of New York

Japanese American General Scholarship

Type of award: Scholarship.
Intended use: For full-time freshman study at accredited 2-year or 4-year institution in United States.
Eligibility: Applicant must be high school senior, of Japanese heritage. Applicant must be U.S. citizen or permanent resident.
Basis for selection: Applicant must demonstrate high academic achievement.
Application requirements: Recommendations, essay and transcript. SAT scores, photograph.
- Amount of award: $1,000-$5,000
- Number of awards: 10
- Number of applicants: 23
- Application deadline: May 15
- Total amount awarded: $18,500

Japanese American Music Award Competition

Type of award: Scholarship.
Intended use: For undergraduate or graduate study.
Eligibility: Applicant must be of Japanese heritage. Applicant must be U.S. citizen or permanent resident.
Basis for selection: Competition in Music performance/composition. Piano or string performance.
Additional information: Competition occurs in odd-numbered years. 1999 competition is for string instruments.
- Amount of award: $1,500
- Number of awards: 5
- Number of applicants: 50
- Application deadline: December 18
- Total amount awarded: $6,000

Contact:
Japanese American Association of New York
15 West 44 Street
New York, NY 10036

Jaycee War Memorial Fund

Jaycee War Memorial Scholarship

Type of award: Scholarship.
Intended use: For full-time undergraduate study at accredited 2-year or 4-year institution.
Eligibility: Applicant must be high school senior. Applicant must be U.S. citizen.
Basis for selection: Applicant must demonstrate leadership, financial need and high academic achievement.
Application requirements: $5 application fee. Transcript.
Additional information: SASE required. Twenty five $1000 scholarships and one $5000 scholarship offered.
- Amount of award: $1,000-$5,000
- Number of awards: 26
- Application deadline: February 1
- Notification begins: May 15
- Total amount awarded: $30,000

Contact:
Jaycee War Memorial Fund
Department 94922
Tulsa, OK 74194-0001

Jeannette Rankin Foundation

Women's Education Fund

Type of award: Scholarship.
Intended use: For undergraduate study at accredited vocational, 2-year or 4-year institution in United States.
Eligibility: Applicant must be female, adult returning student. Applicant must be U.S. citizen.
Basis for selection: Applicant must demonstrate depth of character, leadership, seriousness of purpose, service orientation and financial need.
Application requirements: Recommendations and essay.
Additional information: Application must be requested by January 15. Some financial data requested. This award cannot be used for study towards a second degree.
- Amount of award: $1,500
- Number of awards: 20
- Number of applicants: 900
- Application deadline: January 15
- Notification begins: June 30
- Total amount awarded: $30,000

Contact:
Jeannette Rankin Foundation
P.O. Box 6653
Athens, GA 30604

Jeppesen Dataplan

Jeppesen Meteorology Internship

Type of award: Internship.
Intended use: For non-degree study.
Basis for selection: Major/career interest in atmospheric sciences/meteorology.
Application requirements: resume.
Additional information: Meteorology internship available all year. Salary $8/hr. Must be enrolled in accredited meteorology degree program.

Contact:
Jeppesen Dataplan
121 Albright Way
Attn: Judy Graun, Human Resources
Los Gatos, CA 95030
Phone: 408-866-7611
Website: www.jeppesen.com

Jewish Braille Institute of America

Lazaroff Family Fund

Type of award: Scholarship, renewable.
Intended use: For undergraduate, graduate or postgraduate study.
Eligibility: Applicant must be Jewish.. visually impaired.
Basis for selection: Major/career interest in Jewish studies; religion/theology; education. Applicant must demonstrate financial need.
Application requirements: Interview, recommendations, transcript and proof of eligibility.
Contact:
Gerald M. Kass
Executive Vice President
110 E. 30th St.
New York, NY 10016
Phone: (212) 889-2525
Fax: (212) 689-3692
Website: www.jerishbraille.org

John F. Kennedy Center for Performing Arts

KCACTF/ ChildrenÖs Theatre Foundation Award

Type of award: Scholarship, renewable.
Intended use: For undergraduate study.
Eligibility: Applicant must be enrolled in high school. Applicant must be U.S. citizen or permanent resident.
Basis for selection: Competition in Writing/journalism. Student-written play or adaption on a theme appealing to young people. Major/career interest in theater (artistic); English.
Additional information: A publication contract may be offered to the winning playwright.
   Application deadline: 1
Contact:
Washington, DC 20566
Phone: 202-416-8000
Website: www.kennedy-center.org

John F. Kennedy Center for the Performing Arts

John F. Kennedy Center Performing Arts Internship

Type of award: Internship.
Intended use: For junior, senior, graduate or non-degree study in District of Columbia. Designated institutions: John F. Kennedy Center for the Performing Arts.
Basis for selection: Major/career interest in arts management; arts, general; advertising; marketing. Applicant must demonstrate high academic achievement.
Application requirements: Recommendations, essay and transcript.
Additional information: Internships also in theater, community outreach/education, management information systems, development, education administration, government liaison, symphony/orchestra, press office, programming, public relations, special events, subscriptions. College credit may be available. Writing samples required for government liaison, public relations, or press office placement. Additional deadline is March 1 for summer. Internships are full-time for three to four months.

Amount of award:	$1,950-$2,600
Number of awards:	65
Application deadline:	June 1, November 1
Notification begins:	July 15

Contact:
John F. Kennedy Center for the Performing Arts
Darrell Ayers, Internship Program Manager
Education Department, The Kennedy Center
Washington, DC 20566

KCACTF/ Barbizon Awards for Theatrical Design Excellence

Type of award: Scholarship.
Intended use: For undergraduate study.
Eligibility: Applicant must be U.S. citizen or permanent resident.
Basis for selection: Competition in Theatrical Stage, Lighting and Costume Design. Artistic excellence. Major/career interest in theater (artistic); theater (production/technical).
Application requirements: Portfolio.
Additional information: The three winners will receive an all-expense paid trip to New York City to visit the studios and offices of Barbizon Inc.

Number of awards:	3
Application deadline:	December 1
Total amount awarded:	$1,500

Contact:
Barbizon Awards for Theatrical Design Excellence
Washington, DC 20566
Phone: 202-416-8000
Website: www.kennedy-center.org

KCACTF/ Fourth Freedom Forum Playwriting Award

Type of award: Scholarship.
Intended use: For undergraduate study.
Eligibility: Applicant must be U.S. citizen or permanent resident.
Basis for selection: Competition in Performing arts. Offered to the best play written on the themes of world peace and international disarmament. Major/career interest in English; theater (artistic).
Application requirements: Audition.

Amount of award:	$2,500-$5,000
Number of awards:	2
Application deadline:	December 1
Total amount awarded:	$7,500

Contact:
The Fourth Freedom Award Playwriting Award
JFK Center for Performing Arts
Washington, DC 20566
Phone: 202-416-8000
Website: www.kennedy-center.org

KCACTF/ Irene Ryan Acting Scholarships

Type of award: Scholarship.
Intended use: For undergraduate study at postsecondary institution in United States.
Eligibility: Applicant must be U.S. citizen or permanent resident.
Basis for selection: Competition in Performing arts. Acting ability and talent. Major/career interest in theater (artistic).
Application requirements: Audition and nomination by Each institution nominates up to two actors for their production.
Additional information: Award is for student actors appearing in KC/ACTEF productions.

Amount of award:	$500-$2,500
Application deadline:	December 1

Contact:
The Irene Ryan Acting Scholarships
Washington, DC 20566
Phone: 202-416-8000
Website: www.kennedy-center.org

KCACTF/ Lorraine Hansberry Playwriting Award

Type of award: Scholarship.
Intended use: For undergraduate study.
Eligibility: Applicant must be U.S. citizen or permanent resident.
Basis for selection: Competition in Performing arts. The play that best illustrates the African-American experience will be chosen. Major/career interest in English; theater (artistic).
Additional information: In addition to the cash award, the first place winner will also receive an all expense paid internship. Dramatic Publishing company will publish the winning play. Grants of $750 and $500 will be made to the Theater Departments of the college or university which produces the first and second place play.

Amount of award:	$1,000-$2,500
Number of awards:	2
Application deadline:	December 1
Total amount awarded:	$3,500

Contact:
Washington, DC 20566
Phone: 202-416-8000
Website: www.kennedy-center.org

KCACTF/ Musical Theater Award

Type of award: Scholarship.
Intended use: For undergraduate study.
Basis for selection: Competition in Performing arts. The best musical production will receive the award. Major/career interest in English; theater (artistic).
Application requirements: Audition.
Additional information: The composer, lyricist, author and producing institution of the winning musical will receive $1,000. The musical must be fully produced by a college or university to be considered for this award.

Number of awards:	4
Application deadline:	December 1

Contact:
KCACTF Musical Theater Award
Washington, DC 20566
Phone: 202-416-8000
Website: www.kennedy-center.org

KCACTF/ National AIDS Fund/ CFDA - Vogue Initiative Award for Playwriting

Type of award: Scholarship.
Intended use: For undergraduate study.
Eligibility: Applicant must be U.S. citizen or permanent resident.
Basis for selection: Competition in Performing arts. The selected script must have HIV/AIDS as its main theme. Major/career interest in English; theater (artistic).
Additional information: In addition to the cash award, the winner will also receive a fellowship to attend the Bay Area Playwrights Festival in San Francisco, California.

Application deadline:	December 1
Total amount awarded:	$2,500

Contact:
Washington, DC 20566
Phone: 202-416-8000
Website: www.kennedy-center.org

KCACTF/ National Student Playwriting Award

Type of award: Scholarship.
Intended use: For undergraduate study.
Eligibility: Applicant must be U.S. citizen or permanent resident.
Basis for selection: Competition in Performing arts. Overall quality of submission. Major/career interest in theater (artistic); English.
Additional information: The winner of this award will be eligible to win five more awards and Fellowships.

Amount of award:	$3,600
Number of awards:	20,566
Number of applicants:	500
Application deadline:	1

Contact:
The National Student Playwriting Award
John F> Kennedy Center for the Performing Arts
Washington, DC 20566
Phone: 202-416-8000
Website: www.kennedy-center.org

KCACTF/ Short Play Awards Program

Type of award: Scholarship.
Intended use: For undergraduate study at 4-year institution outside United States.
Basis for selection: Competition in Performing arts. The writers of 2 of the best plays will be given these awards. Major/career interest in theater (artistic); English. Applicant must demonstrate seriousness of purpose.
Additional information: Prize of $1,000 awarded by Playwriting Awards Development Committee. Winners receive publication and listing by Samuel French Incaud membership in the Dramatist Guild.

Amount of award:	$1,000
Number of awards:	3
Number of applicants:	500
Application deadline:	January 1
Total amount awarded:	$3,000

Contact:
The Short Plays Awards Program
John F. Kennedy Center for the Performing Arts
Washington, DC 20566
Phone: 202-416-8000
Website: www.kennedy-center.org

KCACTF/ Short Play Awards Program

Type of award: Scholarship.
Intended use: For undergraduate study.
Eligibility: Applicant must be U.S. citizen or permanent resident.
Basis for selection: Competition in Performing arts. Offered for the best student-written script that explores the human experience of living with a disability. Major/career interest in theater (artistic); English.
Additional information: The play must be produced and entered in the KC/ACTEF. The Dramatist Guild, Inc. and Very Special Arts will participate in the selection of the winning script.

Amount of award:	$2,500
Application deadline:	December 1

Contact:
John F. Kennedy Center for the Performing Arts
Kennedy Center American College Theater Festival.
Washington, DC 20566
Phone: 202-416-8000
Website: www.kennedy-center.org

John F. Kennedy Library Foundation

Archival Internships

Type of award: Internship.
Intended use: For undergraduate or graduate study at 4-year or graduate institution.
Eligibility: Applicant must be Must be studying in USA.
Basis for selection: Major/career interest in history; political science/government; library science; English; journalism; communications. Applicant must demonstrate high academic achievement.
Application requirements: Interview, recommendations and transcript.
Additional information: 12 hours a week, $8 an hour. Provides intern with opportunity to work with projects such as preservation of papers of Kennedy and his administration. Interns given career-relevant archival experience. Limited number of additional Internships may open up during fall, winter, and spring. Library considers proposals for unpaid internships, independent study, work-study and internships undertaken for academic credit.

Application deadline:	February 15
Notification begins:	April 1

Ernest Hemingway Research Grants

Type of award: Research grant.
Intended use: For undergraduate, graduate or postgraduate study.
Eligibility: Must be studying in USA.
Basis for selection: Applicant must demonstrate seriousness of purpose and high academic achievement.
Application requirements: Interview, recommendations and research proposal. Must be used for research in the Hemingway Collection of JFK Library.
Additional information: Preference is given to dissertation research by Ph.D. candidates working in newly opened or relatively unused portions of the collection. Applications received after deadline will be considered for next cycle. Preference is given to projects not supported by large grants from other institutions.

Amount of award:	$200-$1,000
Application deadline:	August 15, October 20
Notification begins:	March 15, April 20

John F. Kennedy Library Foundation/Abba P. Schwartz Research Fellowship

Type of award: Research grant.
Intended use: For undergraduate, graduate or postgraduate study.
Eligibility: Applicant must be Must be studying in USA.
Basis for selection: Major/career interest in political science/government. Applicant must demonstrate seriousness of purpose and high academic achievement.
Application requirements: Recommendations and research proposal. Must be used for research at JFK Library.
Additional information: Intended for the production of work in the areas of immigration, naturalization or refugee policy. Applications received after the deadline will be considered in the next grant cycle. Include writing samples with application. Preference is given to projects not supported by large grants from other insttitutions.

Amount of award:	$3,100
Application deadline:	March 15, May 1
Notification begins:	May 1

John F. Kennedy Library Foundation/Arthur M. Schlesinger Jr. Research Fellowships

Type of award: Research grant.
Intended use: For undergraduate, graduate or postgraduate study.
Eligibility: Applicant must be Must be studying in USA.
Basis for selection: Major/career interest in political science/government. Applicant must demonstrate seriousness of purpose and high academic achievement.
Application requirements: Recommendations and research proposal. Must be used for research at JFK Library.
Additional information: Stipend $7,000 for single recipient or split between two. Intended to support production of works on foreign policy of Kennedy years, or Kennedy's domestic policy, with regard to racial equality and nature conservation. Preference is given to projects not supported by large grants from other institutions. Must submit writing sample.

Amount of award:	$3,500-$7,000
Application deadline:	August 15, October 15
Notification begins:	October 15

Kennedy Library Research Grants

Type of award: Research grant.
Intended use: For undergraduate, graduate or postgraduate study.
Eligibility: Applicant must be Must be studying in USA.
Basis for selection: Major/career interest in political science/government. Applicant must demonstrate seriousness of purpose and high academic achievement.
Application requirements: Recommendations and research proposal. Must be used for research at JFK Library.
Additional information: Preference is given to dissertation research by Ph.D. candidates working either in newly opened collection and to recent Ph.D. recipients who are expanding on their dissertations. Applications received after deadline will be considered for next cycle. Preference is given to projects not supported by large grants from other institutions. Samples of writing are required with applicantion.

Amount of award:	$500-$2,500
Application deadline:	August 15, March 15
Notification begins:	October 20, April 20

Marjorie Kovler Research Fellowship

Type of award: Research grant.
Intended use: For undergraduate, graduate or postgraduate study.
Eligibility: Must be studying in USA.
Basis for selection: Major/career interest in political science/government; international relations. Applicant must demonstrate seriousness of purpose and high academic achievement.
Application requirements: Recommendations and research proposal. Must be used to support research at JFK Library.
Additional information: Intended to support a scholar in the production of substantial work in the area of foreign intelligence and the presidency, or a related topic. Applications received after the deadline will be considered in the next grant cycle. Preference is given to projects not supported by large grants from other instituitions Writing sample must be submitted..

Amount of award:	$2,500
Application deadline:	March 15
Notification begins:	April 20

Theodore C. Sorensen Research Fellowship

Type of award: Research grant.
Intended use: For undergraduate, graduate or postgraduate study.
Eligibility: Must be studying in USA.
Basis for selection: Major/career interest in political science/government; journalism. Applicant must demonstrate seriousness of purpose and high academic achievement.
Application requirements: Recommendations and research proposal. Must be used for research at JFK Library.
Additional information: Intended to support in production of substantial work in the areas of domestic policy, political journalism, polling, press relations or a related topic. Applications received after deadline will be considered in the next cycle. Include writing sample with application. Preference is given to projects not supported by large grants from other institutions.

Amount of award:	$3,600
Application deadline:	March 15
Notification begins:	May 10

Contact:
John F. Kennedy Library Foundation
Columbia Point
Boston, MA 02125-3313
Website: www.cs.umb.edu/jfklibrary

Juilliard School

Juilliard Professional Intern Program

Type of award: Internship.
Intended use: For graduate study.
Basis for selection: Major/career interest in arts management.
Application requirements: $15 application fee. Interview, recommendations and essay.
Additional information: Program provides "hands-on" experience working with professionals and administration in the following fields: production, stage management, public relations, and facilities management.

Amount of award:	$2,592
Number of awards:	2
Number of applicants:	130
Application deadline:	February 5
Notification begins:	April 5

Contact:
The Juilliard School
60 Lincoln Center Plaza
New York, NY 10023-6588
Website: www.lincolncenter.org

Junior Achievement of Maine

Junior Achievement of Maine Scholarship

Type of award: Scholarship.
Intended use: For freshman study at accredited vocational, 2-year or 4-year institution in United States.
Eligibility: Applicant must be high school senior. Applicant must be residing in Maine.
Basis for selection: Major/career interest in business. Applicant must demonstrate high academic achievement.
Application requirements: Recommendations, essay and proof of eligibility.
Additional information: Must have participated in Junior Achievement programs during high school.
    Amount of award: $1,000
    Number of awards: 1
    Number of applicants: 10
    Application deadline: March 12
    Notification begins: May 1
    Total amount awarded: $1,000
Contact:
Chad M. Flynn
185 Lancaster St. Suite 204
Portland, ME 04101
Website: www.ja.org

JVS Community Scholarship Fund

JVS Jewish Community Scholarship Program

Type of award: Scholarship, renewable.
Intended use: For full-time sophomore, junior, senior, graduate or postgraduate study at accredited 4-year or graduate institution in United States. Designated institutions: California.
Eligibility: Applicant must be Jewish. Applicant must be U.S. citizen or permanent resident residing in California.
Basis for selection: Applicant must demonstrate leadership, seriousness of purpose, service orientation and financial need.
Application requirements: Recommendations and transcript.
    Amount of award: $500-$5,000
    Number of awards: 104
    Number of applicants: 170
    Application deadline: April 15
    Total amount awarded: $131,000
Contact:
JVS Community Scholarship Fund
5700 Wilshire Blvd., Suite 2303
Los Angeles, CA 90036

Karla Scherer Foundation

Karla Scherer Foundation Scholarship

Type of award: Scholarship, renewable.
Intended use: For full-time undergraduate, master's or doctoral study at accredited 4-year or graduate institution in United States.
Eligibility: Applicant must be female. Applicant must be U.S. citizen or permanent resident.
Basis for selection: Major/career interest in finance/banking; economics. Applicant must demonstrate depth of character, leadership, seriousness of purpose, service orientation, financial need and high academic achievement.
Application requirements: Recommendations, essay, transcript, proof of eligibility and research proposal.
Additional information: International students must have a U.S. study visa. Must have proof of enrollment in qualified U.S. institution. SASE must accompany application request by March 1st for the following academic year. Only majors in finance and economics with plans for a corporate business career in the private sector need apply.
    Number of awards: 25
    Number of applicants: 25,000
    Application deadline: March 1
Contact:
The Karla Scherer Foundation
737 N. Michigan Ave., Suite 2330
Chicago, IL 60611
Website: www.comnet.org/kschererf

KIMT

KIMT Weather/News Internship

Type of award: Internship.
Intended use: For senior study.
Basis for selection: Major/career interest in atmospheric sciences/meteorology; journalism; radio/television/film.
Application requirements: Resume, non-returnable tape - 3/4" or SVHS.
Additional information: Should have completed junior year, have valid driver's license and good driving record, computer experience, and ability to shoot video. Salary is minimum wage. Pre-employment drug test required. Unpaid internships are also available. Hours are flexible. Student must arrange to receive college credit.
    Number of awards: 2
Contact:
KIMT
112 North Pennsylvania
Attn: Doug Merbach
Mason City, IA 50401

Knights of Pythias, Grand Lodge of Maine

Knights of Pythias Financial Aid Award

Type of award: Scholarship.
Intended use: For full-time freshman study at accredited postsecondary institution.
Eligibility: Applicant must be high school senior. Applicant must be residing in Maine.
Basis for selection: Applicant must demonstrate depth of character, seriousness of purpose, service orientation and financial need.
Application requirements: Essay and proof of eligibility.
   Amount of award: $500
   Number of awards: 4
   Number of applicants: 250
   Application deadline: April 15, April 15
   Notification begins: May 30, May 30
   Total amount awarded: $2,000
Contact:
William W. Clough, P.G.C.
Knights of Pythias
6 McLellan Street
Brunswick, MA 04011
Phone: 207-725-2406

Kosciuszko Foundation

Graduate and Postgraduate Study and Research in Poland

Type of award: Research grant.
Intended use: For full-time graduate or postgraduate study outside United States in Poland. Designated institutions: Must be used at any postsecondary institution in Poland.
Eligibility: Applicant must be U.S. citizen or permanent resident.
Basis for selection: Applicant must demonstrate high academic achievement.
Application requirements: $50 application fee. Recommendations and research proposal.
Additional information: Participants granted tuition waiver, housing and monthly stipend to cover living expenses. Transportation costs are not provided. Must have a working knowledge of Polish language. Must have letter of invitation from a Polish instituteof higher learning. An interview may be required.
   Application deadline: January 16
Contact:
Kosciuszko Foundation
15 East 65th Street
New York, NY 10021
Website: www.kosciuszkofoundation.org

Kosciuszko Tuition Scholarship

Type of award: Scholarship, renewable.
Intended use: For full-time junior, senior, graduate or postgraduate study at 4-year or graduate institution in United States.
Eligibility: Applicant must be of Polish heritage. Applicant must be U.S. citizen or permanent resident.
Basis for selection: Applicant must demonstrate financial need and high academic achievement.
Application requirements: $25 application fee. Recommendations, essay and transcript.
Additional information: Students of other nationalities, doing work in Polish studies, also considered.
   Amount of award: $1,000-$5,000
   Application deadline: January 16
Contact:
Kosciuszko Foundation
15 East 65 Street
New York, NY 10021

Programs in Poland for American Citizens/ Year Abroad

Type of award: Scholarship.
Intended use: For full-time junior, senior study at 4-year institution outside United States in Poland. Designated institutions: Must be used at Jagiellonian University in Poland.
Eligibility: Applicant must be U.S. citizen or permanent resident.
Basis for selection: Applicant must demonstrate high academic achievement.
Application requirements: $50 application fee.
Additional information: Must have interest in Polish subjects and/or involvement in Polish-American community. Foundation pays tuition, housing and provides monthly stipend for living expenses. Travel costs are not covered. Must have a minimum 3.0 GPA. Interview may be required.
   Application deadline: January 16
Contact:
Kosciuszko Foundation
Year Abroad Program
15 East 65th Street
New York, NY 10021
Website: www.kosciuszkofoundation.org

KPMG Peat Marwick Foundation

Peat Marwick Doctoral Scholarship Program

Type of award: Scholarship, renewable.
Intended use: For full-time doctoral study in United States. Designated institutions: Must be used at AACSB accredited schools in the U.S.
Eligibility: Applicant must be of minority background. Applicant must be U.S. citizen or permanent resident.
Basis for selection: Major/career interest in accounting; information systems. Applicant must demonstrate depth of character, leadership, seriousness of purpose, service orientation and high academic achievement.
Application requirements: Resume with cover letter

describing present academic status, field of interest, ethnic background (minority status) and purpose or goals. Curriculum vitae.
Additional information: Must be planning on becoming a full time professor and not entering the corporate world.
    Amount of award: $10,000
    Number of awards: 20
    Number of applicants: 41
    Application deadline: April 1
    Notification begins: April 15
Contact:
KPMG Peat Marwick Foundation
Attn: Tara Perino
Three Chestnut Ridge Road
Montvale, NJ 07645
Phone: 201-307-7932

Kurt Weill Foundation for Music, Inc

Kurt Weill Foundation Dissertation Fellowships

Type of award: Research grant.
Intended use: For doctoral study at accredited graduate institution in United States.
Basis for selection: Major/career interest in music.
Application requirements: Recommendations and research proposal.
Additional information: Provides funds to assist in research activities for dissertations on the work of Kurt Weill.
    Amount of award: $5,000

Research and Travel Grants

Type of award: Research grant.
Intended use: For graduate study at accredited graduate institution in United States.
Basis for selection: Major/career interest in music.
Application requirements: Recommendations and research proposal.
Additional information: Applicants must be researching a topic related to Kurt Weill and/or Lotta Lenya. Provides funds to support specific research expenses. Grants should be requested to reimburse reasonable travel expenses to locations of primary source material.
    Amount of award: $5,000
Contact:
Program Manager
7 East 20th Street
New York, NY 10003-1106
Website: www.kwf.org

Lalor Foundation

Lalor Postdoctoral Research Grants

Type of award: Research grant.
Intended use: For doctoral, postgraduate study.
Basis for selection: Major/career interest in biology. Applicant must demonstrate seriousness of purpose and high academic achievement.
Application requirements: Research proposal.
Additional information: Grants are awarded to institutions for basic postdoctoral research in mammalian reproductive physiology and biochemistry. Funds may be used to cover fellowship stipends, institution overhead and laboratory and miscellaneous expenses. Less money is awarded for projects that require less than one year. Applications must come from tax-exempt institutions.
    Amount of award: $25,000
    Number of awards: 15
    Number of applicants: 85
    Application deadline: January 15
Contact:
Lalor Foundation
Cynthia Patterson
P.O. Box 2493
Providence, RI 02906
Phone: 4012721973

Landscape Architecture Foundation

Aila/Yamagami/Hope Fellowship

Type of award: Scholarship.
Intended use: For master's, doctoral or postgraduate study.
Basis for selection: Major/career interest in landscape architecture.
Application requirements: Essay and proof of eligibility.
Additional information: Fellowship to support landscape architect who has been in practice for a least three years to pursue further education or research.
    Amount of award: $1,000
    Number of awards: 1
    Application deadline: August 1
    Total amount awarded: $1,000
Contact:
Landscape Architecture Foundation
636 Eye St. NW
Washington, DC 20001-3736
Website: www.asla.org

Class Fund Internship Program

Type of award: Internship.
Intended use: For junior, senior study.
Eligibility: Applicant must be residing in California.
Basis for selection: Major/career interest in landscape architecture. Applicant must demonstrate financial need.
Additional information: Internships in Landscape architecture, landscape construction, or related fields. Open to students at the University of California at Irvine, Los Angeles, and Davis, and California Polytechinc at Pomona and San Luis Obispo. Recipients are granted a $2,000 scholarship in addition compensation at $6.00 per hour.

Amount of award:	$2,000
Number of awards:	2
Application deadline:	March 31
Total amount awarded:	$4,000

Contact:
636 Eye Street, NW
Washington, DC 20001
Phone: 202-898-2444
Website: www.asla.org

Class Fund Scholarship Ornamental Horticulture Program

Type of award: Scholarship.
Intended use: For junior, senior study.
Eligibility: Applicant must be residing in California.
Basis for selection: Major/career interest in horticulture.
Application requirements: Recommendations and essay.
Additional information: For Juniors or Seniors enrolled in the ornamental horticulture curriculum at California Polytechnic at Pomona and San Luis Obispo, and at the University of California.

Amount of award:	$1,000
Number of awards:	3
Application deadline:	March 31
Total amount awarded:	$3,000

Contact:
636 Eye Street
Washington, DC 20001
Phone: 202-898-2444
Website: www.asla.org

Class Fund Scholarships

Type of award: Scholarship.
Intended use: For undergraduate study.
Eligibility: Applicant must be residing in California.
Basis for selection: Major/career interest in landscape architecture. Applicant must demonstrate financial need.
Additional information: Open to Students at California Polytechnic at Pomona and San Luis Obispo, and the University of California at Davis.

Amount of award:	$1,500
Number of awards:	6
Application deadline:	March 31
Total amount awarded:	$9,000

Contact:
636 Eye Street, NW
Washington, DC 20001
Phone: 202-898-2444
Website: www.asla.org

David T. Woolsey Scholarship

Type of award: Scholarship.
Intended use: For full-time junior, senior, master's or doctoral study at accredited 4-year or graduate institution.
Eligibility: Applicant must be residing in Hawaii.
Basis for selection: Major/career interest in landscape architecture.
Application requirements: Portfolio, recommendations and essay.

Amount of award:	$1,000
Number of awards:	1
Number of applicants:	4
Application deadline:	March 31
Total amount awarded:	$1,000

Edith H. Henderson Scholarship

Type of award: Scholarship.
Intended use: For undergraduate study.
Basis for selection: Major/career interest in landscape architecture.
Application requirements: Essay.
Additional information: Applicant must be committed to developing practical communication skills in their role as a landscape architect.

Amount of award:	$1,000
Number of awards:	1
Application deadline:	March 31

Contact:
636 Eye Street, NW
Washington, DC 20001
Phone: 202-898-2444
Website: www.asla.org

Edward D. Stone, Jr., and Associates Minority Scholarship

Type of award: Scholarship.
Intended use: For full-time junior, senior study.
Eligibility: Applicant must be of minority background.
Basis for selection: Major/career interest in landscape architecture. Applicant must demonstrate financial need.
Application requirements: Portfolio, recommendations and research proposal. Four to eight 35mm color slides or three to five 8x10 photos of work.

Amount of award:	$1,000
Number of awards:	2
Number of applicants:	6
Application deadline:	March 31
Total amount awarded:	$2,000

Harriett Barnhart Wimmer Scholarship

Type of award: Scholarship.
Intended use: For full-time senior study at accredited 4-year institution.
Eligibility: Applicant must be female.
Basis for selection: Major/career interest in landscape architecture.
Application requirements: Portfolio, recommendations and essay. Photo samples of work.

Amount of award:	$1,000
Number of awards:	1
Number of applicants:	14
Application deadline:	March 31
Total amount awarded:	$1,000

Rain Bird Company Scholarship

Type of award: Scholarship.
Intended use: For full-time junior, senior or post-bachelor's certificate study at accredited 4-year institution.

Basis for selection: Major/career interest in landscape architecture. Applicant must demonstrate financial need.
Application requirements: Essay.
Additional information: Fifth year undergraduates also eligible.

Amount of award:	$1,000
Number of awards:	1
Number of applicants:	30
Application deadline:	March 31
Total amount awarded:	$1,000

Raymond E. Page Scholarship

Type of award: Scholarship.
Intended use: For full-time sophomore, junior or senior study at accredited 4-year institution.
Basis for selection: Major/career interest in landscape architecture. Applicant must demonstrate seriousness of purpose and financial need.
Application requirements: Recommendations and essay.

Amount of award:	$1,000
Number of awards:	1
Number of applicants:	47
Application deadline:	March 31
Total amount awarded:	$1,000

Thomas P. Papandrew Scholarship

Type of award: Scholarship, renewable.
Intended use: For full-time undergraduate study.
Eligibility: Applicant must be Alaskan native, American Indian, African American, Mexican American, Hispanic American or Puerto Rican. Applicant must be residing in Arizona.
Basis for selection: Major/career interest in landscape architecture. Applicant must demonstrate high academic achievement.
Application requirements: Recommendations, essay and transcript.
Additional information: Must be an Arizona resident accepted or enrolled at Arizona State University.

Amount of award:	$1,000
Application deadline:	March 31

Contact:
636 Eye Street, NW
Washington, DC 20001
Phone: 202-898-2444
Website: www.asla.org

William J. Locklin Scholarship

Type of award: Scholarship.
Intended use: For full-time freshman, sophomore, junior, senior, master's or doctoral study at accredited 4-year or graduate institution.
Basis for selection: Major/career interest in landscape architecture; interior design.
Application requirements: Recommendations. Proposal; visual samples.
Additional information: Proposal must be on lighting design project, in process or completed, emphasizing 24-hour lighting in landscape designs. Preference given projects designed to see effect, not source.

Amount of award:	$1,000
Number of awards:	1
Number of applicants:	30
Application deadline:	March 31
Total amount awarded:	$1,000

Contact:
Scholarship Coordinator
636 Eye St. NW
Washington, DC 20001-3736
Website: www.asla.org

Lemmermann Foundation

Lemmermann Scholarship

Type of award: Scholarship, renewable.
Intended use: For graduate study outside United States in Rome, Italy.
Basis for selection: Major/career interest in archaeology; architecture; art, art history; literature. Applicant must demonstrate seriousness of purpose.
Application requirements: Recommendations, proof of eligibility and research proposal. Curriculum vitae and photocopy of passport or a birth certificate.
Additional information: For research and preparation of theses concerning Rome and Roman culture. Must have basic knowledge of the Italian language. Other fields of study include classics, music, history, and philosophy. Duration of scholarship varies from two to six months.

Number of awards:	10
Number of applicants:	75
Application deadline:	September 30, March 15
Notification begins:	October 20, April 10

Contact:
Lemmermann Foundation
c/o: Studio Avvocati Romanelli
via Cosseria 5
Rome, Italy 192
Phone: (39-6) 324.30.23.
Website: vivaldi.nexus.it/altri/lemmermann/index.html

Leo Baeck Institute

David Baumgardt Memorial Fellowship

Type of award: Research grant.
Intended use: For doctoral, postgraduate study. Designated institutions: Requires extensive use of the facilities of the Leo Baeck Institute in New York, particularly the David Baumgardt Collection.
Basis for selection: Major/career interest in Jewish studies.
Application requirements: Recommendations, transcript and research proposal. Curriculum vitae.
Additional information: Awards are provided to research projects connected with the writings of Professor David Baumgardt or his scholarly interests, including ethics,

Wissenschaft de Judentums, and the modern intellectual history of German-speaking Jewry.

- **Amount of award:** $3,000
- **Number of awards:** 1
- **Application deadline:** November 1
- **Notification begins:** January 1

Deutscher Akademischer Austausch Dienst Fellowship

Type of award: Research grant.
Intended use: For doctoral, postgraduate study in United States. Designated institutions: Leo Baeck Institute in New York.
Eligibility: Applicant must be U.S. citizen.
Basis for selection: Major/career interest in Jewish studies.
Application requirements: Recommendations, transcript, proof of eligibility and research proposal. Curriculum vitae.
Additional information: Research project must fall within the field of study served by the Leo Baeck Institute, i.e. the social, communal and intellectual history of German-speaking Jewry.

- **Amount of award:** $2,000
- **Number of awards:** 2
- **Application deadline:** November 1
- **Notification begins:** January 1

Deutscher Akademischer Austausch Dienst Fellowship/Germany

Type of award: Research grant.
Intended use: For doctoral, postgraduate study outside United States. Designated institutions: Research must be done in libraries, archives or research intitutions in the Federal Republic of Germany.
Eligibility: Applicant must be U.S. citizen.
Basis for selection: Major/career interest in Jewish studies.
Application requirements: Recommendations, transcript, proof of eligibility and research proposal. Curriculum vitae.
Additional information: Research must be in the field of study served by the Leo Baeck Institute, i.e. the social, communal and intellectual history of German-speaking Jewry. Monthly stipend of DM 1,700 plus one-time travel amount of DM 1,000. One six-month or two three-month fellowships available.

- **Application deadline:** November 1
- **Notification begins:** January 1

Fritz Halbers Fellowship

Type of award: Research grant.
Intended use: For doctoral, postgraduate study.
Basis for selection: Major/career interest in Jewish studies.
Application requirements: Recommendations, proof of eligibility and research proposal. Curriculum Vitae.
Additional information: For projects connected with the culture and history of German-speaking Jewry.

- **Amount of award:** $3,000
- **Application deadline:** November 1
- **Notification begins:** January 1

Contact:
Leo Baeck Institute
129 East 73 Street
New York, NY 10021-3585
Phone: 212-744-6400

Leopold Schepp Foundation

Leopold Schepp Scholarship

Type of award: Scholarship.
Intended use: For full-time sophomore, junior, senior or graduate study at accredited 4-year or graduate institution in United States.
Eligibility: Applicant must be U.S. citizen or permanent resident.
Basis for selection: Applicant must demonstrate depth of character, financial need and high academic achievement.
Application requirements: Recommendations and research proposal.
Additional information: Age limits for first time applicants: 30 for undergraduates, 40 for graduates. High school students not eligible. The foundation limits the number of grants for graduate study in medical, law and business schools. Write the foundation for further details.

- **Amount of award:** $500-$7,500

Contact:
Leopold Schepp Foundation
551 Fifth Ave., Suite 3000
New York, NY 10176-2597

Library of Congress

AT&T Hispanic Division Fellowship

Type of award: Research grant.
Intended use: For junior, senior or graduate study.
Basis for selection: Major/career interest in library science.
Application requirements: Interview, recommendations and transcript. Cover letter indicating subject area of interest. Application for Federal Employment or resume.
Additional information: Stipend is $1,200 per month. Room and board not covered. Knowledge of Spanish required. Applications by women, minorities, and people with disabilities encouraged. Latin American studies also funded.

- **Number of awards:** 1
- **Application deadline:** April 15
- **Notification begins:** May 11

Contact:
Library of Congress
Hispanic Division
Washington, DC 20540-4580
Phone: 202-707-5400
Website: lcweb.loc.gov/rr/hispanic

Lighthouse, Inc.

Adult Undergraduate Incentive Award

Type of award: Scholarship.
Intended use: For full-time undergraduate study in New York,

New Jersey, Pennsylvania, Connecticut, Massachusetts, Maine, New Hampshire, Rhode Island, Vermont.
Eligibility: Applicant must be adult returning student. Must be visually impaired. Applicant must be U.S. citizen residing in Connecticut or Massachusetts or Maine or New Hampshire or Rhode Island or Vermont or New Jersey or New York or Pennsylvania.
Basis for selection: Applicant must demonstrate high academic achievement.
Application requirements: Recommendations, essay, transcript and proof of eligibility. Documentation of legal blindness from State Commission for the Blind. Recommendations required: one personal, one academic. Personal essay should be at least 500 words. Transcript must be official.
Additional information: This award is for adults in any year of undergraduate study.

Amount of award:	$5,000
Number of awards:	1
Application deadline:	March 31
Notification begins:	April 1
Total amount awarded:	$5,000

Contact:
The Lighthouse
Career Incentive Awards Program
111 East 59 Street
New York, NY 10022

College-Bound Incentive Award

Type of award: Scholarship.
Intended use: For full-time freshman study at accredited 2-year or 4-year institution in New York, New Jersey, Pennsylvania, Connecticut, Massachusetts, Maine, Vermont, New Hampshire, Rhode Island.
Eligibility: Applicant must be high school senior. Must be visually impaired. Applicant must be U.S. citizen residing in Connecticut or Massachusetts or Maine or New Hampshire or Rhode Island or Vermont or New Jersey or New York or Pennsylvania.
Basis for selection: Applicant must demonstrate high academic achievement.
Application requirements: Recommendations, essay, transcript and proof of eligibility. Documentation of legal blindness from State Commission for the Blind. Recommendations required: one personal, one academic. Personal essay should be at least 500 words. Transcript must be official. Letter of acceptance to college.

Amount of award:	$5,000
Number of awards:	1
Application deadline:	March 31
Notification begins:	April 1
Total amount awarded:	$5,000

Contact:
The Lighthouse Women's Committee
Career Incentive Awards Program
111 East 59 Street
New York, NY 10022

Lighthouse Graduate Incentive Award

Type of award: Scholarship.
Intended use: For full-time graduate study. Designated institutions: Must attend an institution in New York, New Jersey, Pennsylvania, or any one of the New England States.
Eligibility: Applicant must be visually impaired. Applicant must be U.S. citizen residing in Connecticut or Massachusetts or Maine or New Hampshire or Rhode Island or Vermont or New Jersey or New York or Pennsylvania.
Basis for selection: Applicant must demonstrate high academic achievement.
Application requirements: Recommendations, essay, transcript and proof of eligibility. Documentation of legal blindness from State Commission for the Blind. Recommendations required: one personal, one academic. Personal essay should be at least 500 words. Transcript must be official.
Additional information: Students may apply anytime prior to or during graduate study.

Amount of award:	$5,000
Number of awards:	1
Application deadline:	March 31
Notification begins:	April 1
Total amount awarded:	$5,000

Contact:
The Lighthouse Women's Committee
Career Incentive Awards Program
111 East 59 Street
New York, NY 10022

Lighthouse Undergraduate Incentive Award

Type of award: Scholarship.
Intended use: For full-time undergraduate study at postsecondary institution in New Jersey, New York, Pennsylvania, Connecticut, Massachusetts, Maine, New Hampshire, Rhode Island, Vermont.
Eligibility: Applicant must be visually impaired. Applicant must be U.S. citizen residing in Connecticut or Massachusetts or Maine or New Hampshire or Rhode Island or Vermont or New Jersey or New York or Pennsylvania.
Basis for selection: Applicant must demonstrate high academic achievement.
Application requirements: Recommendations, essay, transcript and proof of eligibility. Documentation of legal blindness from State Commission for the Blind. Recommendations required: one personal, one academic. Personal essay should be at least 500 words. Transcript must be official.

Amount of award:	$5,000
Number of awards:	1
Application deadline:	March 31
Notification begins:	April 1
Total amount awarded:	$5,000

Contact:
The Lighthouse
Career Incentive Awards Program
111 East 59 Street
New York, NY 10022
Phone: 212-821-9200

Lincoln Center for the Performing Arts, Inc.

Lincoln Center for the Performing Arts Internships in Arts Administration

Type of award: Internship.
Intended use: For graduate study.
Basis for selection: Major/career interest in arts management.
Application requirements: Interview and recommendations.
Additional information: Program features high-level management projects and significant interaction with Lincoln Center's senior staff.

Amount of award:	$6,000
Number of awards:	2
Application deadline:	January 8
Notification begins:	April 7
Total amount awarded:	$12,000

Contact:
Lincoln Center for the Performing Arts, Inc.
70 Lincoln Center Plaza
New York, NY 10023-6583
Website: www.lincolncenter.org

Lisle Fellowship, Inc.

Marion Wright Edelman Scholarship

Type of award: Scholarship.
Intended use: For undergraduate, graduate or postgraduate study.
Eligibility: Applicant must be Foreign nationals residing in the U.S. may apply.
Basis for selection: Applicant must demonstrate depth of character, seriousness of purpose, service orientation and high academic achievement.
Application requirements: Interview, recommendations, essay and transcript.
Additional information: Two- to six-week program that broadens global awareness and appreciation of cultures through programs which bring together persons of diverse religious, sexual, political and racial backgrounds. The scholarship is designated for persons of racial or cultural diversity. Recipient should plan to attend the Lisle Fellowship annual meeting.

Amount of award:	$1,000
Number of awards:	1
Application deadline:	April 1
Total amount awarded:	$1,000

Contact:
Lisle Fellowship, Inc.
Dr. Mark Kinney
433 West Sterns Road
Temperance, MI 48182-9568
Phone: 3138477126
Website: www.lisle.utoledo.edu

Los Angeles Actuarial Club

Actuarial Club Scholarship

Type of award: Scholarship, renewable.
Intended use: For full-time sophomore, junior study at accredited 2-year or 4-year institution in United States.
Basis for selection: Major/career interest in computer and information sciences; mathematics; economics. Applicant must demonstrate seriousness of purpose and high academic achievement.
Application requirements: Interview, recommendations, essay, transcript and proof of eligibility.
Additional information: Minimum GPA of 3.0. Must be attending school in one of the following counties: Los Angeles, Orange, Ventura, Santa Barbara, Riverside, and San Bernadino counties.

Amount of award:	$1,000
Number of awards:	1
Number of applicants:	2
Application deadline:	April 1
Notification begins:	June 1
Total amount awarded:	$1,000

Contact:
Los Angeles Actuarial Club
Attn: Ms. Robin Fichtelberg
Transamerica Life Companies, P.O. Box 2101
Los Angeles, CA 90051-0101

Los Angeles Times

Los Angeles Times Editorial Internships

Type of award: Internship.
Intended use: For junior, senior, master's or doctoral study.
Basis for selection: Major/career interest in journalism.
Application requirements: Interview, portfolio and essay.
Additional information: Intern applicants should have experience as a campus daily and/or a professional daily newspaper, preferably one with a circulation of at least 150,000.

Application deadline:	June 1, October 1

Contact:
Internship Coordinator
Times Mirror Square
Los Angeles, CA 90053
Phone: 213-237-7123

Maine Community Foundation

CMP Scholarships Fund

Type of award: Scholarship.
Intended use: For freshman study at accredited vocational, 2-year or 4-year institution in United States.

Eligibility: Applicant must be high school senior. Applicant must be U.S. citizen or permanent resident.
Basis for selection: Applicant must demonstrate financial need and high academic achievement.
Application requirements: Transcript. Student/Parent must be employed by Central Maine Power.
Additional information: Open to Dependents of Central Maine Power employees, or its subsidiaries, who are high school seniors graduating from a Maine high school. Applications are available from the foundation, Central Maine Power Regional Offices, or by writing Central Maine Power. Governmental and Regulatory Services Dept. 83 Edison Dr. Augusta, Maine 04336.

Amount of award:	$1,000-$5,000
Number of awards:	5
Number of applicants:	33
Application deadline:	May 1

Contact:
Maine Community Foundation
83 Edison Dr.
Augusta, ME 04336

Downeast Feline Fund

Type of award: Scholarship.
Intended use: For first professional study at accredited graduate institution in United States.
Eligibility: Applicant must be U.S. citizen or permanent resident.
Basis for selection: Major/career interest in veterinary medicine. Applicant must demonstrate financial need and high academic achievement.
Application requirements: Transcript.
Additional information: Supports Maine students in their third or fourth year of veterinary school. Must be studying at a New England area institution. Award amount varies. No deadline. Contact the foundation for details.
Contact:
Maine Community Foundation
83 Edison Dr.
Augusta, ME 04336

Gary Merrill Memorial Scholarship Program

Type of award: Scholarship.
Intended use: For sophomore, junior or senior study at accredited 4-year institution in United States. Designated institutions: Maine institutions.
Eligibility: Applicant must be U.S. citizen or permanent resident residing in Maine.
Basis for selection: Major/career interest in political science/government.
Application requirements: Transcript.

Amount of award:	$500-$1,500
Number of awards:	1
Number of applicants:	9
Application deadline:	May 1

Contact:
Maine Community Foundation
83 Edison Dr.
Augusta, ME 04336

Maine Vietnam VeteransÖ Scholarship Fund/ Lest We Forget POW/MIA/KIA Scholarship Fund

Type of award: Scholarship.
Intended use: For undergraduate study at accredited postsecondary institution in United States.
Eligibility: Applicant must be U.S. citizen or permanent resident. Applicant must be veteran, descendant of veteran, child of veteran, deceased veteran or POW/MIA.
Basis for selection: Applicant must demonstrate financial need.
Application requirements: $3 application fee. Transcript and proof of eligibility.
Additional information: Priority is given to Maine veterans of the United States Armed Services who served in the Vietnam Theater and their descendants. If there are no eligible applicants from the first priority category, second priority is children of other Maine veterans of the United States Armed Services. Applications are available from high school guidance offices and the foundation.

Amount of award:	$700-$1,000
Number of awards:	3
Number of applicants:	220
Application deadline:	May 1

Contact:
Maine Community Foundation
83 Edison Dr.
Augusta, ME 04336

R.V. Gadabout Gaddis Charitable Fund

Type of award: Scholarship.
Intended use: For junior, senior study at accredited 4-year institution in United States.
Eligibility: Applicant must be U.S. citizen or permanent resident residing in Maine.
Basis for selection: Major/career interest in English; English literature.
Additional information: Supports Maine Students for the study of outdoor/nature writing. Award amount varies, contact the foundation for details.

Amount of award:	$1,000
Number of awards:	2
Application deadline:	April 1
Total amount awarded:	$2,000

Contact:
Maine Community Foundation
83 Edison Dr.
Augusta, ME 04436

Senator George J. Mitchell Scholarship Fund

Type of award: Scholarship.
Intended use: For full-time freshman study at accredited 4-year institution in United States.
Eligibility: Applicant must be U.S. citizen or permanent resident residing in Maine.
Basis for selection: Applicant must demonstrate service orientation, financial need and high academic achievement.
Application requirements: Transcript.
Additional information: Graduates of a Maine high school

(or legal residents of Maine attending high school outside Maine) planning to attend or be attending an accredited four-year baccalaureate college or university in Maine. Nontraditional students and students who eared their high school diplomas through GED or Job Corps Programs are eligible for consideration.

- Amount of award: $2,500
- Number of awards: 20
- Number of applicants: 268
- Application deadline: April 26

Contact:
Maine Community Foundation
83 Edison Dr.
Augusta, ME ME 04336

Maine Council of Nurse Managers

OMNE/Nursing Leaders of Maine Undergraduate Scholarship

Type of award: Scholarship.
Intended use: For undergraduate study.
Eligibility: Applicant must be U.S. citizen residing in Maine.
Basis for selection: Major/career interest in health-related professions. Applicant must demonstrate seriousness of purpose and service orientation.
Application requirements: Recommendations, transcript and proof of eligibility.
Additional information: Nursing school student. State applicant must attend college in Maine.

- Amount of award: $250-$500
- Number of awards: 2
- Number of applicants: 12
- Application deadline: May 1
- Total amount awarded: $500

Contact:
Redington Fairview General Hospital
P.O. Box 468
Skowhegan, ME 04976

Maine Education Services

Maine Educational Authority Supplemental Loan

Type of award: Loan.
Intended use: For full-time or half-time undergraduate or graduate study at accredited vocational, 2-year, 4-year or graduate institution in United States. Designated institutions: May also be used at Canadian institutions.
Eligibility: Applicant must be residing in Maine.
Application requirements: Proof of eligibility. Income information/credit analysis.
Additional information: Loans available to Maine residents for school of their choice. Out-of-state students attending Maine schools also eligible. May borrow full cost of education minus other financial aid.

- Amount of award: $2,000-$27,000
- Number of awards: 605
- Number of applicants: 871
- Total amount awarded: $53,330,000

Contact:
Maine Education Services
P.O. Box 549
Augusta, ME 04332

Maine Lesbian/Gay Political Alliance

Maine Lesbian/Gay Political Alliance Scholarship

Type of award: Scholarship.
Intended use: For undergraduate study.
Eligibility: Applicant must be high school senior. Applicant must be U.S. citizen or permanent resident residing in Maine.
Basis for selection: Applicant must demonstrate depth of character and service orientation.
Application requirements: Recommendations, essay and proof of eligibility.
Additional information: Open to any senior regardless of sexual orientation. Applicant must have proof of College Acceptance.

- Amount of award: $500-$750
- Number of awards: 2
- Number of applicants: 50
- Application deadline: April 15
- Notification begins: May 15
- Total amount awarded: $1,500

Contact:
Scholship Coordinator
P.O. Box 232
Hallowell, ME 04347

Maine Metal Products Association

Maine Metal Products Scholarship

Type of award: Scholarship, renewable.
Intended use: For undergraduate study in Maine. Designated institutions: Maine Technical College System institutions.
Eligibility: Applicant must be U.S. citizen residing in Maine.
Basis for selection: Major/career interest in engineering. Applicant must demonstrate depth of character, leadership, seriousness of purpose, service orientation and high academic achievement.
Application requirements: Interview, recommendations, essay, transcript, proof of eligibility and nomination by Maine Metal Products Association member.

Amount of award:	$500-$1,500
Number of awards:	9
Number of applicants:	35
Application deadline:	May 1
Notification begins:	June 7
Total amount awarded:	$4,500

Contact:
Maine Metal Products Association
190 Riverside Street
Portland, ME 04103
Phone: 207-871-1032

Maine Osteopathic Association

Andrew M. Longley, Jr., D.O. Scholarship

Type of award: Scholarship.
Intended use: For first professional study. Designated institutions: University of New England College of Osteopathic Medicine.
Eligibility: Applicant must be residing in Maine.
Basis for selection: Major/career interest in medicine, osteopathic. Applicant must demonstrate financial need.
Application requirements: Essay and proof of eligibility.
Additional information: Applicants residing in Maine for sole purpose of postsecondary education not eligible for scholarship. Must show interest in practicing primary osteopathic care in Maine.

Amount of award:	$1,000
Number of awards:	1
Application deadline:	May 1
Total amount awarded:	$1,000

Beale Family Memorial Scholarship

Type of award: Scholarship.
Intended use: For first professional study.
Eligibility: Applicant must be residing in Maine.
Basis for selection: Major/career interest in medicine, osteopathic. Applicant must demonstrate financial need.
Application requirements: Essay and proof of eligibility.
Additional information: Must be second, third or fourth year student and provide proof of enrollment at approved osteopathic college. Residence in Maine for sole purpose of postsecondary education not acceptable for scholarship. Must show interest in practicing in Maine or teaching in osteopathic college in New England. Preference to Bangor area applicants.

Amount of award:	$1,000
Number of awards:	1
Application deadline:	May 1
Total amount awarded:	$1,000

Maine Osteopathic Memorial Scholarship

Type of award: Scholarship.
Intended use: For first professional study.
Eligibility: Applicant must be residing in Maine.
Basis for selection: Major/career interest in medicine, osteopathic. Applicant must demonstrate financial need.
Application requirements: Essay and proof of eligibility.
Additional information: Must be second, third or fourth year student and provide proof of enrollment at approved osteopathic college. Those residing in Maine for sole purpose of postsecondary education not eligible.

Amount of award:	$1,000
Number of awards:	1
Application deadline:	May 1
Total amount awarded:	$1,000

Maine Osteopathic Scholarship

Type of award: Scholarship.
Intended use: For first professional study.
Eligibility: Applicant must be residing in Maine.
Basis for selection: Major/career interest in medicine, osteopathic. Applicant must demonstrate financial need.
Application requirements: Essay and proof of eligibility.
Additional information: Must have resided in Maine three years or more. Those residing in Maine for sole purpose of postsecondary education not eligible.

Amount of award:	$1,000
Number of awards:	1
Application deadline:	May 1
Total amount awarded:	$1,000

Contact:
Maine Osteopathic Association
RR2, Box 1920
Manchester, ME 04351

Maine Recreation and Parks

Maine Recreation and Parks Association Scholarship

Type of award: Scholarship, renewable.
Intended use: For full-time undergraduate or graduate study.
Eligibility: Applicant must be U.S. citizen or permanent resident.
Basis for selection: Applicant must demonstrate depth of character, leadership, patriotism, service orientation and high academic achievement.
Application requirements: Interview, recommendations and transcript. State applicant must attend college in Maine.
Additional information: Students who intend to study physical education or wildlife management are not eligible.

Amount of award:	$750
Number of awards:	3
Number of applicants:	28
Application deadline:	April 1
Total amount awarded:	$2,000

Contact:
Maine Recreation and Parks Association
270 Main St.
Gorham, ME 04038

Maine Restaurant Association

Russ Casey Scholarship

Type of award: Scholarship.
Intended use: For undergraduate or graduate study in United States.
Eligibility: Applicant must be U.S. citizen or permanent resident.
Basis for selection: Major/career interest in hotel/restaurant management; food production/management/services. Applicant must demonstrate high academic achievement.
Application requirements: Recommendations. Student must be entering an institution located in Maine.

Amount of award:	$1,000
Number of awards:	3
Number of applicants:	20
Application deadline:	February 21
Total amount awarded:	$3,000

Contact:
Maine Restaurant Association
P.O. Box 5060
5 Wade St.
Augusta, ME 04332

Maine Society of Professional Engineers

Maine Society of Professional Engineers Scholarship Program

Type of award: Scholarship.
Intended use: For freshman study at 2-year or 4-year institution in United States.
Eligibility: Applicant must be high school senior.
Basis for selection: Major/career interest in engineering.
Application requirements: Recommendations, essay and transcript. Must submit SAT or ACT scores.
Additional information: Applicants must intend to earn a degree in engineering and to enter the practice of engineering after graduation.

Amount of award:	$1,250
Number of awards:	2
Number of applicants:	44
Application deadline:	March 15
Notification begins:	May 30
Total amount awarded:	$2,500

Contact:
Kenneth W. Campbell, Secretary
142 Mills Rd.
Kennebunkport, ME 04046

Maine State Society Foundation

MSSF Scholarship Program

Type of award: Scholarship.
Intended use: For undergraduate study at accredited 4-year institution.
Eligibility: Applicant must be U.S. citizen or permanent resident residing in Maine.
Basis for selection: Applicant must demonstrate depth of character, leadership, patriotism, seriousness of purpose, service orientation and high academic achievement.
Application requirements: Recommendations, essay and transcript. Must attend school in Maine.
Additional information: Undergraduates may apply only after completing first semester.

Amount of award:	$1,000
Number of awards:	2
Number of applicants:	35
Application deadline:	April 1
Total amount awarded:	$2,000

Contact:
Maine State Society Foundation
544 E. Nelson Ave.
Alexandria, VA 22301

Maine Technical College System

Maine PIC/MH/VR/TDC Technical Scholarship

Type of award: Scholarship, renewable.
Intended use: For undergraduate study. Designated institutions: Maine Technical College System institutions.
Eligibility: Applicant must be residing in Maine.
Basis for selection: Applicant must demonstrate financial need.
Application requirements: Proof of eligibility.
Additional information: Applicants must have a recognized mental or physical disability. Award supplements cost of additional services required for disabled student to successfully complete educational goal. Funds disbursed by one of four co-sponsoring agencies: the 16-county job training system, Training and Development Corporation, Vocational Rehabilitation, and Bureau of Mental Health.

Number of awards:	46
Number of applicants:	46
Total amount awarded:	$20,000

Contact:
Maine Technical College System
Division of State and Federal Programs
323 State Street
Augusta, ME 43330
Website: www.famemaine.com

Makovsky & Company Inc.

Public Relations Internship

Type of award: Internship.
Intended use: For junior, senior study.
Eligibility: Applicant must be U.S. citizen.
Basis for selection: Applicant must demonstrate high academic achievement.
Application requirements: Interview.
Additional information: Two to three full-time or part-time positions offered in both the spring and summer. $750/month stipend. Provides opportunity to receive hands-on experience in conducting all facets of public relations under the direction of the forums staff.
    Amount of award: $2,200
    Application deadline: January 15
Contact:
Makovsky & Company, Inc.
575 Lexington Ave.
New York, NY 10022
Website: www.makovsky.com

Manhattan Theatre Club

Manhattan Theatre Club Professional Internship

Type of award: Internship.
Intended use: For undergraduate, graduate, postgraduate or non-degree study.
Eligibility: Applicant must be Must have proper Visas.
Basis for selection: Applicant must demonstrate seriousness of purpose.
Application requirements: Interview and recommendations.
Additional information: Applications accepted year-round. Internships in theater arts and productions are full-time and pay $110 a week. There are four sessions available. Contact office for application and additional information.
    Amount of award: $1,320-$3,960
Contact:
Intern Coordinator
311 W. 43rd St., 8th Floor
New York, NY 10036
Website: www.mtc-nyc.org

Manomet Center for Conservation Sciences

Kathleen S. Anderson Award

Type of award: Research grant.
Intended use: For junior, senior or graduate study in or outside United States. Designated institutions: Institution in the Western Hemisphere.
Basis for selection: Major/career interest in ornithology. Applicant must demonstrate leadership and seriousness of purpose.
Application requirements: Recommendations and research proposal.
Additional information: Either one $1000 award or two $500 awards are given.
    Amount of award: $500-$1,000
    Number of awards: 2
    Number of applicants: 20
    Application deadline: December 1
    Notification begins: February 1
    Total amount awarded: $1,000
Contact:
Manomet Center For Conservation Sciences
Kathleen Anderson Award
81 Stage Point Road, P.O. Box 1770
Manomet, MA 02345
Phone: 508-224-6521

March of Dimes Birth Defects Foundation

Basil O'Connor Starter Scholar Research Award

Type of award: Research grant.
Intended use: For graduate or postgraduate study.
Basis for selection: Major/career interest in science, general. Applicant must demonstrate depth of character, leadership, seriousness of purpose and service orientation.
Application requirements: Recommendations, research proposal and nomination by Deans, Chairmen of Departments or Director of Institutions.
Additional information: Each nomination must be accompanied by the candidate's curriculum vitae (NIH Format). Contact The March of Dimes directly for in-depth and specific instructions.
    Amount of award: $50,000
    Application deadline: February 27

March of Dimes Request for Research Proposals

Type of award: Research grant, renewable.
Intended use: For full-time master's, doctoral, postgraduate or non-degree study at 4-year or graduate institution. Designated institutions: Hospital and Research Centers.
Basis for selection: Major/career interest in science, general. Applicant must demonstrate depth of character, leadership, seriousness of purpose and service orientation.
Application requirements: Research proposal.
Additional information: Applicants must be scientists with faculty appointments or the equivalent. Proposals dealing with infertility will not be accepted. Application requirements are specific. Contact The March of Dime directly for further information.
    Application deadline: March 31
    Notification begins: April 30
Contact:
March of Dimes Birth Defects Foundation
1275 Mamaroneck Ave.
White Plains, NY 10605

Maria Mitchell Observatory

Maria Mitchell Internships for Astronomical Research

Type of award: Internship.
Intended use: For undergraduate study.
Eligibility: Applicant must be Only one position open to non-U.S. citizen residing in Maine.
Basis for selection: Major/career interest in astronomy; physics; mathematics; computer and information sciences. Applicant must demonstrate high academic achievement.
Application requirements: Interview, recommendations and transcript.
Additional information: Positions provide an opportunity for students to conduct independent research and an opportunity to participate in a common project. Students expected to develop their ability to communicate with the public. Furnished housing is available at no cost. Partial travel funds available. Program starts June 1st and continues through August 31st, with a $1,100 a month stipend.

Amount of award:	$3,300
Number of awards:	10
Number of applicants:	150
Application deadline:	February 15
Notification begins:	March 15

Contact:
Maria Mitchell Observatory
3 Vestal St.
Nantucket, MA 02554
Website: www.mmo.org

Marine Corps Scholarship Foundation

Marine Corps Scholarship

Type of award: Scholarship, renewable.
Intended use: For undergraduate study at accredited vocational, 2-year or 4-year institution in United States.
Eligibility: Applicant must be high school senior. Applicant must be U.S. citizen. Applicant must be child of active service person or veteran who served in the Marines. Parent must be Marine, Marine reservist, or honorably discharged from the Marine Corps.
Basis for selection: Applicant must demonstrate financial need.
Application requirements: Transcript and proof of eligibility. First page of family tax statement.
Additional information: Gross family income must not exceed $43,000. Must be a dependant of marine or former marine with an honorable record.

Amount of award:	$500-$2,500
Number of awards:	950
Number of applicants:	1,300
Application deadline:	April 1
Total amount awarded:	$1,130,000

Contact:
Marine Corps Scholarship Foundation
P.O. Box 3008
Princeton, NJ 08543-3008

Mashantucket Pequot Tribal Nation

Public Policy Internship Program

Type of award: Internship.
Intended use: For junior, senior or graduate study.
Eligibility: Applicant must be Alaskan native or American Indian. Applicant must be U.S. citizen.
Basis for selection: Major/career interest in law; public administration/service. Applicant must demonstrate leadership.
Application requirements: Recommendations, essay and transcript.
Additional information: Twelve-week internship. Minimum GPA 2.5. Must be computer literate. Deadlines for application are: Winter term-November 1, Spring term-February 1, Summer term-April 1, and Fall term-July 1. Interns aid with congressional votes analysis, tribal political action forums, political fundraising, issues tracking, and legislative analysis.

Amount of award:	$6,000
Number of awards:	5
Number of applicants:	25
Total amount awarded:	$30,000

Contact:
Chris McNeil, Jr.
1299 Pennsylvania Ave., NW, Suite 1250
Washington, DC 20004

Massachusetts Biotechnology Council, Inc.

Massachusetts Biotechnology Scholars Program

Type of award: Scholarship.
Intended use: For freshman study at accredited 4-year institution.
Eligibility: Applicant must be high school senior. Applicant must be residing in Massachusetts.
Basis for selection: Major/career interest in science, general.
Additional information: Information is sent to counselors at participatory high schools in Massachusetts in Andover, Bedford, Beverly, Boston, Cambridge, Canton, Charlestown, Hopkinton, Framingham, Lexington, Marlborough, Medfield, Needham, Newton, Northboro, Norwell, Norwood, Randolph, Shrewsbury, Walpole, Waltham, Wellesley, West Bridgewater, Woburn and Worcester. See your guidance counselor for further information.

Amount of award:	$1,000

McDonald's

McDonald's RMHC-Hispanic American Commitment to Educational Resources H.S. Program

Type of award: Scholarship.
Intended use: For full-time undergraduate study.
Eligibility: Applicant must be Mexican American, Hispanic American or Puerto Rican. Applicant must be high school senior. Applicant must be U.S. citizen or permanent resident.
Basis for selection: Applicant must demonstrate financial need and high academic achievement.
Application requirements: Recommendations, essay and transcript.
    Amount of award: $1,000-$2,500
    Number of awards: 495
    Application deadline: October 15, February 1
    Notification begins: May 1, August 1
    Total amount awarded: $616,000
Contact:
McDonald's
One Sansome Street
Suite 1000
San Francisco, CA 94104

McDonnell Douglas Aerospace

McDonnell Douglas Internship Program

Type of award: Internship.
Intended use: For junior, senior, master's or doctoral study in United States.
Eligibility: Applicant must be U.S. citizen.
Basis for selection: Major/career interest in aerospace.
Application requirements: Recommendations, transcript and proof of eligibility.
Additional information: Deadlines and compensation varies; contact sponsor for more information.
Contact:
Internship Coordinator
PO Box 516
Mailcode 2761740
St. Louis, MO 63166-0516

MCI Cutting Edge Scholars

MCI Cutting Edge Scholars Internet Project Awards

Type of award: Scholarship.
Intended use: For undergraduate study.
Eligibility: Applicant must be high school senior. Applicant must be U.S. citizen or permanent resident residing in Michigan or Tennessee or Washington.
Basis for selection: Competition in Science project. Must submit a project proposal that demonstrates how internet technology can make a difference in people's lives and communities. Will be judged on originality, practicality, and impact in the "real world.".
Additional information: Must have a GPA of 2.0 or higher, and a proven attendance record in high school. Ten awards will be granted in each of the participating states. In each participating state, nine of the awards will be for individuals, the tenth for a team of up to five people who will divide the award amount evenly.
    Amount of award: $5,000
    Number of awards: 30
    Application deadline: March 31
Contact:
MCI Cutting Edge Scholars
1875 Connecticut Ave. NW
Suite 800
Washington, DC 20009
Website: www.mci.com/cuttingedge

McNeil Consumer Products

Tylenol Scholarship Fund

Type of award: Scholarship.
Intended use: For undergraduate study at accredited vocational, 2-year or 4-year institution in United States.
Basis for selection: Applicant must demonstrate leadership, service orientation and high academic achievement.
Application requirements: Essay and transcript. statement of education and career goals.
Additional information: Number of extracurricular activities and length of commitment important. Awards and honors count for approximately 40 percent of decision, statement of education and career goals for 10 percent, and academic record for 50 percent. Application materials available at participating Tylenol retail stores between late September and mid-October. No application requests after November 1.
    Amount of award: $1,000-$10,000
    Application deadline: November 15
    Notification begins: February 15
    Total amount awarded: $600,000
Contact:
Tylenol Scholarship Fund
P.O. Box 8656
Clinton, IA 52736-8656

Medical Library Association

Medical Library Association Scholarship

Type of award: Scholarship.
Intended use: For graduate study.

Eligibility: Applicant must be U.S. citizen, permanent resident or Canadian citizen.
Basis for selection: Major/career interest in library science. Applicant must demonstrate seriousness of purpose and high academic achievement.
Application requirements: Recommendations and transcript. Statement of career goals.

Amount of award:	$2,000
Number of awards:	2
Number of applicants:	20
Application deadline:	December 1
Notification begins:	March 1
Total amount awarded:	$2,000

Medical Library Doctoral Scholarship

Type of award: Research grant.
Intended use: For doctoral study.
Eligibility: Applicant must be U.S. citizen, permanent resident or Canadian citizen.
Basis for selection: Major/career interest in library science. Applicant must demonstrate high academic achievement.
Application requirements: Recommendations, transcript and research proposal. Detailed budget and statement of career goals.
Additional information: Award is for those studying librarianship in health sciences.

Amount of award:	$2,000
Number of awards:	1
Number of applicants:	20
Application deadline:	December 1
Notification begins:	March 1
Total amount awarded:	$2,000

Medical Library Rittenhouse Award

Type of award: Scholarship.
Intended use: For graduate or non-degree study.
Basis for selection: Competition in Research paper. Thoroughness and relevance of bibliographic research; importance of topic or quality of argument or quality of experimental design; originality of argument or methodological rigor; impact on the field of health sciences; clarity, structure, organization, and style of work. Major/career interest in library science.
Application requirements: Essay. Must provide 6 copies of essay.

Amount of award:	$500
Number of awards:	1
Number of applicants:	20
Application deadline:	October 1
Notification begins:	February 1
Total amount awarded:	$500

Medical Library Scholarship for Minority Students

Type of award: Scholarship.
Intended use: For master's study.
Eligibility: Applicant must be American Indian, Asian American, African American, Mexican American, Hispanic American or Puerto Rican. Applicant must be U.S. citizen or permanent resident.
Basis for selection: Major/career interest in library science. Applicant must demonstrate high academic achievement.
Application requirements: Recommendations and transcript. statement of career goals.

Amount of award:	$2,000
Number of awards:	1
Number of applicants:	20
Application deadline:	December 1
Notification begins:	March 1
Total amount awarded:	$2,000

Contact:
Coordinator
Medical Library Association
6 North Michigan Avenue, Suite 300
Chicago, IL 60602
Phone: 312-419-9094
Website: www.mlanet.org

Menominee Indian Tribe of Wisconsin

Menominee Higher Education Scholarship

Type of award: Scholarship, renewable.
Intended use: For full-time undergraduate study at accredited 2-year or 4-year institution in United States.
Eligibility: Applicant must be American Indian. Must be at least one-quarter degree, tribally enrolled Menominee.
Basis for selection: Applicant must demonstrate financial need.
Additional information: Applications and deadline dates available through college financial aid office.

Amount of award:	$100-$2,200
Number of awards:	97
Number of applicants:	97

Contact:
Menominee Indian Tribe of Wisconsin
P.O. Box 910
Keshena, WI 54135
Phone: 7157995118

Metropolitan Museum of Art

Andrew W. Mellon Conservation Fellowship

Type of award: Internship, renewable.
Intended use: For master's, doctoral study in New York.
Designated institutions: Metropolitan Museum of Art.
Basis for selection: Major/career interest in art, art history. Applicant must demonstrate high academic achievement.
Application requirements: Recommendations and essay.
Additional information: Fellowships for training in conservation of paintings, objects, musical instruments, arms and armor, paper, textiles, costumes, and Asian art.

Amount of award: $20,000
Application deadline: February 1
Contact:
Internship Coordinator
Fellowships in Conservation
1000 Fifth Avenue
New York, NY 10028-0198
Website: www.metmuseum.org

Andrew W. Mellon Fellowship

Type of award: Research grant.
Intended use: For doctoral, postgraduate study in New York. Designated institutions: Metropolitan Museum of Art.
Basis for selection: Major/career interest in art, art history. Applicant must demonstrate high academic achievement.
Application requirements: Recommendations, essay and transcript.
Additional information: Applicant should have received doctorate or completed substantial work toward it. Short-term fellowships available for senior scholars. Applicant should be pursuing research related to museum's collections. Distinguished visiting scholars from United States and abroad who can serve as teachers and advisers are eligible.
Amount of award: $20,000
Application deadline: November 7
Notification begins: February 22
Contact:
Fellowship Program
1000 Fifth Avenue
New York, NY 10028-0198
Website: www.metmuseum.org

Chester Dale Fellowship

Type of award: Research grant.
Intended use: For doctoral, non-degree study in New York. Designated institutions: Metropolitan Museum of Art.
Eligibility: Applicant must be U.S. citizen.
Basis for selection: Major/career interest in art, art history. Applicant must demonstrate high academic achievement.
Application requirements: Recommendations, essay, transcript and research proposal.
Additional information: Preference given to American citizens under age of 40. Grants for research related to fine arts of the western world and cover periods of three months to one year.
Amount of award: $18,000-$26,000
Application deadline: November 7
Notification begins: February 22
Contact:
Research Grant Committee
Fellowship Program
1000 Fifth Avenue
New York, NY 10028-0198
Website: www.metmuseum.org

Classical Art Fellowship

Type of award: Research grant.
Intended use: For doctoral study at graduate institution in New York. Designated institutions: Metropolitan Museum of Art.
Basis for selection: Major/career interest in art, art history. Applicant must demonstrate high academic achievement.
Application requirements: Recommendations, essay, transcript and research proposal.
Additional information: Thesis outline, dealing with Greek or Roman art, must have been accepted by doctoral adviser. Preference given to applicant judged to profit most from utilizing resources of museum's Department of Greek and Roman Art.
Amount of award: $18,000-$26,000
Number of awards: 1
Application deadline: November 7
Contact:
Metropolitan Museum of Art
Fellowship Program
1000 Fifth Avenue
New York, NY 10028-0198
Website: www.metmuseum.org

Cloisters Summer Internship for College Students

Type of award: Internship.
Intended use: For undergraduate study. Designated institutions: Metropolitan Museum of Art: The Cloisters.
Basis for selection: Major/career interest in art, art history.
Application requirements: Recommendations, essay and transcript. Resume, list of art history related coures taken,.
Additional information: Program especially intended for freshmen and sophomores. Nine-week, full-time internship from June to August. Five-day, 35-hour work week.
Amount of award: $2,250
Application deadline: February 7
Notification begins: April 15
Contact:
Fellowship Program
1000 Fifth Avenue
New York, NY 10028-0198
Website: www.metmuseum.org

Jane and Morgan Whitney Fellowship

Type of award: Research grant, renewable.
Intended use: For master's, doctoral study.
Basis for selection: Major/career interest in art, art history. Applicant must demonstrate high academic achievement.
Application requirements: Recommendations, essay and transcript.
Additional information: Awards for study, work or research in fields related to museum's collections. Preference to students in decorative arts who are under 40 years of age.
Amount of award: $21,000
Application deadline: November 7
Notification begins: February 22
Contact:
Fellowship Program
1000 Fifth Avenue
New York, NY 10028-0198
Website: www.metmuseum.org

Metropolitan Museum of Art Graduate Lecturing Internship

Type of award: Internship.
Intended use: For master's, doctoral study at graduate

institution in New York. Designated institutions: Metropolitan Museum of Art.
Basis for selection: Major/career interest in art, art history; arts, general; archaeology.
Application requirements: Recommendations, essay and transcript.
Additional information: Nine-month internship for advanced graduate students from November through July. Lecturers give one hour-long talk per week.

Amount of award:	$3,000
Number of awards:	4
Application deadline:	January 10

Contact:
Fellowship Program
1000 Fifth Avenue
New York, NY 10028-0198
Website: www.metmuseum.org

Metropolitan Museum of Art Nine-Month Art Internship

Type of award: Internship.
Intended use: For non-degree study in New York. Designated institutions: Metropolitan Museum of Art.
Eligibility: Applicant must be of minority background.
Basis for selection: Major/career interest in art, art history. Applicant must demonstrate high academic achievement.
Application requirements: Interview, recommendations, essay and transcript.
Additional information: Internship from September through June. Full-time, five-day, 35-hour week. Eligible applicant is graduating college senior or recent graduate or graduate student in art history, arts administration, conservation, art education.

Amount of award:	$12,000
Number of awards:	3
Application deadline:	February 2
Total amount awarded:	$36,000

Contact:
Metropolitan Museum of Art
Linda Komaroff, Fellowship Program
1000 Fifth Avenue
New York, NY 10028-0198
Website: www.metmuseum.org

Metropolitan Museum of Art Six-Month Art Internship

Type of award: Internship.
Intended use: For senior, master's or doctoral study in New York. Designated institutions: Metropolitan Museum of Art.
Eligibility: Applicant must be of minority background.
Basis for selection: Major/career interest in art, art history. Applicant must demonstrate high academic achievement.
Application requirements: Interview, recommendations, essay and transcript.
Additional information: Internships for graduating college seniors, recent graduates or graduate students in art history or related fields with minority backgrounds. Full-time, five-day, 35-hour week. Program runs from June to December.

Amount of award:	$8,000
Number of awards:	2
Application deadline:	January 31
Total amount awarded:	$16,000

Contact:
Linda Komaroff, Fellowship Program
1000 Fifth Avenue
New York, NY 10028-0198
Website: www.metmuseum.org

Metropolitan Museum of Art Summer Art Internships for College Students

Type of award: Internship.
Intended use: For junior, senior study in New York. Designated institutions: Metropolitan Museum of Art.
Basis for selection: Major/career interest in art, art history; arts, general.
Application requirements: Recommendations, essay and transcript. Resume, list of art-history related courses.
Additional information: Ten week internship at museum from June through August. Also open to recent graduates who have not started graduate school. Full-time, five-day, 35-hour week.

| Amount of award: | $2,500 |
| Application deadline: | January 16 |

Contact:
Fellowship Program
1000 Fifth Avenue
New York, NY 10028-0198
Website: www.metmuseum.org

Metropolitan Museum of Art Summer Art Internships for Graduate Students

Type of award: Internship.
Intended use: For master's, doctoral study in New York. Designated institutions: Metropolitan Museum of Art.
Basis for selection: Major/career interest in art, art history.
Application requirements: Recommendations, essay and transcript. resume, listing of art-history related courses taken.
Additional information: Ten week internship from June to August. Full time, five-day, 35-hour week. Must have completed one year of graduate work in art history or allied field.

| Amount of award: | $2,750 |
| Application deadline: | January 23 |

Contact:
Metropolitan Museum of Art
Fellowship Program
1000 Fifth Avenue
New York, NY 10028-0198
Website: www.metmuseum.org

Polaire Weissman Fund Fellowship

Type of award: Research grant.
Intended use: For doctoral study at graduate institution in New York. Designated institutions: Metropolitan Museum of Art.
Basis for selection: Major/career interest in art, art history. Applicant must demonstrate high academic achievement.

Application requirements: Recommendations, essay and transcript.
Additional information: Generally awarded for nine-month term in alternate years. Preference to applicants interested in pursuing career related to field of costume.
- **Amount of award:** $20,000
- **Application deadline:** November 7

Contact:
Metropolitan Museum of Art
Fellowship Program
1000 Fifth Avenue
New York, NY 10028-0198
Website: www.metmuseum.org

S. Clawson Mills Scholarship

Type of award: Scholarship, renewable.
Intended use: For postgraduate study at graduate institution in New York. Designated institutions: Metropolitan Museum of Art.
Basis for selection: Major/career interest in art, art history. Applicant must demonstrate high academic achievement.
Application requirements: Recommendations, essay and transcript.
Additional information: Award intended for mature scholars of demonstrated ability for study or research in fine arts.
- **Amount of award:** $18,000-$26,000
- **Application deadline:** November 7

Contact:
Fellowship Program
1000 Fifth Avenue
New York, NY 10028-0198
Website: www.metmuseum.org

Starr Asian Painting Conservation Fellowship

Type of award: Internship.
Intended use: For full-time non-degree study in New York. Designated institutions: Metropolitan Museum of Art.
Basis for selection: Major/career interest in art, art history.
Application requirements: Interview, recommendations and essay.
Additional information: Fellowship for training in conservation and mounting of Asian paintings. Before formal application, send brief letter stating particular interest.
- **Application deadline:** January 5

Contact:
Sondra M. Castile, Asian Art Conservation
1000 Fifth Avenue
New York, NY 10028-0198
Website: www.metmuseum.org

Theodore Rousseau Fellowship

Type of award: Internship.
Intended use: For master's, doctoral study.
Basis for selection: Major/career interest in art, art history. Applicant must demonstrate high academic achievement.
Application requirements: Recommendations, essay and transcript.
Additional information: Twelve-month training fellowship for study in Europe awarded to students planning to enter museums as curators of paintings. Must have completed at least one year graduate study in art history. Short-term fellowships available.
- **Amount of award:** $21,000
- **Application deadline:** November 7
- **Notification begins:** February 22

Contact:
Fellowship Program
1000 Fifth Avenue
New York, NY 10028-0198
Website: www.metmuseum.org

Mexican American Grocers Association Foundation

Mexican American Grocers Association Scholarship

Type of award: Scholarship.
Intended use: For full-time sophomore, junior or senior study at accredited 4-year institution in United States.
Eligibility: Applicant must be Mexican American, Hispanic American or Puerto Rican.
Basis for selection: Major/career interest in business; business, management and administration. Applicant must demonstrate financial need and high academic achievement.
Application requirements: Interview, essay and transcript.
Additional information: Must have at least a 2.5 GPA. Application must be postmarked between June 1 and July 31. Send SASE for further information.
- **Amount of award:** $500-$1,500
- **Application deadline:** July 31
- **Notification begins:** August 15

Contact:
Mexican-American Grocers Association Foundation
Attn: Jackie Solis
405 North San Fernando Road
Los Angeles, CA 90031
Phone: 213-227-1565

Mexican American Legal Defense and Educational Fund

Mexican American Law School Scholarship

Type of award: Scholarship.
Intended use: For first professional study at accredited graduate institution in United States.
Eligibility: Applicant must be Mexican American, Hispanic American or Puerto Rican.
Basis for selection: Major/career interest in law. Applicant must demonstrate depth of character, leadership, service orientation, financial need and high academic achievement.
Application requirements: Recommendations, essay,

transcript and proof of eligibility. CSS Profile, resume, photocopy of LSDAS Report with LSAT scores, statement about past activities and importance to the Latino community.
Additional information: Must serve Latino community. Application requests should be made in January.

Amount of award:	$1,000-$2,000
Number of awards:	20
Number of applicants:	100
Application deadline:	June 30
Total amount awarded:	$21,000

Contact:
Mexican American Legal Defense and Educational Fund
Scholarship Program
634 South Spring Street
11th Floor
Los Angeles, CA 90014-1974

Univision-Mexican American Legal Defense Fund Scholarship

Type of award: Scholarship.
Intended use: For graduate study at accredited graduate institution in United States.
Eligibility: Applicant must be Mexican American, Hispanic American or Puerto Rican.
Basis for selection: Major/career interest in communications; journalism; law. Applicant must demonstrate depth of character, leadership, seriousness of purpose, service orientation, financial need and high academic achievement.
Application requirements: Recommendations, essay and transcript. Resume, statement about past activities and importance to the Latino community.
Additional information: Must serve Latino community. Awards for students in communications fields and law students studying communications or entertainment law. Strong writing and interpersonal skills important; bilingual Spanish-English ability encouraged.

Amount of award:	$1,000
Application deadline:	June 30

Contact:
Mexican American Legal Defense and Educational Fund
Communications Scholarship Program
634 South Spring Street
11th Floor
Los Angeles, CA 90014-1974

Michigan Educational Opportunity Fund, Inc.

Michigan Hispanic High School Graduate Award

Type of award: Scholarship.
Intended use: For undergraduate study.
Eligibility: Applicant must be Mexican American, Hispanic American or Puerto Rican. Applicant must be residing in Michigan.

Amount of award:	$1,000-$1,500
Number of awards:	10
Number of applicants:	100
Total amount awarded:	$10,000

Contact:
Michigan Educational Opportunity Fund, Inc.
P.O. Box 19152
Lansing, MI 48901

Michigan Higher Education Student Loan Authority

Michigan Alternative Student Loan (MI-LOAN) Program

Type of award: Loan.
Intended use: For undergraduate or graduate study at 2-year, 4-year or graduate institution in Michigan. Designated institutions: Degree granting colleges & universities located in Michigan.
Eligibility: Applicant must be U.S. citizen or permanent resident residing in Michigan.
Basis for selection: Applicant must demonstrate financial need.
Application requirements: Proof of eligibility.
Additional information: MI-LOAN applications must be received by the servicer no later than the last day of the loan period. Must meet credit standards or provide creditworthy co-signer(s) and not be in default on any federal or state loans. Out-of-state students attending Michigan institutions eligible. Borrowers must reapply annually. MI-LOAN applications must be received by the servicer no later than the last day of the loan period.

Amount of award:	$500-$10,000
Number of applicants:	3,240
Total amount awarded:	$10,212,772

Contact:
Michigan Higher Education Student Loan Authority
Michigan Alternative Student Loan Program
P.O. Box 30051
Lansing, MI 48909
Phone: 888-643-7521

Michigan Society of Professional Engineers

Michigan Society of Professional Engineers

Type of award: Scholarship, renewable.
Intended use: For undergraduate study at accredited 4-year institution in United States. Designated institutions: Must be an ABET accredited school in Michigan.
Eligibility: Applicant must be U.S. citizen residing in Michigan.
Basis for selection: Major/career interest in engineering. Applicant must demonstrate leadership.

Application requirements: Recommendations and transcript. State applicant must attend college in Michigan.
Additional information: Some scholarships for graduating high school seniors and some for undergraduates. Contact information for specific eligibility requirements.
    Amount of award: $1,000-$3,000
Contact:
Scholarship Coordinator
215 N. Walnut St.
P.O. box 15276
Lansing, MI 48901
Website: www.voyager.net.mspe

Microscopy Society of America

Microscopy Presidential Student Award

Type of award: Scholarship.
Intended use: For undergraduate or graduate study.
Basis for selection: Competition in Research paper. Awards are based on the quality of the paper submitted for presentation at the Annual Microscopy and Microanalysis meeting. Applicant must be the first author of the submitted paper. Major/career interest in science, general; biology; chemistry; natural sciences. Applicant must demonstrate seriousness of purpose.
Additional information: Award consists of free registration for the Microscopy and Microanalysis meeting, copy of the proceedings, reimbursement for round trip travel and student housing.
    Amount of award: $775
    Number of awards: 10
    Number of applicants: 24
    Application deadline: February 1
    Notification begins: November 1
    Total amount awarded: $6,000

Microscopy Undergraduate Research Scholarship

Type of award: Research grant.
Intended use: For full-time junior, senior study.
Basis for selection: Major/career interest in science, general; biology; chemistry; natural sciences. Applicant must demonstrate seriousness of purpose.
Application requirements: Recommendations and research proposal. Letter of supervisor of lab where work will be done, curriculum vitae, and explanation letter from scientists or university faculty indicating how budget will be expended.
Additional information: Award for students interested in pursuing microscopy as a career or major research tool.

    Amount of award: $2,500
    Number of awards: 5
    Number of applicants: 10
    Application deadline: December 31
    Notification begins: April 1
    Total amount awarded: $12,500
Contact:
Microscopy Society of America
435 North Michigan Avenue
Suite 1717
Chicago, IL 60611
Phone: 800-538-3672
Website: www.msa.microscopy.com

Miller Brewing Company

Miller Brewing Internship

Type of award: Internship.
Intended use: For graduate study.
Eligibility: Applicant must be residing in Wisconsin.
Basis for selection: Major/career interest in marketing; business; business, international. Applicant must demonstrate high academic achievement.
Application requirements: Interview, recommendations and transcript.
Additional information: Application deadlines are rolling. 10-12 week program at $850 a week. Free housing and free car rental included. Miller hires approximately 50% of interns for full time work. Open to graduate students 21 and over. Occasional world-wide travel required.
    Amount of award: $8,500-$10,200
    Number of applicants: 240
Contact:
Miller Brewing Company
3989 W. Highland Blvd.
Milwaukee, WI 53201

Minnesota GLBT Educational Fund

Minnesota GLBT Educational Fund

Type of award: Scholarship.
Intended use: For undergraduate study.
Eligibility: Gay, Lesbian, Bisexual or Transgender.
Basis for selection: Applicant must demonstrate seriousness of purpose.
Application requirements: Recommendations, essay, transcript and proof of eligibility.
Additional information: Persons must be involved in LGBT community activities and programs. State applicant must attend college in Minnesota.
    Amount of award: $500-$1,000
    Application deadline: April 1
Contact:
Minnesota GLBT Educational Fund
P.O. Box 7275
Minneapolis, MN 55407-0275

Miss America Organization

Miss America Education Scholarship for Post-Graduate Studies

Type of award: Scholarship.
Intended use: For full-time or half-time postgraduate study at accredited graduate institution in or outside United States.
Eligibility: Applicant must be female. Applicant must be U.S. citizen.
Basis for selection: Major/career interest in education. Applicant must demonstrate financial need.
Application requirements: Essay.
Additional information: Applicant must have participated in the Miss America competition at least once.

Amount of award:	$10,000
Application deadline:	June 30
Notification begins:	August 1

Miss America Pageant

Type of award: Scholarship.
Intended use: For undergraduate, graduate or non-degree study at accredited postsecondary institution.
Eligibility: Applicant must be single, female. Applicant must be U.S. citizen.
Basis for selection: Competition in Poise/talent/fitness. Contestants compete in categories of interview, talent, evening wear, and swimsuit. Applicant must demonstrate depth of character, leadership, patriotism, seriousness of purpose and service orientation.
Application requirements: Interview and proof of eligibility.
Additional information: Contestants compete first at local, then state levels. State finalists go to National Competition. Semifinalists in National Competition receive $8,000; each national contestant receives $3,000. Miss America receives $40,000 in scholarship monies. Deadlines for local pageants vary.

Amount of award:	$100-$40,000
Number of awards:	1,000
Total amount awarded:	$32,000,000

Contact:
Miss America Organization
P.O. Box 119
Atlantic City, NJ 08404
Phone: 6093457571
Fax: 6093452716

Missouri League for Nursing

Missouri Nursing Scholarship

Type of award: Scholarship, renewable.
Intended use: For full-time sophomore, junior, senior, master's or non-degree study in Missouri.
Eligibility: Applicant must be U.S. citizen residing in Missouri.
Basis for selection: Major/career interest in nursing. Applicant must demonstrate financial need and high academic achievement.
Additional information: Open only to residents of Missouri. Applications can be obtained from institutions Dean of School of Nursing.

Amount of award:	$500-$2,000
Number of awards:	7
Number of applicants:	29
Application deadline:	November 1
Notification begins:	December 30
Total amount awarded:	$8,000

Contact:
Missouri League for Nursing
PO Box 104476
Jefferson City, MO 65109

Mobility International USA

Mobility Internship Program

Type of award: Internship.
Intended use: For full-time junior, senior or graduate study at accredited 4-year institution in United States.
Eligibility: People with disabilities encouraged to apply.
Basis for selection: Major/career interest in international relations; public relations. Applicant must demonstrate depth of character, leadership and service orientation.
Application requirements: Interview, recommendations, essay and proof of eligibility. Questionnaire completion, resume.
Additional information: Interest in disability issues recommended. Rolling deadline reimbursement stipends provided for full-time, minimum 6 month internships, based on receipts from living expenses. Internships can begin at any time of year and last 3-6 months. Housing is not provided. Internships located in Eugene, Oregon.

Amount of award:	$750

Contact:
Intern Coordinator
P.O. Box 10767
Eugene, OR 97440
Website: www.miusa.org

Mongolia Society, Inc.

Hangin Memorial Scholarship

Type of award: Scholarship.
Intended use: For graduate study at accredited graduate institution in United States.
Eligibility: Applicant must be of Mongolian heritage. Applicant must be Must be an individual of Mongolian ethnic origins who has permanent residency in Mongolia, the People's Republic of China, or the former Soviet Union.
Application requirements: Proof of eligibility and research proposal.

Amount of award: $2,500
Number of awards: 1
Number of applicants: 19
Application deadline: January 1
Notification begins: May 1
Total amount awarded: $2,500

Contact:
Mongolia Society, Inc.
322 Goodbody Hall
Indiana University
Bloomington, IN 47405-2401

Mooney Aircraft Pilot Association Safety Foundation, Inc.

Al and Art Murray Scholarship

Type of award: Scholarship.
Intended use: For full-time undergraduate or graduate study in United States.
Eligibility: Applicant must be U.S. citizen.
Basis for selection: Major/career interest in aviation. Applicant must demonstrate financial need and high academic achievement.
Application requirements: Recommendations, essay and transcript.

Amount of award: $2,500
Number of awards: 1
Number of applicants: 500
Application deadline: September 1
Notification begins: October 1
Total amount awarded: $2,500

Contact:
MAPA Safety Foundation, Inc.
P.O. Box 460607
San Antonio, TX 78246-0607
Phone: 210-525-8008

Morris Arboretum of the University of Pennsylvania

Aboriculture Internship

Type of award: Internship.
Intended use: For undergraduate or graduate study.
Basis for selection: Major/career interest in botany; agriculture; horticulture; forestry; landscape architecture; ecology. Applicant must demonstrate high academic achievement.
Application requirements: Interview, recommendations and transcript.
Additional information: Interns work 40 hrs/week at an hourly rate. Benefits include health insurance and dental plan. Some internships require travel. Strong interpersonal and writing skills are essential. Tree climbing ability is helpful. Drivers license required.
   Application deadline: February 15

Morris Arboretum Education Internship

Type of award: Internship.
Intended use: For undergraduate or graduate study.
Basis for selection: Major/career interest in education; botany; horticulture; forestry; ecology. Applicant must demonstrate high academic achievement.
Application requirements: Interview, recommendations and transcript.
Additional information: Interns work 40hours/week at an hourly wage. Benefits include insurance and dental plan. Some internships require travel. Strong writing and interpersonal skills are essential.
   Application deadline: February 15

Morris Arboretum Horticulture Internship

Type of award: Internship.
Intended use: For undergraduate or graduate study.
Basis for selection: Major/career interest in horticulture. Applicant must demonstrate high academic achievement.
Application requirements: Interview, recommendations and transcript.
Additional information: Interns work 40 hours/week at an hourly wage. Benefits include health insurance and dental plan. Some internships require travel. A drivers license is required.
   Application deadline: February 15

Pennsylvania Internship

Type of award: Internship.
Intended use: For graduate study.
Basis for selection: Major/career interest in biology; botany. Applicant must demonstrate high academic achievement.
Application requirements: Interview, recommendations and transcript.
Additional information: Provides intern with opportunity to contribute to the preparation of a modern state flora. Interns work 40 hours/week at an hourly wage. Benefits include health insurance and dental plan. Valid drivers license and travel may be required.
   Application deadline: February 15

Plant Propagation Internship

Type of award: Internship.
Intended use: For undergraduate or graduate study.
Basis for selection: Major/career interest in botany; agriculture; horticulture; ecology. Applicant must demonstrate high academic achievement.
Application requirements: Interview, recommendations and transcript.
Additional information: Opportunity to explore the use of tissue culture as a propagation technique. Strong background in woody landscape plants, plant propagation and plant physiology required. Interns work 40 hours/week at an hourly rate. Benefits include health insurance and dental plan. Good writing skills helpful. Travel may be required.
   Application deadline: February 15

Plant Protection Internship

Type of award: Internship.
Intended use: For undergraduate or graduate study.
Basis for selection: Major/career interest in horticulture. Applicant must demonstrate high academic achievement.
Application requirements: Interview, recommendations and transcript.
Additional information: Interns work 40 hours/week at an hourly wage. Course work in entomology, mycology and plant pathology required. Provides opportunity to assist Arboretum's plant pathologist with the Integrated Pest Management (IPM) program which includes monitoring of the living collection and communicating information on pests and diseases to staff. Benefits include health insurance and dental plan. Strong writing skills essential. May require some travel.
   Application deadline: February 15

Urban and Community Forestry Internship

Type of award: Internship.
Intended use: For undergraduate or graduate study.
Basis for selection: Major/career interest in forestry; horticulture; landscape architecture; ecology. Applicant must demonstrate high academic achievement.
Application requirements: Interview, recommendations and transcript.
Additional information: Program combines government, botanic garden and community experience in administration, education and outreach. Interns work with USDA Forest Service and Arboretum staff. Work is full time at 40 hours/week with an hourly wage. Benefits include health insurance and dental plan. Experience in interpretation, graphics or publication is useful. A car and license is required for travel purposes.
   Application deadline: February 15
Contact:
Morris Arboretum of the University of Pennsylvania
9414 Meadowbrook Avenue
Philadelphia, PA 19118
Phone: 2152475777
Website: www.upenn.edu

Mother Jones

Mother Jones Art Internship

Type of award: Internship.
Intended use: For graduate study.
Basis for selection: Major/career interest in arts, general. Applicant must demonstrate high academic achievement.
Application requirements: Interview, recommendations and transcript.
Additional information: Deadlines for fall and spring are rolling, for summer April 1, 1999. Internships run four months and require 35 hours a week with $100 stipend. After 4 months interns are reviewed for fellowship program which lasts 8 months with a $937 a month stipend. Must include samples of work with application. Mac skills valuable.
   Amount of award: $400-$3,500

Mother Jones Editorial Internship

Type of award: Internship.
Intended use: For graduate study.
Basis for selection: Major/career interest in journalism. Applicant must demonstrate high academic achievement.
Application requirements: Interview, recommendations and transcript.
Additional information: Deadlines for fall and spring are rolling, for summer April 1, 1999. For graduate students and graduates who have reporting and/or research experience. Internships run four months and require 35 hours a week with $100 stipend. After 4 months interns are reviewed for fellowship program which lasts 8 months with a $937 a month stipend. Must include writing samples with application. Computer skills essential.
   Amount of award: $400-$3,500

Mother Jones MoJo Wire Internship

Type of award: Internship.
Intended use: For junior, senior or graduate study at 4-year or graduate institution.
Basis for selection: Major/career interest in journalism; arts, general; graphic arts and design; computer and information sciences. Applicant must demonstrate high academic achievement.
Application requirements: Interview, recommendations and transcript.
Additional information: Deadlines for fall and spring is rolling, for summer is April 1, 1999. Must submit writing samples. Internships run four months and require a 35 hour week, with $100 a month stipend. After 4 months, interns are reviewed for fellowship program which lasts 8 months, with a $937 a month stipend. Must include samples of work with application. Computer skills essential.
   Amount of award: $400-$3,500

Mother Jones Publishing Internship

Type of award: Internship.
Intended use: For undergraduate or graduate study at 4-year or graduate institution.
Basis for selection: Major/career interest in advertising; communications; finance/banking. Applicant must demonstrate high academic achievement.
Application requirements: Interview, recommendations and transcript.
Additional information: Deadlines for fall and spring are rolling, for summer April 1, 1999. Internships run four months and require 35 hours a week with $100 stipend. After 4 months interns are reviewed for fellowship program which lasts 8 months with a $937 a month stipend. Computer skills helpful.
   Amount of award: $400-$3,500
Contact:
Mother Jones
731 Market St., Suite 600
San Francisco, CA 94103
Website: www.motherjones.com

Muscular Dystrophy Association

Neuromuscular Disease Research Grant

Type of award: Research grant.
Intended use: For doctoral, first professional or postgraduate study.
Basis for selection: Major/career interest in medical specialties/research.
Application requirements: Research proposal.
Additional information: Must be professional or faculty member at appropriate educational, medical, or research institution and be qualified to conduct and supervise original research program. Must have access to institutional resources necessary to conduct project. Proposals from applicants outside the United States considered for projects of highest Muscular Dystrophy Association priority. Request for grant application due one month before application deadlines.
    Amount of award: $35,000
    Application deadline: January 15, July 15
Contact:
Muscular Dystrophy Association
3300 East Sunrise Drive
Tucson, AZ 85718
Phone: 520-529-2000
Website: www.mdausa.org

Museum of Modern Art

Museum of Modern Art Internship Program

Type of award: Internship.
Intended use: For junior, senior or graduate study.
Basis for selection: Major/career interest in arts management; museum studies/administration; arts, general.
Application requirements: Interview, recommendations, essay and transcript.
Additional information: The deadlines are as follows: Fall-July 2, notification on August 9. Spring-November 20, notification January 15. Summer-January 20, notification April 16. Twelve Month Internship-June 4; notification August 2. The Spring and Fall programs are part-time, unpaid internships, for which the students can get undergraduate credit. The Summer and Twelve Month program, the applicant must be a resident or citizen. Fields of study encompass a very broad spectrum of topics. Contact the coordinator for specific information.
    Amount of award: $2,000
    Number of awards: 90
    Number of applicants: 550
    Total amount awarded: $180,000
Contact:
Museum of Modern Art
11 W. 53rd St.
New York, NY 10019
Website: www.moma.org

Music in the Mountains

Kenneth Davenport National Music Competition

Type of award: Scholarship.
Intended use: For undergraduate, graduate or non-degree study.
Eligibility: Applicant must be U.S. citizen or permanent resident.
Basis for selection: Competition in Music performance/composition.
Application requirements: $35 application fee. Proof of eligibility. Recording or score of original musical composition by applicant.
Additional information: Must be able to provide easily legible orchestral parts upon request and free-of-charge. Composer's name may not appear anywhere on score or recording. Enclose SASE for score to be returned. Prize also includes a performance of composition
    Amount of award: $3,000
    Number of awards: 1
    Application deadline: March 31
    Notification begins: May 1
Contact:
Music in the Mountains
School of Fine and Performing Arts, SUNY New Paltz
75 South Manheim Blvd, Suite 9
New Paltz, NY 12561-2443
Phone: 9142573860

Myasthenia Gravis Foundation

Myasthenia Gravis Foundation Kermit E. Osserman Fellowship

Type of award: Scholarship.
Intended use: For postgraduate study in United States.
Basis for selection: Major/career interest in biology; neurology.
Application requirements: Recommendations, transcript and research proposal.
Additional information: For research pertinent to Myasthenia Gravis or related neuromuscular disorders. Research may be concerned with neuromuscular transmission, immunology, molecular or cell biology.
    Amount of award: $30,000
    Application deadline: October 31
Contact:
222 South Riverside Plaza, Suite 1540
Chicago, IL 60606-9524
Website: www.med.unc.edu/mgfa

Myasthenia Gravis Foundation Nursing Research Fellowship

Type of award: Scholarship.
Intended use: For full-time undergraduate or graduate study at accredited 4-year or graduate institution in United States.
Eligibility: Applicant must be U.S. citizen or permanent resident.
Basis for selection: Major/career interest in nursing.
Application requirements: Recommendations, transcript and research proposal.
Additional information: Deadline varies; contact sponsor for information. For nursing students interested in studying problems encountered by patients with Myasthenia Gravis or related neuromuscular conditions.

Amount of award:	$1,500

Contact:
222 South Riverside Plaza, Suite 1540
Chicago, IL 60606-9524
Website: www.med.unc.edu/mgfa

Viets Premedical/Medical Student Fellowship

Type of award: Research grant.
Intended use: For full-time junior, senior or first professional study at accredited 4-year or graduate institution in United States.
Eligibility: Applicant must be U.S. citizen or permanent resident.
Basis for selection: Major/career interest in medicine (m.d.).
Application requirements: Recommendations, transcript, proof of eligibility and research proposal.
Additional information: Focus of research must be myasthenia gravis or related field.

Amount of award:	$3,000
Number of awards:	4
Number of applicants:	10
Application deadline:	March 15
Total amount awarded:	$12,000

Contact:
Research Grant Committee
222 South Riverside Plaza
Chicago, IL 60606-9524
Phone: 312-258-0522
Website: www.med.unc.edu

NAACP Legal Defense and Education Fund, Inc.

Earl Warren Legal Training Program Scholarship

Type of award: Scholarship, renewable.
Intended use: For full-time first professional study at accredited graduate institution in United States.
Eligibility: Applicant must be African American. Applicant must be U.S. citizen.
Basis for selection: Major/career interest in law. Applicant must demonstrate leadership, seriousness of purpose, service orientation, financial need and high academic achievement.
Application requirements: Recommendations, essay, transcript and proof of eligibility. LSAT scores.
Additional information: Must have a minimum 2.70 GPA or above. Should have demonstrated interest in civil rights and public interest practice, exceptional community service. Effort made to involve recipients in current activities and programs of the Legal Defense Fund. Write after November 15 for application/information.

Amount of award:	$3,000-$4,500
Number of awards:	23
Number of applicants:	350
Application deadline:	April 30
Notification begins:	July 31

Contact:
Earl Warren Legal Training Program
NAACP Legal Defense and Educational Fund, Inc.
99 Hudson Street Suite 1600
New York, NY 10013

Herbert Lehman Scholarship for African American Students

Type of award: Scholarship, renewable.
Intended use: For full-time freshman study at accredited 4-year institution in United States.
Eligibility: Applicant must be African American. Applicant must be high school senior. Applicant must be U.S. citizen.
Basis for selection: Applicant must demonstrate depth of character, leadership, seriousness of purpose, service orientation, financial need and high academic achievement.
Application requirements: Recommendations, essay and transcript. Application.
Additional information: For initial application, must be entering first year of college where African Americans are substantially underrepresented. Application request should be made in writing between November 15 and April 1 with statement of career and educational goals, reason why assistance is needed, and name of college to be attended.

Amount of award:	$1,500
Number of awards:	20
Number of applicants:	2,500
Application deadline:	April 15
Notification begins:	July 1
Total amount awarded:	$147,000

Contact:
The Herbert Lehman Fund
NAACP Legal Defense and Educational Fund, Inc.
99 Hudson Street Suite 1600
New York, NY 10013

NASA Space Grant Connecticut Space Grant Consortium

NASA Space Grant Connecticut Undergraduate Fellowship

Type of award: Research grant, renewable.
Intended use: For full-time undergraduate study at accredited 4-year institution in United States.
Eligibility: Applicant must be U.S. citizen.
Basis for selection: Major/career interest in aerospace; engineering; science, general.
Application requirements: Recommendations, transcript and proof of eligibility. State applicant must attend college in Connecticut.
Additional information: Must be used at a Connecticut Consortium member institution. Member institutions include: University of Connecticut, University of Hartford, University of New Haven, Trinity College. The Consortium actively encourages women, minority, and disabled students to apply. Resume required.

Amount of award:	$2,500
Number of awards:	7
Number of applicants:	20
Application deadline:	October 15, April 1
Total amount awarded:	$17,500

Contact:
NASA Space Grant Connecticut Space Grant Consortium
200 Bloomfield Ave., UT Hall
West Hartford, CT 06117
Website: uhavax.hartford.edu/ctspgrant

Nation Institute

I.F. Stone Award for Student Journalism

Type of award: Scholarship.
Intended use: For sophomore, junior or senior study.
Basis for selection: Competition in Writing/journalism. Entries should exhibit the uniquely independent journalistic tradition of I.F. Stone.
Additional information: Contest is open to all undergraduate students enrolled in a U.S. college. Articles can be submitted by the writer or nominated by editors of student publications or faculty members.

Amount of award:	$1,000
Number of awards:	1
Number of applicants:	100
Application deadline:	June 30
Total amount awarded:	$1,000

Contact:
Nation Institute
72 Fifth Avenue
New York, NY 10011

National Academy for Nuclear Training

Nuclear Training Educational Assistance Program

Type of award: Scholarship, renewable.
Intended use: For full-time sophomore, junior, senior or master's study at accredited 4-year or graduate institution in United States. Designated institutions: Institution must have an accredited engineering program.
Eligibility: Applicant must be U.S. citizen.
Basis for selection: Major/career interest in engineering, chemical; engineering, mechanical; engineering, electrical and electronic; engineering, nuclear. Applicant must demonstrate depth of character, leadership, seriousness of purpose, service orientation and high academic achievement.
Application requirements: Recommendations, essay, transcript, proof of eligibility and nomination by department head of school.
Additional information: Minimum GPA of 3.0. Should be considering a career in the nuclear utility industry.

Amount of award:	$2,500
Number of awards:	170
Number of applicants:	100
Application deadline:	February 1
Notification begins:	April 25
Total amount awarded:	$425,000

Contact:
National Academy for Nuclear Training
700 Galleria Parkway
Atlanta, GA 30339-5957
Phone: 800-828-5489

National Academy of American Scholars

American Scholars National Scholarship

Type of award: Scholarship, renewable.
Intended use: For full-time freshman study at accredited 4-year institution in or outside United States.
Eligibility: Applicant must be U.S. citizen or permanent resident.
Basis for selection: Applicant must demonstrate depth of character and high academic achievement.
Application requirements: $1 application fee. Interview, recommendations, essay, transcript and proof of eligibility.
Additional information: Minimum 2.0 G.P.A. Send SASE along with $1.00 handling fee. Applicant must not be a resident of Pittsburgh, PA or an attendee of the Carnegie Mellon University.

Amount of award:	$1,000-$3,000
Number of awards:	1
Application deadline:	March 1

Contact:
National Academy of American Scholars
c/o Scholarship Committee
1249 South Diamond Bar Boulevard, Number 325
Diamond Bar, CA 91765-4122
Phone: 909-621-6856
Website: www.naas.org

R.C. Easley National Scholarship

Type of award: Scholarship, renewable.
Intended use: For full-time freshman study at accredited 4-year institution in or outside United States.
Eligibility: Applicant must be high school senior. Applicant must be U.S. citizen or permanent resident.
Basis for selection: Applicant must demonstrate high academic achievement.
Application requirements: $2 application fee. Interview, recommendations, essay, transcript and proof of eligibility.
Additional information: Must have minimum GPA of 2.0. Send SASE along with $2.00 handling fee to receive application packet.

Amount of award:	$200-$6,000
Number of awards:	13
Number of applicants:	1,100
Application deadline:	February 1
Total amount awarded:	$25,000

Contact:
National Academy of American Scholars
c/o Scholarship Committee
1249 South Diamond Bar Boulevard, Number 325
Diamond Bar, CA 91765-4122
Phone: 909-621-6856
Website: www.naas.org

National Academy of Education

Spencer Postdoctoral Fellowship Program

Type of award: Research grant, renewable.
Intended use: For postgraduate study.
Basis for selection: Major/career interest in education; humanities/liberal arts; social and behavioral sciences.
Application requirements: Research proposal.
Additional information: Must have received Doctoral degree within six years of application.

Amount of award:	$45,000
Number of awards:	30
Number of applicants:	200
Application deadline:	December 10
Notification begins:	April 30

Contact:
National Academy of Education
Stanford University School of Education
520 Galvez, Ceras 108
Stanford, CA 94305-3084
Phone: 650-725-1003

National Air Transportation Foundation

Pioneers of Flight Scholarship Program

Type of award: Scholarship, renewable.
Intended use: For undergraduate study at accredited 4-year institution.
Basis for selection: Major/career interest in aviation.
Application requirements: Nomination by member of National Air Transportation Association.
Additional information: Contact Citizens' Scholarship Foundation of America for further information and application.

Amount of award:	$2,500
Application deadline:	February 1

Contact:
Citizens' Scholarship Foundation of America
Pioneers of Flight Scholarship Program
P.O. Box 297
St. Peter, MN 56082

National Alliance for Excellence, Inc.

Alliance for Excellence Honored Scholars: Academics

Type of award: Scholarship.
Intended use: For full-time freshman, sophomore, junior, senior, master's, doctoral or first professional study at accredited 2-year, 4-year or graduate institution in or outside United States. Designated institutions: Must be foreign study program with degree-granting U.S. institution, or study for credit at approved degree-granting foreign institution.
Eligibility: Applicant must be U.S. citizen.
Basis for selection: Competition in Performing arts. Applicant must demonstrate high academic achievement.
Application requirements: $5 application fee. Transcript. Entrance exam scores (SAT, GRE, LSAT, GMAT, etc.).
Additional information: Must have 3.7 GPA and combined SAT I score of 1200 or ACT composite of 29. Competitions year-round. National Alliance for Excellence, Inc. sponsors competitions in Academics, Performing Arts, and Visual Arts. Send SASE with application request. Students are also eligible for product awards, including software and computers.

Amount of award:	$1,000-$5,000
Number of awards:	20
Number of applicants:	6,000
Total amount awarded:	$45,000

Contact:
National Alliance for Excellence, Inc.
20 Thomas Avenue
Shrewsbury, NJ 07702
Phone: 732-747-0028
Website: www.excellence.org

Alliance for Excellence Honored Scholars: Performing Arts

Type of award: Scholarship.
Intended use: For full-time undergraduate, master's, doctoral or first professional study at 2-year, 4-year or graduate institution in or outside United States. Designated institutions: Must be foreign study program with degree-granting U.S. institution, or study for credit at approved degree-granting foreign institution.
Eligibility: Applicant must be U.S. citizen.
Basis for selection: Competition in Performing arts. Evaluated by panel of advisers in discipline from schools across U.S.
Application requirements: $5 application fee. VHS videotape (up to 10 minutes long) or other evidence of work in performing arts.
Additional information: Competitions year-round. National Alliance for Excellence, Inc. sponsors competitions in Academics, Visual Arts, and Technological Innovations. Awards granted throughout year. Send SASE with application request.
    Amount of award: $1,000-$5,000
    Number of awards: 20
    Number of applicants: 2,000
Contact:
Award Committee
20 Thomas Avenue
Shrewsbury, NJ 07702
Phone: 732-747-0028
Website: www.excellence.org

Alliance for Excellence Honored Scholars: Technological Innovation

Type of award: Scholarship.
Intended use: For full-time freshman, sophomore, junior, senior, master's, doctoral or first professional study at 2-year, 4-year or graduate institution in or outside United States. Designated institutions: Must be foreign study program with degree-granting U.S. institution, or study for credit at approved degree-granting foreign institution.
Eligibility: Applicant must be U.S. citizen.
Basis for selection: Competition in Engineering/architecture. Evaluated by panel of advisers in discipline from schools across U.S.
Application requirements: $5 application fee.
Additional information: For students who excel in design engineering, robotics, architecture or other area that requires design or invention of new technology. Competitions year-round. National Alliance for Excellence, Inc. sponsors competitions in Academics, Performing Arts, and Visual Arts. Send SASE with application request. AutoCAD and 3D studio software, as well as computers given to winners of competition.
    Amount of award: $1,000-$5,000
    Number of awards: 50
    Number of applicants: 500
Contact:
National Alliance for Excellence, Inc.
20 Thomas Avenue
Shrewsbury, NJ 07702
Phone: 732-747-0028
Website: www.excellence.org

Alliance for Excellence Honored Scholars: Visual Arts

Type of award: Scholarship.
Intended use: For full-time freshman, sophomore, junior, senior, master's, doctoral or first professional study at 2-year, 4-year or graduate institution in or outside United States. Designated institutions: Must be foreign study program with degree-granting U.S. institution, or study for credit at approved degree-granting foreign institution.
Eligibility: Applicant must be U.S. citizen.
Basis for selection: Competition in Visual arts. Evaluated by panel of advisers in discipline from schools across U.S.
Application requirements: $5 application fee. Slides, photos, computer disk, or other evidence of work in visual arts. Letters of recommendation required.
Additional information: Competitions year-round. National Alliance for Excellence, Inc. sponsors competitions in Academics, Performing Arts, and Visual Arts. Send SASE with application request.
    Amount of award: $1,000-$5,000
    Number of awards: 20
    Number of applicants: 400
Contact:
National Alliance for Excellence, Inc.
20 Thomas Avenue
Shrewsbury, NJ 07702
Phone: 732-747-0028
Website: www.excellence.org

National Amateur Baseball Federation

Ronald and Irene McMinn Scholarship

Type of award: Scholarship, renewable.
Intended use: For freshman, sophomore, junior or senior study outside United States. Designated institutions: U.S. or Canadian Institutions.
Basis for selection: Applicant must demonstrate financial need and high academic achievement.
Application requirements: Recommendations and proof of eligibility.
Additional information: Must have participated in a National Amateur Baseball Federation event and be sponsored by National Amateur Baseball Federation-member association. Send SASE for application packet.
    Amount of award: $500
    Number of awards: 10
    Number of applicants: 13
    Total amount awarded: $5,000
Contact:
National Amateur Baseball Federation
P.O. Box 705
Bowie, MD 20718

National Art Gallery

National Art Gallery Diversity Internship Program

Type of award: Internship.
Intended use: For graduate study.
Eligibility: Applicant must be of minority background. Applicant must be U.S. citizen.
Basis for selection: Major/career interest in museum studies; art, art history.
Application requirements: Interview, recommendations, essay, transcript and nomination by Must be sent directly by department chair or your institution director. Resume or curriculum vitae along with two letters of recommendation.
Additional information: The internships offer graduate-level students full-time experience for nine months in one department, and a regular program of activities including field trips and weekly seminars on the collections, operations, programs, and departments of the Gallery. Each internship is full time. Health benefits are included.
   Amount of award: $15,000
   Application deadline: February 2
Contact:
Office of Academic Programs
Education Division
Washington, DC 20565
Phone: 202-842-6257
Fax: 202-842-6935

National Art Gallery Graduate Lecturing Fellowships

Type of award: Scholarship.
Intended use: For graduate study.
Eligibility: Applicant must be U.S. citizen.
Basis for selection: Major/career interest in art, art history.
Application requirements: Interview, recommendations, essay and transcript. Resume and summaries of two proposed topics for 40-minute gallery talks.
Additional information: The fellow will deliver a series of gallery talks on the permanent collection and special exhibitions. Fellowship includes a $3,000 stipend for the academic year, supplemented by a $200 travel allowance. Must have completed one year of course work. The Fellowships are part-time. Candidates must be well versed in European or American art or both.
   Amount of award: $3,200
   Number of awards: 2
   Application deadline: February 2
Contact:
Office of Academic Programs
National Art Gallery
Washington, DC 20565
Fax: 202-842-6935

National Association for Community Leadership

National Association for Community Leadership

Type of award: Internship.
Intended use: For junior, senior study.
Eligibility: Applicant must be residing in Indiana.
Basis for selection: Major/career interest in marketing; communications.
Application requirements: Interview.
Additional information: Provides intern with opportunity to gain valuable experience in Communications and Fundraising.
   Amount of award: $2,400-$4,480
Contact:
National Association for Community Leadership
200 S. Meridian St., Suite 250
Indianapolis, IN 46225
Website: www.communityleadership.org

National Association for Public Interest Law

Law Fellowships for Equal Justice

Type of award: Research grant, renewable.
Intended use: For first professional study.
Basis for selection: Major/career interest in law. Applicant must demonstrate service orientation.
Application requirements: Interview, recommendations and research proposal.
Additional information: Awards for lawyers and 3rd year law students. Must develop one- to two-year project to serve underrepresented people or interests. Preference given to projects designed to impact large numbers of people, which can be replicated in other communities, or create lasting institutions. Award amount varies; up to $32,000.
   Number of awards: 70
   Number of applicants: 385
   Application deadline: October 30
   Notification begins: January 31
   Total amount awarded: $2,000,000
Contact:
National Association for Public Interest Law
1118 22 Street NW
Washington, DC
Phone: 202-466-3686
Website: www.napil.org

National Association for the Deaf

William C. Stokoe Scholarship

Type of award: Research grant.
Intended use: For graduate study.
Basis for selection: Applicant must demonstrate seriousness of purpose, service orientation and high academic achievement.
Application requirements: Recommendations, transcript, proof of eligibility and research proposal.
Additional information: Three letters of recommendation are required. Official transcripts of all official undergraduate/graduate institutions attended. 4 copies of the description of the project proposal must be sent, including 4 copies of any visual aids included in the proposal. The award is paid in two parts. 1/2 upon announcement, 1/2 upon project completion.

Amount of award:	$1,000
Application deadline:	March 15
Notification begins:	June 30
Total amount awarded:	$1,000

Contact:
National Association for the Deaf
814 Thayer Ave.
Silver Springs, MD 20910-4500
Phone: 301-587-1788 or TTY: 301-587-1789
Website: www.nad.org

National Association of Black Journalists

Black Journalists College Scholarship

Type of award: Scholarship.
Intended use: For undergraduate, master's, doctoral, first professional or postgraduate study at accredited 4-year or graduate institution.
Eligibility: Applicant must be African American. Applicant must be U.S. citizen.
Basis for selection: Competition in Writing/journalism. Quality of reporting, writing ability, originality, and potential to succeed in journalism career. Major/career interest in journalism.
Application requirements: Recommendations, essay, transcript and nomination by School adviser, Dean or faculty member familiar with student's work.
Additional information: Deadline is in March; contact sponsor for exact date. Article must be 500-800 words on black journalists in applicant's hometown, school, or campus. Work must be original and unpublished. Must submit three samples of work including articles, photos, broadcast scripts, etc. No audio or videotapes. Award based on quality of reporting, writing ability, originality, and potential to succeed in journalism career. Must become member of National Association of Black Journalists before award is given.

Amount of award:	$2,500
Number of awards:	10
Number of applicants:	75
Notification begins:	June 9
Total amount awarded:	$25,000

Contact:
Scholarship Coordinator
3100 Taliaferro Hall
University of Maryland
College Park, MD 20742
Website: nabj.org

Black Journalists Summer Internship

Type of award: Internship.
Intended use: For sophomore, junior, senior or master's study at accredited 4-year or graduate institution in United States.
Eligibility: Applicant must be African American. Applicant must be U.S. citizen.
Basis for selection: Major/career interest in journalism. Applicant must demonstrate high academic achievement.
Application requirements: Recommendations, essay and transcript. Ten clips, articles, photos, or tapes (audio or video).
Additional information: Internships in print, radio, still photography, and television. Must become member of National Association of Black Journalists before award is given. Minimum 2.5 GPA required. Stipend is $325 per week. Internship lasts ten weeks. Deadline varies; contact sponsor for exact date.

Amount of award:	$3,250
Number of awards:	14
Number of applicants:	50
Notification begins:	January 31
Total amount awarded:	$45,500

Contact:
Internship Coordinator
3100 Taliaferro Hall
University of Maryland
College Park, MD 20742
Website: nabj.org

Black Journalists Sustaining Scholarship

Type of award: Scholarship, renewable.
Intended use: For freshman study at accredited 4-year institution in United States.
Eligibility: Applicant must be African American. Applicant must be high school senior.
Basis for selection: Major/career interest in journalism. Applicant must demonstrate high academic achievement.
Application requirements: Recommendations, essay, transcript and nomination by School adviser. Resume, work samples, autobiography, photo.
Additional information: Deadline is in March; contact sponsor for exact date. Must become member of National Association of Black Journalists before award is given. Minimum 2.5 GPA required.

Amount of award:	$2,500
Number of awards:	2
Number of applicants:	50
Notification begins:	June 9
Total amount awarded:	$5,000

Contact:
Scholarship Coordinator
3100 Taliaferro Hall
University of Maryland
College Park, MD 20742
Website: nabj.org

National Association of Latino Elected and Appointed Officials

Latino Summer Legislative Internship

Type of award: Internship.
Intended use: For half-time undergraduate study.
Eligibility: Applicant must be Mexican American, Hispanic American or Puerto Rican. Applicant must be U.S. citizen or permanent resident residing in New York or Florida or Illinois or New Mexico or Arizona or California or Colorado.
Basis for selection: Major/career interest in public administration/service; political science/government; urban planning; Latin American studies. Applicant must demonstrate depth of character, leadership and service orientation.
Application requirements: Recommendations, essay and transcript.
Additional information: Additional field of study includes public policy. Two applicants are chosen from each qualifying state.

Amount of award:	$1,500
Number of awards:	14
Number of applicants:	145
Application deadline:	February 26
Notification begins:	May 1
Total amount awarded:	$21,000

Contact:
National Association of Latino Elected and Appointed Officials
5800 Southeastern Avenue
Suite 365
Los Angeles, CA 90040
Website: www.naleo.org

National Association of Pediatric Nurses and Practitioners

Pediatric Nurses and Practitioners McNeil Scholarship

Type of award: Scholarship.
Intended use: For master's study.
Basis for selection: Major/career interest in pediatric nurse practitioner. Applicant must demonstrate financial need.
Application requirements: Proof of eligibility.
Additional information: Must be a registered nurse with previous experience in pediatrics. Must have documentation of acceptance into a recognized Pediatric Nurses and Practitioners program. The program must be associated with an academic institute authorized to award a master's degree. No previous formal nurse practitioner education necessary. Must state rationale for seeking a Pediatric Nurses and Practitioners education.

Amount of award:	$2,000
Number of awards:	2
Number of applicants:	23
Application deadline:	May 30, September 30
Notification begins:	July 30, November 30
Total amount awarded:	$4,000

Contact:
National Association of Pediatric Nurses and Practitioners
Attn: Renee Wolf
1101 Kings Highway, North, Suite 206
Cherry Hill, NJ 08034-1912
Phone: 6096671773
Website: www.napnap.org

National Association of Plumbing, Heating, Cooling Contractors

Plumbing, Heating, Cooling Contractors Education Foundation Scholarship

Type of award: Scholarship, renewable.
Intended use: For full-time freshman study at accredited 4-year institution in United States.
Basis for selection: Major/career interest in engineering, construction; construction; business, management and administration; construction. Applicant must demonstrate high academic achievement.
Application requirements: Interview, recommendations and transcript. SAT/ACT scores. Career goals summary.
Additional information: Must have experience and interest in plumbing, heating, and cooling contractors industry. High school seniors and college freshman are eligible to apply. Must maintain "C" average to be eligible for renewal.

Amount of award:	$3,000
Number of awards:	12
Number of applicants:	100
Application deadline:	April 1
Notification begins:	July 31
Total amount awarded:	$36,000

Contact:
National Association of Plumbing, Heating, Cooling Contractors
Educational Foundation Scholarship
P.O. Box 6808
Falls Church, VA 22040
Phone: 703-237-8100
Website: www.naphcc.org

National Association of Purchasing Management

Purchasing Management Doctoral Grant

Type of award: Scholarship.
Intended use: For full-time doctoral study at accredited graduate institution in United States.
Eligibility: Applicant must be Must be enrolled at an accredited U.S. institution.
Basis for selection: Major/career interest in business; marketing; economics. Applicant must demonstrate high academic achievement.
Application requirements: Recommendations, transcript and research proposal.

Amount of award:	$5,000-$10,000
Number of awards:	5
Number of applicants:	20
Application deadline:	January 31
Notification begins:	May 15
Total amount awarded:	$40,000

Contact:
National Association of Purchasing Management
Doctoral Grant Program
P.O. Box 22160
Tempe, AZ 85285-2160
Phone: 602-752-6276
Website: www.napm.org

National Association of Secondary School Principals

Prudential Spirit of Community Award

Type of award: Scholarship.
Intended use: For freshman study.
Eligibility: Applicant must be enrolled in high school.
Basis for selection: Applicant must demonstrate service orientation.
Application requirements: Nomination by principal.
Additional information: Recognizes students from middle level and high schools who have demonstrated exemplary community service. Two honorees are named from each state and receive $1,000 each. Ten national honorees each receive $5,000, gold medallion, and trophy.

Amount of award:	$1,000-$5,000
Number of awards:	104
Application deadline:	October 30
Notification begins:	February 4

Secondary School Principals Leadership Award

Type of award: Scholarship.
Intended use: For full-time freshman study at accredited 2-year institution in United States.
Eligibility: Applicant must be high school senior.
Basis for selection: Major/career interest in education; business; political science/government. Applicant must demonstrate depth of character, leadership, seriousness of purpose and high academic achievement.
Application requirements: Recommendations, essay, transcript, proof of eligibility and nomination by high school principal.

Amount of award:	$1,000
Number of awards:	150
Application deadline:	December 13
Notification begins:	April 30

Secondary School Principals National Honor Society Sylvan Scholars Program

Type of award: Scholarship.
Intended use: For freshman study.
Eligibility: Applicant must be high school junior.
Basis for selection: Applicant must demonstrate service orientation and high academic achievement.
Application requirements: Essay.
Additional information: Current events exam given.

Amount of award:	$1,000-$11,000
Total amount awarded:	$72,000

Contact:
National Association of Secondary School Principals
Department of Student Activities
1904 Association Drive
Reston, VA 20191

National Association of Water Companies (NJ Chapter)

Water Companies (NJ Chapter) Scholarship

Type of award: Scholarship.
Intended use: For sophomore, junior, senior or graduate study

at accredited 2-year, 4-year or graduate institution in New Jersey. Designated institutions: Must be used at institutions in New Jersey.
Eligibility: Applicant must be U.S. citizen residing in New Jersey.
Basis for selection: Major/career interest in hydrology; natural resources/conservation; science, general; engineering, environmental; finance/banking; communications. Applicant must demonstrate depth of character, leadership, seriousness of purpose, service orientation, financial need and high academic achievement.
Application requirements: Recommendations, essay and transcript. Essay must illustrate interest in the investor-owned water utility field.
Additional information: Must have 3.0 GPA. Essay must be on Interest in the Water Industry.

Amount of award:	$2,500
Number of awards:	2
Number of applicants:	20
Application deadline:	April 1, April 1
Notification begins:	June 1, June 1
Total amount awarded:	$5,000

Contact:
National Association of Water Companies (NJ Chapter) Attn: Gail Brady
c/o Elizabethtown Water Company
600 South Avenue
Westfield, NJ 07090
Phone: 908-654-1234

National Association of Women in Construction

Women in Construction: Founders' Scholarship

Type of award: Scholarship.
Intended use: For full-time undergraduate or graduate study at accredited postsecondary institution in United States.
Eligibility: Applicant must be of minority background. Applicant must be U.S. citizen.
Basis for selection: Major/career interest in construction; construction management; engineering, construction. Applicant must demonstrate depth of character, leadership, seriousness of purpose, financial need and high academic achievement.
Application requirements: Interview, recommendations and transcript.
Additional information: Must be involved in construction associations. May also be used at Canadian institutions.

Amount of award:	$500-$2,000
Number of awards:	60
Number of applicants:	500
Application deadline:	February 1
Notification begins:	October 1

Contact:
National Association of Women in Construction
327 South Adams Street
Fort Worth, TX 76104
Phone: 800-552-3506

National Basketball Association

NBA Internship Program

Type of award: Internship.
Intended use: For sophomore, junior or senior study.
Basis for selection: Major/career interest in marketing; public administration/service.
Application requirements: Interview. Resume.
Additional information: Interns work 13-18 weeks in either Spring, Summer or Fall sessions. Stipend of $200/week provided. Provides opportunity to work in broadcasting, consumer products, marketing, or public relations in the New York City offices.

Amount of award:	$2,600-$3,600
Application deadline:	August 15, December 15

Contact:
National Basketball Association
645 Fifth Ave
New York, NY 10022

National Black Police Association

Alphonso Deal Scholarship

Type of award: Scholarship.
Intended use: For freshman study at 2-year institution in United States.
Eligibility: Applicant must be high school senior. Applicant must be U.S. citizen.
Basis for selection: Major/career interest in law; criminal justice/law enforcement. Applicant must demonstrate depth of character, seriousness of purpose, service orientation and high academic achievement.
Application requirements: Recommendations, essay and transcript. Applicant must be accepted by a college or university prior to date of award.
Additional information: Award provides higher education training for the betterment of the criminal justice system.

Amount of award:	$500
Number of awards:	2
Number of applicants:	725
Application deadline:	June 1
Total amount awarded:	$1,000

Contact:
National Black Police Association Scholarship Award
3251 Mount Pleasant Street, NW
Washington, DC 20010-2103
Phone: 202-986-2070
Fax: 202-986-0410

National Center for Construction Education and Research

Construction Education and Research Scholarship

Type of award: Scholarship.
Intended use: For full-time sophomore, junior study at accredited 2-year or 4-year institution in United States.
Eligibility: Applicant must be U.S. citizen.
Basis for selection: Major/career interest in construction management. Applicant must demonstrate depth of character, leadership, financial need and high academic achievement.
Application requirements: Recommendations and transcript. Financial information from advisor.
Additional information: Student must be member of Associated Builders and Contractors Student Chapter, if one exists at applicant's institution, and pursue course of study for career in construction management. Open to those pursuing an Associate or Bachelor's degree; must have one year of undergraduate courses in construction management.

Amount of award:	$500-$2,000
Number of awards:	10
Number of applicants:	40
Application deadline:	June 1
Notification begins:	October 1
Total amount awarded:	$10,500

Contact:
National Center for Construction Education and Research
Attn: College Relations Manager
1300 North 17 Street, 8th Floor
Rosslyn, VA 22209

National Collegiate Athletic Association

NCAA Byers Scholarship

Type of award: Scholarship.
Intended use: For senior study.
Basis for selection: Applicant must demonstrate depth of character, leadership and high academic achievement.
Application requirements: Nomination by institutional representative.
Additional information: Awarded to one male and one female student-athlete. Applications available in the fall. Must have minimum GPA of 3.5.

Amount of award:	$12,500
Number of awards:	2
Application deadline:	January 15
Total amount awarded:	$25,000

Contact:
National Collegiate Athletic Association
Stanley Johnson, Dir Professional Devel.
6201 College Boulevard
Overland Park, KS 66211-2422

NCAA Degree Completion Award

Type of award: Scholarship.
Intended use: For senior study. Designated institutions: Colleges in Division I of the NCAA.
Basis for selection: Applicant must demonstrate depth of character, leadership, service orientation and financial need.
Application requirements: Recommendations and proof of eligibility.
Additional information: Must have received athletics-related grant-in-aid at National Collegiate Athletic Association Division I institution. Must be entering at least sixth year after initial collegiate enrollment. Must have less than 30 hours to finish degree. Application materials are also available at Director of Athletics office on member school campuses.

Number of awards:	100
Number of applicants:	250
Application deadline:	October 1, May 1
Notification begins:	November 5, June 5
Total amount awarded:	$550,000

Contact:
National Collegiate Athletic Association
6201 College Boulevard
Overland Park, KS 66211-2422

NCAA Ethnic Minority Internship

Type of award: Internship.
Intended use: For non-degree study.
Eligibility: Applicant must be of minority background.
Basis for selection: Major/career interest in athletic training; sports/sports administration. Applicant must demonstrate high academic achievement.
Application requirements: Interview, recommendations, essay, transcript and proof of eligibility.
Additional information: For applicants seeking careers in athletic administration. Must have at least completed undergraduate degree. Awarded monthly stipend of $1,400.

Number of applicants:	200
Application deadline:	February 15
Notification begins:	June 5

Contact:
National Collegiate Athletic Association
Stanley Johnson, Dir. Professional Devel.
6201 College Boulevard
Overland Park, KS 66211

NCAA Ethnic Minority Postgraduate Scholarship

Type of award: Scholarship.
Intended use: For full-time postgraduate study at accredited graduate institution in United States. Designated institutions: NCAA member institution.
Eligibility: Applicant must be of minority background. Applicant must be U.S. citizen.
Basis for selection: Major/career interest in athletic training; sports/sports administration.
Application requirements: Recommendations, essay and transcript.
Additional information: For applicants seeking careers in athletic administration. Must have or will have completed undergraduate degree. Application materials also available at Director of Athletics office on member school campuses.

Amount of award:	$6,000
Number of awards:	12
Application deadline:	February 15
Notification begins:	June 5
Total amount awarded:	$72,000

Contact:
National Collegiate Athletic Association
6201 College Boulevard
Overland Park, KS 66211

NCAA Freedom Forum Scholarship

Type of award: Scholarship.
Intended use: For junior study.
Basis for selection: Major/career interest in journalism.
Application requirements: Portfolio, recommendations and transcript.
Additional information: One scholarship awarded in each of eight geographical districts of National Collegiate Athletic Association. Winners invited to special programs, National Collegiate Athletic Association office. Expenses paid by Freedom Forum grant. Applications available in October.

Amount of award:	$3,000
Number of awards:	8
Application deadline:	December 15
Total amount awarded:	$24,000

Contact:
National Collegiate Athletic Association
Stanley Johnson, Dir. Professional Devel.
6201 College Boulevard
Overland Park, KS 66211-2422

NCAA Postgraduate Scholarship

Type of award: Scholarship.
Intended use: For full-time master's study at accredited graduate institution in or outside United States.
Basis for selection: Applicant must demonstrate depth of character, leadership and high academic achievement.
Application requirements: Recommendations, transcript, proof of eligibility and nomination by faculty athletics representative or director of athletics of NCAA member institution.
Additional information: Must be in final year of intercollegiate athletics competition under National Collegiate Athletic Association regulations. Must have performed with distinction as member of varsity team in sport in which nominated. Minimum 3.0 GPA. First deadline is for football, second is for basketball. Deadline for other sports is April 27. Nomination materials are sent automatically to member institutions at the appropriate time for sport involved. Thirty-five scholarships are for football, 32 are for basketball (men and women) and the rest are for other sports.

Amount of award:	$5,000
Number of awards:	174
Application deadline:	October 30, March 9

Contact:
National Collegiate Athletic Association
6201 College Boulevard
Overland Park, KS 66211

NCAA Women's Enhancement Postgraduate Scholarship

Type of award: Scholarship.
Intended use: For full-time postgraduate study at accredited graduate institution in United States. Designated institutions: NCAA member institutions.
Eligibility: Applicant must be female. Applicant must be U.S. citizen.
Basis for selection: Major/career interest in athletic training; sports/sports administration.
Application requirements: Recommendations, essay, transcript and proof of eligibility.
Additional information: Must have or will have completed undergraduate degree. Application materials also available at Director of Athletics office on National Collegiate Athletic Association member school campuses.

Amount of award:	$6,000
Number of awards:	12
Application deadline:	February 15
Notification begins:	June 5
Total amount awarded:	$72,000

Contact:
National Collegiate Athletic Association
Stanley Johnson, Dir. Professional Devel.
6201 College Boulevard
Overland Park, KS 66211

NCAA Women's Internship

Type of award: Internship.
Intended use: For graduate or non-degree study.
Eligibility: Applicant must be female.
Basis for selection: Major/career interest in athletic training; sports/sports administration. Applicant must demonstrate high academic achievement.
Application requirements: Interview and proof of eligibility.
Additional information: For applicants seeking careers in athletic administration. Must have at least completed undergraduate degree. Monthly stipend is $1,400.

Number of applicants:	175
Application deadline:	February 15
Notification begins:	June 5

Contact:
National Collegiate Athletic Association
Director of Professional Development
6201 College Boulevard
Overland Park, KS 66211

National Dairy Shrine

Dairy Management Milking Marketing Scholarship

Type of award: Scholarship, renewable.
Intended use: For full-time sophomore, junior or senior study.
Basis for selection: Major/career interest in dairy; marketing; food production/management/services; food science and technology. Applicant must demonstrate financial need and high academic achievement.

Application requirements: Recommendations and proof of eligibility.
Additional information: Minimum 2.5 GPA.

Amount of award:	$500-$1,000
Number of awards:	7
Number of applicants:	37
Application deadline:	March 15
Notification begins:	June 10
Total amount awarded:	$4,000

Dairy Shrine Graduate Student Scholarship

Type of award: Scholarship, renewable.
Intended use: For full-time junior, senior, master's, doctoral or postgraduate study at 4-year or graduate institution.
Basis for selection: Major/career interest in dairy; food production/management/services; food science and technology. Applicant must demonstrate leadership and high academic achievement.
Application requirements: Recommendations and transcript.
Additional information: Juniors and seniors in college must plan to attend graduate school.

Amount of award:	$3,000
Number of awards:	1
Number of applicants:	3
Application deadline:	March 15
Notification begins:	June 10
Total amount awarded:	$3,000

Dairy Shrine Student Recognition Scholarship

Type of award: Scholarship.
Intended use: For senior study.
Basis for selection: Competition in Writing/journalism. Major/career interest in dairy; food production/management/services; food science and technology. Applicant must demonstrate leadership.
Application requirements: Recommendations and nomination by college or university dairy science departments.
Additional information: Must plan career in dairy cattle. One candidate is chosen per institution. National Dairy Shrine chooses final winner.

Amount of award:	$500-$1,500
Number of awards:	9
Number of applicants:	13
Application deadline:	March 15
Notification begins:	June 10
Total amount awarded:	$6,000

Marshall E. McCullough Undergraduate Scholarship

Type of award: Scholarship.
Intended use: For full-time freshman, sophomore, junior or senior study at accredited 4-year institution in United States.
Eligibility: Applicant must be high school senior. Applicant must be U.S. citizen.
Basis for selection: Major/career interest in animal sciences.
Application requirements: Recommendations and essay.
Additional information: Two awards: one for $1500; one for $2,500. Must major in dairy/animal science; applicants with an additional focus on agricultural journalism/communications preferred.

Amount of award:	$1,500-$2,500
Number of awards:	2
Application deadline:	March 15
Notification begins:	June 1

Contact:
National Dairy Shrine
1224 Alton Darby Creek Road
Columbus, OH 43228

National Environmental Health Association

American Academic Sanitarians Scholarship

Type of award: Scholarship.
Intended use: For full-time junior, senior or graduate study at accredited 4-year or graduate institution.
Basis for selection: Major/career interest in environmental science; public health. Applicant must demonstrate seriousness of purpose, financial need and high academic achievement.
Application requirements: Recommendations, transcript and proof of eligibility.
Additional information: Undergraduates must be enrolled in an Environmental Health Accreditation Council accredited school or National Environmental Health Association Institutional/Educational or sustaining member school. Graduates must be enrolled in a graduate program of studies in environmental health science and/or public health.

Amount of award:	$1,000-$2,000
Number of awards:	4
Number of applicants:	14
Application deadline:	February 1
Notification begins:	June 30
Total amount awarded:	$5,000

Contact:
National Environmental Health Association
NEHA/AAS Scholarship/ Veronica White, NEHA
720 South Colorado Boulevard. South Tower, 970
Denver, CO 80246-1925
Phone: 303-756-9090
Website: www.neha.org

National Federation of the Blind

American Action Fund Scholarship

Type of award: Scholarship, renewable.
Intended use: For full-time undergraduate or graduate study.
Eligibility: Applicant must be visually impaired.
Basis for selection: Applicant must demonstrate service orientation, financial need and high academic achievement.
Application requirements: Recommendations, essay, transcript and proof of eligibility.

Amount of award:	$10,000
Number of awards:	1
Application deadline:	March 31
Notification begins:	June 1
Total amount awarded:	$10,000

Computer Science Scholarship

Type of award: Scholarship, renewable.
Intended use: For full-time undergraduate or graduate study.
Eligibility: Applicant must be visually impaired.
Basis for selection: Major/career interest in computer and information sciences. Applicant must demonstrate service orientation, financial need and high academic achievement.
Application requirements: Recommendations, essay, transcript and proof of eligibility.

Amount of award:	$3,000
Number of awards:	1
Application deadline:	March 31
Notification begins:	June 1
Total amount awarded:	$3,000

E.U. Parker Memorial Scholarship

Type of award: Scholarship, renewable.
Intended use: For full-time undergraduate or graduate study.
Eligibility: Applicant must be visually impaired.
Basis for selection: Applicant must demonstrate service orientation, financial need and high academic achievement.
Application requirements: Recommendations, essay, transcript and proof of eligibility.

Amount of award:	$3,000
Number of awards:	1
Application deadline:	March 31
Notification begins:	June 1
Total amount awarded:	$3,000

Educator of Tomorrow Award

Type of award: Scholarship, renewable.
Intended use: For full-time undergraduate or graduate study.
Eligibility: Applicant must be visually impaired.
Basis for selection: Major/career interest in education, teacher. Applicant must demonstrate service orientation, financial need and high academic achievement.
Application requirements: Recommendations, essay, transcript and proof of eligibility.
Additional information: Applicant must be planning career in elementary, secondary, or postsecondary teaching.

Amount of award:	$3,000
Number of awards:	1
Application deadline:	March 31
Notification begins:	June 1
Total amount awarded:	$3,000

Federation of the Blind Humanities Scholarship

Type of award: Scholarship, renewable.
Intended use: For full-time undergraduate or graduate study.
Eligibility: Applicant must be visually impaired.
Basis for selection: Major/career interest in humanities/liberal arts. Applicant must demonstrate service orientation, financial need and high academic achievement.
Application requirements: Recommendations, essay, transcript and proof of eligibility.

Amount of award:	$3,000
Number of awards:	1
Application deadline:	March 31
Notification begins:	June 1
Total amount awarded:	$3,000

Frank Walton Horn Memorial Scholarship

Type of award: Scholarship, renewable.
Intended use: For full-time undergraduate or graduate study.
Eligibility: Applicant must be visually impaired.
Basis for selection: Major/career interest in architecture; engineering. Applicant must demonstrate service orientation, financial need and high academic achievement.
Application requirements: Recommendations, essay, transcript and proof of eligibility.
Additional information: Preference given to students studying architecture or engineering.

Amount of award:	$3,000
Number of awards:	1
Application deadline:	March 31
Notification begins:	June 1
Total amount awarded:	$3,000

Hermione Grant Calhoun Scholarship

Type of award: Scholarship, renewable.
Intended use: For full-time undergraduate or graduate study.
Eligibility: Applicant must be female. Must be visually impaired.
Basis for selection: Applicant must demonstrate service orientation, financial need and high academic achievement.
Application requirements: Recommendations, essay, transcript and proof of eligibility.

Amount of award:	$3,000
Number of awards:	1
Application deadline:	March 31
Notification begins:	June 1
Total amount awarded:	$3,000

Howard Brown Rickard Scholarship

Type of award: Scholarship, renewable.
Intended use: For full-time undergraduate or graduate study.
Eligibility: Applicant must be visually impaired.
Basis for selection: Major/career interest in medicine (m.d.); law; engineering; natural sciences; architecture. Applicant must demonstrate service orientation, financial need and high academic achievement.
Application requirements: Recommendations, essay, transcript and proof of eligibility.

Amount of award:	$3,000
Number of awards:	1
Application deadline:	March 31
Notification begins:	June 1
Total amount awarded:	$3,000

Kucher-Killian Scholarship

Type of award: Scholarship, renewable.
Intended use: For full-time undergraduate or graduate study.
Eligibility: Applicant must be visually impaired.
Basis for selection: Applicant must demonstrate service orientation, financial need and high academic achievement.
Application requirements: Recommendations, essay, transcript and proof of eligibility.

Amount of award:	$3,000
Number of awards:	1
Application deadline:	March 31
Notification begins:	June 1
Total amount awarded:	$3,000

Melva T. Owen Memorial Scholarship

Type of award: Scholarship, renewable.
Intended use: For full-time undergraduate or graduate study.
Eligibility: Applicant must be visually impaired.
Basis for selection: Applicant must demonstrate service orientation, financial need and high academic achievement.
Application requirements: Recommendations, essay, transcript and proof of eligibility.
Additional information: Field of study should be directed toward attaining financial independence.

Amount of award:	$4,000
Number of awards:	1
Application deadline:	March 31
Notification begins:	June 1
Total amount awarded:	$4,000

Mozelle Willard Gold Scholarship

Type of award: Scholarship, renewable.
Intended use: For full-time undergraduate or graduate study.
Eligibility: Applicant must be visually impaired.
Basis for selection: Applicant must demonstrate service orientation, financial need and high academic achievement.
Application requirements: Recommendations, essay, transcript and proof of eligibility.

Amount of award:	$3,000
Number of awards:	1
Application deadline:	March 31
Notification begins:	June 1
Total amount awarded:	$3,000

National Federation of the Blind Scholarship

Type of award: Scholarship, renewable.
Intended use: For full-time undergraduate or graduate study.
Eligibility: Applicant must be visually impaired.
Basis for selection: Applicant must demonstrate service orientation, financial need and high academic achievement.
Application requirements: Recommendations, essay, transcript and proof of eligibility.

Amount of award:	$3,000-$4,000
Number of awards:	15
Application deadline:	March 31
Notification begins:	June 1
Total amount awarded:	$47,000

Contact:
National Federation of the Blind
805 Fifth Avenue
Grinnell, IA 50112

National Foundation for Advancement in the Arts

Arts Recognition and Talent Search

Type of award: Scholarship.
Intended use: For undergraduate certificate, freshman or non-degree study.
Eligibility: Applicant must be high school senior. Applicant must be U.S. citizen or permanent resident.
Basis for selection: Competition in Performing arts. Panel of expert judges in each discipline evaluates entry packets of all applicants and chooses finalists. Finalists participate in week of live adjudications, consisting of auditions, master and technique classes, workshops, studio exercises, and interviews. Major/career interest in arts, general; performing arts; music.
Application requirements: $25 application fee.
Additional information: International applicants in the field of jazz are permitted to apply. Late applications are accepted until October 1. The fee is $35.00

Amount of award:	$100-$3,000
Number of awards:	39
Number of applicants:	8,000
Application deadline:	June 1
Notification begins:	December 20
Total amount awarded:	$35,900

Contact:
Contest Coordinator
800 Brickell Avenue
Suite 500
Miami, FL 33131

National Foundation for Infectious Diseases

Fellowship in Infectious Diseases

Type of award: Research grant.
Intended use: For doctoral study at accredited 4-year or graduate institution.
Eligibility: Applicant must be U.S. citizen.
Basis for selection: Major/career interest in medical specialties/research. Applicant must demonstrate depth of character, leadership, seriousness of purpose and service orientation.
Application requirements: Recommendations, proof of eligibility and research proposal.
Additional information: The applicant must be a physician

who has completed at least three years of postgraduate medical training, and must be sponsored by a university-affiliated medical center.

Amount of award:	$25,000
Application deadline:	January 12
Notification begins:	April 15

John P. Utz Postdoctoral Fellowship in Medical Mycology

Type of award: Research grant.
Intended use: For doctoral study at accredited 4-year or graduate institution.
Eligibility: Applicant must be U.S. citizen.
Basis for selection: Major/career interest in medical specialties/research. Applicant must demonstrate depth of character, leadership, seriousness of purpose and service orientation.
Application requirements: Recommendations, proof of eligibility and research proposal.
Additional information: The applicant must be a physician who has completed at least three years of postgraduate medical training, and must be sponsored by a university-affilitated medical center.

Amount of award:	$25,000
Application deadline:	January 12
Notification begins:	April 15

Postdoctoral Fellowship in Nosocomial Infection Research and Training

Type of award: Research grant.
Intended use: For undergraduate or graduate study at 4-year or graduate institution. Designated institutions: Hospital or Institution with adequate research facilities.
Eligibility: Applicant must be U.S. citizen.
Basis for selection: Major/career interest in medicine (m.d.); epidemiology.
Application requirements: Proof of eligibility and research proposal.

Amount of award:	$25,000
Application deadline:	January 12
Notification begins:	April 15

Young Investigator Matching Grants

Type of award: Research grant.
Intended use: For full-time undergraduate or graduate study at accredited 4-year or graduate institution in United States in Canada.
Eligibility: Applicant must be U.S. citizen, permanent resident or Canadian citizen.
Basis for selection: Major/career interest in medical specialties/research. Applicant must demonstrate depth of character, leadership, seriousness of purpose and service orientation.
Application requirements: Recommendations, proof of eligibility and research proposal.
Additional information: Applicant must be full-time junior faculty at accredited institution in U.S. or Canada.

Amount of award:	$2,000
Application deadline:	February 17
Notification begins:	May 1

Contact:
The National Foundation for Infectious Diseases
4733 Bethesda Ave., Suite 750
Bethesda, MD 30814-5228

National Foundation for Jewish Culture

Doctoral Dissertation Fellowship in Jewish Studies

Type of award: Scholarship.
Intended use: For doctoral study.
Eligibility: Applicant must be U.S. citizen or permanent resident.
Basis for selection: Major/career interest in Jewish studies; Middle Eastern studies; anthropology; sociology.
Application requirements: Recommendations, transcript and research proposal. Dissertation prospectus and bibliography.
Additional information: Must have knowledge of Hebrew and/or Yiddish and intend to pursue career in a Jewish educational field.

Amount of award:	$7,000-$9,000
Number of awards:	12
Number of applicants:	73
Application deadline:	January 5
Notification begins:	May 1
Total amount awarded:	$95,000

Contact:
National Foundation for Jewish Culture
c/o Grants Administrator
330 7 Avenue, 21 Floor
New York, NY 10001
Phone: 212-629-0500, ext. 205

New Play Commissions in Jewish Theater

Type of award: Scholarship.
Intended use: For non-degree study.
Eligibility: Applicant must be U.S. citizen.
Basis for selection: Competition in Writing/journalism. Quality of play, which must reflect Jewish history, tradition or contemporary concerns.
Additional information: If work is adaptation of previous piece, legal rights to work must have been obtained by applicant.

Amount of award:	$2,500-$5,000
Number of awards:	6
Number of applicants:	51
Application deadline:	September 30
Notification begins:	December 1
Total amount awarded:	$25,500

Contact:
National Foundation for Jewish Culture
330 Seventh Avenue
21st Floor
New York, NY 10001
Phone: 212-629-0500, ext. 205

National Gallery of Art

Charles E. Culpeper Art Internship

Type of award: Internship.
Intended use: For graduate study. Designated institutions: National Gallery of Art.
Eligibility: Applicant must be of minority background. Applicant must be . Must be physically challenged. Applicant must be U.S. citizen.
Basis for selection: Major/career interest in museum studies; art, art history; journalism; arts, general. Applicant must demonstrate seriousness of purpose.
Application requirements: Interview, recommendations, essay, transcript, proof of eligibility and nomination by chair of department or head of institution. Resume or curriculum vitae.
Additional information: Internships last nine months with a stipend of $15,000. Call for specific deadline information.
    Amount of award: $15,000
Contact:
National Gallery of Art
Washington, DC 20565
Phone: 202-842-6399
Fax: 2028426935
Website: www.nga.gov

National Gallery of Art, Center for Advanced Study in the Visual Arts

Andrew Mellon Fellowship

Type of award: Research grant.
Intended use: For doctoral study at graduate institution in United States.
Eligibility: Applicant must be U.S. citizen, permanent resident or enrolled in a U.S. institution.
Basis for selection: Major/career interest in art, art history; arts, general.
Application requirements: Interview, recommendations and research proposal. Writing sample.
Additional information: Supports two-year doctoral dissertation research. Must have completed Ph.D. residence/course work requirements and preliminary examinations and have knowledge of two foreign languages related to dissertation. Emphasis on non-Western art. Recipient expected to spend second year at center to complete dissertation. Student should obtain application and sponsorship from dissertation adviser and department chair.

    Amount of award: $32,000
    Number of awards: 1
    Application deadline: November 15
    Total amount awarded: $32,000
Contact:
National Gallery of Art, Center for Advanced Study in the Visual Arts
Fellowship Program
Washington, DC 20565
Phone: 202-842-6482
Fax: 202-842-6733
Website: www.nga.gov

Chester Dale Fellowship

Type of award: Research grant.
Intended use: For doctoral study in or outside United States.
Eligibility: Applicant must be U.S. citizen, permanent resident or enrolled at a U.S. institution.
Basis for selection: Major/career interest in art, art history; arts, general.
Application requirements: Recommendations and research proposal. Writing sample.
Additional information: Award supports a 12-month doctoral dissertation. Must have completed Ph.D. residence/course work requirements, preliminary examinations, have knowledge of two foreign languages related to dissertation. Fellowship intended for completion of dissertation in western art. Applications available through university department head.
    Amount of award: $16,000
    Number of awards: 2
    Application deadline: November 15
    Total amount awarded: $32,000
Contact:
National Gallery of Art, Center for Advanced Study in the Visual Arts
Fellowship Program
Washington, DC 20565
Phone: 2028426482
Fax: 2028426733
Website: www.nga.gov

David Finley Fellowship

Type of award: Research grant.
Intended use: For doctoral study outside United States.
Eligibility: Applicant must be U.S. citizen, permanent resident or enrolled at a U.S. institution.
Basis for selection: Major/career interest in arts, general; art, art history.
Application requirements: Recommendations and research proposal. Writing sample.
Additional information: Applicant must have a significant interest in museum work. Must have completed Ph.D. residence/course work requirements and preliminary examinations and have knowledge of two foreign languages related to dissertation. Three year fellowship with stipend of $16,000 annually. First two years must be used conducting research abroad and last year must be used at Center. Must obtain application and sponsorship from appropriate university department head.

Amount of award:	$48,000
Number of awards:	1
Application deadline:	November 15
Total amount awarded:	$48,000

Contact:
National Gallery of Art, Center for Advanced Study in the Visual Arts
Fellowship Program
Washington, DC 20565
Website: www.nga.gov

Ittleson Fellowship

Type of award: Research grant.
Intended use: For doctoral study in or outside United States.
Eligibility: Applicant must be U.S. citizen, permanent resident or enrolled at a U.S. institution.
Basis for selection: Major/career interest in art, art history; arts, general.
Application requirements: Recommendations and research proposal. Writing sample.
Additional information: Award supports 36-month doctoral dissertation research. Must spend one year at the center. Must have completed Ph.D. residence/course work requirements and preliminary examinations, and also have knowledge of two foreign languages related to dissertation. Must obtain application and sponsorship from university department heads.

Amount of award:	$32,000
Number of awards:	1
Application deadline:	November 15
Total amount awarded:	$32,000

Contact:
National Gallery of Art, Center for Advanced Study in the Visual Arts
Fellowship Program
Washington, DC 20565
Website: www.nga.gov

Mary Davis Fellowship

Type of award: Research grant.
Intended use: For doctoral study in or outside United States.
Eligibility: Applicant must be U.S. citizen, permanent resident or enrolled at a U.S. institution.
Basis for selection: Major/career interest in art, art history; arts, general.
Application requirements: Recommendations and research proposal. Writing sample.
Additional information: Must have completed Ph.D. residence/course work requirements and preliminary examinations, have knowledge of two foreign languages related to dissertation. Focus in Western art. Recipient expected to spend one year on dissertation research, one year at center completing dissertation and doing gallery research projects and gaining curatorial experience. Fellowship lasts two years and pays stipend of $13,000/year and housing stipend of $3,000/year. Must obtain application and sponsorship from university department head.

Amount of award:	$26,000
Number of awards:	1
Application deadline:	November 15
Total amount awarded:	$26,000

Contact:
National Gallery of Art, Center for Advanced Study in the Visual Arts
Fellowship Program
Washington, DC 20565
Website: www.nga.gov

Paul Mellon Fellowship

Type of award: Research grant.
Intended use: For doctoral study in or outside United States.
Eligibility: Applicant must be U.S. citizen, permanent resident or enrolled at a U.S. institution.
Basis for selection: Major/career interest in art, art history; arts, general.
Application requirements: Recommendations and research proposal. Writing sample.
Additional information: Supports doctoral dissertation work allowing candidate to develop expertise in specific city, region or locality abroad. Must have completed Ph.D. residence, course work requirements, and preliminary examinations. Must have knowledge of two foreign languages related to dissertation. Award arranges for one year at center completing dissertation, participation in gallery research projects, and providing curatorial experience. Fellowship lasts three years with a stipend of $16,000 annually. Two years of fellowship must be spent abroad. Must obtain application and sponsorship from university department head.

Amount of award:	$48,000
Number of awards:	1
Application deadline:	November 15
Total amount awarded:	$48,000

Contact:
National Gallery of Art, Center for Advanced Study in the Visual Arts
Fellowship Program
Washington, DC 20565
Website: www.nga.gov

Robert and Clarice Smith Fellowship

Type of award: Research grant.
Intended use: For doctoral study in or outside United States.
Eligibility: Applicant must be enrolled at a U.S. institution.
Basis for selection: Major/career interest in art, art history; arts, general.
Application requirements: Recommendations and research proposal. Writing sample.
Additional information: Field of study emphasis on Dutch or Flemish art. Must have completed Ph.D. residence, course work requirements, and preliminary examinations. Must have knowledge of two foreign languages related to dissertation. Fellowship lasts twelve months with a stipend of $16,000. Applications available through university department heads.

Amount of award:	$16,000
Number of awards:	1
Application deadline:	November 15
Total amount awarded:	$16,000

Contact:
National Gallery of Art, Center for Advanced Study in the Visual Arts
Fellowship Program
Washington, DC 20565
Phone: 2028426482
Fax: 2028426733
Website: www.nga.gov

Samuel H. Kreiss/Alisa Mellon Bruce Paired Fellowship

Type of award: Research grant.
Intended use: For postgraduate study in United States.
Eligibility: Applicant must be U.S. citizen or permanent resident.
Basis for selection: Major/career interest in art, art history; arts, general; architecture; graphic arts and design.
Application requirements: Recommendations and research proposal. A tentative schedule of travel indicating the sites, collections, or institutions most valuable for the proposed research project, copies of selected pertinent publications must be forwarded by deadline.
Additional information: Two paired fellowships (for four individuals) will be awarded annually. Applications are invited from teams consisting of two scholars each, one in the field of art history or another related discipline in the humanities or social sciences, and one in the field of conservation or materials science. Must have held an appropriate terminal degree for five or more years. Additional funds are available for related research travel for the two segments to Washington. The two-month residency period must take place between September 1998 and April 1999.

Amount of award:	$5,500
Number of awards:	4
Application deadline:	March 21
Notification begins:	May 31

Contact:
National Gallery of Art, Center for Advanced Study in the Visual Arts
National Gallery of Art, Center for Advanced Study in the Visual Arts Fellowship Program
Washington, DC 20565
Website: www.nga.gov

Senior Fellowship Program

Type of award: Research grant.
Intended use: For postgraduate study in United States. Designated institutions: Center for Advanced Study of the Visual Arts.
Basis for selection: Major/career interest in art, art history; arts, general; architecture; graphic arts and design. Applicant must demonstrate high academic achievement.
Application requirements: Recommendations and research proposal.
Additional information: Open to scholars who hold appropriate degrees in the field and/or posess an equivalent record of professional accomplishment. Award will include travel, research, housing expenses and two months at the center, followed by two months of travel to visit collections, libraries and other institutions in the United States.

Application deadline:	October 1

Contact:
National Gallery of Art
Center for Advanced Study in the Visual Arts
Fellowship Program
Washington, DC 20565
Website: www.nga.gov

Wyeth Fellowship

Type of award: Research grant.
Intended use: For doctoral study in or outside United States. Designated institutions: Outside Washington DC for 1 year.
Eligibility: Applicant must be U.S. citizen, permanent resident or enrolled at a U.S. institution.
Basis for selection: Major/career interest in art, art history; arts, general.
Application requirements: Recommendations and research proposal. Writing sample.
Additional information: Award for research in American art and to support doctoral dissertation. Must have completed Ph.D. residence, course work requirements, and preliminary examinations. Must have knowledge of two foreign languages related to dissertation. Geographic region unrestricted. Fellow expected to spend second year of fellowship at center to complete dissertation. Must obtain application and sponsorship from university department head. Fellowship is for two years with a stipend of $16,000 annually.

Amount of award:	$32,000
Number of awards:	1
Application deadline:	November 15
Total amount awarded:	$32,000

Contact:
National Gallery of Art, Center for Advanced Study in the Visual Arts
Fellowship Program
Washington, DC 20565
Website: www.nga.gov

National Geographic Society

Geography Research Grants

Type of award: Research grant, renewable.
Intended use: For master's, doctoral, postgraduate or non-degree study.
Basis for selection: Major/career interest in environmental science; geography. Applicant must demonstrate seriousness of purpose.
Application requirements: Research proposal. Curriculum vitae, resume.
Additional information: Grants normally made for field-based research. Priority given to research relating to environmental concerns with relevance to global geographic issues.

Amount of award: $15,000-$20,000
Number of awards: 200
Number of applicants: 750
Total amount awarded: $4,000,000
Contact:
National Geographic Society Committee for Research and Exploration
1145 17 Street, NW
Washington, DC 20036-4688
Website: www.nationalgeographic.com

Geography Students Internship

Type of award: Internship.
Intended use: For junior, senior or master's study in United States.
Basis for selection: Major/career interest in geography; cartography.
Application requirements: Recommendations, essay and transcript. Resume.
Additional information: Spring, summer, and fall internships for 14 to 16 weeks in Washington, D.C. at $425/week. Emphasis on editorial and cartographic research. Contact office for applications and deadline dates.
Amount of award: $5,950-$6,800
Number of awards: 18
Contact:
National Geographic Society
Geography Intern Program/Kristin S. Scott
1145 17 Street, NW
Washington, DC 20036-4688
Website: www.nationalgeographic.com

National Guild of Community Schools of the Arts

Young Composers Award

Type of award: Scholarship.
Intended use: For freshman study.
Eligibility: Applicant must be high school freshman, sophomore, junior, senior. Applicant must be Canadian citizen.
Basis for selection: Competition in Music performance/composition. original musical composition Major/career interest in music.
Application requirements: $5 application fee. Proof of eligibility. Original musical composition written by the applicant.
Additional information: Each applicant may submit only one work. Composer's name may not appear on submission. Pseudonyms required.
Amount of award: $250-$1,000
Application deadline: May 1
Notification begins: June 30
Contact:
National Guild of Community Schools of the Arts
40 North Van Brunt Street, Room 32
P.O. Box 8018
Englewood, NJ 07631
Phone: 201-871-3337

National Hemophilia Foundation

National Hemophilia Foundation/ Judith Graham Pool Postdoctoral Research Fellowship

Type of award: Research grant.
Intended use: For postgraduate study in United States.
Eligibility: Applicant must be U.S. citizen.
Basis for selection: Major/career interest in medical specialties/research (beyond m.d.). Applicant must demonstrate high academic achievement.
Application requirements: Recommendations, transcript, proof of eligibility and research proposal.
Additional information: For research studies relevant to hemophilia. The applicant must enter this fellowship directly from a doctoral, postdoctoral, internship, or residency training program. Fellows are expected to remain at their institution for the duration of the project.
Amount of award: $35,000
Application deadline: December 1, June 1
Contact:
National Hemophilia Foundation
Research Grant Coordinator
110 Greene Street
New York, NY 10012
Website: www.infonhf.org

National Hemophilia Foundation/ Nursing Excellence Fellowship

Type of award: Research grant.
Intended use: For postgraduate study in United States.
Eligibility: Applicant must be U.S. citizen.
Basis for selection: Major/career interest in nursing.
Application requirements: Recommendations, transcript, proof of eligibility and research proposal.
Additional information: Must be a registered nurse currently employed in or interested in hemophilia care. The funds are for nursing research or clinical projects. Endorsement by a federally funded hemophilia treatment center is recommended.
Amount of award: $10,000
Application deadline: May 1
Contact:
National Hemophilia Foundation
Research Grant Coordinator
116 West 32nd Street
New York, NY 10002
Website: www.infonhf.org/resources

National Hispanic Scholarship Fund

Hispanic Fund Scholarships

Type of award: Scholarship.
Intended use: For full-time undergraduate, graduate or non-degree study.
Eligibility: Applicant must be Mexican American, Hispanic American or Puerto Rican. Applicant must be U.S. citizen.
Basis for selection: Major/career interest in business. Applicant must demonstrate leadership, service orientation, financial need and high academic achievement.
Application requirements: Recommendations, essay and transcript.
Additional information: Must send SASE with application request by October 15, 1998. Topics related to business will also qualify. Deadline varies; contact sponsor.

Amount of award:	$1,000
Number of awards:	10
Number of applicants:	4,000
Total amount awarded:	$10,000

Contact:
National Hispanic Scholarship Fund
1 Sansome Street
Suite 1000
San Francisco, CA 94104
Phone: 415-445-9936
Website: www.nhsf.org

National Italian American Foundation

A.P. Giannini Scholarship

Type of award: Scholarship.
Intended use: For graduate study at graduate institution in United States.
Eligibility: Applicant must be of Italian heritage. Applicant must be U.S. citizen or permanent resident.
Basis for selection: Major/career interest in finance/banking. Applicant must demonstrate financial need and high academic achievement.
Application requirements: $10 application fee. Essay and transcript. Photograph, College Scholarship Service Financial Aid Profile.
Additional information: Must have completed 13 hours of community service within the Italian-American community. Send business size SASE for application.

Amount of award:	$1,000
Number of awards:	1
Application deadline:	May 31
Notification begins:	November 15
Total amount awarded:	$1,000

Contact:
National Italian American Foundation
Dr. Maria Lombardo
1860 19 Street NW
Washington, DC 20009
Phone: 202-530-5315

Agnes E. Vaghi-Cornaro Scholarship

Type of award: Scholarship.
Intended use: For undergraduate study at 2-year or 4-year institution in United States.
Eligibility: Applicant must be female, of Italian heritage. Applicant must be U.S. citizen or permanent resident.
Basis for selection: Applicant must demonstrate financial need and high academic achievement.
Application requirements: $10 application fee. Essay and transcript. Photograph, College Scholarship Service Financial Aid Profile.
Additional information: Must submit three-page essay on a famous Italian-American woman. Must have completed 13 hours of community service within the Italian-American community. Send business size SASE for application.

Amount of award:	$2,000
Number of awards:	1
Application deadline:	May 31
Notification begins:	November 15
Total amount awarded:	$2,000

Contact:
National Italian American Foundation
Dr. Maria Lombardo
1860 19 Street NW
Washington, DC 20009
Phone: 202-530-5315

Alyce M. Cafaro Scholarship

Type of award: Scholarship.
Intended use: For undergraduate study at 2-year or 4-year institution in United States.
Eligibility: Applicant must be of Italian heritage. Applicant must be U.S. citizen or permanent resident residing in Ohio.
Basis for selection: Applicant must demonstrate financial need and high academic achievement.
Application requirements: $10 application fee. Essay, transcript and proof of eligibility. Photograph, College Scholarship Service Financial Aid Profile.
Additional information: Must have completed 13 hours of community service within the Italian-American community. Send business size SASE for application.

Amount of award:	$5,000
Number of awards:	1
Application deadline:	May 31
Notification begins:	November
Total amount awarded:	$5,000

Contact:
National Italian American Foundation
Dr. Maria Lombardo
1860 19 Street NW
Washington, DC 20009
Phone: 202-530-5315

Angela Scholarship

Type of award: Scholarship.
Intended use: For freshman study at 2-year or 4-year institution in United States.
Eligibility: Applicant must be high school senior, of Italian heritage. Applicant must be U.S. citizen or permanent resident.

Basis for selection: Applicant must demonstrate service orientation, financial need and high academic achievement.
Application requirements: $10 application fee. Essay and transcript. Photograph, College Scholarship Service Financial Aid Profile.
Additional information: Must be willing to intern at the NIAF for a semester and must have completed 13 hours of community service within the Italian-American community. Send business-size SASE to receive application.

Amount of award:	$2,500
Application deadline:	May 31
Notification begins:	November 15

Contact:
National Italian American Foundation
Dr. Maria Lombardo
1860 19 Street NW
Washington, DC 20009
Phone: 202-530-5315

Antonio and Felicia Marinelli Scholarships

Type of award: Scholarship.
Intended use: For undergraduate study outside United States in Italy. Designated institutions: For students accepted at the American University of Rome.
Eligibility: Applicant must be of Italian heritage. Applicant must be U.S. citizen or permanent resident.
Basis for selection: Applicant must demonstrate financial need and high academic achievement.
Application requirements: $10 application fee. Essay, transcript and proof of eligibility. Photograph, College Scholarship Service Financial Aid Profile.
Additional information: Must have completed thirteen hours of community service within the Italian-American community. Please contact office for further information.

Amount of award:	$1,000
Number of awards:	4
Application deadline:	May 31
Notification begins:	November 15
Total amount awarded:	$4,000

Contact:
National Italian American Foundation
Dr. Maria Enrico
1860 19th Street, NW
Washington, DC 20009
Phone: 202-331-8327

Antonio F. Marinelli Founders Scholarship

Type of award: Scholarship.
Intended use: For undergraduate study at 2-year or 4-year institution in United States.
Eligibility: Applicant must be of Italian heritage. Applicant must be U.S. citizen.
Application requirements: $10 application fee. Essay, transcript and proof of eligibility. Photograph, College Scholarship Service Financial Aid Profile.
Additional information: Applicants parents must belong to the National Utility Contractors Association. Must be studying in the Washington DC area and have completed 13 hours of community service within the Italian-American community. Send business size SASE for application.

Amount of award:	$2,500
Application deadline:	May 31
Notification begins:	November 15

Contact:
National Italian American Foundation
Dr. Maria Lombardo
1890 19th Street, NW
Washington, DC 20009
Phone: 202-530-5315

Assunta Lucchetti Martino Scholarship for International Studies

Type of award: Scholarship.
Intended use: For undergraduate study at 2-year or 4-year institution.
Eligibility: Applicant must be of Italian heritage. Applicant must be U.S. citizen or permanent resident.
Basis for selection: Applicant must demonstrate financial need and high academic achievement.
Application requirements: $10 application fee. Essay and transcript. Photograph, College Scholarship Service Financial Aid Profile.
Additional information: Must be majoring in International Studies. Must have completed 13 hours of communty service within the Italian-American community. Send business size SASE for application.

Amount of award:	$1,000
Application deadline:	May 31
Notification begins:	November 15

Contact:
National Italian American Foundation
Dr. Maria Lombardo
1860 19th Street, NW
Washington, DC 20009
Phone: 202-530-5315

Bolla Wines Scholarship

Type of award: Scholarship.
Intended use: For undergraduate or graduate study at 2-year, 4-year or graduate institution in United States.
Eligibility: Applicant must be of Italian heritage. Applicant must be U.S. citizen or permanent resident.
Basis for selection: Major/career interest in business, international; international relations. Applicant must demonstrate financial need and high academic achievement.
Application requirements: $10 application fee. Essay and transcript.
Additional information: Designated for students in international studies with emphasis on Italian business or Italian-American history. Minimum 3.0 GPA required. Applicants must prepare three page double spaced essay on "The Importance of Italy In Today's Business World." Must have completed 13 hours of community service within the Italian-American community. Send business size SASE for application.

Amount of award:	$1,000
Number of awards:	1
Application deadline:	May 31
Notification begins:	November
Total amount awarded:	$1,000

Contact:
National Italian American Foundation Scholarships
Dr. Maria Lombardo
1860 19th Street, NW
Washington, DC 20009
Phone: 202-530-5315

Capital Area Regional Scholarship

Type of award: Scholarship.
Intended use: For undergraduate study at 2-year or 4-year institution.
Eligibility: Applicant must be of Italian heritage. Applicant must be U.S. citizen or permanent resident residing in District of Columbia or Maryland or Virginia or West Virginia.
Basis for selection: Applicant must demonstrate financial need and high academic achievement.
Application requirements: $10 application fee. Essay and transcript. Photograph, College Scholarship Service Financial Aid Profile.
Additional information: Must have completed 13 hours of community service within the Italian-American community. Send business size SASE to receive application form.

Amount of award:	$2,000-$5,000
Number of awards:	2
Application deadline:	May 31
Notification begins:	November
Total amount awarded:	$7,000

Contact:
National Italian American Foundation
Dr. Maria Lombardo
1860 19 Street NW
Washington, DC 20009
Phone: 202-530-5315

Carmela Gagliardi Fellowship

Type of award: Scholarship.
Intended use: For first professional study at accredited graduate institution in United States.
Eligibility: Applicant must be of Italian heritage. Applicant must be U.S. citizen or permanent resident.
Basis for selection: Major/career interest in medicine (m.d.). Applicant must demonstrate financial need and high academic achievement.
Application requirements: $10 application fee. Recommendations, essay and transcript. Photograph, College Scholarship Service Financial Aid Profile.
Additional information: Must be accepted to or attending an accredited U.S. medical school. Must rank in top 25 percent of class. Must have completed 13 hours of community service within the Italian-American community. Send business size SASE to receive application form.

Amount of award:	$5,000
Number of awards:	5
Application deadline:	May 31
Notification begins:	November
Total amount awarded:	$25,000

Contact:
National Italian American Foundation
Dr. Maria Lombardo
1860 19 Street NW
Washington, DC 20009
Phone: 202-530-5315

Communications Scholarship

Type of award: Scholarship.
Intended use: For undergraduate study at postsecondary institution in United States.
Eligibility: Applicant must be of Italian heritage. Applicant must be U.S. citizen or permanent resident.
Basis for selection: Major/career interest in communications; journalism.
Application requirements: $10 application fee. Essay, transcript and proof of eligibility. Samples of work, Photograph, College Scholarship Service Financial Aid Profile.
Additional information: Must have completed 13 hours of community service within the Italian-American community. Send business size SASE to receive application form.

Amount of award:	$5,000
Number of awards:	1
Application deadline:	May 31
Notification begins:	November
Total amount awarded:	$5,000

Contact:
National Italian American Foundation
Dr. Maria Lombardo
1860 19 Street NW
Washington, DC 20009
Phone: 202-530-5315

Daniel Stella Scholarship

Type of award: Scholarship.
Intended use: For undergraduate or graduate study at 2-year, 4-year or graduate institution in United States.
Eligibility: Applicant must be of Italian heritage. Applicant must be U.S. citizen or permanent resident.
Basis for selection: Applicant must demonstrate financial need and high academic achievement.
Application requirements: $10 application fee. Essay, transcript and proof of eligibility. Photograph, College Scholarship Service Financial Aid Profile.
Additional information: For students with Cooley's Anemia disease. Must have completed 13 hours of community service within the Italian-American community. Send business size SASE for application.

Amount of award:	$1,000
Number of awards:	1
Application deadline:	May 31
Notification begins:	November
Total amount awarded:	$1,000

Contact:
National Italian American Foundation
Dr. Maria Lombardo
1860 19 Street NW
Washington, DC 20009
Phone: 202-530-5315

Dr. William L. Amoroso Jr. Scholarship

Type of award: Scholarship.
Intended use: For undergraduate study outside United States in Italy. Designated institutions: Must be used at the American University of Rome.
Eligibility: Applicant must be of Italian heritage. Applicant must be U.S. citizen or permanent resident.
Basis for selection: Applicant must demonstrate financial need and high academic achievement.
Application requirements: $10 application fee. Essay, transcript and proof of eligibility. Photograph, College Scholarship Service Financial Aid Profile.
Additional information: Must have completed thirteen hours of community service within the Italian-American community. For students accepted into the American University of Rome. Please call Maria Enrico for further information.

Amount of award:	$1,000
Application deadline:	May 31
Notification begins:	November 15

Contact:
National Italian American Foundation
Dr. Maria Enrico
1860 19th Street, NW
Washington, DC 20009
Phone: 301-977-2250

F.D. Stella Scholarship

Type of award: Scholarship.
Intended use: For undergraduate or graduate study at postsecondary institution in United States.
Eligibility: Applicant must be of Italian heritage. Applicant must be U.S. citizen or permanent resident.
Basis for selection: Major/career interest in business. Applicant must demonstrate financial need and high academic achievement.
Application requirements: $10 application fee. Essay, transcript and proof of eligibility. Photograph, College Scholarship Service Financial Aid Profile.
Additional information: Must have completed 13 hours of community service within the Italian-American community. Send business size SASE to receive application form.

Amount of award:	$1,000
Number of awards:	1
Application deadline:	May 31
Notification begins:	November
Total amount awarded:	$1,000

Contact:
National Italian American Foundation
Dr. Maria Lombardo
1860 19 Street NW
Washington, DC 20009
Phone: 202-530-5315

Gianni Versace Scholarship in Fashion Design

Type of award: Scholarship.
Intended use: For undergraduate study at 2-year or 4-year institution in United States.
Eligibility: Applicant must be of Italian heritage. Applicant must be U.S. citizen or permanent resident.
Basis for selection: Major/career interest in fashion design. Applicant must demonstrate financial need and high academic achievement.
Application requirements: $10 application fee. Essay and transcript. Photograph, College Scholarship Service Financial Aid Profile.
Additional information: Must be majoring in fashion design. Must have completed 13 hours of community service within the Italian-American community. Send business size SASE for application.

Amount of award:	$1,000
Application deadline:	May 31
Notification begins:	November 15

Contact:
National Italian American Foundation
Dr. Maria Lombardo
1860 19th Street, NW
Washington, DC 20009
Phone: 202-530-5315

Giargiari Fellowship

Type of award: Scholarship.
Intended use: For first professional study at accredited graduate institution in United States.
Eligibility: Applicant must be of Italian heritage. Applicant must be U.S. citizen or permanent resident.
Basis for selection: Major/career interest in medicine (m.d.). Applicant must demonstrate financial need and high academic achievement.
Application requirements: $10 application fee. Essay, transcript and proof of eligibility. Photograph, College Scholarship Financial Aid Profile.
Additional information: Applicant must be second-, third- or fourth-year medical student. Must have completed 13 hours of community service within the Italian-American community. Applicants must prepare five page double spaced essay on "Italian-Americans in the Medical Field". Send business size SASE to receive application form.

Amount of award:	$5,000
Number of awards:	1
Application deadline:	May 31
Notification begins:	November
Total amount awarded:	$5,000

Contact:
National Italian American Foundation
Dr. Maria Lombardo
1860 19 Street NW
Washington, DC 20009
Phone: 202-530-5315

GRI/ICIF Culinary Scholarship

Type of award: Scholarship.
Intended use: For postgraduate, non-degree study.
Eligibility: Applicant must be of Italian heritage. Applicant must be Must be Italian national.
Basis for selection: Applicant must demonstrate financial need.
Application requirements: Recommendations, essay and transcript. Photograph, College Scholarship Service Financial Aid Profile.
Additional information: Minimum 3.0 GPA and 1,000 hours of work in a commercial kitchen. Must have completed 13

hours of community service within the Italian-American community. Available to culinary school graduates who have met the criteria established by the Italian Culinary Institute for Foriegners (ICIF) and the Gruppi Ristoratori Italiani (GRI). Please call or email Mr. Enrico Bazzoni before applying.

Amount of award:	$6,000
Number of awards:	5
Application deadline:	May 31
Notification begins:	November
Total amount awarded:	$30,000

Contact:
National Italian American Foundation
Contact: Enrico Bazzoni

Phone: 718-875-0547

Italian American Study Abroad Scholarship

Type of award: Scholarship.
Intended use: For undergraduate or graduate study at accredited 4-year or graduate institution Italy outside United States in Italy. Designated institutions: American University of Rome, John Cabot University.
Eligibility: Applicant must be of Italian heritage. Applicant must be U.S. citizen or permanent resident.
Basis for selection: Applicant must demonstrate financial need and high academic achievement.
Application requirements: $10 application fee. Essay, transcript and proof of eligibility. Photograph, College Scholarship Service Financial Aid Profile.
Additional information: Must have completed 13 hours of community service within the Italian-American community. Send business size SASE for application.

Amount of award:	$2,000
Number of awards:	5
Application deadline:	May 31
Notification begins:	November
Total amount awarded:	$10,000

Contact:
National Italian American Foundation
Dr. Maria Lombardo
1860 19 Street NW
Washington, DC 20009
Phone: 202-530-5315

Italian Cultural Society and NIAF Matching Scholarship

Type of award: Scholarship.
Intended use: For undergraduate study at 2-year or 4-year institution in United States.
Eligibility: Applicant must be of Italian heritage. Applicant must be U.S. citizen or permanent resident residing in District of Columbia or Maryland or Virginia.
Basis for selection: Major/career interest in science, general; humanities/liberal arts. Applicant must demonstrate financial need and high academic achievement.
Application requirements: $10 application fee. Essay, transcript and proof of eligibility. Photograph, College Scholarship Service Financial Aid Profile.
Additional information: Available to students from the Washington DC, Maryland and Virginia areas who are majoring in Science or Humanities. Must have completed 13 hours of community service within the Italian-American community. Send business size SASE for application.

Amount of award:	$2,000
Application deadline:	May 31
Notification begins:	November 15

Contact:
National Italian American Foundation
Dr. Maria Lombardo
1860 19th Street, NW
Washington, DC 20009
Phone: 202-530-5315

Italian Regional Scholarship

Type of award: Scholarship.
Intended use: For undergraduate study Italy outside United States in Italy. Designated institutions: Postsecondary institutions located in Italy.
Eligibility: Applicant must be of Italian heritage. Applicant must be Must be Italian national.
Basis for selection: Applicant must demonstrate financial need and high academic achievement.
Application requirements: $10 application fee. Essay and transcript. Photograph, College Scholarship Service Financial Aid Profile.
Additional information: Must have completed 13 hours of community service within the Italian-American community. Send business size SASE to receive application form.

Amount of award:	$2,000-$5,000
Number of awards:	2
Application deadline:	May 31
Notification begins:	November
Total amount awarded:	$7,000

Contact:
National Italian American Foundation
Dr. Maria Lombardo
1860 19 Street NW
Washington, DC 20009
Phone: 202-530-5315

John A. Volpe Scholarship

Type of award: Scholarship.
Intended use: For undergraduate study at 2-year or 4-year institution in United States.
Eligibility: Applicant must be of Italian heritage. Applicant must be U.S. citizen or permanent resident residing in Connecticut or Massachusetts or Maine or New Hampshire or Rhode Island or Vermont.
Basis for selection: Applicant must demonstrate financial need and high academic achievement.
Application requirements: Essay, transcript and proof of eligibility. Photograph, College Scholarship Service Financial Aid Profile.
Additional information: Must have completed 13 hours of community service within Italian-American community. Send business size SASE for application.

Amount of award: $1,000
Number of awards: 1
Application deadline: May 31
Notification begins: November

Contact:
National Italian American Foundation
Dr. Maria Lombardo
1860 19 Street NW
Washington, DC 20009
Phone: 202-530-5315

Louis J. Salerno, M.D. Memorial Scholarship

Type of award: Scholarship.
Intended use: For undergraduate study outside United States in Italy. Designated institutions: Must be used at the American University of Rome.
Eligibility: Applicant must be of Italian heritage.
Basis for selection: Major/career interest in art, art history. Applicant must demonstrate financial need and high academic achievement.
Application requirements: $10 application fee. Essay and transcript. Photograph, College Scholarship Service Financial Aid Profile.
Additional information: Must be an art history major with a minimum GPA of 3.5. Must have completed thirteen hours of community service within the Italian-American community. Send business size SASE for application.

Amount of award: $2,000
Application deadline: May 31
Notification begins: November 15

Contact:
National Italian American Foundation
Dr. Maria Lombardo
1860 19th Street, NW
Washington, DC 20009
Phone: 202-530-5315

Lower Mid-Atlantic Regional Scholarship

Type of award: Scholarship.
Intended use: For undergraduate study at 2-year or 4-year institution in United States.
Eligibility: Applicant must be of Italian heritage. Applicant must be U.S. citizen or permanent resident residing in Delaware or New Jersey or Pennsylvania.
Basis for selection: Applicant must demonstrate financial need and high academic achievement.
Application requirements: $10 application fee. Essay, transcript and proof of eligibility. Photograph, College Scholarship Service Financial Aid Profile.
Additional information: Residents of New Jersey must live south of Trenton. Must have completed 13 hours of community service within the Italian-American community. Send business size SASE to receive application form.

Amount of award: $2,000-$5,000
Number of awards: 2
Application deadline: May 31
Notification begins: November
Total amount awarded: $7,000

Contact:
National Italian American Foundation
Dr. Maria Lombardo
1860 19 Street NW
Washington, DC 20009
Phone: 202-530-5315

Marija Bileta Scholarship

Type of award: Scholarship.
Intended use: For undergraduate study at 2-year or 4-year institution in United States.
Eligibility: Applicant must be of Italian heritage. Applicant must be U.S. citizen or permanent resident.
Basis for selection: Applicant must demonstrate financial need and high academic achievement.
Application requirements: $10 application fee. Essay and transcript. Photograph, College Scholarship Service Financial Aid Profile.
Additional information: Must have completed thirteen hours of community service within the Italian-American community. Send business size SASE for application.

Amount of award: $1,000
Application deadline: May 31
Notification begins: November 15

Contact:
National Italian American Foundation
Dr. Maria Lombardo
1860 19th Street, NW
Washington, DC 20009
Phone: 202-530-5315

Merrill Lynch Scholarship

Type of award: Scholarship.
Intended use: For undergraduate study at 2-year or 4-year institution in United States.
Eligibility: Applicant must be of Italian heritage. Applicant must be U.S. citizen or permanent resident residing in New York.
Basis for selection: Major/career interest in business. Applicant must demonstrate financial need and high academic achievement.
Application requirements: $10 application fee. Essay, transcript and proof of eligibility. Photograph, College Scholarship Service Financial Aid Profile.
Additional information: Must be a business major from the New York State area. Must have completed 13 hours of communty service within the Italian-American community. Send business size SASE for application.

Amount of award: $1,000
Application deadline: May 31
Notification begins: November 15

Contact:
National Italian American Foundation
Dr. Maria Lombardo
1860 19th Street, NW
Washington, DC 20009
Phone: 202-530-5315

Mid-America Regional Scholarship

Type of award: Scholarship.
Intended use: For undergraduate study at 2-year or 4-year institution in United States.
Eligibility: Applicant must be of Italian heritage. Applicant must be U.S. citizen or permanent resident residing in Iowa or Kansas or Missouri or Nebraska or Arkansas or Oklahoma or Colorado.
Basis for selection: Applicant must demonstrate financial need and high academic achievement.
Application requirements: $10 application fee. Essay, transcript and proof of eligibility. Photograph, College Scholarship Service Financial Aid Profile.
Additional information: Must have completed 13 hours of community service within the Italian-American community. Send business size SASE to receive application form.

Amount of award:	$2,000-$5,000
Number of awards:	2
Application deadline:	May 31
Notification begins:	November
Total amount awarded:	$7,000

Contact:
National Italian American Foundation
Dr. Maria Lombardo
1860 19 Street NW
Washington, DC 20009
Phone: 202-530-5315

Mid-Pacific Regional Scholarship

Type of award: Scholarship.
Intended use: For undergraduate study at 2-year or 4-year institution in United States.
Eligibility: Applicant must be of Italian heritage. Applicant must be U.S. citizen or permanent resident residing in California or Hawaii or Nevada or Utah.
Basis for selection: Applicant must demonstrate financial need and high academic achievement.
Application requirements: $10 application fee. Essay, transcript and proof of eligibility. Photograph, College Scholarship Service Financial Aid Profile.
Additional information: Residents of California and Nevada must be from the northern regions. Residents of Guam are also eligible. Must have completed 13 hours of community service within the Italian-American community. Send business size SASE to receive application form.

Amount of award:	$2,000-$5,000
Number of awards:	2
Application deadline:	May 31
Notification begins:	November
Total amount awarded:	$7,000

Contact:
National Italian American Foundation
Dr. Maria Lombardo
1860 19 Street NW
Washington, DC 20009
Phone: 202-530-5315

Mola Scholarship

Type of award: Scholarship.
Intended use: For undergraduate study at 2-year or 4-year institution in United States.
Eligibility: Applicant must be of Italian heritage. Applicant must be U.S. citizen or permanent resident residing in Kentucky or Illinois or Indiana or Iowa or Michigan or Minnesota or North Dakota or Ohio or South Dakota or Wisconsin.
Basis for selection: Major/career interest in Italian. Applicant must demonstrate financial need and high academic achievement.
Application requirements: $10 application fee. Essay, transcript and proof of eligibility. Photograph, College Scholarship Service Financial Aid Profile.
Additional information: Must have completed 13 hours of community service within the Italian-American community. Send business size SASE for application.

Amount of award:	$1,000
Number of awards:	9
Application deadline:	May 31
Notification begins:	November
Total amount awarded:	$9,000

Contact:
National Italian American Foundation
Dr. Maria Lombardo
1860 19 Street NW
Washington, DC 20009
Phone: 202-530-5315

NAIF/FIERI National Matching Scholarship

Type of award: Scholarship.
Intended use: For undergraduate study at 2-year or 4-year institution in United States.
Eligibility: Applicant must be of Italian heritage. Applicant must be U.S. citizen or permanent resident.
Basis for selection: Applicant must demonstrate financial need and high academic achievement.
Application requirements: $10 application fee. Essay and transcript. Photograph, College Scholarship Service Financial Aid Profile.
Additional information: Must have completed 13 hours of community service within the Italian-American community. Send business size SASE to receive application form.

Amount of award:	$1,000
Number of awards:	1
Application deadline:	May 31
Notification begins:	November
Total amount awarded:	$1,000

Contact:
National Italian American Foundation
Dr. Maria Lombardo
1860 19 Street NW
Washington, DC 20009
Phone: 202-530-5315

Nerone/NIAF Matching Art Scholarship

Type of award: Scholarship.
Intended use: For undergraduate or graduate study at 2-year, 4-year or graduate institution in United States.
Eligibility: Applicant must be of Italian heritage. Applicant must be U.S. citizen or permanent resident.
Basis for selection: Major/career interest in art, art history; arts management; arts, general. Applicant must demonstrate financial need and high academic achievement.
Application requirements: $10 application fee. Essay and

transcript. Photograph, College Scholarship Service Financial Aid Profile.
Additional information: Must have completed 13 hours of community service within the Italian-American community. Send business size SASE for application.
- **Amount of award:** $1,000
- **Application deadline:** May 31
- **Notification begins:** November 15

Contact:
National Italian American Foundation
Dr. Maria Lombardo
1860 19th Street, NW
Washington, DC 20009
Phone: 2025305315

New England Regional Scholarship

Type of award: Scholarship.
Intended use: For undergraduate study at 2-year or 4-year institution in United States.
Eligibility: Applicant must be of Italian heritage. Applicant must be U.S. citizen or permanent resident residing in Connecticut or Massachusetts or Maine or New Hampshire or Rhode Island or Vermont.
Basis for selection: Applicant must demonstrate financial need and high academic achievement.
Application requirements: $10 application fee. Essay, transcript and proof of eligibility. Photograph, College Scholarship Service Financial Aid Profile.
Additional information: Must have completed 13 hours of community service within the Italian-American community. Send business size SASE to receive application form.
- **Amount of award:** $2,000-$5,000
- **Number of awards:** 2
- **Application deadline:** May 31
- **Notification begins:** November 15
- **Total amount awarded:** $7,000

Contact:
National Italian American Foundation
Dr. Maria Lombardo
1860 19 Street NW
Washington, DC 20009
Phone: 202-530-5315

NIAF/FIERI D.C. Matching Scholarship

Type of award: Scholarship.
Intended use: For first professional study at graduate institution in United States.
Eligibility: Applicant must be of Italian heritage. Applicant must be U.S. citizen or permanent resident.
Basis for selection: Major/career interest in law. Applicant must demonstrate financial need and high academic achievement.
Application requirements: $10 application fee. Essay and transcript. Photograph, College Scholarship Service Financial Aid Profile.
Additional information: Must be a law student. Must have completed thirteen hours of community service within the Italian-American community. Send business size SASE for application.

- **Amount of award:** $1,000
- **Application deadline:** May 31
- **Notification begins:** November 15

Contact:
National Italian American Foundation
Dr. Maria Lombardo
1860 19th Street, NW
Washington, DC 20009
Phone: 202-530-5315

NIAF/NOIAW Cornaro Scholarship

Type of award: Scholarship.
Intended use: For undergraduate or graduate study at 2-year, 4-year or graduate institution in United States.
Eligibility: Applicant must be female, of Italian heritage. Applicant must be U.S. citizen or permanent resident.
Basis for selection: Applicant must demonstrate financial need and high academic achievement.
Application requirements: $10 application fee. Essay, transcript and proof of eligibility. Photograph, College Scholarship Service Financial Aid Profile.
Additional information: Applicants must write three page double spaced essay on current issue of concern of Italian-American women or on a famous Italian-American woman. Must have completed 13 hours of community service within the Italian-American community. Send business size SASE to receive application form.
- **Amount of award:** $1,000
- **Number of awards:** 3
- **Application deadline:** May 31
- **Notification begins:** November
- **Total amount awarded:** $3,000

Contact:
National Italian American Foundation
Dr. Maria Lombardo
1860 19 Street NW
Washington, DC 20009
Phone: 202-530-5315

North Central Regional Scholarship

Type of award: Scholarship.
Intended use: For undergraduate study at 2-year or 4-year institution in United States.
Eligibility: Applicant must be of Italian heritage. Applicant must be U.S. citizen or permanent resident residing in Ohio or Kentucky or Indiana or Illinois or Wisconsin or Michigan or Minnesota or South Dakota or North Dakota.
Basis for selection: Applicant must demonstrate financial need and high academic achievement.
Application requirements: $10 application fee. Essay and transcript. Photograph, College Scholarship Service Financial Aid Profile.
Additional information: Must have completed thirteen hours of community service within the Italian-American community. Send business size SASE for application.

Amount of award:	$2,000-$5,000
Number of awards:	2
Application deadline:	May 31
Notification begins:	November 15
Total amount awarded:	$7,000

Contact:
National Italian American Foundation
Dr. Maria Lombardo
1860 19th Street, NW
Washington, DC 20009
Phone: 202-530-5315

North Central Regional Scholarship

Type of award: Scholarship.
Intended use: For undergraduate study at 2-year or 4-year institution in United States.
Eligibility: Applicant must be of Italian heritage. Applicant must be U.S. citizen or permanent resident residing in Washington or Oregon or Idaho or Montana or Wyoming or Alaska.
Basis for selection: Applicant must demonstrate financial need and high academic achievement.
Application requirements: $10 application fee. Essay and transcript. Photograph, College Scholarship Service Financial Aid Profile.
Additional information: Must have completed 13 hours of community service within the Italian-American community. Send business size SASE for application.

Amount of award:	$2,000-$5,000
Number of awards:	2
Application deadline:	May 31
Notification begins:	November 15
Total amount awarded:	$7,000

Contact:
National Italian American Foundation
Dr. Maria Lombardo
1860 19th Street, NW
Washington, DC 20009
Phone: 2025305315

Paragano Scholarship

Type of award: Scholarship.
Intended use: For undergraduate study at 2-year or 4-year institution in United States.
Eligibility: Applicant must be of Italian heritage. Applicant must be U.S. citizen or permanent resident residing in New Jersey.
Basis for selection: Major/career interest in Italian. Applicant must demonstrate financial need and high academic achievement.
Application requirements: $10 application fee. Essay, transcript and proof of eligibility. Photograph, College Scholarship Service Financial Aid Profile.
Additional information: Must have completed 13 hours of community service within the Italian-American community. Send business size SASE to receive application form.

Amount of award:	$2,000
Number of awards:	2
Application deadline:	May 31
Notification begins:	November 15
Total amount awarded:	$4,000

Contact:
National Italian American Foundation
Dr. Maria Lombardo
1860 19 Street NW
Washington, DC 20009
Phone: 202-530-5315

Pavarotti Scholarship

Type of award: Scholarship.
Intended use: For undergraduate or graduate study at 2-year, 4-year or graduate institution in United States.
Eligibility: Applicant must be of Italian heritage. Applicant must be U.S. citizen or permanent resident residing in California.
Basis for selection: Major/career interest in music. Applicant must demonstrate financial need and high academic achievement.
Application requirements: $10 application fee. Essay, transcript and proof of eligibility. Cassette tape of performance, Photograph, College Scholarship Service Financial Aid Profile.
Additional information: Must be resident of Southern California. Must have completed 13 hours of community service within the Italian-American community. Send business size SASE to receive application.

Amount of award:	$1,000
Number of awards:	1
Application deadline:	May 31
Notification begins:	November 15
Total amount awarded:	$1,000

Contact:
National Italian American Foundation
Dr. Maria Lombardo
1860 19 Street NW
Washington, DC 20009
Phone: 202-530-5315

Peter Sammartino Scholarship

Type of award: Scholarship.
Intended use: For master's study at graduate institution in United States.
Eligibility: Applicant must be of Italian heritage. Applicant must be U.S. citizen or permanent resident.
Basis for selection: Applicant must demonstrate financial need and high academic achievement.
Application requirements: $10 application fee. Transcript. Photograph.
Additional information: Available to teachers of Italian pursuing their masters degree.

Amount of award:	$2,000
Number of awards:	1
Application deadline:	May 31
Notification begins:	November 15
Total amount awarded:	$2,000

Contact:
National Italian American Foundation
Dr. Maria Lombardo
1860 19 Street NW
Washington, DC 20009
Phone: 202-530-5315

Piancone Family Agriculture Scholarship

Type of award: Scholarship.
Intended use: For undergraduate or graduate study at 2-year, 4-year or graduate institution in United States.
Eligibility: Applicant must be of Italian heritage. Applicant must be U.S. citizen or permanent resident residing in Massachusetts or Delaware or District of Columbia or Maryland or New Jersey or New York or Pennsylvania or Virginia.
Basis for selection: Major/career interest in agriculture. Applicant must demonstrate financial need and high academic achievement.
Application requirements: $10 application fee. Essay, transcript and proof of eligibility. Photograph, College Scholarship Service Financial Aid Profile.
Additional information: Must have completed 13 hours of community service within the Italian-American community. Send business size SASE to receive application form.

Amount of award:	$2,000
Number of awards:	1
Application deadline:	May 31
Notification begins:	November 15
Total amount awarded:	$2,000

Contact:
National Italian American Foundation
Dr. Maria Lombardo
1860 19 Street NW
Washington, DC 20009
Phone: 202-530-5315

Rabbi Feinberg Scholarship

Type of award: Scholarship.
Intended use: For undergraduate or graduate study at 2-year, 4-year or graduate institution in United States.
Eligibility: Applicant must be of Italian heritage. Applicant must be U.S. citizen or permanent resident.
Basis for selection: Applicant must demonstrate financial need and high academic achievement.
Application requirements: $10 application fee. Essay and transcript.
Additional information: Available to any student interested in World War II studies. Applicant must prepare five-page paper on Italian assistance to Jews in Italy and its occupied territories. Must have completed 13 hours of community service within the Italian-American community. Send business size SASE for application.

Amount of award:	$1,000
Number of awards:	1
Application deadline:	May 31
Notification begins:	November 15
Total amount awarded:	$1,000

Contact:
National Italian American Foundation
Dr. Maria Lombardo
1860 19 Street NW
Washington, DC 20009
Phone: 202-530-5315

Ralph Lombardi Memorial Scholarship

Type of award: Scholarship.
Intended use: For first professional study at graduate institution in United States.
Eligibility: Applicant must be of Italian heritage. Applicant must be U.S. citizen or permanent resident residing in District of Columbia.
Basis for selection: Major/career interest in medicine (m.d.). Applicant must demonstrate financial need and high academic achievement.
Application requirements: $10 application fee. Essay, transcript and proof of eligibility. Photograph, College Scholarship Service Financial Aid Profile.
Additional information: Available to medical students in the Washington DC area. Must have completed 13 hours of community service within the Italian-American community. Send business size SASE for application.

Amount of award:	$1,000
Application deadline:	May 31
Notification begins:	November 15

Contact:
National Italian American Foundation
Dr. Maria Lombardo
1860 19th Street, NW
Washington, DC 20009
Phone: 202-530-5315

Recine Scholarship

Type of award: Scholarship.
Intended use: For undergraduate study at 2-year or 4-year institution in New York State.
Eligibility: Applicant must be of Italian heritage. Applicant must be U.S. citizen or permanent resident residing in New York.
Basis for selection: Applicant must demonstrate financial need and high academic achievement.
Application requirements: $10 application fee. Essay, transcript and proof of eligibility. Photograph, College Scholarship Service Financial Aid Profile.
Additional information: Must have completed 13 hours of community service within the Italian-American community. Send business size SASE to receive application.

Amount of award: $2,500
Number of awards: 1
Application deadline: May 31
Notification begins: November 15
Total amount awarded: $2,500
Contact:
National Italian American Foundation
Dr. Maria Lombardo
1860 19 Street NW
Washington, DC 20009
Phone: 202-530-5315

Robert J. Di Pietro Scholarship

Type of award: Scholarship.
Intended use: For undergraduate or graduate study at 2-year, 4-year or graduate institution in United States.
Eligibility: Applicant must be of Italian heritage. Applicant must be U.S. citizen or permanent resident.
Basis for selection: Applicant must demonstrate high academic achievement.
Application requirements: $10 application fee. Essay, transcript and proof of eligibility. Photograph.
Additional information: Applicant must write essay of 400-600 words on how applicant intends to use their ethnicity throughout their chosen field of education to preserve and support their ethnicity throughout life. Must have completed 13 hours of community service within the Italian-American community. Send business size SASE to receive application.
Amount of award: $1,000
Number of awards: 2
Application deadline: May 31
Notification begins: November 15
Total amount awarded: $2,000
Contact:
National Italian American Foundation
Dr. Maria Lombardo
1860 19 Street NW
Washington, DC 20009
Phone: 202-530-5315

Rose Basile Green Scholarship

Type of award: Scholarship.
Intended use: For undergraduate study at 2-year or 4-year institution in United States.
Eligibility: Applicant must be of Italian heritage. Applicant must be U.S. citizen or permanent resident.
Basis for selection: Major/career interest in Italian-American studies. Applicant must demonstrate financial need and high academic achievement.
Application requirements: $10 application fee. Essay, transcript and proof of eligibility. Photograph, College Scholarship Service Financial Aid Profile.
Additional information: Must have completed 13 hours of community service within the Italian-American community. Send business size SASE to receive application.

Amount of award: $1,000
Number of awards: 1
Application deadline: May 31
Notification begins: November 15
Total amount awarded: $1,000
Contact:
National Italian American Foundation
Dr. Maria Lombardo
1860 19 Street NW
Washington, DC 20009
Phone: 202-530-5315

Santavicca Scholarship

Type of award: Scholarship.
Intended use: For undergraduate or graduate study at accredited 2-year, 4-year or graduate institution in United States.
Eligibility: Applicant must be of Italian heritage. Applicant must be U.S. citizen or permanent resident.
Basis for selection: Major/career interest in music. Applicant must demonstrate financial need and high academic achievement.
Application requirements: $10 application fee. Essay, transcript and proof of eligibility. Photograph, College Scholarship Service Financial Aid Profile.
Additional information: Pianist preferred. Must have completed 13 hours of community service within the Italian-American community. Send business size SASE to receive application.
Amount of award: $1,000
Number of awards: 1
Application deadline: May 31
Notification begins: November
Total amount awarded: $1,000
Contact:
National Italian American Foundation
Dr. Maria Lombardo
1860 19 Street NW
Washington, DC 20009
Phone: 202-530-5315

Scalia Scholarship

Type of award: Scholarship.
Intended use: For first professional study at graduate institution in United States.
Eligibility: Applicant must be of Italian heritage. Applicant must be U.S. citizen or permanent resident residing in New York.
Basis for selection: Major/career interest in law. Applicant must demonstrate financial need and high academic achievement.
Application requirements: $10 application fee. Essay, transcript and proof of eligibility. Photograph, College Scholarship Service Financial Aid Profile.
Additional information: 750 word essay on Italian-Americans in law is required with application. Must have completed 13 hours of community service within the Italian-American community. Send business size SASE to receive application form.

National Italian American Foundation: Scalia Scholarship

Amount of award:	$1,000
Number of awards:	1
Application deadline:	May 31
Notification begins:	November 15
Total amount awarded:	$1,000

Contact:
National Italian American Foundation
Dr. Maria Lombardo
1860 19 Street NW
Washington, DC 20009
Phone: 202-530-5315

Sergio Franchi Music Scholarship/ Voice Performance

Type of award: Scholarship.
Intended use: For undergraduate or graduate study at 2-year, 4-year or graduate institution in United States.
Eligibility: Applicant must be of Italian heritage. Applicant must be U.S. citizen or permanent resident.
Basis for selection: Major/career interest in music.
Application requirements: $10 application fee. Audition, essay and transcript. Cassette tape of performance, photograph, College Scholarship Service Financial Aid Profile.
Additional information: Available to students of voice only (tenors). Must have completed 13 hours of community service within the Italian-American community. Send business size SASE to receive application form.

Application deadline:	May 31
Notification begins:	November
Total amount awarded:	$15,000

Contact:
National Italian American Foundation
Dr. Maria Lombardo
1860 19 Street NW
Washington, DC 20009
Phone: 202-530-5315

Silvio Conte Internship

Type of award: Internship.
Intended use: For undergraduate or graduate study.
Eligibility: Applicant must be of Italian heritage. Applicant must be U.S. citizen or permanent resident.
Basis for selection: Applicant must demonstrate financial need and high academic achievement.
Application requirements: $10 application fee. Essay, transcript and proof of eligibility. Photograph, College Scholarship Service Financial Aid Profile.
Additional information: One-semester internship on Capitol Hill. Must include letter of acceptance from a congressional office with application and have completed 13 hours of community service within the Italian-American community. Send business size SASE to receive application.

Amount of award:	$1,000
Number of awards:	1
Application deadline:	May 31
Notification begins:	November
Total amount awarded:	$1,000

Contact:
National Italian American Foundation
Dr. Maria Lombardo
1860 19 Street NW
Washington, DC 20009
Phone: 202-530-5315

South Central Regional Scholarship

Type of award: Scholarship.
Intended use: For full-time undergraduate study at 2-year or 4-year institution in United States.
Eligibility: Applicant must be of Italian heritage. Applicant must be U.S. citizen or permanent resident residing in Alabama or Louisiana or Mississippi or Tennessee or Texas.
Basis for selection: Applicant must demonstrate financial need and high academic achievement.
Application requirements: $10 application fee. Essay, transcript and proof of eligibility. Photograph, College Scholarship Service Financial Aid Profile.
Additional information: Must have completed 13 hours of community service within the Italian-American community. Send business size SASE to receive application.

Amount of award:	$2,000-$5,000
Number of awards:	2
Application deadline:	May 31
Notification begins:	November 15
Total amount awarded:	$7,000

Contact:
National Italian American Foundation
Dr. Maria Lombardo
1860 19 Street NW
Washington, DC 20009
Phone: 202-530-5315

Southeast Regional Scholarship

Type of award: Scholarship.
Intended use: For undergraduate study at 2-year or 4-year institution in United States.
Eligibility: Applicant must be of Italian heritage. Applicant must be U.S. citizen or permanent resident residing in Florida or Georgia or North Carolina or South Carolina.
Basis for selection: Applicant must demonstrate financial need and high academic achievement.
Application requirements: $10 application fee. Essay, transcript and proof of eligibility. Photograph, College Scholarship Service Financial Aid Profile.
Additional information: Must have completed 13 hours of community service within the Italian-American community. Send business size SASE to receive application form.

Amount of award:	$2,000-$5,000
Number of awards:	2
Application deadline:	May 31
Notification begins:	November 15
Total amount awarded:	$7,000

Contact:
National Italian American Foundation
Dr. Maria Lombardo
1860 19 Street NW
Washington, DC 20009
Phone: 202-530-5315

Southwest Regional Scholarship

Type of award: Scholarship.
Intended use: For undergraduate study at 2-year or 4-year institution in United States.
Eligibility: Applicant must be of Italian heritage. Applicant must be U.S. citizen or permanent resident residing in New Mexico or Arizona or California or Nevada.

Basis for selection: Applicant must demonstrate financial need and high academic achievement.
Application requirements: $10 application fee. Essay, transcript and proof of eligibility. Photograph, College Scholarship Service Financial Aid Profile.
Additional information: California and Nevada residents must be from southern areas. Must have completed 13 hours of community service within the Italian-American community. Send business size SASE to receive application form.

    Amount of award: $2,000-$5,000
    Number of awards: 2
    Application deadline: May 31
    Notification begins: November
    Total amount awarded: $7,000

Contact:
National Italian American Foundation
Dr. Maria Lombardo
1860 19 Street NW
Washington, DC 20009
Phone: 202-530-5315

Thomas Joseph Ambrosole Scholarship

Type of award: Scholarship.
Intended use: For undergraduate study at 2-year or 4-year institution in United States.
Eligibility: Applicant must be of Italian heritage. Applicant must be U.S. citizen or permanent resident residing in New York or New Jersey.
Basis for selection: Major/career interest in arts, general; performing arts; humanities/liberal arts. Applicant must demonstrate financial need and high academic achievement.
Application requirements: $10 application fee. Recommendations and essay. Photograph, College Scholarship Service Financial Aid Profile.
Additional information: Must have completed thirteen hours of community service within the Italian-American community. Send business size SASE for application.

    Amount of award: $1,000
    Application deadline: May 31
    Notification begins: November 15

Contact:
National Italian American Foundation
Dr. Maria Lombardo
1860 19th Street, NW
Washington, DC 20009
Phone: 202-530-5315

Upper Mid-Atlantic Regional Scholarship

Type of award: Scholarship.
Intended use: For undergraduate study at 2-year or 4-year institution in United States.
Eligibility: Applicant must be of Italian heritage. Applicant must be U.S. citizen or permanent resident residing in New Jersey or New York.
Basis for selection: Applicant must demonstrate financial need and high academic achievement.
Application requirements: $10 application fee. Essay, transcript and proof of eligibility. Photograph, College Scholarship Service Financial Aid Profile.
Additional information: Residents of New Jersey must live north of Trenton. Must have completed 13 hours of community service within the Italian-American community. Send business size SASE to receive application form.

    Amount of award: $2,000-$5,000
    Number of awards: 2
    Application deadline: May 31
    Notification begins: November 15
    Total amount awarded: $7,000

Contact:
National Italian American Foundation
Dr. Maria Lombardo
1860 19 Street NW
Washington, DC 20009
Phone: 202-530-5315

Vennera Noto Scholarship

Type of award: Scholarship.
Intended use: For undergraduate study at 2-year or 4-year institution in United States.
Eligibility: Applicant must be of Italian heritage. Applicant must be U.S. citizen or permanent resident.
Basis for selection: Major/career interest in business. Applicant must demonstrate financial need and high academic achievement.
Application requirements: $10 application fee. Essay and transcript. Photograph, College Scholarship Service Financial Aid Profile.
Additional information: Must have completed 13 hours of community service within the Italian-American community. Send business size SASE for application.

    Amount of award: $2,000
    Application deadline: May 31
    Notification begins: November 15

Contact:
National Italian American Foundation
Dr. Maria Lombardo
1860 19th Street, NW
Washington, DC 20009
Phone: 202-530-5315

Vincent and Anna Visceglia Fellowship

Type of award: Scholarship.
Intended use: For master's, doctoral study at graduate institution in United States.
Eligibility: Applicant must be of Italian heritage. Applicant must be U.S. citizen or permanent resident.
Basis for selection: Major/career interest in Italian-American studies. Applicant must demonstrate financial need and high academic achievement.
Application requirements: $10 application fee. Essay and transcript. Photograph, College Scholarship Service Financial Aid Profile.
Additional information: Must have completed 13 hours of community service within the Italian-American community. Send business size SASE to receive application form.

Amount of award:	$1,000
Number of awards:	1
Application deadline:	May 31
Notification begins:	November
Total amount awarded:	$1,000

Contact:
National Italian American Foundation
Dr. Maria Lombardo
1860 19 Street NW
Washington, DC 20009
Phone: 202-530-5315

Vincente Minelli Scholarship

Type of award: Scholarship.
Intended use: For undergraduate study at postsecondary institution in United States.
Eligibility: Applicant must be of Italian heritage. Applicant must be U.S. citizen or permanent resident residing in California.
Basis for selection: Major/career interest in performing arts; theater (artistic). Applicant must demonstrate financial need and high academic achievement.
Application requirements: $10 application fee. Essay, transcript and proof of eligibility. Photograph, College Scholarship Service Financial Aid Profile.
Additional information: Must have completed 13 hours of community service within the Italian-American community. Send business size SASE to receive application form.

Amount of award:	$1,000
Number of awards:	1
Application deadline:	May 31
Notification begins:	November 15
Total amount awarded:	$1,000

Contact:
National Italian American Foundation
Dr. Maria Lombardo
1860 19 Street NW
Washington, DC 20009
Phone: 202-530-5315

West Virginia Italian Heritage Festival Scholarship

Type of award: Scholarship.
Intended use: For undergraduate study at 2-year or 4-year institution in United States.
Eligibility: Applicant must be of Italian heritage. Applicant must be U.S. citizen or permanent resident residing in West Virginia.
Basis for selection: Applicant must demonstrate financial need and high academic achievement.
Application requirements: $10 application fee. Essay, transcript and proof of eligibility.
Additional information: Must have completed 13 hours of community service within the Italian-American community. Send business size SASE to receive application.

Amount of award:	$3,500
Application deadline:	May 31
Notification begins:	November
Total amount awarded:	$3,500

Contact:
National Italian American Foundation
Dr. Maria Lombardo
1860 19 Street NW
Washington, DC 20009
Phone: 202-530-5315

Zecchino Postgraduate Orthopaedic Fellowship

Type of award: Scholarship.
Intended use: For postgraduate study at graduate institution outside United States in Italy. Designated institutions: Must be used at Rizzoli Orthopaedic Institute at the University of Bologna.
Eligibility: Applicant must be of Italian heritage. Applicant must be U.S. citizen or permanent resident.
Basis for selection: Major/career interest in medicine (m.d.). Applicant must demonstrate financial need and high academic achievement.
Application requirements: $10 application fee. Recommendations, essay and transcript. Photograph, College Scholarship Service Financial Aid Profile.
Additional information: Fellowship available to graduate M.D. at the completion of four years of orthopaedic residency at a hospital approved by the American Academy of Orthopaedic Surgeons. Must have completed 13 hours of community service within the Italian-American community. Send business size SASE for application.

Amount of award:	$2,000
Application deadline:	May 31
Notification begins:	November 15

Contact:
National Italian American Foundation
Dr. Maria Lombardo
1860 19th Street, NW
Washington, DC 20009
Phone: 202-530-5315

National Journal

National Journal Editorial Internship

Type of award: Internship.
Intended use: For senior or graduate study.
Eligibility: Applicant must be U.S. citizen or permanent resident.
Basis for selection: Major/career interest in political science/government; journalism.
Application requirements: Portfolio.
Additional information: Summer application deadline is 3/15/98. Good writing skills and strong interest in government and politics required.

Amount of award: $2,400-$2,500
Application deadline: July 15, November 15
Contact:
National Journal
1501 M St., NW
Washington, DC 20036

National League of American Pen Women

American Pen Women Award: Arts

Type of award: Scholarship.
Intended use: For non-degree study.
Eligibility: Applicant must be female.
Basis for selection: Competition in Visual arts. quality, originality, workmanship, creativity, and/or performance. Major/career interest in arts, general.
Application requirements: $8 application fee. Portfolio.
Additional information: Awards offered in even-numbered years. Portfolio must include three four-by-six color prints (no slides) in any media. Photographic entries should submit three eight-by-ten color or black and white photographs. Awards to be used to further artistic purpose. Include business-size SASE with all information requests. In order to have pictures returned, applicant should include SASE.
Amount of award: $1,000
Number of awards: 1
Number of applicants: 130
Application deadline: January 15
Total amount awarded: $1,000
Contact:
National League of American Pen Women
Attn: Shirley Helberg
Rd #4 Box 4245
Spring Grove, PA 17362
Phone: 410-522-2557

American Pen Women Award: Letters

Type of award: Scholarship.
Intended use: For non-degree study.
Eligibility: Applicant must be female.
Basis for selection: Competition in Writing/journalism. quality, originality, workmanship, creativity, and/or performance.
Application requirements: $8 application fee. Portfolio.
Additional information: Applicant may submit essay or short story not exceeding 4,000 words, three poems, television script or play, first chapter of a novel with ten page outline, or an editorial. Awards offered in even-numbered years. Awards to be used to further artistic purpose. Include business-size SASE with all information requests. Will not return manuscripts. Will send list of winners if SASE is sent.
Amount of award: $1,000
Number of awards: 1
Number of applicants: 160
Application deadline: January 15
Total amount awarded: $1,000
Contact:
National League of American Pen Women
Attn: Shirley Helberg
Rd #4 Box 4245
Spring Grove, PA 17326
Phone: 410-522-2557

American Pen Women Award: Music

Type of award: Scholarship.
Intended use: For non-degree study.
Eligibility: Applicant must be female.
Basis for selection: Competition in Music performance/composition. quality, originality, workmanship, creativity, and/or performance. Major/career interest in music.
Application requirements: $8 application fee. Portfolio.
Additional information: Applicants must submit two scores of at least 12 minutes and at most 25 minutes. Must not have received previous award for work. One score must have been written within the past five years. Awards offered in even-numbered years. Awards to be used to further creative purpose. Include business-size SASE with information requests. To have score returned include SASE.
Amount of award: $1,000
Number of awards: 1
Number of applicants: 7
Application deadline: January 15
Total amount awarded: $1,000
Contact:
National League of American Pen Women
Attn: Shirley Helberg
Rd #4 Box 4245
Spring Grove, PA 17362
Phone: 410-522-2557

National Medical Fellowships, Inc.

C.R. Bard Foundation Prize

Type of award: Scholarship.
Intended use: For first professional study in United States.
Eligibility: Applicant must be Alaskan native, American Indian, African American, Mexican American or Puerto Rican. Applicant must be U.S. citizen.
Basis for selection: Major/career interest in medicine (m.d.); medicine, osteopathic. Applicant must demonstrate leadership and high academic achievement.
Application requirements: Recommendations, transcript and nomination by medical school dean.
Additional information: Fields of study: Cardiology and Urology. Applicants must be fourth year medical students.

National Medical Fellowships, Inc.: C.R. Bard Foundation Prize

Amount of award:	$5,000
Number of awards:	1
Application deadline:	February 16
Notification begins:	March 16
Total amount awarded:	$5,000

Contact:
National Medical Fellowships, Inc.
110 West 32 Street
8th Floor
New York, NY 10001-3205
Phone: 212-714-0933

Fellowship Program in Academic Medicine

Type of award: Research grant.
Intended use: For first professional study in United States.
Eligibility: Applicant must be Alaskan native, American Indian, African American, Mexican American or Puerto Rican. Applicant must be U.S. citizen.
Basis for selection: Major/career interest in medicine (m.d.); medicine, osteopathic. Applicant must demonstrate leadership and high academic achievement.
Application requirements: Recommendations, essay, transcript, proof of eligibility, research proposal and nomination by medical school deans.
Additional information: Open to second and third-year medical students.

Amount of award:	$6,000
Number of awards:	35
Number of applicants:	49
Application deadline:	December 15
Notification begins:	April 17
Total amount awarded:	$210,000

Contact:
National Medical Fellowships, Inc.
110 West 32 Street
8th Floor
New York, NY 10001-3205
Phone: 212-714-0933

Franklin C. McLean Award

Type of award: Scholarship.
Intended use: For first professional study in United States.
Eligibility: Applicant must be Alaskan native, American Indian, African American, Mexican American or Puerto Rican. Applicant must be U.S. citizen.
Basis for selection: Major/career interest in medicine (m.d.); medicine, osteopathic. Applicant must demonstrate leadership, service orientation and high academic achievement.
Application requirements: Recommendations, transcript and nomination by medical school deans.
Additional information: Applicant must be senior medical student.

Amount of award:	$3,000
Number of awards:	1
Application deadline:	July 30
Notification begins:	September 26

Contact:
National Medical Fellowships, Inc.
110 West 32 Street
8th Floor
New York, NY 10001-3205
Phone: 212-714-0933

Henry G. Award

Type of award: Scholarship.
Intended use: For first professional study in United States.
Eligibility: Applicant must be African American. Applicant must be male. Applicant must be U.S. citizen.
Basis for selection: Major/career interest in medicine (m.d.); medicine, osteopathic. Applicant must demonstrate leadership and financial need.
Application requirements: Recommendations, essay, transcript and proof of eligibility.
Additional information: Applicant must be first year medical student.

Amount of award:	$760
Number of awards:	5
Application deadline:	June 30
Notification begins:	December 15
Total amount awarded:	$3,800

Contact:
National Medical Fellowships, Inc.
110 West 32 Street
8th Floor
New York, NY 10001-3205
Phone: 212-714-1007

Irving Graef Memorial Scholarship

Type of award: Research grant, renewable.
Intended use: For first professional study in United States.
Eligibility: Applicant must be American Indian, African American, Mexican American, Hispanic American or Puerto Rican. Applicant must be U.S. citizen.
Basis for selection: Major/career interest in medicine (m.d.). Applicant must demonstrate leadership, service orientation and high academic achievement.
Application requirements: Recommendations, essay, transcript, proof of eligibility and nomination by medical school dean.
Additional information: Open to third year medical students only.

Amount of award:	$2,000
Number of awards:	1
Number of applicants:	15
Total amount awarded:	$2,000

Contact:
National Medical Fellowships, Inc.
110 West 32 Street
8th Floor
New York, NY 10001
Phone: 212-714-1007

James H. Robinson Memorial Prize in Surgery

Type of award: Research grant.
Intended use: For first professional study in United States.
Eligibility: Applicant must be Alaskan native, American Indian, African American, Mexican American or Puerto Rican. Applicant must be U.S. citizen.
Basis for selection: Major/career interest in medicine (m.d.); medicine, osteopathic. Applicant must demonstrate high academic achievement.
Application requirements: Recommendations, transcript,

proof of eligibility, research proposal and nomination by medical school dean.
Additional information: Applicant must be senior medical student.

Amount of award:	$500
Number of awards:	1
Application deadline:	February 16
Notification begins:	March 16
Total amount awarded:	$500

Contact:
National Medical Fellowships, Inc.
110 West 32 Street
8th Floor
New York, NY 10001-3205
Phone: 212-714-0933

Medical Fellowships General Need-Based Scholarship

Type of award: Scholarship.
Intended use: For full-time first professional study at accredited graduate institution in United States.
Eligibility: Applicant must be Alaskan native, American Indian, African American, Mexican American or Puerto Rican. Applicant must be U.S. citizen.
Basis for selection: Major/career interest in medicine (m.d.); medicine, osteopathic. Applicant must demonstrate financial need.
Application requirements: Recommendations, essay, transcript and proof of eligibility.
Additional information: Applicant must be first- or second-year medical student.

Amount of award:	$500-$6,000
Number of awards:	252
Application deadline:	June 30, August 31
Notification begins:	December 15
Total amount awarded:	$420,900

Contact:
National Medical Fellowships, Inc. - Scholarship Department
110 West 32 Street
8th Floor
New York, NY 10001-3205
Phone: 212-714-1007

Medical Fellowships Special Awards Program

Type of award: Scholarship.
Intended use: For first professional study in United States.
Eligibility: Applicant must be African American. Applicant must be U.S. citizen.
Basis for selection: Major/career interest in medicine (m.d.); medicine, osteopathic. Applicant must demonstrate leadership, financial need and high academic achievement.
Application requirements: Recommendations, essay and transcript.

Amount of award:	$2,250
Number of awards:	11

Contact:
National Medical Fellowships, Inc.
110 West 32 Street
8th Floor
New York, NY 10001
Phone: 212-714-1007

Medical Fellowships Technology Training Program

Type of award: Research grant.
Intended use: For full-time first professional study in United States.
Eligibility: Applicant must be American Indian, African American, Mexican American, Hispanic American or Puerto Rican. Applicant must be U.S. citizen.
Basis for selection: Major/career interest in medicine (m.d.); medicine, osteopathic. Applicant must demonstrate leadership and high academic achievement.
Application requirements: Recommendations and essay.
Additional information: Applicant must have experience in using computers.

Amount of award:	$200-$400
Number of awards:	39
Number of applicants:	45
Total amount awarded:	$14,600

Contact:
National Medical Fellowships, Inc.
110 West 32 Street
8th Floor
New York, NY 10001-3205
Phone: 212-714-1007

Metropolitan Life Foundation Scholarship

Type of award: Scholarship.
Intended use: For first professional study in United States.
Eligibility: Applicant must be American Indian, African American, Mexican American, Hispanic American or Puerto Rican. Applicant must be U.S. citizen.
Basis for selection: Major/career interest in medicine (m.d.). Applicant must demonstrate leadership, financial need and high academic achievement.
Application requirements: Recommendations, essay, transcript and nomination by medical school deans.
Additional information: Applicant must be second- or third-year medical student

Amount of award:	$3,500
Number of awards:	12
Number of applicants:	18
Total amount awarded:	$42,000

Contact:
National Medical Fellowships, Inc.
110 West 32 Street
8th Floor
New York, NY 10001-3205
Phone: 212-714-1007

Ralph W. Ellison Prize

Type of award: Scholarship.
Intended use: For first professional study in United States.
Eligibility: Applicant must be Alaskan native, American Indian, African American, Mexican American or Puerto Rican. Applicant must be U.S. citizen.
Basis for selection: Major/career interest in medicine (m.d.); medicine, osteopathic. Applicant must demonstrate leadership and high academic achievement.
Application requirements: Recommendations, essay, transcript and nomination by medical school deans.

Additional information: Applicant must be graduating medical student.

Amount of award:	$500
Number of awards:	1
Application deadline:	February 16

Contact:
National Medical Fellowships, Inc.
110 West 32 Street
8th Floor
New York, NY 10001-3205
Phone: 212-714-0933

W.K. Kellog Community Medicine Training

Type of award: Research grant.
Intended use: For first professional study in United States.
Eligibility: Applicant must be American Indian, African American, Mexican American or Puerto Rican. Applicant must be U.S. citizen.
Basis for selection: Major/career interest in medicine (m.d.); medicine, osteopathic. Applicant must demonstrate leadership, service orientation and high academic achievement.
Application requirements: Recommendations, essay and transcript.
Additional information: Applicant must be second and third-year student interested in primary care career.

Amount of award:	$10,000
Number of awards:	15
Total amount awarded:	$150,000

Contact:
National Medical Fellowships, Inc.
110 West 32 Street
8th Floor
New York, NY 10001-3205
Phone: 212-714-1007

William and Charlotte Cadbury Award

Type of award: Scholarship.
Intended use: For first professional study in United States.
Eligibility: Applicant must be Alaskan native, American Indian, African American, Mexican American or Puerto Rican. Applicant must be U.S. citizen.
Basis for selection: Major/career interest in medicine (m.d.); medicine, osteopathic. Applicant must demonstrate leadership, service orientation and high academic achievement.
Application requirements: Recommendations, transcript and nomination by medical school dean.
Additional information: Open to senior year medical students.

Amount of award:	$2,000
Number of awards:	1
Application deadline:	July 30
Notification begins:	September 26
Total amount awarded:	$2,000

Contact:
National Medical Fellowships, Inc.
110 West 32 Street
8th Floor
New York, NY 10001-3205
Phone: 212-714-0933

Wyeth-Ayerst Laboratories Prize

Type of award: Scholarship.
Intended use: For first professional study in United States.
Eligibility: Applicant must be Alaskan native, American Indian, African American, Mexican American or Puerto Rican. Applicant must be female. Applicant must be U.S. citizen.
Basis for selection: Major/career interest in medicine (m.d.); medicine, osteopathic. Applicant must demonstrate leadership and high academic achievement.
Application requirements: Recommendations, transcript and nomination by medical school dean.
Additional information: Must study in the field of women's health. Applicant must be fourth-year medical student.

Amount of award:	$5,000
Number of awards:	2
Application deadline:	February 16
Total amount awarded:	$10,000

Contact:
National Medical Fellowships, Inc.
110 West 32 Street
8th Floor
New York, NY 10001
Phone: 212-714-0933

National Merit Scholarship Corporation

National Achievement Scholarship

Type of award: Scholarship.
Intended use: For full-time freshman study at accredited 4-year institution in United States.
Eligibility: Applicant must be African American. Applicant must be U.S. citizen or permanent resident.
Basis for selection: Applicant must demonstrate leadership, service orientation and high academic achievement.
Application requirements: Recommendations and essay.
Additional information: Selection based on academic ability, school and community activities, test scores, and school recommendations. Must take PSAT/NMSQT in junior year. Requirements are published each year in the PSAT/NMSQT Student Bulletin which is sent to high schools for distribution to students in advance of the October test administration. Some 1,500 of the highest scoring participants are named Semifinalists, and those who become Finalists are considered for Achievement Scholarship awards. Approximately 800 Achievement Scholarship awards are offered for full-time undergraduate study. There are 440 $2,000 single-payment awards for which all Finalists compete. The remaining Achievement Scholarship awards are offered to Finalists who have qualifications that particularly interest corporate or college sponsors of the scholarships. Corporate-sponsored scholarships may be designated for Finalists who are children of a company's employees, residents of a sponsor organization's service areas, or Finalists with particular college plans. Permanent residents eligible if in the process of becoming a citizen.

Amount of award:	$2,000
Number of awards:	800
Number of applicants:	100,000
Notification begins:	February 15
Total amount awarded:	$3,000,000

National Merit Scholarship

Type of award: Scholarship, renewable.
Intended use: For full-time freshman study at accredited 4-year institution in United States.
Eligibility: Applicant must be high school junior. Applicant must be U.S. citizen or permanent resident.
Basis for selection: Applicant must demonstrate leadership, service orientation and high academic achievement.
Application requirements: Recommendations and essay.
Additional information: Competition is open to all U.S. high school students who take the PSAT/NMSQT in the proper year in high school and meet other participation requirements. Those requirements are published each year in the PSAT/NMSQT Student Bulletin, which is sent to high schools for distribution to students in advance of the October test administration. Some 15,500 of the highest scoring participants are designated Semifinalists, on a state representational basis. Finalists are considered for Merit Scholarship awards based on academic and other requirements, and winners are chosen on the basis of their abilities, skills, and accomplishments. About 7,600 Merit Scholarship Awards of three types are offered annually. 2,400 single-payment $2,000 scholarships are awarded for which all Finalists compete. More than 4,000 four-year Merit Scholarship awards are financed by colleges and universities for finalists who must attend the sponsor institution. About 1,200 Merit Scholarship awards are sponsored by corporations and other business organizations for Finalists who meet a sponsor's preferential criteria. In addition, approximately 1,400 Special Scholarships for high performers are awarded. Permanent residents eligible if in the process of becoming a U.S. citizen.

Number of awards:	7,400
Notification begins:	March 31
Total amount awarded:	$28,000,000

National Museum of the American Indian

National Museum of the American Indian Internship

Type of award: Internship.
Intended use: For undergraduate, graduate or non-degree study.
Additional information: Internships available at NMAI in Washington, D.C., and New York City. Some positions provide stipends and cover expenses, other do not. Deadlines for summer positions is March 15, for winter is October 15. Applications for positions that do not offer a stipend are accepted at any time of the year. Placement is based on applicant's experience and needs of museum. American Indians and Alaskan natives applicants are preferred for most positions.

Application deadline:	June 15, January 15

Contact:
National Museum of the American Indian
470 L'Enfant Plaza
Suite 7103, MRC 934
Washington, DC 20560
Website: www.si.edu/nmai

National Museum of Women in the Arts

Coca-Cola Internship

Type of award: Internship.
Intended use: For junior, senior, graduate or non-degree study in United States. Designated institutions: National Museum of Women in the Arts.
Basis for selection: Major/career interest in museum studies; education; library science; publishing; womenÖs studies; art, art history. Applicant must demonstrate seriousness of purpose and high academic achievement.
Application requirements: Recommendations, essay and transcript. Resume and a brief writing sample of 1-2 pages in length.
Additional information: Internships lasts 10-12 months. Includes $1500 stipend. Available to students interested in pursuing museum careers. Must have a 3.25 GPA. Application deadline for winter internship is October 30, for summer internship is March 15.

Amount of award:	$1,500
Number of awards:	1
Number of applicants:	113
Application deadline:	June 15
Total amount awarded:	$1,500

Contact:
National Museum of Women in the Arts
1250 New York Avenue, NW
Washington, DC 20005-3920
Website: www.nmwa.org

Lebovitz Internship

Type of award: Internship.
Intended use: For junior, senior, graduate or non-degree study in Washington, DC. Designated institutions: National Museum of Women in the Arts.
Basis for selection: Major/career interest in womenÖs studies; art, art history; business, management and administration; education; arts management; museum studies. Applicant must demonstrate seriousness of purpose and high academic achievement.
Application requirements: Recommendations, essay and transcript. Resume and a writing sample.
Additional information: Ten to 12 month internship to promote careers of young artists. Stipend of $1500. Open to applicants who have not yet entered graduate school. Must have 3.25 GPA. Application deadline for winter internship is October 30, for summer internship is March 15.

Amount of award:	$1,500
Number of awards:	1
Number of applicants:	70
Application deadline:	May 31
Total amount awarded:	$1,500

Contact:
National Museum of Women in the Arts
1250 New York Avenue, NW
Washington, DC 20005-3920
Website: www.nmwa.org

Museum Internships in Washington DC

Type of award: Internship.
Intended use: For junior, senior, graduate or non-degree study. Designated institutions: National Museum of Women in the Arts.
Basis for selection: Major/career interest in museum studies/administration; education; library science; publishing; womenÖs studies; art, art history. Applicant must demonstrate seriousness of purpose and high academic achievement.
Application requirements: Recommendations, essay and transcript.
Additional information: Internships last 10-12 months and are unpaid. Must have 3.0 GPA. Application deadline for winter is October 30th and summer is March 15th.

Application deadline:	May 31

Contact:
National Museum of Women in the Arts
Attn: Andrea Leifer-Schless
1250 New York Ave. NW
Washington, DC 20005-3920
Phone: 202-783-5000
Website: www.nmwa.org

National Organization for Women Legal Defense and Education Fund

National Organization for Women legal defense and Education fund Internships

Type of award: Internship.
Intended use: For junior, senior or graduate study.
Eligibility: Applicant must be Must be studying in the USA.
Basis for selection: Major/career interest in law; public relations. Applicant must demonstrate depth of character, leadership, seriousness of purpose and service orientation.
Application requirements: Recommendations and proof of eligibility.
Additional information: Submit resume and cover letter. Internships are located in New York City and Washington D.C.

Amount of award:	$1,500-$3,500
Application deadline:	March 31, December 1

Contact:
National Organization for Women Legal Defense and Education Fund
Internship Coordinator
99 Hudson St.
New York, NY 10013

National Physical Science Consortium

Physical Science Graduate Fellowship: Minorities and Women

Type of award: Scholarship, renewable.
Intended use: For full-time doctoral study at graduate institution in United States. Designated institutions: Must be an NPSC member institution.
Eligibility: Applicant must be of minority background. Applicant must be U.S. citizen.
Basis for selection: Major/career interest in physical sciences; mathematics; computer and information sciences; chemistry; astronomy; geology/earth sciences; physics. Applicant must demonstrate high academic achievement.
Application requirements: Recommendations and transcript. General GREs.
Additional information: Recruitment emphasis on minorities and women. Additional field of study: materials science. Recipient must work for National Physical Science Consortium employer member during summers preceding and following first year of graduate school. Minimum undergraduate GPA of 3.0.

Amount of award:	$12,500-$15,000
Number of awards:	226
Number of applicants:	278
Application deadline:	November 5
Notification begins:	February 1

Contact:
National Physical Science Consortium
New Mexico State University, MSC 3NPS
University Avenue, Box 30001
Las Cruces, NM 88003-8001
Phone: 800-952-4118
Website: www.nmsu.edu/~npsc

National Research Council

Ford Foundation Dissertation Fellowship: Minorities

Type of award: Research grant.
Intended use: For doctoral study at accredited graduate institution.
Eligibility: Applicant must be Alaskan native, American Indian, Asian American, African American, Mexican American

or Puerto Rican. Applicants of Asian descent must be Pacific Islanders. Applicant must be U.S. citizen.
Basis for selection: Major/career interest in social and behavioral sciences; engineering; mathematics; biology. Applicant must demonstrate high academic achievement.
Application requirements: Recommendations, transcript and research proposal.
Additional information: Fellowships intended for Ph.D. or Sc.D. candidates who have finished all course work, examinations, and requirements. Dissertation topic/proposal must have been approved. Support intended for final year of dissertation writing. Additional fields include Physics and Astronomy, Chemistry, Computer, Life and Earth Sciences. Fellowships last 9 or 12 months.

Amount of award:	$18,000
Number of awards:	29
Number of applicants:	400
Application deadline:	November 15
Notification begins:	April 1
Total amount awarded:	$540,000

Contact:
National Research Council
Fellowship Office
2101 Constitution Avenue
Washington, DC 20418
Website: fellowships.nas.edu

Ford Foundation Postdoctoral Fellowships for Minorities

Type of award: Research grant.
Intended use: For full-time postgraduate study at graduate institution in United States.
Eligibility: Applicant must be Alaskan native, American Indian, Asian American, African American, Mexican American or Puerto Rican. Applicants of Asian descent must be Pacific Islanders. Applicant must be U.S. citizen.
Basis for selection: Major/career interest in social and behavioral sciences; humanities/liberal arts; engineering; mathematics; physical sciences. Applicant must demonstrate high academic achievement.
Application requirements: Recommendations, transcript and research proposal. Current curriculum vitae that lists publications, listing of courses taught in the last five years with teaching load indicated, one-page abstract of the doctoral dissertation, and a working bibliography with annotation of 10 to 12 key sources.
Additional information: Additional field considered: life sciences. Fellowships last nine or twelve months and are to be used at not-for-profit U.S. institutions.

Amount of award:	$32,500
Number of awards:	20
Application deadline:	January 5

Contact:
National Research Council
2101 Constitution Avenue
Washington, DC 20418
Phone: 202-334-2860.
Website: fellowships.nas.edu.

Ford Foundation Predoctoral Fellowship: Minorities

Type of award: Research grant, renewable.
Intended use: For full-time doctoral study at accredited graduate institution in United States.
Eligibility: Applicant must be Alaskan native, American Indian, Asian American, African American, Mexican American or Puerto Rican. Applicants of Asian descent must be Pacific Islanders. Applicant must be U.S. citizen.
Basis for selection: Major/career interest in social and behavioral sciences; mathematics; physical sciences; humanities/liberal arts; chemistry; physics; astronomy; computer and information sciences; geology/earth sciences. Applicant must demonstrate high academic achievement.
Application requirements: Recommendations, essay, transcript and research proposal. GRE test scores.
Additional information: Awards for research-based programs that lead to careers in teaching and research at the university or college level. Award includes an additional $7500 cost of education allowance to applicant's university. Must not have completed more than 30 semester-hours or 45 quarter-hours of graduate level study in field of program. Applicants in life sciences may also apply. Fellowships are funded for three years work and are to be used within five years.

Amount of award:	$14,000
Number of awards:	50
Number of applicants:	500
Application deadline:	November 15
Notification begins:	April 1

Contact:
National Research Council
Fellowship Office
2101 Constitution Avenue
Washington, DC 20418
Website: fellowships.nas.edu

H. Hughes Medical Institute Predoctoral Fellowship

Type of award: Scholarship, renewable.
Intended use: For full-time doctoral study at accredited graduate institution in or outside United States.
Eligibility: Twelve percent of awards given to minorities. Applicant must be International students may study only at U.S. institutions.
Basis for selection: Major/career interest in biology; pharmacy/pharmaceutics/pharmacology; neuroscience; microbiology. Applicant must demonstrate high academic achievement.
Application requirements: Recommendations, transcript and research proposal. GRE general and subject tests.
Additional information: Permanent residents and foreign students must study in U.S. Must not have completed more than one year of graduate study in biological sciences. Award support for study toward Ph.D. or Sc.D. Includes $15,000 cost of education allowance to university. Fellowship initially lasts three years but is open to further study depending on status of research work.

Amount of award:	$15,000
Number of awards:	80
Number of applicants:	1,500
Application deadline:	November 12
Notification begins:	April 1
Total amount awarded:	$1,200,000

Contact:
National Research Council
Hughes Predoctoral Fellowship/Fellowships Office
2100 Constitution Avenue
Washington, DC 20418
Phone: 202-334-2872
Fax: 202-334-3419
Website: fellowships.nas.edu

Integrated Manufacturing Fellowship

Type of award: Research grant.
Intended use: For full-time doctoral study in United States.
Eligibility: Applicant must be U.S. citizen or permanent resident.
Basis for selection: Major/career interest in manufacturing technologies; engineering. Applicant must demonstrate high academic achievement.
Application requirements: Recommendations, transcript and research proposal. Previous research and experience, and four reference report forms.
Additional information: Period of time spent in industrial manufacturing setting is required in research plan. In addition to stipend an allowance of up to $15000 is available to cover tuition and fees. Fellowships are funded for three years of study.

Amount of award:	$20,000
Number of awards:	12
Application deadline:	December 6

Contact:
National Research Council
Fellowships Office
2101 Constitution Avenue
Washington, DC 20418
Phone: 202-334-2872
Fax: 202-334-3419
Website: fellowships.nas.edu

National Restaurant Association Education Foundation

H.J. Heinz Graduate Degree Fellowship

Type of award: Scholarship, renewable.
Intended use: For full-time or half-time master's, doctoral study.
Basis for selection: Major/career interest in food production/management/services; culinary arts; food science and technology; hotel/restaurant management. Applicant must demonstrate financial need and high academic achievement.
Application requirements: Recommendations.
Additional information: Applicant must be high-school or college-level hospitality educator/administrator pursuing a post-graduate degree. Graduate teaching assistants must have taught full-time.

Amount of award:	$2,000
Number of awards:	10
Number of applicants:	75
Application deadline:	February 15
Notification begins:	March 31
Total amount awarded:	$20,000

National Restaurant Association Undergraduate Scholarship

Type of award: Scholarship, renewable.
Intended use: For full-time freshman, sophomore, junior or senior study at vocational, 2-year or 4-year institution in or outside United States.
Basis for selection: Major/career interest in food production/management/services; culinary arts; hotel/restaurant management; dietetics/nutrition. Applicant must demonstrate financial need and high academic achievement.
Application requirements: Recommendations and transcript.
Additional information: Minimum 3.0 GPA and at least 1,000 hours of industry-related work experience required. Must have completed first semester of two- or four-year degree.

Amount of award:	$1,000-$5,000
Number of awards:	100
Number of applicants:	1,000
Application deadline:	March 1
Notification begins:	July 15
Total amount awarded:	$150,000

ProManagement Scholarship

Type of award: Scholarship.
Intended use: For full-time or half-time non-degree study. Designated institutions: School must be a ProManagement partner.
Basis for selection: Major/career interest in food production/management/services; culinary arts; hotel/restaurant management; food science and technology. Applicant must demonstrate seriousness of purpose.
Application requirements: Essay. Applicant must write essay on career goals in food service/hospitality industry.
Additional information: Applicant must be enrolled in and have completed two ProManagement courses (home study accepted). Applicants evaluated on food service/hospitality-related work experience.

Amount of award:	$850
Number of awards:	112
Number of applicants:	250
Application deadline:	November 1, May 1
Notification begins:	December 1, June 1
Total amount awarded:	$112,000

Teacher Work-Study Grant

Type of award: Internship, renewable.
Intended use: For master's, doctoral study.
Basis for selection: Major/career interest in food production/management/services; culinary arts; food science and

technology; hotel/restaurant management. Applicant must demonstrate high academic achievement.
Application requirements: Recommendations and transcript.
Additional information: Applicant must be a full-time high school or college teacher or administrator in hotel, restaurant, institutional management or food production. Applicants must arrange for full-time summer employment in line or staff position in the food service/hospitality industry.

Amount of award:	$750-$3,000
Number of awards:	20
Number of applicants:	90
Application deadline:	February 15
Notification begins:	March 31
Total amount awarded:	$60,000

National Scholarship Trust Fund of the Graphic Arts

National Scholarship Trust Fund of the Graphic Arts

Type of award: Scholarship, renewable.
Intended use: For undergraduate or graduate study at 2-year, 4-year or graduate institution in United States.
Eligibility: Applicant must be U.S. citizen.
Basis for selection: Major/career interest in graphic arts and design; publishing. Applicant must demonstrate depth of character, leadership, seriousness of purpose and high academic achievement.
Application requirements: Recommendations and transcript.
Additional information: Some scholarships require that either student or parent belong to or be employed by specific institutions. Contact office for more information.

Amount of award:	$500-$4,000
Number of awards:	330
Number of applicants:	1,750
Application deadline:	March 1
Notification begins:	June 15
Total amount awarded:	$300,000

National Scholarship Trust Fund of the Graphic Arts Graduate Fellowships

Type of award: Scholarship, renewable.
Intended use: For full-time master's study.
Eligibility: Applicant must be U.S. citizen.
Basis for selection: Major/career interest in graphic arts and design; publishing. Applicant must demonstrate depth of character, leadership, seriousness of purpose, service orientation and high academic achievement.
Application requirements: Recommendations and transcript.
Additional information: Application requirements and criteria may vary by Trust Fund member institution. Contact the coordinator for specific information.

Amount of award:	$2,000-$4,000
Number of awards:	9
Number of applicants:	20
Application deadline:	February 1
Notification begins:	April 28
Total amount awarded:	$30,000

National Scholarship Trust Fund of the Graphic Arts Undergraduate Scholarships

Type of award: Scholarship, renewable.
Intended use: For full-time undergraduate study.
Eligibility: Applicant must be U.S. citizen.
Basis for selection: Major/career interest in graphic arts and design; publishing. Applicant must demonstrate depth of character, leadership, seriousness of purpose, service orientation and high academic achievement.
Application requirements: Recommendations and transcript.
Additional information: Minimum 3.0 GPA preferred. Application deadlines are March 1st for high school seniors and high school graduates not currently attending college, and April 1st for current undergraduate students. Application requirements and criteria may vary by trust fund member institution. Contact the coordinator for specific information.

Amount of award:	$500-$2,000
Number of awards:	304
Number of applicants:	2,000
Application deadline:	June 15
Total amount awarded:	$300,000

Contact:
National Scholarship Trust Fund of the Graphic Arts
200 Deer Run Road
Sewickley, PA 15154
Website: www.gatf.org

National Science Teachers Association

Duracell Competition

Type of award: Scholarship.
Intended use: For non-degree study.
Eligibility: Applicant must be enrolled in high school. Applicant must be U.S. citizen.
Basis for selection: Competition in Science project. creativity, practicality of device and clarity of essay.
Application requirements: Essay. Wiring diagram, photo of device, official entry form.
Additional information: Students design and build working devices powered by Duracell batteries. Awards given in the form of US Series EE savings bonds. Students in grades seven through twelve are eligible to enter.

Amount of award:	$200-$20,000
Number of awards:	100
Number of applicants:	1,542
Application deadline:	January 15
Total amount awarded:	$104,300

Toshiba Exploravision Award

Type of award: Scholarship.
Intended use: For non-degree study.
Eligibility: Applicant must be enrolled in high school. Applicant must be Open to Canadian citizens.
Basis for selection: Competition in Science project. scientific accuracy, creativity, communication and feasibility of vision.
Application requirements: Description paper, series of storyboard frames.
Additional information: Each first place winner receives a $10,000 savings bond, each second place winner receives a $5,000 savings bond, and regional winners receive a $100 savings bond. This competition for grades K through twelve.

Amount of award:	$100-$10,000
Number of awards:	168
Number of applicants:	17,043
Application deadline:	February 3
Notification begins:	March 30
Total amount awarded:	$282,800

Contact:
Toshiba/National Science Teachers Association ExploraVision Awards
1840 Wilson Boulevard
Attn: Pamela Riley
Arlington, VA 22201-3000

National Sculpture Society

Sculpture Society Scholarship

Type of award: Scholarship, renewable.
Intended use: For undergraduate, master's or doctoral study at postsecondary institution in United States.
Eligibility: Applicant must be U.S. citizen or permanent resident.
Basis for selection: Competition in Photography. Slides or photos of work Major/career interest in arts, general. Applicant must demonstrate financial need.
Application requirements: Portfolio, recommendations, essay and proof of eligibility. Eight to ten 8" x 10" photographs of sculpture, proof of financial need, letter of backround and interest in sculpture.
Additional information: Must be studying figurative sculpture.

Amount of award:	$1,000
Number of awards:	3
Number of applicants:	40
Application deadline:	May 31
Notification begins:	June 15
Total amount awarded:	$3,000

Contact:
National Sculpture Society
1177 Avenue of the Americas
New York, NY 10036
Phone: 212-764-5645

National Society for Experiential Education

Experiential Education Internship

Type of award: Internship, renewable.
Intended use: For undergraduate, graduate or non-degree study at accredited postsecondary institution in Raleigh, NC.
Eligibility: Applicant must be of minority background.
Basis for selection: Major/career interest in education; library science; marketing; computer and information sciences. Applicant must demonstrate leadership and seriousness of purpose.
Application requirements: Interview, recommendations and essay. Resume, letter outlining interests, and writing sample.
Additional information: Internships pay $5 to $7 per hour. Experience or interest in experiential education is helpful but not necessary. Strong writing and editing skills essential. Encouraged to arrange for academic credit.
Contact:
National Society for Experiential Education
Internship Program Manager
3509 Haworth Drive, Suite 207
Raleigh, NC 27609-7229
Phone: 919-787-3263
Fax: 919-787-3381
Website: www.nsee.org

National Society of Public Accountants

Public Accountants Scholarship

Type of award: Scholarship.
Intended use: For freshman, sophomore, junior or senior study at accredited vocational, 2-year or 4-year institution in United States.
Basis for selection: Major/career interest in accounting. Applicant must demonstrate leadership, financial need and high academic achievement.
Application requirements: Transcript.
Additional information: Minimum 3.0 GPA. Applicants must be U.S. or Canadian citizens. Evening program students considered full time if pursuing accounting degree. Competition's most outstanding student receives an additional stipend.

Amount of award:	$500-$1,000
Number of awards:	40
Number of applicants:	1,751
Application deadline:	March 10
Notification begins:	July 31
Total amount awarded:	$38,200

Contact:
National Society of Public Accountants
Scholarship Foundation
1010 North Fairfax Street
Alexandria, VA 22314-1574
Website: www.nsacct.org

National Society of the Colonial Dames of America

Colonial Dames of America Indian Nurse Scholarship

Type of award: Scholarship, renewable.
Intended use: For undergraduate, master's or doctoral study at accredited postsecondary institution.
Eligibility: Applicant must be American Indian. Must be enrolled member of a tribe.
Basis for selection: Major/career interest in nursing. Applicant must demonstrate seriousness of purpose, service orientation and financial need.
Application requirements: Recommendations, essay and transcript.
Additional information: Applicant not considered if already receiving an Indian Health Service Scholarship.
   Amount of award: $500-$1,000
   Number of awards: 16
Contact:
National Society of the Colonial Dames of America
Mrs. E. Eugene Trotter
3064 Luvan Blvd. - DeBordieu
Georgetown, SC 29440
Phone: 8035273140

National Space Society

National Space Society Internship Program

Type of award: Internship.
Intended use: For junior, senior, graduate or postgraduate study.
Basis for selection: Major/career interest in communications; aerospace; business, management and administration.
Application requirements: Interview, portfolio and recommendations.
Additional information: The NSS provides a multifaceted intern experience involving everything from special events to educational outreach and grassroots field organization administration. NSS hires interns at all times of the year. Communications and writing skills are essential. Online research skills are a plus.
Contact:
National Space Society
600 Pennsylvania Ave. SE
Suite 201
Washington, DC 20003
Website: www.nss.org

National Speakers Association

National Speakers Association Scholarship

Type of award: Scholarship.
Intended use: For full-time junior, senior or graduate study.
Basis for selection: Major/career interest in communications. Applicant must demonstrate leadership, seriousness of purpose and high academic achievement.
Application requirements: Recommendations, essay and transcript.
Additional information: Applicant must have an above-average academic record.
   Amount of award: $3,000
   Number of awards: 4
   Application deadline: June 1
   Notification begins: July 1
   Total amount awarded: $12,000
Contact:
National Speakers Association
1500 South Priest Drive
Tempe, AZ 85281
Phone: 602-968-2552
Fax: 602-968-0911
Website: www.nsaspeaker.org

National Stone Association

Stone Quarry Engineering Scholarship

Type of award: Scholarship.
Intended use: For full-time undergraduate or graduate study.
Eligibility: Applicant must be U.S. citizen or permanent resident.
Basis for selection: Major/career interest in engineering. Applicant must demonstrate depth of character, leadership, seriousness of purpose, service orientation and high academic achievement.
Application requirements: Recommendations and essay.
   Amount of award: $2,500
   Number of awards: 8
   Number of applicants: 31
   Application deadline: May 31
   Notification begins: June 1
   Total amount awarded: $20,000
Contact:
National Stone Association
Attn: Kash H. McClure
1415 Elliot Place, N.W.
Washington, DC 20007
Phone: 202-342-1100

National Tourism Foundation

Bill Carpenter Memorial Certificate School Scholarship

Type of award: Scholarship.
Intended use: For full-time undergraduate certificate study.
Basis for selection: Major/career interest in tourism and travel; culinary arts. Applicant must demonstrate high academic achievement.
Application requirements: Recommendations, essay, transcript and proof of eligibility. Resume, as well as travel curriculum in which he/she is involved and proof of enrollment.
Additional information: Minimum 3.0 GPA. This award does not apply for students attending a two year or technical institution. This award is for use in certificate schools in the travel and tourism profession only.
  Amount of award: $500
  Application deadline: April 15

Dr. Tom Anderson Memorial Scholarship

Type of award: Scholarship.
Intended use: For full-time junior, senior study.
Eligibility: Applicant must be U.S. citizen, permanent resident or Canadian Citizen.
Basis for selection: Major/career interest in tourism and travel; culinary arts. Applicant must demonstrate high academic achievement.
Application requirements: Recommendations, essay and transcript. Resume.
Additional information: Minimum 3.0 GPA.
  Amount of award: $2,000
  Application deadline: April 15

Eric and Bette Friedhiem Scholarship

Type of award: Scholarship.
Intended use: For full-time junior, senior study.
Eligibility: Applicant must be U.S. citizen, permanent resident or Canadian Citizen.
Basis for selection: Major/career interest in tourism and travel; culinary arts. Applicant must demonstrate high academic achievement.
Application requirements: Recommendations, essay and transcript. Resume.
Additional information: Minimum 3.0 GPA.
  Amount of award: $500
  Application deadline: April 15

H. Neil Mecaskey Scholarship

Type of award: Scholarship.
Intended use: For full-time junior, senior study.
Eligibility: Applicant must be U.S. citizen, permanent resident or Canadian Citizen.
Basis for selection: Major/career interest in tourism and travel; culinary arts. Applicant must demonstrate high academic achievement.
Application requirements: Recommendations, essay and transcript. Resume.
Additional information: Minimum 3.0 GPA. Must be enrolled in a four year institution at time of application.
  Amount of award: $500
  Application deadline: April 15

Louise Dessureault Memorial Scholarship

Type of award: Scholarship.
Intended use: For full-time junior, senior study at 4-year institution in or outside United States.
Basis for selection: Major/career interest in tourism and travel; culinary arts. Applicant must demonstrate high academic achievement.
Application requirements: Recommendations, essay and transcript. Resume.
Additional information: Minimum 3.0 GPA. Must be resident of Canada.
  Amount of award: $500
  Application deadline: April 15

Luray Caverns Grant

Type of award: Scholarship.
Intended use: For graduate study.
Basis for selection: Major/career interest in tourism and travel; culinary arts.
Application requirements: Transcript and research proposal. Resume.
Additional information: Award recipient will receive all expenses paid trip to NTA National Convention.
  Amount of award: $2,500
  Application deadline: April 15

Patrick Murphy Internship

Type of award: Internship.
Intended use: For junior, senior study in Washington, D.C.
Basis for selection: Major/career interest in tourism and travel; political science/government; culinary arts. Applicant must demonstrate high academic achievement.
Application requirements: Resume.
Additional information: Two to three month internship. $1000 stipend. Minimum 3.0 GPA. Must have excellent written, oral and interpersonal skills.
  Amount of award: $1,000
  Application deadline: April 15

Tourism Foundation Alabama-Birmingham Legacy

Type of award: Scholarship.
Intended use: For full-time junior, senior study at 4-year institution in or outside United States.
Eligibility: Applicant must be residing in Alabama.
Basis for selection: Major/career interest in tourism and travel; hotel/restaurant management; culinary arts. Applicant must demonstrate high academic achievement.
Application requirements: Recommendations, essay, transcript and proof of eligibility. Resume.
Additional information: Minimum 3.0 GPA.
    Amount of award: $1,500
    Application deadline: April 15

Tourism Foundation California Scholarship

Type of award: Scholarship.
Intended use: For full-time junior, senior study at 4-year institution in or outside United States.
Eligibility: Applicant must be residing in California.
Basis for selection: Major/career interest in tourism and travel; hotel/restaurant management; culinary arts. Applicant must demonstrate high academic achievement.
Application requirements: Recommendations, essay and transcript. Resume.
Additional information: Minimum 3.0 GPA.
    Amount of award: $500
    Application deadline: April 15

Tourism Foundation Cleveland Legacy 1 Scholarship

Type of award: Scholarship.
Intended use: For full-time junior, senior study at 4-year institution in North America.
Eligibility: Applicant must be U.S. citizen residing in Ohio.
Basis for selection: Major/career interest in tourism and travel; hotel/restaurant management; culinary arts. Applicant must demonstrate high academic achievement.
Application requirements: Recommendations, essay and transcript. Resume.
Additional information: Minimum 3.0 GPA.
    Amount of award: $500
    Application deadline: April 15

Tourism Foundation Cleveland Legacy 2 Scholarship

Type of award: Scholarship.
Intended use: For full-time junior, senior study at 4-year institution in North America.
Eligibility: Applicant must be U.S. citizen residing in Ohio.
Basis for selection: Major/career interest in tourism and travel; hotel/restaurant management; culinary arts. Applicant must demonstrate high academic achievement.
Application requirements: Recommendations, essay and transcript. Resume.
Additional information: Minimum 3.0 GPA. Must be enrolled in a 2 year college at time of application.
    Amount of award: $500
    Application deadline: April 15

Tourism Foundation Connecticut Scholarship

Type of award: Scholarship.
Intended use: For full-time junior, senior study at 4-year institution in North America.
Eligibility: Applicant must be residing in Connecticut.
Basis for selection: Major/career interest in tourism and travel; hotel/restaurant management; culinary arts. Applicant must demonstrate high academic achievement.
Application requirements: Recommendations, essay and transcript.
Additional information: Minimum 3.0 GPA. Must be enrolled in a four year institution at time of application.
    Amount of award: $1,000
    Application deadline: April 15

Tourism Foundation Florida Scholarship

Type of award: Scholarship.
Intended use: For full-time junior, senior study at 4-year institution in or outside United States.
Eligibility: Applicant must be U.S. citizen or permanent resident residing in Florida.
Basis for selection: Major/career interest in tourism and travel; hotel/restaurant management; culinary arts. Applicant must demonstrate high academic achievement.
Application requirements: Recommendations, essay and transcript.
Additional information: Minimum 3.0 GPA. Must be enrolled in a four year institution at time of application.
    Amount of award: $500
    Application deadline: April 15

Tourism Foundation Internship

Type of award: Internship.
Intended use: For full-time sophomore, junior or senior study.
Eligibility: Applicant must be U.S. citizen or open to citizens of countries in North America.
Basis for selection: Major/career interest in tourism and travel; culinary arts. Applicant must demonstrate service orientation and high academic achievement.
Application requirements: Resume.
Additional information: Must have at least a 3.0 GPA on a 4.0 scale and excellent written, oral and interpersonal skills. Interns receive $3000 stipend to offset travel and lodging expenses while in Lexington, KY. Interns also travel to St. Louis, MO for NTA National Convention, all expenses paid.
    Amount of award: $3,000
    Application deadline: April 15

Tourism Foundation Michigan Scholarship

Type of award: Scholarship.
Intended use: For full-time junior, senior study at 4-year institution in Michigan.
Eligibility: Applicant must be residing in Michigan.
Basis for selection: Major/career interest in tourism and travel; hotel/restaurant management; culinary arts. Applicant must demonstrate high academic achievement.

Application requirements: Recommendations, essay and transcript. Resume.
Additional information: Minimum 3.0 GPA. Must be permanent resident of or attending school in Michigan.
    Amount of award: $1,000
    Application deadline: April 15

Tourism Foundation Montana Scholarship

Type of award: Scholarship.
Intended use: For full-time junior, senior study at 2-year or 4-year institution in or outside United States.
Eligibility: Applicant must be residing in Montana.
Basis for selection: Major/career interest in tourism and travel; hotel/restaurant management; culinary arts. Applicant must demonstrate high academic achievement.
Application requirements: Recommendations, essay and transcript. Resume.
Additional information: Minimum 3.0 GPA.
    Amount of award: $500
    Application deadline: April 15

Tourism Foundation Nebraska-Lois Johnson Scholarship

Type of award: Scholarship.
Intended use: For full-time junior, senior study at 2-year or 4-year institution in or outside United States.
Eligibility: Applicant must be residing in Nebraska.
Basis for selection: Major/career interest in tourism and travel; hotel/restaurant management; culinary arts. Applicant must demonstrate high academic achievement.
Application requirements: Recommendations, essay and transcript. Resume.
Additional information: Minimum 3.0 GPA.
    Amount of award: $500
    Application deadline: April 15

Tourism Foundation New Jersey 1 Scholarship

Type of award: Scholarship.
Intended use: For full-time junior, senior study at 4-year institution in or outside United States.
Eligibility: Applicant must be residing in New Jersey.
Basis for selection: Major/career interest in tourism and travel; hotel/restaurant management; culinary arts. Applicant must demonstrate high academic achievement.
Application requirements: Recommendations, essay and transcript. Resume.
Additional information: Minimum 3.0 GPA.
    Amount of award: $1,000
    Application deadline: April 15

Tourism Foundation New Jersey 2 Scholarship

Type of award: Scholarship.
Intended use: For full-time junior, senior study at 2-year institution in or outside United States.
Eligibility: Applicant must be residing in New Jersey.
Basis for selection: Major/career interest in tourism and travel; hotel/restaurant management; culinary arts. Applicant must demonstrate high academic achievement.
Application requirements: Recommendations, essay and transcript. Resume.
Additional information: Minimum 3.0 GPA.
    Amount of award: $500
    Application deadline: April 15

Tourism Foundation New York Scholarship

Type of award: Scholarship.
Intended use: For full-time junior, senior study at 4-year institution in New York.
Eligibility: Applicant must be residing in New York.
Basis for selection: Major/career interest in tourism and travel; hotel/restaurant management; culinary arts. Applicant must demonstrate high academic achievement.
Application requirements: Recommendations, essay and transcript. Resume.
Additional information: Minimum 3.0 GPA. Must be enrolled in four year institution at time of application. Must have essay signed by schools Tour and Travel Department Head. Must be a resident of New York and/or full time student in New York.
    Amount of award: $500
    Application deadline: April 15

Tourism Foundation North Carolina Scholarship

Type of award: Scholarship.
Intended use: For full-time junior, senior study at 4-year institution in or outside United States.
Eligibility: Applicant must be residing in North Carolina.
Basis for selection: Major/career interest in tourism and travel; hotel/restaurant management; culinary arts. Applicant must demonstrate high academic achievement.
Application requirements: Recommendations, essay and transcript. Resume.
Additional information: Minimum 3.0 GPA.
    Amount of award: $500
    Application deadline: April 15

Tourism Foundation Ohio Scholarship

Type of award: Scholarship.
Intended use: For full-time junior, senior study at 2-year or 4-year institution in or outside United States.
Eligibility: Applicant must be residing in Ohio.
Basis for selection: Major/career interest in tourism and travel; hotel/restaurant management; culinary arts. Applicant must demonstrate high academic achievement.
Application requirements: Recommendations, essay and transcript. Resume.
Additional information: Minimum 3.0 GPA.
    Amount of award: $1,000
    Application deadline: April 15

Tourism Foundation Quebec Scholarship

Type of award: Scholarship.
Intended use: For full-time junior, senior, master's or doctoral

study at 4-year or graduate institution in Institutions in Quebec, Canada in Canada.
Eligibility: Applicant must be Residents of Canada.
Basis for selection: Major/career interest in tourism and travel; hotel/restaurant management; culinary arts. Applicant must demonstrate high academic achievement.
Application requirements: Recommendations, essay and transcript. Resume.
Additional information: Minimum 3.0 GPA. For persons residing or studying in Quebec only.
    Amount of award: $500
    Application deadline: April 15

Tourism Foundation Scholarship

Type of award: Scholarship.
Intended use: For full-time freshman study at accredited postsecondary institution.
Eligibility: Applicant must be high school senior. Applicant must be Residents of countries in North America.
Basis for selection: Major/career interest in tourism and travel; hotel/restaurant management; culinary arts. Applicant must demonstrate high academic achievement.
Application requirements: Recommendations, essay and transcript.
Additional information: Minimum 3.0 GPA
    Amount of award: $500
    Number of awards: 1
    Application deadline: April 15

Tourism Foundation Tulsa Scholarship

Type of award: Scholarship.
Intended use: For full-time junior, senior study at 4-year institution in or outside United States. Designated institutions: Must be used at institutions in Oklahoma.
Eligibility: Applicant must be U.S. citizen or permanent resident residing in Oklahoma.
Basis for selection: Major/career interest in tourism and travel; hotel/restaurant management; culinary arts. Applicant must demonstrate high academic achievement.
Application requirements: Recommendations, essay and transcript. Resume.
Additional information: Minimum 3.0 GPA. Must be resident of or studying in Oklahoma and be enrolled in a four year institution at time of application.
    Amount of award: $500
    Application deadline: April 15

Tourism Foundation Wyoming Scholarship

Type of award: Scholarship.
Intended use: For full-time junior, senior study at 2-year or 4-year institution.
Eligibility: Applicant must be U.S. citizen or permanent resident residing in Wyoming.
Basis for selection: Major/career interest in tourism and travel; culinary arts. Applicant must demonstrate high academic achievement.
Application requirements: Recommendations, essay and transcript. Resume.
    Amount of award: $1,000
    Application deadline: April 15

Tourism Foundation Yellow Ribbon Scholarship

Type of award: Scholarship.
Intended use: For full-time undergraduate study at postsecondary institution in or outside United States. Designated institutions: Can be used at any institutions in North America.
Eligibility: Applicant must be high school senior. Must be visually impaired, hearing impaired or physically challenged. Applicant must be U.S. citizen, permanent resident or Canadian Citizen.
Basis for selection: Major/career interest in tourism and travel; culinary arts. Applicant must demonstrate high academic achievement.
Application requirements: Recommendations, essay and transcript. Resume.
Additional information: Minimum 3.0 GPA.
    Amount of award: $3,000
    Application deadline: April 15

Treadway Inns, Hotels, and Resorts Scholarship

Type of award: Scholarship.
Intended use: For full-time junior, senior study at 4-year institution in or outside United States. Designated institutions: Any in North America.
Eligibility: Applicant must be U.S. citizen, permanent resident or Canadian Citizen.
Basis for selection: Major/career interest in tourism and travel; culinary arts. Applicant must demonstrate high academic achievement.
Application requirements: Recommendations, essay and transcript. Resume.
Additional information: Minimum 3.0 GPA. Must be attending four year institution at time of application.
    Amount of award: $500
    Application deadline: April 15

Weeta F. Colebank Scholarship

Type of award: Scholarship.
Intended use: For full-time junior, senior study at 4-year institution in Mississippi. Designated institutions: Must be used at Mississippi schools.
Eligibility: Applicant must be U.S. citizen or permanent resident residing in Mississippi.
Basis for selection: Major/career interest in tourism and travel; culinary arts. Applicant must demonstrate high academic achievement.
Application requirements: Recommendations, essay and transcript. Resume.
Additional information: Minimum 3.0 GPA. Must be a resident of and studying in Mississippi and be enrolled in a four year institution at time of application.
    Amount of award: $1,000
    Application deadline: April 15
Contact:
National Tourism Foundation
546 East Main Street
Lexington, KY 40508
Phone: 800-682-8886
Website: www.ntaonline.com

National Training Systems Association

I/ITSEC Graduate Student Scholarship Program

Type of award: Scholarship, renewable.
Intended use: For graduate study at 4-year or graduate institution in United States.
Basis for selection: Major/career interest in engineering; mathematics; computer and information sciences. Applicant must demonstrate depth of character, leadership, seriousness of purpose and service orientation.
Application requirements: Recommendations, essay, transcript, proof of eligibility and nomination by applicant must be endorsed by the Director of Graduate Programs from the Institution.
Additional information: Applicants must include personal resume of positions held, outstanding awards, publications and leadership capabilities. Applicant must have a stated interest and career goal in the simulation and training systems and/or the education industry. The applicant must have successfully completed undergraduate studies by the end of the spring of 1999. Awardee will attend (expenses paid) the annual meeting of the I/ITSEC.
  Amount of award: $10,000
  Application deadline: February 27
  Notification begins: May 22
Contact:
National Training Systems Association
2111 Wilson Blvd., Suite 400
Arlington, VA 22201-3061

National Urban League

Duracell/Gillette Minority Intern Scholarship

Type of award: Scholarship.
Intended use: For full-time sophomore, junior study at accredited 4-year institution.
Eligibility: Applicant must be of minority background.
Basis for selection: Major/career interest in engineering; marketing; business; finance/banking. Applicant must demonstrate financial need and high academic achievement.
Application requirements: Interview and nomination by Urban League affiliates and Duracell and Gillette Staff.
Additional information: Must rank in top 25 percent of class.
  Amount of award: $10,000
  Number of awards: 10
  Number of applicants: 400
  Application deadline: May 15
  Notification begins: June 30
  Total amount awarded: $100,000
Contact:
National Urban League
Director of Education & Youth Development
120 Wall Street, 8th Floor
New York, NY 10005

National Wildlife Federation

Conservation Internship

Type of award: Internship.
Intended use: For graduate study.
Basis for selection: Major/career interest in environmental science; education.
Application requirements: Interview, audition, portfolio and recommendations.
Additional information: Internship provides experience with environmental issues, such as conservation. Includes research of environmental policy issues. Internships are offered in two sessions of 24 weeks each, which includes stipend of $275 a week. Interns are expected to work full-time. Contact office for detailed information regarding application procedure.
  Amount of award: $13,200
  Application deadline: August 15, March 15
Contact:
Intership Coordinator
1400 Sixteenth St. NW
Washington, DC 20036-2266
Website: www.nwf.org

National Women's Studies Association

Graduate Scholarship in Lesbian Studies

Type of award: Internship, renewable.
Intended use: For full-time master's study.
Basis for selection: Major/career interest in psychology; womenÖs studies. Applicant must demonstrate depth of character, seriousness of purpose and service orientation.
Application requirements: Recommendations, essay, transcript, proof of eligibility and nomination.
Additional information: Candidate must be researching, writing a thesis or dissertation in lesbian studies. Preference given to NWSA members.
  Amount of award: $500
  Application deadline: February 15
Contact:
National Women's Studies Association
7100 Baltimore Ave., Suite 301
College Park, MD 20742

Native American Scholarship Fund

Native American Scholarship

Type of award: Scholarship, renewable.
Intended use: For full-time freshman, sophomore, junior,

senior, master's, doctoral, first professional or postgraduate study at accredited postsecondary institution in United States.
Eligibility: Applicant must be Alaskan native or American Indian. Must be an enrolled member of tribe. Must be one-quarter degree American Indian. Applicant must be U.S. citizen or permanent resident.
Basis for selection: Major/career interest in mathematics; education; science, general; business; engineering; computer and information sciences; humanities/liberal arts; social and behavioral sciences. Applicant must demonstrate depth of character, leadership, patriotism, seriousness of purpose, service orientation and high academic achievement.
Application requirements: Recommendations, essay, transcript and proof of eligibility.
Additional information: Additional fields of study: Fine Arts. Additional deadline: March 15 for summer funding. Applicant must be at least one quarter Native American and enrolled with their tribe. Applicant must be applying to other sources of funding as well.

Amount of award:	$500-$2,000
Number of awards:	162
Number of applicants:	230
Application deadline:	April 15, September 15
Notification begins:	August 1, December 15

Contact:
Native American Scholarship Fund
8200 Mountain Road NE
Suite 203
Albuquerque, NM 87110
Phone: 505-262-2351
Website: www.nasf.com

Navy League of the United States

Samuel Eliot Morison Essay Contest

Type of award: Scholarship.
Intended use: For undergraduate study.
Eligibility: Applicant must be U.S. citizen.
Basis for selection: Competition in Writing/journalism. The best essay on the need to replace the current fleet of U.S. Navy Aircraft Carriers.
Application requirements: Essay.
Additional information: The 17 contest award winners will be selected as regional contest award winners. The national champion will be selected from the regional winners. The regional winners will receive a $400 dollar EE savings bond. The national winner will receive a $3,000 grand prize. Essays must be at least 1,500 words but no longer than 2,000 words.

Amount of award:	$9,800
Number of awards:	18
Number of applicants:	500
Application deadline:	April 1
Total amount awarded:	$9,800

Contact:
The Navy League of the United States
2300 Wilson Blvd.
Arlington, VA 22201

Navy Supply Corps Foundation

Navy Supply Corps Scholarship

Type of award: Scholarship.
Intended use: For full-time undergraduate study at vocational, 2-year or 4-year institution.
Eligibility: Applicant must be single. Applicant must be U.S. citizen. Applicant must be child of active service person or veteran who served in the Navy. Parent, stepparent, or guardian must have served in Navy Supply Corps.
Basis for selection: Applicant must demonstrate depth of character, leadership, service orientation, financial need and high academic achievement.
Application requirements: Transcript and proof of eligibility.
Additional information: Minimum 3.0 GPA required. When requesting information include a business-size SASE.

Amount of award:	$2,500
Number of awards:	60
Number of applicants:	127
Application deadline:	April 10
Notification begins:	June 30
Total amount awarded:	$150,000

Contact:
Navy Supply Corps Foundation
Navy Supply Corps School
1425 Prince Avenue
Athens, GA 30606-2205
Website: www.usnscf.com

Navy-Marine Corps Relief Society

Vice Admiral E.P. Travers Loan

Type of award: Loan, renewable.
Intended use: For full-time undergraduate study.
Eligibility: Applicant must be U.S. citizen. Applicant must be child of active service person, spouse of active service person who served in the Marines or Navy. Current military dependent I.D. required.
Basis for selection: Applicant must demonstrate financial need.
Application requirements: Proof of eligibility.
Additional information: Loan must be repaid in allotments over 24-month period (minimum monthly repayment is $50). Must reapply to renew. Minimum 2.0 GPA required. Must be son, daughter or spouse of retired or active service person.

Amount of award:	$500-$3,000
Application deadline:	October 1

Vice Admiral E.P. Travers Scholarship

Type of award: Scholarship, renewable.
Intended use: For full-time undergraduate study.
Eligibility: Applicant must be U.S. citizen. Applicant must be

child of active service person, spouse of active service person who served in the Marines or Navy. Current military dependent ID required.
Basis for selection: Applicant must demonstrate financial need.
Application requirements: Proof of eligibility.
Additional information: Minimum 2.0 GPA required. Must be son, daughter or spouse of retired or active service person.
Amount of award:	$2,000
Number of awards:	1,000
Application deadline:	March 1

Contact:
Navy-Marine Corps Relief Society
801 North Randolph Street
Room 1228
Arlington, VA 22203

NAWE: Advancing Women in Higher Education

Ruth Strang Women's Research Awards

Type of award: Research grant.
Intended use: For graduate study.
Basis for selection: Major/career interest in womenÖs studies. Applicant must demonstrate seriousness of purpose and service orientation.
Application requirements: Proof of eligibility.
Additional information: Granted ONLY to completed research projects by graduate students or by a person at any career or professional level.
Amount of award:	$750
Number of awards:	2
Number of applicants:	2
Application deadline:	October 1
Notification begins:	January 1
Total amount awarded:	$1,500

Contact:
National Foundation for Infectious Diseases
4733 Bethesda Ave., Suite 750
Bethesda, MD 20814-5228

New Dramatists

New Dramatists Internship

Type of award: Internship.
Intended use: For undergraduate or graduate study.
Basis for selection: Major/career interest in public relations; literature; business, management and administration; performing arts.
Application requirements: Interview.
Additional information: 20 week internship. $25 a week. 40 hours a week. Unpaid part-time internships available. College credit may be available. Computer and writing skills essential. Also open to high school students.

| Amount of award: | $500 |

Contact:
Internship Coordinator
424 West 44th Street
New York, NY 10036
Website: www.itp.tsoa.nyu.edu/~diama/ndintro.html

New England Graphic Arts

New England Graphic Arts Scholarship

Type of award: Scholarship, renewable.
Intended use: For undergraduate study at 2-year or 4-year institution. Designated institutions: Schools recognized by the New England Graphic Arts Committee.
Eligibility: Applicant must be residing in Connecticut or Massachusetts or Maine or New Hampshire or Rhode Island or Vermont.
Basis for selection: Major/career interest in graphic arts and design. Applicant must demonstrate financial need and high academic achievement.
Application requirements: Recommendations and transcript.
Additional information: Must maintain a 2.5 GPA.
Amount of award:	$1,300-$2,000
Application deadline:	May 15
Notification begins:	June 15

Contact:
New England Graphic Arts
P.O. Box 218
Norwood, MA 02062-0218

New England Wild Flower Society

Garden in the Woods Horticultural Internship

Type of award: Internship.
Intended use: For graduate study. Designated institutions: New England Wild Flower Society Garden in the Woods.
Eligibility: Applicant must be U.S. citizen.
Basis for selection: Major/career interest in botany; horticulture; natural resources/conservation. Applicant must demonstrate depth of character and seriousness of purpose.
Application requirements: $8 application fee. Interview and recommendations.
Additional information: Intern must agree to perform manual labor and work a 40-hour week. The six-month positions pay $200 per week; the three-month summer positions pay $160 per week. Two internships begin April 1 and end September. Two begin mid-May and run three months.

Number of awards: 4
Number of applicants: 45
Application deadline: February 15
Notification begins: March 1

Contact:
New England Wild Flower Society
Garden in the Woods Horticultural Internship
180 Hemenway Road
Framingham, MA 01701-2699

New Hampshire Charitable Foundation

New Hampshire Statewide Scholarship Program

Type of award: Scholarship, renewable.
Intended use: For full-time or half-time undergraduate, master's or doctoral study at accredited postsecondary institution.
Eligibility: Applicant must be residing in New Hampshire.
Basis for selection: Applicant must demonstrate depth of character, leadership, seriousness of purpose, service orientation and financial need.
Application requirements: $15 application fee. Recommendations, essay, transcript and proof of eligibility.
Additional information: Adult, non-traditional and vocational/technical students encouraged to apply.

Amount of award: $100-$2,500
Number of awards: 500
Number of applicants: 1,800
Application deadline: April 18
Total amount awarded: $700,000

Contact:
New Hampshire Charitable Foundation
37 Pleasant Street
Concord, NH 03301-4005
Phone: 603-225-6641

New Jersey Society of Architects

American Institute of Architects Scholarship

Type of award: Scholarship.
Intended use: For full-time sophomore, junior, senior or master's study at accredited 4-year or graduate institution in United States.
Eligibility: Applicant must be residing in New Jersey.
Basis for selection: Major/career interest in architecture. Applicant must demonstrate financial need and high academic achievement.
Application requirements: $5 application fee. Portfolio, recommendations, essay and transcript. Photos of projects and FAFSA.

Amount of award: $1,000-$2,000
Number of awards: 10
Number of applicants: 13
Application deadline: April 30
Notification begins: June 30
Total amount awarded: $10,000

Contact:
New Jersey Society of Architects
American Institute of Architects New Jersey Scholarship Foundation, Inc., Attn: Robert Zaccone
212 White Avenue
Old Tappan, NJ 07675
Phone: 201-767-5541

New Jersey State Golf Association Foundation

New Jersey Golf Association Caddie Scholarship

Type of award: Scholarship, renewable.
Intended use: For full-time undergraduate study at accredited 2-year or 4-year institution in United States.
Basis for selection: Applicant must demonstrate depth of character, leadership and financial need.
Application requirements: Recommendations and proof of eligibility.
Additional information: Must have caddied at least one year at New Jersey State Golf Association member golf club. Should have at least a 2.5 GPA. Should be in top 50% of class and have minimum combined SAT I score of 800.

Amount of award: $800-$2,500
Number of awards: 210
Number of applicants: 312
Application deadline: May 1
Notification begins: June 30
Total amount awarded: $215,000

Contact:
New Jersey State Golf Association Foundation
P.O. Box 6947
Freehold, NJ 07728
Phone: 908-780-3562

New Republic

New Republic Internship Program

Type of award: Internship.
Intended use: For sophomore, junior, senior, graduate, postgraduate or non-degree study.
Eligibility: Applicant must be U.S. citizen.
Basis for selection: Major/career interest in journalism. Applicant must demonstrate depth of character and seriousness of purpose.
Application requirements: Recommendations. Must submit resume, cover letter, and 2-5 writing samples.
Additional information: Internships are offered in the

summer (June-August) and during academic year (September-May). Stipend is $200/week. Provides intern with the opportunity to gain editorial experience at a leading opinion magazine. Must have strong writing, administrative and editorial abilities and be willing to work long hours.
- Amount of award: $2,400-$7,200
- Number of applicants: 200
- Application deadline: March 1, April 1

Contact:
New Republic
1220 19th Street, NW, Suite 600
Washington, DC 20036

New Stage Theatre

New Stage Theatre Internship

Type of award: Internship.
Intended use: For undergraduate, graduate or non-degree study.
Basis for selection: Major/career interest in performing arts; theater (production/technical); theater (artistic). Applicant must demonstrate seriousness of purpose.
Application requirements: Interview, audition, portfolio, recommendations, essay and proof of eligibility.
Additional information: Nine month internships starting in August. $140 per week. Acting interns. Travel extensively in Mississippi.
- Amount of award: $4,860
- Application deadline: April 1

Contact:
New Stage Theatre
P.O. Box 4792
Jackson, MS 39296-4792

New York Association of Black Journalists

Stephen H. Gayle Essay Contest

Type of award: Scholarship.
Intended use: For undergraduate study in United States. Designated institutions: Must be located in New York City, Westchester County or Long Island.
Eligibility: Applicant must be enrolled in high school. Applicant must be U.S. citizen residing in New York.
Basis for selection: Competition in Writing/journalism. Essays on a current affairs topic. Criteria include clarity, accuracy, imagination, and excellence of writing. Major/career interest in journalism. Applicant must demonstrate seriousness of purpose.
Application requirements: Essay. Proof of enrollment.
Additional information: Applicants can be in middle school, high school or any year of undergraduate study and must attend school in New York City, Westchester County or Long Island.

- Amount of award: $200-$3,000
- Number of applicants: 35
- Application deadline: October 15, November 20
- Total amount awarded: $9,600

Contact:
New York Association of Black Journalists
P.O. Box 2446
Rockefeller Center
New York, NY 10185

New York State Bar Association, Department of Media Services and Public Affairs

New York State Bar Association Summer Public Relations Internship

Type of award: Internship.
Intended use: For senior study.
Eligibility: Applicant must be U.S. citizen.
Application requirements: Interview and portfolio.
Additional information: For study in the field of public relations. There is a two hour writing test. There is no application per se. Interested students should send a letter detailing their interest and providing specific examples of work-related experience. Three writing samples required.
- Amount of award: $2,450
- Application deadline: April 1

Contact:
New York State Bar Association
One Elk Street
Albany, NY 12207
Phone: 518-463-3200
Website: www.nysba.org

New York Times

New York Times Summer Internship Program for Minorities

Type of award: Internship.
Intended use: For senior, graduate or non-degree study.
Eligibility: Applicant must be of minority background. All minorities qualify.
Basis for selection: Major/career interest in journalism. Applicant must demonstrate seriousness of purpose and service orientation.
Application requirements: Portfolio and proof of eligibility.
Additional information: Applicants must have journalism experience. All queries must be made by mail.
- Amount of award: $7,750

Contact:
The New York Times
229 West 43rd Street
New York, NY 10036

Newberry Library

American Society for Eighteenth Century Studies Fellowship

Type of award: Research grant.
Intended use: For postgraduate study. Designated institutions: The Newberry Library.
Basis for selection: Major/career interest in history.
Application requirements: Recommendations, proof of eligibility and research proposal. Curriculum vitae, proposed project description limited to 1500 words.
Additional information: Must have a Ph.D. or equivalent. For scholars wishing to study in residence at the Newberry Library for study in the period of 1600-1815. Fellowships are available for one to three months. Must be a member in good standing of the American Society for Eighteenth-Century Studies (ASECS) at the time of application.

    Amount of award: $800-$2,400
    Application deadline: March 1

Contact:
Newberry Library
60 West Walton Street
Chicago, IL 60610-3380
Phone: 312-943-9090
Website: www.newberry.org

Audrey Lumsdem-Kouvel Fellowship

Type of award: Research grant.
Intended use: For postgraduate study. Designated institutions: The Newberry Library.
Basis for selection: Major/career interest in history.
Application requirements: Recommendations, proof of eligibility and research proposal. Curriculum vitae, proposed project description limited to 1500 words.
Additional information: For postdoctoral scholars conducting extended research in late medieval and renaissance studies. Applicants must be in continuous residence. Preference given to those who plan longer stays during the academic year or who wish to use the fellowship to extend a sabbatical.

    Amount of award: $1,000-$3,000
    Application deadline: January 20

Contact:
Newberry Library
60 West Walton Street
Chicago, IL 60610-3380
Phone: 312-943-9090
Website: www.newberry.org

Ecole des Chartes Exchange Fellowship

Type of award: Research grant.
Intended use: For doctoral study outside United States. Designated institutions: Ecole Nationale des Chartes. Paris, France.
Eligibility: Applicant must be U.S. citizen.
Basis for selection: Major/career interest in history; literature.
Application requirements: Recommendations, proof of eligibility and research proposal. Proof of French language fluency, curriculum vitae, proposed project description limited to 1500 words.
Additional information: Fellowship lasts for one semester or term. Monthly stipend and free tuition for up to three months at the Ecole Nationale provided. Preference given to students attending institutions that support the Newberry's Center for Renaissance Studies.

    Application deadline: December 12

Contact:
Newberry Library
60 West Walton Street
Chicago, IL 60610-3380
Phone: 312-943-9090
Website: www.newberry.org

Herzog August Bibliothek Wolfenbuttel Fellowship

Type of award: Research grant.
Intended use: For doctoral study outside United States in Germany. Designated institutions: Herzog August Biliothek Wolfenbuttel, Germany.
Basis for selection: Major/career interest in history; literature.
Application requirements: Curriculum vitae, proposed project description limited to 1500 words.
Additional information: Three-month supplemental fellowship in conjunction with other Newberry fellowships. Stipend includes travel expenses.

    Amount of award: $2,000

Contact:
Newberry Library
60 West Walton Street
Chicago, IL 60610-3380
Phone: 312-943-9090
Website: www.newberry.org

Joint Fellowship with the American Antiquarian Society

Type of award: Research grant.
Intended use: For doctoral study. Designated institutions: The Newberry Library and the American Antiquarian Society.
Basis for selection: Major/career interest in history.
Additional information: Must have a Ph.D. or equivalent; doctoral candidates at the dissertation stage eligible.

    Amount of award: $2,400
    Application deadline: January 20

Contact:
Newberry Library
60 West Walton Street
Chicago, IL 60610-3380
Phone: 312-943-9090

Lester J. Cappon Fellowship in Documentary Editing

Type of award: Research grant.
Intended use: For postgraduate study. Designated institutions: The Newberry Library.
Basis for selection: Major/career interest in film/video; history.
Application requirements: Recommendations, proof of

eligibility and research proposal. Curriculum vitae, proposed project description limited to 1500 words.
Additional information: Grant to support editing projects based on Newberry material.
   Amount of award: $800-$2,400
   Application deadline: March 1
Contact:
Newberry Library
60 West Walton Street
Chicago, IL 60610-3380
Phone: 312-943-9090
Website: www.newberry.org

Lloyd Lewis Fellowship in American History

Type of award: Scholarship.
Intended use: For doctoral study. Designated institutions: The Newberry Library.
Basis for selection: Major/career interest in history.
Application requirements: Recommendations, proof of eligibility and research proposal. Curriculum vitae, proposed project description limited to 1500 words.
Additional information: Must have a Ph.D. or equivalent in American history.
   Amount of award: $30,000
   Number of awards: 2
   Application deadline: January 20
Contact:
Newberry Library
60 West Walton Street
Chicago, IL 60610-3380
Phone: 312-943-9090
Website: www.newberry.org

Monticello College Foundation Fellowship for Women

Type of award: Research grant.
Intended use: For postgraduate study. Designated institutions: The Newberry Library.
Eligibility: Applicant must be female. Applicant must be U.S. citizen or permanent resident.
Application requirements: Recommendations, proof of eligibility and research proposal. Curriculum vitae, proposed project description limited to 1500 words.
Additional information: Open to Ph.D holder in early stage of her career. Preference given to applicants whose work is concerned with the study of women. Duration is six months.
   Amount of award: $12,500
   Number of awards: 1
   Application deadline: January 20

National Endowment for the Humanities Fellowship

Type of award: Research grant.
Intended use: For postgraduate study. Designated institutions: The Newberry Library.
Eligibility: Applicant must be must have been living in the U.S. for at least three years.
Basis for selection: Major/career interest in history; music; linguistics; literature.
Application requirements: Recommendations. Curriculum vitae, proposed project description limited to 1500 words.
Additional information: Must have Ph.D. or equivalent. For research projects in any field appropriate to the library's collections. Preference given to applicants who have not held major fellowships or grants for at least three years preceding the proposed period of residency.
   Amount of award: $30,000
   Number of awards: 6
   Application deadline: January 20
   Total amount awarded: $180,000

President Francesco Cossiga Fellowship

Type of award: Research grant.
Intended use: For postgraduate study. Designated institutions: The Newberry Library.
Eligibility: Applicant must be of Italian heritage.
Basis for selection: Major/career interest in history.
Application requirements: Recommendations, proof of eligibility and research proposal. Curriculum vitae, proposed project description limited to 1500 words.
Additional information: For Italian nationals or residents holding the dottorato di recerea. Preference given to applicants whose topic of study includes the historical study of cartography.
   Amount of award: $1,500
Contact:
Ministero Degli Affari Esteri
Direzione Generale della Relazioni Culturali
Ufficio IX
Roma, Italy
Phone: 312-943-9090
Website: www.newberry.org

Short-Term Fellowship in the History of Cartography

Type of award: Research grant.
Intended use: For doctoral, postgraduate study. Designated institutions: The Newberry Library.
Basis for selection: Major/career interest in geography; history.
Application requirements: Recommendations, proof of eligibility and research proposal. Curriculum vitae, proposed project description limited to 1500 words.
Additional information: Applicants must have a Ph.D or be candidates for the Ph.D degree who have completed all requirements except the dissertation. Fellowships of two weeks to two months related to the history of cartography and the library's collection.
   Amount of award: $400-$1,600
   Application deadline: March 1

Short-Term Resident Fellowship for Individual Research

Type of award: Research grant.
Intended use: For master's, doctoral or postgraduate study. Designated institutions: The Newberry Library.
Basis for selection: Major/career interest in history; music; linguistics; literature.
Application requirements: Recommendations, proof of

eligibility and research proposal. Curriculum vitae, proposed project description limited to 1500 words.
Additional information: Must have a Ph.D. or equivalent. Doctoral candidates at the dissertation stage are eligible. Applicants in fields where the Ph.D is not typically available should have the appropriate terminal degree. Preference is given to applicants from outside the greater Chicago area whose research requires study at the Newberry. Fellowships are for two weeks to two months; three months for those traveling from a foreign country. Award is $800 per month.
 Amount of award: $400-$2,400
 Application deadline: March 1

Weinberg Fellowship for Independent Scholars

Type of award: Research grant.
Intended use: For doctoral, non-degree study.
Basis for selection: Major/career interest in history.
Additional information: Award is for independent scholars pursuing historical issues related to social justice and reform.
 Amount of award: $800
 Application deadline: March 1

Weiss Brown Publication Subvention Award

Type of award: Scholarship.
Intended use: For doctoral study.
Basis for selection: Major/career interest in history; humanities/liberal arts; music; literature.
Additional information: Prize to subsidize publication of a scholarly book on European civilization before 1700: music, theatre, French, or Italian literature in cultural studies.
 Amount of award: $15,000
 Application deadline: January 20
Contact:
Fellowship Coordinator
60 West Walton Street
Chicago, IL 60610-3380
Phone: 312-943-9090

Newhouse Foundation

Newhouse Graduate Newspaper Fellowship for Minorities

Type of award: Scholarship.
Intended use: For full-time master's study at graduate institution in United States. Designated institutions: Must be used at Syracuse University Newhouse School of Public Communications.
Eligibility: Applicant must be of minority background. Applicant must be U.S. citizen.
Basis for selection: Applicant must demonstrate depth of character, seriousness of purpose, financial need and high academic achievement.
Application requirements: Recommendations, essay and transcript. GRE scores.
Additional information: Must have an undergraduate degree from an accredited university in a field other than journalism. Fellowships include free tuition, $1,100 a month stipend, health insurance, moving expenses, travel expenses and academic expenses up to $1,000. Upon graduation, interns become full-time paid interns at a Newhouse newspaper for one year. Undergraduate grade average must be at least a B or better.
 Number of awards: 2
 Application deadline: February 10
Contact:
Jane Lorraine, Newhouse School of Public Communications
305 Newhouse I
Syracuse University
Syracuse, NY 13244

Norfolk Chamber Music Festival

Norfolk Chamber Music Festival Summer Fellowship Program

Type of award: Scholarship.
Intended use: For full-time undergraduate, master's, doctoral, first professional, postgraduate or non-degree study. Designated institutions: Must be used at Yale Summer School of Music.
Basis for selection: Major/career interest in music.
Application requirements: Audition, recommendations and essay.
Additional information: Summer fellowships are awarded to individuals with outstanding musical achievement. No phone calls please.
 Amount of award: $4,800
 Number of awards: 60
 Application deadline: January 20

Norfolk Chamber Music Festival Summer Internship Program

Type of award: Internship.
Intended use: For undergraduate, master's, doctoral, first professional, postgraduate or non-degree study.
Basis for selection: Major/career interest in music; arts management.
Application requirements: Recommendations and essay.
Additional information: Summer internships provide opportunity to gain experience in arts administration. Contact office for stipend information. No phone calls please.
 Number of awards: 2
 Application deadline: January 20
Contact:
Norfolk Chamber Music Festival
P.O. Box 208246
New Haven, CT 06520

North American Bluebird Society

Bluebird Research Grant

Type of award: Research grant, renewable.
Intended use: For undergraduate, graduate or non-degree study.
Basis for selection: Major/career interest in ornithology.
Application requirements: Research proposal. Research proposal judged on project design, presentation, relevance of topic and ability of applicant.

Amount of award:	$1,000
Number of awards:	5
Number of applicants:	15
Application deadline:	December 1
Notification begins:	January 15

North American Bluebird Society General Research Grant

Type of award: Research grant, renewable.
Intended use: For graduate or non-degree study.
Basis for selection: Major/career interest in ornithology.
Application requirements: Research proposal. Research proposal judged on project design, presentation, relevance of topic and ability of applicant.

Amount of award:	$1,000
Number of awards:	5
Number of applicants:	24
Application deadline:	December 1
Notification begins:	January 15
Total amount awarded:	$5,000

Student Research Grant

Type of award: Research grant, renewable.
Intended use: For full-time graduate study.
Basis for selection: Major/career interest in ornithology.
Application requirements: Research proposal. Research proposal judged on project design, presentation, relevance of topic and ability of applicant.

Amount of award:	$1,000
Number of awards:	1
Number of applicants:	8
Application deadline:	December 1
Notification begins:	January 15
Total amount awarded:	$1,000

Contact:
North American Bluebird Society
Kevin Berner, Research Committee Chairman
SUNY-Cobleskill
Cobleskill, NY 12043
Phone: 518-234-5252

North American Loon Fund

Loon Fund Grant Program

Type of award: Research grant.
Intended use: For undergraduate, master's, doctoral or non-degree study at accredited postsecondary institution in or outside United States.
Basis for selection: Major/career interest in ornithology; biology; environmental science. Applicant must demonstrate seriousness of purpose.
Application requirements: Research proposal.
Additional information: Enclose SASE with application request. Can also be used at Canadian institutions.

Amount of award:	$100-$3,000
Number of awards:	12
Number of applicants:	12
Application deadline:	December 15
Notification begins:	March 31
Total amount awarded:	$8,000

Contact:
North American Loon Fund
6 Lily Pond Road
Gilford, NH 03246
Phone: 603-528-4711

North Carolina Association of Educators

Mary Morrow-Edna Richards Scholarship

Type of award: Scholarship.
Intended use: For full-time senior study in North Carolina.
Eligibility: Applicant must be residing in North Carolina.
Basis for selection: Major/career interest in education. Applicant must demonstrate depth of character, leadership, service orientation, financial need and high academic achievement.
Application requirements: Recommendations, essay and transcript.
Additional information: Must agree to teach in North Carolina for two years after graduation.

Amount of award:	$1,000
Number of awards:	8
Number of applicants:	40
Application deadline:	January 17
Notification begins:	February 15
Total amount awarded:	$8,000

Contact:
North Carolina Association of Educators
P.O. Box 27347
Raleigh, NC 27611
Phone: 800-662-7924

North Carolina Bar Association

Scholarship for North Carolina Law Enforcement Dependents

Type of award: Scholarship, renewable.
Intended use: For full-time undergraduate, master's, doctoral

or first professional study at accredited postsecondary institution.
Eligibility: Applicant must be residing in North Carolina. Applicant's parent must have been killed or disabled in work-related accident as police officer.
Basis for selection: Applicant must demonstrate financial need.
Application requirements: Essay and transcript.
Additional information: Must apply before 27th birthday.

Amount of award:	$2,000
Number of awards:	17
Number of applicants:	17
Application deadline:	April 1
Notification begins:	May 31

Contact:
North Carolina Bar Association Scholarship Committee
P.O. Box 3688
Cary, NC 27519
Phone: 919-677-0561
Website: www.barlinc.org

North Carolina Botanical Garden

Eight-Month Gardener Internship

Type of award: Internship.
Intended use: For undergraduate, graduate or non-degree study.
Basis for selection: Major/career interest in horticulture; botany; forestry; landscape architecture; education. Applicant must demonstrate depth of character, leadership, seriousness of purpose and service orientation.
Application requirements: Essay. Resume, letter outlining interests.
Additional information: Internship provides experience in research, conservation, and interpretation of horticultural plants. Must have substantial experience in gardening. Position pays $7.50/hour and interns work 40 hours a week. Encouraged to arrange for academic credit. Must be enrolled in or be recent graduate of horticulture or related program.

Amount of award:	$9,600
Number of awards:	3
Number of applicants:	30
Application deadline:	February 14
Notification begins:	March 21

Three-Month Gardener Internship

Type of award: Internship.
Intended use: For undergraduate, graduate or non-degree study.
Basis for selection: Major/career interest in horticulture; botany; forestry; landscape architecture; education. Applicant must demonstrate depth of character, leadership, seriousness of purpose and service orientation.
Application requirements: Essay. Resume, letter outlining interests.
Additional information: Internship provides experience in research, conservation, and interpretation of horticultural plants. Must have substantial experience in gardening. Position pays $7.50 per hour and interns work 40 hrs a week. Must be enrolled in or recent graduate of horticulture or related program. Encouraged to arrange for academic credit.

Amount of award:	$3,600
Number of awards:	1
Number of applicants:	30
Application deadline:	February 14
Notification begins:	March 21

Contact:
North Carolina Botanical Garden James L. Ward, Curator
3375 Totten Center
University of North Carolina
Chapel Hill, NC 27599-3375
Phone: 919-962-0522

North Carolina Department of Community Colleges

North Carolina Community Colleges Sprint Scholarship

Type of award: Scholarship.
Intended use: For full-time freshman, sophomore or non-degree study at 2-year institution in North Carolina.
Eligibility: Applicant must be residing in North Carolina.
Basis for selection: Applicant must demonstrate financial need.
Additional information: Priority given to minorities and "displaced workers." Must be enrolled or planning to enroll in course of study leading to technical degree or vocational diploma at community college located in service area of Carolina Telephone and Telegraph Company. Apply through financial aid office of college.

Amount of award:	$550

Northwest Danish Foundation

Danish Foundation Scholarship

Type of award: Scholarship, renewable.
Intended use: For undergraduate, graduate or non-degree study at postsecondary institution in or outside United States.
Designated institutions: May be used at institutions in Denmark.
Eligibility: Applicant must be of Danish heritage. Applicant must be U.S. citizen or permanent resident residing in Oregon or Washington.
Basis for selection: Applicant must demonstrate depth of character and service orientation.
Application requirements: Recommendations, essay and transcript. three recommendations, personal essay on educational goals, and Danish heritage required.
Additional information: Alternate phone: 800-564-7736. Spouses of persons of Danish descent also eligible. One

recommendation must be from non-family member of Danish community, explaining applicant's involvement in Danish activities/community.

>   Amount of award: $250-$1,000
>   Number of applicants: 35
>   Application deadline: March 15
>   Notification begins: May 1
>   Total amount awarded: $15,000

Contact:
Northwest Danish Foundation
1833 North 105th Street
Suite 203
Seattle, WA 98133-8973
Phone: 206-523-2363

Northwest Journalists of Color

Northwest Journalists of Color Scholarship Program

Type of award: Scholarship.
Intended use: For full-time undergraduate study.
Eligibility: Applicant must be of minority background. Applicant must be residing in U.S. Territories.
Basis for selection: Major/career interest in journalism. Applicant must demonstrate depth of character, seriousness of purpose, financial need and high academic achievement.
Application requirements: Recommendations, essay and transcript.
Additional information: Preference given to applicants from the Pacific Northwest.

>   Amount of award: $1,000-$1,000
>   Number of awards: 4
>   Number of applicants: 4
>   Application deadline: April 30
>   Notification begins: June 30
>   Total amount awarded: $4,000

Contact:
Seattle Times
1120 John Street
Seattle, WA WA 98111
Phone: 2064642916
Fax: 2064642261

Northwest Osteopathic Medical Foundation

Northwest Osteopathic Medical Scholarship

Type of award: Scholarship, renewable.
Intended use: For full-time doctoral study at accredited graduate institution in United States.
Eligibility: Applicant must be U.S. citizen or permanent resident residing in Alaska or Idaho or Montana or Oregon or Washington.
Basis for selection: Major/career interest in medicine, osteopathic. Applicant must demonstrate depth of character, leadership, seriousness of purpose, service orientation, financial need and high academic achievement.
Application requirements: Recommendations, transcript and proof of eligibility. Credit reports and tax forms required.
Additional information: Must have completed one year at American Osteopathic Association-accredited medical school. Preference goes to candidates who want to work in Northwest region after graduation.

>   Amount of award: $5,000
>   Number of awards: 52
>   Number of applicants: 14
>   Application deadline: March 1

Northwest Osteopathic Medical Student Loan

Type of award: Loan, renewable.
Intended use: For full-time doctoral study at accredited graduate institution in United States.
Eligibility: Applicant must be U.S. citizen or permanent resident residing in Alaska or Idaho or Montana or Oregon or Washington.
Basis for selection: Major/career interest in medicine, osteopathic. Applicant must demonstrate depth of character, leadership, seriousness of purpose, service orientation, financial need and high academic achievement.
Application requirements: Recommendations, transcript and proof of eligibility. Credits reports and tax forms required.
Additional information: Must attend American Osteopathic Association accredited institution. Preference goes to candidates who plan to work in Northwest region upon graduation.

>   Amount of award: $500-$1,500
>   Number of awards: 17
>   Number of applicants: 18
>   Application deadline: March 1
>   Notification begins: June 1
>   Total amount awarded: $19,500

Contact:
Northwest Osteopathic Medical Foundation
Suite 780, Tiffany Center
1410 S.W. Morrison Street
Portland, OR 97205
Phone: 503-222-7161
Website: www.osteo.org

Northwest Pharmacists Coalition

Northwest Pharmacists Pre-Pharmacy Scholarship

Type of award: Scholarship, renewable.
Intended use: For less than half-time undergraduate study.
Eligibility: Applicant must be African American. Applicant must be U.S. citizen residing in Washington.
Basis for selection: Major/career interest in pharmacy/pharmaceutics/pharmacology. Applicant must demonstrate depth of character and seriousness of purpose.

Application requirements: Interview, essay and transcript.
Additional information: Must be a Washington state resident either attending school in or out of state.
- Amount of award: $900
- Number of awards: 2
- Number of applicants: 6
- Application deadline: May 1
- Notification begins: June 15

Contact:
Northwest Pharmacists Coalition
P.O. Box 22975
Seattle, WA 98122-0975

Novartis Pharmaceuticals Corporation

Novartis Fellowship of the Immune Deficiency Foundation

Type of award: Research grant.
Intended use: For master's, doctoral or postgraduate study.
Eligibility: Applicant must be U.S. citizen.
Basis for selection: Major/career interest in medicine (m.d.); science, general; medical specialties/research. Applicant must demonstrate seriousness of purpose.
Application requirements: Recommendations, essay and research proposal. Post-doctoral studies in field of Primary Immune Deficiency.
Additional information: Applicants must be pursuing post-doctoral studies in the field of Primary Immune Deficiency Diseases. All research must be done in the United States.
- Amount of award: $25,000
- Application deadline: June 30

Scholarship of the Immune Deficiency Foundation

Type of award: Scholarship, renewable.
Intended use: For undergraduate study.
Eligibility: Applicant must be U.S. citizen.
Basis for selection: Applicant must demonstrate seriousness of purpose and financial need.
Application requirements: Recommendations, essay and proof of eligibility.
Additional information: Student must provide a letter from their immunologist documenting the diagnosis of the student's primary immune deficiency disease. Two letters of recommendation are required.
- Amount of award: $500-$2,000
- Application deadline: June 30

Contact:
Immune Deficiency Foundation
25 W. Chespeake Ave., Suite 206
Towson, MD 21204

Nurses' Educational Funds, Inc.

Carnegie Scholarship

Type of award: Scholarship.
Intended use: For master's, doctoral study in United States.
Eligibility: Applicant must be African American. Applicant must be U.S. citizen.
Basis for selection: Major/career interest in nursing. Applicant must demonstrate depth of character, leadership, seriousness of purpose and service orientation.
Application requirements: $10 application fee. Recommendations, essay, transcript and proof of eligibility. GRE or MAT scores.
Additional information: Applicant must be a registered nurse enrolled in or applying to a National League for Nursing accredited program, and a member of a national, professional nursing organization. Non-citizens who have declared official intention of becoming a U.S. citizen are eligible. Master's students must study full-time.
- Amount of award: $2,500-$10,000
- Number of awards: 16
- Number of applicants: 110
- Application deadline: March 1
- Notification begins: May 1
- Total amount awarded: $64,000

Osborne Scholarship

Type of award: Scholarship.
Intended use: For full-time master's study at accredited graduate institution.
Eligibility: Applicant must be African American. Applicant must be U.S. citizen.
Basis for selection: Major/career interest in nursing. Applicant must demonstrate depth of character, leadership, seriousness of purpose and service orientation.
Application requirements: $10 application fee. Recommendations, essay, transcript and proof of eligibility. Goal statement essay. GRE/MAT scores.
Additional information: Applicant must be a registered nurse enrolled in or applying to a National League for Nursing accredited program, and a member of a national, professional nursing organization. Non-citizens who have declared official intention of becoming a U.S. citizen are eligible.
- Amount of award: $2,500-$10,000
- Number of awards: 16
- Number of applicants: 135
- Application deadline: March 1
- Notification begins: May 1
- Total amount awarded: $64,000

Contact:
Nurses' Educational Funds, Inc.
Barbara Butler, Executive Director
555 West 57 Street, Suite 1327
New York, NY 10019
Phone: 212-399-1428

Oak Ridge Institute for Science and Education

Oak Ridge Institute for Science and Education Professional Internship Program at Federal Energy Technology Centers

Type of award: Internship.
Intended use: For undergraduate or graduate study at accredited postsecondary institution in United States. Designated institutions: Federal Energy Technology Center (Pittsburgh, Pa., and Morgantown, W.Va.).
Eligibility: Applicant must be U.S. citizen.
Basis for selection: Major/career interest in chemistry; computer and information sciences; engineering; environmental science; geology/earth sciences; mathematics; physics.
Application requirements: Recommendations and transcript. Proof of health coverage.
Additional information: Provides opportunities to participate in fossil energy-related research. Three to eighteen consecutive month, full-time or part-time appointments. Weekly stipend of $260 to $350. Limited travel reimbursement (round-trip transportation expenses between facility and home or campus) Off-campus tuition and fees if required by the home institution. Deadlines are February 15, June 1, October 1.

Amount of award:	$3,180-$27,300
Application deadline:	February 15, June 1

Contact:
Intership Coordinator
MS 36, Education Training Division
P.O. Box 117
Oak Ridge, TN 37831-0117
Website: www.orau.gov

Ocean Spray Cranberries, Inc.

Crave To Be Your Best Scholarship

Type of award: Scholarship.
Intended use: For undergraduate study.
Eligibility: Applicant must be female.
Basis for selection: Major/career interest in athletic training. Applicant must demonstrate depth of character, service orientation and high academic achievement.
Application requirements: Application must be completed in full, no attachments (i.e. portfolios, transcripts, pictures, newspaper clips, or covers).

Amount of award:	$500-$10,000
Number of awards:	51
Number of applicants:	2,500
Application deadline:	March 1
Notification begins:	May 1
Total amount awarded:	$48,000

Jean Driscoll Award

Type of award: Scholarship.
Intended use: For undergraduate, graduate or non-degree study.
Eligibility: Applicant must be female. Must be physically challenged.
Basis for selection: Major/career interest in athletic training. Applicant must demonstrate leadership and service orientation.
Application requirements: Application must be completed in full, no attachments (i.e. porfolios, transcripts, pictures, newspaper clips, report covers).
Additional information: Must participate in wheelchair athletic programming. Deadline is in June; contact sponsor for exact date. Must be at least a high school senior to apply.

Amount of award:	$1,000-$5,000
Number of awards:	4
Number of applicants:	70
Notification begins:	August 1
Total amount awarded:	$11,000

Contact:
Jean Driscoll Award
One Ocean Spray Drive
Lakeville, MA 02349
Phone: 800-662-3263 (9 A.M. to 4 P.M.)

Octel Communications

Octel Communications Internship

Type of award: Internship.
Intended use: For senior, graduate or postgraduate study.
Basis for selection: Major/career interest in business; engineering, electrical and electronic. Applicant must demonstrate seriousness of purpose and service orientation.
Application requirements: Essay and proof of eligibility.
Additional information: $480-$640 per week for undergraduates, $720-$1,000 per week for graduate students. All internships located in Milpitas, CA. Resume and cover letter required.

Amount of award:	$4,800-$12,000
Application deadline:	May 15

Contact:
Octel Communications
Internship Coordinator
1001 Murphy Ranch Rd.
Milpitas, CA 95035

Ohio National Guard

Ohio National Guard Tuition Grant

Type of award: Scholarship, renewable.
Intended use: For full-time or half-time freshman, sophomore, junior or senior study at accredited postsecondary institution in Ohio. Designated institutions: Must be approved by Ohio Board of Regents and be degree granting institution in Ohio.
Eligibility: Applicant must be in military service who served

in the Reserves/National Guard. Must enlist, reenlist, or extend current enlistment to equal 6 years with Ohio National Guard. Must remain in good standing.
Application requirements: Proof of eligibility. Must be member of Ohio National Guard. Must not already possess Baccalaureate degree.
Additional information: Must be member of Ohio National Guard and approved by the Ohio Board of Regents. Minimum of 6 credit hours. Must not have Baccalaureate degree. Award covers 60% instructional & general fee for state assisted institutions - average of state assisted universities for proprietary institution. Application deadlines: July 1, November 1, February 1, and April 1.
    Number of awards: 4,200
    Number of applicants: 5,200
    Total amount awarded: $2,858,000
Contact:
Adjutant General's Department
Tuition Grant Program
2825 West Granville Road
Columbus, OH 43235
Phone: 888-400-6484

Ohio Newspapers Foundation

Harold K. Douthit Scholarship

Type of award: Scholarship.
Intended use: For freshman study at 2-year or 4-year institution in United States.
Eligibility: Applicant must be high school senior. Applicant must be U.S. citizen residing in Ohio.
Basis for selection: Major/career interest in journalism. Applicant must demonstrate financial need and high academic achievement.
Application requirements: Recommendations, essay and transcript. Samples of published work.
Additional information: 3.0 GPA required.
    Amount of award: $1,000
    Number of awards: 1
    Application deadline: March 31
    Total amount awarded: $1,000

Ohio Newspapers Minority Scholarship

Type of award: Scholarship.
Intended use: For full-time freshman study in Ohio.
Eligibility: Applicant must be of minority background. Applicant must be residing in Ohio.
Basis for selection: Major/career interest in journalism. Applicant must demonstrate high academic achievement.
Application requirements: Recommendations, essay, transcript and proof of eligibility. Students may include writing samples or articles that have been published.
Additional information: Minimum GPA of 2.5.
    Amount of award: $1,000
    Number of awards: 3
    Number of applicants: 8
    Application deadline: March 31
    Notification begins: May 15
    Total amount awarded: $3,000
Contact:
Ohio Newspapers Foundation
1335 Dublin Road
Suite 216-B
Columbus, OH 43215
Phone: 614-486-6677

Oklahoma Engineering Foundation

Oklahoma Engineering Foundation Scholarship

Type of award: Scholarship.
Intended use: For freshman study at accredited 4-year institution in United States.
Eligibility: Applicant must be high school senior. Applicant must be U.S. citizen residing in Oklahoma.
Basis for selection: Major/career interest in engineering. Applicant must demonstrate depth of character, leadership and service orientation.
Application requirements: Interview, essay and transcript. State applicant must attend college in Oklahoma.
Additional information: Must be used at specific institutions in Oklahoma, Iowa or Kansas. Contact office for more information.
    Amount of award: $500-$1,000
    Application deadline: December 31
    Notification begins: May 30
Contact:
Executive Director
201 Northeast 27th Street
Room 125
Oklahoma City, OK 73105

Oncology Nursing Foundation

Oncology Nursing Bachelor's Scholarship

Type of award: Scholarship.
Intended use: For full-time or half-time undergraduate study at accredited 4-year institution in United States.
Basis for selection: Major/career interest in nursing; oncology. Applicant must demonstrate depth of character, leadership, service orientation and high academic achievement.
Application requirements: $5 application fee. Interview, recommendations, essay, transcript and proof of eligibility. Curriculum vitae.
Additional information: Must be licensed registered nurse

and currently enrolled in or applying to oncology nursing degree program at National League for Nursing-accredited school.

Amount of award:	$2,000
Number of awards:	16
Number of applicants:	50
Application deadline:	February 1
Notification begins:	March 15
Total amount awarded:	$36,000

Contact:
Oncology Nursing Foundation
501 Holiday Drive
Pittsburgh, PA 15220
Phone: 412-921-7373, ext. 231

Oncology Nursing Doctoral Scholarship

Type of award: Scholarship.
Intended use: For full-time or half-time doctoral study.
Basis for selection: Major/career interest in nursing; oncology. Applicant must demonstrate depth of character, leadership and high academic achievement.
Application requirements: $5 application fee. Recommendations, essay, transcript and proof of eligibility.
Additional information: Must be registered nurse and enrolled in oncology program in National League for Nursing-accredited school of nursing. Must have two letters of support.

Amount of award:	$3,000
Number of awards:	5
Number of applicants:	25
Application deadline:	February 1
Notification begins:	March 15
Total amount awarded:	$15,000

Oncology Nursing Master's Scholarship

Type of award: Scholarship.
Intended use: For full-time or half-time master's study at accredited graduate institution in United States.
Basis for selection: Major/career interest in nursing; oncology. Applicant must demonstrate depth of character, leadership, service orientation and high academic achievement.
Application requirements: $5 application fee. Essay, transcript and proof of eligibility. Curriculum vitae.
Additional information: Must be licensed registered nurse. Must be currently enrolled in or applying to graduate master's oncology nursing degree program in National League for Nursing-accredited school.

Amount of award:	$3,000
Number of awards:	16
Number of applicants:	60
Application deadline:	February 1
Notification begins:	March 15
Total amount awarded:	$48,000

Oncology Nursing Post-Master's Nurse Practitioner Certificate

Type of award: Scholarship.
Intended use: For post-bachelor's certificate study at accredited graduate institution in United States.
Basis for selection: Major/career interest in nurse practitioner; nursing; oncology.
Application requirements: $5 application fee.
Additional information: Must be enrolled in or applying to post-master's nurse practitioner certificate academic credit bearing program in National League for Nursing-accredited school of nursing. Must have master's degree in nursing, current registered nurse's license, interest in and commitment to oncology nursing.

Amount of award:	$3,000
Number of awards:	2
Number of applicants:	31
Application deadline:	February 1
Total amount awarded:	$6,000

Oncology Nursing Research Grant

Type of award: Research grant.
Intended use: For master's, doctoral or postgraduate study at accredited postsecondary institution.
Basis for selection: Major/career interest in nursing; oncology. Applicant must demonstrate leadership, seriousness of purpose, service orientation and high academic achievement.
Application requirements: $25 application fee. Recommendations, proof of eligibility and research proposal.
Additional information: Submit abstract of up to 250 words.

Amount of award:	$3,000-$10,000
Number of awards:	30
Application deadline:	November 1
Notification begins:	March 15

Contact:
Oncology Nursing Foundation
Attn: Research Department
501 Holiday Drive
Pittsburgh, PA 15220-2749
Phone: 412-921-7373, ext. 231

Order of American Hellenic Educational Progressive Association

Hellenic Progressive Association Scholarship

Type of award: Scholarship, renewable.
Intended use: For full-time undergraduate or graduate study.
Eligibility: Applicant must be of Greek heritage.
Basis for selection: Applicant must demonstrate depth of character, leadership, patriotism, seriousness of purpose, service orientation, financial need and high academic achievement.
Application requirements: Recommendations, essay, transcript and proof of eligibility. Include recent photograph.
Additional information: Preference given to members of AHEPA and/or those of Greek heritage. High School seniors are welcome to apply.

Amount of award:	$1,000-$2,000
Number of awards:	30
Number of applicants:	1,000
Application deadline:	June 1
Notification begins:	September 1
Total amount awarded:	$70,000

Contact:
AHEPA Educational Foundation--Scholarships
1909 Q Street, NE
Suite 500
Washington, DC 20009
Website: www.ahepa.org

Oregon State Scholarship Commission

American Ex-POW/Peter Connacher Memorial Scholarship

Type of award: Scholarship, renewable.
Intended use: For full-time undergraduate or graduate study at postsecondary institution.
Eligibility: Applicant must be U.S. citizen or permanent resident residing in Oregon. Applicant must be veteran, descendant of veteran.
Basis for selection: Applicant must demonstrate financial need and high academic achievement.
Application requirements: Essay, transcript and proof of eligibility. Documentation of POW status.
Additional information: Must be ex-POW or descendant of POW. Contact high school guidance office, undergraduate financial aid office, or OSSC (send SASE).

Amount of award:	$1,400
Number of awards:	5
Application deadline:	March 1
Total amount awarded:	$7,000

Contact:
Oregon State Scholarship Commission
Grant Department
1500 Valley River Dr. Suite 100
Eugene, OR 97401-2146
Website: www.ossc.state.or.us

Commission State Scholarship Commission/Oregon Public Employees Union

Type of award: Scholarship.
Intended use: For undergraduate or graduate study at postsecondary institution.
Eligibility: Applicant must be residing in Oregon.
Additional information: For Oregon Public Employees Union (OPEU), children, grandchildren, spouses of active or retired members in good standing, dependents of deceased members who were active OPEU members at time of death, and laid-off members. Qualifying members must have been active OPEU members for at least one year. Children, grandchildren of qualifying members must be under age 25 at time of application and will be considered only for undergraduate program. Part-time enrollment (minimum six credit hours) or graduate program enrollment will be considered, only for OPEU active members, spouses, or laid-off members.
Application deadline: March 1
Contact:
Oregon State Scholarship Commission, Attn: Private Awards
Private Awards
1500 Valley River Drive, Suite 100
Eugene, OR 97401-2146
Website: www.ossc.state.or.us

David Family Scholarship

Type of award: Scholarship, renewable.
Intended use: For undergraduate or graduate study at postsecondary institution in United States.
Eligibility: Applicant must be U.S. citizen or permanent resident residing in Oregon.
Basis for selection: Applicant must demonstrate financial need and high academic achievement.
Application requirements: Essay and transcript.
Additional information: Available to residents of Clackmas, Lane, Linn, Marion, Multnomah, Washington and Yamhill counties. Must have minimum 2.50 GPA. First preference to applicants enrolling at least half-time in upper-division or graduate programs at 4-yr colleges (maximum six undergraduate, six graduate quarters); second preference to graduating high school seniors from West Linn-Wilsonville, Lake Oswego, Portland, Tigard-Tualatin, or Beaverton school districts.
Application deadline: March 1
Contact:
Oregon State Scholarship Commission
1500 Valley River Drive, Suite l00
Attn: Private Awards
Eugene, OR 97401-2146
Website: www.ossc.state.or.us

Dorothy Campbell Memorial Scholarship

Type of award: Scholarship, renewable.
Intended use: For full-time undergraduate study at accredited 4-year institution in Oregon. Designated institutions: Four year colleges in Oregon.
Eligibility: Applicant must be female. Applicant must be U.S. citizen or permanent resident residing in Oregon.
Basis for selection: Applicant must demonstrate financial need and high academic achievement.
Application requirements: Essay and transcript.
Additional information: 2.75 GPA required. High school graduates and college undergraduates may apply.
Application deadline: March 1
Contact:
Oregon State Scholarship Commission
1500 Valley River Drive, Suite l00
Attn: Private Awards
Eugene, OR 97401-2146
Website: www.ossc.state.or.us

Ford Opportunity Program

Type of award: Scholarship, renewable.
Intended use: For full-time undergraduate study at accredited

4-year institution in Oregon. Designated institutions: Oregon schools offering four year degrees.
Eligibility: Applicant must be U.S. citizen or permanent resident residing in Oregon.
Basis for selection: Applicant must demonstrate financial need and high academic achievement.
Application requirements: Essay and transcript. Minimum 3.0 GPA, unless accompanied by a counselor recommendation.
Additional information: Must be single head of household with custody of dependent children. Apply to this program OR the Ford Scholars program, not both.

Number of awards:	30
Application deadline:	March 1
Total amount awarded:	$198,870

Contact:
Oregon State Scholarship Commission
1500 Valley River Drive, Suite 100
Attn: Private Awards
Eugene, OR 97401-2146
Website: www.ossc.state.or.us

Ford Scholars Program

Type of award: Scholarship, renewable.
Intended use: For full-time undergraduate study at accredited 4-year institution in Oregon. Designated institutions: Four year colleges in Oregon.
Eligibility: Applicant must be high school senior. Applicant must be U.S. citizen or permanent resident residing in Oregon.
Basis for selection: Applicant must demonstrate financial need and high academic achievement.
Application requirements: Recommendations, essay and transcript. Minimum 3.0 GPA unless accompanied by a counselor recommendation.
Additional information: Individuals who have completed two years at an Oregon community college and are entering junior year at an Oregon four year college are also eligible. Must have 3.0 GPA and/or recommendations.

Number of awards:	120
Application deadline:	March 1
Total amount awarded:	$2,169,079

Contact:
Oregon State Scholarship Commission
1500 Valley River Drive, Suite 100
Attn: Private Programs
Eugene, OR 97401
Website: www.ossc.state.or.us

Ida M. Crawford Scholarship

Type of award: Scholarship, renewable.
Intended use: For full-time undergraduate study at accredited postsecondary institution in Oregon.
Eligibility: Applicant must be U.S. citizen or permanent resident residing in Oregon.
Basis for selection: Applicant must demonstrate financial need and high academic achievement.
Application requirements: Essay and transcript. Minimum 3.5 GPA.
Additional information: Not available to those majoring in medicine, law, theology, teaching, or music. U.S. Bancorp employees, their children and near relatives not eligible. 3.5 GPA required. Award amounts vary.

Application deadline:	March 1

Contact:
Oregon State Scholarship Commission
1500 Valley River Drive, Suite 100
Attn: Private Awards
Eugene, OR 97401-2146
Website: www.ossc.state.or.us

James Carlson Memorial Scholarship

Type of award: Scholarship, renewable.
Intended use: For full-time senior, post-bachelor's certificate study at accredited 4-year or graduate institution.
Eligibility: Applicant must be U.S. citizen or permanent resident residing in Oregon.
Basis for selection: Major/career interest in education, teacher; education; education, special; education, early childhood. Applicant must demonstrate financial need and high academic achievement.
Application requirements: Essay and transcript.
Additional information: Priority in selection process is given to: 1) African-American, Asian, Hispanic, and Native American ethnic groups; 2) dependents of Oregon Education Association members; 3) others commited to teaching autistic children. Award amounts vary.

Application deadline:	March 1

Contact:
Oregon State Scholarship Commission
Attn: Private Awards
1500 Valley River Drive, Suite 100
Eugene, OR 97401
Website: www.ossc.state.or.us

Jeanette Mowery Graduate Scholarship

Type of award: Scholarship, renewable.
Intended use: For full-time first professional study in United States. Designated institutions: Any Oregon law school or Oregon Health Services University.
Eligibility: Applicant must be U.S. citizen or permanent resident residing in Oregon.
Basis for selection: Major/career interest in law; dentistry; medicine (m.d.). Applicant must demonstrate financial need and high academic achievement.
Application requirements: Essay and transcript. FAFSA.
Additional information: TYY 541-687-7357. Send SASE with information request.

Amount of award:	$900
Number of awards:	2
Application deadline:	March 1
Notification begins:	July 31
Total amount awarded:	$1,800

Contact:
Oregon State Scholarship Commission
Grant Department
1500 Valley River Drive, Suite 100
Eugene, OR 97401
Phone: 541-687-7400

Jenkins Scholarship

Type of award: Scholarship, renewable.
Intended use: For full-time or half-time undergraduate study at 2-year or 4-year institution in Oregon.
Eligibility: Applicant must be U.S. citizen or permanent resident residing in Oregon.
Application requirements: Essay and transcript.
Additional information: Open to all graduates of accredited Oregon high schools with preference to graduates of Portland School District 1J high school (especially Jefferson High School). Minimum 3.5 GPA for graduating high school seniors, 3.0 for continuing college students. U.S. Bancorp employees, their children or close relatives not eligible. Send SASE for information.

Amount of award:	$2,000
Number of awards:	54
Application deadline:	March 1
Total amount awarded:	$108,000

Contact:
Oregon State Scholarship Commission
1500 Valley River Drive, Suite 100
Attn: Private Awards
Eugene, OR 97401

Jerome B. Steinbach Scholarship

Type of award: Scholarship, renewable.
Intended use: For full-time sophomore, junior or senior study at accredited 4-year institution in United States.
Eligibility: Applicant must be U.S. citizen or permanent resident residing in Oregon.
Basis for selection: Applicant must demonstrate financial need and high academic achievement.
Application requirements: Essay and transcript.
Additional information: Minimum 3.5 GPA. U.S. Bancorp employees, their children and near relatives not eligible.

Amount of award:	$1,000
Number of awards:	50
Number of applicants:	404
Application deadline:	March 1
Notification begins:	July 31
Total amount awarded:	$50,000

Contact:
Oregon State Scholarship Commission
1500 Valley River Drive, Suite l00
Eugene, OR 97401
Phone: 541-687-7400

Jose D. Garcia Migrant Education Scholarship

Type of award: Scholarship.
Intended use: For full-time or half-time freshman study at 2-year or 4-year institution in Oregon.
Eligibility: Applicant must be U.S. citizen or permanent resident residing in Oregon.
Application requirements: Essay and transcript.
Additional information: Applicant must be participant in Oregon Migrant Education Program.

Amount of award:	$500
Number of awards:	2
Application deadline:	March 1
Total amount awarded:	$1,000

Contact:
Oregon State Scholarship Commission
Attn: Private Awards
1500 Valley River Drive, Suite 100
Eugene, OR 97401

Kaiser Permanente Dental Assistant Scholarship

Type of award: Scholarship, renewable.
Intended use: For full-time undergraduate certificate, freshman or sophomore study at accredited vocational or 2-year institution in United States. Designated institutions: Blue Mountain Community College, Chemeketa Community College, Concorde Career Institute, Lane Community College, Linn-Benton Community College and Portland Community College.
Eligibility: Applicant must be U.S. citizen or permanent resident residing in Oregon.
Basis for selection: Major/career interest in dental assistant. Applicant must demonstrate financial need.

Application deadline:	March 1
Notification begins:	July 31

Contact:
Oregon State Scholarship Commission
1500 Valley River Drive, Suite l00
Eugene, OR 97401

Lawrence R. Foster Memorial Scholarship

Type of award: Scholarship, renewable.
Intended use: For junior, senior or graduate study at accredited 4-year or graduate institution in Oregon.
Eligibility: Applicant must be U.S. citizen or permanent resident residing in Oregon.
Basis for selection: Major/career interest in public health; health-related professions; physician assistant; nursing.
Application requirements: Recommendations, essay and transcript.
Additional information: Preference given to applicant seeking graduate degree in public health.

Amount of award:	$1,800
Number of awards:	1
Application deadline:	March 1
Total amount awarded:	$1,800

Contact:
Oregon State Scholarship Commission
1500 Valley River Drive, Suite 100
Eugene, OR 97401

Maria Jackson--General George White Scholarship

Type of award: Scholarship, renewable.
Intended use: For full-time undergraduate or graduate study at accredited postsecondary institution in Oregon.
Eligibility: Applicant must be U.S. citizen or permanent resident residing in Oregon. Applicant must be child of active

service person, veteran, disabled veteran, deceased veteran or POW/MIA who served in the Army, Air Force, Marines, Navy, Coast Guard or Reserves/National Guard.
Basis for selection: Applicant must demonstrate financial need and high academic achievement.
Application requirements: Essay and transcript.
Additional information: Minimum 3.75 GPA. U.S. Bancorp employees, their children or near relatives not eligible.
   Application deadline: March 1
   Notification begins: July 31
Contact:
Oregon State Scholarship Commission
1500 Valley River Drive, Suite 100
Eugene, OR 97401

Mark Hass Journalism Scholarship

Type of award: Scholarship.
Intended use: For full-time freshman, sophomore, junior or senior study at accredited 4-year institution in United States.
Eligibility: Applicant must be U.S. citizen or permanent resident residing in Oregon.
Basis for selection: Major/career interest in journalism. Applicant must demonstrate financial need.
Additional information: Persons with disabilities contact OSSC Personnel Director, 541-687-7400, TYY 541-687-7357.
   Application deadline: March 1
Contact:
Oregon State Scholarship Commission
1500 Valley River Drive, Suite 100
Eugene, OR 97401

Mentor Graphics Scholarship

Type of award: Scholarship, renewable.
Intended use: For full-time junior, senior study at accredited 4-year institution in United States.
Eligibility: Applicant must be U.S. citizen or permanent resident residing in Oregon.
Basis for selection: Major/career interest in computer and information sciences; engineering, electrical and electronic; engineering, computer. Applicant must demonstrate financial need.
Application requirements: Essay and transcript.
Additional information: TYY 541-687-7357.
   Application deadline: March 1
   Notification begins: July 31
Contact:
Oregon State Scholarship Commission
1500 Valley River Drive, Suite 100
Eugene, OR 97401
Phone: 541-687-7400

Oregon Alpha Delta Kappa/Harriet Simmons Scholarship

Type of award: Scholarship, renewable.
Intended use: For full-time senior, post-bachelor's certificate or master's study at accredited 4-year or graduate institution in United States.
Eligibility: Applicant must be U.S. citizen or permanent resident residing in Oregon.
Basis for selection: Major/career interest in education; education, teacher. Applicant must demonstrate financial need and high academic achievement.

Application requirements: Essay and transcript.
Additional information: Applicants must be elementary or secondary education majors. Persons with disabilities call 541-687-7400, TYY 541-687-7357.
   Application deadline: March 1
   Notification begins: July 31
Contact:
Oregon State Scholarship Commission
1500 Valley River Drive, Suite 100
Attn: Private Awards
Eugene, OR 97401-2146
Website: www.ossc.state.or.us

Oregon Broadcast Journalism Scholarship

Type of award: Scholarship, renewable.
Intended use: For full-time undergraduate study at postsecondary institution in Oregon.
Eligibility: Applicant must be U.S. citizen or permanent resident residing in Oregon.
Basis for selection: Major/career interest in journalism; communications; radio/television/film.
Application requirements: Essay and transcript.
Additional information: Applicants must major in broadcast journalism. Contact high school guidance office for application or additional information.
   Amount of award: $1,000
   Number of awards: 6
   Application deadline: March 1
   Total amount awarded: $6,000
Contact:
Oregon State Scholarship Commission
1500 Valley River Drive, Suite 100
Attn: Private Awards
Eugene, OR 97401
Website: www.ossc.state.or.us

Oregon Collectors Association Bob Hasson Memorial Scholarship

Type of award: Scholarship.
Intended use: For full-time freshman study.
Eligibility: Applicant must be high school senior. Applicant must be U.S. citizen or permanent resident residing in Oregon.
Basis for selection: Applicant must demonstrate financial need.
Application requirements: Essay and transcript. Additional essay: "The Proper Use of Credit.".
Additional information: Children and grandchildren of owners and officers of collection agencies in Oregon not eligible. Persons with disabilities call 541-687-7400, TYY 541-687-7357. Award based on the three to four page essay: "The Proper Use of Credit."
   Application deadline: March 1
   Notification begins: July 31
Contact:
Oregon State Scholarship Commission
1500 Valley River Drive, Suite 100
Attn: Private Awards
Eugene, OR 97401-2146
Website: www.ossc.state.or.us

Oregon Occupational Safety and Health Division Workers Memorial Scholarship

Type of award: Scholarship, renewable.
Intended use: For full-time undergraduate or graduate study.
Eligibility: Applicant must be high school senior. Applicant must be U.S. citizen or permanent resident residing in Oregon. Applicant's parent must have been killed or disabled in work-related accident as fire fighter, police officer or public safety officer.
Basis for selection: Applicant must demonstrate high academic achievement.
Application requirements: Essay, transcript and proof of eligibility. Additional essay: 500 words or less: "How has the injury or death of your parent or spouse affected or influenced your decision to further your education?".
Additional information: Must be dependent or spouse of Oregon worker permanently disabled on the job or receiving fatality benefits as dependent of fatally injured Oregon worker. Contact Oregon Occupational Safety and Health Division or school guidance office or financial aid office of Commission. Send SASE.

Number of awards:	1
Application deadline:	March 1
Total amount awarded:	$4,468

Contact:
Oregon State Scholarship Commission
1500 Valley River Drive, Suite 100
Attn: Private Awards
Eugene, OR 97401-2146
Website: www.ossc.state.or.us

Oregon Private 150 Scholarship

Type of award: Scholarship, renewable.
Intended use: For full-time junior, senior or graduate study at accredited 4-year or graduate institution in Oregon. Designated institutions: Oregon Colleges.
Eligibility: Applicant must be U.S. citizen or permanent resident residing in Oregon.
Basis for selection: Major/career interest in business. Applicant must demonstrate financial need and high academic achievement.
Application requirements: Essay and transcript. Additional essay of 750 words or more "Describe an experience with a company that provides great customer service and what your experience tells you about running a business.".
Additional information: Minimum 3.0 GPA.

Amount of award:	$2,000
Number of awards:	4
Application deadline:	March 1
Notification begins:	July 31
Total amount awarded:	$8,000

Contact:
Oregon State Scholarship Commission
1500 Valley River Drive, Suite 100
Attn: Private Awards
Eugene, OR 97401
Website: www.ossc.state.or.us

Oregon State Occupational Safety Scholarship

Type of award: Scholarship, renewable.
Intended use: For full-time undergraduate or graduate study at accredited postsecondary institution in United States.
Eligibility: Applicant must be U.S. citizen or permanent resident residing in Oregon.
Application requirements: Essay and transcript. Additional essay on how death of parent or spouse has affected decision to futher education.

Application deadline:	March 1
Notification begins:	July 31

Contact:
Oregon State Scholarship Commission
1500 Valley River Drive, Suite 100
Eugene, OR 97401

Oregon State Scholarship Commission/AFL-CIO Scholarship

Type of award: Scholarship.
Intended use: For undergraduate study.
Eligibility: Applicant must be high school senior. Applicant must be residing in Oregon.
Additional information: Preference may be given to applicants from union families. An essay of 500 words or less is required on the following topics: "United Parcel Services use of part-time workers was one of the main issues that led to the nationwide strike of 160,000 teamster union-represented UPS workers for three weeks in the summer of 1997. Can workers and their families survive on part-time work and benefits? Was the teamster union's strike successful?"

Application deadline:	March 1

Contact:
Oregon State Scholarship Commission, Attn: Private Awards
Private Awards
1500 Valley River Drive, Suite 100
Eugene, OR 97401-2146
Website: www.ossc.state.or.us

Oregon State Scholarship Commission/Ben Selling Scholarship

Type of award: Scholarship.
Intended use: For sophomore, junior or senior study.
Eligibility: Applicant must be residing in Oregon.
Additional information: Minimum 3.5 GPA. For Wells Fargo employees, their children, or near relatives. Must provide proof of employment status.

Application deadline:	March 1

Contact:
Oregon State Scholarship Commission, Attn: Private Awards
Private Awards
1500 Valley River Drive, Suite 100
Eugene, OR 97401-2146
Website: www.ossc.state.or.us

Oregon State Scholarship Commission/Bertha P. Singer Scholarship

Type of award: Scholarship.
Intended use: For sophomore, junior or senior study.
Designated institutions: Oregon.
Eligibility: Applicant must be residing in Oregon.
Basis for selection: Major/career interest in nursing.
Additional information: Minimum 3.0 GPA. Employees of U.S. Ben Corp., their children, or near relatives are not eligible.
   Application deadline: March 1
Contact:
Oregon State Scholarship Commission, Attn: Private Awards
Private Awards
1500 Valley River Drive, Suite 100
Eugene, OR 97401-2146
Website: www.ossc.state.or.us

Oregon State Scholarship Commission/Clyde C. Crosby/Joseph M. Edgar Memorial Scholarship

Type of award: Scholarship.
Intended use: For undergraduate study.
Eligibility: Applicant must be high school senior. Applicant must be residing in Oregon.
Additional information: Graduating high school seniors with 3.00+ cumulative GPA who are children or dependent stepchildren of active, retired, disabled or deceased members of local unions affiliated with Joint Council of Teamsters #37. Qualifying members must have been active at least one year.
   Application deadline: March 1
Contact:
Oregon State Scholarship Commission, Attn: Private Awards
Private Awards
1500 Valley River Drive, Suite 100
Eugene, OR 97401-2146
Website: www.ossc.state.or.us

Oregon State Scholarship Commission/Compute Stores Northwest Scholarship

Type of award: Scholarship.
Intended use: For undergraduate study.
Eligibility: Applicant must be high school senior. Applicant must be residing in Oregon.
Additional information: 3.0 GPA minimum. For dependents of Computer Stores Northwest (CSNW) employees enrolled in a tech-related field.
   Application deadline: March 1
Contact:
Oregon State Scholarship Commission, Attn: Private Awards
Private Awards
1500 Valley River Drive, Suite 100
Eugene, OR 97401-2146
Website: www.ossc.state.or.us

Oregon State Scholarship Commission/Friends of Oregon Students Scholarship

Type of award: Scholarship.
Intended use: For undergraduate study.
Eligibility: Applicant must be residing in Oregon.
Additional information: For Oregon residents either with previous college experience working 25+ hours weekly while enrolled full time and planning to continue 25+ hours weekly work or students without previous college planning to work 25+ hours weekly while enrolled full time. Must also meet one of the following: graduate of public alternative Oregon high school or GED recipient or transferring from Oregon community college to a 4-year college. Preference: health, education, social services, and other helping professions.
   Application deadline: March 1
Contact:
Oregon State Scholarship Commission/Friends of Oregon Students Scholarship
Private Awards
1500 Valley River Drive, Suite 100
Eugene, OR 97401-2146
Website: www.ossc.state.or.us

Oregon State Scholarship Commission/Glenn Jackson Scholarship

Type of award: Scholarship.
Intended use: For undergraduate study.
Eligibility: Applicant must be high school senior. Applicant must be residing in Oregon.
Additional information: Dependents of employees or retirees of the Oregon Department of Transportation or Parks and Recreation Department. Employees must have been employed by their departments at least three years. Additional essays: two one-page essays: (1) "How do you plan to finance your college education?" and (2) "If you could have a personal meeting with the Governor of Oregon, what would you talk about and why?" Maximum 12 undergraduate quarters or equivalent; awards at 2-year institutions for no more than six quarters.
   Application deadline: March 1
Contact:
Oregon State Scholarship Commission, Attn: Private Awards
Private Awards
1500 Valley River Drive, Suite 100
Eugene, OR 97401-2146
Website: www.ossc.state.or.us

Oregon State Scholarship Commission/Howard Vollum American Indian Scholarship

Type of award: Scholarship.
Intended use: For undergraduate study.
Eligibility: Applicant must be residing in Oregon.
Basis for selection: Major/career interest in science, general; computer and information sciences; engineering; mathematics.
Additional information: For American-Indian residents of Clackamas, Multnomah, or Washington County in Oregon, or

Clark County, Washington. Submit certification of tribal enrollment or American Indian ancestry: a photocopy of (1) tribal enrollment card that includes enrollment number and/or blood quantum, or (2) Johnson O'Malley student eligibility form, or (3) letter from tribe stating blood quantum and/or enrollment number of parent or grandparent. Additional essay: "How do you view your cultural heritage and its importance to you?" Applicants with a demonstrated commitment to the American Indian community are preferred.

Application deadline: March 1
Contact:
Oregon State Scholarship Commission, Attn: Private Awards
Private Awards
1500 Valley River Drive, Suite 100
Eugene, OR 97401-2146
Phone: 541-687-7395
Website: www.ossc.state.or.us

Oregon State Scholarship Commission/Jean Risley Scholarship

Type of award: Scholarship.
Intended use: For first professional study at accredited graduate institution in United States. Designated institutions: Must be used at the Law Schools of Lewis and Clark, the University of Oregon, or Willamette University. Must be entering the senior year in one of the above law schools.
Eligibility: Applicant must be residing in Oregon.
Additional information: Applicants from Benton, Linn, and Marion counties preferred. For Wells Fargo employees, their children, or near relatives. Must provide proof of employment status.

Application deadline: March 1
Contact:
Oregon State Scholarship Commission, Attn: Private Awards
Private Awards
1500 Valley River Drive, Suite 100
Eugene, OR 97401-2146
Website: www.ossc.state.or.us

Oregon State Scholarship Commission/Oregon Building Industry Association Scholarship

Type of award: Scholarship.
Intended use: For undergraduate study.
Eligibility: Applicant must be residing in Oregon.
Basis for selection: Major/career interest in engineering; construction.
Additional information: Other possible topics of study include housing studies, interior merchandising, building inspection, construction technology, and architectural engineering.

Application deadline: March 1
Contact:
Oregon State Scholarship Commission, Attn: Private Awards
Private Awards
1500 Valley River Drive, Suite 100
Eugene, OR 97401-2146
Website: www.ossc.state.or.us

Oregon State Scholarship Commission/Oregon National Guard Tuition Assistance

Type of award: Scholarship.
Intended use: For undergraduate study. Designated institutions: Oregon.
Eligibility: Applicant must be U.S. citizen residing in Oregon.
Additional information: For Oregon National Guard Members participating in the officer training program, or enlisted members of selected Oregon National Guard units.

Application deadline: March 1
Contact:
Oregon State Scholarship Commission, Attn: Private Awards
Private Awards
1500 Valley River Drive, Suite 100
Eugene, OR 97401-2146
Website: www.ossc.state.or.us

Oregon State Scholarship Commission/Oregon State Personnel Managers Association

Type of award: Scholarship.
Intended use: For undergraduate study.
Eligibility: Applicant must be residing in Oregon.
Additional information: Oregon State Personnel Managers Association: Members of Oregon State Personnel Managers Association entering full-time college in personnel management, personnel administration, human resources management, safety management, labor relations, industrial relations, industrial engineering, business administration, public relations, or closely related fields.

Application deadline: March 1
Contact:
Oregon State Scholarship Commission, Attn: Private Awards
Private Awards
1500 Valley River Drive, Suite 100
Eugene, OR 97401-2146
Website: www.ossc.state.or.us

Oregon State Scholarship Commission/Oregon Trucking Association

Type of award: Scholarship.
Intended use: For undergraduate study.
Eligibility: Applicant must be high school senior. Applicant must be residing in Oregon.
Additional information: For children of Oregon Trucking Association (OTA) members, or children of employees (for at least one year) of OTA members.

Application deadline: March 1
Contact:
Oregon State Scholarship Commission, Attn: Private Awards
Private Awards
1500 Valley River Drive, Suite 100
Eugene, OR 97401-2146
Website: www.ossc.state.or.us

Oregon State Scholarship Commission/Pendleton Postal Workers Scholarship

Type of award: Scholarship.
Intended use: For undergraduate study.
Eligibility: Applicant must be high school senior. Applicant must be residing in Oregon.
Additional information: For graduating high school seniors as well as dependents or descendants of active, retired, or deceased members of Pendleton APWU #110 that have been members for at least one year preceding application deadline. Additional Essay: "What has the labor movement accomplished historically for working people?" One-time award.
Application deadline: March 1
Contact:
Oregon State Scholarship Commission, Attn: Private Awards
Private Awards
1500 Valley River Drive, Suite 100
Eugene, OR 97401-2146
Website: www.ossc.state.or.us

Oregon State Scholarship Commission/Peter Connacher Memorial Scholarship

Type of award: Scholarship.
Intended use: For undergraduate or graduate study at postsecondary institution.
Eligibility: Applicant must be residing in Oregon. Applicant must be veteran, descendant of veteran, child of veteran. For American former prisoners of war and their descendants, submit copy of P.O.W.'s U.S. Armed Forces discharge papers, proof of P.O.W. status, and relationship with P.O.W.
Application deadline: March 1
Contact:
Oregon State Scholarship Commission
Private Awards
1500 Valley River Drive, Suite 100
Eugene, OR 97401-2146
Website: www.ossc.state.or.us

Oregon State Scholarship Commission/Professional Land Surveyors of Oregon Scholarship

Type of award: Scholarship, renewable.
Intended use: For undergraduate study. Designated institutions: Oregon.
Eligibility: Applicant must be residing in Oregon.
Additional information: Professional Land Surveyors of Oregon (OCF): Junior or senior-year students enrolled in curricula leading to land-surveying career. Community college applicants must intend to transfer to eligible 4-year schools. 4-year applicants must intend to take the Land Surveying in Training (LSIT) exam. Additional essay: brief statement of education-career goals relating to land surveying. Oregon colleges; apply-compete annually.
Application deadline: March 1
Contact:
Oregon State Scholarship Commission, Attn: Private Awards
Private Awards
1500 Valley River Drive, Suite 100
Eugene, OR 97401-2146
Phone: 541-687-7395
Website: www.ossc.state.or.us

Oregon State Scholarship Commission/Richard F. Brentano Memorial Scholarship

Type of award: Scholarship.
Intended use: For undergraduate study.
Eligibility: Applicant must be residing in Oregon.
Additional information: Children or IRS-legal dependents (24 years of age and under) of employees of Waste Control Systems, Inc., and subsidiaries. Exception (to maximum age 26) for children or IRS-legal dependents entering U.S. armed forces directly from high school. Must have been employed by Waste Control Systems one year minimum as of application deadline.
Application deadline: March 1
Contact:
Oregon State Scholarship Commission, Attn: Private Awards
Private Awards
1500 Valley Drive, Suite 100
Eugene, OR 97401-2146
Website: www.ossc.state.or.us

Oregon State Scholarship Commission/Teamsters Council #37 Federal Credit Union Scholarship

Type of award: Scholarship.
Intended use: For undergraduate or graduate study at postsecondary institution.
Eligibility: Applicant must be residing in Oregon.
Additional information: For members or dependents of Council #37 credit union who are active, retired, disabled, or deceased members of Teamsters Joint Teamster Council #37. Members must have been active in local affiliated with the Joint Council of Teamster #37 at least one year. Must have cumulative GPA between 2.00-3.00 and be enrolled at least half-time in college. Additional essay: "The Importance of Preserving the Right to Strike in a Free Enterprise System." One-time award.
Application deadline: March 1
Contact:
Oregon State Scholarship Commission, Attn: Private Awards
Private Awards
1500 Valley River Drive, Suite 100
Eugene, OR 97401-2146
Website: www.ossc.state.or.us

Oregon State Scholarship Commission/Teamsters Local 305 Scholarship

Type of award: Scholarship.
Intended use: For undergraduate study.

Eligibility: Applicant must be high school senior. Applicant must be residing in Oregon.
Additional information: For children or dependent stepchildren of active, retired, disabled, or deceased members of Local 305 of the Joint Council of Teamsters Number 37. Members must have been active at least one year.
   Application deadline: March 1
Contact:
Oregon State Scholarship Commission, Attn: Private Awards
Private Awards
1500 Valley River Drive, Suite 100
Eugene, OR 97401-2146
Website: www.ossc.state.or.us

Oregon State Scholarship Commission/Troutman's Emporium Scholarship

Type of award: Scholarship.
Intended use: For undergraduate study.
Eligibility: Applicant must be residing in Oregon.
Additional information: For employees or dependents of employees of Emporium Corp. that have worked there for at least one year. Preference is given to students attending college in Oregon, Washington, Idaho, and California.
   Application deadline: March 1
Contact:
Oregon State Scholarship Commission, Attn: Private Awards
Private Awards
1500 Valley River Drive, Suite 100
Eugene, OR 97401-2146
Website: www.ossc.state.or.us

Oregon Vietnam Era Veterans' Children Scholarship

Type of award: Scholarship.
Intended use: For full-time undergraduate or graduate study at accredited 2-year, 4-year or graduate institution in Oregon. Designated institutions: Oregon colleges.
Eligibility: Applicant must be U.S. citizen or permanent resident residing in Oregon. Applicant must be child of veteran, disabled veteran, deceased veteran or POW/MIA during Vietnam. Must have served between February 28, 1961 and May 7, 1975.
Basis for selection: Applicant must demonstrate financial need.
Application requirements: Essay, transcript and proof of eligibility. Proof of parent's active duty.
Additional information: For dependants of U.S. veterans who served between February 1961 and May 1975.
   Application deadline: March 1
   Notification begins: July 31
Contact:
Oregon State Scholarship Commission
1500 Valley River Drive, Suite 100
Eugene, OR 97401-2146
Website: www.ossc.state.or.us

Ray Kageler Scholarship

Type of award: Scholarship, renewable.
Intended use: For full-time graduate study at accredited graduate institution in United States.
Eligibility: Applicant must be U.S. citizen or permanent resident residing in Oregon.
Basis for selection: Applicant must demonstrate financial need.
Application requirements: Essay and transcript.
Additional information: Applicant must be member of credit union affiliated with the Oregon Credit Union League.
   Application deadline: March 1
   Notification begins: July 31
Contact:
Oregon State Scholarship Commission
1500 Valley River Drive, Suite 100
Attn: Private Awards
Eugene, OR 97401
Website: www.ossc.state.or.us

Walter and Marie Schmidt Scholarship

Type of award: Scholarship, renewable.
Intended use: For undergraduate study in Oregon.
Eligibility: Applicant must be U.S. citizen or permanent resident residing in Oregon.
Basis for selection: Major/career interest in nursing.
Application requirements: Essay and transcript. Must submit essay describing desire to pursue career in geriatric health care.
Additional information: Preference given to students pursuing career in geriatric nursing. U.S. Bancorp employees, their children or near relatives not eligible.
   Amount of award: $1,850
   Number of awards: 27
   Application deadline: March 1
   Notification begins: July 31
   Total amount awarded: $49,950
Contact:
Oregon State Scholarship Commission
Attn: Private Awards
1500 Valley River Drive, Suite 100
Eugene, OR 97401

Osage Tribal Education Committee

Osage Tribal Education Scholarship

Type of award: Scholarship, renewable.
Intended use: For undergraduate or graduate study at accredited postsecondary institution in United States.
Eligibility: Applicant must be American Indian. Must be a member of the Osage Nation of Oklahoma. Applicant must be U.S. citizen.
Basis for selection: Applicant must demonstrate high academic achievement.
Application requirements: Must provide proof of Osage Indian blood and must be enrolled in any post-secondary institution.
Additional information: Must maintain 2.0 GPA. Deadline for summer funding is May 1, 1999.

Osage Tribal Education Committee: Osage Tribal Education Scholarship

Amount of award: $40-$420
Number of awards: 220
Number of applicants: 250
Application deadline: July 1, December 31
Notification begins: August 1, February 1
Contact:
Osage Tribal Education Committee (OTEC)
Oklahoma Area Education Office
4149 Highline Boulevard, Suite 380
Oklahoma City, OK 73108
Phone: 405-945-6051, ext.303 or 304

Pacific Printing and Imaging Association

Pacific Printing and Imaging Scholarship

Type of award: Scholarship, renewable.
Intended use: For full-time undergraduate study at accredited vocational, 2-year or 4-year institution.
Eligibility: Applicant must be residing in Alaska or Hawaii or Idaho or Montana or Oregon or Washington.
Basis for selection: Applicant must demonstrate seriousness of purpose and high academic achievement.
Application requirements: Recommendations, essay, transcript and proof of eligibility.
Additional information: For technical majors in printing and graphic arts. Not for fine arts, graphic design, or graphic illustration.

Amount of award: $750-$2,500
Number of awards: 5
Number of applicants: 10
Application deadline: April 1
Notification begins: April 15
Total amount awarded: $16,250
Contact:
Pacific Printing and Imaging Association
5319 SW Westgate Drive, Suite 117
Portland, OR 97221
Phone: 503-297-3328

Parenteral Drug Association Foundation for Pharmaceutical Sciences, Inc.

Biotechnology Grant

Type of award: Research grant, renewable.
Intended use: For graduate study at graduate institution in United States.
Basis for selection: Major/career interest in medical specialties/research; health sciences; health-related professions. Applicant must demonstrate seriousness of purpose.
Application requirements: Recommendations and research proposal.
Additional information: Money awarded each year for two years. The principal investigator may not be related to any of the directors of the PDAF for Pharmaceutical Sciences and may not receive any other remuneration from the foundation. Must be associated with a tax-exempt institution.

Amount of award: $30,000
Number of awards: 1
Application deadline: July 1
Total amount awarded: $15,000

Millipore/Charles P. Schaufus Grant

Type of award: Research grant, renewable.
Intended use: For doctoral study at graduate institution in United States.
Basis for selection: Major/career interest in health-related professions; health sciences; medical specialties/research. Applicant must demonstrate seriousness of purpose.
Application requirements: Recommendations and research proposal.
Additional information: Award is $10,000 a year for three years and up to $10,000 in Millipore equipment each year. The principal investigator may not be related to any of the directors of the PDAF for Pharmaceutical Sciences Inc. and may not receive any other remuneration from the Foundation. Must be associated with a tax-exempt institution.

Amount of award: $60,000
Number of awards: 1
Application deadline: July 1
Total amount awarded: $60,000

Parenteral Research Grant

Type of award: Research grant.
Intended use: For graduate study at graduate institution in United States.
Eligibility: Applicant must be permanent resident.
Basis for selection: Major/career interest in biology; chemistry; engineering; manufacturing technologies; microbiology; pharmacy/pharmaceutics/pharmacology; science, general. Applicant must demonstrate seriousness of purpose.
Application requirements: Recommendations and research proposal.
Additional information: The principal investigator may not be related to any of the directors of the PDAF for Pharmaceutical Sciences and may not receive any other remuneration from the foundation. Must be associated with a tax exempt instinction.

Amount of award: $15,000
Number of awards: 2
Application deadline: July 1
Total amount awarded: $30,000
Contact:
Parenteral Drug Association Foundation
P.O. Box 242
Garden City, NY 11530
Website: www.millipore.com/corporate/pdaf

Pediatric AIDS Foundation

Elizabeth Glaser Scientist Award

Type of award: Research grant, renewable.
Intended use: For postgraduate study in United States.
Basis for selection: Major/career interest in medical specialties/research (beyond m.d.). Applicant must demonstrate seriousness of purpose.
Application requirements: Research proposal.
Additional information: Must hold an M.D., Ph.D., D.D.S., or D.V.M. degree and be at the assistant professor level or above. $650,000 award is provided for direct costs over a period of five years. Applications available in March.
   Amount of award: $650,000
   Application deadline: October 1
Contact:
Pediatric AIDS Foundation
1311 Colorado Avenue
Santa Monica, CA 90404
Website: www.pedaids.org

Pediatric AIDS Foundation Research Grants

Type of award: Research grant.
Intended use: For postgraduate, non-degree study in United States.
Basis for selection: Major/career interest in medical specialties/research. Applicant must demonstrate seriousness of purpose.
Application requirements: Research proposal.
Additional information: Applicant must have full-time institutional or academic appointment. One-year programs are renewable, two-year programs are not. Provides up to $80,000 per year on direct costs. Research using animals/models may apply for supplemental funds to a total direct cost of $100,000.
   Amount of award: $80,000-$100,000
   Application deadline: November 10
Contact:
Pediatric AIDS Foundation
1311 Colorado Avenue
Santa Monica, CA 90404
Website: www.pedaids.org

Pediatric AIDS Foundation Student Intern Award

Type of award: Internship.
Intended use: For undergraduate or graduate study.
Basis for selection: Major/career interest in medical specialties/research. Applicant must demonstrate seriousness of purpose.
Application requirements: Nomination by Must apply through sponsor (M.D., Ph.D., C.C.S.W.) who have pediatric HIV/AIDS research experience.
Additional information: This program is to encourage students to choose a career in pediatric HIV/AIDS research. Provides $2,000 for 320 hours of work. Must work a minimum of four hours per week. High school seniors, undergraduates, graduates and medical students are eligible. Applications available in January.
   Amount of award: $2,000
   Application deadline: March 27
Contact:
Pediatric AIDS Foundation
1311 Colorado Avenue
Santa Monica, CA 90404
Website: www.pedaids.org

Scholar Awards

Type of award: Research grant, renewable.
Intended use: For postgraduate study in United States.
Basis for selection: Major/career interest in medical specialties/research. Applicant must demonstrate seriousness of purpose.
Application requirements: Research proposal.
Additional information: Must have three years of post doctoral research. Award of $32,000 for first-year, $34,000 for second-year and $36,000 for third-year. Tenured investigators are not eligible. Must be interested in pediatric HIV/AIDS research as a career focus.
   Amount of award: $66,000-$102,000
   Application deadline: November 10
Contact:
Pediatric AIDS Foundation
1311 Colorado Avenue
Santa Monica, CA 90404
Website: www.pedaids.org

Short-Term Scientific Awards

Type of award: Research grant.
Intended use: For non-degree study in United States.
Basis for selection: Major/career interest in medical specialties/research. Applicant must demonstrate seriousness of purpose.
Application requirements: Research proposal.
Additional information: Program provides funding for travel and short-term study to initiate a critical research project, obtain preliminary data, learn new techniques or sponsor a workshop.
   Amount of award: $5,000
   Application deadline: December 10
Contact:
Program Manager Short-term Scientific Awards
1311 Colorado Avenue
Santa Monica, CA 90404
Website: www.pedaids.org

Personnel Magazine Now Workforce Magazine

Personnel Magazines Now Workforce Magazine Internship

Type of award: Internship.
Intended use: For undergraduate or graduate study.
Basis for selection: Major/career interest in journalism. Applicant must demonstrate depth of character, seriousness of purpose and service orientation.

Application requirements: Recommendations and proof of eligibility.
Additional information: Resume and cover letter required.
- **Amount of award:** $3,750
- **Number of awards:** 2
- **Application deadline:** April 15

Contact:
Personnel Magazine Now Workforce Magazine
Internship Coordinator
245 Fischer Avenue, Suite B-2
Costa Mesa, CA 92628

Peter A. McKernan Scholarship Fund

Peter A. McKernan Scholarship

Type of award: Scholarship.
Intended use: For full-time freshman study at vocational, 2-year or 4-year institution in Maine.
Eligibility: Applicant must be high school junior, senior. Applicant must be U.S. citizen residing in Maine.
Basis for selection: Applicant must demonstrate high academic achievement.
Application requirements: Essay, transcript, proof of eligibility and nomination by high school official.
Additional information: Applicant must have "lettered" in a varsity sport, and must have a "c" or above average. Applicant must be graduating from high school. For information contact your high school guidance counselor.
- **Amount of award:** $2,000
- **Number of awards:** 3
- **Number of applicants:** 150
- **Application deadline:** April 15
- **Total amount awarded:** $6,000

Contact:
Peter A. McKernan Scholarship Fund
P.O. Box 5601
Augusta, ME 04332

Pfizer

Pfizer Internships

Type of award: Internship.
Intended use: For master's study.
Basis for selection: Major/career interest in science, general; engineering; medicine (m.d.). Applicant must demonstrate depth of character, leadership, patriotism, seriousness of purpose, service orientation and high academic achievement.
Application requirements: Proof of eligibility.
Additional information: Minimum 3.8 GPA. Resume and cover letter required. Located in CO, CT, IN, MO, NJ and NY.
- **Amount of award:** $10,920-$16,050

Contact:
Pfizer
235 East 42nd Street
New York, NY 10017

PGA Tour

PGA Minority Internship Program

Type of award: Internship.
Intended use: For senior, master's study.
Eligibility: Applicant must be of minority background. Applicant must be U.S. citizen.
Basis for selection: Major/career interest in marketing; business, management and administration. Applicant must demonstrate depth of character, leadership, seriousness of purpose, service orientation and high academic achievement.
Application requirements: Interview, recommendations, essay and transcript.
Additional information: Internship lasts nine weeks at $250/week with an additional $100/month housing stipend. Site locations include California, Connecticut, Florida and Georgia. Also open to Public Relations majors.
- **Amount of award:** $2,250
- **Number of awards:** 20
- **Application deadline:** March 1
- **Notification begins:** April 12

Contact:
PGA Minority Internship Program
Attn: Aleizha Batson
112 TPC Boulevard
Ponte Vedra Beach, FL 32082

Pharmaceutical Research and Manufacturers of America Foundation, Inc.

Advanced Predoctoral Pharmacology and Toxicology Fellowship

Type of award: Research grant, renewable.
Intended use: For full-time doctoral study at accredited graduate institution in United States.
Eligibility: Applicant must be U.S. citizen or permanent resident.
Basis for selection: Major/career interest in pharmacy/pharmaceutics/pharmacology.
Application requirements: Transcript, proof of eligibility and research proposal. GRE.
Additional information: Stipend is $12,000/year for a minimum of one year and a maximum of two years. An additional $500/year is granted for expenses. Program seeks to support predoctoral students who have completed the bulk of pre-thesis requirements and expect to hold a Ph.D. degree within two years. Students entering graduate school are not eligible. Fellowship may not be used as a supplement to other funds.
- **Amount of award:** $12,000-$24,000
- **Application deadline:** September 1
- **Notification begins:** December 15

Medical Student Research Fellowship in Pharmacology/Clinical Pharmacology

Type of award: Research grant.
Intended use: For first professional study at accredited graduate institution in United States.
Eligibility: Applicant must be U.S. citizen or permanent resident.
Basis for selection: Major/career interest in pharmacy/pharmaceutics/pharmacology. Applicant must demonstrate high academic achievement.
Application requirements: Research proposal and nomination by recommendation by faculty member. Curriculum vitae and bibliography.
Additional information: Must be a medical, dental, or veterinary student with substantial interest in research and teaching career in pharmacology or Clinical pharmacology. Fellowships pay $1,000/month for a minimum tenure of three months to a maximum of two years, but stipend will not exceed $12,000. Student may have to interupt scholastic training to complete fellowship requirements.

Amount of award:	$3,000-$12,000
Application deadline:	October 1
Notification begins:	December 15

Morphology Fellowship

Type of award: Research grant.
Intended use: For postgraduate study in United States.
Eligibility: Applicant must be U.S. citizen or permanent resident.
Basis for selection: Major/career interest in pharmacy/pharmaceutics/pharmacology.
Application requirements: Recommendations and research proposal. Curriculum vitae and bibliography.
Additional information: Application must be submitted by institution on behalf of applicant. Fellowship lasts two years. Award amounts vary. In addition to award, a $500/year travel stipend is granted. Eligible students are postdoctoral students who are trained and qualified primarily in pharmacology or in one of the morphologic specialties. Candidates should indicate a strong determination to continue research after fellowship ends.

Application deadline:	January 15
Notification begins:	March 15

Predoctoral Fellowship in Pharmaceutics

Type of award: Research grant, renewable.
Intended use: For full-time doctoral study at accredited graduate institution in United States.
Eligibility: Applicant must be U.S. citizen or permanent resident.
Basis for selection: Major/career interest in pharmacy/pharmaceutics/pharmacology.
Application requirements: Recommendations, transcript, proof of eligibility and research proposal. Curriculum vitae, statement of career plans.
Additional information: Annual stipend of $12,000 for a minimum tenure of one year and a maximum of two years. In addition to stipend, $500/year is provided to help with expenses. Program support is designed to assist full-time, in residence Ph.D. candidates in pharmaceutics who are enrolled in a school accredited by the American Council on Pharmaceutical Education.

Amount of award:	$12,000-$24,000
Application deadline:	October 1
Notification begins:	December 15

Undergraduate Research Fellowship in Pharmaceutics

Type of award: Research grant.
Intended use: For full-time undergraduate study at accredited 4-year institution in United States.
Eligibility: Applicant must be U.S. citizen or permanent resident.
Basis for selection: Major/career interest in pharmacy/pharmaceutics/pharmacology. Applicant must demonstrate high academic achievement.
Application requirements: Proof of eligibility, research proposal and nomination by Application must be made by faculty member on behalf of student. Curriculum vitae, current research support and official copies of GPA and SAT and/or other national achievement test scores.
Additional information: This program seeks to provide selected pharmaceutics faculty with a one year fellowship that can be awarded to qualified undergraduates. Must be faculty at an institution accredited by the American Council of Pharmaceutical Education and be actively undertaking research in one or more areas of pharmaceutics. Each faculty member may apply for up to two one-year undergraduate fellowships. Students chosen must have a 3.0 GPA and acceptable SAT, ACT, PCAT or MCAT scores.

Amount of award:	$5,000
Number of awards:	2
Application deadline:	October 1
Notification begins:	December 15
Total amount awarded:	$10,000

Contact:
Pharmaceutical Research and Manufacturers of America Foundation, Inc.
1100 15th Street NW
Washington, DC 20005
Website: www.phrmaf.org

Phi Beta Kappa Society

Mary Isabel Sibley Fellowship

Type of award: Scholarship.
Intended use: For full-time doctoral, postgraduate study.
Eligibility: Applicant must be single, female.
Basis for selection: Major/career interest in history; archaeology; literature; foreign languages. Applicant must demonstrate high academic achievement.
Application requirements: Recommendations, transcript, proof of eligibility and research proposal.
Additional information: Must have Ph.D. or have completed all requirements for degree except dissertation and be working in Greek studies (in odd-numbered years) or French studies (in

even-numbered years). Applicant must remain unmarried during period of fellowship and devote full-time work to research.

Amount of award:	$20,000
Number of awards:	1
Number of applicants:	44
Application deadline:	January 15
Notification begins:	April 1
Total amount awarded:	$20,000

Contact:
MISF Committee
c/o Phi Beta Kappa Society
1811 Q Street NW
Washington, DC 20009
Phone: 202-265-3808
Website: www.pbk.org

Phi Delta Kappa International

Scholarship Grant for Prospective Educators

Type of award: Scholarship, renewable.
Intended use: For full-time freshman study at accredited postsecondary institution outside United States.
Eligibility: Applicant must be high school senior.
Basis for selection: Major/career interest in education. Applicant must demonstrate leadership, seriousness of purpose, service orientation and high academic achievement.
Application requirements: Recommendations, essay and transcript.
Additional information: Minimum four awards to racial minorities and two to dependents of PDK members. Minimum 3.5 GPA required, 3.7 recommended. Make application to local chapter.

Amount of award:	$1,000-$5,000
Number of awards:	50
Application deadline:	January 31
Notification begins:	June 1
Total amount awarded:	$50,000

Contact:
Phi Delta Kappa Headquarters
George Kersey, Jr
Box 789
Bloomington, IN 47402-0789

Phi Sigma Iota

Phi Sigma Iota Award

Type of award: Scholarship.
Intended use: For junior, senior study at 4-year or graduate institution.
Basis for selection: Major/career interest in foreign languages. Applicant must demonstrate depth of character, leadership, seriousness of purpose, service orientation and high academic achievement.
Application requirements: Recommendations, essay, transcript and nomination by faculty advisor of Phi Sigma Iota chapter at applicant's institution.
Additional information: Must have minimum 3.3 GPA. Must be enrolled in college at time of application. Must be member of Phi Sigma Iota and be nominated by chapter's faculty advisor.

Amount of award:	$500
Number of awards:	7
Number of applicants:	20
Application deadline:	February 1
Notification begins:	April 15
Total amount awarded:	$3,500

Contact:
Dr. Marie-France Hilgar
Phi Sigma Iota
University of Nevada
Las Vegas, NV 89154

Phillips Academy

Phillips Academy Summer Teaching Assistant Internship Program.

Type of award: Internship.
Intended use: For undergraduate, graduate or non-degree study.
Basis for selection: Major/career interest in education.
Application requirements: Essay and transcript.
Contact:
Internship Program
Andover, MA 01810-4166
Website: www.andover.edu

Pickett and Hatcher Educational Fund, Inc.

Pickett and Hatcher Educational Loan

Type of award: Loan, renewable.
Intended use: For full-time freshman, sophomore, junior or senior study at 4-year institution in Alabama, Florida, Georgia, Kentucky, Mississippi, North Carolina, South Carolina, Tennessee, Virginia.
Eligibility: Applicant must be U.S. citizen residing in Alabama or Florida or Georgia or Kentucky or Mississippi or North Carolina or South Carolina or Tennessee or Virginia.
Basis for selection: Applicant must demonstrate financial need and high academic achievement.
Additional information: Not available to law, medicine, or ministry students. Loans renewed up to $22,000. Must have 3.0 GPA.

Amount of award:	$1,000-$5,500
Number of awards:	700
Number of applicants:	1,412
Total amount awarded:	$3,280,286

Contact:
Pickett and Hatcher Educational Fund, Inc.
Loan Program
P.O. Box 8169
Columbus, GA 31908-8169
Phone: 706-327-6586
Fax: 706-324-6788

Pierce Investment Banking

Investment Banking Internship

Type of award: Internship, renewable.
Intended use: For graduate study.
Eligibility: Applicant must be Mexican American, Hispanic American or Puerto Rican.
Basis for selection: Major/career interest in accounting; finance/banking. Applicant must demonstrate depth of character and seriousness of purpose.
Application requirements: Interview. Resume with cover letter.
Additional information: Internship lasts up to 6 months and pays stipend of $600/month. Spanish is required.

Amount of award:	$3,600
Number of awards:	2
Number of applicants:	10

Contact:
Pierce Investment Banking
Luc Agostini
2200 Clarendon Boulevard, Suite 1410
Arlington, VA 22201
Phone: 703-516-7000

Pittsburgh Civic Garden Center

Jane Demaree Internship

Type of award: Internship, renewable.
Intended use: For full-time junior, senior, master's or doctoral study at accredited 2-year, 4-year or graduate institution.
Eligibility: Applicant must be U.S. citizen residing in Pennsylvania.
Basis for selection: Major/career interest in horticulture; landscape architecture; environmental science. Applicant must demonstrate depth of character, leadership, seriousness of purpose, service orientation, financial need and high academic achievement.
Application requirements: Recommendations and transcript.

Amount of award:	$500-$2,500
Number of applicants:	40
Application deadline:	May 31
Notification begins:	June 30
Total amount awarded:	$5,000

Contact:
Education Director
Pittsburgh Civic Garden Center
1059 Shady Avenue
Pittsburgh, PA 15232
Phone: 412-441-4442

Playhouse on the Square

Playhouse on the Square Internship

Type of award: Internship.
Intended use: For undergraduate, master's, postgraduate or non-degree study.
Basis for selection: Major/career interest in performing arts. Applicant must demonstrate depth of character, leadership, seriousness of purpose and service orientation.
Application requirements: Interview, audition, portfolio, recommendations and proof of eligibility.
Additional information: $75 per week, free housing. Internships are located in Memphis, TN and last a full year, beginning in August. Write for an application.

Amount of award:	$3,900
Number of awards:	12

Contact:
Playhouse on the Square
51 South Cooper
Memphis, TN 38014

Population Council

Social Science Fellowship Program

Type of award: Research grant.
Intended use: For full-time doctoral, first professional or postgraduate study at accredited graduate institution in or outside United States.
Basis for selection: Major/career interest in social and behavioral sciences. Applicant must demonstrate depth of character, leadership, seriousness of purpose, service orientation and high academic achievement.
Application requirements: Recommendations, transcript, research proposal and nomination by Nomination must come from student's institution.
Additional information: Preference given to women and students from developing countries. Awards are made for one year and are not renewable. Award amounts are based on type of research, location of research and supply needs.

Number of awards:	21
Application deadline:	January 4
Notification begins:	March 1

Contact:
Population Council
Dag Hammarskjold Plaza
New York, NY 10012
Phone: 212-339-0671

Population Institute

Population Institute Internship

Type of award: Internship.
Intended use: For junior, senior, graduate, postgraduate or non-degree study.
Basis for selection: Major/career interest in public relations. Applicant must demonstrate depth of character, leadership, seriousness of purpose and service orientation.
Application requirements: Interview, recommendations, essay, transcript and proof of eligibility.
Additional information: Resume and cover letter required. $250 per week, 6 months long. Full medical and dental benefits start immediately.
    Amount of award: $6,000
    Number of awards: 12
    Application deadline: April 1, October 1
Contact:
The Population Institute
Internship Coordinator
107 2nd Street, NE
Washington, DC 20002

Presbyterian Church (USA)

Ira Page Wallace Bible Scholarship

Type of award: Scholarship.
Intended use: For undergraduate study in United States. Designated institutions: Barber-Scotia College, Johnson C. Smith University, Knoxville College, Mary Holmes College, Stillman College.
Eligibility: Applicant must be African American. Applicant must be Presbyterian Church (USA). Applicant must be U.S. citizen.
Basis for selection: Major/career interest in religion/theology. Applicant must demonstrate financial need and high academic achievement.
Additional information: Must demonstrate superior academic progress in Bible studies. Contact chairperson of Department of Religion at your school for application information.
    Amount of award: $1,229
    Number of awards: 10
    Number of applicants: 10
    Total amount awarded: $12,289

National Presbyterian College Scholarship

Type of award: Scholarship, renewable.
Intended use: For full-time undergraduate study at 4-year institution in United States.
Eligibility: Applicant must be high school senior, Presbyterian Church (USA). Applicant must be U.S. citizen or permanent resident.
Basis for selection: Applicant must demonstrate financial need and high academic achievement.
Additional information: SAT I/ACT must be taken no later than December 15 of senior year of high school. Must be preparing to enter one of the participating colleges related to the Presbyterian Church (USA). Applications and additional requirements available after December 1.
    Amount of award: $500-$1,400
    Application deadline: December 1
    Notification begins: January 15

Presbyterian Appalachian Scholarship

Type of award: Scholarship, renewable.
Intended use: For full-time or less than half-time undergraduate, non-degree study at postsecondary institution in United States.
Eligibility: Applicant must be Presbyterian Church (USA). Applicant must be U.S. citizen or permanent resident.
Basis for selection: Applicant must demonstrate financial need and high academic achievement.
Application requirements: Transcript and proof of eligibility.
Additional information: Must be member of Presbyterian Church (U.S.A.) and full-time resident of Appalachia. Nontraditional age students with no previous college experience encouraged to apply. Must be high school graduate or GED recipient. Previous recipients must reapply.
    Amount of award: $100-$1,000
    Application deadline: July 1
    Notification begins: August 7

Presbyterian Fund for Graduate Education

Type of award: Scholarship, renewable.
Intended use: For doctoral study at accredited graduate institution in United States.
Eligibility: Applicant must be of minority background. Applicant must be female, Presbyterian Church (USA). Applicant must be U.S. citizen.
Basis for selection: Major/career interest in religion/theology. Applicant must demonstrate financial need.
Application requirements: Recommendations.
Additional information: Must be preparing for or already engaged in teaching/administrative position in Presbyterian college, university, or theological school. Range of award varies. Contact office for applications and award information.
    Application deadline: April 30
    Notification begins: June 7

Presbyterian Grant Program for Medical Studies

Type of award: Scholarship, renewable.
Intended use: For full-time first professional study at accredited graduate institution.
Eligibility: Applicant must be Presbyterian Church (USA). Applicant must be U.S. citizen or permanent resident.
Basis for selection: Major/career interest in health sciences; medicine (m.d.). Applicant must demonstrate financial need.
Application requirements: Recommendations.
Additional information: Must be pursuing course of study related to health field. Recommendations must come from academic advisor and church pastor.
    Amount of award: $500-$1,500
    Number of awards: 57
    Number of applicants: 60
    Total amount awarded: $76,117

Presbyterian Native American Education Grant

Type of award: Scholarship, renewable.
Intended use: For full-time undergraduate or graduate study at accredited 2-year, 4-year or graduate institution in United States.
Eligibility: Applicant must be Alaskan native or American Indian. Applicant must be Presbyterian Church (USA). Applicant must be U.S. citizen or permanent resident.
Basis for selection: Applicant must demonstrate financial need and high academic achievement.
Application requirements: Transcript and proof of eligibility.
Additional information: Must have completed at least one semester at an accredited institution of higher education and have applied for financial aid.

- **Amount of award:** $200-$1,500
- **Application deadline:** June 1
- **Notification begins:** July 7

Presbyterian Native American Seminary Scholarship

Type of award: Scholarship, renewable.
Intended use: For full-time post-bachelor's certificate, master's, doctoral, first professional or non-degree study. Designated institutions: In United States or Canada.
Eligibility: Applicant must be Alaskan native or American Indian. Applicant must be Presbyterian Church (USA). Applicant must be U.S. citizen or permanent resident.
Basis for selection: Major/career interest in religion/theology. Applicant must demonstrate financial need and high academic achievement.
Application requirements: Transcript.
Additional information: Must accept position in Presbyterian Church (USA) upon completion of program. Grants awarded only if all other aid has been exhausted. Must be theological student enrolled as inquirer with or received as candidate by a PC (USA) presbytery, PC (USA) member enrolled in program of theological education by extension or inquirer, candidate, minister, or PC (USA) member in other professional church occupations pursuing program of continuing education. Dollar amounts vary.

- **Application deadline:** June 1

Presbyterian Racial/Ethnic Leadership Supplemental Grant

Type of award: Scholarship, renewable.
Intended use: For full-time first professional study at graduate institution in United States.
Eligibility: Applicant must be of minority background. Applicant must be Presbyterian Church (USA). Applicant must be U.S. citizen or permanent resident.
Basis for selection: Major/career interest in religion/theology. Applicant must demonstrate financial need and high academic achievement.
Application requirements: Recommendations and transcript.
Additional information: Must be enrolled full-time in a prescribed program of study approved by a PC (USA) presbytery. Must accept position with Presbyterian Church (USA) upon completion of program.

- **Amount of award:** $500-$1,000

Presbyterian Service Loan for Undergraduates

Type of award: Loan.
Intended use: For full-time junior, senior study at accredited 4-year institution in United States.
Eligibility: Applicant must be Presbyterian Church (USA). Applicant must be U.S. citizen or permanent resident.
Basis for selection: Applicant must demonstrate financial need and high academic achievement.
Application requirements: Recommendations and transcript.
Additional information: Recommendation must be from campus pastor or chaplain's office of institution. Difficulty of course work considered. In lieu of repayment may perform 250 hours volunteer service in Mission PC (USA), complete a campus or church-related project, or work with a community organization.

- **Amount of award:** $1,500
- **Number of awards:** 38
- **Number of applicants:** 40
- **Application deadline:** April 1
- **Notification begins:** May 1
- **Total amount awarded:** $49,159

Presbyterian Student Opportunity Scholarship

Type of award: Scholarship, renewable.
Intended use: For full-time undergraduate study at accredited 2-year or 4-year institution in United States.
Eligibility: Applicant must be of minority background. Applicant must be high school senior, Presbyterian Church (USA). Applicant must be U.S. citizen or permanent resident.
Basis for selection: Applicant must demonstrate financial need.
Application requirements: Proof of eligibility.
Additional information: Applications available after February 1. Award recipients must reapply on a yearly basis.

- **Amount of award:** $100-$1,400
- **Number of awards:** 142
- **Number of applicants:** 312
- **Application deadline:** April 1
- **Notification begins:** May 7
- **Total amount awarded:** $159,013

Presbyterian Theological Continuing Education Loan

Type of award: Loan.
Intended use: For full-time master's, doctoral study at accredited graduate institution in United States.
Eligibility: Applicant must be Presbyterian Church (USA). Applicant must be U.S. citizen.
Basis for selection: Major/career interest in religion/theology. Applicant must demonstrate financial need and high academic achievement.
Application requirements: Transcript.
Additional information: Must have served a congregation of the Presbyterian Church (USA) with at least 200 members for at least three years. Must be planning study leading to certification or other course work approved by church session, presbytery or synod. Must seek matching funds from other sources. No more than $5,000 may be borrowed. Contact office for current interest rates.
    Amount of award: $200-$5,000
    Application deadline: April 30

Presbyterian Theological Loan

Type of award: Loan, renewable.
Intended use: For full-time master's, first professional study. Designated institutions: In United States or Canada.
Eligibility: Applicant must be Presbyterian Church (USA). Applicant must be U.S. citizen or permanent resident.
Basis for selection: Major/career interest in religion/theology. Applicant must demonstrate financial need and high academic achievement.
Application requirements: Recommendations and transcript.
Additional information: Must accept church position upon completion of program. Must have written verification from committee on preparation for ministry supervising educational preparation and be enrolled as inquirer with or received as candidate by PC presbytery. Must use loan at PC (USA) seminary or theological institution reflecting Presbyterian beliefs. Must be recommended by institutions financial aid officer. Inquirers may apply for up to $6,000 and candidates may apply for up to $10,000 if in final year of study and have not applied for this award in the past. Contact office for interest rates.
    Amount of award: $200-$10,000

Presbyterian Undergraduate and Graduate Loan

Type of award: Loan, renewable.
Intended use: For full-time undergraduate or graduate study at accredited 2-year, 4-year or graduate institution in United States.
Eligibility: Applicant must be Presbyterian Church (USA). Applicant must be U.S. citizen or permanent resident.
Basis for selection: Applicant must demonstrate financial need and high academic achievement.
Additional information: Must establish and maintain minimum 2.0 GPA. Contact office for current interest rates and deferment policies. Must give evidence of financial reliability. Undergraduates can apply for up to $1,000 and graduates for up to $1,500. If last year of study and student has not yet applied for these loans, undergrads can apply for up to $4,000, grads for up to $4,500.
    Amount of award: $200-$4,500
    Application deadline: April 1

Samuel Robinson Award

Type of award: Scholarship.
Intended use: For full-time junior, senior study at 4-year institution in United States. Designated institutions: At one of 69 colleges related to Presyterian Church (USA).
Eligibility: Applicant must be Presbyterian Church (USA). Applicant must be U.S. citizen or permanent resident.
Basis for selection: Competition in Writing/journalism.
Application requirements: Essay.
Additional information: Applicant must successfully recite answers of the Westminster Shorter Catechism and write a 2,000-word essay on assigned topic related to the Catechism.
    Amount of award: $1,000
    Application deadline: April 1
    Notification begins: May 15

Theological Continuing Education Grant

Type of award: Scholarship, renewable.
Intended use: For full-time first professional, postgraduate study at graduate institution in United States.
Eligibility: Applicant must be Presbyterian Church (USA). Applicant must be U.S. citizen or permanent resident.
Basis for selection: Major/career interest in religion/theology. Applicant must demonstrate seriousness of purpose, financial need and high academic achievement.
Application requirements: Recommendations and transcript.
Additional information: Pogram intended to provide funding to professional church workers who have served congregations of 200 or less for at least three years. Must be seeking matching funds from other sources and be taking course of study that leads to certification or be pursuing an advanced degree that will improve work skills.
    Amount of award: $100-$500
    Application deadline: April 30
Contact:
Presbyterian Church (USA)
Financial Aid for Studies
100 Witherspoon Street, M042
Louisville, KY 40202-1396
Phone: 502-569-5760
Fax: 502-569-8766

Princess Grace Foundation-USA

Princess Grace Award

Type of award: Scholarship.
Intended use: For full-time senior, master's study in United States.
Eligibility: Applicant must be U.S. citizen or permanent resident.
Basis for selection: Major/career interest in performing arts; film/video.
Application requirements: Portfolio, recommendations, essay and nomination by Dean or Department Chair.
Additional information: Deadlines are as follows: Theatre- 3/

31, Dance- 4/30, Film- 6/1. Usually given to applicants under thirty years of age.
- **Amount of award:** $2,500-$15,000
- **Number of awards:** 19
- **Number of applicants:** 300
- **Application deadline:** March 31, April 30
- **Notification begins:** July 30
- **Total amount awarded:** $175,000

Contact:
Princess Grace Foundation-USA
150 East 58 St., 21st floor
New York, NY 10155
Phone: 212-317-1470
Website: www.pgfusa.com

Pro-Found Software

Pro-Found Software Internship

Type of award: Internship.
Intended use: For junior, senior, master's or postgraduate study.
Basis for selection: Applicant must demonstrate depth of character, leadership, seriousness of purpose and service orientation.
Application requirements: Recommendations, essay, transcript and proof of eligibility.
Additional information: Must be studying in technical fields and be proficient in "C/C++." $400-$600 per week, located in Teaneck, NJ. Submit cover letter and resume.
- **Amount of award:** $4,800-$14,400
- **Number of awards:** 5
- **Number of applicants:** 250

Contact:
Pro-Found Software
Glenpointe Centre West
500 Frank W. Burr Blvd.
Teaneck, NJ 07666

Professional Engineers of North Carolina

Professional Engineers of North Carolina Engineering Scholarship Program

Type of award: Scholarship, renewable.
Intended use: For freshman, junior study at 4-year institution in United States.
Eligibility: Applicant must be high school senior. Applicant must be U.S. citizen.
Basis for selection: Major/career interest in engineering. Applicant must demonstrate financial need and high academic achievement.
Application requirements: Recommendations and transcript.
Additional information: Must be either graduating high school senior or college sophomore to be eligible to apply.

- **Amount of award:** $500-$2,000
- **Number of awards:** 3
- **Number of applicants:** 20
- **Application deadline:** January 31
- **Notification begins:** June 1
- **Total amount awarded:** $7,500

Contact:
Project Engineer
111 N. Boyland Ave.
Raleigh, NC 27603
Website: www.penc.org

Professional Grounds Management Society

Anne Seaman Memorial Scholarship

Type of award: Scholarship, renewable.
Intended use: For undergraduate or graduate study.
Basis for selection: Major/career interest in horticulture.
Application requirements: Recommendations, transcript and proof of eligibility. Cover letter, resume, and application.
Additional information: Additional fields of study: Turf care and grounds management.
- **Amount of award:** $250-$1,000
- **Number of awards:** 4
- **Number of applicants:** 40
- **Application deadline:** July 5
- **Notification begins:** October 1

Contact:
Professional Grounds Management Society
120 Cockeysville Road, Suite 104
Hunt Valley, MD 21030
Phone: 410-584-9754
Fax: 410-584-9756

Project Excellence

Project Excellence Scholarship

Type of award: Scholarship.
Intended use: For full-time undergraduate study.
Eligibility: Applicant must be African American. Applicant must be high school senior. Applicant must be U.S. citizen or permanent resident.
Basis for selection: Applicant must demonstrate high academic achievement.
Application requirements: Recommendations, essay, transcript and nomination by high school; three nominations per school.
Additional information: Students must be nominated by high school. Open to eligible D.C. residents, and Maryland residents from Prince George's or Montgomery counties only. Virginia residents in Arlington, Alexandria or Fairfax counties also eligible. Award amounts vary from $4,000 up to full, four-year scholarships at participating institutions. Must demonstrate

excellence in use of English language. Applications available from HS administration.

- **Amount of award:** $4,000
- **Application deadline:** February 17

Public Employees Roundtable

Public Service Scholarship

Type of award: Scholarship.
Intended use: For sophomore, junior, senior, master's or doctoral study at accredited 4-year or graduate institution in United States.
Basis for selection: Major/career interest in public administration/service. Applicant must demonstrate depth of character, leadership, patriotism, seriousness of purpose, service orientation and high academic achievement.
Application requirements: Recommendations, essay, transcript and proof of eligibility. Applicant must write a 2-page essay related to future career goals; topic changes each year.
Additional information: Minimum GPA of 3.5. Graduate applicants enrolled at least half-time may apply. Must intend to become public employee at any level of government. Preference given to applicants with previous public service work or volunteer experience. Send SASE to receive application package.

- **Amount of award:** $500-$1,000
- **Number of awards:** 8
- **Number of applicants:** 300
- **Application deadline:** May 10
- **Notification begins:** July 1
- **Total amount awarded:** $8,000

Contact:
Public Employees Roundtable
Scholarship Committee
P.O. Box 44801
Washington, DC 20026-4801

Puerto Rican Legal Defense and Education Fund

Puerto Rican Legal Defense & Educ. Fund-Father Joseph P. Fitzpatrick Scholarship

Type of award: Scholarship.
Intended use: For full-time first professional study.
Eligibility: Applicant must be Mexican American, Hispanic American or Puerto Rican. Applicant must be U.S. citizen or permanent resident.
Basis for selection: Major/career interest in law. Applicant must demonstrate leadership, seriousness of purpose, service orientation, financial need and high academic achievement.
Application requirements: Recommendations, essay and transcript.

Additional information: Must intend to pursue public interest law and be active in Latino community.

- **Amount of award:** $1,000
- **Number of awards:** 5
- **Number of applicants:** 125
- **Application deadline:** April 30
- **Total amount awarded:** $5,000

Contact:
Scholarship Committee
99 Hudson Street
14th Floor
New York, NY 10013

QEM Network

Network Internship or Summer Science Internship

Type of award: Internship.
Intended use: For junior, senior, graduate or postgraduate study.
Basis for selection: Major/career interest in political science/government; science, general. Applicant must demonstrate depth of character, leadership, seriousness of purpose and service orientation.
Application requirements: Recommendations, essay, transcript and proof of eligibility.
Additional information: Minorities encouraged to apply. $3,000 stipend for undergraduates. $4,000 stipend for graduate students. Ten-week summer internships, in Maryland, Virginia and Washington, D.C. Write for application.

- **Amount of award:** $3,000-$4,000
- **Number of awards:** 20
- **Application deadline:** February 15

Contact:
QEM Network
Internship Coordinator
181 N Street, NW, Suite 350
Washington, DC 20036
Website: www.qemnetwork.org

Quill and Scroll Foundation

Edward J. Nell Memorial Scholarship

Type of award: Scholarship.
Intended use: For full-time freshman study at accredited 2-year or 4-year institution in United States.
Eligibility: Applicant must be high school senior. Applicant must be U.S. citizen.
Basis for selection: Major/career interest in journalism. Applicant must demonstrate seriousness of purpose.
Application requirements: Essay. Statement of intent to major in journalism.
Additional information: Open only to winners of Quill and

Scroll Annual National Yearbook Excellence or Writing/Photo Contests at any time during high school career. Yearbook Excellence deadline is November 1. Writing/Photo deadline is February 5.

Amount of award:	$500-$1,000
Number of awards:	10
Number of applicants:	128
Total amount awarded:	$5,500

Lester G. Benz Memorial College Journalism Scholarship

Type of award: Scholarship.
Intended use: For graduate or non-degree study at accredited postsecondary institution.
Eligibility: Applicant must be U.S. citizen or permanent resident.
Basis for selection: Major/career interest in journalism.
Application requirements: Recommendations.
Additional information: For high school journalism teachers, newspaper and yearbook advisers with minimum four years experience and at least six semester hours of completed journalism courses. Must plan taking advanced coursework or workshops to upgrade journalistic skills, teaching methodologies and advising techniques.

Amount of award:	$500
Number of awards:	1
Number of applicants:	15
Application deadline:	April 15
Notification begins:	May 1
Total amount awarded:	$500

Contact:
Quill and Scroll Foundation
School of Journalism
312 West Seashore Hall
Iowa City, IA 52242-1528
Website: www.uiowa.edu/~quill-sc

Radio-Television News Directors Foundation

Abe Schechter Graduate Scholarship

Type of award: Scholarship.
Intended use: For full-time graduate study.
Basis for selection: Major/career interest in journalism; radio/television/film; communications.
Application requirements: Essay, transcript and proof of eligibility. Application form, letter of endorsement from dean or faculty sponsor certifying applicant's eligibility.
Additional information: Previous Radio-Television News Directors Foundation scholarship or internship winners not eligible. Must have at least one full year of school remaining.

Amount of award:	$1,000
Number of awards:	1
Application deadline:	March 2
Notification begins:	May 1
Total amount awarded:	$1,000

Contact:
Radio-Television News Directors Foundation Scholarships
Suite 615
1000 Connecticut Avenue, NW
Washington, DC 20036
Website: www.rtndf.org

Broadcast News Pioneers Undergraduate Scholarships

Type of award: Scholarship.
Intended use: For full-time sophomore, junior or senior study at 2-year or 4-year institution.
Basis for selection: Major/career interest in journalism; communications; radio/television/film. Applicant must demonstrate seriousness of purpose and high academic achievement.
Application requirements: One to three samples showing reporting or producing skills on audio or video tape, accompanied by scripts. Letter of endorsement from Dean or Faculty Advisor certifying proof of eligibility.
Additional information: Previous winners not eligible. Must have at least one full year of school remaining.

Amount of award:	$1,000
Number of awards:	10
Application deadline:	March 2
Notification begins:	May 15
Total amount awarded:	$10,000

Contact:
Radio-Television News Directors Foundation
RTNDF Scholarships
1000 Connecticut Avenue, NW Suite 615
Washington, DC 20036
Website: www.rtndf.org

Carole Simpson Scholarship

Type of award: Scholarship.
Intended use: For full-time sophomore, junior, senior or graduate study at 4-year or graduate institution.
Eligibility: Applicant must be of minority background.
Basis for selection: Major/career interest in journalism; radio/television/film; communications. Applicant must demonstrate depth of character and seriousness of purpose.
Application requirements: Essay, transcript and proof of eligibility. Audio or video tape of one to three work samples, maximum 15 minutes, with accompanying scripts. Statement explaining reasons for seeking career in broadcast or cable journalism, and specific career preferences of radio or television, reporting, producing, or news management. Dean or faculty sponsor letter of endorsement certifying eligibilty.
Additional information: Must have at least one full year of school remaining. Previous Radio-Television News Directors Foundation scholarship or internship winners not eligible.

Amount of award:	$2,000
Number of awards:	1
Application deadline:	March 2
Notification begins:	May 1
Total amount awarded:	$2,000

Contact:
Radio-Television News Directors Foundation
Suite 615
1000 Connecticut Avenue, NW
Washington, DC 20036
Website: www.rtndf.org

Ed Bradley Scholarship

Type of award: Scholarship.
Intended use: For full-time sophomore, junior, senior or graduate study at 4-year or graduate institution.
Eligibility: Applicant must be of minority background.
Basis for selection: Major/career interest in journalism; radio/television/film; communications. Applicant must demonstrate seriousness of purpose.
Application requirements: Essay, transcript and proof of eligibility. Audio or video tape of one to three work samples, maximum length 15 minutes total, with accompanying scripts. Essay explaining reasons for seeking a career in broadcast or cable journalism, and specific career preferences of radio or television, reporting, producing, or news management. Dean or faculty sponsor endorsement letter certifying eligiblity.
Additional information: Must have at least one full year of school remaining. Previous Radio-Television News Directors Foundation scholarship or internship winners not eligible. Preference given to undergraduates.

Amount of award:	$5,000
Number of awards:	1
Application deadline:	March 2
Notification begins:	May 1
Total amount awarded:	$5,000

Contact:
Radio-Television News Directors Foundation
Suite 615
1000 Connecticut Avenue, NW
Washington, DC 20036
Website: www.rtndf.org

Environmental and Science Reporting Fellowship

Type of award: Scholarship.
Intended use: For undergraduate, graduate or non-degree study.
Basis for selection: Major/career interest in journalism; radio/television/film; communications.
Application requirements: Recommendations and proof of eligibility. Script or tape, preferably both, exemplifying best work.
Additional information: Must be employed in electronic news with ten years or less experience. For demonstrated excellence in environmental reporting. Designed to help reporters cover stories about science or the environment.

Amount of award:	$1,000
Number of awards:	1
Application deadline:	March 2
Notification begins:	May 1
Total amount awarded:	$1,000

Contact:
Radio-Television News Directors Foundation
Suite 615
1000 Connecticut Avenue, NW
Washington, DC 20036
Website: www.rtndf.org

Geller Fellowship

Type of award: Scholarship.
Intended use: For undergraduate, graduate or non-degree study.
Basis for selection: Major/career interest in journalism; radio/television/film; communications. Applicant must demonstrate seriousness of purpose.
Application requirements: Recommendations. Script and audio or video tape of best work. Cover letter setting forth reasons for seeking fellowship.
Additional information: For reporters interested in improving their on air skills. Must be employed in the field of electronic journalism with less than ten years of experience.

Amount of award:	$2,000
Number of awards:	1
Application deadline:	March 2
Notification begins:	May 1
Total amount awarded:	$2,000

Contact:
Radio-Television News Directors Foundation
RTNDF Fellowships
1000 Connecticut Avenue, NW Suite 615
Washington, DC 20036
Website: www.rtndf.org

Jacque Minotte Health Reporting Fellowship

Type of award: Scholarship.
Intended use: For undergraduate, graduate or non-degree study.
Basis for selection: Major/career interest in journalism; radio/television/film; communications.
Application requirements: Recommendations, essay and proof of eligibility. Script or tape, preferably both, exemplifying best work. Cover letter outlining reasons for application.
Additional information: For promising young reporters who want to cover health or medical stories.

Amount of award:	$1,000
Application deadline:	March 2
Notification begins:	May 1
Total amount awarded:	$1,000

Contact:
Radio-Television News Directors Foundation
Suite 615
1000 Connecticut Avenue, NW
Washington, DC 20036
Website: www.rtndf.org

Len Allen Award of Merit

Type of award: Scholarship.
Intended use: For full-time sophomore, junior, senior or graduate study at accredited 4-year or graduate institution.
Basis for selection: Major/career interest in journalism; radio/television/film; communications.
Application requirements: Recommendations, essay, transcript and proof of eligibility. Essay explaining reasons for seeking career in radio news management. Dean or faculty sponsor endorsement letter certifying eligibility.
Additional information: Must have at least one full year of school remaining and have career objective of radio news management. Previous Radio-Television News Directors Foundation scholarship or internship winners not eligible.

Amount of award:	$1,000
Number of awards:	1
Application deadline:	March 2
Notification begins:	May 1
Total amount awarded:	$1,000

Contact:
Radio-Television News Directors Foundation
Suite 615
1000 Connecticut Avenue, NW
Washington, DC 20036
Website: www.rtndf.org

Michelle Clark Fellowship

Type of award: Scholarship.
Intended use: For undergraduate or graduate study.
Eligibility: Applicant must be of minority background.
Basis for selection: Major/career interest in journalism; radio/television/film; communications.
Application requirements: Recommendations and essay. Script or tape, preferably both, exemplifying best work.
Additional information: Must be employed in electronic news, with less than ten years experience.

Amount of award:	$1,000
Number of awards:	1
Application deadline:	March 2
Notification begins:	May 1
Total amount awarded:	$1,000

Contact:
Radio-Television News Directors Foundation
Suite 615
1000 Connecticut Avenue, NW
Washington, DC 20036
Website: www.rtndf.org

Oldfield National Security Reporter Fellowship

Type of award: Scholarship.
Intended use: For undergraduate, graduate or non-degree study.
Eligibility: Applicant must be in military service, veteran, disabled while on duty.
Basis for selection: Major/career interest in journalism; radio/television/film; communications.
Application requirements: Recommendations. Script or tape (VHS only), preferably both, exemplifying best work.
Additional information: Must be employed in electronic news with less than ten years experience. Designed to help reporters cover national defense and security stories.

Amount of award:	$1,000
Number of awards:	1
Application deadline:	March 2
Notification begins:	May 1
Total amount awarded:	$1,000

Contact:
Radio-Television News Directors Foundation
Suite 615
1000 Connecticut Avenue, NW
Washington, DC 20036
Website: www.rtndf.org

Presidential Memorial Scholarship

Type of award: Scholarship.
Intended use: For full-time sophomore, junior, senior or graduate study at 4-year or graduate institution.
Basis for selection: Major/career interest in journalism; communications; radio/television/film. Applicant must demonstrate seriousness of purpose and high academic achievement.
Application requirements: Recommendations, essay and transcript. Statement of professional intent.
Additional information: Must be full time student whose career objective is electronic journalism and must have at least one full year of college left.

Amount of award:	$2,000
Number of awards:	1
Application deadline:	March 2
Notification begins:	May 15

Contact:
Radio-Television News Directors Foundation
RTNDF Scholarships
1000 Connecticut Avenue, NW Suite 615
Washington, DC 20036
Website: www.rtndf.org

Radio-Television News Capitol Hill News Internship

Type of award: Internship.
Intended use: For graduate study.
Basis for selection: Major/career interest in journalism; radio/television/film; communications.
Application requirements: Recommendations and essay.
Additional information: Interns receive $1,000 per month for three months and are responsible for housing and living expenses. Must be recent college graduate interested in electronic media in politics. Summer session application deadline is March 2.

Amount of award:	$3,000
Number of awards:	4
Application deadline:	January 15
Notification begins:	May 1
Total amount awarded:	$12,000

Contact:
Radio-Television News Directors Foundation
Suite 615
1000 Connecticut Avenue, NW
Washington, DC 20036
Website: www.rtndf.org

RTNDF Minority News Management Internship

Type of award: Internship.
Intended use: For junior, senior or graduate study.
Eligibility: Applicant must be of minority background.
Basis for selection: Major/career interest in journalism; radio/television/film; communications.
Application requirements: Recommendations and essay. One page essay explaining why applicant seeks career in radio or television news management. Endorsement letter from faculty sponsor regarding applicant's intent on career in news management, and reference letter from someone who knows applicant's work.
Additional information: Six month interns must be recent college graduate (within one year) with degree in electronic journalism. Three month interns can be college junior or senior status. Both positions require that candidates have interest in news management. Each three month internship pays $1,000 per month. Each six-month internship pays $1,300 per month. Interns responsible for housing/living expenses. Interns receive hands-on experience in management related capacity, e.g. production, assignment desk, or administration.
    Amount of award: $3,000-$7,800
    Number of awards: 6
    Application deadline: March 2
    Notification begins: May 1
    Total amount awarded: $18,000
Contact:
Radio-Television News Directors Foundation
1000 Connecticut Avenue, NW
Suite 615
Washington, DC 20036
Website: www.rtndf.org

Sherlee Barish Fellowship

Type of award: Scholarship.
Intended use: For undergraduate, graduate or non-degree study.
Basis for selection: Major/career interest in communications; journalism; radio/television/film. Applicant must demonstrate seriousness of purpose.
Application requirements: Recommendations. Script and audio or video tape of best work. Cover letter explaining reasons for seeking fellowship and intent of use.
Additional information: Award is for television reporters and anchors seeking to improve on air skills. Must be working in electronic journalism and have less than ten years of experience.
    Amount of award: $1,000
    Number of awards: 1
    Application deadline: March 2
    Notification begins: May 1
    Total amount awarded: $1,000
Contact:
Radio-Television News Directors Foundation
RTNDF Fellowships
1000 Connecticut Avenue, NW Suite 615
Washington, DC 20036
Website: www.rtndf.org

Random House

Random House Internship

Type of award: Internship.
Intended use: For junior, postgraduate study.
Basis for selection: Major/career interest in publishing. Applicant must demonstrate depth of character, seriousness of purpose and service orientation.
Application requirements: Recommendations, essay, transcript and proof of eligibility.
Additional information: Open to college juniors and graduate students that still have one year in school after the internships. Ten week assignment at $250 per week in New York City. Submit resume with publishing experience and cover letter.
    Amount of award: $2,500
    Application deadline: March 31
Contact:
Random House
201 E. 50th St.
New York, NY 10022

Raychem

Raychem Internship

Type of award: Internship.
Intended use: For junior, senior or master's study.
Basis for selection: Major/career interest in science, general; marketing; accounting; finance/banking; design; manufacturing technologies; engineering. Applicant must demonstrate depth of character, leadership, seriousness of purpose, service orientation and high academic achievement.
Application requirements: Recommendations, essay, transcript and proof of eligibility.
Additional information: 3.0 minimum GPA. Submit resume and cover letter. $400-$700 per week for undergraduate student, $500-$1,000 per week for graduate student.
    Amount of award: $16,000-$48,000
    Number of awards: 40
    Number of applicants: 2,000
    Application deadline: April 1
Contact:
Raychem
M/S 111/8202
300 Constitution Dr.
Menlo Park, CA 94025-1164

Real Estate Educators Association

Harwood Memorial Scholarship

Type of award: Scholarship, renewable.
Intended use: For full-time undergraduate study in United States.
Eligibility: Applicant must be U.S. citizen.

Basis for selection: Major/career interest in real estate.
Application requirements: Recommendations and transcript.
Additional information: Minimum GPA 3.2. Must have completed two semesters of college work and be currently enrolled in an undergraduate or graduate program, specializing in real estate.

Amount of award:	$250-$500
Number of awards:	7
Number of applicants:	35
Application deadline:	December 30

Contact:
Real Estate Educators Association
100 E. Front St.
Skowhegan, ME 04976

Red River Valley Fighter Pilots Association

Red River Valley Fighter Pilots Scholarship Program

Type of award: Scholarship, renewable.
Intended use: For undergraduate or graduate study at accredited 2-year, 4-year or graduate institution in United States.
Eligibility: Applicant must be U.S. citizen. Applicant must be child of deceased veteran or POW/MIA, spouse of deceased veteran who served in the Army, Air Force, Marines, Navy, Coast Guard or Reserves/National Guard.
Basis for selection: Applicant must demonstrate depth of character, leadership, patriotism, seriousness of purpose, service orientation and financial need.
Application requirements: Transcript and proof of eligibility.
Additional information: Applicant must be the spouse or child of a member of any branch of the U.S. armed forces who is listed as KIA or MIA since August 1964. In addition, the immediate dependants of military aircrew members killed in non-combat missions, as well as dependants of current of deceased River Rats can qualify.

Amount of award:	$2,500-$5,000
Number of awards:	10
Number of applicants:	10
Application deadline:	March 15
Notification begins:	May 15
Total amount awarded:	$35,000

Contact:
Red River Valley Fighter Pilots Association
P.O. Box 1551
North Fork, CA 93643
Phone: 209-877-5000
Fax: 209-877-5001
Website: www.eos.net/rrva

Reforma

Reforma Scholarship Program

Type of award: Scholarship.
Intended use: For half-time master's, doctoral study at accredited graduate institution in United States.
Eligibility: Applicant must be U.S. citizen or permanent resident. Applicant must be descendant of veteran, child of active service person, veteran, disabled veteran or deceased veteran.
Basis for selection: Major/career interest in library science; information systems. Applicant must demonstrate seriousness of purpose and service orientation.
Application requirements: Recommendations, essay, transcript and proof of eligibility.
Additional information: Applicant must have Spanish as his or her first language. Must demonstrate an understanding of and desire to serve the Spanish-speaking community. Award must be used at an ALA accredited program.

Amount of award:	$1,000
Number of awards:	6
Number of applicants:	63
Application deadline:	May 15
Notification begins:	June 30
Total amount awarded:	$6,000

Contact:
Reforma Scholarship Committee
El Paso Community College
P.O. Box 20500
El Paso, TX 79998-0500
Phone: 915-594-2132
Website: clnet.ucr.edu/library/reforma/refoscho.htm

Renew America

Renew America Internship

Type of award: Internship.
Intended use: For graduate study.
Basis for selection: Major/career interest in environmental science. Applicant must demonstrate depth of character, leadership, seriousness of purpose and service orientation.
Application requirements: Interview, recommendations, essay and proof of eligibility.
Additional information: Deadline for summer applicants is March 1. Compensation for 12 week summer program is $3,000, $7,500 for six months. All internships located in Washington, D.C.

Amount of award:	$3,000-$7,500
Number of awards:	6
Number of applicants:	180

Contact:
Renew America
1400 16th St., NW, Suite 710
Washington, DC 20036

Resources for the Future

Gilbert F. White Postdoctoral Fellowship

Type of award: Research grant.
Intended use: For postgraduate study.
Basis for selection: Major/career interest in energy research; environmental science; natural resources/conservation.
Application requirements: Research proposal.
Additional information: Award for social science or public policy programs in the specified fields. Annual stipend of $35,000 plus research support, office facilities at Resources for the Future, allowance up to $1,000 for moving or living expenses. Award for minimum nine months and maximum one year. Candidates must have the Ph.D. degree plus teaching or research experience at the post-doctoral level.

Amount of award:	$35,000
Number of awards:	2
Number of applicants:	30
Application deadline:	March 1
Notification begins:	April 15
Total amount awarded:	$70,000

Joseph L. Fisher Dissertation Award

Type of award: Research grant.
Intended use: For postgraduate study.
Basis for selection: Major/career interest in energy research; environmental science; natural resources/conservation.
Application requirements: Recommendations, transcript and research proposal. Brief letter of application and curriculum vitae, two letters of recommendation from faculty members on the student's dissertation committee. Must submit letter from school verifying PhD. status.
Additional information: Fellowship recipients will not engage in significant employment during fellowship tenure; Resources for the Future will be notified immediately of financial assistance made available from any other source for support of doctoral work. Applicant must be in final year of Ph.D. dissertation.

Amount of award:	$12,000
Number of awards:	5
Application deadline:	March 1
Notification begins:	April 15
Total amount awarded:	$60,000

Contact:
Resources for the Future
1616 P Street NW
Washington, DC 20036
Phone: 202-328-5067
Website: www.rff.org

Rob and Bessie Welder Wildlife Foundation

Rob and Bessie Welder Wildlife Foundation Scholarship

Type of award: Scholarship, renewable.
Intended use: For master's, doctoral study at accredited graduate institution in United States.
Basis for selection: Major/career interest in environmental science. Applicant must demonstrate high academic achievement.
Application requirements: Recommendations, transcript and research proposal.
Additional information: Minimum 3.0 GPA and 1100 GRE required.

Amount of award:	$5,000-$15,000
Number of awards:	20
Number of applicants:	200
Application deadline:	October 15
Notification begins:	November 15
Total amount awarded:	$200,000

Contact:
Rob and Bessie Welder Wildlife Foundation
P.O. Drawer 1400
Sinton, TX 78387
Phone: 512-364-2643

Robert L. Millender Sr. Memorial Fund, Inc.

Robert L. Millender Sr. Memorial Fund Fellowship Program

Type of award: Scholarship.
Intended use: For full-time doctoral, postgraduate study.
Eligibility: Applicant must be African American, Mexican American, Hispanic American or Puerto Rican. Applicant must be residing in Michigan.
Basis for selection: Major/career interest in public administration/service. Applicant must demonstrate high academic achievement.
Application requirements: Interview, recommendations, essay and transcript.

Amount of award:	$20,000
Number of awards:	1
Application deadline:	March 31
Notification begins:	June 30
Total amount awarded:	$20,000

Contact:
Marie Draper Dykes
Wayne State University
4116 Faculty/Administrative Building
Detroit, MI 48202
Phone: 313-577-2023
Fax: 313-577-5666

Rockwell Semiconductor Systems

Rockwell Internship Program

Type of award: Internship.
Intended use: For junior, senior, master's or postgraduate study.
Basis for selection: Major/career interest in electronics; engineering; engineering, electrical and electronic. Applicant must demonstrate depth of character, leadership, seriousness of purpose and service orientation.
Application requirements: Interview, recommendations, essay and proof of eligibility.
Additional information: $400 per week for undergrads, $600 per week for graduate students. 12 weeks during summer in Newport Beach, CA.

Amount of award:	$4,800-$7,200
Number of awards:	40
Number of applicants:	300

Contact:
Rockwell Semiconductor Systems
Mail Stop 501-397, Dept. SH
4311 Jamboree Rd., PO Box C
Newport Beach, CA 92658-8902

Rocky Mountain Coal Mining Institute

Rocky Mountain Coal Mining Scholarship

Type of award: Scholarship, renewable.
Intended use: For full-time sophomore study at 4-year institution in United States. Designated institutions: Mining schools approved by Rocky Mountain Coal Mining Institute.
Eligibility: Applicant must be U.S. citizen residing in North Dakota or New Mexico or Texas or Arizona or Colorado or Montana or Utah or Wyoming.
Basis for selection: Major/career interest in engineering; engineering, mining; geology/earth sciences. Applicant must demonstrate high academic achievement.
Application requirements: Interview and recommendations.
Additional information: Must have interest in western coal mining as possible career. Recommended GPA of 3.0 or above. One new award made per Rocky Mountain Coal Mining Institute member state.

Amount of award:	$1,000
Number of awards:	16
Number of applicants:	55
Application deadline:	February 1
Notification begins:	March 1
Total amount awarded:	$16,000

Contact:
Rocky Mountain Coal Mining Institute
3000 Youngfield
Suite 324
Lakewood, CO 80215
Phone: 303-238-9099
Fax: 303-238-0509

Rodolf Steiner Educational Farming Association

Rodolf Steiner Visiting Students Program

Type of award: Internship.
Intended use: For undergraduate, graduate or postgraduate study.
Eligibility: Applicant must be Must have B-1 Visa.
Basis for selection: Major/career interest in education, teacher; education; agriculture.
Application requirements: Interview, recommendations and transcript.
Additional information: Send resume and cover letter. It is encouraged to visit during application process. Applicants who have worked with children are preferred.

Amount of award:	$400-$1,200

Contact:
Rudolf Steiner Educational Farming Association
Hawthorne Valley Farm
RD 2, Box 225
Ghent, NY 12075

Rotary Foundation of Rotary International

Academic-Year Ambassadorial Scholarship

Type of award: Scholarship.
Intended use: For junior, senior or graduate study at postsecondary institution outside United States in Countries having Rotary Clubs.
Basis for selection: Applicant must demonstrate leadership, seriousness of purpose, service orientation and high academic achievement.
Application requirements: Interview, recommendations, essay, transcript and proof of eligibility. Language certification.
Additional information: Deadlines will be between March and July, as set by the local Rotary clubs. Provides funding for nine months of study in another country, specifically for tuition, room and board, round-trip transportation, and one month of language training if necessary. Must have completed two years of postsecondary work or have appropriate professional experience, and be proficient in the language of the proposed host country. Must be citizen of country that has Rotary clubs. Spouses or descendants of Rotarians ineligible. Check with local Rotary Club for further information and scholarship availability.

Amount of award:	$10,000-$23,000
Number of awards:	1,000
Notification begins:	December 15

Cultural Ambassadorial Scholarship

Type of award: Scholarship.
Intended use: For junior, senior, graduate or non-degree study at postsecondary institution outside United States in Countries having Rotary Clubs.
Eligibility: Applicant must be U.S. citizen.
Basis for selection: Major/career interest in foreign languages. Applicant must demonstrate leadership, seriousness of purpose and service orientation.
Application requirements: Interview, recommendations, essay, transcript and proof of eligibility. Language certification.
Additional information: Deadlines will be between March and July, as set by the local Rotary clubs. Scholarship for three or six months of intensive language study in foreign country at designated language institute. Must have completed two years of postsecondary education or have equivalent work experience. Must have completed at least one year of college-level course work of the language one is planning to study. Spouses or descendants of Rotarians ineligible. Funding covers tuition, round-trip transportation, and homestay expenses ($10,000 for three months study, $17,000 for six months study). Applications will be considered for those interested in studying English, French, German, Hebrew, Japanese, Italian, Mandarin Chinese, Polish, Russian, Portuguese, Spanish, Swahili and Swedish. Check with local Rotary Club for further information.
   Number of awards: 150

Multi-Year Ambassadorial Scholarship

Type of award: Scholarship, renewable.
Intended use: For junior, senior, master's or doctoral study at postsecondary institution outside United States in Countries having Rotary Clubs.
Eligibility: Applicant must be U.S. citizen.
Basis for selection: Applicant must demonstrate leadership, seriousness of purpose and service orientation.
Application requirements: Interview, recommendations, essay, transcript and proof of eligibility. Language certification.
Additional information: Deadlines will be between March and July, as set by the local Rotary clubs. Provides funding for two or three years of degree-oriented study in another country. Must have completed two years of postsecondary work or have appropriate professional experience and be proficient in the language of the proposed host country. Spouse or descendants of Rotarians ineligible. Check with local Rotary Club for further information.
   Amount of award: $11,000
   Number of awards: 100
   Notification begins: December 15
   Total amount awarded: $1,100,000

Sachs Foundation

Sachs Scholarship

Type of award: Scholarship, renewable.
Intended use: For full-time undergraduate study at accredited 2-year or 4-year institution.
Eligibility: Applicant must be African American. Applicant must be high school senior. Applicant must be U.S. citizen or permanent resident residing in Colorado.
Basis for selection: Applicant must demonstrate depth of character, leadership, financial need and high academic achievement.
Application requirements: Interview, recommendations, transcript and proof of eligibility. Financial statement.
Additional information: Must be resident of Colorado for more than five years. Must maintain high academic achievement throughout college for renewal consideration.
   Amount of award: $4,000
   Number of awards: 250
   Number of applicants: 400
   Application deadline: March 1
   Notification begins: April 15
   Total amount awarded: $630,000
Contact:
Sachs Foundation
90 South Cascade Avenue
Suite 1410
Colorado Springs, CO 80903
Phone: 719-633-2353

Saint David's Society

Saint David's Society Scholarship

Type of award: Scholarship, renewable.
Intended use: For full-time or half-time undergraduate, graduate or non-degree study at postsecondary institution outside United States in Wales.
Eligibility: Applicant must be of Welsh heritage.
Basis for selection: Applicant must demonstrate depth of character, seriousness of purpose and high academic achievement.
Application requirements: Recommendations and transcript.
Additional information: Recepients that are Welsh can use this award for any topic of study. Recepients that are not Welsh must use the award for Welsh-related study.
   Amount of award: $250-$1,500
   Number of awards: 12
   Number of applicants: 700
   Application deadline: May 30
   Notification begins: July 15
   Total amount awarded: $12,000
Contact:
Saint David's Society
3 West 51 Street
New York, NY 10019
Phone: 212-397-1346

Samuel H. Kress Foundation

Kress Travel Fellowship

Type of award: Research grant.
Intended use: For doctoral study outside United States.
Eligibility: Applicant must be Must be studying at American institutions.
Basis for selection: Major/career interest in art, art history.
Application requirements: Research proposal and nomination by their art history department; limit of two applicants per department.
Additional information: To support travel abroad to view materials essential for completion of dissertation research. Contact Art History Department for stipend amounts and additional information.
Number of awards:	20
Application deadline:	November 30

Kress Two-Year Research Fellowship at Foreign Institutions

Type of award: Research grant.
Intended use: For doctoral study in Cyprus, Germany, England, France, Italy, Israel or Switzerland outside United States.
Eligibility: Applicant must be Must be studying at an American institution.
Basis for selection: Major/career interest in art, art history.
Application requirements: Research proposal and nomination by their art history department; limit of one per department.
Additional information: Fields of study include art criticism and conservation. Supports advanced dissertation research in association with selected institutes in Florence, Jerusalem, Leiden, London, Munich, Nicosia, Paris, Rome and Zurich. Contact your school's art history department for more information.
Amount of award:	$18,000
Number of awards:	4
Application deadline:	November 30
Total amount awarded:	$72,000

Samuel Lemberg Scholarship Loan Fund, Inc.

Samuel Lemberg Scholarship Loan

Type of award: Loan, renewable.
Intended use: For full-time undergraduate, master's or doctoral study in or outside United States.
Eligibility: Applicant must be Jewish.
Basis for selection: Applicant must demonstrate leadership, financial need and high academic achievement.
Application requirements: Interview, recommendations and transcript.

Amount of award:	$1,000-$5,000
Number of awards:	12
Number of applicants:	250
Application deadline:	April 1
Notification begins:	July 1

Contact:
Samuel Lemberg Scholarship Loan Fund, Inc.
60 E. 42nd Street
Suite 1814
New York, NY 10165

San Francisco Chronicle

San Francisco Chronicle Summer Internship Program

Type of award: Internship.
Intended use: For freshman, sophomore, junior, senior, graduate or postgraduate study.
Basis for selection: Major/career interest in journalism.
Application requirements: Recommendations.
Additional information: Applications for 1999 internships must be postmarked between October 1, 1998 and November 15, 1998. Internships are available to any undergraduate, graduate or college graduates who have been out of school no longer than one year prior to the start of the internship. Applicants must submit a resume, cover letter, at least one letter of recommendation, and the name of three references, and samples of work. The 12 week program begins mid-June and pays approximately $478 a week.
Amount of award:	$5,736
Number of awards:	5
Number of applicants:	700
Total amount awarded:	$5

Contact:
San Francisco Chronicle
Internship Coordinator
901 Mission Street
San Francisco, CA 94103

San Francisco Chronicle Two-Year Internship Program

Type of award: Internship.
Intended use: For undergraduate, graduate or postgraduate study.
Basis for selection: Major/career interest in journalism.
Application requirements: Recommendations.
Additional information: Applications for 1999 must be postmarked between October 1, 1998 and November 15, 1998. Internships are available to any recent college graduates who have been out of school no longer than one year prior to the start of the internship. Applicants must submit a resume, cover letter, at least one letter of recommendation, and the name of three references, and samples of work.
Amount of award:	$28,900-$35,000
Number of awards:	5
Number of applicants:	700
Total amount awarded:	$5

Contact:
San Francisco Chronicle
901 Mission St.
San Francisco, CA 94103

Savvy Management

Savvy Management Internship

Type of award: Internship.
Intended use: For sophomore, junior, senior or graduate study.
Basis for selection: Major/career interest in public relations. Applicant must demonstrate depth of character, leadership, seriousness of purpose and service orientation.
Application requirements: Interview, essay and proof of eligibility.
Additional information: $100/week for 12 weeks; summer, spring or fall in New York City.
    Amount of award: $1,200
    Number of awards: 7
    Number of applicants: 200
Contact:
Internship Coordinator
80 4th Avenue
Suite 800
New Yrok, NY 10003

Schering-Key Pharmaceuticals

"Will to Win" Asthma Athlete Scholarship

Type of award: Scholarship.
Intended use: For full-time freshman study in United States.
Eligibility: Applicant must be high school senior. Must be physically challenged. Applicant must be U.S. citizen.
Basis for selection: Applicant must demonstrate depth of character, leadership, seriousness of purpose, service orientation and high academic achievement.
Application requirements: Recommendations, essay, transcript and proof of eligibility.
Additional information: Applicants must be outstanding athletes who also suffer from asthma.
    Amount of award: $2,500-$10,000
    Number of awards: 130
    Number of applicants: 4,000
    Application deadline: March 31
    Notification begins: May 15
    Total amount awarded: $42,500

Schlumberger

Schlumberger Internship

Type of award: Internship.
Intended use: For senior, graduate or postgraduate study.
Basis for selection: Major/career interest in marketing; physics; geology/earth sciences; engineering, computer; engineering, civil; engineering, chemical; engineering, petroleum. Applicant must demonstrate seriousness of purpose and service orientation.
Application requirements: Interview, recommendations, essay, transcript and proof of eligibility.
    Amount of award: $525-$825
    Number of awards: 100
    Number of applicants: 1,500
    Application deadline: March 31
Contact:
Schlumberger
300 Schlumberger Drive
Sugarland, TX 77478

Scholarships and Loans Department - BPW Foundation

Avon Products Foundation Career Empowerment Scholarship for Adult Women

Type of award: Scholarship.
Intended use: For undergraduate study at accredited vocational, 2-year, 4-year or graduate institution in United States.
Eligibility: Applicant must be female. Applicant must be U.S. citizen residing in California.
Basis for selection: Major/career interest in business; computer and information sciences; health sciences. Applicant must demonstrate financial need.
Application requirements: Transcript.
Additional information: Applicants must be women residents of Los Angeles County who are at least 25 years old. Must be on welfare or public assistance or have been removed in the last 24 months. Must have plans to enter the workforce after attaining degree and be acquiring skills that will increase economic security.
    Amount of award: $500-$1,500
    Number of awards: 40
    Application deadline: April 15
    Notification begins: July 31
Contact:
Scholarships and Loans Department - BPW Foundation
2012 Massachusetts Ave. NW
Washington, DC 20036
Phone: 202-293-1200 ext. 169
Website: www.bpwusa.org/

Scholastic, Inc.

New York Times James B. Reston Writing Portfolio Award

Type of award: Scholarship.
Intended use: For undergraduate study.
Eligibility: Applicant must be high school senior.
Basis for selection: Competition in Writing/journalism.

Originality, technical competence, emergence of personal voice and style. Applicant must demonstrate seriousness of purpose.
Application requirements: $3 application fee. Original signature of student's teacher, guidance counselor or principal.
Additional information: Application deadlines vary, notification begins after May 1. Submission must be collection of nonfiction works intended to instruct, inform, explain, persuade, or entertain, such as essays, journalistic articles or editorials. Portfolios must contain three to eight pieces but cannot exceed 50 pages. Applications available between September and December. Include SASE with all application requests.

Amount of award:	$5,000
Number of awards:	1
Total amount awarded:	$5,000

Scholastic Art Gold Award

Type of award: Scholarship.
Intended use: For freshman study. Designated institutions: 50 participating universities, colleges and art institutes.
Eligibility: Applicant must be high school senior.
Basis for selection: Competition in Visual arts. Applicant must demonstrate seriousness of purpose.
Application requirements: Portfolio, recommendations, essay, transcript and nomination by Scholastic from schools participating in the program. School selects winners. Eight-piece art portfolio with at least 3 drawings. Application must be signed by student's art teacher.
Additional information: Application deadlines vary. Entrant must separately apply and be accepted at awarding schools. Awards range from $100 to full tuition and fees. Eligibility, admissions requirements vary among schools. Applications available between September and December. Include SASE with all application requests.

Amount of award:	$100
Notification begins:	May 1

Scholastic Art Portfolio Award

Type of award: Scholarship.
Intended use: For freshman study.
Eligibility: Applicant must be high school senior.
Basis for selection: Competition in Visual arts. Applicant must demonstrate seriousness of purpose.
Application requirements: Portfolio, essay and transcript. Eight-piece portfolio with at least three drawings. Application form signed by student's art teacher.
Additional information: Application deadlines vary. Applications available between September and December. Include SASE with all application requests.

Amount of award:	$5,000
Number of awards:	4
Notification begins:	May 1
Total amount awarded:	$20,000

Scholastic Photography Portfolio Award

Type of award: Scholarship.
Intended use: For freshman study.
Eligibility: Applicant must be high school senior.
Basis for selection: Competition in Photography. Applicant must demonstrate seriousness of purpose.
Application requirements: Portfolio, recommendations, essay and transcript. Eight-piece photography portfolio in prints, slides or transparencies. Application must be signed by student's art teacher.
Additional information: Applications available between September and December. Deadlines vary. Include SASE with all application requests.

Amount of award:	$5,000
Number of awards:	1
Notification begins:	May 1
Total amount awarded:	$5,000

Scholastic Photography Scholarship

Type of award: Scholarship.
Intended use: For freshman study. Designated institutions: 50 participating universities, colleges and art institutes.
Eligibility: Applicant must be high school senior.
Basis for selection: Competition in Photography. Applicant must demonstrate seriousness of purpose.
Application requirements: Portfolio, recommendations, essay, transcript and nomination by Scholastic from schools participating in the program. School chooses recipient. Eight-piece photography portfolio in prints, slides or transparencies. Application must be signed by student's art teacher.
Additional information: Applications available between September and December. Deadlines vary. Applicant must separately apply and be accepted at awarding school. Awards range from $100 to full tuition. Eligibility, admission requirements vary. Include SASE with all application requests.

Scholastic Writing Gold Award

Type of award: Scholarship.
Intended use: For undergraduate study.
Eligibility: Applicant must be enrolled in high school.
Basis for selection: Competition in Writing/journalism. Originality, technical competence, emergence of personal voice and style. Applicant must demonstrate seriousness of purpose.
Application requirements: $3 application fee. Application must be signed by student's teacher, counselor or principal.
Additional information: Applications available between September and December. Deadlines vary. Awards available in each of the following categories: short story, short-short story, essay/nonfiction/opinion writing, dramatic script, poetry, humor, science fiction/fantasy. Include SASE with all application requests.

Amount of award:	$100
Notification begins:	May 1

Scholastic Writing Portfolio Award

Type of award: Scholarship.
Intended use: For freshman study.
Eligibility: Applicant must be high school senior.
Basis for selection: Competition in Writing/journalism. Originality, technical competence, emergence of personal voice and style. Applicant must demonstrate seriousness of purpose.
Application requirements: $3 application fee. Portfolio and nomination by judges who select 16 portfolios for consideration of four awards. Portfolio of three to eight pieces, not to exceed 50 pages of narratives, individual poems and/or dramatic scripts demonstrating diversity and talent. Excerpts from longer works encouraged. Application signed by student's teacher, counselor or principal.
Additional information: Applications available between

September and December. Deadlines vary. Include SASE with all application requests.
- Amount of award: $5,000
- Number of awards: 4
- Notification begins: May 1
- Total amount awarded: $20,000

Contact:
The Scholastic Art and Writing Awards
555 Broadway
New York, NY 10012

Scoville Peace Fellowship Program

Herbert Scoville Jr. Peace Fellowship

Type of award: Scholarship.
Intended use: For graduate or non-degree study.
Eligibility: Applicant must be U.S. citizen or Only students from countries of proliferation concern to the U.S. are eligible.
Basis for selection: Major/career interest in international relations; political science/government. Applicant must demonstrate high academic achievement.
Application requirements: Interview, recommendations, essay and transcript. curriculum vitae.
Additional information: For explicit detail check web page, call or write. Open to all graduates with any degree.
- Amount of award: $6,000
- Number of awards: 4
- Number of applicants: 100
- Application deadline: March 15, October 15
- Notification begins: May 31, December 31

Contact:
Scoville Peace Fellowship Program
Attn: Paul Revsine
110 Maryland Ave, NE, Suite 201
Washington, DC 20002
Phone: 202-546-2795
Website: www.clw.org/pub/clw/scoville/

Scripps Institute of Oceanography

Scripps Undergraduate Research Fellowship

Type of award: Internship.
Intended use: For full-time junior, senior or graduate study.
Eligibility: Applicant must be U.S. citizen.
Basis for selection: Major/career interest in engineering; physics; mathematics; astronomy; engineering, electrical and electronic; geophysics; oceanography/marine studies; engineering, mechanical. Applicant must demonstrate seriousness of purpose and high academic achievement.
Application requirements: Recommendations and transcript.
Additional information: Provides a nine-week summer internship in marine and earth science research. Stipend of approximately $275/week. Minimum 3.0 GPA.
- Amount of award: $2,500
- Number of awards: 25
- Application deadline: March 12, May 14

Contact:
UCSD Office of Graduate Studies and Research
9500 Gilman Dr. 518 ERC
La Jolla, CA 92093
Website: www.sio.ucsd.edu

Seabee Memorial Scholarship Association, Inc.

Seabee Memorial Scholarship

Type of award: Scholarship, renewable.
Intended use: For full-time undergraduate study at accredited 4-year institution in United States.
Eligibility: Applicant must be U.S. citizen. Applicant must be descendant of veteran who served in the Navy. Applicant must be a child or grandchild of a Seabee or member of Naval Civil Engineer Corps - deceased, retired, reserve, active or honorably discharged.
Basis for selection: Applicant must demonstrate depth of character, leadership, patriotism, seriousness of purpose, service orientation and financial need.
Application requirements: Essay, transcript and proof of eligibility.
- Amount of award: $1,750
- Number of awards: 70
- Number of applicants: 350
- Application deadline: April 15
- Notification begins: June 15
- Total amount awarded: $124,000

Contact:
Scholarship Committee
P.O. Box 6574
Silver Spring, MD 20916
Phone: 301-871-3172
Website: www.seabee.org

Seattle Jaycees

Seattle Jaycees Scholarship

Type of award: Scholarship, renewable.
Intended use: For undergraduate or graduate study at accredited postsecondary institution in United States.
Basis for selection: Applicant must demonstrate depth of character and service orientation.
Application requirements: $5 application fee. Transcript. Resume and proof of community service.
Additional information: Scholarships granted for exemplary civic involvement, volunteerism and community service. Must

attend school in Washington State. Application deadlines vary each year. Send SASE to receive additional information and application.

Amount of award:	$1,000
Number of applicants:	400

Contact:
Seattle Jaycees
Scholarship Committee
109 West Mercer Street
Seattle, WA 98119
Phone: 206-286-2014

Second Marine Division Association Memorial Scholarship Fund

Second Marine Division Scholarship

Type of award: Scholarship, renewable.
Intended use: For full-time freshman, sophomore, junior, senior or non-degree study at accredited vocational, 2-year or 4-year institution.
Eligibility: Applicant must be single. Applicant must be child of active service person, veteran, disabled veteran or deceased veteran who served in the Marines. Parent must be a Second Marine Division, Fleet Marine Force veteran.
Basis for selection: Applicant must demonstrate depth of character, leadership, patriotism, seriousness of purpose, service orientation, financial need and high academic achievement.
Application requirements: Recommendations, essay, transcript and proof of eligibility. Must include SASE when requesting applications.
Additional information: Must be unmarried dependent of individual currently serving or having previously served in Second Marine Division, United States Marine Corps or unit attached thereto; annual family income $30,000 or less. Minimum 2.5 GPA. Letter requesting application must be in handwriting of applicant.

Amount of award:	$800
Number of awards:	32
Number of applicants:	32
Application deadline:	April 30
Notification begins:	September 30
Total amount awarded:	$25,600

Contact:
Second Marine Division Association Memorial Fund
P.O. Box 8180
Camp Lejeune, NC 28547

Seneca Nation of Indians

Seneca Nation Higher Education Program

Type of award: Scholarship, renewable.
Intended use: For undergraduate or graduate study at accredited 2-year, 4-year or graduate institution.
Eligibility: Applicant must be American Indian. Must be an enrolled tribe member of Seneca Nation of Indians.
Basis for selection: Applicant must demonstrate financial need and high academic achievement.
Application requirements: Recommendations, essay, transcript and proof of eligibility. Tribal certificate.
Additional information: Application deadline for summer is May 20th.

Amount of award:	$3,000-$8,000
Application deadline:	July 15, December 31

Contact:
Seneca Nation of Indians
Higher Education Program
P.O. Box 231
Salamanca, NY 14779
Phone: 716-945-1790

Sertoma International

Communicative Disorders Scholarships

Type of award: Scholarship.
Intended use: For full-time master's study at accredited 4-year or graduate institution in or outside United States.
Eligibility: Applicant must be U.S. citizen, permanent resident or Canadian and Mexican citizens.
Basis for selection: Major/career interest in speech pathology/audiology. Applicant must demonstrate seriousness of purpose and high academic achievement.
Application requirements: Recommendations, transcript and proof of eligibility.
Additional information: Statement of Purpose letter required with application. Applicant must have a 3.2 GPA or above. Applicant must be accepted into an accredited Master's degree program in speech language pathology or audiology in the United States, Canada or Mexico.

Amount of award:	$2,500
Number of awards:	30
Number of applicants:	333
Application deadline:	March 31
Total amount awarded:	$75,000

Sertoma Scholarships for Deaf and Hard of Hearing Students

Type of award: Scholarship, renewable.
Intended use: For full-time undergraduate study at 4-year institution in United States.
Eligibility: Applicant must be hearing impaired. Applicant must be U.S. citizen, permanent resident or Canadian citizen.

Basis for selection: Applicant must demonstrate seriousness of purpose and high academic achievement.
Additional information: Applicant must be deaf or hearing impaired. Students who receive funding may reapply and is eligible for funding for up to four years.
    Amount of award: $1,000
    Number of awards: 13
    Number of applicants: 175
    Application deadline: April 15
    Total amount awarded: $13,000
Contact:
Sponsorships Dept.-$1,000 Scholarship
Sertoma International
1912 E. Meyer Blvd.
Kansas City, MO 64132-1174
Website: www.sertoma.org

Service Employees International Union

Service Employees Scholarship

Type of award: Scholarship.
Intended use: For full-time freshman study at accredited 4-year institution in United States.
Eligibility: Applicant must be high school senior. Applicant must be residing in California.
Basis for selection: Applicant must demonstrate financial need and high academic achievement.
Application requirements: Recommendations, essay and transcript.
Additional information: Parent must be a member of the Service Employees International Union.
    Amount of award: $1,000
    Application deadline: March 15
Contact:
Service Employees International Union
1007 7 Street
4th Floor
Sacramento, CA 95814

Service Merchandise

Career Opportunities Through Education Scholarship Program

Type of award: Scholarship.
Intended use: For full-time undergraduate study.
Eligibility: Applicant must be high school senior. Applicant must be U.S. citizen.
Basis for selection: Applicant must demonstrate high academic achievement.
Application requirements: Recommendations, essay and transcript.
Additional information: Applications can only be obtained at a Service Merchandise Catalogue showroom and cannot be requested by mail.
    Amount of award: $500
    Number of awards: 100
    Number of applicants: 2,500
    Application deadline: January 15
    Notification begins: April 15
    Total amount awarded: $50,000

Service Merchandise Company Inc.

Service Merchandise Scholarship

Type of award: Scholarship.
Intended use: For full-time freshman study at accredited 4-year institution.
Eligibility: Applicant must be high school senior. Applicant must be U.S. citizen.
Basis for selection: Major/career interest in business; marketing; economics; accounting. Applicant must demonstrate depth of character, service orientation and high academic achievement.
Application requirements: Essay and transcript.
Additional information: Applications available at all Service Merchandise store locations between October 15 and January 15. Applications will not be mailed.
    Amount of award: $500
    Number of awards: 100
    Number of applicants: 6,000
    Application deadline: January 15
    Notification begins: March 1
    Total amount awarded: $50,000

Seventeen Magazine

Seventeen Magazine Journalism Internship

Type of award: Internship.
Intended use: For undergraduate or graduate study.
Basis for selection: Major/career interest in journalism.
Application requirements: Interview, portfolio and recommendations.
Additional information: Eight week program. $250 a week. Academic interns are granted school credits. Applicant must submit resume, cover letter and writing samples.
    Amount of award: $1,500
    Application deadline: August 15, November 15
    Notification begins: August 31, December 15
Contact:
Seventeen Magazine
850 Third Ave., 8th Fl.
New York, NY 10022

Shop 'N Save Stores

Students Extra Educational Development Scholarship

Type of award: Scholarship.
Intended use: For freshman study at accredited vocational, 2-year or 4-year institution.
Eligibility: Applicant must be residing in Pennsylvania or Ohio or West Virginia.
Additional information: Application materials available after January 1 at Shop 'n Save stores in Ohio, Pennsylvania, and West Virginia. For students with high record of volunteer service.
    Amount of award: $1,000-$5,000
    Application deadline: February 20

Shoshone Tribe

Shoshone Tribal Scholarship

Type of award: Scholarship, renewable.
Intended use: For undergraduate study at accredited vocational, 2-year or 4-year institution in United States.
Eligibility: Applicant must be American Indian. Must be enrolled member of Eastern Shoshone Tribe.
Basis for selection: Applicant must demonstrate financial need.
Application requirements: Transcript and proof of eligibility.
Additional information: Must first apply for Pell Grant and appropriate campus-based aid. Minimum 2.5 GPA required. Application deadline for summer is April 15th.
    Amount of award: $50-$5,000
    Number of awards: 90
    Number of applicants: 100
    Application deadline: June 1, November 15
    Total amount awarded: $300,000
Contact:
Shoshone Education Program
P.O. Box 628
Fort Washakie, WY 82514
Phone: 307-332-3538 ext.15

Sigma Xi The Scientific Research Society

Scientific Research Grant-In-Aid

Type of award: Research grant, renewable.
Intended use: For undergraduate, master's or doctoral study at accredited 4-year or graduate institution.
Basis for selection: Major/career interest in science, general; astronomy; optometry/ophthalmology. Applicant must demonstrate high academic achievement.
Application requirements: Recommendations and proof of eligibility.
Additional information: Student researchers in astronomy or vision research may apply for up to $2,500.
    Amount of award: $1,000
    Number of awards: 691
    Number of applicants: 2,083
    Application deadline: October 15, March 15
    Total amount awarded: $373,132
Contact:
Sigma Xi The Scientific Research Society
99 Alexander Drive
P.O. Box 13975
Research Triangle Park, NC 27709
Phone: 919-549-4691
Website: www.sigmaxi.org

Silicon Graphics Computer Systems

Silicon Graphics Computer Systems Internship Program

Type of award: Internship.
Intended use: For undergraduate or graduate study.
Basis for selection: Major/career interest in computer and information sciences.
Additional information: Deadlines vary; contact sponsor for information. Submit a resume and cover letter to apply. Departments that accept interns include: software development, hardware development, application services, finance, facilities, and purchasing.
    Amount of award: $4,000-$13,600
    Number of applicants: 1,000
    Total amount awarded: $200
Contact:
Silicon Graphics Computer Systems
Internship Coordinator
2011 North Shoreline Boulevard, MS 742
Mountain View, CA 94043

Skadden, Arps, Slate, Meagher and Flom

Skadden, Arps, Slate, Meagher and Flom Law Internship

Type of award: Internship.
Intended use: For junior, senior study.
Basis for selection: Major/career interest in law.
Application requirements: Transcript. Resume and cover letter.
Additional information: Ten to 12 week internship. Stipend of $400 per week. Locations in Boston, New York City and Washington, D.C. Provides opportunity to assist legal assistants and attorneys in various departments. Application deadline for winter session is December 1.

569

Amount of award:	$4,000-$4,800
Application deadline:	August 1, February 1

Contact:
Skadden, Arps, Slate, Meagher and Flom
919 Third Ave.
New York, NY 10022-3897

Smith's Food and Drug Centers Inc.

Personal Best Scholarship

Type of award: Scholarship.
Intended use: For freshman study.
Eligibility: Applicant must be high school senior. Applicant must be residing in New Mexico.
Basis for selection: Applicant must demonstrate financial need.
Application requirements: Recommendations, essay and nomination.

Amount of award:	$1,000
Number of awards:	5
Number of applicants:	70
Application deadline:	April 1
Notification begins:	May 15
Total amount awarded:	$5,000

Contact:
Smith's Food and Drug Centers Inc.
P.O. Box 27020
Albuquerque, NM 87125-7020
Phone: 505-345-8821

Smithsonian Institution

Smithsonian Graduate Student Fellowship

Type of award: Research grant.
Intended use: For master's study. Designated institutions: Smithsonian Institution.
Basis for selection: Major/career interest in science, general; art, art history; anthropology; biology.
Application requirements: Recommendations, transcript and research proposal. curriculum vitae.
Additional information: Research fellowships at Smithsonian Institution for ten weeks in anthropology/archaeology, astrophysics, earth sciences/paleontology, ecology/environmental, behavioral (tropical animals), evolutionary and systematic biology, history of science and technology, history of art (including American contemporary, African, Asian), 20th century American crafts, social and cultural history and folk life of America. Available each semester, including summer. Must be enrolled in Graduate program, completed one semester, and not yet been advanced to candidacy in a doctoral program. For stipend information, contact office. Applications available in September.

Application deadline:	January 15
Notification begins:	April 15

Contact:
Smithsonian Institution
Office of Fellowships and Grants
955 L'Enfant Plaza, Suite 7000 MCR 902
Washington, DC 20560
Phone: 202-287-3271
Website: www.si.edu/research+study

Smithsonian Minority Internship

Type of award: Internship.
Intended use: For undergraduate or graduate study. Designated institutions: Smithsonian Institution.
Eligibility: Applicant must be of minority background.
Basis for selection: Major/career interest in anthropology; science, general; art, art history; history.
Application requirements: Recommendations, essay and transcript.
Additional information: Research Internships at Smithsonian Institution in anthropology/archaeology, astrophysics, earth sciences/paleontology, ecology/environmental, behavioral (tropical animals), evolutionary and systematic biology, history of science and technology, history of art (including American contemporary, African, Asian), 20th century American crafts, social and cultural history and folk life of America. Stipend of $300 a week for ten weeks. February 15th application deadline applies to Fall, Spring and Summer sessions.

Amount of award:	$3,000
Number of applicants:	130
Application deadline:	February 15

Contact:
Smithsonian Institution
Office of Fellowships and Grants
955 L'Enfant Plaza, Suite 7000 MRC 902
Washington, DC 20560
Phone: 202-287-3271
Website: www.si.edu/research+study

Smithsonian Native American Internship

Type of award: Internship.
Intended use: For undergraduate or graduate study. Designated institutions: Smithsonian Institution.
Eligibility: Applicant must be American Indian.
Basis for selection: Major/career interest in Native American studies.
Application requirements: Recommendations, essay and transcript.
Additional information: Internship at Smithsonian Institution in research or museum activities related to Native American studies. Stipend of $300 a week for ten weeks. Summer application deadline is March 1st.

Amount of award:	$3,000
Application deadline:	July 1, November 1

Contact:
Smithsonian Institution
Office of Fellowships and Grants
955 L'enfant Plaza, Suite 7000
Washington, DC 20560
Phone: 202-287-3271
Website: www.si.edu/research+study

Smithsonian Post-Doctoral Fellowship

Type of award: Research grant.
Intended use: For postgraduate study. Designated institutions: Smithsonian Institution.
Basis for selection: Major/career interest in science, general; art, art history; anthropology; biology.
Application requirements: Recommendations and research proposal. curriculum vitae.
Additional information: Fellowships last three to 12 months and are for scholars who have held the doctorate degree for less than seven years. For specific information on program and stipend amounts contact office.
   Application deadline: January 15
   Notification begins: April 15
Contact:
Smithsonian Institution
Office of Fellowships and Grants
955 L'Enfant Plaza, Suite 7000
Washington, DC 20560
Phone: 202-287-3271
Website: www.si.edu/research&study

Smithsonian Pre-Doctoral Fellowship

Type of award: Research grant.
Intended use: For doctoral study. Designated institutions: Smithsonian Institution.
Basis for selection: Major/career interest in anthropology; science, general; art, art history; biology.
Application requirements: Recommendations, essay, transcript and research proposal.
Additional information: Dissertation research fellowships at Smithsonian Institution for three months to a year in: anthropology/archaeology, astrophysics, earth sciences/paleontology, ecology/environmental, behavioral (tropical animals), evolutionary and systematic biology, history of science and technology, history of art (including American contemporary, African, Asian), 20th century American craft's social and cultural history and folk life of America. Applicants must have completed all course work and be currently and engaged in dissertation research. Must have approval from university to conduct research at SI. For stipend inforamation contact office. Applications available in September.
   Number of applicants: 141
   Application deadline: January 15
   Notification begins: April 15
Contact:
Smithsonian Institution
Office of Fellowships and Grants
955 L'Enfant Plaza, Suite 7000 MRC 902
Washington, DC 20560
Phone: 202-287-3271
Website: www.si.edu/research+study

Smithsonian Senior Fellowship

Type of award: Research grant.
Intended use: For postgraduate study. Designated institutions: Smithsonian Institution.
Basis for selection: Major/career interest in science, general; anthropology; art, art history; biology.
Application requirements: Recommendations and research proposal. curriculum vitae.
Additional information: Must have held Ph.D. for more than seven years. Award for research at Smithsonian Institution for three months to a year in: anthropology/archaeology, astrophysics, earth sciences/paleontology, ecology/environmental, behavioral (tropical animals), evolutionary and systematic biology, history of science and technology, history of art (including American contemporary, African, Asian), 20th century American crafts, social and cultural history and folk life of America. For stipend information contact office. Applications may be submitted up to two years in advance. Applications available in September.
   Application deadline: January 15
   Notification begins: April 15
Contact:
Smithsonian Institution
Office of Fellowships and Grants
955 L'Enfant Plaza, Suite 7000 MCR 902
Washington, DC 20560
Phone: 202-287-3271
Website: www.si.edu/research+study

Social Science Research Council

Abe Fellowship Program

Type of award: Research grant.
Intended use: For postgraduate study in Japan.
Eligibility: Applicant must be Open to Japanese citizens or other nationals who demonstrate strong affiliation in research communities of the U.S. or Japan.
Basis for selection: Major/career interest in international relations.
Application requirements: Research proposal.
Additional information: To encourage international multidisciplinary research on topics of pressing global concern. Must hold Ph.D. or terminal degree. Multi/interdisciplinary studies accepted as field of study. One-third of fellowship tenure must be spent in either Japan or U.S. Fellowship tenure need not be continuous, but must be concluded within 24-month period. Language proficiency preferred.
   Application deadline: September 1
Contact:
Social Science Research Council
ATTN: Abe Fellowship Program
810 7th Avenue
New York, NY 10019
Phone: 212-377-2700
Website: www.ssrc.org

Advanced Research Grants: Japan

Type of award: Research grant.
Intended use: For postgraduate, non-degree study outside United States in Japan.
Eligibility: Applicant must be U.S. citizen or permanent resident.
Basis for selection: Major/career interest in international

relations; sociology; Japanese studies; economics; political science/government.
Application requirements: Research proposal.
Additional information: To encourage Japan-related research in social sciences and humanities, including projects which are comparative and contemporary in nature, and have long-term applied policy implications, or which engage Japan in wider regional and global debates. U.S. nationals residing abroad may apply. Emphasis on Japanese fields of study. Special attention given to Japan scholars interested in broadening their skills and expertise through additional training or comparative work in additional geographic area. Award amounts are up to $25,000 with a tenure of two to 12 months.
   Amount of award: $25,000
   Application deadline: December 1
Contact:
Social Science Research Council
ATTN: Japan Program
810 7th Avenue
New York, NY 10019
Phone: 212-377-2700
Website: www.ssrc.org

Advanced Research Grants: Vietnam

Type of award: Research grant.
Intended use: For full-time postgraduate study at accredited graduate institution in Vietnam.
Eligibility: Applicant must be Must be studying in U.S. or Canada.
Basis for selection: Major/career interest in anthropology; humanities/liberal arts; social and behavioral sciences; history; sociology.
Application requirements: Research proposal.
Additional information: Supports scholars and other professionals in conducting research or analyzing previously gathered materials on all aspects of historical or contemporary Vietnam. Must hold Ph.D. or equivalent. Additional fields of study allowed include area, ethnic and cultural studies and Vietnamese studies. Fellowship can be used for 12 consecutive months or two separate six month tenures. Fellows expected to have sufficient knowledge of Vietnamese language.
   Amount of award: $30,000
   Application deadline: December 1
Contact:
Social Science Research Council
ATTN: Fellowships and Grants-Southeast Asia
810 7th Avenue
New York, NY 10019
Phone: 212-377-2700
Website: www.ssrc.org

Berlin Program for Advanced German-European Studies

Type of award: Research grant.
Intended use: For doctoral, postgraduate study outside United States in Berlin, Germany. Designated institutions: Free University of Berlin, Germany.
Eligibility: Applicant must be Canadian citizens eligible.
Basis for selection: Major/career interest in political science/government; social and behavioral sciences; history; economics; anthropology.

Application requirements: Research proposal.
Additional information: Predoctoral applicants must have completed all Ph.D. requirements except for dissertation. Postdoctoral applicants must have received Ph.D. within last two years. Program supports anthropologists, economists, political scientists, sociologists and all scholars in germane social science and cultural studies fields. This includes historians working on the period since the mid-19th century. Award amounts vary.
   Application deadline: February 1
Contact:
Social Science Research Council
ATTN: Fellowships and Grants-Western Europe
810 7th Avenue
New York, NY 10019
Phone: 212-377-2700
Website: www.ssrc.org

Fellowships for Postdoctoral Research: Eastern Europe

Type of award: Research grant.
Intended use: For postgraduate study.
Eligibility: Applicant must be U.S. citizen or permanent resident.
Basis for selection: Major/career interest in humanities/liberal arts; social and behavioral sciences.
Application requirements: Research proposal.
Additional information: Scholars may apply for fellowships of up to $25,000 for a period of six to 12 consecutive months of full time research. Funds may be used to supplement sabbatical salaries or awards from other sources, provided they would further proposed research. Proposals dealing with Albania, Bulgaria, Romania and the former Yugoslavia are especially encouraged.
   Amount of award: $25,000
   Application deadline: November 2
Contact:
American Council of Learned Societies
Office of Fellowships and Grants
228 East 45th Street
New York, NY 10017
Fax: 212-949-8058

International Dissertation Field Research Fellowship Program

Type of award: Research grant.
Intended use: For full-time doctoral study at graduate institution in United States.
Eligibility: Applicant must be Must be enrolled at U.S. institutions.
Basis for selection: Major/career interest in social and behavioral sciences; humanities/liberal arts.
Application requirements: Research proposal.
Additional information: Standard fellowship will provide support for nine to 12 months, plus travel expenses, but will rarely exceed $15,000. Candidate may propose research for less than nine months and no award will be given for less than six months of research. Program invites proposals for field research on all regions of the world. Program is especially interested in proposals that pertain to study of modern world issues (post-1700).

Amount of award: $15,000
Application deadline: November 18
Notification begins: May 1
Contact:
Social Science Research Council
International Dissertation Field Research Program
810 Seventh Avenue
New York, NY 10019
Phone: 212-377-2700
Website: www.ssrc.org

International Predissertation Fellowship Program

Type of award: Research grant.
Intended use: For full-time doctoral study at graduate institution in United States.
Eligibility: Applicant must be U.S. citizen or permanent resident.
Basis for selection: Major/career interest in economics; political science/government; psychology; sociology. Applicant must demonstrate seriousness of purpose.
Application requirements: Research proposal.
Additional information: Applications are sought from enrolled Ph.D students at 23 universities. Students should demonstrate an intent to use fellowship to supplement the normal program of study in preparation for dissertation research. The award is not intended for actual dissertation research. Fellowships will provide 12 months of support for a training program that will prepare fellow to conduct dissertation field research. For specific university participation and deadlines, contact council or refer to web page.
Contact:
Social Science Research Council
810 Seventh Avenue
New York, NY 10019
Phone: 212-377-2700
Website: www.ssrc.org

Language Training Grant: Eastern Europe

Type of award: Scholarship.
Intended use: For full-time master's, doctoral study at graduate institution in United States.
Eligibility: Applicant must be U.S. citizen or permanent resident.
Basis for selection: Major/career interest in foreign languages.
Additional information: Grants of $2,000 are awarded for second year study and $2,500 for intermediate and advanced study. The awards are intended for those who will use the Eastern European languages in their academic and professional careers.
Amount of award: $2,000-$2,500
Application deadline: February 1
Contact:
American Council of Learned Societies
Office of Fellowships and Grants
228 East 45th Street
New York, NY 10017
Fax: 202-949-8058

Melon Minority Fellowship Program

Type of award: Research grant.
Intended use: For full-time sophomore, junior or senior study at accredited 4-year institution in United States. Designated institutions: Program administered at over 40 colleges and universities in the United States. Contact the SSRC for list.
Eligibility: Applicant must be Alaskan native, American Indian, African American, Mexican American, Hispanic American or Puerto Rican. Applicant must be U.S. citizen or permanent resident.
Basis for selection: Major/career interest in English literature; anthropology; geology/earth sciences; mathematics; foreign languages; history; religion/theology; art, art history; anthropology. Applicant must demonstrate high academic achievement.
Application requirements: Recommendations, essay, transcript and research proposal.
Additional information: Fellowship intended to foster graduate study. Additional fields of study include musicology, ecology and physics.
Amount of award: $5,000
Application deadline: October 30
Contact:
Social Science Research Council
ATTN: Fellowships and Grants-Mellon Minority
810 7th Avenue
New York, NY 10019
Phone: 212-377-2700
Website: www.ssrc.org

Mid Career Skills Enrichment Program for Tenured Faculty

Type of award: Research grant.
Intended use: For postgraduate, non-degree study outside United States in Middle East and North Africa but not Afghanistan, Lebanon, Libya, Algeria, Iran or Iraq.
Eligibility: Applicant must be U.S. citizen.
Basis for selection: Major/career interest in humanities/liberal arts; sociology; social and behavioral sciences.
Application requirements: Research proposal.
Additional information: Supports research in Middle Eastern country in which grant recipient has not previously studied, and/or supports training in new field, discipline or method, or enhances ability to conduct research in familiar geographic areas. Fields of study also accepted include area, ethnic and cultural studies and religion/religious studies. Must have held Ph.D. in social sciences/humanities discipline for less than 20 years, and hold rank of associate or full professor. Award varies. Encourage applications focusing on countries, sub-regions currently underrepresented.
Application deadline: December 1
Contact:
Social Science Research Council
ATTN: Fellowships and Grants-Middle East
810 7th Avenue
New York, NY 10019
Phone: 212-377-2700
Website: www.ssrc.org

Postdoctoral Fellowship: Eurasia

Type of award: Research grant.
Intended use: For postgraduate study outside United States in Newly independent states, unrestricted.
Eligibility: Applicant must be U.S. citizen.
Basis for selection: Major/career interest in humanities/liberal arts; social and behavioral sciences.
Additional information: Fellowships last up to two years. To improve employment and tenure opportunities of new Ph.D.'s in any discipline of humanities and social sciences in study of Soviet Union and its successor states. U.S. nationals residing abroad may apply. Must have received Ph.D. after 1991 and be untenured. Fields of study accepted include area, ethnic and cultural studies and Russian and Slavic area studies.
   Amount of award: $24,000
   Application deadline: February 3
Contact:
Social Science Research Council
ATTN: Fellowships and Grants-Eurasia
810 7th Avenue
New York, NY 10019
Phone: 212-377-2700
Website: www.ssrc.org

Postdoctoral Fellowship: Middle East

Type of award: Research grant.
Intended use: For postgraduate, non-degree study outside United States. Designated institutions: American overseas research centers in Middle East and North Africa.
Eligibility: Applicant must be U.S. citizen or permanent resident.
Basis for selection: Major/career interest in arts, general; Middle Eastern studies; linguistics; psychology.
Application requirements: Research proposal.
Additional information: Research not possible in Afganistan, Algeria, Iran, Iraq, Lebanon, or Libya. Promotes integration of area expertise into disciplines currently underrepresented in Middle East studies. Must hold Ph.D. in Middle East social sciences/humanities discipline. Those less than ten years past Ph.D. particularly encouraged to apply. Scholars may propose single country or comparative research, collaborative research, and/or research to acquire familiarity with problems of their disciplines as they apply to Middle East. May request support for language training. Award amounts vary. There are a total of three programs that apply to postdoctoral work in the Middle East. Contact office or refer to web page for further information.
   Application deadline: December 1
Contact:
Social Science Research Council
810 7th Avenue
ATTN: Fellowships and Grants-Middle East
New York, NY 10019
Phone: 212-377-2700
Website: www.ssrc.org

Postdoctoral Sexuality Research Fellowship Program

Type of award: Research grant, renewable.
Intended use: For postgraduate study in United States.
Basis for selection: Major/career interest in anthropology; economics; education; history; womenÖs studies; political science/government; psychology; sociology; social and behavioral sciences. Applicant must demonstrate seriousness of purpose.
Application requirements: Research proposal.
Additional information: This program provides support for up to 24 months and pays $38,000/year to cover costs and living expenses. Applicants should submit research proposals that seek to investigate a wide range of sexuality topics concerning respective discipline and conducted in the U.S. Only joint fellowship applications will be accepted from applicant and research advisor. Botht the advisor and applicant must hold a Ph.D from an accredited institution. Candidates who have conducted research on sexuality for more than eight years will not be considered.
   Amount of award: $38,000
   Application deadline: December 15
   Notification begins: March 1
Contact:
Social Science Research Council
810 Seventh Avenue
New York, NY 10019
Phone: 212-377-2700
Website: www.ssrc.org

Predissertation Fellowship: Bangladesh

Type of award: Research grant.
Intended use: For doctoral study at accredited graduate institution in Bangladesh.
Basis for selection: Major/career interest in humanities/liberal arts; social and behavioral sciences; foreign languages; anthropology; Asian studies; history; sociology.
Application requirements: Research proposal.
Additional information: Supports short-term field trips to Bangladesh designed for preliminary field activities, such as investigate potential research sites and research materials, develop language skills, and establish local research contacts. Must have completed one year graduate study towards Ph.D. at North American university. Fields of study accepted include area, ethnic and cultural studies and religion/religious studies.
   Amount of award: $5,200
   Application deadline: November 1
Contact:
Social Science Research Council
810 Seventh Avenue
ATTN: Fellowships and Grants-Bangladesh
New York, NY 10019
Phone: 212-377-2700
Website: www.ssrc.org

Predissertation Fellowship: Near-Middle East

Type of award: Research grant.
Intended use: For full-time doctoral study outside United States. Designated institutions: American overseas research centers in North Africa, the Middle East, Turkey.
Eligibility: Applicant must be U.S. citizen.
Basis for selection: Major/career interest in anthropology; social and behavioral sciences; humanities/liberal arts; history; Islamic studies; sociology.
Application requirements: Research proposal.
Additional information: Research not possible in Afganistan,

Algeria, Iran, Iraq, Lebanon, or Libya. Fellowships last four to nine months. Supports graduate students engaged in direct preparation for dissertation research through training and study in the Middle East. Must have completed two years coursework, be currently enrolled in Ph.D. program, and not be engaged in dissertation research or writing. Fields of study also accepted include area, ethnic and cultural studies and religion/religious studies. Projects must be concerned with period since beginning of Islam. Award amounts vary.

   Application deadline: November 1

Contact:
Social Science Research Council
ATTN: Fellowships and Grants-Near Middle East
810 7th Avenue
New York, NY 10019
Phone: 212-377-2700
Website: www.ssrc.org

Predissertation Fellowship: South Asia

Type of award: Research grant.
Intended use: For doctoral study Bangladesh, India, Nepal, Pakistan, Ski Lanka in Bangladesh, India, Nepal, Pakistan, Sri Lanka.
Eligibility: Applicant must be U.S. citizen.
Basis for selection: Major/career interest in humanities/liberal arts; social and behavioral sciences; anthropology; foreign languages; Asian studies; history; sociology.
Application requirements: Research proposal.
Additional information: Supports short-term field trips designed for preliminary field activities, such as investigating potential research sites and research materials, development of language skills, and establishing local research contacts. Must have completed one year graduate study towards Ph.D. at U.S. university. Fields of study also accepted are area, ethnic and cultural studies and religion/religious studies. Three types of fellowships available: General (three-month fellowships to explore feasibility of dissertation topics); Underrepresented disciplines; and Languages not taught in the United States.

   Amount of award: $5,000-$11,000
   Application deadline: November 1

Contact:
Social Science Research Council
810 7th Avenue
ATTN: Fellowships and Grants-South Asia
New York, NY 10019
Phone: 212-377-2700
Website: www.ssrc.org

Sexuality Research Dissertation Fellowship Program

Type of award: Research grant.
Intended use: For doctoral study.
Basis for selection: Major/career interest in anthropology; economics; education; history; womenÖs studies; political science/government; psychology; sociology; social and behavioral sciences. Applicant must demonstrate seriousness of purpose.
Application requirements: Research proposal.
Additional information: Grants are awarded for research that will investigate sexuality topics as conceptualized by applicants respective discipline and that are conducted in the United States. Only joint fellowship applications will be considered from applicant an dresearch advisor. Advisor must hold Ph.D. Women and minority groups especially encouraged to apply.

   Amount of award: $28,000
   Number of awards: 10
   Application deadline: December 15
   Notification begins: March 1
   Total amount awarded: $280,000

Contact:
Social Science Research Council
810 Seventh Avenue
New York, NY 10019
Phone: 212-377-2700
Website: www.ssrc.org

SSRC Dissertation Fellowship: Bangladesh

Type of award: Research grant.
Intended use: For full-time doctoral study at graduate institution in Bangladesh, India.
Eligibility: May be Bangladeshi citizen enrolled full-time in Ph.D. program abroad. Applicant must be Bangladeshi citizen.
Basis for selection: Major/career interest in anthropology; humanities/liberal arts; social and behavioral sciences; sociology.
Application requirements: Research proposal.
Additional information: Nine to 15-month fellowships. Supports doctoral students' research in Bangladesh. Award amounts vary. Applicants other than Bangladeshi nationals must be enrolled in a North American institution. May divide time between India and Bangladesh but must spend at least two-thirds of their time in Bangladesh.

   Application deadline: November 1

Contact:
Social Science Research Council
810 Seventh Avenue'
ATTN: Fellowships and Grants-Bangladesh
New York, NY 10019
Phone: 212-377-2700
Website: www.ssrc.org

SSRC Dissertation Fellowship: Eastern Europe

Type of award: Research grant.
Intended use: For doctoral study.
Eligibility: Applicant must be U.S. citizen or permanent resident.
Basis for selection: Major/career interest in social and behavioral sciences; humanities/liberal arts.
Application requirements: Research proposal.
Additional information: Doctoral candidates may apply for up to $15,000 plus expenses for an academic year of research to be undertaken at any university or institution outside of Eastern Europe. Proposals dealing with Albania, Bulgaria, Romania and the former Yugoslavia are especially encouraged.

   Amount of award: $15,000
   Application deadline: November 2

Contact:
American Council of Learned Societies
Office of Fellowships and Grants
228 East 45th Street
New York, NY 10017
Fax: 212-949-8058

SSRC Dissertation Fellowship: Eurasia

Type of award: Research grant.
Intended use: For full-time doctoral study in Newly independent states, unrestricted.
Eligibility: Applicant must be U.S. citizen.
Basis for selection: Major/career interest in humanities/liberal arts; social and behavioral sciences; Russian studies.
Application requirements: Research proposal.
Additional information: Supports students who have completed research for their doctoral dissertations and expect to complete the writing of their dissertations during the next academic year. U.S. nationals residing abroad may apply. Must be doctoral student specializing in any discipline of the social sciences and humanities in the study of Soviet Union and successor states. Fields of study accepted include area, ethnic and cultural studies and Russian and Slavic Area studies.
    Amount of award: $15,000
    Application deadline: February 3
Contact:
Social Science Research Council
ATTN: Fellowships and Grants-Eurasia
810 7th Avenue
New York, NY 10019
Phone: 212-377-2700
Website: www.ssrc.org

SSRC Dissertation Fellowship: Middle East

Type of award: Research grant.
Intended use: For full-time doctoral study at graduate institution outside United States. Designated institutions: American overseas research centers in Middle East and North Africa.
Eligibility: Applicant must be U.S. citizen.
Basis for selection: Major/career interest in Middle Eastern studies; humanities/liberal arts; social and behavioral sciences; sociology; anthropology; foreign languages; history.
Application requirements: Research proposal.
Additional information: Research not possible in Afganistan, Algeria, Iran, Iraq, Lebanon, or Libya. Supports scholars engaged in dissertation research requiring fieldwork in the Middle East. Must complete all Ph.D. requirements except dissertation by June 30 of year abroad. Language training may be required. U.S. nationals residing abroad may apply. Area, ethnic and cultural studies; foreign literatures; and religion/religious studies also accepted fields of study. Award amounts vary.
    Application deadline: November 1
Contact:
Social Science Research Council
ATTN: Fellowships and Grants-Middle East
810 7th Avenue
New York, NY 10019
Phone: 212-377-2700
Website: www.ssrc.org

SSRC Dissertation Fellowship: Middle East

Type of award: Research grant.
Intended use: For full-time doctoral study outside United States. Designated institutions: American overseas research centers in the Middle East and North Africa.
Eligibility: Applicant must be U.S. citizen.
Basis for selection: Major/career interest in social and behavioral sciences; humanities/liberal arts.
Application requirements: Must have completed all Ph.D. requirements except dissertation by June 30 of year abroad. Language training may be required.
Additional information: Research not possible in Afganistan, Algeria, Iran, Iraq, Lebanon, or Libya. Supports single country or comparative dissertation research projects requiring fieldwork in the Middle East. Fields of study accepted include demography/population studies, fine arts and art studies, e.g., underrepresented disciplines. Must complete all Ph.D. requirements except dissertation before June 30, 1999 to be eligible. Award amounts vary.
    Application deadline: November 1
Contact:
Social Science Research Council
ATTN: Fellowships and Grants-Middle East
810 7th Avenue
New York, NY 10019
Phone: 212-377-2700
Website: www.ssrc.org

SSRC Dissertation Fellowship: South Asia

Type of award: Research grant.
Intended use: For full-time doctoral study Bangladesh, Nepal, Pakistan, Ski Lanka outside United States in Bangladesh, Nepal, Pakistan, Sri Lanka.
Eligibility: Applicant must be U.S. citizen.
Basis for selection: Major/career interest in social and behavioral sciences; humanities/liberal arts; architecture; law.
Application requirements: Research proposal.
Additional information: Up to 15-month fellowships for dissertation research. Award amounts vary.
    Application deadline: November 1
Contact:
Social Science Research Council
810 7th Avenue
ATTN: Fellowships and Grants-South Asia
New York, NY 10019
Phone: 212-377-2700
Website: www.ssrc.org

SSRC Dissertation Fellowship: Southeast Asia

Type of award: Research grant.
Intended use: For full-time doctoral study outside United States in Vietnam.
Eligibility: Applicant must be Must be studying at institutions within the U.S. or Canada.
Basis for selection: Major/career interest in history; humanities/liberal arts; social and behavioral sciences; sociology; foreign languages.
Application requirements: Research proposal.
Additional information: Must be enrolled in doctoral program. Supports doctoral dissertation research in social sciences and humanities to be carried out in Vietnam. Fields of study accepted include area, ethnic and cultural studies; foreign

literatures; and Vietnamese studies. Award amounts vary. Must be full-time student enrolled in doctoral program in U.S. or Canada. Tenure is 12 to 24 months.

Amount of award:	$15,000
Application deadline:	December 1

Contact:
Social Science Research Council
ATTN: Fellowships and Grants-Southeast Asia
810 7th Avenue
New York, NY 10019
Phone: 212-377-2700
Website: www.ssrc.org

Society for Technical Communication

Technical Communication Scholarship Program

Type of award: Scholarship.
Intended use: For full-time undergraduate or graduate study at accredited 2-year, 4-year or graduate institution.
Basis for selection: Major/career interest in communications; graphic arts and design. Applicant must demonstrate depth of character, leadership, seriousness of purpose and high academic achievement.
Application requirements: Recommendations, essay and transcript. Must have at least one year of postsecondary education to be eligible.
Additional information: Application must be postmarked by February 12, 1999.

Amount of award:	$2,500
Number of awards:	14
Number of applicants:	80
Application deadline:	February 12
Notification begins:	April 15
Total amount awarded:	$35,000

Contact:
Society for Technical Communication
19 Johnston Avenue
Kingston, NY 12401-5211
Phone: 914-339-4927
Website: www.stc-va.org

Society for the Psychological Study of Lesbian and Gay Issues

Malyon-Smith Scholarship Award

Type of award: Research grant, renewable.
Intended use: For master's study.
Eligibility: Applicant must be U.S. citizen or permanent resident.
Basis for selection: Major/career interest in psychology. Applicant must demonstrate seriousness of purpose and service orientation.
Application requirements: Proof of eligibility and research proposal.
Additional information: Candidate must be enrolled in a Graduate Psychology program. Proposals must concern issues of importance to G, L, B & T individuals, groups or communities.

Amount of award:	$1,000
Application deadline:	February 1

Contact:
The Society for the Psychological Study of Lesbian and Gay Issues
Texas Tech University - Dept. of Psychology
222 Psychology Bldg.
Lubbock, TX 79409-2051

Society for the Psychological Study of Social Issues

Allport Intergroup Relations Prize

Type of award: Scholarship.
Intended use: For graduate or non-degree study.
Basis for selection: Competition in Writing/journalism. The best paper or article of the year on intergroup relations. Major/career interest in psychology; social and behavioral sciences.
Application requirements: Research proposal. Must submit research paper on intergroup relations involving variables of race, sex, age, and socio-economic status.
Additional information: Criteria: the originality of the contribution, whether theoretical or empirical, will be given special weight. The research area of intergroup relations includes such dimensions as age, gender, socio-economic status, as well as ethnicity.

Amount of award:	$1,000
Number of awards:	1
Number of applicants:	60
Application deadline:	December 31
Total amount awarded:	$1,000

Contact:
Society for the Psychological Study of Social Issues
Gordon Allport Intergroup Relations Prize
P.O. Box 1248
Ann Arbor, MI 48106-1248
Phone: 734-662-9130
Website: www.umich.edu/~sociss

Clara Mayo Grants-In-Aid

Type of award: Research grant.
Intended use: For master's, doctoral study.
Basis for selection: Major/career interest in psychology; sociology; political science/government; history.
Application requirements: Research proposal. Budget, curriculum vitae.
Additional information: Grants in support of masters theses or pre-dissertation research on sexism, racism, or prejudice.

Amount of award:	$500-$2,000
Number of awards:	12
Number of applicants:	50
Application deadline:	March 31
Total amount awarded:	$15,000

Contact:
Society for the Psychological Study of Social Issues
Mayo Grants Program
P.O. Box 1248
Ann Arbor, MI 48106-1248
Phone: 313-662-9130
Website: www.umich.edu/~sociss

Klineberg Award

Type of award: Scholarship.
Intended use: For graduate or non-degree study.
Basis for selection: Competition in Writing/journalism. The best paper or article of the year on intercultural or international relations. Major/career interest in psychology; social and behavioral sciences. Applicant must demonstrate high academic achievement.
Additional information: Graduate students encouraged to submit papers. Must provide five copies of paper. The originality of the contribution, whether theoretical or empirical, will be given special weight.

Amount of award:	$1,000
Number of awards:	1
Number of applicants:	35
Application deadline:	February 1
Total amount awarded:	$1,000

Contact:
Society for the Psychological Study of Social Issues
Klineberg Award Committee
P.O. Box 1248
Ann Arbor, MI 48106-1248
Phone: 313-662-9130
Website: www.umich.edu

Louise Kidder Early Career Award

Type of award: Research grant.
Intended use: For postgraduate, non-degree study.
Basis for selection: Major/career interest in psychology; social and behavioral sciences. Applicant must demonstrate seriousness of purpose.
Application requirements: Recommendations and nomination. Curriculum vitae.
Additional information: Nominees should have made substantial contributions to social issues research within five years of receiving graduate degree and have demonstrated potential to continue such contributions.

Amount of award:	$500
Number of awards:	1
Application deadline:	May 1
Total amount awarded:	$500

Contact:
Society for the Psychological Study of Social Issues Kidder Award Committee
P.O. Box 1248
Ann Arbor, MI 48106-1248
Phone: 313-662-9130
Website: www.umich.edu

Social Issues Dissertation Award

Type of award: Scholarship.
Intended use: For full-time graduate study.
Basis for selection: Competition in Writing/journalism. Dissertation must demonstrate scientific excellence and potential application to social problems. Major/career interest in psychology; social and behavioral sciences. Applicant must demonstrate high academic achievement.
Application requirements: Research proposal. Applicant must provide 4 copies of dissertation abstract with all identification deleted, 1 copy of abstract with identification. Must include dissertation advisor acceptance certification.
Additional information: Dissertation must have been accepted between March 1 of the previous year and March 1 of the current year.

Amount of award:	$400-$600
Number of awards:	2
Number of applicants:	50
Application deadline:	April 1
Notification begins:	August 1
Total amount awarded:	$1,000

Contact:
Society for the Psychological Study of Social Issues
Dissertation Award Committee
P.O. Box 1248
Ann Arbor, MI 48106-1248
Phone: 313-662-9130
Website: www.umich.edu

Social Issues Internship Program

Type of award: Research grant.
Intended use: For senior, master's, doctoral or postgraduate study.
Basis for selection: Major/career interest in psychology; social and behavioral sciences. Applicant must demonstrate seriousness of purpose, service orientation and high academic achievement.
Application requirements: Recommendations and research proposal. Proposal must include budget and statement concerning participant protection. Resume.
Additional information: To encourage intervention projects, non-partisan advocacy projects, applied research, writing and implementation of public policy. Award covers research costs and community organization. Proposals are invited for applying social science principals to social issues, in cooperation with a community, city, or state government organization, public interest group, or other not-for-profit entity.

Amount of award:	$1,500-$2,500
Application deadline:	November 1, May 1

Contact:
Society for the Psychological Study of Social Issues Central Office
Attn: Applied Social Issues Internship
P.O. Box 1248
Ann Arbor, MI 48106-1248
Phone: 313-662-9130
Website: www.umich.edu

Social Issues Sages Program

Type of award: Research grant.
Intended use: For non-degree study.
Basis for selection: Major/career interest in psychology; social and behavioral sciences.
Application requirements: Recommendations and research proposal. Curriculum vitae and letter from sponsoring organization. Three copies of project proposal with budget.
Additional information: Applicant must be retired social scientist/scholar or researcher over 60. Proposals are invited for research projects applying social science principals to social issues in cooperation with a community, city, or state, or federal government organization, public interest group, or other not-for-profit entity.

Amount of award:	$2,000
Application deadline:	May 1
Notification begins:	July 1

Contact:
Society for the Psychological Study of Social Issues SAGES Committee
P.O. Box 1248
Ann Arbor, MI 48106-1248
Phone: 313-662-9130
Website: www.umich.edu

Society for the Scientific Study of Sexuality

Scientific Study of Sexuality Student Grant

Type of award: Research grant.
Intended use: For master's, doctoral or first professional study.
Basis for selection: Major/career interest in science, general; social and behavioral sciences.
Application requirements: Research proposal. Letter from chair of department, biographical sketch, proposed project budget.
Additional information: Grant to conduct research; not a scholarship.

Amount of award:	$750
Number of awards:	3
Number of applicants:	30
Application deadline:	September 1, February 1
Notification begins:	November 1, May 1
Total amount awarded:	$2,250

Contact:
Society for the Scientific Study of Sexuality
P.O. Box 208
Mount Vernon, IA 52314-0208
Phone: 319-895-8407
Website: www.ssc.wisc.edu/ssss

Society of Actuaries/ Casualty Actuarial Society

Actuarial Society Minority Scholarship

Type of award: Scholarship, renewable.
Intended use: For full-time freshman, sophomore, junior or senior study at accredited 4-year institution.
Eligibility: Applicant must be Alaskan native, American Indian, African American, Mexican American, Hispanic American or Puerto Rican. Applicant must be U.S. citizen or permanent resident.
Basis for selection: Major/career interest in mathematics; insurance/actuarial science. Applicant must demonstrate financial need and high academic achievement.
Application requirements: Recommendations, transcript, proof of eligibility and nomination by faculty members or actuarial supervisors. SAT or ACT scores. CSS PROFILE application required.

Amount of award:	$1,000-$1,200
Number of awards:	24
Number of applicants:	60
Application deadline:	May 1
Notification begins:	July 15
Total amount awarded:	$23,900

Contact:
Society of Actuaries/Casualty Actuarial Society
475 North Martingale Road
Suite 800
Schaumburg, IL 60173-2226
Phone: 847-706-3543
Website: www.soa.org

Society of Architectural Historians

Architectural Study Tour Scholarship

Type of award: Scholarship.
Intended use: For master's, doctoral study.
Basis for selection: Competition in Visual arts. Major/career interest in architecture. Applicant must demonstrate high academic achievement.
Application requirements: Interview and essay.
Additional information: Scholarship must be used in SAH study tour.

Amount of award:	$800-$1,000
Number of applicants:	4
Total amount awarded:	$800

Edilia and Francois-Auguste de Montequin Fellowship

Type of award: Research grant.
Intended use: For graduate or postgraduate study.

Basis for selection: Major/career interest in architecture. Applicant must demonstrate high academic achievement.
Application requirements: Recommendations and research proposal.
Additional information: Must have an interest in architectural history.
- **Amount of award:** $1,000-$1,000
- **Number of awards:** 1
- **Number of applicants:** 10
- **Application deadline:** December 15
- **Total amount awarded:** $1,000

Rosann S. Berry Annual Meeting Fellowship

Type of award: Scholarship.
Intended use: For master's, doctoral study.
Basis for selection: Major/career interest in architecture. Applicant must demonstrate high academic achievement.
Application requirements: Recommendations and research proposal.
Additional information: Funds cover travel to the SAH annual meeting. Must have an interest in architectural history.
- **Amount of award:** $500-$500
- **Number of applicants:** 8
- **Application deadline:** December 15
- **Total amount awarded:** $500

Rosann S. Berry Annual Meeting Fellowship

Type of award: Scholarship.
Intended use: For freshman, sophomore study.
Basis for selection: Competition in Visual arts. Major/career interest in history. Applicant must demonstrate high academic achievement.
Application requirements: Interview and essay.
Additional information: Funds cover travel to the SAH annual meeting. Must have an interest in architectural history.
- **Amount of award:** $500-$500
- **Number of applicants:** 4
- **Application deadline:** December 15
- **Total amount awarded:** $500

Sally Kress Tompkins Fellowship

Type of award: Internship.
Intended use: For master's, doctoral study.
Basis for selection: Major/career interest in architecture; history.
Application requirements: Recommendations and essay.
Additional information: Must have an interest in architectural history and preservation.
- **Amount of award:** $7,500-$7,500
- **Number of awards:** 1
- **Number of applicants:** 10
- **Application deadline:** January 15
- **Total amount awarded:** $7,500

Contact:
Society of Architectural Historians
1365 N. Astor St.
Chicago, IL 60610-2144
Website: www.sah.org

Society of Automotive Engineers

Automotive Engineers Engineering Scholarship

Type of award: Scholarship, renewable.
Intended use: For full-time undergraduate study at accredited 2-year or 4-year institution in United States.
Eligibility: Applicant must be high school senior. Applicant must be U.S. citizen.
Basis for selection: Major/career interest in engineering. Applicant must demonstrate depth of character, leadership and high academic achievement.
Application requirements: $5 application fee. Essay and transcript.
Additional information: Must have 3.25 GPA and rank in 90th percentile on ACT/SAT I.
- **Amount of award:** $500-$5,000
- **Number of awards:** 60
- **Number of applicants:** 3,000
- **Application deadline:** December 1
- **Notification begins:** May 30
- **Total amount awarded:** $350,000

Society of Automotive Engineers Doctoral Scholars Loan

Type of award: Loan, renewable.
Intended use: For full-time doctoral study at accredited graduate institution.
Eligibility: Applicant must be U.S. citizen, permanent resident or Canadian or Mexican citizen.
Basis for selection: Major/career interest in engineering.
Application requirements: Recommendations, essay and transcript.
Additional information: Applicant must be a U.S., Canadian, or Mexican citizen. Established to assist promising engineering graduate students to pursue careers in engineering teaching at the college level. Must be enrolled in an engineering program accredited by Accreditation Board for Engineering and Technology (ABET), Canadian Accreditation Board (CAB), or the equivalent in Mexico.
- **Amount of award:** $2,500-$5,000
- **Number of awards:** 12
- **Number of applicants:** 30
- **Application deadline:** April 1
- **Notification begins:** May 30
- **Total amount awarded:** $60,000

Yanmar Scholarship

Type of award: Scholarship, renewable.
Intended use: For full-time senior, master's study at 4-year or graduate institution.
Eligibility: Applicant must be U.S. citizen, permanent resident or Canadian or Mexican citizen.
Basis for selection: Major/career interest in engineering.
Application requirements: Essay, transcript and proof of eligibility.
Additional information: Applicant must be a citizen of the

U.S., Canada or Mexico. Must pursue a course of study or research related to the conservation of energy in transportation, agriculture, construction, or power generation. Emphasis is placed on research or study related to the internal combustion engine.

Amount of award:	$1,000
Number of awards:	2
Number of applicants:	20
Application deadline:	April 1
Notification begins:	May 30
Total amount awarded:	$2,000

Contact:
Society of Automotive Engineers
Lori Pail
400 Commonwealth Drive
Warrendale, PA 15096-0001
Phone: 724-772-8534
Website: www.sae.org

Society of Daughters of the United States Army

Daughters of United States Army Scholarship

Type of award: Scholarship, renewable.
Intended use: For full-time undergraduate study at accredited postsecondary institution.
Eligibility: Applicant must be female. Applicant must be descendant of veteran, child of veteran or deceased veteran who served in the Army. Applicant must be a daughter or granddaughter (including step or adopted) of a career warrant (WO 1-5) or commissioned (2nd & 1st LT, CPT, MAJ, COL and BG, MG, LT or full General) officer ofthe U.S. Army who: (1) is currently on active duty, (2) retired after at least 20 years ACTIVE service or for medical reasons before 20 years of ACTIVE service, (3) died while on ACTIVE duty or after retiring with 20 or more years of ACTIVE service. If the retirement is before 20 years, it must be a medical retirement.
Basis for selection: Applicant must demonstrate depth of character, leadership, patriotism, seriousness of purpose, service orientation, financial need and high academic achievement.
Application requirements: Recommendations, essay and transcript. Include resume. Applicant must provide the name, rank, and service number of her qualifying family member, inclusive dates of their active duty, and source of commission.
Additional information: Minimum 3.0 GPA required for at least three years. Send SASE.

Amount of award:	$1,000
Number of awards:	8
Number of applicants:	471
Application deadline:	March 1
Notification begins:	May 1

Contact:
Society of Daughters of the United States Army
Janet B. Otto, Chairman
7717 Rockledge Court
Springfield, VA 22152-3854

Society of Exploration Geophysicists

Society of Exploration Geophysicists Scholarship

Type of award: Scholarship, renewable.
Intended use: For full-time freshman, sophomore, junior, senior or graduate study at 4-year or graduate institution in or outside United States.
Eligibility: Applicant must be high school senior.
Basis for selection: Major/career interest in geophysics; geology/earth sciences; physics. Applicant must demonstrate high academic achievement.
Application requirements: Recommendations, transcript and proof of eligibility.
Additional information: Minimum 3.0 GPA. Must intend to pursue career in exploration geophysics (graduate students in operations, teaching, or research).

Amount of award:	$200-$5,000
Number of awards:	82
Number of applicants:	300
Application deadline:	March 1
Notification begins:	June 1
Total amount awarded:	$97,500

Contact:
Society of Exploration Geophysicists Foundation
P.O. Box 702740
Tulsa, OK 74137-2740

Society of Hispanic Professional Engineers Foundation

Hispanic Professional Engineers Educational Grant

Type of award: Scholarship, renewable.
Intended use: For full-time undergraduate or graduate study at 2-year, 4-year or graduate institution.
Basis for selection: Major/career interest in engineering; chemistry; physics; science, general. Applicant must demonstrate financial need and high academic achievement.
Application requirements: Recommendations and essay.
Additional information: Include SASE with application requests. Applications available in beginning of September.

Amount of award:	$500-$7,000
Number of awards:	274
Number of applicants:	1,001
Application deadline:	April 15
Notification begins:	June 15
Total amount awarded:	$220,000

Contact:
Society of Hispanic Professional Engineers Foundation
5400 East Olympic Boulevard
Suite 210
Los Angeles, CA 90022

Society of Manufacturing Engineers

Caterpillar Scholars Award

Type of award: Scholarship, renewable.
Intended use: For full-time sophomore, junior or senior study at vocational, 2-year or 4-year institution in United States.
Eligibility: Minority students may apply as incoming freshmen.
Basis for selection: Major/career interest in manufacturing technologies; engineering. Applicant must demonstrate high academic achievement.
Additional information: Must have completed 30 credit hours. Minimum 3.0 GPA required.
    Amount of award: $2,000
    Number of awards: 5
    Application deadline: March 1
    Notification begins: June 15
    Total amount awarded: $10,000

Lucile B. Kaufman Women's Scholarship

Type of award: Scholarship, renewable.
Intended use: For full-time sophomore, junior or senior study at vocational, 2-year or 4-year institution in United States.
Eligibility: Applicant must be female.
Basis for selection: Major/career interest in manufacturing technologies; engineering. Applicant must demonstrate high academic achievement.
Additional information: Must have 3.5 GPA. Must have completed minimum of 30 credits.
    Amount of award: $1,000
    Number of awards: 5
    Application deadline: March 1
    Notification begins: June 15
    Total amount awarded: $1,000

M. & E. Walker Scholarship

Type of award: Scholarship, renewable.
Intended use: For full-time sophomore, junior or senior study at accredited vocational, 2-year or 4-year institution in United States.
Basis for selection: Major/career interest in manufacturing technologies; engineering. Applicant must demonstrate high academic achievement.
Additional information: Applicants must have 3.5 GPA. Must have minimum 30 credits.
    Amount of award: $500
    Number of awards: 34
    Application deadline: March 1
    Notification begins: June 15
    Total amount awarded: $17,000

W.E. Weisel Scholarship

Type of award: Scholarship, renewable.
Intended use: For full-time sophomore, junior or senior study at accredited 2-year or 4-year institution in United States in Canada only.
Eligibility: Applicant must be U.S. citizen.
Basis for selection: Major/career interest in manufacturing technologies; robotics; engineering. Applicant must demonstrate high academic achievement.
Additional information: Must have 3.5 GPA and minimum of 30 credits.
    Amount of award: $1,000
    Number of awards: 1
    Application deadline: March 1
    Notification begins: June 15
    Total amount awarded: $1,000

Wayne Kay Graduate Fellowship

Type of award: Scholarship.
Intended use: For full-time master's, doctoral study.
Basis for selection: Major/career interest in manufacturing technologies; engineering. Applicant must demonstrate depth of character, leadership and high academic achievement.
Additional information: Must have 3.5 GPA.
    Amount of award: $5,000
    Number of awards: 10
    Application deadline: March 1
    Notification begins: June 15
    Total amount awarded: $50,000

Wayne Kay Undergraduate Scholarship

Type of award: Scholarship, renewable.
Intended use: For full-time junior, senior study at 2-year or 4-year institution in United States.
Basis for selection: Major/career interest in manufacturing technologies; engineering. Applicant must demonstrate high academic achievement.
Additional information: Applicants must have completed 30 credit hours. Minimum 3.5 GPA required.
    Amount of award: $2,500
    Number of awards: 10
    Application deadline: March 1
    Notification begins: June 15

Contact:
Society of Manufacturing Engineers
Scholarship Review Committee
One SME Drive, P.O. Box 930
Dearborn, MI 48121-0930
Phone: 313-271-1500 x512
Website: www.sme.org/foundation

Society of Nuclear Medicine

Education and Reseach Foundation Tetalman Award

Type of award: Scholarship.
Intended use: For doctoral, first professional, postgraduate or non-degree study.
Basis for selection: Major/career interest in nuclear medicine. Applicant must demonstrate seriousness of purpose, service orientation and high academic achievement.
Application requirements: Recommendations, essay, proof

of eligibility and research proposal. Paper supporting current research efforts, curriculum vitae.
Additional information: Certification in nuclear medicine or nuclear radiology or completion of Ph.D. program within last seven years required. Award based on research accomplishments, teaching, clinical service and administration.

Amount of award:	$1,500
Number of awards:	1
Number of applicants:	5
Application deadline:	March 1
Notification begins:	June 1
Total amount awarded:	$1,500

Contact:
S. Weiss, Administrative Director
CNMT:Children's Mem. Hospital
2300 Children's Plaza, No. 242
Chicago, IL 60614
Phone: 773-880-4416
Fax: 773-880-3839
Website: www.pet.upenn.edu/snmerf

Society of Range Management

Masonic Range Science Scholarship

Type of award: Scholarship.
Intended use: For full-time freshman, sophomore study.
Basis for selection: Major/career interest in agriculture; environmental science; wildlife/fisheries. Applicant must demonstrate leadership and high academic achievement.
Application requirements: Recommendations, essay, transcript and nomination by SRM, NACD or SWCS member.

Amount of award:	$1,000
Number of awards:	1
Number of applicants:	1
Application deadline:	January 15
Notification begins:	February 13
Total amount awarded:	$1,000

Contact:
Society of Range Management
1839 York Street
Denver, CO 80206
Phone: 303-355-7070

Society of Women Engineers

Admiral Grace M. Hopper Scholarship

Type of award: Scholarship.
Intended use: For full-time freshman study at accredited 4-year institution in United States.
Eligibility: Applicant must be female. Applicant must be U.S. citizen or permanent resident.
Basis for selection: Major/career interest in engineering; computer and information sciences.
Application requirements: Recommendations, essay, transcript and proof of eligibility.
Additional information: Applicants must plan to attend an ABET-accredited program or SWE approved school.

Amount of award:	$1,000
Number of awards:	5
Application deadline:	May 15
Notification begins:	September 15
Total amount awarded:	$5,000

Contact:
Society of Women Engineers
120 Wall Street, 11th Floor
New York, NY 10005-3902
Phone: 212-509-9577
Fax: 212-509-0224
Website: www.swe.org

Anne Maureen Whitney Barrow Memorial Scholarship

Type of award: Scholarship, renewable.
Intended use: For full-time freshman study at accredited 4-year institution in United States.
Eligibility: Applicant must be female. Applicant must be U.S. citizen or permanent resident.
Basis for selection: Major/career interest in engineering.
Application requirements: Recommendations, essay, transcript and proof of eligibility.
Additional information: Must attend an ABET-accredited program or a SWE-approved school.

Amount of award:	$5,000
Number of awards:	1
Application deadline:	May 15
Total amount awarded:	$5,000

Contact:
Society of Women Engineers
120 Wall Street, 11th Floor
New York, NY 10005-3902
Phone: 212-509-9577

David Sarnoff Reseach Center Scholarship

Type of award: Scholarship.
Intended use: For full-time junior study at accredited 4-year institution.
Eligibility: Applicant must be female. Applicant must be U.S. citizen.
Basis for selection: Major/career interest in engineering. Applicant must demonstrate high academic achievement.
Application requirements: Recommendations, essay, transcript and proof of eligibility.
Additional information: Applicant must be enrolled in ABET-accredited program or SWE-approved institution. Send SASE for application.

Amount of award:	$1,500
Number of awards:	1
Application deadline:	February 1
Notification begins:	May 1
Total amount awarded:	$1,500

Contact:
Society of Women Engineers
120 Wall Street, 11th Floor
New York, NY 10005-3902
Phone: 212-509-9577
Fax: 212-509-0224

Dorothy Lemke Howarth Scholarship

Type of award: Scholarship.
Intended use: For full-time sophomore study at accredited 4-year institution.
Eligibility: Applicant must be female. Applicant must be U.S. citizen.
Basis for selection: Major/career interest in engineering. Applicant must demonstrate high academic achievement.
Application requirements: Recommendations, essay, transcript and proof of eligibility.
Additional information: Applicant must be enrolled in ABET-accredited program or SWE-approved school. Minimum GPA 3.5. Send SASE for application.

Amount of award:	$2,000
Number of awards:	5
Application deadline:	February 1
Notification begins:	May 1
Total amount awarded:	$10,000

Contact:
Society of Women Engineers
120 Wall Street
New York, NY 10005-3902
Phone: 212-509-9577
Fax: 212-509-0224

Ivy Parker Memorial Scholarship

Type of award: Scholarship.
Intended use: For full-time junior, senior study at accredited 4-year institution in United States.
Eligibility: Applicant must be female. Applicant must be U.S. citizen or permanent resident.
Basis for selection: Major/career interest in engineering. Applicant must demonstrate financial need and high academic achievement.
Application requirements: Recommendations, essay, transcript and proof of eligibility.
Additional information: Must be enrolled in ABET-accredited program or SWE-approved school. Minimum GPA 3.5. Send SASE for application.

Amount of award:	$2,000
Number of awards:	1
Application deadline:	February 1
Notification begins:	May 1
Total amount awarded:	$2,000

Contact:
Society of Women Engineers
120 Wall Street, 11th Floor
New York, NY 10005-3902
Phone: 212-509-9577
Fax: 212-509-0224

Lillian Moller Gilbreth Scholarship

Type of award: Scholarship.
Intended use: For full-time junior, senior study at accredited 4-year institution in United States.
Eligibility: Applicant must be female. Applicant must be U.S. citizen or permanent resident.
Basis for selection: Major/career interest in engineering. Applicant must demonstrate high academic achievement.
Application requirements: Recommendations, essay, transcript and proof of eligibility.
Additional information: Must be enrolled in ABET-accredited program or SWE-approved school. Send SASE for application.

Amount of award:	$5,000
Number of awards:	1
Application deadline:	February 1
Notification begins:	May 1
Total amount awarded:	$5,000

Contact:
Society of Women Engineers
120 Wall Street, 11th Floor
New York, NY 10005-3902
Phone: 212-509-9577
Fax: 212-509-0224

Olive Lynn Salembier Scholarship

Type of award: Scholarship.
Intended use: For undergraduate, graduate or non-degree study at accredited 4-year or graduate institution in United States.
Eligibility: Applicant must be female, adult returning student. Applicant must be U.S. citizen or permanent resident.
Basis for selection: Major/career interest in engineering.
Application requirements: Recommendations, essay, transcript and proof of eligibility.
Additional information: Applicant must have been out of engineering job market for minimum of two years and currently seeking credentials to re-enter job market as engineer. Program must be ABET-accredited or school, SWE-approved. Send SASE for application.

Amount of award:	$2,000
Number of awards:	1
Application deadline:	May 15
Notification begins:	September 15
Total amount awarded:	$2,000

Contact:
Society of Women Engineers
120 Wall Street, 11th Floor
New York, NY 10005-3902
Phone: 212-509-9577
Fax: 212-509-0224

Westinghouse Bertha Lamme Scholarship

Type of award: Scholarship.
Intended use: For full-time freshman study at 4-year institution in United States.
Eligibility: Applicant must be female, high school senior. Applicant must be U.S. citizen or permanent resident.
Basis for selection: Major/career interest in engineering. Applicant must demonstrate high academic achievement.

Application requirements: Recommendations, essay, transcript and proof of eligibility.
Additional information: Applicant must be entering an ABET-accredited program or SWE-approved institution. Send SASE for application.

Amount of award:	$1,000
Number of awards:	3
Application deadline:	May 15
Notification begins:	September 15
Total amount awarded:	$3,000

Contact:
Society of Women Engineers
120 Wall Street, 11th Floor
New York, NY 10005-3902
Phone: 212-509-9577
Fax: 212-509-0224

Women Engineers Chevron Scholarship

Type of award: Scholarship.
Intended use: For full-time sophomore, junior study at accredited 4-year institution in United States.
Eligibility: Applicant must be female. Applicant must be U.S. citizen or permanent resident.
Basis for selection: Major/career interest in engineering, petroleum; engineering, chemical; engineering, mechanical. Applicant must demonstrate high academic achievement.
Application requirements: Recommendations, essay, transcript and proof of eligibility.
Additional information: One award each for sophomore and junior engineering student. Minimum 3.5 GPA. Must be enrolled in ABET-accredited program or SWE-approved school. Send SASE for application.

Amount of award:	$2,000
Number of awards:	2
Application deadline:	February 1
Notification begins:	May 1
Total amount awarded:	$4,000

Contact:
Society of Women Engineers
120 Wall Street, 11th Floor
New York, NY 10005-3902
Phone: 212-509-9577
Fax: 212-509-0224

Women Engineers Chrysler Corporation Re-entry Scholarship

Type of award: Scholarship.
Intended use: For undergraduate study at accredited 4-year or graduate institution in United States.
Eligibility: Applicant must be female, adult returning student. Applicant must be U.S. citizen or permanent resident.
Basis for selection: Major/career interest in computer and information sciences; engineering.
Application requirements: Recommendations, essay, transcript and proof of eligibility.
Additional information: Send SASE for application. Program must be ABET-accredited, or school SWE-approved.

Amount of award:	$2,000
Number of awards:	1
Application deadline:	May 15
Notification begins:	September 15
Total amount awarded:	$2,000

Contact:
Society of Women Engineers
120 Wall Street, 11th Floor
New York, NY 10005-3902
Phone: 212-509-9577

Women Engineers Chrysler Corporation Scholarship

Type of award: Scholarship.
Intended use: For freshman study at accredited 4-year institution in United States.
Eligibility: Applicant must be female. Applicant must be U.S. citizen or permanent resident.
Basis for selection: Major/career interest in computer and information sciences; engineering.
Application requirements: Recommendations, essay, transcript and proof of eligibility.
Additional information: School must be SWE approved, or program of study ABET-accredited. Send SASE for application.

Amount of award:	$1,500
Number of awards:	2
Application deadline:	May 15
Notification begins:	September 15
Total amount awarded:	$3,000

Contact:
Society of Women Engineers
120 Wall Street, 11th Floor
New York, NY 10005-3902
Phone: 212-509-9577

Women Engineers Chrysler Corporation Scholarship (Minorities)

Type of award: Scholarship.
Intended use: For full-time sophomore, junior or senior study at accredited 4-year institution in United States.
Eligibility: Applicant must be of minority background. Applicant must be female. Applicant must be U.S. citizen or permanent resident.
Basis for selection: Major/career interest in computer and information sciences; engineering. Applicant must demonstrate high academic achievement.
Application requirements: Recommendations, essay, transcript and proof of eligibility.
Additional information: Minimum GPA 3.5. Send SASE for application. Must be enrolled in ABET-accredited program or SWE-approved schools.

Society of Women Engineers: Women Engineers Chrysler Corporation Scholarship (Minorities)

Amount of award:	$1,750
Number of awards:	1
Application deadline:	February 1
Notification begins:	May 1
Total amount awarded:	$1,750

Contact:
Society of Women Engineers
120 Wall Street, 11th Floor
New York, NY 10005-3902
Phone: 212-509-9577
Fax: 212-509-0224

Women Engineers General Electric Foundation Scholarship

Type of award: Scholarship, renewable.
Intended use: For full-time freshman study at accredited 4-year institution.
Eligibility: Applicant must be female, high school senior. Applicant must be U.S. citizen.
Basis for selection: Major/career interest in engineering. Applicant must demonstrate high academic achievement.
Application requirements: Recommendations, essay, transcript and proof of eligibility.
Additional information: Must be enrolled in ABET-accredited program or SWE-approved school. Send SASE for application.

Amount of award:	$1,000
Number of awards:	12
Application deadline:	May 15
Notification begins:	September 15
Total amount awarded:	$12,000

Contact:
Society of Women Engineers
120 Wall Street, 11th Floor
New York, NY 10005-3902
Phone: 212-509-9577
Fax: 212-509-0224

Women Engineers General Motors Foundation Graduate Scholarship

Type of award: Scholarship.
Intended use: For full-time master's study at accredited graduate institution.
Eligibility: Applicant must be female. Applicant must be U.S. citizen or permanent resident.
Basis for selection: Major/career interest in engineering, chemical; engineering, electrical and electronic; engineering, materials; engineering, mechanical. Applicant must demonstrate leadership and high academic achievement.
Application requirements: Recommendations, essay, transcript and proof of eligibility.
Additional information: Awarded for first year Master's degree only. Minimum 3.5 GPA. Must hold a position of responsibility in a student organization. Applicant must be enrolled in ABET-accredited program or SWE-approved institution. Send SASE for application.

Amount of award:	$1,500
Number of awards:	1
Application deadline:	February 1
Notification begins:	May 1
Total amount awarded:	$1,500

Contact:
Society of Women Engineers
120 Wall Street, 11th Floor
New York, NY 10005-3902
Phone: 212-509-9577
Fax: 212-509-0224

Women Engineers General Motors Foundation Undergraduate Scholarship

Type of award: Scholarship, renewable.
Intended use: For full-time junior, senior study at accredited 4-year institution in United States.
Eligibility: Applicant must be female. Applicant must be U.S. citizen or permanent resident.
Basis for selection: Major/career interest in engineering, mechanical; engineering, chemical; engineering, electrical and electronic; engineering, materials. Applicant must demonstrate leadership and financial need.
Application requirements: Recommendations, essay, transcript and proof of eligibility.
Additional information: Minimum GPA 3.5. Must be enrolled in ABET-accredited program or SWE-approved school. Send SASE for application.

Amount of award:	$1,500
Number of awards:	4
Application deadline:	February 1
Notification begins:	May 1
Total amount awarded:	$6,000

Contact:
Society of Women Engineers
120 Wall Street, 11th Floor
New York, NY 10005-3902
Phone: 212-509-9577
Fax: 212-509-0224

Women Engineers GTE Foundation Scholarship

Type of award: Scholarship.
Intended use: For sophomore, junior study at accredited 4-year institution in United States.
Eligibility: Applicant must be female. Applicant must be U.S. citizen or permanent resident.
Basis for selection: Major/career interest in engineering, electrical and electronic; computer and information sciences.
Application requirements: Recommendations, essay, transcript and proof of eligibility.
Additional information: Must be enrolled in ABET-accredited program or SWE-approved institution. Send SASE for application.

Amount of award:	$1,000
Number of awards:	9
Application deadline:	February 1
Notification begins:	May 1
Total amount awarded:	$9,000

Contact:
Society of Women Engineers
120 Wall Street, 11th Floor
New York, NY 10005-3902
Phone: 212-509-9577
Fax: 212-509-0224

Women Engineers Men's Auxiliary Memorial Scholarship

Type of award: Scholarship.
Intended use: For full-time sophomore, junior or senior study at accredited 4-year institution in United States.
Eligibility: Applicant must be female. Applicant must be U.S. citizen or permanent resident.
Basis for selection: Major/career interest in engineering; computer and information sciences. Applicant must demonstrate financial need and high academic achievement.
Application requirements: Recommendations, essay, transcript and proof of eligibility.
Additional information: Must be enrolled in ABET-accredited program or SWE-approved institution. Send SASE for application.

Amount of award:	$1,000-$2,000
Number of awards:	3
Application deadline:	February 1
Notification begins:	May 1
Total amount awarded:	$5,000

Contact:
Society of Women Engineers
120 Wall Street, 11th Floor
New York, NY 10005-3902
Phone: 212-509-9577
Fax: 212-509-0224

Women Engineers Microsoft Corporation Scholarship

Type of award: Scholarship.
Intended use: For sophomore, junior, senior or master's study at accredited 4-year institution in United States.
Eligibility: Applicant must be female. Applicant must be U.S. citizen or permanent resident.
Basis for selection: Major/career interest in computer and information sciences; engineering, computer. Applicant must demonstrate high academic achievement.
Application requirements: Recommendations, essay, transcript and proof of eligibility.
Additional information: Minimum GPA 3.5. Must be enrolled in ABET-accredited program or SWE-approved institution.

Amount of award:	$1,000
Number of awards:	9
Application deadline:	February 1
Notification begins:	May 1
Total amount awarded:	$9,000

Contact:
Society of Women Engineers
120 Wall Street, 11th Floor
New York, NY 10005-3902
Phone: 212-509-9577
Fax: 212-509-0224

Women Engineers Microsoft Corporation Scholarship (Graduate)

Type of award: Scholarship.
Intended use: For master's study at accredited graduate institution.
Eligibility: Applicant must be female.
Basis for selection: Major/career interest in computer and information sciences; engineering, computer. Applicant must demonstrate high academic achievement.
Additional information: Program of study must be ABET-accredited, or institution SWE-approved.

Amount of award:	$1,000
Number of awards:	10,000
Application deadline:	February 1
Notification begins:	May 1
Total amount awarded:	$10

Contact:
Scholarship Committee
120 Wall Street, 11th Floor
New York, NY 10005-3902
Phone: 212-509-9577
Fax: 212-509-0224

Women Engineers Rockwell International Corporation Scholarships

Type of award: Scholarship.
Intended use: For full-time junior study at accredited 4-year institution in United States.
Eligibility: Applicant must be female. Applicant must be U.S. citizen or permanent resident.
Basis for selection: Major/career interest in electronics; aerospace. Applicant must demonstrate leadership and financial need.
Application requirements: Recommendations, essay, transcript and proof of eligibility.
Additional information: Minimum 3.5 GPA. Must be enrolled in ABET-accredited program or an SWE-approved school. Send SASE for application.

Amount of award:	$3,000
Number of awards:	2
Application deadline:	February 1
Notification begins:	May 1
Total amount awarded:	$6,000

Contact:
Society of Women Engineers
120 Wall Street, 11th Floor
New York, NY 10005-3902
Phone: 212-509-9577
Fax: 212-509-0224

Women Engineers Stone and Webster Scholarship

Type of award: Scholarship.
Intended use: For full-time sophomore, junior, senior or master's study at accredited 4-year institution in United States.
Eligibility: Applicant must be of minority background. Applicant must be female. Applicant must be U.S. citizen or permanent resident.
Basis for selection: Major/career interest in engineering, chemical; engineering, civil; engineering, electrical and electronic; engineering, environmental; computer and information sciences.
Application requirements: Recommendations, essay, transcript and proof of eligibility.
Additional information: One scholarship each in chemical, civil, electrical, environmental, and mechanical engineering. For minority women only. Must be enrolled in ABET-accredited program or SWE- approved institution. Minimum 3.5 GPA. Send SASE for application.

Amount of award:	$1,000-$1,500
Number of awards:	4
Application deadline:	February 1
Notification begins:	May 1
Total amount awarded:	$4,500

Contact:
Society of Women Engineers
120 Wall Street, 11th Floor
New York, NY 10005-3902
Phone: 212-509-9577
Fax: 212-509-0224

Women Engineers TRW Scholarship

Type of award: Scholarship.
Intended use: For full-time freshman study at accredited 4-year institution in United States.
Eligibility: Applicant must be female, high school senior. Applicant must be U.S. citizen or permanent resident.
Basis for selection: Major/career interest in engineering. Applicant must demonstrate high academic achievement.
Application requirements: Nomination by The student chapter will nominate candidates from the incoming freshman class based on academic performance.
Additional information: Must be entering an ABET-accredited or SWE-approved institution. Send SASE for application. Administered locally by SWE's best national, regional, and new student sections.

Amount of award:	$200-$500
Number of awards:	11
Application deadline:	May 15
Notification begins:	September 15
Total amount awarded:	$2,500

Contact:
Society of Women Engineers
120 Wall Street, 11th Floor
New York, NY 10005-3902
Phone: 212-509-9577
Fax: 212-509-0224

Solomon R. Guggenheim Foundation

Guggenheim Foundation Internship

Type of award: Internship.
Intended use: For junior, senior or graduate study.
Basis for selection: Major/career interest in art, art history; arts management. Applicant must demonstrate depth of character, leadership, seriousness of purpose, service orientation and high academic achievement.
Application requirements: Interview, recommendations, essay and transcript. Include curriculum vitae.
Additional information: Previous museum/gallery experience important. Also open to students in arts education.

Amount of award:	$1,000
Number of awards:	12
Number of applicants:	200
Application deadline:	July 15, November 15
Total amount awarded:	$12,000

Contact:
Internship Coordinator
Internship Program
1071 Fifth Avenue
New York, NY 10128
Phone: 212-423-3557

Peggy Guggenheim Internship

Type of award: Internship.
Intended use: For undergraduate or graduate study.
Basis for selection: Major/career interest in arts, general; art, art history; museum studies. Applicant must demonstrate depth of character, leadership, seriousness of purpose and high academic achievement.
Application requirements: Recommendations and essay. Photograph.
Additional information: One-to-three month internship at Peggy Guggenheim Collection in Venice, Italy. Must be fluent in English and spoken Italian. Interns receive a monthly stipend.

Application deadline:	December 1

Contact:
Peggy Guggenheim Collection
Palazzo Venier dei Leoni
701 Dorsoduro, 30123 VENEZIA, Italy

Phone: 041-520-6288

Solomon R. Guggenheim Museum

Guggenheim Museum Internship

Type of award: Internship.
Intended use: For junior, senior or graduate study.
Basis for selection: Major/career interest in arts management; art, art history; arts, general; film/video; museum studies;

museum studies/administration. Applicant must demonstrate service orientation, financial need and high academic achievement.
Application requirements: Interview, recommendations, essay, transcript and proof of eligibility.
Additional information: Summer application deadline is February 1. Must have taken at least one course in modern art. Summer internship for graduate students only. Museum Internship Program gives preference to minority students who are residents of New York.

Amount of award:	$1,000
Number of awards:	25
Number of applicants:	300
Application deadline:	August 1, December 1
Total amount awarded:	$25,000

Contact:
Solomon R. Guggenheim Museum
1071 Fifth Avenue
New York, NY 10128
Phone: 2124233557
Website: www.guggenheim.org

Sons of Italy Foundation

Henry Salvatori Scholarship

Type of award: Scholarship.
Intended use: For full-time undergraduate study.
Eligibility: Applicant must be high school senior, of Italian heritage. Applicant must be U.S. citizen.
Basis for selection: Applicant must demonstrate depth of character, leadership, patriotism, seriousness of purpose, service orientation and high academic achievement.
Application requirements: $20 application fee. Recommendations, essay, transcript and proof of eligibility. SAT I/ACT scores and two letters of recommendation from public figures who have demonstrated the ideals of liberty, freedom, and equality in their work.
Additional information: Application deadline is in late February; contact sponsor for exact date.

Amount of award:	$5,000
Number of awards:	1
Number of applicants:	94
Total amount awarded:	$5,000

Sons of Italy National Leadership Grant

Type of award: Scholarship.
Intended use: For full-time undergraduate, master's or doctoral study at accredited vocational, 2-year, 4-year or graduate institution in United States.
Eligibility: Applicant must be of Italian heritage. Applicant must be U.S. citizen or Italy.
Basis for selection: Applicant must demonstrate depth of character, leadership, seriousness of purpose, service orientation and high academic achievement.
Application requirements: $20 application fee. Recommendations, essay, transcript and proof of eligibility. SAT I/ACT scores.
Additional information: Deadline is in late February; contact sponsor for exact date.

Amount of award:	$4,000-$5,000
Number of awards:	9
Number of applicants:	600
Notification begins:	April 30

Contact:
Order of Sons of Italy in America
219 E Street NE
Washington, DC 20002
Phone: 202-547-5106
Website: www.osia.org

Sons of Norway Foundation

King Olav V Norwegian-American Heritage Fund

Type of award: Scholarship.
Intended use: For full-time undergraduate, graduate or postgraduate study at accredited postsecondary institution.
Eligibility: Applicant must be Norwegian.
Basis for selection: Major/career interest in Scandinavian studies/research. Applicant must demonstrate depth of character, leadership, service orientation, financial need and high academic achievement.
Application requirements: Recommendations, essay, transcript and proof of eligibility.
Additional information: American applicants must have interest in Norwegian culture; Norwegian applicants must have interest in American culture.

Amount of award:	$500-$2,000
Number of awards:	9
Number of applicants:	100
Application deadline:	March 1
Notification begins:	May 1
Total amount awarded:	$8,000

Contact:
Sons of Norway Foundation
1455 West Lake Street
Minneapolis, MN 55408
Phone: 612-827-3611

Sony Corporation of America

Sony Corporation of America Internship

Type of award: Internship.
Intended use: For junior, senior or graduate study.
Basis for selection: Major/career interest in engineering; marketing.

Additional information: Eight week to One year internships available in electronics engineering, research marketing and sales. $250 to $500 per week. There is no deadline for applications. No formal application form, submit resume and cover letter.
Contact:
Internship Coordinator,. Sony Corporation of America
1 Sony Drive
Park Ridge, NJ 07656-8003

Sony Music Entertainment

SONY Credited Internship

Type of award: Internship.
Intended use: For undergraduate or graduate study.
Basis for selection: Major/career interest in business.
Application requirements: Interview, transcript and proof of eligibility.
Additional information: Full time, non-paid internship. Deadlines for Spring and Fall are rolling. Summer session deadline is March 31. Must be enrolled at an accredited university and provide verification of course credit. Interns are placed in various departments throughout company.
Contact:
Sony Music Entertainment
Credited Internship Program
550 Madison Avenue
New York, NY 10022-3211

SONY Minority Internship

Type of award: Internship.
Intended use: For undergraduate, master's or doctoral study.
Eligibility: Applicant must be American Indian, Asian American, African American, Mexican American, Hispanic American or Puerto Rican.
Application requirements: Resume and cover letter.
Additional information: Ten week internship in New York City. Stipend for undergraduates is $8/hour, graduate stipends are based on past experience. Undergraduates must submit resume and cover letter by March 31, graduates by January 15. Any applicants who wish to be placed at regional sales offices outside of New York must have application materials postmarked by January 31.
    Application deadline: March 31
Contact:
Sony Music Entertainment
Minority Internship Program
550 Madison Avenue
New York, NY 10022-3211

Southern Progress Corporation

Southern Progress Corporation Summer Internship

Type of award: Internship.
Intended use: For junior, senior or graduate study.
Basis for selection: Major/career interest in journalism; graphic arts and design; marketing; advertising; accounting; computer and information sciences.
Application requirements: Interview, recommendations and transcript.
Additional information: Summer application deadline is March 1, 1999. $280-$360 a week. Writing samples encouraged. 12 week internships in editorial, graphic design, market research, photography, advertising and accounting departments.
Amount of award:	$3,360-$4,320
Number of awards:	30
Number of applicants:	400
Application deadline:	July 1, October 1

Contact:
Internship Coordinator
P.O. Box 2581
Birmingham, AL 35209

Southface Energy Institute

Southface Internship

Type of award: Internship.
Intended use: For undergraduate or graduate study at accredited 2-year, 4-year or graduate institution in United States.
Eligibility: Applicant must be U.S. citizen or permanent resident.
Basis for selection: Major/career interest in landscape architecture; hydrology; business, management and administration; environmental science. Applicant must demonstrate high academic achievement.
Application requirements: Interview, recommendations and essay.
Additional information: Three to six month internship. 40 hours week. $335 a month, first 3 months. $50 month increase each month thereafter. Accomodations provided for non-Atlanta residents. Part-time internships available. Application deadlines are rolling. Provides intern with opportunity to work in alternative energy field. Open to high school students.
    Amount of award: $1,000-$2,305
Contact:
Southface Energy Institute
P.O. Box 5506
Atlanta, GA 30307
Website: www.southface.org/home/events/intern.html

Special Libraries Association

Special Libraries Association Affirmative Action Scholarship

Type of award: Scholarship.
Intended use: For master's study at accredited graduate institution. Designated institutions: In United States or Canada.
Eligibility: Applicant must be of minority background.
Basis for selection: Major/career interest in library science. Applicant must demonstrate financial need and high academic achievement.
Application requirements: Recommendations, essay, transcript and proof of eligibility.
Additional information: Special consideration to members of Special Libraries Association and those who have worked in special libraries.

Amount of award:	$6,000
Number of awards:	1
Application deadline:	October 31
Notification begins:	May 15
Total amount awarded:	$6,000

Special Libraries Scholarship

Type of award: Scholarship.
Intended use: For master's study. Designated institutions: In United States or Canada.
Basis for selection: Major/career interest in library science. Applicant must demonstrate financial need and high academic achievement.
Application requirements: Recommendations, essay, transcript and proof of eligibility.
Additional information: Special consideration given to members of Special Libraries Association and persons who have worked in special libraries. Open to undergraduate seniors and to those holding undergraduate degrees.

Amount of award:	$6,000
Number of awards:	3
Application deadline:	October 31
Notification begins:	May 15
Total amount awarded:	$18,000

Contact:
Special Libraries Association
1700 Eighteenth Street NW
Washington, DC 20009
Website: www.sla.org

Spencer Foundation

Aera/Spencer Research Training Fellowship

Type of award: Research grant.
Intended use: For doctoral study.
Basis for selection: Major/career interest in education; education, teacher. Applicant must demonstrate depth of character, leadership, seriousness of purpose and service orientation.
Application requirements: Recommendations, proof of eligibility and research proposal.
Additional information: Eligible scholars can be of any nationality and have completed their doctorate within the last five years and wish to conduct research related to education. Invitation only--Contact Spencer directly for information.
Contact:
The Spencer Foundation
The National Academy of Education
Stanford University, School fo Education, Ceras Bldg., Rm. 108
Stanford, CA 94305-3084

Practitioner Research Communication and Mentoring Grant

Type of award: Research grant.
Intended use: For graduate, postgraduate or non-degree study.
Basis for selection: Major/career interest in education; education, teacher. Applicant must demonstrate depth of character, leadership, seriousness of purpose, service orientation, financial need and high academic achievement.
Application requirements: Recommendations, proof of eligibility and research proposal.
Additional information: Teacher researchers, groups or networks of teacher researchers and collaborative partnerships between teacher researchers and university teachers are all eligible parties for this grant. Call Kerry McGill at ext. 630 for additional deadlines.

Amount of award:	$2,000-$15,000

Contact:
The Spencer Foundation
900 N. Michigan Ave., Suite 2800
Chicago, IL 60611-1542

Small Research Grants Program

Type of award: Research grant.
Intended use: For postgraduate study.
Basis for selection: Major/career interest in education; education, teacher. Applicant must demonstrate depth of character, leadership, seriousness of purpose and service orientation.
Application requirements: Recommendations, proof of eligibility and research proposal.
Additional information: Proposals for support should not exceed 1500 words and should be in the form of statements with relevant attachments. Two copies are required. Complete proposals will receive a response within three months of receipt by The Spencer Foundation. Researchers must have earned a doctorate in an academic discipline or professional field and must have experience in the teaching profession. Researchers must be currently affiliated with a school district or with a College of University; a research facility or a Cultural Institution.

Amount of award:	$1,000-$35,000

Contact:
The Spencer Foundation
900 N. Michigan Ave., Suite 2800
Chicago, IL 60611-1142

Spencer Dissertation Fellowship Program

Type of award: Research grant.
Intended use: For doctoral study at graduate institution in United States.
Eligibility: Applicant must be Candidates for Doctoral degree at a graduate school in the United States.
Basis for selection: Major/career interest in education; education, teacher. Applicant must demonstrate depth of character, leadership, seriousness of purpose and service orientation.
Application requirements: Recommendations, proof of eligibility and research proposal.
Additional information: Eligible scholars can be of any nationality and have completed their doctorate within the last five years and wish to condust research in the USA related to education.

Amount of award:	$20,000
Number of awards:	30
Application deadline:	November 1

Contact:
The Spencer Foundation
900 N. Michigan Ave., Suite 2800
Chicago, IL 60611-1542

Spencer Foundation Major Research Grants

Type of award: Research grant.
Intended use: For postgraduate study.
Basis for selection: Major/career interest in education; education, teacher. Applicant must demonstrate depth of character, leadership, seriousness of purpose and service orientation.
Application requirements: Recommendations, proof of eligibility and research proposal.
Additional information: Proposals for support should not exceed 1500 words and should be in the form of statements with relevant attachments. Researchers must be currently affiliated with a school district, College, University, research facility or a cultural institution. Researchers must have earned a doctorate in an academic discipline and/or professional field and must have experience in the teaching professions. $300,000 is not the guaranteed amount of the award. Award amount will be based on project needs.

Amount of award:	$300,000

Contact:
The Spencer Foundation
900 N. Michigan Ave., Suite 2800
Chicago, IL 60611-1542

Spencer Professional Development Research and Documentation Program

Type of award: Research grant.
Intended use: For master's, doctoral, postgraduate or non-degree study.
Basis for selection: Major/career interest in education; education, teacher. Applicant must demonstrate depth of character, leadership, seriousness of purpose and service orientation.
Application requirements: Recommendations, proof of eligibility and research proposal.
Additional information: Award to be used for studies on the professional development of adults working in elementary and secondary schools. Studies focused on pre-service teacher education programs are not eligible. Applicants, either individual or group, must be affiliated with a not-for-profit agency through which the funds will be distributed.

Amount of award:	$5,000-$500,000

Contact:
The Spencer Foundation
900 N. Michigan Ave., Suite 2800
Chicago, IL 60611-1542

Spencer Support for Scholars at Center for Advanced Study/Behavioral Sciences

Type of award: Research grant.
Intended use: For graduate, postgraduate or non-degree study.
Eligibility: Applicant must be U.S. citizen or permanent resident.
Basis for selection: Major/career interest in medical specialties/research. Applicant must demonstrate depth of character, leadership, seriousness of purpose and service orientation.
Application requirements: Recommendations, proof of eligibility and nomination.
Additional information: 3-5 scholars will be supported for research in issues of education, development, cognition and the social contexts of learning. Invitational program--Contact Spencer for further information.

Number of awards:	5

Contact:
The Spencer Foundation
The Center for Advanced Study in the Behavioral Sciences
202 Junipero Serra Blvd.
Stanford, CA 94305

SPIE - The International Society for Optical Engineering

Educational Optical Engineering Scholarship

Type of award: Scholarship.
Intended use: For undergraduate, graduate or non-degree study at accredited postsecondary institution in United States.
Basis for selection: Major/career interest in engineering; health sciences.
Application requirements: Recommendations.

Amount of award:	$500-$7,000
Number of awards:	25
Number of applicants:	135
Application deadline:	April 1
Notification begins:	September 1
Total amount awarded:	$68,500

Contact:
SPIE
PO BOX 10
Bellingham, WA 98227-0010
Phone: 360-676-3290 x659
Website: www.spie.org

Spina Bifida Association of America

Spina Bifida Association of America Scholarship Fund

Type of award: Scholarship.
Intended use: For undergraduate or graduate study at postsecondary institution in United States.
Basis for selection: Applicant must demonstrate financial need and high academic achievement.
Application requirements: Proof of eligibility.
Additional information: Open to all persons with Spina Bifida who are current members of the Spina Bifida Association of America. May be used for any postsecondary study, vocational or specialized training.

Amount of award:	$500-$1,000
Application deadline:	March 1

Contact:
Scholarship Committee
4590 MacArthur Boulevard, NW
Suite 250
Washington, DC 20007
Website: www.sbaa.org

Spinsters Ink

Young Feminist Scholarship Program

Type of award: Scholarship.
Intended use: For freshman study.
Eligibility: Applicant must be female, high school senior. Applicant must be U.S. citizen.
Basis for selection: Competition in Writing/journalism. Best essay on feminism Major/career interest in womenÖs studies; journalism; English.
Additional information: Winners will have their prize-winning essay published in a national women's magazine.

Amount of award:	$1,000
Number of awards:	1
Application deadline:	January 1
Notification begins:	March 8

Contact:
Spinsters Ink
32 East First St, #330
Duluth, MN 55802-2002

Spoleto Festival USA

Spoleto Festival Administrative Internship

Type of award: Internship, renewable.
Intended use: For undergraduate, graduate or non-degree study in Charleston, SC. Designated institutions: Spoleto Festival U.S.A.
Basis for selection: Major/career interest in arts management. Applicant must demonstrate seriousness of purpose.
Application requirements: Interview, recommendations and essay. Resume, two references, interview recommended.
Additional information: Deadline is February; contact sponsor for exact date. Six week apprenticeship with arts professionals producing and operating international arts festival. Posts available in media relations, development, finance, box office, production, housing, general administration, merchandising, orchestra management, chamber music assistant, and rehearsal assistant. Weekly stipend of $225 and housing included.

Amount of award:	$200-$1,200
Number of awards:	43

Contact:
Spoleto Festival USA
PO Box 157, Apprentice Program
Charleston, SC 29402-0157

Spoleto Festival Apprenticeship Program

Type of award: Internship.
Intended use: For undergraduate, graduate or postgraduate study.
Application requirements: Interview and recommendations.
Additional information: Internship lasts approximately four weeks and pays a stipend of $225 a week. Provides opportunity to work with arts professionals in all areas to assist in production and operation of an international arts festival.

Amount of award:	$900
Application deadline:	February 20

Contact:
Spoleto Festival USA
P.O. Box 157
Charleston, SC 29402

Spoleto Festival Production Internship

Type of award: Internship, renewable.
Intended use: For full-time undergraduate, graduate or non-

Spoleto Festival USA: Spoleto Festival Production Internship

degree study in Charleston, SC. Designated institutions: Spoleto Festival U.S.A.
Eligibility: Applicant must be U.S. citizen.
Basis for selection: Major/career interest in performing arts; electronics; construction; cosmetology/hairdressing. Applicant must demonstrate seriousness of purpose.
Application requirements: Recommendations. Resume, two references, interview recommended.
Additional information: Deadline will be in early February; contact sponsor for exact date. Six week apprenticeship with arts professionals producing and operating international arts festival. Posts available for stage carpenters, stage electricians, sound, properties, wardrobe, wigs and makeup, and production administrators. Must have related experience in technical theater. Weekly stipend of $225 and housing included.

Amount of award:	$200-$1,200
Number of awards:	25

Contact:
Spoleto Festival USA
P.O. Box 157, Apprentice Program
Charleston, SC 29402-0157

State Farm Companies Foundation

State Farm Companies Doctoral Dissertation Award

Type of award: Scholarship.
Intended use: For doctoral study at accredited graduate institution in United States.
Eligibility: Applicant must be U.S. citizen.
Basis for selection: Major/career interest in insurance/actuarial science; business. Applicant must demonstrate high academic achievement.
Application requirements: Recommendations, transcript and research proposal.
Additional information: Provides support to Doctoral candidates whose dissertation topics relate to insurance and risk management or business. Applicants must have completed a major portion of their doctoral program and are at the dissertation stage to be considered for this award. Applicants must be nominated by their supervising professor or faculty advisor.

Amount of award:	$10,000
Number of awards:	3
Number of applicants:	8
Application deadline:	March 31
Total amount awarded:	$7,000

State Farm Companies Exceptional Student Fellowship

Type of award: Scholarship.
Intended use: For junior, senior study at accredited 4-year institution in United States.
Eligibility: Applicant must be U.S. citizen.
Basis for selection: Major/career interest in business; computer and information sciences; mathematics; accounting; finance/banking; insurance/actuarial science. Applicant must demonstrate depth of character and leadership.
Application requirements: Recommendations and transcript.
Additional information: Minimum 3.6 GPA required. Application comes with nomination/recommendation form which must be completed by professor or faculty member. Applications without these forms are not considered. Notifications mailed in March.

Amount of award:	$3,000
Number of awards:	50
Number of applicants:	523
Application deadline:	February 15
Total amount awarded:	$150,000

Contact:
State Farm Companies Foundation
One State Farm Plaza, SC-3
Bloomington, IL 61710-0001
Phone: 3097662039
Website: www.statefarm.com

Strong Museum

H.J. Swinney Internship

Type of award: Internship.
Intended use: For full-time graduate study at graduate institution in Rochester, NY.
Eligibility: Applicant must be U.S. citizen or permanent resident.
Basis for selection: Major/career interest in museum studies; education, early childhood; history. Applicant must demonstrate seriousness of purpose.
Application requirements: Recommendations, essay and transcript. Resume, three letters of recommendation.
Additional information: Two three-month internships for applicants interested in any area of museum work, including American history. Special consideration given to graduate students in museum studies and conservation of historic artifacts and works of art. Sponsor is a museum of American cultural history related to everyday life in the U.S. after 1820. Emphasis currently on exhibits and programs for families and children ages 3-12. Minorities encouraged to apply.

Amount of award:	$4,200
Number of awards:	1
Number of applicants:	7
Application deadline:	December 15
Notification begins:	February 15
Total amount awarded:	$4,200

Contact:
Strong Museum
Education Department
One Manhattan Square
Rochester, NY 14607

Student Aid Foundation

Student Aid Foundation Graduate Loan

Type of award: Loan, renewable.
Intended use: For full-time master's, doctoral or first professional study at accredited graduate institution in United States.
Eligibility: Applicant must be female. Applicant must be U.S. citizen residing in Georgia.
Basis for selection: Applicant must demonstrate seriousness of purpose, financial need and high academic achievement.
Application requirements: Recommendations, essay and transcript.
Additional information: Non-Georgia residents attending Georgia institutions can qualify. Loan not forgivable. Must have financially responsible endorser. Minimum GPA of 3.0. Send SASE with request for application.
    Amount of award: $1,000-$4,000
    Number of awards: 80
    Application deadline: April 15
    Notification begins: June 1
Contact:
Scholarship Coordinator
2520 East Piedmont Road
Suite F180
Marietta, GA 30062
Phone: 770-973-7077

Student Aid Foundation Undergraduate Loan

Type of award: Loan, renewable.
Intended use: For full-time undergraduate, master's, doctoral or first professional study at accredited vocational, 2-year, 4-year or graduate institution in United States.
Eligibility: Applicant must be female. Applicant must be U.S. citizen residing in Georgia.
Basis for selection: Applicant must demonstrate seriousness of purpose, financial need and high academic achievement.
Application requirements: Recommendations, essay and transcript.
Additional information: Non-Georgia residents attending Georgia institutions can qualify. Loan not forgivable. Must have financially responsible endorser. Minimum GPA of 3.0. Send SASE with request for application.
    Amount of award: $3,000
    Number of awards: 100
    Application deadline: April 15
    Notification begins: June 1
Contact:
Student Aid Foundation
2520 East Piedmont Road
Suite F180
Marietta, GA 30062
Phone: 770-973-7077

Sunkist Growers

A.W. Bodine Memorial Scholarship

Type of award: Scholarship, renewable.
Intended use: For full-time undergraduate study.
Basis for selection: Major/career interest in agriculture. Applicant must demonstrate depth of character, leadership, seriousness of purpose, service orientation, financial need and high academic achievement.
Application requirements: Recommendations, essay, transcript and proof of eligibility.
Additional information: Must have a 3.0 GPA. The student, or someone in the student's immediate family must have derived the majority of his/her income from agriculture.
    Amount of award: $3,000
    Number of awards: 20
    Number of applicants: 300
    Application deadline: April 30
    Notification begins: August 30
Contact:
SUNKIST GROWERS A.W. BODINE MEMORIAL SCHOLARSHIP
PO Box 7888
Sherman Oaks, CA 91409-7888

Swiss Benevolent Society

Achievement Award

Type of award: Scholarship.
Intended use: For full-time senior, post-bachelor's certificate, master's, doctoral or first professional study at accredited 4-year or graduate institution in United States.
Eligibility: Applicant must be of Swiss heritage. Applicant must be U.S. citizen or permanent resident residing in Connecticut or Delaware or New Jersey or New York or Pennsylvania.
Basis for selection: Applicant must demonstrate high academic achievement.
Application requirements: Recommendations, transcript and proof of eligibility.
Additional information: Must have a minimum 3.8 GPA.
    Amount of award: $2,500
    Number of awards: 2
    Number of applicants: 5
    Application deadline: March 31
    Notification begins: June 1
    Total amount awarded: $5,000
Contact:
Swiss Benevolent Society
608 Fifth Avenue
Room 309
New York, NY 10020

Medicus Student Exchange

Type of award: Scholarship.
Intended use: For full-time junior, senior, post-bachelor's certificate, master's, doctoral or first professional study at

Swiss Benevolent Society: Medicus Student Exchange

accredited 4-year or graduate institution in Universities and Polytechnic institutes in Switzerland. in Switzerland.
Eligibility: Applicant must be of Swiss heritage. Applicant must be U.S. citizen, permanent resident or Swiss citizen.
Basis for selection: Applicant must demonstrate high academic achievement.
Application requirements: Recommendations, transcript and proof of eligibility.
Additional information: For U.S. students one parent must be a Swiss national. Must have a minimum 3.0 GPA.
- **Application deadline:** March 31
- **Notification begins:** June 1

Contact:
Swiss Benevolent Society
608 Fifth Avenue
Room 309
New York, NY 10020

Pellegrini Scholarship

Type of award: Scholarship, renewable.
Intended use: For undergraduate, graduate or non-degree study at accredited postsecondary institution in United States.
Eligibility: Applicant must be of Swiss heritage. Applicant must be U.S. citizen or permanent resident.
Basis for selection: Applicant must demonstrate financial need and high academic achievement.
Application requirements: Recommendations, transcript and proof of eligibility. Proof of Swiss descent and tax return.
Additional information: One parent must be Swiss. Minimum 3.0 GPA required.
- **Amount of award:** $500-$2,500
- **Number of awards:** 52
- **Number of applicants:** 56
- **Application deadline:** March 31
- **Notification begins:** June 1
- **Total amount awarded:** $73,875

Contact:
Pellegrini Scholarship Fund of the Swiss Benevolent Society
608 Fifth Avenue
Room 309
New York, NY 10020

Tandy Technology Scholars

Tandy Technology Students Award

Type of award: Scholarship.
Intended use: For full-time undergraduate study at accredited 2-year or 4-year institution.
Eligibility: Applicant must be high school senior.
Basis for selection: Major/career interest in mathematics; science, general; computer and information sciences. Applicant must demonstrate service orientation and high academic achievement.
Application requirements: Nomination by Nominated by student's high school.
Additional information: High schools nominate their top senior class mathematics, science, or computer science student; top 100 finalists chosen. Contact high school adviser, counselor, or principal for detailed information.
- **Amount of award:** $1,000
- **Number of awards:** 100
- **Total amount awarded:** $100,000

Tandy Technology Teachers Award

Type of award: Scholarship.
Intended use: For non-degree study.
Basis for selection: Major/career interest in education, teacher. Applicant must demonstrate seriousness of purpose and service orientation.
Application requirements: Recommendations, essay and nomination by Nominated by participating high school. Professional development, continuing education, service to school, profession, community.
Additional information: Enrolled high schools nationwide nominate a mathematics, science or computer science teacher member of their faculty for exhibited outstanding academic excellence. Top 100 finalists selected each receive $2,500 cash award.
- **Amount of award:** $2,500
- **Number of awards:** 100
- **Total amount awarded:** $250,000

Contact:
Tandy Technology Scholars
TCU Box 298990
Fort Worth, TX 76129
Phone: 817-924-4087
Fax: 817-927-1942
Website: www.tandy.com/scholars/

Target

Target All Around Scholarship

Type of award: Scholarship.
Intended use: For undergraduate study at accredited vocational, 2-year or 4-year institution.
Eligibility: Applicant must be high school senior.
Additional information: Information and application available at Target stores.
- **Amount of award:** $1,000-$10,000
- **Application deadline:** September 18

Tau Beta Pi Association

Society of Auto Engineers Engineering Scholarship

Type of award: Scholarship.
Intended use: For full-time freshman study in United States. Designated institutions: The engineering program must be accredited by A.B.E.T. (Accreditation Board for Engineering & Technology).
Eligibility: Applicant must be high school senior. Applicant must be U.S. citizen.
Basis for selection: Major/career interest in engineering. Applicant must demonstrate depth of character, leadership, service orientation and high academic achievement.
Application requirements: $5 application fee. Essay and transcript. ACT/SAT scores required.
Additional information: Minimum 3.75 GPA. 90th percentile on math and verbal ACT/SAT.

Amount of award: $1,000
Number of awards: 6
Number of applicants: 1,000
Application deadline: December 1
Notification begins: May 31
Total amount awarded: $6,000
Contact:
Society of Auto Engineers Educational Relations Division
400 Commonwealth Drive
Warrendale, PA 15096-0001

Tetra Tech

American Indian Fellowship for Environmental Professionals

Type of award: Internship.
Intended use: For graduate or postgraduate study.
Eligibility: Applicant must be Alaskan native or American Indian.
Basis for selection: Major/career interest in environmental science.
Application requirements: Recommendations.
Additional information: Internships may be open to undergraduates with four years of undergraduate course work. The length of internship varies. Compensation ranges from $520 to $600 per week. The deadline is in mid-May of 1999. Call the institution for an exact date. Applicants need not be U.S. Citizens, but must be able to legally work in the U.S.A. The program provides aspiring environmental professionals with technical training and an understanding of how Federal agencies operate.
  Number of awards: 3
  Number of applicants: 5
Contact:
Sue Bartow
10306 Eaton Pl., Suite 340
Fairfax, VA 22030

The GEM Consortium

The GEM Consortium/Doctoral Bridge Projects

Type of award: Scholarship.
Intended use: For full-time doctoral study.
Eligibility: Applicant must be American Indian, African American, Mexican American, Hispanic American or Puerto Rican. Applicant must be U.S. citizen.
Basis for selection: Major/career interest in engineering.
Application requirements: Transcript.
  Amount of award: $60,000-$100,000
  Application deadline: December 1
Contact:
The GEM Consortium Doctoral Bridge Project
PO Box 537
Notre Dame, IN 46556
Phone: 219-631-7771
Website: www.nd.edu/~gem

The GEM Consortium/M.S. Engineering Fellowship

Type of award: Scholarship.
Intended use: For full-time master's study.
Eligibility: Applicant must be American Indian, African American, Mexican American, Hispanic American or Puerto Rican. Applicant must be U.S. citizen.
Basis for selection: Major/career interest in engineering.
Application requirements: Transcript.
Additional information: To be used for M.S. Engineering.
  Amount of award: $26,000-$100,000
  Application deadline: December 1
Contact:
The GEM Consortium M.S. Engineering Fellowship Program
PO Box 537
Notre Dame, IN 46556
Phone: 219-631-7771
Website: www.nd.edu/~gem

The GEM Consortium/Ph.D Science and Engineering Fellowship

Type of award: Scholarship.
Intended use: For full-time doctoral study.
Eligibility: Applicant must be American Indian, African American, Mexican American, Hispanic American or Puerto Rican. Applicant must be U.S. citizen.
Basis for selection: Major/career interest in science, general; engineering. Applicant must demonstrate high academic achievement.
Application requirements: Transcript.
Additional information: M.S. Engineering Fellowship. Ph.D. Science Fellowship. Ph.D. Engineering Fellowship. Doctoral Bridge Project.
  Amount of award: $60,000-$100,000
  Application deadline: December 1
  Notification begins: January 31
Contact:
The GEM Consortium Ph.D Science and Engineering Fellowships
Scholarship Committee
PO Box 537
Notre Dame, IN 46556
Website: www.nd.edu/~gem

The Maine State Society of Washington, DC

The Maine State Society of Washington, DC Foundation Inc. Scholarship Program

Type of award: Scholarship.
Intended use: For full-time undergraduate study.
Eligibility: Applicant must be U.S. citizen residing in Maine.
Basis for selection: Applicant must demonstrate seriousness of purpose and high academic achievement.
Application requirements: Portfolio, essay, transcript and proof of eligibility.
Additional information: Must have been born in Maine or

have been a legal resident of Maine for at least 4 years or have at least one parent who was born in or who has been a legal resident of Maine for at least 4 years. Minimum GPA 03.0.

Amount of award: $1,000
Number of awards: 1
Application deadline: April 1
Total amount awarded: $1,000

Contact:
Scholarship Coordinator
3508 Wilson St.
Fairfax, VA 22030
Phone: 703-237-1031

The National Foundation for Infectious Diseases

Postdoctoral Fellowship in Emerging Infectious Diseases

Type of award: Research grant.
Intended use: For doctoral study.
Eligibility: Applicant must be U.S. citizen.
Basis for selection: Major/career interest in medical specialties/research. Applicant must demonstrate depth of character, seriousness of purpose and service orientation.
Application requirements: Interview, recommendations, proof of eligibility and research proposal.
Additional information: The applicant will be assigned to the national center for infectious diseases, CDC, Atlanta, GA.
Contact:
Grants Manager
4733 Bethesda Ave., Suite 750
Bethesda, MD 20814-5228
Phone: 301-656-0003
Fax: 301-907-0878

Thurgood Marshall Scholarship Fund

Thurgood Marshall Scholarship Award

Type of award: Scholarship, renewable.
Intended use: For full-time undergraduate study. Designated institutions: Any of the 38 Historically Black Universities.
Eligibility: Applicant must be high school senior. Applicant must be U.S. citizen.
Basis for selection: Applicant must demonstrate seriousness of purpose and high academic achievement.
Application requirements: Interview, recommendations, essay and transcript.
Additional information: Must be admitted to one of the 38 historically black colleges and universities before applying. Must have 1100 SAT and 25 ACT and maintain 3.0 GPA throughout college.

Amount of award: $4,200
Number of awards: 45
Number of applicants: 1,000
Total amount awarded: $189,000

Contact:
Thurgood Marshall Scholarship Fund
100 Park Ave., 10th Floor
New York, NY 10017
Website: www.tmsf.org

Transportation Clubs International

Charlotte Woods Memorial Scholarship

Type of award: Scholarship.
Intended use: For junior, senior study.
Basis for selection: Major/career interest in transportation. Applicant must demonstrate depth of character, financial need and high academic achievement.
Application requirements: Recommendations, essay and transcript.
Additional information: Student must be a member or a dependent of a member of the Transportation Clubs International.

Amount of award: $1,000
Application deadline: May 31

Denny Lydic Scholarship

Type of award: Scholarship.
Intended use: For sophomore, junior or senior study.
Basis for selection: Major/career interest in transportation. Applicant must demonstrate depth of character, financial need and high academic achievement.
Application requirements: Recommendations, essay and transcript.

Amount of award: $500
Application deadline: May 31

Ginger and Fred Deines Canada Scholarship

Type of award: Scholarship.
Intended use: For sophomore, junior or senior study. Designated institutions: In United States or Canada.
Eligibility: Applicant must be Canadian citizen.
Basis for selection: Major/career interest in transportation; engineering; engineering, civil. Applicant must demonstrate depth of character, financial need and high academic achievement.
Application requirements: Recommendations, essay and transcript.
Additional information: For a student of Canadian nationality enrolled in a Canadian or U.S. institution.

Amount of award: $500-$1,000
Application deadline: May 31

Ginger and Fred Deines Mexico Scholarship

Type of award: Scholarship.
Intended use: For sophomore, junior or senior study. Designated institutions: In United States or Mexico.
Eligibility: Applicant must be Mexican citizen.
Basis for selection: Major/career interest in transportation; engineering; engineering, civil. Applicant must demonstrate depth of character, financial need and high academic achievement.
Application requirements: Recommendations, essay and transcript.
Additional information: For a student of Mexican nationality enrolled in a Mexican or U.S. institution.
    Amount of award: $500-$1,000
    Application deadline: May 31

Hooper Memorial Scholarship

Type of award: Scholarship.
Intended use: For junior, senior study.
Basis for selection: Major/career interest in transportation; engineering, civil; engineering. Applicant must demonstrate depth of character, financial need and high academic achievement.
Application requirements: Recommendations, essay and transcript.
    Amount of award: $1,500
    Application deadline: May 31

Texas Transportation Scholarship

Type of award: Scholarship.
Intended use: For sophomore, junior or senior study.
Basis for selection: Major/career interest in transportation; engineering; engineering, civil. Applicant must demonstrate depth of character, financial need and high academic achievement.
Application requirements: Recommendations, essay and transcript.
Additional information: Applicant must have been enrolled in a Texas school for some phase of education (elementary through high school).
    Amount of award: $1,000
    Application deadline: May 31
Contact:
Transportation Clubs International
P.O. Box 52
Arabi, LA 70032
Website: www.transclubsintl.org

Travel and Tourism Research Association

J. Desmond Slattery Award: Student

Type of award: Scholarship.
Intended use: For undergraduate study.
Basis for selection: Competition in Research paper. Originality, clarity, overall marketing excellence. Major/career interest in tourism and travel.
Additional information: Must submit original research paper. Paper will be judged on quality of research, originality, creativity, relationship to travel and tourism, applicability, and quality of presentation. Only undergraduate students enrolled in a degree-granting program qualify.
    Amount of award: $700
    Application deadline: March 1

Travel and Tourism Student Research Award

Type of award: Scholarship.
Intended use: For master's study.
Basis for selection: Competition in Research paper. research quality, creativity, relationship to travel/tourism, applicability and presentation. Major/career interest in tourism and travel.
Application requirements: 500-1000 word abstract of completed paper.
Additional information: Must submit paper and abstract of completed, original research study. The paper will be judged on quality of research, creativity of approach, relationship to travel and tourism, applicability, and quality of presentation. Award notification will occur in May.
    Amount of award: $1,000
    Application deadline: March 1

Travel Research Grant

Type of award: Research grant.
Intended use: For undergraduate, graduate or non-degree study.
Basis for selection: Major/career interest in tourism and travel.
Application requirements: Research proposal.
Additional information: Applicant must propose to develop technique or methodology which improves measurement, decreases costs, demonstrates reliability or improves information application and understanding. Grant recipient has three years to complete project. Materials must be submittted in English.
    Amount of award: $1,000
    Application deadline: March 1

William B. Keeling Dissertation Award

Type of award: Scholarship.
Intended use: For doctoral study.
Basis for selection: Competition in Writing/journalism. The best doctoral dissertation on a subject directly related to the travel and tourism fields. Major/career interest in tourism and travel.
Additional information: Award given every three years. Next deadline, March 3, 1999. Only dissertations completed between Jan 1, 1996 and Jan 1, 1999 may be entered. Award will be given biannually in the future.
    Amount of award: $1,000
    Application deadline: March 1
Contact:
Travel and Tourism Research Association
546 East Main Street
Lexington, KY 40508
Phone: 606-226-4344
Fax: 606-226-4355
Website: www.ttra.com

Treacy Company

Treacy Company Scholarship

Type of award: Scholarship, renewable.
Intended use: For full-time freshman, sophomore study at postsecondary institution.
Eligibility: Applicant must be residing in North Dakota or South Dakota or Idaho or Montana.
Basis for selection: Applicant must demonstrate depth of character, leadership, patriotism, seriousness of purpose, service orientation and financial need.
Application requirements: Essay and transcript. Letter stating reason for applying, listing personal information.

Amount of award:	$400
Number of awards:	70
Number of applicants:	100
Application deadline:	June 15
Notification begins:	July 1
Total amount awarded:	$28,000

Contact:
Treacy Company
Box 1700
Helena, MT 59624
Phone: 406-442-3632

Trinity Episcopal Church

Shannon Scholarship

Type of award: Scholarship, renewable.
Intended use: For freshman, sophomore, junior or senior study.
Eligibility: Applicant must be female, Episcopal. Applicant must be residing in Pennsylvania.
Basis for selection: Applicant must demonstrate financial need.
Application requirements: Proof of eligibility.
Additional information: Only open to daughters of Episcopal clergy in state of Pennsylvania. Must apply for state financial assistance first. Previous recipients may reapply.

Amount of award:	$500-$4,000
Number of awards:	12
Number of applicants:	12
Application deadline:	May 15
Total amount awarded:	$34,000

Contact:
Trinity Episcopal Church
200 South Second Street
Pottsville, PA 17901

Truckload Carriers Association

Truckload Carriers Association Scholarship

Type of award: Scholarship, renewable.
Intended use: For full-time junior, senior study at 4-year institution in United States.
Basis for selection: Applicant must demonstrate depth of character, seriousness of purpose, financial need and high academic achievement.
Application requirements: Transcript. Must submit photograph.
Additional information: Must be the child, grandchild or spouse of an employee or an employee of a trucking company, or the child, grandchild or spouse of an independent contractor.

Amount of award:	$1,500-$2,500
Application deadline:	June 6

Contact:
Truckload Carriers Association
2200 Mill Rd.
Alexandria, VA 22314

Twentieth Century Fox

Twentieth Century Fox Internship

Type of award: Internship.
Intended use: For undergraduate or graduate study.
Application requirements: Interview.
Additional information: Internship application deadlines vary; contact sponsor for exact information. Interns work in one of the 19 conglomerate companies of Fox, in such departments as production, programming, legal, accounting, research, finance, sales, and marketing. Duration is from eight to sixteen weeks. Compensation is $300 per week for undergraduates and $450 per week for graduate students. Must submit resume and cover letter.

Amount of award:	$2,400-$7,200
Number of awards:	75
Number of applicants:	800

Contact:
Twentieth Century Fox
Human Resources Department
P.O. Box 900
Beverly Hills, CA 90213

U. The National College Magazine

U. The National College Magazine Scholarship

Type of award: Scholarship.
Intended use: For full-time undergraduate study at accredited 4-year institution.
Eligibility: Applicant must be U.S. citizen or permanent resident.
Basis for selection: Applicant must demonstrate depth of character, leadership, seriousness of purpose, financial need and high academic achievement.
Application requirements: Recommendations, essay, transcript and proof of eligibility. Application, resume, and photo of applicant (optional).
Additional information: Applicant must be enrolled in a US institution and have a minimum of 3.4 GPA. Applicant must demonstrate excellence in one of the following five topics: academic achievement, entrepreneurship, athletics, communication, media, and volunteerism. Please send SASE to receive application. Mail-in application available from website.
  Amount of award: $1,000
  Number of awards: 5
  Number of applicants: 1,000
  Application deadline: June 26
  Notification begins: August 28
  Total amount awarded: $5,000
Contact:
U. The National College Magazine
1800 Century Park East
Suite 820
Los Angeles, CA 90067-1511
Website: www.umagazine.com

U.S. National Arboretum

U.S. National Arboretum Internship

Type of award: Internship.
Intended use: For undergraduate or graduate study.
Eligibility: Applicant must be U.S. citizen or permanent resident.
Basis for selection: Major/career interest in horticulture; botany; agriculture; forestry.
Application requirements: Recommendations and transcript. resume and cover letter.
Additional information: Internships are 40 hours per week, lasts from three months to one year and pays a stipend of $8.25 per hour. Provides opportunity to gain experience in plant research in one of the premier horticultural collections in the country.
  Amount of award: $3,600-$16,500
  Application deadline: January 15, March 1
Contact:
U.S. National Aboretum
3501 New York Ave., NE
Washington, DC 20002
Website: www.ars-grin.gov

Ukrainian Fraternal Association

Eugene and Elinor Kotur Scholarship

Type of award: Scholarship, renewable.
Intended use: For full-time sophomore, junior or senior study.
Eligibility: Applicant must be of Ukrainian heritage.
Basis for selection: Applicant must demonstrate depth of character, financial need and high academic achievement.
Application requirements: Transcript.
Additional information: Must have completed first year of undergraduate studies. Membership in the Ukrainian Fraternal Association is encouraged but not required for this scholarship.
  Amount of award: $1,000-$3,000
  Number of awards: 14
  Number of applicants: 30
  Application deadline: June 30
  Total amount awarded: $19,000
Contact:
Scholarship Coordinator
440 Wyoming Avenue
Scranton, PA 18503

Unico Foundation, Inc.

Alphonse A. Miele Scholarship

Type of award: Scholarship, renewable.
Intended use: For undergraduate study.
Eligibility: Applicant must be high school senior.
Basis for selection: Applicant must demonstrate depth of character, leadership, financial need and high academic achievement.
Application requirements: Recommendations, essay, transcript and proof of eligibility.
Additional information: Student must reside in the corporate limits of a city wherein an active chapter of Unico National is located. Award is for $1000 per year for four years.
  Amount of award: $4,000
  Application deadline: April 15

John Basilone Scholarship

Type of award: Scholarship, renewable.
Intended use: For undergraduate study.
Eligibility: Applicant must be high school senior, of Italian heritage.
Basis for selection: Applicant must demonstrate depth of character, leadership, financial need and high academic achievement.
Application requirements: Recommendations, essay, transcript and proof of eligibility.
Additional information: Student must reside in the corporate limits of a city wherein an active chapter of Unico National is located. Award is for $1000 per year, distributed over four years.
  Amount of award: $4,000
  Application deadline: April 15

Major Don S. Gentile Scholarship

Type of award: Scholarship, renewable.
Intended use: For undergraduate study.
Eligibility: Applicant must be enrolled in high school.
Basis for selection: Applicant must demonstrate depth of character, leadership, financial need and high academic achievement.
Application requirements: Recommendations, essay, transcript and proof of eligibility.
Additional information: Students must reside in corporate limits of a city wherein an active chapter of Unico National is located. Award is distributed in four annual installments of $1000.
    Amount of award: $4,000
    Application deadline: April 15

Theodore Mazza Scholarship

Type of award: Scholarship, renewable.
Intended use: For undergraduate study.
Eligibility: Applicant must be high school senior.
Basis for selection: Major/career interest in architecture; art, art history; music; arts, general. Applicant must demonstrate depth of character, leadership, financial need and high academic achievement.
Application requirements: Recommendations, essay, transcript and proof of eligibility.
Additional information: Student must reside in the corporate limits of a city wherein an active chapter of Unico National is located. Award is distributed in four annual installments of $1000.
    Amount of award: $4,000
    Application deadline: April 15

William C. Davini Scholarship

Type of award: Scholarship.
Intended use: For undergraduate study.
Eligibility: Applicant must be high school senior, of Italian heritage.
Basis for selection: Applicant must demonstrate depth of character, leadership, financial need and high academic achievement.
Application requirements: Recommendations, essay, transcript and proof of eligibility.
Additional information: Students must reside in the corporate limits of a city wherein an active chapter of Unico National is located. Award is distributed in four annual installments of $1000.
    Amount of award: $4,000
    Application deadline: April 15
Contact:
Unico Foundation, Inc.
72 Burroughs Place
Bloomfield, NJ 07003

Unitarian Universalist Association

Unitarian Universalist Stanfield Art Scholarship

Type of award: Scholarship, renewable.
Intended use: For full-time freshman, sophomore, junior, senior, master's or doctoral study.
Eligibility: Applicant must be Unitarian Universalist.
Basis for selection: Major/career interest in art, art history. Applicant must demonstrate depth of character, service orientation, financial need and high academic achievement.
Application requirements: Portfolio, recommendations, transcript and proof of eligibility.
Additional information: Must be preparing for career in fine arts of painting, drawing, or sculpture. Renewable with reapplication.
    Amount of award: $1,900-$12,000
    Number of awards: 6
    Number of applicants: 12
    Application deadline: February 15
    Notification begins: June 15
    Total amount awarded: $24,000
Contact:
Unitarian Universalist Association
25 Beacon Street
Boston, MA 02108

Unitarian Universalist Stanfield Law Scholarship

Type of award: Scholarship, renewable.
Intended use: For full-time first professional study.
Eligibility: Applicant must be Unitarian Universalist.
Basis for selection: Major/career interest in law. Applicant must demonstrate depth of character, service orientation, financial need and high academic achievement.
Application requirements: Recommendations, transcript and proof of eligibility.
    Amount of award: $1,000-$4,000
    Number of awards: 7
    Number of applicants: 10
    Application deadline: February 15
    Notification begins: June 16
    Total amount awarded: $24,000
Contact:
Unitarian Universalist Association
Stanfield Law Scholarship
25 Beacon Street
Boston, MA 02108

United Cerebral Palsy Research and Educational Foundation, Inc.

Ethel Hausman Clinical Research Award

Type of award: Research grant.
Intended use: For postgraduate study in United States.
Basis for selection: Major/career interest in medical specialties/research.
Application requirements: Research proposal. Must used a Outline of Narrative as a format for application.
Additional information: Award is $150,000 (including 10% indirect costs) at $50,000 per year over three years. For scholarly activities in areas of direct relevance to cerebral palsy; activities must include research, teaching, and associated clinical responsibilities. Must have completed formal clinical and research training. Alternate phone number is 800-872-5827, ext.7140.

Amount of award:	$150,000
Application deadline:	February 1
Notification begins:	July 1

Contact:
United Cerebral Palsy Research and Educational Foundation, Inc.
1660 L Street, NW
Suite 700
Washington, DC 20036
Phone: 202-973-7140

United Cerebral Palsy Clinical Fellowship

Type of award: Scholarship.
Intended use: For postgraduate study.
Eligibility: Applicant must be U.S. citizen.
Basis for selection: Major/career interest in medical specialties/research; engineering, biomedical.
Application requirements: Nomination by institution preceptor.
Additional information: Institutional training grant in medical specialty related to cerebral palsy, such as pediatrics, neurology, orthopedic surgery, physical medicine and rehabilitation, pediatric neurobiology. Dentists who have completed graduate curriculum in periodontics, physicians with M.A. in public health, and graduate engineers working in biomedical or rehabilitation engineering eligible. Must have completed clinical residency requirements or, in engineering, a postdoctoral fellowship.

Amount of award:	$15,000
Number of awards:	12
Number of applicants:	18
Application deadline:	December 15
Notification begins:	June 1

Contact:
United Cerebral Palsy Research and Educational Foundation
Medical Director
1660 L Street, NW, Suite 700
Washington, DC 20036
Phone: 202-973-7140

United Cerebral Palsy Research Grant

Type of award: Research grant, renewable.
Intended use: For postgraduate study.
Basis for selection: Major/career interest in medical specialties/research.
Application requirements: Research proposal.
Additional information: Proposed research should be in prevention or improvement in the quality of life of those with cerebral palsy. Award is $50,000 annually for two years.

Amount of award:	$100,000
Number of awards:	15
Number of applicants:	15
Notification begins:	July 1

Contact:
United Cerebral Palsy Research and Educational Foundation
Medical Director
1660 L Street, NW, Suite 700
Washington, DC 20036
Phone: 202-973-7140

United Methodist Church

Bishop James C. Baker Award

Type of award: Scholarship, renewable.
Intended use: For graduate study at graduate institution in United States.
Eligibility: Applicant must be United Methodist. Applicant must be U.S. citizen or permanent resident.
Basis for selection: Major/career interest in religion/theology.
Additional information: Must be campus minister with M. Div. and at least three years professional experience. Must be in higher education doing advanced studies and planning to stay in campus ministry.

Application deadline:	February 1

Contact:
United Methodist Church/Board of Higher Education and Ministry
Office of Loans and Scholarships
P.O. Box 871
Nashville, TN 37202-0871

E. Craig Brandenburg Graduate Award

Type of award: Scholarship, renewable.
Intended use: For full-time graduate study at accredited graduate institution.
Eligibility: Applicant must be United Methodist. Applicant must be U.S. citizen or permanent resident.
Basis for selection: Applicant must demonstrate service orientation.
Additional information: Available to persons wanting to change profession, having interrupted studies, or continuing education. Must be active member of United Methodist Church one year prior to application.

Application deadline: March 1
Contact:
United Methodist Church/Board of Higher Education and Ministry
Office of Scholarships & Loans
P.O. Box 871
Nashville, TN 37202-0871

Georgia Harkness Scholarship

Type of award: Scholarship, renewable.
Intended use: For graduate study.
Eligibility: Applicant must be female, United Methodist. Applicant must be U.S. citizen or permanent resident.
Basis for selection: Major/career interest in religion/theology. Applicant must demonstrate seriousness of purpose and service orientation.
Additional information: Must be a Master of Divinity candidate preparing for ordained ministry as second career. Must be active member of United Methodist Church one year prior to application.
Application deadline: March 1
Contact:
United Methodist Church/Board of Higher Education and Ministry
Division of Ordained Ministry
P.O. Box 871
Nashville, TN 37202-0871

J.A. Knowles Memorial Scholarship

Type of award: Scholarship, renewable.
Intended use: For undergraduate or graduate study in Texas. Designated institutions: One of the eight United Methodist affiliated institutions in Texas.
Eligibility: Applicant must be United Methodist. Applicant must be U.S. citizen or permanent resident residing in Texas.
Basis for selection: Applicant must demonstrate financial need.
Additional information: Must be active member of United Methodist Church one year prior to application. Recipients must attend one of eight United Methodist affiliated institutions in Texas.
Application deadline: June 1
Contact:
United Methodist Church/Board of Higher Education and Ministry
Office of Loans and Scholarships
P.O. Box 871
Nashville, TN 37202-0871

John Q. Schisler Award

Type of award: Scholarship, renewable.
Intended use: For full-time graduate study.
Eligibility: Applicant must be United Methodist. Applicant must be U.S. citizen or permanent resident.
Basis for selection: Applicant must demonstrate depth of character, leadership, seriousness of purpose and service orientation.
Additional information: Scholarship assists professional Christian educators at local church level. Not for students pursuing ordained minister career. Must be active member of United Methodist Church one year prior to application.

Application deadline: February 1
Contact:
United Methodist Church/Board of Higher Education and Ministry
Office of Loans and Scholarships
P.O. Box 871
Nashville, TN 37202-0871

Priscilla R. Morton Scholarship

Type of award: Scholarship, renewable.
Intended use: For full-time undergraduate study at accredited 4-year institution in United States.
Eligibility: Applicant must be United Methodist. Applicant must be U.S. citizen or permanent resident.
Basis for selection: Applicant must demonstrate high academic achievement.
Additional information: Highly competitive academic scholarship. Must be active member of United Methodist Church one year prior to application. Minimum 3.5 college GPA required.
Application deadline: June 1
Contact:
United Methodist Church/Board of Higher Education and Ministry
Office of Loans and Scholarships
P.O. Box 871
Nashville, TN 37202-0871

Rev. Charles W. Tadlock Scholarship

Type of award: Scholarship, renewable.
Intended use: For master's, doctoral or first professional study.
Eligibility: Applicant must be United Methodist. Applicant must be U.S. citizen or permanent resident.
Basis for selection: Major/career interest in religion/theology.
Additional information: Applicant must have completed first year of seminary study. Must be candidate for ministry certified by Annual Conference of United Methodist Church. First preference to United Methodist related seminary.
Application deadline: June 1
Contact:
United Methodist Church/Board of Higher Education and Ministry
Office of Loans and Scholarships
P.O. Box 871
Nashville, TN 37202-0871

United Methodist Bass Scholarship

Type of award: Scholarship, renewable.
Intended use: For full-time undergraduate study at 4-year institution in United States.
Eligibility: Applicant must be United Methodist. Applicant must be U.S. citizen or permanent resident.
Basis for selection: Applicant must demonstrate seriousness of purpose.
Additional information: Preference given to applicants preparing for ministry or other full-time religious work. Must be active member of United Methodist Church one year prior to application.

Application deadline: June 1
Contact:
United Methodist Church/Board of Higher Education and Ministry
Office of Loans and Scholarships
P.O. Box 871
Nashville, TN 37202-0871

United Methodist Church Conference Merit Award

Type of award: Scholarship, renewable.
Intended use: For undergraduate study at 2-year or 4-year institution. Designated institutions: Must be used at United Methodist affiliated college or university.
Eligibility: Applicant must be United Methodist. Applicant must be U.S. citizen or permanent resident.
Basis for selection: Applicant must demonstrate leadership.
Additional information: Must reside and participate in United Methodist Church Annual Conference. Must be full, active member of United Methodist Church one year prior to application. Amount of award and deadline vary. Application and additional information available at Annual Conference office where local church is member.
Contact:
United Methodist Church/Board of Higher Education and Ministry
Office of Loans and Scholarships
PO Box 871
Nashville, TN 37202-0871

United Methodist Church Crusade Scholarship

Type of award: Scholarship, renewable.
Intended use: For full-time graduate study.
Eligibility: Applicant must be United Methodist.
Basis for selection: Applicant must demonstrate leadership and service orientation.
Additional information: Must be active member of United Methodist Church one year prior to application.
Application deadline: February 1
Contact:
United Methodist General Board of Global Ministries
Mission Personnel Resources Program Department
475 Riverside Drive, Room 1470
New York, NY 10115-0871

United Methodist Ethnic Scholarship

Type of award: Scholarship, renewable.
Intended use: For full-time undergraduate study in United States.
Eligibility: Applicant must be American Indian, Asian American, African American, Mexican American, Hispanic American or Puerto Rican. At least one parent of applicant must be 100 percent ethnic minority. Applicant must be United Methodist.
Basis for selection: Applicant must demonstrate financial need.
Application requirements: Recommendations and nomination by applicant's pastor.
Additional information: Must be active member of United Methodist Church for one year prior to application. Applicant must have minimum 2.5 grade point average. If not U.S. citizen or permanent resident must be recommended by president of college/university where enrolled.
Application deadline: May 1
Contact:
United Methodist Church/Board of Higher Education and Ministry
Office of Loans and Scholarships
P.O. Box 871
Nashville, TN 37202-0871

United Methodist Hana Scholarship

Type of award: Scholarship, renewable.
Intended use: For full-time junior, senior, master's, doctoral or first professional study at 4-year or graduate institution in United States.
Eligibility: Applicant must be American Indian, Asian American, Mexican American, Hispanic American or Puerto Rican. At least one parent of applicant must be 100 percent minority. Applicant must be United Methodist. Applicant must be U.S. citizen or permanent resident.
Basis for selection: Applicant must demonstrate leadership, service orientation, financial need and high academic achievement.
Application requirements: Recommendations and transcript.
Additional information: Must be active member of United Methodist Church for one year prior to application. Above average scholarship expected.
Application deadline: April 1
Contact:
United Methodist Church/Board of Higher Education and Ministry
Office of Loans and Scholarships
P.O. Box 871
Nashville, TN 37202-0871

United Methodist Loan Program

Type of award: Loan, renewable.
Intended use: For full-time or half-time undergraduate or graduate study at accredited postsecondary institution in United States.
Eligibility: Applicant must be United Methodist. Applicant must be U.S. citizen or permanent resident.
Additional information: Must be active member of United Methodist Church one year prior to application. May reapply for loan to maximum of $6,000.
Amount of award: $900-$1,200
Contact:
United Methodist Church/Board of Higher Education and Ministry
Office of Loans and Scholarships
P.O. Box 871
Nashville, TN 37202-0871

United Methodist Publishing House Merit Scholarship

Type of award: Scholarship, renewable.
Intended use: For full-time undergraduate study.
Eligibility: Applicant must be of minority background. At

least one parent of applicant must be 100 percent minority. Applicant must be United Methodist. Applicant must be U.S. citizen or permanent resident.
Basis for selection: Applicant must demonstrate high academic achievement.
Application requirements: Transcript.
Additional information: Must be interested in professional lay employment for career with United Methodist Publishing House. Must be active member of United Methodist Church one year prior to application.
   Application deadline: May 1
Contact:
United Methodist Publishing House
United Methodist Church
P.O. Box 871
Nashville, TN 37202-0871

United Methodist Scholarship

Type of award: Scholarship, renewable.
Intended use: For full-time freshman, sophomore, junior or senior study at 2-year or 4-year institution in United States.
Eligibility: Applicant must be United Methodist.
Basis for selection: Applicant must demonstrate financial need and high academic achievement.
Application requirements: Transcript.
Additional information: Available to undergraduate students attending United Methodist affiliated institutions who have been active members of United Methodist Church for one year prior to application. Must have minimum 3.0 GPA. Information and application available through financial aid director at United Methodist institution student plans to attend.
Contact:
United Methodist Church/Board of Higher Education and Ministry
Office of Loans and Scholarships
PO Box 871
Nashville, TN 37202-0871

United Methodist Seminary Award

Type of award: Scholarship, renewable.
Intended use: For master's study. Designated institutions: United Methodist affiliated seminary.
Eligibility: Applicant must be United Methodist. Applicant must be U.S. citizen or permanent resident.
Application requirements: Nomination by seminary faculty member.
Additional information: Must be active member of United Methodist Church one year prior to application. Information and application available through financial aid office at United Methodist seminary student plans to attend.
Contact:
United Methodist Church/Board of Higher Education and Ministry
PO Box 871
Nashville, TN 37202-0871

United Methodist Communications

L.M. Perryman Ethnic Minority Award

Type of award: Scholarship.
Intended use: For full-time junior, senior study at accredited 4-year institution in United States.
Eligibility: Applicant must be of minority background. Applicant must be Christian.
Basis for selection: Major/career interest in journalism; communications. Applicant must demonstrate seriousness of purpose.
Application requirements: Portfolio, recommendations, essay and transcript. Examples of work.
Additional information: Must plan to pursue career in religious journalism or religious communication.
   Amount of award: $2,500
   Number of awards: 1
   Number of applicants: 6
   Application deadline: February 15
   Notification begins: October 1
   Total amount awarded: $2,500
Contact:
United Methodist Communications
Scholarship Committee
PO Box 320
Nashville, TN 37202
Phone: 615-742-5140
Website: www.umc.org/umcom

Stoody-West Fellowship

Type of award: Scholarship.
Intended use: For full-time master's study at accredited graduate institution in United States.
Eligibility: Applicant must be Christian.
Basis for selection: Major/career interest in journalism. Applicant must demonstrate seriousness of purpose.
Application requirements: Portfolio, recommendations, essay and transcript.
Additional information: Must plan to pursue career in religious journalism.
   Amount of award: $6,000
   Number of awards: 1
   Number of applicants: 20
   Application deadline: February 15
   Notification begins: March 30
   Total amount awarded: $6,000
Contact:
United Methodist Communications
Fellowship Committee
Public Media Division, P.O Box 320
Nashville, TN 37202
Phone: 615-742-5140
Website: www.umc.org/umcom

United Negro College Fund

United Negro College Fund Scholarship

Type of award: Scholarship.
Intended use: For undergraduate study in United States.
Eligibility: Applicant must be African American.
Additional information: Must have a minimum 2.5 GPA. Must attend one of the following colleges: Barber-Scotia College, Benedict College, Bennett College, Bethune-Cookman College, Claflin College, Clark Atlanta University, Dillard University, Edward Waters College, Fisk University, Florida Memorial College, Huston-Tillotson College, Interdenominational Theological Center, Jarvis Christian College, Johnson C. Smith University, Lane College, LeMoyne-Owen College, Livingstone College, Miles College, Morehouse College, Morris Brown College, Morris College, Oakwood College, Paine College, Paul Quinn College, Philander Smith College, Rust College, Saint Augustine's College, Saint Paul's College, Shaw University, Spelman College, Stillman College, Talladega College, Tougaloo College, Tuskegee University, Virginia Union University, Voorhees College, Wiberforce University, Wiley College, Xavier University. Exceptions may be made for students at non-qualifying institutions, but such exceptions are very rare. Do not apply to UNCF directly; applicant must make request from the qualifying institution.
   Amount of award: $500-$10,000
Contact:
United Negro College Fund Program Services
8260 Willow Oaks Corporate Drive
P.O. Box 10444
Fairfax, VA 22031-4511
Phone: 8003312244
Website: www.uncf.org

United States Association for Blind Athletes

Arthur E. Copeland Scholarship for Males

Type of award: Scholarship.
Intended use: For full-time freshman study.
Eligibility: Applicant must be male, high school senior. Must be visually impaired. Applicant must be U.S. citizen.
Basis for selection: Open to all majors.
Application requirements: Transcript and proof of eligibility.
Additional information: Applicants who have participated in USABA activities for at least two years are eligible.
   Amount of award: $500
   Application deadline: July 1

Helen Copeland Scholarship for Females

Type of award: Scholarship.
Intended use: For full-time freshman study.
Eligibility: Applicant must be female, high school senior. Must be visually impaired. Applicant must be U.S. citizen.
Basis for selection: Open to all majors.
Application requirements: Transcript and proof of eligibility.
Additional information: Applicants who have participated in USABA activities for at least two years are eligible.
   Amount of award: $500
   Application deadline: July 1
Contact:
Scholarship Director
33 North Institute St.
Brown Hall, Suite 015
Colorado Springs, CO 80903

United States Olympic Committee (USOC)

USOC Student Intern Program

Type of award: Internship.
Intended use: For junior, senior or master's study at accredited 4-year or graduate institution in United States.
Eligibility: Applicant must be be enrolled in an accredited U.S. College or University and have Visa classification.
Basis for selection: Major/career interest in sports/sports administration; computer and information sciences; accounting. Applicant must demonstrate high academic achievement.
Application requirements: Interview, portfolio and proof of eligibility.
Additional information: Accepts applications from eligible students at the following locations: Colorado Springs, Colorado; Lake Placid, New York; and Chula Vista, California. Internships in accounting, broadcasting, computer science, marketing/fundraising, sports administration, and sports science. Internships are paid positions. Housing and meals at an Olympic Training Center plus a small stipend equal minimum wage. Travel expenses to and from the internship site are the responsibility of the student. Late or incomplete applications will be not accepted.
   Number of awards: 35
   Application deadline: June 1, October 1
   Notification begins: July 30, November 30
Contact:
United States Olympic Committee (USOC)
One Olympic Plaza
Colorado Springs, CO 80909-5760
Website: www.olympic-usa.org

University Film and Video Association

Carole Fielding Video Grant

Type of award: Scholarship, renewable.
Intended use: For undergraduate or graduate study at accredited 2-year, 4-year or graduate institution.
Basis for selection: Major/career interest in film/video.

University Film and Video Association: Carole Fielding Video Grant

Application requirements: Application form. Research/production proposal.
Additional information: Project categories include narrative, documentary, experimental, multi-media/installation, animation, and research. Applicant must submit one page resume and summary proposal. Applicant must be sponsored by faculty member who is active member of University Film and Video Association. Number of awards varies. Send five copies of completed application.

Amount of award:	$1,000-$4,000
Number of applicants:	86
Application deadline:	January 1
Notification begins:	March 31
Total amount awarded:	$5,000

Contact:
Julie Simon, University Film and Video Association Grants Chair
University of Baltimore
1420 N. Charles Street
Baltimore, MD 21201
Website: raven.ubalt.edu/staff/simon/ufvagrants.html

UpJohn Company

Upjohn Company Internship

Type of award: Internship.
Intended use: For undergraduate or graduate study.
Basis for selection: Major/career interest in finance/banking; business, management and administration; physical sciences; accounting; chemistry; marketing; agriculture; computer and information sciences.
Application requirements: Transcript and proof of eligibility.
Additional information: Internships last 12 weeks and pay $250-$400 per week. Provides opportunity to gain experience in a number of pharmaceutical fields, including, but not limited to agriculture, chemical engineering, research and quality control. Benefits include discounts on UpJohn over-the-counter products.

Amount of award:	$3,000-$4,800
Number of awards:	10

Contact:
The UpJohn Company
545-88-81, 7000 Portage Rd.
Kalamazoo, MI 49001-0199
Phone: 616-323-4000

Venture Clubs of the Americas

Venture Clubs of America Student Aid Award

Type of award: Scholarship.
Intended use: For full-time undergraduate, graduate, postgraduate or non-degree study at accredited vocational, 2-year, 4-year or graduate institution in United States.
Eligibility: Applicant must be physically challenged. Applicant must be U.S. citizen.
Basis for selection: Applicant must demonstrate financial need.
Application requirements: Recommendations and essay.
Additional information: This award program exists at the club, region, and federation levels. Each club and region determines the amount of its own award. Successful applicants on the seven regional levels are submitted to the federation level. The federation then gives two awards: one first-place ($5,000) and one second-place ($2,500). This award does not specify any particular level of study; however, applicants must demonstrate both financial need and the capacity to profit from further education. Applicants living outside the territorial limits of a Venture Club should apply to the nearest club.

Amount of award:	$2,500-$5,000
Number of awards:	7
Application deadline:	December 31

Contact:
Venture Cubs of the Americas
Soroptimist International
Two Penn Center Plaza, Ste. 1000
Philadelphia, PA 19102-1883

Vermont Golf Association Fund, Inc.

Vermont Golf Association Scholarship

Type of award: Scholarship, renewable.
Intended use: For full-time freshman, sophomore, junior or senior study at 2-year or 4-year institution.
Eligibility: Applicant must be high school senior. Applicant must be residing in Vermont.
Application requirements: Interview, recommendations and transcript. SAR.
Additional information: Must be graduates of a Vermont high school and in top 40% of class. Must demonstrate talent/interest in golf.

Amount of award:	$800
Number of awards:	40
Number of applicants:	35
Application deadline:	April 20
Total amount awarded:	$32,000

Contact:
Vermont Golf Association Scholarship Fund, Inc
c/o Keyser Crowley Carroll George + Memb PC
29 South Main St
Rutland, VT 05701-0280

Veterans of Foreign Wars

Voice of Democracy Scholarship

Type of award: Scholarship.
Intended use: For undergraduate or graduate study at accredited postsecondary institution in United States.

Eligibility: Applicant must be high school sophomore, junior, senior.
Basis for selection: Competition in Writing/journalism. Interpretation of assigned patriotic theme, and content and presentation of recorded 3-5 minute audio-essay. Applicant must demonstrate patriotism.
Application requirements: Essay.
Additional information: Must apply through high school or local Veterans of Foreign Wars Post.

Amount of award:	$1,000-$20,000
Number of awards:	56
Number of applicants:	100,000
Application deadline:	November 1

Contact:
Veterans of Foreign Wars National Headquarters
Voice of Democracy Program
406 West 34 Street
Kansas City, MO 64111
Phone: 816-968-1117
Website: www.vfw.org

Vikki Carr Scholarship Foundation

Vikki Carr Scholarship

Type of award: Scholarship, renewable.
Intended use: For undergraduate study.
Eligibility: Applicant must be Mexican American, Hispanic American or Puerto Rican. Applicant must be U.S. citizen.
Basis for selection: Applicant must demonstrate depth of character, leadership, seriousness of purpose, service orientation, financial need and high academic achievement.
Application requirements: Portfolio and recommendations.
Additional information: Applicants are encouraged to request application forms by August 15, due to a possible change of sponsor address.

Amount of award:	$500-$3,000
Number of awards:	5
Number of applicants:	1,100
Application deadline:	March 1
Notification begins:	July 30

Contact:
Vikki Carr Scholarship Foundation
P.O. Box 16670
Beverly Hills, CA 90210

Virginia Council of Higher Education

Virginia Lee-Jackson Scholarship

Type of award: Scholarship.
Intended use: For full-time freshman study at accredited 2-year or 4-year institution in Virginia.
Eligibility: Applicant must be high school junior, senior. Applicant must be residing in Virginia.
Basis for selection: Competition in Writing/journalism. Awards will be for best essays demonstrating appreciation for virtues exemplified by General Robert E. Lee or General Thomas J. Stonewall Jackson.
Application requirements: Essay and transcript.
Additional information: Awards $1,000 for best of three essays from eight Virginia regions. Additional awards for exceptional essays. Contact high school guidance office for more information.

Amount of award:	$1,000-$10,000

Virginia Museum of Fine Arts

Virginia Museum of Fine Arts Fellowship

Type of award: Scholarship, renewable.
Intended use: For full-time undergraduate or graduate study at accredited 4-year or graduate institution.
Eligibility: Applicant must be high school senior. Applicant must be U.S. citizen residing in Virginia.
Basis for selection: Major/career interest in arts, general; film/video; art, art history. Applicant must demonstrate financial need and high academic achievement.
Application requirements: Portfolio, recommendations and transcript.
Additional information: May apply in one of following categories: crafts, drawing, sculpture, filmmaking, painting, photography, printmaking, video, on the graduate or undergraduate levels. Candidates in art history may apply on the graduate level only. Must submit either ten 35mm slides representing recent work or three of the following: 16mm or video format films, videos, research papers, or published articles.

Amount of award:	$4,000-$5,000
Number of awards:	14
Number of applicants:	600
Application deadline:	March 1
Notification begins:	May 15
Total amount awarded:	$77,000

Contact:
Virginia Museum of Fine Arts Fellowships Division
Education and Outreach Division
2800 Grove Avenue
Richmond, VA 23221-2466
Phone: 804-367-0824

Wal-Mart Foundation

Wal-Mart Competitive Edge Scholarship

Type of award: Scholarship, renewable.
Intended use: For full-time freshman study. Designated institutions: participating universities.
Eligibility: Applicant must be U.S. citizen.
Basis for selection: Major/career interest in computer and

information sciences; engineering, agricultural; engineering, chemical; engineering, civil; engineering, electrical and electronic; engineering, mechanical; mathematics; microbiology. Applicant must demonstrate leadership, service orientation and high academic achievement.
Application requirements: Essay.
Additional information: Must be citizen in the country where university is located. Must have score of at least 27 on ACT or 1100 on SAT. Minimum 3.5 GPA and 90% or higher class rank. Contact university for application requirements. Additional fields of study include: computer information systems and quantitative analysis, industrial and technical education, computer systems engineering, electrical engineering, industrial engineering, and biochemistry.

    Amount of award: $5,000
    Number of awards: 250
    Application deadline: , March 15
Contact:
Wal-Mart Foundation
702 SW 8 Street
Bentonville, AR 72716-8071

Wall Street Journal

Wall Street Journal Internship

Type of award: Internship.
Intended use: For undergraduate or graduate study.
Eligibility: Applicant must be U.S. citizen.
Basis for selection: Major/career interest in journalism; English.
Application requirements: Interview and recommendations.
Additional information: 10-week full-time internship. Previous journalism and/or college newspaper experience helpful. Must submit cover letter, resume and journalistic clips. Interns are paid $550 a week.

    Amount of award: $5,500
    Number of awards: 16
Contact:
The Wall Street Journal
200 Liberty St.
New York, NY 10281

Walt Disney World

Walt Disney Recruiting Program

Type of award: Internship, renewable.
Intended use: For full-time sophomore, junior, senior or graduate study.
Eligibility: Applicant must be U.S. citizen or permanent resident.
Application requirements: Interview.
Additional information: 10 week internship at Walt Disney World. $225 a week, full-time (at least 30 hours per week). Free housing and transportation to and from work. Free admission and discounts. Interns must attend a corporate training program.

    Amount of award: $2,250
    Number of awards: 800
    Number of applicants: 3,000
Contact:
Walt Disney World
P.O. Box 10090
Lake Buena Vista, FL

Walt Disney World Horticulture Summer Internship

Type of award: Internship.
Intended use: For junior, senior study in Lake Buena Vista, FL. Designated institutions: Walt Disney World.
Basis for selection: Major/career interest in landscape architecture; horticulture; entomology. Applicant must demonstrate seriousness of purpose, service orientation and high academic achievement.
Application requirements: Interview, essay and transcript. Resume.
Additional information: Students paid $8.53 per hour.

    Number of awards: 90
    Application deadline: February 1
Contact:
Walt Disney World
Horticulture Creative Services
P.O. Box 10000
Lake Buena Vista, FL 32830-1000

Warwick, Baker and Fiore

Warwick, Baker and Fiore Internship Program

Type of award: Internship.
Intended use: For junior, senior study.
Eligibility: Applicant must be U.S. citizen.
Basis for selection: Major/career interest in advertising. Applicant must demonstrate seriousness of purpose.
Application requirements: Interview and recommendations.
Additional information: Six month internship available to college sophomores and juniors. Must submit resume and cover letter.

    Amount of award: $3,000
    Number of awards: 3
    Number of applicants: 85
    Application deadline: April 14
Contact:
Warwick, Baker and Fiore
100 Avenue of the Americas
New York, NY
Website: www.warwick.com

Washington Crossing Foundation

Washington Crossing Foundation Scholarship

Type of award: Scholarship, renewable.
Intended use: For full-time freshman study at accredited 4-year institution.
Eligibility: Applicant must be high school senior. Applicant must be U.S. citizen.
Basis for selection: Major/career interest in political science/government; public administration/service. Applicant must demonstrate depth of character, leadership, patriotism, seriousness of purpose, service orientation and high academic achievement.
Application requirements: Interview, recommendations, essay, transcript and proof of eligibility. SAT or ACT scores.
Additional information: Applicants must write essay on why they plan a career in government service. One award is reserved for residents of Pennsylvania.
    Amount of award: $1,000-$10,000
    Number of awards: 7
    Number of applicants: 1,500
    Application deadline: January 15, January 15
    Notification begins: April 15, April 15
    Total amount awarded: $46,000
Contact:
Attn: Vice Chairman-Washington Crossing Foundation
6934 N. Radcliffe St
Bristol, PA 19007
Phone: 215-493-6577

Washington Gas

Washington Gas Scholarship

Type of award: Scholarship, renewable.
Intended use: For full-time freshman study at accredited postsecondary institution in or outside United States.
Eligibility: Applicant must be single, high school senior. Applicant must be U.S. citizen or permanent resident.
Basis for selection: Applicant must demonstrate depth of character, leadership, patriotism, seriousness of purpose, service orientation and high academic achievement.
Application requirements: Recommendations and transcript. Brief description of what student wishes to accomplish at school and after graduation. List of community work that student has done.
Additional information: Minimum GPA of 3.0. Program may change; contact sponsor for updated information.
    Amount of award: $1,000
    Number of awards: 16
    Application deadline: February 26
    Notification begins: May 15
Contact:
Washington Gas
1100 H Street, NW
Washington, DC 20008
Phone: 202-624-6758

Washington Internships for Students of Engineering

Washington Internships for Student of Engineering

Type of award: Internship.
Intended use: For senior study.
Eligibility: Applicant must be U.S. citizen.
Basis for selection: Major/career interest in engineering.
Application requirements: Interview, recommendations and transcript.
Additional information: 10 week summer internship available to college seniors. Interns write a required research paper as part of the process. Rund-trip travel allowance.
    Amount of award: $1,750
    Application deadline: October 1
Contact:
Washington Internships for Students of Engineering
1899 L St., SW, Suite 500
Washington, DC

Washington State PTA Financial Grant Foundation

Washington State PTA Financial Grant

Type of award: Scholarship.
Intended use: For full-time freshman study at accredited vocational, 2-year or 4-year institution.
Eligibility: Applicant must be U.S. citizen or permanent resident residing in Washington.
Basis for selection: Applicant must demonstrate depth of character, leadership, seriousness of purpose, service orientation and financial need.
Application requirements: Recommendations, essay, transcript and proof of eligibility.
Additional information: Applicant must be graduate of a Washington state high school. Grant administered according to college's determination. Not transferable to another institution if already enrolled in classes. Applications available after December 1.
    Amount of award: $500-$1,000
    Number of awards: 60
    Number of applicants: 1,500
    Application deadline: March 1
    Notification begins: May 1
    Total amount awarded: $55,000
Contact:
Washington State PTA Financial Grant Foundation
2003 65 Avenue West
Tacoma, WA 98466-6215
Phone: 253-565-2153
Website: www.wastatepta.org

Weather Channel

Weather Channel Meteorology Internship

Type of award: Internship.
Intended use: For senior study.
Basis for selection: Major/career interest in atmospheric sciences/meteorology.
Application requirements: Recommendations and transcript. Include cover letter and resume.
Additional information: Meteorologist intern. Must have completed junior year, taken several meteorology courses, and have interest in operational career. Salary approximately $7 per hour.
    Number of awards: 4
    Application deadline: March 31
Contact:
Weather Channel
300 Interstate North Parkway
ATTN: Kathy Strebe, Meteorology Manager
Atlanta, GA 30339

Wellesley College

M.A. Cartland Shackford Medical Fellowship

Type of award: Scholarship.
Intended use: For full-time first professional study.
Eligibility: Applicant must be female.
Basis for selection: Major/career interest in medicine (m.d.). Applicant must demonstrate financial need and high academic achievement.
Application requirements: Recommendations, essay and transcript. For study of medicine with a view toward general practice (not psychiatry).
Additional information: For the study of medicine with a view to general practice, not psychiatry. Award amount may vary; minimum is $7000. Send SASE or request application by email.
    Amount of award: $7,000
    Number of awards: 1
    Number of applicants: 51
    Application deadline: January 11
    Notification begins: March 1

Mary McEwen Schimke Scholarship

Type of award: Scholarship.
Intended use: For graduate study.
Eligibility: Applicant must be female.
Basis for selection: Major/career interest in literature; history. Applicant must demonstrate financial need and high academic achievement.
Application requirements: Recommendations, essay and transcript.
Additional information: Award is provided for relief from household and child care expenses while pursuing graduate study. Preference given to students of American studies. Applicant must be engaged in graduate study in literature or history. Award amount varies up to $1000.
    Amount of award: $1,000
    Number of awards: 1
    Number of applicants: 11
    Application deadline: January 11
    Notification begins: March 1
Contact:
Wellesley College
Center for Work and Service
106 Central Street
Wellesley, MA 02181
Website: www.wellesley.edu

Western Golf Association

Chick Evans Caddie Scholarship

Type of award: Scholarship, renewable.
Intended use: For full-time freshman, sophomore, junior or senior study at accredited 4-year institution in United States.
Eligibility: Applicant must be high school senior.
Basis for selection: Applicant must demonstrate depth of character, leadership, financial need and high academic achievement.
Application requirements: Interview, recommendations, transcript and proof of eligibility. Tax returns and SAT or ACT test scores required.
Additional information: Scholarship for full tuition plus housing. Must have caddied minimum two years at Western Golf Association affiliated club and rank in top 25 percent of class. Most recipients attend one of the 14 universities where Evans Scholars Foundation owns and operates chapter house.
    Number of awards: 850
    Number of applicants: 1,000
    Application deadline: November 1
Contact:
Scholarship Committee
Western Golf Assoc./Evans Scholars Foundation
1 Briar Road
Golf, IL 60029
Phone: 847-724-4600

Westlake Scholarship Foundation

Westlake Scholarship

Type of award: Scholarship, renewable.
Intended use: For full-time freshman study at accredited 2-year or 4-year institution in United States.
Eligibility: Applicant must be U.S. citizen or permanent resident residing in Missouri.
Basis for selection: Applicant must demonstrate depth of character, leadership, seriousness of purpose, service orientation, financial need and high academic achievement.
Application requirements: Recommendations, essay,

transcript and proof of eligibility. Must submit FAFSA which indicates an EFC of $17,000 or less.
- **Amount of award:** $500-$6,000
- **Number of awards:** 400
- **Number of applicants:** 1,000
- **Application deadline:** March 1
- **Notification begins:** June 1
- **Total amount awarded:** $1,000,000

Contact:
Westlake Scholarship Foundation
8000 Bonhomme Suite 212
Clayton, MO 63105
Phone: 314-725-6410

Whitney Museum of American Art

Critical Studies Program

Type of award: Internship.
Intended use: For undergraduate, graduate or postgraduate study.
Basis for selection: Major/career interest in arts, general; art, art history; museum studies. Applicant must demonstrate high academic achievement.
Application requirements: $15 application fee. Interview, recommendations, transcript and research proposal.
Additional information: Tuition for program is $1,800 a year. Begins in mid-September and concludes at end of following May. Students eligible are graduates, candidates for postgraduate degrees, undergraduates with advanced scholarship, or those who have recently completed formal academic study. Most cooperating schools grant 12-16 credits for participation. Critical studies fellows engage in individual scholarly research and critical writing projects.
- **Application deadline:** April 1
- **Notification begins:** May 1

Curatorial Program

Type of award: Internship.
Intended use: For undergraduate, graduate or postgraduate study.
Basis for selection: Major/career interest in museum studies; arts, general; arts management; art, art history. Applicant must demonstrate high academic achievement.
Application requirements: $15 application fee. Interview, recommendations and transcript.
Additional information: Curatorial fellows collaborate to produce an exhibition. Program begins in mid-September and concludes at the end of following May. Includes $3,500 stipend payable in 3 installments. Must include writing sample and exhibition proposal with application. Students eligible are graduates, candidates for advanced postgraduate degrees, undergraduates with advanced scholarship and those who have recently completed formal academic study. Most cooperating schools grant 12-16 credits for participation.
- **Amount of award:** $3,500
- **Application deadline:** April 1
- **Notification begins:** May 15

Studio Program

Type of award: Internship.
Intended use: For undergraduate, graduate or postgraduate study.
Basis for selection: Major/career interest in arts, general; film/video. Applicant must demonstrate high academic achievement.
Application requirements: $15 application fee. Interview, portfolio, recommendations and transcript.
Additional information: Tuition for program is $1,800 a year. Begins in mid-September and concludes at end of following May. Students eligible are graduates, candidates for postgraduate degrees, undergraduates with advanced scholarship, or those who have recently completed formal academic study. Most cooperating schools grant 12-16 credits for participation. Must include reproductions of examples of work with application.
- **Application deadline:** April 1
- **Notification begins:** April 15

Contact:
Whitney Museum of American Art
384 Broadway, 4th Fl.
New York, NY 10013

Wilhelmina Models

Wilhelmina Models Summer Internship

Type of award: Internship.
Intended use: For undergraduate or graduate study.
Eligibility: Applicant must be U.S. citizen or permanent resident.
Basis for selection: Applicant must demonstrate seriousness of purpose and service orientation.
Application requirements: Recommendations. Resume.
Additional information: Internships available in New York City and Beverly Hills, CA. Stipend of $25 a day to cover lunch and travel expenses. High school students, undergraduates, recent college graduates and graduate students eligible. High school graduates and college graduates of any age are also eligible to work at New York City office only. Interns assist booking agents in the Men's and Women's divisions.
- **Number of awards:** 8
- **Application deadline:** March 3

Contact:
Scholarship Coordinator
300 Park Ave., S.
New York, NY 10010

William Randolph Hearst Foundation

Hearst Journalism Award

Type of award: Scholarship.
Intended use: For full-time or half-time freshman, sophomore, junior or senior study at accredited 4-year institution.
Basis for selection: Competition in Writing/journalism. Newsworthiness, research, excellence of journalistic writing, photo journalism, or broadcast news. Major/career interest in journalism; radio/television/film.
Application requirements: Entries must be submitted by journalism department.
Additional information: Must submit work that has been published or aired to be considered. Entries must be submitted by journalism department. Field of study may also include photojournalism. Institution must be accredited by Accrediting Council on Education in Journalism and Mass Communication. Deadlines vary each month. For additional information, applicants should contact journalism department chair or Hearst Foundation.
   Amount of award: $500-$3,000
   Number of awards: 130
Contact:
W.R. Hearst Foundation, Journalism Awards Program
Suite 1212
90 New Montgomery Street
San Francisco, CA 94105

Hearst United States Senate Youth Program

Type of award: Scholarship.
Intended use: For full-time or half-time freshman, sophomore, junior or senior study at accredited 2-year or 4-year institution in United States.
Eligibility: Applicant must be high school junior, senior. Applicant must be permanent resident.
Basis for selection: Applicant must demonstrate leadership and service orientation.
Application requirements: Nomination by Students are nominated by high school principal based on merit and community service.
Additional information: Must be currently serving in elected capacity as student body officer, class officer, student council representative, or student representative to district, regional, or state-level civic or educational organization.
   Amount of award: $2,000
   Number of awards: 104
   Notification begins: December
   Total amount awarded: $208,000
Contact:
Scholarship Coordinator
Suite 1212
90 New Montgomery Street
San Francisco, CA 94105-4504
Phone: 800-841-7048

Wilson Ornithological Society

Louis Agassiz Fuertes Award

Type of award: Research grant.
Intended use: For master's, doctoral, postgraduate or non-degree study.
Basis for selection: Major/career interest in ornithology.
Application requirements: Recommendations and research proposal.
Additional information: Research grant for studies of birds. Preference given to graduate students and young professionals. The WOS encourages applicants whose first language is not English. Such applicants may send an additional copy of their proposal in their first language to Dr. Jon C. Barlow at the following address: Centre for Biodiversity and Conservation Biology, Royal Ontario Museum, 100 Queen's Park, Toronto, ON, M5S 2C6 Canada. Applicants may also email their first language proposal to jonb@rom.on.ca.
   Amount of award: $600
   Number of awards: 1
   Number of applicants: 55
   Application deadline: January 15
   Notification begins: April 15
   Total amount awarded: $600
Contact:
Dr. Dan Klem
Department of Biology
Muhlenberg College
Allentown, PA 18104

Margaret Morse Nice Award

Type of award: Research grant.
Intended use: For non-degree study.
Basis for selection: Major/career interest in ornithology.
Application requirements: Recommendations and research proposal.
Additional information: Research grant for studies of birds. Award restricted to amateur researchers, including high school students, without access to funds and facilities of academic institutions or governmental agencies.
   Amount of award: $200
   Number of awards: 1
   Number of applicants: 2
   Application deadline: January 15
   Notification begins: April 15
   Total amount awarded: $200
Contact:
Research Grant Committee
Museum of Zoology
University of Michigan
Ann Arbor, MI 48109-1079

Paul A. Stewart Award

Type of award: Research grant.
Intended use: For undergraduate, master's, doctoral, postgraduate or non-degree study.
Basis for selection: Major/career interest in ornithology.
Application requirements: Recommendations and research proposal.
Additional information: Research grant for studies of birds.

Preference given to ornithologists studying bird movements based on banding or on economic ornithology.

Amount of award:	$200
Number of awards:	5
Number of applicants:	7
Application deadline:	January 15
Notification begins:	April 15
Total amount awarded:	$1,200

Contact:
Research Grant Committee
Dr. Dan Klem, Department of Biology
Muhlenberg College
Allentown, PA 18104

Winston Churchill Foundation

Churchill Scholarship

Type of award: Scholarship.
Intended use: For master's, doctoral study in United Kingdom. Designated institutions: University of Cambridge, Churchill College, Cambridge, U.K.
Eligibility: Applicant must be U.S. citizen or permanent resident.
Basis for selection: Major/career interest in mathematics; physical sciences; engineering; biology. Applicant must demonstrate leadership and seriousness of purpose.
Application requirements: Nomination by one of 56 colleges and universities participating in program. Must be enrolled in and nominated by one of 54 participating colleges and universities.
Additional information: Funds cover tuition, living expenses, and travel. To encourage scientific and technological talent and further Anglo-American ties.

Amount of award:	$25,000
Number of awards:	11
Number of applicants:	100
Application deadline:	November 15
Notification begins:	April 15
Total amount awarded:	$250,000

Contact:
Winston Churchill Foundation
P.O. Box 1240
Gracie Station
New York, NY 10028
Phone: 212-879-3450
Fax: 212-879-3480

Wisconsin Dental Foundation

Wisconsin Dental Association Scholarship

Type of award: Scholarship.
Intended use: For half-time freshman, sophomore or junior study at accredited postsecondary institution in United States. Designated institutions: Marquette University and other technical schools in Wisconsin.
Eligibility: Applicant must be residing in Wisconsin.
Basis for selection: Major/career interest in dental hygiene; dentistry. Applicant must demonstrate depth of character, leadership, seriousness of purpose, service orientation, financial need and high academic achievement.
Application requirements: Recommendations and nomination by committees at each campus.

Amount of award:	$250-$500
Number of awards:	13
Number of applicants:	65
Total amount awarded:	$6,000

Contact:
Wisconsin Dental Foundation
111 East Wisconsin Avenue
Suite 1300
Milwaukee, WI 53202
Phone: 414-276-4520

WMTW Channel Eight

Bob Elliot - Channel 8 Journalism Scholarship

Type of award: Scholarship.
Intended use: For undergraduate study.
Eligibility: Applicant must be high school senior. Applicant must be U.S. citizen or permanent resident residing in Maine.
Basis for selection: Major/career interest in journalism; communications.
Application requirements: Recommendations and essay. State applicant must reside in Maine.
Additional information: Only high school seniors in the WMTW viewing area are eligible.

Amount of award:	$1,500
Number of awards:	1
Number of applicants:	500
Application deadline:	April 1

Contact:
WMTW Channel 8
P.O. Box 8
Auburn, ME 04210

Wolf Trap Foundation for the Performing Arts

Wolf Trap Performing Arts Internship

Type of award: Internship.
Intended use: For full-time or half-time sophomore, junior, senior or graduate study in United States.
Eligibility: Applicant must be U.S. citizen, permanent resident or Must meet INS I-9 requirement Wont.
Basis for selection: Major/career interest in arts, general;

music; education; performing arts; accounting; communications; education; information systems. Applicant must demonstrate seriousness of purpose.
Application requirements: Recommendations. Cover letter outlining personal statement and career goals, two recommendations (academic and personal), two contrasting writing samples, resume.
Additional information: The deadline for summer internships is March first. A variety of positions also exist in the development, publications, photography, group sales, and food and beverage departments.

Amount of award:	$700-$1,800
Number of awards:	36
Number of applicants:	200
Application deadline:	July 1, November 1
Notification begins:	August 30, December 15

Contact:
Wolf Trap Foundation For the Performing Arts
Internship Program
1624 Trap Road
Vienna, VA 22182
Phone: 703-255-1933
Fax: 703-255-1924
Website: www.wolf-trap.org

Women Grocers of America

Mary Macey Scholarship

Type of award: Scholarship, renewable.
Intended use: For sophomore, junior, senior, graduate or postgraduate study at accredited 2-year, 4-year or graduate institution in United States.
Basis for selection: Major/career interest in food production/management/services.
Application requirements: Recommendations, essay and transcript.
Additional information: Must plan on a career in any facet of the Grocery industry (retail, wholesale, or manufacturing). Majors in public health and hotel management are not eligible. Must have a GPA of 2.0.

Amount of award:	$1,000-$1,500
Number of awards:	2
Number of applicants:	16
Application deadline:	June 1
Notification begins:	July 1
Total amount awarded:	$6,000

Contact:
Women Grocers of America
1825 Samuel Morse Drive
Reston, VA 20190-5317
Phone: 703-437-5300

Women of the Evangelical Lutheran Church in America

Women of the Evangelical Lutheran Church in America Scholarship

Type of award: Scholarship, renewable.
Intended use: For freshman, sophomore, junior, senior, master's, doctoral or first professional study.
Eligibility: Applicant must be female, adult returning student, Lutheran.
Basis for selection: Applicant must demonstrate service orientation, financial need and high academic achievement.
Application requirements: Recommendations and proof of eligibility.
Additional information: Must be member of Evangelical Lutheran Church in America. Must have interrupted education since high school for at least two years. Must show clear educational goals. Cannot be studying for ordination, diaconate, or church-certified professions. Must be a laywoman, 21 or older.

Amount of award:	$500-$2,000
Number of awards:	16
Number of applicants:	100
Application deadline:	March 1
Notification begins:	June
Total amount awarded:	$25,000

Contact:
Women of the Evangelical Lutheran Church in America
8765 West Higgins Road
Chicago, IL 60631-4189
Website: www.elca.org/wo

Women's Research and Education Institute

Women's Research and Education Congressional Fellowship

Type of award: Internship.
Intended use: For master's, doctoral, first professional or postgraduate study.
Eligibility: Applicant must be U.S. citizen or permanent resident.
Basis for selection: Major/career interest in political science/government; public administration/service; social and behavioral sciences; womenÖs studies. Applicant must demonstrate depth of character, leadership, seriousness of purpose and service orientation.
Application requirements: Interview, recommendations, essay and transcript.
Additional information: Must be enrolled in accredited graduate institution at time of application, and have completed at least nine credit hours of coursework. Must have interest in public policy as it affects women's lives. Applicants in all

fields of study are welcome if their work focuses on women's studies or women's health. Recipient lives in Washington D.C. for nine months and works in either a Congress member's or strategic committee staff member's office. WREI provides up to $1,500 additional funding for independent study at home institution. Send SASE for application, or send request via email.

Amount of award:	$11,500
Number of awards:	7
Number of applicants:	60
Application deadline:	February 15
Notification begins:	May 1
Total amount awarded:	$80,500

Contact:
Congressional Fellowships
Women's Research and Education Institute
1750 New York Avenue, NW, Suite 350
Washington, DC 20006
Website: www.wrei.org

Women's Western Golf Foundation

Women's Western Golf Foundation Scholarship

Type of award: Scholarship, renewable.
Intended use: For full-time freshman, sophomore, junior or senior study at accredited 4-year institution in United States.
Eligibility: Applicant must be female, high school senior. Applicant must be U.S. citizen.
Basis for selection: Applicant must demonstrate depth of character, leadership, seriousness of purpose, financial need and high academic achievement.
Application requirements: Recommendations, essay, transcript and proof of eligibility. SAT/ACT scores, FAFSA. Personal recommendation required from high school teacher or counselor.
Additional information: Must be in top 15 % of class. A 3.5 GPA is recommended. Deadline to request an application is March 1. Must fill out an FAFSA with the U.S. government and provide a copy with the application.

Amount of award:	$2,000
Number of awards:	75
Number of applicants:	75
Application deadline:	April 4
Notification begins:	May 15
Total amount awarded:	$150,000

Contact:
Women's Western Golf Foundation
393 Ramsay Road
Deerfield, IL 60015

Woodrow Wilson National Fellowship Foundation

Andrew W. Mellon Fellowship in Humanistic Studies

Type of award: Scholarship.
Intended use: For full-time doctoral study at accredited graduate institution. Designated institutions: In United States and Canadda.
Eligibility: Applicant must be U.S. citizen or permanent resident.
Basis for selection: Major/career interest in humanities/liberal arts. Applicant must demonstrate seriousness of purpose and high academic achievement.
Application requirements: Interview, recommendations, essay and proof of eligibility.
Additional information: For first year of Ph.D. study. Must plan career in college teaching or scholarship in field of humanities. Application requests must be postmarked by December 7.

Amount of award:	$14,500
Number of awards:	80
Number of applicants:	900
Application deadline:	December 31
Notification begins:	March 29
Total amount awarded:	$1,100,000

Contact:
Woodrow Wilson National Fellowship Foundation
Mellon Fellowships in Humanistic Studies
CN 5329
Princeton, NJ 08543-5329
Website: www.woodrow.org/mellon

Newcombe Doctoral Dissertation Fellowship

Type of award: Scholarship.
Intended use: For full-time doctoral study at accredited graduate institution in United States.
Basis for selection: Major/career interest in education, teacher; humanities/liberal arts; social and behavioral sciences. Applicant must demonstrate high academic achievement.
Application requirements: Recommendations, transcript, proof of eligibility and research proposal. six-page prospectus.
Additional information: Must have completed all pre-dissertation requirements for doctorate and be writing dissertation on ethical or religious values in any field of humanities or social sciences. Applicants who have held a similar award for the final year of dissertation writing (e.g. Whiting, Mellon, NEH, Ford, Pew, Spencer, or AAUW fellowship) are not eligible. Application request deadline November 13. Teacher education must be college level.

Amount of award:	$15,000
Number of awards:	35
Number of applicants:	500
Application deadline:	December 11
Notification begins:	April 15

Contact:
Woodrow Wilson National Fellowship Foundation
Newcombe Fellowships
CN 5281
Princeton, NJ 08543-5281
Website: www.woodrow.org/mellon

Woodrow Wilson Dissertation Grant in Women's Studies

Type of award: Research grant.
Intended use: For doctoral study at accredited graduate institution in United States.
Basis for selection: Major/career interest in womenÖs studies; history; literature. Applicant must demonstrate high academic achievement.
Application requirements: Recommendations, essay, transcript, proof of eligibility and research proposal.
Additional information: For dissertation research. Topic must be relevant to study of women in history, literature, or society. Application must be requested by October 18.

Amount of award:	$1,500
Number of awards:	15
Number of applicants:	314
Application deadline:	November 2
Notification begins:	February 15

Contact:
Woodrow Wilson National Fellowship Foundation
Women's Studies Program
CN 5281
Princeton, NJ 08543-5281
Website: www.woodrow.org/mellon

Woodrow Wilson Program in Public Policy and International Affairs

Type of award: Scholarship, renewable.
Intended use: For full-time junior study.
Eligibility: Applicant must be of minority background. Applicant must be U.S. citizen or permanent resident.
Basis for selection: Major/career interest in international relations; public administration/service.
Application requirements: Recommendations, essay, transcript and proof of eligibility. Include resume.
Additional information: 150 students chosen at end of junior year for three year preparation for careers in public policy and international affairs. All undergraduate majors considered. Must apply as junior for Junior Year Summer Institute; contact foundation for list of institutions holding the institutes. Room, board, travel/living allowance provided. Upon completion, eligible for internship the following summer in policy/international work or Language Institutes Scholarship, and for graduate fellowship in designated master's program. Cannot apply separately for summer programs after senior year or for graduate fellowship.

Number of awards:	150
Number of applicants:	2,000
Application deadline:	March 15
Notification begins:	April 25
Total amount awarded:	$2,700,000

Contact:
Woodrow Wilson National Fellowship Foundation
Public Policy & Int'l Affairs
CN 2434
Princeton, NJ 08543-2434

Worcester County Horticultural Society

Procter-Channin Scholarship

Type of award: Scholarship, renewable.
Intended use: For full-time junior, senior or graduate study at 4-year or graduate institution in United States.
Eligibility: Applicant must be residing in Connecticut or Massachusetts or Maine or New Hampshire or Rhode Island or Vermont.
Basis for selection: Major/career interest in horticulture; landscape architecture. Applicant must demonstrate seriousness of purpose, financial need and high academic achievement.
Application requirements: Recommendations, essay and transcript.
Additional information: Must rank in top third of class, preferably in top quarter.

Amount of award:	$500-$2,000
Number of awards:	2
Number of applicants:	60
Application deadline:	May 1
Notification begins:	June 15
Total amount awarded:	$2,500

Contact:
Scholarship Committee
11 French Drive
P.O. Box 598
Boylston, MA 01503-0598
Phone: 508-869-6111
Fax: 508-869-0314

Y.E.S. To Jobs

Youth Entertainment Summer

Type of award: Internship.
Intended use: For undergraduate study.
Eligibility: Applicant must be enrolled in high school. Applicant must be U.S. citizen.
Basis for selection: Major/career interest in film/video; law; business; computer and information sciences.
Application requirements: Interview, recommendations, essay and transcript.
Additional information: Provides summer employment in various aspects of the entertainment industry.

Amount of award:	$2,000
Number of awards:	350
Number of applicants:	1,300
Application deadline:	April 1
Total amount awarded:	$700,000

Contact:
Program Coordinator
1416 N. La Brea Ave.
Hollywood, CA 90028

Yakama Indian Nation

Yakama Indian Nation Scholarship

Type of award: Scholarship.
Intended use: For freshman, sophomore, junior, senior, master's or doctoral study at accredited 2-year, 4-year or graduate institution.
Eligibility: Applicant must be American Indian. Must be enrolled member of Yakama Indian Nation. Applicant must be U.S. citizen.
Basis for selection: Applicant must demonstrate financial need.
Application requirements: Essay and transcript.
   Amount of award: $1,500
   Number of awards: 270
   Number of applicants: 307
   Application deadline: July 1
   Total amount awarded: $399,000
Contact:
Yakama Indian Nation
P.O. Box 151
Toppenish, WA 98948

Zonta International Foundation

Amelia Earhart Fellowship

Type of award: Scholarship, renewable.
Intended use: For full-time master's, doctoral study at accredited graduate institution.
Eligibility: Applicant must be female.
Basis for selection: Major/career interest in aerospace; engineering. Applicant must demonstrate high academic achievement.
Application requirements: Recommendations, essay, transcript, proof of eligibility and research proposal.
Additional information: Bachelor's degree in science or engineering relating to aerospace sciences required. The recipient must have completed one year of graduate studies in engineering or aerospace by the time the fellowship is awarded.
   Amount of award: $6,000
   Number of awards: 33
   Number of applicants: 186
   Application deadline: November 1
   Total amount awarded: $198,000
Contact:
Zonta International Foundation
Amelia Earhart Fellowship Awards
557 West Randolph Street
Chicago, IL 60661-2206

Private Restricted

1199 National Benefit Fund

Joseph Tauber Scholarship

Type of award: Scholarship, renewable.
Intended use: For full-time undergraduate, non-degree study at accredited vocational, 2-year or 4-year institution outside United States.
Eligibility: Applicant or parent must be member of 1199 National Benefit Fund.
Basis for selection: Applicant must demonstrate financial need.
Application requirements: Transcript and proof of eligibility. High school graduates, post-secondary school students & previous awardees whose parents are in Benefit Fund Wage Class One for one year at the time of application are eligible.
    Amount of award: $750-$8,000
    Number of awards: 1,153
    Application deadline: January 2
    Notification begins: January 8
    Total amount awarded: $3,037,396
Contact:
1199 National Benefit Fund
310 West 43 Street
New York, NY 10036

25th Infantry Division Association

25th Infantry Division Educational Memorial Scholarship

Type of award: Scholarship.
Intended use: For full-time freshman study at accredited 4-year institution in United States.
Eligibility: Applicant or parent must be member of 25th Infantry Division Association. Applicant must be U.S. citizen. Applicant must be in military service, veteran, disabled while on duty, child of active service person, veteran, disabled veteran or deceased veteran who served in the Army. Deceased member must have died on active duty with division or as a result thereof. Veterans must be association members. Applicant on active duty must be scheduled for release/retirement or discharged from division by December 31 of award year.
Basis for selection: Applicant must demonstrate depth of character, leadership, seriousness of purpose, service orientation, financial need and high academic achievement.
Application requirements: Recommendations, essay, transcript and proof of eligibility. SAT or ACT scores.
Additional information: Must be pursuing first bachelor's degree. May not be used at U.S. military academies.
    Amount of award: $1,000-$1,500
    Number of awards: 9
    Number of applicants: 24
    Application deadline: April 1
    Notification begins: June 1
    Total amount awarded: $10,000
Contact:
25th Infantry Division Association
c/o Lawrence Weist
3930 South Bridlewood Drive
Bountiful, UT 84010
Phone: 801-292-7354

A.M. Castle and Company

John M. Simpson Memorial Scholarship

Type of award: Scholarship, renewable.
Intended use: For full-time undergraduate study.
Eligibility: Applicant or parent must be employed by A. M. Castle & Co.
Application requirements: Recommendations, essay and transcript.
Additional information: For children of A.M. Castle and Company employees.
    Amount of award: $2,500
    Total amount awarded: $14,000
Contact:
AMC & Company
3400 North Wolf Road
Franklin Park, IL 60131
Phone: 847-455-7111
Website: www.amcastle.com

Richard G. Mork Scholarship

Type of award: Scholarship, renewable.
Intended use: For full-time undergraduate study.
Eligibility: Applicant or parent must be employed by A. M. Castle & Co. Applicant must be high school senior.
Application requirements: Recommendations, essay and transcript.
    Amount of award: $1,500
Contact:
Scholarship Committee
3400 North Wolf Road
Franklin Park, IL 60131
Phone: 847-455-2240 ext. 42556

Acrometal Management Corporation

Acrometal Family of Companies Scholarship Program

Type of award: Scholarship.
Intended use: For undergraduate study at vocational, 2-year or 4-year institution.
Eligibility: Applicant or parent must be employed by Acrometal Management Corporation. Applicant must be high school senior.
Additional information: For further information or an application contact Acrometal Management Corporation directly.
    Amount of award: $1,000

Adaptec

Adaptec Scholarship

Type of award: Scholarship, renewable.
Intended use: For undergraduate study at accredited postsecondary institution.
Eligibility: Applicant or parent must be employed by Adaptec. Applicant must be high school senior.
Basis for selection: Applicant must demonstrate financial need.
Additional information: For further information or an application contact Adaptec directly.
    Amount of award: $5,000
Contact:
ADAPTEC

Addison Wesley Longman

Melbourne Wesley Cummings Scholarship Program

Type of award: Scholarship, renewable.
Intended use: For undergraduate study.
Eligibility: Applicant or parent must be employed by Addison-Wesley Publishing Company.
Basis for selection: Applicant must demonstrate financial need.
Additional information: For further information or an application contact Addison Wesley Longman directly.
    Amount of award: $500-$2,000

AGL Resources Service Company

AGL Resources Inc. Scholarship

Type of award: Scholarship, renewable.
Intended use: For undergraduate study at vocational, 2-year or 4-year institution.
Eligibility: Applicant or parent must be employed by AGL Resources Service Company. Applicant must be high school senior.
Additional information: For further information or an application contact AGL Resources Incorporated directly.
    Amount of award: $500-$1,000

Air Force Sergeants Association

Air Force Sergeants Association Scholarship

Type of award: Scholarship.
Intended use: For full-time undergraduate study at accredited vocational, 2-year or 4-year institution in or outside United States.
Eligibility: Applicant or parent must be member of Air Force Sergeants Association or Auxiliary. Applicant must be single.
Basis for selection: Applicant must demonstrate depth of character, leadership and high academic achievement.
Application requirements: Recommendations, essay, transcript and proof of eligibility. Minimum 1100 SAT score (high school seniors) and 3.5 GPA.
Additional information: Must be single dependent, including legally adopted child or stepchild, who will not reach 23rd birthday by September 1 of award year. Self-addressed, stamped ($1.47) envelope (9" x 12") required.
    Amount of award: $1,500-$2,500
    Number of awards: 14
    Number of applicants: 200
    Application deadline: April 15
    Notification begins: August 1
    Total amount awarded: $24,000

Capitol College Electronic Engineering Scholarship

Type of award: Scholarship.
Intended use: For full-time freshman, sophomore, junior or senior study. Designated institutions: Capitol College, Laurel MD campus.
Eligibility: Applicant or parent must be member of Air Force Sergeants Association or Auxiliary. Applicant must be single.
Basis for selection: Major/career interest in engineering, electrical and electronic; engineering. Applicant must demonstrate depth of character, leadership and high academic achievement.
Application requirements: Recommendations, essay, transcript and proof of eligibility. Minimum 1100 SAT and 3.5 GPA.
Additional information: Must be single dependent, including

legally adopted child or stepchild, who will not reach 23rd birthday by September 1 of award year. Self-addressed, stamped ($1.47) envelope (9" x 12") required.

Amount of award:	$600
Number of awards:	1
Number of applicants:	9
Application deadline:	April 15
Notification begins:	August 1
Total amount awarded:	$600

Contact:
Air Force Sergeant's Association
AFSA Scholarships
P.O. Box 50
Temple Hills, MD 20757-0050
Phone: 301-899-3500

Air Liquide America Foundation, Inc.

Air Liquide America Foundation Scholarship

Type of award: Scholarship, renewable.
Intended use: For freshman, sophomore, junior or senior study at accredited vocational, 2-year or 4-year institution.
Eligibility: Applicant or parent must be employed by Air Liquide America Corporation.
Basis for selection: Applicant must demonstrate financial need.
Additional information: Must be child of employee of ALAC. For further information or an application contact Air Liquide America Corporation directly.

Amount of award:	$500-$2,000

Air Traffic Control Association, Inc.

Air Traffic Control Children of Specialists Scholarship

Type of award: Scholarship, renewable.
Intended use: For full-time undergraduate or graduate study at accredited 4-year institution.
Eligibility: Applicant or parent must be employed by *Aviation. Applicant must be U.S. citizen.
Basis for selection: Applicant must demonstrate depth of character, seriousness of purpose and financial need.
Application requirements: Recommendations and transcript.
Additional information: Must be natural or adopted child of air traffic control specialist. Applicant's course work must lead to a bachelor's degree or higher.

Amount of award:	$1,500-$2,500
Number of awards:	3
Number of applicants:	200
Application deadline:	May 1
Total amount awarded:	$4,500

Contact:
Scholarship Coordinator
Arlington Courthouse Plaza II
2300 Clarendon Boulevard, Suite 711
Arlington, VA 22201

Air Traffic Control Full-Time Employee/Part-Time Student Scholarship

Type of award: Scholarship.
Intended use: For half-time undergraduate, graduate or non-degree study.
Eligibility: Applicant or parent must be employed by *Aviation. Applicant must be adult returning student. Applicant must be U.S. citizen.
Basis for selection: Applicant must demonstrate depth of character, seriousness of purpose and financial need.
Application requirements: Recommendations, transcript and proof of eligibility.
Additional information: Available only to full-time aviation career professional doing part-time study to enhance job skills. Employee applicant must work full-time in aviation-related field and course work must be deigned to enhance aviation skills. Scholarship must be used within four years of date awarded.

Amount of award:	$600
Number of awards:	3
Number of applicants:	45
Application deadline:	May 1
Notification begins:	September 30
Total amount awarded:	$2,400

Contact:
Air Traffic Control Association Inc.
Arlington Courthouse Plaza II
2300 Clarendon Boulevard, Suite 711
Arlington, VA 22201
Phone: 703-522-5717

Aircraft Electronics Association Educational Foundation

Terra-By-Trimble Avionics Collegiate Scholarship

Type of award: Scholarship, renewable.
Intended use: For full-time undergraduate study at accredited vocational, 2-year or 4-year institution.
Eligibility: Applicant or parent must be member of Aircraft Electronics Association. Applicant must be high school senior. Applicant must be U.S. citizen or permanent resident.
Basis for selection: Applicant must demonstrate depth of character and seriousness of purpose.

Application requirements: Recommendations, essay, transcript and proof of eligibility.
Additional information: Available to high school seniors and college students who are children or grandchildren of employees of AEA regular members. This scholarship can be applied to any field of study. Award is based on an essay completition. Contact the AEA for further details.
- **Amount of award:** $2,500
- **Application deadline:** February 15

Contact:
Scholarship Coordinator
4217 S. Hocker
Independence, MO 64055
Website: www.aeaavneews.org/html/scholarship-info.html

Airgas, Inc.

Airgas Scholarship

Type of award: Scholarship, renewable.
Intended use: For undergraduate study at accredited vocational, 2-year or 4-year institution.
Eligibility: Applicant or parent must be employed by Airgas, Inc.
Basis for selection: Applicant must demonstrate financial need.
Additional information: For further information or an application contact Airgas, Inc. directly.
- **Amount of award:** $500-$2,000

Alco Gravure Education Fund, Inc.

Alco Gravure Scholarship Program

Type of award: Scholarship, renewable.
Intended use: For undergraduate or graduate study.
Eligibility: Applicant or parent must be employed by Quebecor Printing Memphis, Inc.
Additional information: For further information or an application contact Alco Gravure Education Fund, Inc. directly.
- **Amount of award:** $2,500-$5,000

Alcoa Foundation

Alcoa Sons and Daughters Scholarship Program

Type of award: Scholarship.
Intended use: For less than half-time undergraduate study at accredited postsecondary institution.
Eligibility: Applicant or parent must be employed by Aluminum Company of America. Applicant must be high school senior.
Basis for selection: Applicant must demonstrate depth of character, leadership, seriousness of purpose, service orientation and high academic achievement.
Application requirements: Interview, essay, transcript and proof of eligibility.
Additional information: Must have 2.3 GPA or better, or rank in upper half of class. SAT I required.
- **Amount of award:** $7,500
- **Number of awards:** 64
- **Number of applicants:** 424
- **Application deadline:** October 31
- **Notification begins:** March 15
- **Total amount awarded:** $480,000

Contact:
Alcoa Foundation
425 Sixth Ave.
Pittsburgh, PA 15219
Phone: 412-553-4786

Alfa Laval Inc.

Alfa Laval Scholarship Program

Type of award: Scholarship, renewable.
Intended use: For undergraduate study at 2-year or 4-year institution.
Eligibility: Applicant or parent must be employed by Alfa Laval Inc. Applicant must be high school senior.
Additional information: For futher Information or an application contact Alfa Laval Incorporated directly.
- **Amount of award:** $2,000

Allied Group Insurance

Allied Group Scholarship Program

Type of award: Scholarship, renewable.
Intended use: For undergraduate study.
Eligibility: Applicant or parent must be employed by ALLIED Group Insurance.
Basis for selection: Applicant must demonstrate financial need.
Additional information: For further information or an application contact Allied Group Insurance directly.
- **Amount of award:** $500-$1,000

Allstate Foundation

Allstate Scholarship

Type of award: Scholarship, renewable.
Intended use: For undergraduate study at accredited vocational, 2-year or 4-year institution.
Eligibility: Applicant or parent must be employed by Allstate Insurance Company.
Basis for selection: Applicant must demonstrate financial need.

Additional information: For further information or an application contact Allstate Foundation.
    Amount of award: $500-$2,500

Alpha Beta Gamma International, Inc.

Alpha Beta Gamma International Scholarship

Type of award: Scholarship.
Intended use: For full-time junior, senior study at accredited 4-year institution.
Eligibility: Applicant or parent must be member of Alpha Beta Gamma. Applicant must be U.S. citizen.
Basis for selection: Major/career interest in business; business, international; business, management and administration; accounting. Applicant must demonstrate leadership and high academic achievement.
Application requirements: Recommendations. Completed institutional financial forms.
Additional information: Awarded to enrollees of two year schools who have been accepted at four year schools to pursue baccalaureate degrees in business or related professions, including computer and information sciences.
    Amount of award: $500-$10,000
    Number of awards: 300
    Number of applicants: 400
    Total amount awarded: $600,000
Contact:
Alpha Beta Gamma
Scholarship Committee
75 Grasslands Road
Valhalla, NY 10595
Website: www.abg.org

Alpha Mu Gamma National

Alpha Mu Gamma Scholarship

Type of award: Scholarship.
Intended use: For full-time sophomore, junior, senior, master's, doctoral, first professional or postgraduate study at 2-year, 4-year or graduate institution.
Eligibility: Applicant or parent must be member of Alpha Mu Gamma.
Basis for selection: Major/career interest in foreign languages. Applicant must demonstrate seriousness of purpose and high academic achievement.
Application requirements: Recommendations, essay and transcript.
Additional information: Contact the sponsor/adviser of the Local Alpha Mu Gamma Chapter. Minimum 3.2 GPA required.
    Amount of award: $200-$500
    Application deadline: January 10
    Notification begins: March 30
    Total amount awarded: $2,100

American Foundation for Pharmaceutical Education

Phi Lambda Signa First Year Graduate Scholarship

Type of award: Scholarship.
Intended use: For doctoral study.
Eligibility: Applicant or parent must be member of Phi Lambda Sigma. Applicant must be U.S. citizen or permanent resident.
Basis for selection: Major/career interest in pharmacy/pharmaceutics/pharmacology.
Application requirements: Recommendations, essay and transcript. GRE and SAT scores.
Additional information: Must be in final year of pharmacy B.S. or Pharm.D. program.
    Amount of award: $7,500
    Number of awards: 1
    Application deadline: January 15
    Total amount awarded: $7,500
Contact:
Executive Director
Phi Lambda Sigma
3001 Mercer Drive
Atlanta, GA 30341-4155
Phone: 301-738-2160
Fax: 301-738-2161

Rho Chi First-Year Graduate Scholarship Program

Type of award: Scholarship.
Intended use: For doctoral study.
Eligibility: Applicant or parent must be member of Rho-Chi. Applicant must be U.S. citizen or permanent resident.
Basis for selection: Major/career interest in pharmacy/pharmaceutics/pharmacology. Applicant must demonstrate high academic achievement.
Application requirements: Recommendations, essay, transcript and proof of eligibility. GRE and SAT scores.
Additional information: Must be in final year of Pharmacy B.S. or Pharm.D. program.
    Amount of award: $7,500
    Number of awards: 1
    Application deadline: January 15
    Total amount awarded: $7,500
Contact:
Dr. Kenneth W. Kirk-Chairman Rho Chi Graduate Scholarship Committee
c/o St. Louis College of Pharmacy
4588 Parkview Place
St. Louis, MO 63110-1088
Phone: 301-738-2160
Fax: 301-738-2161

American Academy of Physician's Assistants

Physician's Assistants Scholarship

Type of award: Scholarship.
Intended use: For junior, senior study in United States.
Eligibility: Applicant or parent must be member of American Academy of Physician Assistants.
Basis for selection: Major/career interest in physician assistant. Applicant must demonstrate service orientation and financial need.
Application requirements: Transcript and proof of eligibility. Letter from financial aid office verifying aid if any. Passport-type photo.
Additional information: Enrollment in any physician assistant program accredited by Committee on Allied Health Education and Accreditation/Commission on Accreditation of Allied Health Education Programs required. Must be student member of American Academy of Physician Assistants at time of application.

Amount of award:	$2,000-$5,000
Number of awards:	57
Number of applicants:	360
Application deadline:	February 1
Notification begins:	May 15
Total amount awarded:	$128,000

Contact:
Physician Assistant Foundation
American Academy of Physician Assistants
950 North Washington Street
Alexandria, VA 22314
Website: www.aapa.org

American Association for the Advancement of Science

Congressional Science and Engineering Fellowship

Type of award: Research grant.
Intended use: For postgraduate study in United States.
Eligibility: Applicant or parent must be member of American Association of Advancement of Science.
Basis for selection: Applicant must demonstrate depth of character, seriousness of purpose, service orientation and high academic achievement.
Application requirements: Interview and recommendations.
Additional information: Fellows spend one year working on Capitol Hill with members of congress or congressional committees as a special assistant in legislative policy areas requiring scientific and technical input. Employees of AAAS are not eligible.

Amount of award:	$43,000
Number of awards:	2
Number of applicants:	110
Application deadline:	January 15
Total amount awarded:	$86,000

Contact:
American Association for Advancement of Science
1200 New York Avenue, NW
Washington, DC 20005-0000
Website: www.aaas.org

Mass Media Science and Engineering Fellowship

Type of award: Internship, renewable.
Intended use: For junior, senior, master's, doctoral or postgraduate study at accredited 4-year or graduate institution.
Eligibility: Applicant or parent must be member of American Association of Advancement of Science.
Basis for selection: Major/career interest in science, general; engineering; social and behavioral sciences. Applicant must demonstrate depth of character, leadership, service orientation and high academic achievement.
Application requirements: Recommendations, essay and transcript. Resume.
Additional information: Students work for 10 weeks during summer at radio stations, TV stations, newspapers, and magazines in the United States. Weekly stipend prorated by site plus travel expenses paid. Students majoring in English, journalism, or other nontechnical fields not eligible. Employees of AAAS not eligible. Minimum 3.0 GPA required.

Amount of award:	$4,000
Number of awards:	15
Number of applicants:	160
Application deadline:	January 15
Notification begins:	April 15

Contact:
American Association for Advancement of Science
1200 New York Avenue, NW
Washington, DC 20005-0000
Website: www.aaas.org

Technology Policy Fellowship

Type of award: Research grant, renewable.
Intended use: For postgraduate study in Washington, DC. Designated institutions: RAND Critical Technologies Institute.
Eligibility: Applicant or parent must be member of American Association of Advancement of Science. Applicant must be U.S. citizen.
Application requirements: Interview and recommendations.
Additional information: Federal employees ineligible. For postdoctoral to mid-career scientists and engineers to come to Washington, DC, to work in the RAND Critical Technologies Institute only. Applicants must have a minimum of 5 years industrial experience. Stipend, health coverage, and moving allowance are negotiable.

Number of awards:	1
Number of applicants:	35
Application deadline:	January 15

Contact:
American Association for the Advancement of Science
1200 New York Avenue, NW
Washington, DC 20005-0000
Website: www.aaas.org

American Association of Critical Care Nurses

Critical Care Nurses Education Advancement Scholarship (BSN)

Type of award: Scholarship, renewable.
Intended use: For full-time or half-time junior, senior study at accredited 4-year institution in United States.
Eligibility: Applicant or parent must be member of American Association of Critical Care Nurses. Twenty percent of scholarships awarded to minorities. Applicant must be U.S. citizen or permanent resident.
Basis for selection: Major/career interest in nursing.
Application requirements: Essay, transcript and proof of eligibility.
Additional information: Minimum 3.0 GPA required. Must be licensed nurse and American Association of Critical Care Nurses member working in critical care unit with one year experience. Must be enrolled in NLN baccalaureate degree program.

Amount of award:	$1,500
Number of awards:	37
Number of applicants:	104
Application deadline:	May 15
Notification begins:	July 15
Total amount awarded:	$55,500

Critical Care Nurses Education Advancement Scholarship (Graduate)

Type of award: Scholarship, renewable.
Intended use: For full-time or half-time master's, doctoral study at accredited 4-year or graduate institution in United States.
Eligibility: Applicant or parent must be member of American Association of Critical Care Nurses. Twenty percent of scholarships awarded to ethnic minorities. Applicant must be U.S. citizen or permanent resident.
Basis for selection: Major/career interest in nursing.
Application requirements: Essay, transcript and proof of eligibility. Exemplar.
Additional information: Minimum 3.0 GPA required. Must be licensed registered nurse and American Association of Critical Care Nurses member working in critical-care unit with one year experience.

Amount of award:	$1,500
Number of awards:	18
Number of applicants:	119
Application deadline:	May 15
Notification begins:	July 15
Total amount awarded:	$27,000

Contact:
American Association of Critical Care Nurses
101 Columbia
Aliso Viejo, CA 92656-1491
Phone: 800-899-2226
Website: www.aacc.org

American Association of Teachers of Spanish and Portuguese/ Sociedad Honoraria Hispanica

Joseph S. Adams Scholarship

Type of award: Scholarship.
Intended use: For full-time freshman study in United States.
Eligibility: Applicant or parent must be member of Sociedad Honoraria Hispanica. Applicant must be high school senior.
Basis for selection: The SHH Vice President is Chairperson of selection committee. Two $2,000 and six $1,000 awards, at the discretion of committee, are awarded to each of four zones. Applicant must demonstrate depth of character, leadership, patriotism, seriousness of purpose, service orientation and high academic achievement.
Application requirements: Recommendations, essay, transcript and proof of eligibility. Must be presently enrolled in high school Spanish or Portuguese class.
Additional information: Contact SHH sponsor for official application. Applicant must be a senior member of the honor society. One member per chapter may apply. Must apply through local chapter sponsor.

Amount of award:	$1,000-$2,000
Number of awards:	44
Number of applicants:	200
Application deadline:	February 15
Notification begins:	April 15
Total amount awarded:	$52,000

Contact:
John Temple
1015 Hale Street
Durham, NC 27705-4007
Website: www.aatsp.org

American Classical League

David Levy Award

Type of award: Scholarship.
Intended use: For master's, doctoral or non-degree study.
Eligibility: Applicant or parent must be member of American Classical League.
Basis for selection: Major/career interest in classics; education, teacher.
Application requirements: Recommendations. Study program proposal.
Additional information: Must have been member of American Classical League for at least two years, including current school year. Award is for bona fide continued study. Must have B.A. and be classics teacher at elementary or secondary school level.

Amount of award:	$500
Number of awards:	1
Number of applicants:	8
Application deadline:	January 15
Total amount awarded:	$500

Latin Honor Society Scholarship

Type of award: Scholarship.
Intended use: For full-time freshman study at 2-year or 4-year institution.
Eligibility: Applicant or parent must be member of National Junior Classical League. Applicant must be high school senior.
Basis for selection: Major/career interest in classics.
Application requirements: Recommendations, essay and transcript.
Additional information: Must have been member of National Junior Classics League for at least three years and must be enrolled in National Junior Classics League Latin Honor Society for current academic year and at least one preceding year. Must be planning to teach Latin or classics.

Amount of award:	$1,000–$1,500
Number of awards:	1
Number of applicants:	12
Application deadline:	May 1
Total amount awarded:	$1,000

M.V. O'Donnell Memorial Teacher Training Award

Type of award: Scholarship.
Intended use: For junior, senior or master's study at 4-year or graduate institution.
Eligibility: Applicant or parent must be member of American Classical League.
Basis for selection: Major/career interest in education, teacher; classics. Applicant must demonstrate financial need.
Application requirements: Recommendations and transcript.
Additional information: Must be training for certification to teach Latin and have completed a substantial part of these courses.

Amount of award:	$500
Number of awards:	5
Number of applicants:	8
Application deadline:	December 1, March 1
Total amount awarded:	$2,500

McKinlay Summer Award

Type of award: Scholarship.
Intended use: For non-degree study.
Eligibility: Applicant or parent must be member of American Classical League.
Basis for selection: Major/career interest in classics. Applicant must demonstrate financial need.
Application requirements: Recommendations.
Additional information: Must have been member of American Classical League for 3 years preceding application. Must teach classics in elementary or secondary school. May apply for independent study program funding or support to attend American Classical League Institute for first time.

Amount of award:	$1,000
Number of awards:	20
Number of applicants:	20
Application deadline:	January 15
Total amount awarded:	$20,000

National Junior Classical League Scholarship

Type of award: Scholarship.
Intended use: For full-time freshman study at 2-year or 4-year institution.
Eligibility: Applicant or parent must be member of National Junior Classical League. Applicant must be high school senior.
Basis for selection: Major/career interest in classics; humanities/liberal arts. Applicant must demonstrate depth of character, leadership, patriotism, seriousness of purpose, service orientation, financial need and high academic achievement.
Application requirements: Recommendations, transcript and proof of eligibility.
Additional information: Preference is given to applicants who intend to teach Latin, Greek, or classical humanities.

Amount of award:	$500–$1,000
Number of awards:	6
Number of applicants:	100
Application deadline:	May 1
Total amount awarded:	$4,000

Contact:
American Classical League
Miami University
Oxford, OH 45056
Phone: 513-529-7741
Fax: 513-529-7742
Website: www.umich.edu/~acleague

American Congress on Surveying and Mapping

American Congress on Surveying and Mapping

Type of award: Scholarship.
Intended use: For full-time freshman, sophomore, junior or senior study at 2-year or 4-year institution.
Eligibility: Applicant or parent must be member of American Congress of Surveying and Mapping.
Basis for selection: Major/career interest in surveying and mapping. Applicant must demonstrate financial need and high academic achievement.
Application requirements: Recommendations, essay and transcript.
Additional information: Award will be paid to the college or University where the recipient is enrolled and can be applied to tuition, registration, laboratory fees, or books.

Amount of award:	$250
Number of awards:	1
Application deadline:	December 1
Total amount awarded:	$250

American Congress on Surveying and Mapping/National Society of Professional Surveyors Scholarship for Women

Type of award: Scholarship.
Intended use: For full-time freshman, sophomore, junior or senior study.
Eligibility: Applicant or parent must be member of American Congress of Surveying and Mapping. Applicant must be female. Applicant must be U.S. citizen.
Basis for selection: Major/career interest in surveying and mapping. Applicant must demonstrate financial need and high academic achievement.
Application requirements: Recommendations, essay and transcript.
Additional information: Must be enrolled in a four-year Degree Program in surveying.
    Amount of award: $1,000
    Number of awards: 2
    Application deadline: December 1
    Total amount awarded: $2,000

Bernstein International Surveying Scholarship

Type of award: Scholarship.
Intended use: For full-time freshman, sophomore, junior or senior study at 2-year or 4-year institution.
Eligibility: Applicant or parent must be member of American Congress of Surveying and Mapping.
Basis for selection: Major/career interest in surveying and mapping. Applicant must demonstrate financial need and high academic achievement.
Application requirements: Recommendations, essay and transcript.
Additional information: One $500 scholarship to a student in a two-year degree program in surveyors technology, and one $1,500 scholarship for use in four-year degree program. Applicants must prove membership in the ACSM. Incomplete or improperly completed applications will be discarded.
    Amount of award: $500-$1,500
    Number of awards: 2
    Application deadline: December 1
    Total amount awarded: $2,000

Cartographic Association Scholarship

Type of award: Scholarship.
Intended use: For full-time junior, senior study.
Eligibility: Applicant or parent must be member of American Congress of Surveying and Mapping.
Basis for selection: Major/career interest in surveying and mapping. Applicant must demonstrate seriousness of purpose and high academic achievement.
Application requirements: Recommendations, essay and transcript.
Additional information: Must have had minimum of three courses in cartography or other mapping sciences. Open to students enrolled in a four-year or Graduate Degree Program in cartography or geographic information science. Preference will be given to undergraduates with junior or senior standing.
    Amount of award: $1,000
    Number of awards: 1
    Application deadline: January 1
    Total amount awarded: $1,000

Geodetic Surveying Graduate Fellowship

Type of award: Scholarship.
Intended use: For master's study.
Eligibility: Applicant or parent must be member of American Congress of Surveying and Mapping.
Basis for selection: Major/career interest in surveying and mapping. Applicant must demonstrate depth of character and high academic achievement.
Application requirements: Recommendations, essay, transcript and proof of eligibility.
Additional information: Must be enrolled in or accepted to graduate program with significant focus upon geodetic surveying or geodesy. Preference will be given to students with at least two years experience in the surveying profession.
    Amount of award: $2,000
    Number of awards: 1
    Application deadline: December 1
    Total amount awarded: $2,000

Joseph F. Dracup Scholarship

Type of award: Scholarship.
Intended use: For full-time freshman, sophomore, junior or senior study.
Eligibility: Applicant or parent must be member of American Congress of Surveying and Mapping.
Basis for selection: Major/career interest in surveying and mapping. Applicant must demonstrate high academic achievement.
Application requirements: Recommendations, essay and transcript.
Additional information: Must be enrolled in a four-year program with significant focus on geodetic surveying, germatics or surveying engineering.
    Amount of award: $2,000
    Number of awards: 1
    Application deadline: January 1
    Total amount awarded: $2,000

Leica Surveying Scholarship

Type of award: Scholarship.
Intended use: For full-time freshman, sophomore, junior or senior study.
Eligibility: Applicant or parent must be member of American Congress of Surveying and Mapping. Applicant must be U.S. citizen.
Basis for selection: Major/career interest in surveying and mapping. Applicant must demonstrate financial need and high academic achievement.
Application requirements: Recommendations, essay, transcript and proof of eligibility.
Additional information: Must be enrolled in four-year surveying and mapping sciences program and have completed at least one course. Must be member or sponsored by member of American Congress on Surveying and Mapping or

American Society for Photogrammetry and Remote Sensing (ASPRS). Each recipient's school will receive a $2,000 credit toward the purchase of Leica surveying instruments and systems. Additionally, every student majoring in surveying or a related field in the recipients graduating class will receive a $500 credit toward the purchase of Leica surveying equipment and systems. This credit is valid up to six month after the recipient's graduation date and may be used by the graduate's employer.

Amount of award:	$1,000
Number of awards:	2
Application deadline:	December 1
Total amount awarded:	$2,000

National Society of Professional Surveyors Scholarship

Type of award: Scholarship.
Intended use: For full-time freshman, sophomore, junior or senior study.
Eligibility: Applicant or parent must be member of American Congress of Surveying and Mapping. Applicant must be U.S. citizen.
Basis for selection: Major/career interest in surveying and mapping. Applicant must demonstrate financial need and high academic achievement.
Application requirements: Recommendations, essay, transcript and nomination.
Additional information: Must be enrolled in four-year degree program in surveying.

Amount of award:	$1,000
Number of awards:	2
Application deadline:	December 1
Total amount awarded:	$2,000

Schonstedt Surveying Scholarship

Type of award: Scholarship.
Intended use: For full-time junior, senior study.
Eligibility: Applicant or parent must be member of American Congress of Surveying and Mapping.
Basis for selection: Major/career interest in surveying and mapping. Applicant must demonstrate seriousness of purpose and high academic achievement.
Application requirements: Recommendations, essay and transcript.
Additional information: Must have completed at least two years of four-year program leading to surveying degree. The Schonstedt Instrumental Company donates a magnetic locater to the surveying program of the school of the award winner.

Amount of award:	$1,500
Number of awards:	1
Application deadline:	December 1
Notification begins:	January 31
Total amount awarded:	$1,500

Contact:
American Congress on Surveying and Mapping
5410 Grosvenor Lane
Bethesda, MD 20814-2122
Website: www.landsurveyor.com

American Dryer Corporation

American Dryer Corporation Scholarship

Type of award: Scholarship, renewable.
Intended use: For undergraduate or graduate study at accredited vocational, 2-year or 4-year institution.
Eligibility: Applicant or parent must be employed by American Dryer Corporation.
Basis for selection: Applicant must demonstrate financial need.
Additional information: For further information or an application contact American Dryer Corporation directly.

American Express Foundation

American Express Scholarship Program

Type of award: Scholarship, renewable.
Intended use: For freshman study at 2-year or 4-year institution.
Eligibility: Applicant or parent must be employed by American Express Foundation. Applicant must be high school senior.
Additional information: For further information or an application contact American Express Foundation directly.

Amount of award:	$1,000-$3,000

American Federation of State, County and Municipal Employees

State/County/Municipal Employees Family Scholarship

Type of award: Scholarship, renewable.
Intended use: For full-time undergraduate study at accredited 4-year institution.
Eligibility: Applicant or parent must be member of American Fed. of State/County/Municipal Employees. Applicant must be high school senior.
Basis for selection: Competition in Writing/journalism.
Application requirements: Recommendations, essay, transcript and proof of eligibility. SAT or ACT scores.

Amount of award:	$2,000
Number of awards:	40
Number of applicants:	1,500
Application deadline:	December 31
Notification begins:	March 31
Total amount awarded:	$80,000

State/County/Municipal Employees
Jerry Clark Memorial Scholarship

Type of award: Scholarship, renewable.
Intended use: For full-time junior, senior study at accredited 4-year institution.
Eligibility: Applicant or parent must be member of American Fed. of State/County/Municipal Employees.
Basis for selection: Major/career interest in political science/government. Applicant must demonstrate high academic achievement.
Application requirements: Proof of eligibility.
Additional information: Applicant must be a current college sophomore with a declared political science major. Winner given opportunity to intern at International Union Headquarters in Political Action department. Minimum 3.0 GPA required. Award renewable for senior year.

Amount of award:	$10,000
Number of awards:	2
Number of applicants:	100
Application deadline:	July 1
Notification begins:	August 1
Total amount awarded:	$20,000

Contact:
American Federation of State, County and Municipal Employees
Education Department
1625 L Street NW
Washington, DC 20036
Website: www.afscme.org

American Foundation for Pharmaceutical Education

Kappa Epsilon-Nellie Wakeman Fellowship

Type of award: Scholarship, renewable.
Intended use: For senior study.
Eligibility: Applicant or parent must be member of Kappa Epsilon.
Basis for selection: Major/career interest in pharmacy/pharmaceutics/pharmacology.
Application requirements: Recommendations, essay, transcript and proof of eligibility.
Additional information: Applicant must be in good standing with the fraternity and have satisfactorily completed one quarter/semester of advanced studies in the pharmaceutical sciences.

Amount of award:	$4,000
Number of awards:	1
Application deadline:	January 15
Notification begins:	February 28
Total amount awarded:	$4,000

Contact:
American Foundation For Pharmaceutical Education
One Church Street
Suite 202
Rockville, MD 20850
Phone: 301-738-2160
Fax: 301-738-2161

American Health Information Management Association

American Health Information Management Master's Program

Type of award: Loan, renewable.
Intended use: For full-time master's, doctoral, first professional or postgraduate study at accredited graduate institution.
Eligibility: Applicant or parent must be member of American Health Information Management Assoc. Applicant must be U.S. citizen.
Basis for selection: Major/career interest in computer and information sciences; business, management and administration; education; public health. Applicant must demonstrate high academic achievement.
Application requirements: Recommendations, transcript and proof of eligibility.
Additional information: Applicants must be a credentialed health information management professional (RRA, ART, CCS). Must have 2.5 GPA. Loan payments begin six months after graduation at an 8% APR.

Amount of award:	$1,000-$5,000
Application deadline:	May 30, October 30
Notification begins:	June 30, November 1

Contact:
American Health Information Management Association
FORE
919 North Michigan Avenue, Suite 1400
Chicago, IL 60611-1683
Phone: 312-573-8556
Website: www.ahima.org/careers.colleges/scholarships.html

Aspen Systems Awards

Type of award: Scholarship.
Intended use: For full-time graduate study at accredited graduate institution.
Eligibility: Applicant or parent must be member of American Health Information Management Assoc. Applicant must be U.S. citizen.
Basis for selection: Major/career interest in computer and information sciences; business, management and administration; education; public health. Applicant must demonstrate high academic achievement.
Application requirements: Recommendations, transcript and proof of eligibility.
Additional information: Must be credentialed Health Information Management professional (RRA, ART, or CCS) and hold a bachelor's degree and be pursuing at minimum a master's degree in program related to Health Information Management. Must have 2.5 GPA.

Amount of award:	$1,000-$5,000
Number of awards:	1
Application deadline:	May 30
Notification begins:	July 30

Contact:
American Health Information Management Association
FORE
919 North Michigan Avenue, Suite 1400
Chicago, IL 60611-1683
Phone: 312-573-8556
Website: www.ahima.org/careers.colleges/scholarships.html

Barbara Thomas Enterprises Award

Type of award: Scholarship.
Intended use: For undergraduate or graduate study at accredited postsecondary institution.
Eligibility: Applicant or parent must be member of American Health Information Management Assoc. Applicant must be single. Applicant must be U.S. citizen.
Basis for selection: Major/career interest in computer and information sciences; business, management and administration; education; public health. Applicant must demonstrate high academic achievement.
Application requirements: Recommendations, transcript and proof of eligibility.
Additional information: Graduate applicants must be credentialed Health Information Management professional (RRA, ART, or CCS) and hold a bachelor's degree and must be pursuing at minimum master's degree in program related to Health Information Management. Must be a single parent. Must have 2.5 GPA.

Amount of award:	$1,000-$5,000
Number of awards:	1
Application deadline:	May 30
Notification begins:	June 1, July 1
Total amount awarded:	$5,000

Contact:
American Health Information Management Association
FORE
919 North Michigan Avenue, Suite 1400
Chicago, IL 60611-1683
Phone: 312-573-8556
Website: www.ahima.org/careers.colleges/scholarships.html

Coding Specialist Program Loan

Type of award: Loan.
Intended use: For full-time undergraduate or graduate study.
Eligibility: Applicant or parent must be member of American Health Information Management Assoc. Applicant must be U.S. citizen.
Basis for selection: Major/career interest in computer and information sciences; business, management and administration; education; public health. Applicant must demonstrate financial need and high academic achievement.
Application requirements: Recommendations and transcript.
Additional information: Applicant must have 2.5 GPA. Must be enrolled in a coding specialist program. Loan payments start six months after graduation at an 8% APR.

Amount of award:	$1,000-$5,000
Application deadline:	May 30, October 30
Notification begins:	July 30, November 30

Contact:
American Health Information Management Association
FORE
919 North Michigan Avenue, Suite 1400
Chicago, IL 60611-1683
Phone: 312-573-8556
Website: www.ahima.org/careers.colleges/scholarships.html

FORE Graduate Scholarship

Type of award: Scholarship.
Intended use: For full-time graduate study at accredited graduate institution.
Eligibility: Applicant or parent must be member of American Health Information Management Assoc. Applicant must be U.S. citizen.
Basis for selection: Major/career interest in computer and information sciences; business, management and administration; education; public health. Applicant must demonstrate high academic achievement.
Application requirements: Recommendations, transcript and proof of eligibility.
Additional information: Must be credentialed health information management professional (RRA, ART, or CCS) and hold bachelor's degree and be pursuing at minimum master's degree in program related to Health Information Management. Must have 2.5 GPA.

Amount of award:	$1,000-$5,000
Number of applicants:	5
Application deadline:	May 30
Notification begins:	July 1

Contact:
American Health Information Management Association
FORE
919 North Michigan Avenue, Suite 1400
Chicago, IL 60611-1683
Phone: 312-573-8556
Website: www.ahima.org/careers.colleges/scholarships.html

FORE Undergraduate Scholarship

Type of award: Scholarship.
Intended use: For full-time undergraduate study.
Eligibility: Applicant or parent must be member of American Health Information Management Assoc. Applicant must be U.S. citizen.
Basis for selection: Applicant must demonstrate high academic achievement.
Application requirements: Recommendations, transcript and proof of eligibility.
Additional information: Must be enrolled in health information or health information technology program accredited by Committee on Allied Health Education and Accreditation. May be used for Independent Study Program of American Health Information Management Association. Must have 2.5 GPA.

Amount of award:	$1,000-$5,000
Application deadline:	May 30
Notification begins:	June 30

Contact:
American Health Information Management Association
FORE
919 North Michigan Avenue, Suite 1400
Chicago, IL 60611-1683
Phone: 312-573-8556
Website: www.ahima.org/careers.colleges/scholarships.html

HIM PROGRAM

Type of award: Loan, renewable.
Intended use: For full-time undergraduate or graduate study.
Eligibility: Applicant or parent must be member of American Health Information Management Assoc. Applicant must be U.S. citizen.
Basis for selection: Major/career interest in computer and information sciences; business, management and administration; education; public health. Applicant must demonstrate high academic achievement.
Application requirements: Recommendations, transcript and proof of eligibility.
Additional information: Undergraduate applicants must already be accepted into a health information management program. Graduate applicants must be credentialed Health Information Management professionals. Must have 2.5 GPA. Loan payments start six months after graduation at an 8% APR.

Amount of award:	$1,000-$5,000
Application deadline:	May 30, October 30
Notification begins:	June 30, November 1

Contact:
American Health Information Management Association
FORE
919 North Michigan Avenue, Suite 1400
Chicago, IL 60611-1683
Phone: 312-573-8556
Website: www.ahima.org/careers.colleges/scholarships.html

HIT Program

Type of award: Loan, renewable.
Intended use: For full-time undergraduate or graduate study.
Eligibility: Applicant or parent must be member of American Health Information Management Assoc. Applicant must be U.S. citizen.
Basis for selection: Major/career interest in computer and information sciences; business, management and administration; education; public health. Applicant must demonstrate high academic achievement.
Application requirements: Recommendations, transcript and proof of eligibility.
Additional information: Undergraduate applicants must already be accepted into an accredited health information technology program. Must have 2.5 GPA. Loans payments start six months after graduation at an 8% APR.

Amount of award:	$1,000-$5,000
Application deadline:	May 30, October 30
Notification begins:	July 30, November 1

Contact:
American Health Information Management Association
FORE
919 North Michigan Avenue, Suite 1400
Chicago, IL 60611-1683
Phone: 312-573-8556
Website: www.ahima.org/careers.colleges/scholarships.html

Smart Corporation Scholarship

Type of award: Scholarship.
Intended use: For full-time undergraduate study.
Eligibility: Applicant or parent must be member of American Health Information Management Assoc.
Basis for selection: Applicant must demonstrate high academic achievement.
Application requirements: Recommendations and transcript.
Additional information: Must be enrolled in health information management or technology program approved by Committee on Allied Health and Accreditation, or accepted to AHIMA's Independent Study Program. Must have 2.5 GPA.

Amount of award:	$1,000-$5,000
Application deadline:	May 30
Notification begins:	June 30

Contact:
American Health Information Management Association
FORE
919 North Michigan Avenue, Suite 1400
Chicago, IL 60611-1683
Phone: 312-573-8556
Website: www.ahima.org/careers.colleges/scholarships.html

St. Anthony Publishing Graduate Award

Type of award: Scholarship.
Intended use: For full-time graduate study at accredited graduate institution.
Eligibility: Applicant or parent must be member of American Health Information Management Assoc. Applicant must be U.S. citizen.
Basis for selection: Major/career interest in computer and information sciences; business, management and administration; education; public health. Applicant must demonstrate high academic achievement.
Application requirements: Portfolio, transcript and proof of eligibility.
Additional information: Applicant must be a credentialed Health Information Management professional (RRA, ART, CCS) and hold a bachelor's degree in program related to Health Information Management. Must have 2.5 GPA.

Amount of award:	$1,000-$5,000
Application deadline:	May 30
Notification begins:	June 1

Contact:
American Health Information Management Association
FORE
919 North Michigan Avenue, Suite 1400
Chicago, IL 60611-1683
Phone: 312-573-8556
Website: www.ahima.org/careers.colleges/scholarships.html

St. Anthony Publishing Undergraduate Award

Type of award: Scholarship.
Intended use: For full-time undergraduate study at accredited 4-year institution.
Eligibility: Applicant or parent must be member of American Health Information Management Assoc.
Basis for selection: Applicant must demonstrate leadership and high academic achievement.
Application requirements: Portfolio, transcript and proof of eligibility.
Additional information: Must have been accepted to health information management or health information technology program or American Health Information Management Association's Independent Study Program. Must have 2.5 GPA.

Amount of award:	$1,000-$5,000
Application deadline:	May 30
Notification begins:	June 30

Contact:
American Health Information Management Association
FORE
919 North Michigan Avenue, Suite 1400
Chicago, IL 60611-1683
Phone: 312-573-8556
Website: www.ahima.org/careers.colleges/scholarships.html

Transcriptions Limited Graduate Scholarship

Type of award: Scholarship.
Intended use: For full-time graduate study at accredited graduate institution.
Eligibility: Applicant or parent must be member of American Health Information Management Assoc. Applicant must be U.S. citizen.
Basis for selection: Major/career interest in computer and information sciences; business, management and administration; education; public health. Applicant must demonstrate high academic achievement.
Application requirements: Recommendations, transcript and proof of eligibility.
Additional information: Applicant must be a credentialed Health Information Management professional (RRA, ART, CCS) and hold a bachelor's degree in program related to Health Information Management. Must have 2.5 GPA.

Amount of award:	$1,000-$5,000
Application deadline:	May 30
Notification begins:	July 1

Contact:
American Health Information Management Association
FORE
919 North Michigan Avenue, Suite 1400
Chicago, IL 60611-1683
Phone: 312-573-8556
Website: www.ahima.org/careers/colleges/scholarships.html

Transcriptions Limited Undergraduate Scholarship

Type of award: Scholarship.
Intended use: For undergraduate study at accredited postsecondary institution.
Eligibility: Applicant or parent must be member of American Health Information Management Assoc.
Basis for selection: Applicant must demonstrate high academic achievement.
Application requirements: Recommendations, transcript and proof of eligibility.
Additional information: Must be enrolled in health information management or technology program approved by Committee on Allied Health and Accreditation, or accepted into American Health Information Management Association's Independent Study Program. Must have 2.5 GPA.

Amount of award:	$1,000-$5,000
Number of awards:	1
Number of applicants:	11
Application deadline:	May 30
Notification begins:	June 30

Contact:
American Health Information Management Association
FORE of AHIMA Scholarships and Loans
919 North Michigan Avenue, Suite 1400
Chicago, IL 60611-1683
Phone: 312-573-8556
Website: www.ahima.org/careers.colleges/scholarships.html

American Heart Association

Cardiovascular Nursing Award

Type of award: Research grant.
Intended use: For postgraduate study.
Eligibility: Applicant or parent must be member of Council on Cardiovascular Nursing.
Basis for selection: Major/career interest in medical specialties/research; nursing.
Application requirements: Recommendations. Curriculum vitae, abstract of work, manuscript.
Additional information: Must have completed doctoral degree no more than seven years prior to application. Award for basic and clinical research of cardiovascular diseases. Must be a member of Council on Cardiovascular Nursing at time of application.

Amount of award:	$650-$1,500
Number of awards:	3
Application deadline:	May 2
Notification begins:	September 1
Total amount awarded:	$2,900

Contact:
American Heart Association Young Investigators Award
7272 Greenville Avenue
Dallas, TX 75231
Phone: 214-706-1685
Fax: 214-373-3406
Website: www.americanheart.org

Cournand and Comroe Prize

Type of award: Research grant.
Intended use: For postgraduate study.
Eligibility: Applicant or parent must be member of Council on Cardiopulmonary/Critical Care.
Basis for selection: Major/career interest in medical specialties/research.

Application requirements: Recommendations. Curriculum vitae, abstract of work, manuscript.
Additional information: Must be working in any area of research concerned with pulmonary and critical care biology.
- Amount of award: $250-$500
- Number of awards: 3
- Application deadline: May 2
- Notification begins: September 1
- Total amount awarded: $1,000

Contact:
American Heart Association
Young Investigator Award
7272 Greenville Avenue
Dallas, TX 75231-4596
Phone: 214-706-1685
Fax: 214-373-3406
Website: www.americanheart.org

Elizabeth Barrett-Connor Research Award

Type of award: Research grant.
Intended use: For full-time postgraduate study.
Eligibility: Applicant or parent must be member of Council on Epidemiology and Prevention.
Basis for selection: Major/career interest in medical specialties/research.
Application requirements: Recommendations. Letter verifying in-training or full-time student status, manuscript, curriculum vitae, abstract of work.
Additional information: Candidates must be in training program or be full-time matriculated students at the time of application.
- Amount of award: $1,000
- Number of awards: 1
- Application deadline: May 2
- Notification begins: September 1
- Total amount awarded: $1,000

Contact:
American Heart Association
Young Investigator Award
7272 Greenville Avenue
Dallas, TX 75231
Phone: 214-706-1685
Fax: 214-373-3406
Website: www.americanheart.org

Melvin Judkins Award

Type of award: Research grant.
Intended use: For postgraduate study.
Eligibility: Applicant or parent must be member of Council on Cardiovascular Radiology.
Basis for selection: Major/career interest in medical specialties/research.
Application requirements: Recommendations. Curriculum vitae, abstract of work, manuscript.
Additional information: Must be in training or within three years of completion of radiology residency or fellowship. Must be member or fellows of Council on Cardiovascular Radiology, or a letter from a Council member must accompany application.

- Amount of award: $500
- Number of awards: 1
- Application deadline: May 2
- Notification begins: September 1
- Total amount awarded: $500

Contact:
American Heart Association
Young Investigator Award
7272 Greenville Avenue
Dallas, TX 75231
Phone: 214-706-1685
Fax: 214-373-3406
Website: www.americanheart.org

Vivien Thomas Award

Type of award: Research grant.
Intended use: For postgraduate study.
Eligibility: Applicant or parent must be member of Council on Cardio-Thoracic/Vasc. Surgery.
Basis for selection: Major/career interest in medical specialties/research.
Application requirements: Recommendations. Curriculum vitae, abstract of work, manuscript.
Additional information: Candidates must have completed their surgical training (cardio-thoracic, vascular, or anesthesia) no more than five years prior to application. Candidates or their supervisors must be members of the Council on Cardio-Thoracic and Vascular Surgery at time of application.
- Amount of award: $500-$1,500
- Number of awards: 5
- Application deadline: May 2
- Notification begins: September 1
- Total amount awarded: $3,500

Contact:
American Heart Association
Young Investigators Award
7272 Greenville Avenue
Dallas, TX 75231-4596
Phone: 214-706-1685
Fax: 214-373-3406
Website: www.americanheart.org

American Historical Association

American Historical Society Research Grants

Type of award: Research grant.
Intended use: For full-time doctoral study at graduate institution in United States.
Eligibility: Applicant or parent must be member of American Historical Association. Applicant must be U.S. citizen or permanent resident.
Application requirements: Proof of eligibility and research proposal.
Additional information: Preference given to Ph.D. candidates and other junior scholars.

Amount of award:	$1,000
Number of awards:	26
Application deadline:	September 15, February 1
Notification begins:	December 1, April 1
Total amount awarded:	$20,500

Contact:
Research Grant Coordinator
400 A St., SE
Washington, DC 20003
Website: chnm.gmu.edu/aha/

American Holistic Nurses' Association

Holistic Nursing Charlotte McGuire Scholarship

Type of award: Scholarship.
Intended use: For undergraduate or graduate study at accredited 2-year, 4-year or graduate institution.
Eligibility: Applicant or parent must be member of American Holistic Nurses' Association.
Basis for selection: Major/career interest in nursing. Applicant must demonstrate depth of character and seriousness of purpose.
Application requirements: Recommendations, essay, transcript and proof of eligibility. Two recommendations, financial statement required.
Additional information: 3.0 GPA required. Experience in holistic or alternative health care practices preferred. Graduates must be member of AHNA for one year, undergraduates for six months. One reccomendation must be from AHNA member.

Amount of award:	$1,500
Number of awards:	2
Number of applicants:	6
Application deadline:	March 15
Notification begins:	May 15
Total amount awarded:	$3,000

Contact:
American Holistic Nurses' Association
Scholarships
P.O. Box 2130
Flagstaff, AZ 86003-2130
Phone: 8002782462
Fax: 5205262752
Website: www.ahna.org

Holistic Nursing Charlotte McGuire Scholarship (Graduate)

Type of award: Scholarship.
Intended use: For graduate study at accredited graduate institution.
Eligibility: Applicant or parent must be member of American Holistic Nurses' Association.
Basis for selection: Major/career interest in nursing. Applicant must demonstrate depth of character and seriousness of purpose.
Application requirements: Audition, recommendations, essay, transcript and proof of eligibility. Two recommendations, financial statement required.
Additional information: 3.0 GPA required. Experience in holistic or alternative health care practices preferred.

Amount of award:	$1,500
Number of awards:	1
Number of applicants:	6
Application deadline:	March 15
Notification begins:	June 30
Total amount awarded:	$1,500

Contact:
American Holistic Nurses' Association
P.O. Box 2130
Flagstaff, AZ 86003-2130
Phone: 800-278-2462
Fax: 520-787-4916
Website: www.ahna.org

Holistic Nursing Research Grant

Type of award: Research grant.
Intended use: For non-degree study.
Eligibility: Applicant or parent must be member of American Holistic Nurses' Association.
Basis for selection: Major/career interest in nursing. Applicant must demonstrate seriousness of purpose and service orientation.
Application requirements: Proof of eligibility and research proposal.
Additional information: Must be member of AHNA for at least one year and be conducting research on topics related to holistic nursing.

Amount of award:	$1,000-$5,000
Number of awards:	1
Number of applicants:	4
Application deadline:	April 15
Notification begins:	May 15
Total amount awarded:	$5,000

Contact:
American Holistic Nurses' Association
Research Grants
P.O. Box 2130
Flagstaff, AZ 86003-2130
Phone: 8002782462
Fax: 5205262752
Website: www.ahna.org

American Indian Science and Engineering Society

A.T. Anderson Memorial Scholarship

Type of award: Scholarship.
Intended use: For full-time undergraduate or graduate study at accredited postsecondary institution.
Eligibility: Applicant or parent must be member of American Indian Science & Engineering Society. Applicant must be Alaskan native or American Indian. Must be member of a federally recognized tribe.
Basis for selection: Major/career interest in engineering;

medicine (m.d.); business; mathematics; science, general; natural resources/conservation. Applicant must demonstrate depth of character, leadership, seriousness of purpose, service orientation, financial need and high academic achievement.
Application requirements: Recommendations, essay, transcript and proof of eligibility.
Additional information: Minimum 2.0 GPA. Those majoring in science, natural resources, or math and science secondary education also eligible. Graduate student award $2000. Include SASE with all application/information requests. Award may be used at Canadian institutions. Must be a member of AISES.

Amount of award:	$1,000-$2,000
Number of awards:	400
Number of applicants:	600
Application deadline:	June 15
Notification begins:	August 31
Total amount awarded:	$400,000

Contact:
American Indian Science and Engineering Society
Attn: Scholarship Coordinator
5661 Airport Boulevard
Boulder, CO 80301-2339
Phone: 303-939-0023
Website: www.colorado.edu/AISES

Burlington Northern Santa Fe Foundation Scholarship

Type of award: Scholarship, renewable.
Intended use: For full-time freshman, sophomore, junior or senior study at accredited postsecondary institution in United States.
Eligibility: Applicant or parent must be member of American Indian Science & Engineering Society. Applicant must be Alaskan native or American Indian. Must have proof of tribal enrollment with federally recognized tribe. Applicant must be high school senior. Applicant must be U.S. citizen residing in Kansas or Minnesota or North Dakota or South Dakota or New Mexico or Oklahoma or Arizona or California or Colorado or Montana or Oregon or Washington. Applicant must be child of disabled veteran.
Basis for selection: Major/career interest in business; education; science, general; health services administration. Applicant must demonstrate depth of character, leadership, seriousness of purpose, service orientation, financial need and high academic achievement.
Application requirements: Recommendations, essay, transcript and proof of eligibility.
Additional information: Applicants must maintain a 2.0 GPA or higher. Include SASE with all application/information requests. In California, only residents of San Bernardino county eligible. May be used for study in Canadian institutions.

Amount of award:	$1,250-$2,500
Number of awards:	20
Number of applicants:	100
Application deadline:	March 31
Notification begins:	May 15
Total amount awarded:	$31,250

Contact:
Attn: Scholarship Coordinator
5661 Airport Blvd.
Boulder, CO 80301
Phone: 303-939-0023
Website: www.colorado.edu/AISES

American Isuzu Motors, Inc.

J. E. Reilly Scholarship

Type of award: Scholarship, renewable.
Intended use: For undergraduate study at accredited vocational, 2-year or 4-year institution.
Eligibility: Applicant or parent must be employed by American Isuzu Motors, Inc.
Basis for selection: Applicant must demonstrate financial need.
Additional information: For further information or an application contact American Isuzu Motors, Inc. directly.

| Amount of award: | $1,000-$5,000 |

American Legion Arkansas

American Legion Arkansas Scholarship

Type of award: Scholarship.
Intended use: For undergraduate study.
Eligibility: Applicant or parent must be member of American Legion. Applicant must be residing in Arkansas. Applicant must be descendant of veteran.
Application requirements: Proof of eligibility. For child, grandchild, or great-grandchild of American Legion member.

Amount of award:	$500
Number of awards:	4
Total amount awarded:	$2,000

Contact:
American Legion Arkansas
Department Adjutant
Box 1751
Little Rock, AR 72203
Phone: 501-374-5836
Fax: 501-375-4236

American Legion California Auxiliary

American Legion California Auxiliary National President's Junior Scholarship

Type of award: Scholarship.
Intended use: For undergraduate study.
Eligibility: Applicant or parent must be member of American Legion Auxiliary. Applicant must be U.S. citizen residing in California. Applicant must be descendant of veteran during Grenada, Korean War, Lebanon, Panama, Persian Gulf, WW I, WW II or Vietnam.
Application requirements: For current junior league members of at least 3 years standing. Special application.
Additional information: If California's candidate does not

win, a $250 scholarship is awarded by Department of California.
- Amount of award: $1,000
- Number of awards: 1
- Total amount awarded: $1,000

American Legion California Auxiliary Spirit of Youth Scholarship

Type of award: Scholarship.
Intended use: For freshman study.
Eligibility: Applicant or parent must be member of American Legion Auxiliary. Applicant must be high school senior. Applicant must be residing in California.
Application requirements: Request special applicaton.
- Amount of award: $1,000
- Number of awards: 1

Contact:
American Legion California Auxiliary
Junior Activities Chairman
401 Van Ness, No. 113
San Francisco, CA 94102-4586
Phone: 415-431-2400
Fax: 415-255-1571

American Legion Colorado Auxiliary

American Legion Colorado Auxiliary President's Scholarship for Junior Members

Type of award: Scholarship.
Intended use: For undergraduate study in Colorado.
Eligibility: Applicant or parent must be member of American Legion Auxiliary. Applicant must be residing in Colorado.
Application requirements: Must be junior auxiliary member.
- Amount of award: $500
- Number of awards: 1
- Application deadline: March 12

American Legion Colorado Auxiliary/Department President's Scholarship

Type of award: Scholarship.
Intended use: For undergraduate study.
Eligibility: Applicant or parent must be member of American Legion Auxiliary. Applicant must be residing in Colorado. Applicant must be descendant of veteran during Grenada, Korean War, Lebanon, Panama, Persian Gulf, WW I, WW II or Vietnam.

- Amount of award: $250-$500
- Number of awards: 2
- Application deadline: March 12
- Total amount awarded: $750

Contact:
American Legion Colorado Auxiliary
Department Headquarters
3003 Tejon Street
Denver, CO 80211
Phone: 303-477-5752
Fax: 303-477-2950

American Legion Connecticut Auxiliary

American Legion Connecticut Auxiliary Memorial Educational Grant

Type of award: Scholarship.
Intended use: For undergraduate study.
Eligibility: Applicant or parent must be member of American Legion Auxiliary. Applicant must be residing in Connecticut. Applicant must be descendant of veteran, child of veteran.
Basis for selection: Applicant must demonstrate financial need and high academic achievement.
Application requirements: Proof of eligibility.
Additional information: Two awards for descendents of American Legion/Auxiliary members, two awards to children of veteran who is Connecticut resident.
- Amount of award: $500
- Number of awards: 4
- Application deadline: March 1
- Total amount awarded: $2,000

American Legion Connecticut Auxiliary Past President's Parley Education Grant

Type of award: Scholarship, renewable.
Intended use: For undergraduate study.
Eligibility: Applicant or parent must be member of American Legion Auxiliary. Applicant must be residing in Connecticut. Applicant must be descendant of veteran, child of veteran during Grenada, Korean War, Lebanon, Panama, Persian Gulf, WW I, WW II or Vietnam.
Basis for selection: Applicant must demonstrate financial need.
Application requirements: Proof of eligibility.
Additional information: Children and grandchildren of ex-servicewomen who have been American Legion Auxiliary members for five years given preference; children and grandchildren of members or children and grandchildren who themselves are members of five years given second preference.

Amount of award: $500
Application deadline: March 1
Contact:
American Legion Auxiliary, Department of Connecticut
Headquarters
P.O. Box 266
Rocky Hill, CT 06067
Phone: 860-721-5945

American Legion Florida Auxiliary

American Legion Florida Auxiliary Memorial Scholarship

Type of award: Scholarship.
Intended use: For undergraduate study at vocational, 2-year or 4-year institution in Florida.
Eligibility: Applicant or parent must be member of American Legion Auxiliary. Applicant must be female. Applicant must be residing in Florida.
Application requirements: Members, daughters/granddaughters of members with memberships of at least 3 years. Request application by January 1.
Additional information: Junior college and technical school grants not to exceed $500. $1,000 for four-year university.
Amount of award: $500-$1,000
Application deadline: January 1
Contact:
American Legion Auxiliary, Department of Florida
Department Secretary
P.O. Box 547917
Orlando, FL 32854-7917

American Legion Illinois

American Legion Illinois Boy Scout Scholarship

Type of award: Scholarship.
Intended use: For undergraduate study.
Eligibility: Applicant or parent must be member of Boy Scouts of America. Applicant must be male, high school senior. Applicant must be residing in Illinois.
Basis for selection: Competition in Writing/journalism.
Application requirements: Essay and proof of eligibility. Topic: Legion's Americanism and Boy Scout Programs. Explorers also eligible.
Additional information: Boy Scout Scholarship $1,000. Four runners-up receive $200 each.
Amount of award: $1,000
Number of awards: 5
Application deadline: April 30
Total amount awarded: $1,800

American Legion Illinois Scholarship

Type of award: Scholarship.
Intended use: For undergraduate study at accredited vocational, 2-year or 4-year institution.
Eligibility: Applicant or parent must be member of American Legion. Applicant must be high school senior. Applicant must be residing in Illinois.
Basis for selection: Applicant must demonstrate financial need and high academic achievement.
Application requirements: Proof of eligibility.
Additional information: Applications available after September 15.
Amount of award: $1,000
Number of awards: 20
Application deadline: March 15
Total amount awarded: $20,000
Contact:
American Legion Illinois
Department Headquarters
P.O. Box 2910
Bloomington, IL 61702
Phone: 309-663-0361
Fax: 309-663-5783

American Legion Indiana

American Legion Indiana Frank W. McHale Memorial Scholarship

Type of award: Scholarship.
Intended use: For undergraduate study.
Eligibility: Applicant or parent must be member of American Legion, Boys State. Applicant must be male, high school junior. Applicant must be residing in Indiana.
Application requirements: Only Hoosier Boys Staters the year they attend are eligible.
Additional information: Selected by staff at Hoosier Boys State.
Number of awards: 3
Contact:
American Legion Indiana
Americanism Office, Department Headquarters
777 North Meridian Street
Indianapolis, IN 46204
Phone: 317-630-1263
Fax: 317-237-9891

American Legion Indiana Auxiliary

American Legion Indiana Auxiliary Past President's Parley Nursing Scholarship

Type of award: Scholarship.
Intended use: For undergraduate study.
Eligibility: Applicant or parent must be member of American Legion Auxiliary. Applicant must be female. Applicant must be residing in Indiana.
Basis for selection: Major/career interest in nursing.
Application requirements: Must be member of auxiliary. Send SASE to departmental secretary.
    Amount of award: $500
    Number of awards: 1
    Application deadline: April 1
    Total amount awarded: $500
Contact:
American Legion Auxiliary, Department of Indiana
Department Secretary
777 North Meridian Street, Room 107
Indianapolis, IN 46204
Phone: 317-630-1390

American Legion Iowa

American Legion Iowa Boy Scout of the Year Award

Type of award: Scholarship.
Intended use: For undergraduate study.
Eligibility: Applicant or parent must be member of Boy Scouts of America, Eagle Scouts. Applicant must be male. Applicant must be residing in Iowa.
Basis for selection: Applicant must demonstrate service orientation.
Application requirements: Recommendations. Eagle Scout award.
Additional information: Awards: First-$2,000; Second-$600; and Third-$400.
    Amount of award: $400-$2,000
    Number of awards: 3
    Application deadline: February 1
    Total amount awarded: $3,000

American Legion Iowa Outstanding Citizen of Boys State

Type of award: Scholarship.
Intended use: For undergraduate study at postsecondary institution in Iowa.
Eligibility: Applicant or parent must be member of American Legion, Boys State. Applicant must be male, high school senior. Applicant must be residing in Iowa.
Application requirements: Recommendations.
Additional information: Must have completed junior year in high school to attend Boys State. Awarded on recommendation of Boys State.
    Amount of award: $2,500
    Number of awards: 1
Contact:
American Legion Iowa
720 Lyon Street
Des Moines, IA 50309
Phone: 515-282-5068
Fax: 515-282-7583

American Legion Iowa Auxiliary

American Legion Iowa Auxiliary Department of Iowa Scholarship

Type of award: Scholarship.
Intended use: For undergraduate study at postsecondary institution in Iowa.
Eligibility: Applicant or parent must be member of American Legion. Applicant must be residing in Iowa. Applicant must be descendant of veteran, child of veteran during Grenada, Korean War, Lebanon, Panama, Persian Gulf, WW I, WW II or Vietnam.
Application requirements: Member of Legion or Auxiliary, or child, grandchild, or great grandchild of a veteran of WWII, Korea, or Vietnam.
    Amount of award: $200
    Number of awards: 13
    Application deadline: June 1
    Total amount awarded: $2,600
Contact:
American Legion Auxiliary, Department of Iowa
720 Lyon Street
Des Moines, IA 50309
Phone: 515-282-5068
Fax: 515-282-7583

American Legion Kansas

American Legion Kansas Albert M. Lappin Scholarship

Type of award: Scholarship.
Intended use: For undergraduate certificate, freshman, sophomore, junior or non-degree study at accredited vocational, 2-year or 4-year institution in Kansas.
Eligibility: Applicant or parent must be member of American Legion. Applicant must be residing in Kansas.
    Amount of award: $1,000
    Number of awards: 1
    Application deadline: February 15
    Total amount awarded: $1,000
Contact:
1314 SW Topeka Boulevard
Topeka, KS 66612-1886
Phone: 913-232-9315
Fax: 913-232-1399

American Legion Kansas Hugh A. Smith Scholarship

Type of award: Scholarship.
Intended use: For freshman, sophomore or junior study at vocational, 2-year or 4-year institution in Kansas.
Eligibility: Applicant or parent must be member of American Legion. Applicant must be residing in Kansas.
Application requirements: Children or Legion or Auxiliary members.
    Amount of award: $500
    Number of awards: 1
    Application deadline: February 15
    Total amount awarded: $500
Contact:
American Legion Kansas
1314 Southwest Topeka Boulevard
Topeka, KS 66612-1886
Phone: 913-232-9315
Fax: 913-232-1399

American Legion Kansas Ted and Nora Anderson Scholarship

Type of award: Scholarship.
Intended use: For freshman, sophomore or junior study at vocational, 2-year or 4-year institution in Kansas.
Eligibility: Applicant or parent must be member of American Legion. Applicant must be residing in Kansas. Applicant must be child of veteran.
Application requirements: Proof of eligibility. Children of Kansas legion or auxiliary members.
    Amount of award: $500
    Number of awards: 4
    Application deadline: February 15
    Total amount awarded: $2,000
Contact:
American Legion Kansas
1314 Southwest Topeka Boulevard
Topeka, KS 66612-1886
Phone: 913-232-9315
Fax: 913-232-1399

American Legion Maine

American Legion Maine James V. Day Scholarship

Type of award: Scholarship.
Intended use: For freshman study at vocational, 2-year or 4-year institution.
Eligibility: Applicant or parent must be member of American Legion. Applicant must be high school senior. Applicant must be residing in Maine.
Basis for selection: Applicant must demonstrate depth of character, financial need and high academic achievement.
Application requirements: Must be in top half of graduating class.
    Amount of award: $500
    Number of awards: 1
    Application deadline: May 1
    Total amount awarded: $500
Contact:
American Legion Maine
Department Adjutant
P.O. Box 900
Waterville, ME 04903
Phone: 207-873-3229

American Legion Maryland

American Legion Maryland Boys State Scholarship

Type of award: Scholarship.
Intended use: For undergraduate study.
Eligibility: Applicant or parent must be member of American Legion, Boys State. Applicant must be male. Applicant must be residing in Maryland.
Application requirements: Must be Maryland Boys State graduate.
Additional information: Must have graduated from Maryland Boys State.
    Amount of award: $500
    Number of awards: 5
    Application deadline: May 1
    Total amount awarded: $2,500
Contact:
American Legion Maryland
Department Adjutant
War Memorial Building
Baltimore, MD 21202-1405
Phone: 301-752-3104

American Legion Massachusetts

American Legion Massachusetts Nursing Scholarship

Type of award: Scholarship.
Intended use: For freshman study at 2-year or 4-year institution.
Eligibility: Applicant or parent must be member of American Legion. Applicant must be residing in Massachusetts. Applicant must be descendant of veteran, child of veteran.
Basis for selection: Major/career interest in nursing.
Application requirements: Parent or grandparent must be a member in good standing of the Department of Massachusetts Legion.
Additional information: Awards: Six-$1,000; ten-$500; one-$1,000.

Amount of award:	$500-$1,000
Number of awards:	7
Application deadline:	April 1
Total amount awarded:	$7,000

Contact:
American Legion Massachusetts
Department Scholarship Chair
State House, Room 546-2
Boston, MA 02133

American Legion Minnesota

American Legion Minnesota Memorial Scholarship

Type of award: Scholarship.
Intended use: For undergraduate study. Designated institutions: Award may be used at Minnesota institution or in neighboring state with reciprocity agreement.
Eligibility: Applicant or parent must be member of American Legion. Applicant must be U.S. citizen residing in Minnesota. Applicant must be child of veteran, spouse of veteran.
Basis for selection: Applicant must demonstrate financial need.
Application requirements: Child of American Legion or American Legion Auxiliary member.

Amount of award:	$500
Number of awards:	6
Application deadline:	April 1
Total amount awarded:	$3,000

Contact:
American Legion Minnesota
Education Committee
State Veterans Service Building
St. Paul, MN 55155
Phone: 612-291-1800
Fax: 612-291-1057

American Legion Minnesota Auxiliary

American Legion Minnesota Auxiliary Past President's Parley Nursing Scholarship

Type of award: Scholarship.
Intended use: For undergraduate study at postsecondary institution in Minnesota.
Eligibility: Applicant or parent must be member of American Legion Auxiliary. Applicant must be U.S. citizen residing in Minnesota.
Basis for selection: Major/career interest in nursing.

Amount of award:	$500
Number of awards:	3
Application deadline:	March 15
Total amount awarded:	$1,500

Contact:
American Legion Auxiliary, Department of Minnesota
State Veterans Service Building
St. Paul, MN 55155
Phone: 612-224-7634

American Legion Missouri

American Legion Missouri Lillie Lois Ford Boys Scholarship

Type of award: Scholarship.
Intended use: For undergraduate study.
Eligibility: Applicant or parent must be member of Cadet Patrol Academy. Applicant must be male. Applicant must be U.S. citizen residing in Missouri. Applicant must be descendant of veteran, child of veteran.
Basis for selection: Applicant must demonstrate financial need.
Application requirements: Transcript and proof of eligibility. Must have attended a complete session of the Boys State or Cadet Patrol Academy, and must be a dependent child or grandchild of a resident veteran not receiving any other scholarship.

Amount of award:	$900
Number of awards:	1
Total amount awarded:	$900

Contact:
PO Box 179
Jefferson City Jefferson City, MO 65102
Phone: 573-893-2353

American Legion Missouri Lillie Lois Ford Girls Scholarship

Type of award: Scholarship.
Intended use: For undergraduate study.
Eligibility: Applicant or parent must be member of Cadet Patrol Academy. Applicant must be female. Applicant must be residing in Missouri. Applicant must be descendant of veteran, child of veteran.
Basis for selection: Applicant must demonstrate financial need.
Application requirements: Must have attended a complete session of State or Cadet Patrol Academy and be a dependent child or grandchild of a resident veteran and not be receiving any other scholarship.

Amount of award:	$900
Number of awards:	1
Total amount awarded:	$900

Contact:
American Legion Missouri
Department Adjutant
P.O. Box 179
Jefferson City, MO 65102
Phone: 573-893-2353

American Legion National Headquarters

American Legion National Auxiliary President's Scholarship

Type of award: Scholarship.
Intended use: For undergraduate study.
Eligibility: Applicant or parent must be member of American Legion Auxiliary. Applicant must be high school senior. Applicant must be descendant of veteran, child of veteran during Grenada, Korean War, Lebanon, Panama, Persian Gulf, WW I, WW II or Vietnam.
Basis for selection: Applicant must demonstrate depth of character, leadership, financial need and high academic achievement.
Application requirements: Request application from unit auxiliary president auxiliary or department secretary or department education chairman.
Additional information: Request application from community unit president of auxiliary or from Department Secretary or Department Education Chairman.

Amount of award:	$1,500-$2,000
Number of awards:	10
Application deadline:	March 15
Total amount awarded:	$17,500

American Legion National Auxiliary Spirit of Youth Scholarship For Junior Members

Type of award: Scholarship.
Intended use: For undergraduate study.
Eligibility: Applicant or parent must be member of American Legion Auxiliary. Applicant must be high school senior. Applicant must be U.S. citizen.
Basis for selection: Applicant must demonstrate depth of character, leadership, financial need and high academic achievement.
Application requirements: Proof of eligibility. Junior member of 3 years standing. Request application from unit president, community auxiliary, department secretary, or department education chairman.
Additional information: One scholarship available in each of the five divisions.

Amount of award:	$1,000
Number of awards:	5
Application deadline:	March 10
Total amount awarded:	$5,000

American Legion National Eagle Scout of the Year

Type of award: Scholarship.
Intended use: For freshman, sophomore, junior or senior study at postsecondary institution in United States and its possessions.
Eligibility: Applicant or parent must be member of Boy Scouts of America, Eagle Scouts. Applicant must be male, enrolled in high school. Applicant must be U.S. citizen.
Application requirements: Recommendations and nomination by group leaders of religious institution, school, community and scouting. Registered, active members of Boy Scout troop, Varsity Scout team, or Explorer Post sponsored by American Legion Post or Auxiliary Unit. Must be son or grandson of American Legion or Auxiliary member. Request application from state or national headquarters.
Additional information: Applicant must be Eagle Scout, and member of Boy Scout Troop or Varsity Scout Team sponsored by American Legion or Auxiliary, or member of duly chartered Boy Scout Troop or Varsity Scout Team and son or grandson of American Legion or Auxiliary member. Must have received Eagle Scout Award, be an active member of a religious institution, and must have received religious emblem.

Amount of award:	$2,000-$8,000
Number of awards:	4
Total amount awarded:	$14,000

Contact:
American Legion National Headquarters
P.O. Box 1055
Indianapolis, IN 46206
Phone: 317-630-1249

American Legion National Memorial Scholarship of the Twenty and Four

Type of award: Scholarship.
Intended use: For undergraduate or graduate study.
Eligibility: Applicant or parent must be member of American Legion Twenty and Four. Applicant must be female. Applicant must be veteran, descendant of veteran, child of veteran. Applicant must be veteran or descendant of female veteran.
Basis for selection: Applicant must demonstrate financial need and high academic achievement.
Application requirements: Involvement in school activities. Must be child, grandchild, or great-grandchild of living or deceased member in good standing.
Additional information: Memorial to women who served in armed forces during wartime. Age restrictions do not apply to current members of the Twenty and Four. Contact local chapter.

Amount of award:	$500

Contact:
Scholarship Aid
6000 Lucerne Court #2
Meqoun, WI 53092

American Legion Nebraska Auxiliary

American Legion Nebraska Auxiliary Ruby Paul Campaign Fund Scholarship

Type of award: Scholarship.
Intended use: For freshman study at accredited 2-year or 4-year institution.
Eligibility: Applicant or parent must be member of American Legion Auxiliary. Applicant must be high school senior.

Applicant must be residing in Nebraska. Applicant must be descendant of veteran, child of veteran during Grenada, Korean War, Lebanon, Panama, Persian Gulf, WW I, WW II or Vietnam.
Basis for selection: Applicant must demonstrate high academic achievement.
Application requirements: State resident of 3 years. B average during last 3 years of high school and accepted for the fall term at a college or university. Cannot be a nursing student. Legion member for 2 years or child or grandchild of legion member of 2 years standing.
Additional information: Award varies with availability of funding. Not open to applicants enrolled in nursing school.
    Amount of award: $100-$300
    Application deadline: April 10
Contact:
American Legion Nebraska Auxiliary
P.O. Box 5227
Lincoln, NE 68505
Phone: 402-466-1808

American Legion New Hampshire

American Legion New Hampshire Albert T. Marcoux Memorial Scholarship

Type of award: Scholarship.
Intended use: For freshman study.
Eligibility: Applicant or parent must be member of American Legion Auxiliary. Applicant must be U.S. citizen residing in New Hampshire.
Application requirements: Child of living or deceased legion or auxiliary member; graduate of New Hampshire high school, and resident of 3 years. Must be pursuing B.A.
    Amount of award: $1,000
    Number of awards: 1
    Application deadline: May 1
    Total amount awarded: $1,000
Contact:
Department Adjutant
State House Annex, Rm. 431
Concord, NH 03301-6312
Phone: 603-271-2211

American Legion New Hampshire Boys State Scholarship

Type of award: Scholarship.
Intended use: For undergraduate study.
Eligibility: Applicant or parent must be member of American Legion, Boys State. Applicant must be male. Applicant must be U.S. citizen residing in New Hampshire.
Additional information: Award given to participants of Boys State during Boys State Session. Award amount varies every year. Recipient eligible for regional and national awards.
Contact:
American Legion New Hampshire
Department Adjutant
State House Annex, Room 431
Concord, NH 03301-6312
Phone: 603-271-2211

American Legion New Hampshire Auxiliary

American Legion New Hampshire Auxiliary Grace S. High Memorial Child Welfare Scholarship

Type of award: Scholarship.
Intended use: For undergraduate study.
Eligibility: Applicant or parent must be member of American Legion Auxiliary. Applicant must be female. Applicant must be U.S. citizen residing in New Hampshire.
Basis for selection: Applicant must demonstrate financial need.
Application requirements: Must be high school graduate and daughter of legion or auxiliary member.
    Amount of award: $300
    Number of awards: 2
    Application deadline: April 15
    Total amount awarded: $600
Contact:
American Legion Auxiliary, Department of New Hampshire
Department Secretary, Room 432
State House Annex
Concord, NH 03301

American Legion New Jersey

American Legion New Jersey Lawrence Luterman Memorial Scholarship

Type of award: Scholarship.
Intended use: For freshman study.
Eligibility: Applicant or parent must be member of American Legion. Applicant must be high school senior. Applicant must be residing in New Jersey. Applicant must be descendant of veteran, child of veteran.
Additional information: Awards: Two-$4,000 scholarships ($1,000/yr.); two-$2,000; two-$1,000.

Amount of award:	$1,000-$4,000
Number of awards:	6
Application deadline:	February 15
Total amount awarded:	$14,000

Contact:
American Legion Department of New Jersey
Department Adjutant
135 West Hanover Street
Trenton, NJ 08618
Phone: 609-695-5918

American Legion New Jersey Press Club Scholarship

Type of award: Scholarship.
Intended use: For freshman study at accredited 4-year institution.
Eligibility: Applicant or parent must be member of American Legion. Applicant must be residing in New Jersey. Applicant must be descendant of veteran, child of veteran.
Basis for selection: Major/career interest in communications.
Application requirements: Child or grandchild of veteran, or current member of legion or auxiliary--including Sons of American Legion and junior members. Send SASE to education chairman. Must be planning to study communications.

Amount of award:	$500
Number of awards:	1
Application deadline:	July 15
Total amount awarded:	$500

Contact:
Jack W. Keupfer, Education Chairman
American Legion Press Club of New Jersey
68 Merrill Road
Clifton, NJ 07012-1622
Phone: 201-473-5176

American Legion New Jersey Stutz Memorial Scholarship

Type of award: Scholarship.
Intended use: For undergraduate study at vocational, 2-year or 4-year institution.
Eligibility: Applicant or parent must be member of American Legion. Applicant must be high school senior. Applicant must be residing in New Jersey. Applicant must be descendant of veteran, child of veteran.
Application requirements: Must be graduating current year.
Additional information: Award: $1,000 per year for four years.

Amount of award:	$4,000
Number of awards:	1
Application deadline:	February 15
Total amount awarded:	$4,000

Contact:
American Legion New Jersey
Department Adjutant
War Memorial Building
Trenton, NJ 08608
Phone: 609-695-5418

American Legion New York

American Legion New York Association Scholarship

Type of award: Scholarship.
Intended use: For full-time undergraduate study at accredited 4-year institution.
Eligibility: Applicant or parent must be member of American Legion. Applicant must be residing in New York.
Basis for selection: Major/career interest in communications.
Additional information: Applicant must be one of the following: child of Legion or Auxiliary member; junior member; Sons of American Legion member, or graduate of New York Boys State or Girls State.

Amount of award:	$1,000

Contact:
Scholarship Chairman
P.O. Box 1239
Syracuse, NY 13201-1239

American Legion New York Dr. Hannah K. Vuolo Memorial Scholarship

Type of award: Scholarship.
Intended use: For freshman study at accredited 2-year or 4-year institution.
Eligibility: Applicant or parent must be member of American Legion. Applicant must be residing in New York. Applicant must be descendant of veteran during Grenada, Korean War, Lebanon, Panama, Persian Gulf, WW I, WW II or Vietnam.
Basis for selection: Major/career interest in education, teacher. Applicant must demonstrate financial need and high academic achievement.
Additional information: Preference given to state residents.

Amount of award:	$250
Number of awards:	1
Application deadline:	May 1
Total amount awarded:	$250

Contact:
American Legion New York
112 State St., Suite 400
Department Adjutant
Albany, NY 12207

American Legion New York James F. Mulholland Scholarship

Type of award: Scholarship.
Intended use: For freshman study.
Eligibility: Applicant or parent must be member of American Legion. Applicant must be high school senior. Applicant must be residing in New York. Applicant must be child of veteran.
Basis for selection: Applicant must demonstrate financial need and high academic achievement.

Amount of award:	$500
Number of awards:	2
Application deadline:	May 1
Total amount awarded:	$1,000

Contact:
American Legion New York
Department Adjutant
112 State Street, Suite 400
Albany, NY 12207
Phone: 518-463-2215

American Legion North Dakota Auxiliary

American Legion North Dakota Auxiliary Past President's Parley Scholarship

Type of award: Scholarship.
Intended use: For undergraduate study at 2-year or 4-year institution in North Dakota. Designated institutions: Hospital or school of nursing.
Eligibility: Applicant or parent must be member of American Legion Auxiliary. Applicant must be residing in North Dakota.
Basis for selection: Major/career interest in nursing.
Application requirements: Children, grandchildren, or great-grandchildren of legion or auxiliary member in good standing.
Additional information: Apply to your community auxiliary unit. Local unit addresses are available at the contact address.

Amount of award:	$350
Application deadline:	May 15

Contact:
American Legion Auxiliary, Department of North Dakota
Chair of Dept. Parley Scholarship Committee
P.O. Box 250
Beach, ND 58621
Phone: 701-872-3865

American Legion Ohio

American Legion Ohio Scholarship

Type of award: Scholarship.
Intended use: For undergraduate study.
Eligibility: Applicant or parent must be member of American Legion. Applicant must be residing in Ohio. Applicant must be veteran, descendant of veteran, child of veteran during Grenada, Korean War, Lebanon, Panama, Persian Gulf, WW I, WW II or Vietnam.
Additional information: Deadlines and award amounts vary; contact sponsor for information.

Contact:
American Legion Ohio
Department Scholarship Committee
4060 Indianola Avenue
Columbus, OH 43214
Phone: 614-268-7072

American Legion Pennsylvania

American Legion Pennsylvania Joseph P. Gavenonis Scholarship

Type of award: Scholarship.
Intended use: For freshman study at 4-year institution in Pennsylvania.
Eligibility: Applicant or parent must be member of American Legion. Applicant must be high school senior. Applicant must be residing in Pennsylvania. Applicant must be descendant of veteran, child of veteran, deceased veteran or POW/MIA.
Application requirements: One of the following: child or grandchild of legion member in good standing; child of deceased, killed in action, or missing in action legion member.
Additional information: Preference given to children and grandchildren of legionnaires with the most continuous years of membership. Distributed over four years at $1000 per year.

Amount of award:	$4,000
Application deadline:	June 1
Total amount awarded:	$4,000

Contact:
American Legion Pennsylvania
Department Adjutant
P.O. Box 2324
Harrisburg, PA 17105
Phone: 717-730-9100
Fax: 717-975-2836
Website: www.pa-legion.com

American Legion Pennsylvania Robert W. Valimont Endowment Fund Scholarship

Type of award: Scholarship, renewable.
Intended use: For full-time undergraduate certificate, freshman or sophomore study at vocational or 2-year institution. Designated institutions: For two-year technical or vocational schools.
Eligibility: Applicant or parent must be member of American Legion. Applicant must be residing in Pennsylvania. Applicant must be child of veteran, disabled veteran or deceased veteran.
Additional information: Preference given in the following order: legionnaires, veterans, disabled veterans, and deceased veterans.

Amount of award:	$600
Application deadline:	June 1
Total amount awarded:	$600

Contact:
American Legion Pennsylvania
Department Adjutant Attn: Scholarship Secretary
P.O. Box 2324
Harrisburg, PA 17105
Phone: 717-730-9100
Fax: 717-975-2836
Website: www.pa-legion.com

American Legion Sough Dakota Auxiliary

American Legion Sough Dakota Auxiliary College Scholarship

Type of award: Scholarship.
Intended use: For undergraduate study at vocational, 2-year or 4-year institution.
Eligibility: Applicant or parent must be member of American Legion Auxiliary. Applicant must be residing in South Dakota. Applicant must be child of veteran.
Application requirements: Child of either a veteran or an auxiliary member.
    Amount of award: $300
    Number of awards: 2
    Application deadline: March 1
    Total amount awarded: $600
Contact:
American Legion Auxiliary, Department of South Dakota
Department Secretary
P.O. Box 117
Huron, SD 57350
Phone: 605-353-1793

American Legion South Carolina Auxiliary

American Legion South Carolina Auxiliary Gift Scholarship

Type of award: Scholarship.
Intended use: For undergraduate study.
Eligibility: Applicant or parent must be member of American Legion Auxiliary. Applicant must be residing in South Carolina.
Application requirements: Junior member for 3 years.
    Amount of award: $1,000
    Number of awards: 1
    Total amount awarded: $1,000
Contact:
American Legion Auxiliary, Department of South Carolina
Department Secretary
132 Pickens Street
Columbia, SC 29205
Phone: 803-799-6695

American Legion South Dakota

American Legion South Dakota Auxiliary Junior Members Scholarship

Type of award: Scholarship.
Intended use: For freshman study.
Eligibility: Applicant or parent must be member of American Legion Auxiliary. Applicant must be residing in South Dakota.
Application requirements: Junior member for 3 years.
    Amount of award: $300
    Number of awards: 1
    Application deadline: March 1

American Legion South Dakota Auxiliary Nurses Scholarship

Type of award: Scholarship.
Intended use: For undergraduate study.
Eligibility: Applicant or parent must be member of American Legion Auxiliary. Applicant must be residing in South Dakota. Applicant must be child of veteran.
Basis for selection: Major/career interest in nursing.
Application requirements: Child of either a veteran or an auxiliary member.
    Amount of award: $200
    Number of awards: 3
    Application deadline: March 1
    Total amount awarded: $600

American Legion South Dakota Auxiliary Senior America Scholarship

Type of award: Scholarship.
Intended use: For undergraduate study.
Eligibility: Applicant or parent must be member of American Legion Auxiliary. Applicant must be residing in South Dakota.
Application requirements: Senior member for 3 years.
    Amount of award: $300
    Number of awards: 1
    Application deadline: March 1
    Total amount awarded: $300

American Legion South Dakota Auxiliary Vocational Scholarship

Type of award: Scholarship.
Intended use: For non-degree study.
Eligibility: Applicant or parent must be member of American Legion Auxiliary. Applicant must be residing in South Dakota. Applicant must be child of veteran.
Application requirements: Child of either a veteran or an auxiliary member.

Amount of award:	$500
Number of awards:	2
Application deadline:	March 1
Total amount awarded:	$1,000

Contact:
American Legion South Dakota Auxiliary
P.O. Box 117
Huron, SD 57350
Phone: 605-353-1793

American Legion Tennessee

American Legion Tennessee Eagle Scout Award

Type of award: Scholarship.
Intended use: For undergraduate study at postsecondary institution in United States.
Eligibility: Applicant or parent must be member of Boy Scouts of America, Eagle Scouts. Applicant must be male. Applicant must be residing in Tennessee.
Application requirements: Nomination. Tennessee Eagle Scout of the Year winner must be nominated to national level.

Amount of award:	$1,500
Number of awards:	1
Application deadline:	January 1
Total amount awarded:	$1,500

Contact:
American Legion Tennessee
State Headquarters
215 Eighth Avenue, North
Nashville, TN 37203
Phone: 615-254-0568
Fax: 615-255-1551

American Legion Virginia Auxiliary

American Legion Virginia Auxiliary Dr. Kate Waller Barrett Grant

Type of award: Scholarship.
Intended use: For undergraduate study at accredited vocational, 2-year or 4-year institution.
Eligibility: Applicant or parent must be member of American Legion Auxiliary. Applicant must be high school senior. Applicant must be residing in Virginia. Applicant must be veteran, child of veteran.
Basis for selection: Applicant must demonstrate financial need.
Application requirements: Child of veteran or auxiliary member.

Amount of award:	$1,000
Number of awards:	1
Application deadline:	March 15
Total amount awarded:	$1,000

Contact:
American Legion Auxiliary, Department of Virginia
Department Secretary-Treasurer
1805 Chantilly Street
Richmond, VA 23230
Phone: 804-355-6410

American Legion Washington

American Legion Washington Scholarship

Type of award: Scholarship.
Intended use: For undergraduate study at accredited vocational, 2-year or 4-year institution in Washington State.
Eligibility: Applicant or parent must be member of American Legion. Applicant must be high school senior. Applicant must be residing in Washington.
Basis for selection: Applicant must demonstrate financial need.
Application requirements: Child of either Washington legionnaire or auxiliary member, living or deceased.

Amount of award:	$1,000-$1,500
Number of awards:	2
Application deadline:	April 1
Total amount awarded:	$2,500

Contact:
American Legion Washington
Attn: Department Child Welfare Chairman
P.O. Box 3917
Lacey, WA 98509-3917
Phone: 360-491-4373

American Legion Wisconsin

American Legion Wisconsin Eagle Scout of the Year Scholarship

Type of award: Scholarship.
Intended use: For freshman, sophomore, junior or senior study.
Eligibility: Applicant or parent must be member of American Legion/Boys Scouts of America. Applicant must be male, high school senior. Applicant must be residing in Wisconsin.
Basis for selection: Applicant must demonstrate high academic achievement.
Application requirements: Boy Scout, Varsity Scout, or Explorer whose group is sponsored by legion or auxiliary post, or whose father or grandfather is a legion or auxliary member.

Amount of award:	$250
Number of awards:	1
Application deadline:	March 1
Total amount awarded:	$250

Contact:
American Legion Wisconsin
Department Headquarters
812 East State Street
Milwaukee, WI 53202
Phone: 414-271-1940

American Legion Wisconsin Auxiliary

American Legion Wisconsin Auxiliary State President's Scholarship

Type of award: Scholarship.
Intended use: For undergraduate study at accredited postsecondary institution.
Eligibility: Applicant or parent must be member of American Legion Auxiliary. Applicant must be residing in Wisconsin. Applicant must be child of veteran or deceased veteran, spouse of veteran or deceased veteran.
Basis for selection: Applicant must demonstrate financial need and high academic achievement.
Application requirements: Transcript.
Additional information: Minimum 3.5 GPA. Mother of applicant of applicant must be auxiliary member.

Amount of award:	$1,000
Number of awards:	3
Application deadline:	March 15
Total amount awarded:	$3,000

Contact:
American Legion Wisconsin Auxiliary
Department Headquarters
812 East State Street
Milwaukee, WI 53202-3493
Phone: 414-271-0124

American Legion Wyoming

American Legion Wyoming E.B. Blackmore Memorial Scholarship

Type of award: Scholarship.
Intended use: For undergraduate study at postsecondary institution in Wyoming.
Eligibility: Applicant or parent must be member of American Legion. Applicant must be residing in Wyoming. Applicant must be veteran, descendant of veteran, child of veteran.
Application requirements: Legionnaire/children or grandchildren of legionnaire.

Amount of award:	$700
Number of awards:	1
Total amount awarded:	$700

Contact:
American Legion Wyoming
Department Adjutant
P.O. Box 545
Cheyenne, WY 82003
Phone: 307-634-3035

American Medical Women's Association

Medical Women's Carroll L. Birch Award

Type of award: Scholarship.
Intended use: For full-time first professional study in United States.
Eligibility: Applicant or parent must be member of American Medical Women's Association. Applicant must be female. Applicant must be U.S. citizen or permanent resident.
Basis for selection: Competition in Research paper. Major/career interest in medicine (m.d.); medicine, osteopathic.
Application requirements: Three copies of manuscript, letter from facutly sponsor, cover letter, and 250-word abstract repuired with submission.
Additional information: The award is presented to the best research paper written by a student member of AMWA. Applications for membership are available to female medical and osteopathic students.

Amount of award:	$500
Number of awards:	1
Application deadline:	June 30
Total amount awarded:	$500

Contact:
American Medical Women's Association
Carroll L. Birch Award- Medical Education Loans- American Medical Women's Association
801 North Fairfax Street, Suite 400
Alexandria, VA 22314
Phone: 703-838-0500

Medical Women's Education Loan

Type of award: Loan, renewable.
Intended use: For full-time first professional study in United States.
Eligibility: Applicant or parent must be member of American Medical Women's Association. Applicant must be female. Applicant must be U.S. citizen or permanent resident.
Basis for selection: Major/career interest in medicine (m.d.); medicine, osteopathic. Applicant must demonstrate financial need.
Application requirements: Interview, recommendations and proof of eligibility.
Additional information: Award for use at medical or osteopathic medical school. Recipients may reapply but with limit of $5,000 total toward their career.

Amount of award:	$2,000-$5,000
Number of awards:	35
Application deadline:	April 30
Notification begins:	July 30
Total amount awarded:	$70,000

Contact:
American Medical Women's Association
Medical Education Loans- American Medical Women's Association
801 North Fairfax Street, Suite 400
Alexandria, VA 22314
Phone: 703-838-0500

Medical Women's Janet M. Glasgow Essay Award

Type of award: Scholarship.
Intended use: For full-time first professional study in United States.
Eligibility: Applicant or parent must be member of American Medical Women's Association. Applicant must be female. Applicant must be U.S. citizen or permanent resident.
Basis for selection: Competition in Writing/journalism. Essay must be approximately 1,000 words, double-spaced, identifying a woman physician who has been a significant role model and mentor. Major/career interest in medicine (m.d.); medicine, osteopathic.
Application requirements: Essay.

Amount of award:	$1,000
Number of awards:	1
Application deadline:	May 31
Total amount awarded:	$1,000

Contact:
American Medical Women's Association
Janet M. Glasgow Essay Award-Medical Education Loans-
American Medical Women's Association
801 North Fairfax Street, Suite 400
Alexandria, VA 22314
Phone: 703-838-0500

American National Can Company

American National Can Company Scholarship

Type of award: Scholarship, renewable.
Intended use: For freshman study at accredited 2-year or 4-year institution.
Eligibility: Applicant or parent must be employed by American National Can Company.
Basis for selection: Applicant must demonstrate financial need.
Additional information: For further information or an application contact American National Can Company directly.

Amount of award:	$500-$4,000

American Quarter Horse Youth Association

Quarter Horse Youth Scholarship

Type of award: Scholarship, renewable.
Intended use: For full-time undergraduate, non-degree study at accredited vocational, 2-year or 4-year institution in United States.
Eligibility: Applicant or parent must be member of American Quarter Horse Youth Association. Applicant must be high school senior. Applicant must be U.S. citizen.
Basis for selection: Applicant must demonstrate depth of character, leadership, service orientation, financial need and high academic achievement.
Application requirements: Recommendations, transcript and proof of eligibility. Documentation of parents income.
Additional information: Must have been member of American Quarter Horse Youth Association for at least three years. Must be in upper 20 percent of class.

Amount of award:	$1,000
Number of awards:	50
Number of applicants:	120
Application deadline:	May 15
Notification begins:	June 15
Total amount awarded:	$50,000

Contact:
American Junior Quarter Horse Youth Association
Robin Devin
1600 Quarter Horse Drive
Amarillo, TX 79168
Phone: 806-376-4888

American Radio Relay League Foundation, Inc.

Edmond A. Metzger Scholarship

Type of award: Scholarship.
Intended use: For undergraduate, graduate or non-degree study at accredited postsecondary institution in Illinois, Indiana or Wisconsin.
Eligibility: Applicant or parent must be member of American Radio Relay League. Applicant must be residing in Illinois or Indiana or Wisconsin.
Basis for selection: Major/career interest in engineering, electrical and electronic. Applicant must demonstrate financial need.
Application requirements: Recommendations, transcript and proof of eligibility.
Additional information: Must be amateur radio operator with novice license.

Amount of award:	$500
Number of awards:	1
Application deadline:	February 1
Notification begins:	June 30
Total amount awarded:	$500

Contact:
ARRL Foundation Inc. Scholarship Program
225 Main Street
Newington, CT 06111
Phone: 860-594-0200
Fax: 860-594-0259
Website: www.arrl.org/arrlf/scholgen.html

Tom and Judith Comstock Scholarship

Type of award: Scholarship.
Intended use: For undergraduate study at accredited 2-year or 4-year institution in United States.
Eligibility: Applicant or parent must be member of American Radio Relay League. Applicant must be high school senior. Applicant must be residing in Oklahoma or Texas.
Basis for selection: Applicant must demonstrate financial need.
Application requirements: Recommendations and transcript.
Additional information: Must be amateur radio operator holding any class license.

Amount of award:	$1,000
Number of awards:	1
Application deadline:	February 1
Notification begins:	June 30
Total amount awarded:	$1,000

Contact:
ARRL Foundation Inc./Scholarship Program
225 Main Street
Newington, CT 06111
Phone: 860-594-0200
Fax: 860-594-0259
Website: www.arrl.org

You've Got a Friend in Pennsylvania Scholarship

Type of award: Scholarship.
Intended use: For undergraduate, graduate or non-degree study at accredited postsecondary institution in United States.
Eligibility: Applicant or parent must be member of American Radio Relay League.
Basis for selection: Applicant must demonstrate financial need.
Application requirements: Recommendations, transcript and proof of eligibility.
Additional information: Must be amateur radio operator with general license. Preference to Pennsylvania residents.

Amount of award:	$1,000
Number of awards:	1
Application deadline:	February 1
Notification begins:	June 30
Total amount awarded:	$1,000

Contact:
ARRL Foundation Inc./Scholarship Program
225 Main Street
Newington, CT 06111
Phone: 860-594-0200
Fax: 860-594-0259
Website: www.arrl.org/arrlf/scholgen.html

American Society for Microbiology

Robert D. Watkins Minority Graduate Fellowship

Type of award: Scholarship, renewable.
Intended use: For full-time doctoral study at accredited graduate institution.
Eligibility: Applicant or parent must be member of American Society for Microbiology. Applicant must be of minority background. Applicant must be U.S. citizen or permanent resident.
Basis for selection: Major/career interest in microbiology. Applicant must demonstrate high academic achievement.
Application requirements: Recommendations, transcript and research proposal. curriculum vitae.
Additional information: Must have succesfully completed first year of doctoral training. Award cannot be used for tuition and fees. Individuals with medical or veterinary degree are not eligible to apply. Must be a member of American Society for Microbiology. Proposal must be developed in collaboration with mentor or research advisor.

Amount of award:	$24,000
Application deadline:	May 1

Contact:
American Society for Microbiology
Office of Education and Training
1325 Massachusetts Avenue NW
Washington, DC 20005-4171
Website: www.asmusa.org

American Society of Civil Engineers

Trent R. Dames and William W. Moore Fellowship

Type of award: Research grant, renewable.
Intended use: For master's, doctoral, postgraduate or non-degree study.
Eligibility: Applicant or parent must be member of American Society of Civil Engineers.
Basis for selection: Major/career interest in engineering, civil; engineering, environmental; urban planning; environmental science; education. Applicant must demonstrate depth of character, leadership, seriousness of purpose, service orientation and financial need.
Application requirements: Recommendations, essay, transcript, proof of eligibility and research proposal.
Additional information: Application is available on-line. Membership applications may be submitted with scholarhip and/or fellowship application. This award is open to practicing engineers, earth scientists, professors and graduate students.

Amount of award:	$2,000-$6,000
Number of awards:	1
Application deadline:	February 20

Contact:
American Society of Civil Engineers
1801 Alexander Bell Drive
Reston, VA 20191-4440
Website: www.asce.org

American Society of Mechanical Engineers

ASME Student Loan Program

Type of award: Loan.
Intended use: For full-time undergraduate or graduate study.
Eligibility: Applicant or parent must be member of American Society of Mechanical Engineers. Applicant must be Canada & Mexico.
Basis for selection: Applicant must demonstrate depth of character, leadership and financial need.
Application requirements: Recommendations.

Amount of award:	$2,500
Application deadline:	October 15, April 15
Notification begins:	December 15, June 15

Contact:
345 E. 47 St.
New York, NY 10017
Phone: 212-705-8131
Website: www.asme.org/educate/aid

ASME Student Loan Program

Type of award: Loan.
Intended use: For full-time undergraduate or graduate study.
Eligibility: Applicant or parent must be member of American Society of Mechanical Engineers. Applicant must be Canada, Mexico.
Basis for selection: Major/career interest in engineering, mechanical. Applicant must demonstrate depth of character, leadership and financial need.
Application requirements: Recommendations.

Amount of award:	$2,500
Application deadline:	October 15, April 15
Notification begins:	December 15, June 15

Contact:
Nellie Malave
345 E. 47th St.
New York, NY 10017
Phone: 212-705-8131
Website: www.asme.org/educate/aid

F.W. and D.G. Miller Mechanical Engineering Scholarship

Type of award: Scholarship.
Intended use: For full-time junior, senior study.
Eligibility: Applicant or parent must be member of American Society of Mechanical Engineers. Applicant must be U.S. citizen.
Basis for selection: Major/career interest in engineering, mechanical. Applicant must demonstrate depth of character, leadership and high academic achievement.
Application requirements: Recommendations, essay, transcript and nomination. Application must be endorsed by department head.

Amount of award:	$1,500
Number of awards:	2
Number of applicants:	61
Application deadline:	April 17
Notification begins:	June 30
Total amount awarded:	$1,500

Contact:
American Society of Mechanical Engineers
345 East 47 Street
New York, NY 10017-2392
Phone: 212-705-8131
Website: www.asme.org

F.W. Berchley Mechanical Engineering Scholarship

Type of award: Scholarship.
Intended use: For full-time undergraduate study.
Eligibility: Applicant or parent must be member of American Society of Mechanical Engineers.
Basis for selection: Major/career interest in engineering, mechanical. Applicant must demonstrate depth of character, leadership, financial need and high academic achievement.
Application requirements: Recommendations, essay, transcript and nomination. Application must be endorsed by department head.
Additional information: Applicant must be a student member of ASME.

Amount of award:	$1,500
Number of awards:	1
Number of applicants:	48
Application deadline:	April 17
Notification begins:	June 30
Total amount awarded:	$1,500

Contact:
American Society of Mechanical Engineers
345 East 47 Street
New York, NY 10017-2392
Phone: 212-705-8131
Website: www.asme.org

Garland Duncan Mechanical Engineering Scholarship

Type of award: Scholarship.
Intended use: For full-time junior, senior study.
Eligibility: Applicant or parent must be member of American Society of Mechanical Engineers.
Basis for selection: Major/career interest in engineering, mechanical. Applicant must demonstrate depth of character, leadership, financial need and high academic achievement.
Application requirements: Recommendations, essay, transcript and nomination. Application must be endorsed by department head.

Amount of award:	$2,500
Number of awards:	2
Number of applicants:	2
Application deadline:	April 17
Notification begins:	June 30
Total amount awarded:	$5,000

Contact:
American Society of Mechanical Engineers
345 East 47 Street
New York, NY 10017-2392
Phone: 212-705-8131
Website: www.asme.org

John and Elsa Gracik Mechanical Engineering Scholarship

Type of award: Scholarship.
Intended use: For full-time undergraduate study.
Eligibility: Applicant or parent must be member of American Society of Mechanical Engineers. Applicant must be high school senior. Applicant must be U.S. citizen.
Basis for selection: Major/career interest in engineering, mechanical. Applicant must demonstrate depth of character, leadership, financial need and high academic achievement.
Application requirements: Recommendations, essay, transcript and nomination. Application must be endorsed by department head.

Amount of award:	$1,500
Number of awards:	8
Number of applicants:	91
Application deadline:	April 17
Notification begins:	June 30

Contact:
American Society of Mechanical Engineers
345 East 47 Street
New York, NY 10017-2392
Phone: 212-705-8131
Website: www.asme.org/educate/aid

Kenneth Andrew Roe Mechanical Engineering Scholarship

Type of award: Scholarship.
Intended use: For full-time junior, senior study.
Eligibility: Applicant or parent must be member of American Society of Mechanical Engineers. Applicant must be U.S. citizen or permanent resident.
Basis for selection: Major/career interest in engineering, mechanical. Applicant must demonstrate depth of character, leadership, financial need and high academic achievement.
Application requirements: Recommendations, essay, transcript and nomination. Application must be endorsed by department head.

Amount of award:	$6,000
Number of awards:	1
Number of applicants:	60
Application deadline:	April 17
Notification begins:	June 1
Total amount awarded:	$6,000

Contact:
American Society of Mechanical Engineers
345 East 47 Street
New York, NY 10017-2392
Phone: 212-705-8131
Website: www.asme.org

W.J. and M.E. Adams, Jr., Mechanical Engineering Scholarship

Type of award: Scholarship.
Intended use: For full-time undergraduate study in ASME region IX (California, Hawaii and Nevada).
Eligibility: Applicant or parent must be member of American Society of Mechanical Engineers.
Basis for selection: Major/career interest in engineering, mechanical. Applicant must demonstrate depth of character, leadership, financial need and high academic achievement.
Application requirements: Recommendations, essay, transcript and nomination. Application must be endorsed by department head. Must have a student membership in the American Society of Mechanical Engineers.
Additional information: Must have at least 2.5 GPA.

Amount of award:	$1,000
Number of awards:	1
Number of applicants:	9
Application deadline:	April 17
Notification begins:	June 15
Total amount awarded:	$1,000

Contact:
American Society of Mechanical Engineers
345 East 47 Street
New York, NY 10017-2392
Phone: 212-705-8131
Website: www.asme.org/educate/aid

American Society of Safety Engineers

Safety Engineers Academic Scholarship

Type of award: Scholarship.
Intended use: For full-time undergraduate or graduate study at accredited 4-year or graduate institution.
Eligibility: Applicant or parent must be member of American Society of Safety Engineers.
Basis for selection: Applicant must demonstrate seriousness of purpose and high academic achievement.
Application requirements: Recommendations, essay, transcript and proof of eligibility.
Additional information: Must have GPA of 3.25. Must major in occupational safety. Applicant or parent must be member of the American Society of Safety Engineers.

Amount of award:	$2,000-$2,500
Number of applicants:	40
Application deadline:	January 31
Notification begins:	May 1
Total amount awarded:	$12,500

Contact:
Eileen Reiter
American Society of Safety Engineers
1800 East Oakton
Des Plaines, IL 60018
Phone: 847-699-2929
Fax: 800-380-7101
Website: www.asse.org

American Society of Travel Agents Foundation

Arizona Dependent/ Employee Membership Travel Agents Scholarship

Type of award: Scholarship, renewable.
Intended use: For full-time or half-time sophomore, junior or senior study at accredited 2-year or 4-year institution in Arizona. Designated institutions: Applicant must attend a college or university in the state of Arizona.
Eligibility: Applicant or parent must be member of ASTA Arizona Chapter. Applicant must be U.S. citizen or permanent resident.
Basis for selection: Applicant must demonstrate high academic achievement.
Application requirements: Recommendations, essay, transcript and proof of eligibility.
Additional information: Dependents of members and employees of ASTA Arizona chapters eligible. Must submit 500-word essay entitled "My Career Goals." Must be attending an institution in Arizona and enrolled either in final year in two-year college or junior or senior year in four-year university. Minimum 2.5 GPA required. Send SASE. Open to applicants of all majors and fields of study.

Amount of award:	$1,500
Number of awards:	1
Application deadline:	July 28
Notification begins:	December 1
Total amount awarded:	$1,500

Contact:
Scholarship Coordinator
1101 King Street
Alexandria, VA 22314-2944

Amerisure Companies

Amerisure Companies Scholarship

Type of award: Scholarship, renewable.
Intended use: For undergraduate study at accredited vocational, 2-year or 4-year institution.
Eligibility: Applicant or parent must be employed by Amerisure Companies.
Additional information: For further information or an application contact Amerisure Companies directly.
   Amount of award: $1,000

AMP Incorporated

AMP Scholars Program

Type of award: Scholarship, renewable.
Intended use: For undergraduate study at accredited vocational, 2-year or 4-year institution.
Eligibility: Applicant or parent must be employed by AMP Incorporated. Applicant must be high school senior.
Additional information: For further information or an application contact AMP Incorporated directly.
   Amount of award: $3,000

Contact:
AMP Inc.

Appaloosa Youth Foundation

Appaloosa Educational Scholarships

Type of award: Scholarship, renewable.
Intended use: For full-time undergraduate or graduate study at accredited postsecondary institution.
Eligibility: Applicant or parent must be member of Appaloosa Horse Club. Applicant must be U.S. citizen or permanent resident.
Basis for selection: Applicant must demonstrate depth of character, leadership, seriousness of purpose, service orientation, financial need and high academic achievement.
Application requirements: Portfolio, recommendations, essay, transcript and proof of eligibility. Photo, SAT or ACT scores are required.
Additional information: Must be a member of the Appaloosa Horse Club. Must have a GPA of 3.5 for one of the scholarships, 2.5 for rest. Must intend to pursue equine-related studies.

Amount of award:	$1,000-$2,000
Number of awards:	9
Number of applicants:	41
Application deadline:	June 10
Notification begins:	July 15

Contact:
Appaloosa Youth Foundation
5070 Highway 8 West
Moscow, ID 83843
Phone: 208-882-5578
Website: www.appaloosa.com

Aptar Group Charitable Foundation

Seaquist Scholarship for Sons and Daughters

Type of award: Scholarship, renewable.
Intended use: For undergraduate study at accredited vocational, 2-year or 4-year institution.
Eligibility: Applicant or parent must be employed by AptarGroup Charitable Foundation. Applicant must be high school senior.
Basis for selection: Applicant must demonstrate financial need.

Additional information: For further information or an application contact Aptar Group Charitable Foundation.
  Amount of award: $2,000
Contact:
Aptar Group Chartitable Foundation

Arby Construction

Klumb Family Scholarship Program

Type of award: Scholarship.
Intended use: For undergraduate or graduate study at vocational, 2-year, 4-year or graduate institution.
Eligibility: Applicant or parent must be employed by Arby Construction. Applicant must be high school senior.
Additional information: For futher information or an application contact Arby Construction directly.
  Amount of award: $1,500

Armed Forces Communications and Electronics Association

ROTC Scholarships

Type of award: Scholarship.
Intended use: For full-time sophomore, junior study at accredited 4-year institution in United States.
Eligibility: Applicant or parent must be member of Reserve Officers Training Corps (ROTC). Applicant must be U.S. citizen.
Basis for selection: Major/career interest in engineering, electrical and electronic; electronics; computer and information sciences; engineering, computer; physics; mathematics. Applicant must demonstrate depth of character, leadership, patriotism, seriousness of purpose, service orientation and high academic achievement.
Application requirements: Recommendations, transcript and nomination by professor of military science, naval science or aerospace studies. Recommendations from ROTC commander and professor in stated major.
Additional information: For application information, contact commander of ROTC unit. Additional fields of study include mathematics. Send SASE.
  Amount of award: $2,000
  Number of awards: 90
  Number of applicants: 200
  Application deadline: April 1, April 1
  Notification begins: June 1
  Total amount awarded: $180,000
Contact:
Armed Forces Communications and Electronics Association
4400 Fair Lakes Court
Fairfax, VA 22033-3899
Phone: 703-631-6147

Arrow Electronics, Inc..

Tony Winger, Jr., Scholarship

Type of award: Scholarship.
Intended use: For undergraduate study at accredited 4-year institution.
Eligibility: Applicant or parent must be employed by Arrow Electronics, Inc.
Basis for selection: Applicant must demonstrate financial need.
Additional information: For further information or an application contact Arrow Electronics, Inc. directly.
  Amount of award: $500-$3,000

ASCAP Foundation

Rudolf Nissim Composers Competition

Type of award: Scholarship.
Intended use: For non-degree study.
Eligibility: Applicant or parent must be member of American Society of Composers/Authors/Publishers (ASCAP).
Basis for selection: Competition in Music performance/composition.
Application requirements: Proof of eligibility. Must submit an original music composition for a large ensemble which requires a conductor and has not been professionally performed.
Additional information: Applicant must be an ASCAP member.
  Amount of award: $5,000
  Number of awards: 1
  Number of applicants: 260
  Application deadline: November 15
  Notification begins: January 15
  Total amount awarded: $5,000
Contact:
Fran Richard
The ASCAP Foundation
One Lincoln Plaza
New York, NY 10023

Ashland, Inc.

Ashland Scholars Program

Type of award: Scholarship, renewable.
Intended use: For freshman study at accredited 4-year institution.
Eligibility: Applicant or parent must be employed by Ashland Coal, Inc.
Additional information: For further information or an application contact Ashland, Inc. directly.
  Amount of award: $1,500

Association for Library and Information Science Foundation

ALISE Research Grant Award

Type of award: Research grant.
Intended use: For non-degree study.
Eligibility: Applicant or parent must be member of Association for Library/Information Science Educ.
Basis for selection: Major/career interest in library science. Applicant must demonstrate high academic achievement.
Application requirements: Proof of eligibility and research proposal.
Additional information: Must be personal member of ALISE as of deadline date. Research grant award cannot be used to support doctoral dissertation.

Amount of award:	$5,000
Number of awards:	1
Application deadline:	September 15
Total amount awarded:	$5,000

ALISE Research Paper Competition

Type of award: Scholarship.
Intended use: For non-degree study.
Eligibility: Applicant or parent must be member of Association for Library/Information Science Educ.
Basis for selection: Competition in Research paper. Research paper in any aspect of librarianship or information studies. Major/career interest in library science.
Additional information: Research papers concerning any aspect of librarianship or information studies are eligible. Must be personal member of ALISE by deadline date.

Amount of award:	$500
Number of awards:	2
Application deadline:	September 15
Total amount awarded:	$1,000

Contact:
College of Library and Information Science
Robert V. Williams, Chair, ALISE Rsch Cmte
University of South Carolina
Columbia, SC 29208
Website: www.alise.org/awards_main.html

Association of American Geographers

Anne U. White Fund

Type of award: Research grant.
Intended use: For undergraduate, graduate or non-degree study.
Eligibility: Applicant or parent must be member of Association of American Geographers. Applicant must be U.S. citizen.
Basis for selection: Major/career interest in geography.
Application requirements: Research proposal.
Additional information: Must have been member for at least two years at time of application.

Number of awards:	5
Number of applicants:	5
Application deadline:	December 31
Notification begins:	March 1
Total amount awarded:	$2,800

Association of American Geographers Dissertation Research Grant

Type of award: Research grant.
Intended use: For doctoral study.
Eligibility: Applicant or parent must be member of Association of American Geographers.
Basis for selection: Major/career interest in geography.
Application requirements: Research proposal.
Additional information: Must have been member for one year. Candidates must have completed all Ph.D. requirements except dissertation by end of semester following approval of award.

Amount of award:	$1,000
Number of awards:	5
Number of applicants:	6
Application deadline:	December 31
Notification begins:	March 1

Association of American Geographers General Research Grant

Type of award: Research grant.
Intended use: For graduate or non-degree study.
Eligibility: Applicant or parent must be member of Association of American Geographers.
Basis for selection: Major/career interest in geography.
Application requirements: Research proposal.
Additional information: Must have been member for at least two years at time of application. Grant to be used to support research and field work.

Amount of award:	$1,000
Number of awards:	6
Number of applicants:	8
Application deadline:	December 31
Notification begins:	March 1
Total amount awarded:	$4,725

Contact:
Association of American Geographers
1710 16 Street, NW
Washington, DC 20009-3198
Phone: 202-234-1450

Association of Chartered Accountants in the United States

Chartered Accountants Education Award Competition

Type of award: Scholarship.
Intended use: For non-degree study.
Eligibility: Applicant or parent must be member of Beta Alpha Psi.
Basis for selection: Competition in Research paper. Winning paper selection based on creativity, technical content, judgement, readability, relevance Major/career interest in accounting.
Application requirements: Essay.
Additional information: Contact office for essay topics.
    Amount of award: $2,500
    Application deadline: June 30
    Notification begins: September 1
Contact:
Association Of Chartered Accountants In The United States
attn: Mark Merryweather
666 Fifth Avenue, Suite 350
New York, NY 10103

Association of Energy Service Companies

Energy Service Scholarship

Type of award: Scholarship, renewable.
Intended use: For full-time undergraduate, non-degree study at accredited vocational, 2-year or 4-year institution.
Eligibility: Applicant or parent must be employed by Association of Energy Service Companies.
Basis for selection: Applicant must demonstrate depth of character, leadership, service orientation, financial need and high academic achievement.
Application requirements: Essay and transcript.
Additional information: Student or parent must be employed by a member company of the Association of Energy Service Companies.
    Amount of award: $1,000
    Number of applicants: 105
    Application deadline: April 15
    Notification begins: May 1
    Total amount awarded: $32,000
Contact:
Kristen Van Veen Association of Energy Service Companies
6060 North Central Expressway
Suite 428
Dallas, TX 75206
Phone: 800-692-0771 Ext. 25

Association of Former Agents of the U.S. Secret Service

Former Agents of the U.S. Secret Service Scholarship

Type of award: Scholarship.
Intended use: For full-time sophomore, junior, senior, master's or postgraduate study at accredited 2-year, 4-year or graduate institution in United States.
Eligibility: Applicant or parent must be member of Association of Former Agents of the Secret Service. Applicant must be U.S. citizen or permanent resident.
Basis for selection: Major/career interest in criminal justice/law enforcement. Applicant must demonstrate depth of character, leadership, patriotism, seriousness of purpose, service orientation, financial need and high academic achievement.
Application requirements: Recommendations, essay and transcript.
Additional information: Applications accepted from September through April 30. SASE. Unsigned documents will not be accepted.
    Amount of award: $500-$2,500
    Number of awards: 5
    Number of applicants: 90
    Application deadline: May 1
    Total amount awarded: $7,000
Contact:
Scholarship Coordinator
P.O. Box 848
Annandale, VA 22003-0848
Phone: 703-256-0188

Association of the Sons of Poland

Sons of Poland Scholarship

Type of award: Scholarship.
Intended use: For full-time freshman study at accredited 2-year or 4-year institution in United States.
Eligibility: Applicant or parent must be member of Sons of Poland. Applicant must be high school senior, of Polish heritage. Applicant must be U.S. citizen or permanent resident.
Basis for selection: Applicant must demonstrate high academic achievement.
Application requirements: Essay, transcript and proof of eligibility.
Additional information: Must be insured by Association. High GPA and SAT I scores needed. Open to applicants in their senior year of high school.

Amount of award: $100-$1,000
Application deadline: May 14
Notification begins: February 1
Contact:
Association of the Sons of Poland
Achievement Scholarship
333 Hackensack Street
Carlstadt, NJ 07072
Phone: 201-935-2807

Astra Merck

Astra Merck Scholarship Program

Type of award: Scholarship, renewable.
Intended use: For undergraduate study at 2-year or 4-year institution.
Eligibility: Applicant or parent must be employed by Astra Merck. Applicant must be high school senior.
Additional information: For further information or an application contact Astra Merck directly.
Amount of award: $3,000

Atlas Pacific Engineering Company

Atlas Pacific Scholarship Program

Type of award: Scholarship, renewable.
Intended use: For freshman study at vocational, 2-year or 4-year institution.
Eligibility: Applicant or parent must be employed by Atlas Pacific Engineering Company. Applicant must be high school senior.
Additional information: For further information or an application contact Atlas Pacific Engineering Company directly.
Amount of award: $2,500

Avery Dennison

Avery Dennison Scholars Program

Type of award: Scholarship, renewable.
Intended use: For freshman study at accredited 2-year or 4-year institution.
Eligibility: Applicant or parent must be employed by Avery Dennison.
Basis for selection: Applicant must demonstrate financial need.
Additional information: For further information or an application contact Avery Dennison directly.
Amount of award: $500-$2,500

Avnet, Inc.

Avnet Scholarship Program

Type of award: Scholarship, renewable.
Intended use: For undergraduate study at vocational, 2-year or 4-year institution.
Eligibility: Applicant or parent must be employed by Avnet, Inc. Applicant must be high school senior.
Additional information: For futher information or an application contact Avnet Incorporated directly.
Amount of award: $500-$2,000

Baker Manufacturing Company

Baker Scholarship Program

Type of award: Scholarship.
Intended use: For undergraduate study at accredited vocational, 2-year or 4-year institution.
Eligibility: Applicant or parent must be employed by Baker Manufacturing Company.
Additional information: For further information or an application contact Baker Manufacturing Company directly.
Amount of award: $1,000

Bandag, Incorporated

Bandag Scholarship Program

Type of award: Scholarship, renewable.
Intended use: For freshman study at vocational, 2-year or 4-year institution.
Eligibility: Applicant or parent must be employed by Bandag, Incorporated. Applicant must be high school senior.
Additional information: For futher information or an application contact Bandag Incorporated directly.
Amount of award: $500-$1,250

Bank One, Houston

Bank One, Houston Higher Education Scholarship Program

Type of award: Scholarship.
Intended use: For undergraduate study at accredited 2-year or 4-year institution.
Eligibility: Applicant or parent must be employed by Bank One, Houston.
Basis for selection: Applicant must demonstrate financial need.
Additional information: For further information or an application contact Bank One, Houston directly.
Amount of award: $500

BankAmerica Foundation and Bank of America-Giannini Foundation

BankAmerica Scholarship

Type of award: Scholarship.
Intended use: For undergraduate study at accredited vocational, 2-year or 4-year institution.
Eligibility: Applicant or parent must be employed by BankAmerica.
Basis for selection: Applicant must demonstrate financial need.
Additional information: For further information or an application contact Bank America Foundation and Bank of America-Giannini Foundation directly.
    Amount of award: $500-$2,000

Banta Corporation Foundation, Inc.

Banta Scholarship Program

Type of award: Scholarship, renewable.
Intended use: For freshman study at 2-year or 4-year institution.
Eligibility: Applicant or parent must be employed by Banta Corporation Foundation, Inc. Applicant must be high school senior.
Additional information: For futher information or an application contact Banta Corporation Foundation Incorporated directly.
    Amount of award: $2,500

Bardes Fund

Bardes Fund Scholarship

Type of award: Scholarship, renewable.
Intended use: For undergraduate study at accredited vocational, 2-year or 4-year institution.
Eligibility: Applicant or parent must be employed by Bardes Company.
Additional information: For further information or an application contact Bardes Company directly.
    Amount of award: $500-$3,500

Barnes Group Foundation, Inc.

Barnes Group Foundation Scholarship

Type of award: Scholarship, renewable.
Intended use: For undergraduate study at accredited vocational, 2-year or 4-year institution.
Eligibility: Applicant or parent must be employed by Barnes Group.
Basis for selection: Applicant must demonstrate financial need.
Additional information: For further information or an application contact Barnes Group Foundation, Inc. directly.
    Amount of award: $500-$3,500

Barnett Banks, Inc.

Barnett Scholars Program

Type of award: Scholarship, renewable.
Intended use: For undergraduate study at vocational, 2-year or 4-year institution.
Eligibility: Applicant or parent must be employed by Barnett Banks, Inc. Applicant must be high school senior.
Additional information: For further information or an application contact Barnett Banks Incorporated directly.
    Amount of award: $500-$1,500

Bartley Corporation

Marcia Doyle Bartley Scholarship

Type of award: Scholarship, renewable.
Intended use: For undergraduate study at accredited vocational, 2-year or 4-year institution.
Eligibility: Applicant or parent must be employed by Bartley Corporation.
Basis for selection: Applicant must demonstrate financial need.
Additional information: For further information or an application contact Bartley Corporation directly.
    Amount of award: $5,000

Bashinsky Foundation, Inc.

Golden Enterprises Scholarship

Type of award: Scholarship, renewable.
Intended use: For undergraduate or graduate study at accredited vocational, 2-year or 4-year institution.
Eligibility: Applicant or parent must be employed by Golden Enterprises, Inc.

Additional information: For further information or an application contact Golden Enterprises, Inc., or Golden Flake.
    Amount of award: $2,500

Bassett-Walker, Inc.

Barry E. Pruett Scholarship

Type of award: Scholarship, renewable.
Intended use: For undergraduate study at accredited vocational, 2-year or 4-year institution.
Eligibility: Applicant or parent must be employed by Bassett-Walker, Inc.
Basis for selection: Applicant must demonstrate financial need.
Additional information: For further information or an application contact Bassett-Walker, Inc. directly.
    Amount of award: $500

Battle Mountain Gold Company

Battle Mountain Canada Scholarship

Type of award: Scholarship, renewable.
Intended use: For freshman study at 2-year or 4-year institution.
Eligibility: Applicant or parent must be employed by Battle Mountain Gold Company. Applicant must be high school senior.
Additional information: For further information or an application contact Battle Mountain Gold Company directly.
    Amount of award: $2,000

Baxter, Inc. Foundation

Baxter Allegiance Foundation Scholarship

Type of award: Scholarship, renewable.
Intended use: For undergraduate study at accredited vocational, 2-year or 4-year institution.
Eligibility: Applicant or parent must be employed by Baxter International, Inc.
Application requirements: Proof of eligibility.
Additional information: For further information or an application contact Baxter, Inc. Foundation directly.
    Amount of award: $1,000

Bay State Gas Company

Bay State Gas Company Scholarship

Type of award: Scholarship.
Intended use: For full-time undergraduate, non-degree study at vocational, 2-year or 4-year institution in or outside United States.
Eligibility: Applicant or parent must be employed by Bay State Gas Company.
Basis for selection: Applicant must demonstrate depth of character, leadership, seriousness of purpose, service orientation, financial need and high academic achievement.
Application requirements: Recommendations, transcript and proof of eligibility.
Additional information: For further information or an application contact Bay State Gas Company directly.
    Amount of award: $1,000
    Number of awards: 10
    Number of applicants: 57
    Application deadline: April 1
    Notification begins: May 25
    Total amount awarded: $10,000
Contact:
Bay State Gas Company
Human Resource Department
300 Friberg Parkway
Westboro, MA 01581-5039
Phone: 508-836-7155

Beacon Companies

Robert Leventhal Scholars Program

Type of award: Scholarship.
Intended use: For undergraduate study at accredited vocational, 2-year or 4-year institution.
Eligibility: Applicant or parent must be employed by Beacon Companies.
Basis for selection: Applicant must demonstrate financial need.
Additional information: For further information or an application contact Beacon Companies directly.
    Amount of award: $500-$2,000

Bemis Company Foundation

Bemis Company Foundation Scholarship

Type of award: Scholarship, renewable.
Intended use: For undergraduate study at accredited vocational, 2-year or 4-year institution.
Eligibility: Applicant or parent must be employed by Bemis Company.

Additional information: For further information or an application contact Bemis Company directly.
    Amount of award: $500-$3,000

Benchmark Corporation

Benchmark Corporation Scholarship

Type of award: Scholarship, renewable.
Intended use: For undergraduate study at accredited vocational, 2-year or 4-year institution.
Eligibility: Applicant or parent must be employed by Benchmark Corporation.
Additional information: For further information or an application contact Benchmark Corporation directly.
    Amount of award: $2,500

Beta Phi Mu

Frank B. Sessa Scholarship for Continuing Education

Type of award: Scholarship.
Intended use: For graduate or non-degree study.
Eligibility: Applicant or parent must be member of Beta Phi Mu.
Basis for selection: Major/career interest in library science.
Application requirements: Proof of eligibility and research proposal.
Additional information: For members of Beta Phi Mu continuing professional education.
    Amount of award: $750
    Number of applicants: 10
    Application deadline: March 15
    Notification begins: June 1

Harold Lancour Scholarship for Foreign Study

Type of award: Research grant.
Intended use: For master's, non-degree study outside United States.
Eligibility: Applicant or parent must be member of Beta Phi Mu.
Basis for selection: Major/career interest in library science.
Application requirements: Proof of eligibility and research proposal. resume.
Additional information: For a librarian or a library school student to conduct a research project in a foreign country.

    Amount of award: $1,000
    Number of awards: 1
    Number of applicants: 10
    Application deadline: March 15
    Notification begins: June 1
    Total amount awarded: $1,000
Contact:
Beta Phi Mu
School of Information Studies
Florida State University
Tallahassee, FL 32306-2100
Phone: 850-644-3907
Website: www.cas.usf.edu/lis/bpm

Bethlehem Steel Foundation

Bethlehem Steel Scholars

Type of award: Scholarship.
Intended use: For undergraduate study at vocational, 2-year or 4-year institution.
Eligibility: Applicant or parent must be employed by Bethlehem Steel Foundation. Applicant must be high school senior.
Additional information: For further information or an application contact Bethlem Steel Foundation directly.
    Amount of award: $1,000

BetzDearborn Foundation

BetzDearborn Scholarship Program

Type of award: Scholarship, renewable.
Intended use: For freshman, sophomore, junior or senior study at accredited 2-year or 4-year institution.
Eligibility: Applicant or parent must be employed by Betz Laboratories, Inc.
Additional information: For further information or an application contact BetzDearborn Foundation directly.
    Amount of award: $2,000

Bioproducts, Inc.

Bioproducts Scholarship Program for Perdue Farms

Type of award: Scholarship.
Intended use: For freshman study.
Eligibility: Applicant or parent must be employed by Bioproducts, Inc. Applicant must be high school senior.
Additional information: For further information or an application contact Bioproducts Incorporated directly.
    Amount of award: $1,000

Blue Bell Foundation

Red Kap Scholarship

Type of award: Scholarship, renewable.
Intended use: For undergraduate study at accredited vocational, 2-year or 4-year institution.
Eligibility: Applicant or parent must be employed by Red Kap.
Basis for selection: Applicant must demonstrate financial need.
Additional information: For further information or an application contact Red Kap directly.
    Amount of award: $1,000-$2,000

Wrangler Scholarship

Type of award: Scholarship, renewable.
Intended use: For undergraduate study at accredited vocational, 2-year or 4-year institution.
Eligibility: Applicant or parent must be employed by Wrangler.
Basis for selection: Applicant must demonstrate financial need.
Additional information: For further information or an application contact Wrangler directly.
    Amount of award: $1,000-$2,000

Blue Circle America Inc.

Blue Circle America Scholarship Program

Type of award: Scholarship, renewable.
Intended use: For undergraduate study at vocational, 2-year or 4-year institution.
Eligibility: Applicant or parent must be employed by Blue Circle America Inc. Applicant must be high school senior.
Additional information: For further information or an application contact Blue Circle America Incorporated directly.
    Amount of award: $1,000-$2,000

Blue Shield of California Education and Research Foundation

Blue Shield of California Scholarship

Type of award: Scholarship.
Intended use: For freshman, sophomore, junior or senior study at accredited 4-year institution.
Eligibility: Applicant or parent must be employed by Blue Shield of California.
Additional information: For further information or an application contact Blue Shield of California directly.
    Amount of award: $1,500

BNI Coal, Ltd.

BNI Coal Scholarship Program

Type of award: Scholarship.
Intended use: For undergraduate study at accredited vocational, 2-year or 4-year institution.
Eligibility: Applicant or parent must be employed by BNI Coal, Ltd.
Additional information: For further information or an application contact BNI Coal, Ltd. directly.
    Amount of award: $500

Boart Longyear Inc. - Canada

Boart Longyear Scholarship Program

Type of award: Scholarship.
Intended use: For undergraduate study at vocational, 2-year or 4-year institution.
Eligibility: Applicant or parent must be employed by Boart Longyear Inc.- Canada. Applicant must be high school senior.
Additional information: For further information or an application contact Boart Longyear Incorporated - Canada directly.
    Amount of award: $2,500

Bobst Group, Inc.

Jacques Bobst Scholarship

Type of award: Scholarship, renewable.
Intended use: For freshman study at accredited 4-year institution.
Eligibility: Applicant or parent must be employed by Bobst Group Inc.
Additional information: For further information or an application contact Bobst Group Inc. directly.
    Amount of award: $500-$1,000

Boddie-Noell Enterprises, Inc.

James H. Waters Scholarship

Type of award: Scholarship.
Intended use: For undergraduate study at accredited vocational, 2-year or 4-year institution.
Eligibility: Applicant or parent must be employed by Boddie-Noell Enterprises, Inc.
Basis for selection: Applicant must demonstrate financial need.
Additional information: Scholarship open to employees, as

well as children of employees, of Boddie-Noell Enterprises. For more information or an application contact Boddie-Noell Enterprises directly.

Amount of award: $500-$1,000

Boehringer Ingelheim Corporation

Boehringer Ingelheim Corporation Scholarship

Type of award: Scholarship, renewable.
Intended use: For freshman study at accredited vocational, 2-year or 4-year institution.
Eligibility: Applicant or parent must be employed by Boehringer Ingelheim Corporation.
Basis for selection: Applicant must demonstrate financial need.
Additional information: For further information or an application contact Boehringer Ingelheim Corporation directly.

Amount of award: $1,500

Boy Scouts of America

Boy Scouts of America Law Enforcement Assistance Award

Type of award: Scholarship.
Intended use: For undergraduate study at accredited 2-year or 4-year institution.
Eligibility: Applicant or parent must be member of Boy Scouts of America, Explorers. Applicant must be U.S. citizen or permanent resident.
Basis for selection: Applicant must demonstrate depth of character and service orientation.
Additional information: Candidates must have performed "an act which assisted in the prevention or solution of a serious crime or an act which assisted in leading to the apprehension of a felony suspect wanted by a law enforcement agency."

Amount of award: $1,000
Number of awards: 1
Application deadline: March 31
Total amount awarded: $1,000

Contact:
Boy Scouts of America Learning for Life Division S210
1325 West Walnut Hill Lane
P.O. Box 152079
Irving, TX 75015-2079

Boy Scouts of America/Eastern Orthodox Committee on Scouting Scholarship

Type of award: Scholarship.
Intended use: For full-time freshman study at accredited 4-year institution in United States.
Eligibility: Applicant or parent must be member of Boy Scouts of America. Applicant must be male, high school senior, Eastern Orthodox. Applicant must be U.S. citizen or permanent resident.
Basis for selection: Applicant must demonstrate depth of character and service orientation.
Additional information: Offers one $1,000 scholarship and one $500 scholarship upon acceptance to a four0year accredited college or university. The eligible applicant must be a registered member of a Boy Scouts unit; be an Eagle Scout; be an active member of an Eastern Orthodox Church; have received the Alpha Omega Religious Award; have demonstrated practical citizenship in his church, school, Scouting unit, and community.

Amount of award: $500-$1,000
Number of awards: 2
Total amount awarded: $1,500

Contact:
Scholarship Chairman
Eastern Orthodox Committee on Scouting
862 Guy Lombardo Ave.
Freeport, NY 11520
Website: www.ithaca.ny.us/Orgs/Scouts

Boy Scouts of America/Eisenhower Memorial Scholarship

Type of award: Scholarship.
Intended use: For full-time freshman study at accredited 4-year institution in United States.
Eligibility: Applicant or parent must be member of Boy Scouts of America. Applicant must be male, high school senior. Applicant must be U.S. citizen or permanent resident.
Basis for selection: Applicant must demonstrate depth of character and service orientation.
Additional information: Limited to certain Indiana colleges. Applicants are judged on scholastic performance, leadership potential, and promise of becoming opinion leaders. They must have open and inquiring minds, faith in a Divine Being, and a firm belief in the free-enterprise system and the American way of life. Selection is by a rigorous process of competition and screening. Award amount varies, call sponsor for further information.

Amount of award: $1,000

Contact:
Scholarship Chairman
Eisenhower Memorial Scholarship
223 S. Pete Ellis Dr., Suite 27
Bloomington, IN 47408
Website: www.ithaca.ny.us/Orgs/Scouts

Captain James J. Regan Memorial Scholarship

Type of award: Scholarship.
Intended use: For full-time undergraduate study.
Eligibility: Applicant or parent must be member of Boy Scouts of America. Applicant must be male, high school senior. Applicant must be U.S. citizen or permanent resident.
Basis for selection: Major/career interest in criminal justice/law enforcement. Applicant must demonstrate leadership and high academic achievement.
Application requirements: Essay.
Additional information: Program open to law enforcement Explorers.

663

Boy Scouts of America: Captain James J. Regan Memorial Scholarship

Amount of award:	$1,000
Number of awards:	2
Application deadline:	March 31
Total amount awarded:	$2,000

Contact:
Boy Scouts of America Learning for Life - S210
1325 West Walnut Hill Lane
P.O. Box 152079
Irving, TX 75015-2079

Carter Scholarship Grants for New England Scouts

Type of award: Scholarship.
Intended use: For full-time freshman, sophomore study at accredited 4-year institution.
Eligibility: Applicant or parent must be member of Boy Scouts of America. Applicant must be male, high school senior. Applicant must be U.S. citizen or permanent resident residing in Connecticut or Massachusetts or Maine or New Hampshire or Rhode Island or Vermont.
Basis for selection: Applicant must demonstrate leadership, financial need and high academic achievement.
Application requirements: Transcript.
Additional information: Scholarship is for two years at $1,500 per year.

Amount of award:	$3,000
Application deadline:	April 15

Contact:
Mrs. B.J. Shaffer, Adm. Secretary
P.O. Box 527
West Chatham, MA 02669

E. Urner Goodman Scholarship

Type of award: Scholarship.
Intended use: For full-time undergraduate or graduate study.
Eligibility: Applicant or parent must be member of Boy Scouts of America. Applicant must be male. Applicant must be U.S. citizen or permanent resident.
Additional information: Open to Arrowmen planning a career in professional service of the Boy Scouts. Amounts of individual scholarships vary each year. Send SASE with notation on lower left corner, "Order of the Arrow Scholarship Application".

Application deadline:	December 15
Notification begins:	March 1
Total amount awarded:	$20,000

Contact:
Boy Scouts of America National Order of the Arrow S214
1325 West Walnut Hill Lane
P.O. Box 152079
Irving, TX 75015-2079

Frank L. Weil Memorial Scholarship

Type of award: Scholarship.
Intended use: For full-time undergraduate study.
Eligibility: Applicant or parent must be member of Boy Scouts of America. Applicant must be male, Jewish. Applicant must be U.S. citizen or permanent resident.
Additional information: Open to Eagle Scouts who have earned their Ner Tamid emblem.

Amount of award:	$500-$1,000
Number of awards:	3
Application deadline:	January 1

Contact:
Boy Scouts of America National Jewish Committee on Scouting
1325 West Walnut Hill Lane
P.O. Box 152079
Irving, TX 75015-2079

Law Enforcement Explorer Scholarship

Type of award: Scholarship.
Intended use: For full-time undergraduate study.
Eligibility: Applicant or parent must be member of Boy Scouts of America, Explorers. Applicant must be high school senior. Applicant must be U.S. citizen or permanent resident.
Additional information: Must be a registered Explorer active in a law enforcement post.

Amount of award:	$1,000
Number of awards:	1
Application deadline:	March 31

Contact:
Boy Scouts of America
1301 Constitution Avenue
Room 3422
Washington, DC 20299

National Eagle Scout Scholarship

Type of award: Scholarship.
Intended use: For undergraduate study at accredited 2-year or 4-year institution.
Eligibility: Applicant or parent must be member of Boy Scouts of America, Eagle Scouts. Applicant must be single, male, high school senior. Applicant must be U.S. citizen or permanent resident.
Basis for selection: Applicant must demonstrate leadership, financial need and high academic achievement.
Application requirements: Recommendations and transcript.
Additional information: First contact should be at local council office for form 58-702. Must be endorsed by professional or volunteer scout leader. Applicants considered for four kinds of awards: one non-renewable $3,000 award, four awards of $1,000 per year for four years, four awards of $2,000 per year for four years, and one Mabel and Lawrence S. Cooke scholarship of up to $12,000 per year for four years. Award may not be used at military institution. Must have SAT score of at least 1090 or ACT score of 26.

Amount of award:	$3,000-$48,000
Number of applicants:	2,500
Application deadline:	February 28
Notification begins:	June 1
Total amount awarded:	$132,000

Contact:
Boy Scouts of America
1325 West Walnut Hill Lane
Irving, TX 75015-2079

Sheryl A. Horak Law Enforcement Explorer Scholarship

Type of award: Scholarship.
Intended use: For full-time undergraduate study at accredited 2-year or 4-year institution.
Eligibility: Applicant or parent must be member of Boy Scouts of America, Explorers. Applicant must be high school senior. Applicant must be U.S. citizen or permanent resident.
Basis for selection: Major/career interest in criminal justice/law enforcement. Applicant must demonstrate leadership, service orientation and high academic achievement.
Application requirements: Essay.
    Amount of award: $1,000
    Number of awards: 1
    Application deadline: March 31
Contact:
Boy Scouts of America Learning for Life Division S210
1325 West Walnut Hill Lane
P.O. Box 152079
Irving, TX 75015-2079

BP America

BP America Internship

Type of award: Internship.
Intended use: For sophomore, junior study.
Eligibility: Applicant or parent must be employed by BP America, Inc.
Basis for selection: Major/career interest in engineering, chemical.
Application requirements: Interview, recommendations and transcript.
Additional information: Application deadlines and internship compensation varies. Contact sponsor for information.
Contact:
BP America
200 Public Sq., Room 6-3104N
Cleveland, OH 44114

Brake Parts Inc.

Brake Parts Scholarship

Type of award: Scholarship, renewable.
Intended use: For undergraduate study at accredited postsecondary institution.
Eligibility: Applicant or parent must be employed by Brake Parts Inc. Applicant must be high school senior.
Basis for selection: Applicant must demonstrate financial need.
Additional information: For further information or an application contact Brake Parts Inc. directly.
    Amount of award: $1,000
Contact:
Brake Parts, Inc.

Bremer Financial Corporation

Bremer Employee Dependents Scholarship Program

Type of award: Scholarship, renewable.
Intended use: For undergraduate or graduate study at accredited vocational, 2-year or 4-year institution.
Eligibility: Applicant or parent must be employed by Bremer Financial Corporation.
Basis for selection: Applicant must demonstrate financial need.
Additional information: For further information or an application contact Bremer Financial Corporation directly.
    Amount of award: $700-$2,100

Bristol-Myers Squibb Company Foundation, Inc.

Bristol-Myers Squibb Career Education Awards

Type of award: Scholarship, renewable.
Intended use: For freshman study at accredited vocational or 2-year institution.
Eligibility: Applicant or parent must be employed by Bristol-Myers Squibb Company.
Basis for selection: Applicant must demonstrate financial need.
Additional information: For further information or an application contact Bristol-Myers Squibb Company Foundation, Inc. directly.
    Amount of award: $500-$2,000

Brooklyn Hospital Center Employees' Activities Committee

Brooklyn Hospital Center Employees' Activities Committee Award

Type of award: Scholarship.
Intended use: For undergraduate study at accredited postsecondary institution.
Eligibility: Applicant or parent must be employed by Brooklyn Hospital Center.
Additional information: For further information or an application contact The Brooklyn Hospital Center Employees' Activities Committee directly.
    Amount of award: $1,000
Contact:
Brooklyn Hospital Center Employees' Activities Committee

BT Office Products International, Inc.

BT Office Products Scholarship

Type of award: Scholarship.
Intended use: For freshman, sophomore, junior or senior study at accredited vocational, 2-year or 4-year institution.
Eligibility: Applicant or parent must be employed by BT Office Products International, Inc.
Additional information: Must be child of employee of BT Office Products International, Inc. For further information or an application contact BT Office Products directly.
    Amount of award: $2,500

Bureau of Alcohol, Tobacco, and Firearms

Bureau of Alcohol, Tobacco, and Firearms Scholarship

Type of award: Scholarship.
Intended use: For freshman study at accredited 4-year institution.
Eligibility: Applicant or parent must be member of Boy Scouts of America, Explorers. Applicant must be U.S. citizen or permanent resident.
Additional information: Between 1 and 4 scholarships given biannually, on every even year. Open to children of law enforcement officers as well.
    Amount of award: $1,000
    Application deadline: April 1
Contact:
Bureau of Alcohol, Tobacco, and Firearms
Office of Liason and Public Information
650 Massachusetts Avenue, Room 8290
Washington, DC 20226

Business Men's Assurance Company of America

BMA Scholarship for Children of Employees

Type of award: Scholarship, renewable.
Intended use: For undergraduate study at vocational, 2-year or 4-year institution.
Eligibility: Applicant or parent must be employed by Business Men's Assurance Company Of America. Applicant must be high school senior.
Additional information: For further information or an application contact Business Men's Assurance Company of America directly.
    Amount of award: $2,000

Butler Manufacturing Company Foundation

Butler Manufacturing Company Foundation Scholarship

Type of award: Scholarship, renewable.
Intended use: For full-time freshman, sophomore, junior or senior study at accredited 4-year institution.
Eligibility: Applicant or parent must be employed by Butler Manufacturing Co. & subsidiaries. Applicant must be high school senior.
Basis for selection: Applicant must demonstrate depth of character, leadership, service orientation, financial need and high academic achievement.
Application requirements: Recommendations, essay and transcript.
Additional information: SAT I or ACT required. Contact human resources office at parent's work place for information and application. Subsidiaries are: Bucon, Lester Building Systems, Vistawall, Innovative Building Technology, and Butler International.
    Amount of award: $2,500
    Number of awards: 66,000
    Number of applicants: 48
    Application deadline: February 28
    Notification begins: April 15
    Total amount awarded: $64,000
Contact:
Butler Manufacturing Company Foundation
Foundation Administrator
P.O. Box 419917
Kansas City, MO 64141-0917

California Grange Foundation

Deaf Activities Committee Scholarship

Type of award: Scholarship.
Intended use: For undergraduate study at accredited vocational, 2-year or 4-year institution in United States.
Eligibility: Applicant or parent must be member of Fraternal Grange.
Basis for selection: Applicant must demonstrate depth of character, seriousness of purpose and service orientation.
Additional information: This scholarship is for students who are entering, continuing or returning to college to pursue studies that will be of benefit to deaf communities. Award amounts vary. Applications and additional information available after February 1.
    Application deadline: April 1

Doris Deaver Memorial Scholarship

Type of award: Scholarship.
Intended use: For freshman study at accredited vocational, 2-year or 4-year institution in United States.

Eligibility: Applicant or parent must be member of Fraternal Grange. Applicant must be high school senior.
Basis for selection: Applicant must demonstrate service orientation.
Additional information: Award amounts vary. Applications and additional information available after February 1.
   Application deadline: April 1

Peter Marinoff Memorial Scholarship

Type of award: Scholarship.
Intended use: For undergraduate study at accredited vocational, 2-year or 4-year institution in United States.
Eligibility: Applicant or parent must be member of Fraternal Grange.
Basis for selection: Applicant must demonstrate service orientation.
Additional information: Award amounts vary. Available to graduating high school seniors and enrolled undergraduate students. Applications and additional information available after February 1.
   Application deadline: April 1

Sehlmeyer Scholarship

Type of award: Scholarship.
Intended use: For full-time sophomore, junior or senior study at accredited vocational, 2-year or 4-year institution in United States.
Eligibility: Applicant or parent must be member of Fraternal Grange.
Basis for selection: Applicant must demonstrate service orientation.
Additional information: Award amounts vary. Applications and additional information available after February 1.
   Application deadline: April 1
Contact:
Scholarship Committee
2101 Stockton Blvd.
Sacramento, CA 95817

California Teachers Association

California Teachers Association Martin Luther King, Jr., Memorial Scholarship

Type of award: Scholarship.
Intended use: For undergraduate, master's or doctoral study at accredited postsecondary institution.
Eligibility: Applicant or parent must be member of California Teachers Association. Applicant must be of minority background. Applicant must be U.S. citizen.
Basis for selection: Major/career interest in education. Applicant must demonstrate financial need.
Application requirements: Proof of eligibility.
Additional information: Must be active CTA or Student CTA ethnic minority member, or dependent child of active, deceased, or retired-life ethnic minority member. Information may also be obtained from chapter presidents or any Regional Resource Center Office.
   Amount of award: $250-$2,000
   Number of awards: 30
   Number of applicants: 100
   Application deadline: March 15
   Notification begins: May 1

CTA Scholarship for Dependent Children

Type of award: Scholarship, renewable.
Intended use: For full-time undergraduate, master's or doctoral study at accredited postsecondary institution.
Eligibility: Applicant or parent must be member of California Teachers Association. Applicant must be U.S. citizen.
Basis for selection: Applicant must demonstrate high academic achievement.
Application requirements: Proof of eligibility.
Additional information: Must be a dependent child of active, deceased, or retired-life member. Minimum GPA of 3.0. Information may also be obtained from chapter presidents or any Regional Resource Center Office.
   Amount of award: $2,000
   Number of awards: 25
   Number of applicants: 917
   Application deadline: February 15
   Notification begins: May

CTA Scholarship for Members

Type of award: Scholarship, renewable.
Intended use: For full-time master's, doctoral or postgraduate study at accredited postsecondary institution.
Eligibility: Applicant or parent must be member of California Teachers Association. Applicant must be U.S. citizen.
Basis for selection: Major/career interest in education, teacher; education. Applicant must demonstrate high academic achievement.
Application requirements: Proof of eligibility.
Additional information: Must be an active CTA member. Minimum GPA of 3.0 is required. Information may also be obtained from chapter presidents or any Regional Resource Center Office.
   Amount of award: $2,000
   Number of awards: 5
   Number of applicants: 115
   Application deadline: February 15
   Notification begins: March 1
Contact:
California Teachers Association
PO Box 921
Burlingame, CA 94011-0921
Website: www.cta.org/resources98/

Callaway Golf Company Foundation

Callaway Golf Scholarship Program

Type of award: Scholarship, renewable.
Intended use: For undergraduate study at vocational, 2-year or 4-year institution.
Eligibility: Applicant or parent must be employed by Callaway Golf Company Foundation. Applicant must be high school senior.
Additional information: For further information or an application contact Callaway Golf Company Foundation directly.
   Amount of award: $500-$2,000

Cambrex Corporation

Arthur I. Mendolia Scholarship Program

Type of award: Scholarship, renewable.
Intended use: For undergraduate study at accredited vocational, 2-year or 4-year institution.
Eligibility: Applicant or parent must be employed by Cambrex Corporation.
Additional information: For additional information or an application contact Cambrex Corporation directly.
   Amount of award: $1,500

Canned Foods, Inc.

Canned Foods Employees' Children Scholarship

Type of award: Scholarship.
Intended use: For undergraduate study at accredited vocational, 2-year or 4-year institution.
Eligibility: Applicant or parent must be employed by Canned Foods, Inc.
Basis for selection: Applicant must demonstrate financial need.
Additional information: For further information or an application contact Canned Foods, Inc. directly.
   Amount of award: $500-$5,000

Capital Group Companies, Inc.

Capital Group Companies Scholarship Program

Type of award: Scholarship, renewable.
Intended use: For undergraduate study at accredited vocational, 2-year or 4-year institution.
Eligibility: Applicant or parent must be employed by Capital Group, Inc.
Basis for selection: Applicant must demonstrate financial need.
Additional information: For additional information or an application contact Capital Group Companies, Inc. directly.
   Amount of award: $1,000-$3,500

Carolina Power & Light Company

Carolina Power & Light Merit Awards Program

Type of award: Scholarship, renewable.
Intended use: For freshman study.
Eligibility: Applicant or parent must be employed by Carolina Power & Light Company. Applicant must be high school senior.
Additional information: For further information or an application contact Carolina Power & Light Company directly.
   Amount of award: $1,500

Cashiers' Association of Wall Street

Cashiers' Association of Wall Street Scholarship

Type of award: Scholarship.
Intended use: For undergraduate study at accredited vocational, 2-year or 4-year institution.
Eligibility: Applicant or parent must be member of Cashiers' Association of Wall Street.
Additional information: For further information or an application contact Cashiers' Association of Wall Street directly.
   Amount of award: $1,000

Castrol North America

Castrol North America Scholarship

Type of award: Scholarship, renewable.
Intended use: For undergraduate study at accredited 2-year or 4-year institution.
Eligibility: Applicant or parent must be employed by Castrol North America.
Additional information: For further information or an application contact Castrol North America directly.
    Amount of award: $2,000

Catholic Aid Association

Catholic Aid Association Scholarship

Type of award: Scholarship.
Intended use: For full-time freshman, sophomore study at vocational, 2-year or 4-year institution outside United States.
Eligibility: Applicant or parent must be member of Catholic Aid Association. Applicant must be high school senior.
Basis for selection: Applicant must demonstrate depth of character, leadership, seriousness of purpose, service orientation and financial need.
Application requirements: Portfolio, recommendations, transcript and proof of eligibility. Application form and photo of applicant.
Additional information: Open to college freshmen as well as high school seniors. Must have been a member of Catholic Aid Association for two years. Request application between 1/1 and 3/1 of any given year. Application forms change every year.

Amount of award:	$300-$500
Number of awards:	158
Number of applicants:	208
Application deadline:	March 15
Notification begins:	May 15
Total amount awarded:	$55,200

Contact:
Catholic Aid Association
3499 North Lexington Avenue
St. Paul, MN 55126
Phone: 612-490-0170

Catholic Workman Fraternal Life Association

Catholic Workman Fraternal Life Scholarship

Type of award: Scholarship, renewable.
Intended use: For full-time freshman, sophomore, junior, senior or non-degree study at accredited 2-year or 4-year institution in United States.
Eligibility: Applicant or parent must be member of Catholic Workman Fraternal Life Association.
Basis for selection: Applicant must demonstrate leadership, service orientation and high academic achievement.
Application requirements: Recommendations, transcript and proof of eligibility.

Amount of award:	$500-$1,000
Number of awards:	22
Number of applicants:	62
Application deadline:	July 1
Notification begins:	August 25
Total amount awarded:	$15,000

Contact:
Catholic Workman Fraternal Life Association
Scholarship Program
111 West Main
New Pragee, MN 56071
Phone: 800-346-6231

CBS, Inc.

CBS Scholarship

Type of award: Scholarship, renewable.
Intended use: For undergraduate study at accredited vocational, 2-year or 4-year institution.
Eligibility: Applicant or parent must be employed by CBS Inc.
Basis for selection: Applicant must demonstrate financial need.
Additional information: For further information or an application contact CBS Inc. directly.
    Amount of award: $1,000-$5,000

Ceridian Corporation

Ceridian Scholarship Program

Type of award: Scholarship, renewable.
Intended use: For freshman, sophomore, junior or senior study at accredited vocational, 2-year or 4-year institution.
Eligibility: Applicant or parent must be employed by Ceridian Corporation.
Basis for selection: Applicant must demonstrate financial need.
Additional information: For further information or an application contact Ceridian Corporation directly.
    Amount of award: $500-$2,500

Champion International Corporation

Champion International Corporation Scholarship

Type of award: Scholarship, renewable.
Intended use: For freshman study at accredited 2-year or 4-year institution.
Eligibility: Applicant or parent must be employed by Champion International Corporation. Applicant must be high school senior.
Basis for selection: Applicant must demonstrate financial need.
Additional information: Must be child of employee of CIC. For further information or an application contact Champion International Corporation directly.
    Amount of award: $250-$1,000

Chas. Levy Company

Chas. Levy Company Harry Harrington Scholarship

Type of award: Scholarship.
Intended use: For undergraduate study at accredited 2-year or 4-year institution.
Eligibility: Applicant or parent must be employed by Chas. Levy Company.
Basis for selection: Applicant must demonstrate financial need.
Additional information: For further information or an application contact Chas. Levy Company directly.
    Amount of award: $1,000

Chesapeake Corporation Foundation

Chesapeake Corporation Scholarship

Type of award: Scholarship, renewable.
Intended use: For full-time freshman, sophomore, junior or senior study.
Eligibility: Applicant or parent must be employed by Chesapeake Corporation. Applicant must be high school senior.
Basis for selection: Applicant must demonstrate high academic achievement.
Additional information: SAT I or ACT scores required.
    Amount of award: $3,500
    Number of applicants: 50
    Application deadline: November 15
    Total amount awarded: $17,500
Contact:
Chesapeake Corporation Foundation
James Center II, 1021 East Cary Street
Box 2350
Richmond, VA 23218-2350

Chicago Association of Spring Manufacturers

Chicago Association of Spring Manufacturers Scholarship

Type of award: Scholarship.
Intended use: For undergraduate study at accredited vocational, 2-year or 4-year institution.
Eligibility: Applicant or parent must be member of Chicago Association of Spring Manufacturing.
Additional information: Must be child of member of CASMI. For further information or an application contact Chicago Association of Spring Manufacturers directly.
    Amount of award: $1,000

Children's Literature Association

Children's Literature Research Fellowship

Type of award: Research grant.
Intended use: For postgraduate, non-degree study.
Eligibility: Applicant or parent must be member of Children's Literature Association.
Application requirements: Recommendations and research proposal. Projected budget for transportation, mailings, living expenses, and supplies.
    Amount of award: $250-$1,000
    Application deadline: February 1
Contact:
Children's Literature Association
Research Fellowships
PO Box 138
Battle Creek, MI 49016
Phone: 616-965-8180

Margaret P. Esmonde Memorial Scholarship

Type of award: Scholarship.
Intended use: For master's, doctoral, postgraduate or non-degree study.
Eligibility: Applicant or parent must be member of Children's Literature Association.
Basis for selection: Major/career interest in literature.
Application requirements: Recommendations and research

proposal. Projected budget for transportation, mailings, living expenses, and supplies.
Additional information: For proposals that deal with critical or original work in the area of fantasy or science fiction for children.

Amount of award:	$500
Application deadline:	February 1

Contact:
Children's Literature Association
Margaret Esmonde Scholarship Program
PO Box 138
Battle Creek, MI 49016
Phone: 616-965-8180

Chrysler Corporation

Chrysler Corporation Fund Scholarship

Type of award: Scholarship, renewable.
Intended use: For undergraduate study at accredited vocational, 2-year or 4-year institution.
Eligibility: Applicant or parent must be employed by Chrysler Corporation.
Basis for selection: Applicant must demonstrate financial need.
Additional information: May also be used for nursing or secretarial/business schools. Must be child of employee of Chrysler Corporation or its U.S.-based subsidiaries. For further information or an application contact Citizens' Scholarship Foundation of America, administrator of the fund.

Amount of award:	$500-$4,000
Application deadline:	March 15
Notification begins:	May 31

Contact:
Citizens' Scholarship Foundation of America, Inc.
The Chrysler Corporation Fund
P.O. Box 297
St. Peter, MN 56082

Citizens State Bank of Roseau

Citizens State Bank of Roseau Scholarship Fund

Type of award: Scholarship.
Intended use: For freshman study at accredited 2-year or 4-year institution.
Eligibility: Applicant or parent must be employed by Citizen's State Bank of Roseau. Applicant must be high school senior.
Additional information: Must be child of employee of Citizens State Bank of Roseau. For further information and an application contact Citizens State Bank directly.

Amount of award:	$2,000

Citizens Utilities Company

Citizens Utilities Scholarship Fund

Type of award: Scholarship.
Intended use: For freshman study at vocational, 2-year or 4-year institution.
Eligibility: Applicant or parent must be employed by Citizens Utilities Company. Applicant must be high school senior.
Additional information: For further information or an application contact Citizens Utilities Company directly.

Amount of award:	$500-$4,000

Clara Abbott Foundation

Clara Abbott Foundation Educational Grant

Type of award: Scholarship, renewable.
Intended use: For full-time undergraduate study at accredited vocational, 2-year or 4-year institution in or outside United States.
Eligibility: Applicant or parent must be employed by Abbott Laboratories. Applicant must be high school senior.
Basis for selection: Applicant must demonstrate financial need.
Application requirements: Transcript and proof of eligibility. Applicant must provide tax forms (W-2 wage form).
Additional information: Applicant must be a child or dependent of an Abbott Laboratories employee or retiree. Applicant may reapply each year, for a maximum of five years. Deadline for U.S. applicants is March 15, notification by June 1. Deadline for international applicants is August 1, notification by November 1. For Puerto Rican applicants, deadline is February 15, notification June 1. Must have passing grades (usually a "C" average).

Amount of award:	$500-$13,000
Number of awards:	3,250
Number of applicants:	3,800
Application deadline:	March 16
Notification begins:	June 1
Total amount awarded:	$8,282,000

Contact:
Clara Abbott Foundation
200 Abbott Park Road
D-579 J37
Abbott Park, IL 60064-3537

Clark Refining and Marketing, Inc.

Educate Our Children Scholarship

Type of award: Scholarship.
Intended use: For undergraduate study at accredited postsecondary institution.
Eligibility: Applicant or parent must be employed by Clark

671

Refining & Marketing, Inc. Applicant must be high school senior.
Additional information: For further information or an application contact Clark Refining and Marketing, Inc. directly.
Amount of award: $1,000
Contact:
Clark Refining and Marketing, Inc.

Clorox Company Foundation

Clorox Scholarship

Type of award: Scholarship, renewable.
Intended use: For freshman study at 2-year or 4-year institution.
Eligibility: Applicant or parent must be employed by The Clorox Company Foundation. Applicant must be high school senior.
Additional information: For further information or an application contact Clorox Company Foundation directly.
Amount of award: $2,500

CNF Transportation Inc.

CNF Transportation Companies Scholarship

Type of award: Scholarship, renewable.
Intended use: For undergraduate study at accredited vocational, 2-year or 4-year institution.
Eligibility: Applicant or parent must be employed by Consolidated Freightways, Inc.
Basis for selection: Applicant must demonstrate financial need.
Additional information: For further information or an application contact CNF Transportation Inc. directly.
Amount of award: $500-$2,500

Comer Foundation

Comer Foundation Scholarship Fund

Type of award: Scholarship, renewable.
Intended use: For undergraduate study at accredited postsecondary institution.
Eligibility: Applicant or parent must be employed by Lands' End. Applicant must be high school senior.
Basis for selection: Applicant must demonstrate financial need.
Additional information: For further information or an application contact The Comer Foundation directly.
Amount of award: $500-$2,500
Contact:
The Comer Foundation

Communications Workers of America

Foreign Postal Telegraph and Telephone International Affiliates Scholarship

Type of award: Scholarship, renewable.
Intended use: For undergraduate or graduate study.
Eligibility: Applicant or parent must be member of Communications Workers of America. Applicant must be Mexican, Central or South American, and Caribbean citizens.
Additional information: Applicants must be at least either high school graduates or high school students who will graduate during the year in which they apply. Selection is by random drawing. Alternates chosen at time of drawing. Award is $500 per year for four years. Contact CWA Local for applications.
Amount of award: $500
Number of awards: 8
Number of applicants: 125
Application deadline: February 28
Notification begins: June 1
Total amount awarded: $16,000

Joseph Anthony Beirne Scholarship

Type of award: Scholarship, renewable.
Intended use: For full-time undergraduate or graduate study at 2-year, 4-year or graduate institution.
Eligibility: Applicant or parent must be member of Communications Workers of America. Applicant must be U.S. citizen or permanent resident.
Basis for selection: Applicant must demonstrate financial need and high academic achievement.
Additional information: Applicants must be at least either high school graduates or high school students who will graduate during the year in which they apply. Award is paid each year for two years. Second year award is contingent on academic accomplishment of the first year. Contact CWA Local for application.
Amount of award: $3,000
Number of awards: 30
Number of applicants: 1,270
Application deadline: March 31
Notification begins: June 15
Total amount awarded: $180,000

Ray Hackney Scholarship

Type of award: Scholarship, renewable.
Intended use: For full-time undergraduate or graduate study at 2-year, 4-year or graduate institution.
Eligibility: Applicant or parent must be member of Communications Workers of America. Applicant must be U.S. citizen or permanent resident.
Additional information: Applicants must be at least high

school graduates or high school students who will graduate during the year in which they apply. Selection is by random drawing. Alternates chosen at time of drawing. Award is $1000 per year for four years. Contact CWA Local for application.

Amount of award:	$1,000
Number of awards:	8
Number of applicants:	3,185
Application deadline:	February 28
Notification begins:	June 1
Total amount awarded:	$32,000

Compass Foundation

Compass Bancshares-DeWayne C. Cuthbertson Memorial Scholarship

Type of award: Scholarship.
Intended use: For undergraduate or graduate study at accredited vocational, 2-year or 4-year institution.
Eligibility: Applicant or parent must be employed by Compass Bancshares, Inc.
Additional information: For further information or an application contact Compass Bancshares, Inc. directly.
    Amount of award: $1,000

ConAgra Foundation, Inc.

Mike Harper Leadership Scholars Program

Type of award: Scholarship, renewable.
Intended use: For freshman study at accredited vocational, 2-year or 4-year institution.
Eligibility: Applicant or parent must be employed by ConAgra, Inc. Applicant must be high school senior.
Basis for selection: Applicant must demonstrate financial need.
Additional information: For additional information or an application contact ConAgra Foundation directly.
    Amount of award: $1,000-$2,500

Cone Mills Corporation

Cone Mills Scholarship Program

Type of award: Scholarship, renewable.
Intended use: For full-time freshman, sophomore, junior or senior study at accredited vocational, 2-year or 4-year institution in United States.
Eligibility: Applicant or parent must be employed by Cone Mills Corporation. Applicant must be high school senior. Applicant must be U.S. citizen.
Basis for selection: Applicant must demonstrate high academic achievement.
Application requirements: Essay, transcript and proof of eligibility. CSS PROFILE Application required.

Amount of award:	$500-$2,500
Number of awards:	60
Number of applicants:	75
Application deadline:	November 30
Notification begins:	April 30
Total amount awarded:	$30,000

Contact:
Cone Mills Corporation
Scholarship Program
3101 North Elm Street
Greensboro, NC 27415-6540
Phone: 910-379-6252
Fax: 910-379-6930

Consolidated Freightways Corporation

Consolidated Freightways Corporation Scholarship Program

Type of award: Scholarship, renewable.
Intended use: For undergraduate study at vocational, 2-year or 4-year institution.
Eligibility: Applicant or parent must be employed by Consolidated Freightways Corporation. Applicant must be high school senior.
Additional information: For further information or an application contact Consolidated Freightways Corporation directly.
    Amount of award: $500-$2,500

Cushion Cut, Inc.

Lester F. Kuzmick Memorial Scholarship

Type of award: Scholarship.
Intended use: For undergraduate study at accredited vocational, 2-year or 4-year institution.
Eligibility: Applicant or parent must be employed by Cushion Cut Inc.
Additional information: For further information or an application contact Cushion Cut Inc. directly.
    Amount of award: $2,000

CXY Energy, Inc.

CXY Energy Scholarship Program

Type of award: Scholarship, renewable.
Intended use: For freshman study at accredited 4-year institution.
Eligibility: Applicant or parent must be employed by CXY Energy Inc.

Additional information: For further information or an application contact CXY Energy Inc. directly.
    Amount of award: $1,500

Daniel E. O'Sullivan Memorial Scholarship Foundation

Daniel E. O'Sullivan Memorial Scholarship

Type of award: Scholarship.
Intended use: For undergraduate study at accredited vocational, 2-year or 4-year institution.
Eligibility: Applicant or parent must be employed by ULLICO, Inc.
Basis for selection: Applicant must demonstrate financial need.
Additional information: For further information or an application contact Daniel E. O'Sullivan Foundation/Union Labor Life Insurance Company directly.
    Amount of award: $3,300

Data Management Division of Wall Street

Data Management Division of Wall Street Scholarship Program

Type of award: Scholarship.
Intended use: For undergraduate study at accredited vocational, 2-year or 4-year institution.
Eligibility: Applicant or parent must be member of Data Management Division of Wall Street.
Additional information: For further information or an application contact Data Management Division of Wall Street directly.
    Amount of award: $500

Daughters of Penelope

Alexandra A. Sonenfeld Award

Type of award: Scholarship.
Intended use: For undergraduate study at accredited vocational, 2-year or 4-year institution in United States.
Eligibility: Applicant or parent must be member of Daughters of Penelope. Applicant must be high school senior. Applicant must be U.S. citizen.
Basis for selection: Applicant must demonstrate depth of character, financial need and high academic achievement.
Application requirements: Recommendations, essay, transcript and proof of eligibility. Parents IRS forms, Federal Aid Forms, SAT or ACT scores.
Additional information: Immediate family member must be member in good standing of Daughters of Penelope or Order of AHEPA for at least two years. Must be H.S. senior or recent H.S. graduate to be eligible.
    Amount of award: $1,500
    Number of awards: 1
    Application deadline: June 20
    Total amount awarded: $1,500
Contact:
Daughters of Penelope
1909 Q Street, NW
Suite 500
Washington, DC 20009

Daughters of Penelope Graduate Student Award

Type of award: Scholarship.
Intended use: For master's, doctoral or first professional study at accredited graduate institution.
Eligibility: Applicant or parent must be member of Daughters of Penelope. Applicant must be female. Applicant must be U.S. citizen, permanent resident or Canadian citizen.
Basis for selection: Applicant must demonstrate high academic achievement.
Application requirements: Recommendations, essay, transcript and proof of eligibility. GRE scores or other entrance exam scores.
Additional information: Applicant must have a member of immediate family (meaning Father, mother or grandparent) or legal guardian (court appointed) in the Daughters of Penelope, Order of AHEPA, or Maids of Athena in good standing for a minimum of two years. Must be enrolled minimum of nine units per academic year.
    Amount of award: $1,000
    Number of awards: 1
    Application deadline: June 20
    Total amount awarded: $1,000
Contact:
Daughters of Penelope
1909 Q Street, NW
Suite 500
Washington, DC 20009

Daughters of Penelope Past Grand Presidents Award

Type of award: Scholarship.
Intended use: For freshman study at vocational, 2-year or 4-year institution.
Eligibility: Applicant or parent must be member of Daughters of Penelope. Applicant must be female, high school senior. Applicant must be U.S. citizen, permanent resident or Canadian citizen.
Basis for selection: Applicant must demonstrate financial need and high academic achievement.
Application requirements: Recommendations, essay, transcript and proof of eligibility. SAT I or ACT scores, copy of parent's IRS form, federal aid forms.
Additional information: Applicant must be high school senior or recent graduate and have a member in the immediate family (meaning father, mother, or grandparent) or legal guardian (court appointed) in the Daughters of Penelope, Order of AHEPA, or Maids of Athena in good standing for a minimum of two years.

Amount of award:	$1,500
Number of awards:	1
Application deadline:	June 20
Total amount awarded:	$1,500

Contact:
Daughters of Penelope
1909 Q Street NW
Suite 500
Washington, DC 20009

Kottis Family Award

Type of award: Scholarship.
Intended use: For freshman study at vocational, 2-year or 4-year institution.
Eligibility: Applicant or parent must be member of Daughters of Penelope. Applicant must be female, high school senior. Applicant must be U.S. citizen, permanent resident or Canadian citizen.
Basis for selection: Applicant must demonstrate high academic achievement.
Application requirements: Recommendations, essay, transcript and proof of eligibility. SAT I or ACT scores.
Additional information: Applicant must be high school senior or recent graduate and have a member in the immediate family (meaning father, mother, or grandparent) or legal guardian (court appointed) in the Daughters of Penelope, Order of AHEPA or Maids of Athena in good standing for a minimum of two years.

Amount of award:	$1,000
Number of awards:	1
Application deadline:	June 20
Total amount awarded:	$1,000

Contact:
Daughters of Penelope
1909 Q Street, NW
Suite 500
Washington, DC 20009

Mary M. Verges Award

Type of award: Scholarship.
Intended use: For freshman study at vocational, 2-year or 4-year institution.
Eligibility: Applicant or parent must be member of Daughters of Penelope. Applicant must be female, high school senior. Applicant must be U.S. citizen, permanent resident or Canadian citizen.
Basis for selection: Applicant must demonstrate high academic achievement.
Application requirements: Interview, recommendations, essay and transcript. SAT or ACT scores.
Additional information: Applicant must be high school senior or recent graduate and have member in the immediate family (meaning father, mother, or grandparent) or legal guardian (court appointed) in the Daughters of Penelope, order of AHEPA, and Maids of Athena in good standing for a minimum of two years.

Amount of award:	$1,000
Number of awards:	1
Application deadline:	June 20
Total amount awarded:	$1,000

Contact:
Daughters of Penelope
1909 Q Street, NW
Suite 500
Washington, DC 20009

Past Grand Presidents' Award

Type of award: Scholarship, renewable.
Intended use: For freshman study at vocational, 2-year or 4-year institution.
Eligibility: Applicant or parent must be member of Daughters of Penelope. Applicant must be female, high school senior. Applicant must be U.S. citizen, permanent resident or Canadian citizen.
Basis for selection: Applicant must demonstrate high academic achievement.
Application requirements: Recommendations, essay, transcript and proof of eligibility. SAT I or ACT scores.
Additional information: Applicant must be high school senior or recent graduate and have a member of the immediate family (meaning father, mother, or grandparent) or legal guardian (court appointed) in the Daughters of Penelope, Order of AHEPA, or Maids of Athena and in good standing for a minimum of two years.

Amount of award:	$1,000
Number of awards:	1
Application deadline:	June 20
Total amount awarded:	$1,000

Contact:
Daughters of Penelope
1909 Q Street NW
Suite 500
Washington, DC 20009

Sonja Stefanadis Graduate Student Award

Type of award: Scholarship.
Intended use: For full-time master's, doctoral or first professional study.
Eligibility: Applicant or parent must be member of Daughters of Penelope. Applicant must be female. Applicant must be U.S. citizen, permanent resident or Canadian citizen.
Basis for selection: Applicant must demonstrate high academic achievement.
Application requirements: Recommendations, essay, transcript and proof of eligibility. GRE or other entrance exam scores.
Additional information: Applicant must have member of the immediate family (meaning father, mother, or grandparent) or legal guardian (court appointed) in the Daughters of Penelope, Order of AHEPA, or Maids of Athena, and in good standing for a minimum of two years. Must be enrolled minimum nine units per academic year.

Amount of award:	$1,000
Number of awards:	1
Application deadline:	June 20
Total amount awarded:	$1,000

Contact:
Daughters of Penelope
1909 Q Street, NW
Suite 500
Washington, DC 20009

Davis-Roberts Scholarship Fund

Davis-Roberts Scholarship

Type of award: Scholarship, renewable.
Intended use: For full-time undergraduate study at 2-year or 4-year institution.
Eligibility: Applicant or parent must be member of Wyoming Job's Daughters/DeMolay. Applicant must be U.S. citizen.
Basis for selection: Applicant must demonstrate financial need.
Application requirements: Recommendations, essay and transcript. Applicant's photograph.
Additional information: Must be a resident of Wyoming.

Amount of award:	$350-$500
Number of awards:	10
Number of applicants:	15
Application deadline:	June 15
Notification begins:	July 1
Total amount awarded:	$3,500

Contact:
Davis-Roberts Scholarship Fund
c/o Gary D. Skillern
P.O. Box 20645
Cheyenne, WY 82003

Dean Foods

Dean Foods Company Scholarship Program

Type of award: Scholarship, renewable.
Intended use: For undergraduate study at accredited vocational, 2-year or 4-year institution.
Eligibility: Applicant or parent must be employed by Deans Foods Company.
Basis for selection: Applicant must demonstrate financial need.
Additional information: For further information or an application contact Dean Foods directly.

Amount of award:	$1,000-$2,000

Delta Delta Delta Foundation

Delta Delta Delta Graduate Scholarship

Type of award: Scholarship.
Intended use: For graduate study.
Eligibility: Applicant or parent must be member of Delta Delta Delta Fraternity.
Basis for selection: Applicant must demonstrate service orientation, financial need and high academic achievement.
Additional information: Quality of program and goals, and campus, chapter, and community involvement is important. Applications may be obtained by calling Tri Delta's Executive office.

Amount of award:	$3,000
Number of awards:	6
Number of applicants:	35
Application deadline:	January 25
Total amount awarded:	$18,000

Delta Delta Delta Undergraduate Scholarship

Type of award: Scholarship.
Intended use: For junior, senior study.
Eligibility: Applicant or parent must be member of Delta Delta Delta Fraternity. Applicant must be high school junior, senior.
Basis for selection: Applicant must demonstrate service orientation, financial need and high academic achievement.
Additional information: Campus, chapter, and community involvement important.

Amount of award:	$1,000
Number of awards:	36
Number of applicants:	200
Application deadline:	March 1
Total amount awarded:	$36,000

Contact:
Delta Delta Delta Foundation
P.O. Box 5987
Arlington, TX 76005
Phone: 817-633-8001
Website: www.tridelta.org

Delta Gamma Foundation

Delta Gamma Fellowship

Type of award: Scholarship.
Intended use: For graduate study at accredited graduate institution in or outside United States.
Eligibility: Applicant or parent must be member of Delta Gamma. Applicant must be female.
Application requirements: Recommendations, essay, transcript and proof of eligibility.
Additional information: Student must be a member of Delta Gamma.

Amount of award:	$2,500
Number of awards:	22
Number of applicants:	149
Application deadline:	April 1
Notification begins:	June 1
Total amount awarded:	$55,000

Delta Gamma Scholarship

Type of award: Scholarship.
Intended use: For sophomore, junior or senior study at accredited 4-year institution in or outside United States.
Eligibility: Applicant or parent must be member of Delta Gamma. Applicant must be female.
Basis for selection: Applicant must demonstrate high academic achievement.
Application requirements: Recommendations, essay and transcript.
Additional information: Student must be a member of Delta Gamma.

Amount of award:	$1,000
Number of awards:	70
Number of applicants:	155
Application deadline:	February 1
Notification begins:	June 1
Total amount awarded:	$75,500

Delta Gamma Student Loan

Type of award: Loan.
Intended use: For undergraduate or graduate study in or outside United States.
Eligibility: Applicant or parent must be member of Delta Gamma.
Basis for selection: Applicant must demonstrate financial need.
Application requirements: Recommendations and transcript.
Additional information: Children and sisters of members sometimes eligible.

Amount of award:	$1,000-$2,000

Contact:
Delta Gamma Foundation
3250 Riverside Drive
Columbus, OH 43221-0397
Phone: 614-451-8550

Descendents of the Signers of the Declaration of Independence, Inc.

Descendents of the Signers of the Declaration of Independence Scholarship

Type of award: Scholarship, renewable.
Intended use: For full-time freshman, sophomore, junior, senior, master's or doctoral study at accredited 4-year or graduate institution in United States.
Eligibility: Applicant or parent must be member of Descendants of Signers Declaration of Independence.
Basis for selection: Applicant must demonstrate depth of character, leadership, patriotism, seriousness of purpose, service orientation and high academic achievement.
Application requirements: Recommendations, transcript and proof of eligibility.
Additional information: Must be direct lineal descendant of Signer of Declaration of Independence. Submit membership number and ancestor's name with request for application and information with SASE. Preference given to persons involved in community, school activities and volunteer work.

Amount of award:	$1,100-$1,500
Number of awards:	10
Number of applicants:	26
Application deadline:	March 15
Notification begins:	May 1
Total amount awarded:	$12,000

Contact:
Descendents of the Signers of the Declaration of Independence, Inc.
c/o Richard H. Stromberg
609 Irvin Avenue
Deale, MD 20751
Phone: 301-261-5238

DeZurik

AL Kremers Scholarship Program

Type of award: Scholarship.
Intended use: For freshman study at vocational, 2-year or 4-year institution.
Eligibility: Applicant or parent must be employed by DeZurik. Applicant must be high school senior.
Additional information: For further information or an application contact DeZurik directly.

Amount of award:	$1,000

Diemakers, Inc.

Diemakers Scholarship Program

Type of award: Scholarship, renewable.
Intended use: For undergraduate or graduate study at vocational, 2-year, 4-year or graduate institution.
Eligibility: Applicant or parent must be employed by Diemakers, Inc. Applicant must be high school senior.
Additional information: For further information or an application contact Diemakers directly.

Amount of award:	$1,000

Dolphin Scholarship Foundation

Dolphin U.S. Submarine Veterans of World War II Scholarship

Type of award: Scholarship, renewable.
Intended use: For full-time undergraduate study at accredited vocational, 2-year or 4-year institution outside United States.
Eligibility: Applicant or parent must be member of U.S. Submarine Veterans of World War II. Applicant must be single. Applicant must be U.S. citizen. Applicant must be descendant of veteran, child of veteran, disabled veteran or deceased veteran who served in the Navy during WW II.
Basis for selection: Applicant must demonstrate depth of character, leadership, seriousness of purpose, financial need and high academic achievement.
Application requirements: Essay, transcript and proof of eligibility.
Additional information: Address application requests to U.S. Submarine Veterans of World War II Scholarship Program.
    Amount of award: $2,500
    Number of awards: 23
    Number of applicants: 25
    Application deadline: April 15
    Notification begins: May 31
    Total amount awarded: $46,000
Contact:
Dolphin Scholarship Foundation
1683 Dillingham Boulevard
Norfolk, VA 23511
Phone: 757-451-3660
Fax: 757-489-8578

Don Cassidy, Sr., Scholarship Fund

Indiana Builders Association/Don Cassidy, Sr., Scholarship Fund

Type of award: Scholarship.
Intended use: For undergraduate study at accredited vocational, 2-year or 4-year institution.
Eligibility: Applicant or parent must be member of Indiana and Indianapolis Builders' Association.
Additional information: For further information or an application contact Don Cassidy, Sr., Scholarship Fund directly.
    Amount of award: $1,000

Donaldson Foundation

Donaldson Company Scholarship Program

Type of award: Scholarship, renewable.
Intended use: For undergraduate study at accredited vocational, 2-year or 4-year institution.
Eligibility: Applicant or parent must be employed by Donaldson Company, Inc.
Basis for selection: Applicant must demonstrate financial need.
Additional information: For further information or an application contact Donaldson Foundation directly.
    Amount of award: $600-$1,500

Dorr-Oliver Inc.

Dorr-Oliver Scholarship

Type of award: Scholarship, renewable.
Intended use: For undergraduate or graduate study at accredited 4-year institution.
Eligibility: Applicant or parent must be employed by Dorr-Oliver Incorporated.
Additional information: For further information or an application contact Dorr-Oliver Incorporated directly.
    Amount of award: $3,000-$5,000

Dunkin' Donuts Charitable Trust

Allied Domecq Retailing USA Scholarship Program

Type of award: Scholarship.
Intended use: For undergraduate study at vocational, 2-year or 4-year institution.
Eligibility: Applicant or parent must be employed by Dunkin' Donuts Charitable Trust. Applicant must be high school senior.
Additional information: For further information or an application contact Dunkin' Donuts Charitable Trust directly.
    Amount of award: $1,000

F. Ralph Gabellieri Memorial Scholarship Program

Type of award: Scholarship.
Intended use: For undergraduate study at vocational, 2-year or 4-year institution.
Eligibility: Applicant or parent must be employed by Dunkin' Donuts Charitable Trust. Applicant must be high school senior.
Additional information: For further information or an application contact Dunkin' Donuts Charitable Trust directly.
    Amount of award: $1,000

Dynatech Corporation

Dynatech Corporation Scholarship Program

Type of award: Scholarship, renewable.
Intended use: For undergraduate study at vocational, 2-year or 4-year institution.
Eligibility: Applicant or parent must be employed by Dynatech Corporation. Applicant must be high school senior.
Additional information: For futher information or an application contact Dynatech Corporation directly.
    Amount of award: $5,000

E. Stewart Mitchell, Inc.

E. Stewart Mitchell Scholarship Program

Type of award: Scholarship, renewable.
Intended use: For undergraduate study at vocational, 2-year or 4-year institution.
Eligibility: Applicant or parent must be employed by E. Stewart Mitchell, Inc. Applicant must be high school senior.
Additional information: For futher information or an application contact E.Stewart Mitchell Incorporated directly.
    Amount of award: $1,500

E.C. Styberg Engineering Company, Inc.

E.C. Styberg Engineering Company Scholarship

Type of award: Scholarship, renewable.
Intended use: For undergraduate study at accredited vocational, 2-year or 4-year institution.
Eligibility: Applicant or parent must be employed by E. C. Styberg Engineering Co. Inc.
Additional information: For further information or an application contact E.C. Styberg Engineering Company, Inc. directly.
    Amount of award: $1,000

ECM Publishers, Inc.

ECM Publishers Scholarship Program

Type of award: Scholarship.
Intended use: For undergraduate study at accredited postsecondary institution.
Eligibility: Applicant or parent must be employed by ECM Publishers, Inc. Applicant must be high school senior.
Additional information: For further information or an application contact ECM Publishers, Inc. directly.
    Amount of award: $1,000
Contact:
ECM Publisher's Inc.

Edison International

Edison International College Scholarship Program

Type of award: Scholarship, renewable.
Intended use: For freshman study at accredited 4-year institution.
Eligibility: Applicant or parent must be employed by Southern California Edison. Applicant must be high school senior.
Additional information: For further information or an application contact Edison International directly.
    Amount of award: $5,000

Elden and Helen Jones

Crysteel Scholarship Program

Type of award: Scholarship.
Intended use: For undergraduate study at accredited vocational, 2-year or 4-year institution.
Eligibility: Applicant or parent must be employed by Crysteel Manufacturing.
Additional information: For further information or an application contact Elden and Helen Jones directly.
    Amount of award: $500

Electrical Equipment Representatives Association

Sales Engineering Scholarship

Type of award: Scholarship.
Intended use: For undergraduate study at accredited 4-year institution.
Eligibility: Applicant or parent must be member of Electrical Equipment Representatives Association.
Additional information: Must be child of member of Electrical Equipment Representatives Association or of members' employees of Electrical Equipment Representatives Association. For further information or an application contact Electrical Equipment Representatives Association directly.
    Amount of award: $500-$1,000

EMI Music Foundation Inc.

EMI Scholars Program

Type of award: Scholarship.
Intended use: For undergraduate study at 2-year or 4-year institution.
Eligibility: Applicant or parent must be employed by EMI Music Foundation, Inc. Applicant must be high school senior.
Additional information: For further information or an application contact EMI Music Foundation Incorporated directly.
    Amount of award: $2,500

Empire Blue Cross and Blue Shield

Edwin R. Werner Scholarship

Type of award: Scholarship, renewable.
Intended use: For freshman study at accredited 4-year institution.
Eligibility: Applicant or parent must be employed by Empire Blue Cross and Blue Shield.
Basis for selection: Applicant must demonstrate financial need.
Additional information: For further information or an application contact Empire Blue Cross and Blue Shield directly.

F & D Company of Maryland

F & D Companies Scholarship

Type of award: Scholarship, renewable.
Intended use: For undergraduate study at accredited vocational, 2-year or 4-year institution.
Eligibility: Applicant or parent must be employed by Fidelity & Deposit Company of Maryland.
Additional information: For further information or an application contact Fidelity and Deposit Company of Maryland directly.
    Amount of award: $500-$2,000

Fannie Mae Foundation

David O. Maxwell Scholarship

Type of award: Scholarship, renewable.
Intended use: For undergraduate study at accredited 2-year or 4-year institution.
Eligibility: Applicant or parent must be employed by Archibald Candy Corporation.
Basis for selection: Applicant must demonstrate financial need.
Additional information: For further information or an application contact Fannie Mae directly.
    Amount of award: $500-$2,000

Federal Employee Education Assistance Fund

Federal Employee Education and Assistance Fund Scholarship

Type of award: Scholarship, renewable.
Intended use: For undergraduate, master's or doctoral study at accredited 2-year, 4-year or graduate institution.
Eligibility: Applicant or parent must be employed by Federal Employer/U.S. Government.
Basis for selection: Applicant must demonstrate high academic achievement.
Application requirements: Recommendations, essay and transcript.
Additional information: Current civilian federal and postal employees with minimum three years service and their dependents are eligible. Must have 3.0 GPA. Employee applicants eligible for part-time study; dependents must enroll full-time. Send SASE for application materials.
    Amount of award: $300-$1,500
    Number of awards: 401
    Number of applicants: 4,788
    Application deadline: May 8
    Notification begins: August 31
Contact:
Federal Employee Education and Assistance Fund
8441 West Bowles Avenue
Suite 200
Littleton, CO 80123-3245
Phone: 800-323-4140
Website: www.FPMI.com

Federal Signal Corporation

Federal Signal Karl F. Hoenecke Memorial Scholarship

Type of award: Scholarship, renewable.
Intended use: For freshman study at accredited 4-year institution.
Eligibility: Applicant or parent must be employed by Federal Signal.
Additional information: For further information or an application contact Federal Signal Corporation directly.
    Amount of award: $1,000

Financial Management Division of SIA

Financial Management Division of SIA Scholarship

Type of award: Scholarship, renewable.
Intended use: For undergraduate study at accredited 4-year institution.
Eligibility: Applicant or parent must be member of Financial Management Division of SIA.
Additional information: For further information or an application contact Financial Management Division of SIA directly.
    Amount of award: $500-$1,000

First Data Corporation

First Data Corporation Scholarship Awards

Type of award: Scholarship, renewable.
Intended use: For undergraduate study at accredited 2-year or 4-year institution.
Eligibility: Applicant or parent must be employed by First Data Corporation. Applicant must be high school senior.
Basis for selection: Applicant must demonstrate financial need.
Additional information: For further information or an application contact First Data Corporation directly.
    Amount of award: $500-$3,000
Contact:
First Data Corporation

First Marine Division Association, Inc.

First Marine Division Scholarship

Type of award: Scholarship, renewable.
Intended use: For full-time undergraduate study at accredited vocational, 2-year or 4-year institution in United States.
Eligibility: Applicant or parent must be member of First Marine Division. Applicant must be high school senior. Applicant must be U.S. citizen. Applicant must be child of disabled veteran or deceased veteran who served in the Marines. Must be dependent of service person who served with or was attached to 1st Marine Division.
Application requirements: Essay and proof of eligibility.
Additional information: This program is to assist dependants of deceased or 100% permanenetly disabled veterans of service with the First Marine Division in furthering education towards a bachelors degree. Contact office for application deadlines.
    Amount of award: $1,500
    Number of awards: 55
    Number of applicants: 225
    Total amount awarded: $24,000
Contact:
First Marine Division Association, Inc.
14325 Williard Road
Suite 107
Chantilly, VA 21051-2110
Phone: 703-803-3195
Fax: 7038037114
Website: www.erols.com/oldbreed

Fiskars, Inc.

Ed Nielson Scholarship

Type of award: Scholarship.
Intended use: For freshman study at accredited 4-year institution.
Eligibility: Applicant or parent must be employed by Fiskars, Inc.
Additional information: For further information or an application contact Fiskars, Inc. directly.
    Amount of award: $500-$2,000

Florida Rock Industries, Inc.

Florida Rock Industries Scholarship

Type of award: Scholarship, renewable.
Intended use: For undergraduate study at accredited vocational, 2-year or 4-year institution.
Eligibility: Applicant or parent must be employed by Florida Rock Industries, Inc.
Basis for selection: Applicant must demonstrate financial need.
Additional information: For further information or an application contact Florida Rock Industries, Inc. directly.
    Amount of award: $500-$1,500

Flowers Industries, Inc.

Flowers Industries Sons & Daughters Scholarship

Type of award: Scholarship, renewable.
Intended use: For undergraduate study at vocational, 2-year or 4-year institution.
Eligibility: Applicant or parent must be employed by Flowers Industries, Inc. Applicant must be high school senior.
Additional information: For further information or an application contact Flowers Industries Incorporated directly.
    Amount of award: $1,000

Fluor Daniel GTI

Fluor Daniel GTI Scholarship

Type of award: Scholarship, renewable.
Intended use: For undergraduate study at vocational, 2-year or 4-year institution.
Eligibility: Applicant or parent must be employed by Fluor Daniel GTI. Applicant must be high school senior.
Additional information: For further information or an application contact Fluor Daniel GTI directly.
    Amount of award: $1,000-$3,000

Fluor Foundation

Fluor Scholarship (USA)

Type of award: Scholarship, renewable.
Intended use: For undergraduate study at accredited vocational, 2-year or 4-year institution.
Eligibility: Applicant or parent must be employed by Fluor Corporation.
Basis for selection: Applicant must demonstrate financial need.
Additional information: For further information or an application contact Fluor Foundation directly.
    Amount of award: $1,000-$3,000

Foremost Farms USA Employees

Cow-lege Cash Scholarship Fund

Type of award: Scholarship.
Intended use: For undergraduate study at vocational, 2-year or 4-year institution.
Eligibility: Applicant or parent must be employed by Foremost Farms USA Employees. Applicant must be high school senior.
Additional information: For further information or an application contact Foremost Farms USA Employees directly.
    Amount of award: $500

Foss Maritime Company

Foss Maritime Scholarship

Type of award: Scholarship, renewable.
Intended use: For undergraduate study at accredited vocational, 2-year or 4-year institution.
Eligibility: Applicant or parent must be employed by Foss Maritime Co.
Basis for selection: Applicant must demonstrate financial need.
Additional information: For further information or an application contact Foss Maritime Company directly.
    Amount of award: $500-$2,000

Frank D. Visceglia Memorial Scholarship Program

Frank D. Visceglia Memorial Scholarship

Type of award: Scholarship.
Intended use: For full-time freshman study at accredited 4-year institution.
Eligibility: Applicant or parent must be member of Boy Scouts of America, Eagle Scouts. Applicant must be male, high school senior. Applicant must be U.S. citizen or permanent resident.
Additional information: Must be a member of the Eagle Scouts. Preference given to applicants whose service projects relate to the environment and/or the economy.
    Amount of award: $1,000
    Number of awards: 1
    Application deadline: September 30
    Total amount awarded: $1,000
Contact:
Frank D. Visceglia Memorial Scholarship Program
12 Mount Pleasant Turnpike
Denville, NJ 07834

Freightliner Corporation

Freightliner Fund Scholarship

Type of award: Scholarship, renewable.
Intended use: For undergraduate study at accredited vocational, 2-year or 4-year institution.
Eligibility: Applicant or parent must be employed by Freightliner Corporation. Applicant must be high school senior.
Additional information: For further information or an application contact Freightliner Corporation directly.
    Amount of award: $1,000-$5,000
Contact:
Freightliner Corporation

Frontier Insurance Group, Inc.

Frontier Scholarship Program for Children of Employees

Type of award: Scholarship, renewable.
Intended use: For undergraduate study at vocational, 2-year or 4-year institution.
Eligibility: Applicant or parent must be employed by Frontier Insurance Group, Inc. Applicant must be high school senior.
Additional information: For further information or an application contact Frontier Insurance Group Incorporated directly.
   Amount of award: $1,000

Frost National Bank

Tom Frost Scholarship Program for Dependents of Frost National Bank

Type of award: Scholarship, renewable.
Intended use: For undergraduate study at 2-year or 4-year institution.
Eligibility: Applicant or parent must be employed by Frost National Bank. Applicant must be high school senior.
Additional information: For further information or an application contact Frost National Bank directly.
   Amount of award: $5,000

FRP Properties, Inc.

FRP Properties Scholarship Program

Type of award: Scholarship, renewable.
Intended use: For undergraduate study at accredited vocational, 2-year or 4-year institution.
Eligibility: Applicant or parent must be employed by FRP Properties, Inc.
Basis for selection: Applicant must demonstrate financial need.
Additional information: For further information or an application contact FRP Properties, Inc. directly.
   Amount of award: $500-$1,500

GEICO Corporation

GEICO Scholarship Programs

Type of award: Scholarship, renewable.
Intended use: For undergraduate or graduate study at vocational, 2-year, 4-year or graduate institution.
Eligibility: Applicant or parent must be employed by GEICO Corporation. Applicant must be high school senior.
Additional information: For further information or an application contact Geico Corporation directly.
   Amount of award: $500-$4,500

General Mills

General Mills Foundation Scholarship

Type of award: Scholarship, renewable.
Intended use: For undergraduate study at accredited vocational, 2-year or 4-year institution.
Eligibility: Applicant or parent must be employed by General Mills, Inc.
Basis for selection: Applicant must demonstrate financial need.
Additional information: For further information or an application contact General Mills directly.
   Amount of award: $500-$2,500

General Signal Electrical Group

General Signal Electrical Group Scholarship Program

Type of award: Scholarship.
Intended use: For undergraduate study at accredited 2-year or 4-year institution.
Eligibility: Applicant or parent must be employed by O-Z/Gedney Company.
Additional information: For further information or an application contact O-Z/Gedney Company directly.
   Amount of award: $2,000
Contact:
Scholarship Coordinator

General Signal Scholarship

Excel Scholarship

Type of award: Scholarship.
Intended use: For undergraduate study at accredited postsecondary institution.
Eligibility: Applicant or parent must be employed by General Signal Corporation.
Basis for selection: Applicant must demonstrate financial need.
Additional information: For further information or an application contact General Signal Corporation directly.
   Amount of award: $500-$1,500
Contact:
General Signal Corporation

Gerber Foundation

Gerber Scholarship

Type of award: Scholarship, renewable.
Intended use: For full-time undergraduate or graduate study.
Eligibility: Applicant or parent must be employed by Gerber Products Company. Applicant must be high school senior.
Basis for selection: Applicant must demonstrate depth of character and leadership.
Application requirements: Recommendations, essay and transcript. Application and SAT or PSAT scores and counselor's report.
Additional information: Applicant should demonstrate involvement in diverse curricular, extracurricular, and community activities and be the child of a Gerber employee.
    Amount of award: $1,500
    Number of awards: 246
    Number of applicants: 246
    Application deadline: February 28
    Notification begins: May 15
    Total amount awarded: $369,000
Contact:
Gerber Foundation
5 South Division Avenue
Fremont, MI 49412
Phone: 616-924-3175
Fax: 616-924-3660

Gerber Scientific, Inc.

H. Joseph Gerber Vision Scholarship Program

Type of award: Scholarship, renewable.
Intended use: For freshman study at vocational, 2-year or 4-year institution.
Eligibility: Applicant or parent must be employed by Gerber Scientific, Inc. Applicant must be high school senior.
Additional information: For further information or an application contact Gerber Scientific Incorporated directly.
    Amount of award: $2,000

Girls Incorporated

Donna Brace Ogilvie-Zelda Gitlin Poetry Writing Award

Type of award: Scholarship.
Intended use: For undergraduate, non-degree study at 2-year, 4-year or graduate institution in or outside United States.
Eligibility: Applicant or parent must be member of Girls Incorporated. Applicant must be single, female, high school sophomore, junior, senior.
Basis for selection: Competition in Writing/journalism. Clarity, creativity and originality of expression through poetry.
Additional information: Applicant must be a participant in Girls Incorporated Poetry Writing Program.
    Amount of award: $500
    Number of awards: 2
    Application deadline: December 15
    Notification begins: March 1
    Total amount awarded: $1,000
Contact:
Girls Incorporated
120 Wall Street
Third Floor
New York, NY 10005-5394

Girls Incorporated Scholars Program

Type of award: Scholarship.
Intended use: For undergraduate study at 2-year, 4-year or graduate institution in or outside United States.
Eligibility: Applicant or parent must be member of Girls Incorporated. Applicant must be female, high school sophomore, junior, senior.
Basis for selection: Applicant must demonstrate depth of character, leadership, seriousness of purpose and service orientation.
Application requirements: Recommendations, essay and proof of eligibility.
Additional information: Must rank in top 50% of class.
    Amount of award: $1,000-$10,000
    Number of applicants: 47
    Application deadline: December 15
    Notification begins: February 15
    Total amount awarded: $110,000
Contact:
Girls Incorporated
120 Wall Stret
Third Floor
New York, NY 10005-5394

Glaxo Wellcome Inc.

Glaxo Wellcome Employees' Dependents Scholarship

Type of award: Scholarship, renewable.
Intended use: For freshman study at accredited vocational, 2-year or 4-year institution.
Eligibility: Applicant or parent must be employed by Glaxo Wellcome Inc.
Basis for selection: Applicant must demonstrate financial need.
Additional information: For further information or an application contact Glaxo Wellcome Inc. directly.
    Amount of award: $1,000

Golden Key National Honor Society

Art International '98

Type of award: Scholarship, renewable.
Intended use: For undergraduate or graduate study.
Eligibility: Applicant or parent must be member of Golden Key National Honor Society.
Additional information: Must be a lifetime member of Golden Key National Honor Society. One entry per member per category.

Amount of award:	$100-$1,000
Number of awards:	66
Number of applicants:	200
Application deadline:	April 1
Notification begins:	May 15
Total amount awarded:	$12,000

Concepts Literary Contest

Type of award: Scholarship, renewable.
Intended use: For undergraduate study.
Eligibility: Applicant or parent must be member of Golden Key National Honor Society.
Basis for selection: Competition in Writing/journalism.
Additional information: Must be a lifetime member of the Golden Key National Honor Society. Only one entry per member. Entries cannot exceed 1000 words. Applicants are generally notified in September. Check with your local chapter.

Amount of award:	$500-$1,000
Number of awards:	6
Application deadline:	April 1
Total amount awarded:	$3,000

Performing Arts Showcase 1999

Type of award: Scholarship, renewable.
Intended use: For undergraduate study at accredited postsecondary institution.
Eligibility: Applicant or parent must be member of Golden Key National Honor Society.
Basis for selection: Major/career interest in performing arts; music.
Additional information: Must be member of Golden Key National Honor Society. Entry must be submitted on video cassette and not exceed ten minutes in length.

Amount of award:	$1,000
Number of awards:	5
Number of applicants:	118
Application deadline:	April 1
Notification begins:	June 15
Total amount awarded:	$5,000

Pete Marick Scholarship Award

Type of award: Scholarship.
Intended use: For undergraduate study.
Eligibility: Applicant or parent must be member of Golden Key National Honor Society.
Additional information: Application deadline is the same as chapter's membership deadline and varies with school chapters. Two applicants per chapter per school.

Amount of award:	$2,500
Number of awards:	538
Total amount awarded:	$200,000

Contact:
Golden Key National Honor Society
1189 Ponce De Leon Avenue
Atlanta, GA 30306-4624
Phone: 800-377-2401 x228
Website: www.gknhs.gsu.edu

Student Scholastic Showcase

Type of award: Scholarship, renewable.
Intended use: For undergraduate study.
Eligibility: Applicant or parent must be member of Golden Key National Honor Society.
Application requirements: Recommendations and research proposal.
Additional information: Must be member of Golden Key National Honor Society. Only one submission per member will be accepted.

Amount of award:	$500-$1,000
Number of awards:	3
Number of applicants:	87
Application deadline:	April 1
Notification begins:	May 15
Total amount awarded:	$5,500

Contact:
Golden Key National Honor Society
1189 Ponce De Leon Avenue
Atlanta, GA 30306-4624
Phone: 800-377-2401 x228
Website: www.gknhs.gsu.edu

Golf Course Superintendents Association of America

Legacy Awards

Type of award: Scholarship.
Intended use: For full-time undergraduate or graduate study at accredited 2-year, 4-year or graduate institution.
Eligibility: Applicant or parent must be member of Golf Course Superintendents Association of America.
Application requirements: Recommendations and transcript.
Additional information: Applicants must be a child or grandchild of GCSAA members who have been active for at least five years. Must be studying a field unrelated to golf course management.

Amount of award:	$1,500
Application deadline:	April 15

Contact:
Scholarships Coordinator Jonelle O'Neill
1421 Research Park Dr.
Lawrence, KS 66049
Phone: 800-472-7878
Website: www.gcsaa.org

Grace Foundation, Inc.

W.R. Grace Foundation Scholarship

Type of award: Scholarship, renewable.
Intended use: For full-time freshman, sophomore, junior or senior study at accredited 4-year institution in United States.
Eligibility: Applicant or parent must be employed by W. R. Grace & Co. Applicant must be high school senior.
Basis for selection: Applicant must demonstrate high academic achievement.
Application requirements: Transcript.
Additional information: Minimum 2.5 GPA and combined SAT score of 1,100 or Act composite of 25-26 or minimum 3.0 GPA and combined SAT score of 1,000 or an ACT composite of 22-24. For further information contact Citizens' Scholarship Foundation of America, manager of the scholarship program. Parent may be employed by a wholly-owned subsidiary of W.R. Grace and company.

Amount of award:	$2,000
Number of awards:	10
Number of applicants:	126
Application deadline:	June 1
Notification begins:	July 9
Total amount awarded:	$80,000

Contact:
Citizens' Scholarship Foundation of America
W.R. Grace Foundation Scholarship
P.O. Box 297
St. Peter, MN 56082

Graco Foundation

Graco Scholarship

Type of award: Scholarship, renewable.
Intended use: For undergraduate or graduate study at accredited vocational, 2-year or 4-year institution.
Eligibility: Applicant or parent must be employed by Graco.
Basis for selection: Applicant must demonstrate financial need.
Additional information: For further information or an application contact Graco Foundation directly.

Amount of award:	$750-$5,000

Grand Union Company

Michael W. Marris Memorial Scholarship

Type of award: Scholarship.
Intended use: For freshman study at 2-year or 4-year institution.
Eligibility: Applicant or parent must be employed by The Grand Union Company. Applicant must be high school senior.
Additional information: For further information or an application contact Grand Union Company directly.

Amount of award:	$2,000-$4,000

Grange Insurance Association

Grange Insurance Scholarship

Type of award: Scholarship.
Intended use: For full-time undergraduate or graduate study at accredited vocational, 2-year, 4-year or graduate institution.
Eligibility: Applicant or parent must be member of Grange Insurance Association. Applicant must be U.S. citizen or permanent resident residing in California or Colorado or Idaho or Montana or Oregon or Washington or Wyoming.
Basis for selection: Applicant must demonstrate depth of character, leadership, patriotism, seriousness of purpose, service orientation, financial need and high academic achievement.
Application requirements: Recommendations, essay and transcript.
Additional information: Applicant or parents must be permanent residents of the designated state and members of The Grange in that state. Applicant or parents need not have insurance with The Grange.

Amount of award:	$500-$1,000
Number of awards:	36
Number of applicants:	164
Application deadline:	April 1
Notification begins:	December 1
Total amount awarded:	$19,500

Contact:
Grange Insurance Association
Scholarship Coordinator
P.O. Box 21089
Seattle, WA 98111-3089
Phone: 800-247-2643 ext. 2234

GreenPoint Financial

GreenPoint Scholarship

Type of award: Scholarship, renewable.
Intended use: For undergraduate study at accredited postsecondary institution.
Eligibility: Applicant or parent must be employed by GreenPoint Financial. Applicant must be high school senior.
Basis for selection: Applicant must demonstrate financial need.
Additional information: For further information or an application contact GreenPoint Financial directly.

Amount of award:	$5,000

Gregory Poole Equipment Company

Gregory Poole Equipment Scholarship

Type of award: Scholarship.
Intended use: For undergraduate study at accredited vocational, 2-year or 4-year institution.
Eligibility: Applicant or parent must be employed by Gregory Poole Equipment Company.
Additional information: For further information or an application contact Gregory Poole Equipment Company directly.
    Amount of award: $500-$1,000

Guideposts

Norman Vincent Peale Scholarship Program

Type of award: Scholarship.
Intended use: For undergraduate study at vocational, 2-year or 4-year institution.
Eligibility: Applicant or parent must be employed by Guideposts. Applicant must be high school senior.
Additional information: For further information or an application contact Guideposts directly.
    Amount of award: $1,000-$3,500

Gulf States Paper Corporation

Jack & Elizabeth Warner College Scholarship Fund

Type of award: Scholarship, renewable.
Intended use: For undergraduate study.
Eligibility: Applicant or parent must be employed by Gulf States Paper Corporation. Applicant must be high school senior.
Additional information: For further information or an application contact Gulf States Paper Corporation directly.
    Amount of award: $500-$2,500

H&R Block Foundation

H&R Block Scholarship

Type of award: Scholarship.
Intended use: For undergraduate study at accredited vocational, 2-year or 4-year institution.
Eligibility: Applicant or parent must be employed by H&R Block Foundation. Applicant must be high school senior.
Basis for selection: Applicant must demonstrate financial need.
Additional information: For further information or an application contact H&R Block Foundation directly.
    Amount of award: $2,000

H.B. Fuller Company and its International Locations

Elmer and Eleanor Andersen Global Scholarship Program

Type of award: Scholarship.
Intended use: For undergraduate study at vocational, 2-year or 4-year institution.
Eligibility: Applicant or parent must be employed by H.B. Fuller Company and its International Locations. Applicant must be high school senior.
Additional information: For further information or an application contact H.B.Fuller Company and it's International Locations directly.
    Amount of award: $500-$10,000

Hannaford Charitable Foundation

Hannaford Scholarship

Type of award: Scholarship.
Intended use: For undergraduate or graduate study at accredited postsecondary institution.
Eligibility: Applicant or parent must be employed by Hannaford Charitable Foundation. Applicant must be high school senior.
Basis for selection: Applicant must demonstrate financial need.
Additional information: For further information or an application contact Hannaford Charitable Foundation directly.
    Amount of award: $2,000-$5,000
Contact:
Hannaford Charitable Foundation

Harness Tracks of America

Harness Tracks of America Scholarship

Type of award: Scholarship, renewable.
Intended use: For full-time undergraduate or graduate study at accredited postsecondary institution.

Eligibility: Applicant or parent must be member of Harness Racing Industry. Applicant must be permanent resident.
Basis for selection: Applicant must demonstrate depth of character, leadership, patriotism, seriousness of purpose, service orientation, financial need and high academic achievement.
Application requirements: Essay, transcript and proof of eligibility. Student Financial Aid Forms.
Additional information: Must be child of licensed driver, trainer or caretaker (living or deceased) of harness horse or be personally active in harness racing industry. Recommendations not required but considered if included with application.

Amount of award:	$4,000
Number of awards:	5
Number of applicants:	75
Application deadline:	June 15, September
Notification begins:	September 15
Total amount awarded:	$20,000

Contact:
Harness Tracks of America
4640 East Sunrise
Suite 200
Tucson, AZ 85718
Phone: 520-529-2525
Fax: 520-529-3235

Hasbro, Inc.

Hasbro Scholarship

Type of award: Scholarship, renewable.
Intended use: For undergraduate study at accredited postsecondary institution.
Eligibility: Applicant or parent must be employed by Hasbro, Inc. Applicant must be high school senior.
Basis for selection: Applicant must demonstrate financial need.
Additional information: For further information or an application contact Hasbro, Inc. directly.

Amount of award:	$200-$1,500

Hatfield, Inc.

Hatfield Scholarship

Type of award: Scholarship.
Intended use: For undergraduate study at accredited postsecondary institution.
Eligibility: Applicant or parent must be employed by Hatfield Quality Meats, Inc.
Additional information: For further information or an application contact Hatfield Quality Meats, Inc. directly.

Amount of award:	$1,000

Hawaii Community Foundation

E.E. Black Scholarship

Type of award: Scholarship, renewable.
Intended use: For full-time or less than half-time undergraduate or graduate study at accredited postsecondary institution in United States.
Eligibility: Applicant or parent must be employed by BHP Hawaii. Applicant must be U.S. citizen or permanent resident residing in Hawaii.
Basis for selection: Applicant must demonstrate depth of character, leadership, seriousness of purpose, service orientation, financial need and high academic achievement.
Application requirements: Recommendations, essay and transcript. Student Aid Report, personal letter.
Additional information: Minimum 3.0 GPA. CSS Profile. Application required. Award amount varies. Applicants must have permanent address in Hawaii. Applicants who take up mainland residency must have relatives living in Hawaii. Other former Hawaii residents considered on a case by case basis. Notifications mailed between April and July.

Amount of award:	$1,100
Number of awards:	7
Application deadline:	March 2

Contact:
Hawaii Community Foundation
900 Fort Street Mall, Suite 1300
Honolulu, HI 96813
Phone: 808-566-5570

Frances S. Watanabe Memorial Scholarship

Type of award: Scholarship, renewable.
Intended use: For undergraduate or graduate study at accredited postsecondary institution in United States.
Eligibility: Applicant or parent must be member of Dillingham Federal Credit Union. Applicant must be U.S. citizen or permanent resident residing in Hawaii.
Basis for selection: Applicant must demonstrate depth of character, leadership, seriousness of purpose, service orientation, financial need and high academic achievement.
Application requirements: Recommendations, essay and transcript. Student Aid Report, personal letter.
Additional information: CSS PROFILE Application required. Award amount varies. Applicants must have permanent address in Hawaii. Applicants who take up mainland residency must have relatives living in Hawaii. Other former Hawaii residents considered on a case by case basis.

Amount of award:	$500
Number of awards:	3
Application deadline:	March 2

Contact:
Frances S. Watanabe Memorial Scholarship
c/o Hawaii Community Foundation
900 Fort Street Mall, Suite 1300
Honolulu, HI 96813
Phone: 808-566-5570

Hawaii Electric Industries Charitable Foundation

HEI Scholarship

Type of award: Scholarship, renewable.
Intended use: For undergraduate study.
Eligibility: Applicant or parent must be employed by Hawaii Electric Industries, Inc.
Additional information: For further information or an application contact Hawaii Electric Industries Charitable Foundation directly.
    Amount of award: $1,200

Helzberg Diamonds

Helzberg Scholarship Program

Type of award: Scholarship, renewable.
Intended use: For undergraduate study at accredited vocational, 2-year or 4-year institution.
Eligibility: Applicant or parent must be employed by Helzberg Diamonds.
Basis for selection: Applicant must demonstrate financial need.
Additional information: For further information or an application contact Helzberg Diamonds directly.
    Amount of award: $1,000

Henkel Corporation

Henkel Corporation Scholarship

Type of award: Scholarship, renewable.
Intended use: For undergraduate study at accredited vocational, 2-year or 4-year institution.
Eligibility: Applicant or parent must be employed by Henkel Corporation.
Basis for selection: Applicant must demonstrate financial need.
Additional information: For further information or an application contact Henkel Corporation directly.
    Amount of award: $500-$1,500

Herman Miller Inc.

Scholarship Fund for Children of Herman Miller Employees

Type of award: Scholarship, renewable.
Intended use: For undergraduate study at vocational, 2-year or 4-year institution.
Eligibility: Applicant or parent must be employed by Herman Miller Inc. Applicant must be high school senior.
Additional information: For further information or an application contact Herman Miller Incorporated directly.
    Amount of award: $1,000-$5,000

Hershey Foods Corporation

Hershey Foods Corporation Scholars Program

Type of award: Scholarship, renewable.
Intended use: For undergraduate study at accredited 4-year institution.
Eligibility: Applicant or parent must be employed by Hershey Foods Corporation.
Basis for selection: Applicant must demonstrate financial need.
Additional information: For further information or an application contact Hershey Foods Corporation directly.
    Amount of award: $100-$3,000

Hewlettt-Packard Company

Hewlett-Packard Employee Scholarship

Type of award: Scholarship.
Intended use: For full-time freshman study.
Eligibility: Applicant or parent must be employed by Hewlett-Packard Company.
Application requirements: Interview, recommendations, essay and transcript.
    Amount of award: $2,000
    Number of awards: 524
    Number of applicants: 850
    Application deadline: February 27
    Notification begins: May 15
    Total amount awarded: $834,000
Contact:
Hewlett-Packard Company Employee Scholarship Organization
1501 Page Mill Road M/S 4L-9
Palo Alto, CA 94304
Phone: 650-857-6148
Website: ecp.corp.hp.com/scholar/index.htm

Hexcel Corporation

Hexcel Scholarship Program

Type of award: Scholarship, renewable.
Intended use: For undergraduate study at vocational, 2-year or 4-year institution.
Eligibility: Applicant or parent must be employed by Hexcel Corporation. Applicant must be high school senior.
Additional information: For further information or an application contact Hexcel Corporation directly.
    Amount of award: $1,000

Hickory Tech Corporation Foundation

HTC Employees' Daughter & Son Scholarship Program

Type of award: Scholarship, renewable.
Intended use: For undergraduate study at accredited postsecondary institution.
Eligibility: Applicant or parent must be employed by Hickory Tech Corporation. Applicant must be high school senior.
Additional information: For further information or an application contact Hickory Tech Corporation Foundation directly.
    Amount of award: $1,000
Contact:
Hickory Tech Corporation Foundation

Highway AG Services

Highway AG Services Scholarship

Type of award: Scholarship.
Intended use: For freshman study at accredited vocational, 2-year or 4-year institution.
Eligibility: Applicant or parent must be employed by Highway Ag Services. Applicant must be high school senior.
Additional information: Must be child of employee of HAS. For further information and an application contact Highway AG Services directly.
    Amount of award: $500

Hitachi America, Ltd.

HAL USA Scholarship Program

Type of award: Scholarship.
Intended use: For undergraduate study at accredited 4-year institution.
Eligibility: Applicant or parent must be employed by Hitachi America, Ltd.
Basis for selection: Applicant must demonstrate financial need.
Additional information: For further information or an application contact Hitachi America, Ltd. directly.
    Amount of award: $500-$5,000

Hitachi Semiconductor (America) Inc.

Hitachi Semiconductor USA Scholarship

Type of award: Scholarship.
Intended use: For undergraduate study at 2-year or 4-year institution.
Eligibility: Applicant or parent must be employed by Hitachi Semiconductor (America) Inc. Applicant must be high school senior.
Additional information: For further information or an application contact Hitachi Semiconductor (America) Incorporated directly.
    Amount of award: $500-$1,000

Holiday Hospitality, Corporation

Holiday Hospitality Scholarship

Type of award: Scholarship, renewable.
Intended use: For undergraduate study at vocational, 2-year or 4-year institution.
Eligibility: Applicant or parent must be employed by Holiday Hospitality, Corporation. Applicant must be high school senior.
Additional information: For further information or an application contact Holiday Hospitality Corporation directly.
    Amount of award: $3,000

Honor Society of Phi Kappa Phi

Phi Kappa Phi Graduate Fellowship

Type of award: Scholarship.
Intended use: For full-time master's, first professional study at accredited graduate institution in or outside United States.
Eligibility: Applicant or parent must be member of Phi Kappa Phi.
Basis for selection: Applicant must demonstrate high academic achievement.
Application requirements: Recommendations, essay, transcript and nomination by local chapter.
Additional information: For first-year graduate or professional study. Preference to candidates intending to pursue doctorate or advanced professional degree. Students chosen for membership but not yet initiated also eligible. Local chapter deadlines vary. Applications available at local chapters in October.

Amount of award: $1,000-$7,000
Number of awards: 80
Number of applicants: 190
Total amount awarded: $380,000
Contact:
Honor Society of Phi Kappa Phi
P.O. Box 16000
Louisiana State University
Baton Rouge, LA 70893-6000

Horace Mann Companies

Horace Mann Scholarship Program

Type of award: Scholarship, renewable.
Intended use: For full-time undergraduate study at accredited 2-year or 4-year institution.
Eligibility: Applicant or parent must be employed by U.S. public school district or public college/university. Applicant must be high school senior.
Basis for selection: Applicant must demonstrate depth of character, leadership, service orientation and high academic achievement.
Application requirements: Recommendations, essay, transcript and proof of eligibility. Must have B average and score of ACT score of 23 or SAT score of 1,100. List activities and honors.
Additional information: Student must have minimum 3.0 GPA, and score at least a 23 on the ACT or 1100 on the SAT. Parent must be employed by U.S. public school district or public college/university.
Application deadline: February 28
Notification begins: March 31
Contact:
Horace Mann Scholarship Program
P.O. Box 20490
Springfield, IL 62708
Website: www.horacemann.com

Host Marriott-San Francisco International Airport

Host Marriott Scholarship

Type of award: Scholarship, renewable.
Intended use: For undergraduate study at accredited vocational, 2-year or 4-year institution.
Eligibility: Applicant or parent must be employed by Host Marriott-San Francisco Intl Airport. Applicant must be high school senior.
Additional information: For further information or application contact them directly.
Amount of award: $1,000
Contact:
Host Marriott-San Francisco International Airport

Hubbard Farms, Inc.

Hubbard Farms B.U.T.A. Scholarship

Type of award: Scholarship, renewable.
Intended use: For undergraduate study at accredited vocational, 2-year or 4-year institution.
Eligibility: Applicant or parent must be employed by Hubbard Farms Inc.
Basis for selection: Applicant must demonstrate financial need.
Additional information: For further information or an application contact Hubbard Farms Inc. directly.
Amount of award: $300-$1,000

Hugo Neu Corporation

Hugo Neu Corporation Employees Scholarship

Type of award: Scholarship, renewable.
Intended use: For undergraduate study at accredited vocational, 2-year or 4-year institution.
Eligibility: Applicant or parent must be employed by Hugo Neu and Sons, Inc.
Basis for selection: Applicant must demonstrate financial need.
Additional information: For further information or an application contact Hugo Neu Corporation directly.
Amount of award: $500-$7,000

Hydrite Chemical Co.

Richard C. Honkamp Scholarship Award

Type of award: Scholarship.
Intended use: For undergraduate study at vocational, 2-year or 4-year institution.
Eligibility: Applicant or parent must be employed by Hydrite Chemical Co. Applicant must be high school senior.
Additional information: For further information or an application contact Hydrite Chemical Company directly.
Amount of award: $2,500

Ida C. Koran Trust Fund

Ida C. Koran Student Aid Program

Type of award: Scholarship, renewable.
Intended use: For undergraduate study at accredited vocational, 2-year or 4-year institution.
Eligibility: Applicant or parent must be employed by Ecolab Inc.

Ida C. Koran Trust Fund: Ida C. Koran Student Aid Program

Basis for selection: Applicant must demonstrate financial need.
Additional information: For further information and an application contact Ida C. Koran directly.
    Amount of award: $500-$2,500

Ideal Electric Company

Ideal Electric Scholarship

Type of award: Scholarship, renewable.
Intended use: For freshman study at accredited vocational, 2-year or 4-year institution.
Eligibility: Applicant or parent must be employed by Ideal Electric Company.
Additional information: For further information or an application contact Ideal Electric Company directly.
    Amount of award: $1,000

IEEE Computer Society

Lance Stafford Larson Student Scholarship

Type of award: Scholarship.
Intended use: For full-time undergraduate study.
Eligibility: Applicant or parent must be member of IEEE Computer Society.
Basis for selection: Competition in Poise/talent/fitness. Technical content, writing skills and overall presentation Major/career interest in computer and information sciences.
Application requirements: Essay and proof of eligibility.
    Amount of award: $500
    Number of awards: 1
    Application deadline: October 31
    Total amount awarded: $500

Richard E. Merwin Award

Type of award: Scholarship.
Intended use: For full-time junior, senior or graduate study at accredited 4-year or graduate institution.
Eligibility: Applicant or parent must be member of IEEE Computer Society.
Basis for selection: Major/career interest in computer and information sciences; science, general. Applicant must demonstrate seriousness of purpose.
Application requirements: Recommendations and proof of eligibility.
Additional information: Minimum GPA of 2.5 required.
    Amount of award: $3,000
    Number of awards: 2
    Application deadline: May 31
    Total amount awarded: $6,000

Upsilon Pi Epsilon Scholarships

Type of award: Scholarship.
Intended use: For full-time undergraduate or graduate study.
Eligibility: Applicant or parent must be member of IEEE Computer Society.
Basis for selection: Major/career interest in computer and information sciences. Applicant must demonstrate seriousness of purpose and high academic achievement.
Application requirements: Recommendations, transcript and proof of eligibility.
Additional information: Three letters of recommendation on organization letterhead are required. Student winners f the computer society's Richard Merwin or UPE/CS Award for the previous year (13 months) are not eligible.
    Amount of award: $500
    Number of awards: 3
    Application deadline: October 31
    Total amount awarded: $1,500
Contact:
IEEE Computer Society
1730 Massachusetts Ave., NW
Washington, DC 20036-1992
Website: www.computer.org/student/schlrshp.thm

IHOP Corp.

Richard K. Herzer Scholarship for the Study of Entrepreneurial Business

Type of award: Scholarship.
Intended use: For undergraduate or graduate study at vocational, 2-year, 4-year or graduate institution.
Eligibility: Applicant or parent must be employed by IHOP Corp. Applicant must be high school senior.
Additional information: For further information or an application contact IHOP Corporation directly.
    Amount of award: $7,500

Illinois Tool Works

Illinois Tool Works Foundation Scholarship

Type of award: Scholarship, renewable.
Intended use: For undergraduate study at accredited vocational, 2-year or 4-year institution.
Eligibility: Applicant or parent must be employed by Illinois Tool Works Inc.
Basis for selection: Applicant must demonstrate financial need.
Additional information: For further information or an application contact Illinois Tool Works Inc. directly.
    Amount of award: $500-$2,500

Independence Mining Co. Inc. (IMC)

IMC Scholarship Program

Type of award: Scholarship, renewable.
Intended use: For undergraduate study at vocational, 2-year or 4-year institution.
Eligibility: Applicant or parent must be employed by Independence Mining Co. Inc. (IMC). Applicant must be high school senior.
Additional information: For further information or an application contact Independence Mining Company Incorporated directly.
    Amount of award: $500-$3,000

Industrial Electric Wire and Cable Inc.

Ted Krzynski and Harlan Murray Scholarship Program

Type of award: Scholarship, renewable.
Intended use: For undergraduate study at vocational, 2-year or 4-year institution.
Eligibility: Applicant or parent must be employed by Industrial Electric Wire and Cable Inc. Applicant must be high school senior.
Additional information: For further information or an application contact Industrial Electric Wire and Cable Incorporated directly.
    Amount of award: $1,000-$5,000

Inland Steel-Ryerson Foundation

All-Inland Scholarship Program

Type of award: Scholarship, renewable.
Intended use: For full-time undergraduate study at accredited 4-year institution outside United States.
Eligibility: Applicant or parent must be employed by Inland Steel Industries, Inc. Applicant must be high school senior.
Basis for selection: Applicant must demonstrate depth of character, leadership, seriousness of purpose, service orientation, financial need and high academic achievement.
Application requirements: Recommendations, transcript and proof of eligibility. SAT scores, involvement in extracurricular and community activities.
Additional information: Student should be the child or legal ward of an active, retired or deceased employee of Inland Steel Industries, Inc.
    Amount of award: $500-$2,000
    Number of awards: 110
    Number of applicants: 217
    Application deadline: February 17
    Notification begins: April 30
    Total amount awarded: $170,000
Contact:
Inland Steel-Ryerson Foundation
Helen Marich, (MC8-125)
3210 Watling Street
East Chicago, IN 46312
Phone: 219-399-5427

Innovex, Inc.

Innovex Scholarship

Type of award: Scholarship, renewable.
Intended use: For freshman study at vocational, 2-year or 4-year institution.
Eligibility: Applicant or parent must be employed by Innovex, Inc. Applicant must be high school senior.
Additional information: For further information or an application contact Innovex Incorporated directly.

Institute of Food Technologists

Food Packaging Division Graduate Fellowship

Type of award: Scholarship, renewable.
Intended use: For full-time master's, doctoral study.
Eligibility: Applicant or parent must be member of Inst. of Food Technologists/Food Packaging Div.
Basis for selection: Major/career interest in food science and technology. Applicant must demonstrate high academic achievement.
Application requirements: Recommendations, essay, transcript, proof of eligibility and research proposal.
Additional information: Research must be in area of food packaging; institution must be conducting fundamental investigations in the advancement of food packaging. Second-time applicants must be IFT members. Minimum 2.5 GPA required.
    Amount of award: $1,000
    Number of awards: 1
    Application deadline: February 1
    Notification begins: April 15
    Total amount awarded: $1,000
Contact:
Institute of Food Technologists
Scholarship Department
221 North LaSalle Street
Chicago, IL 60601

International Association of Bridge, Structural, Ornamental, and Reinforcing Iron Workers

John Lyons Scholarship

Type of award: Scholarship, renewable.
Intended use: For full-time undergraduate study at accredited 4-year institution. Designated institutions: In United States or Canada.
Eligibility: Applicant or parent must be member of Int'l Assoc. Bridge/Structural/Ornamental Workers. Applicant must be high school senior. Applicant must be U.S. citizen, permanent resident or Canadian citizens.
Basis for selection: Applicant must demonstrate depth of character, leadership and high academic achievement.
Application requirements: Recommendations, essay, transcript and proof of eligibility. SAT I/ACT scores required except for Canadian students who must submit equivalent information.
Additional information: Applicant must rank in top third of graduating class. Parent must be member of International Association with at least five years membership at time of application. Sibling of previous recipient not eligible. Applications may be obtained between January 15 and March 31.

Amount of award:	$2,500
Number of awards:	2
Number of applicants:	225
Application deadline:	March 31
Notification begins:	June 1
Total amount awarded:	$5,000

Contact:
International Association of Bridge, Structural, Ornamental, and Reinforcing Iron Workers
John H. Lyons, Sr. Scholarship Committee
1750 New York Avenue, Suite 400 NW
Washington, DC 20006
Phone: 800-368-0105

International Association of Fire Fighters

W.H. McClennan Scholarship

Type of award: Scholarship, renewable.
Intended use: For full-time undergraduate or graduate study.
Eligibility: Applicant or parent must be member of Int'l Assoc. of Fire Fighters.
Basis for selection: Applicant must demonstrate depth of character, seriousness of purpose, service orientation, financial need and high academic achievement.
Application requirements: Recommendations, essay, transcript and proof of eligibility.
Additional information: Open only to children of firefighters that lost their lives in the line of duty and were members in good standing of the IAFF.

Amount of award:	$2,500
Number of awards:	10
Number of applicants:	14
Application deadline:	February 1
Notification begins:	April 1
Total amount awarded:	$25,000

Contact:
International Association of Fire Fighters
1750 New York Avenue, NW
Washington, DC 20006

International Brotherhood of Teamsters

Teamsters Scholarship Fund

Type of award: Scholarship.
Intended use: For full-time undergraduate study at accredited 4-year institution. Designated institutions: In United States or Canada.
Eligibility: Applicant or parent must be member of International Brotherhood of Teamsters. Applicant must be high school senior. Applicant must be U.S. citizen or Canadian citizens.
Basis for selection: Applicant must demonstrate financial need and high academic achievement.
Application requirements: Transcript and proof of eligibility.
Additional information: Must rank in top 15 percent of class. Available to dependent children/grandchildren of Teamster members. Contact local union office. Fifteen one-time awards of $1000 and ten awards of $6000 distributed evenly throughout the undergraduate years.

Amount of award:	$1,000-$6,000
Number of awards:	25
Number of applicants:	1,300
Application deadline:	December 15
Notification begins:	June 15
Total amount awarded:	$75,000

Contact:
International Brotherhood of Teamsters
25 Louisiana Avenue NW
Washington, DC 20001

International Buckskin Horse Association, Inc.

Buckskin Horse Association Scholarship

Type of award: Scholarship, renewable.
Intended use: For full-time undergraduate study at accredited postsecondary institution in United States.
Eligibility: Applicant or parent must be member of International Buckskin Horse Association. Applicant must be high school senior. Applicant must be U.S. citizen.
Basis for selection: Applicant must demonstrate depth of

character, leadership, seriousness of purpose, financial need and high academic achievement.
Application requirements: Portfolio, recommendations and proof of eligibility. Member for 2 years prior to application.

Amount of award:	$1,000-$1,500
Number of awards:	8
Number of applicants:	10
Application deadline:	February 15
Notification begins:	April 30
Total amount awarded:	$8,700

Contact:
International Buckskin Horse Association, Inc.
P.O. Box 268
Shelby, IN 46377

International Executive Housekeepers Association

Executive Housekeepers Education Foundation Scholarship.

Type of award: Scholarship.
Intended use: For undergraduate, graduate or non-degree study at accredited postsecondary institution.
Eligibility: Applicant or parent must be member of Int'l Executive Housekeepers Assoc.
Basis for selection: Major/career interest in hospitality administration/management.
Application requirements: Essay and transcript.
Additional information: Can be used for International Executive Housekeepers Association Certification program.

Amount of award:	$500-$2,000
Number of awards:	2
Number of applicants:	2
Application deadline:	January 15
Notification begins:	September 1
Total amount awarded:	$2,000

Contact:
International Executive Housekeepers Association
Attn: Tedya Cooper
1001 Eastwind Drive, Suite 301
Westerville, OH 43081-3361
Phone: 800-200-6342
Fax: 614-895-1248
Website: www.ieha.org

International Furnishings and Design Association Educational Foundation

International Furnishings and Design Student Member Scholarship

Type of award: Scholarship.
Intended use: For full-time undergraduate or graduate study at
Eligibility: Applicant or parent must be member of International Furnishings & Design Association.
Basis for selection: Major/career interest in design. Applicant must demonstrate depth of character, seriousness of purpose, service orientation and high academic achievement.
Application requirements: $45 application fee. Recommendations, essay and transcript. Must be a currently enrolled design student.

Amount of award:	$1,500
Number of awards:	1
Number of applicants:	20
Application deadline:	October 15
Notification begins:	November 1
Total amount awarded:	$1,500

Contact:
Jennifer Lewis
IFDA Educational Foundation
1200 19 Street, NW Number 300
Washington, DC 20036-2422
Phone: 202-857-1897

International Multifoods Corporation

International Multifoods Scholarship

Type of award: Scholarship.
Intended use: For undergraduate study at accredited vocational, 2-year or 4-year institution.
Eligibility: Applicant or parent must be employed by International Multifoods Corporation.
Additional information: For further information or an application contact International Multifoods Corporation directly.

Amount of award:	$1,500

International Union of Electronic, Electrical, Salaried, Machine, and Furniture Workers Department of Social Action

James B. Carey Scholarship

Type of award: Scholarship.
Intended use: For full-time undergraduate study in United States.
Eligibility: Applicant or parent must be member of Int'l Union of EESMF Workers, AFL-CIO. Applicant must be high school senior.
Basis for selection: Applicant must demonstrate depth of character and service orientation.

Application requirements: Recommendations, essay, transcript and proof of eligibility. Local Union Seal.
- Amount of award: $1,000
- Number of awards: 9
- Number of applicants: 300
- Application deadline: April 15
- Notification begins: February 1
- Total amount awarded: $9,000

William H. Bywater Scholarship

Type of award: Scholarship.
Intended use: For full-time undergraduate study in United States.
Eligibility: Applicant or parent must be employed by Elected official of Local Union. Applicant or parent must be member of Int'l Union of EESMF Workers, AFL-CIO. Applicant must be high school senior.
Basis for selection: Applicant must demonstrate depth of character and service orientation.
Application requirements: Recommendations, essay, transcript and proof of eligibility. Local Union Seal.
- Amount of award: $3,000
- Number of awards: 1
- Number of applicants: 100
- Application deadline: April 15
- Notification begins: February 1
- Total amount awarded: $3,000

Contact:
Gloria T. Johnson, IUE Department of Social Action
Int'l Union of EESMF Workers, AFL-CIO
1126 16 Street, N.W.
Washington, DC 20036-4866

International Union of Electronic, Electrical, Salaried, Machine, and Furniture Workers Dept. of Social Action

David J. Fitzmaurice Engineering Scholarship

Type of award: Scholarship.
Intended use: For full-time undergraduate study in United States.
Eligibility: Applicant or parent must be member of Int'l Union of EESMF Workers, AFL-CIO. Applicant must be high school senior.
Basis for selection: Major/career interest in engineering. Applicant must demonstrate depth of character and service orientation.
Application requirements: Recommendations, essay, transcript and proof of eligibility. Local Union Seal.

- Amount of award: $2,000
- Number of awards: 1
- Number of applicants: 300
- Application deadline: April 15
- Notification begins: February 1
- Total amount awarded: $2,000

Contact:
Gloria T. Johnson, IUE Department of Social Action
Int'l Union of EESMF Workers, AFL-CIO
1126 16 Street, N.W.
Washington, DC 20036-4866

Interstate Brands Corporation

Interstate Brands Scholarship

Type of award: Scholarship, renewable.
Intended use: For undergraduate study at accredited vocational, 2-year or 4-year institution.
Eligibility: Applicant or parent must be employed by Interstate Brands Corporation.
Basis for selection: Applicant must demonstrate financial need.
Additional information: For further information or an application contact Interstate Brands Corporation directly.
- Amount of award: $300-$2,000

Intuit Scholarship Foundation

Intuit Scholarship

Type of award: Scholarship, renewable.
Intended use: For freshman study at vocational, 2-year or 4-year institution.
Eligibility: Applicant or parent must be employed by Intuit Scholarship Foundation. Applicant must be high school senior.
Additional information: For further information or an application contact Intuit Scholarship Foundation directly.
- Amount of award: $500-$5,000

J. Baker, Inc.

Gertrude Baker Memorial Scholarship

Type of award: Scholarship.
Intended use: For undergraduate study at accredited vocational, 2-year or 4-year institution.
Eligibility: Applicant or parent must be employed by J. Baker, Inc.
Basis for selection: Applicant must demonstrate financial need.

Additional information: For further information or an application contact J. Baker, Inc. directly.
   Amount of award: $1,000

J.C. Penney Company, Inc.

J.C. Penney Scholarship Program

Type of award: Scholarship.
Intended use: For undergraduate study at accredited vocational, 2-year or 4-year institution.
Eligibility: Applicant or parent must be employed by J. C. Penney Company, Inc.
Additional information: For further information or an application contact J.C. Penney Company, Inc. directly.
   Amount of award: $1,500

J.W. Pepper & Son, Inc.

Pepper Employees' Children Scholarship Fund

Type of award: Scholarship.
Intended use: For undergraduate study at vocational, 2-year or 4-year institution.
Eligibility: Applicant or parent must be employed by J.W. Pepper & Sons, Inc. Applicant must be high school senior.
Additional information: For further information or an application contact J.W. Pepper & Son Incorporated directly.
   Amount of award: $250-$5,000

Jaycee War Memorial Fund

Thomas Wood Baldridge Scholarship

Type of award: Scholarship.
Intended use: For full-time undergraduate study at accredited 2-year or 4-year institution.
Eligibility: Applicant or parent must be member of Jaycees. Applicant must be U.S. citizen.
Basis for selection: Applicant must demonstrate leadership.
Application requirements: $5 application fee. Nomination by applicants' state Junior Chamber organization.
Additional information: SASE required.
   Amount of award: $2,500
   Number of awards: 1
   Application deadline: February 1
   Total amount awarded: $2,500
Contact:
Jaycee War Memorial Fund
4 West 21 Street
Tulsa, OK 74114-1116

Jerold B. Katz Foundation

GC Services Scholarship

Type of award: Scholarship, renewable.
Intended use: For freshman study at accredited 2-year or 4-year institution.
Eligibility: Applicant or parent must be employed by GC Services.
Basis for selection: Applicant must demonstrate financial need.
Additional information: For further information or an application contact Jerold B. Katz Foundation or GC Services directly.
   Amount of award: $2,500

Jimmy Treybig Scholarship Fund Endowment

Jimmy Treybig Scholarship Program

Type of award: Scholarship, renewable.
Intended use: For undergraduate study.
Eligibility: Applicant or parent must be employed by Jimmy Treybig Scholarship Fund Endowment. Applicant must be high school senior.
Additional information: For further information or an application contact Jimmy Treybig Scholarship Fund Endowment directly.
   Amount of award: $2,000

Johnson International, Inc.

Johnson International Scholarship Program

Type of award: Scholarship.
Intended use: For undergraduate study at accredited vocational, 2-year or 4-year institution.
Eligibility: Applicant or parent must be employed by Johnson International, Inc.
Basis for selection: Applicant must demonstrate financial need.
Additional information: For further information or an application contact Johnson International, Inc. directly.
   Amount of award: $250-$1,000

Johnson Worldwide Associates, Inc.

JWA Sons and Daughters Scholarship

Type of award: Scholarship, renewable.
Intended use: For undergraduate study at accredited postsecondary institution.
Eligibility: Applicant or parent must be employed by Johnson Worldwide Associates, Inc. Applicant must be high school senior.
Basis for selection: Applicant must demonstrate financial need.
Additional information: For further information or an application contact Johnson Worldwide Associates, Inc. directly.
    Amount of award: $500-$2,500
Contact:
Johnson Worldwide Associates, Inc.

Johnson's Wax Fund, Inc.

Johnson Wax Fund Sons & Daughters Scholarship

Type of award: Scholarship, renewable.
Intended use: For full-time freshman, sophomore, junior or senior study at accredited vocational, 2-year or 4-year institution in or outside United States. Designated institutions: Parent must be working outside U.S. or student must be involved in exchange program.
Eligibility: Applicant or parent must be employed by SC Johnson Wax. Applicant must be single. Applicant must be U.S. citizen.
Basis for selection: Applicant must demonstrate leadership and high academic achievement.
Application requirements: Recommendations and transcript.
Additional information: For further information or an application contact Johnson's Wax Fund, Inc. directly.
    Amount of award: $1,000-$3,000
    Number of awards: 193
    Number of applicants: 210
    Application deadline: January 30
    Notification begins: April 30
Contact:
Johnson's Wax Fund, Inc.
1525 Howe Street
Racine, WI 53403

Juvenile Products Manufacturers Association

JPMA Scholarship Program

Type of award: Scholarship.
Intended use: For undergraduate study at accredited vocational, 2-year or 4-year institution.
Eligibility: Applicant or parent must be employed by Juvenile Products Manufacturers Assoc. Applicant must be high school senior.
Basis for selection: Applicant must demonstrate financial need.
Additional information: For further information or an application contact Juvenile Products Manufacturers Association members directly.
    Amount of award: $2,000
Contact:
Juvenile Products Manufacturers Association

Kappa Omicrom Nu Honor Society

Kappa Omicrom Nu Fellowships and Grants

Type of award: Scholarship.
Intended use: For full-time master's, doctoral study at accredited graduate institution in United States.
Eligibility: Applicant or parent must be member of Kappa Omicron Nu.
Basis for selection: Major/career interest in dietetics/nutrition; home economics; hotel/restaurant management; interior design. Applicant must demonstrate depth of character, leadership, seriousness of purpose and high academic achievement.
Application requirements: Recommendations.
Additional information: Food sciences, family and consumer sciences, family development, and textiles/apparel are also acceptable as fields of study/intended careers.
    Amount of award: $2,000
    Number of awards: 6
    Number of applicants: 12
    Application deadline: January 15, April 1
    Notification begins: April 1, May 15
    Total amount awarded: $12,000
Contact:
Kappa Omicron Nu Honor Society
4990 Northwind Drive
Suite 140
East Lansing, MI 48823-5031

Keane, Inc.

Keane Educational Scholarship

Type of award: Scholarship.
Intended use: For undergraduate study at accredited vocational, 2-year or 4-year institution.
Eligibility: Applicant or parent must be employed by Keane, Inc. Applicant must be high school senior.
Additional information: Must be child of employee of Keane, Inc. For further information or application contact Keane, Inc. directly.
   Amount of award: $10,000

Kinko's

Ryan Orfalea Scholarship

Type of award: Scholarship, renewable.
Intended use: For undergraduate study at accredited vocational, 2-year or 4-year institution.
Eligibility: Applicant or parent must be employed by Kinko's.
Basis for selection: Applicant must demonstrate financial need.
Additional information: For further information or an application contact Kinko's directly.
   Amount of award: $500-$3,000

Knights of Columbus

Bishop Greco Graduate Fellowship

Type of award: Scholarship, renewable.
Intended use: For full-time master's study at graduate institution in United States.
Eligibility: Applicant or parent must be member of Knights of Columbus. Applicant must be Roman Catholic. Applicant must be U.S. citizen.
Basis for selection: Major/career interest in education, special. Applicant must demonstrate seriousness of purpose.
Application requirements: Recommendations, essay, transcript and proof of eligibility.
Additional information: Must be preparing to teach mentally retarded children and be active member, spouse, or child of active or deceased member of Knights of Columbus. Special consideration to applicants attending Catholic graduate school.
   Amount of award: $500-$2,000
   Number of awards: 5
   Number of applicants: 10
   Application deadline: May 1
   Notification begins: June 20
Contact:
Knights of Columbus
Committee on Fellowships
P.O. Box 1670
New Haven, CT 06507-0901
Phone: 203-772-2130

Knights of Columbus Student Loan

Type of award: Loan, renewable.
Intended use: For undergraduate, master's study at vocational, 2-year or 4-year institution.
Eligibility: Applicant or parent must be member of Knights of Columbus. Applicant must be enrolled in high school, Roman Catholic. Applicant must be U.S. citizen or permanent resident.
Basis for selection: Applicant must demonstrate financial need.
Application requirements: Proof of eligibility.
Additional information: Available to Knights of Columbus members, wives, and children of active and deceased members, and Columbian Squires members. Nonmember priests, brothers, nuns, seminarians and postulants at college, seminary, and postgraduate levels also eligible. Contact for loan amounts and interest rates.
Contact:
Knights of Columbus
Student Loan Committee
P.O. Box 1670
New Haven, CT 06507
Phone: 2037722130

Matthews/Swift Educational Trust - Military Dependants

Type of award: Scholarship, renewable.
Intended use: For full-time undergraduate study at 4-year institution in United States. Designated institutions: Catholic.
Eligibility: Applicant or parent must be member of Knights of Columbus. Applicant must be Roman Catholic. Applicant must be U.S. citizen. Applicant must be child of disabled veteran or deceased veteran during Korean War, Persian Gulf, WW II or Vietnam. Parent must have been Knights of Columbus member when killed in action or died as result of service-connected disability. Parent disabled as result of military conflict must have kept Knights of Columbus membership active.
Application requirements: Proof of eligibility.
Additional information: Award pays tuition, room, board, books and incidental fees at a Catholic college. No application deadline.
   Number of awards: 10
   Number of applicants: 10
Contact:
Knights of Columbus
Director of Scholarship Aid
P.O. Box 1670
New Haven, CT 06507-0901
Phone: 203-772-2130

Matthews/Swift Educational Trust - Police/Firefighters

Type of award: Scholarship, renewable.
Intended use: For full-time undergraduate study at 4-year institution in United States. Designated institutions: Catholic.
Eligibility: Applicant or parent must be member of Knights of Columbus. Applicant must be Roman Catholic. Applicant must be U.S. citizen. Applicant's parent must have been killed or disabled in work-related accident as fire fighter or police officer.
Application requirements: Proof of eligibility.
Additional information: Award pays tuition, room, board,

books and incidental fees at a Catholic college. No application deadline.
- **Number of awards:** 10
- **Number of applicants:** 10

Contact:
Knights of Columbus
Director of Scholarship Aid
P.O. Box 1670
New Haven, CT 06507
Phone: 203-772-2130

Pro Deo/Pro Patria Scholarship

Type of award: Scholarship, renewable.
Intended use: For full-time undergraduate study at 4-year institution in United States. Designated institutions: Catholic.
Eligibility: Applicant or parent must be member of Knights of Columbus. Applicant must be high school senior, Roman Catholic. Applicant must be U.S. citizen.
Basis for selection: Applicant must demonstrate high academic achievement.
Application requirements: Recommendations, essay, transcript and proof of eligibility.
Additional information: Must be Knights of Columbus member in good standing, or son or daughter of such a member or deceased member, or a member in good standing of Columbian Squires.

- **Amount of award:** $1,500
- **Number of awards:** 50
- **Number of applicants:** 500
- **Application deadline:** March 1
- **Notification begins:** May 15
- **Total amount awarded:** $297,000

Contact:
Knights of Columbus
Director of Scholarship Aid
P.O. Box 1670
New Haven, CT 06510
Phone: 203-772-2130

Kohler Co.

Kohler Scholarship

Type of award: Scholarship, renewable.
Intended use: For freshman study.
Eligibility: Applicant or parent must be employed by Kohler Co.
Basis for selection: Applicant must demonstrate financial need.
Additional information: For further information or an application contact Kohler Co. directly.
- **Amount of award:** $500-$2,000

Komag

Kids College Scholarship

Type of award: Scholarship.
Intended use: For undergraduate study at accredited vocational, 2-year or 4-year institution.
Eligibility: Applicant or parent must be employed by Komag. Applicant must be high school senior.
Basis for selection: Applicant must demonstrate financial need.
Additional information: Must be child of employee of Komag. For further information or application contact Komag directly.
- **Amount of award:** $500-$2,500

Krause Publications, Inc.

Partners in Publishing Sons and Daughters Scholarship Program

Type of award: Scholarship.
Intended use: For undergraduate study at accredited vocational, 2-year or 4-year institution.
Eligibility: Applicant or parent must be employed by Krause Publications, Inc. Applicant must be high school senior.
Basis for selection: Applicant must demonstrate financial need.
Additional information: For further information or application contact Krause Publication, Inc. directly.
- **Amount of award:** $1,500-$2,000

Laidlaw, Inc.

Laidlaw Scholarship Program

Type of award: Scholarship.
Intended use: For undergraduate study at vocational, 2-year or 4-year institution.
Eligibility: Applicant or parent must be employed by Laidlaw, Inc. Applicant must be high school senior.
Additional information: For further information or an application contact Laidlaw Incorporated directly.
- **Amount of award:** $2,000-$3,000

Lambda Alpha

National Dean's List Scholarship

Type of award: Scholarship.
Intended use: For senior study at accredited 4-year or graduate institution in United States.
Eligibility: Applicant or parent must be member of Lambda Alpha. Applicant must be permanent resident.
Basis for selection: Major/career interest in anthropology.

Applicant must demonstrate seriousness of purpose and high academic achievement.
Application requirements: Recommendations, transcript and nomination by faculty sponsor from department of anthropology. Curriculum vitae.
Additional information: Institution must have chartered Lambda Alpha chapter. Must be life member of Lambda Alpha. Apply in junior year.

Amount of award:	$1,000
Number of awards:	5
Number of applicants:	3
Application deadline:	March 1
Notification begins:	April 1
Total amount awarded:	$5,000

National Scholarship Award

Type of award: Scholarship.
Intended use: For full-time master's, doctoral study at accredited graduate institution in United States.
Eligibility: Applicant or parent must be member of Lambda Alpha. Applicant must be permanent resident.
Basis for selection: Major/career interest in anthropology. Applicant must demonstrate seriousness of purpose and high academic achievement.
Application requirements: Recommendations, essay, transcript and nomination by faculty sponsor from department of anthropology. Curriculum vitae, sample of scholarly writing, statement of professional intent.
Additional information: Institution must have chartered Lambda Alpha chapter. Must be life member of Lambda Alpha. College seniors entering graduate school and graduate students may apply.

Number of awards:	22
Number of applicants:	8
Application deadline:	March 1
Notification begins:	June 1
Total amount awarded:	$4,000

Contact:
Lambda Alpha
Department of Anthropology
Ball State University
Muncie, IN 47306-1099
Phone: 765-285-1577
Website: www.geocities.com/collegepark

Lang Family Foundation, Inc.

Lang Family Foundation Scholarship

Type of award: Scholarship, renewable.
Intended use: For undergraduate study at vocational, 2-year or 4-year institution.
Eligibility: Applicant or parent must be employed by The Lang Family Foundation, Inc. Applicant must be high school senior.
Additional information: For further information or an application contact Lang Family Foundation Incoporated directly.

Amount of award:	$2,000

Latin American Educational Foundation

Latin American Educational Scholarship

Type of award: Scholarship, renewable.
Intended use: For undergraduate, graduate or non-degree study at accredited postsecondary institution in Colorado.
Eligibility: Applicant or parent must be member of Latin American Educational Foundation. Applicant must be residing in Colorado.
Basis for selection: Applicant must demonstrate financial need and high academic achievement.
Application requirements: Recommendations, essay, transcript and proof of eligibility.
Additional information: Must have Hispanic heritage or be actively involved in the Hispanic community. Minimum GPA 3.0 required. SAT or ACT scores required. Recipients must fulfill 10 hours of community service during the award year.

Amount of award:	$200-$500
Application deadline:	March 1
Notification begins:	June 15

Contact:
Executive Director
930 West 7th Avenue
Denver, CO 80204
Website: theedge.com/laef

Leggett & Platt Scholarship Foundation

Leggett & Platt Scholarship Program for Children of Employees

Type of award: Scholarship.
Intended use: For undergraduate study at vocational, 2-year or 4-year institution.
Eligibility: Applicant or parent must be employed by Leggett & Platt Scholarship Foundation. Applicant must be high school senior.
Additional information: For further information or an application contact Leggett & Platt Scholarship Foundation directly.

Amount of award:	$1,000-$1,500

Leroy C. Dettman Foundation, Inc.

Leroy C. Dettman Foundation Scholarship

Type of award: Scholarship.
Intended use: For full-time undergraduate or graduate study at accredited postsecondary institution in United States.

Eligibility: Applicant or parent must be employed by Interim Services. Applicant must be U.S. citizen.
Basis for selection: Applicant must demonstrate financial need and high academic achievement.
Application requirements: Transcript and proof of eligibility.
Additional information: Employees of Interim Services given preference, but anyone can apply. ACT or SAT scores required. Copy of parent's most recent year's income taxes required; copy of own return is required if applicant is financially independent.

Amount of award:	$500-$2,500
Number of awards:	82
Number of applicants:	360
Application deadline:	March 15
Notification begins:	June 15
Total amount awarded:	$70,800

Contact:
Leroy C. Dettman Foundation, Inc.
4401 North Federal Highway
Suite 201
Boca Raton, FL 33431
Phone: 561-367-9811

LeRoy T. Carlson Pioneers Education Foundation

Pioneers Scholarship

Type of award: Scholarship.
Intended use: For undergraduate study at vocational, 2-year or 4-year institution.
Eligibility: Applicant or parent must be employed by LeRoy T. Carlson Pioneers Education Foundation. Applicant must be high school senior.
Additional information: For further information or an application contact LeRoy T. Carlson Pioneers Education Foundation directly.
   Amount of award: $1,500

Levi Strauss Foundation

Levi Strauss Foundation Scholarship

Type of award: Scholarship, renewable.
Intended use: For undergraduate study at accredited vocational, 2-year or 4-year institution.
Eligibility: Applicant or parent must be employed by Levi Strauss & Co.
Basis for selection: Applicant must demonstrate financial need.
Additional information: For further information or an application contact Levi Strauss & Co. directly.
   Amount of award: $750-$2,000

Lew Wasserman Scholarship Foundation-MCA/Universal

Lew Wasserman College Scholarship

Type of award: Scholarship.
Intended use: For undergraduate study at accredited vocational, 2-year or 4-year institution.
Eligibility: Applicant or parent must be employed by Universal Studios - Southern California. Applicant must be high school senior.
Basis for selection: Applicant must demonstrate financial need.
Additional information: For further information or application contact Lew Wasserman Scholarship Foundation-MCA Universal directly.
   Amount of award: $500-$4,000
Contact:
Lew Wasserman Scholarship Foundation

LifeScan

LifeScan Scholarship Program/Dana Pettengill Scholarship Fund

Type of award: Scholarship, renewable.
Intended use: For freshman study at 2-year or 4-year institution.
Eligibility: Applicant or parent must be employed by Lifescan Inc.
Additional information: For further information or an application, contact LifeScan Inc. directly.
   Amount of award: $1,250

Lifetouch

Richard P. Erickson Scholarship Program

Type of award: Scholarship.
Intended use: For undergraduate study at vocational, 2-year or 4-year institution.
Eligibility: Applicant or parent must be employed by Lifetouch. Applicant must be high school senior.
Additional information: For further information or an application contact Lifetouch directly.
   Amount of award: $2,500

Link-Belt Construction Equipment Company

Link-Belt Scholarship Program

Type of award: Scholarship.
Intended use: For undergraduate study at vocational, 2-year or 4-year institution.
Eligibility: Applicant or parent must be employed by Link-Belt Construction Equipment Company. Applicant must be high school senior.
Additional information: For further information or an application contact Link-Belt Constuction Equipment Company directly.
    Amount of award: $750-$1,500

Loctite Corporation

Loctite Scholarship Program

Type of award: Scholarship.
Intended use: For undergraduate or graduate study at accredited vocational, 2-year or 4-year institution.
Eligibility: Applicant or parent must be employed by Loctite Corporation.
Additional information: For further information or an application contact Loctite Corporation directly.
    Amount of award: $500-$2,000

Logan Airport Association, Inc.

Logan Airport Scholarship Trust Scholarship

Type of award: Scholarship.
Intended use: For undergraduate study at vocational, 2-year or 4-year institution.
Eligibility: Applicant or parent must be employed by The Logan Airport Association, Inc. Applicant must be high school senior.
Additional information: For further information or an application contact Logan Airport Association Incorporated directly.
    Amount of award: $1,000-$2,000

Loyal Christian Benefit Association

College Vocational-Technical Scholarship

Type of award: Scholarship, renewable.
Intended use: For full-time freshman, sophomore, junior or senior study at vocational or 4-year institution.
Eligibility: Applicant or parent must be member of Loyal Christian Benefit Association. Applicant must be high school senior.
Basis for selection: Applicant must demonstrate financial need and high academic achievement.
Application requirements: Transcript and proof of eligibility. SAT/ACT scores.
Additional information: Must be LCBA member for one to three years prior to application.
    Amount of award: $1,000
    Number of awards: 20
    Number of applicants: 90
    Application deadline: October 15
    Total amount awarded: $20,000
Contact:
Loyal Christian Benefit Association
P.O. Box 13005
Erie, PA 16514-1305
Phone: 814-453-4331
Fax: 814-453-3211

Nontraditional Undergraduate Grant

Type of award: Scholarship.
Intended use: For freshman, sophomore, junior or senior study at vocational or 4-year institution.
Eligibility: Applicant or parent must be member of Loyal Christian Benefit Association.
Application requirements: Essay and proof of eligibility.
    Amount of award: $500
    Number of awards: 5
    Number of applicants: 5
    Application deadline: November 1
    Total amount awarded: $1,500
Contact:
Loyal Christian Benefit Association
Grant Program
P.O. Box 13005
Erie, PA 16514-1305
Phone: 814-453-4331
Fax: 814-453-3211

Retraining Grant

Type of award: Scholarship.
Intended use: For freshman, sophomore, junior or senior study at vocational or 4-year institution.
Eligibility: Applicant or parent must be member of Loyal Christian Benefit Association.
Application requirements: Essay and proof of eligibility.
Additional information: Must be unemployed at least one

year after holding job for at least two years. Must have been LCBA member for at least two years prior to application and have high school diploma or GED.
- Amount of award: $500
- Number of awards: 5
- Application deadline: June 1
- Total amount awarded: $2,500

Contact:
Loyal Christian Benefit Association
Grant Program
P.O. Box 13005
Erie, PA 16514-1305
Phone: 814-453-4331
Fax: 814-453-3211

Lucent Technologies Business Communications Systems

Arthur Howell and Michael McCarthy Scholarship Award

Type of award: Scholarship.
Intended use: For undergraduate study at vocational, 2-year or 4-year institution.
Eligibility: Applicant or parent must be employed by Lucent Technologies-BCS. Applicant must be high school senior.
Additional information: For further information or an application contact Lucent Technologies Business Communications Systems directly.
- Amount of award: $1,000

John N. Williams Scholarship Award

Type of award: Scholarship.
Intended use: For undergraduate study at vocational, 2-year or 4-year institution.
Eligibility: Applicant or parent must be employed by Lucent Technologies-BCS. Applicant must be high school senior.
Additional information: For further information or an application contact Lucent Technologies Business Communications Systems directly.
- Amount of award: $2,000

Lucent Technologies-BCS

Donald Edwin Lauchner Scholarship

Type of award: Scholarship.
Intended use: For freshman study at vocational, 2-year or 4-year institution.
Eligibility: Applicant or parent must be employed by Lucent Technologies-BCS. Applicant must be high school senior.
Additional information: For further information or an application contact Lucent Technologies-BCS directly.
- Amount of award: $1,000

Luck Stone Corporation

Luck Stone Scholarship

Type of award: Scholarship.
Intended use: For undergraduate study at accredited vocational, 2-year or 4-year institution.
Eligibility: Applicant or parent must be employed by Luck Stone Corporation.
Basis for selection: Applicant must demonstrate financial need.
Additional information: For further information or an application contact Luck Stone Corporation directly.
- Amount of award: $1,000-$3,000

Lund Food Holdings, Inc.

Russell T. Lund Scholarship Program

Type of award: Scholarship.
Intended use: For undergraduate study at vocational, 2-year or 4-year institution.
Eligibility: Applicant or parent must be employed by Lund Food Holdings, Inc. Applicant must be high school senior.
Additional information: For further information or an application contact Lund Food Holdings Incoporated directly.
- Amount of award: $2,000

Lyden Memorial Scholarship Fund

Lynden Memorial Scholarship Program

Type of award: Scholarship.
Intended use: For undergraduate or graduate study at 4-year or graduate institution.
Eligibility: Applicant or parent must be employed by Lynden Memorial Scholarship Fund. Applicant must be high school senior.
Additional information: For further information or an application contact Lyden Memorial Scholarship Fund directly.
- Amount of award: $1,000

MagneTek, Inc.

MagneTek Scholarship

Type of award: Scholarship, renewable.
Intended use: For freshman study at vocational, 2-year or 4-year institution.
Eligibility: Applicant or parent must be employed by MagneTek, Inc. Applicant must be high school senior.

Additional information: For further information or an application contact Magnetek Incorporated directly.
- Amount of award: $1,000-$3,000

Maine Innkeepers Association

Maine Innkeepers Association - Scholarships for Maine Residents

Type of award: Scholarship, renewable.
Intended use: For full-time freshman study at accredited 4-year institution in United States. Designated institutions: Institution with fully accredited programs in Hotel Administration or Culinary Arts.
Eligibility: Applicant or parent must be member of Maine Innkeepers Association. Applicant must be high school senior. Applicant must be U.S. citizen or permanent resident residing in Maine.
Basis for selection: Major/career interest in culinary arts; hotel/restaurant management; hospitality administration/management. Applicant must demonstrate financial need and high academic achievement.
Application requirements: Recommendations, essay and transcript.
Additional information: A minimum GPA of 2.5 is required. Open to graduates and high school seniors who are children of Maine Innkeepers Association members or employees of Maine Innkeepers Association properties.
- Amount of award: $500-$1,500
- Number of awards: 3
- Application deadline: May 1

Contact:
Award Coordinator
305 Commercial St.
Portland, ME 04101

Maine Innkeepers Association Affiliates Scholarship

Type of award: Scholarship.
Intended use: For full-time undergraduate study at accredited 4-year institution in United States.
Eligibility: Applicant or parent must be member of Maine Innkeepers Association. Applicant must be U.S. citizen or permanent resident residing in Maine.
Basis for selection: Major/career interest in culinary arts; hotel/restaurant management; hospitality administration/management.
Application requirements: Recommendations, essay and transcript.
Additional information: Open to members of the immediate family whose property has been an active member of MIA for at least three consecutive years and whose dues are current or a member of the immediate family (owner/manager) of a business of an allied member who has been a member of the MIA for at least three years and whose dues are current or a student of person(s) who have been gainfully employed full-time for at least three years by an active member property or a business of an allied member and endorsed by the owner/manager.
- Amount of award: $500-$1,500
- Number of awards: 4
- Number of applicants: 34
- Application deadline: May 1

Contact:
Executive Director
305 Commercial St.
Portland, ME 04101

Maine State APWU

Maine State APWU Scholarship

Type of award: Scholarship.
Intended use: For freshman study at accredited postsecondary institution.
Eligibility: Applicant or parent must be member of Maine State American Postal Workers Union. Applicant must be high school senior.
Application requirements: Essay, transcript and proof of eligibility.
Additional information: SAT scores required. This scholarship will be payable in 4 equal installments of $375 per annum.
- Amount of award: $1,500
- Application deadline: June 5

Contact:
Scholarship Coordinator
P.O. Box 1964
Portland, ME 04104

Maine State APWU-Portland Local #458

Arthur J. McBride Memorial Scholarship

Type of award: Scholarship.
Intended use: For undergraduate study at accredited postsecondary institution.
Eligibility: Applicant or parent must be member of Maine State American Postal Workers Union. Applicant must be high school senior.
Application requirements: Essay, transcript and proof of eligibility. Portland, Maine area Local APWU.
Additional information: SAT scores required. In any year that a grandchild of Arthur McBride graduates from high school, applies for this scholarship and meets the requirements, that grandchild shall be awarded the scholarship. If feasible, a second scholarship will be made available that year. The scholarship will be for up to $2,000 for a 4-year program, paid at $500 per year. The first $500 shall be sent to the recipient after successful completion of the first year, and will be paid yearly thereafter based on the continuation of acceptable grades.

Amount of award: $2,000
Application deadline: June 5
Contact:
Scholarship Coordinator
P.O. Box 3111
Portland, ME 04104

Mapco Coal Inc. and Affiliates

Mapco Coal Scholars Program

Type of award: Scholarship, renewable.
Intended use: For freshman study at vocational, 2-year or 4-year institution.
Eligibility: Applicant or parent must be employed by MAPCO Coal Inc. and Affiliates. Applicant must be high school senior.
Additional information: For further information or an application contact Mapco Coal Incorporated and Affiliates directly.
Amount of award: $500-$1,000

MAPCO Inc.

MAPCO Scholars Program

Type of award: Scholarship, renewable.
Intended use: For freshman study at accredited vocational, 2-year or 4-year institution.
Eligibility: Applicant or parent must be employed by MAPCO Inc.
Additional information: For further information or an application contact MAPCO Inc. directly.
Amount of award: $500-$1,000

Marion Merrell Dow, Inc.

Dow Educational Assistance Program

Type of award: Scholarship, renewable.
Intended use: For undergraduate study at accredited vocational, 2-year or 4-year institution.
Eligibility: Applicant or parent must be employed by Marion Merrell Dow Inc.
Basis for selection: Applicant must demonstrate financial need.
Additional information: For further information or an application contact Marion Merrell Dow Inc. directly.
Amount of award: $1,000-$4,000

Marten Transport, Ltd.

Randolph L. Marten Scholarship Program

Type of award: Scholarship.
Intended use: For undergraduate study at vocational, 2-year or 4-year institution.
Eligibility: Applicant or parent must be employed by Marten Transport, Ltd. Applicant must be high school senior.
Additional information: For further information or an application contact Marten Transport Ltd. Directly.
Amount of award: $1,000

Marvin Lumber and Cedar Company

Marvin Lumber and Cedar/Marvin Windows Scholarship

Type of award: Scholarship, renewable.
Intended use: For undergraduate study at accredited vocational, 2-year or 4-year institution.
Eligibility: Applicant or parent must be employed by Marvin Lumber & Cedar Co.
Basis for selection: Applicant must demonstrate financial need.
Additional information: For further information or an application contact Marvin Lumber and Cedar Co. directly.
Amount of award: $500-$1,000

Massachusetts Glass Dealers Association

Massachusetts Glass Dealers Scholarship

Type of award: Scholarship.
Intended use: For undergraduate study at accredited vocational, 2-year or 4-year institution.
Eligibility: Applicant or parent must be member of Massachusetts Glass Dealers Association.
Basis for selection: Applicant must demonstrate financial need.
Additional information: For further information or an application contact Massachusetts Glass Dealers Association directly.
Amount of award: $300-$750

Material Sciences Corporation

Material Sciences Corporation Dependent Scholarship Award Program

Type of award: Scholarship.
Intended use: For freshman, sophomore, junior or senior study at accredited vocational, 2-year or 4-year institution.
Eligibility: Applicant or parent must be employed by Material Sciences Corporation.
Additional information: For further information and an application contact Material Sciences Corporation directly.
   Amount of award: $3,000

Materials Research Corporation

MRC Scholar Program

Type of award: Scholarship, renewable.
Intended use: For freshman study at accredited vocational, 2-year or 4-year institution.
Eligibility: Applicant or parent must be employed by Materials Research Corporation.
Additional information: For further information or an application contact Materials Research Corporation directly.
   Amount of award: $2,000

Mattel Inc.

Mattel Foundation Scholarship Program

Type of award: Scholarship, renewable.
Intended use: For undergraduate study at accredited vocational, 2-year or 4-year institution.
Eligibility: Applicant or parent must be employed by Mattel, Inc.
Basis for selection: Applicant must demonstrate financial need.
Additional information: For further information or an application contact Mattel, Inc. directly.
   Amount of award: $500-$2,500

MBK Real Estate Ltd.

MBK Real Estate Ltd. Scholarship Program

Type of award: Scholarship.
Intended use: For undergraduate or graduate study at vocational, 2-year, 4-year or graduate institution.
Eligibility: Applicant or parent must be employed by MBK Real Estate Ltd. Applicant must be high school senior.
Additional information: For further information or an application contact MBK Real Estate Ltd. directly.
   Amount of award: $500-$2,500

McKesson Foundation, Inc.

McKesson Pharmacy Scholarship Program

Type of award: Scholarship, renewable.
Intended use: For full-time junior, senior or first professional study.
Eligibility: Applicant or parent must be employed by McKesson Corporation. Applicant must be U.S. citizen or permanent resident.
Basis for selection: Major/career interest in pharmacy/pharmaceutics/pharmacology.
Application requirements: Recommendations, essay and transcript.
Additional information: For further information or an application contact Mckesson Foundation directly.
   Amount of award: $1,000
   Number of awards: 50,000
   Application deadline: October 1
   Notification begins: November 15

McKesson Scholarship Program

Type of award: Scholarship.
Intended use: For undergraduate study at accredited vocational, 2-year or 4-year institution.
Eligibility: Applicant or parent must be employed by McKesson Corporation.
Basis for selection: Applicant must demonstrate financial need.
Additional information: For further information or an application contact McKesson Foundation, Inc. directly.
   Amount of award: $1,000-$2,500

MDU Resources Foundation

MDU Resources Employees' Scholarship Program

Type of award: Scholarship.
Intended use: For undergraduate or graduate study at accredited vocational, 2-year or 4-year institution.
Eligibility: Applicant or parent must be employed by MDU Resources Group, Inc.
Additional information: For further information or an application contact MDU Resources Foundation directly.
    Amount of award: $1,000

Medical Arts Press, Inc.

MAP Scholarship Program

Type of award: Scholarship.
Intended use: For undergraduate study at vocational, 2-year or 4-year institution.
Eligibility: Applicant or parent must be employed by Medical Arts Press, Inc. Applicant must be high school senior.
Additional information: For further information or an application contact Medical Arts Press Incorporated directly.
    Amount of award: $1,000-$2,500

Medtronic, Inc.

Palmer J. Hermundslie Memorial Scholarship Program

Type of award: Scholarship, renewable.
Intended use: For undergraduate study at vocational, 2-year or 4-year institution.
Eligibility: Applicant or parent must be employed by Medtronic, Inc. Applicant must be high school senior.
Additional information: For further information or an application contact Medtronic Incorporated directly.
    Amount of award: $500-$3,000

Merrill Corporation

Kenneth F. Merrill Scholarship

Type of award: Scholarship.
Intended use: For undergraduate study at accredited postsecondary institution.
Eligibility: Applicant or parent must be employed by Merrill Corporation. Applicant must be high school senior.
Additional information: For further information or an application contact Merrill Corporation directly.
    Amount of award: $1,500

Metal-Matic, Inc.

Jerome J. Bliss Memorial Fund

Type of award: Scholarship.
Intended use: For undergraduate study at accredited vocational, 2-year or 4-year institution.
Eligibility: Applicant or parent must be employed by Metal-Matic, Inc.
Basis for selection: Applicant must demonstrate financial need.
Additional information: For further information or an application contact Metal-Matic, Inc. directly.
    Amount of award: $600-$1,500

Metro Electrical Training Trust

Metro Electrical Training Scholarship

Type of award: Scholarship.
Intended use: For freshman study at 2-year or 4-year institution.
Eligibility: Applicant or parent must be employed by Metro Electric. Applicant must be high school senior. Applicant must be U.S. citizen or permanent resident residing in Oregon.
Basis for selection: Applicant must demonstrate high academic achievement.
Application requirements: Essay, transcript and proof of eligibility.
Additional information: Must have minimum 2.5 GPA. Available to children of Metro employers including those participating in the Metro Electrical Training Trust agreement. Program administered by Oregon State Scholarship Commission. Contact Metro Electric human resources office or Commission (send business-sized SASE).
    Amount of award: $1,000
    Number of awards: 2
    Number of applicants: 24
    Application deadline: March 1
    Notification begins: July 31
    Total amount awarded: $2,000
Contact:
Oregon State Scholarship Commission
Grant Department
1500 Valley River Drive, Suite 100
Eugene, OR 97401

Metropolitan Life Foundation

Pathways Scholarship

Type of award: Scholarship, renewable.
Intended use: For undergraduate study at accredited vocational, 2-year or 4-year institution.
Eligibility: Applicant or parent must be employed by Metropolitan Life Insurance Co.
Basis for selection: Applicant must demonstrate financial need.
Additional information: For further information or an application, contact Metropolitan Life directly.
   Amount of award: $500-$3,000

Michelin Tire Corporation

NTDRA Scholarship

Type of award: Scholarship, renewable.
Intended use: For undergraduate study at accredited vocational, 2-year or 4-year institution.
Eligibility: Applicant or parent must be employed by Michelin/NTDRA. Applicant must be high school senior.
Basis for selection: Applicant must demonstrate financial need.
Additional information: Must be child of member of NTDRA. For further information or application contact NTDRA directly.
   Amount of award: $1,250-$2,500

Michigan Petroleum Assoc./ Michigan Assoc. of Convenience Stores

Michigan Petroleum Asso./ Michigan Asso. of Converntion Store Scholarship Program

Type of award: Scholarship.
Intended use: For undergraduate study at vocational, 2-year or 4-year institution.
Eligibility: Applicant or parent must be employed by Michigan Petroleum Assoc./Michigan Assoc. Of Convenience. Applicant must be high school senior.
Additional information: For further information or an application contact Michigan Petroleum Association/Michigan Association Of Convenience Stores directly.
   Amount of award: $500

Microfibres, Inc.

Microfibres Scholarship Program

Type of award: Scholarship, renewable.
Intended use: For undergraduate study at vocational, 2-year or 4-year institution.
Eligibility: Applicant or parent must be employed by Microfibres, Inc. Applicant must be high school senior.
Additional information: For further information or an application contact Microfibres Incorporated directly.
   Amount of award: $1,500

Midrex Direct Reduction Corporation

Donald Beggs Scholarship

Type of award: Scholarship.
Intended use: For undergraduate study at accredited 4-year institution.
Eligibility: Applicant or parent must be employed by Midrex Direct Reduction Corporation.
Additional information: For further information or an application contact Midrex Direct Reduction Corporation directly.
   Amount of award: $2,000

Midwest Express Airlines

Flying Higher Scholarship Program

Type of award: Scholarship, renewable.
Intended use: For undergraduate study at vocational, 2-year or 4-year institution.
Eligibility: Applicant or parent must be employed by Midwest Express Airlines. Applicant must be high school senior.
Additional information: For further information or an application contact Midwest Express Arilines directly.
   Amount of award: $2,000

Millipore Corporation

Millipore Foundation Scholarship Program

Type of award: Scholarship, renewable.
Intended use: For freshman study at accredited vocational, 2-year or 4-year institution.
Eligibility: Applicant or parent must be employed by Millipore Corporation.
Additional information: For further information or an application contact Millipore Corporation directly.
   Amount of award: $5,000

Minnesota Mutual

Minnesota Mutual Presidents' Scholarship Fund

Type of award: Scholarship, renewable.
Intended use: For freshman study at accredited 4-year institution.
Eligibility: Applicant or parent must be employed by Minnesota Mutual.
Basis for selection: Applicant must demonstrate financial need.
Additional information: For further information or an application contact Minnesota Mutual directly.
   Amount of award: $750-$1,500

Minolta Corporation

Five-Plus Club Scholarship

Type of award: Scholarship.
Intended use: For freshman study at accredited 2-year or 4-year institution.
Eligibility: Applicant or parent must be employed by Minolta Corporation.
Additional information: For further information or an application contact Minolta Corporation directly.
   Amount of award: $3,000-$5,000

Mitsui USA Foundation

Mitsui USA's Sons & Daughters Scholarship Program

Type of award: Scholarship, renewable.
Intended use: For undergraduate study at vocational, 2-year or 4-year institution.
Eligibility: Applicant or parent must be employed by The Mitsui USA Foundation. Applicant must be high school senior.
Additional information: For further information or an application contact Mitsui USA Foundation directly.
   Amount of award: $2,000

Mobile Gas Service Corporation

Blue Flame Scholarship

Type of award: Scholarship, renewable.
Intended use: For freshman, sophomore, junior or senior study at accredited vocational, 2-year or 4-year institution.
Eligibility: Applicant or parent must be employed by Mobil Gas Service Corporation.
Basis for selection: Applicant must demonstrate financial need.
Additional information: Must be child of employee of Mobile Gas Service Corporation. For further information and an application contact Mobile Gas Service Corporation directly.
   Amount of award: $500-$2,000

Moen Incorporated

Bill O'Neill Memorial Scholarship

Type of award: Scholarship.
Intended use: For freshman study at accredited 2-year or 4-year institution.
Eligibility: Applicant or parent must be employed by Moen.
Additional information: For further information or an application contact Moen directly.
   Amount of award: $2,500

Moyer Packing Company

Moyer Packing Company Sons and Daughters Scholarship Program

Type of award: Scholarship, renewable.
Intended use: For undergraduate study at vocational, 2-year or 4-year institution.
Eligibility: Applicant or parent must be employed by Moyer Packing Company. Applicant must be high school senior.
Additional information: For further information or an application contact Moyer Packing Company Sons and Daughters Scholarship Program directly.
   Amount of award: $1,000

NAACP Special Contribution Fund

Agnes Jones Jackson Scholarship

Type of award: Scholarship, renewable.
Intended use: For full-time undergraduate or graduate study at 2-year, 4-year or graduate institution.
Eligibility: Applicant or parent must be member of National Assoc. for Advancement of Colored People.
Application requirements: Recommendations, transcript and proof of eligibility. Financial Aid Forms.
Additional information: Must be current regular member of NAACP for at least one year or fully paid life member. Minimum 2.5 GPA for undergraduates, 3.0 for graduate students. Award amounts: $1,500 undergraduate, $2,500 graduate. Gradutes can be full-time or part-time. Applications may be requested after January 1; include business-sized SASE.
   Amount of award: $1,500-$2,500
   Application deadline: April 30

Roy Wilkins Scholarship

Type of award: Scholarship.
Intended use: For full-time freshman study at accredited 2-year or 4-year institution in United States.
Eligibility: Applicant or parent must be member of National Assoc. for Advancement of Colored People. Applicant must be high school senior.
Application requirements: Recommendations, transcript and proof of eligibility. One recommendation should be from NAACP officer. Financial Aid Forms.
Additional information: Minimum 2.5 GPA. Applications may be requested after January 1. Include business sized SASE.
    Amount of award: $1,000
    Application deadline: April 30

Sutton Education Scholarship

Type of award: Scholarship, renewable.
Intended use: For full-time undergraduate or graduate study at accredited 2-year, 4-year or graduate institution in United States.
Eligibility: Applicant or parent must be member of National Assoc. for Advancement of Colored People. Applicant must be U.S. citizen.
Basis for selection: Major/career interest in education. Applicant must demonstrate high academic achievement.
Application requirements: Recommendations, transcript and proof of eligibility. One recommendation should be from NAACP officer. Financial Aid Forms.
Additional information: For students majoring in field with teacher certification. Undergraduates must have minimum 2.5 GPA, graduate students must have minimum 3.0 GPA. Applications available in January. Include business-sized SASE. Graduate students may be enrolled part-time.
    Amount of award: $1,000-$2,000
    Application deadline: April 30
    Notification begins: July 31

Willems Scholarship

Type of award: Scholarship, renewable.
Intended use: For full-time undergraduate or graduate study at accredited 2-year, 4-year or graduate institution in United States.
Eligibility: Applicant or parent must be member of National Assoc. for Advancement of Colored People. Applicant must be male. Applicant must be U.S. citizen.
Basis for selection: Major/career interest in engineering; chemistry; physics; mathematics. Applicant must demonstrate financial need and high academic achievement.
Application requirements: Recommendations, transcript and proof of eligibility. One recommendation should be from NAACP officer. Financial Aid Forms.
Additional information: Applications may be requested after January 1. Send 9" by 12" SASE. Minimum 2.0 GPA for undergraduates and 3.0 GPA for graduates. Award is $2,000 for undergraduate, $3,000 for graduate students. Graduate students may be enrolled part-time.

    Amount of award: $2,000-$3,000
    Application deadline: April 30
    Notification begins: August 31
Contact:
NAACP Special Contribution Fund
Education Department
4805 Mount Hope Drive
Baltimore, MD 21215-3297

Nash Finch Company

Nash Finch Scholarship Program

Type of award: Scholarship, renewable.
Intended use: For freshman study at accredited vocational, 2-year or 4-year institution.
Eligibility: Applicant or parent must be employed by Nash Finch Company. Applicant must be African American.
Basis for selection: Applicant must demonstrate financial need.
Additional information: For further information or an application contact Nash Finch Company directly.
    Amount of award: $200-$2,500

National Advisory Group

Convenience Stores/Petroleum Marketers Association Scholarship Program

Type of award: Scholarship.
Intended use: For undergraduate study at vocational, 2-year or 4-year institution.
Eligibility: Applicant or parent must be employed by National Advisory Group. Applicant must be high school senior.
Additional information: For further information or an application contact National Advisory Group directly.
    Amount of award: $1,500

National Alpha Lambda Delta Honor Society

Alpha Lambda Delta Fellowship

Type of award: Scholarship.
Intended use: For full-time master's, doctoral or first professional study at accredited graduate institution in United States.
Eligibility: Applicant or parent must be member of Alpha Lambda Delta.
Basis for selection: Applicant must demonstrate depth of character, leadership, seriousness of purpose, service orientation and high academic achievement.
Application requirements: Recommendations, essay, transcript and proof of eligibility.
Additional information: Contribution to Alpha Lambda Delta

Chapter is considered when awarding fellowship. Must have cumulative GPA of 3.5.

Amount of award:	$3,000
Number of awards:	16
Number of applicants:	159
Application deadline:	January 15
Notification begins:	April 1
Total amount awarded:	$48,000

Contact:
National Alpha Lambda Delta
P.O. Box 4403
Macon, GA 31208-4403

National Art Materials Trade Association

National Art Materials Scholarship

Type of award: Scholarship.
Intended use: For full-time or half-time undergraduate or graduate study at accredited postsecondary institution in or outside United States.
Eligibility: Applicant or parent must be member of National Art Materials Trade Association.
Basis for selection: Applicant must demonstrate depth of character, seriousness of purpose, service orientation, financial need and high academic achievement.
Application requirements: Recommendations, essay, transcript and proof of eligibility.

Amount of award:	$1,000
Number of awards:	3
Number of applicants:	83
Application deadline:	March 1
Notification begins:	June 1
Total amount awarded:	$3,000

Contact:
National Art Materials Trade Association
10115 Kincey Avenue
Hunterville, NC 28078
Phone: 800-746-2682

National Association of Black Accountants

National Scholarship Program

Type of award: Scholarship.
Intended use: For full-time sophomore, junior or master's study at 4-year or graduate institution.
Eligibility: Applicant or parent must be member of National Assoc. of Black Accountants. Applicant must be of minority background.
Basis for selection: Major/career interest in accounting; business. Applicant must demonstrate depth of character, leadership and service orientation.
Application requirements: Essay, transcript and proof of eligibility. Personal biography, student aid report.
Additional information: Applicants must have GPA 2.5 or better.

Amount of award:	$500-$6,000
Number of awards:	35
Number of applicants:	120
Application deadline:	December 31
Notification begins:	April 15
Total amount awarded:	$85,000

Contact:
National Association of Black Accountants
National Scholarship Program
7249-A Hanover Parkway
Greenbelt, MD 20770
Phone: 301-474-6222
Website: www.nabainc.org

National Association of Letter Carriers

Costa G. Lemonopoulus Scholarship

Type of award: Scholarship, renewable.
Intended use: For full-time freshman, sophomore, junior or senior study at 4-year institution in Florida. Designated institutions: Any 4-year Florida college or university, or St. Petersburg Junior College.
Eligibility: Applicant or parent must be member of National Association of Letter Carriers.
Basis for selection: Applicant must demonstrate high academic achievement.
Application requirements: Essay and transcript. SAT I scores.
Additional information: High school seniors may apply as well. Three awards reserved for Pinellas County, Florida residents.

Amount of award:	$500-$1,000
Number of awards:	20
Number of applicants:	75
Application deadline:	June 1

Contact:
National Association of Letter Carriers
Thomas R. Bruckman/Pinellas County Community
P.O. Box 205
Clearwater, FL 34617-0205

William C. Doherty Scholarship

Type of award: Scholarship, renewable.
Intended use: For full-time freshman, sophomore, junior or senior study at accredited 4-year institution.
Eligibility: Applicant or parent must be member of National Association of Letter Carriers. Applicant must be high school senior.
Basis for selection: Applicant must demonstrate financial need and high academic achievement.
Application requirements: Recommendations, essay, transcript and proof of eligibility. SAT/ACT scores.
Additional information: For children of active, retired, or

deceased letter carriers. Parent must be National Association of Letter Carriers member in good standing at least one year prior to candidate's application.

Amount of award:	$800
Number of awards:	60
Number of applicants:	1,600
Application deadline:	December 31
Notification begins:	April 15
Total amount awarded:	$48,000

Contact:
National Association of Letter Carriers
100 Indiana Avenue NW
Washington, DC 20001

National Association of Secondary School Principals

Secondary School Principals National Honor Society Scholarship

Type of award: Scholarship.
Intended use: For full-time freshman, sophomore, junior or senior study at accredited 4-year institution in United States.
Eligibility: Applicant or parent must be member of National Honor Society. Applicant must be U.S. citizen or permanent resident.
Basis for selection: Applicant must demonstrate high academic achievement.
Application requirements: Recommendations, essay, transcript and nomination by local National Honor Society chapter.
Additional information: Consult high school National Honor Society adviser for information.

Amount of award:	$1,000
Number of awards:	250
Number of applicants:	3,000
Application deadline:	February 3
Notification begins:	May 8
Total amount awarded:	$250,000

Contact:
National Association of Secondary School Principals
Department of Student Activities
1904 Association Drive
Reston, VA 20191

National Athletic Trainers Association

Athletic Trainers Curriculum Scholarship

Type of award: Scholarship.
Intended use: For full-time undergraduate, master's study at accredited 4-year or graduate institution.
Eligibility: Applicant or parent must be member of National Athletic Trainers Association.
Basis for selection: Major/career interest in athletic training. Applicant must demonstrate high academic achievement.
Application requirements: Recommendations, essay, transcript and proof of eligibility.
Additional information: Minimum 3.0 GPA required. Contact association for list of designated institutions. Must be planning a career in athletic training.

Amount of award:	$2,000
Application deadline:	February 1
Notification begins:	April 15

Contact:
National Athletic Trainers Association
2952 Stemmons Freeway
Dallas, TX 75247

Athletic Trainers Postgraduate Scholarship

Type of award: Scholarship.
Intended use: For full-time graduate study at 4-year or graduate institution.
Eligibility: Applicant or parent must be member of National Athletic Trainers Association.
Basis for selection: Applicant must demonstrate high academic achievement.
Application requirements: Recommendations, essay, transcript and proof of eligibility.
Additional information: Must be a senior planning graduate study. Minimum 3.0 GPA required. Must be planning for a career in athletic training. Must be sponsored by a certified athletic trainer.

Amount of award:	$2,000
Number of awards:	50
Application deadline:	February 1
Notification begins:	April 15
Total amount awarded:	$100,000

Contact:
National Athletic Trainers Association
Research and Education Foundation
2952 Stemmons Freeway
Dallas, TX 75247
Website: www.nata.org

Athletic Trainers Student Writing Contest

Type of award: Scholarship.
Intended use: For undergraduate or graduate study at 2-year, 4-year or graduate institution.
Eligibility: Applicant or parent must be member of National Athletic Trainers Association.
Basis for selection: Competition in Writing/journalism. Must submit paper related to the athletic training profession. Major/career interest in athletic training. Applicant must demonstrate high academic achievement.
Application requirements: Essay and proof of eligibility.
Additional information: Entrants must submit one original and two copies. Topic may be case report, literature review, experimental report, analysis of training room techniques, etc. Must not have been published, or be under consideration for publication.

Amount of award:	$800
Number of awards:	1
Application deadline:	March 1
Notification begins:	April 15

Contact:
National Athletic Trainers Association Student Writing Contest
Deloss Brubaker, EdD, ATC
Life University, 1269 Barclay Circle
Marietta, GA 30060

Athletic Trainers Undergraduate Scholarship

Type of award: Scholarship.
Intended use: For full-time junior, senior study.
Eligibility: Applicant or parent must be member of National Athletic Trainers Association.
Basis for selection: Applicant must demonstrate high academic achievement.
Application requirements: Recommendations, essay, transcript and proof of eligibility.
Additional information: Minimum 3.0 GPA required. Intention to pursue the profession of athletic training as career required. Must be sponsored by a certified athletic trainer.

Amount of award:	$2,000
Number of awards:	50
Application deadline:	February 1
Notification begins:	April 15
Total amount awarded:	$100,000

Contact:
National Athletic Trainers Association
Research and Education Foundation
2952 Stemmons Freeway
Dallas, TX 75247
Website: www.nata.org

National Beta Club

Beta Club Scholarship

Type of award: Scholarship, renewable.
Intended use: For full-time undergraduate, non-degree study at vocational, 2-year or 4-year institution.
Eligibility: Applicant or parent must be member of National Beta Club. Applicant must be high school senior.
Basis for selection: Applicant must demonstrate depth of character, leadership and service orientation.
Application requirements: $10 application fee. Recommendations, essay, transcript and proof of eligibility. SAT I/ACT scores required. Must be Beta Club member. Application and information must be obtained from Beta sponsor at high school.
Additional information: Must be senior member of National Beta Club and reside in state in which Beta membership is held. 171 recipients get one time award of $1,000. Four recipients get larger awards (from $1,000 to $2,500 per year) renewable for three years. Limit of two nominees per school. See school Beta Club sponsor fro more information.

Amount of award:	$1,000-$2,500
Number of awards:	187
Number of applicants:	858
Application deadline:	December 10
Notification begins:	April 6
Total amount awarded:	$199,000

National Black Nurse's Association

Black Nurse's Scholarship

Type of award: Scholarship.
Intended use: For undergraduate or graduate study.
Eligibility: Applicant or parent must be member of National Black Nurses' Association. Applicant must be African American.
Basis for selection: Major/career interest in nursing; nurse practitioner. Applicant must demonstrate seriousness of purpose and service orientation.
Application requirements: Recommendations, essay and transcript. evidence of participation in both student nursing activities and the African-American community.
Additional information: Applicants must be currently enrolled in a nursing program and have at least one full year of school left. Call the association after September 1998 for information on any changes to their program.

Amount of award:	$500-$2,000
Number of awards:	5
Number of applicants:	500
Application deadline:	April 15
Notification begins:	July 1

Contact:
National Black Nurse's Association
1511 K Street N.W.
Suite 415
Washington, DC 20005
Phone: 202-393-6870
Fax: 202-347-3808

National Computer Systems

National Computer Systems Scholarship

Type of award: Scholarship, renewable.
Intended use: For undergraduate study at accredited vocational, 2-year or 4-year institution.
Eligibility: Applicant or parent must be employed by National Computer Systems.
Basis for selection: Applicant must demonstrate financial need.
Additional information: For further information or an application contact National Computer Systems directly.

Amount of award:	$500-$3,000

National Federation of Republican Women

Betty Rendel Scholarship

Type of award: Scholarship.
Intended use: For full-time sophomore, junior or senior study at accredited 4-year institution in United States.
Eligibility: Applicant or parent must be member of Republican Party. Applicant must be female. Applicant must be U.S. citizen.
Basis for selection: Major/career interest in political science/government; economics. Applicant must demonstrate depth of character, leadership, patriotism, seriousness of purpose and high academic achievement.
Application requirements: Recommendations, essay and transcript. Applications are to be sent to the state president (call NFRW or visit the NFRW web page for name and address) who may nominate one candidate for the national competition.
Additional information: All applications are examined by the Federation state president, who will decide whether they go to a committee for a second round of screening.
- Amount of award: $1,000
- Number of awards: 1
- Number of applicants: 15
- Application deadline: August 9
- Notification begins: September 30
- Total amount awarded: $1,000

Contact:
Scholarship Coordinator
National Federation of Republican Women
124 North Alfred Street
Alexandria, VA 22314
Phone: 703-548-9688
Website: www.nfrw.org

Dorothy Andrews Kabis Internship

Type of award: Internship.
Intended use: For full-time junior, senior study at accredited 4-year institution.
Eligibility: Applicant or parent must be member of Republican Party. Applicant must be female. Applicant must be U.S. citizen.
Basis for selection: Major/career interest in political science/government; law; economics; communications. Applicant must demonstrate depth of character, leadership, patriotism, seriousness of purpose and service orientation.
Application requirements: Recommendations, essay and transcript.
Additional information: One month unpaid internship at the national headquarters near Washington, D.C. Airfare and housing paid for. All applications are examined by the Federation state president, who will decide whether they go to a committee for a second round of screening.
- Number of awards: 4
- Number of applicants: 12
- Application deadline: February 1
- Notification begins: , March 14

Contact:
Internship Coordinator
National Federation of Republican Women
124 North Alfred Street
Alexandria, VA 22314
Website: www.nfrw.org

Pathfinder Scholarship

Type of award: Scholarship.
Intended use: For full-time or half-time junior, senior or graduate study at accredited 4-year or graduate institution in United States.
Eligibility: Applicant or parent must be member of Republican Party. Applicant must be female. Applicant must be U.S. citizen.
Basis for selection: Major/career interest in chemistry; mental health/therapy; nursing; psychology. Applicant must demonstrate depth of character, seriousness of purpose and service orientation.
Application requirements: Recommendations, essay and transcript.
Additional information: The applicant must focus on substance abuse prevention. All applications are examined by the Federation state president, who will decide whether they go to a committee for a second round of screening.
- Amount of award: $2,000
- Number of awards: 2
- Number of applicants: 24
- Application deadline: February 1, February 14
- Notification begins: March 14, March 14
- Total amount awarded: $4,000

Contact:
Programs Administrator/Scholarship Coordinator
National Federation of Republican Women
124 North Alfred Street
Alexandria, VA 22314
Phone: 703-548-9688
Website: www.nfrw.org

National Foster Parent Association, Inc.

Benjamin Eaton Scholarship

Type of award: Scholarship.
Intended use: For undergraduate, non-degree study.
Eligibility: Applicant or parent must be member of National Foster Parent Association. Applicant must be high school senior.
Basis for selection: Applicant must demonstrate financial need.
Application requirements: Recommendations, essay and transcript.
Additional information: Preference to applicants with physical disability or handicap. Foster children, adoptive and birth children of foster parents are eligible.

National Foster Parent Association, Inc.: Benjamin Eaton Scholarship

Amount of award:	$1,000
Number of awards:	5
Number of applicants:	60
Application deadline:	March 31
Notification begins:	May 31
Total amount awarded:	$5,000

Contact:
Scholarship Coordinator
I S Office, Benjamin Eaton Scholarship Fund
9 Dartmoor Drive
Crystal Lake, IL 60014
Phone: 800-557-5238
Fax: 815-455-1522
Website: www.nfpninc.org

National Future Farmers of America

National Future Farmers of America Scholarship Program

Type of award: Scholarship.
Intended use: For undergraduate or graduate study at accredited postsecondary institution in United States.
Eligibility: Applicant or parent must be member of National FFA Organization. Applicant must be U.S. citizen or permanent resident.
Basis for selection: Major/career interest in agriculture; agricultural economics; agricultural education; agribusiness.
Additional information: Sponsors over 180 scholarships for members. Eligibility and deadlines vary. Contact FFA for further information.
Contact:
National Future Farmers of America
5632 Mt. Vernon Memorial Highway
P.O. Box 15160
Alexandria, VA 22309
Website: www.agriculture.com/contents/FFA/programs

National Ground Water Association

Ground Water Association Auxiliary Scholarship

Type of award: Scholarship.
Intended use: For full-time undergraduate study at accredited 2-year or 4-year institution.
Eligibility: Applicant or parent must be member of National Ground Water Association.
Basis for selection: Applicant must demonstrate depth of character, leadership, patriotism, seriousness of purpose, service orientation, financial need and high academic achievement.
Application requirements: Essay, transcript and proof of eligibility.
Additional information: Minimum GPA 2.5.

Application deadline:	April 1
Notification begins:	April 30

Contact:
National Ground Water Association
Rosemary Purtee
601 Dempsey Road
Westerville, OH 43081
Phone: 800-551-7379
Website: www.ngwa.org

National Rifle Association

Jeanne E. Bray Law Enforcement Dependents Scholarship

Type of award: Scholarship, renewable.
Intended use: For freshman, sophomore, junior, senior or graduate study at accredited 2-year, 4-year or graduate institution in United States.
Eligibility: Applicant or parent must be member of National Rifle Association. Applicant must be U.S. citizen.
Application requirements: Recommendations, essay, transcript and proof of eligibility.
Additional information: Parent must be active, deceased, discharged, or retired law enforcement officer and member of National Rifle Association. Applicant must also be an NRA member. Minimum 2.0 GPA, SAT I combined score of 950 or ACT score of 25 required.

Amount of award:	$500-$2,000
Number of awards:	3
Number of applicants:	6
Application deadline:	November 15
Notification begins:	February 1

Contact:
National Rifle Association - attn: Sandy S. Elkin
Jeanne E. Bray Memorial Scholarship
11250 Waples Mill Road
Fairfax, VA 22030

National Roofing Foundation

North East Roofing Contractors Association Scholarship

Type of award: Scholarship, renewable.
Intended use: For undergraduate study.
Eligibility: Applicant or parent must be member of National Roofing Contractors Association. Applicant must be U.S. citizen residing in Connecticut or Massachusetts or Maine or New Hampshire or Rhode Island or Vermont or New Jersey or New York or Pennsylvania.
Basis for selection: Major/career interest in architecture; engineering, construction; construction.
Additional information: Request for application must be accompanied by SASE with 64 cent postage. Applicants

pursuing a curriculum related to the roofing industry will be considered.
- **Amount of award:** $1,000
- **Number of awards:** 1
- **Application deadline:** January 10
- **Notification begins:** March 31
- **Total amount awarded:** $1,000

Contact:
National Roofing Foundation
10255 West Higgins Road
Suite 600
Rosemont, IL 60018
Phone: 847-299-9070

Roofing Industry Scholarship

Type of award: Scholarship, renewable.
Intended use: For full-time undergraduate study at vocational, 2-year or 4-year institution.
Eligibility: Applicant or parent must be member of National Roofing Contractors Association.
Basis for selection: Applicant must demonstrate depth of character, seriousness of purpose, financial need and high academic achievement.
Application requirements: Recommendations and essay.
Additional information: Only immediate family of National Roofing Contractors Association members eligible. Requests for application must be accompanied by SASE with 64 cent postage.
- **Amount of award:** $1,000
- **Number of awards:** 2
- **Number of applicants:** 100
- **Application deadline:** January 8
- **Notification begins:** May 1
- **Total amount awarded:** $2,000

Contact:
National Roofing Foundation (NRF)
10255 West Higgins Road
Suite 600
Rosemont, IL 60018
Phone: 847-299-9070

National Scholarship Trust Fund of the Graphic ArtsFoundation

National Scholarship Trust Fund of the Graphic Arts Undergraduate Scholarships and Graduate Fellowships

Type of award: Scholarship, renewable.
Intended use: For full-time undergraduate or graduate study at 4-year or graduate institution in United States.
Eligibility: Applicant or parent must be member of Kappa Kappa Gamma. Applicant must be female. Applicant must be Canada Only.
Basis for selection: Applicant must demonstrate high academic achievement.
Application requirements: Recommendations, essay and transcript.
Additional information: Must be a member of the Kappa Kappa Gamma organization.
- **Amount of award:** $1,000-$1,500
- **Number of applicants:** 200
- **Application deadline:** February 1

Contact:
Kappa Kappa Gamma Foundation
P.O. Box 38
Columbus, GA 43216-0038
Website: www.kappakappagamma.org

National Semiconductor Corporation

Charles E. Sporck Scholarship Program

Type of award: Scholarship, renewable.
Intended use: For freshman study at 2-year or 4-year institution.
Eligibility: Applicant or parent must be employed by National Semiconductor Corporation. Applicant must be high school senior.
Additional information: For further information or an application contact National Semiconductor Corporation directly.
- **Amount of award:** $2,000

National Society of Black Engineers

Fulfilling the Legacy Scholarship

Type of award: Scholarship, renewable.
Intended use: For undergraduate or graduate study.
Eligibility: Applicant or parent must be member of National Society of Black Engineers. Applicant must be U.S. citizen.
Basis for selection: Major/career interest in engineering. Applicant must demonstrate seriousness of purpose and high academic achievement.
Application requirements: Portfolio.
- **Application deadline:** December 1

Contact:
1425 Duke St.
Alexandria, VA 22314
Phone: 703-549-2207

National Society of Black Engineers Oratorical Contest

Type of award: Scholarship.
Intended use: For undergraduate study.
Eligibility: Applicant or parent must be member of National Society of Black Engineers. Applicant must be African American. Applicant must be U.S. citizen.
Basis for selection: Competition in Science project. Diction,

annunciation, clarity of content, eye contact and gestures, demonstrated knowledge of the NSBE.
Additional information: Deadline varies; contact sponsor for information.
Contact:
National Society of Black Engineers
1454 Duke Street
Alexandria, VA 22314
Phone: 703-549-2207
Fax: 703-683-5312
Website: www.nsbe.org

National Society of Black Engineers Scholars Program

Type of award: Scholarship, renewable.
Intended use: For full-time undergraduate or graduate study at accredited 4-year or graduate institution in United States.
Eligibility: Applicant or parent must be member of National Society of Black Engineers. Applicant must be African American. Applicant must be U.S. citizen.
Basis for selection: Major/career interest in engineering. Applicant must demonstrate seriousness of purpose.
Application requirements: Recommendations and transcript.
Additional information: Award amounts vary. Contact office for more information.
- Amount of award: $300
- Number of awards: 700
- Application deadline: May 30

Contact:
Placement Services
1454 Duke St.
Alexandria, VA 22314
Website: www.nsbe.org

National Society of Black Engineers/Boeing Flight Competition

Type of award: Scholarship.
Intended use: For undergraduate study.
Eligibility: Applicant or parent must be member of National Society of Black Engineers. Applicant must be African American. Applicant must be U.S. citizen.
Basis for selection: Competition in Science project. Participants design, construct, and fly airplanes made of balsa wood, which are judged on longest time flown, longest distance flown, and best design.
- Amount of award: $500-$1,000
- Number of awards: 5
- Application deadline: March 11

Contact:
National Society of Black Engineers
1454 Duke Street
Alexandria, VA 22314
Phone: 703-549-2207, ext. 215
Fax: 703-683-5312
Website: www.nsbe.org

National Society of Black Engineers/GE African American Forum Scholarship

Type of award: Scholarship, renewable.
Intended use: For sophomore, junior or senior study.
Eligibility: Applicant or parent must be member of National Society of Black Engineers. Applicant must be African American. Applicant must be U.S. citizen.
Basis for selection: Major/career interest in business; engineering.
Additional information: Minimum GPA 3.2.
- Application deadline: December 5

Contact:
National Society of Black Engineers
1454 Duke Street
Alexandria, VA 22314
Phone: 703-549-2207
Fax: 703-683-5312
Website: www.nsbe.org

National Society of Black Engineers/Undergraduate Students in Technical Research Awards Program

Type of award: Scholarship.
Intended use: For undergraduate study.
Eligibility: Applicant or parent must be member of National Society of Black Engineers. Applicant must be African American. Applicant must be U.S. citizen.
Basis for selection: Competition in Science project. Student research projects will be displayed visually, (via charts, maps, photographs, etc.) and judged based on their content and the result of a question and answer session.
- Amount of award: $50-$1,000
- Application deadline: November 22

Contact:
National Society of Black Engineers
1454 Duke Street
Alexandria, VA 22314
Phone: 703-549-2207
Fax: 703-683-5312
Website: www.nsbe.org

National Society of the Sons of the American Revolution

Sons of the American Revolution Eagle Scout Scholarship

Type of award: Scholarship.
Intended use: For undergraduate study.
Eligibility: Applicant or parent must be member of Boy Scouts of America, Eagle Scouts. Applicant must be male.
Basis for selection: Applicant must demonstrate depth of character, leadership and patriotism.

Application requirements: Essay.
Additional information: Eligible Eagle Scouts must have passed their board of review between July 1 and June 30.
    Amount of award: $1,000-$5,000
    Number of awards: 2
    Application deadline: December 31
    Total amount awarded: $6,000
Contact:
National Society of the Sons of the American Revolution
1000 South Fourth Street
Louisville, KY 40203

Native Daughters of the Golden West

Native Daughters of the Golden West Scholarship

Type of award: Scholarship, renewable.
Intended use: For full-time undergraduate or graduate study at accredited postsecondary institution in California.
Eligibility: Applicant or parent must be member of Native Daughters of the Golden West. Applicant must be U.S. citizen residing in California. Applicant must be in military service, veteran, child of active service person or veteran.
Basis for selection: Major/career interest in business; education; social work; nursing. Applicant must demonstrate depth of character, leadership, patriotism, seriousness of purpose, service orientation, financial need and high academic achievement.
Application requirements: Recommendations, essay, transcript and nomination by local club or parlor.
Additional information: High school seniors may also apply.
    Amount of award: $100-$1,500
    Number of awards: 9
    Number of applicants: 35
    Application deadline: April 15
    Notification begins: May 15
Contact:
Native Daughters of the Golden West
543 Baker Street
San Francisco, CA 94117-1405

NBC News and Tom Brokaw

Tom Brokaw Scholarship Program

Type of award: Scholarship.
Intended use: For undergraduate or graduate study at vocational, 2-year, 4-year or graduate institution.
Eligibility: Applicant or parent must be employed by NBC News and Tom Brokaw. Applicant must be high school senior.
Additional information: For further information or an application contact NBC News and Tom Brokaw directly.
    Amount of award: $5,000

NEC America, Inc.

NEC America Scholarship Program

Type of award: Scholarship.
Intended use: For undergraduate study at accredited vocational, 2-year or 4-year institution.
Eligibility: Applicant or parent must be employed by NEC America, Inc.
Basis for selection: Applicant must demonstrate financial need.
Additional information: For further information or an application contact NEC America, Inc. directly.
    Amount of award: $1,500-$3,000

New England Association of Independent Tire Dealers

New England Association of Independent Tire Dealers Scholarship

Type of award: Scholarship.
Intended use: For undergraduate study at accredited vocational, 2-year or 4-year institution.
Eligibility: Applicant or parent must be member of New England Assoc. of Independent Tire Dealers.
Basis for selection: Applicant must demonstrate financial need.
Additional information: For further information or an application contact New England Association of Independent Tire Dealers directly.
    Amount of award: $500

New Jersey State Policemen's Benevolent Association, Inc.

New Jersey State Policemen's Benevolent Association Scholarship

Type of award: Scholarship.
Intended use: For full-time freshman study at accredited vocational, 2-year or 4-year institution in United States.
Eligibility: Applicant or parent must be member of Patrolmen's Benevolent Association. Applicant must be high school senior. Applicant must be U.S. citizen.
Basis for selection: Applicant must demonstrate financial need and high academic achievement.
Application requirements: Recommendations and transcript.
Additional information: Application available from parent member's police department. Parent must belong to the PBA.

Amount of award: $700
Number of awards: 35
Number of applicants: 150
Application deadline: May 1
Total amount awarded: $24,500

Contact:
New Jersey State Policemen's Benevolent Association, Inc.
158 Main Street
Woodbridge, NJ 07095
Phone: 732-636-8860

New United Motor Manufacturing Scholarship Foundation

New United Motor Manufacturing Scholarship Program

Type of award: Scholarship, renewable.
Intended use: For undergraduate study at vocational, 2-year or 4-year institution in United States.
Eligibility: Applicant or parent must be employed by New United Motor Manufacturing, Inc. Applicant must be high school senior.
Additional information: For further information or application contact New United Motor Manufacturing, Scholarship directly.
Amount of award: $1,500

Contact:
New United Motor Manufacturing, Inc.

New York Operations Division of the Futures Industry Association

Futures Industry Association Scholarship

Type of award: Scholarship.
Intended use: For freshman, sophomore, junior or senior study at accredited 2-year or 4-year institution.
Eligibility: Applicant or parent must be member of New York Operations Division of the Futures Industry.
Application requirements: Proof of eligibility.
Additional information: For further information and an application contact New York Operations Division of the Futures Industry Association directly.
Amount of award: $1,000

New York State Grange

Grange Denise Scholarship

Type of award: Scholarship.
Intended use: For full-time undergraduate study at 2-year or 4-year institution.
Eligibility: Applicant or parent must be member of New York State Grange. Applicant must be residing in New York.
Basis for selection: Major/career interest in agriculture. Applicant must demonstrate financial need.
Application requirements: Recommendations and transcript.
Amount of award: $1,000
Number of awards: 3
Number of applicants: 25
Application deadline: April 15
Notification begins: June 15
Total amount awarded: $3,000

Grange Student Loan Fund

Type of award: Loan.
Intended use: For full-time undergraduate or graduate study.
Eligibility: Applicant or parent must be member of New York State Grange. Applicant must be residing in New York.
Amount of award: $1,000
Application deadline: April 15
Notification begins: June 15

Grange Susan W. Freestone Education Award

Type of award: Scholarship.
Intended use: For full-time undergraduate or graduate study at 2-year or 4-year institution in United States.
Eligibility: Applicant or parent must be member of New York State Grange. Applicant must be residing in New York.
Amount of award: $500-$1,000
Number of awards: 3
Number of applicants: 5
Application deadline: April 15
Notification begins: June 15
Total amount awarded: $2,000

Contact:
New York State Grange
100 Grange Place
Cortland, NY 13045
Phone: 607-756-7553

Newberry Library

South Central Modern Language Association Fellowship

Type of award: Research grant.
Intended use: For doctoral, postgraduate study. Designated institutions: The Newberry Library.
Eligibility: Applicant or parent must be member of South Central Modern Language Assoc.

Basis for selection: Major/career interest in history; music; linguistics; literature.
Application requirements: Recommendations, proof of eligibility and research proposal. Curriculum vitae, proposed project description limited to 1500 words.
Additional information: Must be a doctoral candidate or hold a Ph.D. Applicants from outside the region must have been members for three continuous years to be eligible. Monthly stipends are $800.

Amount of award:	$800-$2,400
Application deadline:	March 1

Contact:
Newberry Library
60 West Walton Street
Chicago, IL 60610-3380
Phone: 312-943-9090
Website: www.newberry.org

NIKE, Inc.

Nike Scholarship Fund

Type of award: Scholarship, renewable.
Intended use: For undergraduate study at accredited postsecondary institution.
Eligibility: Applicant or parent must be employed by Nike, Inc. Applicant must be high school senior.
Basis for selection: Applicant must demonstrate financial need.
Additional information: For further information or an application, contact Nike, Inc., directly.

Amount of award:	$500-$3,000

Non-Commissioned Officers Association

Mary Baracco Scholarship

Type of award: Scholarship, renewable.
Intended use: For full-time undergraduate study at accredited vocational, 2-year or 4-year institution in United States.
Eligibility: Applicant or parent must be member of Non-Commissioned Officers Association. Applicant must be U.S. citizen. Applicant must be child of active service person, veteran or disabled veteran, spouse of active service person, veteran or disabled veteran who served in the Army, Air Force, Marines, Navy, Coast Guard or Reserves/National Guard. Non-commissioned officers.
Basis for selection: Competition in Writing/journalism. Best essay on Americanism.
Application requirements: Recommendations, essay and transcript. 2 letters of recommendation from school, 1 personal letter of recommendation from an adult who is not a relative, autobiography, ACT or SAT scores (for academic applications only), and a 200 word or more composition on Americanism is required.
Additional information: Best essay on Americanism. Recipient is chosen from pool of Non-Commissioned Officers Association scholarship applicants.

Amount of award:	$1,000
Number of awards:	1
Application deadline:	March 31
Notification begins:	May 15
Total amount awarded:	$1,000

Contact:
Non-Commissioned Officers Association
P.O. Box 33610
San Antonio, TX 78265
Phone: 210-653-6161

Non-Commissioned Officers Association Scholarship Fund

Type of award: Scholarship, renewable.
Intended use: For undergraduate study.
Eligibility: Applicant or parent must be member of Non-Commissioned Officers Association.
Application requirements: Recommendations and transcript. A handwritten autobiography. ACT or SAT scores. A composition on Americanism (not less than 200 words). A letter of intent describing degreed course of study, plans for completion of a degreed program, and a closing paragraph on "What a College Degree Means to Me".
Additional information: Children of members must be under age 25 to receive initial grant.

Amount of award:	$900-$1,000
Number of awards:	36
Number of applicants:	500
Application deadline:	March 31

Contact:
Non-Commissioned Officers Association
P.O. Box 33610
10635 IH 35 North
San Antonio, TX 78265
Phone: 210-653-6161

Pentagon Federal Credit Union Grant

Type of award: Scholarship.
Intended use: For full-time undergraduate study at accredited vocational, 2-year or 4-year institution in United States.
Eligibility: Applicant or parent must be member of Non-Commissioned Officers Association. Applicant must be U.S. citizen or permanent resident. Applicant must be child of active service person, veteran or disabled veteran, spouse of active service person, veteran or disabled veteran who served in the Army, Air Force, Marines, Navy, Coast Guard or Reserves/National Guard. Non-commissioned officers.
Basis for selection: Applicant must demonstrate high academic achievement.
Application requirements: Recommendations, essay and transcript. 2 letters of recommendation from school, 1 personal letter of recommendation from an adult who is not a relative, autobiography, scores ACT or SAT (for academic application only), and a 200 word or more composition on Americanism is required.
Additional information: Recipient is chosen from pool of Non-Commissioned Officers Association scholarship applicants. "B" average required.

Non-Commissioned Officers Association: Pentagon Federal Credit Union Grant

Amount of award:	$1,000
Number of awards:	1
Application deadline:	March 31
Notification begins:	May 15
Total amount awarded:	$1,000

Contact:
Non-Commissioned Officers Association
P.O. Box 33610
San Antonio, TX 78265
Phone: 210-653-6161

Scholarship for Children of Members of the Non-Commissioned Officers Association

Type of award: Scholarship, renewable.
Intended use: For full-time undergraduate study at accredited vocational, 2-year or 4-year institution in United States.
Eligibility: Applicant or parent must be member of Non-Commissioned Officers Association. Applicant must be U.S. citizen or permanent resident. Applicant must be child of active service person, veteran or disabled veteran who served in the Army, Air Force, Marines, Navy, Coast Guard or Reserves/National Guard.
Basis for selection: Applicant must demonstrate high academic achievement.
Application requirements: Recommendations, essay and transcript. 2 letters of recommendation from school, 1 personal letter of recommendation from an adult who is not a relative, autobiography, ACT or SAT scores (for academic applications only), and a 200 word or more composition on Americanism is required.
Additional information: Applicant can apply for either academic or vocational grant.

Amount of award:	$900
Number of awards:	22
Number of applicants:	400
Application deadline:	March 31
Notification begins:	May 15
Total amount awarded:	$19,800

Contact:
Non-Commissioned Officers Association
P.O. Box 33610
San Antonio, TX 78265
Phone: 210-653-6161

Scholarship Grant for Spouses of Members of the Non-Commissioned Officers Association

Type of award: Scholarship, renewable.
Intended use: For full-time undergraduate study at vocational, 2-year or 4-year institution in United States.
Eligibility: Applicant or parent must be member of Non-Commissioned Officers Association. Applicant must be U.S. citizen. Applicant must be spouse of active service person, veteran or disabled veteran. Non-commissioned officers.
Basis for selection: Applicant must demonstrate high academic achievement.
Application requirements: Recommendations, essay and transcript. Copy of high school diploma or GED, letter of intent describing degreed course of study, plans for completion of a degreed program, and a closing paragraph on "What a College Degree Means to Me.".
Additional information: Must be spouse of member of Non-Commissioned Officers Association. Recipient must apply for membership in Non-Commissioned Officers Association membership categories.

Amount of award:	$900
Number of awards:	10
Number of applicants:	200
Application deadline:	March 31
Notification begins:	May 15
Total amount awarded:	$9,000

Contact:
Non-Commissioned Officers Association
P.O. Box 33610
San Antonio, TX 78265
Phone: 210-653-6161

William T. Green Grant

Type of award: Scholarship, renewable.
Intended use: For full-time undergraduate study at accredited vocational, 2-year or 4-year institution in United States.
Eligibility: Applicant or parent must be member of Non-Commissioned Officers Association. Applicant must be U.S. citizen or permanent resident. Applicant must be child of active service person, veteran or disabled veteran, spouse of active service person or disabled veteran who served in the Army, Air Force, Marines, Navy, Coast Guard or Reserves/National Guard. Non-commissioned officers.
Basis for selection: Applicant must demonstrate high academic achievement.
Application requirements: Recommendations, essay and transcript. 2 letters of recommendation from school, 1 personal letter of recommendation from an adult who is not a relative, autobiography, copy of ACT or SAT scores (for academic applications only), and a 200 word or more composition on Americanism is required.
Additional information: Awarded for best high-school record. Recipient is chosen from pool of applicants for all Non-Commissioned Officers Association scholarships.

Amount of award:	$1,000
Number of awards:	1
Application deadline:	March 31
Notification begins:	May 15
Total amount awarded:	$1,000

Contact:
Non-Commissioned Officers Association
P.O. Box 33610
San Antonio, TX 78265
Phone: 210-653-6161

NorAm Energy Corporation Endowment

NorAm Employees Scholarship Program

Type of award: Scholarship, renewable.
Intended use: For undergraduate study at vocational, 2-year or 4-year institution.
Eligibility: Applicant or parent must be employed by NorAM Energy Corporation Endowment. Applicant must be high school senior.
Additional information: For further information or application contact NorAm Energy Corporation Endowment directly.
    Amount of award: $2,000

Norand Corporation

George Chadima Memorial Scholarship

Type of award: Scholarship.
Intended use: For undergraduate study at accredited 4-year institution.
Eligibility: Applicant or parent must be employed by Norand Corporation.
Additional information: For further information or an application contact Norand Corporation directly.
    Amount of award: $3,000

North American Limousin Foundation

Limouselle Scholarship

Type of award: Scholarship.
Intended use: For undergraduate study at 2-year or 4-year institution.
Eligibility: Applicant or parent must be member of North American Limousin Junior Association.
Basis for selection: Major/career interest in agriculture; agribusiness; agricultural economics; agricultural education. Applicant must demonstrate depth of character, leadership, patriotism, seriousness of purpose, service orientation, financial need and high academic achievement.
Application requirements: Transcript and proof of eligibility.
Additional information: Must rank in top third of class.
    Amount of award: $500
    Number of awards: 3
    Number of applicants: 16
    Application deadline: June 15
    Notification begins: July 25
    Total amount awarded: $1,500

Limousin Award of Excellence

Type of award: Scholarship.
Intended use: For undergraduate study at 2-year or 4-year institution.
Eligibility: Applicant or parent must be member of North American Limousin Junior Association.
Basis for selection: Major/career interest in agriculture. Applicant must demonstrate depth of character, leadership, patriotism, seriousness of purpose, service orientation, financial need and high academic achievement.
Application requirements: Interview, recommendations and proof of eligibility.
Additional information: Experience with Limousin cattle preferred.
    Amount of award: $750
    Number of awards: 3
    Number of applicants: 4
    Application deadline: May 15
    Notification begins: July 25
    Total amount awarded: $2,250
Contact:
North American Limousin Foundation
7383 South Alton Way
Englewood, CO 80112

North Pacific Lumber Company

Nor Pac Scholarship Program

Type of award: Scholarship, renewable.
Intended use: For freshman, sophomore, junior or senior study at accredited vocational, 2-year or 4-year institution.
Eligibility: Applicant or parent must be employed by North Pacific Lumber Co.
Basis for selection: Applicant must demonstrate financial need.
Additional information: For further information and an application contact North Pacific Lumber Company directly.
    Amount of award: $1,000

Northeastern Loggers' Association

Northeastern Loggers' Association Scholarship Contest

Type of award: Scholarship.
Intended use: For undergraduate study at vocational, 2-year or 4-year institution in United States.
Eligibility: Applicant or parent must be member of Northeastern Loggers' Association.
Basis for selection: Competition in Writing/journalism. 1000 word essay.
Application requirements: Essay and transcript.
Additional information: Applicant must be an immediate

family member of an employee or an individual associate or industrial member of the Northeastern Loggers' Assoc. Decision based largely on quality of 1,000-word essay on "Growing Up in the Forest Industry." Scholarships are given to high school seniors, students in four-year and two-year colleges.

Amount of award:	$500
Number of awards:	3
Number of applicants:	18
Application deadline:	March 31
Notification begins:	May 1
Total amount awarded:	$1,500

Contact:
Northeastern Loggers' Association
P.O. Box 69
Old Forge, NY 13420

Northland Aluminum Products, Inc.

Dalquist Scholarship

Type of award: Scholarship.
Intended use: For undergraduate or graduate study at accredited vocational, 2-year, 4-year or graduate institution.
Eligibility: Applicant or parent must be employed by Northland Aluminium Products, Inc.
Additional information: For further information or an application contact Northland Aluminum Products, Inc. directly.
    Amount of award: $1,000

Northwestern Mutual Life Foundation, Inc.

Northwestern Mutual Life Scholars Program

Type of award: Scholarship, renewable.
Intended use: For undergraduate study at accredited postsecondary institution.
Eligibility: Applicant or parent must be employed by Northwestern Mutual Life Foundation, Inc. Applicant must be high school senior.
Basis for selection: Applicant must demonstrate financial need.
Additional information: For Further information or an application contact Northwestern Mutual Life Foundation, Inc. directly.
    Amount of award: $1,000-$3,000
Contact:
Northwestern Mutual Life Foundation, Inc.

Norwest Foundation

Norwest Scholarship Program

Type of award: Scholarship, renewable.
Intended use: For undergraduate study at accredited vocational, 2-year or 4-year institution.
Eligibility: Applicant or parent must be employed by Norwest.
Basis for selection: Applicant must demonstrate financial need.
Additional information: For further information or an application contact Norwest Foundation directly.
    Amount of award: $500-$1,000

Oak Tree Packaging Corporation

Oak Tree Packaging Corporation Scholarship Program

Type of award: Scholarship.
Intended use: For freshman, sophomore, junior or senior study at accredited 4-year institution.
Eligibility: Applicant or parent must be employed by Oak Tree Packaging Corp.
Basis for selection: Applicant must demonstrate financial need.
Additional information: For further information or an application contact Oak Tree Packaging Corporation directly.
    Amount of award: $1,000-$2,000

Ocean Spray Cranberries, Inc.

Hal Thorkilsen Scholarship Fund

Type of award: Scholarship.
Intended use: For undergraduate study at accredited vocational, 2-year or 4-year institution.
Eligibility: Applicant or parent must be employed by Ocean Spray Cranberries, Inc.
Basis for selection: Applicant must demonstrate financial need.
Additional information: For further information or an application contact Ocean Spray Cranberries, Inc. directly.
    Amount of award: $500-$3,000
Contact:
Ocean Spray Cranberries, Inc.

Phone: 800-662-3263 (9 A.M. to 4 P.M.)

Olympic Steel, Inc.

Olympic Steel Inc. Scholarship Program

Type of award: Scholarship, renewable.
Intended use: For undergraduate study at accredited vocational, 2-year or 4-year institution.
Eligibility: Applicant or parent must be employed by Olympic Steel, Inc.
Additional information: For further information or an application contact Olympic Steel, Inc. directly.
    Amount of award: $1,250

Oral and Maxillofacial Surgery Foundation

Oral and Maxillofacial Surgery Research Endowment Program

Type of award: Scholarship, renewable.
Intended use: For doctoral study at accredited graduate institution in United States.
Eligibility: Applicant or parent must be member of Oral and Maxillofacial Surgery Fdn. Applicant must be U.S. citizen or permanent resident.
Basis for selection: Major/career interest in dental specialties (beyond dds/dmd).
Application requirements: Research proposal.
    Amount of award: $12,000-$100,000
    Number of awards: 53
    Number of applicants: 22
    Application deadline: August 31
    Notification begins: December 1
Contact:
Oral and Maxillofacial Surgery Foundation
Research Endowment Program Coordinator
9700 West Bryn Mawr Ave.
Rosemont, IL 60018-5701
Phone: 847-678-6200

Oregon State Scholarship Commission

Oregon Department of Transportation Glenn Jackson Scholarship

Type of award: Scholarship, renewable.
Intended use: For full-time freshman study at 2-year or 4-year institution.
Eligibility: Applicant or parent must be employed by Oregon Department of Transportation. Applicant must be U.S. citizen or permanent resident residing in Oregon.
Basis for selection: Applicant must demonstrate high academic achievement.
Application requirements: Essay and transcript.
Additional information: Administered by Oregon State Scholarship Commission. Recipient offered summer employment.
    Number of awards: 8
    Application deadline: March 1
    Total amount awarded: $20,000
Contact:
Oregon State Scholarship Commission
1500 Valley River Drive, Suite 100
Eugene, OR 97401

Oregon Metro Federal Credit Union Scholarship

Type of award: Scholarship.
Intended use: For full-time undergraduate study.
Eligibility: Applicant or parent must be member of Oregon Metro Federal Credit Union. Applicant must be high school senior. Applicant must be U.S. citizen or permanent resident residing in Oregon.
Basis for selection: Applicant must demonstrate financial need and high academic achievement.
Application requirements: Essay and transcript.
Additional information: Preference given to high school seniors and applicants planning to attend Oregon public or private college. Contact Oregon State Scholarship Commission or Oregon Metro Federal Credit Union; send SASE.
    Amount of award: $500
    Number of awards: 3
    Application deadline: March 1
    Total amount awarded: $1,500
Contact:
Oregon State Scholarship Commission
1500 Valley River Drive, Suite 100
Attn: Private Awards
Eugene, OR 97401-2146
Website: www.ossc.state.or.us

Oregon Metro Federal Credit Union Scholarship

Type of award: Scholarship, renewable.
Intended use: For full-time undergraduate study at postsecondary institution in United States.
Eligibility: Applicant or parent must be member of Oregon Metro Federal Credit Union. Applicant must be U.S. citizen or permanent resident residing in Oregon.
Basis for selection: Applicant must demonstrate financial need and high academic achievement.
Application requirements: Essay and transcript.
Additional information: Preference given to graduating high school seniors attending Oregon colleges.
    Amount of award: $500
    Number of awards: 1
    Application deadline: March 1
    Total amount awarded: $500
Contact:
Oregon State Scholarship Commission
1500 Valley River Drive, Suite 100
Attn: Private Programs
Eugene, OR 97401-2146
Website: www.ossc.state.or.us

Oregon State Scholarship Commission/Oregon Dungeness Crab Commission

Type of award: Scholarship.
Intended use: For undergraduate study.
Eligibility: Applicant or parent must be employed by Oregon Dungeness Crab Fishermen. Applicant must be high school senior. Applicant must be residing in Oregon.
Additional information: For dependents of licensed Oregon Dungeness Crab Fishermen or Crew.
    Application deadline: March 1
Contact:
Oregon State Scholarship Commission, Attn: Private Awards
Private Awards
1500 Valley River Drive, Suite 100
Eugene, OR 97401-2146
Website: www.ossc.state.or.us

Roger W. Emmons Memorial Scholarship

Type of award: Scholarship.
Intended use: For full-time freshman study at accredited vocational, 2-year or 4-year institution in Oregon.
Eligibility: Applicant or parent must be employed by Oregon Refuse & Recycling Association. Applicant must be high school senior. Applicant must be U.S. citizen or permanent resident residing in Oregon.
Application requirements: Essay, transcript and proof of eligibility.
Additional information: Parents must have been employees of Oregon Refuse & Recycling Association or solid waste company members for at least three years.
    Amount of award: $1,000
    Number of awards: 2
    Application deadline: March 1
    Total amount awarded: $2,000
Contact:
Oregon State Scholarship Commission
1500 Valley River Drive, Suite 100
Attn: Private Awards
Eugene, OR 97401
Phone: 541-687-7400

OSI Industries, Inc.

OSI Group Scholarship Program

Type of award: Scholarship.
Intended use: For undergraduate study at vocational, 2-year or 4-year institution.
Eligibility: Applicant or parent must be employed by OSI Industries, Inc. Applicant must be high school senior.
Additional information: For further information or an application contact OSI Industries Incorporated directly.
    Amount of award: $1,500

Otter Tail Power Company

Otter Tail Power Company Scholarship

Type of award: Scholarship.
Intended use: For undergraduate study at accredited vocational, 2-year or 4-year institution.
Eligibility: Applicant or parent must be employed by Otter Tail Power Company.
Basis for selection: Applicant must demonstrate financial need.
Additional information: For further information or an application contact Otter Tail Power Company directly.
    Amount of award: $250-$500

Pacific Enterprises

Pacific Enterprises Scholarship Program

Type of award: Scholarship.
Intended use: For undergraduate study at vocational, 2-year or 4-year institution.
Eligibility: Applicant or parent must be employed by Pacific Enterprises. Applicant must be high school senior.
Additional information: For further information or an application contact Pacific Enterprises directly.
    Amount of award: $1,000-$4,000

Pacific Life Insurance Company

Pacific Mutual Life Scholarship Program for Children of Employees

Type of award: Scholarship, renewable.
Intended use: For undergraduate study at accredited 4-year institution.
Eligibility: Applicant or parent must be employed by Pacific Mutual Life Insurance Company. Applicant must be U.S. citizen.
Basis for selection: Applicant must demonstrate financial need.
Additional information: For further information or application contact Pacific Mutual Life Insurance Company directly.
    Amount of award: $1,000-$2,000

Payless Cashways, Inc.

Payless Cashways Scholarship Program

Type of award: Scholarship.
Intended use: For undergraduate study at accredited 2-year or 4-year institution.
Eligibility: Applicant or parent must be employed by Payless Cashways, Inc.
Basis for selection: Applicant must demonstrate financial need.
Additional information: For further information or an application contact Payless Cashways, Inc. directly.
    Amount of award: $1,000-$2,500

Pebble Beach Company Foundation

Pebble Beach Scholarship Program for Employees' Children

Type of award: Scholarship, renewable.
Intended use: For undergraduate study at accredited vocational, 2-year or 4-year institution.
Eligibility: Applicant or parent must be employed by Pebble Beach Company Foundation. Applicant must be high school senior.
Additional information: For further information or application contact Pebble Beach Company Foundation directly.
    Amount of award: $1,500
Contact:
Pebble Beach Company Foundation

Pennzoil Company

Pennzoil Scholars Program

Type of award: Scholarship, renewable.
Intended use: For freshman study at accredited 2-year or 4-year institution.
Eligibility: Applicant or parent must be employed by Pennzoil Company.
Additional information: For further information or an application contact Pennzoil Company directly.
    Amount of award: $2,500

Pentair, Inc.

Pentair Scholarship Fund

Type of award: Scholarship, renewable.
Intended use: For undergraduate study at vocational, 2-year or 4-year institution.
Eligibility: Applicant or parent must be employed by Pentair, Inc. Applicant must be high school senior.
Additional information: For further information or an application contact Pentair Incorporated directly.
    Amount of award: $2,000-$5,000

Perkin-Elmer Corporation

Perkin-Elmer Scholarship Program

Type of award: Scholarship, renewable.
Intended use: For undergraduate study at vocational, 2-year or 4-year institution.
Eligibility: Applicant or parent must be employed by Perkin-Elmer Corporation. Applicant must be high school senior.
Additional information: For further information or an application contact Perkin-Elmer Corporation directly.
    Amount of award: $1,000-$5,000

Phi Delta Kappa International

Phi Delta Kappa Graduate Fellowship

Type of award: Scholarship.
Intended use: For full-time master's, doctoral study at accredited graduate institution.
Eligibility: Applicant or parent must be member of Phi Delta Kappa.
Basis for selection: Major/career interest in education. Applicant must demonstrate leadership, seriousness of purpose, service orientation and high academic achievement.
Application requirements: Recommendations, essay, transcript and proof of eligibility. Prospectus for thesis dissertation. Organization: Phi Delta Kappa International.
Additional information: Make application to local PDK chapter or PDK International.
    Amount of award: $500-$1,500
    Number of awards: 6
    Number of applicants: 27
    Application deadline: May 1
    Notification begins: July 1
    Total amount awarded: $4,750
Contact:
Phi Delta Kappa International
P.O. Box 789
Bloomington, IN 47402-0789
Phone: 812-339-1156

PHICO Insurance Company

PHICO Insurance Scholarship for Children of Employees

Type of award: Scholarship.
Intended use: For undergraduate study at accredited vocational, 2-year or 4-year institution.
Eligibility: Applicant or parent must be employed by PHICO Insurance Company.
Additional information: For further information or an application contact PHICO Insurance Company directly.
 Amount of award: $1,000

Philadelphia Drug Exchange

Philadelphia Drug Exchange Scholarship Program

Type of award: Scholarship.
Intended use: For freshman study at 2-year or 4-year institution.
Eligibility: Applicant or parent must be employed by Philadelphia Drug Exchange. Applicant must be high school senior.
Additional information: For further information or an application contact Philadelphia Drug Exchange directly.
 Amount of award: $2,500

Philips Electronics North America

Philips Electronics Scholarship

Type of award: Scholarship, renewable.
Intended use: For full-time undergraduate study at vocational, 2-year or 4-year institution.
Eligibility: Applicant or parent must be employed by North American Philips. Applicant must be U.S. citizen or permanent resident.
Basis for selection: Applicant must demonstrate financial need and high academic achievement.
Application requirements: Recommendations, essay and transcript.
 Amount of award: $500-$3,500
 Number of awards: 52
 Number of applicants: 200
 Application deadline: December 31
 Notification begins: May 1
 Total amount awarded: $270,000
Contact:
Philips Electronics North America
100 East 42 Street
New York, NY 10017

Phillips Petroleum Company

Phillips Petroleum Dependent Scholarship Program

Type of award: Scholarship, renewable.
Intended use: For full-time freshman study at accredited postsecondary institution.
Eligibility: Applicant or parent must be employed by Phillips Petroleum Company. Applicant must be high school senior. Applicant must be U.S. citizen.
Basis for selection: Applicant must demonstrate leadership, seriousness of purpose, financial need and high academic achievement.
Application requirements: Transcript and proof of eligibility.
 Amount of award: $8,000
 Number of awards: 66
 Number of applicants: 320
 Application deadline: February 27
 Notification begins: May 8
 Total amount awarded: $528,000
Contact:
Phillips Petroleum Company
16 Phillips Building
Bartlesville, OK 74004

Pine Tree 4-H Club Foundation

Pine Tree State 4-H Club Foundation Scholarship

Type of award: Scholarship, renewable.
Intended use: For graduate study.
Eligibility: Applicant or parent must be member of Maine Pine Tree 4H Club. Applicant must be high school senior. Applicant must be U.S. citizen.
Basis for selection: Applicant must demonstrate leadership and service orientation.
Application requirements: Recommendations, transcript and by Committee of the 4-H Foundation selects applicants.
Additional information: Applications must be accompanied by a recommendation from a county extension agent or 4-H leader. Applications available at high school guidance offices, county extension offices and the Maine Pine Tree State 4-H Club Foundation.
 Amount of award: $1,000
 Number of awards: 3
 Number of applicants: 200
 Application deadline: April 1
 Total amount awarded: $3,000
Contact:
Maine Pine Tree 4-H Club
5719 Crossland Hall
Orono, ME 04469
Phone: 207-581-3739
Fax: 207-581-3212

Piper Jaffray Companies Inc.

H.C. Piper Scholarship

Type of award: Scholarship.
Intended use: For undergraduate study at accredited vocational, 2-year or 4-year institution.
Eligibility: Applicant or parent must be employed by Piper Jaffray Companies Inc.
Basis for selection: Applicant must demonstrate financial need.
Additional information: For further information or an application contact Piper Jaffray Companies Inc. directly.
    Amount of award: $500-$2,000

Playtex Products, Inc.

Playtex Scholarship

Type of award: Scholarship, renewable.
Intended use: For full-time freshman study at accredited 4-year institution. Designated institutions: In United States or Canada.
Eligibility: Applicant or parent must be employed by Playtex Products, Inc. and subsidiaries. Applicant must be high school senior. Applicant must be U.S. citizen.
Basis for selection: Applicant must demonstrate depth of character, leadership, seriousness of purpose, service orientation and high academic achievement.
Application requirements: Recommendations, essay, transcript and proof of eligibility. SAT I scores.
Additional information: Parent or guardian must have completed one year of continuous service with Playtex by January 1, 1998. Canadian citizens also qualify.
    Amount of award: $2,000
    Number of awards: 7
    Number of applicants: 15
    Application deadline: November 24
    Notification begins: May 1
    Total amount awarded: $10,500
Contact:
Playtex Products Inc. Scholarship Program
300 Nyala Farms Road
Westport, CT 06880

Polaris Industries, Inc.

Polaris Industries Inc. Scholarship Program

Type of award: Scholarship.
Intended use: For undergraduate study at accredited vocational, 2-year or 4-year institution.
Eligibility: Applicant or parent must be employed by Polaris Industries.
Basis for selection: Applicant must demonstrate financial need.
Additional information: For further information or an application contact Polaris Industries directly.
    Amount of award: $1,000

Police and Fire Fighters' Association

Police and Fire Fighters' Association Scholarship

Type of award: Scholarship, renewable.
Intended use: For undergraduate study at accredited 2-year or 4-year institution.
Eligibility: Applicant or parent must be member of Police & Fire Fighters' Association.
Additional information: For further information or an application contact Police and Fire Fighters' Association directly.
    Amount of award: $1,000

Polyfibron Technologies, Inc.

Polyfibron Technologies Scholarship Program

Type of award: Scholarship.
Intended use: For undergraduate study at vocational, 2-year or 4-year institution.
Eligibility: Applicant or parent must be employed by Polyfibron Technologies, Inc. Applicant must be high school senior.
Additional information: For further information or an application contact Polyfibron Technologies Incorporated directly.
    Amount of award: $2,000

Portuguese Continental Union

Portuguese Continental Union Scholarship

Type of award: Scholarship.
Intended use: For undergraduate certificate study at accredited vocational, 2-year or 4-year institution.
Eligibility: Applicant or parent must be member of Portuguese Continental Union.
Basis for selection: Applicant must demonstrate depth of character, seriousness of purpose, financial need and high academic achievement.

Application requirements: Recommendations, essay and proof of eligibility. SAT scores.
Additional information: Must have been PCU member with at least one year in good standing. If not currently enrolled in college or university, must plan to enroll in the current academic year. Award amounts based on individual financial needs.

Number of awards:	13
Number of applicants:	33
Application deadline:	February 15
Notification begins:	April 1
Total amount awarded:	$4,500

Contact:
Portuguese Continental Union
899 Boylston Street
Boston, MA 02115
Website: members.aol.com/upceua

Practitioners Publishing Company

Practitioners Publishing Company Dependents Scholarship

Type of award: Scholarship, renewable.
Intended use: For freshman study at 2-year or 4-year institution.
Eligibility: Applicant or parent must be employed by Practitioners Publishing Company. Applicant must be high school senior.
Additional information: For further information or an application contact Practitioners Publishing Company directly.

Amount of award:	$2,500

Precision Castparts Corporation

Precision Castparts Scholarship

Type of award: Scholarship, renewable.
Intended use: For undergraduate study at accredited vocational, 2-year or 4-year institution.
Eligibility: Applicant or parent must be employed by Precision Castparts Corp.
Basis for selection: Applicant must demonstrate financial need.
Additional information: For further information or an application contact Precision Castparts Corp. directly.

Amount of award:	$1,500

Procter and Gamble Fund

Procter and Gamble Scholarship

Type of award: Scholarship, renewable.
Intended use: For full-time undergraduate study at 4-year institution in United States.
Eligibility: Applicant or parent must be employed by Procter and Gamble.
Basis for selection: Applicant must demonstrate depth of character, leadership and high academic achievement.
Application requirements: Recommendations, transcript and proof of eligibility. CSS PROFILE Application required.
Additional information: Applications available through student's parents.

Amount of award:	$1,000-$4,000
Number of awards:	644
Number of applicants:	600
Application deadline:	November 15
Notification begins:	April 15
Total amount awarded:	$800,000

Contact:
Procter and Gamble Scholarship Fund
P.O. Box 599
Cincinnati, OH 45201-0599
Phone: 513-945-8450
Fax: 513-945-8979

Professional Service Industries, Inc.

PSI Scholarship Program

Type of award: Scholarship.
Intended use: For undergraduate study at accredited vocational, 2-year or 4-year institution.
Eligibility: Applicant or parent must be employed by Professional Service Industries, Inc. Applicant must be high school senior.
Basis for selection: Applicant must demonstrate financial need.
Additional information: For further information or application contact Professional Service Industries, Inc. directly.

Amount of award:	$1,000

Contact:
Professional Service Industries, Inc.

Promus Hotel Corporation Inc.

Promus Hotel Corporation Scholarship Program

Type of award: Scholarship, renewable.
Intended use: For freshman study at accredited 4-year institution.
Eligibility: Applicant or parent must be employed by Promus Hotel Corporation.
Basis for selection: Applicant must demonstrate financial need.
Additional information: For further information or an application contact Promus Hotel Corporation, Inc. directly.
    Amount of award: $2,000-$5,000

Prudential Foundation

Prudential Foundation Scholarship

Type of award: Scholarship, renewable.
Intended use: For freshman study at accredited 4-year institution.
Eligibility: Applicant or parent must be employed by Prudential Foundation.
Basis for selection: Applicant must demonstrate financial need.
Additional information: For further information or an application contact Prudential Foundation directly.
    Amount of award: $300-$3,000

Public Service Company of Colorado

Public Service Company of Colorado Scholarship

Type of award: Scholarship.
Intended use: For undergraduate study at accredited vocational, 2-year or 4-year institution.
Eligibility: Applicant or parent must be employed by Public Service Company of Colorado.
Basis for selection: Applicant must demonstrate financial need.
Additional information: For further information or an application contact Public Service Company of Colorado directly.
    Amount of award: $500-$2,000

Quadion Foundation

Quadion Foundation Scholarship

Type of award: Scholarship.
Intended use: For undergraduate study at accredited vocational, 2-year or 4-year institution.
Eligibility: Applicant or parent must be employed by Quadion.
Additional information: For further information or an application contact Quadion Foundation directly.
    Amount of award: $1,000

Quill Corporation

Quill Scholarship Program

Type of award: Scholarship, renewable.
Intended use: For undergraduate study at accredited vocational, 2-year or 4-year institution.
Eligibility: Applicant or parent must be employed by Quill Corporation.
Additional information: For further information or an application contact Quill Corporation directly.
    Amount of award: $2,500

R. Brouilette Agency, Inc.

Robert B. Brouillette Memorial Tuition Assistance Program

Type of award: Scholarship.
Intended use: For undergraduate study at vocational, 2-year or 4-year institution.
Eligibility: Applicant or parent must be employed by R. Brouilette Agency, Inc. Applicant must be high school senior.
Additional information: For further information or an application contact R.Brouilette Agency Incorporated directly.
    Amount of award: $500-$5,000

Raychem Corporation

Paul M. Cook Scholarship Fund

Type of award: Scholarship, renewable.
Intended use: For freshman study at accredited 4-year institution.
Eligibility: Applicant or parent must be employed by Raychem Corporation.
Basis for selection: Applicant must demonstrate financial need.
Additional information: For further information or an application contact Raychem Corporation directly.
    Amount of award: $1,000-$5,000

Raytheon Company

Raytheon Scholars Program

Type of award: Scholarship, renewable.
Intended use: For freshman study at vocational, 2-year or 4-year institution.
Eligibility: Applicant or parent must be employed by Raytheon Company. Applicant must be high school senior.
Additional information: For further information or an application contact Raytheon Company directly.
    Amount of award: $500-$3,000

Recording for the Blind and Dyslexic

Learning Through Listening Award

Type of award: Scholarship.
Intended use: For full-time undergraduate study at vocational, 2-year or 4-year institution in United States.
Eligibility: Applicant or parent must be member of Recording for the Blind & Dyslexic. Applicant must be high school senior. Must be learning disabled.
Basis for selection: Applicant must demonstrate depth of character, leadership, patriotism, seriousness of purpose, service orientation and high academic achievement.
Application requirements: Recommendations, essay, transcript and proof of eligibility. Must obtain two teacher/school administrator referrals.
Additional information: Must have 3.0 GPA or better in grades 10-12. Must be a registered member of Recording for the Blind & Dyslexic for at least one year prior to the application deadline.
    Amount of award: $3,000-$6,000
    Number of awards: 6
    Number of applicants: 200
    Application deadline: February 21
    Total amount awarded: $24,000
Contact:
Recording for the Blind & Dyslexic
c/o Public Affairs Office
20 Roszel Road
Princeton, NJ 08540
Phone: 609-520-8044
Website: www.rfbd.org

Marion Huber Learning Through Listening Award

Type of award: Scholarship.
Intended use: For undergraduate study at accredited postsecondary institution.
Eligibility: Applicant or parent must be member of Recording for the Blind & Dyslexic. Applicant must be high school senior. Must be visually impaired or learning disabled.
Basis for selection: Applicant must demonstrate leadership and service orientation.
Application requirements: Transcript and proof of eligibility.
Additional information: Award given annually to a total of 6 students in 2 categories: three winners receive $6,000 each; three special honors winners receive $2,000 each. Applicant must be a member of the 1999 graduating class of a public or private high school in the U.S. or its territories. Applicant must have an overall grade average of "B" or above based on grades 10-12. (Or the equivalent if an alternative grading system is used).
    Amount of award: $2,000-$6,000
    Number of awards: 6
    Application deadline: February 1
Contact:
Public Affairs Office
20 Roszel Rd.
Princeton, NJ 08540

Mary P. Oenslager Scholastic Achievement Award

Type of award: Scholarship.
Intended use: For graduate study.
Eligibility: Applicant or parent must be member of Recording for the Blind & Dyslexic. Applicant must be . Must be visually impaired.
Basis for selection: Applicant must demonstrate leadership, seriousness of purpose, service orientation and high academic achievement.
Application requirements: Transcript and proof of eligibility.
Additional information: Applicants must have received a Bachelor's degree from an accredited 4-year college or university in the U.S. or its territories between 7/1/97-6/30/98. Applicants must have an overall academic average for their undergraduate years of 3.0 or more on a 4.0 scale; (or the equivalent if based on a different grading system). Winning categories are as follows: a. Three winners receive $6,000 each. b. Three special honors winners receive $3,000 each. c. Three honors winners receive $1,000 each.
    Amount of award: $1,000-$6,000
    Number of awards: 9
    Application deadline: February 1, February 1
Contact:
Recording for the Blind & Dyslexic
20 Roszel Rd.
Princeton, NJ 08540
Phone: 800-221-4792

Scholastic Achievement Award

Type of award: Scholarship.
Intended use: For senior study.
Eligibility: Applicant or parent must be member of Recording for the Blind & Dyslexic. Applicant must be . Must be visually impaired.
Basis for selection: Applicant must demonstrate depth of character, leadership, patriotism, seriousness of purpose, service orientation and high academic achievement.
Application requirements: Essay and transcript. Two professors/college administrators report forms must be completed.
Additional information: Must have 3.0 GPA. Must be a registered member of Recording for the Blind & Dyslexic for at least one year prior to the application deadline.

Amount of award:	$1,000-$6,000
Number of awards:	9
Number of applicants:	75
Application deadline:	February 21
Notification begins:	, May 31
Total amount awarded:	$30,000

Contact:
Recording for the Blind & Dyslexic
c/o Public Affairs Office
20 Roszel Road
Princeton, NJ 08540
Phone: 609-520-8044
Website: www.rfbd.org

Regions Financial Corporation

Regions Right Way Scholarship

Type of award: Scholarship.
Intended use: For freshman study at accredited 4-year institution.
Eligibility: Applicant or parent must be employed by First Alabama Bancshares, Inc.
Additional information: For further information or an application contact Regions Financial Corporation directly.
Amount of award: $2,000

ReliaStar Foundation

ReliaStar Financial Corporation Scholarship Program

Type of award: Scholarship, renewable.
Intended use: For undergraduate study at accredited vocational, 2-year or 4-year institution.
Eligibility: Applicant or parent must be employed by Northwestern National Life.
Basis for selection: Applicant must demonstrate financial need.
Additional information: For further information or an application contact ReliaStar Foundation directly.
Amount of award: $600-$2,400

Reorganization Division of the Securities Industry

Securities Industry Scholarship

Type of award: Scholarship, renewable.
Intended use: For undergraduate study at accredited 2-year or 4-year institution.
Eligibility: Applicant or parent must be member of Reorganization Division of Securities Industry.
Additional information: Must be child of member. For further information or an application contact Reorganization Division of The Securities Industry directly.
Amount of award: $500

Reserve Officers Association

Henry Reilly Memorial College Scholarship

Type of award: Scholarship, renewable.
Intended use: For full-time junior, senior study at accredited 4-year institution in United States.
Eligibility: Applicant or parent must be member of Reserve Officers Association and ROAL. Applicant must be U.S. citizen. Applicant must be descendant of veteran, child of active service person, veteran, disabled veteran, deceased veteran or POW/MIA, spouse of active service person, veteran, disabled veteran, deceased veteran or POW/MIA.
Basis for selection: Applicant must demonstrate depth of character, leadership, seriousness of purpose and high academic achievement.
Application requirements: Essay, transcript and proof of eligibility.
Additional information: 1200 SAT I or ACT combined English/math score of 55 if taken April 1995 or later. If taken from October 1989 to March 1995, then a 1250 SAT or an ACT score of 62 is required. Minimum GPA of 3.0 required.

Amount of award:	$500
Number of awards:	25
Number of applicants:	25
Application deadline:	April 10
Notification begins:	June 15
Total amount awarded:	$12,500

Contact:
Reserve Officers Association
1 Constitution Avenue, NE
Washington, DC 20002-5655
Website: www.roa.org

Henry Reilly Memorial Graduate Scholarship

Type of award: Scholarship, renewable.
Intended use: For half-time master's, doctoral study at accredited graduate institution in United States.
Eligibility: Applicant or parent must be member of Reserve Officers Association. Applicant must be U.S. citizen. Applicant must be in military service, veteran, disabled while on duty.
Basis for selection: Applicant must demonstrate depth of character, leadership, seriousness of purpose, service orientation and high academic achievement.
Application requirements: Recommendations, transcript and proof of eligibility. Curriculum vitae.
Additional information: Applicant must be a member of the ROA; parental membership is not sufficient. Scholarship will apply to a part-time enrolled student only if that student is also working full-time.

Amount of award:	$500
Number of awards:	25
Number of applicants:	32
Application deadline:	April 10
Notification begins:	June 15
Total amount awarded:	$12,500

Contact:
Reserve Officers Association
1 Constitution Avenue NE
Washington, DC 20002-5655
Website: www.roa.org

Henry Reilly Memorial Scholarship

Type of award: Scholarship, renewable.
Intended use: For full-time freshman, sophomore study at accredited 4-year institution in United States.
Eligibility: Applicant or parent must be member of Reserve Officers Association and ROAL. Applicant must be U.S. citizen. Applicant must be descendant of veteran, child of active service person, veteran, disabled veteran, deceased veteran or POW/MIA.
Basis for selection: Applicant must demonstrate depth of character, leadership, seriousness of purpose and high academic achievement.
Application requirements: Essay, transcript and proof of eligibility.
Additional information: 1250 SAT I or ACT combined English/math score of 55 if taken April 1995 or later. If taken from October 1989 to March 1995, then a 1200 SAT or an ACT score of 62 is required. Open to high school seniors as well as college freshmen and sophomores. Minimum GPA is 3.3 for high school seniors, and 3.0 for college students.

Amount of award:	$500
Number of awards:	50
Number of applicants:	50
Application deadline:	April 10
Notification begins:	June 15
Total amount awarded:	$25,000

Contact:
Reserve Officers Association
1 Constitution Avenue NE
Washington, DC 20002-5655
Website: www.roa.org

Retired Officers Association

Retired Officers Educational Assistance Program

Type of award: Loan, renewable.
Intended use: For full-time undergraduate study at accredited 2-year or 4-year institution in United States.
Eligibility: Applicant or parent must be member of Retired Officers Association. Applicant must be single. Applicant must be U.S. citizen. Applicant must be child of veteran, disabled veteran, deceased veteran or POW/MIA who served in the Army, Air Force, Marines, Navy, Coast Guard or Reserves/ National Guard. Parents should be members of Retired Officers Association.
Basis for selection: Applicant must demonstrate depth of character, leadership, patriotism, seriousness of purpose, service orientation, financial need and high academic achievement.
Application requirements: Transcript and proof of eligibility. Resume, SAT/ACT scores, and first page of most recent federal income tax form from student and parent.
Additional information: Must be child of active serviceperson, active POW/MIA, military retiree, or disabled/deceased military retiree. Students can download application from their website.

Amount of award:	$3,000
Number of awards:	1,000
Number of applicants:	1,100
Application deadline:	March 1
Notification begins:	June 1
Total amount awarded:	$3,000,000

Contact:
Loan Committee
Attn.: EAP
201 North Washington Street
Alexandria, VA 22314-2529
Phone: 703-838-8169
Website: www.troa.org

Rex Lumber Company

Paul Forester, Jr., Scholarship

Type of award: Scholarship, renewable.
Intended use: For freshman study at accredited vocational, 2-year or 4-year institution.
Eligibility: Applicant or parent must be employed by Rex Lumber Company.
Additional information: For further information or an application contact Rex Lumber Company directly.
    Amount of award: $1,000

Reynolds and Reynolds Company Foundation

Reynolds and Reynolds Company Foundation Scholarship

Type of award: Scholarship, renewable.
Intended use: For undergraduate study at accredited vocational, 2-year or 4-year institution.
Eligibility: Applicant or parent must be employed by Reynolds and Reynolds Company.
Additional information: For further information or an application contact Reynolds and Reynolds Company Foundation directly.
    Amount of award: $2,500

Rhone-Poulenc Rorer Inc.

Rhone-Poulenc Rorer Scholarship

Type of award: Scholarship, renewable.
Intended use: For undergraduate study at accredited vocational, 2-year or 4-year institution.
Eligibility: Applicant or parent must be employed by Rhone-Poulenc Rorer Inc.
Basis for selection: Applicant must demonstrate financial need.
Additional information: For further information or an application contact Rhone-Poulenc Rorer Inc. directly.
    Amount of award: $1,000

Richard F. Walsh/Alfred W. Di Tolla Foundation

Richard F. Walsh/Alfred W. Di Tolla Scholarship

Type of award: Scholarship, renewable.
Intended use: For full-time undergraduate study at accredited 4-year institution.
Eligibility: Applicant or parent must be employed by International Alliance of Theatrical Stage Employees. Applicant must be high school senior.
Basis for selection: Applicant must demonstrate high academic achievement.
Application requirements: Recommendations and transcript. SAT, College Entrance Examination, or equivalent examination results.
Additional information: Must be son or daughter of a member in good standing of the International Alliance of Theatrical Stage Employees. Renewable throughout undergraduate studies.

    Amount of award: $1,750
    Number of awards: 2
    Application deadline: December 31
    Notification begins: May 1
    Total amount awarded: $3,500
Contact:
Richard F. Walsh/Alfred W. Di Tolla Foundation
1515 Broadway
Suite 601
New York, NY 10036
Phone: 212-730-1770

Ricoh Corporation

Ricoh Scholarship

Type of award: Scholarship.
Intended use: For undergraduate study at accredited vocational, 2-year or 4-year institution.
Eligibility: Applicant or parent must be employed by RICOH Corporation. Applicant must be high school senior.
Basis for selection: Applicant must demonstrate financial need.
Additional information: Must be child of employee of RICOH Corporation. For further information or application contact RICOH Corporation directly.
    Amount of award: $1,000-$3,000

Robert W. Geyer

Geyer Educational Award Program

Type of award: Scholarship.
Intended use: For undergraduate study at vocational, 2-year or 4-year institution.
Eligibility: Applicant or parent must be employed by Robert W. Geyer. Applicant must be high school senior.
Additional information: For further information or an application contact Robert W. Geyer directly.
    Amount of award: $500-$1,000

Roche Brothers Supermarkets, Inc.

Roche Brothers Supermarkets Scholarship

Type of award: Scholarship.
Intended use: For undergraduate study at accredited vocational, 2-year or 4-year institution.
Eligibility: Applicant or parent must be employed by Roche Bros. Supermarkets, Inc.
Basis for selection: Applicant must demonstrate financial need.
Additional information: For further information or an application contact Roche Brothers Supermarkets, Inc. directly.
    Amount of award: $1,000

Rodale Press, Inc.

Rodale Scholarship Program

Type of award: Scholarship, renewable.
Intended use: For undergraduate study at accredited vocational, 2-year or 4-year institution.
Eligibility: Applicant or parent must be employed by Rodale Press.
Basis for selection: Applicant must demonstrate financial need.
Additional information: For further information or an application contact Rodale Press Inc. directly.
    Amount of award: $500-$2,000

Roger Von Amelunxen Foundation

Roger Von Amelunxen Scholarship

Type of award: Scholarship, renewable.
Intended use: For full-time undergraduate study outside United States.
Eligibility: Applicant or parent must be employed by U.S. Customs.
Basis for selection: Applicant must demonstrate depth of character, leadership, seriousness of purpose, service orientation and high academic achievement.
Application requirements: Recommendations and transcript.
    Amount of award: $750-$4,000
    Number of applicants: 79
    Application deadline: August 1
    Notification begins: August 31
    Total amount awarded: $52,000
Contact:
Roger Von Amelunxen Foundation
8321 Edgerton Boulevard
Jamaica, NY 11432
Phone: 718-641-4800

RoNetco Supermarkets, Inc.

RONECTCO Supermarkets Scholarship Program

Type of award: Scholarship, renewable.
Intended use: For undergraduate study at vocational, 2-year or 4-year institution.
Eligibility: Applicant or parent must be employed by RoNetco Supermarkets, Inc. Applicant must be high school senior.
Additional information: For further information or an application contact RoNetco Supermarkets Scholarship Program directly.
    Amount of award: $500-$1,000

Rosemount Aerospace Inc.

Rosemont Aerospace Scholarship

Type of award: Scholarship.
Intended use: For undergraduate study at accredited postsecondary institution.
Eligibility: Applicant or parent must be employed by Rosemount Aerospace Inc. Applicant must be high school senior.
Additional information: For further information or an application contact Rosemount Aerospace Inc. directly.
    Amount of award: $1,000
Contact:
Rosemount Aerospace Inc.

Rosemount Inc.

Vernon Heath Scholarship Program

Type of award: Scholarship, renewable.
Intended use: For freshman study at 2-year or 4-year institution.
Eligibility: Applicant or parent must be employed by Rosemount Inc. Applicant must be high school senior.
Additional information: For further information or an application contact Rosemount Incoporated directly.
    Amount of award: $1,250

Royal Neighbors of America

Royal Neighbors Fraternal Scholarship

Type of award: Scholarship, renewable.
Intended use: For full-time undergraduate study at accredited 4-year institution in United States.
Eligibility: Applicant or parent must be member of Royal Neighbors of America. Applicant must be high school senior.
Basis for selection: Applicant must demonstrate depth of character, leadership and high academic achievement.
Application requirements: Recommendations, essay, transcript and proof of eligibility. ACT/SAT Test score.
Additional information: Must rank in top 25% of class. Must be a member of Royal Neighbors of America for at least two years.
    Amount of award: $2,000
    Number of awards: 10
    Number of applicants: 105
    Application deadline: January 15
    Notification begins: May 1
    Total amount awarded: $20,000
Contact:
Royal Neighbors of America
National Headquarters
230 16 Street
Rock Island, IL 61201-8645
Phone: 800-627-4762

Royal Neighbors Non-Traditional Scholarship

Type of award: Scholarship.
Intended use: For undergraduate or graduate study at accredited vocational, 2-year, 4-year or graduate institution.
Eligibility: Applicant or parent must be member of Royal Neighbors of America. Applicant must be adult returning student.
Basis for selection: Applicant must demonstrate depth of character, service orientation, financial need and high academic achievement.
Application requirements: Essay, transcript and proof of eligibility.
Additional information: $500 award for part time study,

$1000 for full time study. Must be a member of the Royal Neighbors of America for at least 2 years.
- Amount of award: $500-$1,000
- Number of awards: 15
- Application deadline: January 15
- Notification begins: June 1
- Total amount awarded: $10,000

Contact:
Royal Neighbors of America
230 16 Street
Rock Island, IL 61201-8645
Phone: 800-627-4762

Royal Neighbors State Fraternal Scholarship

Type of award: Scholarship.
Intended use: For full-time freshman study at accredited vocational, 2-year or 4-year institution in United States.
Eligibility: Applicant or parent must be member of Royal Neighbors of America. Applicant must be high school senior.
Basis for selection: Applicant must demonstrate depth of character, leadership and high academic achievement.
Application requirements: Essay and transcript. Must rank in top 33% of the class.
Additional information: Must be a member in good standing of the Royal Neighbors of America for at least two years.
- Amount of award: $500-$1,000
- Number of awards: 29
- Application deadline: January 15
- Notification begins: May 1
- Total amount awarded: $17,500

Contact:
Royal Neighbors of America
National Headquarters
230 16 Street
Rock Island, IL 61201-8645
Phone: 800-627-4762

Rugby Building Products, Inc.

Rugby Building Products Scholarship Program

Type of award: Scholarship, renewable.
Intended use: For undergraduate study at 2-year or 4-year institution.
Eligibility: Applicant or parent must be employed by Rugby Building Products, Inc. Applicant must be high school senior.
Additional information: For further information or an application contact Rugby Building Products Incorporated directly.
- Amount of award: $2,500

Ruud Lighting, Inc.

Ruud Lighting Scholarship

Type of award: Scholarship.
Intended use: For undergraduate study at accredited postsecondary institution.
Eligibility: Applicant or parent must be employed by Ruud Lighting, Inc. Applicant must be high school senior.
Additional information: For further information or an application contact Ruud Lighting, Inc. directly.
- Amount of award: $1,000

S.C. Holman Foundation

S.C. Holman Scholarship

Type of award: Scholarship, renewable.
Intended use: For undergraduate study at accredited vocational, 2-year or 4-year institution.
Eligibility: Applicant or parent must be employed by S. C. Holman.
Basis for selection: Applicant must demonstrate financial need.
Additional information: For further information or an application contact S.C. Holman Foundation directly.
- Amount of award: $250-$2,000

S.J. Electro Systems Foundation

S.J. Electro Systems Foundation Scholarship Program

Type of award: Scholarship.
Intended use: For undergraduate or graduate study at vocational, 2-year, 4-year or graduate institution.
Eligibility: Applicant or parent must be employed by S.J. Electro Systems Foundation. Applicant must be high school senior.
Additional information: For further information or an application contact S.J. Electro Systems Foundation directly.
- Amount of award: $500-$1,000

Safety-Kleen Corporation

Safety-Kleen Corp. Memorial Scholarship Program

Type of award: Scholarship.
Intended use: For undergraduate study at accredited postsecondary institution.
Eligibility: Applicant or parent must be employed by

SAFETY-KLEEN Corporation. Applicant must be high school senior.
Basis for selection: Applicant must demonstrate financial need.
Additional information: For further information or an application contact Safety-Kleen Corporation directly.
   Amount of award: $2,500

Santee Cooper

Santee Cooper Employees' Children Scholarship

Type of award: Scholarship, renewable.
Intended use: For undergraduate study at accredited postsecondary institution.
Eligibility: Applicant or parent must be employed by Santee Cooper. Applicant must be high school senior.
Basis for selection: Applicant must demonstrate financial need.
Additional information: For further information or an application contact Santee Cooper directly.
   Amount of award: $1,000-$2,000

Sargent and Lundy

Sargent and Lundy Centennial Scholarship

Type of award: Scholarship.
Intended use: For undergraduate study at accredited vocational, 2-year or 4-year institution.
Eligibility: Applicant or parent must be employed by Sargent & Lundy.
Additional information: For further information or an application contact Sargent and Lundy directly.
   Amount of award: $500-$2,000

SAS Institute Inc.

SAS Institute Scholar Award Program

Type of award: Scholarship, renewable.
Intended use: For freshman study.
Eligibility: Applicant or parent must be employed by SAS Institute Inc. Applicant must be high school senior.
Additional information: For further information or an application contact SAS Institute Incorporated directly.
   Amount of award: $2,000

SBC Foundation

SBC Foundation Program

Type of award: Scholarship, renewable.
Intended use: For undergraduate study at accredited 4-year institution.
Eligibility: Applicant or parent must be employed by Southwestern Bell.
Additional information: For further information and an application contact SBC directly.
   Amount of award: $3,500

School Food Service Foundation

ConAgra Fellowship in Child Nutrition

Type of award: Research grant, renewable.
Intended use: For doctoral, postgraduate study at accredited graduate institution.
Eligibility: Applicant or parent must be member of School Food Service Foundation.
Basis for selection: Major/career interest in food production/management/services; dietetics/nutrition. Applicant must demonstrate seriousness of purpose, service orientation and high academic achievement.
Application requirements: Recommendations and research proposal. Course descriptions, 2 recommendations.
Additional information: Research in child nutrition and foodservice management relating to school food programs. Appropriate topics include dietary guidelines, comparisons of health status of participants and non-participants of school food programs and analysis of nutrition between school food and food brought from home. Fellowship lasts for 12 months.
   Amount of award: $45,000
   Application deadline: October 1
Contact:
Fellowship Coordinator
1600 Duke Street
7th Floor
Alexandria, VA 22314
Phone: 800-877-8822, ext. 146

Hubert Humphrey Research Grant

Type of award: Research grant.
Intended use: For master's, doctoral, first professional or postgraduate study at accredited graduate institution.
Eligibility: Applicant or parent must be member of School Food Service Foundation.
Basis for selection: Major/career interest in food production/management/services; dietetics/nutrition. Applicant must demonstrate seriousness of purpose and high academic achievement.
Application requirements: Recommendations, transcript, proof of eligibility and research proposal. Applicant must demonstrate competency to conduct research. Recommmendation should be a letter of support.
Additional information: Research must be applicable to child

nutrition and must support SFSF grant program mission. Must be active SFSA member or be supervised on grant by active SFSA member. Must be enrolled in graduate program in related field: foods/nutrition, nutrition education, food service management. Minimum 3.0 GPA required.

    Amount of award: $2,500
    Application deadline: April 30
    Notification begins: August 15

Contact:
Research Grant Committee
1600 Duke Street
7th Floor
Alexandria, VA 22314

Lincoln Food Service Research Grant

Type of award: Research grant.
Intended use: For non-degree study.
Eligibility: Applicant or parent must be member of School Food Service Foundation.
Basis for selection: Major/career interest in dietetics/nutrition; food production/management/services. Applicant must demonstrate seriousness of purpose and high academic achievement.
Application requirements: Proof of eligibility and research proposal. Letter of support.
Additional information: Level of study is nonacademic research (no need to be enrolled in a master's program). Research must be applicable to child nutrition and support SFSF grant program mission. Must be active member of SFSA or be supervised on grant by active SFSA member.

    Amount of award: $2,500
    Application deadline: April 30
    Notification begins: August 15

Contact:
Grant Coordinator
1600 Duke Street
7th Floor
Alexandria, VA 22314
Phone: (800) 877-8822 ext. 146

School Food Service Foundation Professional Growth Scholarship

Type of award: Scholarship.
Intended use: For graduate study.
Eligibility: Applicant or parent must be member of School Food Service Foundation.
Basis for selection: Major/career interest in food production/management/services; food science and technology; dietetics/nutrition.
Application requirements: Recommendations, essay, transcript and proof of eligibility.

    Amount of award: $1,000
    Application deadline: April 15

Tony's Food Service Scholarship

Type of award: Scholarship, renewable.
Intended use: For undergraduate or graduate study at accredited postsecondary institution.
Eligibility: Applicant or parent must be member of School Food Service Foundation.
Basis for selection: Major/career interest in food production/management/services; dietetics/nutrition. Applicant must demonstrate leadership, seriousness of purpose, service orientation and high academic achievement.
Application requirements: Recommendations, essay, transcript and proof of eligibility. Course description, 2 recommendations.
Additional information: No funding for correspondence courses. Must major or intent to pursue a in career in school food service: food science, nutrition, dietetics, food service management. Applicant or parent must be current, active SFSA member for at least one year. Scholarships are primarily for undergraduates; occasionally awarded to graduate students.

    Amount of award: $1,000
    Application deadline: April 15
    Notification begins: May 15

Contact:
Scholarship Coordinator
1600 Duke Street
7th Floor
Alexandria, VA 22314
Phone: 800-877-8822, ext. 146.

Schweitzer-Mauduit International Inc.

Schweitzer-Mauduit Tomorrow's Leaders Scholarship Program

Type of award: Scholarship, renewable.
Intended use: For freshman study at 2-year or 4-year institution.
Eligibility: Applicant or parent must be employed by Schweitzer-Mauduit International Inc. Applicant must be high school senior.
Additional information: For further information or an application contact Schweitzer-Mauduit International Incorporated directly.

    Amount of award: $2,500

Screen Actors Guild Foundation

John L. Dales Scholarship

Type of award: Scholarship.
Intended use: For full-time undergraduate or graduate study at accredited 2-year, 4-year or graduate institution in United States.
Eligibility: Applicant or parent must be member of Screen Actor's Guild.
Basis for selection: Applicant must demonstrate financial need.
Application requirements: Recommendations, essay, transcript and proof of eligibility. Most recent federal income tax return and additional financial information. SAT scores.
Additional information: Must be member of Guild for five

years or child of eight-year Guild member. Guild employees, scholarship committee members, Foundation trustees and their relatives are not eligible.

Amount of award:	$2,000-$3,000
Number of awards:	20
Number of applicants:	50
Application deadline:	April 15
Notification begins:	January 15
Total amount awarded:	$55,000

Contact:
Screen Actors Guild Foundation
John L. Dales Scholarship Fund
5757 Wilshire Boulevard
Hollywood, CA 90036
Phone: 213-549-6773

John L. Dales Transitional Scholarship

Type of award: Scholarship.
Intended use: For full-time undergraduate or graduate study at accredited postsecondary institution in United States.
Eligibility: Applicant or parent must be member of Screen Actor's Guild.
Basis for selection: Applicant must demonstrate financial need.
Application requirements: Recommendations, essay, transcript and proof of eligibility. Most recent federal income tax return and additional financial information. SAT or ACT scores.
Additional information: Must be Guild member for at least ten years. Guild employees, scholarship committee members, Foundation board members, their families, relatives or employees not eligible. Not to be used for a theater or related study degree. For those reentering school to make a transition to another field of study. Award based on financial need.
  Application deadline: April 15
Contact:
Screen Actors Guild Foundation
John L. Dales Scholarship Fund
5757 Wilshire Boulevard
Los Angeles, CA 90036
Phone: 213-549-6773

Seafarers Welfare Plan

Charlie Logan Scholarship

Type of award: Scholarship.
Intended use: For full-time undergraduate or graduate study at accredited postsecondary institution in United States.
Eligibility: Applicant or parent must be member of Seafarers International Union.
Application requirements: Recommendations, transcript and proof of eligibility. Application furnished by seafarers. Must include SAT/ACT scores.
Additional information: Must be eligible for welfare benefits and a member of the Seafarers International Union to be eligible.

Amount of award:	$6,000-$15,000
Number of awards:	7
Number of applicants:	75
Application deadline:	April 15
Notification begins:	May 15
Total amount awarded:	$21,000

Contact:
Seafarers Welfare Plan Scholarship Program
5201 Auth Way
Camp Springs, MD 20746
Phone: 301-899-0675, ext. 4272
Website: www.seafarers.org

Sealed Air Corporation

Sealed Air Corporation Scholarship

Type of award: Scholarship, renewable.
Intended use: For undergraduate study at accredited vocational, 2-year or 4-year institution.
Eligibility: Applicant or parent must be employed by Sealed Air Corporation.
Basis for selection: Applicant must demonstrate financial need.
Additional information: For further information or an application contact Sealed Air Corporation directly.
  Amount of award: $500-$2,000

Securities Operations Division

Securities Operations Division Scholarship Program

Type of award: Scholarship, renewable.
Intended use: For freshman study at accredited vocational, 2-year or 4-year institution.
Eligibility: Applicant or parent must be member of Securities Operations Division.
Additional information: For further information or an application, contact Securities Operations Division directly.
  Amount of award: $500

Service First Financial Corporation

R.J. Johnson Memorial Scholarship

Type of award: Scholarship.
Intended use: For undergraduate study at accredited vocational, 2-year or 4-year institution.
Eligibility: Applicant or parent must be employed by Service First Financial Corporation. Applicant must be high school senior.

Additional information: For further information or application contact Service First Financial Corporation directly.
    Amount of award: $500

Servistar/Coast to Coast Corporation

Melamed Scholarship

Type of award: Scholarship.
Intended use: For freshman study at accredited 2-year or 4-year institution.
Eligibility: Applicant or parent must be employed by ServiStar/Coast to Coast Corp.
Additional information: Parent must be a Coast to Coast store owner. For further information or an application contact ServiStar/Coast to Coast Corporation directly.

    Amount of award: $2,500

Sharp Electronics Corporation

Sharp Electronics Scholarship

Type of award: Scholarship, renewable.
Intended use: For freshman study at accredited vocational, 2-year or 4-year institution.
Eligibility: Applicant or parent must be employed by Sharp Electronics Corporation.
Basis for selection: Applicant must demonstrate financial need.
Additional information: For further information or an application contact Sharp Electronics Corporation directly.
    Amount of award: $500-$2,500

Sid Richardson Memorial Fund

Sid Richardson Scholarship

Type of award: Scholarship, renewable.
Intended use: For full-time undergraduate or graduate study.
Eligibility: Applicant or parent must be employed by Sid Richardson/Bass Companies.
Basis for selection: Applicant must demonstrate financial need and high academic achievement.
Application requirements: Essay and transcript. test scores.
Additional information: Award amount varies. Minimum 2.0 GPA required. Grandchildren of employees also eligible.
    Amount of award: $500-$5,000
    Number of awards: 67
    Number of applicants: 120
    Application deadline: March 31
Contact:
Sid Richardson Memorial Fund
309 Main Street
Fort Worth, TX 76102
Phone: 817-336-0494
Fax: 817-332-2176

SIGECO

SIGECO Scholarship Program

Type of award: Scholarship.
Intended use: For freshman study at vocational, 2-year or 4-year institution.
Eligibility: Applicant or parent must be employed by SIGECO. Applicant must be high school senior.
Additional information: For further information or an application contact SIGECO directly.
    Amount of award: $1,000

Sigma Alpha Epsilon Foundation

Sigma Alpha Epsilon Resident Educational Advisor

Type of award: Internship, renewable.
Intended use: For full-time undergraduate or graduate study at accredited graduate institution.
Eligibility: Applicant must be member of Sigma Alpha Epsilon. Applicant must be male.
Basis for selection: Applicant must demonstrate depth of character, leadership, service orientation and high academic achievement.
Application requirements: Recommendations, essay, transcript and proof of eligibility.
Additional information: Highly qualified undergraduates are accepted, but graduate students are preferred. Applicants must reside in a fraternity house and coordinate educational and academic programs at least 15 hours per week. A $2,000 salary is provided, with a $1,000 bonus when all requirements have been met at the end of the academic year. Room and board provided.
    Amount of award: $2,000-$3,000
    Number of awards: 15
    Number of applicants: 20
    Application deadline: April 15
    Notification begins: May 15
    Total amount awarded: $40,000
Contact:
Christopher Mundy
Sigma Alpha Epsilon Foundation
1856 Sheridan Road
Evanston, IL 60204-1856

Sigma Alpha Epsilon Scholarship

Type of award: Scholarship.
Intended use: For full-time junior, senior or graduate study at accredited 4-year or graduate institution.
Eligibility: Applicant or parent must be member of Sigma Alpha Epsilon. Applicant must be male.
Basis for selection: Applicant must demonstrate depth of character, leadership, service orientation and high academic achievement.
Application requirements: Recommendations, essay, transcript, proof of eligibility and nomination by chapter of fraternity.
Additional information: Grants are awarded to Sigma Alpha Epsilon brothers who are in good standing with the national fraternity office. Applicant must be involved in the fraternity and community.

Amount of award:	$500-$5,000
Number of awards:	15
Number of applicants:	25
Application deadline:	May 15
Notification begins:	August 1
Total amount awarded:	$16,000

Contact:
Sigma Alpha Epsilon Foundation
1856 Sheridan Road
Evanston, IL 60204-1856

Simpson PSB Fund

Simpson PSB Scholarship Program

Type of award: Scholarship, renewable.
Intended use: For undergraduate or graduate study at vocational, 2-year, 4-year or graduate institution.
Eligibility: Applicant or parent must be employed by Simpson PSB Fund. Applicant must be high school senior.
Additional information: Further information or an application contact Simpson PSB Fund directly.
  Amount of award: $2,500

Sippican, Inc.

W. Van Alan Clark Jr./Burgess Dempster Memorial Scholarship

Type of award: Scholarship, renewable.
Intended use: For undergraduate study at accredited vocational, 2-year or 4-year institution.
Eligibility: Applicant or parent must be employed by Sippican, Inc.
Basis for selection: Applicant must demonstrate financial need.
Additional information: For further information or an application contact Sippican, Inc. directly.
  Amount of award: $2,000

Sisters of Charity Health Care System

Regis-St. Elizabeth Scholarship

Type of award: Scholarship.
Intended use: For undergraduate study at accredited vocational, 2-year or 4-year institution.
Eligibility: Applicant or parent must be employed by Sisters of Charity Health Care System. Applicant must be high school senior.
Application requirements: Interview.
Additional information: For further information or application contact Sisters of Charity Health Care System directly.
  Amount of award: $500-$1,000

Sisters of Mercy Health System - St. Louis

Charles E. Thoele Scholarship

Type of award: Scholarship.
Intended use: For undergraduate study at accredited postsecondary institution.
Eligibility: Applicant or parent must be employed by Sisters of Mercy Health System. Applicant must be high school senior.
Additional information: For further information or an application contact Sisters of Mercy Health System - St. Louis directly.
  Amount of award: $1,000

Slope Indicator Co.

Slope Indicator Company Scholarship Program

Type of award: Scholarship.
Intended use: For undergraduate study at accredited postsecondary institution.
Eligibility: Applicant or parent must be employed by Slope Indicator Co. Applicant must be high school senior.
Additional information: For further information or an application contact Slope Indicator Company directly.
  Amount of award: $2,000

Slovak Gymnastic Union Sokol, USA

USA Milan Getting Scholarship

Type of award: Scholarship, renewable.
Intended use: For full-time undergraduate study at accredited 4-year institution.
Eligibility: Applicant or parent must be member of Slovak Gymnastic Union Sokol, USA. Applicant must be high school senior. Applicant must be U.S. citizen.
Basis for selection: Applicant must demonstrate depth of character, leadership, patriotism, seriousness of purpose and high academic achievement.
Application requirements: Recommendations and transcript.
Additional information: Must be a member of Slovak Gymnastic Union Sokol, USA, in good standing for four years. Recipient must attend a four-year college or university. A minimum scholastic average of C+ or equivalent is required. Recipients are chosen on the basis of scholastic merit, leadership, and character.

Amount of award:	$500
Number of awards:	11
Number of applicants:	13
Application deadline:	May 1
Notification begins:	September 30
Total amount awarded:	$5,500

Contact:
Slovak Gymnastic Union Sokol, USA
276 Prospect St.
East Orange, NJ 07017
Phone: 973-676-0280

Slovene National Benefit Society

Slovene Scholarship

Type of award: Scholarship, renewable.
Intended use: For full-time undergraduate, master's or doctoral study at accredited 2-year, 4-year or graduate institution in or outside United States.
Eligibility: Applicant or parent must be member of Slovene National Benefit Society.
Basis for selection: Applicant must demonstrate financial need and high academic achievement.
Application requirements: Transcript and proof of eligibility. Financial information as well as proof of involvement with the SNPJ.
Additional information: Must have been Society member for at least two years. Minimum 2.5 GPA required. Must participate in an Slovene National Benefit Society-approved activity within the Society.

Amount of award:	$250-$500
Number of awards:	120
Number of applicants:	125
Application deadline:	August 1
Notification begins:	October 1

Contact:
Slovene National Benefit Society
Joseph C. Evanish, National President
247 West Allegheny Road
Imperial, PA 15126
Website: www.snpj.com

Slovenian Women's Union of America

Slovenian Women's Union Scholarship

Type of award: Scholarship.
Intended use: For full-time freshman study at vocational, 2-year or 4-year institution in United States.
Eligibility: Applicant or parent must be member of Slovenian Women's Union of America. Applicant must be high school senior.
Basis for selection: Applicant must demonstrate depth of character, leadership, service orientation, financial need and high academic achievement.
Application requirements: Recommendations, essay and transcript. Submit 200-word essay on "Importance of My Heritage and Culture".
Additional information: Must be a Slovenian Women's Union member for at least three years.

Amount of award:	$1,000
Number of awards:	4
Number of applicants:	8
Application deadline:	March 1
Notification begins:	April 20
Total amount awarded:	$4,000

Contact:
Slovenian Women's Union of America
Scholarship Director
52 Oakridge Drive
Marguette, MI 49855
Phone: 906-249-4288

Smith Equipment

Smith Equipment Scholarship Program

Type of award: Scholarship, renewable.
Intended use: For undergraduate study at vocational, 2-year or 4-year institution.
Eligibility: Applicant or parent must be employed by Smith Equipment. Applicant must be high school senior.
Additional information: For further information or an application contact Smith Equipment directly.

Amount of award:	$1,500

743

SmithKline Beecham Clinical Laboratories

Dr. Vincent P. Perna Science Award

Type of award: Scholarship.
Intended use: For undergraduate study at accredited 4-year institution.
Eligibility: Applicant or parent must be employed by SmithKline Beecham Clinical Laboratories. Applicant must be high school senior.
Basis for selection: Applicant must demonstrate financial need.
Additional information: For further information or an application contact SmithKline Beecham Clinical Laboratories directly.
   Amount of award: $2,000

Society for Human Resource Management Foundation

Society for Human Resource Management Sons and Daughters Scholarship

Type of award: Scholarship, renewable.
Intended use: For undergraduate study at accredited 4-year institution.
Eligibility: Applicant or parent must be member of Society for Human Resource Management.
Additional information: For further information or an application contact Society for Human Resource Management directly.
   Amount of award: $1,500

Society of Automotive Engineers

American Engineers Longterm Member Scholarship

Type of award: Scholarship.
Intended use: For full-time senior study.
Eligibility: Applicant or parent must be member of Society of Automotive Engineers.
Basis for selection: Major/career interest in engineering. Applicant must demonstrate leadership.
Application requirements: Proof of eligibility and nomination by SAE Faculty Advisor, SAE or Section Chair or Vice Chair for Student Activities must submit a nomination form. SAE student member.
Additional information: Nominee must be an SAE student member. Selection is based on the nominee's support of SAE, the SAE collegiate chapter on campus, and the local SAE section.

Amount of award:	$1,000
Number of awards:	2
Number of applicants:	15
Application deadline:	April 1
Notification begins:	May 30
Total amount awarded:	$5,000

Contact:
Society of Automotive Engineers
Lori Pail
400 Commonwealth Drive
Warrendale, PA 15096-0001
Phone: 724-722-8534
Website: www.sae.org

Society of Naval Architects and Marine Engineers

Naval Architects and Marine Engineers Graduate Scholarship

Type of award: Scholarship.
Intended use: For master's study at graduate institution in United States.
Eligibility: Applicant or parent must be member of Society of Naval Architects and Marine Engineers. Applicant must be U.S. citizen or Canadian citizen.
Basis for selection: Major/career interest in engineering, marine; oceanography/marine studies; engineering. Applicant must demonstrate depth of character, leadership, seriousness of purpose, financial need and high academic achievement.
Application requirements: Recommendations, essay, transcript and proof of eligibility.
Additional information: Must be a member in good standing for at least one year prior to application. May be used at U.S. or Canadian institutions.

Amount of award:	$4,000-$12,000
Number of awards:	7
Number of applicants:	9
Application deadline:	January 31
Notification begins:	March 30
Total amount awarded:	$36,000

Contact:
Society of Naval Architects and Marine Engineers
601 Pavonia Avenue, Suite 400
Jersey City, NJ 70306

Society of Physics Students

Physics Students Leadership Scholarship

Type of award: Scholarship.
Intended use: For full-time junior study.

Eligibility: Applicant or parent must be member of Society of Physics Students.
Basis for selection: Major/career interest in science, general; physics. Applicant must demonstrate leadership, financial need and high academic achievement.
Application requirements: Recommendations and transcript.
Additional information: Must demonstrate interest in physics and be active participant of Society of Physics Students. One $4,000 award, two $2,000 awards and eleven $1,000 awards granted.
- Amount of award: $1,000-$4,000
- Number of awards: 15
- Number of applicants: 35
- Application deadline: February 15
- Notification begins: May 15
- Total amount awarded: $19,000

Contact:
Society of Physics Students
1 Physics Ellipse
College Park, MD 20740
Phone: 301-209-3007

Society of Women Engineers

Judith Resnik Memorial Scholarship

Type of award: Scholarship.
Intended use: For full-time senior study at accredited 4-year institution.
Eligibility: Applicant or parent must be member of Society of Women Engineers. Applicant must be female. Applicant must be U.S. citizen or permanent resident.
Basis for selection: Major/career interest in engineering; aerospace. Applicant must demonstrate high academic achievement.
Application requirements: Recommendations, essay, transcript and proof of eligibility.
Additional information: Must plan to pursue career in space industry. Must be enrolled in ABET-accredited program or SWE-approved school. Minimum GPA 3.5. Send SASE for application.
- Amount of award: $2,000
- Number of awards: 1
- Application deadline: February 1
- Notification begins: May 1
- Total amount awarded: $2,000

Women Engineers Northrop Corporation Founders Scholarship

Type of award: Scholarship.
Intended use: For full-time sophomore study at accredited 4-year institution in United States.
Eligibility: Applicant or parent must be member of Society of Women Engineers. Applicant must be female. Applicant must be U.S. citizen.
Basis for selection: Major/career interest in engineering. Applicant must demonstrate high academic achievement.
Application requirements: Recommendations, essay, transcript and proof of eligibility.
Additional information: Must be student member of SWE. Must be enrolled in ABET accredited program or SWE-approved school. Send SASE for application.
- Amount of award: $1,000
- Number of awards: 1
- Application deadline: February 1
- Notification begins: May 1
- Total amount awarded: $1,000

Contact:
Society of Women Engineers
120 Wall Street, 11th Floor
New York, NY 10005-3902
Phone: 212-509-9577
Fax: 212-509-0224

Women Engineers Texaco Scholarship

Type of award: Scholarship, renewable.
Intended use: For full-time junior study at accredited 4-year institution in United States.
Eligibility: Applicant or parent must be member of Society of Women Engineers. Applicant must be female. Applicant must be U.S. citizen or permanent resident.
Basis for selection: Major/career interest in engineering, chemical; engineering, mechanical. Applicant must demonstrate high academic achievement.
Application requirements: Recommendations, essay, transcript and proof of eligibility.
Additional information: Must rank in top 20 percent of class to qualify for scholarship renewal. $500 travel grant awarded separately for travel to National Convention/Student Conference. Must be enrolled in ABET- accredited program or SWE-approved school. Send SASE for application.
- Amount of award: $2,000
- Number of awards: 4
- Application deadline: February 1
- Notification begins: May 1
- Total amount awarded: $8,000

Contact:
Society of Women Engineers
120 Wall Street, 11th Floor
New York, NY 10005-3902
Phone: 212-509-9577
Fax: 212-509-0224

Soil and Water Conservation Society

Soil and Water Conservation Research Scholarship

Type of award: Research grant.
Intended use: For graduate study.
Eligibility: Applicant or parent must be member of Soil and Conservation Society.
Basis for selection: Major/career interest in natural resources/conservation.

Application requirements: Research proposal.
Additional information: Funds will be awarded for an investigation to determine deterrents to be overcome and improvements needed to effectively manage ecosystems with the objective of sustainability.

Amount of award:	$1,300
Number of awards:	1
Application deadline:	March 1
Total amount awarded:	$1,300

Soil and Water Conservation Student Leader Scholarship

Type of award: Scholarship.
Intended use: For full-time or half-time senior, master's study.
Eligibility: Applicant or parent must be member of Soil and Conservation Society.
Basis for selection: Major/career interest in natural resources/conservation; agricultural economics; forestry; engineering, agricultural; hydrology. Applicant must demonstrate high academic achievement.
Additional information: Must have been member of and held office in student chapter of SWCS for more than one year. Chapter must have had at least fifteen members. Those studying soils, planned land use management, wildlife biology, rural sociology, agronomy, or water management also eligible. May not be combined with other SWCS scholarships.

Amount of award:	$900
Number of awards:	2
Total amount awarded:	$1,800

Soil Conservation Scholarship

Type of award: Scholarship.
Intended use: For undergraduate study.
Eligibility: Applicant or parent must be member of Soil and Conservation Society.
Basis for selection: Major/career interest in natural resources/conservation. Applicant must demonstrate financial need.
Additional information: Must demonstrate integrity, ability, and competence in line of work. Must have completed at least one year of full-time employment and be currently employed in a natural resource conservation endeavor.

Amount of award:	$1,500
Number of awards:	3
Application deadline:	March 1
Total amount awarded:	$4,500

Contact:
Soil and Water Conservation Society
7515 Northeast Ankeny Road
Ankeny, IA 50021-9764
Website: www.swcs.org

Sons of Norway Foundation

Astrid G. Cates Fund

Type of award: Scholarship.
Intended use: For undergraduate study at vocational, 2-year or 4-year institution.
Eligibility: Applicant or parent must be member of Sons of Norway. Applicant must be U.S. citizen.
Basis for selection: Applicant must demonstrate service orientation, financial need and high academic achievement.
Application requirements: Recommendations, transcript and proof of eligibility.
Additional information: Applicant eligible if parent or grandparent is member of Sons of Norway.

Amount of award:	$500
Number of awards:	6
Number of applicants:	99
Application deadline:	March 1
Notification begins:	May 1
Total amount awarded:	$3,000

Contact:
Sons of Norway Foundation
c/o Sons of Norway
1455 West Lake Street
Minneapolis, MN 55408
Phone: 612-827-3611

Nancy Lorraine Jensen Memorial Scholarship

Type of award: Scholarship, renewable.
Intended use: For full-time freshman, sophomore, junior or senior study.
Eligibility: Applicant or parent must be member of Sons of Norway. Applicant must be female. Applicant must be U.S. citizen.
Basis for selection: Major/career interest in chemistry; physics; engineering, electrical and electronic; engineering, mechanical. Applicant must demonstrate depth of character, seriousness of purpose and high academic achievement.
Application requirements: Recommendations, essay, transcript and proof of eligibility.
Additional information: Employees of NASA Goddard Space Flight Center, Greenbelt, Maryland, and granddaughters of members of Sons of Norway (for three years) are also eligible. Minimum SAT score of 1200 or ACT score of 26.

Number of awards:	1
Application deadline:	March 1, March 1

Contact:
Sons of Norway Foundation
1455 West Lake Street
Minneapolis, MN 55408
Phone: 612-827-3611

Sony Music Entertainment, Inc.

Sony Music Scholarship Program

Type of award: Scholarship, renewable.
Intended use: For undergraduate study at accredited vocational, 2-year or 4-year institution.
Eligibility: Applicant or parent must be employed by Sony Music Entertainment Inc.
Basis for selection: Applicant must demonstrate financial need.
Additional information: For further information or an application contact Sony Music Entertainment Inc. directly.
    Amount of award: $500-$2,000

Soo Line Credit Union

SLCU Y.E.S. Scholarship Program

Type of award: Scholarship.
Intended use: For undergraduate study at vocational, 2-year or 4-year institution.
Eligibility: Applicant or parent must be employed by Soo Line Credit Union. Applicant must be high school senior.
Additional information: For further information or an application contact Soo Line Credit Union directly.
    Amount of award: $500

South-Western/ITP Publishing Company

International Thompson Publishing Scholarship

Type of award: Scholarship, renewable.
Intended use: For undergraduate study at accredited vocational, 2-year or 4-year institution.
Eligibility: Applicant or parent must be employed by South-Western Publishing Company.
Basis for selection: Applicant must demonstrate financial need.
Additional information: For further information or an application contact South-Western/ITP Publishing Company directly.
    Amount of award: $500-$3,000

Southeastern Claim Executives Association

Southeastern Claim Executives Association Scholarship

Type of award: Scholarship.
Intended use: For undergraduate study at accredited 2-year or 4-year institution.
Eligibility: Applicant or parent must be member of Southeastern Claim Executives Association.
Additional information: For further information or an application contact Southeastern Claim Executives Association directly.
    Amount of award: $1,500

Southwest Research Institute

Southwest Research Institute Dependents Scholarship Program

Type of award: Scholarship, renewable.
Intended use: For undergraduate study at 2-year or 4-year institution.
Eligibility: Applicant or parent must be employed by Southwest Research Institute. Applicant must be high school senior.
Additional information: For further information or an application contact Southwest Research Institute directly.
    Amount of award: $5,000

Space Center Company/ McNeely Foundation

Space Center Company/McNeely Foundation Scholarship

Type of award: Scholarship.
Intended use: For undergraduate or graduate study at accredited vocational, 2-year or 4-year institution.
Eligibility: Applicant or parent must be employed by Space Center Company.
Additional information: For further information or an application contact Space Center Co./McNeely Foundation directly.
    Amount of award: $1,000-$2,500

Spear, Leeds and Kellogg Foundation

Spear, Leeds and Kellogg Scholarship Award

Type of award: Scholarship, renewable.
Intended use: For undergraduate study at accredited vocational, 2-year or 4-year institution.
Eligibility: Applicant or parent must be employed by Spear, Leeds, and Kellogg.
Basis for selection: Applicant must demonstrate financial need.
Additional information: For further information or an application contact Spear, Leeds and Kellogg directly.
    Amount of award: $2,000-$8,000

Special Libraries Association

Mary Adeline Connor Professional Development Scholarship

Type of award: Scholarship.
Intended use: For post-bachelor's certificate, doctoral study.
Eligibility: Applicant or parent must be member of Special Libraries Association.
Basis for selection: Major/career interest in library science. Applicant must demonstrate seriousness of purpose, financial need and high academic achievement.
Application requirements: Recommendations, essay, transcript and proof of eligibility.
Additional information: Must have M.L.S. degree and have worked in special libraries for at least five years.
    Amount of award: $6,000
    Number of awards: 1
    Application deadline: October 31
    Notification begins: June 15
    Total amount awarded: $6,000

Special Libraries Institute for Scientific Information Scholarship

Type of award: Scholarship.
Intended use: For doctoral study.
Eligibility: Applicant or parent must be member of Special Libraries Association.
Basis for selection: Major/career interest in library science; information systems. Applicant must demonstrate seriousness of purpose, financial need and high academic achievement.
Application requirements: Recommendations, essay, transcript and proof of eligibility.
Additional information: Must be beginning doctoral candidate enrolled in library sciences program. Must have worked in special library. Medical librarian applicants ineligible.
    Amount of award: $1,000
    Number of awards: 1
    Application deadline: October 31
    Notification begins: May 15
    Total amount awarded: $1,000
Contact:
Special Libraries Association
1700 Eighteenth Street NW
Washington, DC 20009
Website: www.sla.org

Special Libraries Plenum Scholarship

Type of award: Scholarship.
Intended use: For doctoral study.
Eligibility: Applicant or parent must be member of Special Libraries Association.
Basis for selection: Major/career interest in library science; information systems. Applicant must demonstrate seriousness of purpose, financial need and high academic achievement.
Application requirements: Recommendations, essay, transcript and proof of eligibility. Proof of dissertation topic approval.
Additional information: Medical librarian applicants not eligible. Must be enrolled in graduate program leading to Ph.D. in library sciences.
    Amount of award: $1,000
    Number of awards: 1
    Number of applicants: 66
    Application deadline: October 31
    Notification begins: May 15
    Total amount awarded: $1,000
Contact:
Special Libraries Association
1700 Eighteenth Street NW
Washington, DC 20009-2508
Website: www.sla.org

St. Patrick Hospital

St. Patrick Hospital Sons and Daughters Scholarship Program

Type of award: Scholarship.
Intended use: For undergraduate study at vocational, 2-year or 4-year institution.
Eligibility: Applicant or parent must be employed by St. Patrick Hospital. Applicant must be high school senior.
Additional information: For further information or an application contact St Patrick Hospital directly.
    Amount of award: $500

Stanadyne Automotive Corporation

Stanadyne Automotive Corporation Scholarship Program

Type of award: Scholarship.
Intended use: For freshman study at accredited 4-year institution.
Eligibility: Applicant or parent must be employed by Stanadyne Automotive Corp.
Additional information: For further information or an application contact Stanadyne Automotive Corporation directly.
   Amount of award: $2,500

Stanhome, Inc.

Stanhome Scholarship

Type of award: Scholarship.
Intended use: For freshman study at accredited 2-year or 4-year institution.
Eligibility: Applicant or parent must be employed by Stanhome, Inc. Applicant must be high school junior, senior.
Basis for selection: Applicant must demonstrate leadership, seriousness of purpose, service orientation and high academic achievement.
Application requirements: Recommendations, essay and transcript. SAT I or PSAT scores.
Additional information: For children of full-time or regular part-time associates of Stanhome or affiliated company. Pre-application must be submitted in early September. The Entry Form must then be submitted to high school counselor by November 1.
   Amount of award: $2,500-$10,000
   Number of awards: 10
   Contact:
Scholarship Coordinator
Karen Gallo
333 Western Avenue
Westfield, MA 01085
Phone: 413-562-3631

Stanley Works

Stanley Sons and Daughters Scholarship Program

Type of award: Scholarship.
Intended use: For undergraduate study at accredited postsecondary institution.
Eligibility: Applicant or parent must be employed by Stanley Works. Applicant must be high school senior.
Basis for selection: Applicant must demonstrate financial need.
Additional information: For further information or application contact Stanley Works directly.
   Amount of award: $500-$2,500

Star Tribune/Cowles Media Company

Charles A. Freeman Memorial Scholarship

Type of award: Scholarship.
Intended use: For undergraduate or graduate study at accredited 4-year institution.
Eligibility: Applicant or parent must be employed by Star Tribune/Cowles Media Company.
Basis for selection: Applicant must demonstrate financial need.
Additional information: For further information or an application contact Star Tribune/Cowles Media Company directly.
   Amount of award: $2,000

Sto Corporation

Sto Corporation Scholarship Fund

Type of award: Scholarship.
Intended use: For undergraduate study at vocational, 2-year or 4-year institution.
Eligibility: Applicant or parent must be employed by Sto Corp. Applicant must be high school senior.
Additional information: For further information or an application contact Sto Corp. directly.
   Amount of award: $1,500

Stone Container Corporation

Stone Foundation Scholarship

Type of award: Scholarship, renewable.
Intended use: For undergraduate study at accredited vocational, 2-year or 4-year institution in or outside United States. Designated institutions: Must be affiliated with a school in the U.S.
Eligibility: Applicant or parent must be employed by Stone Container Corp. Applicant must be high school senior.
Basis for selection: Applicant must demonstrate depth of character, seriousness of purpose, service orientation and high academic achievement.
Application requirements: Recommendations, essay and transcript.
Additional information: Must be child of full-time employee (of at least two years) or of a company acquired by Stone. Children of Long-Term Incentive Plan participants not eligible. Scholarship renewals at the discretion of the Scholarship Committee and based on maintaining minimum 2.0 GPA. Must state career objectives. Applications available from any Stone Container office manager or personnel representative.

Stone Container Corporation: Stone Foundation Scholarship

Amount of award: $2,000
Number of awards: 10
Application deadline: March 31
Notification begins: May 30
Contact:
Stone Container Corporation/Stone Foundation Scholarship
Human Resources, ATTN: Nicole Stevens
150 North Michigan Avenue
Chicago, IL 60601

Stratus Computer, Inc.

Daniel M. Clemson Scholarship for Young Engineers

Type of award: Scholarship.
Intended use: For undergraduate or graduate study at accredited postsecondary institution.
Eligibility: Applicant or parent must be employed by Stratus Computer, Inc.
Additional information: For further information and to receive application contact Stratus Computers, Inc. directly.
Amount of award: $5,000

Stratus Scholarship Program

Type of award: Scholarship.
Intended use: For undergraduate study at accredited vocational, 2-year or 4-year institution.
Eligibility: Applicant or parent must be employed by Stratus Computer, Inc.
Basis for selection: Applicant must demonstrate financial need.
Additional information: For further information or an application contact Stratus Computers, Inc. directly.
Amount of award: $1,000

Sub-Zero Freezer Company, Inc.

Walter Wiest Scholarship Program

Type of award: Scholarship, renewable.
Intended use: For freshman study at vocational, 2-year or 4-year institution.
Eligibility: Applicant or parent must be employed by Sub-Zero Freezer Company, Inc. Applicant must be high school senior.
Additional information: For further information or an application contact Sub-Zero Freezer Company Incorporated directly.
Amount of award: $1,000

Suddath Companies

Richard H. Suddah Scholarship Foundation

Type of award: Scholarship, renewable.
Intended use: For freshman study at 2-year or 4-year institution.
Eligibility: Applicant or parent must be employed by The Suddath Companies. Applicant must be high school senior.
Additional information: For further information or an application contact Suddath Companies directly.

Supreme Guardian Council, International Order of Job's Daughters

Supreme Guardian Council, International Order of Job's Daughters Scholarship

Type of award: Scholarship.
Intended use: For freshman, sophomore, junior or senior study at postsecondary institution outside United States.
Eligibility: Applicant or parent must be member of International Order of Job's Daughters. Applicant must be single, female.
Basis for selection: Applicant must demonstrate depth of character, leadership, patriotism, seriousness of purpose, service orientation and financial need.
Application requirements: Recommendations and transcript.
Amount of award: $750
Application deadline: April 30
Notification begins: August 1
Contact:
Supreme Guardian Council
International Order of Job's Daughters
233 West 6 Street
Papillion, NE 68046
Phone: 402-592-7987
Fax: 402-592-2177
Website: www.iojd.org

Sykes Enterprises Incorporated

Sykes Student Scholarship

Type of award: Scholarship, renewable.
Intended use: For undergraduate study at 2-year or 4-year institution.
Eligibility: Applicant or parent must be employed by Sykes Enterprises, Incorporated. Applicant must be high school senior.

Additional information: For further information or an application contact Sykes Enterprises Incorporated directly.
    Amount of award: $2,000

SYSCO Corporation

John F. Eula Mae Baugh SYSCO Scholarship Program

Type of award: Scholarship, renewable.
Intended use: For undergraduate study.
Eligibility: Applicant or parent must be employed by SYSCO Corporation. Applicant must be high school senior.
Additional information: For further information or an application contact SYSCO Corporation directly.
    Amount of award: $1,000-$12,000

T.D. Williamson, Inc.

T.D. Williamson, Jr., Scholarship

Type of award: Scholarship.
Intended use: For undergraduate study at accredited vocational, 2-year or 4-year institution.
Eligibility: Applicant or parent must be employed by T. D. Williamson, Inc.
Additional information: For further information or an application contact T.D. Williamson, Inc. directly.
    Amount of award: $500-$1,000

T.J. Hale Company

T.J. Hale Company Scholarship

Type of award: Scholarship.
Intended use: For undergraduate study at accredited postsecondary institution.
Eligibility: Applicant or parent must be employed by T.J. Hale Company. Applicant must be high school senior.
Additional information: For further information or an application contact T.J. Hale Company directly.
    Amount of award: $1,500
Contact:
T.J. Hale Company

Talbots

Talbots Scholarship Fund

Type of award: Scholarship.
Intended use: For undergraduate study at accredited vocational, 2-year or 4-year institution.
Eligibility: Applicant or parent must be employed by Talbots.
Basis for selection: Applicant must demonstrate financial need.
Additional information: For further information or an application contact Talbots directly.
    Amount of award: $2,000

Target

Target Team Member Scholarship

Type of award: Scholarship.
Intended use: For freshman study at vocational, 2-year or 4-year institution.
Eligibility: Applicant or parent must be employed by Target. Applicant must be high school senior.
Additional information: For further information or an application contact Target directly.
    Amount of award: $1,000

Tau Beta Pi Association

Tau Beta Pi Fellowship

Type of award: Scholarship.
Intended use: For full-time graduate study at graduate institution in or outside United States.
Eligibility: Applicant or parent must be member of Tau Beta Pi.
Basis for selection: Major/career interest in engineering; engineering, civil; engineering, electrical and electronic; engineering, mechanical. Applicant must demonstrate depth of character, leadership, seriousness of purpose, service orientation and high academic achievement.
Application requirements: Recommendations, essay and proof of eligibility.
Additional information: Students planning to study chemical, nuclear, biomedical or environmental engineering also eligible. For application information send SASE.
    Amount of award: $10,000
    Number of awards: 35
    Number of applicants: 220
    Application deadline: January 15
    Notification begins: March 31
    Total amount awarded: $200,000
Contact:
Tau Beta Pi Association
P.O. Box 2697
Knoxville, TN 37901-2697
Phone: 423-546-4578
Website: www.tbp.org

Taylor Packing Corporation Inc.

Taylor Packing Corporation Scholarship Program

Type of award: Scholarship, renewable.
Intended use: For undergraduate study at vocational, 2-year or 4-year institution.
Eligibility: Applicant or parent must be employed by Taylor Packing Co., Inc. Applicant must be high school senior.
Additional information: For further information or an application contact Taylor Packing Company Incorporated directly.
    Amount of award: $1,000

TCF Foundation

TCF Scholarship Program

Type of award: Scholarship.
Intended use: For undergraduate study at vocational, 2-year or 4-year institution.
Eligibility: Applicant or parent must be employed by TCF Foundation. Applicant must be high school senior.
Additional information: For further information or an application contact TCF Foundation directly.
    Amount of award: $500-$2,500

TDS Corporate Scholarship Program

Telephone and Data Systems, Inc.

Type of award: Scholarship.
Intended use: For undergraduate study at accredited vocational, 2-year or 4-year institution.
Eligibility: Applicant or parent must be employed by TDS Telecom. Applicant must be high school senior.
Additional information: For further information or application contact TDS Telecom directly.
    Amount of award: $1,500

Techneglas

Techneglas Scholarship Program

Type of award: Scholarship, renewable.
Intended use: For freshman study at vocational, 2-year or 4-year institution.
Eligibility: Applicant or parent must be employed by Techneglas. Applicant must be high school senior.
Additional information: For further information or an application contact Techneglas directly.
    Amount of award: $1,000

Telephone and Data Systems, Inc.

TDS Corporate Scholarship Program

Type of award: Scholarship.
Intended use: For undergraduate study at vocational, 2-year or 4-year institution.
Eligibility: Applicant or parent must be employed by Telephone and Data Systems, Inc. Applicant must be high school senior.
Additional information: For further information or an application contact Telephone and Data Systems Incorporated directly.
    Amount of award: $2,500

Tennant

Tennant Scholarship

Type of award: Scholarship, renewable.
Intended use: For undergraduate study at accredited vocational, 2-year or 4-year institution.
Eligibility: Applicant or parent must be employed by TENNANT.
Additional information: For further information or an application contact Tennant directly.
    Amount of award: $1,100

Tescom Corporation

Tescom Scholarship

Type of award: Scholarship, renewable.
Intended use: For undergraduate study at accredited vocational, 2-year or 4-year institution.
Eligibility: Applicant or parent must be employed by Tescom Corporation.
Additional information: For further information or an application contact Tescom Corporation directly.
    Amount of award: $1,500

Tesoro Petroleum Corporation

Tesoro Petroleum Corporation Scholarship Program

Type of award: Scholarship, renewable.
Intended use: For undergraduate study at accredited vocational, 2-year or 4-year institution.
Eligibility: Applicant or parent must be employed by Tesoro Petroleum Companies, Inc.

Basis for selection: Applicant must demonstrate financial need.
Additional information: For further information or an application contact Tesoro Petroleum Companies, Inc. directly.
    Amount of award: $500-$1,250

Textilease Corporation

Oscar Stempler Scholarship

Type of award: Scholarship, renewable.
Intended use: For undergraduate study at accredited vocational, 2-year or 4-year institution.
Eligibility: Applicant or parent must be employed by Textilease Corporation.
Basis for selection: Applicant must demonstrate financial need.
Additional information: For further information or an application contact Textilease Corporation directly.
    Amount of award: $600-$2,000

Theodore R. and Vivian M. Johnson Scholarship Foundation

Theodore and Vivian Johnson Scholarship

Type of award: Scholarship, renewable.
Intended use: For undergraduate study at accredited 2-year or 4-year institution.
Eligibility: Applicant or parent must be employed by United Parcel Service--Florida.
Basis for selection: Applicant must demonstrate financial need.
Additional information: For further information or an application contact UPS-Florida directly or write to Citizens' Scholarship Foundation of America.
    Amount of award: $750-$4,500
Contact:
Citizens' Scholarship Foundation of America
Theodore R. and Vivian M. Johnson Scholarship
P.O. Box 297
St. Peter, MN 56082

Third Marine Division Association

Third Marine Division Memorial Scholarship Fund

Type of award: Scholarship, renewable.
Intended use: For undergraduate study at accredited vocational, 2-year or 4-year institution in United States.
Eligibility: Applicant or parent must be member of Third Marine Division Association. Applicant must be U.S. citizen. Applicant must be child of active service person or veteran who served in the Marines.
Basis for selection: Applicant must demonstrate financial need.
Application requirements: Proof of eligibility.
    Amount of award: $500-$1,250
    Number of applicants: 48
    Application deadline: April 15
    Total amount awarded: $32,250
Contact:
Third Marine Division Association
P.O. Box 634
Inverness, FL 34451-0634

Time Warner Inc.

Time Warner Academic Award

Type of award: Scholarship, renewable.
Intended use: For undergraduate study at accredited vocational, 2-year or 4-year institution.
Eligibility: Applicant or parent must be employed by Time Warner Inc.
Basis for selection: Applicant must demonstrate financial need.
Additional information: For further information or an application contact Time Warner Inc. directly.
    Amount of award: $500-$5,000

TJX Companies, Inc.

TJX Companies Scholarship Program

Type of award: Scholarship.
Intended use: For undergraduate study at vocational, 2-year or 4-year institution.
Eligibility: Applicant or parent must be employed by The TJX Companies, Inc. Applicant must be high school senior.
Additional information: For further information or an application contact TJX Companies Incorporated directly.
    Amount of award: $1,000

TMI Companies

Larry R. Strand Memorial Scholarship Program

Type of award: Scholarship.
Intended use: For undergraduate study at vocational, 2-year or 4-year institution.
Eligibility: Applicant or parent must be employed by TMI Companies. Applicant must be high school senior.
Additional information: For further information or an application contact TMI Companies directly.
    Amount of award: $750

Tri-Gas Inc.

Tri-Gas Scholarship Program

Type of award: Scholarship, renewable.
Intended use: For undergraduate study at vocational, 2-year or 4-year institution.
Eligibility: Applicant or parent must be employed by Tri-Gas Inc. Applicant must be high school senior.
Additional information: For further information or an application contact Tri-Gas Incorporated directly.
    Amount of award: $2,000

Trustmark Foundation

Trustmark Foundation College Scholarship Program

Type of award: Scholarship, renewable.
Intended use: For undergraduate study at accredited vocational, 2-year or 4-year institution.
Eligibility: Applicant or parent must be employed by Trustmark Foundation.
Additional information: For further information or an application contact Trustmark Foundation directly.
    Amount of award: $1,000

Tultex Foundation

Tultex Foundation Scholarship Program

Type of award: Scholarship, renewable.
Intended use: For undergraduate study at accredited vocational, 2-year or 4-year institution.
Eligibility: Applicant or parent must be employed by Tultex Corporation.
Additional information: For further information or an application contact Tultex Foundation directly.
    Amount of award: $1,200

Tuttle-Click Automotive Group

Tuttle-Click Automotive Group Education Assistance Program

Type of award: Scholarship, renewable.
Intended use: For undergraduate study at accredited vocational, 2-year or 4-year institution.
Eligibility: Applicant or parent must be employed by Tuttle-Click Automotive Group. Applicant must be high school senior.
Additional information: For further information or application contact Tuttle-Click Automotive Group directly.
    Amount of award: $3,000

Twin City Fan & Blower Co.

Twin City Fan & Blower Co. Scholarship Program

Type of award: Scholarship.
Intended use: For undergraduate study at accredited vocational, 2-year or 4-year institution.
Eligibility: Applicant or parent must be employed by Twin City Fan & Blower Co.
Additional information: For further information or an application contact Twin City Fan and Blower Company directly.
    Amount of award: $500-$1,000

Two/Ten International Footwear Foundation

Two/Ten International Footwear Foundation Scholarship

Type of award: Scholarship, renewable.
Intended use: For full-time undergraduate study at accredited vocational, 2-year or 4-year institution.
Eligibility: Applicant or parent must be employed by Footwear/Leather Industry. Applicant must be high school senior. Applicant must be U.S. citizen.
Basis for selection: Applicant must demonstrate depth of character, leadership, seriousness of purpose, financial need and high academic achievement.
Application requirements: Recommendations, essay, transcript and proof of eligibility.
Additional information: Must have worked 500 hours in footwear or leather industries or have a parent currently employed in this field for a minimum of one year. Open to high school seniors and students who have graduated high school in the past four years and are returning or applying to college full time in the fall.
    Amount of award: $200-$2,000
    Number of awards: 572
    Number of applicants: 977
    Application deadline: December 15
    Notification begins: June 15
Contact:
Two/Ten International Footwear Foundation
Attn: Scholarship Department
56 Main Street
Watertown, MA 02172
Phone: 800-346-3210

U.S. Bancorp

U.S. Bancorp Educational Awards Program

Type of award: Scholarship, renewable.
Intended use: For undergraduate study.
Eligibility: Applicant or parent must be employed by First Bank System, Inc.
Additional information: For further information or an application contact U.S. Bancorp directly.
    Amount of award: $500-$1,000

Ukrainian Fraternal Association

Ukrainian Fraternal Association Scholarship

Type of award: Scholarship, renewable.
Intended use: For full-time sophomore, junior or senior study.
Eligibility: Applicant or parent must be member of Ukrainian Fraternal Association. Applicant must be of Ukrainian heritage.
Basis for selection: Applicant must demonstrate financial need and high academic achievement.
Application requirements: Essay and transcript.
Additional information: Must have completed first semester of undergraduate study.
    Amount of award: $200-$1,000
    Number of awards: 50
    Application deadline: June 30
    Total amount awarded: $10,000
Contact:
Scholarship Scholarship Coordinator
440 Wyoming Avenue
Scranton, PA 18503

Ullico Inc. Family of Companies

Ullico Scholarship

Type of award: Scholarship.
Intended use: For undergraduate study at accredited vocational, 2-year or 4-year institution.
Eligibility: Applicant or parent must be employed by ULLICO, Inc.
Basis for selection: Applicant must demonstrate financial need.
Additional information: For further information or an application contact Ullico directly.
    Amount of award: $500-$1,000

Ultramar Diamond Shamrock Corporation

Ultramar Diamond Shamrock Student Educational Loan Program

Type of award: Loan.
Intended use: For freshman, sophomore, junior or senior study at accredited vocational, 2-year or 4-year institution.
Eligibility: Applicant or parent must be employed by Diamond Shamrock Refining & Marketing Co.
Basis for selection: Applicant must demonstrate financial need.
Additional information: For further information and an application contact Ultramar Diamond Shamrock Corporation directly.
    Amount of award: $1,500-$2,500

Union Pacific Corporation

Union Pacific Scholarship

Type of award: Scholarship, renewable.
Intended use: For full-time undergraduate study at 2-year or 4-year institution.
Eligibility: Applicant or parent must be employed by Union Pacific Corporation. Applicant must be high school junior.
Basis for selection: Applicant must demonstrate high academic achievement.
Application requirements: Transcript. SAT or ACT scores.
Additional information: Program not open to dependents of elected railroad officers. Applicant must be the son or daughter of a full-time, retired, or deceased employee of Union Pacific. Applicants must be in top quarter of class.
    Amount of award: $1,000
    Number of awards: 50
    Number of applicants: 550
    Application deadline: January 1
    Notification begins: April 1
Contact:
Scholarship Administrator, Union Pacific Corporation
1700 Farnam Street
10th Floor North
Omaha, NE 68102
Phone: 402-271-3233

Unique Industries, Inc.

Unique Industries Inc. Scholarship Program

Type of award: Scholarship.
Intended use: For undergraduate study at accredited postsecondary institution.
Eligibility: Applicant or parent must be employed by Unique Industries, Inc. Applicant must be high school senior.

Basis for selection: Applicant must demonstrate financial need.
Additional information: For further information or an application Unique Industries, Inc. directly.
 Amount of award: $2,000-$10,000

Unite

Unite National Scholarship

Type of award: Scholarship, renewable.
Intended use: For full-time freshman study at accredited 2-year or 4-year institution.
Eligibility: Applicant or parent must be member of Unite.
Application requirements: Proof of eligibility. Proof of college acceptance.
Additional information: Parent must be a Unite union member in good standing for at least two years. Children of officers or employees of Unite not eligible. Award is given over a period of four years.
 Amount of award: $325
 Number of awards: 25
 Number of applicants: 300
 Application deadline: June 30
Contact:
Unite
Scholarship Program/Education Department
1710 Broadway
New York, NY 10019

United Commercial Travelers of America

Retarded Citizens' Teachers Scholarship

Type of award: Scholarship, renewable.
Intended use: For junior, senior, master's or doctoral study at 4-year or graduate institution. Designated institutions: In United States and Canada.
Eligibility: Applicant or parent must be member of United Commercial Travelers of America.
Basis for selection: Major/career interest in education, special.
Application requirements: Transcript and proof of eligibility. Resume, statement of further education and/or career plans.
Additional information: Area of study special education, specifically mental retardation. Applicants must be of service to mentally handicapped in the US or Canada.
 Amount of award: $100-$750
 Number of applicants: 438
 Notification begins: January 15
 Total amount awarded: $154,256
Contact:
Scholarship Committee
632 North Park Street
Columbus, OH 43215-8619

United Food and Commercial Workers Union

United Food and Commercial Workers Union Scholarship Program

Type of award: Scholarship.
Intended use: For full-time undergraduate study at accredited 4-year institution.
Eligibility: Applicant or parent must be member of United Food and Commerical Workers. Applicant must be single, high school senior.
Application requirements: Transcript. Complete Biographical Questionaire. SAT or ACT scores.
Additional information: Applicant's parent must be member of United Food and Commercial Workers Union for one year priof to application.
 Amount of award: $4,000
 Number of awards: 7
 Number of applicants: 4,000
 Application deadline: December 31, March 15
 Total amount awarded: $28,000
Contact:
United Food and Commercial Workers Union
1775 K Street, N.W.
Washington, DC 20006
Phone: 202-223-3111

United Paperworkers International Union

United Paperworkers International Union Scholarship

Type of award: Scholarship.
Intended use: For full-time freshman study at 4-year institution in United States.
Eligibility: Applicant or parent must be member of United Paperworkers International Union. Applicant must be high school senior. Applicant must be U.S. citizen or permanent resident.
Basis for selection: Applicant must demonstrate depth of character, leadership, patriotism, seriousness of purpose, service orientation, financial need and high academic achievement.
Application requirements: Transcript.
Additional information: Scholarship recipients required to take one course in labor relations.

Amount of award: $1,000
Number of awards: 22
Number of applicants: 1,800
Application deadline: March 15
Notification begins: June 15
Total amount awarded: $22,000
Contact:
Scholarship Coordinator
United Paperworkers International Union
P.O. Box 1475
Nashville, TN 37202
Phone: 615-834-8590

United Parcel Service Foundation

George D. Smith Scholarship Program

Type of award: Scholarship, renewable.
Intended use: For freshman study at accredited vocational or 2-year institution.
Eligibility: Applicant or parent must be employed by United Parcel Service--Florida.
Basis for selection: Applicant must demonstrate financial need.
Additional information: For further information or an application contact United Parcel Service Foundation directly.
Amount of award: $500-$2,000

United Piece Dye Works, L.P.

United Piece Dye Works Scholarship Program

Type of award: Scholarship, renewable.
Intended use: For undergraduate study at accredited postsecondary institution.
Eligibility: Applicant or parent must be employed by United Piece Dye Works, L.P. Applicant must be high school senior.
Additional information: For further information or an application contact United Piece Dye Works, L.P. directly.
Amount of award: $7,000

United Service Automobile Association

United Service Automobile Association Scholarship

Type of award: Scholarship, renewable.
Intended use: For freshman study at accredited 4-year institution.
Eligibility: Applicant or parent must be employed by United Services Automobile Association.
Basis for selection: Applicant must demonstrate financial need.
Additional information: For further information or an application contact USAA directly.
Amount of award: $1,500

United States Cellular Corporation

USCC Scholarship Program

Type of award: Scholarship.
Intended use: For undergraduate study at vocational, 2-year or 4-year institution.
Eligibility: Applicant or parent must be employed by United States Cellular Corporation. Applicant must be high school senior.
Additional information: For further information or an application contact United States Cellular Corporation directly.
Amount of award: $2,500

United States Golf Association

United States Golf Association Education Assistance Program

Type of award: Scholarship, renewable.
Intended use: For undergraduate or graduate study at vocational, 2-year, 4-year or graduate institution.
Eligibility: Applicant or parent must be employed by United States Golf Association. Applicant must be high school senior.
Additional information: For further information or an application contact United States Golf Association directly.
Amount of award: $2,000-$15,000

United Transportation Union Insurance Association

United Transportation Union Insurance Association Scholarship

Type of award: Scholarship, renewable.
Intended use: For full-time undergraduate study at accredited vocational, 2-year or 4-year institution in or outside United States.
Eligibility: Applicant or parent must be member of United Transportation Union. Applicant must be high school senior. Applicant must be U.S. citizen or permanent resident.
Application requirements: Proof of eligibility.
Additional information: Members and direct descendants of living or deceased members eligible. Scholarships awarded by lottery.

Amount of award:	$500
Number of awards:	128
Number of applicants:	2,400
Application deadline:	March 31
Notification begins:	May 1
Total amount awarded:	$68,000

Contact:
United Transportation Union Insurance Association
14600 Detroit Ave.
Cleveland, OH 44107-4250

Univest Corporation

Univest Corporation Scholarship Program

Type of award: Scholarship.
Intended use: For undergraduate study at vocational, 2-year or 4-year institution.
Eligibility: Applicant or parent must be employed by Univest Corporation. Applicant must be high school senior.
Additional information: For further information or an application contact Univest Corporation directly.
    Amount of award: $1,000-$2,500

Unocal Foundation

Unocal Foundation Scholarship

Type of award: Scholarship, renewable.
Intended use: For freshman study at accredited 2-year or 4-year institution.
Eligibility: Applicant or parent must be employed by Unocal Corporation.
Basis for selection: Applicant must demonstrate financial need.
Additional information: Available to children of employees only. For further information or an application contact Unocal Foundation directly.
    Amount of award: $500-$3,000

Unum Foundation

Unum Foundation Scholarship

Type of award: Scholarship, renewable.
Intended use: For undergraduate study at accredited 2-year or 4-year institution.
Eligibility: Applicant or parent must be employed by UNUM.
Basis for selection: Applicant must demonstrate financial need.
Additional information: For further information or an application contact Unum Foundation directly.
    Amount of award: $1,000-$5,000

UPS Foundation

James E. Casey Canadian Scholarship

Type of award: Scholarship, renewable.
Intended use: For freshman study at accredited 4-year institution.
Eligibility: Applicant or parent must be employed by United Parcel Service--Florida.
Basis for selection: Applicant must demonstrate financial need.
Additional information: For further information or an application contact UPS Foundation directly.
    Amount of award: $2,000-$6,000

USF&G Foundation, Inc.

USF&G Foundation Scholarship

Type of award: Scholarship, renewable.
Intended use: For freshman study at accredited vocational, 2-year or 4-year institution.
Eligibility: Applicant or parent must be employed by USF&G.
Basis for selection: Applicant must demonstrate financial need.
Additional information: For further information or an application contact USF&G Foundation, Inc. directly.
    Amount of award: $500-$2,500

UST

UST Sons and Daughters Scholarship

Type of award: Scholarship, renewable.
Intended use: For undergraduate study at accredited vocational, 2-year or 4-year institution.
Eligibility: Applicant or parent must be employed by UST.
Basis for selection: Applicant must demonstrate financial need.
Additional information: For further information or an application contact UST directly.
    Amount of award: $200-$2,500

USX Foundation Inc.

U.S. Steel Scholarship

Type of award: Scholarship, renewable.
Intended use: For undergraduate study at accredited vocational, 2-year or 4-year institution outside United States.
Eligibility: Applicant or parent must be employed by USX Foundation, Inc. Applicant must be high school senior.
Basis for selection: Applicant must demonstrate financial need.
Additional information: Must be child of employee of USX Foundation, Inc. For further information or application contact the foundation directly.
    Amount of award: $2,500
Contact:
USX Foundation, Inc.

Varian Associates, Inc.

Edward L. Ginzton Scholars Program

Type of award: Scholarship, renewable.
Intended use: For freshman study at accredited 4-year institution.
Eligibility: Applicant or parent must be employed by Varian Associates, Inc.
Additional information: For further information or an application contact Varian Associates, Inc. directly.
    Amount of award: $2,500

Veeder-Root Company

Wilbur C. Stauble Trust Scholarship

Type of award: Scholarship.
Intended use: For freshman study at accredited 4-year institution.
Eligibility: Applicant or parent must be employed by Veeder-Root Company.
Additional information: For further information or an application contact Veeder-Root Company directly.
    Amount of award: $500-$1,500

Vesuvius Americas

Vesuvius Americas Scholarship Fund

Type of award: Scholarship.
Intended use: For undergraduate or graduate study at accredited postsecondary institution.
Eligibility: Applicant or parent must be employed by Vesuvius USA. Applicant must be high school senior.
Basis for selection: Applicant must demonstrate financial need.
Additional information: For further information or an application contact Vesuvius USA directly.
    Amount of award: $500-$1,000
Contact:
Vesuvius Americas

VF Corporation

VF Corporation Scholarship for Children of Employees

Type of award: Scholarship, renewable.
Intended use: For undergraduate study at accredited 2-year or 4-year institution.
Eligibility: Applicant or parent must be employed by VF Corporation.
Additional information: For further information or an application contact VF Corporation directly.
    Amount of award: $1,000-$2,000

Voith Hydro, Inc.

Voith Companies Scholarship

Type of award: Scholarship.
Intended use: For undergraduate study at accredited vocational, 2-year or 4-year institution.

Eligibility: Applicant or parent must be employed by Voith Companies.
Basis for selection: Applicant must demonstrate financial need.
Additional information: Must be child of employee of Voith Companies. For further information or an application contact Voith Hydro, Inc. directly.
    Amount of award: $2,000-$2,500

Voith Sulzer Paper Technology North America, Inc.

Voith Sulzer Scholarship

Type of award: Scholarship.
Intended use: For undergraduate study at accredited vocational, 2-year or 4-year institution.
Eligibility: Applicant or parent must be employed by Voith Sulzer.
Additional information: For further information or an application contact Voith, Inc. directly.
    Amount of award: $1,000

Vollrath Company, L.L.C.

Vollrath Company Scholarship Program

Type of award: Scholarship, renewable.
Intended use: For freshman study at accredited vocational, 2-year or 4-year institution.
Eligibility: Applicant or parent must be employed by Vollrath Company, Inc.
Additional information: For further information or an application contact Vollrath Company, L.L.C. directly.
    Amount of award: $1,000-$2,000

Volvo Cars of North America, Inc.

Volvo Scholars Program

Type of award: Scholarship, renewable.
Intended use: For undergraduate study at accredited postsecondary institution.
Eligibility: Applicant or parent must be employed by Volvo Cars of North America, Inc. Applicant must be high school senior.
Additional information: For further information or an application contact Volvo Cars of North America, Inc. directly.
    Amount of award: $2,000
Contact:
Volvo Cars of North America, Inc.

VPI Foundation Inc.

VPI Foundation Scholarship for Sons and Daughters

Type of award: Scholarship, renewable.
Intended use: For undergraduate study at vocational, 2-year or 4-year institution.
Eligibility: Applicant or parent must be employed by VPI Foudation, Inc. Applicant must be high school senior.
Additional information: For further information or an application contact VPI Foundation directly.
    Amount of award: $1,000-$2,000

VVP America, Inc.

S.E. Binnswanger Memorial Scholarship

Type of award: Scholarship.
Intended use: For full-time undergraduate study at accredited vocational, 2-year or 4-year institution in United States.
Eligibility: Applicant or parent must be employed by VVP America, Inc. Applicant must be U.S. citizen.
Basis for selection: Applicant must demonstrate depth of character, leadership, seriousness of purpose, service orientation, financial need and high academic achievement.
Application requirements: Portfolio, recommendations, essay and transcript.
Additional information: Parent must obtain application from branch office.
    Amount of award: $1,000-$2,500
    Number of awards: 8
    Number of applicants: 25
    Application deadline: March 15
    Notification begins: May 1
    Total amount awarded: $12,000
Contact:
VVP America, Inc.
965 Ridge Lake Boulevard
Memphis, TN 38120

W.E. Lahr Co.

William E. Lahr Scholarship Program

Type of award: Scholarship.
Intended use: For undergraduate study at vocational, 2-year or 4-year institution.
Eligibility: Applicant or parent must be employed by W.E. Lahr Co. Applicant must be high school senior.
Additional information: For further information or an application contact W.E. Lahr Company directly.
    Amount of award: $500-$3,000

Wakefern Food Corporation

Shoprite Scholarship Program

Type of award: Scholarship, renewable.
Intended use: For undergraduate study at accredited vocational, 2-year or 4-year institution.
Eligibility: Applicant or parent must be employed by Wakefern Food Corporation.
Additional information: For further information or an application contact Wakefern Food Corporation directly.
    Amount of award: $1,000-$3,000

Wal-Mart Foundation

Walton Foundation Scholarship

Type of award: Scholarship, renewable.
Intended use: For full-time freshman, sophomore, junior or senior study at 2-year or 4-year institution.
Eligibility: Applicant or parent must be employed by Wal-Mart Stores, Inc. Applicant must be high school senior.
Basis for selection: Applicant must demonstrate leadership and financial need.
Application requirements: Recommendations, transcript and proof of eligibility. SAT/ACT scores.
Additional information: $6,000 scholarship payable over four years. Applicant's parent (associate) must have been employed with Wal-Mart full-time at least one year as of March 1. Applications available in December from store or by calling/writing the Wal-Mart Foundation.

Amount of award:	$6,000
Number of awards:	70
Number of applicants:	1,250
Application deadline:	March 1
Total amount awarded:	$420,000

Contact:
Wal-Mart Foundation
702 SW 8 Street
Bentonville, AR 72716-8071

Walker Forge, Inc.

Walker Forge Scholarship Program

Type of award: Scholarship, renewable.
Intended use: For undergraduate study at accredited vocational, 2-year or 4-year institution.
Eligibility: Applicant or parent must be employed by Walker Forge, Inc.
Basis for selection: Applicant must demonstrate financial need.
Additional information: For further information or an application contact Walker Forge, Inc. directly.
    Amount of award: $500-$1,000

Walter O. Wells Foundation

Walter O. Wells Foundation Scholarship Program

Type of award: Scholarship.
Intended use: For undergraduate study at vocational, 2-year or 4-year institution.
Eligibility: Applicant or parent must be employed by Walter O. Wells Foundation. Applicant must be high school senior.
Additional information: For further information or an application contact Walter O. Wells Foundation directly.
    Amount of award: $500-$1,500

Washington Osteopathic Foundation

Washington Osteopathic Loan

Type of award: Loan, renewable.
Intended use: For full-time first professional study in United States. Designated institutions: Institution must be accredited by the American Osteopathic Association.
Eligibility: Applicant or parent must be member of Washington Osteopathic Medical Association.
Basis for selection: Applicant must demonstrate financial need and high academic achievement.
Application requirements: Recommendations, transcript and proof of eligibility.
Additional information: 3.0 GPA recommended. Recipients must begin practice within 30 days of completing their internship/residency and practice for three years in Washington state. Application deadlines are as follows: 2/15, 5/15, 8/15, 11/15.

Amount of award:	$5,000
Number of awards:	1
Number of applicants:	1
Application deadline:	February 15, May 15
Total amount awarded:	$5,000

Contact:
Washington Osteopathic Foundation
P.O. Box 16486
Seattle, WA 98116
Phone: 206-937-5358

Waters Corporation

Waters Scholarship Program

Type of award: Scholarship, renewable.
Intended use: For freshman study.
Eligibility: Applicant or parent must be employed by Waters Corporation. Applicant must be high school senior.
Additional information: For further information or an application contact Waters Corporation directly.
    Amount of award: $5,000

Watlow Electric Manufacturing

Watlow Employee Children Scholarship Fund

Type of award: Scholarship.
Intended use: For undergraduate study at vocational, 2-year or 4-year institution.
Eligibility: Applicant or parent must be employed by Watlow Electric Manufacturing Co.
Additional information: For further information or an application contact Watlow Electric Manufacturing directly.
   Amount of award: $1,500

Wells Fargo

Wells Fargo Employees' Dependent Children Scholarship

Type of award: Scholarship.
Intended use: For undergraduate study at accredited vocational, 2-year or 4-year institution.
Eligibility: Applicant or parent must be employed by Wells Fargo Bank.
Basis for selection: Applicant must demonstrate financial need.
Additional information: For further information or an application contact Wells Fargo directly.
   Amount of award: $500-$3,000

Wendell J. Kelley Scholarship

Illinois Power Company Wendell J. Kelley Scholarship

Type of award: Scholarship, renewable.
Intended use: For full-time undergraduate study at accredited 4-year institution in Illinois. Designated institutions: Any of 15 institutions within Illinois Power Service territory.
Eligibility: Applicant or parent must be employed by Illinois Power Company. Applicant must be residing in Illinois.
Basis for selection: Applicant must demonstrate high academic achievement.
Application requirements: Transcript.
Additional information: For further information or an application contact Wendell J. Kelley Scholarship directly.

   Amount of award: $2,000
   Number of awards: 24
   Number of applicants: 700
   Application deadline: January 6
   Notification begins: July 7
   Total amount awarded: $48,000

West Company, Inc.

Herman O. West Scholarship

Type of award: Scholarship, renewable.
Intended use: For full-time undergraduate study at accredited 2-year or 4-year institution.
Eligibility: Applicant or parent must be employed by West Company. Applicant must be high school senior. Applicant must be U.S. citizen.
Basis for selection: Applicant must demonstrate high academic achievement.
Application requirements: Proof of eligibility.
Additional information: Parent must be employee of The West Company, Inc. Award is renewable annually for a maximum of four years.
   Amount of award: $2,500
   Number of awards: 27
   Number of applicants: 24
   Application deadline: February 28
   Notification begins: May 1
   Total amount awarded: $44,797
Contact:
West Company, Inc.
H.O. West Foundation
101 Gordon Drive
Lionville, PA 19341-0645

West Group

West Group Scholarship Program

Type of award: Scholarship, renewable.
Intended use: For undergraduate study at accredited vocational, 2-year or 4-year institution.
Eligibility: Applicant or parent must be employed by West Publishing Company.
Additional information: For further information or an application contact West Group directly.
   Amount of award: $2,000

Western Beef

Western Beef Scholarship Program

Type of award: Scholarship.
Intended use: For undergraduate study.
Eligibility: Applicant or parent must be employed by Western Beef. Applicant must be high school senior.
Additional information: For further information or an application contact Western Beef directly.
    Amount of award: $1,000

WestPlains Energy

WestPlains Energy Scholarship

Type of award: Scholarship, renewable.
Intended use: For undergraduate study at accredited vocational, 2-year or 4-year institution.
Eligibility: Applicant or parent must be employed by WestPlains Energy.
Additional information: For further information or an application contact WestPlains Energy directly.
    Amount of award: $500-$1,500

Weyerhaeuser Company Foundation

Weyerhaeuser Community Education Scholarship Program

Type of award: Scholarship, renewable.
Intended use: For freshman study at accredited vocational or 2-year institution.
Eligibility: Applicant or parent must be employed by Weyerhaeuser Company.
Basis for selection: Applicant must demonstrate financial need.
Additional information: For further information or an application, contact Weyerhaeuser Company Foundation directly.
    Amount of award: $500-$4,000

Wheaton Franciscan Services, Inc.

Sister Rose Mary Pint Scholarship Program

Type of award: Scholarship.
Intended use: For undergraduate study at vocational, 2-year or 4-year institution.
Eligibility: Applicant or parent must be employed by Wheaton
Additional information: For further information or an application contact Wheaton Franciscan Services Incorporated directly.
    Amount of award: $3,000

William Beaumont Hospital

William Beaumont Hospital Scholarship Program

Type of award: Scholarship, renewable.
Intended use: For undergraduate study at vocational, 2-year or 4-year institution.
Eligibility: Applicant or parent must be employed by William Beaumont Hospital. Applicant must be high school senior.
Additional information: For further information or an application contact William Beumont Hospital directly.
    Amount of award: $1,000

William S. Davila Scholarship Fund Endowment

William S. Davila Scholarship

Type of award: Scholarship.
Intended use: For freshman study at accredited 4-year institution.
Eligibility: Applicant or parent must be employed by Food Industry. Applicant must be residing in California or Nevada.
Additional information: Must work in the food industry or be son or daughter of person working in the food industry, including retail supermarket companies, manufacturers, brokers and distributors of food products sold in retail stores. Must attend public high school in one of the following Southern California counties: Los Angeles, Orange, San Diego, Fresno, Kearns, Tulare, San Luis Obispo, Santa Barbara. Students in Clark County, Nevada also eligible. Further information and application available from high school guidance office.
    Amount of award: $1,000-$2,500

Williams Steel and Hardware

Williams Steel and Hardware Scholarship

Type of award: Scholarship, renewable.
Intended use: For undergraduate study at accredited vocational, 2-year or 4-year institution.
Eligibility: Applicant or parent must be employed by Wiliams Steel & Hardware.
Basis for selection: Applicant must demonstrate financial need.

Additional information: For further information or an application contact Williams Steel and Hardware directly.
Amount of award: $300-$1,200

Willis Corroon

Robert F. Corroon Legacy Scholarship

Type of award: Scholarship.
Intended use: For undergraduate study at accredited vocational, 2-year or 4-year institution.
Eligibility: Applicant or parent must be employed by Willis Corroon. Applicant must be high school senior.
Additional information: Must be child of employee of Willis Corroon. For further information or application contact Willis Corroon directly.
Amount of award: $2,500
Contact:
Scholarship Coordinator

Winegard Company

Winegard Company Scholarship

Type of award: Scholarship.
Intended use: For undergraduate or graduate study at accredited postsecondary institution.
Eligibility: Applicant or parent must be employed by Winegard Company. Applicant must be high school senior.
Additional information: Must be child of employee of Winegard Company. For further information or application contact Winegard Company directly.
Amount of award: $1,500
Contact:
Winegard Company

Wisconsin Central Ltd.

Wisconsin Central Ltd. & Algoma Central Railway Scholarship

Type of award: Scholarship.
Intended use: For undergraduate study at accredited vocational, 2-year or 4-year institution.
Eligibility: Applicant or parent must be employed by Wisconsin Central Ltd.
Additional information: For further information or an application contact Wisconsin Central Ltd. directly.
Amount of award: $1,000

Wisconsin Energy Corporation Foundation, Inc.

Wisconsin Energy Corporation Daughters & Sons Scholarship

Type of award: Scholarship, renewable.
Intended use: For undergraduate study at vocational, 2-year or 4-year institution.
Eligibility: Applicant or parent must be employed by Wisconsin Energy Corporation Foundation, Inc. Applicant must be high school senior.
Additional information: For further information or an application contact Wisconsin Energy Corporation directly.
Amount of award: $500-$5,000

Wisconsin Power and Light Foundation

Wisconsin Power and Light Scholarship

Type of award: Scholarship, renewable.
Intended use: For freshman study at accredited vocational, 2-year or 4-year institution.
Eligibility: Applicant or parent must be employed by Wisconsin Power & Light.
Additional information: For further information or an application contact Wisconsin Power and Light Foundation directly.
Amount of award: $1,000

Witco Corporation

Witco Corporation Scholarship Program

Type of award: Scholarship, renewable.
Intended use: For undergraduate study at vocational, 2-year or 4-year institution.
Eligibility: Applicant or parent must be employed by Witco Corporation. Applicant must be high school senior.
Additional information: For further information or an application contact Witco Corporation directly.
Amount of award: $2,500

World Federalist Association

"Builders of a Better World" Scholarship Program

Type of award: Scholarship, renewable.
Intended use: For undergraduate study at accredited 2-year or 4-year institution in or outside United States.
Eligibility: Applicant or parent must be member of World Federalist Association.
Basis for selection: Applicant must demonstrate depth of character, leadership, seriousness of purpose and service orientation.
Application requirements: Recommendations, essay, transcript, proof of eligibility and research proposal.
Additional information: Applicants must be members before applying--student membership dues are $5 and must be received by February 1st of 1999.
    Amount of award: $500-$1,500
    Number of awards: 5
    Application deadline: April 15
    Notification begins: August 30
Contact:
World Federalist Association
418 7th St., SE
Washington, DC 20003-2796

Yankee Gas Services Company

Yankee Gas Scholarship Program

Type of award: Scholarship, renewable.
Intended use: For undergraduate study at accredited postsecondary institution.
Eligibility: Applicant or parent must be employed by Yankee Gas Services Company. Applicant must be high school senior.
Basis for selection: Applicant must demonstrate financial need.
Additional information: For further information or an application contact Yankee Gas Services Company directly.
    Amount of award: $1,000
Contact:
Yankee Gas Services Company

YKK Corporation of America

YKK Dependent Children Scholarship Program

Type of award: Scholarship, renewable.
Intended use: For undergraduate study at accredited vocational, 2-year or 4-year institution.
Eligibility: Applicant or parent must be employed by YKK Corporation of America. Applicant must be high school senior.
Additional information: For further information or application contact YKK Corporation of America directly.
    Amount of award: $750-$1,500
Contact:
YKK Corporation of America

Zee Medical, Inc.

Tomlinson Memorial Scholarship Program

Type of award: Scholarship.
Intended use: For undergraduate study at accredited vocational, 2-year or 4-year institution.
Eligibility: Applicant or parent must be employed by Zee Service, Inc.
Additional information: For further information or an application contact Zee Medical Inc. and its distributors directly.
    Amount of award: $1,000

Program Index

"Builders of a Better World" Scholarship Program, 765
"Will to Win" Asthma Athlete Scholarship, 564
1890 National Scholars Program, 228
1st Infantry Division/Lieutenant General C. R. Huebner Scholarship, 247
25th Infantry Division Educational Memorial Scholarship, 621
3M Internship, 247
A.J. "Andy" Spielman Travel Agents Scholarship, 344
* A.P. Giannini Scholarship, 491
A.T. Anderson Memorial Scholarship, 636
A.W. Bodine Memorial Scholarship, 595
* AAUW Educational Foundation International Fellowship Program, 263
Abbie Sargent Memorial Scholarship, 247
* Abe Fellowship Program, 571
* Abe Schechter Graduate Scholarship, 555
Aboriculture Internship, 469
Academic-Year Ambassadorial Scholarship, 561
Academy of Television Arts and Sciences Summer Student Internship, 247
Achievement Award, 595
Acrometal Family of Companies Scholarship Program, 622
Actuarial Club Scholarship, 454
Actuarial Society Minority Scholarship, 579
Adaptec Scholarship, 622
* Adelle and Erwin Tomash Fellowship, 378
ADHA Institute for Oral Health Minority Scholarship, 249
ADHA Institute for Oral Health Part-Time Scholarship, 249
Admiral Grace M. Hopper Scholarship, 583
Adult Undergraduate Incentive Award, 452
* Advanced Predoctoral Pharmacology and Toxicology Fellowship, 546
* Advanced Research Grants: Japan, 571
* Advanced Research Grants: Vietnam, 572
* Advanced Research Program, 437

Advertising Internship for Minority Students, 261
Advertising/Public Relations Internship, 366
* Aera/Spencer Research Training Fellowship, 591
Aeronautics and Astronautics Undergraduate Scholarship, 281
* Aerospace Graduate Research Fellowship Program, 172
Aerospace Undergraduate Scholarship Program, 173
* AFOSR Summer Research Program, 53
* African-American Doctoral Teacher Loan / Scholarship, 140
AGC of Maine Scholarship Program, 357
Aging Research Scholarship, 272
AGL Resources Inc. Scholarship, 622
Agnes E. Vaghi-Cornaro Scholarship, 491
Agnes Jones Jackson Scholarship, 710
Aiea General Hospital Association Scholarship, 419
* Aila/Yamagami/Hope Fellowship, 449
Air Force Aid Society Education Grant, 251
Air Force Four-Year Scholarships(Types # 1,2 and Targeted), 217
Air Force Sergeants Association Scholarship, 622
Air Liquide America Foundation Scholarship, 623
Air Safety Foundation D.B. Burnside Scholarship, 256
Air Safety Foundation McAllister Memorial Scholarship, 256
Air Traffic Control Children of Specialists Scholarship, 623
Air Traffic Control Full-Time Employee/Part-Time Student Scholarship, 623
Air Traffic Control Half/Full-Time Student Scholarship, 251
Air Travel Card Travel Agents Scholarship, 344
Airgas Scholarship, 624
Airport Executives Scholarship, 261
Al and Art Murray Scholarship, 469
AL Kremers Scholarship Program, 677
* Alabama Chiropractic Scholarship, 256
Alabama GI Dependents Educational Benefit, 55

Alabama Junior/Community College Academic Scholarship, 54
Alabama Junior/Community College Athletic Scholarship, 54
Alabama Junior/Community College Leadership Scholarship, 54
Alabama Junior/Community College Performing Arts Scholarship, 55
Alabama National Guard Educational Assistance Award, 53
Alabama Nursing Scholarship Program, 55
Alabama Robert C. Byrd Honors Scholarship, 54
Alabama Scholarship for Dependents of Blind Parents, 54
Alabama Student Assistance Program, 53
Alabama Student Grant, 53
* Alabama Technology Scholarship for Alabama Teachers, 53
Alaska Airlines Travel Agents Scholarship, 344
Alaska Brindle Memorial Scholarship Loan, 257
Alaska Educational Aid For Dependents of POWS/MIAs, 56
Alaska Educational Incentive Grant, 55
Alaska Family Education Loan, 55
Alaska Student Loan, 56
Alaska Teacher Scholarship Loan, 56
* Albania: Full Grant (Fulbright), 77
Alco Gravure Scholarship Program, 624
Alcoa Sons and Daughters Scholarship Program, 624
Alexander Graham Bell Association for the Deaf Scholarship, 257
* Alexander Hollaender Distinguished Postdoctoral Fellowship, 197
Alexandra A. Sonenfeld Award, 674
Alfa Laval Scholarship Program, 624
* Alfred P. Sloan Foundation Fellowship in Molecular Evolution, 179
* Alice Smith Fellowship, 221
* ALISE Dissertation Competition, 359
* ALISE Methodology Paper Competition, 359
* ALISE Research Grant Award, 656
* ALISE Research Paper Competition, 656
All-Inland Scholarship Program, 693
Allen Lee Hughes Fellows Program, 353
* Allen Lee Hughes Internship, 353

*Graduate/nondegree study

Program Index

Alliance for Excellence Honored Scholars: Academics, 474
Alliance for Excellence Honored Scholars: Performing Arts, 475
Alliance for Excellence Honored Scholars: Technological Innovation, 475
Alliance for Excellence Honored Scholars: Visual Arts, 475
Allied Domecq Retailing USA Scholarship Program, 678
Allied Group Scholarship Program, 624
*Allport Intergroup Relations Prize, 577
Allstate Scholarship, 624
Alma White--Delta Chapter, Delta Kappa Gamma Scholarship, 419
Alpha Beta Gamma International Scholarship, 625
*Alpha Lambda Delta Fellowship, 711
Alpha Mu Gamma Scholarship, 625
Alphonse A. Miele Scholarship, 601
Alphonso Deal Scholarship, 480
Alpine Club A.K. Gilkey and Putnam/Bedayn Research Grant, 259
Alwin B. Newton Scholarships, 341
Alyce M. Cafaro Scholarship, 491
Ambucs Scholarship, 257
*Amelia Earhart Fellowship, 619
*Amer. Fdn. For Pharm. Educ./Clinical Pharmacy Post-Pharm.D. Fellowship In The Biomedical Research Sciences, 272
*American Foundation for Pharmaceutical Education Predoctoral Fellowship, 258
American Academic Sanitarians Scholarship, 483
*American Academy in Rome/Rome Prize Fellowships in the School of Fine Arts, 57
*American Academy in Rome/Rome Prize Pre- and Post-Doctoral Fellowship, 57
American Action Fund Scholarship, 483
*American Art Dissertation Fellowship, 270
*American Association for the Advancement of Science Risk Assessment Science & Engineering Fellows Program, 260
*American Association for the Advancement of Science Royer Revelle Fellowship in Global Stewardship, 261
American Association of Japanese University Women Scholarship, 262
American Association Of Medical Assistants Endowment (AAMA)/Maxine Williams Scholarship Program, 262

American Association of Pharmaceutical Scientists Gateway Scholarship, 272
*American Association of University Women International Fellowship, 264
*American Bar Doctoral Dissertation Fellowship, 265
*American Cancer Society Doctoral Degree Scholarship in Cancer Nursing, 266
*American Cancer Society Training Grants In Clinical Oncology Social Work (Tgcosw), 266
*American College of Musicians Musical Composition Test, 268
American Congress on Surveying and Mapping, 628
American Congress on Surveying and Mapping/Allen Chelf Scholarship, 268
American Congress on Surveying and Mapping/McDonnel Memorial Scholarship, 269
American Congress on Surveying and Mapping/National Society of Professional Surveyors Scholarship for Women, 629
American Conservatory Theater Production Internships, 269
*American Dissertation Fellowship, 264
American Dryer Corporation Scholarship, 630
American Electroplaters and Surface Finishers Society Scholarship, 272
American Engineers Longterm Member Scholarship, 744
American Ex-POW/Peter Connacher Memorial Scholarship, 535
American Express Card Scholarship Program, 280
American Express Scholarship Program, 630
American Express Travel Agents Scholarship, 344
*American Foundation for Urologic Disease Health Policy Research Program, 274
*American Foundation for Urologic Disease Intramural Urologic Oncology Ph.D./ Post-Doctoral Research Training Program, 275
*American Foundation for Urologic Disease Intramural Urologic Oncology Research Training, 275
*American Foundation for Urologic Disease Intramural Urology Research Training Program, 275
*American Foundation for Urologic Disease MD Post-Resident Research Program, 275

*American Foundation for Urologic Disease MD/Ph.D. One Year Research Program, 275
*American Health Information Management Master's Program, 631
*American Heart Association Beginning Grant-in-Aid Program, 278
*American Heart Association Grant-In-Aid, 278
*American Heart Association Postdoctoral Fellowship, 279
*American Heart Association Predoctoral Fellowship, 279
American Heart Association Student Research Program, 279
*American Historical Society Research Grants, 635
*American Indian Fellowship for Environmental Professionals, 597
*American Indian Graduate Fellowship, 280
American Institute of Architects Fellowship in Health Facilities Design, 282
American Institute of Architects for Professional Degree Candidates, 282
American Institute of Architects Minority/Disadvantaged Scholarship, 283
American Institute of Architects Scholarship, 523
*American Institute of Architects Scholarship for Advanced Study and Research, 283
American Institute of Architects The RTKL Traveling Fellowship, 283
*American Institute of Certified Public Accountants' Minority Doctoral Fellowship, 284
American Legion Alabama Auxiliary Scholarship, 287
American Legion Alabama Oratorical Contest, 287
American Legion Alabama Scholarship, 287
American Legion Alaska Auxiliary Scholarship, 287
American Legion Alaska Oratorical Contest, 287
American Legion Arizona Auxiliary Health Occupation Scholarship, 288
American Legion Arizona Auxiliary Nurses' Scholarship, 288
American Legion Arkansas Auxiliary Academic Scholarship, 288
American Legion Arkansas Auxiliary Nurse Scholarship, 288
American Legion Arkansas Oratorical Contest, 288
American Legion Arkansas Scholarship, 637

American Legion California Auxiliary Department of Education Scholarship I, 289
American Legion California Auxiliary Department of Education Scholarship II, 289
American Legion California Auxiliary High School Scholarship, 289
American Legion California Auxiliary National President's Junior Scholarship, 637
American Legion California Auxiliary National President's Scholarship, 289
American Legion California Auxiliary Spirit of Youth Scholarship, 638
American Legion California Oratorical Contest, 289
American Legion Colorado Auxiliary President's Scholarship for Junior Members, 638
American Legion Colorado Auxiliary/ Department President's Scholarship, 638
American Legion Colorado Auxiliary/ Past President's Parley Nurse's Scholarship, 290
American Legion Connecticut Auxiliary Memorial Educational Grant, 638
American Legion Connecticut Auxiliary Past President's Parley Education Grant, 638
American Legion Delaware Auxiliary Past President's Parley Nursing Scholarship, 290
American Legion District of Columbia Oratorical Contest, 290
American Legion Florida Auxiliary Memorial Scholarship, 639
American Legion Florida Auxiliary Scholarship, 291
American Legion Florida Oratorical Contest, 290
American Legion Georgia Auxiliary Past President's Parley Nursing Scholarship, 291
American Legion Georgia Auxiliary Scholarship, 291
American Legion Idaho Auxiliary Nursing Scholarship, 291
American Legion Illinois Auxiliary Ada Mucklestone Memorial Scholarship, 292
American Legion Illinois Auxiliary Marie Sheehe Trade School Scholarship, 292
American Legion Illinois Auxiliary Mildred R. Knoles Opportunity Scholarship, 292
American Legion Illinois Auxiliary Special Education Teaching Scholarship, 292

American Legion Illinois Auxiliary Student Nurse Scholarship, 292
American Legion Illinois Boy Scout Scholarship, 639
American Legion Illinois Oratorical Contest, 292
American Legion Illinois Scholarship, 639
American Legion Indiana Auxiliary Edna M. Barcus Memorial Scholarship, 293
American Legion Indiana Auxiliary Past President's Parley Nursing Scholarship, 640
American Legion Indiana Frank W. McHale Memorial Scholarship, 639
American Legion Indiana Oratorical Contest, 293
American Legion Iowa Auxiliary Department of Iowa Scholarship, 640
American Legion Iowa Auxiliary Harriet Hoffman Memorial Scholarship, 293
American Legion Iowa Auxiliary Mary Virginia Macrea Memorial Nurses Scholarship, 294
American Legion Iowa Boy Scout of the Year Award, 640
American Legion Iowa Oratorical Contest, 293
American Legion Iowa Outstanding Citizen of Boys State, 640
American Legion Iowa Outstanding Senior Baseball Player, 293
American Legion Kansas Albert M. Lappin Scholarship, 640
American Legion Kansas Dr. Click Cowger Scholarship, 294
American Legion Kansas Hugh A. Smith Scholarship, 641
American Legion Kansas John and Geraldine Hobble Licensed Practical Nursing Scholarship, 294
American Legion Kansas Music Scholarship, 294
American Legion Kansas Oratorical Contest, 294
American Legion Kansas Ted and Nora Anderson Scholarship, 641
American Legion Kentucky Auxiliary Laura Blackburn Memorial Scholarship, 295
American Legion Kentucky Auxiliary Mary Barrett Marshall Scholarship, 295
American Legion Kentucky Auxiliary Mary Barrett Marshall Student Loan Fund, 295
American Legion Maine Auxiliary General Scholarship, 296
American Legion Maine Auxiliary President's Parley Nursing Scholarship, 296

American Legion Maine Children and Youth Scholarship, 295
American Legion Maine Daniel E. Lambert Memorial Scholarship, 295
American Legion Maine James V. Day Scholarship, 641
American Legion Maryland Auxiliary Nursing Scholarship, 297
American Legion Maryland Auxiliary Scholarship, 297
American Legion Maryland Boys State Scholarship, 641
American Legion Maryland General Scholarship, 296
American Legion Maryland Oratorical Contest, 296
American Legion Maryland Science/ Math Scholarship, 296
American Legion Massachusetts Auxiliary Past President's Parley Scholarship, 298
American Legion Massachusetts Auxiliary Scholarship, 298
American Legion Massachusetts Nursing Scholarship, 641
American Legion Massachusetts Oratorical Contest, 297
American Legion Massachusetts Past County Commander's Scholarship, 297
American Legion Michigan Auxiliary Memorial Scholarship, 299
American Legion Michigan Auxiliary National President's Scholarship, 299
American Legion Michigan Auxiliary Scholarships For Nurses, Physical Therapists, and Respiratory Therapists, 299
American Legion Michigan Guy M. Wilson Scholarship, 298
American Legion Michigan Oratorical Contest, 298
American Legion Michigan William D. Brewer--Jewell W. Brewer Scholarship Trusts, 298
American Legion Minnesota Auxiliary Department Scholarship, 300
American Legion Minnesota Auxiliary Past President's Parley Nursing Scholarship, 642
American Legion Minnesota Legionnaire Insurance Trust Scholarship, 299
American Legion Minnesota Memorial Scholarship, 642
American Legion Minnesota Oratorical Contest, 299
American Legion Mississippi Auxiliary Scholarship, 300
American Legion Missouri Auxiliary Past President's Parley Scholarship, 301

Program Index

American Legion Missouri Auxiliary Scholarship, 301
American Legion Missouri Lillie Lois Ford Boys Scholarship, 642
American Legion Missouri Lillie Lois Ford Girls Scholarship, 642
American Legion Missouri M.D. "Jack" Murphy Memorial Nursing Scholarship, 300
American Legion Missouri Oratorical Certificates, 300
American Legion National Auxiliary President's Scholarship, 643
American Legion National Auxiliary Spirit of Youth Scholarship For Junior Members, 643
American Legion National Eagle Scout of the Year, 643
*American Legion National Eight and Forty Lung and Respiratory Nursing Scholarship Fund, 301
American Legion National High School Oratorical Contest, 301
American Legion National Memorial Scholarship of the Twenty and Four, 643
American Legion Nebraska Auxiliary Practical Nurse Scholarship, 302
American Legion Nebraska Auxiliary Roberta Marie Stretch Memorial Scholarship, 302
American Legion Nebraska Auxiliary Ruby Paul Campaign Fund Scholarship, 643
American Legion Nebraska Auxiliary Student Aid Grant - Vocational Technical Scholarship, 302
American Legion Nebraska Maynard Jensen Memorial Scholarship, 301
American Legion Nebraska Oratorical Contest, 302
American Legion New Hampshire Albert T. Marcoux Memorial Scholarship, 644
American Legion New Hampshire Auxiliary Grace S. High Memorial Child Welfare Scholarship, 644
American Legion New Hampshire Auxiliary Marion J. Bagley Scholarship, 303
American Legion New Hampshire Auxiliary Past President's Parley Nursing Scholarship, 303
American Legion New Hampshire Boys State Scholarship, 644
American Legion New Hampshire Christa McAuliffe Scholarship, 302
American Legion New Hampshire Department Scholarship, 302
American Legion New Hampshire Department Vocational Scholarship, 303
American Legion New Hampshire Oratorical Contest, 303

American Legion New Jersey Auxiliary Claire Oliphant Memorial Scholarship, 304
American Legion New Jersey Auxiliary Department Scholarship, 304
American Legion New Jersey Auxiliary Past President's Parley Nursing Scholarship, 304
American Legion New Jersey David C. Goodwin Scholarship, 303
American Legion New Jersey David C. Goodwin Scholarship, 304
American Legion New Jersey Lawrence Luterman Memorial Scholarship, 644
American Legion New Jersey Oratorical Contest, 304
American Legion New Jersey Press Club Scholarship, 645
American Legion New Jersey Stutz Memorial Scholarship, 645
American Legion New Mexico Auxiliary Teachers of Exceptional Children Scholarship, 305
American Legion New York Association Scholarship, 645
American Legion New York Auxiliary Medical & Teaching Scholarship, 305
American Legion New York Auxiliary Nannie W. Norfleet Loan Fund, 306
American Legion New York Auxiliary Past President's Parley Nursing Scholarship, 305
American Legion New York Auxiliary Scholarship, 305
American Legion New York Dr. Hannah K. Vuolo Memorial Scholarship, 645
American Legion New York James F. Mulholland Scholarship, 645
American Legion New York Oratorical Contest, 305
American Legion North Dakota Auxiliary Past President's Parley Scholarship, 646
American Legion North Dakota Auxiliary Scholarship, 306
American Legion North Dakota Oratorical Contest, 306
American Legion of Kansas General Scholarship, 294
American Legion Ohio Auxiliary Scholarship, 306
American Legion Ohio Auxiliary Scholarship For Nurse's Training or Medical Field, 307
American Legion Ohio Scholarship, 646
American Legion Oklahoma Auxiliary Student Education Loan, 307

American Legion Oregon Auxiliary Department Nurses Scholarship, 307
American Legion Oregon Auxiliary Department Scholarship, 307
American Legion Oregon Auxiliary National President's Scholarship, 307
American Legion Oregon Auxiliary One-Time Grant, 308
American Legion Oregon Oratorical Contest, 307
American Legion Pennsylvania Auxiliary Scholarship, 308
American Legion Pennsylvania Auxiliary Scholarship For Children of Deceased/Disabled Veterans, 308
American Legion Pennsylvania Joseph P. Gavenonis Scholarship, 646
American Legion Pennsylvania Robert W. Valimont Endowment Fund Scholarship, 646
American Legion Puerto Rico Auxiliary Nursing Scholarship, 308
American Legion Sough Dakota Auxiliary College Scholarship, 647
American Legion South Carolina Auxiliary Floyd Memorial Scholarship Fund, 309
American Legion South Carolina Auxiliary Gift Scholarship, 647
American Legion South Carolina Robert E. David Children's Scholarship, 308
American Legion South Carolina Scholarship, 309
American Legion South Dakota Auxiliary Junior Members Scholarship, 647
American Legion South Dakota Auxiliary Nurses Scholarship, 647
American Legion South Dakota Auxiliary Senior America Scholarship, 647
*American Legion South Dakota Auxiliary Vocational Scholarship, 647
American Legion South Dakota Educational Loan, 309
American Legion South Dakota Oratorical Contest, 309
American Legion Tennessee Auxiliary Vara Gray Nursing Scholarship, 310
American Legion Tennessee Auxiliary Vara Gray Scholarship, 310
American Legion Tennessee Eagle Scout Award, 648
American Legion Tennessee Oratorical Contest, 309
American Legion Texas Auxiliary General Scholarship, 310
American Legion Texas Auxiliary Nurses Scholarship, 310
American Legion Texas Oratorical Contest, 310

*Graduate/nondegree study

American Legion Utah Auxiliary National President's Scholarship, 311
American Legion Vermont Scholarship, 311
American Legion Vermont Scholarship Program, 311
American Legion Virginia Auxiliary Dr. Kate Waller Barrett Grant, 648
American Legion Virginia Oratorical Contest, 311
American Legion Washington Auxiliary Education Scholarship, 311
American Legion Washington Auxiliary Florence Lemcke Fine Arts Scholarship, 312
American Legion Washington Auxiliary Margarite McAlpin Nursing Scholarship, 312
American Legion Washington Auxiliary Susan Burdett Scholarship, 312
American Legion Washington Scholarship, 648
American Legion West Virginia Auxiliary Scholarship, 312
American Legion West Virginia Oratorical Contest, 312
American Legion Wisconsin Auxiliary Badger Girls State Scholarships, 313
* American Legion Wisconsin Auxiliary Child Welfare Scholarship, 313
American Legion Wisconsin Auxiliary H.S. and Angeline Lewis Scholarship, 313
American Legion Wisconsin Auxiliary Health Careers Award, 313
American Legion Wisconsin Auxiliary King-Hahn Scholarship, 313
American Legion Wisconsin Auxiliary M. Louise Wilson Educational Loan, 314
American Legion Wisconsin Auxiliary Merit and Memorial Scholarship, 314
American Legion Wisconsin Auxiliary Registered Nurse Degree Award, 314
American Legion Wisconsin Auxiliary State President's Scholarship, 649
American Legion Wisconsin Baseball Player of the Year Scholarship, 312
American Legion Wisconsin Eagle Scout of the Year Scholarship, 648
American Legion Wyoming Auxiliary Past Presidents' Parley Scholarship, 314
American Legion Wyoming E.B. Blackmore Memorial Scholarship, 649
American Legion Wyoming Oratorical Contest, 314

* American Library Association Doctoral Dissertation Fellowship, 315
* American Liver Foundation Postdoctoral Fellowship, 317
* American Museum of Natural History Graduate Student Fellowship Program, 321
* American Museum of Natural History Research Fellowships, 321
American National Can Company Scholarship, 650
American Nuclear Society Environmental Sciences Division Scholarship, 322
American Nuclear Society Washington Internship for Students of Engineering, 322
American Numismatic Society Fellowship in Roman Studies, 326
* American Numismatic Society Frances M. Schwartz Fellowship, 326
American Numismatic Society Shaykh Hamad Fellowship in Islamic Numismatics, 326
* American Pen Women Award: Arts, 505
* American Pen Women Award: Letters, 505
* American Pen Women Award: Music, 505
American Physical Society Minorities Scholarship, 329
* American Political Science Association Minority Fellows, 330
American Scholars National Scholarship, 473
* American Schools of Oriental Research/Annual Professorship, 334
American Schools of Oriental Research/Endowment for Biblical Research and Travel Grant, 335
* American Schools of Oriental Research/Harrell Family Fellowship, 335
American Schools of Oriental Research/Jennifer C. Groot Fellowship, 335
* American Schools of Oriental Research/Kenneth W. Russell Fellowship, 267
* American Schools of Oriental Research/National Endowment for the Humanities Fellowship, 335
* American Schools of Oriental Research/Samuel H. Kress Fellowships, 335
* American Schools of Oriental Research/United States Information Agency Fellowship, 336
American Soc. Heating/Refrigeration/Air-Conditioning Engineers Technical Scholarship, 337

American Soc. Heating/Refrigeration/Air-Conditioning Engineers Undergraduate Scholarship, 337
* American Society for Eighteenth Century Studies Fellowship, 525
* American Society Interior Designers Education Foundation/Dora Brahms Award, 342
American Society of Magazine Editors Internship, 343
* American Speech-Language-Hearing Graduate Scholarship, 347
* American Speech-Language-Hearing International/Minority Student Scholarship, 347
* American Speech-Language-Hearing Student with Disability Scholarship, 347
* American Speech-Language-Hearing Young Minority Scholars Award, 347
American Welding Society District Scholarship, 349
* American Welding Society Graduate Fellowship, 349
Amerisure Companies Scholarship, 654
AMP Scholars Program, 654
Amtrol Ground Water Research Scholarship, 277
* Amy Louise Hunter Fellowship, 221
* Andrew M. Longley, Jr., D.O. Scholarship, 457
* Andrew Mellon Fellowship, 487
* Andrew W. Mellon Conservation Fellowship, 462
* Andrew W. Mellon Fellowship, 463
* Andrew W. Mellon Fellowship in Humanistic Studies, 617
Angela Scholarship, 491
Angelo S. Biseti Scholarship, 323
Anna K. Meredith Fund Scholarship, 434
* Anne and Oliver C. Colburn Fellowship, 351
Anne Maureen Whitney Barrow Memorial Scholarship, 583
* Anne S. Chatham Fellowship in Medicinal Botany, 410
Anne Seaman Memorial Scholarship, 553
Anne U. White Fund, 656
Annis I. Fowler/Kaden Scholarship, 220
* Antiquarian Society Short-Term Fellowship, 259
Antonio and Felicia Marinelli Scholarships, 492
Antonio F. Marinelli Founders Scholarship, 492
Appaloosa Educational Scholarships, 654
Applegate/Jackson/Parks Future Teacher Scholarship, 383

*Graduate/nondegree study

Program Index

* Applied Health Physics Fellowship, 197
* Architectural Study Tour Scholarship, 579
  Archival Internships, 445
* Argentina: Full Grant (Fulbright), 77
  Arizona Chapter Gold Travel Agents Scholarship, 344
  Arizona Dependent/ Employee Membership Travel Agents Scholarship, 654
  Arizona Registration Fee Waiver Police/Fire Children, 60
  Arizona State Student Incentive Grant, 61
  Arizona Tuition and Registration Fee Waiver and Grant, 60
  Arizona Tuition Waiver Program, 61
  Arkansas Emergency Secondary Education Loan, 61
  Arkansas Freshman/Sophomore Minority Grant, 61
  Arkansas Law Enforcement Officers' Dependents Scholarship, 61
* Arkansas Minority Master's Fellowship, 61
  Arkansas Minority Teachers Loan, 62
  Arkansas Missing/Killed in Action Dependents Scholarship, 62
* Armed Forces Educational Foundation Fellowship, 353
* Armenian Relief Graduate Scholarship, 354
  Armenian Relief Undergraduate Scholarship, 354
  Armenian Union Awards for Students on Non-U.S. Soil, 354
* Armenian Union U.S. Graduate Loan, 354
  Army Emergency Relief Scholarship, 355
* Army Research Laboratory - Postdoctoral Fellowship, 338
  Arnell BJUGSTAD Scholarship, 220
  ARRL General Fund Scholarship, 330
  ARRL League Ph.D. Scholarship, 330
  ARRL Mississippi Scholarship, 330
  Art International '98, 685
  Arthur and Doreen Parrett Scholarship, 355
  Arthur E. Copeland Scholarship for Males, 607
  Arthur Howell and Michael McCarthy Scholarship Award, 704
  Arthur I. Mendolia Scholarship Program, 668
  Arthur J. McBride Memorial Scholarship, 705
* Arthur S. Tuttle Memorial National Scholarships, 340
  Artistic Internships, 269
  Arts Recognition and Talent Search, 485
  Ashland Scholars Program, 655

  Asia-Pacific Undergraduate Scholarship, 434
* Asian Art and Religion Fellowship Program, 356
* Asian Humanities Fellowship Program, 356
* Asian Language Fellowship, 369
  ASM Foundation Undergraduate Scholarship, 357
  ASME Student Loan Program, 652
  ASME Student Loan Program, 652
* Aspen Systems Awards, 631
  Associated General Contractors James L. Allhands Essay Competition, 357
  Associated Press/APTRA-CLETE Roberts Memorial Journalism Scholarship, 358
  Association for Women in Communications Scholarship, 359
* Association of American Geographers Dissertation Research Grant, 656
* Association of American Geographers General Research Grant, 656
  Assunta Lucchetti Martino Scholarship for International Studies, 492
  Astra Merck Scholarship Program, 658
  Astrid G. Cates Fund, 746
  AT&T Hispanic Division Fellowship, 452
  Athletic Trainers Curriculum Scholarship, 713
* Athletic Trainers Postgraduate Scholarship, 713
  Athletic Trainers Student Writing Contest, 713
  Athletic Trainers Undergraduate Scholarship, 714
  Atlas Pacific Scholarship Program, 658
* Atmospheric Research Graduate Fellowship, 177
  Atmospheric Science Internship, 251
* Audrey Lumsdem-Kouvel Fellowship, 525
* Australia: Full Grant (Fulbright), 77
* Austria: Full Grant (Fulbright), 77
* Austria: IFK Grants, 78
* Austria: Study Grant English Language Teaching Assistantship, 78
* Austrian Cultural Institute Fine Arts and Music Grant, 362
* Austrian Research and Study Scholarship, 362
  Automotive Engineers Engineering Scholarship, 580
  Avery Dennison Scholars Program, 658
  Aviation Distributors and Manufacturers Scholarship, 362
  Aviation Scholarship and Work Studies Program, 394

* Avis Rent-a-Car Travel Agents Scholarship, 345
  Avnet Scholarship Program, 658
  Avon Products Foundation Career Empowerment Scholarship for Adult Women, 564
  B. Charles Tiney Memorial ASCE Student Chapter Scholarships, 340
* Bahrain: Full Grant (Fulbright), 78
  Baker Scholarship Program, 658
  Bandag Scholarship Program, 658
* Bangladesh: Full Grant (Fulbright), 78
  Bank One, Houston Higher Education Scholarship Program, 658
  BankAmerica Scholarship, 659
  Banta Scholarship Program, 659
  Barbara Carlson Scholarship, 363
  Barbara Thomas Enterprises Award, 632
  Bardes Fund Scholarship, 659
  Barnes Group Foundation Scholarship, 659
  Barnett Scholars Program, 659
  Barry E. Pruett Scholarship, 660
  Barry M. Goldwater Scholarship, 62
* Basil O'Connor Starter Scholar Research Award, 459
  Battle Mountain Canada Scholarship, 660
  Baxter Allegiance Foundation Scholarship, 660
  Bay State Gas Company Scholarship, 660
* Beale Family Memorial Scholarship, 457
  Bechtel Corporation Summer Intern Program, 363
* Behavioral Sciences Research Fellowship, 401
  Behavioral Sciences Student Fellowship, 401
* Belgium and Luxembourg: Full Grant (Fulbright), 79
* Belgium and Luxembourg: Teaching Assistantship (Fulbright), 79
* Belgum and Luxembourg: Center for European Studies Award, 79
  Bemis Company Foundation Scholarship, 660
  Benchmark Corporation Scholarship, 661
  Benedict Cassen Post-Doctoral Fellowship, 396
* Benin: Full Grant (Fulbright), 79
  Benjamin Eaton Scholarship, 715
* Berlin Program for Advanced German-European Studies, 572
  Bernstein International Surveying Scholarship, 629
  Beta Club Scholarship, 714
* Beta Phi Mu Blanche E. Woolls Scholarship for School Library Media Service., 367

772   *Graduate/nondegree study

Program Index

* Beta Phi Mu Doctoral Dissertation Scholarship, 367
Bethesda Lutheran Homes and Services Cooperative Program Internship, 368
Bethlehem Steel Scholars, 661
Betty Rendel Scholarship, 715
BetzDearborn Scholarship Program, 661
BF Goodrich Collegiate Inventors Program, 363
Biblical Research Travel Grant, 336
Bill Carpenter Memorial Certificate School Scholarship, 516
Bill O'Neill Memorial Scholarship, 710
Billy Barty Financial Assistance Program, 368
Bioproducts Scholarship Program for Perdue Farms, 661
* Biotechnology Grant, 544
* Bishop Greco Graduate Fellowship, 699
* Bishop James C. Baker Award, 603
Black & Veatch Summer Internship in Engineering, Construction, and Architecture, 368
Black Journalists College Scholarship, 477
Black Journalists Summer Internship, 477
Black Journalists Sustaining Scholarship, 477
Black Nurse's Scholarship, 714
Black Nursing Faculty Scholarship, 360
Blanche Fearn Memorial Award, 409
Blossom Kalama Evans Memorial Scholarship, 419
Blue Circle America Scholarship Program, 662
Blue Flame Scholarship, 710
Blue Shield of California Scholarship, 662
Bluebird Research Grant, 528
BMA Scholarship for Children of Employees, 666
BNI Coal Scholarship Program, 662
Boart Longyear Scholarship Program, 662
Bob Elliot - Channel 8 Journalism Scholarship, 615
Boehringer Ingelheim Corporation Scholarship, 663
Bok Tower Gardens Internship, 369
* Bolivia: Full Grant (Fulbright), 80
Bolla Wines Scholarship, 492
Bose Corporation Scholarship, 252
* Boston Globe One-Year Internship, 369
Boston Globe Summer Internship, 370
Bosworth Smith Trust Fund, 435
* Botswana: Full Grant (Fulbright), 80

* Bound to Stay Bound Books Scholarship, 315
Boy Scouts of America Law Enforcement Assistance Award, 663
Boy Scouts of America/Eastern Orthodox Committee on Scouting Scholarship, 663
Boy Scouts of America/Eisenhower Memorial Scholarship, 663
BP America Internship, 665
* Brain Tumor Research Fellowship, 265
Brake Parts Scholarship, 665
* Brazil: Full Grant (Fulbright), 80
Bremer Employee Dependents Scholarship Program, 665
Bristol-Myers Squibb Career Education Awards, 665
* Bristol-Myers Squibb Outstanding Resident Award, 329
Broadcast Education Association Scholarship, 371
Broadcast News Pioneers Undergraduate Scholarships, 555
Brooklyn Hospital Center Employees' Activities Committee Award, 665
BT Office Products Scholarship, 666
Bucks County Courier Times Minority Internship, 371
Buckskin Horse Association Scholarship, 694
Bud Glover Memorial Scholarship, 252
* Bulgaria: Full Grant (Fulbright), 80
* Bulgarian Studies Grant, 438
Bureau of Alcohol, Tobacco, and Firearms Scholarship, 666
Bureau of Indian Affairs-Oklahoma Area Grant, 371
Bureau of Indian Affairs-Oklahoma Area Scholarship, 63
* Burkina Faso: Full Grant (Fulbright), 81
Burlington Northern Santa Fe Foundation Scholarship, 637
Butler Manufacturing Company Foundation Scholarship, 666
C.G. Fuller Foundation Scholarship, 373
* C.R. Bard Foundation Prize, 505
California Association of Realtors Scholarship, 374
California Assumption Program Loans for Education, 63
California Child Development Teacher and Supervisor Grant Program, 63
California Farm Bureau Scholarship, 374
California Grant Program, 63
California Junior Miss Competition, 375
California Law Enforcement Personnel Dependents Scholarship, 64

* California Library Scholarship for Minority Students, 375
California Masonic Foundation Scholarship, 375
California Robert C. Byrd Honors Scholarship, 64
California State Work-Study Program, 64
California Teachers Association Martin Luther King, Jr., Memorial Scholarship, 667
Callaway Golf Scholarship Program, 668
* Cameroon: Full Grant (Fulbright), 81
* Canada: Full Grant (Fulbright), 81
* Canada: Native North American Scholarship (Fulbright), 81
* Cancer Research Fellowship, 441
* Cancer Society Postdoctoral Fellowship, 266
* CANFIT Program Graduate Scholarship, 373
CANFIT Program Undergraduate Scholarship, 374
Canned Foods Employees' Children Scholarship, 668
Capital Area Regional Scholarship, 493
Capital Group Companies Scholarship Program, 668
Capitol College Electronic Engineering Scholarship, 622
Captain James J. Regan Memorial Scholarship, 663
* Cardiovascular Nursing Award, 634
Career Advancement Scholarship, 372
* Career Development Grant, 264
Career Opportunities Through Education Scholarship Program, 568
* Carillon Fellowship, 369
Carl F. Dietz Memorial Scholarship, 364
* Carmargo Foundation Fellowship, 376
* Carmela Gagliardi Fellowship, 493
* Carnegie Scholarship, 531
Carole Fielding Video Grant, 607
Carolina Simpson Scholarship, 555
Carolina Power & Light Merit Awards Program, 668
Carter Scholarship Grants for New England Scouts, 664
Cartographic Association Scholarship, 629
Cashiers' Association of Wall Street Scholarship, 668
Castle & Cooke George W.Y. Yim Scholarship Fund, 420
Castleberry Instruments Scholarship, 252
Castrol North America Scholarship, 669
Caterpillar Scholars Award, 582
* Catherine Beattie Fellowship, 410

*Graduate/nondegree study

Program Index

Catholic Aid Association Scholarship, 669
Catholic Workman Fraternal Life Scholarship, 669
CBS Scholarship, 669
Centenary Scholarship, 435
Center for Defense Information Internship, 377
Ceramic Manufacturers Scholarship, 377
Ceridian Scholarship Program, 669
*Certified Public Accountants' John L. Carey Scholarship, 284
Certified Public Accountants' Minorities Scholarship, 284
*Chad: Full Grant (Fulbright), 82
Chairscholars Scholarship, 378
Champion International Corporation Scholarship, 670
Charles A. Freeman Memorial Scholarship, 749
Charles Clarke Cordle Memorial Scholarship, 330
*Charles E. Culpeper Art Internship, 487
Charles E. Sporck Scholarship Program, 717
Charles E. Thoele Scholarship, 742
Charles N. Fisher Memorial Scholarship, 331
Charlie Logan Scholarship, 740
Charlotte Woods Memorial Scholarship, 598
Charter Fund Scholarship, 378
*Chartered Accountants Education Award Competition, 657
Chas. Levy Company Harry Harrington Scholarship, 670
Chemical Society Minority Scholarship, 267
Chesapeake Corporation Scholarship, 670
*Chester Dale Fellowship, 463
*Chester Dale Fellowship, 487
*Chesterfield Writers Film Project, 379
Cheyenne-Arapaho Tribe Department of Education Scholarship, 379
Cheyenne-Arapaho Tribe Higher Education Scholarship, 379
Chicago Association of Spring Manufacturers Scholarship, 670
Chicago FM Club Scholarship, 331
Chick Evans Caddie Scholarship, 612
Chief Master Sergeants of the Air Force Scholarship, 256
*Children's Literature Research Fellowship, 670
*Chile: Full Grant (Fulbright), 82
*Chinese American Medical Society Scholarship, 379
Choate Rosemary Hall Internship, 380
Choctaw Nation Higher Eduation Grant, 65

Christian Record Services Scholarship, 380
Chronicle of the Horse Summer Internship, 380
Chrysler Corporation Fund Scholarship, 671
Chuck Peacock Honorary Scholarship, 252
*Churchill Scholarship, 615
CIA Undergraduate Scholarship, 64
*CIC/GE Predoctoral Fellowship, 382
Citizens State Bank of Roseau Scholarship Fund, 671
Citizens Utilities Scholarship Fund, 671
City University Seek/College Discovery Program, 189
*Civil Engineering Graduate Scholarship, 361
Clara Abbott Foundation Educational Grant, 671
*Clara Mayo Grants-In-Aid, 577
Clare Brett Smith Scholarship, 434
Clarke Internship Program, 380
Class Fund Internship Program, 449
Class Fund Scholarship Ornamental Horticulture Program, 450
Class Fund Scholarships, 450
*Classical Art Fellowship, 463
*Clinical Cancer Research Fellowship, 259
*Clinical Pathology Student Scholarship, 341
*Clinical Psychology Training Minority Fellowship, 58
*Clinical Rehabilitation Audiology Research Grant, 348
Cloisters Summer Internship for College Students, 463
Clorox Scholarship, 672
Clyde Russell Scholarship Fund, 380
CMP Scholarships Fund, 454
CNF Transportation Companies Scholarship, 672
Coca-Cola Internship, 509
Coca-Cola Scholars Program, 381
Coding Specialist Program Loan, 632
Colgate "Bright Smiles, Bright Futures" Minority Scholarships, 249
Colgate-Juliette A. Southard/ Oral B Laboratories Scholarship, 271
*Collection Study Grants, 321
College of Aeronautics Scholarship, 253
College Television Award, 248
College Vocational-Technical Scholarship, 703
College-Bound Incentive Award, 453
*Colombia: Full Grant (Fulbright), 82
Colonial Dames of America Indian Nurse Scholarship, 515
Colorado CPAs Ethnic Scholarship, 381

Colorado CPAs Ethnic-College and University Scholarship, 381
Colorado CPAs Gordon Scheer Scholarship, 381
Colorado CPAs High School Scholarship, 382
Colorado Diversity Grant, 65
*Colorado Graduate Fellowship, 65
*Colorado Graduate Grant, 65
Colorado Masons Scholarship, 381
Colorado Nursing Scholarship, 65
Colorado Part-time Student Grant, 66
Colorado Society of CPAs Educational Foundation Scholarship, 382
Colorado Student Grant, 66
Colorado Student Incentive Grant, 66
Colorado Undergraduate Merit Award, 66
Colorado Work-Study Program, 66
Comer Foundation Scholarship Fund, 672
Commission State Scholarship Commission/Oregon Public Employees Union, 535
Communications Scholarship, 493
*Communicative Disorders Scholarships, 567
Community College Scholarship, 166
Community College Scholarship Program, 173
Community College Transfer Scholarships, 173
Compass Bancshares-DeWayne C. Cuthbertson Memorial Scholarship, 673
Computer Science Scholarship, 484
Computing Research Association Outstanding Undergraduate Award, 383
*ConAgra Fellowship in Child Nutrition, 738
Concepts Literary Contest, 685
Cone Mills Scholarship Program, 673
Congressional Black Caucus Foundation Spouses' Scholarship, 383
Congressional Hispanic Caucus Internship, 383
*Congressional Science and Engineering Fellowship, 626
Connecticut Aid for Public College Students, 66
Connecticut Aid to Dependents of Deceased/Disabled/MIA Veterans, 67
Connecticut Building Congress Scholarship, 384
Connecticut Independent College Student Grant, 67
Connecticut Nursing Scholarship, 384
Connecticut Robert C. Byrd Honors Scholarship, 67

*Graduate/nondegree study

Connecticut Scholastic Achievement Grant, 67
Connecticut Tuition Set Aside Aid, 67
Connecticut Tuition Waiver for Senior Citizens, 67
Connecticut Tuition Waiver for Veterans, 67
Connecticut Tuition Waiver for Vietnam MIA/POW Dependents, 67
*Conservation Internship, 520
Consolidated Freightways Corporation Scholarship Program, 673
Construction Education and Research Scholarship, 481
Consulting Engineers Scholarship, 270
Convenience Stores/Petroleum Marketers Association Scholarship Program, 711
Cooperative Education Program, 363
Cooperative Education Program, 62
Cooperative Education Program, 62
Cora Aguda Manayan Fund, 420
*Corning Inc. Optometric Scholarship, 328
Costa G. Lemonopoulus Scholarship, 712
*Costa Rica: Full Grant (Fulbright), 82
Council of Energy Resource Tribes Summer Intern Program, 385
*Council of Jewish Federations Scholarship, 385
*Council of Learned Societies Fellowship, 270
*Cournand and Comroe Prize, 634
Cow-lege Cash Scholarship Fund, 682
Crave To Be Your Best Scholarship, 532
Creede Repertory Theatre Summer Internship, 386
Critical Care Nurses Education Advancement Scholarship, 262
Critical Care Nurses Education Advancement Scholarship (BSN), 627
*Critical Care Nurses Education Advancement Scholarship (Graduate), 627
Critical Studies Program, 613
*Croatia: Full Grant (Fulbright), 83
Crysteel Scholarship Program, 679
CTA Scholarship for Dependent Children, 667
*CTA Scholarship for Members, 667
Cultural Ambassadorial Scholarship, 562
Curatorial Program, 613
Cushman School Internship, 387
CXY Energy Scholarship Program, 673
Cymdeithas Gymreig (Welsh Society) Philadelphia Scholarship, 387
*Cyprus: Full Grant (Fulbright), 83
*Cystic Fibrosis Clinical Research Grant, 387

*Cystic Fibrosis First and Second Year Clinical Fellowship, 387
*Cystic Fibrosis Pilot and Feasibility Award, 388
*Cystic Fibrosis Postdoctoral Research Fellowship, 388
*Cystic Fibrosis Research Grant, 388
Cystic Fibrosis Student Traineeship, 388
*Cystic Fibrosis Summer Scholarship in Epidemiology, 388
*Cystic Fibrosis Third and Fourth Year Clinical Fellowship, 389
*Czech Republic: Full Grant (Fulbright), 83
Dairy Management Milking Marketing Scholarship, 482
Dairy Product Marketing Scholarship, 390
Dairy Shrine Graduate Student Scholarship, 483
Dairy Shrine Student Recognition Scholarship, 483
Dalquist Scholarship, 724
Dam Safety Officials Scholarship, 361
*Damon Runyon Scholar Award, 376
Daniel E. O'Sullivan Memorial Scholarship, 674
Daniel M. Clemson Scholarship for Young Engineers, 750
Daniel Stella Scholarship, 493
Danish Foundation Scholarship, 529
Data Management Division of Wall Street Scholarship Program, 674
Datatel Scholarship, 390
*Daughters of Penelope Graduate Student Award, 674
Daughters of Penelope Past Grand Presidents Award, 674
Daughters of Penelope Re-entry Grant, 390
Daughters of United States Army Scholarship, 581
David and Dovetta Wilson Scholarship, 391
David Arver Memorial Scholarship, 253
*David Baumgardt Memorial Fellowship, 451
David Family Scholarship, 535
*David Finley Fellowship, 487
*David H. Clift Scholarship, 315
*David Hallissey Memorial Travel Agents Scholarship, 345
David J. Fitzmaurice Engineering Scholarship, 696
*David Levy Award, 627
David O. Maxwell Scholarship, 680
*David Rozkuszka Scholarship, 315
David Sarnoff Reseach Center Scholarship, 583
David T. Woolsey Scholarship, 450
Davis-Roberts Scholarship, 676

Deaf Activities Committee Scholarship, 666
*Deafness Research Foundation Otological Research Fellowship, 391
Dean Foods Company Scholarship Program, 676
Delaware B. Bradford Barnes Scholarship, 68
Delaware Christa McAuliffe Scholarship Loan, 69
Delaware Diamond State Scholarship, 69
Delaware Education Fund for Children of Deceased Military Personnel/State Police, 69
Delaware Engineering Society Undergraduate Scholarship Program, 392
Delaware Herman M. Holloway, Sr. Memorial Scholarship, 69
Delaware Nursing Incentive Program, 70
Delaware Scholarship Incentive, 70
*Delaware Speech Language Pathologist Incentive Program, 70
Delayed Education Scholarship for Women, 323
Dell Computer Internship, 392
Deloitte And Touche Summer Internship Program, 392
*Delta Delta Delta Graduate Scholarship, 676
Delta Delta Delta Undergraduate Scholarship, 676
*Delta Gamma Fellowship, 676
Delta Gamma Memorial Scholarship, 273
Delta Gamma Scholarship, 677
Delta Gamma Student Loan, 677
*Denmark: Aalborg University Grant (Fulbright), 83
*Denmark: Full Grant (Fulbright), 84
Denny Lydic Scholarship, 598
Dental Assisting Scholarship, 271
Dental Hygiene Scholarship, 248
Dental Laboratory Technician Scholarship, 248
*Dental Student Research Fellowship, 260
*Dental Student Scholarship, 248
Dependent Children Scholarship, 222
Descendents of the Signers of the Declaration of Independence Scholarship, 677
*Deutscher Akademischer Austausch Dienst Fellowship, 452
*Deutscher Akademischer Austausch Dienst Fellowship/Germany, 452
Diemakers Scholarship Program, 677
*Dirksen Research Grant Program, 392
Discover Card Tribute Award, 263
District of Columbia Student Incentive Grant, 70

*Graduate/nondegree study

Program Index

* Doctoral Dissertation Fellowship in Jewish Studies, 486
* Doctoral Fellowship in Accounting, 392
  Dog Writers Educational Trust Scholarship, 393
  Dolly Ching Scholarship Fund, 117
  Dolphin Scholarship, 393
  Dolphin U.S. Submarine Veterans of World War II Scholarship, 678
* Dominican Republic: Full Grant (Fulbright), 84
  Donald Beggs Scholarship, 709
  Donald Edwin Lauchner Scholarship, 704
  Donald F. Hastings Scholarship, 349
  Donaldson Company Scholarship Program, 678
  Donna Brace Ogilvie-Zelda Gitlin Poetry Writing Award, 684
* Dora Brahms Interior Design Award, 342
  Dorice & Clarence Glick Classical Music Scholarship, 420
  Doris Deaver Memorial Scholarship, 666
  Dorothy Andrews Kabis Internship, 715
  Dorothy Campbell Memorial Scholarship, 535
  Dorothy Lemke Howarth Scholarship, 584
  Dorr-Oliver Scholarship, 678
  Dosatron International Scholarship, 364
  Dow Educational Assistance Program, 706
* Downeast Feline Fund, 455
  Dr. Alfred C. Fones Scholarship, 249
  Dr. Hans and Clara Zimmerman Foundation Health Scholarship, 420
  Dr. Harold Hillenbrand Scholarship, 250
  Dr. James L. Lawson Memorial Scholarship, 331
  Dr. Tom Anderson Memorial Scholarship, 516
  Dr. Vincent P. Perna Science Award, 744
  Dr. William L. Amoroso Jr. Scholarship, 494
* Dupont Fellowship, 417
* Duracell Competition, 513
  Duracell Internship Program, 393
  Duracell/Gillette Minority Intern Scholarship, 520
  Dutch and Ginger Arver Scholarship, 253
  Dynatech Corporation Scholarship Program, 679
* E. Craig Brandenburg Graduate Award, 603
  E. Stewart Mitchell Scholarship Program, 679

E. Urner Goodman Scholarship, 664
E.C. Styberg Engineering Company Scholarship, 679
E.E. Black Scholarship, 688
E.L. Peterson Scholarship, 394
E.U. Parker Memorial Scholarship, 484
* Earl Warren Legal Training Program Scholarship, 472
  Earl J. Small Growers Scholarship, 364
* Early American Industries Grants-In-Aid Program, 394
* Early Childhood Language Research Grant, 348
  Easter Seal Scholarship, 394
  Easter Seal Society of Iowa Disability Scholarship, 395
* Eastern Europe Dissertation Fellowship, 270
* Eastern Europe Postdoctorate Fellowship, 270
  Eastman Kodak Student Program, 395
  ECM Publishers Scholarship Program, 679
  Ecolah Scholarship Program, 280
* Ecole des Chartes Exchange Fellowship, 525
* Ecuador: Full Grant (Fulbright), 84
  Ed Bradley Scholarship, 556
  Ed Markham International Scholarship, 364
  Ed Nielson Scholarship, 681
* Edgar Pam Fellowship, 435
* Edilia and Francois-Auguste de Montequin Fellowship, 579
  Edison International College Scholarship Program, 679
  Edith H. Henderson Scholarship, 450
  Edmond A. Metzger Scholarship, 650
  Edmund F. Maxwell Foundation Scholarship, 396
  Educate Our Children Scholarship, 671
* Education and Reseach Foundation Tetalman Award, 582
* Education and Research Junior Graduate Award, 358
* Education and Research Outstanding Educators Award, 358
  Education and Research Undergraduate Scholarship, 358
  Educational Communications Scholarship, 397
  Educational Optical Engineering Scholarship, 592
  Educator of Tomorrow Award, 484
  Edward D. Stone, Jr., and Associates Minority Scholarship, 450
* Edward H. Hatton Awards Competition, 260
  Edward J. Brady Scholarship, 349
  Edward J. Nell Memorial Scholarship, 554

Edward L. Ginzton Scholars Program, 759
Edwin R. Werner Scholarship, 680
EED Scholarship Program, 357
* Egypt: Full Grant (Fulbright), 84
  Eight-Month Gardener Internship, 529
* El Salvador: Full Grant (Fulbright), 84
* Electrochemical Society Summer Fellowship, 397
  Elie Wiesel Prize in Ethics, 398
* Elizabeth Barrett-Connor Research Award, 635
  Elizabeth Dow Internship Program, 398
* Elizabeth Glaser Scientist Award, 545
  Elizabeth Greenshields Grant, 399
  Elks Most Valuable Student Scholarship, 399
  Elks Undergraduate Disabled Student Scholarship, 376
  Ellison Onizuka Memorial Scholarship, 421
  Elmer and Eleanor Andersen Global Scholarship Program, 687
* Embassy of France Office for Science and Technology Chateaubriand Fellowship, 399
  EMI Scholars Program, 680
  Employee Communication Internship, 391
  Energy Service Scholarship, 657
  Engineers Foundation of Ohio Scholarship, 399
* English-Speaking Union Graduate Scholarship, 400
  Enology and Viticulture Scholarship, 339
  Entertainment Weekly Internship, 401
  Entomological Society Undergraduate Scholarship, 401
  Environmental and Science Reporting Fellowship, 556
* Environmental Protection Agency Environmental Science and Engineering Fellowship, 57
* Epilepsy Clinical Training Fellowship, 401
* Epilepsy Research Training Fellowship, 402
* EPSCoR Graduate Fellowship Program, 161
  EPSCoR Undergraduate Scholarship Program, 161
  Eric and Bette Friedhiem Scholarship, 516
  Eric Delson Memorial Scholarship, 377
* Eritrea: Full Grant (Fulbright), 85
  Ernest Hemingway Research Grants, 445
  Ernst and Young Internship, 402
  ESPN Internship, 402
  ESPN2 Sports Figures Scholarship, 402

*Graduate/nondegree study

Essay Contest, 414
Essence Internship, 402
*Estonia: Full Grant (Fulbright), 85
*Ethel Hausman Clinical Research Award, 603
*Ethel Marcus Memorial Fellowship in American Jewish Studies, 285
*Ethiopia: Full Grant (Fulbright), 85
Eugene and Elinor Kotur Scholarship, 601
*European Union: Full Grant (Fulbright), 85
*Everitt P. Blizard Scholarship, 323
Excel Scholarship, 683
Executive Housekeepers Education Foundation Scholarship., 695
Executive Women International Scholarship, 403
Experiential Education Internship, 514
*Exploration Fund, 403
Explorers Club Youth Activity Fund, 403
F & D Companies Scholarship, 680
F. Charles Ruling N6FR Memorial Scholarship, 331
*F. Maynard Lipe Scholarship, 267
F. Ralph Gabellieri Memorial Scholarship Program, 678
F.D. Stella Scholarship, 494
F.M. Becket Summer Research Award, 397
F.M. Peacock Native Bird Habitat Scholarship, 411
F.W. and D.G. Miller Mechanical Engineering Scholarship, 652
F.W. Berchley Mechanical Engineering Scholarship, 652
Family Education Loan Program, 384
*Federal Chancellor Scholarship, 56
Federal Direct Student Loans, 229
Federal Employee Education and Assistance Fund Scholarship, 680
Federal Family Education Loan Program, 229
Federal Pell Grant Program, 229
Federal Perkins Loan, 229
Federal Plus Loan, 229
Federal Reserve Summer Internship, 71
Federal Signal Karl F. Hoenecke Memorial Scholarship, 680
Federal Supplemental Educational Opportunity Grant Program, 230
Federal Work-Study Program, 230
Federation of the Blind Humanities Scholarship, 484
*Fellowship Grants to Asian Individuals, 356
*Fellowship in Infectious Diseases, 485
*Fellowship Program in Academic Medicine, 506
*Fellowships for College Teachers and Independent Scholars, 177

*Fellowships for Postdoctoral Research: Eastern Europe, 572
*Fellowships for University Teachers, 177
Ferdinand Torres AFB Scholarship, 273
Field Aviation Co., Inc. Scholarship, 253
*Fight-For-Sight Postdoctoral Research Fellowship, 404
Fight-For-Sight Student Research Fellowship, 404
Filoli Center Garden Internship, 404
Financial Management Division of SIA Scholarship, 681
*Financial Markets Center Henry B. Gonzalez Award, 405
Financial Women International Scholarship, 421
*Finland: Full Grant (Fulbright), 86
First Data Corporation Scholarship Awards, 681
First Marine Division Scholarship, 681
Fisher Broadcasting Minority Scholarship, 405
Five-Plus Club Scholarship, 710
Florida Academic Scholars Award, 71
Florida Children of Deceased/Disabled Veterans/POW/MIA Scholarship, 71
Florida Critical Teacher Shortage Student Loan Forgiveness, 72
*Florida Critical Teacher Shortage Tuition Reimbursement, 72
*Florida Education Fund McKnight Doctoral Fellowship, 405
*Florida Education Fund Minority Participation in Legal Education Law School Scholarship, 76
Florida Education Fund Minority Pre-law Scholarships, 76
Florida Educational Assistance for the Blind, 76
*Florida Exceptional Student Education Training Grant, 72
Florida Gold Seal Vocational Scholars Award, 72
Florida Jose Marti Scholarship Challenge Grant, 72
Florida Limited Access Competitive Grant, 73
Florida Mary McLeod Bethune Scholarship, 73
Florida Merit Scholars Award, 73
*Florida Nursing Loan Forgiveness, 76
*Florida Occupational/Physical Therapist Loan Forgiveness Program, 73
Florida Occupational/Physical Therapist Scholarship Loan Program, 73
*Florida Occupational/Physical Therapist Tuition Reimbursement, 74

Florida Resident Access Grant, 74
Florida Robert C. Byrd Honors Scholarship, 74
Florida Rock Industries Scholarship, 681
Florida Rosewood Family Scholarship, 74
Florida Seminole and Miccosukee Indian Scholarship, 74
Florida Student Assistance Grant, 75
Florida Teacher Scholarship and Forgivable Loan (Freshmen/Sophomores), 75
*Florida Teacher Scholarship and Forgivable Loan (Graduate), 75
Florida Teacher Scholarship and Forgivable Loan (Juniors/Seniors), 75
Florida Work Experience, 75
Flowers Industries Sons & Daughters Scholarship, 681
Floyd Qualls Memorial Scholarship, 271
Fluor Daniel GTI Scholarship, 682
Fluor Scholarship (USA), 682
Flying Higher Scholarship Program, 709
Food Engineering Division Junior/Senior Scholarship, 432
*Food Packaging Division Graduate Fellowship, 693
Food Service Communicators Scholarship, 436
Forbes Internship, 406
*Ford Foundation Dissertation Fellowship: Minorities, 510
*Ford Foundation Postdoctoral Fellowships for Minorities, 511
*Ford Foundation Predoctoral Fellowship: Minorities, 511
Ford Opportunity Program, 535
Ford Scholars Program, 536
*FORE Graduate Scholarship, 632
FORE Undergraduate Scholarship, 632
Foreign Postal Telegraph and Telephone International Affiliates Scholarship, 672
*Foreign Scholar Research Fellowships, 257
Foreign Study/Minority Scholarship Strategic Studies Award, 281
Former Agents of the U.S. Secret Service Scholarship, 657
Foss Maritime Scholarship, 682
Fossil Energy Technology Internship, 197
Fran Johnson Non-traditional Scholarship, 364
*France: Full Grant (Fulbright), 86
*France: Government Teaching Assistantship (Fulbright), 86
*France: Lusk Memorial Fellowship (Fulbright), 86

*Graduate/nondegree study

Frances S. Watanabe Memorial Scholarship, 688
Francis Ouimet Scholarship, 407
*Frank B. Sessa Scholarship for Continuing Education, 661
Frank D. Visceglia Memorial Scholarship, 682
Frank L. Weil Memorial Scholarship, 664
*Frank M. Chapman Memorial Grants, 321
Frank Walton Horn Memorial Scholarship, 484
*Franklin C. McLean Award, 506
Franklin D. Roosevelt Library/ Roosevelt Internship, 408
Franklin Lindsay Student Aid, 408
Fred G. Zahn Foundation Scholarship, 408
Fred R. McDaniel Memorial Scholarship, 331
*Frederic G. Melcher Scholarship, 316
Frederick A. Downes Scholarship, 273
*Freeman Fellowship, 340
Freightliner Fund Scholarship, 682
*Friedrich Ebert Advanced Graduate Fellowship, 409
*Friedrich Ebert Doctoral Research Fellowship, 409
*Friedrich Ebert Postdoctoral Fellowship, 409
Friends of the National Zoo Research Traineeships, 410
*Fritz Halbers Fellowship, 452
Frontier Scholarship Program for Children of Employees, 683
FRP Properties Scholarship Program, 683
Fuel Cycle and Waste Management, 323
*Fulbright - USIA U.K. Zeneca Award, 87
*Fulbright Program/USIA - U.K. Calvin Klein/Harvey Nichols Award in Fashion, 410
Fulfilling the Legacy Scholarship, 717
Fund for Lesbian and Gay Students Scholarship, 410
Futures Industry Association Scholarship, 720
*G. Vernon Hobson Bequest, 436
*Gabriel Prize, 370
Garden Club of America Summer Environmental Awards, 411
*Garden in the Woods Horticultural Internship, 522
Garland Duncan Mechanical Engineering Scholarship, 652
Gary Merrill Memorial Scholarship Program, 455
Gateway Pharmaceutical Research Scholarship, 273
GC Services Scholarship, 697
GEICO Scholarship Programs, 683

Geller Fellowship, 556
*Gem Consortium Scholarship, 412
Gene Baker Honorary Scholarship, 253
General Emmett Paige Scholarship, 353
General John A. Wickham Scholarship, 353
General Mills Foundation Scholarship, 683
General Mills Internship Program, 412
General Motors Corporation Education Relations Internship, 114
General Signal Electrical Group Scholarship Program, 683
Gensler and Associates Intern Program, 412
*Geodetic Surveying Graduate Fellowship, 629
Geoffrey Foundation Undergraduate Scholarship, 412
*Geography Research Grants, 489
Geography Students Internship, 490
Geological Institute Minority Participation Program, 276
*Geological Society Research Grant, 413
*George A. Barton Fellowship, 267
George Chadima Memorial Scholarship, 723
George D. Smith Scholarship Program, 757
George M. Brooker Collegiate Scholarship for Minorities, 435
George Reinke Travel Agents Scholarship, 345
Georgia Governor's Scholarship, 114
*Georgia Harkness Scholarship, 604
Georgia Hope Scholarship - GED Recipient, 114
Georgia Hope Scholarship - Private Institution, 115
Georgia Hope Scholarship - Public College or University, 115
Georgia Hope Scholarship - Public Technical Institution, 115
*Georgia Hope Teacher Scholarship, 115
Georgia Law Enforcement Personnel Dependents Grant, 115
*Georgia Osteopathic Medical Loan, 116
Georgia Promise Teacher Scholarship, 116
Georgia Regents Scholarship, 116
Georgia Robert C. Byrd Scholarship, 116
Georgia Service-Cancelable Stafford Loan, 116
Georgia Student Incentive Grant, 117
Georgia Tuition Equalization Grant, 117
Gerber Scholarship, 684

*German Academic Exchange Service Grant (Fulbright), 87
*Germanistic Society of America Quadrille Grant (Fulbright), 87
*Germany: Bavarian State Government Grant (Fulbright), 87
*Germany: Full Grant (Fulbright), 88
*Germany: Government Teaching Assistantship (Fulbright), 88
*Germany: Travel Grant (Fulbright), 88
Gertrude Baker Memorial Scholarship, 696
*Gertrude Elion Cancer Research Award, 259
*Getty Postdoctoral Fellowship, 413
Geyer Educational Award Program, 735
*Ghana: Full Grant (Fulbright), 88
Gianni Versace Scholarship in Fashion Design, 494
*Giargiari Fellowship, 494
*Gilbert F. White Postdoctoral Fellowship, 560
*Gillian Award, 434
Ginger and Fred Deines Canada Scholarship, 598
Ginger and Fred Deines Mexico Scholarship, 599
Girls Incorporated Scholars Program, 684
Gladys C. Anderson Memorial Scholarship, 274
Glaxo Wellcome Employees' Dependents Scholarship, 684
Golden Enterprises Scholarship, 659
*Golden Key Scholar Awards, 414
Golden State Minority Scholarship, 414
Golf Course Superintendents Association Scholars Program, 414
*Gordon C. Oates Award, 282
Gore Family Memorial Foundation Scholarships, 415
Governor's Commission on People with Disabilities Scholarship Fund, 415
Graco Scholarship, 686
*Graduate & Professional Degree Loan / Scholarship, 140
*Graduate and Postgraduate Study and Research in Poland, 448
Graduate and Undergraduate Fellowships, 155
*Graduate Scholarship in Lesbian Studies, 520
Grand Army of the Republic Living Memorial Scholarship, 390
Grange Denise Scholarship, 720
Grange Insurance Scholarship, 686
Grange Student Loan Fund, 720
Grange Susan W. Freestone Education Award, 720
*Grant for Research in Venice, 413

Program Index

Grant Program for Physically Disabled Students in the Sciences, 407
Grants-In-Aid for Research on the Roosevelt Years, 408
Greater Kanawha Valley Scholarship Program, 416
*Greece: European Banking Grant (Fulbright), 89
*Greece: Full Grant (Fulbright), 89
GreenPoint Scholarship, 686
Gregory Poole Equipment Scholarship, 687
*GRI/ICIF Culinary Scholarship, 494
Ground Water Association Auxiliary Scholarship, 716
GTE Internship Program, 416
*Guatemala: Full Grant (Fulbright), 89
Guggenheim Foundation Internship, 588
Guggenheim Museum Internship, 588
*Guinea: Full Grant (Fulbright), 89
Gulf Coast Avionics to Fox Valley Technical College Scholarship, 254
Gulf Coast Research Laboratory Minority Summer Grant, 140
H&R Block Scholarship, 687
*H. Hughes Medical Institute Predoctoral Fellowship, 511
H. Joseph Gerber Vision Scholarship Program, 684
H. Neil Mecaskey Scholarship, 516
*H. Thomas Austern Writing Award, 405
H.C. Piper Scholarship, 729
*H.J. Heinz Graduate Degree Fellowship, 512
*H.J. Swinney Internship, 594
*Hagley Museum and Library Grant-In-Aid, 417
Haines Memorial Scholarship, 219
*Haiti: Full Grant (Fulbright), 90
Hal Thorkilsen Scholarship Fund, 724
HAL USA Scholarship Program, 690
Hallmark Corporate Staffing Program, 417
*Hangin Memorial Scholarship, 468
Hannaford Scholarship, 687
Harness Horse Youth Scholarship, 418
Harness Tracks of America Scholarship, 687
Harold Bettinger Memorial Scholarship, 365
Harold K. Douthit Scholarship, 533
*Harold Lancour Scholarship for Foreign Study, 661
*Harriet and Leon Pomerance Fellowship, 352
Harriett Barnhart Wimmer Scholarship, 450
*Harry Frank Guggenheim Dissertation Fellowship, 418
*Harry Frank Guggenheim Dissertation Fellowships, 418

*Harry Shwachman Clinical Investigator Award, 389
Harry Truman Scholarship, 117
Harwood Memorial Scholarship, 558
Hasbro Scholarship, 688
Hatfield Scholarship, 688
Hawaii Community Margaret Jones Memorial Nursing Scholarship, 421
Hawaii Student Incentive Grant, 118
Hawaii Tuition Waiver, 118
*Hawaii Veterans Memorial Fund, 421
Hawk Mountain Internship Program, 425
*HDSA Fellowship Program, 430
Health Career Scholarship, 437
*Health Education Scholarship, 260
*Health Sciences Student Fellowship, 402
Healy Travel Agents Scholarship, 345
Hearst Journalism Award, 614
Hearst United States Senate Youth Program, 614
*Heed Ophthalmic Scholarship, 425
HEI Scholarship, 689
Helen Copeland Scholarship for Females, 607
*Helen M. Woodruff Fellowship, 352
*Helicopter Mechanic Technician Scholarship, 426
Hellenic Progressive Association Scholarship, 534
Helzberg Scholarship Program, 689
Henkel Corporation Scholarship, 689
*Henry A. Murray Research Center Dissertation Award, 426
Henry and Dorothy Castle Memorial Scholarship, 421
*Henry Belin DuPont Dissertation Fellowship, 417
*Henry G. Award, 506
Henry Reilly Memorial College Scholarship, 733
*Henry Reilly Memorial Graduate Scholarship, 733
Henry Reilly Memorial Scholarship, 734
Henry Salvatori Scholarship, 589
Herbert Lehman Scholarship for African American Students, 472
*Herbert Scoville Jr. Peace Fellowship, 566
Herman O. West Scholarship, 762
Hermione Grant Calhoun Scholarship, 484
Herschel C. Price Educational Scholarship, 427
Hershey Foods Corporation Scholars Program, 689
*Hertz Foundation Fellowship, 404
*Herzog August Bibliothek Wolfenbuttel Fellowship, 525
Hewlett-Packard Employee Scholarship, 689
Hexcel Scholarship Program, 689

Higher Education Legislature Plan for Needy Students, 141
Higher Education Undergraduate Grant Program, 58
Highway AG Services Scholarship, 690
Highway Engineers/Carolina Triangle Section Scholarship, 342
HIM PROGRAM, 633
Hispanic Association of Colleges and Universities Internship, 228
Hispanic Fund Scholarships, 491
Hispanic Professional Engineers Educational Grant, 581
*History of Pharmacy Grant-In-Aid, 285
HIT Program, 633
Hitachi Semiconductor USA Scholarship, 690
*HIV/AIDS Research Training Minority Fellowship, 58
Hoffman-La Roche Student Internship, 428
Holiday Hospitality Scholarship, 690
Holistic Nursing Charlotte McGuire Scholarship, 636
*Holistic Nursing Charlotte McGuire Scholarship (Graduate), 636
*Holistic Nursing Research Grant, 636
Holland America Line-Westours Travel Agents Scholarship, 345
*Honduras: Full Grant (Fulbright), 90
*Hong Kong: Full Grant (Fulbright), 90
Hooper Memorial Scholarship, 599
*Hoover Presidential Library Fellowship/Grant, 427
Hopi BIA Higher Education Scholarship, 428
Hopi Scholarship, 428
Hopi Supplemental Grant, 428
Hopi Tribal Priority Scholarship, 428
*Hopi Tuition-Book Scholarship, 429
Horace Mann Scholarship Program, 691
Horizons Foundation Scholarship, 429
*Horton Geophysical Research Grant, 276
Host Marriott Scholarship, 691
Howard Brown Rickard Scholarship, 484
Howard E. Adkins Memorial Scholarship, 350
HTC Employees' Daughter & Son Scholarship Program, 690
Hubbard Farms B.U.T.A. Scholarship, 691
*Hubert Humphrey Research Grant, 738
Hugo Neu Corporation Employees Scholarship, 691
*Hungary: Government Grant (Fulbright), 90
*Hungary: Teaching Assistantship (Fulbright), 91

*Graduate/nondegree study

Program Index

* Hungary: Travel Grant (Fulbright), 91
* Huntington British Academy Exchange Fellowship, 430
* Huntington Fellowship, 430
* Huntington National Endowment for the Humanities Fellowship, 431
* Huntington W.M. Keck Foundation Fellowship for Young Scholars, 431
I.F. Stone Award for Student Journalism, 473
* I/ITSEC Graduate Student Scholarship Program, 520
IBM Internship & Co-Op Program, 431
* Iceland: Full Grant (Fulbright), 91
* Iceland: Travel Grant-Government Grant (Fulbright), 91
Ida C. Koran Student Aid Program, 691
Ida M. Crawford Scholarship, 536
Idaho Education Incentive Loan Forgiveness Program, 118
Idaho Minority and At-Risk Student Scholarship, 118
Idaho Paul A. Fowler Memorial Scholarship, 119
Idaho Robert C. Byrd Honors Scholarship, 119
Idaho Student Incentive Grant, 119
Ideal Electric Scholarship, 692
Illinois D.A. DeBolt Teacher Shortage Scholarship, 119
Illinois Descendents Grant Program, 120
Illinois Incentive for Access, 120
Illinois Merit Recognition Scholarship, 120
Illinois Minority Teachers Scholarship, 120
Illinois Monetary Award, 121
Illinois National Guard Grant, 121
Illinois Power Company Wendell J. Kelley Scholarship, 762
Illinois Robert C. Byrd Honors Scholarship, 121
Illinois Student-to-Student Grant, 121
Illinois Tool Works Foundation Scholarship, 692
Illinois Veteran Grant, 121
IMC Scholarship Program, 693
* India: Full Grant (Fulbright), 91
Indiana Builders Association/Don Cassidy, Sr., Scholarship Fund, 678
Indiana Higher Education Grant, 122
Indiana Hoosier Scholar Program, 122
Indiana Minority Teacher Scholarship, 122
Indiana Nursing Scholarship, 122
Indiana Special Education Services Scholarship, 122
Indianapolis Newspapers Fellowship, 431
Indians Higher Education Grant Program, 231

* Indonesia: Full Grant (Fulbright), 92
* Industrial Hygiene Graduate Fellowship Program, 197
Innovex Scholarship, 693
Inroads Internship, 432
* Institut Francais de Washington Fellowship, 432
Institute for Humane Studies Fellowship, 432
Institute of Food Technologists Freshman Scholarship, 433
* Institute of Food Technologists Graduate Fellowship, 433
Institute of Food Technologists Junior/Senior Scholarship, 433
Institute of Food Technologists Sophomore Scholarship, 433
* Integrated Manufacturing Fellowship, 512
Intel Science Talent Search, 436
INTELSAT Summer Intern Program, 436
* International Dissertation Field Research Fellowship Program, 572
* International Educational Exchange Graduate Scholarship/Russia, 68
International Educational Exchange Scholarship/China, 68
International Educational Exchange/R.B. Bailey Minority Scholarship, 68
International Furnishings and Design Student Member Scholarship, 695
* International Graduate Student Fellowship, 321
International Incentive Award, 434
International Management Group Summer Intern Program, 436
International Multifoods Scholarship, 695
* International Predissertation Fellowship Program, 573
* International Research and Exchanges Board Travel Grant, 438
International Semester Scholarship, 281
International Summer Scholarship, 281
International Thompson Publishing Scholarship, 747
* International Water Conference Merit Award Scholarship, 400
* Interns for Peace Internship, 439
Interstate Brands Scholarship, 696
Intuit Scholarship, 696
* Investment Banking Internship, 549
Iowa Grant, 123
Iowa National Guard Tuition Aid Program, 123
Iowa Robert C. Byrd Honor Scholarship, 123
Iowa Tuition Grant, 123
Iowa Vocational-Technical Tuition Grant, 123

Iowa Work Study, 124
Ira Page Wallace Bible Scholarship, 550
* Ireland: Full Grant (Fulbright), 92
Irene E. Newman Scholarship, 250
* Irvine H. Page Arteriosclerosis Award, 277
* Irving Graef Memorial Scholarship, 506
Irving W. Cook WAOCGS Scholarship, 331
Irwin Scholarship Trust Fund, 422
* Israel: Full Grant (Fulbright), 92
* Israel: Postdoctoral Award (Fulbright), 93
Italian American Study Abroad Scholarship, 495
Italian Catholic Federation Scholarship, 439
Italian Cultural Society and NIAF Matching Scholarship, 495
Italian Regional Scholarship, 495
* Italy: Full Grant (Fulbright), 93
* Italy: Miguel Vinciguerra Fund Grant (Fulbright), 93
* Italy: Travel Grant (Fulbright), 93
* Ittleson Fellowship, 488
* Ivory Coast: Full Grant (Fulbright), 94
Ivy Parker Memorial Scholarship, 584
* J. Carew Memorial Scholarship, 365
J. Desmond Slattery Award: Student, 599
J. E. Reilly Scholarship, 637
J. Paul Getty Trust Internship Program, 440
J.A. Knowles Memorial Scholarship, 604
J.A. Young Memorial Education Recognition Award, 333
J.B. Cornelius Foundation Grants Program, 440
J.C. Penney Scholarship Program, 697
J.K. Rathmell, Jr., Memorial for Work/Study Abroad, 365
J.W. Saxe Memorial Prize, 440
Jack & Elizabeth Warner College Scholarship Fund, 687
* Jack E. Leisch Memorial National Scholarships, 340
Jackie Robinson Scholarship, 440
Jacob Van Namen/Vans Marketing Scholarship, 365
Jacque Minotte Health Reporting Fellowship, 556
Jacques Bobst Scholarship, 662
* Jamaica: Full Grant (Fulbright), 94
James A. Turner, Jr., Scholarship, 350
James B. Carey Scholarship, 695
James Carlson Memorial Scholarship, 536
James E. Casey Canadian Scholarship, 758
James F. Byrnes Scholarship, 441
* James F. Schumar Scholarship, 323

*Graduate/nondegree study

Program Index

*James H. Robinson Memorial Prize in Surgery, 506
James H. Waters Scholarship, 662
James L. & Lavon Maddon Mallory Disability Scholarship, 395
*James Madison Memorial Junior Fellowship, 124
*James Madison Memorial Senior Fellowship, 124
James R. Vogt Scholarship, 323
*Jane and Morgan Whitney Fellowship, 463
Jane Demaree Internship, 549
*Japan Foundation Doctoral Fellowship, 441
*Japan-United States Arts Program, 356
*Japan: Fellowship for Graduating Seniors (Fulbright), 94
*Japan: Full Grant (Fulbright), 94
Japanese American General Scholarship, 442
Japanese American Music Award Competition, 442
Jaycee War Memorial Scholarship, 442
Jean Driscoll Award, 532
Jean Fitzgerald Scholarship Fund, 422
*Jeanette Mowery Graduate Scholarship, 536
Jeanne E. Bray Law Enforcement Dependents Scholarship, 716
*Jeanne Humphrey Block Dissertation Award, 426
Jenkins Scholarship, 537
*Jeppesen Meteorology Internship, 442
Jerome B. Steinbach Scholarship, 537
Jerome J. Bliss Memorial Fund, 708
Jerry Baker Scholarship, 365
Jerry Wilmot Scholarship, 366
Jimmy Treybig Scholarship Program, 697
Joel Garcia Memorial Scholarship, 374
John A. Volpe Scholarship, 495
John and Elsa Gracik Mechanical Engineering Scholarship, 653
John and Muriel Landis Scholarship, 324
John Basilone Scholarship, 601
*John C. Geilfuss Fellowship, 221
John C. Lincoln Memorial Scholarship, 350
John Cook Honorary Scholarship, 254
John Dawe Fund, 422
John F. Eula Mae Baugh SYSCO Scholarship Program, 751
John F. Kennedy Center Performing Arts Internship, 443
John F. Kennedy Library Foundation/ Abba P. Schwartz Research Fellowship, 445

John F. Kennedy Library Foundation/ Arthur M. Schlesinger Jr. Research Fellowships, 446
John L. Dales Scholarship, 739
John L. Dales Transitional Scholarship, 740
John Lyons Scholarship, 694
John M. Simpson Memorial Scholarship, 621
John N. Williams Scholarship Award, 704
*John O. Butler Graduate Scholarships, 250
*John P. Utz Postdoctoral Fellowship in Medical Mycology, 486
*John Q. Schisler Award, 604
John R. Lamarsh Scholarship, 324
*John Randall Scholarship, 324
John Ross Foundation, 422
John W. McDermott Scholarship, 423
*Johnson and Johnson Dissertation Grants in Women's Health, 244
Johnson International Scholarship Program, 697
Johnson Wax Fund Sons & Daughters Scholarship, 698
*Joint Fellowship with the American Antiquarian Society, 525
*Jordan: Full Grant (Fulbright), 95
Jose D. Garcia Migrant Education Scholarship, 537
Joseph Anthony Beirne Scholarship, 672
Joseph F. Dracup Scholarship, 629
*Joseph L. Fisher Dissertation Award, 560
Joseph Levendusky Memorial Scholarship, 400
Joseph R. Dietrich Scholarship, 324
Joseph R. Stone Travel Agents Scholarship, 346
Joseph S. Adams Scholarship, 627
Joseph Tauber Scholarship, 621
JPMA Scholarship Program, 698
Judith Resnik Memorial Scholarship, 745
*Juilliard Professional Intern Program, 446
Juliette M. Atherton Scholarship, 423
Junior Achievement of Maine Scholarship, 447
*Junior Investigator Epilepsy Research Grant, 402
Junior Miss Scholarship, 258
Junior/Senior Scholarship Program, 165
JVS Jewish Community Scholarship Program, 447
JWA Sons and Daughters Scholarship, 698
K.M. Hatano Scholarship, 423
K2TEO Martin J. Green, Sr. Memorial Scholarship, 331

Kaiser Permanente Dental Assistant Scholarship, 537
Kaiulani Home for Girls Trust Scholarship, 423
Kansas Ethnic Minority Scholarship, 125
Kansas Nursing Scholarship, 125
*Kansas Optometry Program, 125
*Kansas Osteopathic Program, 125
Kansas Regents Supplemental Grant, 125
Kansas State Scholarship, 126
Kansas Teacher Scholarship, 126
Kansas Tuition Grant, 126
Kansas Vocational Education Scholarship, 126
Kappa Epsilon-Nellie Wakeman Fellowship, 631
*Kappa Omicrom Nu Fellowships and Grants, 698
*Karen D. Carsel Memorial Scholarhip, 274
Karla Scherer Foundation Scholarship, 447
Katherine F. Gruber Scholarship, 369
Katherine M. Grosscup Scholarship, 411
Kathleen S. Anderson Award, 459
Kathryn D. Sullivan Science and Engineering Undergraduate Fellowship, 169
Kawasaki-McGaha Scholarship Fund, 423
KCACTF/ Barbizon Awards for Theatrical Design Excellence, 443
KCACTF/ ChildrenÖs Theatre Foundation Award, 443
KCACTF/ Fourth Freedom Forum Playwriting Award, 443
KCACTF/ Irene Ryan Acting Scholarships, 444
KCACTF/ Lorraine Hansberry Playwriting Award, 444
KCACTF/ Musical Theater Award, 444
KCACTF/ National AIDS Fund/ CFDA - Vogue Initiative Award for Playwriting, 444
KCACTF/ National Student Playwriting Award, 444
KCACTF/ Short Play Awards Program, 445
KCACTF/ Short Play Awards Program, 445
Keane Educational Scholarship, 699
Kemper Scholars Grant Program, 441
*Kenan T. Erim Award, 352
Kennedy Library Research Grants, 446
Kenneth Andrew Roe Mechanical Engineering Scholarship, 653
Kenneth Davenport National Music Competition, 471
Kenneth F. Merrill Scholarship, 708

*Graduate/nondegree study

Program Index

Kentucky College Access Program (CAP) Grant, 126
Kentucky Teacher Scholarship, 127
Kentucky Tuition Grant, 127
Kentucky Work-Study Program, 127
*Kenya: Full Grant (Fulbright), 95
Kids College Scholarship, 700
KIMT Weather/News Internship, 447
King Olav V Norwegian-American Heritage Fund, 589
*Klineberg Award, 578
Klumb Family Scholarship Program, 655
Knights of Columbus Student Loan, 699
Knights of Pythias Financial Aid Award, 448
Knights Templar Educational Foundation Loan, 416
Kohler Scholarship, 700
Koloa Scholarship, 424
*Korea: Full Grant (Fulbright), 95
*Korea: Teaching Assistantship (Fulbright), 95
*Korea: Travel Grant (Fulbright), 96
Kosciuszko Tuition Scholarship, 448
Kottis Family Award, 675
*Kreiss Art History and Archaeology Fellowship, 333
*Kress Travel Fellowship, 563
*Kress Two-Year Research Fellowship at Foreign Institutions, 563
Kucher-Killian Scholarship, 485
*Kurt Weill Foundation Dissertation Fellowships, 449
*Kuwait: Full Grant (Fulbright), 96
L. Gordon Bittle Memorial Scholarship for Student CTA, 375
L. Phil Wicker Scholarship, 332
L.M. Perryman Ethnic Minority Award, 606
Laidlaw Scholarship Program, 700
*Lalor Postdoctoral Research Grants, 449
Lance Stafford Larson Student Scholarship, 692
Lang Family Foundation Scholarship, 701
*Language Training Grant: Eastern Europe, 573
Larry R. Strand Memorial Scholarship Program, 753
Latin American Educational Scholarship, 701
Latin Honor Society Scholarship, 628
Latino Summer Legislative Internship, 478
*Latvia: Full Grant (Fulbright), 96
Laura N. Dowsett Fund, 118
Law Enforcement Explorer Scholarship, 664
*Law Fellowships for Equal Justice, 476
*Law Internship Program, 198

Law/Social Sciences Summer Research Fellowship for Minority Undergraduates, 265
Lawrence R. Foster Memorial Scholarship, 537
Lazaroff Family Fund, 443
Learning Through Listening Award, 732
Lebovitz Internship, 509
Legacy Awards, 685
Legal Medicine Student Writing Competition, 268
Leggett & Platt Scholarship Program for Children of Employees, 701
Leiber and Stoller Scholarship, 355
Leica Surveying Scholarship, 629
*Lemmermann Scholarship, 451
Len Allen Award of Merit, 557
Leon Harris/Les Nichols Memorial to Spartan School of Aeronautics, 254
Leopold Schepp Scholarship, 452
*Lerner-Gray Grants for Marine Research, 322
Leroy C. Dettman Foundation Scholarship, 701
*Leroy Matthews Physician/Scientist Award, 389
Lester F. Kuzmick Memorial Scholarship, 673
*Lester G. Benz Memorial College Journalism Scholarship, 555
*Lester J. Cappon Fellowship in Documentary Editing, 525
Levi Strauss Foundation Scholarship, 702
Lew Wasserman College Scholarship, 702
*Library and Information Science Grant, 438
*Library and Information Technology Association/GEAC-CLSI Scholarship, 316
*Library and Information Technology Association/LSSI Minority Scholarship, 316
*Library and Information Technology Association/OCLC/Minority Scholarship, 316
Library of Congress Junior Fellows Internship, 127
LifeScan Scholarship Program/Dana Pettengill Scholarship Fund, 702
*Lighthouse Graduate Incentive Award, 453
Lighthouse Undergraduate Incentive Award, 453
Lillian Moller Gilbreth Scholarship, 584
Lilly for Learning Diabetes Scholarship, 398
Limouselle Scholarship, 723
Limousin Award of Excellence, 723

*Lincoln Center for the Performing Arts Internships in Arts Administration, 454
*Lincoln Food Service Research Grant, 739
*Lindbergh Foundation Grant, 378
Link-Belt Scholarship Program, 703
*Lithuania: Full Grant (Fulbright), 96
*Liver Scholar Award, 317
*Lloyd Lewis Fellowship in American History, 526
Loctite Scholarship Program, 703
Logan Airport Scholarship Trust Scholarship, 703
Loon Fund Grant Program, 528
Los Angeles Times Editorial Internships, 454
*Louis Agassiz Fuertes Award, 614
Louis J. Salerno, M.D. Memorial Scholarship, 496
*Louis N. and Arnold M. Katz Research Prize, 277
Louise Dessureault Memorial Scholarship, 516
*Louise Giles Minority Scholarship, 316
*Louise Kidder Early Career Award, 578
Louisiana Innovative Professional Development/Teacher Tuition Exemption, 128
Louisiana Rockefeller Wildlife Scholarship, 129
Louisiana Social Services Rehabilitation/Vocational Aid For Disabled Persons, 128
Louisiana State Student Incentive Grant, 129
Louisiana Tuition Opportunity Program Award, 129
Louisiana Tuition Opportunity Program Performance Award, 129
Louisiana Veterans Affairs Educational Assistance for Dependent Children, 128
Louisiana Veterans Affairs Educational Assistance for Surviving Spouse, 128
Lowell Gaylor Memorial Scholarship, 254
*Lowenstein-Wiener Fellowship in American Jewish Studies, 285
Lower Mid-Atlantic Regional Scholarship, 496
Lucile B. Kaufman Women's Scholarship, 582
Luck Stone Scholarship, 704
*Luise Meyer-Schutzmeister Award, 360
*Lung Association Career Investigator Award, 317
*Lung Association Clinical Research Grant, 318

782   *Graduate/nondegree study

Program Index

*Lung Association Dalsemer Research Dissertation Grant, 318
*Lung Association Research Grant, 318
*Lung Association Research Training Fellowship, 318
*Lung Health Research Dissertation Grant, 318
*Luray Caverns Grant, 516
Lynden Memorial Scholarship Program, 704
Lynn Marie Vogel Scholarship, 395
M. & E. Walker Scholarship, 582
*M.A. Cartland Shackford Medical Fellowship, 612
M.B. Duggan, Jr., Memorial Education Recognition Award, 333
M.V. O'Donnell Memorial Teacher Training Award, 628
*Mabelle Wilhelmina Boldt Interior Design Scholarship, 342
*Madagascar: Full Grant (Fulbright), 97
MagneTek Scholarship, 704
Maine Educational Authority Supplemental Loan, 456
Maine Innkeepers Association - Scholarships for Maine Residents, 705
Maine Innkeepers Association Affiliates Scholarship, 705
Maine Lesbian/Gay Political Alliance Scholarship, 456
Maine Metal Products Scholarship, 456
*Maine Osteopathic Memorial Scholarship, 457
*Maine Osteopathic Scholarship, 457
Maine PIC/MH/VR/TDC Technical Scholarship, 458
Maine Recreation and Parks Association Scholarship, 457
Maine Robert C. Byrd Honors Scholarship, 130
Maine Rural Rehabilitation Fund Scholarship, 221
Maine Society of Professional Engineers Scholarship Program, 458
Maine State APWU Scholarship, 705
Maine Veterans Services Dependents Educational Benefits, 129
Maine Vietnam VeteransÖ Scholarship Fund/ Lest We Forget POW/MIA/KIA Scholarship Fund, 455
Major Don S. Gentile Scholarship, 602
*Malawi: Full Grant (Fulbright), 97
*Malaysia: Full Grant (Fulbright), 97
*Mali: Full Grant (Fulbright), 97
*Malyon-Smith Scholarship Award, 577
Manhattan Theatre Club Professional Internship, 459
MAP Scholarship Program, 708

Mapco Coal Scholars Program, 706
MAPCO Scholars Program, 706
Marc A. Klein Playwriting Award, 377
*March of Dimes Request for Research Proposals, 459
Marcia Doyle Bartley Scholarship, 659
Margaret E. Swanson Scholarship, 250
*Margaret Morse Nice Award, 614
*Margaret P. Esmonde Memorial Scholarship, 670
Marguerite R. Jacobs Memorial Award in American Jewish Studies, 286
Maria Jackson--General George White Scholarship, 537
Maria Mitchell Internships for Astronomical Research, 460
Marija Bileta Scholarship, 496
Marine Corps Scholarship, 460
Marion Huber Learning Through Listening Award, 732
Marion MacCarrell Scott Scholarship, 424
Marion Wright Edelman Scholarship, 454
Marjorie Kovler Research Fellowship, 446
Mark Hass Journalism Scholarship, 538
Marlin R. Scarborough Memorial Scholarship, 219
Marshall E. McCullough Undergraduate Scholarship, 483
Marshall Scholarship, 370
Martin McLaren-Interchange Fellowship in Horticulture and Landscape Design, 411
Martin R. Scarborough Memorial Scholarship, 220
Marvin Lumber and Cedar/Marvin Windows Scholarship, 706
*Mary Adeline Connor Professional Development Scholarship, 748
Mary Baracco Scholarship, 721
*Mary Davis Fellowship, 488
*Mary Isabel Sibley Fellowship, 547
Mary Lou Brown Scholarship, 332
Mary M. Verges Award, 675
Mary Macey Scholarship, 616
*Mary McEwen Schimke Scholarship, 612
Mary Morrow-Edna Richards Scholarship, 528
*Mary P. Oenslager Scholastic Achievement Award, 732
Maryland Child Care Provider Scholarship, 130
Maryland Delegate Scholarship, 130
Maryland Distinguished Scholar: Academics, 130

Maryland Distinguished Scholar: National Merit Finalists, 131
Maryland Distinguished Scholar: Talent, 131
Maryland Distinguished Scholar: Teacher Education Program, 131
Maryland Distinguished Scholar: Visual Arts, 131
Maryland Educational Assistance Grant, 131
Maryland Edward T. Conroy Memorial Grant--Disabled Public Safety Employees, 132
Maryland Edward T. Conroy Memorial Scholarship Program, 132
*Maryland Family Practice Medical Scholarship, 132
Maryland Guaranteed Access Grant, 132
Maryland Jack F. Tolbert Memorial Grant, 133
*Maryland Loan Assistance Repayment Program, 133
*Maryland Loan Assistance Repayment Program/Primary Care Services, 133
Maryland Part-Time Grant Program, 133
Maryland Physical/Occupational Therapists and Assistants Grant, 134
Maryland Professional School Scholarship, 134
Maryland Reimbursement of Firefighters, 134
Maryland Senatorial Scholarship, 134
Maryland Sharon Christa McAuliffe Memorial Teacher Education Award, 135
Maryland State Nursing Scholarship and Living Expenses Grant, 135
Maryland Tuition Reduction for Out-of-State Nursing Students, 135
Masonic Range Science Scholarship, 583
Mass Media Science and Engineering Fellowship, 626
Massachusetts Biotechnology Scholars Program, 460
Massachusetts Christian A. Herter Memorial Scholarship Program, 135
Massachusetts Gilbert Grant, 135
Massachusetts Glass Dealers Scholarship, 706
Massachusetts Massgrant Program, 135
Massachusetts No Interest Loan, 136
Massachusetts Public Service Program, 136
Massachusetts Robert C. Byrd Honors Scholarship, 136
Massachusetts Tuition Waver, 136
*Master's Degree Scholarship in Cancer Nursing, 266

*Graduate/nondegree study

Material Sciences Corporation Dependent Scholarship Award Program, 707
Mattel Foundation Scholarship Program, 707
Matthews/Swift Educational Trust - Military Dependants, 699
Matthews/Swift Educational Trust - Police/Firefighters, 699
*Mauritius: Full Grant (Fulbright), 98
Maxine Williams Scholarship, 263
MBK Real Estate Ltd. Scholarship Program, 707
McAllister and Burnside Scholarship, 351
McDonald's RMHC-Hispanic American Commitment to Educational Resources H.S. Program, 461
McDonnel Memorial Scholarship, 269
McDonnell Douglas Internship Program, 461
McFarland Charitable Foundation Scholarship, 419
MCI Cutting Edge Scholars Internet Project Awards, 461
McKesson Pharmacy Scholarship Program, 707
McKesson Scholarship Program, 707
*McKinlay Summer Award, 628
MDU Resources Employees' Scholarship Program, 708
*Medical Fellowships General Need-Based Scholarship, 507
*Medical Fellowships Special Awards Program, 507
*Medical Fellowships Technology Training Program, 507
*Medical Library Association Scholarship, 461
*Medical Library Doctoral Scholarship, 462
*Medical Library Rittenhouse Award, 462
*Medical Library Scholarship for Minority Students, 462
*Medical Student Research Fellowship in Pharmacology/Clinical Pharmacology, 547
Medical Technologists Scholarship, 319
*Medical Women's Carroll L. Birch Award, 649
*Medical Women's Education Loan, 649
*Medical Women's Janet M. Glasgow Essay Award, 650
*Medical Women's Wilhelm-Frankowski Scholarship, 319
Medicus Student Exchange, 595
Melamed Scholarship, 741
Melbourne Wesley Cummings Scholarship Program, 622

Melon Minority Fellowship Program, 573
Melva T. Owen Memorial Scholarship, 485
*Melvin Judkins Award, 635
*Melvin L. Marcus Award, 277
Menominee Adult Vocational Training Scholarship, 136
Menominee Higher Education Scholarship, 462
Mental Retardation Nursing Scholastic Achievement Scholarship, 367
Mental Retardation Scholastic Achievement Scholarship, 368
Mentor Graphics Scholarship, 538
*Merck Research Scholarship Program, 273
Merrill Lynch Scholarship, 496
Meteorological Society Father James B. MacElwane Annual Award, 319
*Meteorological Society Industry Graduate Fellowship, 320
Meteorological Society Industry Undergraduate Scholarship, 320
Meteorological Society Minority Scholarship, 320
Meteorological Society Undergraduate Scholarship, 320
Metro Electrical Training Scholarship, 708
*Metropolitan Life Foundation Scholarship, 507
*Metropolitan Museum of Art Graduate Lecturing Internship, 463
*Metropolitan Museum of Art Nine-Month Art Internship, 464
Metropolitan Museum of Art Six-Month Art Internship, 464
Metropolitan Museum of Art Summer Art Internships for College Students, 464
*Metropolitan Museum of Art Summer Art Internships for Graduate Students, 464
Mexican American Grocers Association Scholarship, 465
*Mexican American Law School Scholarship, 465
*Mexico: Binational Business Grants (Fulbright), 98
*Mexico: Garcia Robles Grant (Fulbright), 98
Michael W. Marris Memorial Scholarship, 686
Michael J. Flosi Memorial Scholarship, 332
Michelle Clark Fellowship, 557
Michigan Adult Part-Time Grant, 137
Michigan Alternative Student Loan (MI-LOAN) Program, 466
Michigan Competitive Scholarship, 137
Michigan Educational Opportunity Grant, 137

Michigan Educational Opportunity Scholarship, 137
Michigan Hispanic High School Graduate Award, 466
Michigan Petroleum Asso./Michigan Asso. of Convervntion Store Scholarship Program, 709
Michigan Robert C. Byrd Honors Scholarship, 137
Michigan Society of Professional Engineers, 466
Michigan Tuition Grant, 137
Michigan Work-Study Program, 138
Microbiology Summer Research Fellowship for Minority Students, 339
Microfibres Scholarship Program, 709
Microscopy Presidential Student Award, 467
Microscopy Undergraduate Research Scholarship, 467
*Mid Career Skills Enrichment Program for Tenured Faculty, 573
Mid-America Regional Scholarship, 497
Mid-Continent Instrument Scholarship, 254
Mid-Pacific Regional Scholarship, 497
Midwest Student Exchange Program, 138
Mike Harper Leadership Scholars Program, 673
Mildred Towle Trust Fund Scholarship, 424
*Miller Brewing Internship, 467
Miller Electric Manufacturing Company Ivic Scholarship, 350
Millipore Foundation Scholarship Program, 709
*Millipore/Charles P. Schaufus Grant, 544
*Mining Club Award, 435
Minnesota Educational Assistance for Veterans, 138
Minnesota Educational Assistance for War Orphans, 138
Minnesota GLBT Educational Fund, 467
Minnesota Mutual Presidents' Scholarship Fund, 710
Minnesota Non-Aid to Families with Dependent Children Child Care Grant, 139
Minnesota Nursing Grant for Persons of Color, 139
Minnesota Safety Officers Survivors Program, 139
Minnesota State Grant Program, 139
Minnesota Student Educational Loan Fund, 139
Minnesota Work-Study Program, 140
*Minority Dental Student Scholarship, 248

* Miss America Education Scholarship for Post-Graduate Studies, 468
Miss America Pageant, 468
* Mississippi Dental Education Loan/Scholarship, 141
Mississippi Eminent Scholars Grant, 141
* Mississippi Graduate Teacher Summer Loan/Scholarship Program, 141
Mississippi Health Care Professional Loan/Scholarship, 141
Mississippi Law Enforcement Officers/Firemen Scholarship, 142
* Mississippi Medical Education Loan/Scholarship, 142
Mississippi Nursing Education Loan/Scholarship, 142
* Mississippi Nursing Teacher Stipend Program, 142
Mississippi Psychology Apprenticeship Program, 142
* Mississippi Public Management Graduate Internship, 143
Mississippi Resident Tuition Assistance Grant, 143
Mississippi Southeast Asia POW/MIA Scholarship, 143
* Mississippi Southern Regional Education Board Loan/Scholarship, 143
Mississippi Space Grant Consortium, 159
Mississippi Student Incentive Grant, 143
Mississippi William Winter Teacher Scholar Loan Program, 144
Missouri Higher Education Academic Scholarship, 144
Missouri Minority Teaching Scholarship, 145
Missouri Nursing Scholarship, 468
Missouri Public Service Survivor Grant, 144
Missouri Robert C. Byrd Honors Scholarship, 145
Missouri Student Grant, 145
Missouri Teacher Education Scholarship, 145
Mitsui USA's Sons & Daughters Scholarship Program, 710
Mobility Internship Program, 468
Mola Scholarship, 497
Montana Student Incentive Grant, 146
Montana Tuition Fee Waiver for Dependents of POW/MIA, 146
Montana Tuition Fee Waiver for Veterans, 146
Montana University System Community College Honor Scholarship, 146
Montana University System High School Honor Scholarship, 146
Monte R. Mitchell Global Scholarship, 255

Montgomery GI Bill (MGIB), 227
Montgomery GI Bill Plus Army College Fund, 227
* Monticello College Foundation Fellowship for Women, 526
Morocco: Full Grant (Fulbright), 98
* Morphology Fellowship, 547
Morris Arboretum Education Internship, 469
Morris Arboretum Horticulture Internship, 469
* Morton Gould Young Composers Award, 355
Mortuary Education Grant, 428
* Mother Jones Art Internship, 470
* Mother Jones Editorial Internship, 470
Mother Jones MoJo Wire Internship, 470
Mother Jones Publishing Internship, 470
Moyer Packing Company Sons and Daughters Scholarship Program, 710
* Mozambique: Full Grant (Fulbright), 99
Mozelle Willard Gold Scholarship, 485
MRC Scholar Program, 707
MSSF Scholarship Program, 458
Multi-Year Ambassadorial Scholarship, 562
Museum Internships in Washington DC, 510
Museum of Modern Art Internship Program, 471
Music Assistance Fund, 348
* Myasthenia Gravis Foundation Kermit E. Osserman Fellowship, 471
Myasthenia Gravis Foundation Nursing Research Fellowship, 472
NAIF/FIERI National Matching Scholarship, 497
* Namibia: Full Grant (Fulbright), 99
Nancy Lorraine Jensen Memorial Scholarship, 746
NASA Academy Internship, 167
NASA Space Grant Alabama Graduate Fellowship, 146
NASA Space Grant Alabama Undergraduate Scholarship Program, 147
* NASA Space Grant Alaska Graduate Fellowship, 147
NASA Space Grant Alaska Undergraduate Scholarship, 147
* NASA Space Grant Arizona Graduate Fellowship, 148
NASA Space Grant Arizona Undergraduate Research Internship, 148
* NASA Space Grant Arkansas Graduate Fellowship, 148
NASA Space Grant Arkansas Undergraduate Scholarship, 148

* NASA Space Grant California Fellowship Program, 149
NASA Space Grant California Undergraduate Scholarship, 149
NASA Space Grant Colorado Graduate Fellowship, 149
NASA Space Grant Colorado Undergraduate Scholarship, 149
* NASA Space Grant Connecticut Graduate Fellowship, 150
NASA Space Grant Connecticut Undergraduate Fellowship, 473
* NASA Space Grant Delaware Space Graduate Student Fellowship, 150
NASA Space Grant Delaware Undergraduate Summer Scholarship, 150
NASA Space Grant Delaware Undergraduate Tuition Scholarship, 150
NASA Space Grant District of Columbia Undergraduate Scholarship, 151
* NASA Space Grant District of Columbia Graduate Fellowship, 151
* NASA Space Grant Florida Fellowship Program, 151
* NASA Space Grant Florida Fellowship Program, 151
NASA Space Grant Florida Undergraduate Space Research Participation Program, 152
NASA Space Grant Georgia Fellowship Program, 152
* NASA Space Grant Hawaii Graduate Fellowship, 152
NASA Space Grant Hawaii Undergraduate Scholarship, 153
NASA Space Grant Hawaii Undergraduate Traineeship Program, 153
* NASA Space Grant Idaho Graduate Fellowship, 153
NASA Space Grant Idaho Undergraduate Scholarship Program, 153
* NASA Space Grant Illinois Graduate Fellowship, 154
NASA Space Grant Illinois Undergraduate Scholarship, 154
* NASA Space Grant Indiana Graduate Fellowship, 154
NASA Space Grant Indiana Summer Undergraduate Research Program, 154
NASA Space Grant Indiana Undergraduate Scholarship, 154
NASA Space Grant Kansas Graduate Fellowship, 155
NASA Space Grant Kansas Undergraduate Scholarship, 155
* NASA Space Grant Kentucky Graduate Fellowship, 155

*Graduate/nondegree study

Program Index

NASA Space Grant Kentucky Undergraduate Scholarship, 156
NASA Space Grant Louisiana LaSPACE Graduate Fellowship Program, 156
NASA Space Grant Louisiana LaSPACE Undergraduate Scholarship Program, 156
*NASA Space Grant Maine Graduate Fellowship, 157
*NASA Space Grant Maine Research Acceleration Grant Program, 157
NASA Space Grant Maine Undergraduate Internship Award, 157
NASA Space Grant Maine Undergraduate Scholarship Program, 157
*NASA Space Grant Maryland Graduate Fellowship, 157
NASA Space Grant Maryland Undergraduate Scholarship, 157
*NASA Space Grant Massachusetts Graduate Fellowships, 158
NASA Space Grant Massachusetts Summer Jobs for Students, 158
NASA Space Grant Massachusetts Undergraduate Research Opportunities, 158
*NASA Space Grant Michigan Graduate Fellowship, 158
NASA Space Grant Michigan Undergraduate Fellowship, 159
*NASA Space Grant Minnesota Graduate Fellowship, 159
NASA Space Grant Minnesota Internship Program, 159
NASA Space Grant Minnesota Undergraduate Scholarship, 159
*NASA Space Grant Missouri Summer Jobs for Students, 160
NASA Space Grant Missouri Summer Undergraduate Internship, 160
*NASA Space Grant Montana Graduate Fellowship, 160
NASA Space Grant Montana Undergraduate Scholarship Program, 160
*NASA Space Grant Nevada Graduate Fellowship, 161
NASA Space Grant Nevada Undergraduate Scholarship, 162
NASA Space Grant New Hampshire Undergraduate Scholarship, 162
*NASA Space Grant New Hampshire Graduate Fellowship, 162
NASA Space Grant New Jersey Undergraduate Summer Fellowship, 162
*NASA Space Grant New Mexico Graduate Fellowship, 163
NASA Space Grant New Mexico Undergraduate Scholarship, 163

NASA Space Grant New York Graduate Fellowship, 163
NASA Space Grant New York Undergraduate Internship, 163
*NASA Space Grant North Carolina Graduate Fellowship, 164
NASA Space Grant North Carolina Undergraduate Scholarship Program, 164
*NASA Space Grant North Dakota Graduate Fellowship, 164
NASA Space Grant North Dakota Undergraduate Scholarship, 164
*NASA Space Grant Ohio Fellowship Program, 165
*NASA Space Grant Oklahoma Space Grant Consortium Graduate Fellowship, 166
NASA Space Grant Oklahoma Undergraduate Scholarship, 166
*NASA Space Grant Oregon Graduate Fellowship, 166
NASA Space Grant Oregon Undergraduate Scholarship, 166
*NASA Space Grant Pennsylvania Graduate Fellowship, 167
NASA Space Grant Pennsylvania Undergraduate Scholarship, 167
*NASA Space Grant Puerto Rico Graduate Fellowship, 167
NASA Space Grant Puerto Rico Summer Internship Program, 168
NASA Space Grant Puerto Rico Undergraduate Scholarship, 168
*NASA Space Grant Rhode Island Graduate Fellowship, 168
NASA Space Grant Rhode Island Summer Undergraduate Scholarship Program, 168
NASA Space Grant Rhode Island Undergraduate Academic Year Scholarship Program, 169
NASA Space Grant Rocky Mountain Graduate Fellowship, 169
NASA Space Grant Rocky Mountain Undergraduate Scholarship, 169
*NASA Space Grant South Carolina Graduate Fellowship, 170
NASA Space Grant South Carolina Undergraduate Academic Year Research Program, 170
NASA Space Grant South Carolina Undergraduate Research Summer Scholarship, 170
NASA Space Grant South Carolina Undergraduate Scholarship Program, 170
*NASA Space Grant Tennessee Graduate Fellowship, 171
NASA Space Grant Tennessee Undergraduate Scholarship, 171
*NASA Space Grant Texas Graduate Fellowship, 171

NASA Space Grant Texas Undergraduate Scholarship Program, 172
*NASA Space Grant Vermont Space Graduate Research Assistantship, 172
NASA Space Grant Vermont Undergraduate Scholarships, 172
*NASA Space Grant Washington Graduate Fellowships at the University of Washington, 174
NASA Space Grant Washington Undergraduate Scholarship Program, 174
*NASA Space Grant West Virginia Graduate Fellowship, 174
NASA Space Grant West Virginia Undergraduate Fellowship Scholarship, 175
NASA Space Grant West Virginia Undergraduate Scholarship, 175
*NASA Space Grant Wisconsin Graduate Fellowship, 175
NASA Space Grant Wisconsin Space Other Student Awards, 175
NASA Space Grant Wisconsin Undergraduate Research Awards, 176
NASA Space Grant Wisconsin Undergraduate Scholarship, 176
*NASA Space Grant Wyoming Space Graduate Research Fellowships, 176
NASA Space Grant Wyoming Undergraduate Research Fellowships, 177
*NASA Space South Dakota Graduate Fellowship Space Grant, 171
Nash Finch Scholarship Program, 711
Nathan Burkan Memorial Competition, 356
National Achievement Scholarship, 508
*National Art Gallery Diversity Internship Program, 476
*National Art Gallery Graduate Lecturing Fellowships, 476
National Art Materials Scholarship, 712
National Association for Community Leadership, 476
National Computer Systems Scholarship, 714
National Dean's List Scholarship, 700
*National Defense Science and Engineering Graduate Fellowship Program, 70
National Eagle Scout Scholarship, 664
*National Endowment for the Humanities Fellowship, 526
*National Endowment for the Humanities Postdoctoral Fellowship, 60

786

*Graduate/nondegree study

Program Index

* National Endowment for the Humanities Summer Stipends Program, 177
National Federation of the Blind Scholarship, 485
National Future Farmers of America Scholarship Program, 716
National Health Services Corps Scholarship, 230
* National Hemophilia Foundation/Judith Graham Pool Postdoctoral Research Fellowship, 490
* National Hemophilia Foundation/Nursing Excellence Fellowship, 490
* National Institute of Justice Graduate Research Fellowship, 178
* National Institutes of Health Funding Award, 389
National Journal Editorial Internship, 504
National Junior Classical League Scholarship, 628
National Merit Scholarship, 509
National Museum of the American Indian Internship, 509
National Network for Environmental Management Studies Internship, 71
National Organization for Women legal defense and Education fund Internships, 510
National Peace Essay Contest, 231
National Presbyterian College Scholarship, 550
National Restaurant Association Undergraduate Scholarship, 512
* National Scholarship Award, 701
National Scholarship Program, 712
National Scholarship Trust Fund of the Graphic Arts, 513
* National Scholarship Trust Fund of the Graphic Arts Graduate Fellowships, 513
National Scholarship Trust Fund of the Graphic Arts Undergraduate Scholarships, 513
National Scholarship Trust Fund of the Graphic Arts Undergraduate Scholarships and Graduate Fellowships, 717
* National Science Foundation Graduate Fellowship, 179
* National Science Foundation Minority Graduate Fellowship, 180
* National Science Foundation Minority Postdoctoral Fellowship, 180
* National Science Foundation Postdoctoral Research Fellowship, 180
National Security Agency Undergraduate Tuition Assistance Program, 180
National Society of Black Engineers Oratorical Contest, 717

National Society of Black Engineers Scholars Program, 718
National Society of Black Engineers/Boeing Flight Competition, 718
National Society of Black Engineers/GE African American Forum Scholarship, 718
National Society of Black Engineers/Undergraduate Students in Technical Research Awards Program, 718
National Society of Professional Surveyors Scholarship, 630
National Space Society Internship Program, 515
National Speakers Association Scholarship, 515
National Student Nurses Association Scholarship, 407
Native American Scholarship, 520
Native Daughters of the Golden West Scholarship, 719
* Naval Architects and Marine Engineers Graduate Scholarship, 744
Naval Engineers Scholarship, 343
* Naval Research Laboratory - Postdoctoral Fellowship, 338
Navy Supply Corps Scholarship, 521
NBA Internship Program, 480
NCAA Byers Scholarship, 481
NCAA Degree Completion Award, 481
* NCAA Ethnic Minority Internship, 481
* NCAA Ethnic Minority Postgraduate Scholarship, 481
NCAA Freedom Forum Scholarship, 482
* NCAA Postgraduate Scholarship, 482
* NCAA Women's Enhancement Postgraduate Scholarship, 482
* NCAA Women's Internship, 482
* Near and Middle East Research and Training Act Predoctoral Fellowship, 336
* Near and Middle East Research and Training Act Senior Post-Doctoral Research Grant, 336
* Nebraska Medical Student Scholarship Program, 181
Nebraska Postsecondary Education Award, 181
Nebraska Robert C. Byrd Honors Scholarship, 182
Nebraska Scholarship Assistance Program, 181
Nebraska State Scholarship Award, 181
NEC America Scholarship Program, 719
Ned McWherter Scholarship, 222
Nemal Electronics Scholarship, 332
* Nepal: Full Grant (Fulbright), 99

Nerone/NIAF Matching Art Scholarship, 497
* Netherlands: America Foundation Grant (Fulbright), 99
* Netherlands: Full Grant (Fulbright), 100
Network Internship or Summer Science Internship, 554
* Neuromuscular Disease Research Grant, 471
* Neuroscience Training Minority Fellowship, 59
Nevada Robert C. Byrd Honors Scholarship, 182
Nevada Student Incentive Grant, 182
New Dramatists Internship, 522
New England Association of Independent Tire Dealers Scholarship, 719
New England Femara Scholarship, 332
New England Graphic Arts Scholarship, 522
New England Higher Education Regional Student Program, 182
New England Regional Scholarship, 498
New Hampshire Alternative Loans for Parents and Students, 416
New Hampshire Incentive Program, 182
New Hampshire Nursing Scholarship Program, 183
New Hampshire Scholarship for Orphans of Veterans, 183
New Hampshire Statewide Scholarship Program, 523
* New Investigators Program, 273
* New Jersey C. Clyde Ferguson Law Scholarship, 183
New Jersey Class Loan Program, 184
New Jersey Educational Opportunity Fund Grant, 184
New Jersey Edward J. Bloustein Distinguished Scholars, 184
New Jersey Garden State Scholars, 184
New Jersey Golf Association Caddie Scholarship, 523
* New Jersey Minority Academic Career Program, 185
New Jersey POW/MIA Program, 183
New Jersey Public Tuition Benefits Program, 185
New Jersey Scholarship Foundation, 283
New Jersey State Policemen's Benevolent Association Scholarship, 719
New Jersey Tuition and Grants, 185
New Jersey Tuition Credit Military and Veterans Affairs, 183
New Jersey Urban Scholars, 185

*Graduate/nondegree study

Program Index

New Mexico Allied Health Student Loan for Service Program, 186
New Mexico Athlete Scholarship, 186
* New Mexico Graduate Scholarship: Minorities/Women, 186
New Mexico Legislative Endowment Program, 186
New Mexico Medical Student Loan, 186
New Mexico Minority and Handicapped Teachers Scholarship: Southeast, 186
* New Mexico Minority Doctoral Assistance Loan for Service, 187
New Mexico Nursing Student Loan for Service, 187
* New Mexico Osteopathic Student Loan for Service, 187
New Mexico Scholars Program, 187
New Mexico Student Choice Program, 187
New Mexico Student Incentive Grant, 188
New Mexico Three Percent Scholarship, 188
New Mexico Vietnam Veteran's Scholarship, 188
New Mexico Work Study Program, 188
* New Play Commissions in Jewish Theater, 486
New Republic Internship Program, 523
New Stage Theatre Internship, 524
New United Motor Manufacturing Scholarship Program, 720
New York Life Foundation Health Professions Scholarship, 372
New York State Aid for Part-Time Study Program, 189
New York State Bar Association Summer Public Relations Internship, 524
New York State Child of Correction Officer Award, 189
New York State Child of Veteran Award, 189
New York State Education Opportunity Program, 190
New York State Higher Education Opportunity Program, 190
New York State Memorial Scholarship for Families of Deceased Police/Firefighters, 190
New York State Native American Student Aid Program, 191
New York State Primary Care Service, 189
New York State Readers Aid Program, 188
New York State Regents Award for Children of Correction Officers, 190

* New York State Regents Health Care Professional Opportunity Scholarship, 190
New York State Robert C. Byrd Honors Scholarship, 190
* New York State Senate Graduate/Post-Graduate Fellows Programs, 191
* New York State Senate/Richard J. Ross Journalism Fellowship, 191
New York State Tuition Assistance Program, 191
New York State Vietnam Veteran Tuition Award/Persian Gulf Veteran Award, 191
New York Times James B. Reston Writing Portfolio Award, 564
New York Times Summer Internship Program for Minorities, 524
* New Zealand: Full Grant (Fulbright), 100
* Newcombe Doctoral Dissertation Fellowship, 617
* Newhouse Graduate Newspaper Fellowship for Minorities, 527
Newspaper Editing Intern Program, 393
* NIAF/FIERI D.C. Matching Scholarship, 498
NIAF/NOIAW Cornaro Scholarship, 498
* Nicaragua: Full Grant (Fulbright), 100
* Niger: Full Grant (Fulbright), 100
* Nigeria: Full Grant (Fulbright), 101
* NIH Postgraduate Research Training Award, 178
NIH Summer Internship Program, 178
NIH Undergraduate Scholarship Program, 178
Nike Scholarship Fund, 721
* NNEMS Graduate Fellowship, 179
NNEMS Undergraduate Fellowship, 179
Non-Commissioned Officers Association Scholarship Fund, 721
Nontraditional Undergraduate Grant, 703
Nor Pac Scholarship Program, 723
NorAm Employees Scholarship Program, 723
Norfolk Chamber Music Festival Summer Fellowship Program, 527
Norfolk Chamber Music Festival Summer Internship Program, 527
Norman Vincent Peale Scholarship Program, 687
* North American Bluebird Society General Research Grant, 528
North American Indian Scholarship, 437
* North Carolina Board of Governors Dental Scholarship, 234
* North Carolina Board of Governors Medical Scholarship, 234

North Carolina Botanical Garden Internship Program, 192
* North Carolina Community Arts Administrative Internship, 192
North Carolina Community College Scholarship, 192
North Carolina Community Colleges Masonry Contractors Scholarship, 192
North Carolina Community Colleges Petroleum Marketers Association Scholarship, 193
North Carolina Community Colleges Southern Bell Telephone/Telegraph Scholarship, 193
North Carolina Community Colleges Sprint College Transfer Scholarship, 193
North Carolina Community Colleges Sprint Scholarship, 529
North Carolina Community Colleges Wachovia Technical Scholarship, 193
North Carolina Contractual Scholarship Fund, 194
North Carolina Legislative Tuition Grant, 194
North Carolina Nurse Education Scholarship Loan, 195
North Carolina Nurse Scholars Program, 195
North Carolina Prospective Teacher Scholarship Loan, 193
North Carolina Robert C. Byrd Honors Scholarship, 193
North Carolina Scholarships for Children of War Veterans, 194
North Carolina Student Incentive Grant, 65
North Carolina Student Loans for Health/Science/Mathematics, 195
North Carolina Teacher Assistant Scholarship Loan, 194
North Carolina Vocational Rehabilitation Award, 194
North Central Regional Scholarship, 498
North Central Regional Scholarship, 499
North Dakota Indian Scholarship Program, 196
North Dakota Scholars Program, 196
North Dakota State Grant, 196
North East Roofing Contractors Association Scholarship, 716
Northeastern Loggers' Association Scholarship Contest, 723
Northern Airborne Technical Scholarship, 255
Northern California/Epping Travel Agents Scholarship, 346
Northern Cheyenne Higher Education Program, 196

788

*Graduate/nondegree study

Program Index

Northwest Journalists of Color Scholarship Program, 530
*Northwest Osteopathic Medical Scholarship, 530
*Northwest Osteopathic Medical Student Loan, 530
Northwest Pharmacists Pre-Pharmacy Scholarship, 530
Northwestern Mutual Life Scholars Program, 724
*Norway: Full Grant (Fulbright), 101
Norwest Scholarship Program, 724
*Novartis Fellowship of the Immune Deficiency Foundation, 531
NROTC Express Scholarship, 231
NTDRA Scholarship, 709
*Nuclear Medicine Pilot Research Grant, 396
Nuclear Medicine Student Fellowship Award, 396
Nuclear Operations Division Scholarship, 324
Nuclear Training Educational Assistance Program, 473
*Numismatic Graduate Fellowship, 327
*Numismatic Graduate Seminar, 327
*Nurses Clinical Training Fellowship, 327
*Nurses Health Policy Research Institute Fellowship, 327
*Nurses Research Training Fellowship, 328
*Nurses Substance Abuse Fellowship, 328
O.H. Ammann Research Fellowship in Structural Engineering, 340
Oak Ridge Institute for Science and Education Energy Research Undergraduate Laboratory Fellowship, 198
*Oak Ridge Institute for Science and Education Fossil Energy Postgraduate Research, 198
*Oak Ridge Institute for Science and Education Fusion Energy Postdoctoral Research, 198
Oak Ridge Institute for Science and Education Historically Black Building Technology Summer Research Participation, 199
Oak Ridge Institute for Science and Education Historically Black Colleges Nuclear Energy Training Program, 199
Oak Ridge Institute for Science and Education Historically Black Nuclear Energy Training Program, 199
*Oak Ridge Institute for Science and Education Magnetic Fusion Energy Technology Fellowship, 199
*Oak Ridge Institute for Science and Education Magnetic Fusion Science Fellowship, 199
*Oak Ridge Institute for Science and Education National Library of Medicine Associate Fellowship, 200
Oak Ridge Institute for Science and Education National Oceanic and Atmospheric Administration Student Program, 200
*Oak Ridge Institute for Science and Education Nuclear Engineering Health Physics Fellowship, 200
*Oak Ridge Institute for Science and Education Oak Ridge National Laboratory Postdoctoral Research, 200
Oak Ridge Institute for Science and Education Office of Biological and Environmental Research Historically Black Colleges and Universities Student Research Participation, 201
Oak Ridge Institute for Science and Education Office of Civilian Radioactive Waste Management Historically Black Colleges and Universities Undergraduate Scholarship Program, 201
Oak Ridge Institute for Science and Education Office of Fossil Energy Historically Black Colleges and Universities Student Research Participation, 201
Oak Ridge Institute for Science and Education Office of Nuclear Energy Undergraduate Scholarship, 201
*Oak Ridge Institute for Science and Education Postgraduate Environmental Management Participation at the U.S. Army Environmental Center, 202
*Oak Ridge Institute for Science and Education Postgraduate Internship at the Office of Ground Water and Drinking Water, 202
*Oak Ridge Institute for Science and Education Postgraduate Internship at the U.S. Army Center for Health Promotion and Preventive Medicine, 202
*Oak Ridge Institute for Science and Education Postgraduate Research at the Agency for Toxic Substances and Disease Registry, 202
*Oak Ridge Institute for Science and Education Postgraduate Research at the Center for Biologics Evaluation and Research, 202
*Oak Ridge Institute for Science and Education Postgraduate Research at the Center for Devices and Radiological Health, 203
*Oak Ridge Institute for Science and Education Postgraduate Research at the Center for Drug Evaluation and Research, 203
*Oak Ridge Institute for Science and Education Postgraduate Research at the Centers for Disease Control and Prevention, 203
Oak Ridge Institute for Science and Education Postgraduate Research at the Department of Veterans Affairs, Birmingham Education Center, 203
*Oak Ridge Institute for Science and Education Postgraduate Research at the National Center for Toxicological Research, 204
*Oak Ridge Institute for Science and Education Postgraduate Research at the National Exposure Research Laboratory, 204
*Oak Ridge Institute for Science and Education Postgraduate Research at the National Risk Management Research Laboratory, 204
*Oak Ridge Institute for Science and Education Postgraduate Research at the Oak Ridge National Laboratory, 204
*Oak Ridge Institute for Science and Education Postgraduate Research at the Savanah River Site, 204
*Oak Ridge Institute for Science and Education Postgraduate Research at the St. Louis District, U.S. Army Corps of Engineers, 205
*Oak Ridge Institute for Science and Education Postgraduate Research at the U.S. Army Aviation and Troop Command, 205
*Oak Ridge Institute for Science and Education Postgraduate Research at the U.S. Army Construction Engineering Research Laboratory, 205
*Oak Ridge Institute for Science and Education Postgraduate Research at the U.S. Army Depot, Anniston, 205
*Oak Ridge Institute for Science and Education Postgraduate Research at the U.S. Army Directorate of Environment-Fort McClellan, 205
*Oak Ridge Institute for Science and Education Postgraduate Research at the U.S. Army Edgewood Research, 206
*Oak Ridge Institute for Science and Education Postgraduate Research at the U.S. Army Environmental Policy Institute, 206
*Oak Ridge Institute for Science and Education Postgraduate Research at the U.S. Army Garrison, Aberdeen, 206
*Oak Ridge Institute for Science and Education Postgraduate Research at the U.S. Army Medical Research Institute of Chemical Defense, 206

*Graduate/nondegree study

Program Index

*Oak Ridge Institute for Science and Education Postgraduate Research at the U.S. Army National Guard Bureau, 207
*Oak Ridge Institute for Science and Education Postgraduate Research at the U.S. Navy Commander Fleet, Okinawa, 207
Oak Ridge Institute for Science and Education Professional Internship Program at Federal Energy Technology Centers, 532
Oak Ridge Institute for Science and Education Professional Internship Program at the Oak Ridge National Laboratory, 207
Oak Ridge Institute for Science and Education Professional Internship Program at the Savannah River Site, 207
Oak Ridge Institute For Science and Education Student Environmental Management Participation for the U.S. Army Environmental Center, 208
Oak Ridge Institute for Science and Education Student Internship at the U.S. Army Center for Health Promotion and Preventive Medicine, 208
Oak Ridge Institute for Science and Education Student Research at the Agency for Toxic Substances and Disease Registry, 208
Oak Ridge Institute for Science and Education Student Research at the U.S. Army Aviation and Troop Command, 208
Oak Ridge Institute for Science and Education Student Research at the U.S. Army Environmental Policy Institute, 209
Oak Ridge Institute for Science and Education Student Research at the U.S. Army Garrison, Directorate of Safety, Health and the Environment, 209
Oak Ridge Institute for Science and Education Student Research Participation at the Centers for Disease Control and Prevention, 209
Oak Ridge Institute for Science and Education Student Research Participation at the National Center for Toxicological Research, 209
Oak Ridge Institute for Science and Education Student Research Participation at the U.S. Army Aviation and Troop Command, 210
Oak Ridge Institute for Science and Education Student Research Participation at the U.S. Army Edgewood Research, Development and Engineering Center, 210

Oak Ridge Institute for Science and Education Student Research Participation at the U.S. Army Environmental Policy Institute, 210
Oak Ridge Institute for Science and Education Technology Internship Program at the Oak Ridge National Laboratory, 210
Oak Ridge Institute for Science and Education U.S. Department of Energy/NAACP, 210
Oak Ridge Institute for Science and Education U.S. Geological Survey Earth Sciences Internship, 211
Oak Ridge Institute for Science and Education U.S. Nuclear Regulatory Commission Historically Black Colleges and Universities Student Research Participation, 211
Oak Ridge Institute for Science and Education University Coal Research Internship, 211
Oak Tree Packaging Corporation Scholarship Program, 724
Octel Communications Internship, 532
*Office of Naval Research - Postdoctoral Fellowship, 338
Ohio Academic Scholarship, 212
Ohio Instructional Grant, 212
Ohio National Guard Tuition Grant, 532
Ohio Newspapers Minority Scholarship, 533
Ohio Nurse Education Assistance Loan Program, 212
Ohio Safety Officers College Memorial Fund, 212
Ohio Student Choice Grant, 212
Ohio War Orphans Scholarship, 212
Oklahoma Academic Scholars Program, 213
*Oklahoma Chiropractic Education Assistance, 213
Oklahoma Engineering Foundation Scholarship, 533
Oklahoma Future Teachers Scholarship, 213
*Oklahoma Minority Doctoral Study Grant, 214
*Oklahoma Minority Professional Study Grant, 214
Oklahoma Tuition Aid Grant, 214
Oldfield National Security Reporter Fellowship, 557
Olive Lynn Salembier Scholarship, 584
*Olivia James Traveling Fellowship, 352
Olympic Steel Inc. Scholarship Program, 725
*Oman: Full Grant (Fulbright), 101
OMNE/Nursing Leaders of Maine Undergraduate Scholarship, 456

Oncology Nursing Bachelor's Scholarship, 533
*Oncology Nursing Doctoral Scholarship, 534
*Oncology Nursing Master's Scholarship, 534
*Oncology Nursing Post-Master's Nurse Practitioner Certificate, 534
*Oncology Nursing Research Grant, 534
*Oral and Maxillofacial Surgery Research Endowment Program, 725
Oral-B Laboratories Dental Hygiene Scholarship, 250
*Orchid Research Grant, 328
Oregon Alpha Delta Kappa/Harriet Simmons Scholarship, 538
Oregon Broadcast Journalism Scholarship, 538
Oregon Collectors Association Bob Hasson Memorial Scholarship, 538
Oregon Department of Transportation Glenn Jackson Scholarship, 725
Oregon Disabled Peace Officer Grant Program, 214
Oregon Metro Federal Credit Union Scholarship, 725
Oregon Metro Federal Credit Union Scholarship, 725
Oregon Occupational Safety and Health Division Workers Memorial Scholarship, 539
Oregon Private 150 Scholarship, 539
Oregon Robert C. Byrd Honors Scholarship, 214
Oregon State Need Grant, 215
Oregon State Occupational Safety Scholarship, 539
Oregon State Scholarship Commission/AFL-CIO Scholarship, 539
Oregon State Scholarship Commission/Ben Selling Scholarship, 539
Oregon State Scholarship Commission/Bertha P. Singer Scholarship, 540
Oregon State Scholarship Commission/Clyde C. Crosby/ Joseph M. Edgar Memorial Scholarship, 540
Oregon State Scholarship Commission/Compute Stores Northwest Scholarship, 540
Oregon State Scholarship Commission/Friends of Oregon Students Scholarship, 540
Oregon State Scholarship Commission/Glenn Jackson Scholarship, 540
Oregon State Scholarship Commission/Howard Vollum American Indian Scholarship, 540

*Graduate/nondegree study

*Oregon State Scholarship Commission/Jean Risley Scholarship, 541
Oregon State Scholarship Commission/Oregon Building Industry Association Scholarship, 541
Oregon State Scholarship Commission/Oregon Dungeness Crab Commission, 726
Oregon State Scholarship Commission/Oregon National Guard Tuition Assistance, 541
Oregon State Scholarship Commission/Oregon State Personnel Managers Association, 541
Oregon State Scholarship Commission/Oregon Trucking Association, 541
Oregon State Scholarship Commission/Pendleton Postal Workers Scholarship, 542
Oregon State Scholarship Commission/Peter Connacher Memorial Scholarship, 542
Oregon State Scholarship Commission/Professional Land Surveyors of Oregon Scholarship, 542
Oregon State Scholarship Commission/Richard F. Brentano Memorial Scholarship, 542
Oregon State Scholarship Commission/Teamsters Council #37 Federal Credit Union Scholarship, 542
Oregon State Scholarship Commission/Teamsters Local 305 Scholarship, 542
Oregon State Scholarship Commission/Troutman's Emporium Scholarship, 543
Oregon Vietnam Era Veterans' Children Scholarship, 543
Osage Tribal Education Scholarship, 543
*Osborne Scholarship, 531
Oscar Stempler Scholarship, 753
OSI Group Scholarship Program, 726
*Osteopathic Foundation Student Loan Program, 329
*Otologic Research Grant, 391
Otter Tail Power Company Scholarship, 726
Pacific Enterprises Scholarship Program, 726
Pacific Mutual Life Scholarship Program for Children of Employees, 726
Pacific Printing and Imaging Scholarship, 544
*Pakistan Studies Fellowship, 284
*Pakistan: Full Grant (Fulbright), 101

Palmer J. Hermundslie Memorial Scholarship Program, 708
*Panama: Full Grant (Fulbright), 101
Paragano Scholarship, 499
*Paraguay: Full Grant (Fulbright), 102
*Parenteral Research Grant, 544
Paris Fracasso Production Floriculture Scholarship, 366
Part-Time Student Instructional Grant Program, 212
Partners in Publishing Sons and Daughters Scholarship Program, 700
Past Grand Presidents' Award, 675
Pathfinder Scholarship, 715
Pathways Scholarship, 709
Patrick Murphy Internship, 516
*Paul A. Greebler Scholarship, 324
Paul A. Stewart Award, 614
Paul and Blanche Wulfsberg Scholarship, 255
Paul and Helen L. Grauer Scholarship, 332
Paul Cole Scholarship, 397
Paul Douglas Teacher Scholarship, 230
Paul Forester, Jr., Scholarship, 734
Paul M. Cook Scholarship Fund, 731
*Paul Mellon Fellowship, 488
Pavarotti Scholarship, 499
Payless Cashways Scholarship Program, 727
Pearl I. Young Scholarship, 165
*Peat Marwick Doctoral Scholarship Program, 448
Pebble Beach Scholarship Program for Employees' Children, 727
*Pediatric AIDS Foundation Research Grants, 545
Pediatric AIDS Foundation Student Intern Award, 545
*Pediatric Nurses and Practitioners McNeil Scholarship, 478
Peggy Guggenheim Internship, 588
Pellegrini Scholarship, 596
Pennsylvania Grant Program, 215
*Pennsylvania Internship, 469
Pennsylvania Robert C. Byrd Honors Scholarship, 215
Pennsylvania Work-Study Program, 215
Pennzoil Scholars Program, 727
Pentagon Federal Credit Union Grant, 721
Pentair Scholarship Fund, 727
Pepper Employees' Children Scholarship Fund, 697
Performing Arts Showcase 1999, 685
*Periodontology Student Loan, 258
Perkin-Elmer Scholarship Program, 727
Personal Best Scholarship, 570
Personnel Magazines Now Workforce Magazine Internship, 545
*Peru: Full Grant (Fulbright), 102

Pete Marick Scholarship Award, 685
Peter A. McKernan Scholarship, 546
Peter Kaufman Memorial Scholarship, 412
Peter Marinoff Memorial Scholarship, 667
*Peter Sammartino Scholarship, 499
*Petroleum Geologists Grant-in-Aid, 263
*Pfizer Internships, 546
PGA Minority Internship Program, 546
PGH Foundation Scholarship, 424
*Phi Delta Kappa Graduate Fellowship, 727
*Phi Kappa Phi Graduate Fellowship, 690
*Phi Lambda Signa First Year Graduate Scholarship, 625
Phi Sigma Iota Award, 548
PHICO Insurance Scholarship for Children of Employees, 728
Philadelphia Drug Exchange Scholarship Program, 728
*Philippines: Full Grant (Fulbright), 102
Philips Electronics Scholarship, 728
Phillips Academy Summer Teaching Assistant Internship Program., 548
Phillips Petroleum Dependent Scholarship Program, 728
*Physical Science Graduate Fellowship: Minorities and Women, 510
Physician's Assistants Scholarship, 626
*Physician's Research Development Grant, 317
Physics Students Leadership Scholarship, 744
Piancone Family Agriculture Scholarship, 500
*Piano Teachers Scholarship, 268
Pickett and Hatcher Educational Loan, 548
*Pilot Training Scholarship, 255
*Pine Tree State 4-H Club Foundation Scholarship, 728
Pioneers of Flight Scholarship Program, 474
Pioneers Scholarship, 702
Pittsburgh Local Section of the James R. Vogt Scholarship, 325
Plane and Pilot Magazine/Garmin Scholarship, 255
Plant Propagation Internship, 469
Plant Protection Internship, 470
Plasma Physics National Undergraduate Fellowship Program, 216
Playhouse on the Square Internship, 549
Playtex Scholarship, 729

*Graduate/nondegree study

Program Index

Plumbing, Heating, Cooling Contractors Education Foundation Scholarship, 478
*Polaire Weissman Fund Fellowship, 464
*Poland: Government Grant (Fulbright), 102
Polaris Industries Inc. Scholarship Program, 729
Police and Fire Fighters' Association Scholarship, 729
Police/Firefighters' Survivors Educational Assistance, 54
Polish Culture Scholarship, 285
Pollard Travel Agents Scholarship, 346
Polsky-Fixtures Furniture Award, 342
*Polsky-Fixtures Furniture Prize, 343
Polyfibron Technologies Scholarship Program, 729
Population Institute Internship, 550
Porter McDonnell Memorial Scholarship, 269
Portugal: Full Grant (Fulbright), 103
Portuguese Continental Union Scholarship, 729
*Postdoctoral Cancer Research Fellowship, 376
*Postdoctoral Fellowship in Emerging Infectious Diseases, 598
Postdoctoral Fellowship in Nosocomial Infection Research and Training, 486
*Postdoctoral Fellowship: Eurasia, 574
*Postdoctoral Fellowship: Middle East, 574
*Postdoctoral Microbiology Research Program, 339
*Postdoctoral Sexuality Research Fellowship Program, 574
Power Division Scholarship, 325
*Practitioner Research Communication and Mentoring Grant, 591
Practitioners Publishing Company Dependents Scholarship, 730
Praxair International Scholarship, 350
*Pre-Dissertation Fellowship for Research in Europe, 384
Precision Castparts Scholarship, 730
*Predissertation Fellowship: Bangladesh, 574
*Predissertation Fellowship: Near-Middle East, 574
*Predissertation Fellowship: South Asia, 575
*Predoctoral Clearinghouse Application Fee Waiver, 382
*Predoctoral Fellowship in Pharmaceutics, 547
Presbyterian Appalachian Scholarship, 550
*Presbyterian Fund for Graduate Education, 550

*Presbyterian Grant Program for Medical Studies, 550
Presbyterian Native American Education Grant, 551
*Presbyterian Native American Seminary Scholarship, 551
*Presbyterian Racial/Ethnic Leadership Supplemental Grant, 551
Presbyterian Service Loan for Undergraduates, 551
Presbyterian Student Opportunity Scholarship, 551
*Presbyterian Theological Continuing Education Loan, 552
*Presbyterian Theological Loan, 552
Presbyterian Undergraduate and Graduate Loan, 552
*President Francesco Cossiga Fellowship, 526
*Presidential Management Program, 228
Presidential Memorial Scholarship, 557
Princess Cruises and Tours Travel Agents Scholarship, 346
Princess Grace Award, 552
Priscilla R. Morton Scholarship, 604
Pro Deo/Pro Patria Scholarship, 700
Pro-Found Software Internship, 553
Procter and Gamble Scholarship, 730
Procter-Channin Scholarship, 618
Professional Engineers of North Carolina Engineering Scholarship Program, 553
Programs in Poland for American Citizens/ Year Abroad, 448
Project Excellence Scholarship, 553
*ProManagement Scholarship, 512
Promus Hotel Corporation Scholarship Program, 731
Prudential Foundation Scholarship, 731
Prudential Spirit of Community Award, 479
PSI Scholarship Program, 730
*Psychology Research Training Minority Fellowship, 59
Public Accountants Scholarship, 514
Public Policy Internship Program, 460
Public Relations Internship, 459
Public Service Company of Colorado Scholarship, 731
Public Service Scholarship, 554
*Puerto Rican Legal Defense & Educ. Fund-Father Joseph P. Fitzpatrick Scholarship, 554
Puerto Rico Robert C. Byrd Honors Scholarship, 216
*Purchasing Management Doctoral Grant, 479
*Qatar: Full Grant (Fulbright), 103
Quadion Foundation Scholarship, 731
Quality Assurance Division Junior/ Senior Scholarship, 433

Quarter Horse Youth Scholarship, 650
Quill Scholarship Program, 731
R.C. Easley National Scholarship, 474
R.J. Johnson Memorial Scholarship, 740
R.L. Gillette Scholarship, 274
R.M. Lawrence Education Recognition Award, 334
R.V. Gadabout Gaddis Charitable Fund, 455
Rabbi Feinberg Scholarship, 500
*Rabbi Frederic A. Doppelt Memorial Fellowship in American Jewish Studies, 286
*Rabbi Levi A. Olan Memorial Fellowship in American Jewish Studies, 286
*Rabbi Marc H. Tannenbaum Foundation Fellowships, 286
*Radcliffe Research Support Program Award, 427
*Radio-Television News Capitol Hill News Internship, 557
Rain Bird Company Scholarship, 450
*Raissa Tselentis J. S. Bach Scholarship, 268
*Ralph Lombardi Memorial Scholarship, 500
*Ralph W. Ellison Prize, 507
Randolph L. Marten Scholarship Program, 706
Random House Internship, 558
*Rapoport Fellowships in American Jewish Studies, 286
Ray Hackney Scholarship, 672
*Ray Kageler Scholarship, 543
Raychem Internship, 558
Raymond DiSalvo Scholarship, 325
Raymond E. Page Scholarship, 451
Raytheon Scholars Program, 732
Recine Scholarship, 500
Red Kap Scholarship, 662
Red River Valley Fighter Pilots Scholarship Program, 559
*Reforma Scholarship Program, 559
*Regents Graduate/Professional Fellowship, 213
Regions Right Way Scholarship, 733
Regis-St. Elizabeth Scholarship, 742
ReliaStar Financial Corporation Scholarship Program, 733
*Renew America Internship, 559
*Rennie Taylor/Alton Blakeslee Fellowship, 385
*Research and Travel Grants, 449
*Research Center in Egypt Fellowship, 59
Research Experiences for Undergraduates, 322
*Research Institute in Turkey Fellowship, 333
*Research Training Fellowships for Medical Students, 430

792   *Graduate/nondegree study

Program Index

Retarded Citizens' Teachers Scholarship, 756
Retired Officers Educational Assistance Program, 734
Retraining Grant, 703
Reuben Trane Scholarship, 337
*Rev. Charles W. Tadlock Scholarship, 604
Reynolds and Reynolds Company Foundation Scholarship, 734
*Rho Chi First-Year Graduate Scholarship Program, 625
Rhode Island Government Intern Program, 216
Rhode Island Higher Education Assistance Authority State Grant, 216
Rhode Island State Government Internship Program, 216
Rhone-Poulenc Rorer Scholarship, 735
Richard C. Honkamp Scholarship Award, 691
Richard E. Merwin Award, 692
Richard F. Walsh/Alfred W. Di Tolla Scholarship, 735
Richard G. Mork Scholarship, 621
Richard H. Suddah Scholarship Foundation, 750
Richard K. Herzer Scholarship for the Study of Entrepreneurial Business, 692
Richard P. Erickson Scholarship Program, 702
Ricoh Scholarship, 735
*Risk Assessment Science and Engineering Fellowships, 261
*Rob and Bessie Welder Wildlife Foundation Scholarship, 560
*Robert A. Dannels Scholarship, 325
*Robert and Clarice Smith Fellowship, 488
Robert B. Brouillette Memorial Tuition Assistance Program, 731
Robert C. Byrd Honors Scholarship, 122
Robert C. Byrd Honors Scholarship, 213
*Robert D. Watkins Minority Graduate Fellowship, 651
Robert F. Corroon Legacy Scholarship, 764
Robert G. Lacey Scholarship, 325
Robert J. Di Pietro Scholarship, 501
*Robert L. Millender Sr. Memorial Fund Fellowship Program, 560
Robert Leventhal Scholars Program, 660
Robert T. Liner Scholarship, 326
Roche Brothers Supermarkets Scholarship, 735
Rocket Program Internship, 147
Rockwell Internship Program, 561
Rocky Mountain Coal Mining Scholarship, 561

Rodale Scholarship Program, 735
Rodolf Steiner Visiting Students Program, 561
Roger Von Amelunxen Scholarship, 736
Roger W. Emmons Memorial Scholarship, 726
Rolfe B. Karlsson Scholarship, 395
*Romania: Government Grant (Fulbright), 103
*Ron Brown Fellowship Program, 438
Ronald and Irene McMinn Scholarship, 475
RONECTCO Supermarkets Scholarship Program, 736
Roofing Industry Scholarship, 717
*Rosann S. Berry Annual Meeting Fellowship, 580
Rosann S. Berry Annual Meeting Fellowship, 580
Rose Basile Green Scholarship, 501
Rosemont Aerospace Scholarship, 736
ROTC Scholarships, 655
ROTC/ Air Force Three-Year Scholarships Types 2 And Targeted, 217
ROTC/Navy Marine Two-Year Scholarship Program, 233
ROTC/Navy Nurse Corps Scholarship Program, 233
ROTC/Navy/Marine Four-Year Scholarship, 233
ROTC/United States Army Four-Year Historically Black College/Univ. Scholarship, 217
*Rotch Traveling Scholarship, 370
Roy Wilkins Scholarship, 711
Royal Neighbors Fraternal Scholarship, 736
Royal Neighbors Non-Traditional Scholarship, 736
Royal Neighbors State Fraternal Scholarship, 737
RTNDF Minority News Management Internship, 558
*Rudolf Nissim Composers Competition, 655
Rudolph Dillman Memorial Scholarship, 274
Rudolph Dillman Memorial Scholarship Based on Need, 274
Rugby Building Products Scholarship Program, 737
*Rural Special Education Scholarship, 271
Russ Casey Scholarship, 458
*Russel C. McCaughan Education Fund Scholarship, 329
Russell Leroy Jones Memorial Scholarship (Colorado Aero Tech), 255
Russell T. Lund Scholarship Program, 704
*Ruth Satter Memorial Award, 360

*Ruth Strang Women's Research Awards, 522
Ruud Lighting Scholarship, 737
Ryan Orfalea Scholarship, 699
*S. Clawson Mills Scholarship, 465
S. Harris Memorial Interior Design Scholarship, 343
S.C. Holman Scholarship, 737
S.E. Binnswanger Memorial Scholarship, 760
S.J. Electro Systems Foundation Scholarship Program, 737
Sachs Scholarship, 562
Safety Engineers Academic Scholarship, 653
Safety-Kleen Corp. Memorial Scholarship Program, 737
Saint David's Society Scholarship, 562
Sales Engineering Scholarship, 679
*Sally Kress Tompkins Fellowship, 580
*Sammy Cahn Award, 356
*Samuel A. Levine Young Clinical Award, 278
Samuel Eliot Morison Essay Contest, 521
*Samuel Fletcher Tapman ASCE Student Chapter/Club Scholarship, 340
*Samuel H. Kreiss/Alisa Mellon Bruce Paired Fellowship, 489
Samuel Lemberg Scholarship Loan, 563
Samuel Robinson Award, 552
San Francisco Chronicle Summer Internship Program, 563
San Francisco Chronicle Two-Year Internship Program, 563
Santavicca Scholarship, 501
Santee Cooper Employees' Children Scholarship, 738
*Sarah Rebecca Reed Scholarship, 367
Sargent and Lundy Centennial Scholarship, 738
SAS Institute Scholar Award Program, 738
*Saudi Arabia: Full Grant (Fulbright), 103
Saul Jakel Memorial Award, 409
Savvy Management Internship, 564
SBC Foundation Program, 738
*Scalia Scholarship, 501
Schlumberger Internship, 564
*Scholar Awards, 545
*Scholar Exchange Program, 438
Scholarship for Children of Members of the Non-Commissioned Officers Association, 722
Scholarship for North Carolina Law Enforcement Dependents, 528
Scholarship for People with Disabilities, 386
Scholarship Fund for Children of Herman Miller Employees, 689

*Graduate/nondegree study

Scholarship Grant for Prospective Educators, 548
Scholarship Grant for Spouses of Members of the Non-Commissioned Officers Association, 722
Scholarship of the Immune Deficiency Foundation, 531
Scholarships at Seattle Central Community College, 174
Scholastic Achievement Award, 732
Scholastic Art Gold Award, 565
Scholastic Art Portfolio Award, 565
Scholastic Photography Portfolio Award, 565
Scholastic Photography Scholarship, 565
Scholastic Writing Gold Award, 565
Scholastic Writing Portfolio Award, 565
Schonstedt Surveying Scholarship, 630
School Division Internship, 429
* School Food Service Foundation Professional Growth Scholarship, 739
Schuyler Meyer Junior Scholarship, 280
Schweitzer-Mauduit Tomorrow's Leaders Scholarship Program, 739
* Science and Technology Fellowship, 264
* Science, Engineering, and Diplomacy Fellowship, 57
Scientific Research Grant-In-Aid, 569
* Scientific Study of Sexuality Student Grant, 579
Scotts Company Scholars Program, 415
Scripps Undergraduate Research Fellowship, 566
Sculpture Society Scholarship, 514
Seabee Memorial Scholarship, 566
Sealed Air Corporation Scholarship, 740
Seaquist Scholarship for Sons and Daughters, 654
* Sears-Roebuck Graduate Business Studies Loan Fund, 372
Seattle Jaycees Scholarship, 566
Second Marine Division Scholarship, 567
Secondary School Principals Leadership Award, 479
Secondary School Principals National Honor Society Scholarship, 713
Secondary School Principals National Honor Society Sylvan Scholars Program, 479
Securities Industry Scholarship, 733
Securities Operations Division Scholarship Program, 740
Sehlmeyer Scholarship, 667
* Selected Professions Fellowship, 265

Selected Reserve Montgomery GI Bill, 228
Senator Barry Goldwater Scholarship, K7UGA, 332
Senator George J. Mitchell Scholarship Fund, 455
Seneca Nation Higher Education Program, 567
* Senegal: Full Grant (Fulbright), 104
* Senior Fellowship Program, 489
Sergio Franchi Music Scholarship/Voice Performance, 502
Sertoma Scholarships for Deaf and Hard of Hearing Students, 567
Service Employees Scholarship, 568
Service Merchandise Scholarship, 568
Seventeen Magazine Journalism Internship, 568
* Sexuality Research Dissertation Fellowship Program, 575
Shannon Scholarship, 600
Sharp Electronics Scholarship, 741
Sherlee Barish Fellowship, 558
Sheryl A. Horak Law Enforcement Explorer Scholarship, 665
Shoprite Scholarship Program, 761
* Short-Term Fellowship in the History of Cartography, 526
* Short-Term Resident Fellowship for Individual Research, 526
* Short-Term Scientific Awards, 545
Shoshone Tribal Scholarship, 569
Sid Richardson Scholarship, 741
SIGECO Scholarship Program, 741
Sigma Alpha Epsilon Resident Educational Advisor, 741
Sigma Alpha Epsilon Scholarship, 742
Sigma Phi Alpha Graduate Scholarship, 250
Sigma Phi Alpha Undergraduate Scholarship, 251
Silicon Graphics Computer Systems Internship Program, 569
Silvio Conte Internship, 502
* Simmons Travel Agents Scholarship, 346
Simpson PSB Scholarship Program, 742
* Singapore: Full Grant (Fulbright), 104
Sister Rose Mary Pint Scholarship Program, 763
Six Meter Club of Chicago Scholarship, 333
Skadden, Arps, Slate, Meagher and Flom Law Internship, 569
SLCU Y.E.S. Scholarship Program, 747
Slope Indicator Company Scholarship Program, 742
* Slovak Republic: Full Grant (Fulbright), 104
Slovene Scholarship, 743
* Slovenia: Full Grant (Fulbright), 104

Slovenian Women's Union Scholarship, 743
* Small Research Grants Program, 591
Smart Corporation Scholarship, 633
Smith Equipment Scholarship Program, 743
Smithsonian Environmental Research Work/Learn Program, 218
* Smithsonian Graduate Student Fellowship, 570
Smithsonian Minority Internship, 570
Smithsonian Native American Internship, 570
* Smithsonian Post-Doctoral Fellowship, 571
* Smithsonian Pre-Doctoral Fellowship, 571
* Smithsonian Senior Fellowship, 571
SOARS - Significant Opportunities in Atmospheric Research and Science, 233
* Social Health Postdoctorate Research Fellowship in Sexually Transmitted Diseases, 338
* Social Issues Dissertation Award, 578
Social Issues Internship Program, 578
* Social Issues Sages Program, 579
* Social Science Fellowship Program, 549
* Social Work Clinical Fellowship, 386
* Social Work Minority Research Fellowship, 386
Society for Human Resource Management Sons and Daughters Scholarship, 744
Society of Auto Engineers Engineering Scholarship, 596
* Society of Automotive Engineers Doctoral Scholars Loan, 580
Society of Exploration Geophysicists Scholarship, 581
* Society of Flavor Chemists Memorial Graduate Fellowship, 433
* Sociological Association Minority Fellowship, 60
* Soil and Water Conservation Research Scholarship, 745
Soil and Water Conservation Student Leader Scholarship, 746
Soil Conservation Scholarship, 746
* Sonja Stefanadis Graduate Student Award, 675
Sons of Italy National Leadership Grant, 589
Sons of Poland Scholarship, 657
Sons of the American Revolution Eagle Scout Scholarship, 718
Sony Corporation of America Internship, 589
SONY Credited Internship, 590
SONY Minority Internship, 590
Sony Music Scholarship Program, 747
* South Africa: Full Grant (Fulbright), 105

Program Index

South Carolina Teacher Loans, 219
South Carolina Tuition Grants, 219
* South Central Modern Language Association Fellowship, 720
South Central Regional Scholarship, 502
South Dakota National Guard Tuition Assistance, 220
South Dakota Robert C. Byrd Honors Scholarship, 220
Southeast Regional Scholarship, 502
Southeastern Claim Executives Association Scholarship, 747
Southern California/Hawaiian Holidays Travel Agents Scholarship, 347
Southern Progress Corporation Summer Internship, 590
Southface Internship, 590
Southwest Regional Scholarship, 502
Southwest Research Institute Dependents Scholarship Program, 747
Space Center Company/McNeely Foundation Scholarship, 747
* Spain: Full Grant (Fulbright), 105
* Spain: Government Grant (Fulbright), 105
* Spain: Professional Grant in Journalism (Fulbright), 105
Spear, Leeds and Kellogg Scholarship Award, 748
* Special Libraries Association Affirmative Action Scholarship, 591
* Special Libraries Institute for Scientific Information Scholarship, 748
* Special Libraries Plenum Scholarship, 748
* Special Libraries Scholarship, 591
* Special Medical Education Loan / Scholarship, 144
Spence Reese Scholarship, 370
* Spencer Dissertation Fellowship Program, 592
* Spencer Foundation Major Research Grants, 592
* Spencer Postdoctoral Fellowship Program, 474
* Spencer Professional Development Research and Documentation Program, 592
* Spencer Support for Scholars at Center for Advanced Study/Behavioral Sciences, 592
Spina Bifida Association of America Scholarship Fund, 593
Spoleto Festival Administrative Internship, 593
Spoleto Festival Apprenticeship Program, 593
Spoleto Festival Production Internship, 593

* Sri Lanka: Full Grant (Fulbright), 106
* SSRC Dissertation Fellowship: Bangladesh, 575
* SSRC Dissertation Fellowship: Eastern Europe, 575
* SSRC Dissertation Fellowship: Eurasia, 576
* SSRC Dissertation Fellowship: Middle East, 576
* SSRC Dissertation Fellowship: Middle East, 576
* SSRC Dissertation Fellowship: South Asia, 576
* SSRC Dissertation Fellowship: Southeast Asia, 576
* St. Anthony Publishing Graduate Award, 633
St. Anthony Publishing Undergraduate Award, 634
St. Patrick Hospital Sons and Daughters Scholarship Program, 748
Stanadyne Automotive Corporation Scholarship Program, 749
Stanhome Scholarship, 749
Stanley E. Jackson Award for Gifted/Talented Minorities with Disabilities, 406
Stanley E. Jackson Scholarship Award for Ethnic Minority Students., 406
Stanley E. Jackson Scholarship Award for Gifted/Talented Students with Disabilities, 406
* Stanley Elmore Fellowship Fund, 435
Stanley Sons and Daughters Scholarship Program, 749
* Starkoff Fellowship in American Jewish Studies, 286
* Starr Asian Painting Conservation Fellowship, 465
* State Farm Companies Doctoral Disseration Award, 594
State Farm Companies Exceptional Student Fellowship, 594
* State Medical Education Board of Georgia Scholarship, 221
State of Idaho Scholarship, 119
State of Iowa Scholarship, 124
State/County/Municipal Employees Family Scholarship, 630
State/County/Municipal Employees Jerry Clark Memorial Scholarship, 631
Stephen H. Gayle Essay Contest, 524
Sto Corporation Scholarship Fund, 749
Stone Foundation Scholarship, 749
Stone Quarry Engineering Scholarship, 515
* Stoody-West Fellowship, 606
Stratus Scholarship Program, 750
Strong Foundation Interest-Free Student Loan, 418
* Student Aid Foundation Graduate Loan, 595

Student Aid Foundation Undergraduate Loan, 595
Student Assistance Award, 222
Student Employment and Educational Program, 427
* Student Loan, 348
* Student Ministry Fund, 437
Student Paper Competition, 400
* Student Research Grant, 528
* Student Research Grant, 317
Student Scholastic Showcase, 685
Students Extra Educational Development Scholarship, 569
Studio Program, 613
* Study in Scandinavia Grant, 351
Supreme Guardian Council, International Order of Job's Daughters Scholarship, 750
Surgical Technologists Scholarship Fund, 361
Sutton Education Scholarship, 711
* Swaziland: Full Grant (Fulbright), 106
* Sweden: Full Grant (Fulbright), 106
* Switzerland: Government Grant (Fulbright), 106
* Switzerland: Seydel Fellowship (Fulbright), 107
Sykes Student Scholarship, 750
* Syria: Government Grant (Fulbright), 107
T.D. Williamson, Jr., Scholarship, 751
T.J. Hale Company Scholarship, 751
* Taiwan: Full Grant (Fulbright), 107
* Taiwan: Teaching Assistantship-Internship (Fulbright), 107
Talbots Scholarship Fund, 751
Tandy Technology Students Award, 596
* Tandy Technology Teachers Award, 596
* Tanzania: Full Grant (Fulbright), 108
Target All Around Scholarship, 596
Target Team Member Scholarship, 751
* Tau Beta Pi Fellowship, 751
Taylor Packing Corporation Scholarship Program, 752
TCF Scholarship Program, 752
TDS Corporate Scholarship Program, 752
Teacher Education Scholarship Program, 173
Teacher Preparation Scholarship, 361
* Teacher Work-Study Grant, 512
Teamsters Scholarship Fund, 694
Techneglas Scholarship Program, 752
Technical Communication Scholarship Program, 577
* Technology Policy Fellowship, 626
Ted Krzynski and Harlan Murray Scholarship Program, 693
Telephone and Data Systems, Inc., 752
Tennant Scholarship, 752

*Graduate/nondegree study

Program Index

Tennessee Minority Teaching Fellows Program, 223
Tennessee Robert C. Byrd Honors Scholarship, 223
Tennessee Teaching Scholarship, 223
Terra-By-Trimble Avionics Collegiate Scholarship, 623
Tescom Scholarship, 752
Tesoro Petroleum Corporation Scholarship Program, 752
Texas Aid to Families with Dependent Children (AFDC) Students Exemption, 224
Texas American Hemisphere Student Scholarship, 224
Texas Children of Disabled Firefighters/Peace Officers Tuition Exemption, 224
Texas College Work-Study Program, 224
Texas Early High School Graduation Scholarship, 224
Texas Fifth-Year Accountancy Scholarship Program, 224
Texas Foster Care Students Exemption, 225
Texas General Scholarship for Nursing Students, 225
Texas Hazlewood Act Tuition Exemption: Dependents, 225
Texas Hazlewood Act Tuition Exemption: Veterans, 225
Texas Highest Ranking High School Graduate Tuition Exemption, 225
Texas Licensed Vocational Nurses Becoming Professional Nurses Scholarship, 225
Texas Outstanding Rural Scholar Program, 223
Texas Public Educational Grant, 225
Texas Robert C. Byrd Honors Scholarship, 226
Texas Rural Bachelors or Graduate Nursing Students Scholarship, 226
Texas Rural Nursing Students Scholarship, 226
Texas Student Incentive Grant, 226
Texas Transportation Scholarship, 599
Texas Tuition Assistance Grant, 226
Texas Tuition Equalization Grant, 226
Texas Tuition Exemption for Blind and Deaf Students, 226
Texas Tuition Exemption for Children of POW/MIAS, 227
*Thailand: Full Grant (Fulbright), 108
*The GEM Consortium/Doctoral Bridge Projects, 597
*The GEM Consortium/M.S. Engineering Fellowship, 597
*The GEM Consortium/Ph.D Science and Engineering Fellowship, 597
The Governor James G. Martin College Scholarship, 195

The Maine State Society of Washington, DC Foundation Inc. Scholarship Program, 597
*The North Carolina Nurse Scholars Program MasterÖs Program, 195
Theodore and Vivian Johnson Scholarship, 753
Theodore C. Sorensen Research Fellowship, 446
Theodore Mazza Scholarship, 602
*Theodore Roosevelt Memorial Grants, 322
*Theodore Rousseau Fellowship, 465
*Theological Continuing Education Grant, 552
Think Automotive Scholarship, 362
Third Marine Division Memorial Scholarship Fund, 753
Thomas Joseph Ambrosole Scholarship, 503
Thomas P. Papandrew Scholarship, 451
Thomas Wood Baldridge Scholarship, 697
Three-Month Gardener Internship, 529
Thurgood Marshall Scholarship Award, 598
Thz Fo Farm Fund, 118
Time Warner Academic Award, 753
Timothy Bigelow Scholarship, 429
TJX Companies Scholarship Program, 753
*Togo: Full Grant (Fulbright), 108
Tom and Judith Comstock Scholarship, 651
Tom Brokaw Scholarship Program, 719
Tom Frost Scholarship Program for Dependents of Frost National Bank, 683
Tomlinson Memorial Scholarship Program, 765
Tony Winger, Jr., Scholarship, 655
Tony's Food Service Scholarship, 739
Top Ten College Women Competition, 413
*Toshiba Exploravision Award, 514
Tourism Foundation Alabama-Birmingham Legacy, 517
Tourism Foundation California Scholarship, 517
Tourism Foundation Cleveland Legacy 1 Scholarship, 517
Tourism Foundation Cleveland Legacy 2 Scholarship, 517
Tourism Foundation Connecticut Scholarship, 517
Tourism Foundation Florida Scholarship, 517
Tourism Foundation Internship, 517
Tourism Foundation Michigan Scholarship, 517
Tourism Foundation Montana Scholarship, 518

Tourism Foundation Nebraska-Lois Johnson Scholarship, 518
Tourism Foundation New Jersey 1 Scholarship, 518
Tourism Foundation New Jersey 2 Scholarship, 518
Tourism Foundation New York Scholarship, 518
Tourism Foundation North Carolina Scholarship, 518
Tourism Foundation Ohio Scholarship, 518
Tourism Foundation Quebec Scholarship, 518
Tourism Foundation Scholarship, 519
Tourism Foundation Tulsa Scholarship, 519
Tourism Foundation Wyoming Scholarship, 519
Tourism Foundation Yellow Ribbon Scholarship, 519
*Transcriptions Limited Graduate Scholarship, 634
Transcriptions Limited Undergraduate Scholarship, 634
*Travel and Tourism Student Research Award, 599
Travel Research Grant, 599
Treacy Company Scholarship, 600
Treadway Inns, Hotels, and Resorts Scholarship, 519
*Trent R. Dames and William W. Moore Fellowship, 651
Tri-Gas Scholarship Program, 754
*Trinidad and Tobago: Full Grant (Fulbright), 108
*Tropical Botany Award, 411
Tropical Garden Summer Internship, 403
Troy Barboza Education Fund, 425
Truckload Carriers Association Scholarship, 600
Truman D. Picard Scholarship, 439
Trustmark Foundation College Scholarship Program, 754
Tultex Foundation Scholarship Program, 754
*Tunisia: Full Grant (Fulbright), 109
*Turkey: Full Grant (Fulbright), 109
*Turkey: Teaching Assistantship (Fulbright), 109
Turkish Language Summer Scholarship, 60
Tuttle-Click Automotive Group Education Assistance Program, 754
Twentieth Century Fox Internship, 600
Twin City Fan & Blower Co. Scholarship Program, 754
Two/Ten International Footwear Foundation Scholarship, 754
Tylenol Scholarship Fund, 461
U. The National College Magazine Scholarship, 601

*Graduate/nondegree study

* U.S. Army Center of Military History Dissertation Fellowship, 227
U.S. Bancorp Educational Awards Program, 755
U.S. Department of Agriculture Summer Intern Program, 228
U.S. Department of Commerce/Ron Brown Fellowship, 244
U.S. Department of Education Robert C. Byrd Honors Scholarship, 230
* U.S. Department of Energy Summer Research Fellowships, 398
U.S. Department of State Foreign Affairs Fellowship, 245
U.S. Department of Vocational Rehabilitation Scholarship, 231
* U.S. English Foundation Award (Fulbright), 109
* U.S. Information Agency Predoctoral/Postdoctoral Fellowship, 336
U.S. National Arboretum Internship, 601
U.S. Navy-Marine Corps Immediate Selection Decision Scholarship, 232
U.S. Steel Scholarship, 759
* Uganda: Full Grant (Fulbright), 110
Ukrainian Fraternal Association Scholarship, 755
Ullico Scholarship, 755
Ultramar Diamond Shamrock Student Educational Loan Program, 755
Uncommon Legacy Foundation Scholarship, 351
Undergraduate Microbiology Research Fellowship, 339
Undergraduate Research Fellowship in Pharmaceutics, 547
Union Pacific Scholarship, 755
Unique Industries Inc. Scholarship Program, 755
Unitarian Universalist Stanfield Art Scholarship, 602
* Unitarian Universalist Stanfield Law Scholarship, 602
Unite National Scholarship, 756
* United Arab Emirates: Full Grant (Fulbright), 110
* United Cerebral Palsy Clinical Fellowship, 603
* United Cerebral Palsy Research Grant, 603
United Food and Commercial Workers Union Scholarship Program, 756
* United Kingdom: British-American Chamber of Commerce Award (Fulbright), 110
* United Kingdom: British-American Tobacco Industries Award (Fulbright), 110
* United Kingdom: Cambridge University Research Scholarship (Fulbright), 111

* United Kingdom: Full Grant (Fulbright), 111
* United Kingdom: Marks and Spencer Award (Fulbright), 111
* United Kingdom: Oxford University Scholarship (Fulbright), 111
* United Kingdom: Sussex University Research Scholarship (Fulbright), 112
* United Kingdom: University College London Scholarship (Fulbright), 112
* United Kingdom: University of East Anglia Research Scholarship (Fulbright), 112
United Methodist Bass Scholarship, 604
United Methodist Church Conference Merit Award, 605
* United Methodist Church Crusade Scholarship, 605
United Methodist Ethnic Scholarship, 605
United Methodist Hana Scholarship, 605
United Methodist Loan Program, 605
United Methodist Publishing House Merit Scholarship, 605
United Methodist Scholarship, 606
* United Methodist Seminary Award, 606
United Negro College Fund Scholarship, 607
United Paperworkers International Union Scholarship, 756
United Piece Dye Works Scholarship Program, 757
United Service Automobile Association Scholarship, 757
United States Army Four-Year Nursing Scholarship, 218
United States Army Four-Year Scholarship, 218
United States Department of State Internships, 232
United States EPA Tribal Lands Environmental Science Scholarship, 58
United States Golf Association Education Assistance Program, 757
United States Holocaust Memorial Museum Internship, 232
United States Information Agency Summer Internship, 232
United Transportation Union Insurance Association Scholarship, 758
University of North Carolina Incentive Scholarship, 234
* University of North Carolina Minority Grant: Doctor/Lawyer/Veterinary Medicine, 234
University of North Carolina Minority Presence Grant: General, 234

University of North Carolina Native American Incentive Graduate Scholarship, 235
University of North Carolina Native American Incentive Merit Scholarship, 235
University of North Carolina Native American Incentive Undergraduate Scholarship, 235
Univest Corporation Scholarship Program, 758
* Univision-Mexican American Legal Defense Fund Scholarship, 466
Unocal Foundation Scholarship, 758
Unum Foundation Scholarship, 758
Upjohn Company Internship, 608
Upper Mid-Atlantic Regional Scholarship, 503
Upsilon Pi Epsilon Scholarships, 692
Urban and Community Forestry Internship, 470
* Urologic Disease Ph.D. Research Scholarship, 276
* Uruguay: Full Grant (Fulbright), 112
US Department of State Internships, 235
USA Milan Getting Scholarship, 743
USCC Scholarship Program, 757
USF&G Foundation Scholarship, 758
USOC Student Intern Program, 607
UST Sons and Daughters Scholarship, 759
Utah Career Teaching Scholarship/T.H. Bell Teaching Incentive Loan, 236
Utah Robert C. Byrd Honors Scholarship, 236
Utah State Student Incentive Grant, 236
Valderrama Award, 415
* Van Schaik Dressage Scholarship, 320
* Venezuela: Full Grant (Fulbright), 113
Vennera Noto Scholarship, 503
Venture Clubs of America Student Aid Award, 608
Vermont Extra Loan (Supplemental), 236
Vermont Golf Association Scholarship, 608
Vermont Incentive Grant, 236
* Vermont Non-Degree Program, 236
Vermont Part-Time Grant, 237
Vermont Robert C. Byrd Honors Scholarship, 237
* Verne R. Dapp Scholarship, 326
Vernon Heath Scholarship Program, 736
Vertical Flight Foundation Scholarship, 279
Vesuvius Americas Scholarship Fund, 759
* Veterinary Medicine Minority Loan / Scholarship, 144
* Veterinary Student Scholarship, 348

*Graduate/nondegree study

Program Index

VF Corporation Scholarship for Children of Employees, 759
Vice Admiral E.P. Travers Loan, 521
Vice Admiral E.P. Travers Scholarship, 521
*Vietnam: Full Grant (Fulbright), 113
Viets Premedical/Medical Student Fellowship, 472
Vikki Carr Scholarship, 609
*Vincent and Anna Visceglia Fellowship, 503
Vincente Minelli Scholarship, 504
Virgin Islands Music Scholarship, 237
Virgin Islands Student Incentive Grant, 237
Virgin Islands Territorial Grants Scholarship, 237
Virgin Islands Territorial Loan Scholarship, 238
Virginia Academic Common Market Program, 238
Virginia Assistance for the Visually Handicapped, 238
Virginia College Scholarship Assistance, 238
Virginia Eastern Shore Tuition Assistance, 238
Virginia Graduate and Undergraduate Assistance, 238
Virginia Lee-Jackson Scholarship, 609
*Virginia Medical Scholarship Program, 222
Virginia Museum of Fine Arts Fellowship, 609
Virginia Nursing Scholarship Program, 222
Virginia Regional Contract Program, 238
Virginia Rehabilitative Services College Scholarship, 239
*Virginia Rural Dental Scholarship Program, 222
Virginia Student Financial Assistance Program, 239
Virginia Transfer Grant, 239
Virginia Tuition Assistance Grant, 239
Virginia Undergraduate Student Financial Aid, 239
*Vision Awareness Educational Grant, 276
*Vivien Thomas Award, 635
*Vocal Competition for North American Operatic Artists, 363
Vocational Horticulture Scholarship, 366
Voice of Democracy Scholarship, 608
Voith Companies Scholarship, 759
Voith Sulzer Scholarship, 760
Vollrath Company Scholarship Program, 760
Volvo Scholars Program, 760
VPI Foundation Scholarship for Sons and Daughters, 760

W. Van Alan Clark Jr./Burgess Dempster Memorial Scholarship, 742
W.E. Weisel Scholarship, 582
*W.F. Miller Postgraduate Education Recognition Award, 334
W.H. McClennan Scholarship, 694
W.J. and M.E. Adams, Jr., Mechanical Engineering Scholarship, 653
*W.K. Kellog Community Medicine Training, 508
W.M. Burgin, Jr., Scholarship, 334
W.R. Grace Foundation Scholarship, 686
Wal-Mart Competitive Edge Scholarship, 609
Walker Forge Scholarship Program, 761
Wall Street Journal Internship, 610
Walt Disney Recruiting Program, 610
Walt Disney World Horticulture Summer Internship, 610
Walter and Marie Schmidt Scholarship, 543
*Walter Meyer Scholarship, 326
Walter O. Wells Foundation Scholarship Program, 761
Walter Wiest Scholarship Program, 750
Walton Foundation Scholarship, 761
Warwick, Baker and Fiore Internship Program, 610
Washington Crossing Foundation Scholarship, 611
Washington Gas Scholarship, 611
Washington Internships for Student of Engineering, 611
*Washington Osteopathic Loan, 761
Washington State American Indian Endowed Scholarship, 239
Washington State Educational Opportunity Grant, 240
Washington State Health Professions Loan/Scholarship, 240
Washington State Need Grant, 240
Washington State PTA Financial Grant, 611
Washington State Scholars Program, 240
*Washington State Work-Study Program, 240
Water Companies (NJ Chapter) Scholarship, 479
*Water Works Fellowship, 348
Waters Scholarship Program, 761
Watlow Employee Children Scholarship Fund, 762
*Watson Fellowships, 415
*Wayne Kay Graduate Fellowship, 582
Wayne Kay Undergraduate Scholarship, 582
Weather Channel Meteorology Internship, 612
Weeta F. Colebank Scholarship, 519

*Weinberg Fellowship for Independent Scholars, 527
*Weiss Brown Publication Subvention Award, 527
Wells Fargo Employees' Dependent Children Scholarship, 762
West Group Scholarship Program, 762
West Virginia Higher Education Grant, 241
West Virginia Italian Heritage Festival Scholarship, 504
*West Virginia Medical Student Loan Program, 241
West Virginia Robert C. Byrd Honors Scholarship, 241
West Virginia Underwood-Smith Teacher Scholarship, 241
West Virginia War Orphans Educational Assistance, 241
Western Beef Scholarship Program, 763
Westinghouse Bertha Lamme Scholarship, 584
Westlake Scholarship, 612
WestPlains Energy Scholarship, 763
Weyerhaeuser Community Education Scholarship Program, 763
*Whitney Postdoctoral Research Fellowship, 426
Wilbur C. Stauble Trust Scholarship, 759
Wilhelmina Models Summer Internship, 613
Willems Scholarship, 711
*William and Charlotte Cadbury Award, 508
William and Dorothy Lanquist Foundation, 425
*William B. Keeling Dissertation Award, 599
William Beaumont Hospital Scholarship Program, 763
William C. Davini Scholarship, 602
William C. Doherty Scholarship, 712
*William C. Stokoe Scholarship, 477
William E. Lahr Scholarship Program, 760
William H. Bywater Scholarship, 696
William J. Locklin Scholarship, 451
William S. Davila Scholarship, 763
William T. Green Grant, 722
*William T. Piper Award, 282
Williams Steel and Hardware Scholarship, 763
*Willis H. Carrier Graduate Fellowship, 341
Winegard Company Scholarship, 764
*Winterthur Fellowship, 417
Wisconsin Academic Excellence Scholarship, 243
Wisconsin Central Ltd. & Algoma Central Railway Scholarship, 764
Wisconsin Dental Association Scholarship, 615

*Graduate/nondegree study

Wisconsin Energy Corporation Daughters & Sons Scholarship, 764
Wisconsin Higher Education Grant, 243
Wisconsin Minority Retention Grant, 243
Wisconsin Minority Teacher Loan Program, 243
Wisconsin Native American Student Grant, 244
Wisconsin Power and Light Scholarship, 764
Wisconsin Talent Incentive Program, 244
Wisconsin Tuition Grant, 244
Wisconsin Veterans Affairs Economic Assistance Loan, 242
Wisconsin Veterans Affairs Part-Time Study Grant, 242
Wisconsin Veterans Affairs Retraining Grant, 242
Wisconsin Veterans Affairs Tuition and Fee Reimbursement Grant, 242
Wisconsin Visual and Hearing Impaired Program, 244
Witco Corporation Scholarship Program, 764
Wolf Trap Performing Arts Internship, 615
Women Engineers Chevron Scholarship, 585
Women Engineers Chrysler Corporation Re-entry Scholarship, 585
Women Engineers Chrysler Corporation Scholarship, 585
Women Engineers Chrysler Corporation Scholarship (Minorities), 585
Women Engineers General Electric Foundation Scholarship, 586
*Women Engineers General Motors Foundation Graduate Scholarship, 586
Women Engineers General Motors Foundation Undergraduate Scholarship, 586
Women Engineers GTE Foundation Scholarship, 586
Women Engineers Men's Auxiliary Memorial Scholarship, 587
Women Engineers Microsoft Corporation Scholarship, 587
*Women Engineers Microsoft Corporation Scholarship (Graduate), 587
Women Engineers Northrop Corporation Founders Scholarship, 745
Women Engineers Rockwell International Corporation Scholarships, 587
Women Engineers Stone and Webster Scholarship, 588

Women Engineers Texaco Scholarship, 745
Women Engineers TRW Scholarship, 588
Women in Architecture Scholarship, 359
Women in Business Scholarship, 372
Women in Construction: Founders' Scholarship, 480
Women in Engineering Studies Loan Fund, 372
*Women in Science Education Research Grant, 360
Women of the Evangelical Lutheran Church in America Scholarship, 616
*Women Pilots Airline Scholarship, 438
*Women Pilots Financial Scholarship, 439
Women's Education Fund, 442
*Women's Research and Education Congressional Fellowship, 616
Women's Western Golf Foundation Scholarship, 617
*Woodrow Wilson Dissertation Grant in Women's Studies, 618
Woodrow Wilson Program in Public Policy and International Affairs, 618
*Woodruff Dissertation Research Fellowship, 352
Wrangler Scholarship, 662
*Wyeth Fellowship, 489
*Wyeth-Ayerst Laboratories Prize, 508
*Wyeth-Ayerst Laboratories Scholarship, 373
Wyoming State Student Incentive Grant, 245
Yakama Indian Nation Scholarship, 619
Yale R. Burge Interior Design Competition, 343
Yankee Gas Scholarship Program, 765
Yanmar Scholarship, 580
*Yemen: Full Grant (Fulbright), 113
YKK Dependent Children Scholarship Program, 765
Yosemite National Park Internships, 245
You've Got a Friend in Pennsylvania Scholarship, 651
Young Composers Award, 490
Young Feminist Scholarship Program, 593
Young Investigator Matching Grants, 486
*Young Investigator Prize in Thrombosis, 278
Young Writers Contest, 417
Youth Entertainment Summer, 618
Youth Scholarship, 321
*Zambia: Full Grant (Fulbright), 113
*Zecchino Postgraduate Orthopaedic Fellowship, 504

*Zeneca Pharmacy Underserved Healthcare Grant, 329
*Zimbabwe: Full Grant (Fulbright), 114

*Graduate/nondegree study

Sponsor Index

1199 National Benefit Fund, 621
1st Infantry Division Foundation, 247
25th Infantry Division Association, 621
3M, 247
A.M. Castle and Company, 621
Abbie Sargent Memorial Scholarship Fund, 247
Academy of Television Arts and Sciences, 247
Acrometal Management Corporation, 622
ADA Endowment and Assistance Fund, Inc., 248
Adaptec, 622
Addison Wesley Longman, 622
ADHA Institute for Oral Health, 249
Aeromet, Inc., 251
AFOSR/Air Force Office of Scientific Research, 53
AGL Resources Service Company, 622
Air Force Aid Society, 251
Air Force Sergeants Association, 622
Air Liquide America Foundation, Inc., 623
Air Traffic Control Association, Inc., 251, 623
Aircraft Electronics Association Educational Foundation, 252, 623
Aircraft Owners and Pilots Association Air Safety Foundation, 256
Airgas, Inc., 624
Airmen Memorial Foundation, 256
Alabama Commission on Higher Education, 53
Alabama Department of Education, 54
Alabama Department of Postsecondary Education, 54
Alabama Department of Veterans Affairs, 55
Alabama Legislature, 55
Alabama State Chiropractic Association, 256
Alaska Commission on Postsecondary Education, 55, 257
Alaska Division of Veterans Affairs, 56
Alco Gravure Education Fund, Inc., 624
Alcoa Foundation, 624
Alexander Graham Bell Association for the Deaf, 257
Alexander Von Humboldt Foundation, 56, 257
Alfa Laval Inc., 624

Allied Group Insurance, 624
Allstate Foundation, 624
Alpha Beta Gamma International, Inc., 625
Alpha Mu Gamma National, 625
Ambucs Living Endowment Fund, Inc., 257
America's Junior Miss Pageant, Inc., 258
American Foundation for Pharmaceutical Education, 258, 625
American Academy in Rome, 57
American Academy of Periodontology, 258
American Academy of Physician's Assistants, 626
American Alpine Club, 259
American Antiquarian Society, 259
American Association for Cancer Research, Inc., 259
American Association for Dental Research, 260
American Association for Health Education, 260
American Association for the Advancement of Science, 57, 260, 626
American Association of Advertising Agencies, 261
American Association of Airport Executives, 261
American Association of Critical Care Nurses, 262, 627
American Association of Japanese University Women, 262
American Association of Medical Assistants Endowment, 262
American Association of Medical Assistants' Endowment, 263
American Association of Petroleum Geologists Foundation, 263
American Association of School Administrators/ Discover Card, inc., 263
American Association of Teachers of Spanish and Portuguese/ Sociedad Honoraria Hispanica, 627
American Association of University Women, 263
American Association of University Women Educational Foundation, 264
American Bar Foundation, 265
American Brain Tumor Association, 265
American Cancer Society, 266

American Cancer Society Extramural Grants, 266
American Center of Oriental Research, 267
American Chemical Society, 267
American Classical League, 627
American College of Chiropractic Orthopedists, 267
American College of Legal Medicine, 268
American College of Musicians/ National Guild of Piano Teachers, 268
American Congress on Surveying and Mapping, 268, 628
American Conservatory Theater, 269
American Consulting Engineers Council, 270
American Council of Learned Societies, 270
American Council of the Blind, 271
American Council on Rural Special Education, 271
American Dental Assistants Association/ Oral B Laboratories, 271
American Dental Association Endowment and Assistance Fund, Inc.., 271
American Dryer Corporation, 630
American Electroplaters and Surface Finishers Society Scholarship Committee, 272
American Express Foundation, 630
American Federation of State, County and Municipal Employees, 630
American Foundation for Aging Research, 272
American Foundation for Pharmaceutical Education, 272, 631
American Foundation for the Blind, 273
American Foundation for Urologic Disease, 274
American Foundation for Vision Awareness, 276
American Geological Institute, 276
American Geophysical Union, 276
American Ground Water Trust, 277
American Health Information Management Association, 631
American Heart Association, 277, 634
American Heart Association Western States Affiliate, 278
American Helicopter Society, Inc., 279
American Historical Association, 635

Sponsor Index

American Holistic Nurses' Association, 636
American Hotel Foundation, 280
American Indian Graduate Center, 58, 280
American Indian Science and Engineering Society, 58, 280, 636
American Institute for Foreign Study, 281
American Institute of Aeronautics and Astronautics, 281
American Institute of Architects, 282
American Institute of Certified Public Accountants, 284
American Institute of Pakistan Studies, 284
American Institute of Polish Culture, 285
American Institute of the History of Pharmacy, 285
American Isuzu Motors, Inc., 637
American Jewish Archives, 285
American Legion Alabama, 287
American Legion Alabama Auxiliary, 287
American Legion Alaska, 287
American Legion Alaska Auxiliary, 287
American Legion Arizona Auxiliary, 288
American Legion Arkansas, 288, 637
American Legion Arkansas Auxiliary, 288
American Legion California, 289
American Legion California Auxiliary, 289, 637
American Legion Colorado Auxiliary, 290, 638
American Legion Connecticut Auxiliary, 638
American Legion Delaware Auxiliary, 290
American Legion District of Columbia, 290
American Legion Florida, 290
American Legion Florida Auxiliary, 291, 639
American Legion Georgia Auxiliary, 291
American Legion Idaho Auxiliary, 291
American Legion Illinois, 292, 639
American Legion Illinois Auxiliary, 292
American Legion Indiana, 293, 639
American Legion Indiana Auxiliary, 293, 640
American Legion Iowa, 293, 640
American Legion Iowa Auxiliary, 293, 640
American Legion Kansas, 294, 640
American Legion Kansas Auxiliary, 294

American Legion Kentucky Auxiliary, 295
American Legion Maine, 295, 641
American Legion Maine Auxiliary, 296
American Legion Maryland, 296, 641
American Legion Maryland Auxiliary, 297
American Legion Massachusetts, 297, 641
American Legion Massachusetts Auxiliary, 298
American Legion Michigan, 298
American Legion Michigan Auxiliary, 299
American Legion Minnesota, 299, 642
American Legion Minnesota Auxiliary, 300, 642
American Legion Mississippi Auxiliary, 300
American Legion Missouri, 300, 642
American Legion Missouri Auxiliary, 301
American Legion National Headquarters, 301, 643
American Legion Nebraska, 301
American Legion Nebraska Auxiliary, 302, 643
American Legion New Hampshire, 302, 644
American Legion New Hampshire Auxiliary, 303, 644
American Legion New Jersey, 303, 644
American Legion New Jersey Auxiliary, 304
American Legion New Mexico Auxiliary, 305
American Legion New York, 305, 645
American Legion New York Auxiliary, 305
American Legion North Carolina Auxiliary, 306
American Legion North Dakota, 306
American Legion North Dakota Auxiliary, 306, 646
American Legion Ohio, 646
American Legion Ohio Auxiliary, 306
American Legion Oklahoma Auxiliary, 307
American Legion Oregon, 307
American Legion Oregon Auxiliary, 307
American Legion Pennsylvania, 646
American Legion Pennsylvania Auxiliary, 308
American Legion Puerto Rico Auxiliary, 308
American Legion Sough Dakota Auxiliary, 647
American Legion South Carolina, 308
American Legion South Carolina Auxiliary, 309, 647

American Legion South Dakota, 309, 647
American Legion Tennessee, 309, 648
American Legion Tennessee Auxiliary, 310
American Legion Texas, 310
American Legion Texas Auxiliary, 310
American Legion Utah Auxiliary, 311
American Legion Vermont, 311
American Legion Virginia, 311
American Legion Virginia Auxiliary, 648
American Legion Washington, 648
American Legion Washington Auxiliary, 311
American Legion West Virginia, 312
American Legion West Virginia Auxiliary, 312
American Legion Wisconsin, 312, 648
American Legion Wisconsin Auxiliary, 313, 649
American Legion Wyoming, 314, 649
American Legion Wyoming Auxiliary, 314
American Library Association, 315
American Liver Foundation, 317
American Lung Association, 317
American Medical Technologists, 319
American Medical Women's Association, 319, 649
American Meteorological Society, 319
American Morgan Horse Institute, 320
American Museum of Natural History, 321
American National Can Company, 650
American Nuclear Society, 322
American Numismatic Society, 326
American Nurses Association, 327
American Optometric Foundation, 328
American Orchid Society, 328
American Osteopathic Foundation, 329
American Physical Society, 329
American Political Science Association, 330
American Psychological Association, 58
American Psychological Association/MFP, 59
American Quarter Horse Youth Association, 650
American Radio Relay League Foundation, Inc., 330, 650
American Research Center in Egypt, 59
American Research Institute in Turkey, 60, 333
American Respiratory Care Foundation, 333
American Schools of Oriental Research, 334

Sponsor Index

American Soc. Heating/Refrigeration/Air-Conditioning Engineers, Inc., 337
American Social Health Association, 338
American Society for Engineering Education, 338
American Society for Enology and Viticulture, 339
American Society for Microbiology, 339, 651
American Society of Civil Engineers, 340, 651
American Society of Clinical Pathologists, 341
American Society of Heating/Refrigeration/Air-Conditioning Engineers, Inc., 341
American Society of Highway Engineers, 342
American Society of Interior Designers Educational Foundation, 342
American Society of Magazine Editors, 343
American Society of Mechanical Engineers, 652
American Society of Naval Engineers, 343
American Society of Safety Engineers, 653
American Society of Travel Agents Foundation, 344, 654
American Society of Travel Agents Scholarship Foundation, 345
American Sociological Association, 60
American Speech-Language-Hearing Foundation, 347
American Symphony Orchestra League, 348
American Veterinary Medical Foundation, 348
American Water Works Association, 348
American Welding Society Foundation, Inc., 349
American-Scandinavian Foundation, 351
Amerisure Companies, 654
AMP Incorporated, 654
An Uncommon Legacy Foundation, Inc., 351
Aopa Air Safety Foundation, 351
Appaloosa Youth Foundation, 654
Aptar Group Charitable Foundation, 654
Arby Construction, 655
Archaeological Institute of America, 351
Arena Stage, 353
Arizona Board of Regents, 60
Arizona Commission for Postsecondary Education, 61

Arkansas Department of Higher Education, 61
Armed Forces Communications and Electronics Association, 353, 655
Armenian General Benevolent Union, 354
Armenian Relief Society of North America, Inc., 354
Army Emergency Relief, 355
Arrow Electronics, Inc.., 655
Arthur and Doreen Parrett Scholarship Trust Fund, 355
ASCAP Foundation, 355, 655
Ashland, Inc., 655
Asian Cultural Council, 356
ASM Foundation for Education and Research, 357
ASQ EED, 357
Associated Constructors of Maine, Inc. Educational Foundation, 357
Associated General Contractors Education and Research Foundation, 357
Associated Press, 358
Association for Library and Information Science Foundation, 359, 656
Association for Women in Architecture, 359
Association for Women in Communications, 359
Association for Women in Science Educational Foundation, 360
Association of American Geographers, 656
Association of Black Nursing Faculty, 360
Association of Chartered Accountants in the United States, 657
Association of Drilled Shaft Contractors, 361
Association of Energy Service Companies, 657
Association of Former Agents of the U.S. Secret Service, 657
Association of State Dam Safety Officials, 361
Association of Surgical Technologists, 361
Association of the Sons of Poland, 657
Association of Washington School Principals/PEMCO Financial Center, 361
Astra Merck, 658
Atlas Pacific Engineering Company, 658
Austrian Cultural Institute, 362
Automotive Hall of Fame, 362
Avery Dennison, 658
Aviation Distributors and Manufacturers Association, 362
Avnet, Inc., 658

B.F. Goodrich Collegiate Inventors Program, 363
Baker Manufacturing Company, 658
Baltimore Opera Company, 363
Bandag, Incorporated, 658
Bank One, Houston, 658
BankAmerica Foundation and Bank of America-Giannini Foundation, 659
Banta Corporation Foundation, Inc., 659
Bardes Fund, 659
Barnes Group Foundation, Inc., 659
Barnett Banks, Inc., 659
Barry M. Goldwater /Excellence In Education Foundation, 62
Bartley Corporation, 659
Bashinsky Foundation, Inc., 659
Bassett-Walker, Inc., 660
Battle Mountain Gold Company, 660
Baxter, Inc. Foundation, 660
Bay State Gas Company, 660
Beacon Companies, 660
Bechtel Corporation, 363
Bedding Plants Foundation, Inc., 363
Bemis Company Foundation, 660
Benchmark Corporation, 661
Bernstein-Rein, 366
Beta Phi Mu, 367, 661
Bethesda Lutheran Homes and Services, 367
Bethesda Lutheran Homes and Services, inc., 368
Bethlehem Steel Foundation, 661
BetzDearborn Foundation, 661
Billy Barty Foundation, 368
Bioproducts, Inc., 661
Black & Veatch, 368
Blakemore Foundation, 369
Blinded Veteran's Association, 369
Blue Bell Foundation, 662
Blue Circle America Inc., 662
Blue Shield of California Education and Research Foundation, 662
BNI Coal, Ltd., 662
Board of Governors of the Federal Reserve System, 62
Boart Longyear Inc. - Canada, 662
Bobst Group, Inc., 662
Boddie-Noell Enterprises, Inc., 662
Boehringer Ingelheim Corporation, 663
Bok Tower Gardens, 369
Boston Globe, 369
Boston Society of Architects, 370
Boy Scouts of America, 663
Boys and Girls Clubs of San Diego, 370
BP America, 665
Brake Parts Inc., 665
Bremer Financial Corporation, 665
Bristol-Myers Squibb Company Foundation, Inc., 665
British Government, 370
Broadcast Education Association, 371

Sponsor Index

Brooklyn Hospital Center Employees' Activities Committee, 665
BT Office Products International, Inc., 666
Bucks County Courier Times, 371
Bureau of Alcohol, Tobacco, and Firearms, 666
Bureau of Indian Affairs-Oklahoma Area Education Office, 63, 371
Business and Professional Women's Foundation, 372
Business Men's Assurance Company of America, 666
Butler Manufacturing Company Foundation, 666
C.G. Fuller Foundation, 373
California Adolescent Nutrition and Fitness (CANFIT) Program, 373
California Association of Realtors Scholarship Foundation, 374
California Chicano News Media Association, 374
California Farm Bureau, 374
California Grange Foundation, 666
California Junior Miss Program, 375
California Library Association, 375
California Masonic Foundation, 375
California Student Aid Commission, 63
California Teachers Association, 375, 667
California/Hawaii Elks Major Project, Inc., 376
Callaway Golf Company Foundation, 668
Camargo Foundation, 376
Cambrex Corporation, 668
Cancer Research Fund, 376
Canned Foods, Inc., 668
Capital Group Companies, Inc., 668
Caremark Therapeutic Services, 377
Carolina Power & Light Company, 668
Case Western Reserve University, 377
Cashiers' Association of Wall Street, 668
Castrol North America, 669
Catholic Aid Association, 669
Catholic Workman Fraternal Life Association, 669
CBS, Inc., 669
Center for Defense Information, 377
Central Intelligence Agency, 64
Ceramic Manufacturers Association, 377
Ceridian Corporation, 669
Chairscholars Foundation, Inc., 378
Champion International Corporation, 670
Charles A. and Anne Morrow Lindbergh Foundation, 378
Charles Babbage Institute, 378
Charter Fund, 378
Chas. Levy Company, 670

Chesapeake Corporation Foundation, 670
Chesterfield Film Company, 379
Cheyenne-Arapaho Tribe, 379
Chicago Association of Spring Manufacturers, 670
Children's Literature Association, 670
Chinese American Medical Society, 379
Choate Rosemary Hall, 380
Choctaw Nation of Oklahoma, 65
Christian Record Services, 380
Chronicle of the Horse, 380
Chrysler Corporation, 671
Citizens State Bank of Roseau, 671
Citizens Utilities Company, 671
Clara Abbott Foundation, 671
Clark Refining and Marketing, Inc., 671
Clarke and Company, 380
Clorox Company Foundation, 672
Clyde Russell Scholarship Fund, 380
CNF Transportation Inc., 672
Coca-Cola Scholars Foundation, 381
College Foundation, Inc., 65
Colorado Commission on Higher Education, 65
Colorado Masons Benevolent Fund Association, 381
Colorado Society of CPAs Educational Foundation, 381
Comer Foundation, 672
Committee on Institutional Cooperation, 382
Communications Workers of America, 672
Compass Foundation, 673
Computing Research Association, 383
ConAgra Foundation, Inc., 673
Concerned Educators Against Forced Unionism, 383
Cone Mills Corporation, 673
Congressional Black Caucus Foundation, Inc., 383
Congressional Hispanic Caucus Institute, 383
Connecticut Building Congress Scholarship Fund, 384
Connecticut Department of Higher Education, 66
Connecticut Higher Education Supplemental Loan Authority, 384
Connecticut League for Nursing, 384
Consolidated Freightways Corporation, 673
Council for European Studies, 384
Council for the Advancement of Science Writing, Inc., 385
Council of Energy Resource Tribes, 385
Council of Jewish Federations, 385
Council on International Educational Exchange, 68

Council on Social Work Education, 386
Courage Center Vocational Services-United Way Organization, 386
Creede Repertory Theatre, 386
Cushion Cut, Inc., 673
Cushman School, 387
CXY Energy, Inc., 673
Cymdeithas Gymreig/Philadelphia, 387
Cystic Fibrosis Foundation, 387
Dairy Management, Inc., 390
Daniel E. O'Sullivan Memorial Scholarship Foundation, 674
Data Management Division of Wall Street, 674
Datatel Scholars Foundation, 390
Daughters of Penelope, 390, 674
Daughters of Union Veterans of the Civil War 1861-1865, Inc., 390
David and Dovetta Wilson Scholarship Fund, 391
Davis Hays and Company, 391
Davis-Roberts Scholarship Fund, 676
Deafness Research Foundation, 391
Dean Foods, 676
Delaware Engineering Society (DES), 392
Delaware Higher Education Commission, 68
Dell Computer, 392
Deloitte and Touche, 392
Deloitte and Touche Foundation, 392
Delta Delta Delta Foundation, 676
Delta Gamma Foundation, 676
Department of Defense, 70
Descendents of the Signers of the Declaration of Independence, Inc., 677
DeZurik, 677
Diemakers, Inc., 677
Dirksen Congressional Center, 392
District of Columbia Office of Postsecondary Education, 70
Dog Writers Educational Trust, 393
Dolphin Scholarship Foundation, 393, 678
Don Cassidy, Sr., Scholarship Fund, 678
Donaldson Foundation, 678
Dorr-Oliver Inc., 678
Dow Jones Newspaper Fund, 393
Dunkin' Donuts Charitable Trust, 678
Duracell, 393
Dynatech Corporation, 679
E. Stewart Mitchell, Inc., 679
E.C. Styberg Engineering Company, Inc., 679
EAA Aviation Foundation, 394
Early American Industries Association, 394
Easter Seal Society of Iowa, Inc., 394
Eastman Kodak Company, 395
ECM Publishers, Inc., 679

Edison International, 679
Edmund F. Maxwell Foundation, 396
Education and Research Foundation, Society of Nuclear Medicine, 396
Educational Communications Scholarship Foundation, 397
Elden and Helen Jones, 679
Electrical Equipment Representatives Association, 679
Electrochemical Society, Inc., 397
Eli Lilly & Company, 398
Elie Wiesel Foundation for Humanity, 398
Elizabeth Dow Ltd., 398
Elizabeth Greenshields Foundation, 399
Elks National Foundation, 399
Embassy of France, Office of Science and Technology, 399
EMI Music Foundation Inc., 680
Empire Blue Cross and Blue Shield, 680
Engineers Foundation of Ohio, 399
Engineers Society of Western Pennsylvania, 400
Engineers' Society of Western Pennsylvania, 400
English-Speaking Union, 400
Entertainment Weekly, 401
Entomological Society of America, 401
Environmental Protection Agency, 71
Epilepsy Foundation of America, 401
Ernst and Young, 402
ESPN Inc., 402
Essence Magazine, 402
Executive Women International, 403
Explorers Club, 403
F & D Company of Maryland, 680
Fairchild Tropical Garden, 403
Fannie and John Hertz Foundation, 404
Fannie Mae Foundation, 680
Federal Employee Education Assistance Fund, 680
Federal Reserve Bank of New York, 71
Federal Signal Corporation, 680
Fight-For-Sight, 404
Filoli Center, 404
Financial Management Division of SIA, 681
Financial Markets Center, 405
First Data Corporation, 681
First Marine Division Association, Inc., 681
Fisher Broadcasting Inc., 405
Fiskars, Inc., 681
Florida Department of Education, 71
Florida Department of Health Professional Recruitment, 76
Florida Division of Blind Services, 76
Florida Education Fund, 76, 405
Florida Rock Industries, Inc., 681

Flowers Industries, Inc., 681
Fluor Daniel GTI, 682
Fluor Foundation, 682
Food and Drug Law Institute, 405
Forbes Magazine, 406
Foremost Farms USA Employees, 682
Foss Maritime Company, 682
Foundation for Exceptional Children, 406
Foundation for Science and Disability, 407
Foundation of the National Student Nurses Association, Inc., 407
Francis Ouimet Scholarship Fund, 407
Frank D. Visceglia Memorial Scholarship Program, 682
Franklin and Eleanor Roosevelt Institute, 408
Franklin D. Roosevelt Library, 408
Franklin Lindsay Student Aid Fund, 408
Fred G. Zahn Foundation, 408
Freedom from Religion Foundation, 409
Freightliner Corporation, 682
Friedrich Ebert Foundation, 409
Friends of the National Zoo, 410
Frontier Insurance Group, Inc., 683
Frost National Bank, 683
FRP Properties, Inc., 683
Fulbright Program/USIA - U.S. Student Program, 410
Fulbright Program/USIA-U.S. Student Programs, 77
Fund for Gay and Lesbian Scholarships Whitman-Brooks Scholarship Fund, 410
Garden Club of America, 410
Gay & Lesbian Education Commission, 412
GEICO Corporation, 683
Gem Consortium, 412
General Mills, 412, 683
General Motors Corporation, 114
General Signal Electrical Group, 683
General Signal Scholarship, 683
Gensler and Associates/Architects, 412
Geoffrey Foundation, 412
Geological Society of America, 413
Georgia Student Finance Commission, 114
Gerber Foundation, 684
Gerber Scientific, Inc., 684
Getty Grant Program, 413
Girls Incorporated, 684
Gladys Krieble Delmas Foundation, 413
Glamour Magazine, 413
Glaxo Wellcome Inc., 684
Golden Key National Honor Society, 414, 685
Golden State Minority Foundation, 414

Golf Course Superintendents Association of America, 414, 685
Gore Family Memorial Foundation, 415
Governor's Commission on People with Disabilities, 415
Grace Foundation, Inc., 686
Graco Foundation, 686
Grand Encampment of Knights Templar of the USA, 416
Grand Union Company, 686
Grange Insurance Association, 686
Granite State Management and Resources, 416
Greater Kanawha Valley Foundation, 416
GreenPoint Financial, 686
Gregory Poole Equipment Company, 687
GTE, 416
Guideposts, 417, 687
Gulf States Paper Corporation, 687
H&R Block Foundation, 687
H.B. Fuller Company and its International Locations, 687
Hagley Museum and Library, 417
Hallmark Cards, 417
Hannaford Charitable Foundation, 687
Harness Horse Youth Foundation, 418
Harness Tracks of America, 687
Harry Frank Guggenheim Foundation, 418
Harry Truman Scholarship Foundation, 117
Hasbro, Inc., 688
Hatfield, Inc., 688
Hattie M. Strong Foundation, 418
Havana National Bank, 419
Hawaii Community Foundation, 117, 419, 688
Hawaii Electric Industries Charitable Foundation, 689
Hawaii Postsecondary Education Commission, 118
Hawk Mountain Sanctuary, 425
Heed Ophthalmic Foundation, 425
Helen Hay Whitney Foundation, 426
Helicopter Association International, 426
Helzberg Diamonds, 689
Henkel Corporation, 689
Henry A. Murray Research Center, 426
Herbert Hoover Presidential Library Association, Inc., 427
Herman Miller Inc., 689
Herschel C. Price Educational Foundation, 427
Hershey Foods Corporation, 689
Hewlett-Packard, 427
Hewlettt-Packard Company, 689
Hexcel Corporation, 689
Hickory Tech Corporation Foundation, 690

Sponsor Index

Highway AG Services, 690
Hilgenfeld Foundation for Mortuary Education, 428
Hitachi America, Ltd., 690
Hitachi Semiconductor (America) Inc., 690
Hoffman-La Roche, 428
Holiday Hospitality, Corporation, 690
Honor Society of Phi Kappa Phi, 690
Hopi Tribe Grants and Scholarship Program, 428
Horace Mann Companies, 691
Horizons Foundation, 429
Horticulture Research Institute, 429
Host Marriott-San Francisco International Airport, 691
Houghton Mifflin Company, 429
Howard Hughes Medical Institute, 430
Hubbard Farms, Inc., 691
Hugo Neu Corporation, 691
Hungtington's Disease Society of America, 430
Huntington, 430
Hydrite Chemical Co., 691
IBM, 431
Ida C. Koran Trust Fund, 691
Idaho State Board of Education, 118
Ideal Electric Company, 692
IEEE Computer Society, 692
IHOP Corp., 692
Illinois Student Assistance Commission, 119
Illinois Tool Works, 692
Independence Mining Co. Inc. (IMC), 693
Indiana Student Assistance Commission, 122
Indianapolis Newspapers, Inc., 431
Industrial Electric Wire and Cable Inc., 693
Inland Steel-Ryerson Foundation, 693
Innovex, Inc., 693
Inroads, Inc., 432
Institut Francais de Washington, 432
Institute for Humane Studies, 432
Institute of Food Technologists, 432, 693
Institute of International Education, 434
Institute of Mining and Metallurgy, 435
Institute of Real Estate Management Foundation, 435
Institution of Mining and Metallurgy, 435
Intel Corporation, 436
INTELSAT, 436
International Association of Bridge, Structural, Ornamental, and Reinforcing Iron Workers, 694
International Association of Fire Fighters, 694
International Brotherhood of Teamsters, 694

International Buckskin Horse Association, Inc., 694
International Executive Housekeepers Association, 695
International Food Service Editorial Council (IFEC), 436
International Furnishings and Design Association Educational Foundation, 695
International Management Group, 436
International Multifoods Corporation, 695
International Order of the King's Daughters and Sons, 437
International Research and Exchanges Board, 437
International Society of Women Airline Pilots, 438
International Union of Electronic, Electrical, Salaried, Machine, and Furniture Workers Department of Social Action, 695
International Union of Electronic, Electrical, Salaried, Machine, and Furniture Workers Dept. of Social Action, 696
Interns For Peace, 439
Interstate Brands Corporation, 696
Intertribal Timber Council, 439
Intuit Scholarship Foundation, 696
Iowa College Student Aid Commission, 123
Italian Catholic Federation, 439
J. Baker, Inc., 696
J. Paul Getty Trust, 440
J.B. Cornelius Foundation, Inc., 440
J.C. Penney Company, Inc., 697
J.W. Pepper & Son, Inc., 697
J.W. Saxe Memorial Fund, 440
Jackie Robinson Foundation, 440
James F. Byrnes Foundation, 441
James Madison Memorial Fellowship Foundation, 124
James S. Kemper Foundation, 441
Jane Coffin Childs Memorial Fund for Medical Research, 441
Japan Foundation, 441
Japanese American Association of New York, 442
Jaycee War Memorial Fund, 442, 697
Jeannette Rankin Foundation, 442
Jeppesen Dataplan, 442
Jerold B. Katz Foundation, 697
Jewish Braille Institute of America, 443
Jimmy Treybig Scholarship Fund Endowment, 697
John F. Kennedy Center for Performing Arts, 443
John F. Kennedy Center for the Performing Arts, 443
John F. Kennedy Library Foundation, 445
Johnson International, Inc., 697

Johnson Worldwide Associates, Inc., 698
Johnson's Wax Fund, Inc., 698
Juilliard School, 446
Junior Achievement of Maine, 447
Juvenile Products Manufacturers Association, 698
JVS Community Scholarship Fund, 447
Kansas Board of Regents, 125
Kappa Omicrom Nu Honor Society, 698
Karla Scherer Foundation, 447
Keane, Inc., 699
Kentucky Higher Education Assistance Authority, 126
KIMT, 447
Kinko's, 699
Knights of Columbus, 699
Knights of Pythias, Grand Lodge of Maine, 448
Kohler Co., 700
Komag, 700
Kosciuszko Foundation, 448
KPMG Peat Marwick Foundation, 448
Krause Publications, Inc., 700
Kurt Weill Foundation for Music, Inc, 449
Laidlaw, Inc., 700
Lalor Foundation, 449
Lambda Alpha, 700
Landscape Architecture Foundation, 449
Lang Family Foundation, Inc., 701
Latin American Educational Foundation, 701
Leggett & Platt Scholarship Foundation, 701
Lemmermann Foundation, 451
Leo Baeck Institute, 451
Leopold Schepp Foundation, 452
Leroy C. Dettman Foundation, Inc., 701
LeRoy T. Carlson Pioneers Education Foundation, 702
Levi Strauss Foundation, 702
Lew Wasserman Scholarship Foundation-MCA/Universal, 702
Library of Congress, 127, 452
LifeScan, 702
Lifetouch, 702
Lighthouse, Inc., 452
Lincoln Center for the Performing Arts, Inc., 454
Link-Belt Construction Equipment Company, 703
Lisle Fellowship, Inc., 454
Loctite Corporation, 703
Logan Airport Association, Inc., 703
Los Angeles Actuarial Club, 454
Los Angeles Times, 454
Louisiana Department of Education, 128

Sponsor Index

Louisiana Department of Social Services, 128
Louisiana Department of Veterans Affairs, 128
Louisiana Office of Student Financial Assistance, 129
Loyal Christian Benefit Association, 703
Lucent Technologies Business Communications Systems, 704
Lucent Technologies-BCS, 704
Luck Stone Corporation, 704
Lund Food Holdings, Inc., 704
Lyden Memorial Scholarship Fund, 704
MagneTek, Inc., 704
Maine Community Foundation, 454
Maine Council of Nurse Managers, 456
Maine Division of Veterans Services, 129
Maine Education Services, 456
Maine Finance Authority, 130
Maine Innkeepers Association, 705
Maine Lesbian/Gay Political Alliance, 456
Maine Metal Products Association, 456
Maine Osteopathic Association, 457
Maine Recreation and Parks, 457
Maine Restaurant Association, 458
Maine Society of Professional Engineers, 458
Maine State APWU, 705
Maine State APWU-Portland Local #458, 705
Maine State Society Foundation, 458
Maine Technical College System, 458
Makovsky & Company Inc., 459
Manhattan Theatre Club, 459
Manomet Center for Conservation Sciences, 459
Mapco Coal Inc. and Affiliates, 706
MAPCO Inc., 706
March of Dimes Birth Defects Foundation, 459
Maria Mitchell Observatory, 460
Marine Corps Scholarship Foundation, 460
Marion Merrell Dow, Inc., 706
Marten Transport, Ltd., 706
Marvin Lumber and Cedar Company, 706
Maryland Higher Education Commission/State Scholarship Administration, 130
Mashantucket Pequot Tribal Nation, 460
Massachusetts Biotechnology Council, Inc., 460
Massachusetts Board of Higher Education, 135
Massachusetts Department of Education, 136

Massachusetts Glass Dealers Association, 706
Material Sciences Corporation, 707
Materials Research Corporation, 707
Mattel Inc., 707
MBK Real Estate Ltd., 707
McDonald's, 461
McDonnell Douglas Aerospace, 461
MCI Cutting Edge Scholars, 461
McKesson Foundation, Inc., 707
McNeil Consumer Products, 461
MDU Resources Foundation, 708
Medical Arts Press, Inc., 708
Medical Library Association, 461
Medtronic, Inc., 708
Menominee Indian Tribe of Wisconsin, 136, 462
Merrill Corporation, 708
Metal-Matic, Inc., 708
Metro Electrical Training Trust, 708
Metropolitan Life Foundation, 709
Metropolitan Museum of Art, 462
Mexican American Grocers Association Foundation, 465
Mexican American Legal Defense and Educational Fund, 465
Michelin Tire Corporation, 709
Michigan Educational Opportunity Fund, Inc., 137, 466
Michigan Higher Education Assistance Authority, 137
Michigan Higher Education Student Loan Authority, 466
Michigan Petroleum Assoc./Michigan Assoc. of Convenience Stores, 709
Michigan Society of Professional Engineers, 466
Microfibres, Inc., 709
Microscopy Society of America, 467
Midrex Direct Reduction Corporation, 709
Midwest Express Airlines, 709
Midwestern Higher Education Commission, 138
Miller Brewing Company, 467
Millipore Corporation, 709
Minnesota Department of Veteran's Affairs, 138
Minnesota GLBT Educational Fund, 467
Minnesota Higher Education Services Office, 139
Minnesota Mutual, 710
Minolta Corporation, 710
Miss America Organization, 468
Mississippi Office of State Student Financial Aid, 140
Missouri Coordinating Board for Higher Education, 144
Missouri Department of Elementary and Secondary Education, 145
Missouri League for Nursing, 468
Mitsui USA Foundation, 710
Mobile Gas Service Corporation, 710

Mobility International USA, 468
Moen Incorporated, 710
Mongolia Society, Inc., 468
Montana Board of Regents of Higher Education, 146
Mooney Aircraft Pilot Association Safety Foundation, Inc., 469
Morris Arboretum of the University of Pennsylvania, 469
Mother Jones, 470
Moyer Packing Company, 710
Muscular Dystrophy Association, 471
Museum of Modern Art, 471
Music in the Mountains, 471
Myasthenia Gravis Foundation, 471
NAACP Legal Defense and Education Fund, Inc., 472
NAACP Special Contribution Fund, 710
NASA Space Grant Alabama Space Grant Consortium, 146
NASA Space Grant Alaska Space Grant Consortium, 147
NASA Space Grant Arizona Grant Consortium, 148
NASA Space Grant Arizona Space Grant Consortium, 148
NASA Space Grant Arkansas Space Grant Consortium, 148
NASA Space Grant California Space Grant Consortium, 149
NASA Space Grant Colorado Space Grant Consortium, 149
NASA Space Grant Connecticut Space Grant Consortium, 150, 473
NASA Space Grant Delaware Space Grant Consortium, 150
NASA Space Grant District of Columbia Space Grant Consortium, 151
NASA Space Grant Florida Space Grant Consortium, 151
NASA Space Grant Georgia Space Grant Consortium, 152
NASA Space Grant Hawaii Space Grant Consortium, 152
NASA Space Grant Idaho Space Grant Consortium, 153
NASA Space Grant Illinois Space Grant Consortium, 154
NASA Space Grant Indiana Space Grant Consortium, 154
NASA Space Grant Iowa Space Grant Consortium, 155
NASA Space Grant Kansas Space Grant Consortium, 155
NASA Space Grant Kentucky Space Grant Consortium, 155
NASA Space Grant Louisiana Space Grant Consortium, 156
NASA Space Grant Maine Space Grant Consortium, 157
NASA Space Grant Maryland Space Grant Consortium, 157

Sponsor Index

NASA Space Grant Massachusetts Space Grant Consortium, 158
NASA Space Grant Michigan Space Grant Consortium, 158
NASA Space Grant Minnesota Space Grant Consortium, 159
NASA Space Grant Mississippi Space Grant Consortium, 159
NASA Space Grant Missouri Space Grant Consortium, 160
NASA Space Grant Montana Space Grant Consortium, 160
NASA Space Grant Nebraska Space Grant Consortium, 161
NASA Space Grant Nevada Space Grant Consortium, 161
NASA Space Grant New Hampshire Space Grant Consortium, 162
NASA Space Grant New Jersey Space Grant Consortium, 162
NASA Space Grant New Mexico Space Grant Consortium, 163
NASA Space Grant New York Space Grant Consortium, 163
NASA Space Grant North Carolina Space Grant Consortium, 164
NASA Space Grant North Dakota Space Grant Consortium, 164
NASA Space Grant Ohio Space Grant Consortium, 165
NASA Space Grant Oklahoma Space Grant Consortium, 166
NASA Space Grant Oregon Space Grant Consortium, 166
NASA Space Grant Pennsylvania Space Grant Consortium, 167
NASA Space Grant Puerto Rico Space Grant Consortium, 167
NASA Space Grant Rhode Island Space Grant Consortium, 168
NASA Space Grant Rocky Mountain Space Grant Consortium, 169
NASA Space Grant South Carolina Space Grant Consortium, 169
NASA Space Grant South Dakota Space Grant Consortium, 171
NASA Space Grant Tennessee Space Grant Consortium, 171
NASA Space Grant Texas Space Grant Consortium, 171
NASA Space Grant Vermont Space Grant Consortium, 172
NASA Space Grant Virginia Space Grant Consortium, 172
NASA Space Grant Washington Space Grant Consortium, 173
NASA Space Grant West Virginia Consortium, 174
NASA Space Grant Wisconsin Space Grant Consortium, 175
NASA Space Grant Wyoming Space Grant Consortium, 176
Nash Finch Company, 711
Nation Institute, 473
National Academy for Nuclear Training, 473
National Academy of American Scholars, 473
National Academy of Education, 474
National Advisory Group, 711
National Air Transportation Foundation, 474
National Alliance for Excellence, Inc., 474
National Alpha Lambda Delta Honor Society, 711
National Amateur Baseball Federation, 475
National Art Gallery, 476
National Art Materials Trade Association, 712
National Association for Community Leadership, 476
National Association for Public Interest Law, 476
National Association for the Deaf, 477
National Association of Black Accountants, 712
National Association of Black Journalists, 477
National Association of Latino Elected and Appointed Officials, 478
National Association of Letter Carriers, 712
National Association of Pediatric Nurses and Practitioners, 478
National Association of Plumbing, Heating, Cooling Contractors, 478
National Association of Purchasing Management, 479
National Association of Secondary School Principals, 479, 713
National Association of Water Companies (NJ Chapter), 479
National Association of Women in Construction, 480
National Athletic Trainers Association, 713
National Basketball Association, 480
National Beta Club, 714
National Black Nurse's Association, 714
National Black Police Association, 480
National Center for Atmospheric Research, 177
National Center for Construction Education and Research, 481
National Collegiate Athletic Association, 481
National Computer Systems, 714
National Dairy Shrine, 482
National Endowment for the Humanities, 177
National Environmental Health Association, 483
National Federation of Republican Women, 715
National Federation of the Blind, 483
National Foster Parent Association, Inc., 715
National Foundation for Advancement in the Arts, 485
National Foundation for Infectious Diseases, 485
National Foundation for Jewish Culture, 486
National Future Farmers of America, 716
National Gallery of Art, 487
National Gallery of Art, Center for Advanced Study in the Visual Arts, 487
National Geographic Society, 489
National Ground Water Association, 716
National Guild of Community Schools of the Arts, 490
National Hemophilia Foundation, 490
National Hispanic Scholarship Fund, 491
National Institute of Justice, 178
National Institutes of Health, 178
National Italian American Foundation, 491
National Journal, 504
National League of American Pen Women, 505
National Medical Fellowships, Inc., 505
National Merit Scholarship Corporation, 508
National Museum of the American Indian, 509
National Museum of Women in the Arts, 509
National Network for Environmental Management Studies, 179
National Organization for Women Legal Defense and Education Fund, 510
National Physical Science Consortium, 510
National Research Council, 510
National Restaurant Association Education Foundation, 512
National Rifle Association, 716
National Roofing Foundation, 716
National Scholarship Trust Fund of the Graphic Arts, 513
National Scholarship Trust Fund of the Graphic ArtsFoundation, 717
National Science Foundation, 179
National Science Teachers Association, 513
National Sculpture Society, 514
National Security Agency, 180
National Semiconductor Corporation, 717

Sponsor Index

National Society for Experiential Education, 514
National Society of Black Engineers, 717
National Society of Public Accountants, 514
National Society of the Colonial Dames of America, 515
National Society of the Sons of the American Revolution, 718
National Space Society, 515
National Speakers Association, 515
National Stone Association, 515
National Tourism Foundation, 516
National Training Systems Association, 520
National Urban League, 520
National Wildlife Federation, 520
National Women's Studies Association, 520
Native American Scholarship Fund, 520
Native Daughters of the Golden West, 719
Navy League of the United States, 521
Navy Supply Corps Foundation, 521
Navy-Marine Corps Relief Society, 521
NAWE: Advancing Women in Higher Education, 522
NBC News and Tom Brokaw, 719
Nebraska Coordinating Commission for Postsecondary Education, 181
Nebraska Department of Health and Human Services, 181
Nebraska State Department of Education, 182
NEC America, Inc., 719
Nevada Department of Education, 182
New Dramatists, 522
New England Association of Independent Tire Dealers, 719
New England Board of Higher Education, 182
New England Graphic Arts, 522
New England Wild Flower Society, 522
New Hampshire Charitable Foundation, 523
New Hampshire Postsecondary Education Commission, 182
New Jersey Department of Military and Veterans Affairs, 183
New Jersey Office of Student Assistance, 183
New Jersey Society of Architects, 523
New Jersey State Golf Association Foundation, 523
New Jersey State Policemen's Benevolent Association, Inc., 719
New Mexico Commission on Higher Education, 186
New Republic, 523

New Stage Theatre, 524
New United Motor Manufacturing Scholarship Foundation, 720
New York Association of Black Journalists, 524
New York Operations Division of the Futures Industry Association, 720
New York State Bar Association, Department of Media Services and Public Affairs, 524
New York State Education Department, 188
New York State Grange, 720
New York State Health Department, 189
New York State Higher Education Services Corporation, 189
New York State Native American Education Unit, 191
New York State Senate, 191
New York Times, 524
Newberry Library, 525, 720
Newhouse Foundation, 527
NIKE, Inc., 721
Non-Commissioned Officers Association, 721
NorAm Energy Corporation Endowment, 723
Norand Corporation, 723
Norfolk Chamber Music Festival, 527
North American Bluebird Society, 528
North American Limousin Foundation, 723
North American Loon Fund, 528
North Carolina Arts Council, 192
North Carolina Association of Educators, 528
North Carolina Bar Association, 528
North Carolina Botanical Garden, 192, 529
North Carolina Department of Community Colleges, 192, 529
North Carolina Department of Public Instruction, 193
North Carolina Division of Veterans Affairs, 194
North Carolina Division of Vocational Rehabilitation Services, 194
North Carolina State Education Assistance Authority, 194
North Dakota University System, 196
North Pacific Lumber Company, 723
Northeastern Loggers' Association, 723
Northern Cheyenne Tribal Education Department, 196
Northland Aluminum Products, Inc., 724
Northwest Danish Foundation, 529
Northwest Journalists of Color, 530
Northwest Osteopathic Medical Foundation, 530
Northwest Pharmacists Coalition, 530

Northwestern Mutual Life Foundation, Inc., 724
Norwest Foundation, 724
Novartis Pharmaceuticals Corporation, 531
Nurses' Educational Funds, Inc., 531
Oak Ridge Institute for Science and Education, 197, 532
Oak Tree Packaging Corporation, 724
Ocean Spray Cranberries, Inc., 532, 724
Octel Communications, 532
Ohio Board of Regents, 212
Ohio National Guard, 532
Ohio Newspapers Foundation, 533
Oklahoma Engineering Foundation, 533
Oklahoma State Regents for Higher Education, 213
Olympic Steel, Inc., 725
Oncology Nursing Foundation, 533
Oral and Maxillofacial Surgery Foundation, 725
Order of American Hellenic Educational Progressive Association, 534
Oregon State Scholarship Commission, 214, 535, 725
Osage Tribal Education Committee, 543
OSI Industries, Inc., 726
Otter Tail Power Company, 726
Pacific Enterprises, 726
Pacific Life Insurance Company, 726
Pacific Printing and Imaging Association, 544
Parenteral Drug Association Foundation for Pharmaceutical Sciences, Inc., 544
Payless Cashways, Inc., 727
Pebble Beach Company Foundation, 727
Pediatric AIDS Foundation, 545
Pennsylvania Higher Education Assistance Agency, 215
Pennzoil Company, 727
Pentair, Inc., 727
Perkin-Elmer Corporation, 727
Personnel Magazine Now Workforce Magazine, 545
Peter A. McKernan Scholarship Fund, 546
Pfizer, 546
PGA Tour, 546
Pharmaceutical Research and Manufacturers of America Foundation, Inc., 546
Phi Beta Kappa Society, 547
Phi Delta Kappa International, 548, 727
Phi Sigma Iota, 548
PHICO Insurance Company, 728
Philadelphia Drug Exchange, 728

809

Sponsor Index

Philips Electronics North America, 728
Phillips Academy, 548
Phillips Petroleum Company, 728
Pickett and Hatcher Educational Fund, Inc., 548
Pierce Investment Banking, 549
Pine Tree 4-H Club Foundation, 728
Piper Jaffray Companies Inc., 729
Pittsburgh Civic Garden Center, 549
Playhouse on the Square, 549
Playtex Products, Inc., 729
Polaris Industries, Inc., 729
Police and Fire Fighters' Association, 729
Polyfibron Technologies, Inc., 729
Population Council, 549
Population Institute, 550
Portuguese Continental Union, 729
Practitioners Publishing Company, 730
Precision Castparts Corporation, 730
Presbyterian Church (USA), 550
Princess Grace Foundation-USA, 552
Princeton Plasma Physics Laboratory, 216
Pro-Found Software, 553
Procter and Gamble Fund, 730
Professional Engineers of North Carolina, 553
Professional Grounds Management Society, 553
Professional Service Industries, Inc., 730
Project Excellence, 553
Promus Hotel Corporation Inc., 731
Prudential Foundation, 731
Public Employees Roundtable, 554
Public Service Company of Colorado, 731
Puerto Rican Legal Defense and Education Fund, 554
Puerto Rico Department of Education, 216
QEM Network, 554
Quadion Foundation, 731
Quill and Scroll Foundation, 554
Quill Corporation, 731
R. Brouilette Agency, Inc., 731
Radio-Television News Directors Foundation, 555
Random House, 558
Raychem, 558
Raychem Corporation, 731
Raytheon Company, 732
Real Estate Educators Association, 558
Recording for the Blind and Dyslexic, 732
Red River Valley Fighter Pilots Association, 559
Reforma, 559
Regions Financial Corporation, 733
ReliaStar Foundation, 733

Renew America, 559
Reorganization Division of the Securities Industry, 733
Reserve Officers Association, 733
Resources for the Future, 560
Retired Officers Association, 734
Rex Lumber Company, 734
Reynolds and Reynolds Company Foundation, 734
Rhode Island Higher Education Assistance Authority, 216
Rhode Island State Government, 216
Rhone-Poulenc Rorer Inc., 735
Richard F. Walsh/Alfred W. Di Tolla Foundation, 735
Ricoh Corporation, 735
Rob and Bessie Welder Wildlife Foundation, 560
Robert L. Millender Sr. Memorial Fund, Inc., 560
Robert W. Geyer, 735
Roche Brothers Supermarkets, Inc., 735
Rockwell Semiconductor Systems, 561
Rocky Mountain Coal Mining Institute, 561
Rodale Press, Inc., 735
Rodolf Steiner Educational Farming Association, 561
Roger Von Amelunxen Foundation, 736
RoNetco Supermarkets, Inc., 736
Rosemount Aerospace Inc., 736
Rosemount Inc., 736
Rotary Foundation of Rotary International, 561
ROTC, 217
Royal Neighbors of America, 736
Rugby Building Products, Inc., 737
Ruud Lighting, Inc., 737
S.C. Holman Foundation, 737
S.J. Electro Systems Foundation, 737
Sachs Foundation, 562
Safety-Kleen Corporation, 737
Saint David's Society, 562
Samuel H. Kress Foundation, 563
Samuel Lemberg Scholarship Loan Fund, Inc., 563
San Francisco Chronicle, 563
Santee Cooper, 738
Sargent and Lundy, 738
SAS Institute Inc., 738
Savvy Management, 564
SBC Foundation, 738
Schering-Key Pharmaceuticals, 564
Schlumberger, 564
Scholarships and Loans Department - BPW Foundation, 564
Scholastic, Inc., 564
School Food Service Foundation, 738
Schweitzer-Mauduit International Inc., 739

Scoville Peace Fellowship Program, 566
Screen Actors Guild Foundation, 739
Scripps Institute of Oceanography, 566
Seabee Memorial Scholarship Association, Inc., 566
Seafarers Welfare Plan, 740
Sealed Air Corporation, 740
Seattle Jaycees, 566
Second Marine Division Association Memorial Scholarship Fund, 567
Securities Operations Division, 740
Seneca Nation of Indians, 567
Sertoma International, 567
Service Employees International Union, 568
Service First Financial Corporation, 740
Service Merchandise, 568
Service Merchandise Company Inc., 568
Servistar/Coast to Coast Corporation, 741
Seventeen Magazine, 568
Sharp Electronics Corporation, 741
Shop 'N Save Stores, 569
Shoshone Tribe, 569
Sid Richardson Memorial Fund, 741
SIGECO, 741
Sigma Alpha Epsilon Foundation, 741
Sigma Xi The Scientific Research Society, 569
Silicon Graphics Computer Systems, 569
Simpson PSB Fund, 742
Sippican, Inc., 742
Sisters of Charity Health Care System, 742
Sisters of Mercy Health System - St. Louis, 742
Skadden, Arps, Slate, Meagher and Flom, 569
Slope Indicator Co., 742
Slovak Gymnastic Union Sokol, USA, 743
Slovene National Benefit Society, 743
Slovenian Women's Union of America, 743
Smith Equipment, 743
Smith's Food and Drug Centers Inc., 570
SmithKline Beecham Clinical Laboratories, 744
Smithsonian Environmental Research Center, 218
Smithsonian Institution, 570
Social Science Research Council, 571
Society for Human Resource Management Foundation, 744
Society for Technical Communication, 577
Society for the Psychological Study of Lesbian and Gay Issues, 577

Society for the Psychological Study of Social Issues, 577
Society for the Scientific Study of Sexuality, 579
Society of Actuaries/Casualty Actuarial Society, 579
Society of Architectural Historians, 579
Society of Automotive Engineers, 580, 744
Society of Daughters of the United States Army, 581
Society of Exploration Geophysicists, 581
Society of Hispanic Professional Engineers Foundation, 581
Society of Manufacturing Engineers, 582
Society of Naval Architects and Marine Engineers, 744
Society of Nuclear Medicine, 582
Society of Physics Students, 744
Society of Range Management, 583
Society of Women Engineers, 583, 745
Soil and Water Conservation Society, 745
Solomon R. Guggenheim Foundation, 588
Solomon R. Guggenheim Museum, 588
Sons of Italy Foundation, 589
Sons of Norway Foundation, 589, 746
Sony Corporation of America, 589
Sony Music Entertainment, 590
Sony Music Entertainment, Inc., 747
Soo Line Credit Union, 747
South Carolina Commission on Higher Education, 219
South Carolina Higher Education Tuition Grants Commission, 219
South Dakota Board of Regents, 219
South Dakota Board of Regents Scholarship Committee, 220
South Dakota Department of Education and Cultural Affairs, 220
South-Western/ITP Publishing Company, 747
Southeastern Claim Executives Association, 747
Southern Progress Corporation, 590
Southface Energy Institute, 590
Southwest Research Institute, 747
Space Center Company/McNeely Foundation, 747
Spear, Leeds and Kellogg Foundation, 748
Special Libraries Association, 591, 748
Spencer Foundation, 591
SPIE - The International Society for Optical Engineering, 592
Spina Bifida Association of America, 593

Spinsters Ink, 593
Spoleto Festival USA, 593
St. Patrick Hospital, 748
Stanadyne Automotive Corporation, 749
Stanhome, Inc., 749
Stanley Works, 749
Star Tribune/Cowles Media Company, 749
State Farm Companies Foundation, 594
State Historical Society of Wisconsin, 221
State Medical Education Board of Georgia, 221
State of Maine-Department of Agriculture, Food and Rural Resources, 221
State of Virginia, 222
Sto Corporation, 749
Stone Container Corporation, 749
Stratus Computer, Inc., 750
Strong Museum, 594
Student Aid Foundation, 595
Sub-Zero Freezer Company, Inc., 750
Suddath Companies, 750
Sunkist Growers, 595
Supreme Guardian Council, International Order of Job's Daughters, 750
Swiss Benevolent Society, 595
Sykes Enterprises Incorporated, 750
SYSCO Corporation, 751
T.D. Williamson, Inc., 751
T.J. Hale Company, 751
Talbots, 751
Tandy Technology Scholars, 596
Target, 596, 751
Tau Beta Pi Association, 596, 751
Taylor Packing Corporation Inc., 752
TCF Foundation, 752
TDS Corporate Scholarship Program, 752
Techneglas, 752
Telephone and Data Systems, Inc., 752
Tennant, 752
Tennessee Student Assistance Corporation, 222
Tescom Corporation, 752
Tesoro Petroleum Corporation, 752
Tetra Tech, 597
Texas Center for Rural Health Initiatives, 223
Texas Higher Education Coordinating Board, 224
Textilease Corporation, 753
The GEM Consortium, 597
The Maine State Society of Washington, DC, 597
The National Foundation for Infectious Diseases, 598
Theodore R. and Vivian M. Johnson Scholarship Foundation, 753

Third Marine Division Association, 753
Thurgood Marshall Scholarship Fund, 598
Time Warner Inc., 753
TJX Companies, Inc., 753
TMI Companies, 753
Transportation Clubs International, 598
Travel and Tourism Research Association, 599
Treacy Company, 600
Tri-Gas Inc., 754
Trinity Episcopal Church, 600
Truckload Carriers Association, 600
Trustmark Foundation, 754
Tultex Foundation, 754
Tuttle-Click Automotive Group, 754
Twentieth Century Fox, 600
Twin City Fan & Blower Co., 754
Two/Ten International Footwear Foundation, 754
U. The National College Magazine, 601
U.S. Army Center of Military History, 227
U.S. Army Recruiting Command, 227
U.S. Bancorp, 755
U.S. Department of Agriculture, 228
U.S. Department of Education, 229
U.S. Department of Health and Human Services, 230
U.S. Department of Interior-Bureau of Indian Affairs, 231
U.S. Department of Vocational Rehabilitation, 231
U.S. Institute of Peace, 231
U.S. National Arboretum, 601
U.S. Navy-Marine Corps, 231
Ukrainian Fraternal Association, 601, 755
Ullico Inc. Family of Companies, 755
Ultramar Diamond Shamrock Corporation, 755
Unico Foundation, Inc., 601
Union Pacific Corporation, 755
Unique Industries, Inc., 755
Unitarian Universalist Association, 602
Unite, 756
United Cerebral Palsy Research and Educational Foundation, Inc., 603
United Commercial Travelers of America, 756
United Food and Commercial Workers Union, 756
United Methodist Church, 603
United Methodist Communications, 606
United Negro College Fund, 607
United Paperworkers International Union, 756
United Parcel Service Foundation, 757
United Piece Dye Works, L.P., 757

Sponsor Index

United Service Automobile Association, 757
United States Association for Blind Athletes, 607
United States Cellular Corporation, 757
United States Department of State, 232
United States Golf Association, 757
United States Holocaust Memorial Museum, 232
United States Information Agency, 232
United States Navy/Marine NROTC College Scholarship Program, 233
United States Olympic Committee (USOC), 607
United Transportation Union Insurance Association, 758
University Corporation for Atmospheric Research, 233
University Film and Video Association, 607
University of North Carolina General Administration, 234
Univest Corporation, 758
Unocal Foundation, 758
Unum Foundation, 758
UpJohn Company, 608
UPS Foundation, 758
US Department of State, 235
USF&G Foundation, Inc., 758
UST, 759
USX Foundation Inc., 759
Utah State Board of Regents, 236
Utah State Office of Education, 236
Varian Associates, Inc., 759
Veeder-Root Company, 759
Venture Clubs of the Americas, 608
Vermont Golf Association Fund, Inc., 608
Vermont Student Assistance Corporation, 236
Vesuvius Americas, 759
Veterans of Foreign Wars, 608
VF Corporation, 759
Vikki Carr Scholarship Foundation, 609
Virgin Islands Board of Education, 237
Virginia Council of Higher Education, 238, 609
Virginia Museum of Fine Arts, 609
Voith Hydro, Inc., 759
Voith Sulzer Paper Technology North America, Inc., 760
Vollrath Company, L.L.C., 760
Volvo Cars of North America, Inc., 760
VPI Foundation Inc., 760
VVP America, Inc., 760
W.E. Lahr Co., 760
Wakefern Food Corporation, 761
Wal-Mart Foundation, 609, 761

Walker Forge, Inc., 761
Wall Street Journal, 610
Walt Disney World, 610
Walter O. Wells Foundation, 761
Warwick, Baker and Fiore, 610
Washington Crossing Foundation, 611
Washington Gas, 611
Washington Internships for Students of Engineering, 611
Washington Osteopathic Foundation, 761
Washington State Higher Education Coordinating Board, 239
Washington State PTA Financial Grant Foundation, 611
Waters Corporation, 761
Watlow Electric Manufacturing, 762
Weather Channel, 612
Wellesley College, 612
Wells Fargo, 762
Wendell J. Kelley Scholarship, 762
West Company, Inc., 762
West Group, 762
West Virginia Division of Veterans Affairs, 241
West Virginia State College and University Systems, 241
Western Beef, 763
Western Golf Association, 612
Westlake Scholarship Foundation, 612
WestPlains Energy, 763
Weyerhaeuser Company Foundation, 763
Wheaton Franciscan Services, Inc., 763
Whitney Museum of American Art, 613
Wilhelmina Models, 613
William Beaumont Hospital, 763
William Randolph Hearst Foundation, 614
William S. Davila Scholarship Fund Endowment, 763
Williams Steel and Hardware, 763
Willis Corroon, 764
Wilson Ornithological Society, 614
Winegard Company, 764
Winston Churchill Foundation, 615
Wisconsin Central Ltd., 764
Wisconsin Dental Foundation, 615
Wisconsin Department of Veterans Affairs, 242
Wisconsin Energy Corporation Foundation, Inc., 764
Wisconsin Higher Educational Aid Board, 243
Wisconsin Power and Light Foundation, 764
Witco Corporation, 764
WMTW Channel Eight, 615
Wolf Trap Foundation for the Performing Arts, 615
Women Grocers of America, 616

Women of the Evangelical Lutheran Church in America, 616
Women's Research and Education Institute, 616
Women's Western Golf Foundation, 617
Woodrow Wilson National Fellowship Foundation, 244, 617
Worcester County Horticultural Society, 618
World Federalist Association, 765
Wyoming Community College Commission, 245
Y.E.S. To Jobs, 618
Yakama Indian Nation, 619
Yankee Gas Services Company, 765
YKK Corporation of America, 765
Yosemite National Park, 245
Zee Medical, Inc., 765
Zonta International Foundation, 619